GREAT RIVER

The Rio Grande
in North American History

GREAT

The Rio

VOLUME ONE

Indians and Spain

VOLUME TWO

Mexico and the United States

RIVER

Grande

in

North American

History

by PAUL HORGAN

HOLT, RINEHART AND WINSTON
New York · Chicago · San Francisco

works by Paul Horgan

Novels

The Fault of Angels
No Quarter Given
Main Line West
A Lamp on the Plains
Far From Cibola
The Habit of Empire
The Common Heart

Shorter Fiction

The Return of the Weed
Figures in a Landscape
The Devil in the Desert
One Red Rose for Christmas

History and Belles-Lettres

Men of Arms *(juvenile)*
From the Royal City
New Mexico's Own Chronicle *(with Maurice Garland Fulton)*
Biographical Introductions to Volumes 1 and 2 of Diary and Letters of
        Josiah Gregg *(edited by Maurice Garland Fulton)*
Great River: The Rio Grande in North American History
    VOLUME ONE: Indians and Spain
    VOLUME TWO: Mexico and the United States

to Charles Arthur Henderson

a letter of dedication to serve as a preface

Dear C.,

let me give you this book, which has been in the making so long a time—ever since, really, I was brought to the Rio Grande at Albuquerque as a small boy in 1915. You were an earlier immigrant to New Mexico—where, as in our continent, everybody, far enough back, was an immigrant—and from you I have learned much about my subject, particularly about the spirit behind the image of man so small and so great, so various and so tenacious, against the river empire where for centuries there was no such thing as a short journey.

Neither in these volumes is my passage through the river's story a short one. How could it be? The river is nearly two thousand miles long, its historical course takes us through something over ten centuries of time and through the chronicles of three cultures. To do it anything like justice, I have wanted to produce a sense of historical experience, rather than a bare record. This required me wherever possible to see events, societies, movements, through human characters in action. Without, I hope, departing from the inflexible limits of respectful scholarship, I took every opportunity to stage a scene. What this may have cost in brevity was perhaps made up for by a presentation of experience with which the reader might be able to identify himself. If here and there I halted the narrative of events to describe various ways and customs of the peoples, then I had precedent for it; for Herodotus did this, to our enrichment. Only when events are rooted in the soil of the culture might they seem to have true reality.

Perhaps it would interest you to see a few comments on the writing of history which have seemed to clarify for me my own view

vii

of the task. Here is one which I found in an essay on *The Literary Historian* in the *London Times Literary Supplement* for January 16, 1953:

> Macaulay wrote to stimulate the reader, not to contribute an original piece of research. He wrote, in fact, much as he talked. . . .

Here is another, out of Aldous Huxley's essay *Vulgarity in Literature:*

> What is the smallest amount of simplification compatible with comprehensibility, compatible with the expression of a humanly significant meaning? It is the business of the non-classical naturalistic writer to discover. His ambition is to render, in literary terms, the quality of immediate experience. . . .

And in his *Journal* for July 21, 1850, Eugène Delacroix gave me comfort for those passages in which I may have translated the experience of the past with an accent other than that of conventional historiography:

> The historian's task appears to me to be the most difficult of all because he needs to give unceasing attention to a hundred and one things at the same time, and must preserve through quotations, precise recitals of events, and facts that are only relatively important, the enthusiasm that gives life to his story and makes it something more than an extract from the newspapers. . . . We need to be very bold. Without daring, without extreme daring, even, there is no beauty. . . . (Translated by Lucy Norton. London, Phaidon Press, 1951.)

For I agree with Professor Nevins that the writing of history, in addition to being a technical craft, is also an art. Its proper aim is to produce, in literary form, to whatever degree the author may command, a work of art.

To realize this purpose may require the historian to invoke certain flexibilities of method. Here's one that I've invoked in order to give the reader an immediate sense of locality in the vastly scattered backgrounds of the river empire. To accomplish this I have in many cases used recent or modern place names in speaking of persons and events belonging to earlier times. For example, "Mexico" properly speaking was not the name of a nation, or a whole national region, until 1821; but I use it for events in its area before that date rather than the officially correct designation "New Spain" because by doing so I hope to give the modern reader a more ready sense of where he is on the map. Similarly, pressing ahead with narratives of events occurring near the sites of modern river towns, I use their modern names—e.g., "near Eagle Pass"—as a quick means of orientation, trusting to the reader to understand my freedom with historical time.

Perhaps you will notice that in the flow of the narrative I have not used footnotes or running references with superior numbers to identify sources. I followed this course not because I did not have precise references for my facts, or because I did not want to share these with the reader; but because it seemed to me more to the reader's advantage to give him the story without diverting his interest to the anatomy of my framework. But of course I must identify my sources, under two obligations: one is to acknowledge my debt to those authors whose works I have consulted; the other is to provide anyone interested in the source material—its range and authenticity—with general evidence for my statements. Accordingly, such information appears in brief form at the end of each volume, with the sources listed by chapters, from which the reader may refer to the complete bibliography at the end of volume two, in Appendix C.

I am, of course, deeply indebted to a great number of men and women who have helped me in every phase of my long task. Contributing much to whatever successes my work may show, they are in no wise responsible for its failures. Let me list such benefactors, many of whom you will know.

For help in locating source materials and for other good acts of guidance I thank United States Senator Clinton P. Anderson, and Mrs. Luna Diamond of his office staff; Ernst Bacon, who helped me to travel the river's source country; the Most Reverend Dr. Edwin V. Byrne, Archbishop of Santa Fe, and his predecessor, the Most Reverend Rudolf A. Gerken, who gave me access to various records of the Church in New Mexico; Kenneth Chapman and Stanley Stubbs of the Laboratory of Anthropology at Santa Fe; J. Frank Dobie, of Austin, who gave me both books and advice; Edward Corrigan, of Laredo, who directed me to information about the Republic of the Rio Grande, an elusive subject; Colonel Martin L. Crimmins, of San Antonio, who shared with me his information on the forts of the Rio Grande; Major General and Mrs. Hunter Harris, Jr.; Dr. Rex Z. Howard, of Fort Worth, who supplied me with useful photographs of Saint Bernard's Mission at Guerrero, Coahuila; Peter Hurd, who gave me valuable materials, whether published or remembered out of his own experience; William A. Keleher, of Albuquerque, who gave me the freedom of his library and of his judgment in literary and historical matters; Victor J. Smith, of Alpine, Texas; James L. Threlkeld, of Albuquerque, who lent me his support as a bookman; Mrs. J. P. White, of Roswell, who let me study her folio copy of the Percier designs after Isabey for the *Sacre* of Napoleon; and Mrs. John Boylan, who typed many of my source notes.

You can imagine how much I owe to libraries and librarians. I must pay my grateful respects to William Dix and members of his staff at the Princeton University Library; Mrs. Dollis Stevens, librarian of the New Mexico Military Institute, and her predecessor, Mrs. Charlotte Gaylord; Mrs. Albert Ely, formerly librarian of the Museum of New Mexico, and Augustus Gaylord, a later incumbent of the position; Arthur McAnnally, former librarian of the University of New Mexico, and Miss Ruth Russell and Miss Williams of his staff; Miss Haydée Noya of the Henry E. Huntington Memorial Library at San Marino; Miss Fannie Ratchford, Miss Winnie Allen, and other officers of the University of Texas Library; Miss Erin Humphrey of the Reference Department of the El Paso Public Library; and Miss Katherine Brand of the Manuscripts Division of the Library of Congress. I must give my thanks to these officers and library staff members of the United States Department of Agriculture at Albuquerque: Miss Marian W. Dorroh, Al Jarrett, Mrs. Clemmie Shirley, Harper Sims; and to Hubert Ball, chief engineer of the Middle Rio Grande Conservancy District.

You'll find a detailed record of my great indebtedness to authors of printed works in the General Bibliography (Appendix C). Here I must mention with particular admiration and gratitude certain works appearing in the bibliography which were of recurrent value to me: Charles Wilson Hackett's edition of Mr. and Mrs. Adolph Bandelier's *Historical Documents Relating to New Mexico, Nueva Viscaya and Approaches Thereto, to 1773,* of which, by the way, you gave me your copies; Eugene C. Barker's edition of *The Austin Papers;* the publications issued through the University of New Mexico Press by the Coronado Cuarto Centennial Commission, and those of the Quivira Society; the works of Herbert C. Bolton; Carlos E. Castañeda's *Our Catholic Heritage in Texas, 1519-1936;* the works of J. Frank Dobie; the *Report* of Commissioner William H. Emory; the works of Cleve Hallenbeck; the works of Edgar L. Hewett and Bertha Dutton; the southwestern books of Erna Fergusson; General Tom Green's *Journal of the Texian Expedition Against Mier;* Joseph C. McCoy's *Historic Sketches of the Cattle Trade;* Salvador de Madariaga's volumes on the Spanish American empire; Tocqueville's *Democracy in America;* Twitchell's catalogue of the *Spanish Archives of New Mexico,* and his *Leading Facts of New Mexican History;* the two volumes of the *Diary and Letters of Josiah*

Gregg, discovered and edited by Maurice Garland Fulton; Cleofas M. Jaramillo's *Shadows of the Past (Sombras del pasado);* William A. Keleher's *Turmoil in New Mexico, 1846-1868;* Constance Rourke's *American Humor* and *The Roots of American Culture;* Bancroft's *History of the North Mexican States and Texas;* Rives's *The United States and Mexico, 1821-1848;* Yoakum's *History of Texas;* and *Coahuila y Texas en la época colonial,* by Vito Alessio Robles.

In addition to people whose printed works gave me so much that was useful there were many others whose conversation contributed to my work. Among these were Judge Harbert Davenport, of Brownsville; Dr. Bertha Dutton, of Santa Fe; the late Mrs. Clara M. Fergusson, of Albuquerque; Brigadier General William J. Glasgow, of El Paso; J. Brinckerhoff Jackson, of Santa Fe; Mrs. D. S. McKellar and Sheriff Lehman, of Eagle Pass; Virgil Lott, of Roma, Texas; Stuart Rose, of Philadelphia; John Sinclair, of Tiguex, at Bernalillo; and Seb. S. Wilcox, of Laredo.

As you know, I turned to historical motion picture film to find impressions of living character in the animated images of certain figures who appear near the end of my story. I thank the Film Division of the National Broadcasting Company for help in locating, through Lloyds Film Storage Company of New York, and in making available for study, historic film footage showing Villa, Pershing, Carranza, Wilson, Funston, Obregón, and an episode of desert fighting during the Punitive Expedition of 1916. I wonder if my bibliography is the first to list factual motion pictures as serious historical reference material. I should like to think so. But even if it is not, I shall rest content to be among the earliest of historians to show the way to scholarly use of such a vivid medium of enlivening the past.

I am glad to record that I profited from critical readings given variously to portions, or to all, of my typescript by the Rev. Fray Angélico Chavez, O.F.M., Carl Carmer, and Allan Nevins. During my labors I was often given a chance to read aloud to friends from the work in progress, so to weigh my effects and discover lacks. For such help I thank Henriette, Peter, and Peter Wyeth Hurd; Robert and Barbara Anderson; Constance and Vernon Knapp; Dwight Starr; and Remi and Thomas Messer. Henriette Wyeth Hurd, Margaret Duffield, Mary C. Nicholas, Stuart Rose, Virginia Rice, and Daniel Longwell read the whole work in typescript, and their comments were of much value to me. I am grateful to Edward Nicholas for hospitality he gave me while I was at work on the last phase of the book.

To three superintendents of the New Mexico Military Institute I give full thanks for their consideration of me. During the last years of my service as an officer of the school, Colonel D. C. Pearson and General Hugh M. Milton II both granted me extended leaves of absence from my duties to permit me to give all my time to this book, and General Milton further helped me with gifts of source material. Colonel Charles Francis Ward, in a gesture of true generosity, permitted me to use his edited manuscript, yet unpublished, of his great-grandfather's Mexican War diary.

Part of my study was done under the auspices of the John Simon Guggenheim Memorial Foundation. I warmly thank Dr. Henry Allen Moe, Secretary-General of the Foundation, for his sensitive and generous administration of my Guggenheim Fellowship.

Finally, to my agent, Virginia Rice, who sustained me with more than merely professional confidence throughout my years of work on this book, I offer all gratitude.

Here, then, in whatever part I have managed to divine its meaning and stay its likeness, is your country and mine.

P. H.

Roswell, New Mexico,
16 March 1954.

Contents

VOLUME ONE: *Indians and Spain*

Prologue: Riverscape

   1. Creation   3
   2. Gazetteer   5
   3. Cycle   7

Book One: The Indian Rio Grande

   1. The Ancients   13
   2. The Cliffs   17
   3. To the River   19
   4. The Stuff of Life   23
        i. Creation and Prayer   23
        ii. Forms   33
        iii. Community   37
        iv. Dwelling   48
        v. Garments   51
        vi. Man, Woman and Child   53
        vii. Farmer and Hunter   59
        viii. Travel and Trade   68
        ix. Personality and Death   75
   5. On the Edge of Change   79

Book Two: The Spanish Rio Grande

   1. The River of Palms   83
   2. Rivals   89
   3. Upland River   95

4. The Travellers' Tales   100
5. Destiny and the Future   109
6. Faith and Bad Faith   113
7. Facing Battle   119
8. Battle Piece   124
9. The Garrison   127
10. Siege   130
11. The Eastern Plains   136
12. Prophecy and Retreat   142
13. Lords and Victims   147
14. The River of May   151
15. Four Enterprises   153
16. Possession   160
17. The River Capital   166
18. Collective Memory   174
     i. Sources   174
     ii. Belief   175
     iii. The Ocean Masters   177
     iv. The King and Father   180
     v. Arts   187
     vi. Style and Hunger   190
     vii. The Swords   192
     viii. Soul and Body   193
19. Duties   195
20. A Dark Day in Winter   199
21. The Battle of Acoma   203
22. Afterthoughts   210
23. Exchange   211
24. The Promises   215
25. The Desert Fathers   219
26. The Two Majesties   238
27. The Hungry   256
28. "This Miserable Kingdom"   268
29. The Terror   274
30. Limit of Vision   293
31. A Way to the *Texas*   298

Contents

32. The Great Captain   305
33. Fort St. John Baptist   323
34. Early Towns   328
35. Colonial Texas   331
36. Mexico Bay   340
37. Forgotten Lessons   346
38. Hacienda and Village   352
       i. Land and House   352
      ii. Fashion   358
     iii. Family and Work   360
      iv. Mischance   367
       v. Feast Days   368
      vi. Wedding Feast   371
     vii. Mortality   374
    viii. The Saints   383
      ix. Provincials   387
39. The World Intrudes   390
40. The Shout   422
41. The Broken Grasp of Spain   436

Appendix A: Sources for Volume One, by chapters   443

Maps

1. Pueblos and Early Settlements   10–11
2. Spanish Expeditions   82

Contents

VOLUME TWO: *Mexico and the United States*

Book Three: The Mexican Rio Grande

1.	A Colony for Mexico	453
2.	A Wild Strain	460
3.	The Twin Sisters	469
4.	Last Return	473
5.	The Spark	474
6.	The *Ariel*	481
7.	Slavery	485
8.	Bad Blood	491
9.	The Mexico Trade	495
10.	Tormented Loyalties	505
11.	"God and Texas"	513
12.	From Mexico's Point of View	519
13.	Fortunes of New Mexico	541
	i. Peoples and Towns	541
	ii. Politics	544
	iii. Defense	545
	iv. Church and School	547
	v. Foreigners	549
14.	Revolt Up River	551
15.	The River Republic	559
16.	The Santa Fe Pioneers	569
17.	Border Smoke	585
18.	To Mier and Beyond	592
19.	Diplomacies	601
20.	The United States to the River	609

Contents   xvii

Book Four: The United States Rio Grande

   1. "Way, You Rio"   617
   2. Collective Prophecy   619
       i. New Man and New Principles   619
      ii. Frontier Attitudes   628
     iii. Woman and Home   631
     iv. Community Expression   635
      v. Language   638
     vi. Arts and Utility   642
    vii. Light in the Clearing   644
   viii. Sons of Harmony   647
     ix. Knacks and Crafts   651
      x. First Interpreters   655
     xi. The American Art   658
   3. Bivouac   660
   4. The Army of the Rio Grande   662
   5. The Cannonade   668
   6. Fort Texas   673
   7. The Listeners   679
   8. Palo Alto   682
   9. Resaca de la Palma   685
  10. The River Dead   689
  11. The Nation's War   692
  12. Invasion Summer   696
  13. Recurrent Frontier   701
  14. Upstream and Inland   709
  15. The Army of the West   716
  16. The Secret Agent   721
  17. Bloodless Possession   728
  18. The Army of Chihuahua   736
  19. The Free Missourians   742
  20. Brazito and the Pass   747
  21. Counterdance   753
  22. The Avengers   762
  23. Massacre at Taos   764
  24. Chihuahua   768

25. Trial at Taos   770
26. All on the Plains of Mexico   774
27. El Dorado   784
28. Contraband   788
29. A Thread of Spirit   793
30. Boundaries   799
31. Flag and Lamplight   806
32. The Rio Grande Divided   819
33. The Desolate   831
34. Confederate Border   834
35. The Second Mexican Empire   839
36. The Mexico Moon   845
37. Bad Men and Good   853
38. The Last Wagons   868
39. The Last Frontiersman   871
40. Treasure   887
41. The Last Earth Secrets   894
42. Revolution and Reflex   904
43. Utility and Vision   940
        i. Utility   940
       ii. Vision   944

Appendix B: Sources for Volume Two, by chapters   949

Appendix C: General Bibliography   957

Appendix D: The Names of the Rio Grande   981

Index   985

Maps
1. Texas and Mexico   450–451
2. New Mexico   614–615

Riverscape

*". . . Since I offered to narrate
the story, I shall start at the
beginning, which is as follows."*

—PEDRO DE CASTAÑEDA, OF NÁXERA

I.

Creation

Space.
Abstract movement.
The elements at large.

Over warm seas the air is heavy with moisture. Endlessly the vast delicate act of evaporation occurs. The seas yield their essence to the air. Sometimes it is invisible, ascending into the upper atmosphere. Sometimes it makes a shimmer in the calm light that proceeds universally from the sun. The upper heavens carry dust—sea dust of salt evaporated from ocean spray, and other dust lingering from volcanic eruption, and the lost dust of shooting stars that wear themselves out against the atmosphere through which they fly, and dust blown up from earth by wind. Invisibly the volume of sea moisture and dust is taken toward land by prevailing winds; and as it passes over the coast, a new condition arises—the wind-borne mass reflects earth temperatures, that change with the earth-forms inland from the sea. Moving rapidly, huge currents of air carrying their sea burdens repeat tremendously in their unseen movement the profile of the land forms over which they pass. When land sweeps up into a mountain, the laden air mass rolling upon it must rise and correspond in shape.

And suddenly that shape is made visible; for colder air above the mountain causes moisture to condense upon the motes of dust in the warm air wafted from over the sea; and directly in response to the presence and inert power of the mountain, clouds appear. The two volumes—invisible warm air, immovable cold mountain—continue to meet and repeat their joint creation of cloud. Looking from afar calm and eternal, clouds enclose forces of heat and cold, wind and inert

3

matter that conflict immensely. In such continuing turbulence, cloud
motes collide, cling together, and in the act condense a new particle of
moisture. Heavier, it falls from cold air through warmer. Colliding with
other drops, it grows. As the drops, colder than the earth, warmer than
the cloud they left, fall free of cloud bottom into clear air, it is raining.

Rain and snow fall to the earth, where much runs away on the
surface; but roots below ground and the dense nerve system of grasses
and the preservative cover of forest floors detain the runoff, so that
much sky moisture goes underground to storage, even through rock;
for rock is not solid, and through its pores and cracks and sockets
precipitation is saved. The storage fills; and nearing capacity, some of
its water reappears at ground level as springs which find upward release
through the pores of the earth just as originally it found entry. A flowing
spring makes its own channel in which to run away. So does the melt
from snow clinging to the highest mountain peaks. So does the sudden,
brief sheet of storm water. Seeking always to go lower, the running water
of the land struggles to fulfill its blind purpose—to find a way over,
around or through earth's fantastic obstacles back to the element which
gave it origin, the sea.

In this cycle a huge and exquisite balance is preserved. Whatever
the amount of its element the sea gives up to the atmosphere by evaporation, the sea regains exactly the same amount from the water which
falls upon the earth and flows back to its source.

This is the work, and the law, of rivers.

2.

Gazetteer

Out of such vast interaction between ocean, sky and land, the
Rio Grande rises on the concave eastern face of the Continental Divide
in southern Colorado. There are three main sources, about two and a

half miles high, amidst the Cordilleran ice fields. Flowing from the west, the river proper is joined by two confluents—Spring Creek from the north, and the South Fork. The river in its journey winds eastward across southern Colorado, turns southward to continue across the whole length of New Mexico which it cuts down the center, turns southeastward on reaching Mexico and with one immense aberration from this course—the Big Bend—runs on as the boundary between Texas and Mexico, ending at the Gulf of Mexico.

In all its career the Rio Grande knows several typical kinds of landscape, some of which are repeated along its great length. It springs from tremendous mountains, and intermittently mountains accompany it for three fourths of its course. It often lies hidden and inaccessible in canyons, whether they cleave through mountains or wide level plains. From such forbidding obscurities it emerges again and again into pastoral valleys of bounty and grace. These are narrow, at the most only a few miles wide; and at the least, a bare few hundred yards. In such fertile passages all is green, and the shade of cottonwoods and willows is blue and cool, and there is reward for life in water and field. But always visible on either side are reaches of desert, and beyond stand mountains that limit the river's world. Again, the desert closes against the river, and the gritty wastelands crumble into its very banks, and nothing lives but creatures of the dry and hot; and nothing grows but desert plants of thirsty pod, or wooden stem, or spiny defense. But at last the river comes to the coastal plain where an ancient sea floor reaching deep inland is overlaid by ancient river deposits. After turbulence in mountains, bafflement in canyons, and exhaustion in deserts, the river finds peaceful delivery into the sea, winding its last miles slowly through marshy bends, having come nearly one thousand nine hundred miles from mountains nearly three miles high. After the Mississippi-Missouri system, it is the longest river in the United States.

Along its way the Rio Grande receives few tributaries for so long a river. Some are sporadic in flow. Reading downstream, the major tributaries below those of the source are Rock Creek, Alamosa Creek, Trinchera Creek and the Conejos River in Colorado; in New Mexico, the Red River, the Chama River, and four great draws that are generally dry except in storm when they pour wild volumes of silt into the main channel—Galisteo Creek, the Jemez River, Rio Puerco and Rio Salado; and in Texas and Mexico, the Rio Conchos (which renews the river as it is about to die in the desert), the Pecos River, the Devil's River, (another) Rio Salado and Rio San Juan. The river commonly does not

carry a great volume of water, and in some places, year after year, it
barely flows, and in one or two it is sometimes dry. Local storms will
make it rush for a few hours; but soon it is down to its poor level again.
Even at its high sources the precipitation averages only five inches year-
round. At its mouth, the rainfall averages in the summer between twenty
and thirty inches, but there the river is old and done, and needs no
new water. In January, at the source the surface temperature is fourteen
degrees on the average, and in July fifty degrees. At the mouth in the
same months the averages read fifty and sixty-eight. In the mountainous
north the river is clear and sparkling, in the colors of obsidian, with
rippling folds of current like the markings on a trout. Once among the
pastoral valleys and the desert bench terraces that yield silt, the river is
ever after the color of the earth that it drags so heavily in its shallow
flow.

Falling from so high to the sea, and going so far to do it, the
river with each of its successive zones encounters a new climate. Winter
crowns the source mountains almost the whole year round, in the longest
season of cold in the United States. The headwaters are free of frost for
only three months out of the year, from mid-June to mid-September.
Where the river carves its way through the mesas of northern New
Mexico, the seasons are temperate. Entering the Texas desert, the river
finds perennial warmth that rises in summer to blasting heat. At its
end, the channel wanders under the heavy moist air of the tropics, mild
in winter, violently hot in summer.

3.

Cycle

Landscape is often seen as static; but it never is static. From its
first rock in the sky to its last embrace by the estuary at the sea, the
river has been surrounded by forces and elements constantly moving

and dynamic, interacting to produce its life and character. It has taken ocean and sky; the bearing of winds and the vagary of temperature; altitude and tilt of the earth's crust; underground waters and the spill of valleys and the impermeable texture of deserts; the cover of plants and the uses of animals; the power of gravity and the perishability of rock; the thirst of things that grow; and the need of the sea to create the Rio Grande.

The main physical circumstances of the Rio Grande are timeless. They assume meaning only in terms of people who came to the river.

BOOK ONE

The Indian Rio Grande

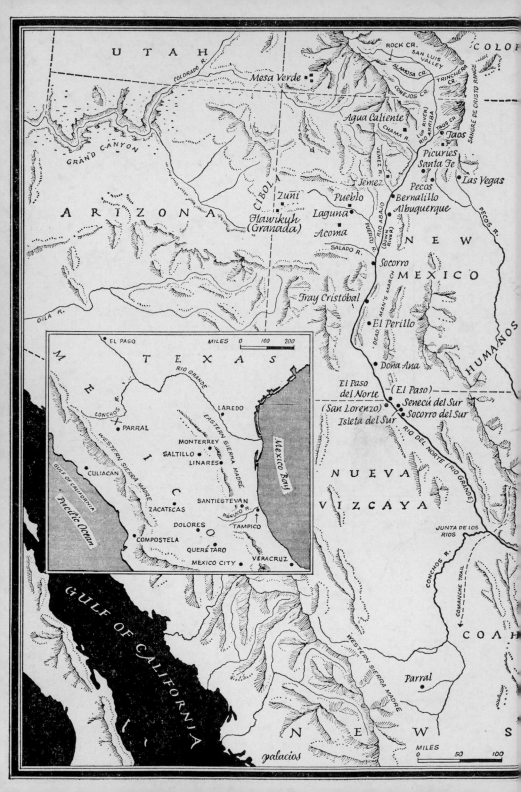

I.

The Ancients

THERE WAS NO RECORD BUT MEMORY and it became tradition and then legend and then religion. So long ago that they did not know themselves how long, their ancestors, the ancient people, moved. They went with the weather. Seasons, generations, centuries went by as each brought discovery of places farther toward the morning, across vacant Asia. They were guided that way by the lie of mountains, whose vast trough lay northeastward and southwestward. There was toil enough for people in taking their generations through valleys, without crossing the spines of mountains. But valleys end at the sea, and finally the people saw it too. The Asian continent ended, except for an isthmus of land or ice that remained above the waters. They crossed it, not in a day, or a year perhaps; perhaps it took lifetimes to find and keep what the bridge led to. But lost memory has no time, only action; and they came to North America, bringing their animals, their blind history, their implements and the human future of two continents. Once again they encountered mountains which became their immovable guides. The entire vast new land lay on an axis of north and south, and its greatest mountains did also. Having entered at the north, the people must move southward, between the sea and the mountains.

Movement, however laborious, slow and lost in dangers it may have been, was the very nature of their lives. Through age after age it took them down the continent, across another isthmus, and into the great continent to the south, until the antipodean ice fields were joined by the disorderly but urgent line of mankind. Movement was what kept them alive, for they lived by hunting animals that followed the seasons.

They knew how to twist vegetable fibres until they had string.

They could bend a branch until it made a bow by which a string could be tautly stretched. With bow, then, and arrow, they brought down game. There was another weapon, a throwing stick, with which to kill. Fish in the streams were taken with the harpoon. Its points, and those of arrows, were chipped from stone; often from glittering, sharp volcanic glass. Birds and fish were snared with nets. These measures travelled easily. They were light, efficient, and imaginative.

There were others called alive in their consequence. To make fire, the ancient people set a wooden drill into a socket in a small wooden hearth, and rotated the drill with their palms. Smoke came. They blew upon it. Coals glowed and under breath burst into flame. It was possible to cook. They heated stones and in vessels of wood or bark, even of animal hide dried and toughened, cooked the booty of the hunt. When it was time again to move, valuable leftovers could be carried in baskets invented and woven as baggage. With them travelled, or crouched to eat, a clever, fond and valiant friend whose ancestors too had made the timeless migration. He was the dog.

Throughout ages of lost memory the people possessed the new continents and found great regions within which to rove, above and below the equator, as loosely scattered groups. Vast localisms determined their ways—whether they pursued animals on plains, or hunted for berries in mountains, or clung to the unvarying climate of warm zones in one luxuriant wilderness after another. It took a mystery of the vegetable world to unfold for them in slow discovery a new way of life. There was a seed which could be eaten. It could be planted. It could be watered and made to grow at the hunter's will. It could multiply. It could be carried far and planted elsewhere. Wherever it took root it afforded food. It made a place where the people could stay season after season. It kept the hunters home, and their women and children and dogs, relieved of their wandering in search of life itself. Up from the warm zones of the earth it travelled from tribe to tribe, until most of the people who lived in the huge valleys and basins of the cordilleras knew how to use it, and using it, gradually discovered the arts of living together. Their histories were changed by it. The laws of its growth created their dwellings, their sense of property and brought them their gods, and its crushed seed became their most habitual and sacred offering in prayer. It was maize, or Indian corn.

In becoming farmers the ancient people looked for the most suitable places in which to remain. Corn needed water. Water flowed down the mountains making streams. In the grand valleys were many isolated mountain fragments standing separate whose heights were secure against animal and human dangers. When people could stay where they chose to stay there was time, there was imagination, to improve their conditions of life. A surplus of corn required some place in which to store it, safe against waste and thieving little animals. Dry caves in rocky cliffs seemed made by nature for the purpose. But food was wealth and people protected it in the caves by hauling stones, making enclosures which they sealed with clay which dried solid. The wall of a bin protecting food could be extended to make walls which gave shelter. Boldly beautiful rooms were made in the cliffs, some of masonry, some carved with obsidian knives out of rich soft yellow tufa itself. Arising independently, some at the same time, some at other times, and almost all on the western slopes of the continental divide in the American Southwest, many such cliff cities of the high plateaus were settled and developed by hunters who learned how to become farmers. After thousands of years of migration across continents in search of the always moving forms of live food, it took only a few hundred years of settled agriculture for the ancient people to discover how to satisfy their prime hunger, and find time and ways in which to recognize other hungers and give form to their satisfaction, socially, morally and spiritually. And though in their slowly developed mastery of how to grow corn they needed not only the seed but also water, they established their plateau cities not by the banks of the three or four great rivers that rose in the mountain system that had pointed the path for their ancestors, but on mesas and in valleys touched by little streams, some of them not even perennial in their flow.

Nor did all of the ancient people find the secret of maize. Some who found eastern gateways in the mountains spread themselves out on the great plains where for long succeeding centuries they continued to rove as hunters, governed by solstice and the growing seasons of animal feed. In time the wanderers heard of the plateau cities and their riches stored against hunger and the hardships of travel. Raids resulted, and battle, devastations and triumphant thefts, leaving upon the withdrawal of the nomads new tasks of rebuilding and revival according to the customs of the farmers who long ago had given up the bare rewards of the chase for hard but dependable and peaceful cultivation of the land.

If there was little regular communication between the scattered cliff cities of southwestern Colorado, northeastern Arizona, and northern New Mexico, and if there were local differences between their ways,

still they solved common mysteries in much the same fashion and in
their several responses to the waiting secrets of earth, sky and mind, they
made much the same fabric of life for people together.

2.

The Cliffs

The fields were either on the mesa top above the cliff cities or
on the canyon floor below. At sunup the men went to cultivate their
crops. Corn was planted a foot deep, and earth was kept piled up about
the stalks, to give them extra growing strength and moisture. Every
means was used to capture water. Planting was done where flood waters
of the usually dry stream beds came seasonally. But there were long
summers without rain. The winter snows filtered into porous sandstone
until they met hard rock and found outlets in trickles down canyon
walls. The people scooped basins out of the rock to collect such precious
flow, from which they carried water by hand to the growing stalks.
The mesa tops were gashed at the edges by sloping draws which fell
away to the valley floor, like the spaces between spread fingers. Between
the great stone fingers the people built small stone dams to catch storm
waters running off the plateau. Occasionally springs came to the surface
in the veined rock of the cliffs and were held sacred.

Seeds were planted and crops cultivated with a stick about a
yard long which could poke holes in the earth or turn it over. The
prevailing crop was red corn, and others were pumpkin, beans and
cotton. Wild sunflowers yielded their seeds which were eaten. When
the crop was harvested it became the charge of the women, who were
ready to receive it and store it in baskets which they wove to hold about
two bushels. Flat stone lids were fashioned to seal the baskets, which
went into granaries built by the men. Part of the seed was ground between suitably shaped stones, and part was kept for planting. If meal

was the staff of life, it was varied by meat from wild game including
the deer, the fox, the bear, the mountain sheep and the rabbit.

As they lived through the centuries learning how to work and
build together, the ancient people made steady and continuous progress
in all ways. If their first permanent houses had only one room with a
connecting underground ceremonial chamber and storeroom, they increasingly reflected the drawing together of individuals into community
life in a constantly elaborated form of the dwelling. The rooms came
together, reinforcing one another with the use of common walls, and
so did families. The rooms rose one upon another until terraced houses
three and four stories high were built. The masonry was expert and
beautiful, laid in a variety of styles. The builders were inventive. They
thought of pillars, balconies, and interior shafts for ventilation. They
made round towers and square towers. And they placed their great house-
cities with an awesome sense of location, whether on the crown of a mesa
or in the wind-made architectural shell of a long arching cave in the
cliffside. The work was prodigious. In one typical community house
fifty million pieces of stone were quarried, carried and laid in its walls.
Forests were far away; yet thousands of wooden beams, poles and joins
were cut from timber and hauled to their use in the house. From the
immediate earth untold tons of mortar were mixed and applied—and
all this by the small population of a single group dwelling.

The rooms averaged eight by ten feet in size, with ceilings reaching from four feet to eight. There were no windows. Doors were narrow
and low, with high sills. The roof was made of long heavy poles laid
over the walls, and thatched with small sticks or twigs, finally covered
with mud plaster in a thick layer. The floor was of hard clay washed
with animal blood and made smooth, in a shiny black. Walls were
polished with burnt gypsum. Along their base was a painted band of
yellow ochre, taken as raw mineral from the softly decaying faces of the
cliffs where great stripes of the dusty gold color were revealed by the
wearing of wind and water. Round chambers of great size and majesty
were built underground for religious and ceremonial use. Many cities
had a dozen or more such rooms, each dedicated to the use of a separate
religious cult or fraternity. One had a vault with a covering of timber
which resounded like a great drum when priests danced upon it.

In the ceremonial kivas men kept their ritual accessories and the
tools of their crafts. They made tools out of bones—deer, rabbit, bird,
and of deerhorn and mountain sheep horn. Their knives and hunting
points and grinding tools and scraping tools for dressing skins and

gravers for carving and incising and axes and chisels for cutting and shaping wood and mauls for breaking rock were made out of stone.

Baskets were woven for light, mobile use at first, when the people kept moving, and as they found ways to settle in their cities they continued to use baskets for cooking, storage and hauling. But more durable and more widely useful vessels could be made out of clay; and so the women developed in connection with domestic arts the craft of pottery. Their early attempts imitated the construction of basketry, with long clay ropes coiled into enclosing form which was not smoothed over on the surface. But for greater comeliness and better protection against leakage and breakage the surfaces of pots were eventually made smooth and fired with glazes. Natural mineral pigments gave each locality its characteristic pottery style—now red clay, again ochre, white gypsum, iron-black.

In warm weather the people lived naked; in cold they wore fur-cloth and feather-cloth robes and leggings, and dressed skins. Thread was made from yucca fibre. Both men and women wore ornaments created out of beads—stone, shell, bone. Feather tassels, bright with color, hung from garments. Small pieces of chipped or cut turquoise were put together in mosaic for pendants and bracelets. Fashion had its power, modifying out of sheer taste rather than utility various details of dress. The sandal fringe of one period was missing from the next.

For hundreds of years this busy life with all its ingenuities, its practices whose origins lacking written record were lost among the dead ancestors, its growing body of worship of all creation, its personal and collective sorrows, its private and communal joys, rose and flourished with the affirmative power of living prophecy. Were they being readied to imagine a greatness beyond themselves in the future? Already they had found for the material face of life a grace and beauty whose evidence would endure like the mountain stuff out of which they had made it. The people grew their nourishment on plateaus that reached toward the sun. They put about themselves like garments the enfolding substances of cliffs. They looked out in daylight upon breathtaking views of intercourse between sky and ground, where light and shadow and color and distance in their acts of change made in every moment new aspects of the familiar natural world. Amidst the impassive elegance of mountains, valleys and deserts they fulfilled their needs with intimacy and modesty in their use of natural things. With no communication through time but the living voice, for they had no records but their own refuse, the power of their hooded thoughts brought them a long

way from the straggle out of Asia tens of centuries before to the flowering
civilization of the cliffs, the plateaus and the canyons.

And at just the long moment in their story when all material
evidence seemed to promise life more significant than that which they
had so laboriously made so beautiful, mysteriously, in city after city
among the plateaus, they left it never to return.

3.

To the River

Their departures were orderly. Not all occurred at the very same
instant, but all took place late in the thirteenth century and early in
the fourteenth, and all gave evidence of having been agreed upon. Their
houses were left standing. Their rooms were neat and emptied of
possessions needed for travel and new life elsewhere. But for occasional
bits of corn and stalk and tassel the food bins were bare. The dead
were left in peaceful burial according to regular custom. Few personal
objects—clothing, jewelry, ceremonial effects—were left behind. Fires died
in their proper places. There was no sign of the applied torch. Sudden
natural calamity—earthquake, flood, lightning-set holocaust—played no
part. The cities, one by one, at the point of their highest development,
were left to time and the amber preservative of dry sunlit air.

Again the people left no record, and carried none with them,
written, or even pictorial, to explain these abandonments. Perhaps for
a few generations memory told the story, until gradually it was lost in
the recesses of time. The only records which can be consulted are those
of the natural world. They have been much invoked and disputed by
experts.

The trees have testified. By counting the rings of annual growth
in the cross section of a trunk, a system of dating has been devised. By
comparing the thickness and thinness of the successive rings, periods of

relative wetness or dryness have been tabulated. According to such information the century of the migrations from the plateaus coincided with a period of increasing dryness, until crops could no longer be watered, and the people were faced with living on the seed corn and finally starvation. A search for new watered lands was the only recourse.

Erosion has been blamed. Too much timber was cut for building use. Bared forest lands permitted too rapid runoff of storm-water. Gullies were lengthened until their waters became ungovernable for flood-farming. Old fields had to be abandoned and new ones begun farther from the houses and from water sources.

But erosion presupposes flow of water, and the drought theory contradicts the erosion theory. And though some scientists say that the entire region during its whole period of occupation by people has been slowly growing drier, they say further that the rate of desiccation would not in itself account for these migrations. And one of the greatest of the communities—in Chaco Canyon—was abandoned a century before the tree-ring evidence of the great drought. On top of this, lately, the whole responsibility of the tree-ring theory has been shaken by comparison of ancient rings formed when there were no written records with more recent rings which when checked against modern meteorological records show no consistent correlation with thickness and thinness of the rings in wet and dry periods as scientifically recorded. The drought theory holds no firm answer.

In the canyon of the Rito de los Frijoles the river is an ever-flowing stream. Yet the cliff dwellings there and the houses of the canyon floor were abandoned just like communities near streams which were intermittent and for the most part dry. Lack of water was not a motive for the silencing of the Rito.

The mystery has been attacked in other ways.

Did the soft rock of the cliff dwellings disintegrate too fast and force the people to move? But the rooms are still intact today.

Were there epidemics of other disease? Burials reveal no evidence of unusual numbers of deaths in any one period.

Was the prevailing diet of corn meal—hard and coarse, and especially when old as hard as gravel—the cause of disease? Recovered skulls show teeth ground down to the bone as a result of chewing the tough meal. Tooth decay led to abscesses, lodged poisons, rheumatism, arthritis and diet deficiencies. Did the people go to look in new places for other foods? But wherever they resettled, corn remained their staple food, and does today.

Did nomadic enemies cut off water supplies and drive the people from their towns? There would have been battles, and if defeated, the city dwellers would have left their homes in disarrayed flight. There was no evidence to indicate siege and defeat.

Did the pattern of community life become so complex as the towns grew that political quarrels between clans and religious fraternities broke apart the order of existence and made communal life impossible and migration imperative? If so, then why did not one or more clans survive dissension and continue in possession of the houses? But no one was left behind. And when the people found their new homesites, they recreated the same social pattern they had expressed in the cliff cities, in some instances building even larger cities with greater populations and more group divisions.

All efforts to explain the mystery on the basis of physical or material motives come to nothing. What is left? Where might the explanation lie? The people left beautiful cities and looked for new places to live. Consulting the favor of the natural world, many of them came at last through the barrier mountains to the river, the big river, P'osoge, or the big water, Hanⁿyap'akwa, or just the river, Tšina, where they found scattered settlements of people raising corn and living in primitive pit-houses. Life was already blessed there. The new settlers joined the old. The Pueblos of the Rio Grande were founded. What drove the people from the silent cities they had left behind them might well have been something they carried within themselves; something with more power over their acts than heat or cold, rain or dust, sickness or war or dissension. If they had reason to believe that their gods had abandoned them where they lived, the people would have had to go and find them again, in order to live at peace with the world of nature. As everything had its abiding spirit, not only things that grew, but inanimate things, and places, so with the loss of that spirit would be lost blessing, protection, safety. In fear and trembling the people would have had to abandon a place, no matter how splendid, from which the ruling deity had withdrawn. Any event, natural or imaginary, which would withdraw the gods of a place would make it accursed, and dangerous to life; and no matter how great hitherto it may have become, it would be abandoned.

They told stories through the centuries of such a motive for migration from various places. What was believed true of one place could be so of another.

In cliff towns of the Pajarito Plateau west of the river the people

said that A-wan-yu lived among them, their deity. He was the plumed
snake, creature of both air and land. A time came when they lost favor
with him. He abandoned them, retired to the sky, and became the
major galaxy of stars which reached across the central heavens as the
Milky Way. Without him the people were at a loss. They gathered their
life and its objects and, leaving their rooms in modest order, went away
to build new cities on the river.

At the greatest of cliff cities (Mesa Verde) the people began to
build a temple to the sun. It sat upon a crown of the mesa between
valley and sky. Using the skin-colored stone of the place, they quarried
and shaped their blocks and raised their walls in expert masonry. The
temple contained many rooms. The largest was a round one in the center.
Little junipers whose shape echoed the pull of the wind grew all about
the temple. Close to its doors the mesa's cliffs swept away to the valley
floor far below. It was a noble site facing the rising sun. To reach it
with stone and timber took prodigious work. The work went slowly. The
walls rose carefully to the same successive heights day by day or year
by year. But they were never finished. Before they could be, all human
life departed from the mesa, with its fields on top, its farms below in
the valley, and its magnificent community houses high up in the faces
of the cliffs. What if before the sun temple could be completed there
was no god to receive in it? The people could only leave what they had
partially done, with all of its walls unfinished at the same height, and
go away.

Long later, in another ancient town, east of the river, the people
kept a great black snake in the kiva, who had power over their life. They
fed him the fruits of the hunt—deer, antelope, rabbit, bison, birds. From
him they received all they needed to eat and to wear—corn, squash,
berries, fruit of the yucca and cactus; shoes, leggings, shirts of soft deerskin. One night at midnight he left them. In the morning they found
that he was gone. He left his track and they followed it. It took them
down a dry river of white stones and clay (Galisteo Creek) which at last
entered into the big river (Rio Grande), where the track was lost in the
ever-flowing water. They returned to their town and discussed their
trouble. "The snake has gone. What are we going to have of those things
which he gave us? He has gone away. Now we also must be going away,"
they said. They worked together at the sorrowful job of taking up their
things, and went down the dry river to the big river, where they found
another town already living. There they took up their lives again amidst
the gods of that place.

Fear of their gods may well have sent the cliff people from the mesas to the river. Bringing their high culture from the plateaus, the people wedded it to the primitive human ways they found along the Rio Grande, and once again with the approval of the gods made for themselves a settled life, sure of land, water, and corn, and of what explained fear and what creation.

4.

The Stuff of Life

i. creation and prayer

Most intimately they could watch creation as a child was born. So from the womb of the earth itself they said all life came forth long ago. The underworld was dark and mysterious. People and animals lived there and knew their mother, who was kind and loving, even though she remained far from the daily lives of her children. So they accounted for the impersonality of nature. As all life came from the underworld, so it returned there in death. To come in life and go in death, people and animals had to pass through a lake between the underworld and the world. The first people climbed up a great fir tree through the waters of the lake and entered this world. The place where they emerged was in the north and was called Shipapu.* Emergence into the world was a tremendous act, full of awe for what was left behind, and of fear and respect for what was found above, on the earth and in the sky. A thing ever afterward could be made sacred simply by saying "It came up with us."

With them came spirit, and could dwell in everything upon the

---

* With many variants, like all proper names in the myths.

earth. All spirit was like that of people. Rock, trees, plants; animals, birds, fish; places, directions, the bodies and acts of the sky; the live and the dead; things found or things made—all had the same spirit and behaved in the same ways as men and women. Some spirit was good and some bad, and accordingly had to be propitiated or guarded against. And sometimes spirit would leave its visible form and be gone. If it was bad spirit, people could rejoice; if good, they must mourn at having lost favor with the powers of their lives.

Everything in the world was part of the same living force, whether thought, action, object or creature. Of all this the earth was the center, and all things existed in order to help people to live upon it. And the center of the earth—earth's navel—was in the center of each group of people and their own city. All things reached out in widening circles of awareness from the very point of the self, individual, and the group, collective. From the center, then, of person and place, reached the six directions, each with its animal deity: north, with the mountain lion; west, with the bear; south, with the badger; east, with the wolf; the zenith, with the eagle; and the nadir, with the shrew. North and west produced the snow; south and east the rain. So the reach of Pueblo belief went across the earth, and into the depths underground and into the heights of the sky, and all tied to the place of emergence which was imitated with a stone-lined pit in the center of each ceremonial chamber, and sometimes out in the open in the very center of the town placita itself. All forces interacted to make life; and of these, none was greater in effect, sacredness and poetry than the sky, with its heroes, goddesses, and ancestors.

"Our Father Sun," they said. Some said that even the sun had ancestors—two mothers, who before the people came from the underworld saw that people must have light in order to see. The mothers fashioned the sun out of a white shell, a pink abalone shell, a turquoise and a red stone. They carried him to the east and in the morning climbed a high mountain. They dropped the sun behind the mountain; and presently he began to rise, taking his way over trails that ran above the waters of the sky, toward the evening. He set toward the lake which lay between the world and the underworld. He went down through the lake and when it was night on the earth he shone dimly below in the underworld. In the morning again he arose and again the people saw him with joy. What they saw was not the sun himself but a large mask that covered his whole body. By his light everyone saw that the world was large and beautiful. The sun saw and knew, like any other person.

And others said that he walked through the sky dressed in white deer-skin which flashed with countless beads. His face, hidden by a mask, was beautiful. They said he was the father of the twin boys, Masewi and Oyoyewi, the young gods of war, who protected the people by killing their enemies. The concept of evil, menace, hugeness of danger was defeated by the dream of small, immature mortals—the very cast of hope in people who first imagined their survival and triumph, then willed it, and then achieved it through the spirit which towered to victory over threatening forces. Power and strength came from the sun, as they could plainly see in the daily life all about them. "Our Father Sun" governed the overworld.

But when he went down through the sacred lake at evening the world was dark. He needed a companion god in the sky at night. So they said that the two mothers who made the sun also made the moon, taking a dark stone, different kinds of yellow stone, turquoise and a red stone, and placed it in the sky, where it followed by night the same trails which the sun followed by day. The moon was a mystery, and some said it was a man, others a woman.

Because the moon travelled slowly, not always giving light, the stars were needed, and were made out of crystal which sparkled and shone. At morning a great star shone into the dawn, and at evening another flashed slowly in the west even before the daylight was all gone at the place where the sun went below. They were clear in the heavens, along with many others, hanging near in power and beauty when the night was clear and dark, making at least some things certain and pure in a world where evil spirit could bring about change among people and things, and cause fear.

When clouds came, they brought rain, which blessed the earth and made things grow. Who loved the people and blessed them? The dead ancestors, who once were people, and who came back as clouds to do good for those whose life they already knew, with its constant hope, need and prayer for rain. Clouds were prayed to. The prayers took many forms. Feathers were used to imitate clouds and were put on top of headdresses and sacred masks. Visible prayers were put together out of little sticks decorated with feathers. These could be set about and left as invocations from earth to sky. The dead who departed to life in the clouds were in some places prepared with white paint on the forehead, and feathers and cotton placed in the hair, so that cloud would go to cloud and come back bringing rain.

Lightning, they said, was born of mischief by Masewi and Oyoyewi.

The twin war godlings once came to an empty kiva in a village of another world. While all the people were elsewhere the boys stole bows and arrows from the kiva wall and tried to escape unnoticed; but they were seen, their theft discovered, and they were chased by outraged people. Just where they had come from their own world to the other one, and as they were about to be taken, the adventurers were picked up by a whirlwind and thrust back into their own world, where they went home. On the way, Masewi sent an arrow high up to the sky. It made a grand noise. The womenfolk saw it and fainted. The boys shot many more arrows. These were the first bolts of lightning known by the people. Some days later here came rainclouds, bringing the arrows back and delivering rain with many flashes and noises. Arrows fell. The twins were glad their arrows came back to them. Sky arrows were holy to hunters, who prayed to lightning when they got ready to hunt. Thunder was made by an old goddess. They said medicine men could send for thunder and receive it at any time. The wind had a divinity, too, sometimes man, sometimes woman. There was an aged god of the rainbow. When the war twins wanted to visit their father the sun, they walked on the rainbow which quickly took them to him in mid-sky.

The Pueblos said, then, recognizing the exchange of influences and acts between earth and sky, that the Old Man of the Sky was the husband of the Old Woman of the Earth. All things came from their union, just as the child came from the union of man and woman. Mankind and the animals, the earth and the sky with all their elements, all had the same kind of life; and a person must be in harmony with the life in all things. The way to find it was in religion. Prayer and observances were part of all daily life. Bound upon the earth with other living things, the Pueblos said that the same life belonged in everything, and that life was either male or female. Everything they believed came within the frame of those two ideas.

Prayer took many forms.

Sometimes it was only the person who prayed; and sometimes the whole family, or fraternity, or town. Prayers were always visible, a stuff was used, in an act, to make plain the desire locked in the heart. Of all prayer substances, the most common was meal, ground once, from white corn. It had life in it, it came from something that once grew, it fed life in people, its seed made more life in the ground. The Pueblo person took it in his hand and breathed upon it as he prayed. "Eat" he said to it, and then he sprinkled it into the air, or over the ground, or upon the person, place, thing, or animal he wanted to bless. At sunrise he would go out and sprinkle meal and say a prayer. When holy men, or hunters, or warriors went by his house before or after doing their work, he would come to his wall, breathe upon meal, and sprinkle it before their steps. His fingers were bunched at his lips holding the pinch of meal. In breathing upon it he gave his living essence to it. His inward prayer made an arc of spirit from him to all godliness; and his arm when he swept it widely to sprinkle the meal had a noble reach in it; for a gesture can always be bigger than the little member which makes it.

Sometimes pollen from flowers was used and spread in prayer in just the same way.

Another form of prayer, one which lasted longer, and could be left to bear testimony and intercede by itself, was the prayer stick. It was used in every group ceremonial in some pueblos, and often a whole ritual was built around it. It was also used privately. Much care, ingenuity and taste went into its making. The prayer stick was as long as from the wrist to the end of the middle finger. It was cut from oak, willow, spruce or cottonwood. Its stem was richly painted with colors taken from the earth. There was turquoise color, made out of malachite or copper ore mixed with white bean meal. Yellow ochre came from canyon or gully faces, exposed in stripes by long weather. Shale made black. Pale clay made white, iron-stained sandstone made red, and from cactus flowers or purple cornhusk came violet. The colors were mixed with water from sacred springs, and with flowers from the bee-plant. Honey was sprayed on the paint after it was applied. The sky was called by feathers bound onto the prayer stick. Turkey, duck, hawk and eagle; flicker, jay, bluebird, oriole, towhee, yellow warbler feathers were used. To speak to cloud spirits, downy or breast feathers were bound in with the feather bundles. Beads were added sometimes.

When the prayer stick was made, it was prayed over and exposed to smoke. It was breathed upon and given its intention. Then it was taken to do its work. Perhaps it was set up in the house where it would stay for life, expressing its prayer forever. It might be taken to the fields and buried; or set in the riverbank; or taken to a holy spring and established at its lip; or carried high into the mountains to make a remote shrine; or put away with stored food; or sealed up in the wall of a new house; or carried in the hand during ceremonials; or put to earth with the dead. If a prayer stick was left in an exposed place, they could tell by whether it stood or fell how the spirit of its maker was. If it fell, he must have had bad thought while making it, and his offering was in consequence rejected.

Sometimes prayer and its acts were delegated. Certain persons became priests and acted for everyone else. It was agreed that nature did what the priests told it to do. The priests spoke to the world in grander ways than anyone else. When they meant "four years" they would say "four days," for example. But everyone knew what they meant when they sounded special. It was part of their having power. People watched to see that the priests used their power when it was needed, such as those times every year when the sun had to be turned back. All summer long the sun moved farther to the south, toward the badger. The weather was colder. Every year, in the same month, there came a point beyond which the sun must not be permitted to go. They would know by watching the sun come to a natural landmark when the limit of his southern journey was reached. At that point, on that day, it was the duty of the priests to halt the sun; and with prayer, ceremony and power, make the sun start northward in the sky once again, in its proper way. Half a year later, when the sun touched the point to the north, with the mountain lion, beyond which it must never be allowed to go, the priests brought it back toward the south again. So the natural cycles were preserved. What nature had already ordered was ordered once again by the people in their prayers. To rise above, govern and hold the natural world they imagined their own control of it and solemnly sanctioned the inevitable.

Other ways to pray and gain favor were found in imitating what nature looked like and did. And here the great group prayer was made, when the people came together in ceremony to tell nature what it must do for their lives.

They gave great splendor to the group prayer, and prepared for it with rigor, always in the same ways which had come down to them out of memory. A certain society of men learned invocations and chants which lasted for hours, and had to be word-perfect. They learned choruses and strict drumbeats to accompany them. Sacred costumes were made, and the materials for them came from expeditions, often to the mountains and even farther—boughs of the pine tree, skins of the fox and the rabbit, the deer, the buffalo, the bobcat; feathers from eagles, the bright parrots of the south; and from nearer home, gourds to dry and fill with pebbles from the arroyos, cornhusks to weave into headdresses, paint to put on the body. Groups of men and groups of women worked at practicing over and over the steps of the dance to be used in the ceremony. They must stand—the men separate from the women—just so, and to the beat of the drum, they must lift and put down their feet so, all exactly together; they must turn, and pause, and advance, facing

newly, and the women's bare feet must be lifted only a little and put
down again mildly, while the men must smartly raise their feet in their
soft deerskin shoes and bring them down to pound on the ground with
power. The singers and the dancers and the drummers learned perfect
accord. Implements were ma_e in the ceremonial chambers to be used
on the day of the group prayer which was held in the plaza of the town.
All persons, young and old, worked toward the day. Men and women
could not lie together for a certain period before it. Only certain foods
might be eaten. For several days before, those who were going to take
part made sure to vomit many times a day. The dancing ground was
swept clean. If there was any refuse about the houses it was taken away.
Thoughts were put in order too. Some of the figures in the dance were
going to be the clowns, the spirits who mocked and scolded humanity,
whose very thoughts they could see. And above all, there would be certain masked figures who came there from the other world. All the women
knew that these were gods themselves—the spirits of rain and growth—
who wore wooden coverings on their heads, trimmed with downy
feathers, painted to represent the deities of the sky. These were the most
mysterious and powerful of all the dancers. They had naked arms and
breasts and legs like any other men, and wore foxtails on their rumps.
and had pine boughs banded upon their arms, and wore the woven belts
and the rabbit-fur baldrics and deerskin shoes, and used the gourds like
the real men, but the women said they were not real men, they were
actual gods, called the kachinas, and upon them depended the rainfall,
the crops and the yield of the hunt. All year, said the women, their
masks were kept in the ceremonial chamber, and when time came for
the group prayer, they came like gods and put them on, and appeared
in the ceremony. The men knew something else. They knew that long
ago, before anybody could remember, or think of it, the kachinas really
came and danced with the people. But for a long time they had not
really come. It was actually certain men who put on the masks and
appeared as the kachinas. But they never told the women of the substi-
tution. Children did not know of it, either; and only boys, when they
reached a certain age, learned of it, and kept the secret among their sex.
If the gods were properly imitated, then they would do as their imitators
did, and make the motions which would produce rain, growth and
game.

When the day came the whole pueblo was ready. Those who did
not dance sat in silence upon the rooftops or against the walls upon the
ground. All was still in the early sunlight. The houses, made of earth,

looked like mesas, and cast strong shadows. People waited as nature
waited for whatever might come. The ground before the houses was
empty and clean, dazzling in the light. What would break the silence,
and release the bodies full of prayer?

It was a thunderclap which came suddenly and rocked from wall
to wall, in the voice of the drums. The drums told the thunder what to
do; and thunder, born of storm, would bring rain.

At once the first dancers came like creatures of the air out of the
door in the flat roof of the ceremonial chamber; and at the same instant
song began and the drums sounded with it. The chorus appeared from
between two houses and came to the plaza.

Then the dancers came, great ranks of them, the men in front,
the women behind them, led by a man holding a long pole into the air,
decorated with eagle feathers that spoke to the sky, as from one cloud
to another. They all advanced as slowly as a shadow from a high cloud
on a still day; but they never ceased their movement. The men pounded
the stamped ground. The women padded softly upon it. The men commanded nature. The women waited to receive it. Slowly the long columns
reached out and out into the dancing-ground until they were all seen.
They crossed it. They faced and returned. The chorus and the drummers sang and beat without falter. Everyone was exactly together in
rhythm and action. The evolutions of the dancing and singing groups
were made so gradually and in such slowly changed relation to one
another that they seemed like the slow wheeling of the stars overhead
at night.

In their right hands the men held the rattles of dried gourds
containing seed pods or pebbles. With these at intervals they clattered
upon the ground the sound of seeds falling; and again they showered
together upon the earth the sound of falling rain.

In their left hands the men and women carried bunches of eagle
feathers which like those on the banner that towered above them and
went with them in their grave evolutions invoked the clouds of the sky.

In their left hands the women carried pine boughs; and pine
boughs were bound upon the arms of the men. These were a prayer for
everlasting life, for the pine tree was always green.

The men proclaimed by their presence the seed, and invoked it,
and wet it, pounding their power into the earth, and ordered that it
live and grow.

The women impassively like the earth itself showed by their
presence how the seed was received and nurtured.

With their pine boughs spaced throughout the ranks, they looked like a little forest. Advancing powerfully against the light they were like a movement of the earth in an analogy of slow time. The voices of the singers barked together and made order out of the sounds of the animal kingdom. The arms moved, the legs rose and fell, the bodies travelled in such unanimity and decorum that they all seemed like a great woven construction, something man-made, some vast act of basketry, the parts tied and yet flexible in supple buckskin; again, moving against the sidelines, they seemed like a cliff advancing; or if the watchers shut their eyes and only listened for a moment, they heard the singing voices clapping flatly back from the facing houses, and the clatter of seeds, the swipe of rain, the breeze of pine trees, the rattle of little shells tied to costumes, and in all of it the spacious and secret sound of the sky into which all other sounds disappeared and were taken to the gods.

All day long the insistent pounding of the prayer went on.

The clowns—koshare—played about the undisturbed edges of the formal dancing groups. They were painted white, with here and there a black stripe. They were naked, and used their nakedness in comic outrage and in joking punishment of generative power. They leaped and ran. They now went soberly by the dancers and jogged like them and then broke away to enact a burlesque at a corner of the dancing-ground. A little boy or two, painted like them, capered along with them learning the mocking idiom of the people's self-critics. Against so much work and preparation and proper devoutness in the great dance, it was necessary to send a different kind of prayer through the antics of the koshare—all the things the people knew about themselves but would not say separately. Fun included hurting. About that there was nothing odd. Much of life hurt.

The masked gods moved with the men.

The singers and drummers, massed closely together, turned and changed formation, now into a solid square, now a circle, but so slowly that the watchers hardly saw the change take place, but only realized it the next time they looked. The drums smote the air every time the dancing feet charged the ground with the day's stern message, in beat, beat, beat. Every now and then, as dictated by the words of the chant, and the phases of prayer, the whole united government of bodies and voices and shaken air would suddenly break, missing a beat, and break again, missing another, making a clap of silence, a falter like a loss of light, a chasm in design, until, still in absolute union, legs, arms, voices, drums would resume the steady pounding by which the power of that town was driven, beat, beat, beat, into the earthen and airy body of nature.

And the whole day long it pounded.

According to the season, the dance took its theme from different gods. With them all, it practiced imitation of nature to influence nature. The rainbow dance with its arches of willows carried by women suggested rain as the rainbow could never appear in a dry sky. The turtle dance reminded the powers of water, for water came with turtles. The corn dance showered the sound of seeds and rain on the ground. The parrot dance with its blaze of feathers woven on costumes made nature think of the warm south where the parrots lived, and the hot sun, also, which made crops grow. The eagle dance, in which men soared along the ground with eagle wings tied to their arms, reminded of how strong an eagle was, and how such strength could cure anything. Before huntsmen set out, the dance would imagine and predict success for them— sometimes in the deer dance, with men garbed in deerskin and hunted down by other dancers as heroes; or the antelope, the elk, the buffalo, all costumed accordingly, and full of respect for the habits of the beloved adversary and victim who would be brought to death in order that the people might live. In the animal dances, little boys sometimes went costumed as bobcats and coyotes, jogging under the dancing bodies of men who impersonated deer or buffalo. Sometimes a boy dancer was a turkey, bridling and flaring with a suit of feathers.

To imitate was to induce, in gesture, sound and article.

To impersonate was to become.

To endure ordeal was to know not exhaustion but refreshment.

For when evening came the dancers, the singers and drummers were not tired. They were stronger than ever. They were lifted up. In giving they had received. The great ranks ended their slow stately evolutions, and the men retired to the kiva. The women sought their houses. The chorus broke formation and entered the kiva. The clowns went trotting lazily over the town. They capered benignly now. Dwellers came forward from their rooms and breathing upon corn meal dusted it into the air before the clowns who took the tribute with a kindly bend of painted nakedness. The spectators drifted to their rooms.

Such a pueblo typically sat on an eminence above the river, and near to it. The river was a power which like the light of the sky was never wholly lost. It came from the north beyond knowing, and it went to the south nobody knew where. It was always new and yet always the same. It let water be taken in ditches to the lowest fields. Trees grew along its banks—willows, cottonwoods, young and old, always renewing themselves. The water was brown, as brown as a body, and both lived on earth as brown. The river was part of the day's prayer.

Evening came down over the west, like thin gray smoke pulled over color, and the evening star stood like a great trembling drop of water on the soft darkness of the sky.

Before daylight was all gone, the pueblo was silent but for the little sounds of ordinary life—voices lost in narrow walls, a dog, someone breaking branches for firewood, children. The twilight was piercingly sweet and clear. The river went silent and silken between its low banks where grasses grew and saplings and little meadows sprung up out of mudbanks. Sky and town and valley were united in deep peace after the hard wonders of the dancing day. And at that hour the men of the dance came through the sapling groves to the river. The deepening yellow dusk put color on the water. The men came in their ceremonial dress. They took it off and went naked to the river's edge. There they breathed upon the pine boughs which they had worn, and the baldrics of rabbit fur, and sometimes the gourd rattles, and cast them upon the sliding surface of the water. They sent their prayers with the cast-off branches and the skins which, wherever they were borne by the river wherever it went, would go as part of that day's pleading will. Then entering the river the men bathed. The brown water played about them and over them and they thanked it and blessed it. Silken as beavers they came out and dried. Now their voices rang and they laughed and joked and gossiped about the long hard day, for its ceremony was over, and its make-believe, and could be talked about quite ordinarily. They felt strong and refreshed. It was good to have such a river, and such a town, and to have done such a work as that of today. Everything about it told nature what to do; everything was done in exactly the right way; all the ways were right, because, said the men, "they came up with us."

So the idea of creation, and so the ways of propitiating the creators.

ii. forms

There in that long stretch of New Mexico valley (which even so was but one seventh of the whole length of the river) the Pueblo Indians ordered the propriety of their life to the landscape that surrounded them.

This act was implicit in all their sacred beliefs. It recognized the power, nearness and blaze of the sky; the clarity of the air; the colors of the earth; the sweep of mountain, rock, plain; and the eternity of the river. Environment directly called forth the spirit and the creations of the people. The weather had direct effects upon vegetable growth, and the life of waterways, and the change in land forms. It had equally direct effect upon the human personality and its various states and views of life. The presence of mountains; the altitude of the very valley itself; the outlying deserts beyond; the effects created by the interchange of influence and response between that particular land and that particular sky—all had effect and expression in the Pueblo world.

The natural forms rising from a landscape created by surface water action, and wind, and volcanic fury—that is to say, river, desert and mountain—bore intimate fruits in their imitation by the forms of Pueblo life. The cave became a room. The room became part of a butte. The butte, joined with others like it, resembled a mesa, terraced and stepped back. The Pueblo town looked like a land form directly created by the forces that made hills and arroyos and deserts. Daylight upon the face of a pueblo looked the same as daylight upon the face of a cliff. Who knew how much this was accidental, and how much devised by the Indian in his sense of propriety in the natural world, his reverence for all its aspects, and his general application in imitative symbols of all the living and enduring forms he knew about him? Even where his town stood above the river, the river dictated his farming methods; for the irrigation ditch leading from the river to the fields below the town was in itself but a tiny river in form, with the same general laws of flow, and reach, and structure as the big river. People not too long the owners of such a concept would not find it a naive one, to be taken for granted. It would instead be a grave and reassuring fact, to be thankful for along with all of the other energetic expressions of the landscape, among which the Pueblo Indian prayed passionately to be included as a proper part— not a dominant part, not a being whose houses and inventions and commerce would subject the physical world until he rose above it as its master; but as a living spirit with material needs whose modest satisfaction could be found and harmonized with those of all other elements, breathing or still, in the dazzling openness all about him, with its ageless open secrets of solitude, sunlight and impassive land.

So every act and relationship of Pueblo life included the intention to find and fulfill such harmony. The whole environment found its way by spiritual means into all of Pueblo life. Works of art captured the animal and vegetable and spiritual world—always in objects meant for use, never display for its own sake. The work of art, in the sense that all elements were brought together—colors, emotions, ideas, attitudes—in harmonious proportion and mixed with fluent skill, the work of art was the act of living, itself. No one part of it had significance alone, just as each feature of the landscape by itself meant less than what all meant and looked like together.

Worship entered into every relation between the people and their surroundings. The mountains were holy places; temples standing forever which held up the sky. Gods lived in them, and other supernaturals. The priests of the people went to the mountains to call upon the deities of the four points of the compass. The various pueblo groups identified their sacred mountains differently. For one of them, the northern one was Truchas Peak; the eastern one was the Lake Peak of the Santa Fe range; the southern one was the Sandia range, which they called Okupi^{n}n, turtle mountain; the western one was Santa Clara Peak of the Jemez range, which they called the mountain covered with obsidian. All of them rose far back and above the Rio Grande, into whose valley they all eventually shed water.

The action of the river upon land forms was recognized at times by the Indians. Near the pueblo of San Ildefonso is a great black mesa on the west of the river, faced across the river on the east by high ground. This place they called P'o-woge, "where the water cut through." In the midst of supernatural explanations of natural conditions this was suddenly a cool and observant conclusion; not, however, to the disadvantage of another idea, which was that in the great cave on the north side of the black mesa there once lived (they said) a cannibal giant. His cave was connected with the interior of the vast, houselike mesa by tunnels which took him to his rooms. His influence upon the surrounding country was heavy. Persons did the proper things to avoid being caught and eaten by him.

Lakes and springs were sacred too, and natural pools. They were doorways to the world below. If everything originally "came up" with the people through the sacred lake Shi-pap, the same action could be imagined for other such bodies of water. Many of these were springs which fed the river. Gods and heroes were born out of springs, and ever afterward came and went between the above and below worlds through their pools. Every pueblo had sacred springs somewhere near-by. There was every reason to sanctify them—physical, as life depended upon water; spiritual, as they had natural mystery which suggested supernatural qualities; for how could it be that when water fell as rain, or as snow, and ran away, or dried up, there should be other water which came and came, secretly and sweetly, out of the ground and never failed?

Some of the rivers that went into the Rio Grande dried up for months at a time. In the Pueblo world, the most important tributaries were Taos, Santa Cruz, Pojuaque, Santa Fe and Galisteo Creeks on the east, and on the west, Jemez Creek, the Chama River. Of these only the last one had perennial flow. Its waters were red in melting season and colored the Rio Grande for many miles below their confluence. But the courses of them all bore the valley cottonwood. It was the dominant and most useful tree in all the Pueblo country. Its wood was soft and manageable, and it supplied material for many objects. Its silver bark, its big, varnished leaves sparkling in the light of summer and making caverns of shade along the banks, its winter-hold of leaves the color of beaten thin gold lasting in gorgeous bounty until the new catkins of spring—all added grace to the pueblo world. The columnar trunks were used to make tall drums, hollowed out and resonated with skins stretched over the open ends. The wood was hot fuel, fast-burning, leaving a pale, rich ash of many uses. Even the catkins had personal use—eaten raw, they were a bitter delicacy in some towns. And in that arid land, any tree, much less a scattered few, or a bounteous grove, meant good things— water somewhere near, and shade, and shelter from the beating sun, and talk from trifling leaves.

The feeling, the sense, of a place was real and important to the people. Almost invariably for their towns they chose sites of great natural beauty. The special charm of a place was often commemorated in what they named it. On the river's west bank stood a pueblo called Yunge, which meant "Western mockingbird place." The name was a clue to the sense of the place, for above its graces of flowing water, rippling groves and the high clear valley with its open skies would rise the memory of the May nights when the prodigal songs of the mockingbirds year after year sounded all night long in the moonlight. The birds sang so loudly as to awaken people from sleep. Night after night a particular voice seemed to come from the very same tree with the same song. It was like a blessing so joyful that it made an awakened sleeper laugh with delight, listening to that seasonal creature of the river's life. In the daytime little boys on rooftops caught moths which also appeared in May and whistling to the mockingbirds released the moths which the birds in an accurate swoop caught in midair with their bills.

Everything in the landscape was sacred, whether the forms of nature, or those made by people—altars, shrines, and the very towns which were like earth arisen into wall, terrace, light and shadow, enclosing and expressing organized human life.

iii. community

It was an organized life whose ruling ideas were order, moderation, unanimity. All ways were prescribed, all limits set, and all people by weight of an irresistible power took part in the town life. Examples of such controls elsewhere suggested that they must come from a ruler, a presiding head of state whose decrees could only be obeyed, on pain of despotic gesture. But the Pueblo people had no ruler; no despot. The irresistible power which ordered their communal life was the combined and voluntary power of the people—all the people, in each town, giving continuity to inherited ways by common agreement.

Everybody, together, in a pueblo, owned all the land, all the religious edifices and ritual objects. Assignment of use was made by a council of elders. Heads of families were granted the use of portions of land, which could be reallotted every year, according to change in families through marriage or death. Religious properties were assigned to proper organizations.

Crops grown by families upon their assigned plots belonged to them alone. Families owned objects which they made for their own use. Families were given permanent possession of rooms in the pueblo for as long as the family existed and could build additional space as needed. When a family died out its apartments were abandoned and went into ruins.

Since property was entirely for use, and not for sale or trade within the pueblo, everybody lived upon the same scale. Their rooms were alike. Their holdings in food, clothing, furniture, were about the same. Living closely together, they interfered very little with their immediate neighbors, though within the family there was no privacy and no desire for any. Outbursts of feeling, emotion, violence, were bad form, and so was indulgence in authority for its own sake, instead of for the propriety it was meant to preserve. Nobody was supposed to stand out from everyone else in any connection but that which had to do with official duties. Everyone understood that certain work—official or religious—had to be done by someone who was given, by common consent, the authority to do it. But nobody was supposed to propose himself for the job, or go out after it. If he was chosen for it, a man with real reluctance but equally real obedience to the wishes of his associates accepted it and did his serious best while in office. If anybody in such a position showed the wrong attitude, or indeed, if anyone at all transgressed against the accepted way of things, he was shown his error in the ridicule he received from other people. He did not like to be laughed at in the town, or made sport of by the clowns in the dances, and he would mend his ways if he had gone too far out of line. There was no excuse for him to feel differently from anybody else, and to behave accordingly. As there was a proper way to perform all acts, everyone not only understood ritual but performed it. United in gesture, the pueblo had a strong sense of its own identity. Everyone agreed how things were and had to be and should be. Understanding so, there could be few disappointments in life, and few complete bafflements.

Certain towns had thin, narrow, long stones which rang with a clear song when struck. They were hung by deerskin thongs to the end, outdoors, of a roof beam. The singing stones could be heard in the town and the near-by fields. To summon men for meetings, the stones were struck. Meetings were held often, for the town had many organizations, each with particular work to do.

In some towns, all people were divided into two cults—the Summer, or Squash, People; and the Winter, or Turquoise, People. Other towns knew four seasons of the year, and organized accordingly. All towns had secret societies with particular social duties, all religious in form. At the head of the pueblo, as guardian of all spiritual lives, was the cacique. He served for life. He had many duties, for no important act was ever done without ritual, and it was he who blessed and approved all ceremonies. In his own life he invoked holiness with fasting and prayer. That he might be free entirely for his sacred offices he was relieved of all other work. His house was built for him. Other people planted for him and cultivated his crops and made his harvests. In his shrines he kept fetishes which had to be fed with rabbit meat. Men went on special hunts to bring him rabbits, and the sacred food was prepared by his appointed helper, who cooked the rabbits, and also kept his house for him, making fires, sweeping the packed earthen floor, and ministering to his needs.

The cacique made important appointments to the priesthood. Two of these were the war priests, named for the twin boy-gods Masewi and Oyoyowi. They held office for a year. Part of their duty was to observe the cacique in the performance of his duties, and to admonish him if he was negligent. Each year he appointed ten assistants to the war priests. His influence was great, his position among the people that of the fountainhead of all spiritual belief and practice. He was both father and mother to them, a living analogue of the source of their lives. Upon his death his successor was chosen by the war priests from his own secret society.

The cult was a medium through which the people could formally take part in the religious life of the pueblo. Everyone belonged to one or another of the cults in the town. Membership was hereditary, except that a girl who married entered the cult of her husband. If she was widowed she could choose between remaining in the cult of her husband or returning to that of her father. The cult had a head who was in charge of all its activities. The most sacred of objects were the masks used in the kachina dances—those great group prayers in which the gods of rain were believed by women and children to be actually present in the dance. These masks, and the costumes that went with them, and the miniature carved figures representing the godly kachinas, were kept by the cult leader as his own personal duty. He alone could mix the turquoise green paint used in decorating the masks. Not everyone could have masks. Only married men of mature experience could have them. With the mask came powers—the wearer turned into someone else. His real person was hidden not only from the spectator but delivered from himself. Behind the mask he was the godlike being which the people saw. He escaped into a new and sacred dignity, leaving behind him the weak man of every day to whom he must return when he doffed his mask again but surely with some lingering joy and a new strength.

The cult had its ceremonial home in the large chamber of the kiva, sacred to its own members. It was usually circular, sometimes underground, generally above ground. Here was the very house of power and ritual. It was entered through a hatch in the roof, by a tall ladder which leaned down to the floor. A small altar stood in the room, sometimes against the wall, sometimes free. Before it was a small round hole. This was called by the same name as the original place where the people came up into the world—Shipapu. A shaft built into the wall brought air to the altar, and with it could come and go the spirits addressed in prayer. Smoke from fires built before the altar was carried out through the entrance hatch in the roof by the spirits of the kachinas. On another plane of experience and discovery, the air descending through the shaft

made the fire draw, and set up circulation which drew smoke to the roof
and out into the air through the hatchway. At about the height of a
kneeling man, a deep shelf or seat ran around the wall of the interior.
The wall was sometimes painted with sacred images and symbols of
weather, animals, birds, plants, and human actions, all with ritual
purposes.

The whole kiva itself was a powerful symbol. It was like a small
butte with a flat top, a land form often seen. In its interior it gave
passageway to the two worlds—the earth-world above, through the hatch
to natural life of land, creatures and sky; and the netherworld below,
through the portal of the world's womb from which all had come so long
ago. Both worlds were made to join in the kiva. Here the holy pigments
were prepared, and the costumes for the dances. Inherited rituals were
studied and learned here. Sacred objects remained in the kiva when
not in use out of doors. Fetishes were fed there. Boys were initiated there
into knowledge and power of which they had known only animal intimations. There dancers painted and dressed for their outdoor ceremonials,
and when readied came in a crowding line up the ladder through the
hatch, over the roof and down to the ground. To perpetuate the kiva
in filling vacant kiva offices, there the members met in conclave. There
in the significant number of four times—invocation of the whole world
through its four quarters—ceremonies were prepared during four days
of vomiting and other purifications.

Each kiva group was dedicated to the ceremonial work of one
of the seasons. Since ritual and its texts were elaborate, and long, and
transmitted only by memory with no written records, and since every
phase of community life was accompanied by its ceremonial observance,
no one cult could learn and execute the liturgy for all occasions. Yet
certain events, like the great corn dance, called upon two or more cults
to perform in the plaza, alternately throughout the day-long invocation
of the spirits of fertility and growth, when one group would dance
while the other waited to take its place, with all joining at the end.

So the religious life of the people was formalized in groups that
separately represented neither the whole town nor a single clan but
drew symmetrically upon the population until all were included, empowered in the same terms, and actors of the same myths. Religion was
not a thing apart from daily life. It *was* daily life, a formalization, an
imitation of nature, an imagined control of the elements, and of what
was obscure in the spirit of men and women.

In addition to the major divisions of the kiva groups, which cut boldly through the whole company of the town for organized religious acts, there were smaller groups with specialized missions whose members were not chosen along the lines of kiva organization. These were the secret societies. Each had its unique purpose. There was one in charge of war. Another appointed all holders of major nonreligious offices. Another comprised the koshare, the clowns of the dances who served also as the disciplinarians, through censure or ridicule, of individuals who offended against the unspoken but powerful sense of restraint and decorum that governed behavior. Several others were curing societies, and together constituted the medicine cult. And another embraced the hunters of the town. All selected and initiated their own members throughout the generations.

Of the secret societies those which did battle on behalf of the people against illnesses of body and spirit had the largest number of members. Their work was highly specialized and in much demand. Almost everywhere there was reason to call upon them, for even a suspicion of illness was enough to invoke the powers of the curing societies. It all related to what the people said was behind illness—any illness but the little commonplace ones that came and went in a day. No, there were other kinds that came from nowhere, lasted a long time, and had strange effects. They were not accounted for in ordinary ways. Something was at work, something wicked, something unseen, and clever, and dangerous because it might be right here, anywhere, abiding for the while in a bird, or an animal, or a person, or a rock, none of whom knew it. Possibly an ant, or a toad, or a buzzing insect contained the responsible thing. One day well, the next day sick—the invalid, they said, must have received the sickness in his sleep when nobody was watching, and the awful thing had its chance to happen. Once again they had struck, those powers of evil and illness, of whom everybody knew, and sooner or later encountered. They were witches, male and female, who were invisible, who put themselves into innocent creatures and objects, and who did their worst work in all success because people could not recognize them and prevent them from creating harm and havoc. All witches worked upon the same purpose—to make people sicken and die. Sometimes they put spells also upon useful animals to make them die. The danger was so real and so prevalent that everyone kept a sharp watch for suspicious behavior on the part of persons, animals and things. And yet much else had to be done, daily, and so the people gave to the curing societies the special responsibility of keeping vigil against witches, and of taking proper action when the blow fell.

It was they said most fortunate that the doctors of the medicine societies were able to receive extraordinary powers from the real medicine men of the spirit world—the ones who were animal-gods and heroes, whose benign influence reached to all the quarters of the world, and to the zenith and the nadir too: the mountain lion, the bear, the badger, the eagle, the wolf, and the shrew. Thanks to these powers, the doctors were able to recognize witches where no other person could possibly do so. Once identified, the witches could be unmasked and worked against. It was hard work, calling for exactly learned methods, and sadly enough there was always the possibility of failure. Still, everything possible had to be done, and if in the end the doctors lost their patient, the people did not hold it against them, but realized that in this case the opposing powers were the stronger, and could not but prevail. Witches were powerful, that was just the point of being so careful about them, and working so energetically against them. Witches especially tried to destroy the young men. It was particularly evil of them thus to strike against the strength of the present and the seed of the future.

When a person was bewitched into sickness, great forces went to work to save him. His people sent for the doctor of a medicine society who came to the house. Family and friends were there. The prevalence of witches was of much concern to everyone. The doctor followed a procedure known to all, for it was established long ago. He removed his clothes, returning to his animal estate naked. He went to the patient whom he examined with thorough care, feeling him all over his naked body to determine the location of the malevolence which had invaded him. He prayed. If there was a fracture he made splints and set the bone. If there was lameness he massaged. If there was an eruption he lanced it with a flint knife. If no visible ailment showed he administered medicines brewed of herbs and water. He anointed the sick body with his curative saliva. He was disembodied from his daily self. The patient and the people knew him as a power in tune with greater powers, and as he worked, they felt in themselves the energy he brought and the conviction of recovery he carried. Hope arrived with him. Witches might be strong, but here was strength too, in every curative gesture, word and thought. At the end of the treatment, the doctor resumed his clothes and left, with instructions to summon him again if the patient did not improve rapidly.

If he was needed again, he then assembled all the other members of his own medicine society and unless the patient was critically ill, the doctor worked with them for four days in ritualistic preparation for the major cure which they were to undertake. If the patient seemed to be dying, they went to him in the first evening. Otherwise on the evening of the fourth day (the people said great virtue resided in the number four) they went to the house of sickness. The doctors undressed. To frighten the witches they painted their faces black. Over their heads from ear to ear they each fastened a band of white eagle-down, and around their necks hung necklaces of bear claws. Each doctor held two eagle wing feathers and a gourd rattle. The medicine society was ready to go to work.

The doctors in turn came to the patient and felt over his body to determine the seat of illness. When they found it they would know into what member the witches had shot their evil, and what was its nature. The whole cure led to the extraction of the evil object from the patient's body.

Meantime there were prayers and chants. Paintings of colored meal were laid upon the swept floor by a medicine priest. He sprinkled grains of color through his fingers, drawing lines with delicacy. He aimed the dropping meal with his thumb that sifted it, to compose in flax yellow, turquoise blue, berry red, skin brown, black, and white, a design full of magic power against sickness and witches. Before he changed from one color to another, he cleaned his fingers by twiddling them in a little pile of clean sand, like the sand that was spread down as the general background of the painting. It was almost hypnotic, to see the curative design come to being out of the little pouring streams of colored motes. Where nothing was, now power dwelt. How fortunate to know that it came manifest on the side of good, against evil! And then medicines were mixed and administered. The doctors partook of them along with the patient.

The proceedings were dangerous, they said, because such a gathering of virtue and opposition would in itself attract witches who would do their utmost to defeat the forces of good. Therefore, the war priests attended also, Masewi and Oyoyewi, to defend the doctors at their hopeful work. They stationed their assistants outside the house of illness with bows and arrows with which to shoot the witches if they came close. Nobody was in any doubt—the witches were there, and the last act of the curing drama was soon to come, after everything proper had been done in the sickroom. It was sober and urgent in feeling—so many personalities, so much gesture, such powerful singing, all the medicines—and the patient alone and bare in the midst of it felt these forces pulling at him and empowering him to recover. The doctors labored mightily.

Feeling the flesh of the patient, one of them found what they had all
searched for—the place of illness, and the physical cause of it: turning
to the assembled powers, he indicated the place, and then he bent to it
and sucked upon the skin, or he operated with his hands, until he was
able to come away from the sufferer and show everyone the cause of
the trouble which had been stricken into the sick man by the witches.
It was sometimes a thorn; again, a little snake, or a lizard, or piece of
rag, or a pebble; any small foreign substance might turn out to be the
seat of trouble. Only a trained doctor, they agreed, could ever find it,
and bring it forth for everyone to see.

    And now it was time to do battle directly with the witches who
lurked outside. Already they had been partially defeated with the discovery of their projectile in the flesh of their victim. The doctors would
finish the cure by physically punishing the witches so they would hardly
dare to repeat their wickedness soon again.

    Taking up each a sleeve made of the skin of a bear's leg (the
power of the deity of the West) the doctors covered their left arms and
took flint knives in their right hands. Linking arms they went out into
the dark of the night in the open air before the house, and there as they
knew they would they came upon the witches, who were invisible to all
but them. A fearful struggle followed, as the people could hear in the
sickroom. The patient could hear how mightily he was being avenged
and—all hoped—freed of his trouble. There were shrieks and thunders,
blows and wounds and imprecations without, as the doctors fought in
the dark. The whole town was aware of the battle. The witches were
strong and terrible. They might lead the doctors away. The sounds of
the fight came and went. Now and then there was a human scream as a
witch killed a doctor, who fell down dead, in proof that the enemy was
formidable and the cure hazardous. Gradually all sounds whimpered
down to nothing, and the guardian war priests went to look at the evidence of the struggle. On the ground they found the dead doctors. The
other doctors who survived on their feet helped to carry the dead ones
back to the curing chamber. There, with measures known to the doctors
as part of their powers, the dead men were revived.

    But the witches were repulsed. Sometimes a witch was killed by
a shot through his heart with a flint-tipped arrow. Witches were known
to have escaped the very grasp of a doctor, leaving only their clothes in
the doctor's hands—but that was proof, anyway, of how close the battle
was. There was much to talk about when the whole thing was over. The
medicine meal had to be swept up, the pictures destroyed, the ceremonial

equipment taken away. The Masewi always stood up, at the end of the curing labor, and told all how the patient had been cured. How strenuous the efforts; how huge and powerful the witches; how deep-seated the disease, and how wise the doctors to find it; how satisfactory the way in which all had participated; how fortunate the patient.

Then with the luxurious thoughts of the aftermath, the people went home. Now and then for the next several days one or another of the doctors would call informally upon the patient until he was well entirely, or dead. If it was death instead of cure, everyone however saddened knew where it came from and sighed over the awful power and strength of the witches, whose thundering blows and calls and general tumult they had heard through the darkness several nights before in the town. No wonder the doctors had not prevailed. If it was cure, that was not surprising, they said, for who did not recall the fury of the encounter with the witches, the valor of the doctors, the expertness of their ritual? No wonder witches could not endure such powerful attacks.

Thus comfort through organized observances.

The whole year had its cycle of them.

All winter the river ran shallow and lazy from the faraway north, and deep against the sky of the whole valley the snow was locked on the peaks by cold air. The fields by the pueblo were dry and the irrigation ditches which ran to them from the river were overgrown with the dry golden stalks, the pink brush, of the past year's weeds. In March* it was time to clean the ditches and then with prayer, dancing and prayer sticks, open the ditches to bring the river water in upon the spring plantings. The masked gods came from the otherworld to attend. They were seen right there in their masks among the dancers.

In April with four days of preparations the assembled kiva groups of the pueblo held a dance for the blessing of corn, which would come to summer harvest. Water, rain, were the greatest of blessings, and all was asked in their name, and in their image, gesture, and sound. The curing societies during this month went into retreat for purification and for prayer, again invoking rain, upon whose coming the lives of plant and person and animal alike depended. They retreated to their houses which they called, during the retreat, Shipapu, the same as the place of origin, through which everyone had come up. The retreat over, dances

---

* For convenience I have used modern calendric names, which of course were not accessible to the Pueblo Indians of the Rio Grande in the period before recorded history.

followed, again with the gods in their masks, who also had spent the
same time in retreat at the real Shipapu. Well into the summer, retreats
and emergence ceremonies continued.

In early summer the ceremony was held by the curing societies to
pull the sun to the south, where his hot light would make long days
and help things to grow.

In full summer they danced again for corn. Sometimes they
started out in clear day, with all the kiva groups in fullest magnificence
under a spotless blue sky which gave back heat like stone near fire. Rain
could never come from such a sky. But all day they pounded the prayer
into the ground and showered the sound of falling drops of rain from
the air to the earth while the heat grew and grew and the shadows of
the houses stood like triangles painted on pottery in black paint; and
presently they might see without giving any sign what loomed in the
north and the west against the ringing blue—dazzling white thunderheads
marching slowly and powerfully over the sky toward this town, these
fields and seeds. The blessings were vast and visible; and late in the day
as the prayer still beat its way into the ground, the light might change,
and the clouds meet over all, and brown color of the bodies and the
town and the earth all alike would turn dark like the river as rain came
and fell upon them and answered them and the sparkling green shoots
of the corn in the fields. Sometimes it rained so hard and long that the
earth ran and the gullies deepened, and new cracks appeared leading to
them, and rocks rolled scouring new ways to the river, and the river rose
and flowed fast carrying unaccustomed things sideways in the queer
sailing current of flood.

In September as the border of summer and winter was reached
the Summer People and the Winter People both held dances. Autumn
brought hunting dances too, and some of them were given later in
wintertime. In November came the feast of the dead, when all the
ancestors came back to the pueblo to visit for a day and a night. It was
a blessed occasion and a happy one. And before long it was time to urge
the four curing societies to watch the sun, and call it back to the north
before it went too far southward.

In midwinter the kiva groups chose their officers for the next
year, and held dances to honor them, to bless them and to make them
know the right ways. The curing societies now frequently in the winter
held general cures for everyone. People could come to the curing ceremonies with their ailments and have them included with the other ills
against which the doctors gave battle. They purged everyone, the whole

town, of evil spirits. Again they cried out and struck blows against the witches, while all heard the encounters, and were reassured.

In February the koshare danced, the clowns, the critics, who hazed the people, sometimes to laughter, sometimes to shame, the spirit of irony and perversity thus accounted for and made useful.

And it was by then observed that the sun was safely on his way north again, and there was a ceremony to confirm this and give thanks.

Then the winter's weeds stood thick again in the ditches, and the path of life from the river to the fields had to be readied. Once again it was time to burn the weeds away, clean the ditches, let the river in, and set the plantings of another year.

It was an organized life based upon the desire for peace. The Pueblos rarely went to war unless they had to resist attack. The war society with its chief captains Masewi and Oyoyewi maintained the magic necessary to use in times of crisis from without the town. The war society was also a medium for the forgiveness of killing. Its members—all men —were those who had brought upon themselves the danger of having killed someone. This danger was the same whether the killing was accidental, murderous, or in sanctioned conflict. If there was blood upon a man he had to join the war society to wipe it out. He then became a defender of his people. He was confirmed with ceremony. After his initiation he went—like all boys and men after initiations and dances— to the river to bathe his body and his thoughts.

As for thoughts, when grave matters were in the air, requiring the judgment of the cacique and his council, these leaders fasted. They did penance the better to make wise decisions. Their fasting was known about. At home they abstained. In the kiva they abstained. They spoke to no one of what lay heavily upon their thoughts, but their concern was plain to all. Soon there was wonder, and gossip, worry; something was brewing; what would it be; was there anywhere to turn but once again to blind Nature?

But at last the council would speak to them. At evening, the town crier went to his rooftop. Perhaps the sky was yellow behind him and the house fires sent their smokes upward in unwavering lines of pale blue above the earth's band of twilight. The murmur of talk was like the sound of the river beyond its groves. Facing four ways in succession, the crier told four times what the council had decided and what it wanted of the people. On their roofs, or by their walls, or in their fields, the people heard him, and gave no kind of response; but they all heard and in proper order and time did what was asked of them.

iv. dwelling

When the Pueblo builders came to the river they found dwellers
in little shelters built of upright poles stuck in the ground with brush
woven among them and covered with dried mud. The walls of the cliff
cities which had been left behind were of chipped flat stone anchored
with earth. Now by the river there was no stone to be had, and the
outlines, the terraces, the pyramids of the cliff towns were reproduced
in the river material—clay, adobe, mixed with brush or straw from dried
grasses native to the valley. At first even the upright poles of the scattered *jacales* along the river were used, in modified design. The poles
were set close together in double rows. Between the rows wet earth was
poured. The faces of the walls, outdoors and in, were built up with
adobe scooped together a handful at a time and patted, puddled, into
place. Layers were allowed to dry, and new layers for strength and
thickness were added. When a wall was thick enough it could support
beams; cross branches could be laid on the beams and plastered over,
to make a ceiling, and a roof. Once a smooth level was managed on the
roof, it could serve as a floor for a second storey, which in turn could
support a third, and a fourth, until the great hive with all its cells had
a porous strength shared by all its supporting uprights and laterals.
There was no entrance at ground level. Ladders took the dweller from
ground to all levels above.

The cities were much alike in form, varying most in color. The
Rio Grande long ago cut down through different layers of buried color,
revealing each at widely separated places along its course. The local soil
made the walls, and gave them their color. The prevailing hue was pale,
the Indian tan of dried river mud, wherever the pueblos sat on or near
the river course in its most pastoral character. Where lava still showed
in the soil in spite of centuries of weathering after forgotten upheavals,
the earth, and the town, had a gray look, as at San Ildefonso. Up the
Chama river, the ancient pueblo of Abiquiu had a dusty vermilion
adobe, taken from the red hills and cliffs. A faint pink clay went into
the pueblos of the Piros farther down the Rio Grande near Socorro.

The form of the pueblos was found not only on the Rio Grande.
Those cities, and the typical life they showed, were common to great
areas and long gaps of time. Just as certain tribes of Pueblo Indians

came to the river to resettle, so others went westward and grew their cities in northwestern New Mexico and northeastern Arizona. Even deep in Mexico, and long before them in time, the Rio Grande Pueblos had their counterparts among the Aztecs, whose houses, temples, rituals and organization suggested theirs. Much came northward with the seed of corn and of ways to cultivate, invoke and protect it.

In the community house each family had a room. It was private, for its only entrance was through a hatch in the roof, entered by a long ladder. It was small—about twelve by fourteen by seven or eight feet. The walls were painted with gypsum and water whitewash. Much gypsum was available in the river country. The beams overhead were brought from forests far away. The length of the timbers determined the size of the room. Smoke from fires built on the floor went up through the hatch in the ceiling. Little openings in the walls let a draft in and gave a view outward, and in times of trouble served as a hole through which to fly arrows. Blankets of cotton and yucca fibre mats made beds and places to sit upon. There were also drum-shaped stools carved out of cottonwood trunks, and hollowed out on top.

If the family grew, a room next door was built, connected by a low opening to the first room. Each family prepared its own food. Food and water were kept in pottery vessels, and cooked in them. Pottery bowls were used to eat from. The pots were more than just receptacles. They were works of art, and more, they were made as acts of devotion, just as the poetry and song and drama and design of the dances were. All imaginative creation and skilled craftsmanship went to fulfill a direct purpose which was partly religious, partly esthetic and always utilitarian. A pot was made in a certain size and shape for a certain purpose; beyond that it was decorated with designs which spoke of the potter's desire for blessings from the natural world and its gods. By representing the forms of life associated with fertility, rain and growth, the Indian painter called them into being on his own behalf. Handling pots decorated with such symbols, the family had daily communion with the powers. The designs were without meaning for their own sake. Their value was not inherent in their lines, masses and colors, but dwelt in their spiritual message. They were outpourings of wish, not of artistic pleasure. As all forms of art and craft went to express the unanimous belief and observance of the people, so every person was in some degree an artist or a craftsman. The arts like all other phases of Pueblo life were communal in their purpose and realization.

The people of the Rio Grande had no metal crafts. Their products

were all made with stone or bone tools, and with fingers. Raw material
and finished object remained close to each other. What was inherent in
the one determined the form of the other.

Pueblo symbols for bird, or cloud, lightning or rain, animal, or
man, or mountain, were used by all makers. There was a common
graphic language in each tribe. Its designs were not meant to be realistic,
nor were they purposely grotesque. They were stylized images hallowed
by long usage and accepted as descriptive. The typical Pueblo pot carried
bands of design around its circumference combining specific symbols
with abstract lines and spaces. Even these last had a suggestive power.
Though they represented nothing, they seemed to recreate the spaces
and the angles, the sweep and line of the Southwest, the shafting of light
in the sky, the bold mesa, the parallels of rain and the dark spots of
juniper on hills otherwise bare. There was a genius common to all
Indian artisans—a tepee recalled a pine tree, a pueblo was a mesa, a
clay cist was a seed pod. Whatever its conscious motive, however symbolic its style, the impulse to record life was an ancient one; and in
any degree of its fulfillment always respectable as art.

The needs of daily use called forth in the Rio Grande town
Indians a profuse and vigorous creation of pottery. They took the same
material of which they made their houses and with it made their vessels,
and somewhat by the same method, building up surfaces of moist earth,
letting them dry, adding more, and exposing the final form, in the one
case, to the baking sun, and in the other, to the fire of the kiln. The
decorations of the pottery were rich, often using two or three colors,
some of which had a glazed finish. Black, white, red and natural clay
color were the most common. A syrup of the yucca fruit was used with
paint and water. The designs were painted with a brush made of yucca
leaves. The line was flowed firmly, the sense of balance and proportion
was exquisite, and the use of color was both strong and delicate. In
such artistry there seemed to be an impersonal obedience to laws of
harmony and grace which dwelled deep in the common spirit of the
people. They said that life existed in everything; and that when they
made a pot, they gave personal life to it, just as all creatures, places
and things had personal life. Believing so, they knew a responsibility not
to art and its abstract aims, but to life and its hope of perfection. They
dared not make even a pot with less than their utmost skill if it was
to live a good life. Allowance was invariably made for its spirit to breathe
and come and go in the painted design on its surface. Somewhere in
the decoration there was always left an opening in the design, a gap,

a space not closed, so that life might enter there or flow from it. Wherever
decorative design appeared—on textiles, walls, or on the half-sections of
gourds fashioned into ladles—the ceremonial gap was represented.

v. garments

The pueblo people wove cloth and wore it hundreds of years
before they came to the river. They made thread from the native cotton,
and used a true loom, and whether they invented it or acquired it from
Mexico no one can say. Cloth came from yucca fibres, too. On their
clothing they painted or embroidered designs, much like those which
they used in making baskets and pottery. Their costumes were rich and
complete, according to the season. In summertime, the children went
naked, and the men and women wore as little as necessary. In cold
weather they had plenty to cover themselves with, some of it magnificent.
They domesticated the wild turkey for the use of his feathers. Turkey
tail feathers were part of the dance paraphernalia, and the soft little
feathers of breast and body were tied with yucca fibres to make rich,
warm blankets that could be worn as cloaks or slept in. Turkeys evidently had no other use, for the Pueblos did not eat them; but a glaring
and straining bunch of live turkeys tied together by the legs made a
ceremonial gift to visitors who came to the pueblo.

The people's clothes took their prevailing color from the natural
hues of cotton and yucca fibre. Designs were added in colors taken from
the earth and plants. There was a rich red, from clay. Mustard yellow
came from rabbit brush, and a soft golden yellow came from ochreous
earth. Larkspur and blue beans yielded a delicate blue stain, and copper
sulphate gave again the brilliant blue-green dye which prevailed in the
kachina masks.

A man dressed himself in a breechclout of cloth when he wore
no other clothing. Otherwise, he wore a broad kilt wrapped about his
waist. It was held in place by a richly decorated sash whose ends hung
down. His shirt was a square of cloth with a hole cut for the head.
Around his head he wore a cloth bandeau. His legs were sometimes
covered by the superb buckskin leggings which he imitated from those
of the hunting Plains Indians. The leggings were not joined, but hung
separately from the sash or breechclout by leather thongs, from the

crotch to the ankle. They were often gathered at the knee with ties of rawhide. On his feet he wore soft skin mocassins. Over all he wore a robe or cloak, now of turkey feathers, again of rabbit fur cut in strips and laced together with yucca thread. Tied to interesting points of his costume he wore, if he was fortunate, a number of the little copper bells and beads made far away in Mexico, and very rare in his river country. But some of the bells came northward in trade, and possibly some were made by wandering metalworkers from far to the south who came to the river and used local metals; but without leaving their skill behind them, for the pueblo people had no metal crafts in that time. Such an ornamental bell was about an inch, open at the bottom, and had a pebble strung on a thread for its clapper. The beads were an inch long and shaped in tight little cylinders. The bells seemed to be cast by some lost method and the beads were hammered. The man wore jewels, too, as many as he could contrive out of strings of turquoise, bone inlaid with bright stones, black, red, or blue; and bits of shined rock in any beautiful color. He wore strings of precious color about his neck, and hung them from his ears, and wrapped them about his arms. Finally, on many occasions, he used paint on his skin as decoration, whether in the dance, in ceremonies for the sick, in rites of the hunt, or in war.

A woman wore a mantle four or five feet long, and about three feet wide, which she wrapped about herself under the left arm and over the right shoulder and held together with a long decorated belt that went several times around her waist. She wore nothing on her head and, except in bad weather when she used mocassins, nothing on her feet. Like her husband she wore as much jewelry as she could get, and in her uses of the dance and other ceremonies, she wore paint, but only on her face.

As among people anywhere, the children wore miniature imitations of adult costumes, except in hot weather, when they wore nothing at all.

The skins of the people were the color of moist river-earth. Their eyes were black and so was the thick hair of their heads. In general they were not tall. The men, from the exercises of their rituals, the ordeals of work, were lean and muscular. The women early lost the figures of maidenhood and grew heavy, moving modestly and calmly about their duties, fixed in their pivotal positions as the bearers of life, the holders of all that brought stability to the family.

vi. man, woman and child

For in the analogy of woman as the repository of continuing life, it was the wife and mother who was custodian of the family dwelling, and all communal property. Growing up among her relatives, she was courted by her suitor, who sometimes played to her upon the flageolet in the evening on the hills at a little distance from the town, when the fading light was still clear, and the day's sounds were dying away. If she heard him with favor, and took him as her husband, he joined her in the circle of her blood relations, who helped her with materials to build new rooms for her own life. She herself made the walls out of earth long ago laid down by the passage of the river. She received her husband in the shelter of her own life, with her person, her house and her years. It was hers to make all the enfolding and conserving gestures of life, whether as maker of shelter, of children, or of pottery. She took her husband for life and he understood that he was to have no other woman. A daughter born meant that the mother's family was increased, for the child would in her time bring a suitor to the same family premises; while a son born meant that one day he would leave and find his mate in another settled family bound together by its matron. From mother to daughter the home was passed on; not from father to son.

The father and mother rarely separated from one another; but if it came to pass that the marriage must end, it was the man who was removed, leaving the dominion of the family secure with the mother and her relations. He would one day find his few personal possessions set out upon the doorstep of his home by his wife, whereupon he would weep, take up his things, and return to the house of his mother. For it was there that he went at important times; and if his mother was dead, he would find his sister there, to whom he gave his ancestral allegiance.

A woman in her house produced the clothes worn by her husband and children. She prepared the food and cooked it. The staple of the diet was corn, and she ground the meal, often before sunrise. While her husband sang to her a song which celebrated the act of grinding corn, or beat upon a drum, she worked the kernels in time with his rhythm. She put the corn upon a large flat stone and ground it with a smaller bar of stone, and in time the first was hollowed out like a dish and the second was rounded off at the edges by the work. Her hands grew hard and big and her fingernails wore down as she labored. For each batch of meal she used several different stones, going from coarse to smooth, always refining the flour and roasting it after each grinding. Sometimes several women ground corn together at night. If a woman wanted to make a gift to a man, she would give corn bread or any cooked food.

She kept her house immaculate and the roof above it and the space before it. Her broom was made of slender branches of Apache plume (or poñil) bound to a willow stick. When she swept her floor she first sprinkled it with water or blew a spray of water from her mouth. Her soap was made from yucca roots. To make cord or rope she boiled the succulent leaves of the yucca and when they cooled she chewed them until they were soft, and then drew out the stringy fibers which she worked together.

Her day was busy and her duties were serious. Much depended upon her, not only what needed to be done, but also how. From her mother she had learned the proper ways of life, and it was her own obligation to transmit these to her own daughters. Even hopes and desires had their proper gestures, to be made in the image of what she wanted. If she wanted a son and had none, she went to find a stone that had the shape of a man's generative member. From this she scraped a little stone dust and put it into water and drank. She prayed. She deeply knew her animal womanhood and enacted its appointed nature in harmony with what she saw of life all about her.

A man's purposes and duties were all plain, too.

If he owned no house, anyhow he governed the town. He explained life through religion and ordered, preserved and executed the ceremonies which he said kept the year and its seasons in their proper passage. He provided raw food by farming and hunting. Like the seed for children, the seed corn belong to him. All the powers latent in the fields were his, and so was the rubble after harvest. Harvested food and stored corn was, he said, "my wife's." If he wanted to make a gift to a woman, he gave the products of his work—game, firewood, embroidered or woven cloth, which it was his to produce. He ruled the river and brought its water to the fields for irrigation. And in times of danger from other peoples, he made war.

The Pueblo people were peaceful. They said they never carried war to others, but gave battle only in defense of their own lands, towns and families. One Pueblo tribe sang a song of war which told of no glory, no brag, no zest for a fight.

> So we have bad luck
> For we are men.
> You have good luck
> For you are women.
> To Navaho camps we go
> Ready for war. Good-bye.

Bad luck—but ready, they sang, with realism and a larger bravery.

The Pueblo warriors painted themselves, for there was power in paint, and to go out to save their community life was in itself a ceremony. The surface of their bodies, perceptive of touch, caress and wound, was beautified with designs that came alive with movement—the lift and fall of breathing, the haul and suck of the belly in exertion, the climb and pound of limbs. Flesh became a living temple of esthetic and spiritual feeling. It was an act of both art and religion, and the warrior's mortal humanity, his bodily stuff dear because it was not immortal, was the very material of his craft. Using the colors of the earth itself, the great source and repository both, the act of devotion combined in tragic wholeness the Pueblo man's concepts of himself and his gods. Upon his own nakedness he used his earth in the symbols of what he believed in.

First he put on his skin a layer of tallow. Over this went the colors—gypsum white that clothed but did not conceal his legs; red, from clay or crushed amaranth blossoms, on arms and chest; lines of soot black edging designs; yellow from the dust of sunflower petals. He ceremonially washed his hair in yucca suds. Wearing only invocations as armor, he went to the enemy carrying his loins wrapped in buckskin. A buckskin baldric hung over the left shoulder, and above the left shoulder peered the bow case and the quiver, from which arrows could be slipped with the right hand, the left holding the bow. From a tight belt were slung a stone knife and a club, a pouch of sacred objects to bring power, and a little bag of ground meal to be used with water as food on the campaign. Bad luck—but ready for war. The Pueblo men were devoted to their soil. Their towns rose from the river earth like shapes of nature. Their fields were cunningly cultivated. The seed corn secured them life. Their wives gave houses to live in to generation upon generation. There was every reason to stay at home and live well. But their most powerful enemies came from the plains where nothing grew but food for the wandering herds of buffalo, whose flesh made meals for the marauders, whose droppings gave them fire, whose vast seasonal whims took them drifting like cloud shadows over the exposed prairies. The invaders had little to lose and much to gain. But the pueblo people had everything to lose and they fought for it and kept it. Their ways came up with them from a long time ago, and gave them strength.

They lost few of their reluctant prehistoric wars, though perhaps a town here, a scatter of houses there, might suffer and be abandoned. They could come home and make sacrifices of thanksgiving with ceremonies, smoking clay pipes filled with red willow bark, and telling of battle. They had earned their ease. When they wanted to relax and gossip, and be purified, the men took sweat baths together, putting heated stones in a closed room, and pouring water upon them, and finally going to the river to bathe. The river always purified. It seemed to bring some thoughts from far above, who knew from where, and carry others far downstream, who knew whither. Using the river, a person could dream awake, like a child.

The people treated their children tenderly, from the time of birth to the entrance into adult societies. Ceremony and symbol accompanied the child into the world, and at every stage of life thereafter attended him.

The mother unbraided her hair and wore her clothing unknotted that her unborn child might learn to come easily without stricture into the world. A midwife delivered him. In slow or dangerous deliveries, medicine priests might be sent for. They had measures. With invocations, they would hold the laboring woman up by her hips. Again, they would burn pine-nut shells on live coals in a medicine bowl, placing it under her blankets to sweat her. They would massage her belly and call forth the child.

When the baby was born, the midwife cut its cord and wiped its eyes. If a boy, she put his legs and feet into a black pottery bowl so that he might have a heavy voice, and then handed him to his maternal grandfather. If a girl, the midwife put her in the grinding bin for a moment to make her a proper woman, and handed her to her maternal grandmother. The midwife took the afterbirth to the river and threw it into the water which took it away in purification. For her help she received a gift of fine meal.

The paternal grandmother or aunt took up corn meal and with it sprinkled on each wall of the room four little parallel lines, saying to the infant, "Now I have made you a house, and you shall stay here." In his blankets the baby was laid between two unblemished ears of corn that would guard him until he was given his name. His mother chose a woman to name him, which would be done after four sunrises. Before dawn on the fifth day the sponsor came to the baby's house. Taking

him up, and accompanied by the mother, she went outdoors just before
sunrise and as the sun rose she presented him to the light, and spoke
his name. The sun was his spiritual father. All then returned to the
house and feasted. The sponsor was given a gift of meal. The child was
given an ear of corn so that he might always know plenty. Then he was
put upon his cradleboard and was so carried on her back by his mother
for the first year of his life. Thereafter he was taken from it and taught
to walk. Young girls and old men helped to take care of him in his
infancy. Through him, the one could learn motherhood, the other
could contemplate the cycle of life.

A girl grew up learning the ways of the household from her
mother.

Between five and nine years of age, a boy was taken by the men
for schooling in the man's duties of government and ceremony. He was
initiated into a kiva. He was too small to learn anything of the ritual
or to understand the revelations that awaited him later, and that in
their stunning force would bring him almost at one stroke from the
sweet useless thoughts and illusions of boyhood to the purposeful im-
postures used by men. As a little boy in the kiva, he was brought into
direct relation with the spirit powers, and given strength. He learned
through fear and pain, for the masked kachinas came to his initiation
bearing yucca whips with which they whipped him until he cried. Their
lashes drove out the badness in him and made him ready for a good
future. His elders nodded and approved as he cried under the punishment of his innocence. Now he had his allegiance, and though understanding nothing of what he did, perhaps he might impersonate an
animal in one of the dances, and trot cleverly among the legs of the
dancing men.

At adolescence, ready with new powers and desires, the boy was
again the victim of a kiva rite. Again the masked gods came and whipped
him, harder than before. He venerated them. He felt that the greatest
power in the world was chastising him directly. He knew the gods, for
they danced in their masks at all the great ceremonials. He knew they
came from the sacred lake far underground to the north, where all life
had come up. He knew the gods had come down to be about him on
this day. It was terrible to be so near to the gods and to receive punishment from their own hands. But he bent himself under the painful honor
and valiantly endured what he must.

And then more horrifying than any of the blows he had taken,
more shocking than any other discovery of growth, an incredible thing

happened to him. The masked gods who were savagely whipping him suddenly stopped, faced him, and lifted from their heads and shoulders their bright copper-green wooden masks with feathers and designs, and showed themselves to be men—neighbors, or uncles, people whom the boy had always known and taken for granted.

The boy was stupefied with terror and amazement.

Then the dances? Who were the gods there?

They were the same men who here, at the kiva ceremony, now removed all their masks. All were men. None was a god. But only men knew this. Women and children still believed that it was the real gods who came masked to the pueblo. Here: let the boy learn how mortal the masked figures were: take this whip. The boy was made to whip the unmasked gods who had whipped him. They put a mask on him and he knew how it felt to be the impersonator of a god from the sacred lake. When he learned enough he would be able to act out what all the other people believed of the gods. He now owned a tremendous secret which he must never, never betray. They spoke of one boy who had told, and what had happened to him. It appeared that they had cut off his head and then, using it like a ball in a game, had kicked it to the sacred underworld.

There would be much learning and several years to go through before they were men; but boys passing the stage of discovering the gods were no longer children. There were other stages. They could not smoke until they had qualified in the hunt, killing deer, buffalo, rabbit and coyote. If before this anyone found them smoking, they were thrown into the river, in punishment.

Though punishment played less part in the lives of children than fear. Unless children behaved well, they would be in danger from giants and bogeymen who knew all. Once a year the bogeymen, wearing fearful masks, came to the pueblo and knew exactly which children to visit and scold. They knew all the bad things that parents had been harping on. They appalled the children, who had heard of one giant, for example, who went every day to a pueblo near the black mesa in which he lived, and stole children, took them home, and ate them. The bogeymen made threats. The children shivered. And then their parents in anguish begged them not to take the children or hurt them, they were sure the children would be better boys and girls from now on, wouldn't they, children? With sobs and shudders the children promised. The bogeymen rattled their masks. No, who could be sure. Threats and horrors were renewed.

The parents pleaded. Promises were repeated. At last the dreadful visitors consented to go, for this time. But remember and beware!

Happier children were favored with the protection of the masked gods, the kachinas, who rewarded their goodness.

In the morning, waking up, one of the children in the family was sent out to make a prayer, sprinkling sacred meal or pollen to the sun. Then came duties, and then play. The boys tried all the games played by the men. They practiced the kick-race, which the men ran on a course sometimes as long as forty miles, circling out by landmarks and back to the pueblo. Two teams played, each kicking a lump about five inches in size made of hair stuck with pinyon gum. The men could kick the ball twenty yards. The boys tried. They also played a game using a curved stick with which they knocked a deerskin ball filled with seeds. The winner was the one who broke the ball. They liked to run relay races, wearing tufts of down to make them light as birds. All running games were valuable, they said, because they kept the sun running in its course. The boys pitched little stones at a larger target stone. They threw darts and practiced with bow and arrow. Boylike, they discovered things to do with things, and took the fruit of the ground-tomato which had a puffy envelope over it and, by smacking it against their foreheads, made a fine loud pop.

Children were desired and cherished and given all that their families could give, of things and powers and certainties. The blessings of life came from the parents, the ancestors, to whom gratitude and veneration were due. On the hot afternoons of the summer, when the sky blue had golden shimmers over it from heat, and the cottonwoods were breathless and the river ran depleted in and out of their shade, there rose on the hot silver distance the big afternoon rain clouds, with their white billows and black airy shadows. They had promise and blessing in them—rain and life. The people pointed to them and said to the children with love and thanks, "Your grandfathers are coming."

vii. farmer and hunter

The people did not consider that the cloud that made the rain that fell on the mountain thus made the river. Long ago, when they lived on the mesas and plateaus, far from the valleys, they needed water direct from the clouds to make their crops grow. In dry times they took water out to the plants in jars and spilled it carefully on the roots. Sometimes when heavy rain brought fast floods, they channelled the runoff to their fields. Running waters took usually the same channel, deepening it, widening it, turning its soil over. The people began to use such places in which to plant, so that their crops would receive the water that fell and ran.

When they came to the river and through generations settled their life along its farming plain, they saw that if water could run into the river from all the uplands, then on the immediate floor of the valley it was in many places possible to run water out of the river to the fields. Nearly a thousand years ago Pueblo people were irrigating their fields through well-laid canals and ditches. The river had in some places sharp steep deep walls of rock which ran for many miles. But most of these hard-buried canyons opened out as the river went downstream into wide flat valleys whose floor on each side of the riverbed was lush with growing grasses, plants and trees. In such places the people placed many of their towns. The river was accessible. They used it and it sustained them.

There were thirty thousand people, living in at least thirty, perhaps up to seventy, towns on the Rio Grande of central and northern New Mexico. They cultivated in all about twenty-five thousand acres, through irrigation from the river and its tributaries, and by the use of controlled floodwater. They grew corn, beans, pumpkins, gourds and cotton. They said it was the leaves that made the plants grow, because when the leaves dropped off, the plants stopped growing. The leaves could be watched. Roots were below ground and could not be watched. But even things that could be watched might mean nothing. Pollen from corn was sacred and used in many a prayer; it was part of the great plant which gave life; but nobody noticed what pollen did to make more corn.

Seed corn was kept into the second season before it was planted. Each town used its own, and refused to plant that of other towns, for, they said, the corn was the same as the people. Sowing was assisted by much prayer. Under the waxing moon of April the corn was planted, so it would grow as the moon grew, for under a waning moon the corn paused in its growth. Each farmer made his own prayer, and conducted his own ritual. One said this:

Mother, Father, you who belong to the great Beings, you who belong to the storm clouds, you will help me. I am ready to put down yellow corn and also blue corn, and red corn and all kinds of corn. I am going to plant today. Therefore, you will help me and you will make my work light. You will not make it heavy and also you will make the field not hard. You will make it soft.

The river water was let into the ditches to run to the fields. As the sluices were opened, the farmers prayed and threw feathers upon the first seeking ruffles of the muddy water in the dry ditches whose winter reeds had been burned down. As plants grew the farmers cultivated them with sharpened sticks. Each plant had its own little crater of shaped earth to conserve water. The fields were laid in long narrow strips touching at their ends to the river course so that each would have access to water. The farming lands were owned by the town, and each family man's share was assigned to his use by the cacique's council.

The growing plants had enemies that had to be watched out for. So, in a place commanding a good view of the fields and the country beyond them, the old men who could no longer do the work of irrigating and cultivating served as guardians of the fields. For this duty a lookout was built, eight or ten feet square and two stories high. Four posts held up the deck of the second floor and a brush roof over the top. There were no side walls, for the view had to be clear. But brush was sometimes set along one side as a windbreak. Under the platform, in the ground, there was a first floor made of a shallow pit with a fireplace and food storage. The guard sat up on top. Women came and prepared his food in the pit below him, while he kept up his watch against enemies. Sometimes they were Navahos, Apaches, Comanches who grew no food for themselves but knew where to find it all done for them. Sometimes it was birds who came to flock through the tender new plants and strip them clean. Small riverside animals sometimes found a crop to their taste and had to be scared away. The watchman often had a dog with him who could give chase, or bark an alarm, or simply doze and scratch companionably and affirm by his devoted presence how suitably things were arranged, with one to lead and one to follow, and behind both, the need, the power and the responsibility of the earthen town whose life came from the river.

As crops matured, the people danced for rain in late spring, full summer, and early fall. Then came the harvest. First the melons were taken in and stored, and then the corn. In many towns the ground was swept clean before the corn was brought through the streets from the fields. Everyone, men, women and children, took part in the harvest, which lasted for several days. It was a happy time, full of social exchange and pleasure. Neighbors helped one another. The storage bins were ready. The year's hard work was over for a spell. Peace and plenty repaid virtue. The winter was coming when nothing would grow. The days would be bright, the nights cold, sometimes there would be ice on the river. The cottonwoods would turn golden and keep their dried leaves. The stalks and grasses by the water would be rods of rusty brown and black and pink and pale gold. In the fields, the corn husks would dry and crackle in the wind. The ditches would be clogged with withered weeds. Vegetation did not rot. It dried up. A seed planted then would be lost. But it did not matter, for now in harvesttime there was enough food to last through the coming months, and people could live.

If the summer was the man's season, then winter was the woman's. For the harvest was hers, and she knew what to do with it to make all its produce into good dishes to eat. There were two meals a day to prepare, the first in midmorning, when everyone had already been at work for several hours; the second in late afternoon, when smoke from cooking fires stood plain against the setting sunlight. The mother and her girls prepared the food. They had to have enough on hand in case anyone appeared at mealtime. This often happened. Brothers and sisters, aunts and uncles, grandparents, felt free to go visiting and to take a meal in the family at any time. Friends sometimes came, too, with the unspoken question, What do you suppose she is going to serve this evening? They would find out, and whatever it was, they would know it represented the best the family could offer, for the news would travel fast if the guest found any evidence of poverty, carelessness or clumsiness in the meal. The company sat in a circle on the floor. The tone was one of gaiety and good humor, for it was not good manners to be gloomy or disagreeable while dining. The room was small, the air smoky, the floor hard, but with much to say, and plenty to taste, they all enjoyed themselves.

The staff of life was maize. It was prepared in many ways. It was boiled in the whole ear, or the ear was toasted over charcoal fire, and the corn was eaten off the cob. It was ground into meal and cooked as a mush and eaten hot. For anniversaries and dances and weddings, corn bread was made in fancy shapes called flowers, with fluted designs, or shell-coils, or petals, or little hunks pinched out into spikes. Thin large wafers of corn dough mixed with fine cottonwood ashes were baked into tortillas. Corn meal, ground fine, and toasted three times, was carried by travelers, who needed only to add water to it to have a nourishing dish called pinole.

Roots of wild onion and mariposa lily were cooked for green vegetables. Milkweed was eaten raw or boiled. Seed pods were boiled, and seeds often made into dumplings with corn dough. The berries of the ground-tomato and nuts from the oak and pine were eaten raw. Pumpkins were given as presents, and served uncooked, and also could be preserved. The housewife cut off the rind, opened one end of the pumpkin and scraped out seeds and pithy fibres, and put the pumpkin to dry overnight. The next day she tore it carefully into long, spiral strips, and hung each strip to dry on a cottonwood sapling which she had trimmed as a drying rack. When the pumpkin meat was dry, it could be bundled together and stored, until it was wanted for stewing and making into pies.

The people had meat on special occasions. They liked mountain sheep, deer, squirrel, prairie dog, mountain lion, badger, fox and the fat field mouse. Meat was cut into little strips and, unsalted, hung out in the sun to dry, after which it could be stored without spoiling. Fresh meat was cooked on sticks held over a fire of coals, or included in a stew with vegetables. Fat and marrow were the tastiest parts. When the ducks came down the river in the fall, or went back up in the spring, they snared them and cooked them between hot stones. They did not eat fish, for this reason: they said that two pueblos faced each other across the Rio Grande near the confluence of the Chama and the main river. The towns belonged to two groups of the same ancestry. Desiring intercourse, they said they would see that a bridge was built over the river between them. Their medicine men built it, reaching out from one bank with parrot feathers, and magpie feathers from the other. When the feather spans met, people used the bridge until evil witches one day overturned it, causing people to fall into the river, where they became fishes. The people said they must not eat their own bewitched relations.

They made tea from the leaves of coyote plant, coreopsis, mistletoe, and thelesperma, and if they wanted the bitter brew sweetened, they used corn syrup. Young girls whose mouths were pure were chosen to make the sweet syrup. For days before they worked, they kept spurge root in their mouths to clear their breaths. Then they chewed fine corn meal until it became a paste. This was added to a mixture of water and corn meal, and the cornstarch and the saliva of the maidens combined to make sugar. There was no alcoholic drink.

The people took much of their food from wild nature. After the corn harvests they went to the mountains to gather the little sweet nuts from the piñon tree, and crops of acorns and wild plum. Men and women, young and old, went on the expeditions, and for the young, these were occasions of love-making and courtship. To the children who stayed home in the pueblo the elders would bring back sticky juniper boughs loaded with frost-purple berries.

The pueblos never domesticated animals for food. One tribe did not even have a word meaning animal. Each kind of animal had a specific name, and each creature had its own identity, like a living person. The dogs they lived with, perhaps the domestic mouse, the turkeys they kept for feathers, could no more be eaten than a person (for it was a long time since human sacrifice had taken place among them, even though to the south in Mexico it still was performed daily in untold numbers). But the wild animal was fair game, and the hunt was one of a man's glories. It made him not only a provider, proud to bring home that which kept life going. It gave him a challenge, and it told him of his own animalhood which he must use with all his craft and power if he was to succeed over other creatures. The mountain lion was his hunting god, a symbol of the killer who saw with a piercing yellow stare, who moved as softly as cloud, and who killed with claws like lightning. On a mountaintop above one abandoned plateau city, hunters had long ago carved two stones into the likenesses of the mountain lion, and later hunters carried little images of him in clay or stone when they went out.

Some useful animals were found near home—the prairie dog, whose bark the men could imitate to perfection, the beaver along the river, whose meat was good to eat, whose fur was needed in dance costumes. All the animals they hunted had many uses—food, hides and fur for clothes, bone for instruments, sinew for stitching and for bowstrings, leather for drumheads, pouches, bags. They said in one of the towns to the north that the animals of the hunt lived together far off to the west in a great kiva, and when the people needed them, they were sent out to be hunted. They were clever, and every skill had to be shown by the people, and by their dogs. Before a good hunting dog went out with his master, he was given food containing powdered bumblebees which would buzz and sting inside him and give him power.

Some hunts took place far away and lasted several days, some just for a day, near-by.

The deer hunt was often sacred if the meat was to be used in a ceremony. The deer was hunted by many men, who scattered until they could surround him. They closed toward him. They forced him to a trap, made of a great snare of yucca fibres, sometimes over two hundred feet long. They took him alive, and smothered him to death, so that his blood would not be spilled and his meat contaminated and made useless in the rites for which they took him. If the deer was captured for food and other use, he was killed with a knife. So with other animal victims too. When they came back dead with the hunting parties, they were received in the pueblo with great respect. Many more animals would be needed for food, and if they heard from the spirits of those already taken and killed how gentle the people were, how respectful of the loved creatures whom they had killed out of need, then when the hunters went out again, the wild quarry would be kind and come to be captured and killed and given honor. So they laid the bodies of the deer, and the other animals, on fur rugs, and covered them with blankets, and hung precious ornaments on them of turquoise and shell. The animal dead lay for a little while in pathetic splendor before being put to many uses.

Deer hunts were held in fall and spring, rabbit hunts many times a year, and for several different purposes. The ceremonial treasures of the kiva had to be fed—the kachina masks, the scalps collected in warfare, the sacred fetishes made by the medicine priests. Rabbit meat went for that, and the hunts were held in spring and fall. Other rabbit hunts were held in honor of the cacique and the war captain, to supply them with food and fur. The men alone hunted for these. In the fall, when harvesttime brought high spirits and symbolized sharp change in the year's life, rabbit hunts were held for the girls, in which they were permitted to join. The koshare were in charge of the hunt, and, holding authority from all the people and the gods, performed without resistance from the people whom they mocked, chastised and humiliated. They seemed to act on witless impulse, and they also gave freedom to the spirit of the perverse and the sardonic which lived somewhere in everyone, and never otherwise escaped into comic mockery of life and its origin. The power of the koshare was absolute when they took charge. They called the girls and men and boys to the hunt, telling them the time and place to assemble. Woe to them if they were late. What happened to them was the worst kind of punishment—they were made objects of derision. The koshare watched for those who came late, had them lined up in the presence of all the other hunting men and girls, and ordered them to show their sexual parts to everyone. The victims were half-ashamed, half-satisfied at making a sensation, and all went on the hunt in high spirits.

The men were armed with throwing sticks with which to kill rabbits. The girls did not kill. They all walked to the hunting place. Girls brought food along for lunch. When a man killed a rabbit, all the girls broke loose in a run and each tried to be first to pick up the dead game. Whoever touched it first could keep it, and take it home. At lunchtime she was the one who had to feed the man who killed the rabbit. The koshare watched to see that all was properly conducted. After lunch the hunt was resumed. The party spread out and drove the rabbits within an always contracting circle. Now and then someone, a man, a girl, would be far out on the circle, and might disappear together behind a protecting bush or rock. If they were certain they had not been noticed, they had forgotten the koshare, who came to see what they were doing. If they were coupled together carnally, the koshare broke them apart, and took them back to the party in captivity for the rest of the day. News of the arrest, and what for, would spread, and everyone with amusement would wait for what came next, for all knew what must follow. At the day's end, when the hunt was over, and the whole party gathered together to return to the pueblo, the koshare produced their prisoners and had them resume and complete before everyone the act which had been interrupted. After this, all went home. The girls took their trophy rabbits with them, and cooked them for their families to eat.

On the hunts they encountered members of the reptile creation, but did not fear them. The rattlesnake was the only poisonous snake in that part of the river world, and though the people knew of its dangerous nature, they did not regard it with horror. Some of them used the murderous snake in ceremonies as messenger to the cardinal points of the world. The swift, a little gilded lizard, was the supernatural of the sixth, or downward, point of direction. Turtles sometimes lay in their path. They saw many of the harmless horned lizard, or horned toad, and blue and green racer snakes, brown bull snakes, little water snakes with black and gold stripes running the length of their bodies. Deep and dim was the memory of past life which came stepping down the generations in talk; the people knew of a curious mixture in nature between snake and bird, each of whom was born in an egg. They made prayers to their image of the feathered serpent, and believed prodigies of a bird that could crawl and a snake that could fly. Land and sky with all their separate mysteries were brought together in that god, and in thread and paint the people made his picture again and again.

To find certain game the hunters had to go far away from home. For the big bear they went deep into the mountains to the north, and for the bison whose robe was so rich, whose meat was so good, and whose head and horns were such mighty ornaments for the dance, the men of the pueblos went to the eastern plains. Out of their own valley of the Rio Grande, they followed a pass eastward to the valley of another river, the Pecos, which began its life between high mountain walls. But the eastern wall ended more or less due east from the central Rio Grande world, and the hunters came up a grand escarpment to the plains not long after crossing the Pecos. They had to go carefully in some years, for the plains people sometimes came that far west, and not always for peaceful purposes. But with care and good fortune, the Pueblo men could advance to the immensity of flat land and hunt the buffalo. They could see, it seemed, forever, if time and distance there became one. The horizon was clear and flat and the light was stunning. Stiff grass grew everywhere, and in dry years was brittle and yellow. From time to time they would see far away what looked like a grove of trees. But there were no trees on that plain. Those tree trunks, rising to dark blurs of joined treetops were actually the legs of buffalo against the white lower sky, and the heavy tree crowns were their bodies—all optically enlarged in the shining air. The buffalo at first were not afraid. Sometimes they moved off in answer to scents on the wind. Sometimes they watched the hunters approach. When the attack came they would heave and run away together. The hunters had their plans. They set great snares and then as in the rabbit and deer hunts they separated and began to drive the buffalo inward to the trap. They set fires around the circle they made and the big herds ran against them in confusion and were turned back as the burning circle narrowed. In high weather, the sky was blinding blue and the sunlight white. Strenuous buffalo-colored smoke blew upward in rolling clouds. Fire in daylight at the edge of the hunt showed yellow and red and brighter than the air. There were yells and commotion. Silvery waves of heat arose. The buffalo stormed from side to side. Their eyes glared sidewise in terror as they fled to their doom. Behind them came the naked hunters shining with sweat and triumph, making calls and motions of menace. Blue, black, straw, curly smoke and pelt, running flame and figure—the picture ended with the capture and the kill.

It was a different picture when they hunted buffalo in the winter. They found the great herds black against the snow and searched until they found deep drifts piled up on unseen obstacles by the hard north wind that made storm on those plains. Spreading out on the white flat land, in a thin line of dark dots, the hunters began to drive the herd toward the drifts of snow. In the end, the buffalo got in deeper and deeper, until at last they could flounder no more and were caught for red slaughter on the white drift.

There were years when plains people, the Comanches, came west bringing buffalo furs and horns to the river people to exchange for corn, corn meal and other precious things. Products and stories, habits and words, beliefs and wonders—there was much to trade.

viii. travel and trade

The Rio Grande pueblo world had corridors to other worlds. Mountain passes to the east gave upon the great prairies. Deserts and mountain parallels to the west finally led to the sea. The river's own valley led south to Mexico through a pass which opened on a vast plain just as the river turned southeastward on the course which finally took it to the sea. With these roads open, the people yet did not travel them very far, and only the hunt took them away from their pueblo world. The river towns knew one another, and exchanged visits, and took part in one another's dances, and showed, and sometimes traded, curious rare objects that had come from nobody knew just where, or by what crawling pace, through what perilous distance. A stranger now and then appeared, walking, moving into the sight at first like a fleck of dust that bobbed on the glaring distance and seemed to come hardly nearer. He would be noticed. Someone saw him and told. Without seeming to, many people watched, as they went on with their work. Where was he from. What would he want. What did he bring. Was he alone. Perhaps he finally arrived half a mile away and sat down and stared at the pueblo for a while and rested. And then moving gradually so as not to be noticed, he came closer, and was at last where people could hear him, and see his ingratiating nods, as he unpacked his pouch and revealed bits of color.

Perhaps he came from northern Mexico, where he obtained from another man who got it from another farther south who in turn had it from a hunting party in the jungle a bundle of macaw feathers—sunflower yellow, scarlet, sky blue, copper green. For their rarity, beauty and sacred meaning, they were wanted for ceremonial use on masks, headdresses, robes. Sometimes the trader brought with him a live macaw with its feathers still in place. That was a treasure. The bird changed hands and after an honored lifetime of yielding its blazing feathers to the needs of ritual, was buried in the pueblo with ceremony, prayers and fetishes.

Perhaps he came from the deserts to the west, bringing a rare red paint, chips of agate, and fine baskets which had come to him through many hands.

If he came from the plains, the trader might have with him not only the useful products of the buffalo, but also worked buckskin, moccasins, odd foods.

The pueblos were a thousand miles from the sea, with every danger of weather, distance, time, human and animal conflict, desert and mountain between. Yet the trader, walking, for there was no other way to travel, might have with him a pouch of little sea shells that came either from the ocean to the west or the gulf to the southeast. The trader may never have seen the sea; but others had, and what they found came slowly and through many relays to the upper river whose origin and whose end, in relation to its populated part, none of the people knew. The shells were acquired and made into necklaces, pendants, fringe. From the western sea came over sixty species of shells, and from the gulf, nearly a dozen. Red coral beads came through tribe after tribe, from the seacoast inland.

The trader may have brought stone tools to offer, or a few pots to exchange for the kind made by the women here in the town.

And beyond all that, there was much to tell about and to hear.

The walking trader might come alone, but often he had company. Even so, in such a wilderness, reaching so far and open without forest and with little water, it took an intermittent multitude toiling on foot in tiny, scattered bands across rocky space immeasurable time to make their mark. But they made it. Trails were established, first in relayed knowledge of landmarks, and then in barely worn but visible pathways that were like the first tributaries of communication struggling to feed a stream of knowledge.

The incoming traders looked for things to take back with them when they left. News of what was to be had always took people to coun-

try strange to them. In the river towns, traders saw the accumulated
produce of the pueblo farms. There was corn meal to be had, either
coarse, or ground fine in pinole. Dried pumpkin seeds, squash were
bartered. Irrigation ditches ran to cotton fields, and picked cotton was
made into cloth, and cloth could be carried away in bulk, or in the form
of shirts, kilts, sashes, or shawls. Mineral and vegetable dyes were used
to decorate such garments. The traders might trade for the knowledge
of how to use such colors.

There was one color and substance they wanted most, for the
river pueblos had much of it, and prized it dearly. It was turquoise, and
the people knew of a place, the only place in the river world, where it
could be found in the earth. South of the site of Santa Fe, they mined
turquoise for centuries in undisputed ownership. They made necklaces
and ear pendants of the rich green-blue stone, usually carving little
discs which they pierced and strung on yucca fibre. It was their principal jewel, and as such it was given to the gods in costumes, vessels,
masks, fetishes with sacred meaning—and sometimes with magnificence:
in one ancient town there was a superb basket, made in the shape of a
cylinder, paved with 1,214 turquoises. If the people had treasure to bury,
it was turquoise, and bits of red coral, which they put into large jars and
hid in the earth.

Not only trade from far away made trails. The river people themselves went travelling to fulfill their needs, one of which was salt. They
knew where to find it, in great deposits across the mountains to the
east of the Rio Grande, and about in a line with the southernmost of
the river pueblos. There, across that mountain range from the river
valley, lived other town people who spoke a different language. They
occupied ten or more communities, and their life faced out across the
great plains to the east. Mountains behind them divided them from
the river world. Precariously they survived the wandering fighters of
the plains who came periodically to make war. Their bleak riches were
the salt deposits which lay in a series of shallow, white lakes surrounded
by low curving hills whose skyline seemed like the idling path of a
circling and banking vulture. In some years the lakes were dry and the
salt glistened dry at the sun. In others, a milky water filmed over the
beds and rippled like cotton cloth when the wind came. Little vegetation grew about the lakes. They were like part of the underworld exposed. Nobody stayed by the brackish water for very long, but gathered
up salt, and made whatever trade was necessary, and returned on the
trail through the mountains to the river.

They saw much along the way. There were long-abandoned towns here and there, and from the ruins the travellers could learn something about the vanished inhabitants. Wanderers sometimes came to the pueblo world from down south on the river where, they said, there once flourished life in river caves that was long since gone. The river went more or less straight south, as you left the pueblo cities, and for the most part, the best—though not very good—trails were along the west side, for on the east, mountains came very close to the river and made travel difficult if not impossible. But finally after its usual succession of canyons and flat, fertile valleys, and after finding a pass between the ends of two mountain ranges, the river turned southeastward across a hard desert. Travellers had little reason to go there. They said that as far away as many days of walking, the river entered mountains which no man could enter, and disappeared between high rock walls into deep shadow. There were few people there.

But news of the other people who had once lived in river caves far away drifted with the wanderers. (These were the caves of the Big Bend and below.) The Pueblo dwellers listened, though the facts were scattered and few. Still, they could recognize by their own ways what other people must have been like.

The caves were in a great rocky wall of a river far to the southeast. (Was it the same river? It might be. And yet it was very far away. Rivers came from many places. Who could be sure?) The rocks were marked with lines like the flow of water. Water once made the caves and filled them and then left them as the river deepened. People came to live in them for part of the year, passing the rest of the seasons on the flat plain above the river cliffs. On the cave walls and on near-by rocks they made pictures by scratching with hard stone. They drew animals and the four directions and made marks to show time passing, and more often than anything else they drew hands in outline on the rock. There: hand, meaning a person was here; the thumb spread, the fingers straight. On a wall, hand. On a flat stone up on the plain, hand. I, long ago, hand now, and forever, said the rocks, without saying who, exactly.

From the river they took smooth large pebbles the size of the palm of your hand and painted upon them various yellow, blue and gray lines and made certain spaces which sometimes looked like a man, sometimes like nothing to see but like something to think. They carried these, or made offerings of them in ceremonies, or buried them. They took their colors from rock and berry. With a hollowed bone from a deer's leg filled with color that could ooze from a little hole in the end, they drew their shapes and spaces.

They had no corn, but near their places up on the plain above the cliff they gathered berries and yucca and ate of them. In time bushes and stalks grew nearer to the cave entrances, as seeds were dropped near the shelter. Paths and toe holds—the only way to the caves—led from the plain above. The men fished in the river where they could get to it. They used hooks made from bent thorns of devil's-head cactus, and yucca fibre nets weighted with round stones, and stone fish-knives. With a throwing stick from which they discharged spear and arrow they hunted running animals. With bone daggers they struck a wounded animal to death.

There were not many caves—less than a dozen, and only one family lived in each, at a time. They built fires under the overhang of rock, using long slender wooden drills which they palmed to spinning against a wooden hearth to make smoke, spark and flame. From the dry hard brush of the plain they gathered little bundles of kindling.

Like many people they wore few clothes in warm seasons, when the men went bare, and the women wore skirts made of yucca fibre that was corded and woven into matting. In cold times, they all wore blankets of lechuguilla fibre twisted with strips of rabbit fur. Traders rarely came their way, and so they had no turquoise, no red coral for necklaces. Instead, they strung together something that made beads, that was fairly hard to get, even dangerous, and was therefore valuable and not entirely commonplace. It was the vertebrae of the rattlesnake.

What they used more than anything else were baskets and other articles woven from fibre or straw or tender twigs. They made no pottery. But baskets served to cook in and eat from. The children had toy baskets to play with. Even bracelets were made of basketwork. They came to know, as anyone might, how to make baskets from watching birds. The parent birds brought little twigs and bits of grass to make a nest, twining them in and out until a little cup-shaped wall was made. There the nestlings were safe as they grew. A woman of the river caves in time would have her nestling and must carry him with her and keep him. If she wove a nest for him out of fibres, she might make other things in the same way.

As children grew within each family, they met new times of life during ceremonies which told them fearful things and made them able. The gods lived in the sun, in fire and in the snakes of the canyon and the plain. People of the river, and those far away to the south beyond the river in Mexico, prayed to the same powers. Shaped stones and modelled clay represented other powers to help men make and keep life through the day's hard work of providing shelter and food—coyotes, bears, lions, frogs, wolves.

All about them on both sides of the river, ranged other people who hunted everywhere, never staying to live and worship and grow in one place; but always prowling to kill. They were Comanches, Apaches, Lipans. Lipantitlan was the rippling name of the domain where they roved. They came to the caves, perhaps many times, and in the end, they finished forever what was trying to fix its life there above the river in the rocky walls. It was like much life in many other places of the desert and mountain land. It did not last very long, but it made signs, even in death.

A body was buried in rock shelters or under piled rocks in the open. Its limbs were gathered against itself and bound. A few of its meagre possessions were placed with it—things to work with and to pray. Woven fibre matting was wrapped around all, and where at last it lay, a blanket of cactus leaves, thick and bristling with sharp needles, was put to protect and cover all. On a flat rock face near-by was a picture that said "Hand," and meant "Forever."

Below, in its rocky trough, the river went on and presently—not very far off—was joined by another big river from the north—the Pecos of today. The two streams came along the flat sides of a great rock wedge that ended sharply, like a stone hatchet. They went on as one river when they met below the hatchet edge.

All along the river there were wandering people, even at the coast where the brown water went into the green sea. People travelling inland followed rivers, and those by the sea followed the shore. Out of Mexico went travellers up along the coast, coming to the mouth of the river, crossing it, and going on beyond to see what they could find. The travellers met trouble at times, for the people who roved the great vaporous sea-plain were hostile. They were naked hunters, always moving, and they attacked not only animals but people, and when they made any kill, they ate of it. Otherwise on the sandy plain where the sky all day long changed from thick to thin and back again, there was little to be had except roots in the sand and food from the sea. They snatched the white crabs of the beach and fished in the surf and in the end-waters of the river that passed through empty wilderness to meet the tide.

In news that came to the river pueblos from travellers who had seen, or heard, all of it, there was little of any other cities that lived anywhere else along the river. Towns at the river's mouth were made of sand grasses that blew away in hurricane or fell down dry if the rovers left them for long. A few dug-out pits roofed with yucca stalks clung to the river in the middle desert (southeast of the site of El Paso) whose people grew corn and went to the buffalo plains to hunt. But it was much harder country than the pueblo valleys up north—rockier, hotter, barer, dryer. Sometimes the desert part of the river failed to run. Its mountains were too far away to renew it. It was, there below, a river to cross, not to live along. The pueblo people were the only ones, with their many towns up and down the green, gold, blue, black and pink valley of their world, to whom the river through a thousand years gave continuing life, and connection with one another.

People from the farthest north pueblo, Taos, which was on a plateau too high for the growing of cotton, came south to the central towns below the volcanic canyons of the river, where the land forms stepped down immensely and the farms lay two thousand feet lower in altitude, and traded for cotton cloth.

During November men from the red rocks and plains of the west came on travels to see dances and to make trades, and went home again to their own towns, that were made of shale and mud plaster.

Other travellers, the Navahos, wandered with the seasons, and sometimes reached the western edge of the river world. If fixed with the spirit of war, they struck, thieved, and fled. If at peace, they threw up their mud cells, like wasps' hives, and dwelled in them awhile. If someone died in a Navaho hut, it was fearfully abandoned and a new one built by the survivors. The house meant nothing in itself. Thus, neither did a town, or a place. The Navaho moved, always just ahead of his hunger and his fear.

Stable, relatively secure amidst all such movements and motives, the river people received the trails as they were made, and maintained themselves at home by their work, their search for harmony with the visible world, and their endless propitiation of forces of whose existence they dreamed but whose nature they did not know.

ix. *personality and death*

Imprisoned in their struggle with nature, the people sought for an explanation of the personality they knew in themselves and felt all about them, and came to believe in a sorcery so infinitely distributed among all objects and creatures that no act or circumstance of life was beyond suspicion as evil or destructive. Neighbors might be trusted; but they had also to be watched in secret, for who knew who among them might finally turn out to be a witch? If every object, every animal, every man and woman quivered with the same unseen personal spirit, to whom prayers might be said, and of whom in anxiety blessings could be asked, then they could also and with terrible swiftness turn out to be agents for evil. Long ago, they said, the young war gods Masewi and Oyoyewi, the powerful twins, lived amongst the people, and protected them by killing witches and giants. Nature was vast and people were little and danger was everywhere. But (in the universal canon of faith which brings to every Goliath his David) there was the very cast of hope in the people who imagined their survival and triumph in the midst of menace, then willed it, and even by implausible means achieved it.

But at great cost.

Anyone suspected of sorcery was put to death, often in secret, often by individuals acting without formal sanction. What would identify a witch? A vagrant idea in someone's head; a dream (for dreams were always seen as truth, as actual life encountered by the spirit freed from the sleeping body); a portent in nature; perhaps a conspicuous act, aspect or statement, anything too unusual, too imaginative in unfamiliar terms; persistent misfortune or sickness among the people which must be blamed upon someone—the notion could come from anywhere. If only one or two people knew of the witch, he might be secretly killed. If everyone suspected him and knew about him, he would be accused and pressed to confess. In their search for a victim the people sometimes fixed upon an ancient person who had outlived his family and, obtaining a confession through torture, exiled him to another pueblo or simply killed him. Sometimes people in one town would discover a witch in another town who was causing them grief, and would murder him virtuously. Retaliation, inspired by the highest motives, would follow.

The killing of witches at times reached such numbers that whole towns were nearly wiped out by it.

Otherwise believers in peace, and calm, measured life, the people sanctioned their only outbreak of violence in connection with punishment of witches, whose machinations, they said, threatened the communal safety of life. Was that very communality itself an expression not so much of the dignity of men and women as their fear—a fear which put them always on guard, created a propriety of the commonplace, and held as its core a poisonous distrust of one another? The old people told the children that no one could know the hearts of men: there were bad people—witches—everywhere. Evil resided in them, and never came from the gods. The gods were exempted from doubt or blame. All believed so and, believing, all followed the same superstitions in the same strength of mind. Such strong beliefs, laced through with such compelling fears, created a personality common to the people as a whole.

Men went out during the night to encounter the spirits at sacred sites. They went in fear and returned trembling, whatever their experience, for they went to garner omens for themselves. Going home from the shrine they must not look behind them, no matter what might seem to be following them. They would consider gravely before they would tell what they had encountered, for what had been gained could be lost if not kept secret. It would not be a sin to tell—there was no guilt in the people since they were not responsible for what nature did to them—but in telling a secret, new power against menace might be lost. Ordeals were spiritual rather than physical. Endurance of torture was demanded only of witches.

The personality had many private faces, each with a new name. A man had his name given at birth as a child of the sun. When he joined a kiva, he received another, and another when he entered any organization, and he was nicknamed after his various duties and kinds of work. The personality was renewed and purified by ritual acts, such as vomiting. Before all ceremonial dances, all taking part were required to vomit in the early morning for four days (four was a powerful number in all ways). They said that those who vomited breathed differently from those who had not. "After you vomit four days you're *changed.*" A man thus purged left the daily world and entered the supernatural.

The personality was clever. A man prowling in hostile country wore sandals made of wooden hoops wound with thongs of rabbitskin. His footprints were round; from them, he was sure, nobody would tell which way he was coming or going.

The personality could be shared: images of men or animals were made in gestures of menace, to frighten trespassers away from property.

And the personality was vain, for the people of this town looked down upon the people of that town, saying that those others did not hunt so well, or farm, or fight, or sing, or dance, or race, so well as we do, the poor crazy things, with their silly ways, and their bad imitations of what we do which they stole by watching us secretly. But this was a pitying superiority, without anger or quarrel.

The most immediate medium of personality was talk. The people of the river world did not all speak the same language, but were divided into two general groups, Keres and Tewa, each of which had its localized variations. But all derived from the same mother tongue long ago far in Mexico, and ventured northward with the farming people and their maize. In spite of differences in language the river pueblos with minor local variations lived under much the same beliefs, customs and ways of work. Their language was expressive and exact. The men spoke it with voices that seemed to try to escape from smothering. They formed some words deep in the throat. Others were framed lightly on the lips. Some ideas were given through little pauses in a series of sounds, and a tiny round-mouthed silence became eloquent. Their words were never written even though in Mexico the mother tongue of the Aztec people was used in written form. The pueblo people taught all their knowledge by word of mouth. The greatest body of it had to do with ceremony and ritual. "One who knows how"—that was a man of power who remembered all that had been told to him. For the dances those "who knew how" had to memorize tremendous amounts of ritual, word-perfectly. Such men showed great powers of mind which their life in other directions hardly equalled. The great movements of time and the seasons, the acts of life and work, the inherited stories of the gods, the forms of prayers, all had to be stored in mind, along with their many variations and combinations, until a vast body of knowledge rested trembling and precarious on the spoken thread of the generations that was spun from elder to youth. Thus even the act of literature was not individual but co-operative, since it took one to tell, and another or more to listen, and remember. Much of what was so recorded in memory was to be kept secret among those "who knew how." If a man betrayed them, he was punished. The war captains put him naked within a circle drawn upon the ground. He must not lie down, but stand or sit. If he moved to step across the circle he was shot with arrows by the captains.

People within a language group visited one another's towns.

Before he went, a man had his hair washed by the women of his family
before sunrise, and his body bathed in yucca suds. They gave him a
new name for his venture. At the end of his journey, if he found a friend
awaiting him, he took his hand and breathed upon it, and clasping it
with both hands lifted it toward the sky without words, for joy muted
his speech.

"May I live so long," prayed the people, "that I may fall asleep
of old age." The personality ended with death and had to be exorcised
from living memory, and become one with all ancestry, impersonal,
benign and beyond fear. When a man lay dying among his relatives
they sent for the doctors of the curing society that combatted witches.
Then doctors came and undressed the dying man to examine him carefully. If he was already dead, they put a cotton blanket over him. His
people brought all his clothes to the doctors who tore little holes in
each garment to let its life, too, escape and leave the dead cloth. They
folded the arms of the dead across his breast, tying his wrists together.
His legs they closed up against his body. They wrapped him in this
huddled position with cotton blankets. His clothes were included. A
feather robe was folded about him next, and lastly, a yucca matting was
bundled over all, and tied with a woman's sash. Crouched in silence
within its wrappings the body was a restatement of the attitude of birth,
when the unborn infant was folded within the womb; and bound by a
mother's cincture to the womb of all it was now returned. The doctors
rinsed their mouths and washed their hands, saying to each other,

"Now he is gone."

"Yes, he is gone back to Shipapu."

"The place from where all emerged."

"He is gone back to Shipapu."

The family took the body out of doors to burial in the open ground,
or in a rocky crevice, or in a midden. With it were placed water and
food. The food was cooked, so the dead could feed on its aroma. The
dead man's turquoises, his weapons, his tools were buried with him,
for he was now about to set out on his journey to the underworld from
which all life had come, and his spirit would need the spirits of all such
articles to use in the life that awaited him. He was on his way to be
one with the gods themselves. At the end of his journey he would take
up again what he did in the world, whether as hunter, farmer, priest,
or dancer.

Four days after his burial, his personality was finally expunged
with ceremony. The doctors returned to his house and arranged an altar

on which they laid sacred ears of corn, bear paws, a medicine bowl and kachinas. They sang songs and ceremonially cooked food for the ghost to smell. They made a painting on the floor with colored corn meal. He was gone, and to confirm this and help him where he now would be forever, they made a bundle of offerings containing moccasins in which he might journey, a dancer's kilt and turtleshell rattle and parrot feathers and necklace which he might use to start rain from the ghostly world. They buried this out of doors. Underground, he would find it. Doctors then dipped eagle feathers into the medicine bowl on the altar and sprinkled the meal painting, the sacred implements and the people. They swept the walls of the dead man's room with the eagle feathers to brush away his spirit, and they went to other houses where he had last been seen and did the same. Returning to the house of the ghost, they sang again, and all settled down to a feast provided by the family. A few morsels were thrown aside by the doctors for the spirits. At the end of the repast, the doctors arose and were given finely ground grain for their services. They destroyed the painting and took up its colored meal in a cloth which they gave to a woman, who carried it to the river. There she threw it into the water which for all his life had flowed by the dead man, had sustained him, purified him, and which now took away his last sign forever, through the shade of cottonwoods and into the sweet blue light of distant mountains beyond the pale desert.

5.

On the Edge of Change

So the Pueblo people agreed without exception in their worship, their work, their designs for making things in the largest to the smallest forms, their views of property, the education of their children, the healing of their sick, and their view of death.

A clear and simple and within its limits a satisfactory plan of

living together was understood by everybody, and complied with. But
tragically it lacked the seed of fullest humanity. Mankind's unique and
unpredictable gift was not encouraged to burgeon in Pueblo society.
Individuality, the release of the separate personality, the growth of the
single soul in sudden, inexplicable flowering of talent or leadership or
genius, were absent. In harmony with all nature but individual human
nature, the people retained together a powerful and enduring form of
life at the expense of a higher consciousness—that of the individual free
to unlock in himself all the imprisoned secrets of his own history and that
of his whole kind, and by individual acts of discovery, growth and ability,
to open opportunities that would follow upon his knowledge for all who
might partake of them. It was costly, that loss of the individual to the
group. The essential genius of humanity, with all its risks, and yet too
with its dazzling fulfillments, was buried deep in the sleeping souls of
the Indians by the Rio Grande.

They solved with restraint and beauty the problem of modest
physical union with their mighty surroundings.

But only to their gods did they allow the adventure, the brilliance,
the gift of astonishment that came with individuality. Those mythic
heroes, those animal personifications ranged sky and earth and underworld performing prodigies, releasing dreams for the dreamers, perhaps
beckoning inscrutably toward some future in which the people too
might find freedom before death to be individuals in nature instead of
units among units in a perfected animal society whose loftiest expression
of the human properties of mind and soul was an invisible tyranny of
fear that bent them in endless propitiation before inanimate matter.

The deep alien sadness of such a life was born with dignity. They
lived like figures in a dream, waiting to be awakened. Possibly if left
to their own time and development, they would have awakened by themselves to discover another and greater environment than the physical one
to which they were already accommodated with economy and tenacity.
The inner environment of the conscience, the responsible and endlessly
replenished human soul, the recognition of God within mankind above
a multitude of gods without—these might have come as their own discoveries to those people who already had climbed far from forgotten
antiquity.

But men of another order were making ready to come to the
river as ministers of enlightenment and shock and the strongest necessity of their epoch.

BOOK TWO

The Spanish Rio Grande

I.

The River of Palms

AS IT CAME TO THE SEA AT THE GULF OF MEXICO the river turned from side
to side in looping bends and dragging effort like a great ancient dying
snake. The land was white with sea shells and crusty with salty sand.
On the low dunes hard tall ranks of grass stood up in thin blades that
cut if touched. The sky was low, even in sunlight. Air over the sea
thickened and thinned as wind and moisture played. Someone watching
the sea where the river flowed its brown water into salty gray waves that
broke shoreward forever, someone looking and idly turning his head,
saw the low lines of the whole world—pale horizon, vapory sky, wide-
shadowed green sea, the mist-white shore with its reed huts scattered
close to the river, and the drying nets, and the powdery browns of the
people moving at what they did. Warm in the fall, the days expected
nothing new. The search for clams, crabs, oysters went on, and the
dwellers watched for signs that the edible root of the sand dunes was
coming into season. Now and then a memory of outrage by other people
inland, or from up and down the coast, returned and brought caution.
Enemies always came on foot. Sometimes all their dogs and children and
women came too, and waited in the land haze for the outcome of battle.
On some days the distance was blue with misty heat and the aisles of
palm trees along the river could be taken for smoke far away.

Looking to the land for food and protection, and to the sky for
weathers that told the immediate future, the beach people kept no guard
seaward, where the water birds dived with sounds like splintering rock,
and the clouds now met and hung over everything and again separated
and travelled like misty pearls and trailed shadows like mother of pearl

over the waters that were never still, and yet always the same, forever long as anyone remembered, forever and forever.

Yet the sea, the light, the clouds, had the power of making image and marvel out of nothing, phantoms to loom and fade. Perhaps it was so with the vision of change that became visible on the sea one day.

One, then another, and another, and another, sharp cloud came clear of the horizon. They moved close on the surface of the water. They rested on dark bulks. They came toward shore, all four of them. They were not clouds, then, but houses on the water, with trees standing out of them holding up great mats in the air. All four moving slowly could turn in accord like birds. Each time they turned they crossed a line nearer to the beach. Before long they were moving in the water that was made brown by the run of the river into the sea. The mats were shaken and changed, the bulks drifted, and all four came into the arms of the river, and in the moving houses were men amazingly decorated. Voices stranger than any before echoed across the water.

Twenty-seven years after Columbus's first discoveries, it was a day in the autumn of 1519 Anno Domini when four ships of Jamaica stood in through the veils of sea air to the mouth of the Rio Grande, and the point of view was about to be changed for the next three hundred years from that of the river Indian to that of the European soldiers, sailors, civil servants and friars—for surely chaplains came too—on board the little fleet.

With their coming, the golden haze of the Indian story along the river began to lift. Hitherto, the river people had been without individuality. Time was unrecorded and experience was halted within each generation. There was no way of setting down the past and of letting it recede. The ancient people were trapped in an eternity of the present tense.

Now against the moving backdrop of the civilized world, the little fleet dropped anchor in the brown river water, and someone on board recorded the act. Leo X was Pope, the earthly source of all legitimate authority. The Emperor Charles V, King of Spain, was planning to go to Germany to preside at hearings of Martin Luther. In England Henry VIII was King, and the righteous author of an essay condemning Luther for defection from the Faith. In France, as guest and employee of Francis I, Leonardo da Vinci died. Ferdinand Magellan was nearing Tierra del Fuego in his first voyage around the globe. There were no European colonies anywhere in North America. Deep in Mexico, to

the south, the passion to conquer smoldered like hidden coals under
the courtesy with which the Captain-General Hernando Cortés approached the Emperor Montezuma high in his capital.

The four ships of the little fleet were under the command of
Captain Alonso Alvarez de Pineda. With him were two hundred and
seventy Spanish men-at-arms. They had been afloat since the previous
spring. Their orders, issued by Francisco Garay, governor of Jamaica,
directed them to coast along the shores of Florida as far as they might
in order to find a water passage to the Orient. For a while the term
Florida signified the whole immense crescent of the Gulf of Mexico.
Pineda logged rivers and bays, but he had not found the strait for
Cathay when in August he came upon other Spaniards already ashore
at Veracruz.

There was an incident at Veracruz. Pineda anchored his fleet
in the harbor. The ships were reported to the Spanish commander ashore
—Cortés, who at once went with fifty soldiers to investigate. No newcomers
were welcome on that shore. Cortés had already sunk his own ships. His
men were ready with his own spirit to take Mexico, for by now they
had seen with him the gifts brought with soft messages by ambassadors
from Montezuma; and they lusted for such a country. The feathered
ambassadors had laid before Cortés an image of the sun, beautifully
chased, of pure gold, the size of a carriage wheel, alone worth more than
twenty thousand crowns; a larger disc, of silver, which was the moon;
a helmet full of raw gold to the value of three thousand crowns; thirty
excellently modelled gold figures of ducks, dogs, lions, deer, monkeys and
tigers; ornaments—rods, collars, plumes of feathers, fans, all done in gold
or silver; headdresses of precious green parrot feathers. The Emperor's
messages in presenting the gifts said that he would not welcome the
Spaniards in his capital. In return, Cortés gave the ambassadors three
shirts of Holland cloth and a Venetian glass cup to take to their lord,
with the answer that having come so far, he could not fail his own
monarch the Emperor Charles V by not pressing forward to visit the
ruler of Mexico in his palace. Mexico was rich. The soldiers knew it
now for a fact in their own terms. Was every unknown land in the new
world a treasure house? An ancient theme sounded again fatefully.
Cortés wanted none to help, and none to share, in the ravishment of
Mexico. Coming to the Veracruz beach with his soldiers to see who
anchored offshore and what was wanted, he did not see Pineda, but met
a notary and two soldiers from the anchored fleet, who in ceremony took
possession of these lands for Governor Garay of Jamaica.

Cortés at once had them arrested and denuded. Putting three of his own men in the clothes of the captives, he sent them in the landing-party's own boat to hail the ships to send ashore. A small boat with twelve men in it put in to the beach, and four came from it through the surf carrying crossbows and guns. Cortés's men sprang out of hiding and surrounded them. The small boat pushed off in alarm, and as it reached the nearest anchored ship, the fleet was already making sail. It departed.

So Cortés knew from his captives that the coasting expedition was also charged with laying claim to lands; and Pineda knew that a ruthless and powerful campaign was afoot in Mexico. Plunging heavily northward, the four ships travelled along the barren coast which at that season was also mild. There were no signs of other Spaniards, there were nothing but naked brown staring creatures as Pineda brought the squadron to the mouth of the river that reached inland and showed its course by its aisle of palm trees. The tallest masts of the vessels reached as high as the highest palms. At rest, the ships looked heavy and swollen, with their high bows and bulging sides and tall, suddenly narrowed housing at the stern where rows of windows framed in gilt carving flashed slowly when the hulls veered. Either under sail, or with sail furled as now, the ships looked to be nodding forward, across their own bowsprits.

Seen close to, their mystery vanished. Their clinker-built planking was crusted with barnacles. When an unloading port in the side was opened, and men leaned out gazing, a wave of foul air was let go. What looked like a cloud on the horizon was dirty coarse sailcloth with faded heraldic painting on it. The hulls were perhaps a third as long as the masts were high. A small boat was launched over the side to bring Pineda ashore. It was then proper style to step into the surf when the boat grounded and, drawing a sword, slash the blade into the waves, stating at the same time that these waters, and this land, and all in their provinces, now came under the possession of His Most Catholic Majesty.

Company from the ships followed the captain ashore. They were in general slender and muscular people, not very tall, but finely proportioned. Their heads were narrow, their faces oval, their hands and fingers long, their shoulders sloping. Moving with grace, and a certain suggestion of repose, they yet could in an instant flare into violence, sparring with blade or pike swift and deadly. Their skin was tough and swarthy, taking the light with a faint tarnish of gold, and turning in shadow with warm darks that suggested embers buried but alive and ardent. They kept their dark hair cropped like caps hugging their tall skulls. Many of them, even youths, wore mustaches that curved out about the mouth to meet sharply pointed beards under the lower lip. The lips were exposed, ruddy and sharply scrolled. These swarthy faces flashed alive with startling whites—the whites of eyes set off by the piercing black of their pupils, and the whites of teeth showing through lips parted for the breath of interest. Their eyes were set deep and often showed black shadows under the carved shell of their brows. In the faces of old men, the eyes were like black gems that reflected suffering, resignation and irony from the world all about them. The eyelids roofed over from a little curved fold deep in the socket. In the faces of young men, the eyes, suggesting a taste for life to be both given and taken, shone with calm animal charm. Above metal gorget or velvet collar a white ruffle of starched linen, sometimes edged with lace, gleamed along the dark jaws, bony or bearded, of those lean, perfervid faces.

Those men were not all dressed alike. Some—the leaders, the elders—wore shining pieces of armor at the neck, the breast, the arms, the thighs. Others wore chain-mail shirts, hauberks, under their ordinary shirts of Holland linen. Some had jackets of many layers of quilted cotton, that could turn or break the blow of an arrow. Some wore metal helmets shaped like deep slices of melon, that were morions, and others had hats of leather and felt shaped like little round boxes with tufted brims and jeweled brooches and expensive feathers from eastern Africa. There were suits of brocade or velvet, stained and worn from travel, padded and puffed at the shoulders and elbows. The hips and loins were covered with trunks made of leather or heavy cloth, slashed and puffed to show other stuff and color beneath. Their legs looked long and slender and ceremonial, encased in tight thick hose that reached to the groin. Soft leather boots were worn either rippled up tight on the thighs or loosely pulled down about the calves in many folds. Shoes were flat-soled-and-heeled, and had puffed and slashed toes revealing contrasting color. Everyone had cloaks, some with embroidery of gold and silver bullion, some plain, but all voluminous and expressive in gesture, whether thrown about the face for warmth or secrecy, or lifted by a sword at the rear like the rooster's tail, and all hanging as richly from the shoulders of a hungry private soldier as from those of a hereditary gentleman.

At the waist, aslant the codpiece, nestled the dagger with hilt turned to receive the left hand instantly. At the left side, from a baldric of leather studded variously with precious stones, or gold, silver or brass rivets, hung the sword with basket guard, silver wire-wrapped hilt, and a cross guard below the grip that signified when necessary the crucifix. The private soldiers carried a variety of tall weapons—pikes, halberds, spears, lances—and some had maces, including the morning star from Germany with its long-spiked ball dangling from a length of chain. A platoon handled the heavy crossbows that with their carved and colored ornaments, graceful curved bows and stout thongs at a glance suggested some sort of plectral instrument for music. A few elite soldiers handled the heavily chased flintlock muskets bound to walnut or blackthorn stocks with thick bands of copper, brass and silver. A hardly bearded youngster in white hose and quilted body mail, with indifference masking pride, might carry the royal standard on a tall pole tipped with silk streamers and a sharp iron point.

They gave in the light every color as they came out of the foul ships and crossed to the shore. They found the Indians friendly in their leathery nakedness. A sizable squatters' town reached along the river at the mouth. Supplies must be at hand. The beach was wide and sloped gently, so gently that the tidal marks of certain seasons showed far back in the sharp-grassed marshes. The air was balmy. As far inland as could be seen the ground was flat and easy to explore. Pineda's ships were ready for overhaul. Here he ordered them careened.

The Spanish company spent forty days about the mouth of the Rio Grande, which they called the Rio de las Palmas. While some of the men worked on the ships—scraping barnacles, recaulking, repairing— others went into the country. They traded with the Indians, though for what and with what nobody said. Travelling eighteen miles upriver from the mouth, they found forty Indian towns—wattled reed and mud houses to come to for sea food seasons, and to leave when the roots and berries inland were ready to be eaten. There was no report of seeds planted and crops raised for food. Pineda told in sweeping general terms of the whole land he had seen, from Florida to Veracruz, and found it good, at peace, productive, healthful. He saw Indians with gold ornaments but did not say where. But of all the places he had seen he chose the River of Palms to recommend for colonization when at the end of forty days, the ships were floated, and the expeditioners embarked for their return to Jamaica, four and a third centuries ago, laden with the most desirable cargo of their time—knowledge of new lands. They were the first Europeans to see any part of the Rio Grande.

2.

Rivals

A year later in the summer Spaniards came back, again by sea, to the mouth of the Rio de las Palmas. News of this swiftly crossed the wilderness to the south, where the chief of the Pánuco River was a native ally of Cortés. It was not long until in Mexico City Cortés received an inquiry to know whether the cacique Pánuco should be friend or foe to the white men at the Rio de las Palmas. Pending an answer from Cortés, he would send the strangers at the north some women and food. If the answer ever came, it was not preserved.

There were a hundred and fifty foot soldiers, seven cavalrymen, some brass cannon, and building brick and lime, with several masons, in three ships under Diego de Camargo on the lower river in that summer of 1520. Again the visitors came from Governor Garay of Jamaica, who declared in his official reports to the crown that the men of the previous year had been eager to return to their river; that they had promised the natives to do so; that it was important to keep their word to the Indians; that the Indians longed for Christianizing; and that three ships were idle and available at Jamaica for the venture. Behind the florid virtue of colonial prose lay harder fact. Cortés had made plain in his encounter with Pineda's men that other claimants to Mexico would be briskly handled. A colony, an organic evidence of true claim, would have to underlie any argument that might arise over frontiers. The Rio de las Palmas lay conveniently north of Cortés, and yet near enough to the river Pánuco where a position could be taken, and an attitude struck, to bound Cortés on the north, and extend Garay to the south. And what professional colonizer in a time of colonial genius forgot the rewards that came to the successfully bold? Literally lord of frontiers, of marches, such a one could hope to be created marquis, and know glory, before wearing a carved coronet on his tomb.

Camargo sailed up the Rio de las Palmas for about twenty miles,

winding on the long and repeated curves of the river, above whose low
banks that seemed like the sea floor his fat heavy little ships bulged like
sea monsters cast out of their element, and could be seen from miles
away on the flat coastal wilderness. The masts moved slowly among the
palms, and came to rest between Indian towns on the banks.

The stone masons, the bricks and lime, in the ships were intended
for the building of a fort as the first unit of civilization on the river for
defense against Indians and, possibly against other Spaniards from the
south, should the boundary challenge ever be given.

Perhaps motives were never really concealed.

The Indians were friendly as Camargo and his people landed.
Pineda had come and gone in peace, while the Indians watched what
he did, and gave him their frail products in return for his cheap colors
and shines and pretties, and let him march, if he would, seeing and seeing
as if he hungered with his eyes.

Now Camargo settled heavily among the river Indians. He would
have food from their stores, for his men. Superior strength in armament
at times felt like personal virtue, justifying all, as in a police psychology.
Other Indian possessions may have seemed suitable to take—dwellings,
women, lordship, honor, liberty. The record of provocations on the one
hand, and of treacheries on the other, was meagre. But one day a group
of Indians turned against the Spaniards, and open hostility flared on
both sides. Camargo made a show of arms, but the river people fought
back, and a battle driving them to the ships in the river cost the
Spaniards eighteen men and all seven horses of the cavalry. Abandoning
one of their ships, the Spaniards weighed anchor in the other two and
headed downriver. Indians pursued them in a great fleet of canoes. The
clumsy towering ships like great bullheaded fish, imprisoned by the
meanders of the river, were exposed to the stinging missles and cries of
the Indians in the canoes, and others on the low banks. The distance they
had to travel to reach the sea was twice as long by water as by land. But
at last they came to the roiled water of the mouth, crossed the shallow
bar, and headed south following the coast.

The ships were in bad repair. Unlike Pineda, these expeditioners
had not careened their vessels, which—"idle and available" at Jamaica—
may have been no good to start with. On board were few stores, because
of the unexpected flight from the river country. The stoutest men on
board ship were permitted to land on the coast, to make their way overland to Veracruz, foraging for their keep, and heading for the promises
of Mexico. The ships went on for Veracruz by sea. The same ambitions

filled their companies. Nearing Veracruz, and other Spaniards, one of
the ships had to be abandoned. It sank, after the men on board had safely
moved to the other ship, which reached Veracruz only to settle and
sink in the harbor after ten days.

A little while later, reinforcements came from Jamaica to join
Camargo's colony on the river. It was nowhere to be seen. But the passion
of Cortés, shaking the Mexican kingdoms for their gold and glory, called
to the men of Garay's second expeditionary force who, when they had to
leave the Rio de las Palmas, turned southward, irresistibly drawn into
hardship, catastrophe—and unity with the power of their time.

Three years later, on July 25, in 1523, Governor Francisco Garay
himself finally arrived at the Rio de las Palmas from Jamaica with an
army of seven hundred and fifty officers and men in sixteen ships, armed
with two hundred guns, three hundred crossbows, and artillery. A town
was to be founded here and called Garay. The civil administration had
already been established, and the alcaldes and councilmen appointed,
before the Governor's expedition had left Jamaica. He had never heard
from his other two forces of 1520; but he believed that their attempts to
found a colony were successful. His purpose was not only to make his
capital on the River of Palms, but also to make good his claims—based
on Pineda's voyage in 1519—to all the region reaching south to the
Pánuco River, despite the fiery shadow of Cortés which had already fallen
across the territory. Cortés, Cortés—the name, the legend reached into
the mind and affairs of every man who turned himself and his fortunes
toward the New World.

Garay sent a subordinate up the river to fix upon a proper site
for his city. The Governor waited at the arms of the river for a report.
It came in four days, when his scouting officer returned to say that what
he had seen made him conclude that the river country was unsuitable
for the founding of the city of Garay.

Many men were dismayed when the Governor, almost as though
seizing upon a pretext for his action, abandoned the plan to settle the
Rio de las Palmas. Some urged him to remain. But he turned his face
toward the south where on the Pánuco River, as he already knew, Cortés
had established the town of Santiestevan. Was this to be endured by that
officer of the crown who swore he had a claim to the Pánuco prior to
the claim of Cortés? Garay was heard to declare that he would fight for
his claim, and ordered the bulk of his army ashore, to join him in an
overland march from the Rio de las Palmas to the Pánuco. The fleet he
directed to follow the coast. Through hardship and loss, both land and

sea forces made their way south to give battle. But what genius of success attended Cortés? On his very way to oppose Garay by force of arms rather than by legal sanction, he received in the jungle a new royal grant giving him jurisdiction over the Pánuco, superseding the one earlier made to Garay, who came only to be swept magnetically into the power of Cortés—Cortés, to whom Garay's soldiers and sailors were eager to desert, Cortés, who never forgot anything, Cortés, to whom the Rio de las Palmas at the north was an outpost, possibly strategic, to be kept sharply in a corner of his mind, and be done about when the time came.

Garay bowed to the royal cédula and in due course was kindly, even sumptuously, received by Cortés in Mexico. There in the court of New Spain, he met another of the conqueror's defeated rivals—Pánfilo de Narváez, who had undertaken to represent the Governor of Cuba in a matter of landing in Mexico and arresting Cortés—a venture which had cost Narváez his small army, his reputation, his freedom, and one of his eyes. The two prisoners, given every privilege, exchanged old hopes and severed dreams. To proud men, the very kindness of Cortés could be terrible; for only to rivals rendered harmless could he show so much. Governor Garay died before the new year, of a broken heart it was said, after leaving Cortés as executor of his will, and Narváez as the inheritor of his hope to colonize the River of Palms.

It was the destiny of this river from the first to be a frontier of rivalries, a boundary of kingdoms, a dividing line between opposing ambitions and qualities of life. During the next three years, three Spanish leaders considered themselves the rightful masters of the Rio de las Palmas.

Cortés planned to settle a colony there in 1523, to help in carrying out the Emperor's command to find the Strait of Anian, which all believed to open from the coast between Florida and the Rio de las Palmas and to lead by water to Cathay. But affairs in central Mexico took all his attention.

Intrigue in the colonies and at Court worked away to crumble Cortés from below. As a result of representations made to him, the Emperor in 1525 removed the Pánuco from the jurisdiction of Cortés and created a new province of Pánuco-Victoria Garayana, reaching all the way to Florida and including the Rio de las Palmas. Nuño de Guzmán, appointed governor, sailed for his new province which he reached over a year later.

And meantime, with the return of Narváez to Spain petitioning for command of the lands once granted to Garay, the Emperor made still another grant, establishing the province of Florida, reaching from the Atlantic coast to the Rio de las Palmas. Narváez was made adelantado.

Messages, even royal commands, with their replies, took a year for the round trip, for the fleet sailed from Spain in April and returned from Veracruz in the fall. To such delay, again subject to the vagaries of the ocean, and the soundness of little ships and of men, there was added the formal obstructionism of government with its dedicated waste of time. It was no wonder that for years Cortés knew nothing of the royal patents made to Guzmán and Narváez.

Once in residence at the Pánuco, Guzmán established slave trade among the Indians of his region, and word traveled swiftly through the Indian jungles and deserts and river valleys of the cargoes of stolen Indians shipped out at fat prices for the enrichment of the Governor and his followers. He knew of the forty and more reed towns on the Rio de las Palmas; what was more, Pineda had seen Indians wearing golden ornaments somewhere along the Gulf Coast. Guzmán sent his cousin Sancho de Caniedo north to the River of Palms with orders to found a town on its course, reconnoitre the country, and claim it for Guzmán in the name of the King. It was an act of typical ruthlessness, for Guzmán knew then that Narváez by royal authority had been given command of the land taking in this river. He held to his prior claim. There was no news of Narváez. Slaves and gold to the north—let his brave cousin march. Caniedo went overland and spent five months exploring the territory. But where were they, the forty towns on the river? And where the people, with or without golden jewels? He found no towns and no tribes, only a few roving Indians who said yes, there were people, but they had scattered themselves away from the river, far away from what they knew about. To the south, Indian men and women of tribes persecuted in the slave trade had vowed to have no children rather than let them grow up to be captives for sale. Such news travelled. Caniedo returned from the empty lowlands of River of Palms to Guzmán at the Pánuco with neither slaves, gold, nor establishment of a city. Guzmán was later transferred to a command in the western coastal region of Mexico, where after a successful campaign he became the cruel governor of Nueva Galicia.

On September 3, 1526, from the city of Tenochtitlan, where he had come after months of arduous pacification of Yucatan and Guatemala, Cortés wrote to the King, ". . . I have a goodly number of people ready to go to settle at the Rio de las Palmas . . . because I have been informed

that it is good land and that there is a port. I do not think God and
Your Majesty will be served less there than in all the other regions
because I have much good news concerning that land. . . . " That
announcement had the air of forestalling in the King's mind any rival's
similar plans for the River of Palms. On the great map of New Spain
Cortés laid a paw here, a dagger point there, a knee elsewhere, a scowl
yonder; while he pursued whatever local battle required his presence.
Now deep in the tropics, away from communication for two years, he
finally heard from a loyal friend in Mexico the capital that his government had proved treacherous; that his death and his army's had been
proclaimed and all their possessions confiscated; and that Narváez, his
miserable, once-disposed-of rival, had been granted the River of Palms.
For a whole day the great commander kept to himself. His soldiers outside
his tent could hear that "he was suffering under the greatest agitation."
After Mass the following morning he told them the terrible news, and in
the midst of their dejection made plans for a secret return to Mexico, to
confound his traitors, regain his empire, and once more beguile the
Emperor with triumphs. But in his large affairs, as in his small, a spell
seemed to have been broken. The genius for success had abandoned
him. Soon he was in Spain arguing for more power; the Emperor deliberated, complimented him, relieved him of his major command, and
created him Marquis of the Valley of Oaxaca. He returned to Mexico,
a lion still hungry but with claws drawn. He never saw the Rio de las
Palmas; for, a decade later when he asked for another part of the same
long river, far to the north, he was denied in favor of a young officer, a
late-comer to Mexico, of whom nobody among the veterans of the
Conquest had ever heard.

Meanwhile, Pánfilo de Narváez with his royal charter, four hundred men, eighty-two horses, four ships and a brigantine rode out of the
harbor of Xagua in Cuba. His course was charted for the mouth of the
Rio de las Palmas. His pilot had been there before, with Garay, and
was believed to know the whole crescent of the great Gulf, from Pánuco
to Florida. But it was a year of storms, and in early April of 1528
Narváez and his company were driven from their course by a wild south
wind that blew them into the west coast of Florida, where they landed
on the fifteenth. They were far—how far they could not know—from the
River of Palms; but amidst hostile demonstrations by Indians, who yet
wore a few golden trinkets, and discoveries of the wrecked ship and the
deerskin-wrapped corpses of earlier Spaniards, Narváez concocted high
plans. The fleet was to proceed along the Gulf Coast to the Rio de las

Palmas, while he and the cavalry and the bulk of the footmen marched
to the same future capital by land. There they would meet, and the
city would rise, and it would not be Cortés who built it, or poor Garay,
but the Adelantado Pánfilo de Narváez, with his failures in Mexico
wiped out, his one eye flashing enough for the other one which Cortés
had cost him, his marvelous deep commanding voice proper to a wise
governor of fabulous lands united to Spain and ennobled by his own
courage and zeal. The fleet caught the wind to sea, and in due course,
Narváez moved overland into the wilderness, according to plan. He
never reached the river that was the western boundary of his vast province.
The ships of his original fleet looked for the River of Palms, there to
meet him, but either did not sail far enough or passed the lazy waters
of its bar-hidden estuary at night, for they never found it. They returned
to their starting point on the Florida coast, but there was no sign of their
captain-general. They sailed back and forth for nearly a year searching
for him and the three hundred men who had disembarked with him;
but to no avail; and in the end they gave up and sailed for Veracruz, in
New Spain.

For seven years nothing was known of the fate that befell the
remainder of the Narváez command. But when the news finally came,
those who heard it were lost in marvelling at how it arrived.

3.

Upland River

A thousand miles upland from the mouth of the Rio de las Palmas,
dug-out villages roofed with straw, twig and mud sat by the banks of the
river. It was the same river, though nobody then knew this. The riverbanks were low, here and there shaded by willows and cottonwoods.
A little distance back on either side, the ground was hard with gravel.
Narrow deserts reached to mountains that lay parallel to the river. The

leaves were turning yellow, for the first frost had come, and the hunting parties from the villages had already left for the buffalo plains to the northeast, leaving only a few people at home to care for old persons and to guard the stored harvest of beans, squashes and corn. In mid-November, if the wind was from the north, hard dust was blown up to sting the face, and the sky was wan with long white streaks. If the breeze was southerly, midday was warm and blazed with empowering light out of the blue, and sharp, dry scents came off the scaly desert and somehow told of well-being.

To the most northerly of these river villages, near the site of modern El Paso, now came walking in mid-November, 1535, two Indian women, one of whom was the returning daughter of a man who lived there. With them were two extraordinary persons, a man whose skin was light, though burned by sun and wind, and a man whose skin was black. These men showed signs of having suffered from near-starvation over a long period. They were sparsely clothed in animal skins. The women said that three days away were two other white men, escorted by a large throng of Indians of the prairies who dared not approach closer because of long-standing enmities with the village people. There was much to tell the villagers about the strangers, who were great doctors able to cure the sick and raise the dead. If the two already there in the town by the river were made welcome, the other two who waited three days away would come also. Yes, let them come, said the town people. With that, accompanied by many of the river people, the strangers set out to join their companions. Toward the end of the three days' journey, the white man, with five or six of the villagers, went ahead to prepare the meeting, and a few miles later met the other two white men who waited in the desert with their crowd of roving prairie people. The white strangers greeted one another with joy, sharing the news of settled towns where food was to be had. They then proceeded to meet the gift-laden procession that was approaching, and with which walked the black man.

The meeting in the desert was ceremonious. The river dwellers brought gifts of beans, squashes, gourds, robes of buffalo fur, and other things. These were bestowed upon the strange doctors in friendship. Now the plains people and the river people confronted one another. They did not speak one another's tongues, and were enemies. The doctors gathered up the gifts they had just received and gave them to the roaming people who had come there as escorts, and asked them to go back to their own people and away from their enemies, which they did.

With the others, the doctors then marched to the river dwellings, and as night came with the November chill they reached the houses. Great celebrations were held for the visitors, who gave thanks in prayer for having found those people, with whom they stayed all night and a day. On the second morning they began to travel again, accompanied by the people, going up the river which ran brown and shallow between earthen banks below two mountains that made a pass. Messengers went ahead. On the streambanks beyond the mountains the doctors found other towns where they were received with different signs of friendship. When the strangers came into houses they found the people seated facing the wall, with lowered heads, and their hair hiding their faces. In tribute to the visitors the householders had heaped all their possessions in the middle of the room from which, when greetings had been exchanged, they gave presents of robes and animal skin. The people were strong and energetic, with beautiful bodies and lively intelligence. The young and able men went wholly naked, the women and old feeble men clothed in deerskin. They freely and aptly answered questions put to them by the strangers.

Why did they not plant corn?

Because all they had left was seed corn on which they were living.

How was this?

Because there had been no rain for two years. Seed put into the fields was stolen by the moles, who could find nothing else to eat, since nothing grew in the dry years. The summer sun destroyed what the winter cold had not killed. The people begged the doctors to invoke rain for them from the sky, and the doctors acquiesced.

Where did the corn come from?

From that place where the sun went down.

Ah. And how did a man reach that place?

The shortest way to it was in that very direction, to the west, but the proper way was to go up the river toward the north. Even so, anyone would have to walk for seventeen days before finding anything to eat except chacan (juniper berries) which even when ground between stones was too dry and bitter to enjoy, though birds ate it, and brown bears in the mountains. Here, they said, try it, producing some. The strangers tried, but could not eat it.

And the river trail, then, how was it?

Passable, until the river turned west at the point of a mountain which could not be followed, for it came sharply down to the river and there was no path. All the way there were many people who spoke the same language as here, but who were enemies. They likewise, in towns, had little food in the dry years, but they would be friendly to the doctors, and present them with gifts of their riches, such as hides and cotton cloth. But it would be wise not to go that way, but take another journey toward the buffalo plains where the village hunters were.

Hunger was everywhere in the immense land, through which the river crawled brown by day, white in the twilight, shadowed by the vast moving clouds, walled now near, now far, by mountains of bare rock against which the pale dust stirred upward off the deserts whose constant change in motion could be seen only from great distance. Which way to turn? The strangers debated, remaining two days with their informers, who gave them beans and squash to live on, and who showed them how to cook. They took a large dried gourd which they half-filled with water from the river, and making fire with a hard wooden drill which they rapidly palmed to make its point turn in a small pit let into a flat piece of wood from which embers would presently come, they heated small stones readily picked up from the crusty gravel of the desert. When the stones were hot they were taken up with sticks and dropped into the water in the gourd. When the water boiled, the cooks dropped their raw food into it, and replaced stones that cooled with others just heated.

There was much to consider if the strangers were to take their way safely toward the goal they blindly sought. At the end of two days they made up their minds not to go directly to the west, or to cross the deserts northeastward toward the hunting plains, but in spite of the advice they had received, to go up the river as far as possible, and then turn west for the corn country; for it was in going always toward the sunset that they believed their salvation lay. Leaving the people, who would not go with them, they walked on the trail up the river's east bank. Every night they came to other people who received them with gifts of buffalo robes, and offered them chacan, which they did not eat, but lived instead on little stores of deer suet that they had hoarded against starvation. For fifteen, sixteen, or seventeen days the three white men and the black man made their way along the depleted river from village to village. And then, below the shoulder of the mountain that made them change their course (the southern tip of the Caballo range) they crossed over to the other bank, and diminishing as they toiled away from the river until they were mere specks in that speckled land, they finally vanished into the west.

Behind them were seven years of impossible endurance and deter-mination to survive—impossible, except that they endured and survived; for these four were all that remained free and alive in 1536 out of the whole armored and bannered company that had landed in April of 1528 on the west shore of Florida with Pánfilo de Narváez, by royal charter hereditary Grand Constable, Governor, Captain-General and Adelantado of that kingdom in fantasy. The mission of Narváez—to know the country from Florida to the Rio de las Palmas—was at last carried out by members of his company, however unexpectedly.

One of the four starving travellers was the royally appointed Treasurer of the Rio de las Palmas. His name was Alvar Núñez Cabeza de Vaca, and he came from Jerez de la Frontera in Spain. He did not know his own river when he found it. The others were Captain Alonso del Castillo Maldonado, of Salamanca, and Andres Dorantes de Carr- ança, of Béjar, who owned the last man of the four, the Moorish Negro slave Estebanico.*

The river saw them no more. But with them they carried its image and its legend. Weeks later they came among people who told them more of life to the north. There was a great river—and again it was the same river—where lived many people in big towns with immense houses. They were people of wealth, and had many fine and desirable things, like these blue stones, and these green arrowheads, five of them—here, take them—which, the Spaniards thought, shone like emeralds. Emeralds treated like common flint for arrowheads! For such treasures, Indians went on a long trail crossing the deserts and mountains to the great house-cities of the north on the river, and traded yellow, scarlet, blue and orange macaw feathers, and the tiny green breast feathers of little parrots for them. At the right times of the year the trail was well-travelled.

The four travellers followed it to the south, and took with them in experience and memory all they had seen and all they had been told, that would soon reveal a whole new world to those whom they at last met—Spanish soldiers bearded and helmeted, mounted on horses, armed with swords and lances, at the outposts of the slave trade in the province of New Galicia whose governor was the former governor of the River of Palms, Nuño de Guzmán.

They were delivered from their prison of space. The wilderness of their tremendous passage ceased to be an abstraction as soon as they found succor amongst those who could hear what they had to tell, Spaniard to Spaniard.

---

* One more survivor of the Narváez entry was still alive, a prisoner of Indians in Florida. He was Juan Ortiz, who suffered abominable captivity before his rescue a few years later by De Soto, and died before seeing his Spanish homeland again.

4.

The Travellers' Tales

They were given clothes to wear, and after seven years of nakedness they could scarcely endure the feeling of cloth. They were given beds
to sleep in, but for many nights could not sleep anywhere but on the
ground. Their rescuers wept and prayed with them giving thanks for
their delivery out of the barbarian lands. But there were bitter discoveries to make again of rapacity and greed among their own kind as
represented by Governor Guzmán's men at Culiacan. Still, every sense of
the value inherent in their extraordinary—and exclusive—news of vast
new kingdoms helped to urge Núñez Cabeza de Vaca and his companions
on to the city of Mexico, where they arrived on Sunday, July 25, 1536.
Here there were two men who, more than anyone else, wanted to see
them, to question them, and to glean their treasure of information.

One was the Viceroy, Don Antonio Mendoza, maintaining in his
palace a state proper to the direct representative of the Emperor
Charles V, with sixty Indian servants, three dozen gentlemen in his
bodyguard, and trumpets and kettledrums.

The other—how could it have been otherwise so long as he
breathed?—the other was the Marquis of the Valley of Oaxaca, Cortés,
starving for a renewal of conquest, and gnawing on his pride like a dog
on a bare bone. Still restless, he still saw the new continent as exclusively
the vessel of his aging energies.

The sabbatical refugees were splendidly received, now by the
Viceroy, now by Cortés, and given fine clothes and other gifts. On the
feast day of St. James the Apostle, a bull fight was arranged with a fiesta
to honor the heroes. Núñez Cabeza de Vaca was put up at the viceregal
palace. Interesting interviews followed.

What was the extent of the seven-year journey?

The travellers drew a map for the Viceroy and on it traced their
immense passage that spanned the continent from ocean to ocean.

And what had befallen them in that seven-year passion of survival? The travellers had much to tell:

How seven years before with the whole company they had set out with the Grand Constable in Florida to find the rich inland country of Apalachen where they were promised gold and food, and how when they got there all they saw was a starving tribe of belligerent Indians; how days of roaming brought them nothing better; how the Governor fell ill and irresolute; how they tried to find the sea again and, having found it, how they wondered whether they could build boats in which to go by water to the River of Palms; how they had no tools or crafts with which to build boats; and yet how one day a soldier volunteered to make pipes out of tree branches and bellows out of deerskins; how they turned their stirrups, spurs, crossbows into nails, axes, saws and other tools, and set to work; how in twenty days with only one real carpenter among their number they constructed five boats about thirty feet long, caulked with palm fibre, and rigged with ropes made from horsehair, and sails made from Spanish shirts, and oars carved out of willow; how two hundred and two men embarked for the River of Palms in the five boats on the twenty-second of September in 1528, and how when all were loaded, the sea reached to within the spread of a thumb and little finger of the gunwales, and how men could hardly move for fear of swamping; how nobody in the party knew navigation; how they drifted west in hunger, and thirsted when the water containers made from the whole skins of horses' legs rotted and would not serve further; how it was when men died from drinking sea water; how when they landed now and then to forage they were attacked by Indians; how winds and currents drove the boats apart from one another; how the Captain-General dissolved his command, saying it was each man for himself, and how he himself in his boat vanished out to sea one night in high weather and was never again seen; how two of the boats were blown ashore and broken on a barren island near the coast; how those who escaped, now only eighty in number, came to land naked and skeletal; how they passed the winter there amidst Indians, digging in the shallows for roots until January; how with spring all went to hunt blackberries; how they agreed to demands by Indians to effect cures of the sick, praying the Pater Noster and the Ave Maria, which healed the infirm; how certain Indians on meeting one another sat and wept for half an hour, then how he who was visited rose and gave the visitor all he owned who went away often without a word; how they were enslaved as root diggers by the Indians; how Núñez Cabeza de Vaca became a

trader between coastal and inland people, taking from the shore such
things as sea snail, conch shell for use as knives, sea beads, and berries,
and bringing from inland in return skins, reeds or canes to make arrows
of, hide thongs, ochre for face-painting, and tassels of deer hair; how
one of their companions refused to leave the island to try for freedom
overland, and how Núñez Cabeza de Vaca tried each year for several
years to persuade him, and, having succeeded, only saw him give up and
return to the island where he died; how others of the company died until
eighty became fifteen, and those became four, threatened and terrorized
by Indians through the years of captivity and constant movement from
sea to plains, from plains to rivers, according to the seasons of food; how
the company sliced and dried the flesh of their companions who died,
and ate it to live; how the Indian people ate ant eggs, and spiders, worms,
lizards, poisonous snakes (even those that bore at the tips of their tails
little horny pods that shook with the sound of castanets), the droppings
of animals, powdered fishbones, and other things to be remembered but
not told; how the mosquitoes caused such torment that the people at
times set fire to forests and grasses to drive them off; how they saw
buffalo, some tawny, some black, with small horns; how the ground
fire-hot from the sun in summer burned their bare feet as they wandered
naked; how the four friends were separated many times when their
Indian masters of different tribes met and parted; how one day after
years they heard of the remains of one of the five poor boats and were
shown by Indians the weapons and clothes of the occupants who had
been too weak to resist as they were killed by the people of the coast;
how the friends escaped and came to friendlier tribes inland among
whom they became, all four of them, powerful doctors of medicine,
making cures by the grace of God, and even as Núñez de Cabeza de Vaca
did, restoring to life an Indian admitted to be dead; how after six months
with those people, in famine, they found the prickly pears ripening and
regaled themselves though the fruit was green and so milky it burned
their mouths; how when the Indians set them to scraping skins to cure
they scraped diligently and ate the scraps which would sustain them
for two or three days; how going naked under the sun they shed their
skins twice a year like snakes, and carried open sores on their shoulders
and breasts, and were torn by thorns in the heavy brush of the inland
country; how they came to be with other Indians who were astonished by
their appearance and who overcoming their first fear put their hands
on the faces and bodies of the strangers and then on their own faces
and bodies almost as though to banish the mystery of human separate-

ness in a gesture of common identity; how the Indians saw and heard better and had sharper senses than any other people they had ever seen; how one day they were given two gourd rattles by Indian doctors who said these had come floating by a river from the north; how another day they saw a hawk's-bell of copper, carved with a face, which they were told came from a country where there was much copper; how in a new tribe they came among, the men hunted rabbits driving the animal ever closer to each other and finally striking it with a club most accurately thrown; how these people were hospitable and hunted deer, quail and other game for them, and at night made them shelters of mats; how as they moved, the people, three or four thousand strong, went with them and asked of them cures, blessings, and breathings of sanctification upon their very food, until their duties became a great burden; how these people never spoke to one another, and silenced a crying child by scratching it from shoulder to calves with the sharp teeth of a rat in punishment; how through the summers and winters of seven years these and countless other memories came with them in their powerful will to keep walking to the west, to the west; how they avoided the courses of rivers that flowed south and east which would return them to the miseries of the seacoast and its barbarians; and how they looked for rivers that flowed south and west, which might lead them out of the unknown land toward the mapped places of New Spain. . . .

And by the grace of God, they had indeed found their countrymen. Now—continued the voice of government—after all the abuses and hardships so admirably survived, was there then information as to the material resources seen along the journey?

Nothing but the utmost in degrading poverty for the first six years, until the travellers moved westward through mountains, and encountered the river where the corn-raisers lived. Given rain, it must be good country. They saw it.

Was that all?

Not all, for though they did not actually see, they heard of great cities on the river to the north, with many storied houses, where there were great riches, according to the people who told them so, and in fact, there was some evidence, for the people gave them some turquoises, and five arrowheads carved out of emerald.

Emerald? Where were these? Could they be examined?

Unfortunately, they had been lost in a frontier fracas with Governor Guzmán's men, but were perfectly real, a bright, polished, though not transparent, green.

And these fabulous arrowheads came from the cities to the north, on the river?

Yes, and had been obtained by trade with southerly Indians, who bartered parrot feathers for them. There were other things of interest, and possibly of value—beautifully made shawls better than those made in Mexico, bangles and ornaments of beads, including coral that was traded inland from the South Sea, that great ocean lying to the west.

Yes, yes, shawls and beads—was there by any chance any sign of gold and silver and other metals?

Not directly, save for a copper hawk's-bell come upon in the prairies far inland. The trading Indians were asked, as of course all people were asked every time they met anyone, whether gold and silver were in use in the great river houses. The reply was no, they did not seem to place much value on such substances. However, in the mountains through which they had come, reported Núñez Cabeza de Vaca, he and his friends had themselves seen many signs of "gold, antimony, iron, copper, and other metals."

In other words, though the natives did not employ them, there were deposits of natural wealth?

So the trading Indians had said.

This was curious, in the face of earlier reports that came officially to the viceregal government, through an Indian belonging to Governor Guzmán, who said that as a child he had gone with his father—a trader—to those northern river cities, and he well remembered them, there were seven of them, where there were whole streets made up of the shops of gold- and silversmiths. Still. They might well be the same cities. —What was the way like? A road? Landmarks? A trail?

A trail, principally, once past the northern outposts of Governor Guzmán. It was employed for the travel of traders. There were many such guiding paths to be seen, made by the people who went from place to place for food and barter.

Could the way be followed by strangers to the land?

Probably—certainly, if anyone went along who had once travelled it.

Good. The refugees would please prepare a written report of all they had seen, as fully as possible, to be forwarded to the home government.

It was like the imperceptible rising of a pall of smoke from unknown land which became slowly visible.

All the evidence was translated into visions of wealth. But after

all, experience made it seem plausible that the northern country should
be another Mexico, another Peru, where in their own terms of gold and
silver the conquerors had found wealth so real and heavy that the
treasure ships returning to Spain with only the King's fifth of all colonial
income were worth whole fleets of raiders to the French and British.
From the very first evidence at the tropical coast, with Montezuma's gifts
to Cortés of golden suns the size of carriage wheels and the rest, there
was promise in every report of an unknown land.

Cortés believed that he held moral and legal right to all new
conquests in the continent he had been the first to overcome. He spoke
privately and urgently with Núñez Cabeza de Vaca, and was not amazed
at what he heard. In 1528, had he not already petitioned the Emperor
for a patent to the northern lands, where this river was that they spoke of?
Now it must certainly be his to exploit. Everything would appear to
justify his selection as commander of an expedition to the great house-
towns of the north—experience, ability, seniority, not to mention what
might be due to him in gratitude for his past discoveries, pacifications
and enrichments.

But the Viceroy had been given a firm understanding of the
crown policy toward Cortés. All honor, consideration, respect—but no
power. Power in the hands of the Marquis of the Valley tended to become
too personal; too possibly enlarged until the crown itself might in its
colonial relationship come to appear somewhat diminished, which would
be unsuitable. As interest grew in the conquest of the north, there was
talk that the Spanish Governor of New Galicia, Francisco Vásquez de
Coronado, would be named by the Viceroy to organize and command the
new colonization. He had come to Mexico in the suite of the Viceroy a
year or so before, and had shown himself to be an able man of government. The Viceroy conversed with him—secretly, for fear of Cortés—and
arrived at a plan for further investigation of the north before the full
expedition should be sent. The Bishop of Mexico had a remarkable
guest, a certain Franciscan friar, called Marcus of Nice, who was known
to be bold, saintly and selfless. Let him go north to find, if he could,
the seven cities of Cíbola, of which such firm evidence had already been
noted, and let him pacify the Indians as he went, and return with news.
To guide him, the Moor Estebanico, who had already walked on much
of the traders' trail in the northern wilderness, would be sent along.
Núñez Cabeza de Vaca had earlier declined an invitation to return to
the north, and had sailed for Spain. The other two survivors were settled
in Mexico. The Moor was the best one to go.

The plan was agreed upon in the summer of 1538, and from
New Galicia Francisco Vásquez de Coronado dispatched the friar and
the Moor, with Indians who knew the immediate north, in the mid-
spring of 1539. Fray Marcus was robed in a gray zaragoza cloth habit.
Estebanico, fleetly accompanied by two greyhounds, went clad in bright
clothes with jingle bells at his wrists and ankles, carrying as a badge of
importance one of the gourd rattles long ago acquired in the inland
plains whither it had floated by river. The party travelled on foot. The
Viceroy's orders to the friar said, in part, "You shall be very careful to
observe the number of people that there are, whether they are few or
many, and whether they are scattered or living together. Note also the
nature, fertility, and climate of the land; the trees, plants, and domestic
and wild animals there may be; the character of the country, whether it is
broken or flat; the rivers, whether they are large or small; the stones and
metals which are there; and of all things that can be sent or brought,
send or bring samples of them in order that His Majesty may be informed
of everything. . . . Send back reports with the utmost secrecy so that
appropriate steps may be taken, without disturbing anything. . . ."

Would Cortés be listening?

The faithful friar was back in Mexico by early summer, making
his reports first to Governor Vásquez de Coronado at Compostela, and
later to the Viceroy in the capital. He told a temperate story, as full of
fear as of conjecture, and earnestly hopeful of truth, in spite of its
hearsay with occasional exaggerations and inaccuracies. It was a story
with its regrets, too. He had gone faithfully northward, observing the
land, passing from people to people, by whom he was cordially received,
with food, triumphal arches, and requests for blessings. Estebanico he
sent ahead with Indian guides, who were to return on the trail to tell
the friar what his black man had seen: a small cross if he had seen a
moderate-sized settlement, two crosses if a larger one, a great large cross
if a big city. Day by day the messengers came back with ever larger
crosses, until they bore one as high as a man. The great cities so long
imagined must surely be coming into view. . . .

Meantime, Indians from the west coast brought shells of the kind
known to contain pearls. There were deserts to cross, but the land became
gentle again, and the journey was feasible. Finally one day came weeping
messengers with bloody wounds who told of how Estebanico had halted
at a great city at the base of a high mound. There he sent to the chief
his ceremonial gourd rattle with its copper jingle bells. On seeing this,

the chief hurled it to the ground, crying that it belonged to people who were his enemies and ordering its bearers to retire from the land. But Estebanico had refused, an attack had followed, the Moor had been killed by arrows, along with many of his Indian party. Those who returned to report declared that this took place before the first of the cities of Cíbola, which they said had many stories with flat roofs, doorways paved with turquoise, and other signs of wealth.

Friar Marcus then believed all was lost. His Indian companions were angered against him, for he had led them into a land of danger where many of their relatives had been killed along with Estebanico. He opened his sacks containing articles of trade, gifts received farther back on the trail, and made them presents, and declared that faithfully he would go forward and see but not enter the city of Cíbola. Two of the Indians finally agreed to go with him, and at last he saw the city with his own eyes, from a safe distance. It looked as he had expected—terraced, made of stone, and larger than the city of Mexico, which itself had over a thousand souls. Even so, the Indians told him it was the smallest of the seven cities. Giving thanks to God, he named it the new kingdom of Saint Francis, built a cairn of rocks surmounted by a cross, and solemnly possessing the whole of Cíbola for the Emperor and the Viceroy, retreated to his waiting party.

One more matter needed observation—a valley many days' journey to the east, where he was told that in well-populated towns there was much gold which the people used for vessels, for ornaments of their persons, and for little blades with which they scraped away the sweat of their bodies. He believed that he saw only the mouth of that valley which lay at the end of the mountains of the north. There he planted two crosses and took formal possession, and hurried back to Compostela and Governor Vásquez de Coronado.

What he told was fitted ardently into the statements of Núñez Cabeza de Vaca, and into the long-sustained expectation of a true discovery of the lost cities of Atlantis—a dream kept alive in a time of marvels and credulities by Europeans whose exploits had already been marvellous enough to render any rumor plausible.

Excitement was high and gossip general. The Viceroy sent to Cortés, as a common courtesy, a brief of the friar's report. From his hacienda at Cuernavaca, the Marquis replied with thanks and a formidable offer to co-operate in any expedition of settlement sent to Cíbola. Presently he was in the capital, scornfully letting it be known that in

fact he had himself supplied Friar Marcus with most of the information
which other people accepted as having been gathered at great personal
risk by the Franciscan in his northern journey. The feeling of movement
was in the air.

People felt which way the wind was blowing. Cortés called upon
Francisco Vásquez de Coronado, whom he knew to be in the confidence
of the Viceroy, and proposed himself for the expedition to conquer,
settle and exploit Cíbola. Vásquez de Coronado faithfully reported the
hungry offer to the Viceroy, who rejected it sharply, and gave his young
provincial governor a wigging into the bargain. It was as well to have the
position made clear: he had already recommended Vásquez de Coronado
to the Emperor for appointment to the command of the expedition to
the north; and with no further word to the great, the difficult, the restless
Marquis, the Viceroy by royal authority on January 6, 1540, issued the
commission to Vásquez de Coronado, with the order "that no impediment
or hindrance whatsoever be placed in your way in the discharge and
exercise of the office of captain-general in the said lands, that everyone
accept your judgment, and render and have others render you, without
any excuse or delay, all the assistance that you may demand from them
and that you may need in the performance of the duties of your
office. . . ."

It was time to move rapidly.

Cortés was only waiting for the spring sailings from Veracruz to
hurry back to Spain, where he meant to press his claims personally upon
Charles V.

Already a fleet and an army had left Spain once again for Florida.
Núñez Cabeza de Vaca had hoped to return to the new kingdom of his
long suffering as commander of the present Florida fleet, but he was too
late with his petition to the King. A veteran of the Peruvian campaign,
Don Hernando de Soto, had already received the commission. De Soto
sailed with much of Núñez Cabeza de Vaca's information in his head,
imagining that he understood the country of his grant, all the way from
Florida to the Rio de las Palmas.

Núñez Cabeza de Vaca was a fateful man; for in Compostela, and
Culiacán, and the city of Mexico, another expedition in consequence of
what he had seen, heard, and suffered, now made ready for the north,
where waiting to be found in the distance of time and rumor, beyond
the cities of Cíbola, was the valley of the long river, with its people who
grew corn and wore mantles of cotton.

5.

Destiny and the Future

In midsummer of 1540 the Pueblo World of the river had the news of what was happening at the rocky towns to the west, in the deserts, where Zuñi people lived. New men had come, in shining garments, with tremendous animals on whose backs they rode. It seemed that these animals, with their great teeth in their long bony heads, ate people. There was a battle at the town of Hawikuh, where before the town the Indians made a line of sacred meal on the ground which they told the newcomers not to cross. One of the strangers advanced and made a long statement with a one-handed gesture to his brow, his breast, and each shoulder. More came up behind him. The Zuñis sounded their war horn, and were ready, with leather shields and bows, arrows, lances and maces. The women and the little ones and the old ones were sent many hours before to the hills beyond the town. The war captain gave the signal and arrows flew. Then came the men with the high animals, and gave war, making loud sudden noises with flashes of fire and smoke, and thrusting with hard knives as long as a leg. The Zuñis broke and ran to their town, the invaders followed, and a hot fight brought the surrender of the town in a little while. The new men broke into the food stores and ate like starving dogs. They made peace, and treated everyone kindly, though they had killed twenty Zuñis in the battle. Their chief was a grand lord who had been hurt in the fight, wearing a helmet of gold. He now recovered, and remained with his men at Hawikuh. Various chiefs from other pueblos went to see him, bringing him gifts of turkeys, animal skins and food. To them he gave marvellous little things never before seen, some to be worn, either as ornaments, like the flashing beads, or on the head, like the red caps, others to be played with, like the little bells. He made much of a sign to be given with fingers, crossed one over another, squarely, or fixed in wooden pieces.

It was the mark by which they did everything. They could always be recognized by it.

Nobody knew who the newcomers were, with their light coloring, their immense animals, and their frightful noises. They brought with them a great amount of things they needed, and they sat down and put their legs one over the other as though to stay.

Long ago this world had heard of a white lord who would come to rule them. He would come from the south, as these men had come. Was this he?

There were people always moving on the long trails that went from the western deserts to the eastern plains. The news came along steadily.

One day in August of that summer the old chief of the pueblo of Pecos,* that stood at the gateway to the plains to the east of the river, came to the river pueblos on a journey. With him he brought a few of his people, including a young chief who wore long mustaches. He had heard of what had happened to the Zuñis, and he was going to see for himself. Word had travelled that the new man at Hawikuh would be glad to see chiefs from the country. The newcomers at Hawikuh were strange people, and bold men, and should be met and examined. Travelling by the pueblos on the river, the chief from Pecos and his party crossed over to the west and made their way in the August heat over the desert to the town where the amazing thing had happened.

When he arrived with his party at Hawikuh, he was without delay taken to see the commander of the invasion, whose name was given as General Don Francisco Vásquez de Coronado. The travellers identified themselves. The old chief of the pueblo of Pecos, because of his position, was at once called Cacique, and the young chief, because of his long mustaches, was called Bigotes. Friendly greetings were exchanged and gifts—on the one hand little glass dishes, and pearl beads, and little bells; on the other, dressed animal skins, and leather shields, and head-dresses.

Bigotes spoke for the callers. He was a tall, handsomely made young man, a person of authority. He said they had come in response to the General's invitation to the people of this land to meet him as friends. He put his hands on himself and then toward the General. If the other soldiers and the General wished to come to his own land—he pointed to the east—then they would be welcomed, and in the air he made designs to enlarge his meaning.

---

* Pecos was then called **Ciqúique**.

The General was touched, and showed his gratitude. He was himself a tall and handsome young man, with dark gold hair, mustaches and beard, and blue eyes. He gave himself a fine bearing and was beautifully dressed, with leather, velvet, brocade and linen. He indicated that he would know more of the lands from which Bigotes and his friends came.

There to the east, told Bigotes with word and hand, lay the plains, so wide, so flat, so far, where the cattle were, with great bodies, little hooves, heads lowered, short curled horns, and beards, thus, from the chin.

The General knew of those before, from the reports of Núñez Cabeza de Vaca. One by one the pieces of the map fell into place. He wondered if the hides that had come as gifts might be from such cattle? But the hair on them was so matted and snarled that it was impossible to picture from them the appearance of those plains cows.

Bigotes could show them. He took one of his men and turned him so that all could see his nakedness. There on his body was a painted picture of one of the cows. On his breathing skin they could see how the cattle were.

The General and his men were delighted. The interview continued, with descriptions of the trails to the east, towns to see, one on a vast high rock, a river with more towns, and then mountains, with the plains beyond. The General for his part explained who he was, for whom he came here, his purpose in the land, the power of the Emperor, and the will of God, whose Son to save the world died on the Cross: thus: cross.

Now it was clear that there was much to see and the General wanted to ask one of his first captains to go to see it. He presented Captain Hernando de Alvarado, commander of the artillery. Captain de Alvarado, with twenty soldiers, and the chaplain Fray Juan Padilla, was to accompany the Indian visitors on their return to their homelands, and take up to eighty days if necessary to make a proper reconnaissance of the territory to the east.

Bigotes and Cacique found that this could be arranged, and at once proposed to accompany Alvarado as his guides and to sponsor him in friendship among the people they would meet and whose towns they must pass as they went, toward the land of the cattle.

So it was settled. The General had already sent other expeditions to the west and the northwest, who would report back to Hawikuh which he now called Granada, both because it somewhat resembled the

town in Spain, and also to honor the Viceroy, who came from the old
Granada. Captain de Alvarado now with his little force of sixteen
cavalry, four dismounted crossbowmen and a chaplain, along with the
Indian party would be able to furnish much information. The General
would remain at Granada until he received all reports from his scouting
forces in the field. Then, in a position to move wisely, he would decide
where to take the bulk of the army, which awaited his word in the Sonora
Valley to the south, and establish its winter quarters.

The General saw Alvarado and his company off to the east on
Sunday, August 29, 1540, which was the feast day of the beheaded
St. John. The unknown lay vastly all about him to the west, the north
and the east. His health was restored to him after the wounds he had
suffered in the battle for Hawikuh, when because of his gilded armor
and his place of command in the vanguard of his troops he had been
the chief target of the Indian defenders. Storming the walls among his
men, he had suffered piercing arrows and a rain of heavy stones thrown
down from the parapets. Alvarado and another captain, García de
Cárdenas, had saved his life and borne him away unconscious, and for
the duration of the battle they had thought he must die.

But now the town was at peace, the Indians made paintings for
him on hides, showing the animals of the region, that he could send to
the Viceroy, and he worked on his reports, and awaited news from his
field forces.

Not too many years before an odd thing had happened in Salamanca, his home in Spain. It was the kind of thing to which thought now
and then returned. It seemed that in his young days he had a friend who
was an adept in mathematics and other sciences. One day they had a
conversation in which destiny and the future came up. The mathematician looked at him and told him that he was destined in the future
to find himself in faraway lands.

Faraway?

Yes, and furthermore, that he would become a man of high position and much power.

Position? Power?

Yes, but alas, he was to suffer a fall from which he would never
recover.

A fall?

The mathematician told him no more; but already at Granada
in the Indian wastes of the most remote northerly marches of the Indies
of the Ocean Sea, the General of the Army Francisco Vásquez de

Coronado was undertaking new kingdoms for the Crown. Was the prophecy two-thirds fulfilled?

6.

Faith and Bad Faith

On the evening of September 7, 1540, Alvarado and his company on the way to the plains came to a river which Indians called P'osoge, or Big River. Upstream, they said, were many towns, and downstream a few others. Here the banks were gentle, with cottonwoods and willows and wild fields of grass. On the west side were gravelly terraces and on the east, a band of desert rising far away into a long range of blue mountains parallel to the river. The evening light there arched yellow and vast overhead and the full river ran brown and silky to the south. The Spaniards were near the site of the modern Indian town of Isleta.

The river they named the River of Our Lady, because they had discovered it on the eve of her feast day—the Rio de Nuestra Señora.

Alvarado ordered his tent pitched, and at once sent Indian guides bearing a cross to the river towns of the north, to announce his coming. The march from Vásquez de Coronado's headquarters at Granada had taken a week, during which they had passed other towns, notably Ácoma, the citadel on the rock. Alvarado declared that it was one of the strongest ever seen. The town, of three- and four-storied houses, sat on a great mesa of red rocks four hundred feet high, or, as Spaniards measured, about as many feet as a shot from a harquebus would travel. The ascent was so difficult that, he said, they were sorry they tried it. It was a well-provisioned town, with corn, beans and turkeys. They passed on eastward and came to a big lake with abundant trees that reminded them of those of Castile. And then they reached the river.

On the next day came Indians from twelve pueblos with friendly greetings. They formed a little procession and came to Alvarado's tent,

the group from each pueblo following in turn. An Indian played on a
flute as they marched. After circling the tent, they entered and presented
the Captain with food, skins and blankets, and an old man spoke for
all of them. In return Alvarado gave them little gifts, and they withdrew.

Alvarado pursued such a good beginning. His party moved northward along the river. They saw its groves of cottonwoods and its wide
fields, and the twelve towns of the province where they were, which
was called Tiguex, and the two-storied houses built of mud. In the fields
by the towns they saw cotton plants, and they took notice of the rich
produce of melons, beans, corn, turkeys and other foods that the people
raised, and they saw that the people, following the ways of the farmer,
were more peaceable than warlike. Here the people did not go naked,
but wore mantles of cotton and robes of dressed hides, and cloaks of
turkey feathers. Their hair was worn short. Among them, the governing
power lay with the elders of the town, who made certain odd statements,
such as that they could rise to the sky at their pleasure. Alvarado believed
that they must be sorcerers.

Lying all about the river country were other provinces with eighty
scattered towns. From these the leaders came to greet Alvarado in peace.
With Bigotes guiding him, he continued his progress up the river from
town to town until he came to a black canyon cutting through a high
plain. He ascended the plain for there was no passage in the canyon.
On the plain he came to a town remarkable for its size and the number
of its stories, and for the fact that it lay in two parts, with a creek
running between. He understood it to be called Braba, and was invited
to lodge there. But he declined with thanks, and camped without. It
was the pueblo of Taos. He thought it had fifteen thousand people.
The weather was cold. It appeared that the people worshipped the sun
and the water.

Wherever they went, Alvarado's company planted crosses and
taught the people to venerate them. In the bare ground before the towns,
the large crosses stood, and to them the Indians prayed in their fashion.
They freed sprinkles of corn meal and puffs of pollen before the crosses.
They brought their prayer sticks of feathers and flowers. To reach the
arms of the cross, an Indian would climb on the shoulders of another,
and others brought ladders which they held while another climbed, and
then with fibres of yucca they were able to tie their offerings to the
cross, bunches of sacred feathers and wild roses. . . .

All this Captain de Alvarado and Fray Juan de Padilla wrote to
the General at Granada, telling him of good pasture land for the horses

and domestic animals, and sending him a buffalo head and several loads of Indian clothing and animal skins, and a map of the country they had seen, and advising him to bring the army to the River of Our Lady for the winter, as it was much the best country they had yet seen. The report was dispatched by courier.

With this first duty done, Alvarado with his own men and the Indian guides departed from the river to go east to see the cattle plains.

His report to the General brought early and positive results. Don García López de Cárdenas, captain of cavalry, with thirteen or fourteen cavalrymen and a party of Indian allies from Mexico and Hawikuh, came to the river with orders to prepare winter quarters for the whole army. The main body of the army was moving up from northern Mexico to join the General at Granada, and would come to the river in good order and season when preparations were completed. The campaign was proceeding in all propriety.

Cárdenas came to the twelve towns of Tiguex, and near the most southerly, on the west bank, he began to prepare campsites in the open, opposite the site of modern Bernalillo. It was October, and the bosky cottonwoods were turning to pale bronze above the brown run of the river. The days were golden and warm, but the nights were beginning to turn cold. The soldiers shivered in their open camp.

Now and then, when the light was gone, and all was quiet, and the smokes of evening no longer dawdled in the still air above the pueblo near-by, an Indian here, and another there, would quietly appear among the soldiers in their camp. They looked to see where the sentries were, and if they were on guard. In their expressionless way the Indians would seek out soldiers and communicate a suggestion to them. Did they want to wrestle? And a soldier or two, off duty, would get up, and with every appearance of good will, take up the challenge. The wrestling pairs went at their game. Something about the way of the Indian wrestlers made the Spaniards think. It was almost as though the Indians with a buried idea were trying out the strength of the soldiers. The nights were cold. The soldiers shivered.

A hard winter was coming. One October night the snow fell on the soldiers in the open fields. What would the whole army do when it arrived to camp on the river?

Cárdenas presented himself to the chief of the near-by pueblo on the west bank, which was called Alcanfor, and asked him to move his people into other pueblos of the province, to leave the Spaniards a town to themselves. where not only the small advance guard but the main

body of the army, when it arrived, could be given shelter. The Indian
governor gazed upon him and finally agreed to do as he asked. Taking
nothing but their clothes the Indians left their houses, and the soldiers
moved in, settling themselves and making arrangements for the arrival
of the General. The garrison—only fourteen cavalry soldiers and a handful of Indian infantry from the west and south—hoped for the early
arrival of the General and the whole army. Amidst the pueblos they
felt alien and uneasy.

One day an Indian from Arenal, a town a few miles up the river,
came to Alcanfor accompanied by the elders of his pueblo. He asked to
see Captain López de Cárdenas. He was received, and at once launched
into a vigorous complaint, making eloquent signs and enactments with
his hands, his arms, his body. The elders with him seemed to sustain his
case. Cárdenas strained to understand, and gradually the story of the
visitors began to come clear.

They said that a soldier came on a horse to Arenal and presently
rode up to the walls and saw a woman on the terrace with her husband.
The soldier dismounted and called up to the man if he would come
down and hold his horse for him. The man went down the ladder to
the ground to hold the horse, and watched as the soldier climbed up to
the roof. Since all rooms were entered from the roof, the man was not
surprised when the soldier like all visitors went there and vanished into
a room from the top. The man patiently waited holding the horse. He
heard a commotion somewhere in the pueblo, but thought nothing of
it at the time. In a while, the soldier reappeared, came down the ladder,
mounted his horse and rode away. The man then went to his part of the
pueblo and found to his horror that his wife had been carnally assaulted
by the soldier. When she resisted, there followed the commotion heard
below and outside. The soldier seized at her garments as if to tear
them from her. He had presented himself violently upon her, and if he
had not actually ravished her, he had tried to. It was an outrage. The man
who told the story, here with the elders, was the woman's husband. He
demanded punishment and redress. The elders supported him.

It was grave news for Cárdenas to hear. He agreed that if true,
the outrage must be redressed. Did the husband believe he would know
the soldier?

Yes, yes.

Cárdenas sent for the whole garrison of Spaniards, and when the
fourteen were all present, he asked the Indian from Arenal to point to
the guilty man.

The Indian searched the faces and examined the clothes of the soldiers, but could not recognize his man. He angrily told how impossible it would be to find him if the soldier had meantime changed his costume. But having held the horse, the Indian would never forget how it looked, and he now demanded to see all the horses of the garrison.

Cárdenas obliged him. The party moved to the horse stalls on the ground below, and the Indian went down the line until he came to a dappled gray covered with a blanket. That was the horse, he was certain of it.

It belonged to Juan de Villegas, who owned three horses, one coat of mail, one buckskin coat, and pieces of armor. What did Villegas have to say to the charge?

He denied it. He reminded the Captain that the Indian had not been able to recognize the man whom he accused, and asked if it was any more reasonable to think the Indian was any more certain about the horse?

The argument had weight. Captain López de Cárdenas was obliged in the face of no better evidence to drop the matter. The Indians went away with their story dishonored.

There was, somehow, a feeling of more trouble in the air. It was something of a relief when Captain de Alvarado returned to the river from the eastern cattle plains. He came dragging four people in iron collars and chains, and he had an animated story of his adventures to tell Cárdenas and the others at Alcanfor:

Eastward, through a mountain pass, beyond which were many other pueblos in ruins, and a turquoise mine, and another spine of mountains, there was the largest town yet to be seen by any of the explorers. It was Pecos, where Bigotes and Cacique had come from. There the chiefs and their Spanish friends were received with drums and flageolets, and gifts of clothing and turquoises. There the soldiers rested for a few days, feasting, and listening to stories of the kingdoms of the plains that lay beyond.

The stories were told by two captive Indian slaves who came from the plains and belonged to Bigotes and Cacique. One, a young man, was called Isopete. The other, because he looked like one, was named the Turk by Alvarado. These two must be the guides for a march to the cattle country. Bigotes decided to stay behind when the rest of them set out.

They went south by a river (the Pecos) with red rock and water and then left it to follow a smaller river, eastward. The Turk learned to speak a little Spanish. With that, and by gestures, he began to talk about a land of Quivira far to the east. Gold, silver, silks. Rich harvests. Great towns. Alvarado listened as they travelled. Soon they were in sight of endless herds of buffalo, and they hunted among them, bringing the big running bulls down with lances. Several horses were killed by the charging buffalo and others were wounded. If the cattle stood and stared with their bulging eyes sidewise, the soldiers killed them with harquebuses.

Gold, continued the Turk, and for proof, there was a gold bracelet that he himself had brought from Quivira when captured by Bigotes.

Where was the bracelet then?

Bigotes had it, at home, in Pecos.

Was he sure?

Very sure, and he added other details of precious wealth in the far plains kingdom.

Alvarado's commission of eighty days was then over half spent, and he decided to turn back to Pecos to take from Bigotes the Turk's golden bracelet as proof of what lay waiting for the General in Quivira. He ordered his party back to Pecos. The Turk cautioned him. He must on no account mention the bracelet to Bigotes. But on arrival, after receiving new gifts of provisions, Alvarado demanded the bracelet.

Bigotes and Cacique were bewildered. What bracelet?

The bracelet of gold they had taken from the arm of the Turk, here.

They declared that the Turk was lying. There was no such bracelet.

With that, Alvarado retired to his tent, and sent for Bigotes and Cacique. When they appeared, he had them clapped into chains for denying him what he asked for, and ordered the Turk to be kept in arrest as a witness. Trouble followed. The people of Pecos hearing what had happened to their chiefs came to Alvarado's camp crying bad faith, and discharging arrows. Presently the Turk escaped. A parley followed. Alvarado agreed to release the captive Cacique if he and his men would bring back the Turk. When they did so, Alvarado put them back in chains again, and again there was an outcry from the Indians. And then the land of Pecos was threatened by enemy Indians from another province. Alvarado and his men helped the Indian war party to go and defeat the enemy. The captive chiefs were released for the campaign, but in the course of it, the Turk once again escaped, taking Isopete with him. Once again Bigotes and Cacique were sent to recapture the slaves, and returning without them, were still again put in chains.

"I will keep you so until the Turk is delivered to me," declared
Alvarado, whereupon the fugitives were brought back by other Indians.
The battle campaign was abandoned as suddenly as it had been started,
and Alvarado, bringing his four prisoners in iron collars and chains,
marched westward to report to the General at Granada. But coming to
the River of Our Lady he found Cárdenas and the others already at
Alcanfor, and heard that the General himself with a large advance guard
was on his way to the river. Alvarado halted there to wait for him with
the enlivening news of the golden bracelet and all that it must mean.

7.

Facing Battle

At Granada, to the west, by late November, the main body of the
army had arrived from the south under command of Captain Tristan de
Arellano. The General received them warmly, and gave orders that they
should rest for twenty days and then follow him east to the river, for
he was leaving with thirty men to establish his winter headquarters at
Alcanfor. He took a different trail from that of Alvarado and Cárdenas,
striking to the southeast, meeting cold weather and for three days finding no water. Just before coming to the river he passed through a
province of eight pueblos called Tutahaco, where the people were peaceable. Hearing of further towns down the river, the General sent Captain
Francisco de Ovando, perhaps his most popular officer, to explore them
and rejoin him at Alcanfor in the Tiguex province. Then turning upstream the General made his way in the winter valley, with all its dry
golden, earthen pink and river-brown colors, to the town commandeered
by his advance guard, where he arrived in the afternoon of an early
December day, pleased to see the garrison established under Cárdenas,
and especially pleased to find Alvarado already returned from the cattle
plains. The very first evening, the General sent for Alvarado to tell his

story. Alvarado, who brought the Turk with him, made his report. The General then turned to the Turk. What, then, was this country like to the east of the cattle?

Oh, there was a vast river, two leagues across, where the fish were as big as the Spanish horses. On it floated great numbers of long canoes, carrying sails, with more than twenty oarsmen on each side. At their prows were large golden eagles. Under canopies at the stern the lords of the country took their ease. The ruler of that kingdom slept in the afternoons under a large tree in whose branches were hung countless little golden bells which beguiled him as they rang in the breeze.

The Turk spoke earnestly and openly. It was impossible not to believe him.

Was he sure of what he meant by gold?

Acochis, he replied. That was gold.

The General showed him some ornaments made of tin. Was this gold?

The Turk leaned over and smelled of the tin, and said that of course it was not gold, he knew gold and silver very well, and in fact, did not, as it happened, himself, care for any other metals.

Then there was silver, too?

Yes, all the ordinary table service was of silver, and larger pieces, like pitchers, bowls and platters, were of gold.

(Hardly thirty years before, the Emperor Montezuma had sent Cortés, at the seacoast, an image of the sun as large as a carriage wheel, and all of solid gold. . . .)

The General was enthralled.

What of the golden bracelet, then?

The Turk repeated that it had been wrested from him by Bigotes, and hidden at Pecos.

How could it be obtained?

Why, if they would let him go there alone, without Bigotes, the Turk would find it and bring it straight back to prove all he had been saying.

The General excused him, and he was led away. Alvarado advised strongly against releasing the Turk. He had long tried to escape from his enslavement; now could he be trusted to do as he promised? Bigotes, with the other captives, was at Alcanfor and could be questioned. With the advice of Fray Juan de Padilla, the General ordered him and Alvarado together to question Bigotes further. Much depended upon what they could learn from the young chief.

That night the Captain and the friar took the prisoner to the fields near the pueblo and interrogated him. Bigotes denied everything all over again. They concluded that he was lying. Alvarado knew what was commonly done in cases of that sort. He ordered some of the army's dogs turned loose upon Bigotes. But even though bitten on an arm and both legs, the prisoner refused to confirm the Turk's story. Later, the lacerated Bigotes, with Isopete and the Turk, was delivered in shackles to Cárdenas for safekeeping. Cacique, the fourth prisoner, an old man, though not chained was also retained in custody. The news of their treatment filtered through the pueblo settlements, behind whose impassive walls it made bitterness among the river people.

But now for the moment the General had more immediate problems to solve. The garrison was growing, and in less than three weeks his main force would arrive. Most of them were used to warmer southern climates. Already some of the Mexican Indians and Negroes with the army had died of the freezing weather. It was a sharp December in the river valley. He would need additional clothing for his troops. The Indian people seemed to have ample supplies of cloth of their own manufacture—cotton, and yucca fibre in which strips of rabbit fur were twisted. A requisition would have to be levied.

The General sent for an Indian who was called Juan Alemán, after a man in Mexico of the same name whom he resembled. Juan was a chief of Moho, a pueblo fifteen miles up the river. He had shown himself to be friendly. The General now asked him to collect from all twelve towns of Tiguex a requisition of three hundred articles of clothing or cloth with which to dress the soldiers.

Juan Alemán replied that he was unable to speak for more than one pueblo, as each was independently governed and would have to be approached separately.

With this, the General designated officers to visit the pueblos one by one and collect the levy. The order was promptly carried out. Some of the Spaniards did their duty considerately, others roughly. But in all cases the Indians had no chance to prepare for the demand, and time and again submitted by taking the clothes off their backs to hand to the soldiers, some of whom while foraging also took the opportunity to come away with corn, turkeys and other edibles. The river people lived from season to season, for the most part. Privation for them must follow the stern removal of their modest possessions, even though, in obedience to the strict command of the Viceroy, nothing was taken from the native people without reimbursement. But beads and little bells would not keep the people of Tiguex warm as winter fell, or feed their mouths as their harvest, gleaned with dances of thanksgiving, was so fast depleted by the strangers in their midst.

Thought moved behind the earthen brows within the earthen walls.

The soldiers were but men like others, as the playful wrestling had shown on those autumn evenings in the Spanish camp. Any man could die like another; but not so readily if he rode a huge beast that could trample over obstacles and people with furious power, and bear away its rider to safety faster than a man could run.

One day there came running from the Spanish pastures near Alcanfor a Mexican Indian wounded and bleeding who was one of the guards with the garrison's herd of horses. He cried that another guard had been killed by arrows, and that the horses were being driven across the river and north toward the pueblo of Arenal by men of Tiguex.

In a very real sense the horses could mean life itself to the Spanish. Cárdenas, taking some men with him, galloped out in pursuit. Footprints led him across the river and as he went he came upon many horses already killed with arrows. Others were alive and scattering in the river groves. He rounded up all he could and started back to the corrals, passing the pueblo of Arenal, which was barricaded behind new palisades. Within there was a wild concert of yells, exhortations, sportive chorus. He heard captured horses braying and dashing wildly about. The Indians were driving them as in a bull ring, and shooting arrows at them. He made a demonstration outside the palisades, and got their attention. He offered them forgiveness and peace. They reviled him and mocked him with obscene motions. He returned to his own pueblo with the rescued portion of the herd and reported to the General.

Vásquez de Coronado called his staff together for a council of war. His captains and his two Franciscan chaplains sat with him. All factors were weighed. The main army was not yet at the river, though surely it must by then be on the march. With the river towns in revolt, it would be impossible to conduct any explorations of the cattle plains and beyond, where the real objective of the whole expedition seemed now to lie. The uprising must be put down or between the prizes of Quivira and the long road home to Mexico there would be unpredictable dangers. The advance garrison was not large; there was risk in giving battle at this point; yet there seemed greater risk in not doing so. The General asked for votes. Each captain in turn, and the friars, voted to make one more offer of peace and, if it were rejected, to fight.

Captains Diego López and Maldonado were ordered to go respectively to the pueblos of Arenal and Moho. There they made announcements in official style offering peace and asking for specific complaints as to any individual misbehavior on the part of the army. If evidence supported charges, the guilty soldiery would be punished in the presence of the Indians.

In answer, the Indians, from their terraces where they seethed in tumultuous crowds, with their ladders drawn up, cried their defiance to the sky and brandished like flags the tails of the Spanish horses they had killed. After the officers were nearly killed at both pueblos through trickery, they returned to the General and war orders went out.

Captain Don García López de Cárdenas would command a force to subdue and capture the pueblo of Arenal, without delay. Attention would be turned later to Moho and other rebellious towns.

Sixty cavalry, and an infantry detachment, including Mexican Indians, were ordered in readiness. Veterans of Mexico and Cortés among them knew all over again the feelings facing battle. All night long before great battles the soldiers one by one moved slowly forward in line to confess their sins to the chaplains with the army. Loosely buckled great rowelled spurs chased in gold and silver on metal openwork clanged and tinkled as the horsemen moved up in line to the field confessionals. When had Indians first learned that Spaniards could be killed like other men? Perish it, whenever! After battles in the war of Mexico the soldiers used to dress their own wounds with the fat of Indians. Who remembered the hot jungle night when it rained just before a battle in Mexico—against Narváez and his invaders who sought to overthrow Cortés—and how just at that instant in the heavy air above the ground, a multitude of fireflies appeared in the wet darkness, and to the soldiers of Narváez looked like the lighted matches of Cortés's musketry, and seemed like a vast force?

In the cold valley of the Tiguex river hovered absolution and memory on the one hand, and on the other, a passion to protect an ancient breathing life within the hard-walled hives of the pueblos.

8.

Battle Piece

In daylight, the east mountains of bare rock looked near. Below them lay the band of desert; below that, the sandy terraces to the river, edged with groves brittle in winter. The pueblo rose in cubes of earth, casting sharp triangles of ink-blue shadow. The roof terraces were peopled. The ladders were up. Silence held the strain of looking. Presently from the south there was movement through the dry trees and out to the opening about the celled house. The light stung itself on metal and broke in rays as the column turned and halted. One man went forward and motioned a few others to follow him. They advanced quite clear of the troops and halted facing the plain walls along whose tops clung the minutely striving creatures dimly glistening like bees in great swarm. To them the man spoke out. At a distance his voice sounded thin but earnest. He motioned with his arms, offering. The swarm buzzed in rage from the roofs and replied with threatening motions. The man cried out again. Again the clustered bodies of the hive showed defiance. For two hours the exchange of offer and refusal continued. The man on the ground then returned to the mounted column and all rested motionless for a few moments. Then a movement began to detach one horseman after another from the column, as they set out and formed a circle all around the pueblo. When the movement was completed, there followed another pause and then came a long valiant cry that weakened as it went through the air until it might have been a wail, crying "Santiago . . ." and the men outside the pueblo began to advance on horseback and on foot against it. From the roofs downward: arrows and stones, wild dancing convulsions loathing and loathly, handfuls of powdered mud from puddled walls, screamed incantations. From the ground upward: slicing flights of arrows from crossbows, and volleys of lead bullets lumbered in gentle arcs by the harquebuses, and charges forward on horseback to cover efforts on the ground against the very walls. The walls were not excessively high, for the bodies of a few men leaning upon them, and the feet and hands of others climbing upon these, and holding, and the scramble of a few more upon those, let the top of the first rise of wall be reached. There swords flew, flashing, and wooden maces beat against them and upon helmets. The clinging strife against the wall fell down and rose again and fell and rose, and through the hours prevailed with its armored bodies flowing at last over the roof edge to stay, like a stain that once spilled would spread and flow until it stained all. Colors changed. Fluid crimson altered the rooftop as it altered naked earthen brown. Sounds wound on the air, the break of wood and steel, bone and life. With failing light and yellow evening the men from the ground were everywhere on the rooftops, and the people of the hive, but for their dead, were vanished below within the cells, into which the long delicate prongs of their ladders were drawn after them. Silence came with night, and hardly a movement, save that of the calm river going in its shallow valley. With morning, on the roofs, the leader of the armored men made another scene of exhortation, casting his voice awide and turning himself to be heard down below in the pits of darkness where remained silence and defiance. After an interval, then, separate small storms followed when the attackers tried to capture each cell by itself with its occupants. But the structure was thick, the entrances small, the cells many and interconnected, and advance was slow. There was a pause for a new undertaking, directed from the captured terraces, and then, below, on the ground, came men bearing a heavy burden against the walls. It was a huge log. With its end they began to thunder upon the ground wall of the big house slowly, in regular rhythm, shaking the earth house as if with deep drumbeat. Behind the battering ram there was a gathering of dry winter brush and bough. Fires sprang alive in the daylight and carried smoke into the blue. The giant drumming went on and wall-earth began to crumble. Cakes of earth fell aside, then whole clods, sliding like talus, then white dust shaken from the interior walls, and the hive was opened at its lowest level. Now the fires were taken brand by brand to the breach, and thrown in, and wood brought, and added, and the air shuddered in and out as drafts fought, but finally the whole cellular house acted as a chimney, and the smoke was drawn whistling from the banked fire on the ground outside through the rooms and out onto the roof terraces. With it were drawn the people inside, stumbling and crying, who clawed at themselves to see, and hugged themselves to breathe. They swarmed to the edges of the roof, where many were thrust by swords. Some hung down from the roof and dropped and ran and were ridden down by mounted men. Others were stopped as they ran on the ground, and were laid low by swords or bullets. Still others, taken as they fled from the walls, were made to keep running but tightly held until they reached the roaring fires into which they were thrown and in which they were kept at the points of long lances that spitted them if they strove to reach the cool air. Near-by there were stakes driven into the ground with faggots piled about them. To these many captives were dragged and tied, and the fires lighted about them. All appeared to happen with speed, wild understanding and inevitability. A tent for the mounted commander stood safely apart. Into it a large throng of escaped or surrendered people were put. The burning bodies at the stakes were in their view. Seeing those they tried to break from the tent to escape again but from outside men with blades thrust at them through the walls of the tent and those who survived to throw themselves forth were seized and piled onto the fires that grew and grew making flame and smoke high in the air by the mild river below the sandy sweeps that reached to the bare rock mountain on the east. Presently the mountain grew dim and the smoke from the fires seemed heavy in its rise. Winds swept over the reeking ground. The air turned colder. A thick snow began to fall upon the flames, the dying who still moved, the open dead at quiet, the excited animals and the armored men at their last tasks. The snowfall was gentle and sober. It softened broken edges and darkened the day and fell so fast that it muffled the hooves of the mounts as the column of troopers assembled from their various works about the little plain of the terraced city and with movements now modest and slow rode away southward through the thickened air. By evening all was quiet and no fires burned, and late in the night a handful of last inhabitants in the hive found their way safely out and ran away in the shadows of their house which was destroyed by the events of those two days.

　　　Returning at the head of his troops through the snowfall from the ruins of Arenal, Don García López de Cárdenas was met outside the headquarters at Alcanfor by the General himself, who embraced him heartily and approved his whole action in the victorious battle.

9.

The Garrison

The snow was still falling on the next day when the main body of the army under Captain de Arellano arrived from the west to join the General at Alcanfor. It was a dry snow that fell thickly but lay lightly and soldiers in the open field slept warmer all night for the cover silently made upon them.

The General's forces were now all with him but for a small rear guard left in the northern march of Mexico in the Sonora Valley. The army could look up the river and see the thickened air above Arenal still smoking from yesterday's battle. They were eager for news, and heard all, especially the Turk's promises of the great wealth that awaited them in the eastern kingdom of Quivira. When would they leave? When the river of Tiguex, as they now called it, was pacified. They would be on the river for a while. A self-supporting army in the field moved slowly at best.

There were three hundred and forty men-at-arms enrolled in the now-assembled force, including two hundred and thirty cavalry, and sixty-two infantrymen. These were all of European blood, mostly Spanish, but with an occasional foreigner, like the five men from Portugal, and the Scotsman, and the German bugler from Worms, and the Sicilian, the Genoan, and the Frenchman. Like a bridge between the Old World and the New, a native of the island of Hispaniola was on the muster roll. These were young soldiers. The youngest was seventeen, most of them were barely over twenty, hardly any over thirty. The General himself at thirty was an elder of the army. Many of them were nobles and gentlemen, come to seek their fortunes in the New World. Their blood pounded with longing and promise. By their young beards they looked older than they were, and by their cap-cropped hair younger. In their great appetite for the unknown they went to take more than to give; and like all youth what they desired most if they did not say it was experience, without

which there was shame before other men, and inequality of opinion.
Many of them were fellows of high spirits and wild behavior, and there
was talk in Mexico that as they were unmarried and dissolute, without
work or property, and with nothing to do but eat and loaf, and make
trouble for more settled people, it was a good thing that they went with
the army and left the city in peace. It was legally noted that they left
of their own will and happily.

They were armed variously with double-edged swords, crossbows,
daggers, lances, harquebuses and maces; and protected, some with pieces
of plate armor, gorget, cuirass, corselet; others with coats of mail, breeches
of mail, one with only sleeves of mail; and helmets of casque, morion
and sallet design, the last with beaver to protect the jaw and chin; and
steel gauntlets and shields. Such equipment ranged in value from the
splendor of the General's gilt armor with its plumed sallet to the buckskin coat worn by most. They brought with them a few bronze mortars
that discharged stones.

Three of the private soldiers brought their wives. One of these
men was a tailor. His wife served as nurse and seamstress, and rode
seven thousand miles with the expedition on a horse. The military company were served by close to a thousand Mexican Indians, many of whom
were accompanied by their wives and children. With the main body of
the army came the flocks of sheep—over five thousand rams, ewes and
lambs. The pace and distance of the daily marches of the army were
determined by how steadily and at what speed those grazing little animals
could move. The army brought five hundred head of cattle. Six hundred
pack mules carried supplies and equipment. Five hundred and fifty-two
horses belonged to the soldiers.

Alcanfor received the army shortly before the new year of 1541.
The pueblo was crowded but as a fortress it was also safe. The herds
and the flocks were guarded in corrals and pastures outside the walls.
The snow continued to fall. Spanish soldiers whiled away their off-duty
time. They would talk with the chaplains—Fray Juan de Padilla and
Fray Luis de Escalona. Fray Juan had been a soldier himself in his
youth. He knew how to talk with them. There were two Indian lay
assistants with him, the oblates Sebastián and Lucas. The soldiers went
to confession, heard Mass, attended vespers, and cooked, and some wrote
letters that two years later would be received in Spain, if ever. Playing
cards could be made out of the heads of drums. They gambled at cards,
playing "first" and "triumph," which were not prohibited by the com-

mand, and "doubles" and "lamb-skin-it," which were. Throwing dice was also forbidden and popular.

Captain de Ovando was back from the explorations downstream, to report that he had found four towns, built like the ones at Tiguex, occupied by friendly Indians. He saw no wild people, but as he had stayed with the river, this was not surprising, for the wandering Indians seemed to keep to the plains.

Heavy snowfall kept the garrison confined at Alcanfor, though the General had determined to demand the submission of the rest of the Tiguex nation and to obtain it if necessary with further battle. About a week after the arrival of the army it was possible to send Captain de Cárdenas and a party of forty horsemen and some infantry up the river with the ultimatum. They crossed to the eastern bank and presently came among the upriver towns which they found abandoned. At one of these they discovered a number of dead horses. In retaliation, Cárdenas burned the town and returned to headquarters. Word presently came that the Indians driven from their refuge in the bare and frigid hills were collecting at the pueblo of Moho, on the west bank about ten miles north of Alcanfor. In common defense, the river people, though accustomed to live under local rule in each town, now gathered under the general rule of Juan Alemán. Again and again the General sent his message of clemency and power, calling for all to submit to His Holy Catholic Caesarian Majesty. Captain de Maldonado took it to Moho first, only to return with reports of treachery and defiance. Cárdenas went forth once more with his cavalry and infantry, and found the Indians clustered on their roof edges at Moho waiting for him with Juan Alemán to speak for them.

Arriving within earshot, Cárdenas made his proclamation with large gestures.

Alemán responded. It was good to have the Captain there. Much could be settled without war. Let the Captain dismount and come forward alone, and he would meet him likewise on the ground before the pueblo.

Cárdenas gave his sword, lance and horse to an orderly to hold for him and went forward, but not without a few guardsmen following him. Alemán advanced from the pueblo unarmed, but also followed by his bodyguard. As the two leaders met, Alemán held out his arms with a smile and embraced Cárdenas about the body—and tightly held him immovable. The Indian bodyguard sprang forward and rang blows

with wooden maces on the Captain's helmet. They took him away from
their chief and carried him rapidly toward a narrow opening in the
palisade. People on the roof crying execrations sent arrows and stones
down on the visitors. At the entrance, Cárdenas freed himself enough to
brace against its sides as the Indians worked to drag him through into
captivity and death. Three of his horsemen rallied and charged to the
palisade to rescue him. They brought him free of danger. He was
wounded in the leg by an arrow.

But in spite of his wound and the weather he went upstream to
the next pueblo, after leaving a detachment on guard at Moho. Once
again he met abuse, arrows and defiance. He returned to Moho, gathered up his rear guard, and followed the trail in the snow back to
Alcanfor. The General then determined to give battle with his whole
army.

10.

Siege

They came in full array a few days later to Moho, and made
camp about the spring outside the pueblo. The German bugler from
Worms sounded his trumpet. The call to surrender and the offer of
amnesty were given in the proper form, with the notary officiating. The
frieze of defenders on the terraces became animated with obscene mockery. The General gave an order. The troops moved out to surround the
town which stood on a level plain of barren gravel from which the wide
slow curves of the river could be seen to the north and south. Stout tree
trunks were planted deep in the earth to form a palisade before the walls.
The defenses were better than at Arenal, for the walls themselves were
built of upright timbers solidly side by side and woven with willow
branches from the riverbanks, and thickly plastered over with river silt.
Here the town had not one continuous terrace of roof at each level,

but several platforms separated by wide gaps. There were towers with portholes near their tops. It was a large town with deep granaries well-filled.

On the second morning, and on almost every day thereafter until the issue was decided, the General repeated the overtures for peace, but without submission by the Indians. With the battle cry invoking Saint James of Compostela, the patron of Spain, the army attacked from all sides.

Recalling the stratagem of Arenal that brought victory, they breached the palisade and brought battering rams to the walls. But the stout construction of the first storey defeated the attempt to open a hole and set fires. The Indian force was larger than at Arenal, with people from many towns gathered within. Moho was more than a single hive, it was several, as the plan of the clustered rooms with spaces between clusters revealed. Small battles took place in separate places at the same time against the fortress.

Stones flew down on the attackers who tried to climb the walls. Many soldiers fell, hurt and stunned. On one wall, soldiers raised ladders and fifty reached a roof terrace. They fought across gaps firing at Indians on the same level. From higher terraces stones fell and arrows whistled. To help them in their preparations for war the Indians called upon deathly nature. They shut rattlesnakes into willow cages and thrust arrows among the snakes who striking at the arrowheads flooded their venom on the flint or obsidian points, where it dried in tiny crystals but did not lose its power. Now from the portholes in the towers they sent the poisoned arrows and where these struck they left festering wounds that killed or disfigured.

A soldier ascended to one of the portholes bringing wet mud with which he tried to plaster it shut. He was killed outright by an arrow that quivered deep into his eye.

Another was struck in an eyebrow by a poisoned arrow, but lived, saying that he was saved by his devotion to the rosary.

Nearly a hundred soldiers were wounded by arrows in this first day.

When the cold night fell the soldiers retired to their camp where the physician went to work on the living casualties, who numbered nearly a third of the army. It was costly; too costly. The General resolved on a siege of the pueblo. He controlled the water supply. How long could the Indians live on whatever water they had stored?

The army lived in the field, and its tents and settled ways and traffic of supply between the camp and Alcanfor suggested the existence of a new town. The besiegers were as troubled as the besieged. The weather continued cold. It was wearing to be vigilant yet inactive. Twice it appeared that the water within Moho must be all gone, and that peace would follow at once; and twice, the Indians were saved by what gave the soldiers such discomfort: it snowed. The Indians melted the snow and stored the water in their clay vessels.

Life for the army became a routine.

Every day the invocation to surrender and come forth peacefully was made.

Daily the Indians refused. Their argument was that the Spaniards had broken their trust, they still kept Bigotes, Cacique, the Turk, and Isopete as prisoners, they would not keep their promises.

Keeping siege, the General yet had time for other duties. One of these was to listen to the Turk, who still a prisoner continued to show great eagerness to interest his jailers. What he said filtered through the camp. The siege of Moho seemed to be an irritating obstacle in the way of the proper business of the army, which lay to the east, in the land called Quivira, where——

Why, yes, there was gold, the Turk said, there was so much of it that they could load not only horses with it, but wagons.

What else?

In Quivira, on a lake, the royal canoes had golden oarlocks. The ruler lived in a great palace, hung with cotton cloth.

Quivira?

Yes, Quivira where there was much gold and silver, but not as much as could be seen even farther east, in other kingdoms, called Harahey and Guaes.

Even more? It sounded like the richest country of all the Indies so far, including Mexico and Peru.

Yes, even more, and in that land lived the king—the Turk even knew his name, which was Tatarrax—who said his prayers from a book, and addressed them to a woman who was queen of heaven.

Then it was, surely it was, a Christian country?

During the siege of Moho the General made a friendly trip to Pecos. When the war on the river should be ended, he would start for Quivira. Pecos lay on the way. It would be well to resume friendly relations with so powerful a city on his line of march. He took with him the aged Cacique whom he restored to his people amid their acclamations. But where, they wondered, was Bigotes, and where the Turk and Isopete, the slaves?

He could answer that. They were still at the great river, but had actually presented him with a plan to lay before their countrymen, which was this: if the people of Pecos helped in the conquest of Tiguex, the General would reward them with the gift of one of the conquered pueblos. At the victorious end of the war, Bigotes and the others would be released.

The people thought, and replied that it was not convenient to do as he proposed. It was early spring. The planting had begun with prayer and observance. But if he commanded them, they would obey.

The General did not insist since they hesitated to volunteer. He returned to the river where he found his people suffering from the cold, and inaction, and impatience. In the third week of February, 1541, he ordered another attack upon Moho. It was inconclusive, like the first, and it lost the army five killed, including its well-loved young Captain Francisco de Ovando, who while crawling on his hands and knees toward an opening in the defenses was seized by the enemy and taken within the walls where he was put to death, despite the efforts of his soldiers to save him.

This event was sad, and it became mysterious, and all things seemed related in odd powerful ways when something was discovered about the Turk in connection with it.

Cervantes, a soldier who was the guard at the Turk's prison, looked in at him one day, whereupon the Turk asked how many Spaniards had been killed in a recent fight.

Cervantes stonily replied that no soldiers had been killed.

No, said the Turk, Cervantes was lying, for the Indians had killed five Christians, including a captain.

Yes, admitted the guard, now that he was forced to say so, the Turk was correct. But how could it be? The Turk was under lock and key, he saw no one, talked to no one, heard nothing.

All the Turk would say was that he knew it already, and needed no one else to tell him.

Cervantes was not satisfied, and when opportunity came, he spied upon the Turk and was dumfounded at what he saw, and saw at once that it explained everything. He swore under oath that he saw the Turk talking to the Devil who was enclosed in a jug filled with water. It must have been the Devil who told him what he knew. What a mystery. What if everything else the Turk knew—gold, silver, little bells in trees, wagons full of treasure—were just as true as the death of Captain de Ovando, whom all knew as a distinguished young fellow, very honorable, gracious and well-beloved?

The siege dragged on. Soldiers experimented with building some cannons out of heavy timber, thickly bound with ropes. But these were a failure.

The General sent to the pueblo of Zia, to the west of the river, asking for clothing for his shivering army. The people were generous, and sent back some cloaks, hides and blankets.

In the middle of March the Indians at last asked for a truce in which to discuss a proposal. It was granted. The Indians declared that their water supply was falling rapidly. They believed the Spanish did not harm women and children. Would the General consent to accept theirs, and let the siege be resumed? He agreed. Soldiers rode forward and escorted Indian women and youngsters out of the walls. Young Captain Lope de Urrea, from Aragón, went back and forth on his horse, without his helmet, receiving Indian babies in his arms, and delivering them to safety. His men warned him to wear his helmet, but he refused. When all who were coming out had come (some women with their children refused to leave the besieged town), the Captain rode back to the walls and asked on behalf of his General for surrender and peace, promising all fair treatment. The Indians became angered and warned him to withdraw. He persisted. The Indians threatened. Soldiers called to Urrea to put on his helmet, he was in danger, and he called back that the Indians would not harm him, and took up his persuasions again. An Indian sprang an arrow toward the feet of Urrea's horse with a last warning that next time he would aim to kill. The Captain shrugged. He gently turned his horse and rode at a walk away from the walls, putting on his helmet indifferently. As he passed beyond the range of arrows, the Indians began to howl and fire vollies. The siege was resumed.

But spring was advancing. The snowfalls ended. The water supply in the crippled town was finally vanishing. Moreover, the season of planting and propitiation, the birth of the future, were passing by, and if unattended, would end in physical hardship and spiritual sorrow for the Indians. One night at the end of March they began to steal away out of their walls toward the river. Forty mounted soldiers were on guard. The alarm was given. An Indian arrow pierced a soldier's heart and he died at once. Another soldier was seized and taken and was never seen again. The soldiers attacked, the camp was aroused, and a battle

followed in the darkness. Many Indians were killed, and soldiers were
wounded, as the Indian retreat continued toward the river. The water
was high and cold, the current fast. Hurrying for freedom, the Indians
came to the bank and were pursued by the cavalry, and few escaped
wounds or death. The river took away the bodies and blood of those
killed while trying to cross. Some reached the east bank in the dark. It
was an icy night, filled with the sounds of arms and voices. The investment of Moho was over. It had lasted fifty days.

In the morning, soldiers went over the river and found wounded
and half-frozen Indians lying there, whom they brought back to be
restored and treated as servants. Other soldiers entered the pueblo to
see what they could find, for all provisions were to be gathered for the
commissary. Soldiers looked out for jewels and other treasures, and discovered instead the ashes of mantles, feathers and turquoise strings
burned to save them from the Spaniards. They found stores of maize, and
recognized again that Indians of the river did not own anything except
their food and their cotton clothes and their robes made of turkey
feathers and rabbit fur.

The soldiers found something that, had it succeeded, might have
prolonged the war indefinitely. It was a well, dug within the protection
of the walls of Moho, but the well had caved in, and thirty Indians
had died in it.

They explored further. In one section of the surrendered town
there was a small group of people who still resisted. They would be
taken in a matter of days.

And somewhere in the fallen town, the soldiers came upon a sight
that awed them. They found the body of Captain Francisco de Ovando,
dead forty days, naked, whole but for the wound of his death, white
as snow, and incorrupt, "with no bad odor."

The General commanded a portion of the pueblo of Moho burned
as a warning to the people of Tiguex. He sent for Bigotes, the Turk and
Isopete so they too might see. His policy was prevailing everywhere, for
farther up the river during the last days of the siege, another pueblo
had been taken by a mounted detachment who forced the Indians to
abandon it. After a few days, in early April, the General heard that the
people were returning to some of the upriver towns to fortify them. He
sent Captain de Maldonado to do what needed to be done. A day or so
later, the General saw smoke in the north over the valley, and asked
what it meant. He was informed that Captain de Maldonado had burned
a town. With that image—distant smoke rising from the mud-plastered

timbers of a Rio Grande pueblo in the springtime groves of willows
and cottonwoods far below the air-blue mountains—the Tiguex war
was won.

I I.

The Eastern Plains

The weather warmed, and then froze again, and solid ice reached
across the river. If they were all going east it would be well to start while
they could cross on the ice, the whole army of fifteen hundred people,
and a thousand horses, and five hundred cattle, and five thousand sheep.
On April 23, 1541, the train passed from Alcanfor over the frozen river
and began the long march to the eastern plains in search of Quivira
and its treasures. Bigotes and Isopete, freed of their collars and chains,
were on their way to be restored to their pueblo of Pecos. The Turk was
the principal guide, still raving of wonders to come. The slow procession
went north along the east bank, passing the burned town of Arenal,
empty like all the other pueblos of Tiguex. Rounding the northern end
of the Sandia mountains, the army drew away eastward and out of sight
of the river.

Seventy-seven days later, all but the General, his chaplain, and
thirty mounted men and six footmen returned to the river to settle once
again at Alcanfor. The town was still empty of Indians, like all the others,
and so long as these Spaniards were in the nation of Tiguex, no Indians
ever came back to live there.

The army returned in low spirits and unwillingly. On their
march to the plains with the General they had met one disappointment
after another, though they saw strange sights of passing interest. Farther
and farther east the visions of the Turk had taken them to the very
limit of caution. They left Bigotes at Pecos, and moved out to the plains
where they saw Indians who lived in tents and used dogs as beasts of

burden, and noticed that if his load was badly balanced the dog barked for someone to come and set it right. They heard of a big river to the east and many canoes. It was all familiar—the Turk had mentioned such. They came to flat highlands in whose irregular faces were deep-slashed canyons of red rock and scrub oak. In such places, the plains cattle stampeded, the army lost horses, Captain de Cárdenas broke his arm. Now and then they encountered groups of Indians who lived in straw huts on the prairies and hunted the buffalo for materials of food, shelter and arms. Among such a people they found an old blind man who told them something amazing. Six years ago, as they figured it, he and his people had been farther to the south, and there they were visited by four great doctors, one of them black, the other three white, who gave blessings, healed the sick and wanted to go toward the sunset. The army knew who these were—Núñez Cabeza de Vaca and his companions. They were awed that in so great a wilderness they should come upon the trace of the man long gone who more than any other seemed responsible for their whole hard journey now.

What was wrong? Where was the gold? The Turk took them now in one direction, now in another, keeping up a flow of promises and explanations for his change of plans.

Isopete, the Indian slave brought from Pecos, declared that the Turk was lying. There was such a country as the Turk said, but there was nothing in it that the General sought.

But still they marched, seeing in one place a white woman with painted chin, and in another a wild hailstorm. The stones, as big as oranges, dented armor and killed animals. Trembling, the people wept and prayed and made vows. Each day they heard how far they had gone according to the soldier whose duty it was to count steps by which the leagues could be computed. In all that wilderness, they were appalled at how little mark so great a throng of men and women and beasts made upon the grasses of the plain. They left no trail, for the grass in the wind waved over their path like the sea over a galleon's wake.

One day the General called a halt for a council of his captains. The leaders agreed upon a decision. The army was to turn back to the Tiguex River, there to settle at Alcanfor once again, and scour the valley for supplies against the next winter. The General and thirty picked horsemen and a handful of infantry, together with Fray Juan de Padilla, and Isopete, and the Turk, once again in chains for his ineffectual performance of his duties as guide, would go farther to the east to see what they could see. The General's smaller force could proceed more swiftly than the long lumbering straggle of the burdened army, and could live off the animals of the plains more readily. The army begged to be taken along, saying they would rather die with the General than return to the river without him who might never return. He was firm, though he promised to send swift couriers to fetch them after him again if he came upon the treasure of Quivira. They saw him go, and waited a fortnight for word from him, while they hunted the buffalo, and killed five hundred bulls whose meat they dried for winter storage. The hunters often lost their way back to camp, for the land was so flat and so barren of marks that in midday with the sun overhead there was no way to know where to turn. At the end of every day the army in camp built fires, blew horns, beat drums, fired their muskets to guide the huntsmen home. Only at sundown could they get their bearings.

But no word came from the General, and at last the army turned to the west. Plains Indians served as guides. Each sunrise a guide watched where the sun rose, and then facing westward sprang an arrow whose course they followed. Before they overtook it, they let go another, and so each day they drew the line of their course through the air until they came once again to the river, on the ninth of July.

Captain de Arellano was in command of the army. He lost little time in sending out detachments to forage for the winter supplies, one to the north, one to the south, both to follow the river.

Captain Francisco de Barrionuevo led his men to the province of Jemez, containing seven pueblos, where the people were generous and gave supplies. This lay on a stream that entered the Tiguex River from the west. On the main stream, at a powerful tributary with red water which they called the Chama, the soldiers came to two cities called Yuque-Yunque whose people fled to the mountains at the approach of the mounted strangers. These towns were on opposite banks of the river and in Indian tales were once connected by a bridge of parrot feathers, that had been upset by witches so that many people fell into the river and were drowned and became fish. Here the soldiers made an abundant haul of food and pottery with a high glaze over many curious designs. Some of the pots held a shiny metal—they thought it might be silver, and their hearts leaped—used for the glaze. Following the main river again, Barrionuevo came to Taos, where Alvarado had been before him a year ago.

To the south another officer led a party to the towns previously seen by Ovando. Going farther than his lost fellow officer, he followed the river until, as he reported later, it disappeared in the ground. He

stated that it made him think of the Guadiana River in Estremadura, in
Spain, and that it made him quite homesick. The people down the river
told him that much farther down, it reappeared with much water. It
was the country of drought where Núñez Cabeza de Vaca had seen the
low or dry river, like travellers in certain years long later. Where the
river reappeared, it was brought back to life by the never-failing, full
and clear green water of the Rio Conchos out of Mexico.

The garrison at Alcanfor gathered their stores and explored the
silent towns of Tiguex, and saw the kivas underground, some round,
some square, with their walls painted in sorcerers' markings, and some
large enough in which to have a game of ball. They saw how the floors
were paved with smooth stones, which reminded them of the sunken
baths of Europe. They foraged in the fields where the Indians sowed their
seed corn without plowing, but only waiting for the snows that would
cover the earth in winter, and fatten the seed out of which would break
the sprouts in summer. The snow clouds came off the mountains by the
river and nourished the valley floors. Great flocks of cranes, wild geese,
crows and thrushes came to eat the seed, and even so, the crop of one
year was enough to last for seven, with a litter of ungathered corn left
in the fields. Corn was the staff of life for the river people. They did not
eat human flesh, or sacrifice it, like the Mexicans of twenty years before,
who took youths to the tops of their temples and under the open sun tore
their living hearts out with obsidian knives, in such quantity that at a
certain temple the conquerors had seen one hundred thousand corpses
near the walls. As well as they could tell, the army at Tiguex accounted
for the existence of sixty-six towns in the new land, with Tiguex in the
center of them all. They believed the Indian population to number
twenty thousand.

The pueblo people and their ways were so different from all others
so far met with in the Indies of the Ocean Sea, remarked the soldiers,
that surely they must have come from the coast of Greater India, that lay
to the west of this land. The soldiers declared that the river rose in the
mountains to the northeast, and that the towns were settled all along
it until it disappeared underground. There was speculation. Might it not
have been better to go north, rather than follow the Turk eastward?
To be sure, the land between Norway and China, they realized, was very
far up. But as something was known of Greater India, its treasure should
perhaps have been attempted instead of that lying across the barren
cattle plains. . . .

In Tiguex, as they stated, there was not even anything to steal, though the jars and pots made by the women of the pueblos were fanciful and curious, but otherwise the rooms in the towns were bare and clean. They could only hope that when the General returned to the river he would bring the news all had sought so hard.

Toward the end of summer Captain de Arellano decided to go to look for the General. Picking forty men, and giving the command of the army on the river to Captain de Barrionuevo, he started east. At Pecos he found the people unfriendly. There was a skirmish near the town and two Indians were shot. The misfortunes of Bigotes and Cacique were not forgotten. Pecos stood near the pass through which the General's return must come. Why did he not come? It was late in August, and the rains were falling everywhere, the rivers would rise, the homeward travellers would have trouble crossing them if they waited much longer. But at last word came by Indian traveller that the General was actually on his way. Arellano decided to wait for him at Pecos, to protect the pass if need be, and by his presence keep the people of Pecos subdued.

During the second week of September the General's cavalcade came into view. Arellano and his men welcomed it with great joy. The General paid a visit to Pecos, and was politely received by the people, for he knew what he knew, now, and they realized it. He then pushed on rapidly to the river, and the soldiers of his party mingled with Arellano's, and the General talked with his officers, and on reaching Alcanfor everybody had something to ask and to answer. Those starved for news were fed by those who had meagre news to share, and most of that outrageous.

What was King Tattarax like: Montezuma?

They saw a chief, an old naked wretch with white hair and a copper bangle around his neck, that was his whole wealth, and they were not even sure he was King Tattarax.

And the canoes with golden eagles? The gold bells in the trees? The wagons full of gold?

No gold anywhere.

But the Turk said?

The Turk was dead, garrotted one night in silence in the tent of Captains López and Zaldívar, and buried in a hole already dug for him, before anybody woke with the morning watch.

But why?

Treachery. He lied and lied. He plotted the destruction of the whole army from the first. Going east through Pecos, he arranged with the people to lead the army astray and exhaust them and remove them from food supply, so their horses would die, and if they straggled back from the plains, the Pecos warriors could easily dispose of them in their weakness.

But Pecos? Why would they agree to this?

Bigotes. The iron collar and chain, the dogs that bit him when ordered to. Cacique's captivity.

But the country? The wealth?

Immense plains, people with grass-roofed huts, people who ate meat raw and carried a freshly butchered cow-gut around their necks from which they drank blood and stomach juice when thirsty, people who did everything with little flint knives set in wooden handles, who sharpened the blades rapidly against their own teeth, like monkeys that put everything to the mouth.

And the Turk knew all the time there was nothing else?

He must have known, though he kept saying to the end that just a way farther there really was the other great river, with all its gold and silver and jewels and royal splendor. But then, he had said that about every place at which they had stopped, and where they had found nothing.

Why was he not killed much sooner then?

The General was partial to him. Everybody knew it and resented it. Finally, of course, the General ordered the execution himself.

How miserable. And there was nothing else in the country of Quivira?

Big wolves, and white-pied deer, and rabbits that a man on foot could never catch but that never moved from the path of a horse, so that you could lance them from your saddle with no trouble. And grapes grew there, nuts, mulberries, and plums like those in Castile. As for riches and comforts and fine living—when you got off your horse at the end of a hard day and had to get some supper to satisfy your hunger, you cooked whatever you had, and you cooked it on a fire made of the only thing to be found, which was cow droppings. That was Quivira.

12.

Prophecy and Retreat

The Turk lied and died for it, at the hands of outraged Europeans. But it was more than individuals, it was two kinds of life that told on the one hand, and punished on the other. The quest for wealth led to different answers in each case. To the Indian, wealth meant all that both pueblo and plain offered—rain and grass and primal acts of work and of the fruits of the earth only sufficient to sustain life equally for all. To the Spaniard it meant money and all that lay behind it: to purchase instead of to make, and of the world's wealth, all that a man could possibly gather and keep far beyond the meeting of his creature needs. The logical extension of the Indian's view would in time produce the wealth sought by the Spaniard, but only through work and cultivation of the humble stuff of the earth. But the Spaniard's hope had a simple logic that ended with the ravishment of wealth already existing in forms dependent upon civilization for their pertinence—gold and silver instead of grass and rain.

The General went among his people hiding his disappointment as well as he could, and giving them heart against the problems of the winter by a promise of renewed hope. Now that he knew the plains so well, and would not have to count upon treasonable Indian guides, he would lead the army out again in the spring, for it was entirely possible that by going just a little farther to the east, the rich kingdoms would at last appear before their eyes.

Some of the soldiers could kindle to this hope; others could not. It was going to be another cold year, the food stocks were not any too full, and the silent towns of the river no longer supplied clothing, even under force. Even keeping warm by fire was not easy. The General wrote to the Emperor Charles about Tiguex and its problems. Of all the lands he had seen, he wrote on October 20, 1541, "the best I have found is this Tiguex river, where I am camping, and the settlements here. They are not suitable for settling, because, besides being four hundred leagues from the North sea, and more than two hundred from the South sea, thus prohibiting all intercourse, the land is so cold, as I have related to your Majesty, that it seems impossible for one to be able to spend the winter here, since there is no firewood or clothing with which the men may keep themselves warm, except for the skins that the natives wear, and some cotton blankets, few in number."

(Eighteen years before, far away at the mouth of the same river, another captain-general had concluded that the river lands he saw were not suitable for settling, either.)

The winter garrison was increased by the arrival of Captain Pedro de Tovar and a small force from the base camp far away in Sonora. He brought letters, including one that announced to Captain de Cárdenas that his brother in Spain was dead and that he had succeeded to titles and properties at home. There was also news of disorders and rebellions among the detachment at Sonora. Tovar's party looked about eagerly for the treasures of the northern conquest and, finding none, could not hide their sharp disappointment which was like a reproof to the long-disillusioned garrison. But Tovar's men kept their high spirits, for they could hardly wait until spring, and the second march into Quivira, with all its promises of adventure and wealth. The garrison let them hope. For the present all suffered together from cold and hunger and lice. Try as they would, they could not rid themselves of the lice. Some people were colder than others, for the distribution of Indian garments when they could be had was not always fair. The soldiers said the officers took more than their share, or gave more than was just to those whom they favored. Yes, and certain ones were excused from sentry duty and other hard jobs. All of this in the face of Quivira, the famous swindle. It was a hard winter in the soldier's heart as well as in his stomach and on his shivering skin. When Captain de Cárdenas, with permission, departed on the long trip home to assume his inheritance, and took with him a few who were no longer able-bodied fighters, there was many another soldier who would have gone too, but did not ask, for fear of being thought cowardly. Bad feeling ate at the core of the command. If things went wrong, who was responsible? The General himself, no matter how much he had once been respected and loved.

But as winter wore on the General once again was setting things in motion for the return to Quivira. Few of the soldiers wanted to go. Most of those who were eager to go were officers. Preparations went ahead with commands given by enthusiastic officers to men in low spirits.

Christmas came and went, with the friars leading in the observance of the Feast of the Nativity.

The army had time on its hands, and all sought diversion as they could. The General liked to ride. He had twenty-two horses with him, and often went out riding with one of his close friends. On December 27, 1541, he took riding with him Captain Rodrigo de Maldonado, who was the brother-in-law of the Duke of Infantado. Riding side by side, the two officers were soon in a race. The General's horse was spirited. The contest was lively. The General was leading. Suddenly his saddle girth broke. He fell. As he struck the ground, there was no time to throw himself out of the path of Maldonado's horse, or for Maldonado to check his mount. The Captain tried to jump his horse in order to miss the General, but one of its flying hoofs struck the General in the head.

The garrison was horrified at the calamity. They took the General to his quarters and laid him in bed. He was close to death. How could it have happened? The saddle girth, long among his effects, must have rotted without anyone's knowing, the servants or anyone. For days his life was given up for lost. When at last he began to recover, and was able to be up again, they had to give him bad news.

Captain de Cárdenas on his way to Mexico to sail for Spain, had returned in flight to the Tiguex River with news of Indians in rebellion in Sonora, and Spanish soldiers stationed there dying from arrows poisoned by the yerba pestifera of that land. The homeward path to Mexico was endangered.

The General turned faint at the story and took to his bed again. And there he had time for a terrible reflection.

He spoke of how a long time ago in Salamanca his mathematical friend had prophesied for him that he would one day find himself in faraway lands (which had come true), and that he would become a man of high position and power (which had come true), and that he would suffer a fall from which he would never recover (and was this coming true now?).

He spoke of his wife and children, saying that if he were to die, let him be with them.

The doctor taking care of him repeated outside what he had heard in the sickroom. Those who meant to return to Quivira were angered at the thought of giving up the expedition, and the doctor carried to the General reports of what they said. In his weakness the General was pressed by all—those who wanted to go to Quivira, and those who longed, like him, to return to Mexico. He kept to his rooms, saw few people, and sent word that if, as was claimed, the army wanted now only to go home, he must have proof of this will in a written petition, signed by all their captains and leaders.

This was given to him, and he hid the folded paper under his mattress. If enemies should steal his strongbox to recover the paper and destroy it for bad ends, they would be fooled. The General then sent forth an order announcing the return of the entire army to New Spain.

But once the decision was made to abandon the poor realities of Tiguex and the vision of Quivira, some officers changed their minds and proposed compromises. Let the General go with sixty men, leaving all the rest to make a colony. But few of the bulk of the army would agree to this. Then let the General take the main body and leave sixty men here until the Viceroy could send reinforcements. But the General disapproved all such suggestions, and held legal proof in the petition which all had signed that his order to retreat from the hard country was by the agreement of all. Somehow in spite of the guards posted in his quarters and outside, an attempt was made to rob him of the petition. The thieves got his strongbox, but not the paper, and only knew afterward where he had kept it.

Visions were lost, and fealties broken, and as the army came to readiness to depart in April of 1542, the dissident officers showed disrespect to the General and carried out his orders with poor grace, if at all. He relied on the common soldiers to sustain him, and they did, and all that remained to do before he led the army home was to take leave of his friends and counsellors, the Franciscans, who were not going with him.

During the season of Lent in 1542, Fray Juan de Padilla preached a sermon at Mass attended by the army. In a time of penance and rededication he spoke of his duty, based on Scriptural authority, to bring eternal salvation to those whom he could reach. Amidst the sorrows and furies of life in the kingdom of these lands, there had been small opportunity to go among the people and preach the word of God. Now that the army was returning home, it was his firm decision, and likewise that of his fellow Franciscans, the lay brother Fray Luís de Escalona, and the oblates Lucas and Sebastián, to remain here in the service of their Divine Lord. They would live among the Indians and convert them and give them peace. He declared that he had received permission from the General to take this course, though such permission was not necessary, as he drew his authority from the superior of the Franciscans in Mexico.

The soldiers listening to him knew well enough the images of the land he chose for his own.

Fray Juan was going back to Quivira, where he had been with the General. Indian guides from the plains would return with him. One of the army's Portuguese soldiers, Andres Do Campo, volunteered to go with him too, and a free Negro, a Mexican Indian and the two oblates. The General gave them sheep, mules and a horse. Fray Juan carried his Mass vessels.

Fray Luís de Escalona chose Pecos for his mission. He owned a chisel and an adze, and with these, he said, he would make crosses to place in the towns. He was not an ordained priest, and so could not administer the sacraments, except, as he said, that of baptism, which he would give to Indian children about to die, and so send them to heaven. Cristóbal, a young servant, volunteered to stay with him.

In their blue-gray robes, the little company of Franciscans set out for the east, escorted as far as Pecos by a detachment from the army. At Pecos, Fray Juan and his companions took leave of Fray Luís and advanced into the open prison of the plains.

A few days later a handful of soldiers went back to Pecos from Tiguex to deliver some sheep to Fray Luís, to keep as his own flock. Before they reached Pecos, they met him walking accompanied by Indians. He was on his way to other pueblos. The soldiers talked with him, and hoped that he was being well treated and that his Indians listened to his word. He replied that he had a meagre living, and that he believed the elders of the pueblo, at first friendly, were beginning to desert him. He expected that in the end they would kill him. The soldiers saw him as a saintly man, and said so many times. They never saw him again, or ever heard of him further, or of Cristóbal, his servant.

In the battles of Arenal and Moho the army had taken many Indian prisoners. The General now ordered these released. It was his last official act as lord of that river province. Early in April, 1542, the command was given to begin the long march down the river to the narrows of Isleta, and there turn west over the desert to retrace the trail to Mexico. Aside from a few Mexican Indians who decided in the end to remain in the Tiguex nation, the expedition had lost in its two years of movement and battle and privation no more than twenty men out of the whole fifteen hundred.

Travelling at times by litter, the General left behind him a vision changed and gone like a cloud over the vast country of the Spanish imagination in his century. A faith of projected dreams and heroic concepts gave power to the men of the Golden Age, a few of whom found even more than they imagined. The General, like many, found less. Having searched for the land of his imagining, and not finding it, he could have said, as Don Quixote later said, ". . . I cannot tell you what country, for I think it is not in the map. . . ."

The army, as it descended into Mexico, began to disintegrate. Officers and men fell away as it pleased them to find other occupations at Culiacán, Compostela, and all the way to the city of Mexico.

In due course reports of the expedition went to Madrid and came before the Emperor. The royal treasuries had supported the expenses of the undertaking. On learning of its outcome, Charles V ordered that no further public monies were to be allocated to such enterprises.

As for the governor of the Seven Cities, the Tiguex River and Quivira, the Emperor received another report during a legal inquiry a few years later. The Judge Lorenzo de Tejada, of the Royal Audiencia of Mexico, wrote on March 11, 1545:

"Francisco Vásquez came to his home, and he is more fit to be governed in it than to govern outside of it. He is lacking in many of his former fine qualities and he is not the same man he was when your Majesty appointed him to that governorship. They say this change was caused by the fall from a horse which he suffered in the exploration and pacification of Tierra Nueva."

13.

Lords and Victims

If the early governors of the river came to poor ends, they were not alone in their last bitterness at the inscrutability of strange lands, the resistance of betrayed natives and the ingratitude of governments. There was hardly a conqueror for the Spanish crown who after his prodi-

gies (whether of success or failure did not matter, for the very scale of
colonial operations was prodigious in itself) was not stripped of power,
or tried, or impoverished by fines, or imprisoned, or subjected to all
these together. What amounted each time to a passion for probity in
the crown's affairs reached out to take hold of the adventurous lords of
the conquests—but only after they had done their grandiose best or worst.

Of the administrators of the Rio de las Palmas, two were saved
by death—Garay in the terrible mercies of Cortés, Narváez in the tempests
of the Gulf.

Of the others, Nuño de Guzmán died first, in 1544, in Spain,
penniless, while attempting to defend himself against grave charges of
maladministration. Cortés was in Spain at the time and, hearing of the
trials of his old rival who hated him, offered him money. In bitter
pride the offer was refused.

The years between 1540 and 1547 Cortés passed in Spain on the
profitless enterprise of trying to recall himself to the memory of a king
who as a matter of policy preferred to forget him. If the Marquis of
the Valley of Oaxaca was a great man before whom a hemisphere had
trembled, he was yet not so great a man as the Emperor of the Holy
Roman Empire and King of Spain. In vain Cortés submitted plans for
new conquests, petitioned, presented himself at court, reminded the
currents of cold air about the throne of what he had accomplished.
The court officials were sensitive members that extended the monarch's
capacity to know; and in just the same relation carried as in gelid
nerves the monarch's messages to enact. Cortés never reached the Emperor—until one day as the royal coach was passing through the streets
he detached himself from the crowd and before he could be prevented
threw himself upon it, clinging to its leather straps, at last face to face
again with the source of power or misery.

"Who is this man?" inquired the king who years before had seated
him at his right hand, had ennobled him, and had known him well
enough to deprive him of power.

"I am the man who brought Your Majesty more kingdoms than
your father left you towns," cried the desperate old conqueror.

The embarrassing scene ended quickly. The coach jolted on.
Cortés fell back among the street idlers. However much longer he
might live, he had come to the end. On December 2, 1547, in the village
of Castillejo de la Cuesta, near Seville, while on his way to embark
again for Mexico, he died at the age of sixty-two.

And in Mexico, where out of all his preferments he was left with

only his membership on the city council, the Captain-General Francisco
Vásquez de Coronado lived for twelve years after his return from the
river. He was tried on various charges of crime and error in the conduct
of his command, but was absolved, and the attorney for the Crown was
enjoined by the court "to perpetual silence, so that neither now nor at
any time in the future may he accuse or bring charges against him for
anything contained . . . in this our sentence." The judgment was handed
down in February, 1546.

In the following year an amazing creature appeared in the streets
of Mexico City. His hair was extraordinarily long, and his beard hung
down in braids. What he had to tell soon became news everywhere.
He was Andres Do Campo, the Portuguese soldier from the Tiguex
River who had gone to the plains with Fray Juan de Padilla when the
General turned toward home. For five years he had struggled to return
to Mexico. One year he spent in captivity, the rest in wandering ever
southward. He could speak of having witnessed a martyrdom, for five
years before, when the Franciscan's party were come to the land of
Quivira, they encountered Indians who made it plain that they were
going to kill the hardy priest. Fray Juan ordered his companions to
retire out of reach of danger. They fell back to a little rise of land,
and watched what followed. Falling to his knees Fray Juan began to
pray, and prayed until pierced with arrows he fell dead upon the earth.
His companions were permitted to return and bury him where he fell.
Ten months later Do Campo and the oblates Lucas and Sebastián,
escaped with two dogs. On their backs the fugitives carried wooden
crosses with which to invoke grace for themselves and for the Indians
whom they met in their travels. Their dogs hunted rabbits for them.
Somewhere near the site of Eagle Pass they came to the lower reaches
of the same long river in whose pueblo valley far away they had spent
two wretched winters. Making their way southeast across Mexico, they
reached the coast, and the town of Pánuco, and civilization.

The General must have heard the story, for it was discussed
widely. It was the last report of his venture, and it reminded its hearers
of the tales of Núñez Cabeza de Vaca, by which the venture had been
conceived.

Some years later other news of the river was talked about in
Mexico. A certain group of twenty ships had left Veracruz for Cuba
and Spain with the spring sailings of 1553. They touched at Havana
and sailed again, but were blown from their course by a furious storm
that drove them almost all the way back across the Gulf of Mexico.

Only three of the ships ever got to Spain, one returned to Veracruz, and the remainder were lost at sea or wrecked on the Gulf Coast. Three hundred survivors, including five Dominican friars, found themselves ashore without food and poorly clad. They started to march on foot to the south following the coast, hoping to reach the Pánuco and safety. To protect their large company of men, women and children the only arms they had were two crossbows. Indians soon discovered the toiling procession and followed it making little attacks. Crossing a stream, the fugitives lost their crossbows, and now the Indians knew the strangers to be defenseless. Two days later they captured two Spaniards and took away their clothes, sending them back naked to their friends.

What did this mean? Did it mean that the Indians, naked themselves, resented anyone else clothed? The Spaniards thought so, and in confusion and desperation all stripped themselves naked and left their clothes for the Indians to find. But the sacrifice of modesty was useless, for the attacks continued, and many people fell from Indian arrows, illness, despair, until there were only two hundred left. They came along the coast to the mouth of a large river. It was the Rio de las Palmas. On the near bank they found a canoe and used it to help ferry some of the company across, while the Indians attacked in great fury. It was a running fight which continued on the other bank, for the Indians crossed over also leaving many dead and wounded Spaniards behind.

Among these were two badly wounded Dominican friars, Fray Diego de la Cruz and Fray Hernando Méndez. They saw the party vanish along the misty beach to the south and resolved to recover from their wounds and remain on the River of Palms to find and convert the Indians who lived on its banks in little villages. When they could, the two friars returned to the northern bank of the river to start their mission, but Fray Diego could not go on. He lay down in weakness. Fray Hernando gave him the Last Sacraments and, when he died, buried him on the bank of the river, and went on his way.

Up the river he met another survivor, a man named Vásquez, and later the two met a third, a Negress. In spite of her shame at their common nakedness, they joined forces and went along the river digging for roots. Fray Hernando was growing weaker from his wounds, and they fed him what they could, but he died and they buried him. The Negress was killed by Indians. Vásquez left the river to overtake his retreating companions.

Meanwhile the two Dominican fathers were missed among the party of exhausted and hurrying Spaniards along the beaches. The other

three friars turned back to find them, accompanied by two sailors. They
returned to the cross of the river, found the same canoe as before, and
climbed in to paddle upstream. Coming to two small islands where they
would feel safe resting for a while, they touched shore on one to land,
when the islands sank with commotion, capsizing the canoe and throwing the men into the river. They then saw with astonishment that the
islands reappeared, and were two whales, which swam down the river
toward the sea. The Spaniards swam to another island which was real,
and on it fell exhausted. The next day they contrived a raft out of drift-
wood, crossed to the south bank, and set out from the Rio de las Palmas
to overtake the party moving south on the shore. After they joined their
countrymen, all faced another hard Indian attack in which many more
were killed, including two of the three remaining Dominicans. The
remaining one, Fray Marcos de Mena, survived to reach Mexico City,
and to tell this tale.

If the General heard it, it was the last story he ever heard out
of the wilds. He had never regained his health, and he died an old man
in his forty-fourth year on the night of September 22, 1554, and was
buried in the church of Santo Domingo in the city of Mexico.

14.

The River of May

In the autumn of 1568 the Rio de las Palmas was crossed somewhere in its lower reaches near the sea by three destitute men who were
walking to the northeast. They were David Ingram, Richard Browne
and Richard Twide, English sailors who had come to the New World
with the fleet of Captain Sir John Hawkins. At Veracruz where six
English ships had put in for refuge from storm and a haven for overhaul,
they had done battle with Spanish vessels in the roadstead. Only two
English ships escaped. One, captained by a certain Francis Drake who

would richly fulfill a later opportunity for revenge, sailed directly for
England. The other, under Hawkins, overloaded with survivors, bore
north along the Gulf Coast and at their own request landed one hundred
and fourteen men on the beach thirty miles above Tampico, and then
stood out to the long voyage across the Atlantic.

The shore party were attacked by Indians, and presently divided,
one group going north, another south. The northern marchers lost more
men through attack, and others through faintness of heart that made
some turn back to overtake those moving southward, and still others
who abandoned themselves to the countryside. The three who came to
the river referred to it as the River of May, where "the ground and
countrey is most excellent, fertile and pleasant," more so than country
they had already crossed, "for the grasse of the rest is not so greene, as
it is in these parts, for the other is burnt away with the heate of the
Sunne. And as all the Countrey is good and most delicate, having great
plaines, as large and as fayre in many places as may be seene, being as
plaine as a board. . . ."

They examined trees and bushes, identifying many, and tasting
the bark of one which bit like pepper, and seeing "a great plentie of
other sweete trees" to them unknown. Of all, the fruitful palm tree
yielded most interest, for it carried "hayres on the leaves thereof, which
reach to the ground, Whereof the Indians doe make ropes and cords
for their Cotton beds, and doe use the same to many other purposes."
Further, "The which Tree, if you picke with your knife, about two foote
from the roote, it will yeelde a wine in color like whey, but in taste
strong and somewhat like Bastard, which is most excellent drinke. But
it will distemper both your head and body, if you drinke too much
thereof. . . ." The palm tree gave not only drink but meat, since "the
branches of the top of the tree, are most excellent meat raw, after you
have pared away the bark." Finally, the useful and beautiful tree could
save life, for "Also there is a red oyle that commeth out of the roote of
this tree, which is most excellent against poisoned arrowes and weapons:
for by it they doe recover themselves of their poysoned wounds."

As for "Tempests and other strange monstrous things in those
partes," the sailor saw it "lighten and Thunder in sommer season by the
space of foure & twentie houres together," and concluded that the cause
for this was the heat of the climate. They saw "Furicanos," and "Turna-
dos," with "a Cloud sometime of the yeere seene in the ayre, which
commonly turneth to great Tempests," and again, "great windes in
maner of Whirlewindes."

They crossed the great River of May whose gulf land they saw so clearly, and went on their way until a year after the beginning of their misadventure they arrived at New Brunswick, having walked the whole shape of the American coast from Mexico east and north. In 1569 they were safe again in England.

15.

Four Enterprises

For nearly forty years after Coronado's retreat no organized Spanish entries were made into the country of the Rio Grande. As Garay had abandoned the river at its mouth, so Coronado had abandoned its pueblo valley. What these explorers knew about the river was not lost, yet neither was it part of common knowledge. The river had to be discovered over and over again. From time to time little streams of information came out of the blind north country along Indian trails and aroused speculation as though no Spaniard had ever been there before. No comprehensive theory of the river's course was yet held; but Indians told of how the big Rio Conchos, flowing northeast from the Mexican Sierra Madre, made a junction—La Junta de los Rios the Spaniards called it—with the long river whose valley twisted and turned and led northward to the pueblos. The Conchos suggested a new route to the north, more direct than the wide swing westward up the Mexican coast and across Arizona to approach the river from the west as Coronado had done; and finally like all roads it called to be taken. From 1581 to 1593 four small expeditions went to the river from the vast empty highlands of Northern Mexico.

Marching northward along the Conchos, three Spanish Franciscan friars, nine soldiers and sixteen Mexican servants arrived on July 6, 1581, at the junction with the Rio Grande, which they called the Guadalquivir, and also the Rio de Nuestra Señora de la Concepción. The

founder of this expedition was Fray Agustín Rodríguez. His squad of
soldiers was commanded by Francisco Sánchez Chamuscado. They were
on their way to convert the pueblos in the north. Guided by river
dwellers they marched northwest following the valley, and turned with
it northward, coming at last among the nation of towns that Coronado
had known as Tiguex. One of the friars, Juan de Santa Maria, who was
an adept in astrology, there resolved to return to Mexico with reports
of what the party had seen; and despite warnings of his comrades
departed alone for the south.

The rest of the company explored the land east of the river,
passing through Pecos to the buffalo plains and returning; visiting the
salines east of the Sandia and viewing the rosy stone town of Abo; and
marching to the west past Ácoma as far as Zuñi, where a December
snowfall forced them back to the river. There the two other Franciscans
declared they would stay to preach the word of God. A handful of Indian
servants elected to stay with them at the pueblo of Puaray, not far from
Coronado's capital of Alcanfor. Chamuscado gave them a few goats,
horses and articles of barter, and left them there. With his reduced party
he went down the river retracing his course. He was sixty, an old man,
exhausted and ill from his hardships. He never reached his home in
Santa Barbara near the headwaters of the Conchos, but died a few days'
journey from it.

In the following year another small troop took the same passage
up the river. This party of thirteen soldiers and various Indian servants
was commanded by a merchant of New Spain, Antonio de Espéjo, who
was a fugitive from justice under charge of having murdered one of his
ranch hands. Its real authority was its spiritual leader, Fray Bernardino
Beltrán. Their mission was to bring aid to the two friars who had
remained the year before at Puaray, and to look for the astrologer, Fray
Juan de Santa María, who had never arrived in Mexico. Coming on
December 9, 1582, to the Rio Grande, which they called the Rio del
Norte, for the direction of its source, and the Rio Turbio, for its heavy
flow of mud, the soldiers were welcomed by people who greeted them
with odd, sweet music, which they made with their mouths, and which
sounded like the tones of flutes. Along the river Espéjo came upon the
memory of Núñez Cabeza de Vaca who with his one black and two white
companions was still spoken of among the little towns of willow switches,
mud and straw above the *junta de los rios*. The river flowed in silence
even in its larger passages. Some of the inhabitants went naked with

strings tied upon their prepuces. Other peoples farther north were fully
clothed.

The soldiers proceeded up the river in December 1582, passing
crosses that still stood since the year before. On occasions Indians whom
they met sat at night around a great bonfire and clapped their hands in
music, while some rose to dance in pairs, fours or eights. In curiosity
and delight the Indians touched the soldiers with their hands, fond-
ling them, and their horses. Gifts were brought to the travellers—food,
blankets, hides. Tanned deerskins reminded the soldiers of soft Flemish
leather. The Indian weapons were wooden clubs and "Turkish" bows,
both fashioned from mesquite. The soldiers made new stocks for their
harquebuses of the same wood.

Wherever they stopped the Spaniards erected crosses, and took
possession of the lands of the river with properly notarized documents.
After turning due north on the river, they met an Indian who told them
that one of friars of the year before had been killed (was this the
astrologer on his way alone to Mexico?) and that the other two still
lived (and were these the two left at Puaray in Tiguex?). Coming into
the country of the three-and-four-storey pueblos, they marvelled at their
size and permanence after the half-dugout, perishable houses below them
in the valley. At Puaray, not far from Coronado's old headquarters of
Alcanfor across the river, they learned the worst. The two missionaries
had been slain, presumably for their possessions—the goats, the horses,
the little metal hawk's-bells, the beads, and the red caps, of barter.

Espéjo and Fray Bernardino had completed their mission, but like
all of their kind before and after them, turned to explore the lands east
and west of the river. Near Pecos, they found that Fray Juan was indeed
also dead. He had been murdered before the expedition of the year
before had even left the pueblo valley. They went on to the plains and
saw the buffalo herds, and they returned to the river, crossing it and
marching to the west. They saw Ácoma, and beyond, in the pueblos far
from the river, they found that Coronado was remembered, and in one
of them, Espéjo came upon an old, small travelling chest and a book
that the General had left there. They collected mineral specimens from
mines even farther west, and turned back to the river, where since their
passage the towns had become rebellious.

Espéjo met his own battles, too, in the upriver pueblos, and with
spirit. "The Lord willed this that the whole land should tremble for
ten lone Spaniards, for there were over twelve thousand Indians in the

province with bows and arrows. . . ." declared his chronicler, and yet
when reports came of Indian peoples waiting to attack the travellers,
". . . trusting in God we always marched to the place where we were
told the largest number of people awaited us." Espéjo was obliged at one
point to burn a town and execute by the garrote sixteen Indians, not
to mention those who burned to death. A soldier reflected that "this was
a strange deed for so few people in the midst of so many enemies."
He knew too what it was to come before a walled town and find it empty,
its people immured in the mountains, full of distrust and fear.

In Indian grottoes or caves the soldiers saw prayer sticks with
feathers and bits of cooked meat and concluded that there the Devil
came to take his ease and feed himself and speak with the Indians.
Once they saw in a cage what looked like a Castilian parrot. They
noticed that the women of the river were whiter of skin than the Indian
women of Mexico, and that the pueblo people did not stink like Indians
met with earlier. They remarked much "game of foot and wing, rabbits,
hares, deer, native cows, ducks, geese, cranes, pheasants, and other birds,"
and spoke, like connoisseurs, of "good mountains," and Espéjo euphori-
cally cited "millions of souls" for conversion.

When they turned toward home, the company divided and followed two routes. Fray Bernardino and one group went down the river
as all had come. Espéjo and his soldiers returned to Pecos and marched
southward along the Rio de la Vacas, which was the Pecos River. Indians
whom they met told how this River of Cows joined with another large
river flowing eastward which in turn formed a junction with a large
river flowing from the north. They knew then that they were once again
near the Rio del Norte and its meeting with the Conchos. Turning west
they found the river and were given a joyful reception by the people,
who performed dances, and fed the soldiers with a feast of green corn,
cooked and raw squashes, and cat, and other river fish. The welcome
was so friendly that the soldiers put aside arms and armor, going about
"almost in shirt sleeves." On August 21, 1583, they came to the *junta de
los rios,* where people of another town greeted them warmly, and gave
the news that Fray Bernardino and his party had already passed safely
by there. The river was now too high to ford. The soldiers rested there
for three days, and all traded for blankets, buffalo robes, and Indian
bows reinforced with rawhide, and received supplies of squash, beans
and corn. Those Indians, thought a soldier, were "fine and elegant
people who would readily accept the Holy Faith."

On the twenty-sixth the little troop started homeward up the

Conchos into Mexico. They had failed of their first purpose, but once again knowledge of the river and its lands went to the authorities in New Spain, who noted among other details that Espéjo spoke of a kingdom of New Mexico, which in honor of his native soil he preferred to call New Andalusia.

Again the country of the north, New Mexico in particular, emerged in both fact and dream. Coronado's failure was forgotten, his hope remembered. Explorers were still talking of the vast river (the Mississippi) beyond the plains, adding now that it was salty, and spoke of a great lake with canoes whose prows carried decorations of "brass-colored" metal. The South Sea (the Pacific) was assuredly rich in pearls. New Mexico, as it lay between all these promises, must be worth the labor, the distance, the danger, to colonize as a base of operations. The government in Mexico City was besieged with applications to forward to the Crown, each begging for the honor and opportunity of leading a colony to New Mexico, and serving God and the King at private expense as governor and captain-general, and signed with piety, humble duty and rubric, duly notarized. Strict laws governed the terms by which a colony might be launched forth. Applicants made elaborate cases for themselves. All papers went to Madrid to pass over the worktable of King Philip II to await, sometimes for months, his personal attention. News of his pleasure, coming by sea, subject to the winds, could be hurried or delayed, or lost in disaster. The applicants could only wait.

But seven years after Espéjo with his soldiers marched down the Pecos on his way home, another, and much larger, procession followed it to the north. Acting apparently in good faith under the colonial laws which with certain requirements allowed any governor to settle lands already discovered, Gaspar Castaño de Sosa came to the Rio del Norte near the site of modern Del Rio in September, 1590, with one hundred seventy people, a long supply train, and two brass fieldpieces. The company were the whole population of the mining town of Almaden, now Monclova in Nuevo Leon. Castaño de Sosa was lieutenant governor of his province. At the river he found no settlements. He camped for three weeks in the low sandy hills and heavy greenery of late summer along the banks. On the first of October he started out again, following the south bank until near Eagle Pass he found the ford, crossed over, and went upstream to the Pecos. The canyon of this tributary was too deep to follow from this point to the north. He forded it, marched on to the passes of the Davis mountains, and found the Pecos again in its high plains character, and followed it to the pueblo of Pecos where he halted

toward the end of December. His supplies were depleted, the weather
was bitter, and it was time to be made welcome, but the people of Pecos
were defiant before his resounding overtures of colonial kindliness.
Night fell before the negotiations were completed, and when day came
again, the colonists saw that the town had been silently abandoned during
the dark. Entering in, Castaño de Sosa found rich supplies of corn in
the storage cists of the cellular houses. Taking what they needed, the
invaders went on their way westward to the Rio Grande del Norte. Once
again the river towns submitted to Spanish expeditioners, let them have
food, clothing, watched them raise crosses, saw them go exploring east
and west of the river. Now and then there was hostility—at a parley
before a pueblo, a soldier of Castaño de Sosa's company spoke out for
peace, at which an Indian came forth on his terrace, with throngs of his
own people clustered about him on the rooftops, and in a gesture small
in size but great in power, threw a pinch of ashes at the soldier. At this,
as on a signal, the other Indians raised their voices in imprecation, and
the soldier departed.

Near the pueblo later called Santo Domingo the new colony
made its capital in camp. Castaño de Sosa, sure of his governorship now,
sent couriers with news of his march and achievement to the Viceroy at
Mexico City, to claim that what no one had yet done, he had succeeded
in doing. In his river capital there were men, women and children,
domestic animals, a government, a new land—in fact, a colony. Farms
must come, he saw Indians growing cotton and several kinds of beans.
In reporting to the Viceroy, he was complying with one of the most
important requirements of the laws of colonial administration. Knowing its importance, he had been careful to acquaint the Viceroy of all his
plans even before leaving Almaden. His report of later progress could
only improve his position with the Viceregal Court. With it he sent
requests for reinforcements—more soldiers, more families, more supplies.

Meanwhile, at his river outpost Castaño de Sosa was scrupulous
to enforce all regulations protecting native peoples. Many of his followers
wanted to use their superior armaments and habitual sense of command
to despoil the Indians of property and require labor of them. The leader
refused to approve such plans. As a result his life was in danger from
his own people. A plot to kill him was exposed. He gave any man or
woman freedom to return to Mexico as they liked, but he would remain.
The cabal died away. He went to Pecos again for more corn from the
stores. He explored his country north on the river, and west, and
returned to his capital which was no better fed or clothed or protected

against all strangenesses than Coronado's Alcanfor. There he had news of a Spanish detachment marching up the river and went out rejoicing to meet his reply from the Viceroy—the reinforcements, the honors, he must have.

What he met instead was a warrant of arrest at the hands of an officer, Juan Morlete, who came to take him prisoner and to disband his colony. His report to the Viceroy from the river had been the first word of his adventures, his presumptions, to reach the government. The law was plain. He had entered the north without a royal commission, such as even then many great captains were hoping to receive from the King. They had been waiting for it, and would be waiting for it, for years. Castaño de Sosa's disgrace was inescapable. Captain Juan Morlete led him down the river. His people were dispersed—Thomas and Christopher, two Mexican Indians, remained at Puaray to live, the rest straggled back to old homes and lost satisfactions. Castaño de Sosa was entered into the infinitely slow mercies of viceregal justice, which was merely a lever touched by the royal hand in Madrid.

> The King: to the president and oidores of my royal audiencia which resides in the City of Mexico in New Spain: I have been informed that Gaspar Castaño . . . entered New Mexico with a company which he collected upon his own authority without order or license to do so. This having come to the attention of yourself, the viceroy, and you learning that those men had committed many disorders and abuses and had taken certain Indians as slaves, you sent in pursuit of them Captain Juan Morlete, who entered New Mexico and took prisoners Captain Gaspar Castaño and his companions. Since it is just that such a bold and dishonorable act should be punished, I command you to . . . proceed against them judicially. . . . Dated at Madrid, January 17, 1593. I THE KING.

Castaño was tried, found guilty, and exiled to China.

In the same year, two officers led a small detachment of soldiers on a mission to subdue Indian disorders in northern Mexico. The task accomplished, they were supposed to return south to their home garrison; but across the deserts of northern Mexico was the river, and up the river was what so many had gone for—Coronado, Chamuscado, Espéjo, Castaño —and the two officers proposed to their men that they too, though without orders, enter the north. Some of the men refused. Others agreed, and followed Captain Francisco Leyda de Bonilla and Captain Antonio

Gutierrez de Humaña along the Conchos, up the Rio del Norte, and out of living knowledge. Word of their defection was circulated; they were famous deserters, lawbreakers. Their capture or voluntary return was awaited with all propriety. They would not be forgotten by the courts.

The courts, in fact, also remembered Castaño de Sosa and his case. Before a final decision was made in respect to applications before the King for the governorship of New Mexico, the case of Castaño was revived. Reconsideration of all its aspects led to a reversal of the earlier verdict. He was exonerated and ordered home from exile to become the first royally authorized governor of New Mexico. His recall went to China, where it arrived too late. He had been killed shortly before while dealing with a mutiny on a Chinese junk.

So through many weighings, intrigues, hesitations and refinements of policy, the question of the colony for New Mexico aged with the last decade of the sixteenth century; until the decision was finally made, the captain-general named once and for all, the expedition authorized, and the northward toil undertaken over a new route to the river in 1598.

16.

Possession

Late one morning in April, 1598, a party of eight armed and mounted men came to the river from the south through heavy groves of cottonwoods. They were emaciated and wild with thirst. On seeing the water they lost their wits, men and horses alike, and threw themselves into it bodily. The current was swift. Two of the horses thundered too far into the stream and were carried away and drowned. Two others drank so much so fast that, as they staggered to the bank from the shallows, their bellies broke open and they died.

The men drank and drank in the river. They took the water in through their skins and they cupped it to their mouths and swollen

tongues and parched throats. When they could drink no more they went
to the dry banks and fell down upon the cool sand under the shade of
the big trees. In their frenzied appetite for survival itself, they had become bloated and deformed, and they lay sprawled in exhaustion and
excess. One of their company, looking upon himself and them, said
they were all like drunkards abandoned on the floor of an inn, and
that they looked more like toads than like men.

Numbed with simple creature pleasures they took their ease in
the shade. In the bounteous trees overhead many birds sang. There were
bees in the wildflowers of spring, and the surviving horses grazed in
near-by meadows. The river looked calm and peaceful. All such sounds
and sights were deeply restful to the squad of men. Their clothes were
ragged, their boots were worn through, and their bellies were hungry;
for they had come for fifty days through deserts with thorns, mountains
with rocks, and nothing to eat but roots and weeds. For the last five days
they had not had a drop of water. In finding the river, they not only
saved their lives; they fulfilled their assignment—to break a new trail
to the Rio del Norte from the south, that would bypass the Junta de los
Rios, to bring the colony directly to its New Mexican kingdom with
one hundred and thirty families, two hundred and seventy single men,
eighty-three wagons and carts, eleven Franciscan friars, seven thousand
cattle herded by drovers on foot, and all commanded by the Governor,
Captain-General and Adelantado Don Juan de Oñate.

The little advance detachment was headed by Vicente de Zaldívar,
sergeant major of the colony, and nephew of the Governor. Among his
seven men was Captain Don Gaspar Pérez de Villagrá, from Salamanca,
a former courtier of King Philip II, and a scholar with a classical education who later wrote the history of the colony's first year in thirty-four
rhymed Virgilian cantos. When they set out on their mission Villagrá
said they were all without scientific knowledge of the heavens by which
to set their course. He doubted if there was one among them who, "once
the sun had set, could with certainty say, 'There is east, there is west'."
They marched with hunger and thirst and once were captured by Indians
who freed them unharmed having enjoyed their fright. But with the next
dawn the eight Spaniards charged the large camp of their tormentors
from all sides, firing their arms, and scattering all but a handful of
Indians, whom they captured, holding two as guides, releasing the others.
Now they also had rations—venison, badger, rabbit meat, along with
herbs and roots. They moved on to the north, again running out of
water. The guides brought them to six shallow water holes where all

horses and men drank selfishly and greedily but one—Zaldívar, the
leader, who waited till all were done, at the risk of there being no water
left; then last in turn by his own choice, he drank his fill. Advancing
over a plain where they could see far, they asked the guides where lay
the river they sought? One did not understand. The other smoothed
the ground and at once drew a circle, and "marked the four cardinal
points . . . the two oceans, the islands, mountains, and the course of
the river we sought. He seemed to act with the knowledge and experience of an expert cosmographer. As we watched him it seemed as though
he was tracing the Arctic and Antarctic seas, the signs of the Zodiac,
and even the degrees and parallels. He marked the different towns of
New Mexico and the road we should follow and where along the journey
we should find water. He then explained to us the direction we should
take and where we would be able to ford the mighty river." It was reassuring to have such a guide; but by the next day the Indians had
escaped and the Spaniards were adrift in the desert, "trusting in God
to bring us with safety to the river's shore." There was always too much
water or too little. They passed through a whole week of uninterrupted
rain; and then there was thirst again, like that of the last five days that
brought them to the river.

But now they rested and recovered their strength. They fished in
the river, and shot ducks and geese, and on April 20, saw with pride
and joy the best results of their efforts, for then arrived the mounted
vanguard of the main body, led by the Governor. The wagons and the
herds were following more slowly. That evening the trail blazers and the
Governor's great cavalcade celebrated their meeting with a feast. They
built a roaring fire, and in it roasted meat and fish. Afterward there were
speeches. The Sergeant Major described the adventures of his little party.
The Governor then rose to tell of all that his people had endured, and
they listened thirstily to his accounts of their heroism, and knew all
over again the burning days, the cold nights, the thorns, the hunger, the
fear, the bewildered privation of children, the courage of women, and
the power of prayer to bring them rain when they were parched. At the
end of his speech, the Governor was pleased to make them all a gift
which only he could make. It was a whole day of rest in which all might
do as they wished, to recover themselves before the journey up the river
was resumed.

On April 26 the rest of the expedition arrived. All were reunited,
and moved together up the south bank of the river a few more leagues.
There was a sense of great occasion in this arrival and encamp-

ment at the Rio del Norte. The wastes of northern Mexico were behind them all now, and the path to the north was more familiar from this point on. To select the ford to the north bank the Sergeant Major detailed a party of five men, all good swimmers. They found a shallow wide place, and returning to make their report met with an Indian encampment where four friendly Indians agreed to return with them. The Governor received the Indian visitors, gave them clothes and many gifts to take back to their people. It was not long before the Indians were back again, with many of their friends, bringing fish in quantities, which were welcome for the celebrations and feasts that were approaching. The river flowed through the gates of the kingdom of New Mexico. The army would enter through them only after suitable observances.

Under a river grove they built an altar. There on the morning of the last day of April in the presence of the whole army and the families, a solemn High Mass was sung by the Franciscan priests. Candle flames dipped and shone in the dappled shady light under the trees that let moving discs of sunlight in upon the gold-laced vestments, the bent heads of the people, their praying hands. At Mass the Father Commissary, Fray Alonso Martinez, preached a learned sermon.

After Mass came an entertainment. It was a play composed for the occasion by Captain Don Marcos Farfán de los Godos, who came from Seville and in his forty years had seen much of the theatre. He understood the drama as a habit of occasion, a proper part of any festival. He was a man of good stature, with a chestnut-colored beard, and his sense of amenity was becoming to a soldier who was also a colonist. His play, hurriedly prepared and rehearsed, showed how the Franciscan fathers came to New Mexico; crossed the land, so; met the poor savages, so; who were gentle and friendly, and came on their knees, thus, asking to be converted; and how the missionaries then baptized them in great throngs. So the colony showed to themselves a great purpose of their toil. The audience adjourned in high spirits to prepare for the next episode of the celebrations.

Men with horses now went to mount, and came in formation shining with arms, armor and all their richest dress. The rest of the colony took up formal ranks, and when all was ready the Governor came forward accompanied by the crucifer, the standard-bearer, the trumpeters and the royal secretary of the expedition to perform the most solemn of acts.

All knew what a great man the Governor was. He was supposed to be one of the five richest men in Mexico. His father the Count de

Oñate had been a governor before him—in New Galicia. During the four years of preparations, delays, starts and stops which the expedition had already endured, they said the Governor had spent one million dollars of his own fortune, for salaries, supplies, equipment, and running expenses. The Governor was magnificent on both sides of his household, for his wife was a granddaughter of the Marquis of the Valley, Cortés, the conqueror; and the great-granddaughter of the Emperor Montezuma himself. Her father was Don Pedro de Tovar, who had gone and returned with Coronado. As a child she must have heard him tell of his adventures in the north. All such great connections were matters of pride to the colony, but since opinion was always divided in human affairs, there were those who had heard things. They said the Governor had squandered and mismanaged his great patrimony so that he actually owed more than thirty thousand dollars, all of it borrowed in bad faith, with the creditors evaded by tricks ever since. Everybody knew he was only a private individual, and thus had no place in the government to command respect for him. How would anybody obey him? In fact, once before, leading soldiers, he had been treated disrespectfully and disobeyed. Would anybody but wastrels and thugs enlist to go with him? But for all such opinion there was plenty of the opposite, which held that the delays and frustrations that had so many times during the past four years prevented the Governor from actually marching forth with his army had come from the Devil, whose purpose it was to prevent the colony from going to convert the heathen Indians, and it was plain that those who worked against the Governor worked for the Prince of Darkness. Many said that nobody was better fitted for the command than the Governor, with his virtue, his human understanding and the nobility of his character; his efficiency and his place in the affections of the soldiers; and the fact that he was the son of his father, who was the beloved "refuge of soldiers and poor gentlemen in this kingdom."

When he now came forward to face the army and with them all to signalize their common achievement, all hearts lifted to him in unity. He was a fine-looking man in middle life, wearing one of his six complete suits of armor. He held many closely written pages of parchment on which were written over three thousand words of solemn proclamation. Bareheaded, in the presence of the cross and the royal standard, he began to read aloud.

He invoked the trinity in "the one and only true God . . . creator of the heavens and earth . . . and of all creatures . . . from the highest cherubim to the lowliest ant and the smallest butterfly." He called upon

the Holy Mother of God and upon Saint Francis. He set forth the legal
basis of his authority, and declared, ". . . finding myself on the banks
of the Rio del Norte, within a short distance from the first settlements
of New Mexico, which are found along this river . . . I desire to take
possession of this land this 30th day of April, the feast of the Ascension
of Our Lord, in the year fifteen hundred and ninety-eight. . . ." He
commemorated the Franciscan martyrs of earlier years up the river, and
showed how their work must be taken up and continued. Turning to
other purposes of his colony, he listed many—the "need for correcting
and punishing the sins against nature and against humanity that exist
among these bestial nations"; and the desirable ends "that these people
may be bettered in commerce and trade; that they may gain better ideas
of government; that they may augment the number of their occupations
and learn the arts, become tillers of the soil and keep livestock and
cattle, and learn to live like rational beings, clothe their naked; govern
themselves with justice and be able to defend themselves from their
enemies. . . . All these objects I shall fulfill even to the point of death,
if need be. I command now and will always command that these objects
be observed under penalty of death." Mentioning the presence of his
reverend fathers and of his officers, and the name of the King, he
declared:

"Therefore . . . I take possession, once, twice, and thrice, and
all the times I can and must, of the . . . lands of the said Rio del Norte,
without exception whatsoever, with all its meadows and pasture grounds
and passes . . . and all other lands, pueblos, cities, villas, of whatsoever
nature now founded in the kingdom and province of New Mexico . . .
and all its native Indians. . . . I take all jurisdiction, civil as well as
criminal, high as well as low, from the edge of the mountains to the
stones and sand in the rivers, and the leaves of the trees. . . ."

He then turned and took the cross beside him, and advancing to
tree he nailed the cross to it and knelt down to pray, "O, holy cros-
divine gate of heaven and altar of the only and essential sacrifice of the
blood and body of the Son of God, pathway of saints and emblem of
their glory, open the gates of heaven to these infidels. Found churches
and altars where the body and blood of the Son of God may be offered
in sacrifice; open to us a way of peace and safety for their conversion,
and give to our king and to me, in his royal name, the peaceful possession
of these kingdoms and provinces. Amen."

And the royal secretary then read his certification of the deed, and
the trumpets blew a tremendous voluntary, and the harquebusiers fired

a salute together, and the Governor planted with his own hands the
royal standard in the land near the river.

17.

The River Capital

Four days later, on May 4, the army arrived upriver at the ford
discovered by the five swimmers a week before. There the river flowed
from between two mountains whose flanks it had for aeons worn away
in its search for the sea, still so distant. All went to work to get the train
across. The ford was close to the site of modern El Paso-Juarez. The
most noble youth sweated himself like the commonest half-breed, hauling at the heavy carts, calling to the cattle, riding back and forth from
dust to dust on each side of the river. A man's worth was in how much
he worked when the time came. The Governor's nephews, Juan and
Vicente de Zaldívar, were among the worthiest.

Once across on the left bank, the colony moved on to the pass
through the mountains, which they called now the North Pass, El Paso
del Norte. Wandering Indians watched them, Mansos, naked and passive,
but known to be capable of great ferocity. They had no fixed dwellings
or planted fields, but ate berries and whatever they could catch that
jumped or ran, such as toads, lizards and vipers, and other animals, all
of which they ate raw.

The colony moved safely on with all its burdens on pack animals
and in the two-wheeled wagons. The wheels were made of cross sections
of cottonwood trunks, joined by a pine-log axle on which rested the
wagon bed four feet square. The wagon sides were made of slender
branches lashed upright. The shaft of the wagon was of pine, and to it
were chained the yokes of the oxen. There went all the household
treasures and trifles, the possessions that meant personality and home

and ways of doing things, from sacred images to dishes to books and clothing, whether humble or grand.

A servant of one of the officers was in charge of his master's arms and wardrobe, which included a captain's lance of silver with tassels of gold, yellow and purple silk; three suits of armor; three Madrid harquebuses, with powder horns, firelocks, and bullet moulds; three sets of buckskin armor for horses; a sergeant's halberd with yellow and purple velvet tassels; a Toledo sword and a dagger inlaid with soft gold, with silk belts; four Cordovan leather saddles; a bed with two mattresses and coverlet, sheets, pillowcases, pillows. The Captain owned a suit of blue Italian velvet faced with wide gold lace; another of lustrous Castilian satin, rose-colored, with a short gray cloak trimmed in long silver and gold fringe, and rose-colored silk stockings and striped rose-colored taffeta garters; another of straw-colored Castilian satin, slashed over crimson Castilian taffeta with matching garters and stockings; another of purple Castilian cloth with cape, garters and stockings to match, all trimmed in gold; another of chestnut-colored London cloth embroidered in silver; another of flowered silk from China, tan and green, trimmed in gold; two doublets of soft kid leather decorated with gold and silver lace; another doublet of royal lion skin with gold and purple braid and buttons to match. The Captain had a gray rain-cloak, and two Rouen linen shirts with collars and cuffs of Dutch cambric, six handkerchiefs of Rouen linen, eight pairs of linen drawers with socks (plain), six pairs of Rouen linen drawers (trimmed), eight pairs of Cordovan leather boots, four pairs of sole leather and buckskin boots, four pairs of laced gaiters, fourteen pairs of Cordovan leather shoes, white and black. He had three hats, one black trimmed around the crown with a silver cord, with purple, white and black feathers; another gray with purple and yellow feathers; and the last of purple taffeta with blue, purple and yellow feathers and trimmed with gold and silver braid. For riding (he was a captain of cavalry), he had four pairs of spurs, two for short stirrups, two for long stirrups, and some Moorish spurs with silken tassels and cords. And to house himself and his establishment in camp (he had a wife and family and two young Spanish servants, and thirty war horses) there were fifty yards of striped Mexican canvas for a tent, with all the gear with which to set it up, including forked stakes.

The train stretched out for nearly four miles along the road it was making as it went. Drovers and mounted soldiers did their best to keep the animals, the carts, the walking people closed up in manageable formation. It was often hard to do. Animals strayed. Horses would run away and their soldiers grumbled at continuing on foot. The Governor had much to think about on the route. The Viceroy was known to be against him. When the expedition found its settling place, it was possible that another man might arrive by the fleet (for surely the river in the north was near enough to the sea for shipping to ply between New Mexico and Acapulco as all the best cosmographers believed?), and would produce a royal commission to take over the governorship. But perhaps not, if all went well in the meantime. If, for example, there was much of interest discovered east and west of the river, and if there were many conversions, and if the renegade explorers, Bonilla and Humaña, were at last found and captured, and returned to the proper authorities to be punished with "pain of death or mutilation of members," as the familiar legal expression put it. It was one of the duties specified in the Governor's commission that he find and capture the two deserters believed to be "in that country . . . wandering about there."

He hoped also to find one if not both of the Mexican Indians, Thomas and Christopher, who had remained along the river when Castaño de Sosa's column returned to Mexico.

Leaving the North Pass behind them the Governor's train marched up the wide flat valley where they met wandering Indians who lived a carefree existence, "far removed from the bustle and hurry of our great cities," and a former courtier noted that the Indians were "ignorant of court life." Soon they heard that the first of the river towns lay ahead. The Governor sent a detachment under Captain de Aguilar to scout the town, with orders, under penalty of death, not to enter the town for any reason whatsoever, but to see it from afar and return to report.

At a point sixty miles above the North Pass, the army came to the great westward turn in the river caused by the end of a mountain range. It was the same place where Nuñez Cabeza de Vaca had turned west. The river could not be followed in its valley there, for on the east bank mountains sloped almost directly into it, and on the west bank the land fell to the river in such a repeated tumble of gullies and arroyos, with rising and falling hills between, that no road could be made over it with the tools and equipment owned by the army. And where the river went west, the army wanted to go north. There was only one thing to do, which was to leave the river and continue overland on the northward course, and presently—ninety miles upstream—the river would be accessible again. For all the intervening distance, bare, high and abrupt mountains separated the travellers from the river, and their course would lie over a desert plain flat enough for the carts and wagons.

Just as the colony was about to leave the river and enter the journey over the north-lying desert, Captain de Aguilar returned to report to the Governor.

He had seen the town?

Yes.

How far away was it?

About ninety miles—near the end of the desert passage.

And there were people?

Yes, he talked with them.

Talked with them?

The Governor was enraged. Did the Captain disobey orders and enter the town, then?

Yes. He had done so.

The Governor stormed on. Did the Captain not suppose that the Governor had full and sufficient reasons for giving orders not to enter the town? It was a known habit of those Indian people to gather their possessions and abandon their towns when they heard of an army's approach. Such behavior would defeat the Governor's purpose. If they now through the Captain's disobedience had news of the approaching caravan, a proper beginning for the colony might be impossible. The Captain's grave offense must not go unnoticed. The Governor hardly pausing to catch his breath commanded that he be executed at once, for outright disobedience to orders.

The sentence aroused the colony. The Captain's men came to plead with the Governor for his life. The Governor listened to all who asked to be heard. Had he been hasty? But he was not entirely alone in his decision. Juan Piñero, an ensign of the army, who had gone north with the Captain, stated that he for one had wished to obey the Governor's orders exactly. He had been overruled, and he now repeated that the orders should have been obeyed. He would not plead against the punishment. But in the end the Governor yielded to all the others and spared the Captain.

But he felt obliged now to take a mobile and light detachment of thirty horsemen and go ahead himself, to meet the Indians in the pueblos, and pacify them, and keep them in their houses. He gave command of the army to a senior officer and by forced marches crossed the desert passage leaving the army to follow him in its trudging.

They made their course by the stars at night. The desert was

bounded on east and west by long mountain ranges between which the
river had once run. In the summer daytime the heat was great. Mountains
seemed to waver on their bases in the desert shimmer. A knife, a sword,
any metal thing, or even leather, if it was shined and hard-finished, was
actually too hot to handle if exposed to the sun. The mountains between
the desert and the river held the colors of dead fire—dusty reds, yellows,
clinker purple, ash violet, and burned blacks; and at sundown for a few
moments seemed to fire alive again on the surface as once they must
have been fired within.

On May 21, Pedro Robledo, one of the soldiers, died and was
buried near the end of the mountain range on the west, which was
named for him. Two days later the Governor's party was in distress from
lack of water. They had advanced only six leagues since the twenty-first.
Man, horse and dog (there was a little dog travelling with the party)
searched for a water hole in any likely place. On the twenty-third the
little dog disappeared and awhile later returned to his soldiers. They
took him up and spoke to him, but he had already answered them, for
all his paws were freshly muddy, and there must be water near-by.
Everyone looked again, and the dog helped, and presently Captain Pérez
de Villagrá found a water hole a little way toward the mountain barrier
of the river, and soon after that a soldier named Cristóbal Sanchez found
another, and all drank, some too much, including the Father President
Fray Alonso Martinez, who drank until he was ill. They named the
place Perillo Spring, after the little dog, and marked it for those following. It was for generations the only place where travellers could find
water in the whole desert passage between the outlying mountains. Later
Spaniards named the ninety-mile desert the Jordada del Muerto, the
Dead Man's March—the name by which it was finally to be known.

Where the river came back from the west and joined the northward route, ending the Dead Man's March, the Governor found a good
campsite. In honor of one of his Franciscan chaplains, the place, and
the mountains that rose above it, were given the chaplain's name—Fray
Cristóbal—when on a later passage he died near there.

And north of there on the river's west bank clear in the diamond
sunlight was the first of the towns. As the Governor approached with his
men the sky went suddenly black with clouds. How could it be, when a
moment ago the sky was clear? A torrent fell on the instant. The soldiers
trembled. There was no shelter. They prayed. It was certainly the Devil
who had done this, to keep the army from its good task. Hail followed the
rain and wild shattering thunder. Lifting their crucifixes the friars

replied to the storm with the terrible prayers of exorcism. What happened instantly was almost more fearful than the storm. The sky cleared, the rain stopped, the clouds vanished in silence, and the sun shone forth. As the soldiers rode forward to the pueblo they saw that the Indians too were amazed at the sudden end of the tempest.

The Indians came out to meet them, took them into the pueblo, gave them rooms, food and comforts. Seeing the crucifixes on the long rosaries of the friars the Indians took them up and kissed them. On the walls of the little cubed rooms the soldiers saw paintings of the Indian gods—gods of water, mountain, wing, seed, all fierce and terrible. In honor of the day, for it was the Feast of Saint John the Baptist, June 24, the Governor ordered a military display and sham battle. He divided the command into two sides, both mounted, and put his nephews Juan and Vicente in charge as opposing leaders. The brothers gave a brave show, and all handled their horses with skill and their weapons with dexterity. Indians watched. There was much meaning to the tournament.

When it was over the Governor went among the soldiers speaking about the games. Presently three naked Indians came up to him, and one declared loudly, in Spanish:

"Thursday, Friday, Saturday and Sunday!"

What was that?

The Governor and all others were astonished. As a soldier later said, it was like hearing the serpent bark like a dog, after the defeat of the Tarquinians, in Roman history.

The Indian would not repeat what all were sure he had said, and therefore the Governor had him and his companions seized. Then, terrified, the Indian spoke again.

"Thomas and Christopher!" he shouted.

What?—And by much questioning with signs, and indications upon the ground, the soldiers found that he was telling them of two men named Thomas and Christopher who lived at a town two days away, who had been there for seven years, ever since the last time the valley had seen men with horses, armor and guns.

This could only mean the two Mexican Indians who had stayed behind after Castaño de Sosa. The Governor needed them as interpreters, for they could speak Spanish, and having lived in the pueblos they must now speak Indian languages. Their capture was essential to his mission. He took leave of this first town and hurried north with his cavalcade to look for Thomas and Christopher two days' journey away.

On the following day he came to Puaray and with all his men

was hospitably received. They were conducted into the pueblo where passing through a room they saw something that made their hearts turn over. It was a wall painting which had been lately whitewashed, as though in hasty response to a warning. But the effacement was not complete, and the Governor and his men could see that the mural painting represented the murder with stones and arrows of two Franciscan fathers. Now it was plain that seventeen years ago Fray Agustín Rodríguez and Fray Francisco López had died there in that fashion. With his eye the Governor warned his people not to give any sign. They accepted rooms for the night, but did not sleep, and late in the darkness while the whole pueblo slept, the Spaniards led by the Governor withdrew in dead quiet.

Early the next morning at the pueblo which the Spaniards named El Agua de Santo Domingo they met the Indians as friends and asked if Thomas and Christopher were here.

Yes, they were here, but still in bed.

Just where?—and the soldiers found them, brought them to the Governor, and they spoke freely with him.

They said they were Christian Indians who had come from New Spain with Castaño. When he was taken away, they had stayed here of their own will, were now married to pueblo women, and were happy. They could speak the Mexican, Spanish and the local Indian tongues. From that time on, they belonged to the Governor, and played a vital part in his government, for through them he could now make his way into the understanding of the people of his river.

At Santo Domingo the Governor received seven chiefs representing thirty-four pueblos. With fuller communication achieved through Thomas and Christopher, a solemn ceremony was held in the great kiva of Santo Domingo in which the chiefs swore allegiance to God and the king of the Christians on the seventh of July.

The Governor moved upriver again, and on the eleventh arrived near the two pueblos of Yuque and Yunque which faced each other across the river just below the confluence of the Chama with the Rio del Norte. These were the same towns seen fifty-seven years before by Captain Barrionuevo of Coronado's army. From the nearer one of these pueblos —the one on the east bank—the people came out to give their submission to the Governor, and peaceably evacuated their houses to let him and his soldiers move in. In memory of the first Spaniards who had erected the cross there years before, the Governor named his town San Juan de los Caballeros, and designated it as his capital.

Captain Vicente de Zaldívar, the Sergeant Major, was sent down-

stream to meet and escort the heavy train of the wagons and the cattle
to the new capital, while the Governor with a small party rode to the
north as far as Taos, and to the east as far as Pecos.

At Pecos a man was brought forward who could speak in a sort
of Spanish. His name was Joseph. After a few words he struck deep into
the interest of his hearers. Another mystery of the north was partly solved
as he talked. Five years ago Joseph was taken from the Rio del Norte
with other Indians to guide some Spanish soldiers eastward to the plains.
He spoke the names of Captain Francisco Leyda de Bonilla and Captain
Antonio Gutierrez de Humaña.

The Spaniards quickened at this mention of the deserters, the
leaders of an illegal entry, whom it was the Governor's assigned duty to
arrest, and for whom he had been looking ever since his arrival in
New Mexico.

But go on: where were they now?

Joseph continued. They had gone together eastward, and for six
or seven weeks travelled past pueblos, rivers, great herds of buffalo, until
one day Gutierrez de Humaña turned on Leyda de Bonilla and killed
him on the plains.

So! Gutierrez de Humaña was not only a deserter but also a murderer. What else?

After that, the party came to a large river, and there Joseph and
five other Indians ran away and tried to go back to the Rio del Norte.
He alone got back, and then only after a year's captivity by plains
Apaches.

And Gutierrez de Humaña and the rest of his soldiers?

They had never returned from the plains. There were several possibilities. They might be living there as conquerors. They might be
captive slaves of buffalo-hunting Indians. They might be dead.

Joseph, after his escape, hearing that there were other Spaniards
on the river, went to meet them, and there, at Pecos, found them. The
Governor was glad to take him into his service as interpreter, guide and
geographer. Turning back to the Rio del Norte, the Governor's party
crossed westward and explored the Jemez province.

In his absence from the capital, other soldiers, with fifteen hundred
Indians, undertook to build the first municipal works—an irrigation ditch
—for the river city of San Juan. At that point the valley was wide, with
many grand steps in the land rising away from the river, through river
terraces of pinkish sand, and Indian-colored foothills carved by the wind
into fantastic shapes, and high flat mesas, to mountains whose forests

turned the clear air blue as smoke. The river course was edged with
trees.

Here on August 19 the wagon train arrived to be reunited to the
Governor and his command, and to stay on the river as no colony had
yet stayed. They brought more than their lashed and lumbering cargoes
to the capital high on the river, more than their toiling bodies. They
brought all that had made them, through the centuries. If their heritage
was a collective memory, it remembered for all more than any one man
could know for himself. It shone upon their inner lives in another light
than the light of the material world, and in countless hidden revelations
suggested what brought them where they were.

18.

Collective Memory

i. *sources*

Brown plains and wide skies joined by far mountains would always
be the image of home to them, the image of Spain, that rose like a castle
to inland heights from the slopes of the Mediterranean, and gave to the
offshore wind the fragrance of ten thousand wild flowers that mariners
smelled out at sea.

The home of the Spanish spirit was Rome. When Spain was a
province of the Caesarian Empire her promising youths went to Rome,
to make a name for themselves, to refresh the life of the capital with the
raw sweetness of the country, and to help form the styles of the day in
the theatre, like Seneca of Cordoba, and make wit acid as wine, like
Martial of Bilbilis, and elevate the public art of speech, like Quintillian
from Calahorra, and even become Emperor, like Trajan, the Spanish
soldier. Rome gave the Spaniards their law; their feeling for cliff and

wall, arch and cave, in building; and their formal display of death in the arena, with its mortal delights, its cynical esthetic of pain and chance. Martial said it:

> Raptus abit media quod ad aethera taurus harena,
> non fuit hoc artis sed pietatis opus. . . .

A bull, he said, taken up from the center of the arena rises to the skies, and this was not act of art, but of piety. . . . It remained an act of passion when Spanish piety turned to Christianity.

It was an empowering piety that grew through fourteen centuries, the last eight of which made almost a settled condition of life out of war with the Moslems of the Spanish peninsula. It was war both holy and political, striving to unify belief and territory. Like all victors the Spaniards bore lasting marks of the vanquished. Perhaps in the Moors they met something of themselves, long quiet in the blood that even before Roman times flowed in Spanish veins from Africa and the East, when the ancient Phoenicians and the Carthaginians voyaged the Latin sea and touched the Spanish shore and seeded its life. From the Moslem enemy in the long strife came certain arts—numbers, the mathematics of the sky, the art of living in deserts, and the virtue of water for pleasure, in fountains, running courses and tiled cascades. That had style: to use for useless pleasure in an arid land its rarest element.

Hardly had they made their home kingdom secure than the Spaniards put themselves and their faith across the world. They fought the infidel wherever they could find him, they ranged toward the Turk, and the Barbary Coast, and for them an admiral mercenary in 1492 risked sailing west until he might fall over the edge of the world and be lost. But however mockingly he was called a man of dreams, like many such he was a genius of the practical, and as strong in his soul as in his heart; for he believed as his employers believed.

ii. belief

They believed in God, the Father Almighty, Creator of heaven and earth; and in Jesus Christ His only Son their Lord, Who was conceived by the Holy Ghost, born of the Virgin Mary, suffered under

Pontius Pilate, was crucified, died and buried. He descended into hell;
the third day He rose again from the dead; He ascended into heaven to
sit at the right hand of God the Father Almighty from thence to come
to judge the living and the dead. They believed in the Holy Ghost, the
Holy Catholic Church, the communion of saints, the forgiveness of sins,
the resurrection of the body, and life everlasting. Amen, they said.

So believing, it was a divine company they kept in their daily
habit, all, from the monarch to the beggar, the poet to the butcher. The
Holy Family and the saints inhabited their souls, thoughts and words.
They believed that with the love of God, nothing failed; without it,
nothing prospered. Fray Juan of the Cross said it for them:

> Buscando mis amores,
> Iré por esos montes y riberas,
> No cogeré las flores,
> Ni temeré las fieras,
> Y pasaré los fuertes y fronteras.

Thus seeking their love across mountain and strand, neither gathering
flowers nor fearing beasts, they would pass fortress and frontier, able to
endure all because of their strength of spirit in the companionship of
their Divine Lord.

Such belief existed within the Spanish not as a compartment where
they kept their worship and faith, but as a condition of their very being,
like the touch by which they felt the solid world, and the breath of life
they drew until they died. It was the simplest and yet most significant
fact about them, and more than any other accounted for their achievement of a new world. With mankind's imperfect material—for they knew
their failings, indeed, revelled in them and beat themselves with them
and knew death was too good for them if Christ had to suffer so much
thorn and lance and nail for them—they yet could strive to fulfill the
divine will, made plain to them by the Church. Relief from man's faulty
nature could be had only in God. In obedience to Him, they found their
greatest freedom, the essential freedom of the personality, the individual
spirit in the self, with all its other expressions which they well knew—
irony, extravagance, romance, vividness and poetry in speech, and honor,
and hard pride.

If they were not large men physically, they were strong, and their
bodies which the King commanded and their souls which God commanded were in harmony with any task because both God and King
gave the same command. It was agreed that the King held his authority

and his crown by the grace of God, communicated to him by the sanction of the Church. This was clear and firm. Thus, when required to serve the King in any official enterprise, great or small, they believed that they would likewise serve God, and had doubled strength from the two sources of their empowerment.

But if the King was divinely sanctioned he was also a man like all; and they knew one another, king and commoner, in the common terms of their humanity. To command, to obey; to serve, to protect— these were duties intermixed as they faced one another. The King was accountable to the people as well as to God; for they made the State, and the State was in his care. *Del rey abajo ninguno,* they said in a proverb, Between us and the King, nobody. So they spoke to him in parliaments. Representative government began with the Spaniards. All, noble or commoner, had equality before the law. They greatly prized learning and respected those who owned it, such as lawyers. Indeed, the law was almost another faith, with its own rituals and customs, and even its own language, closed to uninitiated eyes and ears. Learning being scarce must also have seemed precious, and beyond the grasp of many a hungry mind. Yet with other peoples of the Renaissance, the sixteenth-century Spanish had intimations of world upon world unfolding, and they could not say what their children would know except that it would be greater than what they the fathers knew, watching the children at play with their little puppets of friars made from bean pods, with the tip broken and hanging down like a cowl, and showing the uppermost bean like a shaven head.

iii. the ocean masters

The year after the astounding first voyage of Admiral Christopher Columbus came the Bull of Pope Alexander VI giving the King and Queen of Spain for themselves, their heirs and successors, all the lands of the New World known and still to be known. Given the unexempted belief of all civilized society in the reality of the Pope's spiritual and temporal power, this was an act of unquestionable legality. (In making his proclamation at the Rio del Norte, the Governor cited it, outlining briefly the divine origin of the Papacy through the story of Christ.) Thus the Americas came to belong to Spain, and to reach those lands she

became a great sea power, for a time the greatest in the world. Schools
of navigation and piloting were founded at Ferrol, Cádiz and Cartagena.
Universities maintained professorial chairs in cosmography. The great
lords of Spain were given command of the fleets that plied to the Indies,
though some had no qualities for the ocean but rank and magnificence,
like the old marquis, a certain governor of the Armada, who through
gout could not take off his own hat or feed his own lips, but had to have
his courtesy and his food handled for him by servants. But still the
Spanish sailed, and sailed well, and their fleets were prodigious at their
greatest, like the one that bore the King to marry the Princess of England—gilded carving on the stern galleries, and sails painted with scenes
from ancient Rome, and fifteen thousand banners at the masts, and
damask, cloth of gold and silk draping the rails, and the sailors in
scarlet uniforms, and all the ships standing to one another in such perfect
order as to remind those who saw it of the buildings of a city, and the
music of silver trumpets coming from the ships as they sailed.

To recruit the Indies fleets, a public crier and his musicians went
from town to town, mostly in Andalusia that bordered on the sea. The
drums rolled in the plaza, the fifes whistled a bright tune, calling a
crowd. Then the crier bawled out his news. He told the sailing date of
the next fleet, how great the ships were, some of one hundred twenty
tons burden and sixty feet long, how skilled the captains, what opportunities oversea awaited the able-bodied young man between twenty-five
and thirty years of age with a taste for adventure and good pay. And
many a youth saw in his mind the great lands lifting over the ocean, with
their Amazons who invited and broke men, and the golden treasuries
waiting to be shipped home, and shapeless but powerful thoughts of
how a fortune waited only to be seized, and a fellow's excellence recognized, his body given content, his pride matched with hazard, his dear-
ness to himself made dear to all whom he should newly encounter.
Many answered the fifes, the drums, and the crier. But if the recruitment
was not great enough under the regulations which forbade signing on
heretics and foreigners, then the merchant marine took on Jews, Moors,
Frenchmen, Italians, Englishmen, Scotchmen, Germans, for the fleets
had to sail and men had to sail them.

They sailed twice a year from Seville, in April and August, after
three inspections held in the Guadalquivir. Crewmen signed on in the
ship's register, took an oath of loyalty to the captain or the owner, and
were bound for the voyage. Some were paid by the month, some by the
mile, some with shares in the cargo. A sailor could not go anywhere

without the commander's consent, and unless in port for the winter could not even undress himself without permission. If he did so, he was punished by being ducked in the sea three times at the end of a rope from the yardarm. The crew's rations left them hungry enough at times to catch rats and eat them. The ship provided beef, pork, rice, fish, spices, flour, cheese, honey, anchovies, raisins, prunes, figs, sugar, quinces, olive oil and wine, but in poor quantities, and very little water. The officers fared better, dining apart.

The passengers prepared their own meals out of the stores they had brought along, mostly hardtack and salted beef. They were almost always thirsty. Some slept on deck, some in little cabins five feet square, on mats stuffed with a thin layer of doghair, and under a blanket of worked goatskin. Below decks all day it was nearly dark. They could hear cockroaches and rats at restless work, and feel lice multiplying. There was no place in which to walk around. They could only lie down or sit, day and night. In storm the alcázar at the stern swayed as if to fall off the ship, and the blunt prows under their heavy castle shook like shoulders burrowing into the deep. The pumps at work spewed up bilge water as sickening as the air below decks, and all remained above whenever possible—the pilot navigating, the captain inspecting the artillery and other defenses, the master of the treasure that was packed in the hold, the cargo-master, the barber-surgeon, the caulker, the engineer, the cabin boys, the seamen.

But on busy days when the weather was blessed, the company was busy with interests. So long as they lasted uneaten, cocks were set to fighting on deck for an audience that took sides and made bets. A young fellow would become a bull and another would pretend to fight him with cape and sword. Clever people got up plays and gave them. Others sang ballads to the music of the vihuela. Others read poetry aloud or improvised rhymes about the people on board. There were always some who brought the latest books printed by the Crombergers of Seville, and sat reading by the hour. The fleet might be becalmed, and then boys and men went over the side to swim near the ships. And when the wind came alive again, the painted sails swelled out, and the hulls leaned, and their sodden timbered breasts pushed heavily against the waves, while the cabin boy sang out the devotions of praise and thanks, "Amen: God give us a happy voyage, may the ships make a good passage, captain, master, and your lordships, good day my lords, from stern to prow," and at evening they cried, "Evening chow, ready now," and "Long live the King of Castile on land and sea," and all bowed and said "Amen."

So they sailed and were sailed, taking two to three months to come to New Spain, where, like Juan Ponce de León, when he saw Florida, they said, "Gracias le sean dadas, Señor, que me permites contemplar algo nuevo," giving thanks to God that He granted them to see the new.

And some amongst them feeling if they could not speak the wonder of the New World, where dangers and hardships in the end bound them more closely to her than easy victories ever could have, exclaimed in their hearts, with love, in their various ways, "Oh, Virgin of the World, innocent America!"

That the Spaniards take her lawfully, with care, and with conscience, the Spanish kings of the Golden Age worked without cease.

iv. the king and father

Not all Spaniards had seen the King, but in every large company there was always one who had seen him, or knew someone who served him closely, and remembered much to tell. Anything they could hear of the King was immensely interesting and important. He was their pride even as he was their master. He commanded them by the power of God, and yet as they were so was he, a man, their common image, but with the glory and dignity of the crown over his head, and so, over theirs. What he was had greatly to do with what they were, as in all fatherhood. So, his image passed through them to the Indies, wherever they went, beyond cities and maps, however far along remote rivers. Even the gossip about great kings created the character of their subjects.

King Charles, who was also the Holy Roman Emperor, lived and worked in hard bare rooms with no carpets, crowding to the fire in winter, using the window's sunshine in summer. The doctors of medicine stated that the humors of moisture and of cold dominated his quality. His face was fixed in calm, but for his eyes, that moved and spoke more than his gestures or his lips. His face was pale and long, the lower lip full and forward, often dry and cracked so that he kept on it a green leaf to suck. His nose was flat and his brows were pitted with a raised frown that appeared to suggest a constant headache. He held his shoulders high as though on guard. He would seem to speak twice, once within and fully, and then outwardly and meagrely. But his eyes showed his mind, brilliant, deep and always at work. He loved information for its own sake, was always reading, and knew his maps well. They said he saw the Indies better than many who went there, and held positive views on all matters concerning the New World and its conquerors.

But if his opinions were strong, so was his conscience. He said once that it was his nature to be obstinate in sticking to his opinions. A courtier replied that it was but laudable firmness to stick to good opinions. To this the Emperor observed with a sigh that he sometimes stuck to bad ones. Much contemplation rested behind such a remark. He was in poor health for most of his life, and as a result considered himself in many aspects. In his young days he was a beautiful rider, with his light legs and his heavy lifted shoulders. He once liked to hunt bear and boar; but illness and business put an end to it. He worked all day and much of the night, until his supper at midnight, at which he received ambassadors, who were amazed at his appetite. Matters of state went on even then, by candlelight, as the platters were passed, and the baskets of fruit, and the water bowls. He wore his flat black cap, his black Flemish velvet doublet and surcoat with the collar of Germany-dressed marten skins, and his chain of the Golden Fleece. The letters of Cortés from New Spain had good talk in them, and the Emperor later had them published in print.

Whether or not America, so far away, was a matter of policy instead of feeling, Charles required justice for the Indians of the New World. Before 1519 he was sending people to the Indies to study and report to him upon the conditions of the natives. Uppermost was his desire that their souls be saved through Christianity. It was of greater moment that Indians became Christians than that they became Spaniards. So as the conquerors made cities in the New World they made schools, colleges and universities for the Indians, in which to teach them—often in Latin but more often in the Indian tongues which the friars learned rapidly—salvation in Christ. The Emperor held that through such salvation all else of life must naturally take its course and would come. He strongly supported the missioners in the Indies, and inspired them and many laymen to build the Church in the New World even as ominous cracks ran up its walls in the Old.

But from the first, and increasingly, another spirit worked against the Indians. The military, the landowners, the civil officials believed that conversion was a proper thing, but once out of the way, let the natives be useful to them in labor and arms. But the priests meant what they preached, just as much as the men of the world meant what they ordered. Both said they served the Crown as it desired to be served. Both appealed to the King.

His Holy Caesarian Catholic Majesty (for so he was addressed in documents) wished to know an all-determining truth. Was the Indian a man, as many claimed? Or was he an animal, as many others insisted? Could he understand Christianity? Did he deserve better than the yoke of slavery?

Commissions investigated, passions rose, and humanity triumphed. The Cardinal Adrian in Spain preached that the Indians were free and must be treated as free men, and given Christianity with Christian gentleness. The Emperor acted, and the laws for the Indies were decreed in that spirit. The Crown gave its approval to the ideals of the missionary priests who ever afterward, over new land, went with the armies not only to convert but to protect Indians.

When he left Spain for Germany, and after his retirement from the throne in mid-century, the Emperor kept the problem in mind, for he wrote to his son Prince Philip to caution him that he must be vigilant to prevent oppressions and injustices in the Colonies, saying that only through justice were sound business and prosperity possible. It was a cold and impassive statement of policy, but in it (as in the brilliant black and white flash of those eyes in his pallid face that found it so difficult otherwise to express itself) true humanity shone behind expediency.

When the Emperor abdicated to become a country gentleman at Yuste near Placencia, there was still much to hear about him, even as he invented ways to pass the time. He made a garden. He designed and fashioned mechanical works, including a hand mill to grind meal, and a marvellous set of little clockwork soldiers that performed military drills. Visitors brought him watches and clocks upon which he delighted to work. The joke went around that one time when he complained of his food, he was told by the majordomo that the only thing that would please his palate then would be a stew of watches. He laughed heartily at this.

From his early days in the Italian campaigns he loved the arts of music and painting. In his military travels, even to Africa, he took along his choir—the best choir in Europe—and pipe organs. His ear was true, he remembered music as well as he did facts, and he loved to sit and listen to a French air, *Mille regrets.* At Placencia he had his nine favorite paintings by Titian with him.

With a few guests in his party, he would go wandering through the woods with his harquebus in hand, watching for game. But the joy he took from this sport in his old age was more that of watching birds, and little animals, and their quick mysterious commerce, than that of killing them. He would shoot now and then, but his friends said that the pigeons pretended out of courtesy to be frightened of his blasts, and perhaps he was an old man hunting for life, not death.

But his piety kept death before him. He was read aloud to from the *Confessions of Saint Augustine,* and he could nod in recognition of anybody who turned sharply away from the great world to lead a modest life of outer trifles and inner mysteries of faith and conscience. It was talked of everywhere, for thousands were there, when he had a Requiem Mass sung to rehearse his own funeral. It was just as though it were the actual funeral. There before the altar was the catafalque swept in black draperies and silver lace, with thousands of candles burning at all the altars and shrines, and the prelates and priests singing the pontifical Mass, and the Emperor's wonderful music in the stalls with the organ, and there in the middle of it wearing a black mantle was the Emperor himself, praying for the repose of his soul before it left his body.

The Spaniards knew the same thing in themselves—the strength and the countenance to stare upon contrition and death. For, in their belief, what could anyone do enough to mortify himself, if he was to be worthy of salvation by the sufferings of the Son of Man upon the cross? The Emperor had a flail with which he would whip himself so hard that the thongs showed his blood. After his death it became known that in his will he left this flail to his son Philip, for him to prize all his life and in his turn to pass on as a beloved heirloom, a relic of the blood of the father. . . .

Philip II spared himself no less, and left his image no less in the Indies, though in somewhat different manner. People missed the occasional humor and grace of the Emperor, even though under him they had had to work just as hard as under his son. But there was as it were a darkening of life that came when the Emperor retired and, dying in retirement, left all power to the new King. But the King demanded more of himself than of anyone else. New Spain and all the other Indies became greater, quieter, richer, and as the conquests receded, the work of government grew enormously. The whole world wrote to Spain. Her ships carried not only the treasure of the New World, they took also reports, contracts, budgets, petitions, court records, confidential intelligence, complaints and all manner of papers to Madrid. And there, the

King himself read them, all of them, and marked his wishes upon their margins.

Secretaries came to him in the morning as he dressed, and after dinner at midday, and again to spend the long evening, while he dictated, initialled, weighed, decided; held in abeyance, revived for discussion, or postponed again; examined for policy or referred for further study dozens, and hundreds, and tens of thousands of papers through a lifetime of late-working nights. Besides all that, there were the endless committees to receive, who sat through hours of giving all aspects proper consideration. Minutes of such meetings were kept, and, doubling the ecstasy of administrative indulgence, could always be referred to later. It was a poor business if anyone sought to relieve the King of any small details of his official burden. Some of the best men in the land were called to court for appointment to important posts, and then denied the use of their faculties of originality and initiative. No detail was too small to interest the King. If he was King and was to sign, then what he signed must be exquisitely proper; and he would put all the power, weight and style of his office into a debate upon the nicety of a word to employ in a certain phrase to be written down in a state paper. He would refuse to be hurried, but would spend himself twice over on a matter rather than settle it out of hand. Don Pedro Ponce de León (he was Governor Oñate's most serious rival for the appointment) wrote to the King from Mexico asking for the command of the entry into New Mexico to colonize the Rio del Norte, and as the ocean passage of letter and reply would take eight months more or less, he expected to hear nothing for a while. But time passed, and no answer came to him from the King, whereupon he wrote again, begging in all respect for a reply to his earlier petition. The reply when it came said, "Tell him it will take a year to decide."

There was much to decide at home. The King saw with sorrow the disorderly and frivolous nature of the populace, and, asking less actually of them than of himself, issued decrees of prohibition upon conduct, possessions and belief. It was unseemly and therefore forbidden by royal edict to wear luxurious dress; to live amidst lavish surroundings; to use private carriages or coaches except under certain stated conditions; to employ courtesy titles; to seek education beyond the frontiers of Spain; to open the mind to the inquiries of science; or otherwise fail in proper humility and self-discipline. It was a grief to Philip that despite his endless efforts to guide his great family of subjects in ways of piety and decorum all manner of license grew and continued. Rich and clever people found ways to evade the laws, while poor people could not even qualify under them to commit the crimes of indulgence they forbade. Orders might come in a stream of papers from the palace, but Madrid remained a mudhole, the filthy streets choked with carriages and palanquins, bearing rich ladies who accosted men unknown to them, and of whom they invited proposals of shame. How could this be in a land where women were previously sacred and guarded within the family walls as the very Moors had done before them?

How could it be when any man worked so hard that he should be visited with so many sorrows and reverses? The King bent his head and spoke of the will of God. There were endless tales of his natural piety, that sustained him in the hours of humiliation that came to Spain. The Dutch wars went against the Spanish forces. They were defeated in France. The English under an infidel Queen broke Spain's greatest fleet and a year later raided, burned and robbed Cádiz, Spain's richest city. Spanish ships were attacked homeward bound from the Indies. The King suffered all with courage, determined to be an example to all in adversity, that they might keep their faith. He declared that it was better not to reign at all than to reign over heretics. Of these there were not many, then, and those few learned or vanished, though the question remained whether the delicate seed of faith that could grow to such mighty power could truly prosper through the habits of brutality of all agencies of discipline, such as the army, the constabulary, the office of the Inquisition, and the law courts alike. And still the King worked, writing orders to govern how many horses and servants a man could maintain with seemliness; how funerals should be conducted, and how weddings; what public amusements might be countenanced and what not. And while he slaved at concerns so alarming and dear to him, there went unanswered pleas from his ambassadors overseas and viceroys desperate for Crown policies ("tell him it will take a year"), and groaning supplications from fiscal officers who expected mutinies unless the armies were paid.

How could a man's goodness be so crushing?

Those who saw him come to the throne saw his father's son, in the tall forehead, the vivid black and white eyes, the lower lip permanently outthrust. Even then, as a young man, there was no mark of humor in his face, which was furrowed beside the nose and under the cheekbone. Yet it was a head of grace and distinction, lean above the ruffed collar of Brabant linen, and the puffed doublet worked in gold. His beard and hair, that had a little wave in it, were a golden brown.

And then those who saw him long later saw a heavy face, with sallow color, and sacs about the eyes, now smaller and heavier-lidded. His dress was different, he wore a tall black cap and black garments relieved only by the starch-white of his collar. His spirit was heavy, too, and sallow, if souls had color. The feature most unchanged in his face was the deep cleft between his eyes, that made a scowl of abnegation natural to him in youth when he first renounced so much for himself, and that cut deeper in age, when he renounced so much in their own lives for others.

An image of his quality was the palace of the Escorial which he built on the sweeping plain outside Madrid, below the mountains. It was as big as a palisaded mesa. The plain was as barren as a desert. In New Spain and New Mexico was much country of which that was the miniature. The palace rose in a great square of ochreous gray walls. It was so vast that human silence seemed a very part of its design. What no man could see but which the profuse flocks of little martins and swallows could see as they circled over it was that within the great square stood inner walls, crisscrossing one another in the form of a gridiron or grill. It was believed that this was built in imitation and endless reminder of the grill upon which St. Lawrence met his death. Thus Philip could have constant point for contemplation. Within the palace the long corridors that followed the lines of the grill were low and narrow, showing the bare granite of their walls. The floors were of unfinished stone. Coming in from even a hot summer's day the courtier met indoors the chill of the tomb. The palace was so made that a great portion of its internal volume was taken by a dark church whose dome and towers rose above the enclosing walls. The King's own bedroom, a cell, was placed so that he could look out from it through an indoor window and see the Mass at the high altar, which was just below. Church, monastery, palace and tomb, that tenebrous heart of the Empire expressed in all its purposes the sacred and profane obsessions of the King its builder.

And if the monarch had his palatial rack designed after a saint's, the soldiers, the traders, the shopmen, the scholars, the voyagers of Spain each had his Escorial of the soul, where to endure the joys and the pains of his spiritual exercises he entered alone and in humility.

Perhaps the deeper a man's humility in the privacy of his soul, the more florid his pride in public. All Spaniards, high or low, could use a spacious manner. Its principal medium was the Spanish language. Not many could read; but all could speak like lords or poets. The poorest soldier in the farthest outlandish expedition of New Mexico might be a chip floating beyond his will on the stream of history, but still he could make an opinion, state it with grace and energy, and even, in cases, make up a rhyme for it. He spoke his mind through a common language that was as plain and clear as water, yet able to be sharp as a knife, or soft as the moon, or as full of clatter as heels dancing on tile. Like Latin, from which it came, it needed little to say what it meant. It called less upon image and fancy than other tongues, but made its point concretely and called forth feelings in response to universal commonplaces rather than to flights of invention. With that plain strength, the language yet could show much elegance, and such a combination—strength with elegance—spoke truly for the Spaniards and of them. The Emperor once said that to speak to horses, the best tongue to use was German; to talk with statesmen, French; to make love, Italian; to call the birds, English; and to address princes, kings, and God, Spanish. In the time of Cicero the Spanish town of Córdoba was famous for two things, its poetry and its olive oil. He said the poetry sounded as though it were mixed with the oil.

v. arts

A passion for study filled the century of the Golden Age. In Spain, thirty-four universities were at work, and others were founded in the New World within a few years of the conquest. The German Jacob Cromberger and his sons established their printing house at Seville in 1500, reading became an indispensable part of living, and all because a complicated machine held together many rows of reversed little metal letters and pressed them into damp paper, again and again, until many copies of the same words and ideas were at hand. Because her language went everywhere with Spain's power, printers in Italy, France, the Netherlands and the Indies printed books in Spanish.

Everything found its way into print, even the ballads that previously passed through generations by word of mouth. People made them up in inns and on travels and marching in wars, telling droll stories or love stories or wicked scandals, and the rude narratives were sung wherever somebody had an instrument to pluck. Seeing how such efforts looked in print, men of letters began to write ballads in the style of the old popular ones, that had gone always changing as one man's memory

revised the residue of another's. The new poetic ballads sang of the
courts of chivalry; imaginary histories that revealed Spanish ideals of
noble kingship, knightly valor, reverence for womanhood and death to
monsters. True histories were also written in rhyme, long chronicles of
heroes, as when Captain Pérez de Villagrá, the alumnus of the University of Salamanca, sat down to write the history of Oñate's first year on
the Rio del Norte, he wrote it in heroic verse. The Spanish world grew
not only in range but also in meaning as the people saw its likeness in
all that was made by writers and artists.

As his father the Emperor admired Titian of Venice, so King
Philip admired and employed Domenico Theotocopuli, known as The
Greek, who came from Greece by way of long studies and labors in
Venice and Rome. He was a learned man and a pious one, and for the
Escorial and churches elsewhere he painted many pictures that swept
the eye and mind of the beholder upward to heaven. Often even the
very eyes of the kings and saints he painted were gazing heavenward
and shining with great diamond tears of desire, and seeing them so,
the beholder cast his desires upward also. The skies of his pictures of
martyrdoms and sufferings and triumphs were like the skies of Good
Friday afternoon, torn apart and blowing aloft in black and white clouds
through which the Spanish temperament could see the immortal soul of
Christ as it flew to His Father from the cross. The Greek painted many
likenesses of people of circumstance, who without their starch and black
velvet and swords, their armor and ribbons, or their violet mantelletas
and trains, would have looked very much like everybody else in the
Spanish populace, even those on the northern river of the latest and
farthest Crown colony. All countenances which he limned were grave
and melancholy, even that of the Madonna in the Nativity. The Spaniards were a people who did not often smile, but more often laughed
outright or possessed their faces in calm, when most faces look sad. The
Greek was much seen at Toledo, where he painted the town many times,
making odd changes in exactly how it looked, yet by so doing, making
the city's image combine with the beholder's feeling to produce a rise
of the soul.

It was the same rise that Spaniards knew from music in the High
Mass, when the dark high vaults of the church where candlelight never
reached would be filled with the singing of choirs, plain, without instruments. They heard the masses composed by the great Tomás Luís de
Victoria of Ávila, and Cristóbal of Morales, and Francisco Guerrero. The
voices of boys came like shafts of heaven, and in the polyphonic style,

the voices of men rose under them and turned with melody, and the two qualities met and divided, the one qualifying the other, now with one long note held against several notes in a figure, again with highs against lows, and again with syllables against whole words, and loud against soft, so that in heavenly laws known to music alone an experience of meaning and delivery struck all who truly listened, and the stone arches and the drift of incense and the possibility of divinity in mankind and the Mass at the altar all became intermingled with the soul that rose. How, lost in dark choir stalls under lofting stone, could boys, having yet had so little of life, strike so purely to the darkest self with their shining voices that seemed to come from beyond all flesh?

And there was other music that used the very flesh itself, spoke to it, enlivened it, cozened it with coarse jokes, and pulled its nose and made the hearers laugh and clap and stamp their feet. It was heard at the inns, in public squares, and in the theatres, when ballads were sung or skits and plays given by actors and dancers. They came out on a stage bringing sackbuts, or dulcimers, harps, lutes or vihuelas, or combinations of all these, and struck up a tune to which they sang a story with many verses. They plucked, beat, blew and nodded together, and often repeated with each verse a clever effect in which one musician gave a little variation at the same place each time, so that the audience listened for it in following verses. Such players entertained anyone who called for them and displayed a coin. They went from one tavern to another, ready to stand in a half-circle facing a table and play to a private party much to the advantage of any others in the place. Their music went with the Spaniards wherever in the world they might go.

If popular balladry was the poor man's comfort, there was much to sing about as the world moved and poor times befell Spain in her might. Great fortunes shrank, and the high state of many nobles lost its quality because it could not be paid for, and wage earners found their coins worth very little, and poor people lived always hungry. It was the very outpourings of wealth from the new world that caused such trouble. When so much more gold than usual came to be circulated, each little coin or bit of gold spent in trade was worth much less than usual, as gold itself became too common. In giving civilization to the New World, Spain seemed to give up its own strength as the new land found the lusty power to grow by itself. In the home kingdom, while all graces were maintained, the substance behind them shrank, and for great numbers of Spaniards the graces which they aired came to be pretensions and little else.

vi. style and hunger

And yet there was that in the Spanish spirit which made of each
Spaniard his own castle, and it was very like them all that as the wealth
that sustained public nobility began to shrink, and as every hidalgo by
birth disdained to reveal his poor estate, so many another man who had
no title or claim to nobility adopted the airs and styles of the hidalgo,
until the land became a parade of starving lords, real and false, who
the lower they fell in worldly affairs, the more grandly they behaved.
Going hungry, they would loll against a wall in public, picking their
teeth to convince the passer-by that they had just dined on sweet carrots
and turnips, sharp cheese, pungent bacon, fresh eggs, crusty roast kid,
tart wine from Spanish grapes, and a covered dish of baked gazpacho,
that was made out of wheat bread, olive oil, vinegar, onions, salt, and
red peppers hot enough to make the eyes water.

There was little else for such a gentleman to do. If he had talents
that could be employed, there was hardly anybody to pay him for them.
He was a man of honor and to make a living could not stoop to improper
ways, which no matter how hard the times seemed always to prosper. If
his shanks were thin and bare, and his sitting bones almost showed in
his threadbare breeches, and his belly was puffy with windy hunger,
then he still had his ragged cloak to throw about such betrayals. Within
his cloak he could stand a noble stance, and at a little distance, who
was the wiser? As the proverb said, "Under a bad cloak there may hide
a good drinker," which gave comfort to fallen swagger; and to comfort
the dream of impossible valor, there spoke another proverb, saying,
'Under my cloak I kill the king."

But no patch ever failed to show, however lovingly stitched, even
a patch on a man's pride. To cloak his spirit, the mangy gentleman had
another sort of possession left to him from his better days. This was the
high thought of chivalry, that gave to human life, all human life, so
great a dignity and such an obligation of nobility on behalf of all other
persons. There was a poor sweetness in this extravagant spending of
spirit, that the more a man lacked simply to keep him alive, the more
he disdained his own trouble and grandly swore to demolish the trouble
of another. In his ironic self-knowledge the Spaniard knew such men,

and smiled at the antic capers they cut in their hungry pretensions. And yet he bowed to their spirit which stated that "he is only worth more than another who does more than another." It was no surprise to him that a champion should vow the rescue of anyone in distress, without reference to rank or station. If there were different levels of life, then one man in his own was worth as much as another in his, and was free to state as much, and act accordingly. And as every soul originated in God, and so was equal to every other in worth, so its offerings on earth deserved succor without discrimination. The Spaniard knew that the grandeur of God did not disdain the humblest surroundings, and could say with Saint Teresa of Ávila, *Entre los pucheros anda el Señor*—God moves among the kitchen pots.

But all came back to hunger. Private soldiers who went to the Americas were experienced in that condition. It was a marvel how far they could march, how hard they could fight, and how long they could cling to unknown country on empty stomachs. Nuñez Cabeza de Vaca, Coronado's soldiers, Castaño de Sosa pillaging at Pecos, Zaldívar crawling over deserts toward the river, all gnawed on tradition when rations were low. Certainly the adventurers did not enlist for the pay, for the pay was meagre and always in arrears, even that owed to the commanders in silver-gilt armor. Nor did they venture forth for commerce as it could affect the ordinary individual, for the risks were too great for uncertain profits, and in any case the Spanish gift for business fulfilled itself not in the largest but in the smallest affairs, face to face with another man. For the pleasures of business were firstly social—little exchanges of desire and deceit, indifference and truth, the study of human nature, the flourish of bargaining, the satisfaction of the righteous swindle, in buyer and seller alike. Nor was it inordinate love of adventure that took Spaniards past oceans and shores, and up the river, for adventure could be had anywhere, even at home. Perhaps more than any one other motive it was a belief in their own inherent greatness that took the men of the Golden Age to their achievements in geography and colonization.

For to them it was finer to make greatness than to inherit it; and after they made it, they could in all justice cry with the True Chronicler of the conquest of Mexico, "I say again that I—I, myself—I am a true conqueror; and the most ancient of all . . . and I also say, and praise myself thereon, that I have been in as many battles and engagements as, according to history, the Emperor Henry the Fourth." In such spirit, what they did with so little, they did with style.

vii. the swords

Even the swords that were extensions not only of their right arms
but also of their personalities came out of humble means through fire
and water to strength and beauty. Ovid sang the praises of Toledo
blades, the best of which were made of old used metal, such as horseshoes. The Spaniard's sword was born at nighttime, through fire, of a
river and the south wind.

In the city hall of Toledo the master steelworkers—Sahagún the
Elder, Julian del Rey, Menchaca, Hortuño de Aguirre, Juanes de la
Horta—kept their metal punches when these were not in use to stamp
the maker's name on a new blade. Every blade had its *alma,* and this
soul was the core of old iron on whose cheeks were welded new plates
of steel. Standing ready were the two gifts of the river Tagus that flowed
below the high rocks of Toledo. These were its white sand and its clear
water. The blades were born only in the darkest nights, the better to let
the true or false temper of the steel show when red-hot; and of the
darkest nights, only those when the south wind blew, so that in passing
the blade from fire to water it might not cool too rapidly as a north
wind would cool it. The clumsy weld was put into the coals where the
bellows hooted. When it came red-hot the master took it from the fire.
It threw sparks on meeting the air. Casting river sand on it which extinguished the sparks, the master moved to the anvil. There with taps of
hammer and sweeps of the steel against the anvil he shaped the blade,
creating a perfectly straight ridge down the center of each side, until
squinted at endwise the blade looked like a flattened lozenge. Now the
blade was put again into the fire and kept there until it began to color
again, when the master lifted it into the darkness to see if it showed
precisely cherry-red. If so, it was ready for the river. There stood handy
a tall wooden pail filled with water from the Tagus. Into this, point
down, went the blade for its first immersion. To keep the exact right
time for each immersion, and to bring blessings, the master or one of
his boys sang during the first one, "Blessed be the hour in which Christ
was born," and then the blade was lifted out. Heated again, it was
returned to the water, and they sang, "Holy Mary, Who bore Him!" and
next time they sang, "The iron is hot!" and the next, "The water hisses!"
and the next, "The tempering will be good," and the last, "If God wills."

Then once more the blade went to the fire, but this time only until it became dull red, liver-colored. Then with pincers the master held it by the tang which would later fit into the hilt, and had the boy smear the blade with raw whole fat cut from the sac about the kidneys of a male goat or a sheep. The fat burst into flame. They took the blade to the rack and set it there against the wall point downward. The fat burned away, the blade darkened and cooled through several hours. In daytime they sharpened and polished it, and if it was to bear an inscription, it went to the bench of the engraver, who chiselled his letters on one of the flat faces, or perhaps both, spelling out a pious or patriotic motto, like one on a sword found in Texas not far from the Rio Grande, that read, on one side, "POR MY REY," and on the other, "POR MY LEY," thus swearing protection to king and law. The hilt, with guard and grip, then was joined to the tang, and those for plain soldiers were of well-turned iron, but without inlays of gold or silver, or studdings of smooth jewels, or wrappings with silver-gilt wire that variously went onto the swords of officers and nobles.

And at last the maker sent for his stamp from the city hall and let his device be punched into the blade at its thickest part near the guard, and the proud work was done, and the Spanish gesture could be sharpened and elongated across the world.

viii. soul and body

Both within the Spaniard and without him lay the country which Lope de Vega called "sad, spacious Spain." If Spaniards enacted their literature, it was because, like all people, they both created literature and were created by it. So it was with memories and visions in the colony of the river wilderness. Their hopes of what to be were no less full of meanings than their certainties of what they had done, and both found their center of energy in a moral sense that gave a sort of secret poetry to the hard shape of life. The Spaniard was cruel but he loved life, and his melancholy brutality seemed to issue forth almost involuntarily through the humanitarian laws and codes with which he surrounded himself. If his nature was weak his conscience was strong, and if he sinned his first act of recovery must be to recognize his guilt. When one of the most brutal of the conquerors of the New World was dying of wounds given to him by Indians he was asked where he ached, and he replied, "In my soul."

So the baggage of personality brought by the colonists told of their origin, their faith, the source of their power, the human types by which they perpetuated their tradition; and forecast much about how they would live along the river.

But in that very summer of 1598 when the newest colony of the Spanish Empire was settling on the Rio del Norte in northern New Mexico, the Empire was already ailing. Its life stream carried human tributaries to the river, but already at its source, in Madrid, the springs of Spanish energy were starting to go low. It was an irony of history that just as the American continent was being comprehended, the first great power that sought it began to lose the force to possess it. It would take two more centuries for the flow to become a trickle that barely moved and then altogether stopped. But the Spanish effectiveness in government, society and commerce began to lose power in the New World with the failure of life in the last of the kings of the Golden Age.

Laboring inhumanly to govern his world-wide kingdoms for goodness and prosperity, Philip II left them a complicated legacy of financial ruin, bureaucratic corruption and social inertia. After a dazzling conjugation of *to do,* the destiny of Spain seemed to turn toward a simple respiration of *to be.* One was as true of the Spanish temperament as the other.

If Philip left to his peoples anything in the way of a true inheritance, one that expressed both him and them, and that would pass on through generations, it was his example in adversity, his patience facing a hideous death, and his submission to the will of God.

He lay through the summer of 1598 in the Escorial holding the crucifix that his father the Emperor had held on his own deathbed. The son in an agony of suppurating tumors repeatedly gnawed upon the wood of the cross to stifle his groans. His truckle bed was run close to the indoor window through which he could look down upon the big altar of the Escorial church. In the early mornings he could hear the choir singing in the dark stalls and watch the Holy Sacrifice of the Mass performed for the repose of his soul whose liberation was nearing. But it came slowly. On August 16 he received the pontifical blessing from Rome. A fortnight later he took the last sacraments, and afterward spoke alone to his son and heir on the subject of how reigns ended and crowns passed and how instead came shrouds and coarse cinctures of rope in which to be buried. For days and nights the offices of the dying were chanted by priests in his cell. If momentarily they paused, he whispered, "Fathers, continue, the nearer I come to the fountain, the greater my thirst." Before four in the morning on September 13 he asked for a blessed candle to hold. Its calm light revealed a smile on his face. His father's crucifix was on his breast; and when he gasped faintly three times, and died, and was enclosed in a coffin made of timbers from the *Cinco Chagas,* a galleon that had sailed the seas for him, the crucifix was still there. By his will the blood-crusted flail left to him by his father now passed to the new ruler, King Philip III. In the austere grandeurs of such a scene the deathly luxuries of the Spanish temperament, as well as the dying fall of the Empire, found expression. At San Juan de los Caballeros, in the valley of the Rio del Norte, near the junction with the Chama, where willows and cottonwoods along bench terraces of pale earth all imaged the end of summer, the Crown's new colony was at work on a matter of enduring importance to their settlement. By order of Governor de Oñate they were already building their church.

19.

Duties

It was a dry summer. Late in August, 1598, the Governor was at his mess table one day when he heard unearthly wailing from many voices. He sent an officer to inquire who returned to report that the Indians were making lamentations to their gods because there had been no rain, in spite of the many dances for rain that the pueblo had performed during the summer. It was already very late, and the crop of corn would wither and die and the people would hunger unless rain came. Through four centuries it was a familiar condition along the river in certain years.

The Father President and his assistant Fray Cristóbal spoke to the Indians and calmed them, saying that he and his brothers would offer prayers to God that rain might come and the corn be saved. An officer heard the promise, and sarcastically remarked that the Indians ceased their frightful wailing immediately, "like little children who hush when they are given the things they have cried for." All the rest of the day, and that night, and the following day, the Indians watched the sky, which was "as clear as a diamond," until suddenly it rained. Torrents fell. They were moved and awed. The corn was saved.

But the Indians were not the only residents of San Juan who showed dissatisfaction and fear on occasion. Some forty-five soldiers and officers, including Captain de Aguilar who had once had his life spared by the Governor's clemency, felt aggrieved on several counts. The Governor was aware of their feelings. They had come expecting to get rich, and they were not rich. He said, with his heavy irony, that they expected to find whole platters of silver lying on the ground waiting to be picked up. Failing that, they were not even allowed to take what they liked of the Indian properties, or do as they wished with the Indian persons. They were disgusted with the country, or, said the Governor, "to be more exact, with me," and they resolved to mutiny and desert the colony, stealing slaves and clothing in their flight. The plot failed. The Governor put Aguilar and two soldiers in arrest, and condemned them to die by the garrote. It was a shocking event with which to begin life in the new capital, and once again, as at the entrance to the Dead Man's March, down the river, the Governor was entreated to pardon the condemned.

Life was as easily spared as taken. He consented, ordered a week of jubilee, and work on the church was hastened, and on the eighth of September, the first Mass was sung before San Juan's own altar. The heads of all the pueblos had been invited to the celebrations. A messenger had visited them all in their provinces, carrying with him the Governor's diary, which the Indian chiefs acknowledged as his emblem of office—the pages bearing the marks of his own hands. All had accepted the Governor's invitation but the chief of Ácoma, who chose to be represented in another way. He sent spies who lost themselves among the other Indians but saw everything.

The colonists gave a new comedy specially written for the feast (was Captain Farfán at work again?) and a mounted tournament was staged, and bullfights, and a pageant and sham battle representing the wars of the Moors and Christians, in which brave salvos of firearms were discharged, concluding with a "thunderous discharge of artillery"—but all with gunpowder without shot.

The Ácoma spies watched. How was it that though the soldiers fired, nobody fell and died? The firearms of the white men, though noisy and smoky, must be harmless. It was useful to Ácoma to know this. . . .

On the following day, September ninth, a solemn event was celebrated in the church. The Governor rose to address the chiefs of the Indian provinces. Behind him were the Father President and the other priests. As the Governor spoke the royal secretary noted down his words.

He spoke of his love for the Indian people, and came to them with a grave duty. He must tell of his Divine Lord, and the rewards of heaven, and the punishments of hell, that came to all according as they chose well or ill in the life of the world. But man needed guidance and was provided with God's ministers who could give it. To receive it, all must swear allegiance to the royal crown, and could never after withdraw. Many benefits of body and spirit would come to those who swore. Would they swear?

The Indian leaders would swear.

The secretary then prepared the necessary papers, and all were appropriately signed "amid great rejoicings."

Now the Father President came forward and proposed their salvation to them, in the name of "Christ, God and man, who died and was buried for the redemption of mankind." Would they be saved?

They considered, and presently gave their answer. First, they desired to be instructed in all he had proposed; and second, if they liked what they learned, they would gladly follow his teachings; but third, if they did not like them, it would not do to be forced to accept something they did not understand.

The example of the apostles was before the Franciscans. It was enough. The Father President, Fray Alonso Martinez, rededicated his brother Franciscans in their calling, and assigned to them one by one the parishes over which each would preside. He called them forward in turn:

"Father Fray Francisco de Miguel"—and to him gave the province of Pecos that lay beyond the mountains to the east, and included forty towns, the roving peoples of the cow plains, and the great salines where the Indians went for salt;

"Father Fray Juan Claros"—and to him, all the towns of the Tigua language along the Rio del Norte to the south in number close to sixty;

"Father Juan de Rosas"—the province of the Keres language, on the river and westward, excepting Ácoma, which was assigned to another parish;

"Father Fray Cristóbal de Salazar"—the Tewa towns to the north;

"Father Fray Francisco de Zamora"—the province of the Picuries, and Taos, and the river towns to the north, together with the Apaches north and east of the snowy mountains;

"Father Fray Alonzo de Lugo"—the Jemez province of nine towns and all the Apaches west of the river;

"Father Fray Andres Corchado"—the city of Ácoma on its rock, the Sia province, and the towns of the Zuñis and Hopis far to the west.

Each was to go alone with only Indians to his parish, which was so vast that it could contain mountain, desert and river, all three; and so far from the comfort of familiar life and reassuring knowledge common to all, that a journey of many days by horse or weeks on foot would be needed to bring the priest from his parish to the capital.

They prayed at San Juan, received their commissions and, guided by Indians who had attended the Governor's convocation, went forth into wilderness through their own human trepidation empowered by that which was greater than both.

Four other men left the colony soon after. They were horse thieves and deserters, unreconciled since the Aguilar mutiny. The Governor could not countenance insurrection and the loss of horses. He sent two captains, Pérez de Villagrá and Márques, to arrest the fugitives and bring them back. Expecting them to return in a day or two, the Governor waited at San Juan. But they did not come. He busied himself with organizing an expedition to go east to the buffalo plains, under the command of Vicente de Zaldívar, with "many droves of mares and other supplies," which departed on September sixteen, to look for all that nobody before them had ever found. September passed, and the first days of October, and still the fugitives had not been returned in arrest. The Governor could wait no longer. He was ready to go forth himself to visit the salines east of the mountains, and then turn west across the river and explore possible trails to the South Sea where there were certain to be pearls. He left orders. Pérez de Villagrá was to overtake him after arriving at San Juan with the prisoners. Juan de Zaldívar would stay at San Juan in command until his brother Vicente returned, and then turning over the command to him, would set out with a mounted squad and ride to meet the Governor in the west.

The Governor left San Juan de Nuevo Mexico (as he headed his letters) on October sixth.

20.

A Dark Day in Winter

The Zaldívar brothers were reunited on the eighth of November, when Vicente returned to San Juan after fifty-four days of travel to and from the buffalo plains. He had seen nothing that earlier travellers had not seen, but he was the first to try to capture the buffalo herds into cottonwood corrals which he built near a river. He could not take the cows and bulls, but calves were captured. He thought to domesticate and raise them. But they all "died of rage" within an hour. He brought none back.

Juan now set about arranging to leave with thirty soldiers to reinforce the Governor in the west. In a few days Captain Márques returned to the river capital from his long expedition with Pérez de Villagrá to overtake and bring back the four men who had stolen horses and flown in September. He was alone, for down the river at Puaray on the way back, he and Villagrá, coming home together, had met young Francisco de las Nievas, who said that the Governor had been there only the day before on his way west from the saline provinces. Villagrá believed he should join the Governor without delay, and saying good-bye to Márques, had struck westward alone across the river from Puaray to pick up the Governor's trail, going by way of Ácoma.

And the prisoners? Where were they?

Márques shrugged. Two had escaped. He and Villagrá had trailed the other two almost all the way to Santa Barbara on the Conchos River in Mexico, and on finding them, had taken such action as had seemed in the judgment of Villagrá, who was in authority, to be suitable. They had executed the prisoners, cutting off their heads, and dutifully had made haste to return, themselves, to San Juan. Captain Márques took up new duties under Vicente de Zaldívar at the capital.

In about the third week of November Juan took leave of his younger brother. Both wore beards the color of chestnuts. Juan was

twenty-eight, Vicente twenty-five. Juan was the taller of the two, but
both had good stature. They were from Zacatecas in Mexico. At the head
of his thirty troopers Juan rode out and down the river. They were on
their way to find the Governor in the western wilderness.

Cold was coming down the river from the northern mountains.
Huge geese went south in great high flocks, making their hornlike calls
that came muted to earth. Faster little ducks went plummeting south
too, landing at times on the river like bullets, and talking in circles, and
rising away again. Soldiers shot them as they could, and feasted the home
garrison. On some mornings there was snow on the riverbanks, which
made the brown water look darker than usual. Winter wood was being
gathered to burn in the pueblo rooms, whose thick walls could hold
cold or heat for so long. The river cottonwoods were heavy gold, keeping
their leaves, and the bare willow groves looked from a little distance
like smoke. Winter was coming and even in so open a valley cutting
through such vast plains, there was a sense of days closing in, and vistas,
as November passed and early December came crisply along in golden
chilly days, so far away from other homes in other winters.

One day—it must have seemed ever afterward a dark day no
matter what the weather—there returned to San Juan from a forced
march on spent horses three exhausted soldiers who had gone out a few
weeks before with Juan de Zaldívar. Vicente received them and stood
as they told sorely what they knew. He was dazed. He crossed his
arms on his breast and bowed his head; and then he groaned and began
to sob.

The soldiers said that on December first they arrived with Juan
de Zaldívar at the base of the rocks of Ácoma, under a cold, cloudy sky.
The rock mesa was nearly four hundred feet high, from afar it looked
like a palace, a fortress, a city, all of it; only on coming near could you
see that the city was on the very top, a line of low clay houses against
the sky. The walls of the mesa were cliffs, in all places but one, and there
a trail led up through slopes of sand and finally it too became a cliff
with toeholds cut in the stone. The Indians could swarm up and down
the difficult approach like monkeys. They all came below to welcome
everyone on that first of December, and when Zaldívar asked for food,
they said that if he camped here below that night, he and everyone could
ascend in the morning, and would be given provisions. So the soldiers
made their camp and slept in peace.

In the morning they went up. It was awkward. They had to hang
their swords behind. Armor was stiff and heavy to climb in. They were

laughing and wheezing by the time they got over the edge and walked about on the high island of dusty red stone surrounded by an empty valley. They saw that Ácoma was made not of one rock but two, separated by a chasm of varying width. Down below they could see the horses and the squad of soldiers left to guard them. They looked like toys. The men on the rock turned and went into the town, guided by a chief, Zutucapan, who was all courtesy. Food, their needs, he indicated, would be taken care of at various houses, there, there, and there—and Zaldívar sent soldiers separately to the places indicated.

And as soon as they were separated, the soldiers were lost. A fearsome cry sounded over the stone plateau. It came from Zutucapan crying for battle. The Indians began to gather in menace. Zaldívar yelled with warning and encouragement to those few men remaining by him. They sprang their swords (". . . the tempering will be good . . .") and Zaldívar called out asking if they should retire to the plain below and later inflict punishment for treachery. One soldier objected. He said he would be glad to take on the Indian mob alone, and after he had disposed of it, see that the soldiers could then in their own good time leave the rock. There was a dead moment of wonder and indecision. It was a fateful pause. The Indians poured out of their housetops and streets and closed in. Zaldívar keeping the peace cried to his men to take aim but hold fire. But the Indians flew arrows, lances and even their wooden clubs at Zaldívar's small band, and the soldiers at his order fired. In another moment the fight was joined. Over a thousand Indians broke upon the soldiers in wild combat.

It lasted three hours.

Zaldívar was prodigious. His men fell wounded and dead and three jumped from the cliff and were killed and all fought who could in hand-to-hand combat, and one soldier with his belly ripped open as he died cut his enemy's body awide with his dagger so that the two men fell with their entrails mingling. Zaldívar fell three times only to rise and fight, until he fell forever, when the Indians stormed upon him and destroyed him obscenely. There were five soldiers left on top then, and seeing that Zaldívar was dead and mutilated they battled their way to the edge of the island and jumped out into the air, whether to live or die they didn't know.

One died striking rocks as he fell. The other four landed hundreds of feet below in long sand drifts against the base of the island. From the camp came the guard who had remained with the horses, and three soldiers who had already escaped from the rock. They revived the four who had jumped and all hurried to the camp. They made quick decisions. The survivors were divided into three parties, one to hurry westward to inform the Governor; one to take advice to the isolated fathers in their lonely missions to return with speed to the capital; and one to ride hard to San Juan de Nuevo Mexico to tell the colony.

Vicente de Zaldívar was in command at San Juan. He received the names of those killed at Ácoma. He went to the families and told them and comforted them. He ordered Requiem Masses for the faithful departed. The colony on the river was in mortal danger, and all knew it.

Presently came home the soldiers who had left Ácoma to overtake the Governor. They had not been able to find his trail. It was of the first importance that he hear immediately what had happened. Vicente de Zaldívar sent a new detachment to find him at all costs. They rode out immediately heavily armed. Nobody knew if the revolt would spread. The garrison at San Juan lived at the alert waiting for the Governor.

He arrived four days before Christmas with his troops, including Pérez de Villagrá. The Governor already had the news. The soldiers from the capital told how they had met him returning from his western explorations in a pleased frame of mind. In spite of having had reason to suspect disloyalty if not treachery at Ácoma on his way west in November, he had planned to spend the night there homeward bound. But the messengers with their awful news had saved him. In the open land by his camp they gave him a description of the massacre, for some of them had been there. He listened on horseback. When they were done, he dismounted and went to his knees and prayed aloud. Then in grief he walked to his tent, leading his horse, and ordered Pérez de Villagrá to make a rude cross of lashed branches. This was taken into his tent, where he asked to be left alone.

In the morning he ordered a formation and came out to speak to the men. His eyes were swollen and his face was haggard from lack of sleep. He had prayed all night for wisdom and guidance in the danger about them. Facing the soldiers he tried three times to speak, but could not, until at last he was able to say that they had all suffered a terrible loss in their comrades, who died martyrs. He spoke of dangers to come that must be met bravely, and he invoked their faith by saying that all knew it to be true that the more they suffered the greater would be their heavenly reward, and he placed all trust in God. He lifted up the soldiers' hearts.

With that he gave marching orders and the exploring party turned toward the capital. It snowed. They drank melted snow from their helmets. It was hard marching in December on the friendless plains.

When he arrived home the Governor found all turned out to wait for him. They were weeping. He went to them, and in silence embraced each one of his people. He then led them into the church where he greeted the friars with his embrace, and the Father President led the priests who chanted in chorus the Te Deum Laudamus in thanks for the Governor's safe return with his men.

The city of San Juan de Nuevo Mexico was in the form of a great square with four gates at which sentinels were now posted. All people carried arms. The Governor retired to his quarters and did not put away his belt and baldric, his sword and dagger, all night. He had a heavy decision to contemplate. Its basis in law was already, at his request, being considered by the Father President and the other friars.

21.

The Battle of Ácoma

He received their official opinion on the following day.

"What conditions," he had asked them, "are necessary in order to wage a just war? In the event of such a war, what steps may be taken against those warred upon and against their possessions?"

In reply to the first question the learned friars made several points.

To begin with, there must be authority to wage war, as in the cases of popes, emperors and kings, *and those acting in their stead*. The Governor was a delegate of the Crown. Plainly, he had authority.

And then there must be a just cause. The friars listed "to punish those who are guilty of wrongdoing, or have violated the laws of the land," which clearly covered the crime of treacherous insurrection. The friars added that the final just cause for war was to establish peace, "for

peace is the principal object of war." The Governor could feel that he
had more than one just cause.

Moreover, they stated, war must be waged with good faith, and
without covetousness, malice, hate, or ambition for power. The Governor examined his conscience.

As to the second question, though several points were analyzed,
the pertinent one seemed to be that about war against wrongdoers, and
the opinion declared that "they and their possessions are at the mercy
of their conqueror according to the laws of the land," and could be
"treated by divine and civil law, as law and justice require," but any
punishment visited upon the vanquished must be taken "to carry into
effect the requirements of justice." The Governor noted this respect
for due process.

Finally, said the friars, "as the purpose of war is to establish peace,
then it is even justifiable to exterminate and destroy those who stand
in the way of that peace."

The Governor could hear his duty clearly. If he had known
doubt before he knew none now. He ordered public proclamation in
the capital that "war by blood and fire" was declared against the Indians
of Ácoma, and announced that he would himself lead the punitive army.
Immediate protests of concern for his safety made him change his mind
about taking personal command, and instead he named Vicente de
Zaldívar to lead the return to Ácoma.

On the same day—December 22, 1598—a Requiem Mass was held
for Juan de Zaldívar and all who had died with him. The cold, narrow,
dark, clay church above the riverbanks resounded with the offices of
the dead. It was, the church, as plain as a coffin and the spirit of all
there that day filled it with fierce thoughts and prayers upon the reality
of death.

But three days later came the great feast of Christmas, and the
birth of life and purity in the world. All worked hard, and rededicated
themselves in the midst of hazard, loneliness and loss; and resolve grew
with the preparations for war.

Seventy picked soldiers made up the army against Ácoma. Each
had his coat of mail, double strength. They had shields which when
not in use hung from the shoulder. The lancers carried many designs
in their tall weapons. Some had points called partisans, like sharp leaves
facing both ways. There were glaives, which carried a plain, long knife
with a sudden curve at the tip like an eagle's beak. The halberds had

an axe facing one way, a steel beak another, and at the very top, a long sharp point. All these the soldiers polished and tightened and sharpened. The firearms were taken apart, the springs tested, oiled and reassembled. Some musketeers carried the harquebus, others the petronel, which was fired with its butt against the breast. Colonel de Zaldívar had two pieces of brass artillery to take with him—culverins with the Spanish Crown engraved above their touchholes. The artillerymen polished them inside and out until they shone green with the blue sky. Gunpowder was sifted and spread thin to dry in the sun. The heavy fixed maces and the morning stars from Germany with a spiked ball hung by a short chain from the mace-staff were scrubbed with river sand. All riding equipment was inspected, repaired with rawhide thongs, and inspected again—bridles, reins, saddles, stirrups. The horses had heavy steel breastplates, and these were burnished. Every man's knapsack was filled with his issue of emergency rations, gunpowder, bullets. With so much at stake, proper preparation was essential. As the men worked day by day, after Christmas, and into the New Year, they came to love their weapons and equipment. They worked as absorbed as children in ritual play. Their common purpose, their similar tasks, the buried excitement of awaiting danger, made them happy in a way that they could never expose. They were soldiers getting ready for a soldier's job.

By order of the Governor all men went to confession and communion before leaving with the army—all but one, "who, despite the urgings of his commander, would have nothing to do with the holy sacraments." He was called "an abandoned wretch."

On the morning of January 12, 1599, the army against Ácoma left the capital on the river. It took nine or ten days to reach Ácoma. On arriving, Vicente de Zaldívar was under orders to call upon the Ácomese for peace and submission. If these were denied, he was to attack. It would take nine or ten days for news to come back to the river after that. The Governor and the colony could only wait, hope and pray as January passed.

On the night of the twenty-first while the Governor was in his quarters at San Juan disturbances broke out among the Indians in the twin pueblo over the river. Sentries reported hostile announcements. Defiant reports came of how all the pueblos of the river country were marching in arms to destroy the Spanish colony. The Governor personally took charge of doubling the sentinels on guard, with a captain at each of the four gates to San Juan. Fires were lighted to see by. It was a cold night. The army must have just about then come to Ácoma, for they had left nine days before. Here on the river, and there far to the west, were they all in danger tonight?

The Governor making his rounds saw the rooftops of his own town full of people who should be inside. Who were they? He sent two officers to find out. They returned to report that the roofs were thronged by the wives, the mothers, the widows of the colony, under the leadership of Doña Eufemia de Sosa Peñalosa, wife of the royal ensign. They had all decided that they must in the common peril help their soldier menfolk to defend their common home, the capital city. The Governor was touched at such spirit, and confirmed Doña Eufemia's command of the roofs. The women of the garrison "walked up and down the housetops with proud and martial step."

The vigil lasted all night, but no attack came, then, or in the days following. It was hard to wait and to wonder, but they could do nothing else at San Juan, though a curious thing happened in the late afternoon of January twenty-fourth. A very old Indian woman came to see the Governor and was admitted. She was accustomed to the respect which her people always gave to the aged and the ancestors, and she expected it from the Spaniards. She had something to tell the Governor and she told it with gravity. She made references to distance, westward, wide country, vastly high rock, so, long and sheer. Her little crabbed hands whirled in gestures of battle and strife one against the other. The war at Ácoma. The soldiers with brave swords, the Indians with arrows, the air full of fury. The battle came and went. It lasted three long days. It was over just today, she said. There was much death amidst the Indians. There came smoke, the town was burning. There was a vision in the air. Quiet came. The soldiers were victorious. She nodded many times, nodding with her whole drawn, eroded and folded person in emphatic confirmation of what she knew and told.

The Governor thanked her and dismissed her. Her recital hardly allayed his impatience to hear what really had happened.

But at last nine days afterward, the quartermaster Diego de Zubia came riding to San Juan from the battle of Ácoma with information and two prisoners. The prisoners he put into a kiva under guard and went to report to the Governor. He announced an overwhelming victory at once. The details followed.

Late in the afternoon of January twenty-first the army was greeted at Ácoma by fearful sights and sounds. On the rock overhead, the Indians, men and women, were naked, figuring obscene gestures, and shrieking like devils out of hell. Vicente de Zaldívar sent the secretary and Thomas, the interpreter, to demand peaceful submission and delivery of the murderers of December, only to be greeted with vileness and scorn. Night falling, the army camped below the rock while Zaldívar completed his battle plan. When the sun rose on the morning of January twenty-second he took eleven men unseen to one of the rocks of Ácoma while the rest of the army marched in plain view to the other announcing their attack. The Indian defenders swarmed to fight the main army, while Zaldívar and his little squad scaled the far rock to gain an all-important foothold. Four hundred Indians discovered them and attacked them with stones and arrows, but without driving them off the cliff. Zaldívar called on his patron Saint Vincent and gave battle. Soon he saw an Indian dressed in his brother Juan's clothes, and in valorous rage he killed him with one blow. The army at the other rock, and other soldiers on the ground far below, attacked with all their power so that the Indians found themselves defending three fronts. Many Indians were killed by fire from below, and fell from the edge of the island "leaving their miserable souls up in their lofty fortress." The battle raged all the first day and was ended only by the cold January nightfall, with Vicente down on the ground in camp again, making plans for the second day, while his squad retained their safe position on top of the first rock. The army once more confessed to the chaplain, all but the "abandoned wretch," and received communion from the Father President before sunrise on the second morning, January twenty-third. A large force then went to the first rock, scaled the cliff and were received by the soldiers on top. The pueblo on the islands looked deserted. Thirteen soldiers carrying a heavy timber to bridge the chasm between the rocks advanced and crossed, and pulled their bridge with them to use again farther ahead. The Indians then broke from hiding to attack. The rest of the army saw their comrades cut off from them beyond the abyss. Captain Pérez de Villagrá superbly ran, leaped the chasm and heaved the great log up, restoring it as a bridge, upon which the soldiers crossed to the reinforcement of their fellows, while the trumpeter blew his trumpet and all felt great new strength. A harquebusier, firing wildly, shot four times through the body of his comrade the "abandoned wretch," who then called for God's forgiveness and heroically made his way to the camp below, where he confessed to the Father President and died. The two brass culverins were brought up, and each was loaded with two hundred balls and fired into a front of three hundred Indians who were advancing, and did fearful damage.

A squad of soldiers went behind the battle and set fire to the city of
Ácoma, so that smoke and flame rose to obscure the sun. Peace demands
were made repeatedly by the attackers and refused. Some Indians in
despair threw themselves from the rock, and others walked into the
burning houses to die, and others hanged themselves. In the third day
an Ácoma ancient came forward walking with a staff, pleading for peace,
offering the surrender for his people, which was accepted by the Colonel.
Zaldívar asked what had happened to the bodies of the soldiers murdered in December, and the old man led him to the place where all
had been gathered and burned in a savage funeral pyre. There Zaldívar
prostrated himself to weep and pray, saying to the soldiers with him,
"Here is another Troy." He raised a cross at the site. After the surrender
of every Indian was certain, the soldiers saw the women of the pueblo
rush forward with sticks and fall to beating a dead body that lay on
the stone until it was a mound of formless flesh. They explained in
their rage that they were punishing Zutucupan, the treacherous chief
who had led the Ácomas into the terrible revolt from the beginning.
Finally as the stillness of the third evening came, the Indians asked the
soldiers who was the mighty warrior who rode to battle above them in
the sky, mounted on a white charger, carrying a fiery sword, wearing a
long white beard, and accompanied by a maiden of heavenly beauty,
robed in blue and crowned with stars. Hearing this Zaldívar and his
men made the sign of the cross and declared that their arms had been
triumphant through the support of Saint James of Compostela on his
white horse, and of the Queen of Heaven herself. Colonel de Zaldívar
shortly afterward sent the news of all these events to the Governor at
San Juan by his courier the quartermaster Diego de Zubia, who reported
thus. Zaldívar, the army and their captives would arrive in a few days.

Governor de Oñate could be proud and thankful. The victory
was prodigious—seventy soldiers against thousands of Indians on their
rocky fastness. He marvelled. Almost a thousand Indians were killed,
and only two soldiers. And the city burning, and the vision in the sky?
The Governor regarded all Indians, including that old woman who had
come to him on the twenty-fourth, as superstitious creatures. How had
she known on the very last day of battle what the courier took nine days
to bring him? The Indians believed all old people wise unless crazy.
Who knew?

He thanked the quartermaster, who mentioned the two Indian
prisoners whom he had brought and who were now detained in a kiva
at San Juan.

Who were they and what were they about?

Zubia explained that he had taken them as they were fleeing Ácoma. They told him they were Indians from elsewhere who had been attacked and robbed by the Ácomas. They asked him for food and help. He gave them what they needed and they were now awaiting attention in the kiva.

The Governor made inquiries. Friendly Indians reported to him that the two men in the kiva were not fugitives from Ácoma at all, but were actually two Ácoma Indians who had not surrendered. An extraordinary affair followed, a miniature of the battle of Ácoma itself. The two in the kiva when asked to come out refused. For three days they threw stones at all who tried to reach them. They lurked in the dark kiva emanating baleful energy, like wild animals dangerously trapped. Finally their bodies yielded but not their wild spirits. They asked for daggers with which to kill themselves, as they disdained to surrender to the Spaniards. The Governor and his Indian friends besought them to come out and be baptized. The reply came in vile abuse from the dark round cave. The Governor shrugged, and ordered then that instead of daggers, ropes be thrown to them, with which if they chose they might hang themselves. Silence followed for some time. The soldiers stood listening in the bright sunlight while mortal exasperation gathered its powers out of sight in the kiva. At last there was a sound, the scratch of body on packed clay, and the two emerged wearing their nooses already around their necks. Permitted to pass, they went to a sizable cottonwood tree like all those that cast shade by the river. In and out of sunlight they climbed to a topmost branch where the golden winter leaves quivered about their dry brown bodies. Knotting their ropes to the tree, they were silent, and after that they stared at the Governor and the others who watched from below. Finally one of the Ácomas spoke. With pride and scorn he declared that the two of them would die and dying would leave the soldiers free to ravage the land. "Our towns, our things, our lands are yours," he said bitterly, and promised vengeance, if anyone could ever return from the dead. And with that, he and his comrade dropped from their bough with the spittle of fury on their lips. They hung swaying and ugly with bent necks and swollen faces as they died.

Looking up in awe and fascination, the soldiers, the Governor, witnessed there in the river cottonwood at San Juan the end of the battle of Ácoma.

22.

Afterthoughts

Though there were afterthoughts that wanted expression in the official terms of legal government, and found it. The battle, the war was won, but the Governor set about confirming the gains already made in his province by civilization as he represented it. If he re-examined the legal opinion of December twenty-second, he found full justification to punish the leaders of the insurrection, so long as "divine and civil" law were properly administered. It was therefore with every proper observance of the Spanish passion for legality in its finest details that he ordered a trial at the pueblo of Santo Domingo down the river of those captives brought from Ácoma by Vicente de Zaldívar.

The prisoners were charged with killing eleven Spaniards and two Indian servants in the massacre of December; and further charged with refusal to submit peacefully, deliver the murderers, and accept due punishment when the army went in January to Ácoma to accomplish these ends.

The trial was held in early February, 1599, with the Governor presiding. It was a medium through which the Spaniards heard once again the chronicle of Ácoma treachery and Spanish valor. The prisoners—a throng of them—had no advocate. Witnesses described known perfidies. The corporate indignation of the stronger of two societies energized itself emotionally. Who could doubt that punishment—any conceivable punishment—paled beside the acts that cried for it? Virtue was not a strand of life interwoven with evil. It was a dogmatic posture which for its own protection could justly resort to any devices of pain and mutilation. The law took for granted in the last year of the sixteenth century that acts of crime done by a human body called for the break-ing of such a body in degrees varying with the offense. Such degrees could hardly be arrived at without due process of law, and the Governor heard the witnesses one by one as they came in their soldierly leather,

steel, feather and linen and wool to speak. The testimony was all in by
the eleventh, and on the twelfth of February, the head of the government was ready to respond with the sentences, which would be properly
recorded and notarized.

The Governor ordered that: all male Ácomese prisoners over
twenty-five years old be condemned to have one foot cut off and to give
twenty years of personal service (assignments to be made later) ; all
males over twelve and under twenty-five years of age, to give twenty
years of personal service; all females over twelve years of age, to give
twenty years of personal service; and two Indians from the towns in the
far west who had been captured at Ácoma, to have their right hands
cut off and to be sent to their western homes to warn others of the power
that dwelled upon the river.

The expression "personal service" with its limitation of term
was preferred to the term slavery. Among the assignments made later was
that of sixty girls of Ácoma who, escorted by Captain Pérez de Villagrá,
were sent to the viceroy in Mexico for distribution among the convents,
to be educated and converted, in alien peace. Pérez left in March, 1599,
bearing a letter to the Viceroy from the Governor, asking for reinforcements in men with families "who are the solid rock upon which new
republics are permanently founded," and arms, and ammunition; while
the colony got on with the spring planting.

23.

Exchange

With each day that passed the colony more deeply established
its roots, bringing new ways to the Indian people, and in turn acquiring from them some of the old habits of living along the river.

The river lands met now a new use on a larger scale than ever
before. The Spaniards set their cattle, sheep, horses and goats out to

graze on the slopes of the valley above the irrigated fields—the slopes where storm water ran, and according as it was detained by vegetation made great or little damage in the face of the earth. Nobody could see in the first years or even generations, as the grass came back every spring, whether or not there was less of it showing each time; and whether gullies formed and grew faster than before. It was an immemorial process, the grazing of animals, and the land had always fed them. There were no thoughts of river life and valley character and land use as related to one another by all the fateful possibilities that lay within change wrought by man.

Vásquez de Coronado had brought his sheep along to be eaten. Oñate's sheep gave not only mutton but wool. Indian weavers prepared the wool just as they had their cotton and used the same looms and methods with the new material. New garments began to appear among the Indians, which could be acquired by the Spaniards in turn through sale or force.

Foods were exchanged. The Indian chocolate, that had come from the Aztec, and the tomato, were already in the Spanish household. Indian hunting drives to the foothills after piñon nuts brought a rich little nibble to the colonists. On such expeditions they saw many piñon trees ruined by the heavy antics of bears—the silver-tip, the brown bear and the black bear—who loved to gather the clustered nuts but broke whole limbs away doing it. In return the Indian farms came to plant new foods brought by the colonists—wheat, oats, barley, chile, onions, peas, watermelon, muskmelon, peaches, apricots, apples and certain varieties of beans. The irrigated fields of both Indian and Spaniard showed new plants. The honey of the Indians was "very white," as the Governor wrote to Mexico. He detailed much of the wild life, the vegetation, the untouched mineral riches of the land; and he found the Indians much like those of Mexico in coloring, disposition and all but speech.

Colonists went looking at their new land. They saw the abandoned cliff cities west of the river, and came upon the two stone panthers in a mountain shrine above the Rito de los Frijoles. The carved animals were four feet long with tails two feet longer than that. They were crouched as if to spring. A circle of large rocks surrounded them. Traces of red ochre showed on the cats' heads—devotional signs made by Indians. The Spaniards watched how the Indians fished, using long nets of yucca fibre stretched from bank to bank across a shallow place. Great hauls were taken, most of them thrown away. So too the Indians killed game far beyond their needs. The soldiers marvelled at the quantity of deer in the country. They would capture fawns and train them to pull little toy carts for the Spanish children. Later, grown deer were broken to harness and used to draw full-sized vehicles. Indians now had wheels to use. The vast land began to lose its secrets. The Governor thought there were about seventy thousand people in the pueblos.

As to where they were, the people of the river colony had firm notions. They thought it was nonsense to say, as some people said, that the New World had been peopled in the beginning by a landing of King Solomon's armada on the coast of Peru. Such a theory was held by certain scholars, but it was demolished by others who pointed out that King Solomon sailed from the Red Sea on a cruise of three years, from which he returned with gold, silver and ivory. There were neither elephants nor ivory in Peru. What seemed plain was that he had actually been in the Orient, China. As for where the earliest people came from— somewhere in the north there was a strait, and they came across it from China. China, Japan Island, India, were not far distant in the seas to the west, and only awaited the discovery of suitable harbors on the coast of New Mexico for the birth of lively overseas trade. The Governor had a clause in his royal contract granting him the right to bring two ships annually direct to New Mexico. He looked forward with confidence to trade with China, so close in the west, and with Mexico and Peru to the south. He saw world enterprises centering upon his city of San Juan on the river. Already capital of so much land, who knew what remained to be brought loyally to it? The western sea shored along the provinces of "the Californios." Reports compared the climate there to that of New Castile, and added further that "their states are the best managed of those thus far discovered," resembling, indeed, "Roman republics." In the summer of 1600 Vicente de Zaldívar led a troop of soldiers to find so promising a sea. On his way out he marched first to the saline pueblos beyond the mountains east of the river, to gather provisions for his journey. At one town where he asked for maize and beans the Indians gave him stones. He sent word of this to the capital and went on his way.

The Governor acted upon his message. Taking fifty soldiers he went to the transmontane pueblo, gave battle in which six Indians died, and later hanged two chiefs. He then burned part of the town, but in a manner "tactful and gentle," and returned to San Juan.

Zaldívar was home before autumn to report that though he had come within three days of the sea he had not been able to reach it

through hostile Indian country and high mountains. It was a setback
for an impatient Governor, who had problems of discipline to contend
with besides. During that autumn two captains of the army were murdered—Aguilar, who had twice made trouble for the Governor, and
Sosa Albernoz. There was talk. The Governor was supposed to have
ordered the killings.

But Christmas came and with it a new train from Mexico. It
arrived at the capital on Christmas Eve bringing new families, new
soldiers, six new friars; quantities of arms and ammunition; blankets
and clothing, and shoes for everyone. Bonfires of celebration were
lighted, and there was music and singing, and at midnight everyone
went to Mass to give thanks. With his new resources the Governor
could now plan to explore in strength his lands to the east and to
the west.

Once again Quivira glowed in the civilized mind. Joseph, the
Indian who had escaped from Bonilla and Humaña on those same plains,
beguiled the Governor as the Turk had beguiled Vásquez de Coronado.
It had long been a common form of Indian politeness to say that which
the hearer would like to hear, the truth to the contrary notwithstanding.
By his questions a Spanish general could kindle the answers he longed
to receive. Gold, like this? Silver? Cities? A great house, a palace? Bounty
in all things? Joseph had much to promise, and recited his wonders,
ending with an account of a city he himself had not happened to see,
but which he well knew from descriptions by other plains people—a city
nine leagues long, two leagues wide, filled with marvels. There wasn't
a city in all Spain as big as that. The Governor commanded that preparations be launched for his entry into Quivira in the springtime.

But once again his peaceful purposes of acquisition were interrupted by calamitous news, when three soldiers came home to San Juan
to say that two of their comrades had been killed by the same insolent
Indians over the mountains to the east. Zaldívar once again led a
punitive force against the guilty pueblo. The Indians massed at Quarai,
one of the three large towns in the saline district. A battle of five nights
and days followed before the town, deprived of its water supply by the
soldiers, surrendered. Forty soldiers were wounded. Zaldívar had an
arm broken and carried two wounds besides. Nine hundred Indians were
killed. Their town was burned and two hundred prisoners were taken
to the capital. Two months behind schedule, the Governor marched for
Quivira with nearly a hundred soldiers, and pack animals, and cottonwood carts, in June, 1601. His sense of high fortune was at its fullest.

Crossing the vast eastern land would be like the act of rolling up a map after it had served its simple purpose.

24.

The Promises

Close to eight hundred people were left at the river capital. Not long after the Governor's departure they began to air certain disagreements.

First of all, the friars spoke out against the cruelties shown by the Governor to the Indians, and the robberies of Indian food, clothing and other possessions which many of the colonists seemed to consider privileged acts. Certainly no firm action against such unjust behavior was taken by the government. The Indians were close to starvation because the colonists had despoiled them of so much food. It was not to be condoned. Better no city, no province at all, than one so godless.

Other complaints came from other sources. There were charges of misrepresentation of the whole nature of New Mexico and even of the purpose of the expedition. Where was the quick return in wealth and personal fortune that all had believed in? A man put all he owned into a venture of this sort, and he deserved a proper return on his risk and his investment. What did he get here? He owed something to himself and his family. Back in Mexico, they had at least had a home of their own and something to eat.

Many men disdained to work in the colony to develop its modest but life-sustaining yield. They had come to make a fortune, not an irrigation ditch, a bean patch or a slaughter pen.

It appeared to the majority that one after another, the Governor's explorations up the river, west of the river, east of the river, all founded on promises, showed nothing in the end but battle and burning pueblos. He himself seemed disappointed, but that helped nobody, for his temper

only grew shorter, his rule more strict, and his methods more cruel.
(After all, if what was going around was true, *somebody* had ordered
the assassination of Aguilar and Sosa Albernoz.) Perhaps he was desperate to prove his whole venture a success. The question remained as
to how long others should be expected to pay for things as they were.

In July a mass meeting was called at San Juan to give all such
opinion a chance to crystallize. The Governor had his defenders who
pointed out the happier facts overlooked by the discontented—there was
plenty of food if farmers farmed, the plains were stocked with buffalo if
hunters hunted, wheat and corn crops of the year were excellent.

Very well, cried the opposition, if the colony could be sustained
on its river, then let the Governor stay at home, keep his soldiers here,
and work hard to develop the new city where people could live decently.
All those forays over the country brought nothing, took away man power,
interrupted family life, and led to conflicts with the Indians.

The Governor's supporters picked up the attacks of the friars and
flung them back. If the friars stormed over the treatment of the Indians,
some of the friars themselves were not doing their whole duty in their
far-flung missionary parishes. Let them go back to their outlying pueblos,
and do their work, and then talk.

The debates were full and bitter, and out of them came two
documents. One, representing the great majority, filed fifty-seven charges
against the Governor. The other, signed by his supporters, defended
him. Both papers were sent by courier to the Viceroy in Mexico, and
through the remaining weeks of summer, all but a small part of the colony
made ready to take the road down the river to Mexico and older homes.
At the end of September, 1601, they departed. Their journey took them
two months, and as they arrived home at Santa Barbara near the head
of the Conchos River in Mexico, the Governor was approaching his
capital from yet another crossing of the plains of Quivira.

He brought a meagre return for all his pains. In his fifty-nine
days of travel he saw nothing that had not been reported before. He
learned one thing he was eager to know, and that was the fate of
Humaña, the murderer, and his fellow deserters. Indians far eastward
told how the Spanish renegades had been captured, surrounded with
fire on the plains, and burned to death. *Pace.* For the rest of it, spirit
and courage had run out of Oñate's men, who hearing warnings of
hostile Indians in vast numbers farther east presented a written petition
to the Governor to turn homeward, as the "horses and mules were tired
out and exhausted." The petition bravely went on to say that in any

case, "the chief purpose of our journey had been achieved," which was merely to learn "the wonders of this land," so they could be reported to the King in Madrid. The wonders were now detailed in terms not of gold, silver and jewels but of soil and innumerable cattle, yielding suet, hides and tallow. Confronted by homely realities, the Governor assented. Turning homeward, his party had to battle an Indian ambush. Many soldiers were wounded, many Indians killed. One Indian was taken prisoner, assigned the name Michael, and carried back to New Mexico to "give information." He made a map of Quivira and described its treasures. Once again an Indian talked about gold in the east and Spaniards listened. But they continued westward toward the river. There remained little else to say of the plains, except that "the carts went over the country . . . very nicely," which would interest anyone who had not heard that the plains were flat.

And now arriving at San Juan on November twenty-fourth the Governor found his capital deserted by all but a few loyal families and officials. His lieutenant governor was still there, and the Father President. As to the others two months gone he could hardly believe his ears. In rage he commanded Zaldívar to ride out with a troop, overtake the deserting colonists and return them to San Juan for punishment. He filed legal charges against them. It was all useless. The Mexican authorities ruled that the returned colonists need not go back to New Mexico, though the colony as presently constituted was to be continued.

The Governor found himself with a skeleton town, a mere cadre for an army, and a waning reputation. His fortunes were reversed. He had promised wealth out of the north, the east and the west. Only the west remained. There beckoned the pearl fisheries of the Californios of which Indians gave reports, and the harbors for the Orient trade, where surely the Governor's own ships could unload treasure. These things had to be real. He proceeded in the certainty that they were. But to make them come true, he would need more people—soldiers, and pilots, and men with special skills; and he would need money and supplies. There was small chance that the Viceroy of Mexico would grant him what he asked. There remained only one to whom to turn, and in 1602, from the little clay hive on the banks of the Rio del Norte in remotest New Mexico, the Governor sent Vicente de Zaldívar, who had never failed him, to the great city of Madrid across the ocean to see the King.

Zaldívar pursued his mission in the chambered perspectives of the Madrid government. He asked for four hundred soldiers, a detachment of skilled shipbuilders to construct vessels for the New Mexico-

Orient trade, a money loan, and men with families. Papers passed from the Council of the Indies to the Casa de Contratación, and the four hundred became forty, and difficulties developed about ocean passage for men with families, and affairs sometimes required reconsideration. Meanwhile, in secret, the Crown had ordered an investigation into the charges brought against the Governor. The very existence of the colony trembled in the balance. Now it was abolished by royal decree, and again it was confirmed. Zaldívar returned to his uncle empty-handed. The reduced colony and the small army then were made to serve one more reach that never found its grasp. In the autumn of 1604 the Governor led a detachment westward determined to find pearls and harbors. He returned to San Juan in April, 1605, having reached the Gulf of Lower California at the mouth of the Colorado River. It was his last expedition and like his others it was a failure, in terms of what he sought.

In the following year King Philip III instructed the Viceroy in Mexico to order all exploration to cease in New Mexico. It was a profitless region and the colony was a poor enterprise—though it should not be abolished. "And," continued the royal letter, "you shall, with tact and discretion, cause the said Don Juan de Oñate to be recalled for some sufficient reason, as seems best to you, so that he may come without disturbance; as soon as he has come you will detail him in the City of Mexico, disband whatever military force he may have, and appoint a satisfactory governor, discreet and Christian, to govern what has been discovered in the said New Mexico, and you will endeavor to maintain it in justice and peace, and to protect and treat with kindness the native Indians, providing them with religious fathers to instruct them, and if any of these wish to go into the interior of the country to teach with Christian zeal you will permit it, so that fruit may be drawn from it and by this means certain information of what is to be found in that province may be had without recourse to arms. . . ."

There were delays, suspicions, acts of obedience and revolt and again submission, but the end so inexorably spelled out by the royal letter came to pass. The Governor left San Juan forever. Going south to oblivion he suffered yet one more blow from the hard country of his lost dominion. As he crossed the Dead Man's March with his little company, he encountered Indians who gave challenge. In the skirmish that followed a young soldier was killed. He was the Governor's only son. The father buried him there and moved on to Mexico and the courts. Behind him, up the river, his colony survived him. In 1610 a new governor took the capital away from the river to a mountain plateau

to the east, where he founded Santa Fe. The period of exploration after
treasure was at an end. Another motive began to know its own full
expression.

25.

The Desert Fathers

An early Franciscan on the river said that its human life seemed
to show on a map the shape of a cross. The upright stem, north and
south, was the river itself along which clustered the great house-towns,
and the arms reached east and west to settlements of other Indian people.
It was an approximate image, but it expressed the dedication of the
friars to their inner and immaterial motive. Their spirit and their flesh
were one in purpose. They came to take nothing and they brought with
them nothing that could be measured. Like the founder of their order,
Saint Francis of Assisi, they could have said that they "had been called
to the way of simplicity," and that they always "wished to follow the
'foolishness of the cross,' " by which they meant the innocence that made
worldly men smile. Certainly it was the act of a fool, in terms of shrewd
mankind, to go into barbarian wilderness at times alone and unprotected to preach the love of Christ. The Castilian Saint John of the Cross
said, "Where there is no love, bring love and you will find love." The
martyrs of Puaray, and Fray Juan de Padilla in Quivira, had made their
ultimate demonstration. "They killed him," said another Franciscan of
Fray Agustín Ruíz, "and threw his body into the Rio del Norte, which
flows along the edge of this pueblo." And at Taos, when Fray Pedro de
Ortega came to offer his faith to the Indians, he was refused a place to
live, and to eat was given tortillas made of corn meal and the ground-up
flesh of field mice, mixed with urine. These he ate with words of relish,
remarking that for "a good appetite there is no bad bread." The Indians
marvelled. "They go about poor and barefoot as we do," said Indians

elsewhere, "they eat what we eat, sit down among us, and speak to us gently."

In one respect the Indians and the friars were close together from the beginning. Both had profoundly religious character, and saw life's essentials best explained through the supernatural. But as the friars believed that their faith enclosed all faiths and purified them in the fire of divine love, until God's relation to man shone forth in the image of Christ Who was the Son of Man, so did they think to bring love to replace the fear that animated all objects, creatures and forces in the Indian's pagan world. The gift they sought to give the Indian was the sense of his individual human soul, and the need, and the means, of its salvation.

But if the friar in himself was poor and managed with very little, his work in the aggregate required extensive organization. The friar's immaterial mission was enclosed in a system that rested on a rigid hierarchy and showed itself in massive monuments. At the pueblo of El Agua de Santo Domingo, that stood on the banks of Galisteo Creek a short way east of the river, the Franciscan order established the religious headquarters of the whole kingdom of New Mexico. There resided the Father President, and there he held his yearly chapters when all his friars would come in from their lonely posts in the outlying missions. Santo Domingo was a little Rome, the seat of an authority that bowed to no secular power in matters of the spiritual welfare of men and women. In the mountains to the northeast was the new political capital of the colony at Santa Fe, founded in 1610, after Oñate's recall. Between the river pueblo and the mountain capital much was in dispute throughout the seventeenth century and would be composed only in slowly gathering tragedy.

Meanwhile the work of the religious reached into the river towns to the north and south; into the pueblos of the west, and to the saline towns over the eastern mountains. Nominally, even the Apache nations who roamed the plains and alternately traded with and attacked the settled pueblo people were part of a missionary parish. The Apaches, wrote a Father President in his report, "are very spirited and belligerent . . . a people of a clearer and more subtle understanding, and as such laugh at other nations that worship idols of wood and stone. The Apaches worship only the sun and the moon. . . . They pride themselves on never lying but always speaking the truth." It was an optimistic vision of mass murderers of whole towns. To such peoples went "missions of penetration," consisting of a travelling friar who preached, converted where he could, and if he lived, returned to Santo Domingo, or to the settled "mission of occupation" to which he was assigned; for many of the outlying missions in Indian towns were organized as field headquarters from which faith and civilization were carried to other towns that had no permanent pastor. Such other towns were designated *visitas.*

Fifty churches were built in New Mexico by twenty-six friars in the first quarter of the seventeenth century. First came the word of God and the conversion of the Indians; and then, with no other power but example and patience, the solitary Franciscan father led his parishioners in building a church. In choosing the site for his church he considered many things. He looked into the hearts of the Indians and seeing all that mankind was capable of in good and evil, he felt that a church surrounded by the town was subject to being overwhelmed from within. He looked at the country beyond the town and he saw that the strongest fortress should stand first in the way of invaders. Considering ceremony, he saw how a church must have approaches for processions, and remembering functions, he knew it must be close to community life. Accordingly, at the edge of the pueblo he marked out a site for the church where it could stand by itself, yet be tied to the walls of the town.

He had large papers scratched with drawings. The people looked from these to his face and then to the straggled marks on the baked ground. He was all things; architect, engineer, carpenter, mason, foreman, building master to apprentices who themselves were masters of a building style. He did not scorn their methods or their designs. He saw their perfect economy of material and purpose in what they built. Remembering vast vaults of stone, the flutings of arches and echoing heights, sombre color in glass and every intricacy of grille and recess and carved screen, he saw that reduced to essentials, even the great churches of Europe and Mexico had a plain strong purpose, which was to enclose the attention of men and women in safety and direct it toward the altar. Here were wanted walls and roof as soon as possible. They must be made of materials already used and understood by the people, and to them must be added new methods understood by the friar. He had with him, assigned by the Father President at Domingo, and paid for by the King of Spain, ten axes, three adzes, three spades, ten hoes, one medium-sized saw, one chisel, two augers, and one plane; six thousand nails of various sizes, a dozen metal hinges, two small locks, several small latches, and one large latch for the main church door. With him, too, he brought the principle of the lever, the windlass and the block and fall. Out of his belief and his technique, combined with native

materials and the Indian's reproduction of earth forms in building,
a new style was ready to come, massive, stark, angular, and powerfully
expressive of its function.

Until they worked under Spaniards, the Indians built their walls
of puddled clay and rock. Now the first lesson of the friar was to teach
the making of adobes—earthen bricks. Clay was disintegrated rock. The
adobe was a restoration of clay to coherent form—a sort of return to rock.
With their new hoes, people went to work mixing water and earth in
an excavated tray. Only Indian women did this work, for as theirs was
the ancient task of enclosing life so they had always made the dwelling
rooms of the family. Men, as craftsmen of arms and tools, learned carpentry, and made wooden molds after the friar's instructions. Into the
wet clay, straw was mixed as a binder, and the clay was then pressed
into the molds to take the shape of large bricks. A brick weighed sixty
pounds, and measured ten by eighteen by five inches. It was about all
the load a man or woman could carry over and over, as the rows of
drying bricks grew longer.

Sometimes foundations were dug and filled with loose stone foot-
ings, sometimes the walls rose directly from unopened ground. The
walls were deep—six to nine feet thick, and one side wall was several
feet thicker than the other. The people wondered why this was as the
width was marked out on the ground, and as the walls rose they discovered why, but meanwhile the dried bricks were brought by a long
line of workers, and laid in place. The entire pueblo worked on the
church. While women mixed earth, and men molded bricks, other men
and boys went to the mountains to bring back timbers. With rock and
chisel they shaped these. The friar drew patterns for them to follow
and out of the wood came beams, corbels, door panels, doorframes,
window embrasures. If someone knew where deposits of selenite or mica
were to be found, men were sent to bring in a supply so that thin layers
of the translucent mineral could be worked into windowpanes. The days
were full and the walls rose slowly but all could see progress, and it
made them one in spirit. The church was from twenty to forty feet wide,
and sixty to a hundred feet long. Its ceiling was to occur at about thirty
feet. On one of its long flanks, against the thicker of the two walls, were
laid out living quarters for the friar and his Indian staff in a row of
little square rooms with low roofs. These formed one side of a patio,
the other sides of which held more rooms or a covered cloister. In certain
towns the walls of the convent quadrangle took in a round sunken kiva
previously used by the Indians. Rooms in the patio were planned for

teaching classes, for cooking, dining, and storage of grain and other supplies.

Nowhere in the church or its convento was there a curved wall line, or arch, or dome. As the walls rose to their limit, the purpose of the wider wall became plain. Down on the ground the great tree beams were about to be hoisted up to span the church. Their weight needed a heavy support, and the dozens of men on top of the wall working to bring them up needed room to stand. The wide wall made a fulcrum for the great levers of the beams, and served as a broad platform on which men could work. Scaffolding was little used. Indians had ladders by which to enter their houses and kivas from the roof, and these were put to work too in acts of building. As the church walls achieved their height, carved wooden corbels were laid into the bricks to support cross-beams. Oxen dragged one timber at a time to the base of the walls and men hauled it upright, tipping it against the massive fulcrum at the top, and laying it across the nave. Such beams, or vigas, were of unequal length. Their ends projected beyond the walls and were often left so. Now between the beams were placed branches of uniform size to close the ceiling, and above these rose the parapet of the walls high enough to hide a man. Crenellations were let into the parapet for sighting with musketry or arrows. Over the whole roof went load after load of loose earth, which was packed down by feet, and hardened by water and sun.

The river churches followed two designs. One was that of a long narrow straight box; the other that of a cross, with shallow transepts. Where transepts occurred, the builders lifted a higher roof over them and the sanctuary in a gesture of grace; for where this higher portion rose above the long nave, they placed a clerestory window reaching the width of the nave that took in the light of the sky and let it fall upon the altar, while the rest of the interior remained in shadow. The only other occasional windows were two or three small, high openings in the thinner of the long side walls.

Entering by the main door anyone had his attention taken to the altar by many cunningly planned devices of which the first was the pour of wide and lovely light from the clerestory whose source was hidden by the ceiling of the shadowy nave. The builders used the science of optical illusion in false perspectives to make the nave seem longer, the approach to heaven and altar more august and protracted. The apse, tall and narrow, tapered toward the rear wall like the head of a coffin. Where there were transepts, the body of man was prefigured all-evidently—the head lying in the sanctuary, the arms laid into the transepts, and all the length of the nave the narrow-ribbed barrel and the thin hips and the long legs inert in mortal sacrifice. Many churches added one further symbol and illusion: the rear wall of the sanctuary was built upon another axis than that of the nave. It suggested two things— the fall of Christ's head to one side as he hung on the cross; the other, a farther dimension to the house that honored Him. All such variation of symmetry, and modulation of perspective, combined with inexact workmanship and humble materials, resulted in an effect of spontaneity and directness, like that in a drawing made by a child to fulfill a great wish. The wish, the emotion, transcended the means, and stood embodied forth in grave impersonal intimacy.

Over the adobe texture was placed by the women a plaster of mud. They applied it with the palms of their hands and sometimes smoothed it with a patch of sheepskin bearing fleece. The outer walls in time bore the same marks of the weather as the ancient natural forms of earth all about—little watercourses that ran making wrinkles which when dry came to resemble the marks of life in an old sun-browned face. And yet with even such sensitive response to the elements, an unattended adobe building weathered down only one inch in twenty years. In any proper town the walls were replastered after every rainy season. The walls were renewed so long as human life used them. Some stood for centuries after being abandoned, and still stand in part, above talus of their own yielding as they go ever so slowly back to the earth.

The interior walls received a coat of whitewash and on this in pure colors the people painted designs, as though they were decorating great unrolled surfaces of clay pots. Scrolls, parrots, columns; flowers and cornstalks; symbols of sun, rain, lightning, thunder and the oblique slantings of terraced forms that took an impression of the landscape receding from the river. Many of the frescoes had not only an Indian but also a strangely Byzantine air, as though a new hybrid culture must turn back to relive all the stages of its various influences.

Finally, before the front of the church a walled enclosure was completed where the blessed dead could lie, and where, against the façade an outdoor altar could be set in a sort of atrium to accommodate large crowds on feast days and Sundays.

From a little distance then the finished building gave its purpose with hard grandeur in its loom and weight, its grace of plain angular shadow, and the wide sunlight on its unbroken faces, where the shadows of the vigas bladed down the walls making a sundial that told not hours but centuries. The whole mission with church, convento, cloister and

walled burial field seemed like a shoulder of earth emerging out of the
blind ground as a work of living sculpture. To see the true beauty of
those structures it was necessary first of all to love and to believe in their
purpose.

With the establishment of the "missions of occupation" came the
need of a train to bring supplies from Mexico every three years. An
invoice of 1620 showed aside from common tools and builders' supplies
a variety of foodstuffs, clothing, and articles of religious use. The Father
President at Domingo received for distribution many boxes of salt pork,
cheese, shrimps, haddock, dogfish; lima beans, lentils, frijoles; rosemary
and lavender; white sugar, salt, pepper, saffron and cinnamon; preserved
peaches and quinces and sweetmeats; noodles, Condado almonds, Cam-
peche honey, Castile rice, cloves, ginger and nutmeg; and wine, olive oil
and Castile vinegar. On his lists he checked frying pans, brass mixing
mortars, tin wine vessels with pewter dishes, and leather wine bags. To
clothe his friars he noted Córdoban shoes, Mexican sandals, leggings,
kidskin hats with cords, sackcloth and Rouen linen in bolts, and to work
these materials, papers of pins, sixteen hundred needles, twenty-four
pounds of thread and fifty-two pairs of scissors. To take the missioners
on their visits he issued travelling bags for bedding, and leather saddlebags and saddles and heavy Michoacan cloth of tents, and tin boxes in
which to carry the Host. For the infirmaries he checked one hundred
and seven Mexican blankets.

To furnish the altars he distributed frontals of Chinese damask,
with borders of brocatel and fringes of silk, and lined with Anjou linen;
figures of Christ on crosses four and a half feet high; pairs of brass
candlesticks and snuffing scissors; an octagonal wooden tabernacle over
six feet tall lined with gold leaf and its panels painted in oil with sacred
likenesses; several large paintings framed in gold; a pall of red damask
edged with brocade; vessels of tin, silver and copper for water and wine;
and handbells for the consecration. He bestowed silver chalices lined
with gold plating, and gold patens, and bound missals "recently revised,"
and tin chrismatories, and processional candelabra of gilt wood, and
choir books, and a brass lamp. For sanctuary floors he sent Turkish
carpets. The Father President assigned vestments to the missions—
chasubles, stoles, maniples, dalmatics and copes, of various materials:
velvets from Granada and Valencia, brocades from Toledo, enriched with
designs by the embroiderers whose craft came long before from the
Netherlands; "small shirts of Chinese goods to be used as surplices" by
altar boys; and for the friars albs and surplices of Rouen linen and lace.

He gave them rosaries and breviaries and little iron molds in which to take the wafers of the Host. For the towers he sent bronze bells, and for High Mass sets of musical instruments—flageolets, bassoons and trumpets; and incense, and wax, and four quires of paper, and oddments like a gross of little bells, and macaw feathers, and twelve bundles of glass beads, and ecclesiastical certificates on which to record the large stages of life, and twelve plowshares with steel edges to help all become self-sustaining on their riverside fields. The Father President's catalog was a history in itself.

And when the mission was built and furnished it was both fortress and sanctuary. When outside its blind heavy walls a wind rose, there within were peace and security, where the many candle flames never wavered as they shone on flowers of colored paper. "It all looked very holy," remarked a friar of such a church in 1634. And yet, if he knew Spain, and its sacred treasures, he perhaps looked upon his mud walls and his rough-chiselled timbers and bitterly told himself that here he had contrived no beauty or splendor, remembering such an altar vessel as the monstrance of Toledo that took nine years to fashion out of three hundred and thirty pounds of silver, until it was eight and a half feet high, with two hundred and sixty small statues amongst jewelled pillars, so that in its exposition the Blessed Sacrament appeared to hover in midair surrounded by a shining cloud. He could only say to himself that there was work to be done as well as possible with the materials at hand. Ending his day only to dedicate the morrow, he recited the prayer written by his founder Saint Francis that said ". . . grant that I may not so much seek to be consoled as to console; to be understood as to understand; to be loved as to love; for it is in giving that we receive; it is in pardoning that we are pardoned; and it is in dying that we are born to eternal life."

And when the morrow came, there were many tasks to guide. The convento and the church were staffed by Indians—a bell ringer, a cook, two or three sacristans, a porter, two boys who kept order in the friars' cells, some women to grind corn, an old man who scratched at the beginnings of a garden within the clay walls of the patio. Without seeing themselves so, the Franciscan priests of the early river were great artists of community life. If they desired to bestow and maintain the standards of civilization in their wilderness, they had first to show the Indians the whole image of the cultivated life that came from Europe. Many of the friars were extraordinarily versatile, and most of them were wholly without that pride of learning which in the universities and coteries of the day often allowed both the scholar and his knowledge to die unused by life. The friars put their learning to work.

Lessons were organized and conducted with discipline. At dawn every day but Sunday the bellman went to ring the church bell for Prime. The pupils, young and old, came to the classrooms which they at once swept out. They then took their places and the pastor came to teach.

He was quick at languages, and for immediate understanding of the Indians, learned the native tongues rapidly, and taught the Christian story in the people's own words. The earliest book to be printed in the New World appeared in Mexico in 1539 under the imprimatur of Zumárraga, the first Bishop of Mexico. It was a catechism in Spanish and Nahuatl. Some of the friars came to the river after preaching for years in Mexico in the native dialects. Once having reached the understanding of the Indian, they developed it with classes in many subjects. They first taught Latin, so that the responses at Mass and vespers could properly be made. Eventually they taught Spanish so that daily life might link the wilderness people to the all-powerful source of national life in Madrid. The Indians learned to speak and to write in those new ways, through which such amazing information came to them. The past found a way to exist in the Indian mind.

Along with words, the Indians learned music. Boys were formed into choirs and trained in the sacred chants of the Church. In one pueblo, out of a thousand people who went to school the pastor chose and trained a "marvelous choir of wonderful boy musicians." In another, the singing boys "with their organ chants . . . enhanced the divine service with great solemnity." Winter and summer, in the river dawns and twilights the heavenly traceries of the polyphonic style rose to the blunt clay ceilings of the coffinlike churches; and the majestic plainness of antiphonal chants echoed from sanctuary to nave as the people together stolidly voiced the devotions composed by Fray Geronimo Ciruelo and shipped north to the river in 1626. A little organ with gilt pipes went to Santa Fe in 1610, and a few decades later eighteen of the kingdom's churches had organs. The friars taught how to play them, and how to make and play stringed musical instruments, and flutes, and bassoons, and trumpets, after the models shipped in from abroad. On great feast days, the level Indian voices were enriched by ardent stridencies from pierced cane, hollowed gourd, and shaped copper. A tradition lasting centuries had an imitation of nature at work in the worship of the Mass. From the choir loft over the main door of the church came first softly then mounting in sweet wildness the sounds of a multitude of little birds calling and trilling in controlled high spirits. On the gallery floor a dozen little boys lay before pottery bowls half-filled with water. Each boy had a short reed pierced at intervals which he fingered. He blew through one end while the other rested in the water, from which rose the liquid notes of songbirds adoring God. At the elevation of the Host or other moments of high solemnity it was proper on great feast days to fire a salute of musketry amid the rolling of the bells.

The Franciscan school taught painting. Indians learned not so much how to hold a brush or use color—they knew that—as how to see, look, formalize a representation. A whole new notion of what the world looked like came to the Indians; yet without greatly affecting their decorative styles, for they continued to draw more the spirit, the idea of a subject, than its common likeness.

Joy and laughter were praised by Saint Francis, and there was no reason why the river fathers should not by these means as well as any other reach into the minds and hearts of their taciturn children. The Spanish delight in theatre, scarcely a hundred years old, was already a deeply rooted taste; and the friars, like the lay colonists, gave plays on suitable occasions. In the pueblos, the comedies were meant to instruct as well as entertain. Ancient Nativity stories were acted out by well-rehearsed Indians, who took the parts not only of the Holy Family and their ecstatic attendants but also represented a little party of Indians in their own character. When in the play it was asked who were these strangers come to attend the birth of the Infant Savior, the answer said that they too were men for whom the Son of God was born on earth that He might save them. A dignifying love reached out to the Indians in the audience. Sometimes the plays were hilarious, and all could laugh at the embarrassments and defeats cleverly visited upon Satan, whose exasperation would know no bounds. Any play telling the story of people brought a sense of community and self-discovery.

The Franciscan teaching turned everywhere, lifted up the soil, planted new seeds, and put the soil back. Among the first new crops was one directly related to the Mass. Cuttings of fine grapevines were brought across the sea from Spain and sent up the long trail from Mexico—a light red grape and a purple one, from which the fathers made sacramental white and red wines. New fruits were set out in orchards— peaches, apples, pears, plums, cherries, quinces, figs, dates, pomegranates, olives, apricots, almonds, pecans, walnuts. Later when the missions rose by the river at the gateway to Mexico, lemons and nectarines were planted to thrive in the mild winters, and oranges, which had first been planted in the New World by Bernal Díaz del Castillo landing with Cortés. Together with the fields of newly introduced vegetables, the orchards were irrigated from the river with improved methods long known to the friars from their Mediterranean culture. With the foundation of horses, cows and sheep brought by the colony, the friars taught the Indians how to herd and how to breed the animals for improvement of the stock. There were workable resources in the kingdom observed by the well-educated priests, who said that with patience and labor much could be done with the ores in the mountains. The treasure hunters had come and gone, unwilling to work for what they wanted. New Mexico was officially reported as a poor country. But a Father President of the Franciscan province in 1629 disagreed: "As for saying that it is poor, I answer that there nowhere in the world has been discovered a country richer in mineral deposits." He listed the very localities of the river kingdom where he had seen deposits, and went on scornfully to say that all such news meant nothing to the Spaniards in Mexico, who if they had merely a good crop of tobacco to smoke were content. It seemed odd to him that they should be so indifferent, when Spaniards "out of greed for silver and gold would enter Hell itself to get them."

But the chance and toil of the freight trains to and from Mexico could not be lightly ignored. The regular service to supply the missions was established in 1617. Trains left for the north every three years, and took the better part of a year to complete the journey. Escorted by a handful of hard soldiers and driven by Mexican Indians about thirty cottonwood carts drawn by oxen came over the gritty trail in movements as slow as the high turns of astronomy by which like ships at sea they made their course. They passed among enemies and at the Northern Pass came to the Rio del Norte, whose source, they said, was at the North Pole. This was easy to believe, in the absence of maps visualizing the unknown country above New Mexico, for the river had an arctic character, "during the months of November, December, January and February . . . frozen over so solid that iron-bound wagons, heavily laden," crossed on the ice, and "vast herds of cattle" went over it at full gallop. "To the same extreme," they noted, "this land suffers from the heat during the months of June, July and August, for even in the shade of the houses tallow candles and salt pork melt."

The freighters saw the Manso Indians about the river at the Pass, who ate their fish and meat raw and bloody, not even cleaning the entrails, but devoured it all "like animals." With mineral powders of

different colors rubbed on their nakedness they looked fierce, despite
their "good features." As the years passed, and the trains came and
went in their crawling regularity, these people about the ford at the
Pass came to know the Franciscans and in them grew the desire to be
Christians. In time they were taken farther north on the river, near to
the Piro pueblos which were the first of the river towns reached by
northbound travellers, from Nuñez Cabeza de Vaca to the supply
trailers of the seventeenth century; and there they found their mission.
It was the policy of the religious province wherever possible to bring
together compatible Indian peoples, the better to instruct large numbers, and to insure common defense. Pueblos grew. Ways were traded.
New dimensions of human life reached out from the river. Tucked away
in the lumbering carts were richly printed little gazettes and random
news sheets from the printing shops in Mexico. So came news of the
great world, the gossip of government and religion and solemn bulletins
in science and philosophy, to the remote fastnesses of spirit and education
in the river kingdom of the north.

Knowledge, a full mind, made a companion in the empty wilds
when the friars went forth from their clay citadels to preach among the
Indians far east or west of the river. They might be accompanied by a
dozen soldiers "more," as a Father President said, "for the pious sentiment of not abandoning such a sacred enterprise than for protection
or defense, which would have been very limited considering the large
number of people they were to meet, all as skilful at arms as they were
tenacious in their wars." The friars, he said, "know much hardship in
crossing the river each time their ministering demands it, since the river
is very swift and subject to bad floods." But all was endurable in the
natural world for the sake of that which came to pass in the spirits of
those whom they sought in simplicity and love. An Indian cacique
came to a father missioner bringing him a marvelously tanned buffalo
hide. Unfolding it, the friar saw a painting that showed a green sun
and a gray moon, and above them each a cross.

"What does this painting mean?" he asked, and the cacique
replied,

"Father, until now we have not known other benefactors greater
than the sun and the moon. They light us and warm us, and make our
plants produce and the flowers germinate. Thus because of so many
benefits we have worshipped them as the arbiters of our lives. But since
we heard you tell us who God is who created the sun and the moon, in
order that you may know that we now worship only God, I had these

crosses, which are the emblem of God, painted above the sun and the moon."

And there were other simple evidences of the new reach of spirit and understanding. If once the Indians were creatures of blind destiny denied by fear the state of the responsible individual, they now had an instrument of self-knowledge and mercy and they used it serious as children. "When they come to confession," wrote a pastor, "they bring their sins, well studied, on a knotted string, indicating the sins by the knots. . . ."

Again, encouragement of their efforts seemed to come in "a very special manner" to the laboring friars in 1629. Its awesome source was in itself enough to overwhelm them with a renewal of the humility that was their spiritual food. One day in the church at the ancient pueblo of San Felipe on the west shore of the river below a dark mesa, Father Fray Cristóbal Quirós was busy baptizing a large group of Indians. He was an old man, though his tonsure was not gray, and his long face had a ruddy complexion. The stone baptismal font stood at the rear of the nave to the right of the main door. Many Indians crowded into the door but hung back in diffidence from taking their proper places. The throng grew. The old priest would have them come forward to help him expedite the ceremonies. They hardly moved until suddenly there was a surge in the crowd and each row turned around to see who pushed. Even the people in the last row turned around, for they had felt the push harder than anybody. When all saw that no one was behind the rearmost people, who yet were thrust forward by an invisible force, they laughed out loud, and continued to push those ahead of them until all were in their places and old Fray Cristóbal was satisfied. Though mysterious and amusing, the incident by itself would not have seemed significant. But other interesting events followed.

On July 22, 1629, at the pueblo mission of Isleta fifty Humanos Indians appeared on what had been for several summers an annual excursion. They invariably brought the same request. Would not the fathers come to their country east of the river over the waste of plains, and convert them to the Christian faith? Summer after summer the request was received with a stir of interest. It was odd that those people should come from so far away, already aware of Christianity. Yet each year the fathers had to deny them what they asked for, because so much work for so few priests was already called for in the river kingdom. The Humanos presently would go away unsatisfied. It was sad for all. They were so persistent. They were so ignorant and so hopeful.

A few days later in July, 1629, the first supply train in four years drew into view through the glassy curtain of the river heat, and with it arrived thirty friars. They brought letters and news from Spain, and fresh supplies of food, and holy oil for the tin chrismatories, and many other supplies, and reinforcement in their persons for the field forces of the missions. And they brought an interesting assignment from Don Francisco Manzo y Zúñiga, the new archbishop of Mexico. It was a professional matter, and the newly arrived religious settled down with their hosts to discuss it fully.

It seemed that for the past several years, there was much talk in Spain of how the Reverend Mother Superior of the Discalced Nuns of the order of Saint Francis at Agreda, on the borders of Castile and Aragón, had been miraculously transported over and over again from Spain to New Mexico to preach the Catholic doctrine to the savage Indians. Her name was Mother María de Jesús, though in the gossip that aroused such interest everywhere she was more commonly mentioned as María de Agreda. Her whole family were widely known for their unusual piety. On a single day in 1619, she and her mother entered a convent, and her father and two brothers took their first vows as Franciscan friars. She became abbess of her convent in Agreda at the age of twenty-five. Her leadership was exemplary, and under her rule the convent became fervent and prosperous. People said she was planning to write an extraordinary book, to be called "The Mystical City of God, A Divine History of the Virgin Mother of Christ." In it she was to give detailed accounts of her puzzling visits to other kingdoms, including Spain's farthest colony on the Rio del Norte. How could it be? She never left Agreda, yet was able at the same time to be in a far corner of the earth. The Bishop of Viseo in Spain heard of her aetherial journeys. Learned theologians spoke of "bilocation," a miraculous faculty with subtle distinctions as to whether it was the physical body that was transported, or the spiritual essence, which then projected the image of its body's likeness María de Agreda spoke of being transported to the Orient, and to New Mexico, which she visited as often as four times in one day. She gave descriptions of her visits—how she spoke to the Indians in their own tongue, though at home in Spain she could not speak a word of theirs; how she was lifted and taken by angels; how the people needed instruction and of what kinds of country and customs would be found by the missioners when at last they went among them. The whole affair was fascinating, even though as usual in newly reported supernatural matters the Church preserved an official skepticism pending

further investigation. News of the marvellous mother superior came to
Mexico, and the Archbishop now wished to know whether in the country of the Rio del Norte there had been any evidence of her visits, or
"flights," as they were spoken of.

The pueblo friars looked at one another and racked their brains.
To men of their fervid belief, whose very canon of faith proclaimed the
possibility of the miraculous, it was an exalting thought that they and
their works may have been visited by Divine Favor through the occasional presence of the zealous nun. And yet nobody could recall out of
the dangers and labors of every day a bit of evidence that she had indeed
been with them. If only they might see her, speak with her, ask her
what of the river kingdom she had observed, to test her knowledge! The
matter must be deeply looked into. What had the Archbishop written?
The Father President Alonso de Benavides had the paper in his own
hands: ". . . do hereby urgently recommend this inquiry to the reverend
custodian and fathers" of New Mexico "in order that they may carry it
out with the solicitude, faith and devotion as the case demands, and
that they duly inform us concerning its results, so that they may be
verified in legal form." The whole thing deeply stirred the religious New
Mexicans. They had never before heard of Mother María de Jesús, or
suspected the existence of her influence.

But a thought struck them. What of the pathetic trudging visits,
summer after summer, of the Humanos people from far over the plains?
Why had they come back faithfully after so many discouragements? Was
it possible—who could dare hope so—was it even likely that they had
been inspired by someone from far away? The fifty Humanos petitioners
were still lingering in the pueblo of Isleta before setting out in disappointment once again for their homeland. The pastor of Isleta, Fray
Estevan de Perea, sent for a group of their spokesmen. They came where
he and the other friars now sat in the common room of the convento.

Why, asked the pastor, had the Humanos come year after year to
ask with such insistency for baptism?

The Indians pointed to a painting that hung on the wall of the
refectory. It was a portrait of a famous old nun, Mother Luisa de Carrión,
in the full habiliments of her order.

"A woman in similar garb," they said, "wanders among us over
there, always preaching, but her face is not old like this, but young."

The inquirers leaned forward with quickened interest. But why,
demanded the pastor, had the Humanos never mentioned this before?,
and they replied,

"Because you did not ask us, and anyway, we thought she was around here, as well."

It was astounding. It demanded action. The religious community immediately decided to send two friars from the river province to the Humanos kingdom. Without delay, Fray Juan de Salas and Fray Diego López set out with the Humanos for the east. In a week or two they were back to call for more workers, "as the harvest was great." They told how crossing the plains of the Apache buffalo country they travelled one hundred leagues by the time they came among the Humanos nation. There the people came forward in procession to meet the friars, calling aloud for baptism. They carried a large cross garlanded with wild flowers. Mothers with babies at their breasts held the infants aloft and begged that they be baptized too. The friars were enchanted. Where had the people gained knowledge of the cross? The Indians replied that the same young woman in nun's robes had told them how they must go in procession to meet the friars, and herself had helped to decorate the cross with its garlands. For several days the friars prayed with the people about the cross which they set in the ground. There was more to hear about the visitation. To the Indians she was flesh and blood like another woman. They all saw her, though this joy was denied to the friars. The Indians told how she taught them in their own language, and reproved them for laziness that they did not go more often to seek the priests of the Rio del Norte. The friars were moved. What was known of this matter in Spain now began to be supported by what was becoming known of it in this last wilderness of the New World. One day while Fray Juan and Fray Diego were with the Humanos, messengers from two other Indian nations to the east arrived asking for baptism. A white woman, young, pretty, in gray, black and white robes, with a blue cloak, had been among them preaching and urging them to seek the desert fathers. It was bewildering. The Franciscans made ready to return to the river to ask for more help in the great task. The Humanos chief begged that before they went they would bless the sick. Two hundred invalids were brought to the cross, and the friars told the other missioners at Isleta on the river how they had immediately arisen, "well and healed."

There was much to report to the Archbishop of Mexico. Fray Alonso de Benavides, the Father President of the river province, resolved to go to Mexico, and—there was much other administrative business to justify the decision as well—even to Spain, where he hoped to obtain permission to pay a call upon Mother María de Jesús himself. To his brothers on the river he would report the outcome as soon as possible.

He left New Mexico in the summer of 1629, in time to make the spring sailings from Veracruz in 1630.

It took nearly two years for his report to come back to the river. Affairs of the church and the government moved slowly across time and distance. But at last it came. Fray Alonso submitted his findings in detail, in a letter written at Madrid on May 15, 1631.

"Most dear and beloved father custodian and other friars of our father, Saint Francis, of the holy custodia of the Conversion of Saint Paul in the kingdoms and provinces of New Mexico," he wrote, "I give infinite thanks to the divine majesty for having placed me, unworthy as I am, among the number enjoying the happy good fortune of your paternities, since you are so deserving of heavenly favor that the angels and our father, Saint Francis, aid you. They personally, truly, and actually carry the blessed and blissful Mother María de Jesús, discalced Franciscan of the order of Concepción, from the town of Agreda, which is in the limits of Castile, to help us with her presence and preaching in all these provinces and barbarous nations."

Having first stated his tremendous conclusion he went on to the absorbing details. He arrived in Spain on August 1, 1630, and in due course was received by the Bishop of Viseo, who at the moment was governing the Franciscan order. They exchanged their knowledge of Mother María de Jesús. The Bishop had been familiar for years with the matter, had been to see her, and only looked for confirmation of her claims. Fray Alonso told him of what had occurred in New Mexico, which seemed to supply it. The Bishop authorized him to go to Agreda, there "to constrain the blessed nun through obedience to reveal . . . all that she knew about New Mexico." He kissed the bishop's ring and by the last day of April, 1631, was in Agreda, where the Mother Superior was waiting.

She could not, he thought, be as old as twenty-nine. Her face was beautiful, white except for a faint rosy tinge. She had large black eyes under heavy, high-arched eyebrows. Her costume consisted of coarse gray sackcloth worn next to the skin, and over that a habit of coarse white sackcloth with a scapulary of the same stuff. She wore the white cloth tucked up so that much of the gray showed. Around her neck was a heavy rosary. At the waist she wore the Franciscan cord. Her face was framed in a winding of white cloth over which she wore a black veil. To her feet were tied hemp sandals. Her cloak was of heavy blue sackcloth. If her eyes were darkly calm, her mouth had a little smile of sweetness and humor. She talked freely.

She said that all her life she had suffered for those who did not know God, especially the heathen peoples whose ignorance was not their own fault. She had had made known to her in revelations all those lands which did not know God. To them she had been repeatedly transported by her guardian angels, whom she identified as Saint Michael and Saint Francis of Assisi. As for New Mexico, she had been expressly called for by the custodian angels of that kingdom, who had come to get her by divine command. She went there the first time in 1620, and continued to go ever since. On some days she went three or four times in less than twenty-four hours.

So much for the general claims. As to particulars, she said that when Fray Alonso himself had gone to baptize the Piro pueblos, she had been there. She recognized him now.

On another occasion somewhat similar, she said, when a father was baptizing Indians in a pueblo church, the people all crowded about the door. With her own hands she pushed them on. They looked to see who was pushing "and they laughed when they were unable to see who did it." She described the officiating pastor—an old man but without gray hair, who had a long face and a ruddy complexion. It was a clear description of Father Cristóbal Quirós, who was known to all the province.

She told in detail about how Fray Juan de Salas and Fray Diego López went from the river to the Humanos nation, and said that it was she who had sent the Indians to fetch them. She described the two priests, and declared that she helped them herself in their work. When the messengers came to them from the other tribes farther out on the plains, it was because she had sent them. Her descriptions of the country were so accurate and detailed that they recalled to Fray Alonso much that he had seen and forgotten.

Fray Alonso asked her "why she did not allow us to see her when she granted this bliss to the Indians?" and she "replied that they needed it and we did not, and that her blessed angels arranged everything."

He then asked her "most earnestly" if she would not make herself plain to the friars still in New Mexico, and "she promised that she would ask God, and that if He granted it, would do it most willingly." Fray Alonso wrote that he trusted that "by the time this letter reaches the hands of your paternities some of you will have succeeded in seeing her." They could not say that they had.

She went on to tell of other savage kingdoms which she had

visited, and of dangers, conversions, and martyrdoms. She herself, in her other person, had been martyred "and received many wounds, and her heavenly angels crowned her. . . ."

When the interview was over, Fray Alonso showed her what he had written down of their exchange, and asking her whether it was the truth he "invoked the obedience from our most reverend father general that I carried for this purpose." Her confessor was also present and he called down upon her the same powerful sanction. In her own hand she addressed to the friars of the New Mexican river a confirmation of all that Fray Alonso had put down in his notebooks. ". . . I saw and did all that I have told the father," she wrote, and in a final summation of his view, the priest declared, "She convinced me absolutely by describing to me all the things in New Mexico as I have seen them myself, as well as by other details which I shall keep within my soul. Consequently, I have no doubts in this matter whatsoever."

In her written statement to the friars, Mother María de Jesús spoke gently of the nature of the Indians, and of the measures to be taken for their salvation. It grieved her to see them "continue in darkness and blindness and . . . deprived of the . . . immaculate, tender and delightful law." The friars must work tirelessly, and in their work must be aided and protected by "soldiers of good repute and habits, men who forbear patiently the abuse that may come upon them." All must "exercise the greatest possible charity with these creatures of the Lord, made in His image and likeness with a rational soul to enable them to know Him." It was a view of the Indian that was by no means universally held. But she was firm. "God," she wrote, "created these Indians as apt and competent beings to serve and worship Him. . . ."

When Fray Alonso asked her whether in the river kingdom of New Mexico all were "proceeding in the right way" in the work of conversions, she replied that "everything was pleasing to our Lord, as it was all directed to the aim of the conversions, which is the greatest charity." But she also said that she had taken it upon herself to pray for "the peace and harmony between the governors and the friars . . . so that friars, governors, Spaniards and Indians together and in harmony may worship and praise the Lord. . . ."

With those words, and in her baffling knowledge of the river kingdom of the seventeenth century, Mother María de Jesús de Agreda went to the heart of a problem that was charged with passion and violence.

26.

The Two Majesties

For in the seventeenth century the river colony was like a man in whom raged opposing desires, good and bad. These forces contended so long and so hard that they nearly tore apart forever the social body in which they were inescapably joined. The body and the soul were at war—life temporal and life spiritual. In her cry for harmony Mother María had fearfully seen who were the contenders. They were the governors at Santa Fe, with their corrupt little garrisons and their comic vanity and their bald cleverness at scraping private gain from the impoverished province; opposed by the friars in their fortress-missions, with a grim strength of spirit, and arrogance on behalf of Almighty God, and certain convictions as to human nature which keeping faith they could not recant. With but a few brief peaceful interludes the struggle raged for seven decades, and was resolved only in a disaster which falling equally upon both contenders was the bitter product of their strife.

In a certain sense the conflict was an outgrowth of the Spanish character. The agents of both civil and religious government used to speak of "the two Majesties" in whose name all affairs were conducted; and they meant God and the King of Spain. The Spanish character in which these two majesties were polarized was able at times to be furiously partisan. The armored captain-general saw himself as the inhabitant and example of that majesty which had created the New World under Charles V and Philip II. The friar in his proud rags no less strongly saw in himself the representative of a divine prototype, his Lord Jesus Christ. But each believed not only in his own majesty, but also in the other's, so that the internal conflict was complicated; and yet each claimed the superior right and glory of his own motives, and was obliged to illustrate them in physical acts which often took hard effect upon many human beings outside the quarrel—the Indians.

Behind the open strife between church and state in the river

kingdom lay the whole Spanish conquest, with its mixed motives. These
were never more bluntly exposed than by the old warrior of Cortés,
Bernal Díaz del Castillo, when he said, "We came here to serve God,
and also to get rich." If these purposes were equal, they became less
so as Spain's red and yellow royal colors moved northward on the map
of the New World, until on the Rio del Norte a bare subsistence for the
colony was to be had, while the harvest of souls among the Indians
was almost inexhaustible to those who believed in its actuality and
desirability.

The fight between governors and friars in the river colony
revolved around a number of issues, all of which had to do with limits
of authority, but one rising above the others related to jurisdiction over
the native peoples. It was an issue so sharpened by prejudice and conviction and inherited attitudes that it too struck more than merely the
local factors, and reached back to the earliest thoughts about the Indian
—his nature, his purpose and his right. The struggle between the body
and the soul of the colony was essentially about human relations.

What was an Indian? The question had been asked so long ago
as the reign of King Ferdinand, when the Laws of Burgos, regarding
Indians, were enacted in 1512. The Emperor Charles V saw it raised
again, and serious debate was carried on as to whether an Indian was
an animal or a human being, or if a mixture, just how much of one and
which nature dominated to what extent. Possibly, thought some philoso-
phers, he represented neither man nor animal but some intermediate
species. Or if Indians were animals, then as such, they might enjoy the
faculty of reason in various low degrees. The question was, how much,
if at all? For the purposes of inquiry, some even supposed that the
Indian might be a rational being, though barbarian. Where had the
Indians come from, anyhow? It was a striking possibility that they had
wandered into the New World as descendants of the lost ten tribes of
Israel. But if thus they were human beings, how was it that they seemed
to be indifferent to the mining of gold, which was assuredly a human
preoccupation, and preferred simply to eat, which was both human
and animal? Further, if they were human beings, were they free or
slave? It was all a most involved and serious question, and it was endlessly explored in written works and before boards of inquiry and courts
of law. What lay at the heart of it was whether or not the Spanish conquest, in its treatment of Indians, was just. It was not long until the
various speculations crystallized into two opposing views, held with
vigor on the one hand by the Spanish civil powers and on the other by

the Church. The Crown, to its credit, required full examination of its
own conduct of the conquest in respect to the Indian, but it was forced
to do so by the impassioned outcries of the clergy on behalf of the
despoiled native. Mercy and protection for the Indian might be translated into law (and they were) but established attitudes were hard to
change.

For the Spanish civil view of the Indians, brutally clear in the
colonization, was that they were as different from Spaniards as monkeys
from men. They were miserable, glum, vicious and lazy. They could not
read or write, they had no laws, or private property, or respect for
human life. Their religion was idolatrous and obscene. They practiced
incest and sodomy. They were so thick-skulled that if a soldier struck
one of them on the head with his sword, the tempered steel of Toledo
would be dulled. It was absurd to imagine that such a creature was
capable of living in freedom. Even if he were sentimentally called a
man, it would be far more suitable, as a Spaniard said, for him to live
as a slave man than as a free beast. Aristotle's *Politics* was quoted to
prove that some men were slaves by nature. If all this was true, how could
anyone hope that the Indian any more than another beast of burden
could be saved? That was how most of the colonial administrators, and
military officers, and landholders felt about the matter.

The Church felt differently. Even if all such charges against the
Indian were true, they could be nullified if the Indian were educated,
trained, given freedom, and brought to Christianity. The champion of
this view was a Dominican friar who as a young propertyholder had
seen both sides of the conquest in Cuba in the early sixteenth century.
He was Fray Bartolomé de las Casas, later Bishop of Chiapas. He himself had owned Indian slaves, whom he used for the working of mines
on his land, even after he had taken holy orders. But preparing a sermon
to deliver on Whitsunday in 1514, he came upon the text in Ecclesiastes
that read, "He that sacrificeth of a thing wrongfully gotten, his offering
is ridiculous, and the gifts of unjust men are not accepted." His thoughts
were sober and long, but they led him to the inevitable conclusion, and
he announced "that everything done to the Indians thus far was unjust
and tyrannical." The remainder of his life was given to the cause he
proclaimed, which repeatedly took him from the colonies to the Court
of Madrid and back. He faced powerful adversaries, but the Emperor
Charles ordered that he be heard, and Spain listened to the conscience
of the conquest.

Aristotle, he conceded in the context of his times, might be right about the condition of natural slavery; but if they existed, natural slaves were few in number, and were to be regarded as mistakes of nature rather than as an order of beings. No, all the peoples of the world belonged to mankind; all had understanding and free will; all had the same senses, and were equally moved by the objects of these, took comfort from goodness, felt pleasure with happy and delicious things, and regretted and turned from evil. All men and their nations no matter how barbaric or corrupt were capable of improvement and susceptible of acquiring the virtues of domestic, political and rational man. The way to such human achievement was not through armed conquest; but through peaceable preaching of the love of God and the brotherhood of mankind. The way to imperial conquest was not by war but by peace.

No enduring society could be built upon the shaky foundation of the Spanish treatment of Indians. Its chief feature was the *encomienda* system, or provision of guardianships by which each Spanish landholder had "commended" to him the Indians who lived on his land. He was to be responsible for them, in their spiritual and physical welfare. In return, their work was owed to him and their defense of the land. Ideally the design was that of a family, which was what was intended when Pope Alexander VI deeded the western hemisphere to the King and Queen of Aragón and Castile. But in practice the guardians were slaveholders and the entrusted children of the wilds were slaves. From the days of the earliest conquerors onward—beginning with Columbus himself—the persons and products of the Indians were considered practical spoils of conquest. Forced labor in pearl fisheries and mines and farming fields and domestic life and concubinage and armed forces was the lot of the Indian wards. As early as 1509 the Church asked that Indians not be required to serve their guardians for longer than a year or two, instead of for life. The Crown so ordered, but the order was flouted, and before long new regulations were won by the landholders that permitted guardianships to descend by inheritance, with the practical result that not only the current generation of Indians but even future ones must know bondage.

In 1520 the Emperor Charles issued a memorial requiring that the Indians be treated as free men, and in 1523 he directed Cortés to assign no more Indians to guardianships. Neither proclamation had any practical effect, and in 1526 the guardianship system was legalized for Mexico with the provision—meant to be ameliorative—that no guardian might receive more than three hundred Indians. The colonists pressed at every opportunity for laws that gave them complete and perpetual jurisdiction over the native peoples. Government officials—even, it was whispered, some in the Council of the Indies itself—took bribes to influence policies in favor of the slaveholding class. To protect their material holdings, the lords of the Indies used their consciences loosely, and took comfortable refuge in theories of Indian inferiority. Las Casas gave them no rest. He wrote, he spoke, he memorialized the Crown. The Emperor had already proved himself sympathetic to his views. The issue was the liveliest one of its time, and decades later its energy was to reach even the remotest colony on the farthest river of the Crown's dominions. Throughout the Empire, in spite of royal and even papal declarations of policy, the protective laws for Indians remained only ideal and never knew the simple reality of obedience. But the agencies of human charity never ceased to do their duty.

If the arguments of Las Casas, "Apostle to the Indians," carried much weight with the Emperor Charles it may be imagined how thoughtfully he took notice of a bull, *"Sublimis Deus,"* which was issued by Pope Paul III in 1537, at the very height of the controversy. The Pontiff was explicit in the utterance of his exalted conclusion: "The sublime God so loved the human race that . . . all are capable of receiving the doctrines of the faith." Lest anyone might choose to exclude certain types from the human race, he thundered on saying that the Evil One himself had inspired those who, "to please him, have not hesitated to publish abroad that the Indians of the West and the South . . . should be treated as dumb brutes created for our service, pretending that they are incapable of receiving the Catholic faith." It should have made the enslavers of the Indian tremble. The Pope proceeded: "We . . . consider, however, that the Indians are truly men and that they are not only capable of understanding the Catholic faith but, according to our information, they desire exceedingly to receive it. . . . We declare . . . that, notwithstanding whatever may have been or may be said to the contrary, the said Indians and all other people who may later be discovered by Christians, are by no means to be deprived of their liberty or the possession of their property, even though they be outside the faith of Jesus Christ: and that they may and should, freely and legitimately, enjoy their liberty and the possession of their property; nor should they be in any way enslaved; should the contrary happen it shall be null and of no effect." Having thus laid the foundation for granting legal personality to the Indian, Paul III concluded that august and compassionate charter by declaring that "the said Indians and other peoples should be converted to the faith of Jesus Christ by preaching the word of God and by the example of good and holy living."

How in the face of such a document, and against his known piety, the Emperor could increasingly make legal concessions to the big and little estateholders of the Colonies it was hard to understand. Under the law itself the encomienda system grew worse instead of better, and the whole vast spectacle of abuse and injustice in the New World was more than a devoted follower of Christ could endure. The Holy Father's intention in giving the new lands and their peoples into the care of the Crown had been betrayed. The conquest instead of being a glory to God was a fulfillment of evil. If the encomienda system was inevitably the accompaniment of conquest, then there was but one thing left to do, and Las Casas demanded that it be done. He called upon the Emperor to order a halt to all further wars and conquests in the Indies, so that the existing evil of Indian bondage might at least grow no greater. On April 16, 1550, Charles V to the astonishment of the world commanded that all conquests in the Spanish empire be halted until a royal board of inquiry, composed of church doctors and political scientists, could propose an acceptable scheme of waging war and conquest with justice. There was splendor in this act, and its extreme simplicity could come only from an absolute morality. Right and wrong was the issue, and not even vast expedients and material commitments—on a scale of continents—were to justify an improper humanity.

But as before, the fiery ideal was lost sight of in smoky argument. Old abuses gradually crept forward again, though a framework of regulations for the conduct of wars of conquest was set up requiring that commanders must have the approval of proper ecclesiastical authority before opening battle against the Indians. (Hence Oñate consulting his chaplains for official opinion before moving against pueblos.) Colonists were to be responsible for the welfare of their Indians, and must explain to them the advantages of coming under the government of the Crown— think, they said, of the new things brought by the Spaniards: horses, cows, silk, iron tools, firearms, wine, oil, roads, wheeled vehicles, and the supreme gift of the Holy Faith. If the Indian worked for the Spaniards, they would see that he was fed and clothed, and he would give them his labor and the products of it. If asked to work on the land, the colonist, like Cortés, would reply, "But I came to get gold, not to till the soil like a peasant."

After over half a century of debate and legislation, the Indian laws of Philip II were in practice even less protective than those of his father the Emperor. The moral force of the clergy had resulted in a great statement of principle; but the heavy inertia of those men who by their courage and ambition had continued the conquest was more powerful than any ideal. With their methods of gunfire and slavery, the practical men of affairs prevailed over the friars' promise of peace and prosperity through the word of God. The result was unceasing strife, and a slow process of organic death for the empire and its most outlandish colonies, where even so, the claim could be made in good sense that in their daily living, the Indians in pueblos were closer to Christian simplicity and perfection than many a Spaniard, who ravaged them in the name of the Two Majesties. Las Casas saw the Indians as compact of all virtues. They are "more delicate than princes and die easily from work or illness. They neither possess nor desire to possess worldly wealth. Surely these people would be the most blessed in the world if only they worshipped the true God."

On the regal and viceregal level the view of the Indian was beneficent and gentle. Mendoza, the first viceroy of Mexico, advised his successor in office to accept neither one nor the other extreme opinion as to what an Indian was. "Treat them," he declared, "like any other people, and do not make special rules and regulations for them. There are few persons in these parts who are not motivated, in their opinions of the Indians, by some interest, whether temporal or spiritual, or by some passion or ambition, good or bad."

Few on either side of the controversy were as wise as he; and on the river in New Mexico where the struggle over the Indian went on at a lower level, fury replaced amenity, and poverty settled its dust over the meagre stakes.

For it had been a long time since New Mexico was hopefully regarded as another treasure house, and all large-scale exploitation of its resources by the Crown had been abandoned. The kingdom was regarded essentially as a missionary field. The civil authority, the armed garrison, were to exist primarily to protect the friars at their hazardous work, whose object was the peaceful conversion of the Indian. But the position of the Indian under the guardianship of the encomienda was poison at the heart of the province; and with their attitudes of mind inherited through history the governors who favored the Indian civil system and the friars who abhorred it must only come to blows. Carefully as it was worked out through experiment and altruism, imagination and a royal sense of honor, the legal frame of the occupation of the colonies could not stand against the force that worked to tear it down. This

was, once again, the Spanish character. "Spaniards always end by devouring their institutions with the acid of their corrosive individualities."*
The two governments of New Mexico—the provincial majesties of the Church and the State—poured forth streams of accusations, complaints, scandals against one another to the viceroys of the seventeenth century in Mexico. These mostly had to do with circumstances of the Indians, though side issues were often too outrageous to miss. The freight wagons crawled out of Santa Fe on their triennial voyages to Mexico City bearing packets of official letters wrapped in antelope skin. Often by the very same train the friars and the governors dispatched their dossiers against each other. Personalities changed, governors came and went every three years with the supply trains, and new fathers president were assigned nearly as often. Details varied, and the scenes of conflict, but the bitter lack of harmony continued from about 1613, shortly after the establishment of Santa Fe as the civil capital, until the eighth decade of the century.

The deeply rooted disagreement in policy broke into the open in May, 1613, when Governor Peralta sent a squad of soldiers to Taos to collect tribute owed by the Indians under the official encomienda. Fray Isidro Ordóñez, the Father President, was in Taos at the time. He came out of the pueblo, dispersed the Indians who were waiting to deliver their levy, and commanded the Governor's troops to return empty-handed to the capital. The Governor was outraged and when he persisted in his orders, Fray Isidro invoked against him the terrible wrath of excommunication, calling him "a heretic, a Lutheran and a Jew." Peralta was at that time beginning the construction of the Palace of the Governors in the new city of Santa Fe, which had been established on the site of a long-abandoned pueblo. Indian laborers were used in the work. Fray Isidro denounced the Governor for using the natives as a press gang, and the Governor on meeting the friar later on during the summer fired at him with a flintlock pistol, missing him but slightly, and hitting another friar and a civilian. For this Fray Isidro demanded that the Santa Fe town council arrest the Governor, but to no avail. The Governor's chair was thrown out of the parochial church. When it was certain that news of the squabble must be sent to the Viceroy in Mexico, Fray Isidro promised to excommunicate anyone bearing dispatches for the Governor, who then moved to go to report in person, and started down the river road. At Isleta he was captured by agents of the Father President who threw him in chains into a cell at the convent of Sandía. Fray Isidro was

_____
* Salvador de Madariaga, in *Rise of the Spanish Empire.*

for the moment triumphant. His position was particularly strange since there was some question as to the validity of his appointment and his credentials as Father President. Some of the friars under him were in revolt against him. None was permitted to leave the kingdom, and Fray Isidro's furious dispatches describing his own hardships of spirit and person went to Mexico by fast courier. The Governor escaped from Sandía and returned to Santa Fe, only to be clapped into prison again on reduced rations. His friends were powerless, and the state of the province was critical, for under what purported to be a royal order Fray Isidro had published permission for all colonists and soldiers to return to Mexico if they wanted to do so. As a result the Spanish lay population of Santa Fe dropped to forty-seven persons, and the continued life of the colony was precarious.

In May, 1614, a new governor, Admiral Bernardo de Ceballos, arrived to take office. Peralta was sent on his way south. He was ruined, and even the last legal recourse that might have proved him right in his report to the Viceroy was snatched from him. At the Perillo Spring in the Dead Man's March, he was once more confronted by Fray Isidro's partisans and robbed of his papers before being permitted to proceed to his obscure fate in Mexico. But a refugee friar managed to reach Mexico in the same year, and there he made charges against the Father President. The Viceroy acted at once to appoint another friar already in New Mexico to succeed Fray Isidro, who was recalled to Mexico City to face the Holy Office of the Inquisition.

The whole affair was all too typical, with its angry challenges of authority between the two majesties, its infinitely laborious intrigues across desert kingdoms and quires of parchment, its squalid local reprisals. The Indians strove to keep their ancient ways of life while submitting to the physical and spiritual demands of the warring powers, and the colonists subsisted on their national traditions while watching the energies that might have worked for peace and plenty spend themselves in cease-less recrimination. One after another, the successive regimes in the Governor's Palace and the Chapter House of Santo Domingo poured forth for vice-regal consumption the accounts of each other's infamies.

Governor Eulate, cried the friars, in 1619 sent permission to the Indians to revive the pagan religious practices which the friars had worked hard to supplant with the rituals of Christianity. It was an official act designed to divide the allegiance of the Indians from the friars who lived and worked among them. The same governor, against the royal edict that prohibited governors from engaging in trading enterprises, raised livestock to be exported at profit to himself. Another governor closed the river highway to friars who wanted to send little herds of sheep to be sold in Mexico for "ornaments, decorations for the churches and other necessities." When they protested to him, the governor replied "that churches with decorations and costly ornaments were not necessary; that a few huts of straw and some cloth ornaments, with spoken [as against sung] Masses, were ample." He did not or would not understand: the friars pleaded that "these things are what we have the most care for, and procure at our expense and labor, for, if precept and virtue teach these natives, they are all influenced as well by the decency, ornamentation, and ritual of the churches." The governor cared as little for the health and safety of the Indians. From the rich salt lakes beyond the eastern mountains of the river, the native people were forced to bring like beasts of burden great cargoes of salt, and this, wrote the friars to the viceroy, "has occasioned among the natives serious illnesses and convulsions, some of them being permanently incapacitated . . . both on account of the haste and the misfortunes attending their departure, and because of the long distance which they carried the salt." By 1630 the garrison at Santa Fe had again increased, and two hundred and fifty soldiers were paid, declared the father president of the time, through a levy on the Indians of a yard of cotton cloth for each Indian house and a bushel of corn.

Against these and other abuses the friars pleaded with the King to command relief. The guardianship system was wholly corrupt. Royal decrees specified that no Indians could be given in encomienda until after baptism. And yet, "even before the pueblos are converted, the governor himself gives them out in encomienda without notifying the father president or the viceroy. Even before they are converted and baptized, when they are only pacified, they constrain them to pay tribute and do personal service, taking them far from their pueblos and treating them badly. As a result, the heathen Indians who have not yet been converted or even pacified say that they do not want to become converted, or even pacified, that they do not want to become Christians, in order not to pay tribute or serve. They have even been sent to be sold as slaves in New Spain. . . . They escape these and other abuses as long as they remain free and do not become Christians." And the friars, in whom the justice of Las Casas was still alive, prayed the King to order that "the Indians of New Mexico be not given in encomienda by the governors of New Mexico until five years after the whole pueblo has been baptized."

Every request they made of the King revealed a new abuse.

Pray, let the King order that no landholder or any other Spaniard be allowed to live in the Indian pueblos "without the consent of the Indians themselves." If every Indian house had to pay the governors a cotton blanket and five bushels of corn per year, let the king issue orders against charging the tribute against individuals who lived in, or moved into, the house. Let Indians move freely to whatever pueblos they chose to live in, and not be bound to the land where they were discovered. Command that Indians who are officials in their own pueblos be excused from personal service, and prohibit the practice of taking Indian boys and girls from their homes on the pretext that they are orphans and must be given care, which invariably is seen to be for what it is, the position of slaves. Indians captured in wars should not be sold far away as slaves, but should be given to the convents for teaching faith and industry. Grant that the royal power move against the way Indians were forced off their lands. Order that the governors be required to obey the decree against raising of cattle to be exported for their private gain, a practice bad in many ways. To drive the cattle to Mexico, the governors "send along the best Indians of the land who then are left stranded because the distance is so great . . . and unable to return to their country and homes." And others connive to send cattle with the governors' herds, "and in particular female cattle, whereby the land is impoverished." It should be ordered that the right of sanctuary in the churches be respected. "This will afford some protection and relief to the helpless Spaniards who live there as in a walled prison." And the friars looked to the future of the kingdom and requested "that if anyone should wish to found at his own cost a town at the pass of the Rio del Norte, which is midway to New Mexico," the viceroy should be given power to encourage this, for "that pass is extremely important, both for keeping open that trail and for the conversion of the many savage nations in that region. Your Majesty would be greatly benefitted by the foundation of such a town and by the production of the mines and farms that may be established there."

The complaints of the clergy went up through the years like sighs. A state official at Santa Fe travelled to the Apache nation to buy buckskins for the governor. He informed the Indians that his father had begotten a son among them and he wished to do the same. The Indians withdrew and discussed his statement and came to understand what he wanted. Accordingly, at four in the afternoon they erected a tent for him, made it comfortable with skins, and seated him on a new hide spread out. "Then they began their wedding dance as they call it, and when it was finished they brought to him a young maiden, and he admitted her and slept with her. In the morning the Apaches came and seeing that he had known her, they anointed his breast with her blood." It was—but only to the Indians—a marriage contract.

Another civil official "of large body, coarse, and somewhat brown," came one time to the pueblos over the mountains to the east where Indians in the choir were assembled to sing the High Mass. For this by his order they were to be given fifty lashes each, and "the poor things have not since then dared to take part in any sung Mass, wherefore the divine service has been impeded." In the pueblo of Quarai the same man was once sitting in the very cell of a friar who was making him a cup of chocolate when the Indian officers of the pueblo came in to say that they were sorry to see their pastor go out alone to the wheat fields to reap the harvest singlehanded. They asked for permission to help him. The visiting official flew into a rage and ordered the Indians "not to reap the wheat nor serve the father, for if they did he would give them one hundred lashes; for such," he roared, "was the command of his governor. . . ."

Anything was to be expected as the governors and their men worked to discredit the clergy and the church. At a western pueblo certain captains from Santa Fe spoke to the Indians. "One of them went out proclaiming that the people should come together, for he had some things to tell them which were very sweet, very pleasant, and very much in accord with their desires." Nobody knew what was said to the Indians, "but from that time they did not ring the Ave Maria, or the evening bells, nor did they attend the teaching of the doctrine or the choir, but acted as if they had never been converted. . . ."

Another officer went to a pueblo, assembled the people, and insisted to the Indians that they make charges against their priest, who was ninety years old. An Indian woman finally rose to state that he had violated her. The Indians burst into roars of laughter, jeering at the name of the priest, who was ordered to pay the woman a fine of a piece of cloth worth a dollar. Someone went to the friar's cell where he had remained reading his breviary during the scene, and asked why he did not come out to defend himself. The old man replied "that it was of more consequence to him to continue reciting the divine office . . . than to notice all that."

There seemed no end to the irresponsibility of the governors. There was one who sent all his troops to capture slaves whom he could sell. "The army went away at the time when the corn was maturing, and there are eight hundred and forty fields left to go to ruin without their owners, at the mercy of bears and other wild beasts, which constantly destroy the crops." This occurred at a time when the "poor kingdom" had just been through a serious famine during which Indians had to live on grass seeds and harmful herbs, and everybody in Santa Fe ate "bran, quilites, green barley, and other herbs which they happily were able to find."

One of the charges made most bitterly by the friars was that more than one governor since Eulate did his utmost to revive the pagan dances of the Indians. The friars believed these to be diabolic in their nature, and believing so, were compelled to suppress them at all costs. The Indian communal dance, they said, consisted first of an invocation of the devil in unknown tongues during which he was offered the fruits of the earth; and second, of a growing frenzy so that "they appear beside themselves, though no drinking has taken place whereby they may have become intoxicated. Sometimes they go from this dance and enter any house they wish, and take pleasure from any Indian woman they desire— even," they said, daughters, mothers, sisters, "no attention being paid to relationship." No wonder it was a shock to Fray Salvador de Guerra, pastor of Isleta, to see his people performing the dances from which he had believed them converted. Not being able to make them desist in any other way, he "went throughout the pueblo with a cross upon his shoulders, a crown of thorns, and a rope about his neck, beating his bare body, in order that they might stop the dance." When he reached a certain part of the pueblo "they came after him weeping, and saying they were not to blame, because the governor had commanded them to do as they were doing."

What could be hoped for from such a ruler, who was heard to declare loudly in the corridor of his palace at Santa Fe that "if it were not for the necessity of upholding his dignity as governor, he would himself go out and perform the dances, and for a little he would do it anyway"? When assured that the dances were superstitious, he replied that he could see no superstition in them, and he doubted whether anyone else could either. If any could, let them say so. After all, the Indian chorus in the dance sang "something which sounded like 'Hu-hu-hu.'"

"Look here," said the governor, "this dance contains nothing

more than this 'Hu-hu-hu,' and these thieving friars say it is superstitious."

The friars looked around and "knew from the faces of those who
were present that they were much affected by this action, but offered
no opposition to it because the speaker was their governor and captain-
general." And so the authority of the kingdom was torn apart over yet
another issue, and the Indians were offered both restraint and license,
and the dances went on in the earthen plazas along the river, and at
Pojuaque they danced at night so bedevilled and rapt that when the
horses of some Spaniards stumbled over them they did not feel it, and
at Taxique in the mountains when the snow was heavy on the ground
the people went to the church roof to dance and the Spanish mayor
went to the priest and mocked him, asking how it happened that he
had ordered the Indians to "dance the catzinas on the roof of the
church. . . ." It was a curiously prophetic episode, for centuries later
the modified Indian dances were to be approved by the pastors, and on
occasions permitted in the very churches; and it also recalled how in
the fourth century, Priscillian the Heretic introduced dancing into the
services of the Church, with lasting effect, for even centuries later the
Dance of the Seises was still given before the high altar in the cathedral
at Seville.

In the long roll of the contentious governors, Peralta, Eulate,
de Rosas and Mendizabel were the most reckless in their hatred of the
other majesty until the arrival in New Mexico in 1660 of Governor
Diego Dionysio de Peñalosa Briceña y Bertugo, who from the first
moment in his new kingdom showed himself master of a particularly
malicious style in government. He sent word ahead that all settlers
for fifty leagues around must come to meet him at Senecu, the first pueblo
on the river above the Northern Pass, and accompany him from there
to Santa Fe. Some two hundred colonists responded. As he approached
the pueblo and convent of Senecu, the friars there paid him due cour
tesies of an official nature. The bells pealed and the pastor in canonicals
accompanied by a crucifer bearing a large cross went forth to meet him
at the gate of the holy field of the cemetery. The new governor halted his
cavalcade to berate Father Fray Benito de la Natividad for not having
advanced down the road six miles to receive him. "What ridiculous pretensions for his reception!" exclaimed the priest in a protest to the
authorities in Mexico. From Senecu the governor proceeded up the
river in a royal progress, pausing at the convents with his huge court to
be fed and entertained and bedded without remuneration to the

frantic clergy, who having no resources equal to such privileged invasion, cried out that his vanity "exhausted the convents through no fault
but his own, for they were ruined by such great expense."

The new administration was off to an unhappy start. Peñalosa,
once installed in Santa Fe, commanded that from each pueblo convent
a trumpeter must come every week to the capital to "play for him in his
palace when he eats or rises, using for his own ostentation that which
the clergy employ" to dignify the church services in the missions. His
incumbency was one long scandal, public and private, and he enlivened
it by new hostilities against the Church. In his clay palace, ruling a
province suffering from famine, drought and rising threats of Indian
aggression, and supported by a half-intimidated, half-cynical official
circle, he was heard to murmur grandly that he had "secret instructions
from the Duke of Albuquerque to put the clergy to the garrote, or hang
them, and haul their corpses away ignominiously on pack saddles." A
friar went to Taos to rebuild a church that had been destroyed and
whose pastor had been murdered. Peñalosa appointed as governor of the
pueblo the same Indian who had murdered the priest, and decreed that
under penalty of death no Taos Indian was to help the new pastor to
rebuild the church. The pastor was forced to resign and work elsewhere.
Even though Taos was readily accessible from Santa Fe by the river road,
Peñalosa never visited that most important of the northern pueblos.

All the familiar issues between the two majesties reappeared
under Peñalosa, and the father president Fray Alonso de Posada, who
was also the resident commissioner of the Holy Office of the Inquisition,
opposed him with increasing vigor throughout the three years of the
administration. In 1663 the climax came. Francisco de Madrid, captain
of the governor's cavalry, appeared at the church capital of Santo
Domingo one day bringing two prisoners, Don Pedro Duran y Chavez
and his nephew Cristóbal, on the way to Santa Fe. They installed themselves in the convent that fronted on the plaza of the pueblo. Seeing
that his guards were inattentive, Don Pedro told one of his Indian
servants to take him up and carry him into the pueblo church where
he hoped to enjoy the right of sanctuary. The Captain saw too late what
had happened. Reluctant to violate the church on his own responsibility,
he sent a courier to the Governor asking for orders. As soon as possible
additional troops arrived from Santa Fe with an order to take Don
Pedro from the church. Having demanded the keys from the pastor, after
Mass on Sunday, August 23, 1663, they entered and took the refugee by
force. Word of the outrage came to Fray Alonso who was at Pecos. He

called upon the Governor to release the prisoner, threatening him with excommunication if he refused. The governor was heard to say that "he recognized no judge in this country who could excommunicate him, neither ecclesiastic, bishop, nor archbishop," and in his most florid style added that "I was a cleric in my own country, a padre, and I married when I was ordained as subdeacon, and I sang and intoned nicely a gloria, a credo and a prefacio." His next move was to gather up the father president at Pecos, remove him to Santa Fe and make him a prisoner in the palace. He then looked about to find witnesses to justify his actions.

But none came forward. The city—it was then the only Spanish city in New Mexico—and the river missions stirred with excitement. It was unheard of, to throw a prelate and a commissioner of the Inquisition into jail. Peñalosa searched for a diplomatic formula that would allow him to climb down with dignity. Surely the friars would petition him to free their president, whereupon he would do so with clemency? But the clergy kept an offended silence. Finally desperate, he wrote in October to the pastor of Isleta, asking him to call. With a show of diplomatic mediation, the incarcerated commissioner was released, and promptly made charges to the Holy Office in Mexico. Peñalosa decided to vacate his office voluntarily, and returned to Mexico, where the Inquisitors dealt with him in an exhaustive inquiry. He received the heaviest sentence ever imposed by the Inquisition in the New World—he was ordered to perform an act of faith by walking, bareheaded and barefoot, in a penitent's robe, and carrying a lighted green candle, through the streets of Mexico City; to pay a fine of five hundred pesos and all the costs of the case; to be ineligible ever to hold political or military office; to perpetual banishment from the New World; to make various holy devotions for one year; and to quit New Spain within a month. In the end the Inquisition had to lend him the money to pay for his passage to Europe, where he sought the ear first of Charles II in England and then of Louis XIV in France with a traitorous scheme to conquer New Spain.

If such were highlights of the religious case against the governors, equally profuse and even more violent charges were made throughout the century against the friars. In their hatred the governors accused the protectors of the Indian and of the common colonists of every conceivable crime. The quarrel was morally unequal, for the clergy in their ire were motivated in behalf of the human conscience; while the governors in their attacks upon the only valuable possession of the friars—their purity of purpose and repute—were moved by an exasperated venality. A gov-

ernor stated that some of the friars he knew were "sailors, artillerymen,
and men of ill-repute, engaged in evil pursuits; they took the habit in
order to go to the provinces of New Mexico. They served no novitiate,
and were without religion, which they did not understand." They
"took holy orders only to avoid work and live with greater liberty
than in worldly pursuits." The town council of Santa Fe in 1639
charged that the friars exploited the Indians for their own rich gain, and
caused anguish to the Spaniards by refusing them the sacraments, even
in Lent. ". . . On the doors of the churches there are posted more excom-
munications than bulls," and ". . . the worst thing about it is that usually
they take action against the governors and justices . . . and since all the
religious belong to the same Order, quarrels or contentions with one
mean trouble for all. . . . Thus the royal jurisdiction is much humbled
and violated and the few inhabitants who uphold their governor, besides
suffering poverty greater than that of Haman, are afflicted and snubbed
and addressed by the religious with ugly and insulting words, and even
forbidden to fight in the field."

The issues complained of by the friars were reinterpreted by
laymen. To keep the Spaniards from "holding or establishing farms,
under the excuse of protecting the cornfields of the Indians [the friars]
find sufficient reason for interfering with the Spanish inhabitants, even
though the latter settle two or three leagues away from the Indian
pueblos. . . . When they can do no more they even burn the farms, as
they have done in some cases." Let the Viceroy "consider, for the love
of God, that this is a very poor land, with few people, and that the
measures were taken in passion and with great harshness." The maintenance of civil order was impossible if the clergy were able to harbor
criminals in the sanctuaries of the chapels, which were becoming "asy-
lums and refuges" for "delinquent." The convents, declared the councilmen, maintained large farms and herds, and the Indians were abused
by being put to work with them, and the pastors in their stables kept
"three or four saddle horses very daintily, for they are quite valuable and
are taken to be sold in New Spain." Worst of all, and almost incredible,
was that the clergy "hold most of the arms that there are in the country, for they have armor for the horses, leather jackets, swords, harquebuses, and pistols," and the council begged that these arms be ordered
turned over to the governors to issue in times of trouble, "for there
are none in the storehouse." Did a friar steal most of a shipment of
iron intended for horseshoes? Did he sell a herd of oxen intended for
the use of Indians in tilling their fields? Were even religious articles

meant for the chapels sold for private gain by the Franciscans? The councilmen bitterly said so.

Some of the charges made by the officials were appalling. At a certain pueblo the resident friars took much cloth and other tribute from the people, who sent a delegation to complain to the authorities. Upon their return the pastor had them brought before him for questioning. He then went to their houses and searching them found "some feathers, or idols"—the usual Indian katchinas. He flew into a passion and confronting his people again he sent for turpentine, threw it upon them and put the torch to them. Many people were badly burned. One died of the effects. The resident friars were ordered to Santa Fe to be disciplined by the father president. But soon they were again in favor and assigned religious duties.

The indictments streamed on—friars whipped Indians; sometimes cut off the hair of Indian women; put prisoners whom they detained into a little cell "not even large enough or decent enough for a good-sized pig"; were frauds, hypocrites and drunkards. As for Indian dances, the friars were willing enough to let them be danced if they needed the Indians to sow the fields or do other jobs. Most fervently of all, the civil charges complained of religious abuses by the friars. They refused confession at a whim, excommunicated for nonreligious reasons, suspended the saying of Mass thus anguishing many more persons than the one or two they meant to deprive, and again, "would say Mass in the house of any mulatto or kept woman, according to their pleasure." The laymen repeatedly begged that clergy be sent to them who would restore the sacraments of which they were deprived and of which they felt such profound need. The faith itself was never threatened; only its priesthood, whom the governors chose to judge by its least instead of its most worthy members. Even a certain friar said to one of the governors, "Sir, the ignorance of these fathers is immense. God take me away from here." But this governor was a poor witness, for like all the others who accused the friars of heinous deeds he was himself a man of low character.

So in bitter animation of the whole tiny society, the two majesties took issue for generations over the prerogatives of the soul and of the civil power. Against the sparse and lonely background of the narrow river valley, the Indians in their towns, far from the great world, were the victims of a divided authority which they had never invited over them. The stalemate between church and state, with its postures of mutual defiance, was symbolized in a story believed in 1660. Told that

the father commissary of the Holy Office of the Inquisition was coming
to arrest him, Governor López de Mendizabel "said that before that
commissary could seize him, he would hang him to a tree (indicating
with his hand a tree which was there). Then, though the sky was serene,
clear and without clouds, a little cloud came up with a tempest and
a ray of lightning fell, which reduced the entire tree to ashes. . . ."

27.

The Hungry

Trouble of another kind, vast and impersonal, came to the whole
river kingdom and its outlying unknown lands and peoples in the middle
of the seventeenth century. The plains Apaches and Comanches roved
under the weather, obeying its great movements like shadows obeying
clouds. Where the grass was ripe the cows went, and the Indian rovers
followed to hunt and eat them, and to pick berries and herbs that prospered as the grasses did, when the rains fell on all things and made life.
All depended on the rains. The plains people had no storage. Their food
grew before them, and they took it, and used it, and moved on to the
next living supply.

In the land of the pueblos, and farther south, below the North
Pass, where the river turned east and south for its last thousand miles,
were people who planted crops and harvested them, saving against the
future what they did not need each year. The lower river people were
seen in 1653 by Captain Alonso de León who with thirty soldiers came
to the river from the settlement called Cerralvo in the province of Nuevo
León. He was under orders to find the mouth of the Rio de las Palmas
from its inland approach. Since the efforts of more than a century
before no foreign travellers had sought the lower river. De León came
to its bank a few hundred miles from the sea and followed its course
toward the mouth. He passed through a green land, saw many fish in the

river, and found many Indian settlements whose people were friendly, unlike "their forebears, who killed a large number of Spaniards who attempted to settle in that country" generations before. Life seemed abundant on the River of Palms, which once again had been discovered.

But in the middle decades of the century a vast restraint of nature came upon the whole Southwest, plain and river alike, and brought suffering for people. It was drought. In the long valley of New Mexico the Spaniards recognized drought when it came, for the rivers of Spain mostly went dry in summer, and the white riverbeds and the gray grasses and the staring empty sky and the winds that hauled away the surface of the land and the endless question waiting to be answered out of the hot light of day were doubly familiar to them where they now lived. The river Indians knew it too and eyed their storage cists whose seed corn, held sacred for planting, would be eaten only in desperation. In the farms of pueblo and encomienda alike lay the hope of the future—feed for the cattle, crops for the people, seed for the next year.

With the plains Indians the problem had a different solution. Their roving life reached in an immense crescent from the unknown lands north of the river to the low gulf lands of the east and south. In the long years of drought the plains cattle and the people alike had little food. They had to forage far and wide for what had failed them in their own sweeping country. The great crescent contracted. The hunters turned to the river, where in its northern reaches lived people with stored food, and where across its long southeastward passage were increasing settlements of farmers and cattle raisers from New Spain. The Apache and Comanche raids, always a sporadic menace to the river dwellers, grew with each passing year of the drought.

In 1660 war parties of the plains people crossed the southeastward river and struck at the frontier posts of New Spain—Cerralvo, Saltillo and Monterrey, even going as far inland as Chihuahua and Cases Grandes. They drove off herds of cattle and retreated swiftly to the plains. The widely separated towns took joint action to punish the raiders, and by October, 1663, an expedition was ready to leave Monterrey with a hundred men, eight hundred horses, eighty loads of flour and other provisions. Under the command of Sergeant Major Juan de la Garza the volunteer army marched to the river, which they called the Rio Bravo, and crossed near the site of Eagle Pass. They found the enemy Indians defensively gathered in a rancheria, and battle followed, in which a hundred Indians were killed and a hundred and twenty-five men, women and children were captured. Six months after they had set

out, the soldier-farmers returned to Monterrey. Many of their prisoners
were sent to work as slaves in the mines of Zacatecas.

Two years later the pattern was repeated. The Indians came,
plundered, retreated, and again the towns mustered a force to overtake
them, this time with the help of three hundred Bobole Indians of
Coahuila. Seventy-five miles north of the Rio Bravo the fight was joined.
An old Indian woman played a flute to hearten her tribesmen. The
Indian allies of the Spaniards begged for permission to capture her and
eat her. Their request was not granted. But at night, when the battle
was over, and the Indians were defeated without loss to the Spaniards,
a captive boy was taken by the Boboles, sacrificed and eaten—"a matter
which could not be remedied."

So the necessities of defense took the first Spaniards to the river
in its southeastward inland stretches, showed them the country beyond
it to the north, and acquainted them with the Indians who lived along
it on both sides. In the years following, another necessity brought
repeated delegations of Indians from the plains river to the northern
settlements of New Spain. Like the Humanos to the north, they came
asking for conversion, remembering the appearances among them of a
woman in a blue cloak. Their appeals were finally heard by Fray Juan
Larios, who came from Guadalajara to Coahuila and spent three years
among the Indians south of the river. In 1673 he went home to recruit
missionary help and returned with two other friars, one of whom, Fray
Manuel de la Cruz, in the following year crossed the river alone to recon-
noiter the opportunities among Indians in the northern plains. Once
again Indians asked for instruction, but nations beyond the river were
not always at peace with one another. The little frontier outposts in
Mexico, with their armed garrisons, were creeping nearer to the river
where it cut its long way through harsh highlands, and now the missionary purposes and those of civil government combined to make a
reconnaissance in force. Under orders of the governor of Coahuila,
Lieutenant Fernando del Bosque set out with an observation party on
April 30, 1675. With him were Father Fray Juan Larios and Father Fray
Dionysio de San Buenaventura, ten Spaniards, two Indian chiefs and
twenty-one Indian allies. The company was augmented later by another
hundred Indians recruited as they went north.

They crossed the high wastes of northern Mexico where the pale
ground was dotted with dusty scrub groves of mesquite. Encountering
Indians almost every day they made addresses, took possession and
planted crosses, duly notarizing these actions. They passed over many

little rivers, some dry, some flowing, and arrived on the eleventh of May, 1675, at a "very copious and very wide river," nearly four hundred yards across, bordered by "fine pastures of green grass . . . which the Indians said was called the Rio del Norte." A scattering of people lived there in grass huts. They searched for a ford and found none, and finally crossed at a place where the river had three channels, the first of which was as deep as the "hind bow of the saddle," and the second of which, too deep to ford, they managed with an improvised raft. In artless words that caught the picture of how the river looked in countless places, the Lieutenant spoke of "willow and osier brush on a little island which is in the middle," and said that the banks of the river were "very pleasing, and it had many fish, such as catfish, *piltontes,* very large turtles, and eels." He claimed the river for the Crown, named it the San Buena Ventura, and planted a large cross.

Two days later the scouting party moved inland going north and east. Once again they passed among little scattered nations of hunting Indians, and promised them baptism when they should have learned their prayers, and set up crosses, and saw the buffalo which gazed at the people sidewise "like wild hogs, with hair abristle," scolded tribes that would not befriend one another and ordered them to settle together in peace which they promised to do. The Lieutenant made notes of the country and its products. In a certain encampment on the sixteenth of May an Indian "made a demonstration" and brought him "a Spanish boy apparently about twelve years old, with a black streak on his face running from forehead to nose, and one on each cheek, like o's, and many rows of them on the left arm and one on the right." Questioned, the boy replied that his mother had raised him, and had given him to the Indians years ago. As far as he knew, he came from near Parral, in Mexico. His Indian masters said that "although they loved him like a brother," they would give him up to the Lieutenant who could take him home to his relatives. Asked if there were any other captive Spaniards, they answered that there were none at present, though years ago a boy prisoner had been killed with arrows, "praying till he died," and that a girl prisoner, after dying the same death, had been left where she fell, and for two years her body did not decay and no animals touched it. "In view of this, they took it and carried it to a cave, where it now is; and (said) that it has long hair; and that this is the truth."

On the same day a portable altar was set up, the small bell was rung, and the first sung Mass was held in the Indian wilderness above the southeasterly river in Texas.

By May twenty-ninth, the combined military and religious expedition was again on the Rio de San Buena Ventura, returning to Mexico. In June Bosque submitted his report with his recommendations. He proposed three settlements, widely separated, with four friars for each group, and a district garrison of seventy soldiers, for it would be impossible "for any officer of his Majesty to keep them in order and under instruction unless he has forces for it, although he may have to use much love and blandishment when having to correct them, for since they are vicious people and not habituated to labor to sustain themselves, they will return to their natural habits, and greater damages will result," such as the murderous and thieving raids over the river of the 1660s.

It was not long until four mission outposts, with their protective garrisons, were established in central Coahuila which though not on the river itself worked to educate and stabilize the Indians on both sides of the river frontier.

Far to the west and north, the same vocations were already implanted. At the Northern Pass of the river in 1659 "a church of branches and mud and a monastery thatched with straw" had been erected on the south bank of the river where the Mansos Indians lived, and where the supply trains between Mexico and New Mexico made a station on their long hauls north and south. In 1668 a new church was completed. At its ceremonies of dedication, a group of Indian women were baptized at one door and a group of men at another. Entering, then, the men and women were married before the altar during a nuptial Mass. The church was named Our Lady of Guadalupe of El Paso. It stood on a slight eminence about a mile from the south bank of the river. The heavy beams for its ceiling were brought from mountains far away, and were richly incised, and set upon corbels that were beautifully scrolled. Above the beams ran the ceiling in a herringbone pattern of peeled sapling branches. The Indians stood and gazed at the length of the ceiling and felt a mysterious joy in the perfect regularity and repetition of the polished timbers, in so high and so wide and so long a place. The thick walls were plastered inside and out. Before the church the dead were buried. About its walls in the open wilderness the living came together and made houses—the first wholly Spanish town on the river. For its first decade the settlement existed almost entirely to meet the needs of the mission—its irrigated fields, vineyards and pastures. These, like the whole land, suffered in the drought. It was a small settlement referred to as The Pass, and roads drew toward it from all directions. Of these the one most travelled was that which connected the two Mexicos, old and

new, north and south. In the 1670s the town grew, and parish books
recorded weddings, baptisms and burials of Spanish settlers. Friars on
ecclesiastical business from Santo Domingo up the river brought news
of the capital, where the small garrison was helpless to control the local
Indian aggressions that broke out in widely separated places like fires
kindled on dry wooded mountainsides by the pitiless sun, which as
they burnt out left an acrid trace in the air like a troublesome reminder.
Travellers from the south told of the settlements in Coahuila and Nuevo
León that reached nearer and nearer toward the river to bring conversion and peace where starving atrocity roved. Every traveller could recite
more calamities than joys.

It was possible that only an epidemic of smallpox in 1641, in
which many thousands of Indians had died of the imported disease,
prevented a general uprising of the native peoples against their new
masters who quarrelled so bitterly among themselves. There were whispers of revolt among the Piro pueblos, who were conspiring with the
ancient Apache enemy to turn against the settlers. Soldiers went out
from Santa Fe to put down the disturbance. There were skirmishes and
a few were killed. The Apache had entered the pueblos as a confederate.
Withdrawing, he was like the fox who had been guest in the farmyard.
He knew his hunger and he knew where to take his fill.

The great Piro pueblos of the Salines province stood in a long
line below the fine sweeping eastern approaches to the Manzanos mountains east of the river. They were cities of stone. Behind them rose the
mountains whose air, sweetened by the moist breath of forests, was a
living blue. Before them to the east stretched golden-grassed plains
where no natural barriers divided them from the country of the hunters.
Twenty miles away in a straggling line thirty miles long from north to
south lay the shallow white lakes of salt which gleamed amid low crusty
dunes. The three southernmost of the saline pueblos—Quarai, Abó and
Tabira (the Gran Quivira)—had the largest churches of New Mexico.
These like the towns they served were made of the native sandstone,
ranging in color from a gray rose at Quarai, to a deep coral at Abó, and
at Tabira a speckled gray and tan like the skin of a rattlesnake. The
friars went to these towns in the 1620s, made their conversions and led
the people in building the missions. Each church and its convent were
made of millions of pieces of shaped sandstone, set layer by layer in
earth mortar. The thick walls, heavily buttressed, had almost no outside
windows. In a great square growing from a side wall of the church were
enclosed the living quarters, the storerooms, the patio and the corral of

the mission, with no separate outside gate. At Tabira the livestock was driven along the interior cloister to reach the corral. Light entered the rooms from the patio, and in the center of the patio as if to be enfolded by the teaching of the church was the sunken kiva for the male cults of the pueblo. It was a kiva without the supernatural shipapu, or passage-way to the nether world, such as the kivas of the ancients always had.

Large as they were—the nave at Quarai was one hundred two feet long and fifty-seven wide—the churches were built with false per-spective so that the nave would seem even greater. White plaster with colored decorations made the interior brilliant. Light fell upon the altar from a transverse clerestory window above the transept. Wooden beams, altars and corbels were carved and painted and touched with gilt. The ceiling was between thirty and forty feet above the floor. The Indians had never seen any such building: its size, its hinged doors, carved wood-work, staircases, balconies, windows, bell towers, enclosed fireplaces and chimneys; though into it went ancient devices of their own, like the ceiling with its willow wands reaching from beam to beam, and its open-hearth fireplaces in the convent kitchen, where on earthen ledges rested the table service and cooking pots. These were assorted. There was one Indian ware of the red clay found right outside the building, and there was another of pale clay decorated in black also made at home. There were rich pots from the river, brought in trade, done in black, red, and tan. From Mexico there was flowered Majolica ware and from China there was porcelain, jade green on one side and white on the other, brought north in the mission freight trains. The water for such establishments flowed in stone-lined ditches from springs or seasonal pools that lay outside the walls. In the years of drought these sources dwindled, and at Tabira Spaniards noticed that Indians saved their own urine for use in mixing plaster.

But however primitive that life, it was complete; and however isolated from civilized delights it knew a natural one in the space and color of its setting, with blue quiver of mountain air, pale gold of prairie grass, sparkle of dense cottonwood groves, and far away the pearly clouds and their wandering shadows on the plains, where hidden in space lived the quick and starving enemy. The people of Tabira looking south from their hill could see fifty miles away in its ever-changing atmosphere the range of the Sierra Blanca. There lived the Mescalero Apaches, an interior pocket of menace quite as grave as that of the eastern plains.

To those Saline pueblos, reaching from Tabira in the south to

Taxique and Chilili in the north, came drought and the threat of famine. They had no spare stores to use in trade when the inquiring Apaches came to see them. The Apaches might withdraw in peace once or twice; but as the dry years pressed hotly upon the whole kingdom they came again when the meagre harvests were ready, and stole what the towns needed to live on through the winter. They came and went, relenting long enough to let the townspeople get their hopes up and set another year's planting; and then at the ripeness of corn and fruit, they struck once more. They could lay siege to the towns by bracketing water supplies until tribute was forthcoming. Any Christian Indian venturing beyond his walls was walking into his death. "The whole land is at war with the widespread heathen nations of Apache Indians," wrote a friar in 1669, "who kill all the Christian Indians they can find. . . . No road is safe; everyone travels at the risk of his life." From the forests in the mountains about the pueblo of Taxique the Apaches would burst forth and capture Christian Indians and carry them off to their own distant encampments. "There they build a great fire, near which they bind the person whom they have captured; they then dance around him, cutting off parts of his body, which they cook and eat, until they entirely consume him, cutting him to pieces alive." More than one kind of hunger was fed but not appeased.

As the murderous raids continued, there were only five Spanish soldiers at each frontier station to combat them, and any soldiers on a mission went armored with leather shields and rode horses wearing armor. As they marched in 1668 they saw innumerable Indians "lying dead along the roads, in the ravines, and in their huts." In one pueblo more than four hundred and fifty died of hunger. A friar reported that there was "not a fanega of corn or of wheat in the whole kingdom." Indians and Spaniards alike fought starvation by eating leather. Taking hides and even the straps off their carts, they soaked and washed them, rolled them in corn meal, and toasted them in the fire, or boiled them with herbs and roots. In 1671 "a great pestilence carried off many people and cattle," and in the following year, with the province at its weakest, the Apaches struck again and again, taking away cattle and sheep until hardly any were left to the Spanish population that numbered less than twenty-five hundred.

Against such privations and dangers the stone cities of the Salines could not prevail. In the early 1670s their people crept away forever leaving their magnificent churches, their clustered houses and their lyric fields. The rust-red city of Abó was pillaged and the convento burned. Fray Pedro de Ayala was stripped naked, tied with a rope around his neck, viciously flogged, and finally killed with a blow from a stone axe. He was left with his body intact and surrounded by dead white lambs and his sex covered, a seeming respect that astonished the defeated Indians who crawled back after the battle and saw him so, for they knew "the ferocity of these Indian barbarians, who kill one another for a piece of meat. . . ."

The refugees from eastern pueblos went through the mountains to the river where some settled among kinsmen at Socorro and Senecu, and others fled downstream to El Paso. The Salines cities were never really inhabited again. The winds took them and the earth rose slowly about them. The ceilings of the great naves fell. The walls in a shudder that took centuries crumbled from the top. Weeds grew high on the exposed masonry filled with clay. Above the common, mounded grave of each town loomed like a sepulchre the great fragment of its church.

But even where they sought sanctuary by the river the transmontane Piros were not safe. In 1675 the Apaches streaked out of the mountains on the twenty-third of January and attacked the pueblo of Senecu. The pastor, Fray Alonso Gil de Ávila, showed himself in a window holding a crucifix. He was killed by an arrow in his heart, and more than half the people died that day. The remainder fled up the river to Socorro. Senecu was never resettled, though the Father President at Santo Domingo drew up plans for the reoccupation of all the Piro towns. There was no possibility of military protection from Santa Fe. In 1675 the government could hardly have been more disorganized under the forces of disaster, physical and spiritual—drought, famine, Indian atrocities, on the one hand, and on the other, a breakdown in moral authority resulting from the long quarrel between the two majesties.

Though the quarrel had been left passive ever since a strange event given credence in the middle 1670s. One day the Blessed Virgin Mary appeared in a vision to a dying young girl and cured her, saying, "My child, go and tell everyone that the kingdom will soon be destroyed because of the lack of reverence shown to my priests. . . ." Miraculously cured, the girl told her story, and fear seized the province. A special Mass was sung, and the civil majesty ceased its attacks upon the friars. But the damage was long since done, and the Indians in their impassivity seemed somehow alarming, and now and then their open return to communion with the superstitious powers of their ancient days affected the settlers. There was an odd strength to the Indian attitude and belief. Most fearful of all was that which defied understanding.

The Spanish governor, trying to undo the effects of earlier permissions by his predecessors, ordered the Indian rituals and incantations discontinued, and sent his cavalry to take prisoner as many of the pueblo medicine doctors as possible. Forty-seven were arrested and dragged to Santa Fe, where they were charged with witchcraft and sorcery—a crime so serious that even the Spaniards were tried for it whenever it appeared in their own life by the Holy Office of the Inquisition. Three of the Indian doctors were hanged and the others were severely whipped and jailed. Bitterly the river towns from which they came spoke against such action. They felt their own sacred forces to have been profaned, and without their doctors of magic they were defenseless against the invisible powers of evil. Once willing to come like children to Christianity, in fact, to ask for it, now in consequence of corruption and persecution within the Spanish vision of life they were clinging more fearfully than ever to their ancestral explanation of the world.

Seventy Indians from the Christianized pueblos of the Tewa nation on the river came to Santa Fe to see the Governor. They demanded the release of their doctors, and declared that unless this were granted, their people would abandon their towns and flee to the Apaches, or together rise up and make war upon the colonists. The Governor yielded. With his twenty-five hundred colonists, he could not hope to prevail for long against an angry pueblo population of between sixteen and twenty thousand. The liberated doctors returned to their towns. Among them was one from San Juan named Popé, whose bitterness was as great as that of his fellows, and whose strength was greater. With a fiery vision burning in his mind he returned home making threats and summoning powers. What he saw for the future did not seem so difficult to bring about.

Santa Fe, the capital, was the only Spanish town in the kingdom other than the tiny post on the overland march at El Paso. It lay in a wide shallow cup among mountains and it drank from a little creek that flowed west to the Rio del Norte thirty miles away. It was not a river town, it was a mountain town, and all its relation to the actual river life was administrative. A plaza twice as long as wide lay east and west. Clay houses were scattered close to the plaza, where the Palace of the Governors on the north side was the center of all office and authority. This was a long low building between towers, in one of which was a chapel, in the other a powder magazine and a prison. The official residence and offices were between in the long low rooms with connecting doors. Behind the Palace was a garden with a well, and beyond this, the

cavalry horses were stabled, and the state coach was kept, and the guard
was quartered. Cultivated fields stretched away to the north beyond the
buildings. To the west of the Palace were the barracks for the garrison.
On the east side of the plaza stood the parish church and convento of
Saint Francis, in whose tower was the voice of the colony, ringing for
daybreak, for Mass, for noon, for evening vespers, and for jubilation
when appointed, and for sorrowful news in affliction. Across the creek
to the south stood the chapel of Saint Michael surrounded by fields.

Each house was set in its farm field. Plows now and then turned
up reminders of how people long ago had lived there in an ancient
pueblo, and had breathed the delicious air, had raised their faces to the
golden sunlight's vast clear jewel, and had known the unspoken joys
of nature's beauty. For the rest, life was different, it meant to be better,
it could hardly have been more severe, and its troubles of body seemed
to produce there as well as everywhere in the kingdom trials, and even
absurdities, of soul.

For the evils of superstition were not invited by the Indians alone.
In Santa Fe private sorceries ate away at the edges of society, and scared
people, and made them gossip and doubt. No force seemed absent from
the hungry little colony that could help to disunify it and promise its
destruction, if not yet from without the human spirit, then in time from
within. When Indians worked as house servants, they brought into the
Spanish mind much of their view of life, including their constant commerce with the occult. Spanish women implored Indians to bring them
love potions. One such feared to lose the love of the man with whom
she lay illicitly, and begged an Indian for "some herbs" which would
cause her lover to "love her very much and never forget her." The Indian
agreed, "but first he desired to speak to her privately." They went away
together to the garden and there the Indian spoke to her, but nobody
ever knew what he said. Presently they returned, and much later it was
known that "the Indian gave her the herbs, that he is now dead and
that the woman is now married to the same man."

The same Indian failed another supplicant. A certain Spaniard
asked for herbs that would make the Governor like him very much, and
was given them. Not long afterward the man was arrested by the Governor who threatened to have his throat cut. The prisoner sent back the
herbs to the Indian with the message that "he was a dog of an enchanter,
that there his herbs were, and that they had no effect at all."

Love and success, health and the recovery of lost articles and
magic protection—all the immemorial desires ached again and were

approached through sorceries. A Spanish official living in a pueblo heard
that his ten-year-old son Francisco went with his young uncle to the kiva
where several Indians let them in. There the young man pricked himself with an awl but without any effect. At another time in the presence
of the boy and two women, he had stabbed himself with a dagger and a
knife, but without making wounds. It was astonishing and frightening.
Asked for an explanation, the young uncle said that at Mass one day
while he was up in the choir loft, a German trader from Sonora who
travelled with the supply trains had come up the stairs and had written
something on some slips of paper. These, said the German, if you ate
them, would make you "invulnerable for twenty-four hours." The young
man at once swallowed one and could not then hurt himself with a
blade. The papers read:

$$\text{"+ A.B.V.A. \quad + \quad A.D.A.V. +"}$$

The Spanish official was horrified and hastened to the Father President
at Santo Domingo to denounce the German sorcerer, who was arrested
after further testimony and charges, and imprisoned for trial. After
several months in jail he escaped with the aid of an Indian, and fled
south on the river road. Five soldiers were sent to pursue him and his
accomplice. The case was closed with the report of one of the pursuers.
Near the spring of El Perillo in the long desert passage separated from
the river by mountains they found a dead roan horse tied to a tree.
Near it were a pair of blue trousers and a blue doublet lined with otter
fur. A little farther away they came upon hair and bones—the bones had
been gnawed by animals—and the soldiers identified the remains as those
of the German witch, and said they supposed he had been killed by the
Indian who was travelling with him. And now they named the desert
passage after the lost German—the Jornada del Muerto, the Dead Man's
March. The whole story was a parable of moral confusions as they
showed in the actions and the guilts of the Christian, the heathen, the
Spaniard, the Indian.

But if the Indian failed in his grasp of Spanish and Christian
civilization, who was to blame but the colonizer himself? "It is a shame,"
wrote a friar, "to see how we tell them one thing and then do the opposite, and the poor ignorant Indian sees very well what I do and forgets
what I say." It was again the voice of the Spanish conscience, accusing
its own "base sinners and their bad example." The hour was late, in the
river kingdom of New Mexico in the 1670s, for its salvation through

the spirit. The two majesties of God and King could only look desperately for aid on the physical level, and were lucky enough to find a good man in a hard job who saw what was needed and did his utmost to get it.

28.

"This Miserable Kingdom"

He was the Father Quartermaster of the Franciscan province of New Mexico, Fray Francisco de Ayeta. In 1674 the supply system dating from 1609, whereby freighters took contracts to operate the wagon trains, was ended, and the religious establishment on the one hand, and the civil power on the other, were obliged if they needed supplies to go in their resepective persons to fetch them. Every three years the Crown granted alms to the missions, by which was meant an aggregate of money, foodstuffs, livestock, and various matériel. Fray Francisco came with the cargo to Santa Fe in 1674 on the first of his several trips. The oxen, mules, wagons, carts and all travelling gear now belonged to the Franciscan Order. In the hard times which he found prevailing in the kingdom, much of what he brought was needed for distribution to relieve the suffering population outside the missions. He was shocked by what he found, and his energies of mind and body—both exceptional —began to work first on understanding the serious problems all about him, and next on their relief. It was fortunate that he was so robust for his age, that his nature was generous, and that with his gifts as a bookkeeper he combined a sense of humor. Such qualities were crucially valuable in the midst of the hardships of the trail and of the land at its end. "This miserable kingdom!" exclaimed the governor's papers again and again in communication with the viceregal offices of Mexico City.

Fray Francisco de Ayeta brought his train up the valley road in the dry summer. His only reliefs were the little pauses he would make— like all voyagers—at the haciendas along the river, where each clustered around the life of a family that had chosen to live away from the mountain capital of Santa Fe. Each was a walled sanctuary against the dangers of distance and unconverted Indians. Widely separated from its nearest neighbor, the estate had to be self-sustaining in all things. Owners, relatives, servants, Indian slaves, all lived like one family, taking life itself from the river water, and insuring it in the tending of farm fields and animal herds. Constant vigilance was the price of bare survival. Yet with the graces of bounteous shade from cottonwood groves, modest satisfaction in daily work, and faith in Providence, the haciendas seemed to have much to offer the infrequent passer-by, as he came to one after another in the long valley where the scattered pueblos were the only other dwellings. The valley of New Mexico was separated into two districts, as seen from Santa Fe. These were called the Rio Arriba, the Upriver—above Santa Fe; and the Rio Abajo, or Downriver—below Santa Fe. Coming north the wagon train entered into the Downriver district where most of the haciendas were strung out, and Fray Francisco broke his journey at many of them. There were the establishments of the matriarch Doña Luisa de Trujillo, and of Don Alonso García, the lieutenant general of the kingdom, and of the Gonzales Bernal family who called their place Bernalillo. The train rested at Don Cristóbal de Anaya's place, which stood near the river in a narrow part of the valley where the desert heights crowded close, and went on to the estate of Captain Agustín de Carbajal and his wife Doña Damiana Dominguez de Mendoza, who had a grown daughter and several sons. Farther along were the houses and corrals of Pedro de Cuellar.

The Father Quartermaster saw that life in such places was in danger now from many forces. One was the drought. One was the intermittent threat of the Apaches. One was the gossip going around that made much uneasiness over the other Indians in the pueblos, who here and there and in ways hard to define portended trouble. A number of families—he eventually heard of forty—talked of banding together for the purpose of quitting the northern river altogether, and returning to Mexico in a spirit of outright failure. Such a movement, if it gathered momentum, might lead to the abandonment of the whole province. And yet who could blame those who felt undefended, hungry and at the mercy of the merciless sky?

In 1675 at San Juan pueblo the Indian doctor Popé, ever since his release from punishment and prison at Santa Fe, did his best to make trouble among the other Indians whom he exhorted to rebel. The Spanish authority of San Juan watched him narrowly, and curtailed his do-

ings until in exasperation he moved to Taos to continue his campaign.
He had ominous information to give to the Taos people. It was his
distinction that extraordinary powers had been revealed to him. He was
able to say that Montezuma, their ancient war god, in his other-kingdom
of Po-he-yemu, was gathering all his forces to lead the Indian people in
revolt against the Spaniards. Popé was in direct communication with
him through three spirits of the underworld who regularly came to him
in the kiva and told him what to do. He could tell their names. They
were Caudi, Tilini and Tleume.

Rumors of such machinations came in driblets to the Spaniards
through Christianized Indians, and caused uneasiness, and yet with a
garrison of only ten regular soldiers in the capital, what could be done,
even if volunteers took up arms? There were precious few arms to wield.
The Indians were superstitious. Popé was a disgruntled hothead. Perhaps
it would rain, and all would be well. . . .

Arrived at Santa Fe, Ayeta saw how in places the walls of the
Governor's Palace were falling down and how the main entrance leading through a covered passage to the patio had no doors. He heard how
five whole settlements had been destroyed by Apaches, and churches
burned, and their sacred images profaned. Friars had been murdered at
their altars. The contempt shown for the friars through so many years
by the local government was ripening in bitter fruit, for the Indians in
general seemed to have lost all respect for the teachings which they had
once so hungrily and so simply taken. It was an appalling situation, and
Ayeta must have wondered how it happened that nobody, from the
Governor down, had made vigorous moves to save it. He would soon
return to Mexico. Let him present to the Viceroy a clear picture of
what was needed to save the province from utter collapse. He was empowered to act for the colony, and with his creaking vehicles and his
trudging oxen he went slowly, but with rapid thoughts, back to the
source of power.

In early September, 1676, he made his petition, supporting it by
scholarly references to earlier royal decrees pertaining to the frontier,
and arguing with a show of reason on behalf of an issue vital to his
emotion. It was all precarious. If he asked for too little—which might
be easy to get—life itself might be the cost in New Mexico. If he asked
for too much, the mind of government would decide that any real need
hidden beneath extravagant demands was not worthy, and he would
get nothing. On September twenty-second he was informed that he would
receive almost exactly what he asked for, and this on the authority of

the Viceroy, without reference to the Crown in Madrid. The memorandum provided for fifty soldiers to guard the frontiers; eight women to accompany the train to make tortillas and cook for the men; one thousand horses; twelve men to drive the horses; supplies for the caravan sufficient to last six months; and other miscellaneous provisions. The total cost was 14,700 pesos. He went to work at once to fill the bill.

Man power was the first need. He published calls for volunteers. Enlistments were not forthcoming, and he petitioned the government to fill his lists with men chosen from the usual source. Eventually he was granted forty-seven convicts, who "were condemned to serve His Majesty in New Mexico." They were to receive a pittance as pay, and be commanded by an officer and a sergeant. Freed from jail to march northward for the defense of a threatened province, the criminals for the most part accepted their fate calmly. At the last minute, three young men volunteered, and received sixty pesos each forthwith. On February 27, 1677, with his people and his animals and his cargo, Fray Francisco left Mexico again for Santa Fe. He had his problems on the way. At El Parral one of his convicts, an epileptic, who had repeatedly tried to commit suicide, and who suffered from the grand mal, falling from his cart time and again, finally ran away. At the ford of El Paso where the party was long delayed by flood waters, six convicts assigned to guard duty deserted their posts and ran away and were never heard of again. They stole fifty-seven horses, three harquebuses and six saddles. The Father Quartermaster had been given supplies to last the caravan through a journey of six months, but delays on the way stretched it to nine, and it was November before the train crawled into Santa Fe, to be joyfully received.

In December the whole population was assembled in open meeting to hear Fray Francisco's official report of what he had obtained for them. Governor Antonio de Otermín presided. Fray Francisco reported that he had brought one hundred new harquebuses with locks; one hundred new hilts for swords and daggers; fifty saddles, and a thousand saddle horses (at three pesos each). For the use of the city of Santa Fe, he assigned fifty head of cattle, and one hundred thirty fanegas of provisions, and twenty soldiers whom he armed with twenty leather jackets of six thicknesses and twenty leather shields, and sets of armor for two of their horses. On his way up the river he had paused here and there to relieve suffering by unloading supplies. At the despoiled pueblo of Senecu, where he found an attempt at resettlement, he left four hundred fanegas of provisions, two hundred goats and sixty head of cattle. At Galisteo he unloaded over four hundred fanegas of food, and cut out four hundred goats and sixty head of cattle from the caravan herds to leave behind. What was more, he reported that he had fed the troops out of his mission stores during the extra three months consumed on the journey. To keep his accounts straight, he asked that this be acknowledged, and that general receipts be issued covering all his deliveries. These the Governor was glad to authorize "on common paper because stamped paper is not current in these provinces." Stating plainly that without Fray Francisco's help the soldiery "in the defense of these provinces could not have been maintained," the receipt was witnessed by the clerk of the council, and then the clerk's witness was witnessed by the Governor. In an atmosphere of compliments and thanks and solemn legalities the kingdom took heart from its new resources.

But what were fifty men and a thousand horses and a hundred sword hilts in that land where there were thirty missions to guard, and dozens of pueblos to watch, and cloud-shadowed empires to scan for the Apache marauders who could appear and disappear like streaks of shadow on the plains? What good were so few sacks of grain to farmers who knew that the future depended not on laboriously shipped supplies but on green fields at home every year after rain? What could be done for people who let the walls of their capitol building fall down without repairing them? The drought's vast lassitude seemed to have entered into men and women. Proverbs and prayers—what else was there to try? Fray Francisco was not finished, however. If he had not asked for enough last time, he would ask again. Providence, in which he strongly believed, could operate not only outside but inside a man. Let him not wait and observe, but go to work again in the elaborate and familiar approaches to government.

In 1679 he was again in Mexico City, and again he wrote and wrote. He told the Viceroy what had already been granted, and what had been done with it, and what now remained to be done. He reminded him of how the King had approved the relief granted in 1676, and he told how the savages had been deterred since its application. Fawning almost desperately upon the Viceroy (who was an Archbishop), he recalled to His Excellency His Excellency's gift for seeing "misfortunes before they come in order to avert them." And then he had to say that whatever had been done before, it was not enough. He gave details and statistics, and labored to bring into the remote mind of authority an image of the space, the sparsity of mankind, and the poverty, of New Mexico. "There can be no remedy except to increase the number of people, so that everywhere," he said in dignity and courage, "when the offender arrives he will find the defender."

And then he asked for fifty more soldiers to assign to frontier posts, and fifty to be garrisoned in Santa Fe. He anticipated the recoil waves of such a demand, and cushioned them by quoting earlier decrees of the Crown, variously dated 1602, 1664, 1670, 1671. He was trying to influence bureaucracy with its own methods and styles of argument.

But to no avail.

On May 16, 1679, a reply from the government found his frantic appeals "not sufficiently convincing," and pointed out that only three years had passed since His Majesty had granted earlier aid. In view of this, the new requested relief would, it was feared, seem to His Majesty "to be a useless and unnecessary expense." Fray Francisco's poor wilderness reality had run into abstract policy at the viceregal capital. However, the government mused, when looked at closely there was one aspect of the matter which might be referred to Madrid after all. The New Mexican requirements were actually in two categories—one, the mission alms which were granted every triennium as a matter of course; the other, the military aid newly asked for, and on which all else seemed perhaps to revolve. Having approved military aid three years before on its own authority, with later approval by the Crown, the viceregal court was at this time unwilling to assume the responsibility for assigning more soldiers and their pay to New Mexico. Still, it would forward the inquiry to Madrid, and leave the decision, this time, to His Majesty.

Fray Francisco was left with only his mission caravan to outfit. He spent the summer buying and packing and loading. Again he hoped to be in Santa Fe in six months, and with twenty-eight wagons and small herds of animals whose count he would increase with purchases among the ranches of the trail, he left Mexico City on September 30, 1679. Heaven only knew what was being done with his petition for armed assistance against the human troubles of the north. He marched without the usual meagre protection himself. Heaven only knew what he would find when he came to the river, after months of travel at the pace of the slowest hoofs in his care.

From Parral, the capital of the province of Nueva Vizcaya south of New Mexico, he wrote to Governor Otermín at Santa Fe by courier to tell him of the failure to get new additional military aid; but assured him that he was coming with full wagons, though slowly. He expected to reach the Rio del Norte in August.

When he saw it from the south bank in that month, the waters

were high and he could not cross, but not too high to prevent a detachment of twenty-seven soldiers commanded by Pedro de Leiva to ford the
stream and report to him. They had been ordered to meet him and escort
him to Santa Fe by Governor Otermín. The cargo was too precious to
risk in any way. Too much could befall an unprotected food train. By
the muddy river in flood, at the church and settlement of Our Lady of
Guadalupe of the Pass of the Northern River, Fray Francisco and his
wagons and Pedro de Leiva and his soldiers waited till they could cross
to the north together. They were patient, for the rhythm of travel was
entirely timed by conditions of nature, and rivers rose when snow melted
in far mountains or storms broke on the dry tributaries. They were among
friends, for there were several friars and a number of lay families clustered about the big mission. If one day was much like another, that was
what their world was made of and they were at home in it.

But early in the morning of August 25, 1680, two Indian couriers
appeared at the Pass from across the river, and going to the convent
asked for Fray Francisco, and gave him two letters, and reading them
he saw that what he had so labored to save, the Spanish world of the
Rio del Norte, was lost.

29.

The Terror

He sent for the officers of the escort from Santa Fe. At eight o'clock
they appeared in the cell he occupied in the Guadalupe mission. Showing the two letters he told who had sent them. One was from Fray Diego
de Mendoza, the pastor at Socorro, up the river, and it enclosed another
from a man named Juan Severino Rodríguez de Suballe, a farmer in the
Downriver district. Suballe's letter was shocking. The Indians of the
pueblos had risen, the farming families of the Downriver were driven
away and were coming south looking for safety. Haciendas like those

of the Anayas and the Carbajals were destroyed and everyone on them
killed. The people from Bernalillo were able to escape and were marching with the rest down the valley. Nobody was left above Sandía, and
below Sandía everyone fell in with the refugee column as it passed.
Suballe did not know what was happening at Santa Fe, or whether the
governor were alive or dead, but he thought it most likely that he was
dead. He wrote his letter on August eighteenth at Tomé.

Fray Diego de Mendoza had received it on the twentieth, and
immediately forwarded it to Fray Francisco at El Paso. In his note, Fray
Diego asked for relief in the way of food and protection by soldiers. He
proposed an armed march to Santa Fe "to see if all who are in the town
have perished, for it is not right to leave them to their fate." He went on
to tell that he knew of four friars already murdered in the uprising, and
he wondered about many others. He ended by saying that among the
refugees there were many small children, and everyone, women and children included, was travelling on foot.

The officers fingered the letters, and spoke of "the disaster which
has threatened so many times." Their families were in the north. None
of them knew what might have befallen them. Pedro de Leiva, "General
of the kingdom and commander of twenty-seven men" in the armed
escort at El Paso, became the spokesman, and asked Fray Francisco for
permission to take the letters away and discuss them with the soldiers
in a formal meeting, for he recognized "the common desire to proceed
juridically." Fray Francisco approved the request. There was much wild
feeling and grief, and, as he said later, "The confusion . . . that has
passed over my small forces since eight o'clock in the morning of the
25th could not be described on many reams of paper."

At nine o'clock the call for a war council went out. At ten, it
assembled, with the soldiery and Fray Francisco attending. General
de Leiva read the fatal letters aloud. Discussion followed. The first desire
of everyone was to go to the rescue of the refugees on the road, and then
of the Governor and all in the capital, if further news should justify it.
As far as they could estimate matters now, if everyone north of Sandía
was lost, then the Governor and the whole council and thirty-six priests
out of forty were dead. This left a vital consideration unanswered: who
was the government, and where? Without organized heads, there was
no kingdom. Suffering as they were, and hungry for action that would
relieve both the victimized population and their own feelings, the little
knot of Spaniards at the Pass that day must restore first of all the comfort and the propriety of the Two Majesties, which had come to such

grief. Fray Francisco proposed an election to be held the same day in which a provisional governor would be elected, whom he would serve, whoever was elected, as "his Majesty's humblest vassal."

He made his pledge sternly, to set an example, for he saw that there were some who opposed the election "not from dislike of the person elected but for private reasons." He saw jealousy and possibly anarchy looming. "Certain interested individuals" asked why a governor should be elected. Fray Francisco answered them grimly, "in a clear voice, in the presence of all," so that the more who heard him the better:

"So that, in case by some chance any of the same ones who cast their votes should fall short in the duties of vassal and in military obedience, he who may be elected by your honors yourselves may execute the offender summarily, according to military usage and without wasting a great deal of paper in writing, for unless an officer with sufficient authority goes, it will be impossible, in case the governor is dead, to avoid the inconveniences that will arise from every one wishing to be the head."

This appeared to answer the question, and given pause, all agreed upon the proper course, and the election was called for the afternoon.

Then before adjourning, Fray Francisco launched the first of his practical plans to succor the victims. The wagons were to be unloaded immediately of their long-stowed Mexico cargo, and emergency supplies were to be packed in them. Space was to be left for exhausted boys and girls and women to ride in. Two hundred head of cattle were to be driven ahead to afford extra provisions. Forced marches were to be laid out. He would go himself as chaplain and take along four other friars "experienced in hardships." All agreed with his vigorous proposals, and the meeting broke up to set them in motion.

Between one and two o'clock that afternoon a drum rolled and a trumpet flourished, "according to military usage," and the party reassembled for the election. It was quickly over, with unanimous votes for General de Leiva. Fray Francisco sent for a chair, and seated the new provisional governor in it. All then paid homage and swore loyalty. With that, the General was offered "a baton of wood with a blue ribbon as a sign of his election as chief. After making very courteous responses and admitting himself to be the most unworthy member of the group, he received it, in the name of his Majesty, our king and lord, Charles II, whom God keep." By order of the new governor, three volleys were fired.

For the next three days the wagons were unloaded and loaded, and the nature of the first relief debated. The soldiers unencumbered could ride twice as far in a day as the wagons could travel. The first thought of everyone was to rescue the Governor at Santa Fe and put down the revolt by military action. Leiva was to order the refugees whom he met to hurry on to El Paso, sending a small armed escort with them, while he and the rest of his men drove ahead northward for the capital. Wagonloads of relief supplies would go out from El Paso to meet the colonists.

Leiva's soldiery had brought servants and horse-handlers with them from Santa Fe. These—mostly young men—were now armed by Fray Francisco with harquebuses, so that with Leiva's original twenty-seven, and the newly armed fifty-one, the armed force numbered seventy-eight. Fray Francisco provisioned them all "generously, for in such cases niggardliness and calculation are not becoming, and so I gave each one what he asked." One man came back three times, but giving no sign the friar let him have what he took, and reflected, "I acted simply and generously, this being my natural inclination." The soldiers were each equipped with two pounds of powder and a hundred shot. If there was not enough armor to go around for every man and horse, the detachment still had eleven entire sets of armor for horses, and a number of helmets and coats of mail for men. There was a reserve supply of four thousand shot and two casks of powder.

By order of the provisional governor, whom he had sworn to obey, Fray Francisco was not permitted to march with the soldiery, but was to remain at El Paso, for two reasons. One was that he would best be able to succor the refugees as they began to arrive at the Guadalupe Mission. The other was that news of the revolt in the north having reached the local Indians, there was danger of uprisings about El Paso and to the south. If any broke out, General de Leiva thought the Father Quartermaster would be the man to control them. So he stayed behind when the column moved out on August thirtieth. "All are going absolutely raging," noted Fray Francisco. "I believe under God that each one must be reckoned as ten men." All knew in sickening detail what Indian warfare meant. According to what news they had received, many of the officers and men had lost everything in the north—Leiva his wife, three daughters, three sons, eight grandchildren, and a farm; another officer, his mother, three sisters, and much property; another, his wife and children at home. They went over the high waters of the river to take back what was left to them and to avenge what was gone forever.

At the mission, the work of disaster relief went on. The friars and their laymen ground corn, and prepared dried beef, and made bis-

cuits; and as rations for the enemy, they went on making shot. Fray
Francisco was everywhere, and his thoughts were far ahead. He saw that
there was danger that the colonists, on arriving at El Paso, might not
be content to stop there, collect themselves, and undertake what was
needed to restore themselves in their kingdom. He feared that they
would instead go right on south, through New Biscay, to their old source
of life and tradition in Mexico. The entire north would be lost to the
Two Majesties. It was a calamitous problem, and its solution was complicated, but he did his best to solve it.

His labors cost him peace of mind and health. He said he knew
He wrote to the governor of New Biscay, asking for "a dozen
vagrants" to help in the defense of the Pass if uprisings occurred. He
informed him of the danger that Indian revolt might quickly spread
to the south, with the loss of northern Mexico. He wrote to the Viceroy
in Mexico City outlining the same argument, and begged that the provisional governor be confirmed in office, so that order and continuity in
the life of the kingdom would be assured. He pointed out to the Viceroy
that the vital need was to detain and reform the colony at El Paso. The
governor must have the authority to command people to stay. If it were
not done at El Paso, which was "the key," with "lands and water sufficient for a large settlement," then revolt could be looked for in all the
Indian nations about, and all Spain would be lost in the northern
provinces There was one difficulty he had to mention—it was a legal
one, but he thought it had a legal remedy. El Paso was not in the jurisdiction of New Mexico. If her residents, fleeing south, entered New
Biscay across the Rio del Norte, then the Governor of New Mexico
would have no authority over them. They would be then under the baton
of the governor of New Biscay. It occurred to the Father Quartermaster
to propose that the Viceroy issue a decree stating that though colonists
from New Mexico might sojourn in New Biscay, they would still be
under the legal jurisdiction of the Governor of New Mexico. There was
no other way to quarantine the revolt and save the colony. Otherwise,
he could promise political, moral and religious disaster. It was a persuasive case and he sent it off with a prayer that the decision would come
his way.

His labors cost him peace of mind and health. He said he knew
neither what he was saying nor doing. He had no news from the north
for days, and then on September eighth he received letters by runner
from Don Alonso García, the lieutenant general of New Mexico, who
was a resident of the pastoral valley of the haciendas, and from Fray
Antonio de Sierra who was travelling with him. Fray Francisco devoured

the letters, for they brought more news of the terrifying upheaval in the north.

The news was better than he expected. Governor Otermín was alive, having escaped with a large number of families from the Upriver district, and together they were marching, hungry, in rags and exhausted, down the valley to overtake the families that had fled from the Downriver. Fray Francisco was overjoyed to "taste the sweetness" of this information. The two parties of refugees were referred to as the First Division, which was García's, now waiting for the Governor at Fray Cristóbal at the head of the Dead Man's March; and the Second Division, composed of the Upriver people under Otermín.

The story was enlarged with sorrowful details. The Governor was wounded, along with many of his men. There had been a warning at Santo Domingo on August the eighth, and on Saturday the tenth the rebellion broke into the open in all the northern pueblos at the same time. The Governor and his people were besieged in the palace at Santa Fe, and the town was burned about them by the rebels. Eventually the Governor led his forces in an escape from the palace and began his destitute march downriver. As far as they knew all the churches had been destroyed and their vestments and vessels profaned. The Father President had been killed at Santo Domingo. Only eleven priests had escaped. Three hundred Indians had been killed in battles and the count of Spanish dead now showed seventy-six. Both the First and Second Divisions were desperately in need of food and other supplies, and the Father Quartermaster was begged to prepare relief as soon as possible. The Governor had asked that the request be relayed to him at El Paso without delay.

The whole story was not yet told, and Fray Francisco longed for certain further details and instructions. If there had been some warning given of the impending revolt, how had it come, and what had been done as a consequence? How long was the siege in the Palace at Santa Fe and how had the defenders escaped? How was it possible for all the pueblos to rise at the same moment? What a conspiracy. Who had organized it? If Santa Fe went up in flames was there anything left? If the columns of refugees came down the river how had they managed to travel through Indian country and survive? What was the Father Quartermaster to do to relieve the travellers? Where were they going? Were they going to stop somewhere up the river and "make a stand"? What was the outlook for the future? He wrote to Governor Otermín immediately.

News of the Governor's survival and of the escape of the Upriver
families was "very delightful to me," he wrote, "at a time when I and
my brothers had been mourning for you." He had never ceased to hope
that his patron Saint Anthony "would protect so many poor people . . .
from the infernal fury of paganism." As for exactly what he was now
supposed to do to help alleviate the tragedy, he wrote: ". . . I find myself confused by not having information of your lordship's decision, in
order to know what I ought to do." Once given orders, he was ready to
act, for "I have made all arrangements and the wagons are ready to
leave." He wished the Governor would come with a guard to meet him
so that they could "consult on some matters pertaining to the service of
both Majesties," and explained that he planned to leave for Mexico to
tell the viceroy and the government what had taken place in the river
kingdom, "for not everything should be told in writing, nor is it possible
to do so." He added, "I find myself in very poor health," and closed
with a solemn assurance: "Your lordship may believe that you are among
the chosen."

On the same day Fray Francisco wrote this letter, the Governor
with his people arrived at a place near Fray Cristóbal. From there the
Governor wrote Fray Francisco further news and asked him to come
immediately with the wagons. General de Leiva and his men had met
the Governor, and he was sending them back to the Pass to serve as
escort to the relief train. The letter took several days to reach the
Guadalupe mission. On September sixteenth the Father Quartermaster
had his wagons in motion heading up the river toward the ford called
La Salineta. He watched them start on their lumbering way, and as he
watched he wrote to the Viceroy with the latest reports, announcing that
he was sending supplies north, and was going himself. "I shall travel day
and night, since for the sake of speed each wagon carries less than half
an ordinary load." He was sorry that he could not take all thirty of his
carts, but "the men belonging to six of them ran away last night, apparently having little liking for going to war." Alas, they stole some horses
as they went. He was prepared to throw his great influence into the
struggle to reassure the fugitive colonists, to encourage them to make a
halt at a suitable place and preserve the kingdom, and "to placate and
persuade them" he was taking in the wagons "a very handsome portion"
of goods and provisions. Was this a device? He shrugged. With all sympathy, it was as well to recognize human nature. He glanced up from
his pages and saw that the wagons were ready to cross the river, and
wrote that he must "go to overtake them," and closed by kissing his

excellency's hands. He sealed his packet, gave it to the courier, sent him off, and went down to the river to direct a troublesome job.

The river was still in flood from late summer rains, but far away across its course an urgent need allowed of no further delay. The lowlands by the river were flooded on both sides of the current. Twenty-four wagons stood waiting for him. His drivers looked to him for instructions. If the long drought was broken, it was a mercy, though perhaps one too violent, like many acts of wide nature in that country of narrow valley, hard desert and bare, cloud-making mountains. The carts were all but mired and those men riding horses sank in the mud to the animals' bellies. But the wagons had to move and if nobody else would move them the Father Quartermaster would show the way. He ordered six spans of mules to be harnessed to the first wagon, entered it himself, and taking up the reins drove the mules forward into the flowing seep of the south bank. The mud dragged at his solid cotton-wood wheels. Helped by some Indian swimmers he lurched into the channel where the sailing heavy current pulled at his cart with wild power. The mules struggled. Water poured over the bed of the wagon, and in midstream the wagon stuck. Its high wheels were entirely under water. It was two o'clock in the afternoon. Those watching saw the brown ruffled water breaking about the stranded wagon and knew that the Father Quartermaster was in danger.

At that moment appeared on the muddy north bank a small party of horsemen. They were thin and exhausted, having travelled from upriver fifty-four leagues in three days, subsisting off dates of the yucca palm. They were Governor Otermín, and twelve soldiers, and Fray Francisco's courier. They saw the mules in the river barely holding their footing on the river bed. The animals would drown there. Fray Francisco cut them loose of their harness and they scrambled for the bank. He was alone in the flood.

Throwing off their clothes some of the Governor's men swam out to the wagon and found their precarious footing beside it. They lifted Fray Francisco out and took him on their shoulders to the north shore and the Governor. The Two Majesties were united in disaster. Nothing now concerned them but to work together for the rescue of the two divisions of starving and frightened people who were coming down the river. The Father Quartermaster in spite of his narrow escape from the flood insisted that all the wagons even at the risk of losing some must attempt the crossing. The Governor proposed instead that supplies be reloaded on pack animals, and this was done. Men worked all the rest of daylight swimming horses across with packs on them. In the packs were maize, flour, chocolate, sugar and biscuits. Seeing how the loading went, Fray Francisco said, "I do not know whether gold dust will ever be bestowed in the pockets of the bearers as carefully as were the biscuits." With nightfall a squad with pack mules was sent northward to meet the hungry. The friar's wagon, from the middle of the river, was brought finally to the north shore and its cargo laid out to dry. On the next day another pack train was sent out, and more provisions were brought to the north shore. For fifteen days the Governor and the friar remained in camp there. It was not long until the refugees began to arrive in little groups. Fray Francisco, moved with pity and horror as he saw them, could not find words to express himself at "such great unhappiness and pitiful tragedy, with the need corresponding to the great numbers, and the poor women and children on foot and unshod, of such a hue that they looked like the dead. . . ."

When they had eaten and rested a little the people came to the Father Quartermaster with a petition. His worst fears were justified. Appalled by the disaster that had befallen them, they declared that it was impossible to stay in the kingdom. They begged him as a merciful minister of God to see them on their way south to Mexico. In their misery they were even arrogant. How long could they be expected to sit on the riverbank barely existing on the supplies there?

Fray Francisco's foresight was what saved him, and the kingdom, even as he was wondering what to say to the desperate population. For before they had finished with their appeal to him, he was handed a dispatch from the Governor of New Biscay, written in reply to his report of the revolt and the dangers that followed it. It was "a most strict dispatch." Fray Francisco ordered a roll on the drums, and when all had gathered to hear, the communication from New Biscay was read aloud. It stated that any refugees from New Mexico who passed from that kingdom without a written permission from Governor Otermín would be ordered by all civil officials of New Biscay to return to New Mexico under "penalty of his life and of treason to the king." Any who resisted were to be delivered to the Governor of New Biscay for punishment. The fleeing colonists were trapped. It was a hard condition. But Fray Francisco said, "We have come to the point where we must act or abandon everything." And abandonment, he knew, would "necessarily expose the missions at one blow," not only those in New Mexico, but all other missions already established on the lower river, in New Biscay and in

Sonora. "Thus is seen," he declared, "the importance of maintaining the people at that place as a check, and of controlling them."

For the time being, his energetic grasp of policy prevailed. To gather enough additional supplies soldiers were sent to neighboring settlements to buy what they could. He induced Governor Otermín to ford the river on his horse and inspect the stores at Guadalupe so that he might order proper distribution of what there was there—grain, beef and mutton. Gradually order was restored to the wretched company. The colony took a look at itself in a three-day count during which all passed muster, identified themselves and told off their poor possessions, and those who could signed their names.

Gregorio Valdés "passed muster with five horses useless for service, an harquebus, a sword, a dagger, and a leather jacket. He is married, with two sons, a little girl, and an Indian servant woman. He was robbed by the enemy; and he signed it. . . ."

Sargento Luis Granillo "passed muster with nine very hard-used horses. . . . He is married, without children, and has three grown brothers able to bear arms, but having none, nor any horses. . . . He was robbed by the enemy; and he signed it. . . ."

Captain Alonso del Rio, "married and without children, passed muster with three lean and worn-out horses. . . . He was robbed by the enemy; and he signed it. . . ."

Behind their count was the full story of the shock that had struck them all in the events of the revolt, which Fray Francisco heard in detail for the first time from the Governor and others.

For some time there had been no disturbances among the converted Indians or even among the heathen Apaches. Nevertheless, the Governor had ordered repairs on the crumbling Palace at Santa Fe, and the walls were strengthened, the missing gates and doors restored, until the whole government house and its corrals could safely accommodate more than a thousand people, five thousand head of sheep and goats, four hundred horses and mules, and three hundred head of beef cattle "without crowding."

Late in the day of August 9, the Indian governors of Pecos and Taos appeared at the Palace to see the Governor. They told him that they had been asked by Indians from Tesuque pueblo to join in a general rebellion of all the pueblos. They stated that they "now regarded the Spaniards as their brothers" and did not wish to join in the revolt, but came instead to give warning. The Governor thanked them and told them to go home and "remain quiet." He then sent warnings to the officials in all Spanish districts, and especially to the lieutenant general Don Alonso García, at his farms in the Downriver, the district where most settlers lived. He asked them to muster aid and come to the defense of the capital. Many on receiving the message did not put much faith in it. The country seemed quiet in the hot summer.

But the next morning, St. Lawrence's Day, as the Governor was on his way to Mass, a man named Pedro Hidalgo came to him and gasped out a dreadful story. The Indians of Tesuque only nine miles north of Santa Fe had that morning risen and murdered their pastor who said to them just before, "What is this, children; are you mad? Do not disturb yourselves; I will help you and die a thousand deaths for you." They tried to kill Hidalgo himself. He had seen it all. The Indians sacked the convent and drove all its horses and cattle into the mountains. The Governor sent a squad of soldiers to Tesuque to verify the tale and to put down any disobedience there. They returned on the same day to say that the report was true, and that other outrages had happened besides. The pastors of Nambé and San Ildefonso were dead, and whole families in the country places had been massacred, including Doña Petronila de Salas with ten sons and daughters, and the churches had been profaned and the farmhouses robbed.

(Thomé Dominguez de Mendoza passed muster who with his sons was "robbed by the enemy of cattle, houses, crops . . . The rebels killed thirty-eight Spanish persons, all being his daughters, grandchildren, sons-in-law, sisters, nephews, nieces and sisters-in-law. . . . He signs it. . . ." Pedro de Leiva—"The enemy killed his wife, two grown daughters, and two soldier sons, three grandchildren and a daughter-in-law . . . and of thirty servants whom he had, the enemy left him three, robbing him and his sons of all their property. He signed it. . . ." Captain Juan Luís, the elder, "with a worn-out mare and a broken harquebus. . . . He is married, has a grown son without any equipment, two children—correction, three—and a servant. He was robbed. . . . and he signed it. . . .")

Again the Governor sent out warnings and ordered local officials to gather their people together for common defense, and to bring as many as possible to find haven in the Palace. All day word of disaster poured in. Santa Clara had risen, Pecos and Taos too, in spite of the warning from their leaders, and Galisteo and Santo Domingo. Seven friars were killed in those places, and many civil officials and families. No word came from the lieutenant general. The Governor thought he might be dead with most of the residents of the Downriver. To Taos he sent an armed squad to save the residents and the pastors, and also protect the herds of cattle and horses that might be found there. They returned to tell that the Taos and Picuries pueblos, allied with Apaches, had already done their part in the uprising. Three priests were murdered and many families.

It was clear then that the revolt had been planned as a coordinated effort, and the Governor was certain that the Indians meant to destroy every Spaniard in the kingdom. He summoned all who could to come to the Palace. By Monday night, the twelfth of August, many people had come to take refuge from Indians who now when reasoned with said they wanted "to die and go to hell."

At nine the next morning, across the Santa Fe creek in the fields around the chapel of Saint Michael moved what the watchers barricaded in the Palace dreaded to see. Rattling through the cornfields came a painted host, some on horseback, some on foot, making cries for blood. They were armed with native weapons and with Spanish harquebuses, lances, swords and padded jackets which they had taken from the dead. There were dwellings in the fields and these the invading Indians entered and sacked, making barracks of them where they would await reinforcements from other pueblos. One of them was an Indian called John whom the Spaniards knew. The Governor sent an escort of soldiers to bring him to the Palace under safe-conduct. Riding his horse, and wearing about his waist a red taffeta ribbon which had been torn from the missal of Galisteo, he was outfitted with a full complement of Spanish arms. Carrying two crosses, one white, one red, he came to speak to the Governor in the patio of the Palace.

"John," said the Governor, "why have you too gone crazy when you are an Indian who speaks our tongue, who are so intelligent, who have lived all your life in the capital with us, where I placed so much confidence in you? And now look at you: a leader of the Indian rebels!"

"They elected me their captain," replied John. "They sent these two crosses to show you. This one"—the white—"means peace. And the other one, war."

"Well?"

"If you choose the white there will be no war but you must all leave the country. If you choose the red, you must all die, for we are many and you are few. Having killed so many Spaniards and priests, we will kill all the rest."

The Governor spoke to him "very persuasively," saying:

"Now John, you and the rest of your followers are all Catholic Christians. How do you expect to live without your friars? Even if you have committed so many crimes already, there can still be pardon, if you will return to obedience. Now go back and tell your friends, in my name, what I have said, and tell them they should accept it, and go to their homes quietly. And then come back and tell me what they say."

John left and returned. His answer was dishonest, asking that all classes of Indians in the Spanish service be given up, that his wife and children be allowed to join him, and that all Apache men and women who were prisoners of the Spanish be released, as Apaches among the rebels were asking for them. Lacking these things, war would follow immediately. But there were no Apaches among them, and the Governor knew it. John was only playing for time until allies arrived to join him from Taos, Picuries and the Tewa pueblos. The Governor dismissed him to go back and say that unless the outrages in the fields of San Miguel ceased at once, the soldiers would be ordered forth to attack. John went back across the creek with this word, and when he spoke it, the Indians joined in a howl of rage, and rang the bells of Saint Michael's, and blew trumpets, in defiance, and moved toward the Palace.

The soldiers met them in a battle that lasted almost all day, driving them back to the houses in the fields, which were finally burned about them, so that they fled to the foothills. But as they fled, the Indian allies arrived from the Tewas, and Taos, and Picuries, who attacked from another side, and when darkness fell, occupied a high place overlooking the Palace. Many Indian dead lay about. There was one soldier dead in the garrison, with fifteen wounded.

(". . . passed muster with ten lean beasts . . . the enemy killed thirty-two persons of his family; . . . passed muster . . . two sons, naked and without equipment . . . eight more small children; . . . passed muster . . . with twelve children, including four sons of military age, all naked and extremely poor; . . . passed muster . . . the enemy carried off his wife and daughter; . . . on foot, naked, without arms or anything except himself. He signed it. . . .")

On the fourteenth and fifteenth of August the enemy kept to the high ground and the soldiers under the command of the Governor patrolled all day to save the town from being burned. On the following day, Friday the sixteenth, the Indians attacked in a mass of twenty-five hundred warriors, having received more reinforcements during the night. They took positions in all the houses and roads, and in swift moves broke the ditch that brought water from the creek to the Palace, and

set fire to the parish church in the plaza and several houses. The garrison
made sallies to regain the ditch but failed, and retired within the Palace
walls. About noon the Indians swarmed against the Palace chapel with
its tower at one end of the building, and tried to burn it. Facing hot
vollies from the Spanish firearms in the hands of the rebels, the whole
garrison went out to save the chapel, and fought all afternoon. By nightfall almost every soldier was wounded, and when the army barricaded
itself once more it was to suffer the first miseries of thirst.

With gunshot, arrows and stones, the Indians attacked on Saturday the seventeenth, shouting that now there was no hope for the
garrison, because the Apaches were coming to join the siege. In one of
the Spanish sorties of that day the Governor was wounded, ·twice in the
face by arrows, once in the breast by a shot from a harquebus. Late in
the day the Indians took both positions at the gates where the royal brass
cannon were trained on the ends of the plaza. To keep these from being
turned on their own walls, the Governor ordered a desperate sally to
recover them and bring them into the patio. Guarding the cannon all
night, the soldiers fought off attacks. The Indians raised a song of victory,
believing it all but won. As the Spaniards watched in helpless anguish,
the whole town of Santa Fe excepting houses fortified by the rebels was
set afire, and pagan chants mingled with the smoke and flame, and the
parish church was burned, and its fittings thrown about, and the "whole
villa was a torch." The Indians mockingly sang the Latin liturgy.

There was nothing to do on Sunday but make a final effort. After
a night of fear and thirst for the thousand people in the Palace where
many animals were dead without feed or water, and following Mass at
dawn, the garrison in a last show of strength threw itself at the Indians
in the streets with resolve to win or lose all. Their spirit triumphed, for
masses of Indians, after hot fighting at first, began to break and run,
leaving only scattered resistance in fortified houses which were burned
about their defenders, who either died or were taken prisoner. Three
hundred Indians were dead in the capital after the battles of the week.

Hurriedly the ditch was repaired and water was run into the
Palace courtyard for the people and the animals. Freedom was restored
—but little else. The city was a ruin. There was no food supply. The
Indians had withdrawn but might come again. Nothing had been heard
from the Downriver, where the great estates were, whose people would
surely have come to the rescue had they been able. Dealing with forty-
seven rebel prisoners, the Governor found out that the revolt had been
ordered by the gods of Po-he-yemu, who promised to kill instantly any

Indian refusing to join in it. Thus all agreed to destroy all male Spaniards, even to suckling boys, leaving only women and girls. All remaining Spanish men were still to be killed under orders of the powers in the northern underworld. As for the results of the insurrection—the prisoners reported that from Taos to Isleta there was nobody left of the Spanish colony, excepting those who had gathered in the Palace at Santa Fe to defend themselves. The information was officially noted, and the forty-seven prisoners were executed.

At Isleta, as far as could be learned, the families of the Down-river had gathered and fortified themselves. The kingdom was divided in two, and the Governor saw that it was his duty to unite it again. There was no hope of doing this at Santa Fe. After discussions with his clergy and his staff, he resolved for "the better service of both Majesties and the safety of the people, arms, horses, and cattle which have remained where it is not possible to maintain them," to abandon the capital and to march "in military formation" to Isleta. There was nothing to take with them except a trust in Providence, and they left "without a crust of bread or a grain of wheat or maize, and with no other provision for the convoy of so many people except four hundred animals and two carts belonging to private persons, and, for food, a few sheep, goats, and cows."

They came down off the great highlands of Santa Fe on August twenty-fourth and sought the river with its narrow boskied passage below the desert benches, lava flows and mountains that looked down upon it. The country was pale with heat as the fugitives hastened (but nightmarishly at foot-pace) down the river. They were not alone in the land. As they struggled southward, by day and evening, they saw signal smokes on the mesas above the river. They saw lines of Indian warriors drawn up to watch their going. In the dawns the watchers were still there as the column moved starving down the valley. Apart from a few skirmishes there were no attacks; only an alien watchfulness between rock and sky that made them shiver. Among their most grievous losses was the loss of a common ground of understanding between them and the people who had been given to them, and then fought over, in guardianship.

Yet atrocity and delicacy were bafflingly mixed. When the refugees reached the sacerdotal seat of Santo Domingo, they found a common grave holding the bodies of three friars, and signs of fighting all about, and the bodies of five lay Spaniards; but the church, the convent and the sacristy were closed, and on being opened revealed that all the sacred articles were undisturbed—six silver chalices, a hand basin, a salver, seven cruets for wine and water, a thurible, a vessel, a lamp, and "other things of silver." One of the refugee chaplains took possession of these things.

They came to one after another of the estates downriver where in the thick-walled cool rooms still lay the naked dead bodies of families.

(". . . enemy killed two of her nephews, and more than thirty relatives. She does not sign because of not knowing how; . . . a widower with one child three or four years old; . . . robbed of all his property and the enemy carried off or killed his wife, three children, twenty-eight servants, another woman, and a son of his. He signed it; . . . with harquebus and sword. He is more than eighty years old, with a family of nine persons. He signed it. . . .")

During a halt near the hacienda of the Anaya family an Indian escaped from the rebels came to give information to the Governor. Asked why the pueblos had risen, he answered that "they were tired of the work they had to do for the Spaniards and the clergy," who "did not allow them to plant, to do other things for their own needs; and that being weary they had rebelled." As to incidents of the uprising, he spoke of priests who had been killed, churches and homes destroyed, and three Spanish women who had been taken captive—they were of the Leiva family—and used until word came that men from the pueblo where they were held had been killed and wounded in the battle at Santa Fe, whereupon the three women, Lucía, María and Juana, had been killed in retaliation. He himself had had his wife taken away as he escaped to join the Governor.

On the twenty-sixth of August the column reached Sandía. The church was closed. Within, they found wreckage. Everything had been broken and stolen, and the nave piled with straw which had been set on fire, but the choir was all that burned. There were brief skirmishes with Indians at Sandía and below. The column crawled on, longing for the safety of numbers and of the provisions which the Downriver people could surely afford them once they were reunited at Isleta. They saw many estates in ruins on both sides of the swollen river, including that of Don Luís Carbajal on the east bank. When they came upon a mounted Indian in their path, they captured him for interrogation. He was an old man over eighty who came from the place of Alameda. Their hopes sank at what he finally had to say.

First, as to why the revolt had happened, he declared that for as long as he could remember, the Indians had talked bitterly among themselves of what the Spaniards had tried to take from them—the ways of the ancestors, the right ways that had "come up with us," the power and the magic belonging to those "who know how." By these were meant the practices which to the Spanish were sorceries and idolatries, and to the Indians, safety through power and magic. The revolt itself had been secretly talked of for twelve years. What it was moved by went back as early as the first Spanish day in the kingdom. He himself had not taken part in any of the outrages.

Last, as to whether he knew anything of a gathering of Spanish families, soldiers and religious at Isleta down the river, he said yes, some days before a number of friars and Spanish families had come to Isleta, but they had not stayed long. Gathering up everything they could take, they had gone away down the valley leaving the town empty.

This was a hard blow, and perhaps even, in the official view, an act of insubordination had occurred. The Governor pushed on with his party to Isleta, and there indeed found nothing and no one. All that could be done now was to hurry on to overtake the first division before all in the second fell from starvation. The Governor sent four soldiers ahead with a message to Lieutenant General García to halt his march and await the rest of the fugitive kingdom. The Lieutenant General was to return to report to the Governor.

On September sixth García appeared from the south and met the Governor at the farm of the Valencia family, a short distance above Socorro. The Governor ordered him in arrest and gave the signal for legal deliberations to be held. Why had he not come to the rescue at Santa Fe with men and supplies from the Downriver? Why had he left Isleta instead of waiting to determine whether he could help those who might be following? Once again the kingdom, now in its last rags, was torn within. García, experienced in the ways of official life, came prepared to defend himself with thirteen written folios of depositions, properly witnessed. All that he had done he had done according to his best judgment and in the interests of both Majesties. To begin with, he had never received any of the three appeals for help sent to him from Santa Fe by the Governor. The people of his own district had besieged him with cries for help, and he had done his best to bring everyone together for common defense. He and his sons had tried to get word through to Santa Fe but without success. When they heard that everyone in the north had been murdered and the settlements destroyed, he and his wisest advisers had agreed that they must try to save the kingdom by saving themselves, and had gone south along the river. His patriotism had been sufficiently proved in the past. Let him, he petitioned, be cleared of charges and given his freedom.

The Governor studied the case, and in the end was convinced that his lieutenant general had acted properly under the circumstances. He ordered him cleared and released. The march was resumed. García's division was encamped at Fray Cristóbal, on the river, at the northern end of the Dead Man's March, where mountains forced the river to turn west and the land-travellers east.

Later in the same day something was seen on the southern horizon. It was a cloud of dust, and for a little while caused concern; but before long the marchers saw that it was a troop of more than forty mounted soldiers, accompanied by four friars, bringing emergency rations under Pedro de Leiva, now no longer provisional governor. When the two parties met, the soldiers fired their harquebuses in a joyful volley. Together all moved on southward toward Fray Cristóbal and the other division.

A day or so later the Governor received a letter from Fray Diego de Parraga who was at Fray Cristóbal, asking one of two things: either let the Governor send ahead enough provisions for the fifteen hundred people at Fray Cristóbal, for they were starving, or order them to go at once to El Paso without waiting for him. Fray Diego received a sharp reply. Where, asked the Governor, would he get enough food in the desert to feed anybody in addition to the thousand mouths of his own wretched division? Already "straining every nerve" to join the other division and thus provide safety to all in united numbers against the Apaches, how could it be asked now that the first division be allowed to run away—especially, wrote Otermín, when "I am so near to accomplishing the purpose that has brought me, of uniting the two forces. . . . My father, if your reverence wishes to go alone, do what seems best to you, but it is not conducive to the service of God or of his Majesty for that camp to do so. . . ."

At Fray Cristóbal on September thirteenth the forces were united in privation and spirit. The Governor called a council of war to discuss whether they should try to root themselves where they were, but all agreed that in the hardest land in the miserable kingdom they must find nothing but woe, and that the reconquest of the northern river could only be managed after the colony had been reinforced with men and supplies sent from Mexico. While at Fray Cristóbal the Governor received Fray Francisco de Ayeta's urgent request that he hurry south-

ward for consultations, and with his armed escort of twelve men he went
ahead, leaving the column to follow to El Paso, where there were food
and rest, and where the muster could be taken and concluded.

On October third the rolls were closed when "Juan Sanchez
Cabello passed muster on foot with harquebus, leather jacket, and sword
belonging to His Majesty. He is married, with a family of six persons.
He signed it."

Of the twenty-five hundred colonists and servants who had fled
the rebellion, only nineteen hundred and forty-six were recorded on the
rolls taken opposite El Paso. Hundreds had already escaped into Mexico
undetected. But there was official confidence and pride in what remained,
with "a hundred and fifty-five persons capable of bearing arms, including
youths who are expert horsemen, and four hundred and seventy-one
horses and mules; and there are munitions and provisions of meat and
maize." And what if some of the harquebuses are out of repair? "They
can be mended, cleaned, and made useful; and although some soldiers
are without equipment of arms and horses, they can aid and assist one
another in such an important matter in the service of the two Majesties,
they being such good servants of his Majesty, deserving, noble, loyal,
and zealous in the royal service, in imitation of their ancestors, the conquerors and founders. . . ."

It was a busy autumn at the entrance to New Mexico. On October
ninth the Governor moved all his forces to the south bank and settled
them in three camps neighboring the Guadalupe mission. The Father
Quartermaster moved from camp to camp to say Mass, using a little
cart as his church. Everyone thought of the encampments as temporary
bases from which one day to undertake the reconquest of the north;
but no one could say when that might come, though a council of war
decided that it was already too late in that autumn to undertake an
expedition. The colony made a town where they were. Its huts were
"built in an orderly manner, each one living in the house which he has
made with his own hands of sticks and branches," as the Father Quartermaster said. For the time being the kingdom could remain alive at
El Paso, which was now more than a village.

But its larger future depended upon powers, resources and decisions in Mexico. Soldiers and arms were needed to establish a fort at
El Paso. Legal jurisdiction of a governor over his subjects in another
state must be settled. The whole chance for continued existence rested
on how clearly the Viceroy and his government could be made to see the
true dimensions of what had happened on the Rio del Norte. Once

again the Father Quartermaster knew that he must go and work for the
miserable kingdom he had already served so mightily. He had told
them before, and they had not believed him, but had sent him north
with empty hands.

Now in December with a story of shock and blood and horror,
he went to renew his pleadings before the impervious bastions of Spanish
officialdom. He arrived at Mexico City in January, 1681, and hurried to
the government palace. There he was handed a document dated, at
Madrid, June twenty-fifth of the previous year. The paper ordered all
to be done that was necessary to save the river kingdom. It was the royal
reply to his urgent plea of a year and a half ago, when he was moving
heaven and earth—but not the Viceroy—to obtain the means to prevent
the disaster that he had foreseen, and that had come. The Crown document was issued in the name of Charles II, great-grandson of the selfless
procrastinator, Philip II. Four years later, in 1685, in spite of all there
was to tell, it had not yet been answered by the viceregal government
in Mexico City.

30.

Limit of Vision

The thoughts of the settlers at El Paso could not but turn toward
the north. Their hearts ached when they thought of what had there
befallen so many whom they loved—little sons and daughters, wives,
fathers, grandparents, friends, devoted servants. Remembering life as it
had been, they wondered what it was now. What were the Indians
doing? What was the present image of familiar and beloved places?
Who still lived as captives and what was their lot? The answers lay
beyond the limit of vision to the north. Useless to stare at the horizon
until the sky seemed to be made of slowly moving motes of dusty gold
light. And yet the last thing the majority of settlers wanted to do was

return. It was therefore disconcerting when the Father Quartermaster
arrived at El Paso from Mexico City in September, 1681, with supplies,
a handful of new settlers, and viceregal orders to undertake a re-entry
into New Mexico. The Indians were to be punished and reconverted.
Information was to be forwarded to the royal offices. Not everyone was
as dedicated to duty as Fray Francisco. In Mexico he had been officially
thanked "for the kindness and promptness with which he has acted in
order to maintain and save the said people." He then was notified of
his promotion in the Franciscan Order to the office of Father Quartermaster for the entire western hemisphere, and ordered home to Spain
for discussions. It was high recognition of his tremendous labors. But
when the Viceroy determined on sending supplies back to New Mexico,
it was clear that only Fray Francisco, so well acquainted with the dreadful
conditions in the north, could be confidently trusted to control them.
He must postpone his sailing to assume his new honors in Spain and go
instead to El Paso. The Father Quartermaster replied "that he obeyed
with entire willingness that which he was ordered," and added that he
he would loyally go north even if it cost him his new office in the end.

  With his customary energy and optimism he did all he could to
inspire the settlers in their new orders. But even Governor Otermín
was without enthusiasm, though he scrupulously carried out every proper
detail in ordering the new expedition. He knew that he was poorly
equipped for a major military operation. The viceregal government had
not sent the garrison to found a permanent fort at El Paso, though it
approved the establishment otherwise. The men he had available to
him were for the most part untrained and ill-equipped, and many were
boys, and hardly any wanted to go. A poor example was set by certain
prominent men who failed to volunteer for the march, and refused to
accept the royal issue of farming and building equipment which would
bind them to the duty of reconquest. Such action unloosed another
torrent of legal depositions, charges, defenses. Old sores were raked open
—the very ones who now refused to go were those who on the flight
south before the storm had clutched their own wealth to themselves
refusing to succor their less fortunate fellows. Yet they brazenly demanded royal protection for themselves, their family and their herds.
Some had enough cattle to drive off, illegally, many head into New
Biscay to be sold for private profit. The animals were so sorely needed
to feed the settlers at El Paso that in desperation and contempt the friars
bought them and drove them back to the hungry camps at the Guada-

lupe mission. While the rest starved, such enterprising men now owned "more than they did in the said New Mexico."

Yet somehow the Governor assembled a hundred and forty-six soldiers, a hundred and twelve Indian allies from local tribes, twenty-eight servants, and nine hundred and forty-eight horses, mules and cattle. On November 5, 1681, the silken royal banners were shaken out, trumpets played, and the army crossed the river going north. Without loss of a man, they were back by early February, 1682, with one hundred and three folios of written records of the enterprise.

They found all the pueblos south of Isleta deserted, and many sacred objects partially destroyed. These were gathered up and burned by the Father Quartermaster. As Isleta the Indians were present, and received the column peaceably, coming forth in tears and responding to prayers, and obeying orders to bring forth "the idols, feathers, powders, masks, and every other thing pertaining to their idolatry and superstition" which were "piled in a heap and burned." The Governor sent word ahead by Indian runners to upriver pueblos to stay in their towns and submit. When after two days he received no reply he sent his lieutenant Juan Dominguez de Mendoza with seventy soldiers to investigate. impose discipline, and return to report.

It was a hard winter. Snow and sleet storms swept down the valley. In many a camp firewood was scarce. The troops suffered privation during the whole expedition. Until he reached Cochiti, Mendoza found all pueblos empty except for an occasional old man or woman too feeble to go very far who had been abandoned by their people, and who weeping and bewildered asked for absolution. In the churches there was havoc among the Christian objects, and stores of pagan articles were found in the convent cells. All profaned sacred materials and Indian fetishes were burned. Mendoza's men plundered and burned ten abandoned pueblos.

On the hills signal smokes showed that the Indians were watching the Spanish advance, and at Cochiti, the Indians gathered in defiance. Parleys were opened. The Indians reviled the Spaniards as "horned, bleating he-goats"—a serious insult in Spanish. But gradually the Indian mood softened. A chief came forward and when offered absolution wept for his terrible sins. Plans were made for peaceful return to their pueblos of the Indians who in great numbers had fled to the icy rocks of the mountains. And at last on December eighteenth colonists heard the details of how the revolt had been started, and by whom.

The leader who inspired them all, "who had made them crazy and was like a whirlwind," was the Indian doctor Popé, who had moved from San Juan to Taos, where he talked with the three gods, Caudi, Tilini and Tleume, who had come into the kiva at Taos and were never seen to leave. They ordered him to restore Indian life to the ways of the ancestors, as it had been when all issued out of the sacred entrance lake in the north. Emitting fire from all extremities of their bodies, they told him to make a cord of maguey fibres "and tie some knots in it which would signify the number of days" for each pueblo to "wait before the rebellion." Each knot was a day apart from the next one. The cord was taken to the pueblos by the swiftest young Indian runners. Each pueblo agreeing to the revolt untied its own knot and lit smoke signals and the runners went on to the next. When his son-in-law the Governor of San Juan threatened to reveal the plot to the Spaniards, Popé killed him. Fearing premature exposure from other sources, Popé moved up the date of the rebellion two days and the fury broke out everywhere at once, with Indians crying, "Now the God of the Spaniards who was their father, and Saint Mary who was their mother, and the saints, who were rotten pieces of wood, are dead," and again only the Indian gods lived. The pueblo people were ordered to go to the river and there with the suds of the yucca root to enter and wash away from their skin the touch of baptism, and from their clothes the character of Christians. Popé now lived at Santa Fe in the Palace where he ruled like a governor. The story of the revolt was complete.

Mendoza at Cochiti received agreements to peace pacts from other pueblos. Indians came and wept for the sacraments, and borrowed horses, and gunpowder, and told how in a day or two the pueblos would all be peacefully repopulated. But a former Indian servant of one of the soldiers came to say that all this was deceit. The Indians meant to steal all the Spanish horses, and then at their own convenience massacre the trapped soldiers. The girls of Cochiti were told to go and bathe and scent themselves and on a certain night enter the soldier camp and beguile the men in their flesh until the Indians could come to kill them all. The professions of faith and the tears of penitence were only what the Indians knew the Spaniards wanted to inspire. The whole seventy men were in mortal danger. Mendoza withdrew them and returned to join the Governor in the south.

Through bitter cold and over the riverside country of ruined haciendas Mendoza and Otermín advanced to meet each other, and met in ill will. The Governor believed his lieutenant had not done enough to subjugate the Indians and, above all, had not sent him frequent and proper written reports. Mendoza replied that there had been no time for paper work, and that he stood on his record. The sorry expedition retreated to Isleta. Gathering up three hundred and eighty-five Indians there they took them, restored in faith, to El Paso where the Isletans founded a new pueblo called Isleta del Sur.

The north was still lost. Bitterness and feelings of futility more than ever divided the colony. Even under military discipline the soldiers were lawless. On the winter march to the north and back, though they were ordered to deliver to the Governor all loot or recovered Spanish possessions for proper distribution for the benefit of all, including the original owners, they had taken to themselves whatever they had found, and had kept it "with audacious impudence and effrontery." The Governor hopelessly noted that "this . . . is an offense so general that at present there is no remedy for it." The expedition was a failure. Indeed, its purpose would never be achieved without large forces, said the Governor sombrely, and paid his respects to the fierce individualism of the Spanish character by reporting to the Viceroy that his people "are accustomed to live very much as they please in everything and at long distances from each other—which was the cause of the loss of New Mexico. . . ." He concluded his report with a request for leave of absence to go south for medical treatment, saying, "My health, Sir, what with continuous attacks of headache which I have experienced on this occasion, contracted from the severe cold and extremes of weather in this kingdom, is much impaired and requires some remedy."

His report was grimly reviewed by the viceregal officials. Ignoring the hard conditions under which he had struggled, they found him wanting in proper leadership. The whole rebellion of the Indians, concluded the government in Mexico, rose "from the many oppressions which they receive from the Spaniards." Mention was made of the Indian difficulty in wearing "the yoke of the church." A new attempt at reconquest just now was useless, since the last one was "so unsatisfactory, and the people engaged in it being suspect and discredited, and having little respect and obedience for those who govern them." Governor Otermín's request for leave was disapproved. His term of office expired in the following year, 1683, and his replacement, a veteran of Spain's campaigns in Europe, General Domingo Jironza Petriz de Cruzate, came to preside over local problems at El Paso and to forward the reach of colonial life down the river in its southeastward stretches, where the identity of a people, and a place, called Texas, came to knowledge.

31.

A Way to the Texas

General de Cruzate arriving on August 30, 1683, found his official
residence at El Paso to be a twig and timber hut built by the council of
Santa Fe. His people were scattered along the river in camps. The land
was dry with velvety dust that lay in great flats on the river's south
shore. It was sweet dust and when kicked up by hoof or wind put a
parched scent in the air, part of the river smell. Sweet under the summer
moonlight, too, the dust looked like snow, and cottonwoods made cool
sounds and breathed through sparkling leaves. In the wide turn of the
valley there were softened signs of the river's old excursions out of its
course. Cruzate studied the lie of the land and set about bringing his
settlers nearer to the Guadalupe Mission and closer to his government.
As Otermín had noticed, most Spaniards preferred to live apart from
one another.

Cruzate improved his dignity, buying land from the Manso
Indians at El Paso and building a new Government House of earthen
brick, containing an audience hall, the secretary's office and dwelling
room, a cellar vault for munitions, and another bedroom. Kitchens and
pantry formed one side of the patio. Four other adjacent houses belonging to the Indians were purchased and provided a jail, a guardroom and
eight bedrooms. To these royal buildings came reports of Indian disturbances in the north Mexico provinces, where the Indian triumphs of New
Mexico and the sorry estate of the hungry, poor and meagrely armed
colony at El Paso were familiar news. There was occasional talk of reconquering the north, but until the Crown should afford enough soldiers,
munitions and pay, even a veteran field commander like Cruzate could
not conceive of such a mission. On the contrary, most people still wanted
to abandon the kingdom, and said so. And yet the very purpose of the
Spaniards in the north was once again underscored when a party of
seven people arrived at the Government Houses in El Paso on October
15, 1683.

They were Indians from down the river, the region called the Junta de los Rios, where so many expeditioners from Mexico coming down the Conchos had met the Rio del Norte and turned northwestward to the northern pass. These people came to ask again what they had asked before. Their spokesman was a Mexican Indian from Parral named Juan Sabeata, already a Christian. He asked for missionaries to go among the people of the Junta country, and even beyond, over the river, to the immense plains of the northeast, where lying like a tremendous leaf the land was veined by countless streams that all ran in the same direction toward the sea. He mentioned more than thirty tribes of that land, and the Spaniards understood him to speak of "the great kingdom of the Texas," which was ruled by a powerful monarch. The Texas were farmers, and raised grain in such abundance that even their horses ate it. Quivira, to the north, lay next to them. Once again a colony on the river was tempted and heartened by the glow of fortune, both worldly and divine, over the edge of the eastern world.

The Father President was Fray Nicolás López. While the Governor wrote to the Viceroy of the new possibilities of the Texas, Fray Nicolás instructed Sabeata and the delegates to return to their homes, and there, if they meant to keep faith, to build a church where the fathers could say Mass if they came. If he expected to see them falter, they did not. They went to the Guadalupe Mission, measured it, and left El Paso. Twenty days later sixty Indians were back to say that the church was already going up, and would be ready by the time the father could travel to it. Fray Nicolás clasped his hands together with rapture. They had kept faith and he would go to them. Not waiting for a military escort, he took two of his friars, and on December first set forth down the river, going barefoot on the harsh desert. For thirteen days the three priests, guided by the Indian party, walked along the river, crossing to the north bank at a convenient ford. The river fell lower and lower as they went until toward the end of their journey there was almost no water in it. But where the Conchos entered from Mexico the river sprang back to life again with renewed flow from the great tributary; and similarly the life of faith was redoubled again in the friars when they came to the first Indian town in the Junta country and saw the first church built for their reception. It was built of reeds, and it had an altar the size of the altar in the Guadalupe. A little farther downriver was another basketry church, larger, and equipped with living quarters for the friars.

The Father President and his aides, heartened by such proofs of sincerity, "began at once to baptize the children, because their parents offered them with singular love to our holy faith." Word came from inland towns that there too churches had been prepared. What accounted for all such zeal? Had any friars ever been there before? The Indians replied that years before, at different times, two priests had been to see them and had promised to return; but never had. There had also been visits years ago by a lovely white-faced lady in blue robes who "came down from the heights" and taught them lessons and urged them to ask for further teaching. The old people remembered her and spoke of her. She had come many times; but for a generation now she had not come any more. So once again the missioners encountered the powers of María de Agreda.

Fray Nicolás sent enthusiastic reports to Cruzate at El Paso, and on December fifteenth a military party of twenty-six men under Captain Juan Dominguez de Mendoza rode down the river, joined the priests and went with them among the Texas. Six months later the soldiers and friars were again at the Junta, having been far inland to the northeast. On June 13, 1684, the country across the Rio del Norte, the land of the Texas, was officially and legally taken possession of by Mendoza, for the jurisdiction of New Mexico. He and the Father President were both deeply taken by the lands they had seen, and desired to hurry back to report to the Governor at El Paso, the sooner to confirm the establishment of permanent missions at the Junta, and to colonize New Mexico's vast new Texas possession.

They were unable to return by the river trails to El Paso, for Indians were in revolt along its course. Mendoza and Fray Nicolás and their followers went south in a great arc and approached El Paso from deep in New Biscay. They found the colony harried by Indian threats and divided by opposing desires to retreat and to stay. An Indian uprising had been betrayed and prevented in March, 1684. The frontier was dotted with small outbreaks like fires in dry years, and signal smokes stood inscrutably in the dry skies. Yet in the face of such conditions, and with barely enough resources to hold what they held at El Paso, Mendoza and Fray Nicolás with the Governor's permission were eagerly off to Mexico in 1684 to petition the Viceroy for authority and means to go with cross and banner over the river to civilize Texas.

It was a land for which they longed, ". . . the richest land in all New Spain," said Mendoza, "for it abounds in grapes, nuts, acorns, berries, plums, buffaloes, rivers with pearls [the Concho], and mountains full of minerals." Yes, and "the variety of fruits," cried Fray Nicolás, and the "diversity of fish, the abundance of prairie chickens, quail, partridges, and especially the grapevines." Mendoza would accept the governorship, and Fray Nicolás would return as the church father of the new kingdom, pointing out that he already spoke the local Indian tongue, "having a very large vocabulary in the said tongue, as had been legally declared" by those who heard him preach.

And there was another inducement meant in its time to be irresistibly persuasive. Near the Pecos River, Mendoza and Fray Nicolás had met Indians—a tribe known as the Stinking Ones—who carried a painted cross and a white taffeta flag on which, beautifully sewed, were two blue crosses. It could only have been a foreign flag. It was a French flag. Somehow into far west reaches of the Texas kingdom had come evidence that the French were somewhere in its eastern parts.

In 1686 the Spanish Empire was bringing its European resources of espionage, and its colonial naval and land power, to the job of finding the French who were rumored to be threatening New Spain from the unknown country between Florida and the River of Palms. Fray Nicolás urged that the Texas peoples be taken for Spain before the French might chance to take them. Acting now, the ingress of the French "may be prevented with two hundred men," where later it would take "millions" of pesos to repair the damage. Mendoza for his part announced himself as "the only one for this affair . . . in order to force out the French (who may now be settled there), for he is fully experienced in matters of war, and moreover, is known to be a man of singular good fortune in it."

It was not to be. The Viceroy, acting more swiftly than was the custom of his office, analyzed the French menace in dispatches to the Crown offices in Madrid, and resolved to attack it with expeditions by sea in the Gulf, and by land, from Coahuila, across the Rio del Norte, far southeast of the point already established by the El Pasoans as their crossing.

Between 1685 and 1690 the knowledge of the river in its long Texas diagonal was increased by many expeditions, on land and sea, in pursuit of the French to the east. A commission to conquer Spain's northern American colonies for Louis XIV was in the hands of Robert Cavalier, Sieur de LaSalle. Another mission was planned for a filibustering attack on the mouth of the Pánuco, where French soldiers would land and march inland. This latter enterprise was the outcome of intrigues pursued at Versailles by the disgraced former governor of New Mexico, Peñalosa, who now styled himself as the Count of Santa Fe. LaSalle from the north, Peñalosa from the coast, were to combine

their forces inland, and march brilliantly on Mexico City—where the
Count of Santa Fe had suffered such great humiliation—and take it
for the glorious warrior cushioned at Versailles. In the end, though
his scheme was modified to fit in with LaSalle's, Peñalosa did not sail
for his vengeance in the New World. LaSalle alone commanded the
French threat. In 1682 at the mouth of the Mississippi he had already
claimed for Louis XIV "this country of Louisiana" along the Gulf Coast
"to the mouth of the River of Palms."

In July, 1686, an officer of Coahuila, Alonso DeLeón, led a mission
in search of the French colony which, according to Spanish intelligence,
was established somewhere near the coast in the Texas kingdom. He
came to the river by following its Mexican tributary the San Juan, and
marched along the south bank to the gulf. The river was wide, muddy
and swift, but unpopulated until near the coast DeLeón captured
three Indians who had fled their reedy town. They told him there were
other white soldiers living to the northeast, across the river, but could
not say just where. Were these the French? He could not say. After
examining the country of palms at the river's mouth, and recording
the wide lazy issuance of the brown waters into the sea, which was rough,
and the clean beach, and the far tidal marks upon it, he turned south
along the coast. There he saw broken planking, and pieces of mast
timber, and other vestiges of shipping wrecked on the shore, including
cannon wheels, small boats and a corked bottle of soured wine. He
returned to Coahuila by overland trails without proof of the French
occupation. Seven months later DeLeón returned to cross the river
and explore the coast north of the River of Palms, but again without
finding what he sought.

But even in so wide a land, without civilized commerce, news
travelled. Knowing nothing of the Spanish attempts to pierce the distance and discover the French aggressors, the Indians of the Junta
country innocently told of strangers in the East, whom they referred
to as other "Spaniards." The Junta Indians had heard of them while
on trading journeys among the Texas, and told their missionary friar
about them in the fall of 1687. Would he give them a letter to take
to the strangers when next they went to trade? He smiled with skepticism.
Let the strangers send him a letter first, he said. They would bring it,
they said.

In 1688, DeLeón, now governor of Coahuila, was at Monclova
when strange news was brought to him by one of his Indian allies who
had seen a white man across the river in Texas, living naked and

painted as the lord of an Indian nation who paid him royal honors. He gave DeLeón's scout a handful of printed pages. Their text was in French. When DeLeón saw these he acted at once. With a small force of soldiers and a Franciscan chaplain he set out for the river, crossed on May 25, 1688, and sixty miles farther found the man amidst his Indian subjects. He was seated on a throne covered with buffalo hides. Beside him were Indian servants who fanned him and standing about him as his bodyguard were forty warriors. "I am French," he said to his visitors, "Yo francés," and gave his name as Jean Géry. He was about fifty years old. Recognizing the chaplain's calling, he knelt to kiss his robes. DeLeón ordered him politely to return to Mexico with him, and Géry with odd docility obeyed, leaving his subjects behind. Once in Mexico, he was sent to the capital for interrogation.

Meanwhile the government was pursuing the French by sea, but without finding anything except some uncertain wreckage on the Gulf Coast. Late in the afternoon of September 1, 1688, two Spanish pirogues entered the mouth of the River of Palms. There, it seemed to the viceregal view, surely there was where any invading colony would try to settle? But when the Spanish sailors tried to cross rough surf of the bar at the river's mouth in small boats, they encountered angry Indians. The sailors offered them gifts of bread, tobacco and honey, which the Indians threw upon the beach. The shore party withdrew. Heavily armed, another landing party in two small boats explored the river upstream for the next five days. A long drought was again over the river, and the winding stream in the coastal plain was very low. In a penetration of one hundred miles the sailors found nobody but unfriendly Indians who had come to the river's lower reaches in search of seasonal food—roots and shell fish. The sailors returned to their ships and sailed away.

Later in the same month, upstream nearly a thousand miles, the Junta Indians returned home from their next trading journey. Though they brought no letter from the white strangers whom they had spoken of a year before, they came with an animated story of a lively colony in the eastern kingdom. There were wooden houses and enclosures not far from the sea, they said. Other wooden houses sat upon the waters of the sea, though one of these had gone under the sea. The white people wore armor like that of the Spaniards, and traded many of their strange possessions with the Indians for food and skins. They meant to make friends with the Indians, telling them that the Spaniards of New Biscay were bad people whom they would soon go to destroy.

It sounded like definite proof of a French establishment, with a fortress and ships, and the information was immediately forwarded to the Mexican authorities by the friars of the Junta.

Not long after, the friars themselves followed their news to Mexico, for the Junta Indians rebelled. Toward the end of the year Captain Juan de Retana marched for the Junta to subdue the Indians and enlist Indian guides who could take him across Texas to the French colony. Before he could leave for his eastern expedition, Juan Sabeata, the Junta chief, arrived from the east with a tale that changed all his plans. There was no longer a French colony by the sea. It had been wiped out, with massacre and torch, by eastern Indians. Sabeata gave Captain de Retana a few scraps of paper which he had obtained from Indians of the massacre. They were written pages in the handwriting of LaSalle, describing part of his voyage to the Texas coast. One of the pages carried a drawing of a French ship with a French verse on its sail. Retana cancelled his plans and reported what he had heard to his chief in Mexico, sending him LaSalle's manuscripts.

Now armed with the information taken from Géry in Mexico, and with Retana's news, Governor DeLeón marched out for the fourth time to find LaSalle's settlement. Géry went with him as guide. They went over the river on April 1, 1689, crossed many more streams going east, and on April twenty-second (after many false directions given by Géry who they decided was insane), coming downstream along a small creek, they saw at last what it had taken them years to find. It was Fort Saint Louis, empty, silent, charred and strewn with human remains and the wreckage of possessions.

DeLeón explored the coast, and scouted the inland country where he found two survivors of Fort Saint Louis. One of these was Jacques Grollet. The other was Jean L'Archevêque, who in March, 1687, had assisted at the murder of his commander, LaSalle. They were taken as prisoners to give information in Mexico. Before turning homeward the expedition heard the pleas of a Texas chief for conversion. He showed them his altar, with a figure of Christ on a cross, and four painted saints, and a light that he kept burning as in a sanctuary night and day. He had long known the usages of the Christians. Where had his knowledge come from? He replied that though he had never seen her himself, his forefathers had seen her, and had kept her instructions and her memory alive among them. She was a woman in a robe like that of DeLeón's chaplain, over which she wore a blue cloak. The chaplain, Fray Damián Massanet, recognized María de Agreda from the description, for she was now famous throughout the Indies. He promised to return with his brothers and all that would be needed to establish missions in the eastern kingdom. DeLeón led his party back to Coahuila.

He returned in the following year with Fray Damián and a full complement of friars and soldiers. Two missions were established, and for the next few years held the wilderness against rumors of renewed aggressions by the French. Texas became an official province of Spain. Meagre pack trains with a handful of armed guards went back and forth on the long journey from Coahuila across the Rio del Norte. But the tendrils of Spain at their farthest tips received little nourishment from the main source of energy, for Spain was at war with France, and missions without fortresses of soldiers in the wilderness could not long survive. In 1692 and 1693 the Texas missions were abandoned. Yet a way to Texas had been marked out across the river through the hard brush country; and dotted by quill pens in guizache ink on dried skin maps the way remained to be followed again.

An older kingdom, settled for almost a century, and lost for a decade, still called for reconquest. At El Paso, the entrance to New Mexico, Spaniards looked north along their river again.

32.

The Great Captain

In the autumn of 1692 the cold came earlier than usual, and on the plain of Santa Fe smokes from hearth fires stood together in airy columns above the city, where the victorious Indians had lived for twelve years. The palace was partly a ruin, partly a pueblo. All Spanish furnishings had been burned. Rooms had been added, and battlements. Other communal dwellings had been built until there were four, with cells for a thousand people. The church on the plaza and Saint Michael's across the creek were open to the sky. Their doors were long since

burned. Cattle and sheep were corralled within the charred walls of
the churches. The plaza was bare of all but refuse. Spanish trees had
been hauled out by the roots, Spanish flower beds dug up. Orchards
were ruined and fields where once wheat and melons grew, grapes and
any other product of Spain, were long since ravaged, in Santa Fe as in the
river pueblos. Dogs and turkeys wandered freely in the plaza dust. The
city was neither pure pueblo nor Spanish capital, but a heap of occupied
ruins of both kinds of life that told the worst about each. Only the
act of rebellion had been a success for the Indians. Having known a
century or more of a new life, they could never wholly return to the
way of the elders in all the fearful magic of its animal doom. Shreds of
the new life clung, even if they were only the bitterest shreds. The
primal glories of the Indian past, where were they? Under Popé,
governing a pueblo federation, the golden age was supposed to have
dawned. Imitating the Spanish governor, he gave himself state at Santa
Fe. One time with savage hilarity he enacted a furious burlesque
of Spanish manners, religious and official. At the pueblo of Santa Ana
he presided over a feast, with a long table laid in the Spanish style. He
sat at one end as the Governor, and at the other he placed another
Indian as the Father President. From the fouled treasures of a mission
church he sent for two chalices. With one of these, Popé gave a toast,
bowing down the table, and saying, "To your Paternal Reverence's
health." The other Indian rose and lifting the other chalice, replied in
mock courtesy, "Here is to your Lordship's health, my Lord Governor,"
and all roared with laughter. But Popé was a worse tyrant even than
any Spanish governor and by his very pretensions as prophet, a failure.
His promises of rain that would fall on dead Spaniards and live Indians
were lies. The rivers continued to dry up, and if the ancestors came
to show themselves in vast thunderheads over the mountains, no rain
fell from their hands. Popé died but his successor improved nothing.
The Pueblo federation broke up. Rule returned wholly to the separate
pueblos. Neither the old nor the new gave comfort. The Spanish farms
and orchards downriver, the Spanish meadows upriver, were wild and
profitless, except to an occasional Indian who rode by and for his
journey picked a handful of cherries, plums, peaches or apples. The
land and the people were so poor that half the pueblos, undefended by
Spain, were abandoned under Apache pressure against their dwindling
food stores. The baptisms were washed off in the brown river, cribs
of Spanish wheat were burned, pigs and chickens were exterminated,
the many gods were lifted in place of the One, in the plaza of Santa Fe

a kiva was built, and with pity locked in their jaws and in misery
under the sun the rebels were left with the forlorn consequences of their
triumph.

It was very cold and dark in Santa Fe before dawn on September
13, 1692, and the fields about the town were quiet when suddenly, at
something after four o'clock in the morning, the voices of two hundred
men rose toward the sleeping walls and together shouted out five times
in Spanish, "Glory be to the blessed Sacrament of the altar!"

At once Indians came to the tops of their walls, men and women,
youths and children. They peered into the darkness of the fields where
the shouting came from. Who was there? they demanded, and a voice
answered in the Indian tongue that these were Spaniards, come back
to forgive and to resume what was theirs. No, cried the Indians, that was
a lie, it was a war party of Pecos and Apache Indians who shouted in
the fields. At this the Gloria was repeated, and after a pause, the Indians
asked, if it was Spaniards who called from the fields, why they did not
fire a harquebus? To this a commanding voice replied:

"Be calm. I am a Catholic, and when the sun rises you will see
the image of the Blessed Virgin on my banner."

It was the voice of Don Diego de Vargas Zapata Luján Ponce de
León, the new Governor and Captain-General of New Mexico. The
banner he carried was the same one that had come up the river with
Oñate in 1598, and had gone down the river with Otermín in 1680.

In the darkness the Indians could not be sure, and asked that
a Spanish trumpet be played in proof. In answer, the trumpet sounded
and a long roll on the military drums. The Indians on the roofs called
back that they were ready to fight for five days, and would kill every
Spaniard, allowing none to escape next time. Their words stung their own
spirits into frenzy. They all turned up their faces and pointed their
jaws like foxes, coyotes, wolves and dogs, and beginning to howl in fury,
kept it up for more than an hour, while dawn approached, and soldiers
went to take up strategic stations at the entrances and corners of the city,
and Indians dragged stones to block openings in their walls, and piled
others to use as missiles. As the gray light turned to white, and then gold,
they could all see each other. At sunrise Vargas, with his interpreter and
two officers, rode forward twenty paces and identified himself. Showing
the banner with the arms of the king on one side and Our Lady of Remedies on the other, he called for peace and promised amnesty. They asked
him to remove his helmet so they could see him better. He turned to his
arms bearer, and asked for his hat. Then Vargas rode forward, taking off

his helmet and the scarf beneath it and showed himself, repeating his promises and invitations.

The Indians were clustered with drawn bows on the roofs. They quickened tensely at every random move made by a soldier. They countered promises of peace by saying that years ago the Spaniards offered peace to Apaches and then killed them. Vargas answered that the Apaches were traitors who used guile to enter in order to kill. He rose in his stirrups and showed a rosary and a cross, and he took his banner and held it aloft. He pointed to his three chaplains who stood with the soldiers. They would absolve the rebels and all would be at peace.

An Indian on the walls acted as spokesman. His name was Bolsa, The Pouches, because of his big cheeks. He said that all the governor said might be true, and yet if they came down, wouldn't the Indians be ordered to rebuild the churches and houses of the Spaniards? If they did not do as they were told, they would be whipped. Didn't they remember? They had not forgotten Xavier, Quintana, and Diego López. Were these men with the soldiers now? Vargas replied that they were not and promised that they would never come back to New Mexico.

In the full daylight the Spanish supply train and two pieces of bronze artillery on carts came over the fields and made camp. Every soldier had strict orders to make no hostile move, and fire no gun, even into the air, unless Vargas gave the signal to attack, which would be the drawing of his sword. Bolsa on the wall declared that those who were to blame for the revolt were all dead. Vargas repeated his pardon and lifted his banner. An armed Indian came forward from the gate in defiance. He refused to give Vargas his hand. Indians on the walls told him to ask for something, and he did so, asking that two friars come inside with him. Hearing him, two Franciscans dismounted and were ready to go but Vargas detained them. Not yet, he said. The friars obeyed him. Spanish sentry calls sounded from the corners of the pueblo.

Vargas turned to see throngs of Indians coming off the heights above Santa Fe, some on foot, some mounted. "Now you will see!" cried the people on the walls. Vargas sent a squad to each side of the town to hold the Indian reinforcements at bay. On the roofs the people dragged up more stones and made their walls higher. They painted themselves with vermilion and called all animal powers to war for them, reviling the captain-general for his pleas and pledges. He called a detachment of Indian allies and soldiers. Pointing to the ditch that took water into the walls he ordered them to break it and divert the flow. It was quickly done. An outcry arose from the walls. Vargas proclaimed that water would be restored, and peace made certain, if the Indians came down to render obedience. He gave them one hour in which to agree, and retired to his camp for a breakfast of biscuits and a drink of chocolate, which was served to all the soldiers.

Vargas was busy for the next two hours. He ordered the two cannon dragged in their carts by mules to a position facing the Palace. Powder stores were brought up to be used as mines against the walls. Indian delegates from other pueblos arrived and were kindly received, promised peace and told to go to the besieged people with calming messages. The soldiers worked mightily at their tasks, and in the face of overwhelming enemy forces, "showed no concern for the risk and danger of their lives." Vargas was proud of them and loved them as a commander loved good soldiers.

There was movement behind the battlements of the Palace. Seeing the artillery now trained on them, all but the archers at the loopholes were leaving the Palace at the rear. An Indian messenger came to Vargas to say that he had done all he could, but without success, and he believed he could do no more. Vargas talked with him at length in the open space before the town. Seeing the two engaged so in conversation, the people began to return to the Palace in wonder. Vargas for the last time seized his banner, his rosary and his cross, and went before the walls to deliver a final exhortation before giving battle.

And now the Indians accepted peace, provided he would pull back his troops to the supply camp, remove his cannon, and come unarmed himself to receive them, who would also lay down their arms.

So the long day of haranguing was over. Two unarmed Indians came forward. Vargas dismounted and embraced them. The Franciscan fathers now went into the Palace. Indians streamed forth to make peace with Vargas, which he "extended to all of them with great love, as I stood there dismounted, embracing them, shaking hands with them, and speaking to them with tender and loving words. . . ." Giving orders that Indians must hang crosses about their necks, and erect a large cross in the patio of the Palace, Vargas some twelve hours after his first call in the fields before dawn retired to camp, leaving soldiers on guard against treachery. But gazing across the fields toward the Palace he made a sudden resolve. "I decided to place some trust in fate," he said, and ordered all soldiers to return to camp, bringing the artillery with them, and leaving the town free and open for whatever the Indians resolved upon. It was a lofty demonstration of good faith. It was supported by good military sense in camp, where Vargas "ordered that

tonight the horses and mules be provided with a guard of two squads
and that they might not be permitted to separate." Two other squads
were armed and at the alert with their mounts saddled, "in case of
any sudden attack." Night fell cold on the peaceful reconquest of the
capital of the restored kingdom.

Vargas was the son of a great family close to the throne in Spain.
From the time of his birth it was taken for granted that he would enter
public service, and his career was a pleasant chronicle of progress from
one responsible preferment to another. He fought with the Spanish
armies in the kingdoms of Naples and Italy, and in 1672, like many
another less illustrious scion, turned his ambitions toward the New
World, which he entered as a diplomatic courier. In Mexico he filled
a succession of political posts, always with distinction and honor. In
1688 he was given the governorship and captain-generalcy of New Mexico by the King, and when talk of a reconquest arose there were under-
standings that so great a young lord (he was in his late forties) would
be willing to outfit an expedition at his own cost, on the revenues derived
from his rich holdings—palaces and houses and villas at Madrid, Granada
and Mexico City; grainfields, olive orchards, vineyards, pigeon lofts and
arable lands at Torrelunga, Buytrago, Miraflores, and Salamanca; the
salt works at Orcaña, and the rest. He took command at El Paso in 1691.
Facing north, he had the full support of the viceregal government, for
it was now understood that New Mexico must be regained on two new
accounts—one was the necessity of a northern buffer against the French,
or any other power that might look for an easy conquest of a vast
kingdom; the other was the rumor that quicksilver existed in rich
commercial quantities in a range of mountains called, in a general
poetry of the region, the Sierra Azul—Blue Range. Beyond such purposes, there resided always the earnest belief that for their own souls'
sakes the apostate Indians must be restored in the Holy Faith.

There had been earlier attempts at a reconquest. While Texas
was coming to light across the lower river, the El Pasoans went north
in 1687 and again in 1688. The first of these two forays yielded nothing;
the second resulted in a pitched battle against the Pueblo of Zia, on the
Jemez creek, in which six hundred Indians were killed and the houses
were burned. It looked like the beginning of a reconquest, but without
additional arms and men to exploit it, the venture had to stand by
itself, a futile and costly but proud effort to move against the rebels.

And then before Vargas in his turn could take the river trail he
was obliged to remain at the entrance of New Mexico and from there

to lead missions of punishment against the Indians of northern Mexico
who were in sporadic revolt, and who unsuppressed would be a danger
to his base at the Pass and his communications to the rearmost echelon
of the colonial command at Mexico City. At last in the summer of 1692
he was ready to go north. Fifty soldiers from Parral were to join him at
El Paso, but as the hot months wore on they did not come, and he went
without them, leaving orders for them to overtake him in New Mexico.
On August twenty-first he led his column of two hundred men, gathered from among Indian allies and Spanish colonists at the Pass, across
the river into the silvery wavers of the desert heat. The departure, at
four in the afternoon, was ceremonious, with banners shaken out and
military music.

Vargas was a tall man. His long hair and large eyes were dark, his
face was a long oval with a straight nose, and his mustaches and beard
were slender. He wore a morion and body armor. His horse-stained boots
were wrinkled up about his thighs when mounted, and folded down
below his knees when dismounted. In his luggage he carried court dress
of much splendor, including Dutch linen shirts with shoulder-wide
collars and long ballooned sleeves; knee-length vests embroidered and
edged with gold lace; slashed doublets outlined with fur and tied with
ribbons; knee breeches with bullion garters and bows; white silk hose;
low shoes tied with double bows of silk ribbons; dark velvet hats
crowned with plumes and faced under the brims with ermine; and stiff
taffeta baldrics to carry his light dress rapier. These proclaimed estate.
Within he carried the essence of it. His mind was orderly, clear and grave.
He was without fear of all things short of God. He rode northward into
experiences which, however familiar they were to men before his time,
were new to him and charged with peril. Many of the soldiers with him
were returning to the lands they had fled twelve years before.

They crossed northward along the Dead Man's March, moving
slowly because of the dragging pace of the supply train and its animals,
and came to the first pueblos, Senecu and Socorro, which were empty.
Going up the east bank of the river they passed by the first of the
abandoned and overgrown haciendas where the air was hot and sweet
with the summer breath of the narrow valley in its wide desert—the
smell of warm river mud, and of varnished cottonwood leaves, and of
marshy fields busy with droning life in their low air. Vargas at one of
the estates left behind him the larger part of the supply train with an
officer who was to await the reinforcements from Parral, and moved on
through the next pueblos toward Cochiti. There he expected the fullest

strength of the Indians to meet him, since all other pueblos were abandoned.

But when on September eleventh he came to Cochiti, it was, like all those towns downriver, empty, and he went to Santo Domingo on the Galisteo creek. It too was abandoned, and only Santa Fe lay ahead. On the twelfth the column with much difficulty climbed an abandoned and eroded path up the escarpment of La Bajada and stood on the wide plain looking toward the Sangre de Cristo mountains at whose base lay the capital. Vargas halted there until sundown, resting his men and animals. He ordered an assembly and spoke to the soldiers of their duty and responsibility in upholding both Majesties in the encounter that surely lay ahead, for Indians from the empty towns behind them must have gathered at Santa Fe. At eleven o'clock he gave the command to move forward in the cold dark night. Later he halted again and designated three o'clock in the morning as the moment to advance against the city. When that time came, he was to be notified by certain officers who would know the hour, "through their knowledge, by the position of the stars." They moved on at three and halted once again to receive absolution from the chaplains. The soldiers were forbidden to fire or make any gesture of war unless they saw the captain-general draw his sword. At another signal, once they had come to the open fields by the walls, all were to cry out the Gloria. Bound together by command, understanding and excitement, the shivering column crept forward to the surprise of Santa Fe and its peaceful recapture after the long day's debate outside the walls.

On guard by the horses in the Spanish camp, the soldiers saw people coming and going all night long at the Palace gates. In the morning, word was sent that the Indians would be given absolution in the patio of the fortified buildings. Vargas laid aside his armor, his rough campaign clothes. His page opened a brass-studded leather trunk and brought out a suit of court dress which Vargas put on. So arrayed "in gala," as he said, but bearing arms, he went to witness the sacrament in the palace. The Indians asked that he come without soldiers, for the women and children were afraid. His officers warned him against going without armor and alone. But he saw the Indians holding bars of timber across the gates, and he went forward unescorted. "So," he said, "I gratified them, so that they would not think that I was afraid," and they lowered their bars, and he entered the patio where he saw that a large cross had been erected. The friars went with him. The people, reassured, in great numbers began to come down from their high roofs on their

ladders made of poles. The royal banner was raised three times, and
three times the multitude repeated after the captain-general the cry of
"Long live the King," and all cheered, and knelt down while the reconquering fathers intoned the Te Deum Laudamus. The absolution, with
all kneeling, followed. Santa Fe was again a royal city.

In the next few days, not waiting for the reconquering governor to
come to them, the governors of several pueblos appeared one by one at
Santa Fe to render obedience. San Lázaro, San Cristóbal, Tesuque, San
Juan and Picuries were represented. One of the pueblo lords wore animal
skins and around his head a yucca palm bandeau to which a heart-
shaped shell was affixed, "all of which resembled a diadem." Advancing
toward the Captain-General he three times fell to one knee, "to make
three courtesies." He displayed a few Christian objects. Invited into the
headquarters tent, he drank chocolate with the Spaniards and was
lavished with "affectionate words." On the following day he called
again upon the Captain-General with something on his mind. It appeared
that his people and certain other pueblos were at war with one another.
He asked the Spanish commander to defeat his enemies, among whom
were the pueblos of Pecos and Taos. Vargas gazed at him, who was a
known traitor, though now restored and absolved. The fifty soldiers
from Parral were not yet arrived in Santa Fe. Their presence might tip
the scales in any conflict with Indians. Making a sudden decision, and
"trusting in Blessed Mary, our Queen, Our Lady and Advocate of
Remedies," Vargas promised to march for Pecos.

He waited five days for the Parral company, but they did not
come, and leaving orders for them to follow, he set out on Sunday, September twenty-first, and camped that night in an arroyo near Galisteo.
As he was mounting his horse the next morning to resume his march,
he heard two signal shots, and in a few minutes the guards challenged
seven mounted men who rode up with jingling accoutrements. They
were the first of the relief party from Parral. The rest were following
from Santa Fe. By late afternoon the command was complete. Together,
they moved out and marched until ten o'clock at night. Ahead of them
was Pecos in the dark.

When they came to it on the following morning, they saw "two
curls of smoke" rising above the rosy clay city and when they moved
closer they saw that it was abandoned. Vargas remained for five days,
scouting the country, and capturing twenty-seven Indians who said only
that their people had fled to the mountains and were not ready to make
peace. With the captives was another, a Spanish youth, who was the

son of Cristóbal de Anaya. He had been held captive ever since the day in 1680 when his father had been murdered at the family estate down-river. He was taken in charge by his uncle, Francisco Lucero de Godoy, who was with Vargas as captain of the artillery, and who now under-took to have the boy taught the trade of armorer. Vargas freed the Pecos prisoners with messages of amnesty. He left the pueblo intact, neither burning it nor sacking its stores of grain, and returned to Santa Fe.

Between the twenty-ninth of September and the eighth of October the army marched into all the northern pueblos and received their obedi-ence, including that of Taos. Ceremonies of rededication to both "the divine and the human Majesties" were held, absolutions granted, and baptisms performed, in peace. At Taos, Indian travellers told Vargas that they had lately returned from the far western pueblo of Zuñi where a council of war had been held with the object of organizing the annihi-lation of the Spaniards. He marched at once for Santa Fe, and left there immediately to make his appearance in all the pueblos not yet visited. Going by way of Pecos, he found now a full population who came out to meet him and to submit, secure in the possession of their city which he had not burned, their storerooms and kivas which he had not sacked. Surrounded by guns and gunpowder, armor and tough horses and an impregnable sense of righteousness, the Captain-General found enough strength aside from these powers to do his duty and fulfill his orders with merciful humanity. It was the strength of a perfect, an unquestioned aristocracy in which official obligation was matched by an imaginative grasp of human nature. He received the submission of Pecos and turned west to the pueblos across the Rio del Norte, where again he entered and left in peace—Zia and Jemez, though at the last of these there were precarious moments when dancing and shouting and arrayed for war the Indians seemed alive with menace under their festive airs. Jemez had attended the murderous council at Zuñi, and Vargas knew it. He entered the milling crowd on foot with only a handful of soldiers, and gravely and calmly ordered the women and children to come down to him from the roofs, and the men to put down their weapons at their feet, and give him their hands, and listen to him, as he walked about among them saying what they must hear and must do. Once again by the richness of his inner powers he prevailed. Jemez kneeled down under his voice, his eye, and his hand.

Now for the march to the far western provinces where revolt was organized, he needed a light force of high mobility. At the end of October the weather was already wintry. His pack train, the people with

it, had already suffered from the cold, including many Spaniards and
the surviving households who had been freed from captivity in the tour
of the pueblos. Facing what was possibly to be his most dangerous
march, Vargas yet dismissed his artillery, his wagons and a squad of his
soldiers, ordering them to lead the delivered colonists to their kinsmen
and friends at El Paso. He gave them meat and pinole, biscuits, chocolate, sugar, tobacco and soap. Then he left them to make their slow way
southward, while with his cavalry he rode on to Isleta, which he found
empty and in ruins, where only the walls of the church were standing.
Turning to the west he left the river on October thirty-first. Far across the
wintry deserts were the pueblos in league against him—Zuñi, Oraibi,
Walpi—and there too were the mountains where quicksilver was supposed to be seen in an earth called vermilion with which the Indians
painted themselves, and "which leaves a purplish luster, greasy and
buttery when rubbed in the palm of the hand, and which is good for
cold eyes, preserves the condition of the face, and removes the marks
of small-pox. . . ."

On December tenth he brought his men back to the river near
Socorro. They had marched in blizzards and in thirsty dryness. The
western pueblos ready for war had resisted, one by one, but not for
long. The Captain-General spoke to them at length, and walked inadequately guarded upon their mesas, and here and there occurred those
episodes of suspense in which for a crystalline instant the forces within
the Indian mind seemed about to crack toward violence; but piled stones
were not hurled, arrows were lowered, and the lonely cry of the Te Deum
Laudamus ascended from the rocky plazas in the bitter wilderness.

They hastened south now along the river toward El Paso.
Attacked by Apaches, they captured two, one of whom was killed.
Vargas intervened before the other was killed, and asked for a statement from him. Had the Apaches entered El Paso to steal and destroy?
The Apache replied that during the same moon, "he and a companion
had entered and stolen two horses, that this was all he knew." Vargas
then turned to his chaplain, asking him to tell the Indian that he should
become a Christian and that, after he had agreed, he would be shot.
The chaplain talked with the Indian who accepted baptism, and the
name of Agustín. In his conviction of performing a virtuous service,
both compassionate and stern, Vargas, in the Spanish renaissance, was
concerned for the economy, the health, of the soul at the moment of
dying. He watched the dealings of the friar and the Apache to their
finish, "and this having been done," he said, "I ordered the lieutenant

of cavalry to have four soldiers take the said Indian off to one side and
shoot him forthwith, giving him a good death." The march continued
and on December 20, 1692, after four months in the northern river
kingdom, the expedition arrived at El Paso.

What they had accomplished was proudly reported to the Viceroy, and a sample of vermilion earth was sent to Mexico to be assayed
for quicksilver. Twenty-three pueblos were pacified and restored to the
official faith. Over two thousand Indians had been baptized. No soldier
had been killed, and no Indian, other than Apaches. At Zuñi a treasure
of sacred vessels and vestments and books belonging to the friars murdered in the great rebellion was recovered and brought to El Paso,
and was handed over to the Father President. Haciendas and churches
were in ruins, and most of Santa Fe, but with peace restored, there was
yet much to rebuild the Spanish kingdom on. Indians could still read
and write Spanish, and still knew the responses in hymns, litanies and
prayers. Except for the salaries of the fifty men from Parral, the enterprise in all its march of nearly two thousand miles had cost the Crown
not a single maravedi. The kingdom now awaited only the return of
families, the rebuilding of the capital, the resettlement of the rankly
overgrown haciendas. The Captain-General had plans for his second
entry into New Mexico.

Vargas's news overjoyed the city of Mexico. The cathedral was
outlined with illuminations and bells were rung in all the churches.
His report was forwarded to Madrid. Commendations were voted to
him, and were sent to him by viceregal courier. The mail also brought
instructions for him to return the fifty soldiers from Parral to their home
garrison, as he would have no need of them now. One more detail was
reported on in the papers that came by official pouch to Vargas at El
Paso. "With regard to the matter of the red vermilion referred to in
his letter, let him be notified that the examination has been made and
that it has been found to have no quicksilver content."

But if one of the purposes of a reconquest was suddenly thus
undone, the others remained; and on October 4, 1693, ninety-six years
after Oñate's entry, and thirteen after the murderous revolt, the old
colony left El Paso for the north. All their difficulties in the undertaking
were by now familiar ones, and one by one in laborious and familiar
measures they were met. Vargas had asked for soldiers, and had been
assigned a troop which brought his armed component up to one hundred men. "You might as well," he wrote in the level tone of his day,
"you might as well try to convert Jews without the Inquisition as

Indians without soldiers." The colony embraced a wide range of qualities, from Spanish lords, learned friars, taciturn mercenaries and gently
bred ladies to half-breed Indians, jailbirds under orders, licensed lawyers
and worried merchants; and it included L'Archevêque, one of LaSalle's
murderers, who had come from Mexico to enroll. There were seventy
families, eighteen friars, and many Indian allies. The train included
eighteen wagons pulled by mules and horses and three cannon in carts.
A thousand mules, two thousand horses and nine hundred cattle were
herded along the way. Leaving Guadalupe mission with buccinal music
and flags that bobbed in the air at the rate of a horse's walk, the column
went to the river where they knew much delay and bother in crossing,
but finally crossed and drew away northward through the Pass. A week
later Vargas and his staff left the mission and overtook the column on
the road. With him was his official standard, making its third ascent of
the river. He inspected his people, and rode on ahead with a light escort
to test the temper of the pueblos.

He found that once again all but a few of them were hostile. A
friendly chief offered to help him with messages to Santa Fe. Vargas
rejoined his main column. Thirty women and children had died in
crossing the Dead Man's March. Slowly the remainder advanced to the
heights of Santa Fe and on December sixteenth faced the city. The assembled Indian population awaited him in silence. Fifteen friars chanting
hymns walked into the plaza. Vargas dismounted and followed. As he
passed into the gate he "made due obeisance" to the Indian precincts
he was entering, and those following him did the same—the Spanish town
council of Santa Fe, the standard-bearer and officers. There was a moment
of tension, and then the Father President, "attuning his voice," began
to sing the Te Deum, and the moment broke with relief, and all rejoiced.
Afterward, with the lessons of a century behind him, Vargas proclaimed
that all he came to do was bring Christ to the Indians and not to take
from them anything rightfully theirs. He gave the Spanish city back
to the Spanish aldermen; and then though the ground was covered with
snow, he retired his forces from the city and camped at a little distance
in "a despicable dwelling place" to afford the Indians a reasonable time
to make way for the colonists in their ruined capital.

But the Indians now showed no disposition to move. Twenty-one
Spaniards died of exposure in the snowy campground during the following two weeks, while the Indians were seen to be barricading the walls.
On the twenty-eighth they felt their strength and shouted defiance to
the Spaniards. With weariness and patience in the name of their pur-

poses, the soldiers attacked, and by dawn of the thirtieth were masters
of the town. Patience was not to be confused with weakness. Vargas
commanded the execution of seventy Indian leaders. The cannon, the
animals and the families came into the plaza, and the carts, in one of
which was the statue of La Conquistadora, the patroness of the expedition who was returned to her city at last. The Indians fled downriver
to the high gravelly benches and the canyon rims of the west side. Their
fires burned on the plateau, and smoke talked, and by New Year's Day
the kingdom was once again everywhere flaring with promises of war.
The Captain-General could count on only four pueblos—Santa Ana,
Zia, San Felipe and Pecos. All the rest had to be subdued one by one, in
images of violence long familiar in the thin green valley with its tawny
wastes beyond—siege assaults, burning rafters, commandeered maize,
dried watercourses, hundreds of dead natives, and handfuls of lost
Spaniards.

     Peace of a sort was restored, and friars moved out to the missions
and began to rebuild what had worn so hard in the worst weather between
two orders of men. New families arrived from Mexico. The haciendas
were resettled, and the first Spanish towns outside of Santa Fe and El
Paso came to life in the river kingdom. "With sails full we forge ahead,"
wrote Vargas to Mexico. Santa Cruz was established with sixty-six new
families on April 22, 1695, and more came in May. In the autumn a
town took root at the old site of the Bernal family downriver, on the
estate called Bernalillo, opposite the long-abandoned and disappearing
pueblo of Tiguex where Coronado had bivouacked in hard winter one
hundred and fifty-three years before.

     The winter of 1695-96 was no easier. War and drought had pre-
vented good crops from being sowed and stored against the cold months.
Indians and colonists suffered alike. The friars in the missions felt
danger brooding behind the impassive Indian life. They warned Vargas
and some even left their parishes to take refuge in Santa Fe. There was
a sense of storm building up and on June 4, 1696, it broke with fury:
five priests and twenty-one soldiers were massacred when a number of
pueblo populations, in a co-ordinated movement, rebelled, burned and
outraged their churches, and escaped to the mountains. But if the outbreak recalled the horrors of 1680, it was not so widespread. Pecos and
a few other towns were loyal, and warrior Indians from those helped
Vargas to suppress the rebellion. The Indian federation was again divided
against itself but for the first time the balance of power among them was
on the side of the Two Majesties. Vargas moved severely and fast against

the miscreant towns. By the end of the year the danger was over. Indians came down off the mesas and mountains to dwell again under the walls of their mission churches, where peace and forgiveness awaited them, and learning. Why, asked the conquerors, why had the revolt of 1696 taken place? and an Indian of Nambé, one of the rebellious towns, answered (and no one knew whether it was the truth or an evasive pretext) that "the sole cause of the uprising of the Indians was the fact that a Spaniard had said, while in Cochiti . . . that the governor of New Mexico had determined that in the month of June of the same year all the adult men of that kingdom were to be killed, reserving only the boys. . . ."

The Pueblo Indians submitted, then, forever. The battles were over between the Spaniards and their Christian wards. Vargas was ready to move into a second term as governor to protect all his people, Indian and Spanish alike, against the enemy who was left, the travelling Apaches and Comanches, and those others of whom rumors now and then dawned out of the east, who were, more than likely, Frenchmen from the lower banks of the river called the Espiritu Santo and, again, the Micipipi.

But his petition to be appointed to a second term in the river kingdom which he had restored to the Crown moved too slowly in the channels of government. In January, 1697, a new governor arrived at Santa Fe, Don Pedro Rodríguez Cubero. Honoring his credentials, Vargas turned the office over to him and remained at Santa Fe to offer himself for the usual hearings required of all outgoing officials. He asked that these be expedited but there were delays. Suddenly, on October second, a squad of soldiers arrested him by order of the Governor and imprisoned him in one of the towers of the Palace at Santa Fe. He was denied communication with the colonists whom he had led and protected. The town council, at the pleasure of the new governor, drew up a heavy bill of indictments against him. If he had any friends left they were powerless to help him. He was fined four thousand pesos. He lost all his property by confiscation. A year passed, and another, and part of another, while he lived isolated in his cell like a criminal. Mexico City and Madrid knew nothing of his condition. No inquiries came from the Viceroy. No one was allowed to see Vargas where he existed in one end of the Palace, while Governor Cubero reigned in the other. People peering in at the Governor's office saw Cubero writing, writing, one official paper after another, almost without cease, like Philip II, while affairs outside were neglected, and the dirt walls of the Palace itself were allowed to crumble. It was whispered that the new Governor was a

drunkard. Suspicious of everyone, he was victim of that temperament
which fearing to be last respected was first to accuse. In 1700 his treatment of the prisoner finally met open opposition, when the Father
President of New Mexico, whom Governor Cubero dared not restrict,
went to the Viceroy in Mexico with the story. A report went to the King.
Vargas was ordered free to leave Santa Fe without bail. He hurried to
Mexico City. There he was heard. His record was cleared. He was reap-
pointed governor and captain-general of New Mexico. He was created
a marquis by the King—Marqués de la Nava Brazinas, a title by which
thereafter he was known. In July, 1703, he left again for Santa Fe.
Cubero, having word of such reversals, announced that he was about to
be absent from the northern capital on an expedition against certain
Apaches; marched out; and, having allied tact with speed, never came
back. The Marquis arrived in November at the Royal City which, with
its kingdom, he had won back to security, using the means and laws
of his time, according to the powers of his belief. The aldermen of Santa
Fe waited upon his excellency's pleasure.

They soon learned it in resounding terms. To the same town
council which a few years before had drawn up a bill of accusations
against his conduct of official affairs he now made a statement in which
he thundered, "It is justice for which I ask." In a single passionate sentence of almost a thousand words he first reviewed his accomplishments
and then ticked off the disasters that had befallen the kingdom under
his successor and jailer. The Palace and fortress of Santa Fe, restored by
Vargas to strength and comfort, was allowed by Cubero to go to ruins,
so that the capital was defenseless. The army, once in tiptop condition,
was now scattered, indifferent and plagued by desertions. New towns,
like Santa Cruz, founded with joy and hope, were unprotected, and therefore abandoned, their crops run to weed, their buildings empty and
falling. Why had Cubero treated him and all his works so, "with what
intention and malice?" The Marquis did not know. He could only say
that it had been the purpose of Cubero to "destroy all I had done and
leave no memory of it," even to the dishonoring of land grants already
in legal process, and assigning of them to new owners. The Marquis was
concerned not only for his own personal redress but for the proper
recording of acts of bad government, and the due responsibility for
them. Much work had to be done over again. The reasons why must be
set down. He asked the aldermen for an endorsement, in triplicate, of all
his claims to merit, and of all his charges against Cubero.

They obliged overnight. The Lord Marquis, they said, by his

"ability and resolution" had won Santa Fe and the kingdom from the apostates. He had indeed made the Palace a great fort, and had given his people shelter for their bodies and souls, in house and church. As for Santa Cruz and other places, Cubero had allowed them to go to rack and ruin, a dreadful fact "to be explained by the great enmity and dis-affection he has toward the said Lord Marquis, trying by every means to show his malice. . . ." It was all true, as the Lord Marquis had charged, and Cubero, who was now so plainly to be seen as a wretch, "in all the time of his government, was solely occupied in drinking and writing papers with no reason whatever," said the aldermen who had served him earlier, and in "imagining things he had no business to imagine, ascrib-ing faults and crimes to those who had not committed them, like that which he attributed to the said Lord Marquis." The Council could not contain its moral indignation. It was, it said, "sure of the high sense of duty of the said Lord Marquis in the interest of all that was and has been under his charge." It was now their duty, the aldermen insisted, "to give him fully and completely the satisfaction he demands and should have." Bridling with courage, the Council touched upon the charges made against the Lord Marquis, and now flatly declared that "the same were made up, hatched and invented" by the vanished Cubero and his secretary. To the Lord Marquis, then, the Council offered "entire and full satisfaction," signed, sealed and witnessed, with three copies. With these in his pocket, he could now set about his job.

There was work to do on the government houses and on Saint Michael's chapel across the creek. Winter days were clear topaz and nights were cold and brilliant. All was made of earth. Elsewhere he owned palaces, parts of towns, whole lordships where people toiled over crops and enlarged his accounts and supported his noble estate. An altar in Madrid, alive in candlelight with gold and silver, perpetuated his family name, in its place alongside the kings of Spain in history. And yet it was to Santa Fe, lost in the north, that he wanted to return. That was the town where, disdaining armor, he had entered alone in soft velvet, fur and silk, smiling at danger, and declaring, "He who takes no risks to win an immortal name accomplishes nothing." He was most at home where he had most triumphed and most suffered.

The winter months of 1704 went by rapidly. The army was reorganized none too soon. In March came appeals for help, war "with fire and sword," against the Apaches who were sweeping into the central valley farms of the Garcías and the Chaveses, and stealing animals. They came from beyond the Sandía and Manzanos mountains, now around the

northern tip, again through the zigzag canyon that was cut, as though by
tijeras—scissors—between the two ranges, and they struck haciendas at
Bernalillo, Alameda, and below. The Marquis made his plans. Orders
were published on the parade ground in the Santa Fe plaza. Fifty officers
and men from the capital garrison would move out on March twenty-
seventh, to join a selected detachment of Indian allies at Bernalillo on
the following day. The Governor and Captain-General himself went in
command, at the work he liked best, amidst shining arms and armor,
scrubbed saddles, a campaign in the field.

At Bernalillo the troops were mustered and he inspected them.
The Indian thieves had gone into the mountains that lay parallel to the
river. He sent a scouting force to observe them, and received a report
that they seemed to be going under mountain cover toward Tijeras
Canyon, where they would escape through the pass to the great yellow
plain of their cloud-shadowed empire. With the main body he marched
down the river road. On Tuesday, April first, the Apaches were seen
at a watering place at the edge of the Plain of the Inferno, near the
village of Taxique. In the distance gleamed the pale salt lakes. The
Captain-General marched on the following day to join his scouts.
The Apache band were skirting the eastern base of the Manzanos mountains and leaving a clear trail, a fact which was noted in the day's
campaign journal by the Captain-General commanding.

It was the last entry he dictated. In the thin mountain air he
halted. He felt distress in his breathing. He was feverish and in pain.
He was suddenly weak. There was a tightness in his chest. His officers
consulted together and he gave permission to do what they asked. They
took him back to Bernalillo to the house of Don Fernando Durán y
Chaves, the Mayor, travelling slowly. There he went to bed. He saw all
that was done for him, and he knew in a very few days what was coming
to pass. On April seventh he sent for his military and civil secretary,
to whom he gave dictation. Beginning with the words, "In the name of
God Almighty," he commended his soul for a "most clear career of salvation," and his body "to the earth from which it was made." He gave
orders for his funeral, and he divided his arms, his garments of state,
his favorite saddles and other personal objects, between his two natural
sons. With their sister in Mexico City they were to share equally in cash
bequests. His silverware in heavy profusion, bearing his coat of arms,
and his diamond and emerald and pearl jewelry, were to be sold. He
gave freedom to two slaves, his body servants, and a sum of money to
each. He listed debts to be paid. He ordered two hundred Masses for

himself, and three hundred "for the souls of the poor who died in the
conquest of this kingdom," his old comrades with whom thus he would
be once more united. He signed with the large capitals, the generously spaced light and firm letters of his writing, "The Marquis de la
Brazinas." Five officers witnessed the instrument. On the following day,
April 8, 1704, he died.

If his wishes were obeyed, a Mass was said for him there at Bernalillo before his soldiers brought him up over the mesa of La Bajada for
his last return to Santa Fe, and once there he was laid on his bed
'selected as a bier," which was covered with "honest woollen cloth."
With military rites he was conveyed from the clay Palace to the temporary clay parish church of St. Francis which stood behind the Palace
on the road to Tesuque, close to the north city wall which Cubero had
demolished not long before. Two horses, caparisoned in the same woollen
cloth, were led before him, while the "title ceremonies and privileges of
Castile" were observed over him. He was buried "at the principal altar
under the platform where the priest stands." On the day of his funeral
fifty measures of corn and twelve head of cattle were distributed for
him among the poor of Santa Fe. The earth for which he fought and
which he defended was over him in peace, and, in the peace that he had
brought to it, the upper river kingdom lived.

33.

Fort St. John Baptist

From high above the map in the last years of the seventeenth
century, the way from Mexico City to the Rio Grande was seen as a
single stem, winding this way and that around mountains and through
valleys and across plains, pausing at watering places and isolated missions
with their little forts, touching alive as it went an occasional provincial
capital where commerce and religion found rewards, and ending at

Santa Fe. But now at the outset of the eighteenth century a new branch
began to grow, reaching northeastward toward Texas and stopping at
the southern bank of the river. The northward reach of Colonial Spain
took the form of a great Y. No Spanish settlements had been made in
Texas since the abandonment of the mission frontier against the French
in 1693. But in the Mexican provinces south of the Texas Rio Grande
the mission establishments crept closer and closer to the river. Roaming
Indians were gathered into villages, converted and taught Spanish ways
of work, not only for the peace of their souls, but for the pacification of
the frontier. In 1699 Mexico heard that the French were settling colonies
in Louisiana. Once again from the east arose the threat that in one or
another form would challenge and call forth defensive expansion by the
Spaniards for the next century. The mission of San Juan Bautista, first
founded on the Sabinas river in northern Coahuila in 1699, was suddenly moved in the following year to the plains of the right bank of the
Rio Grande. With it came its Indians, friars and farmers, and in the
next three years, with strategic foresight, it was augmented through
the foundation of two more missions—San Francisco Solano and San Bernardo—and the establishment of a fortified garrison of thirty troops in
a "Flying Company" under the command of Captain Diego Ramón.
The whole cluster of barracks, dwellings, Indian huts and three mission
churches with their convents was called the Presidio de San Juan
Bautista del Rio Grande—Fort St. John Baptist of the Rio Grande.
It stood six miles from the river on the vast plain of northern Coahuila,
which in dry weather was deep with gray dust, and in wet was a great
mire of bottomless mud. Thickets of mesquite forced the road to turn
and twist. Underground shelves of porous yellow-gray rock emerged
toward the river to make its walls. The fort was placed near one of the
river's best fords. It was the way over which most of the expeditions had
marched to the northeast since the 1650s, in search of the French. The
ford was known for many decades as the Paso de Francia—France Way.

The three missions stood in a triangle a mile or two apart, with
the fort in the center. Each had its settlements and its farming fields. San
Juan and San Francisco were built of clay. San Bernardo, or Saint Bernard's, the largest, was made of river stone, in massive magnificence. Its
largest foundation blocks were cubes of two and three feet cut from the
soft yellow-gray limestone that hardened when put into the walls. The
scale of Saint Bernard's was grand for its time and place. Baptistry,
sacristy, refectory, convent, travellers' rooms, storerooms and corral, grew
from one another with uninterrupted walls, and all clung heavily about

the main volume of the church. The nave was one hundred two feet long and twenty-four feet wide, except at the cruciform transepts, which reached from side to side for fifty-seven feet. Built with square corners that threw sharp diagonals of shadow on jutting outer walls, the build ing had many levels of roof and angles of wall. It had a stern splendor, like a monument to the anonymous labor and the tireless belief from which it was born in the river wilderness. Light entered into it in thin rays through small, high, square windows too deep to transit a firearm through more than a narrow arc. But above such weight, such massive secrecy and dedication of its inner life, Saint Bernard's lifted in 1703 a grace new to the river, for with its creation the curve arrived in the Spanish architecture of the Rio Grande. The circle was fragmented and used in the stone arches of the great doorways, the barrel vaultings of the nave and the refectory, and the stone dome of the baptistry. High on the nave were long moldings of carved stone that followed the angles of the walls. The Franciscan style was now formed, and while it spoke with echoes of Rome, Byzantium, North Africa and Spain, it spoke also of the river's rocky walls and ledges, the lateral stretch of plains, and the aboriginal temper it sought to enclose in peace and had to withstand in war. The limestone was pitted. Its colors carried aloft the gray of the plain and the dusty yellow of the mesquite bloom, and even in little fossil shells an ancient undersea white, and all weathered in the speckled richness of tapestry. Across the wastes of Mexico Saint Bernard's high walls and baptistry dome were a signal of haven for wayfarers coming to the wide valley from the south.

A short walk away from the walls was a clear deep pool walled by a little cliff of shelving rock and screened with feathery willows. Into it poured with enlivening voice a pale green fall of water that came over the cliff from a stone irrigation trough above. There missioners and travellers bathed. Canals brought farming water from the river upstream and activated the fields and made a park about the mission. Water entered the plaza of the garrison, and in one corner a pond collected where Indian women washed the soldiers' clothes.

At Fort St. John Baptist in the early eighteenth century all the old tasks of pacifying, teaching and overseeing labor were carried on in all the missions. The friars learned first to speak the Indian languages, and how it hurt the tongue to make it reproduce their clicks, swallowed syllables, and enclosed explosions. With communications established, they had then to explain systematic work to Indians who had never known any. Two soldiers were assigned to each mission to supervise the fields where Indian men learned to plow, Indian women to plant and cultivate. In time Indians were trained to become supervisors. If harvests were bountiful, the common stores held enough food to be distributed to all in bounty. If they failed in dry seasons, and stores were low, Indians ran away, and when overtaken could most readily be lured home again with gifts of Mexican tobacco which the missions kept on hand. From the mission herds a beef was slaughtered every fortnight and all received a share, which was not large, and was quickly gone. In a year of surplus crops, farm products were traded in Mexico for cloth which the friars gave to Indians to clothe themselves.

At morning and evening the mission bell sounded and all came for devotions, followed by religious instruction. Attendance was counted. Only the sick were excused. An Indian otherwise absent was hunted out and taken to the mission graveyard, there to kneel before a cross in penance as an example to others. If he persisted in absenting himself from indoctrination he was whipped in the presence of all the converts. The old life of the plains often called to such a one and he ran away. It called too in hunting season when far over the river in Texas the buffalo were coming south before the continental winter, and Indians were stirred in their old nature and in the nighttime quietly were gone, hollow-bellied with desire for the chase, the kill, the feasts and the orgies of lust that followed in violent satisfaction and gave them animal ease oblivious of sin. Many came back and meeting the mission fathers who had come in search of them fell to their knees and wept for forgiveness and lifted up were accompanied to Fort St. John Baptist where pressing like endless waves the repeated acts of a new way of life prevailed on the frontier shores of Texas.

For even if at the outpost there were hardship and poverty, it was sustained by resources of all kinds deep in the interior. Supplies, armaments, and ideas came from official quarters in Mexico, the sources of which moved forward in settlement as the frontier advanced. Even priests were supplied by colleges that were established far north of the viceregal capital. Many of those friars who came to work at Fort St. John Baptist near the river received their training in the seminaries of Querétaro and Zacatecas. For decades this garrison with its missions was the focus and concentrate of Spanish colonial life on the Texas Rio Grande. It was the foundation of the town long later called Guerrero, thirty miles down the river from Piedras Negras, Coahuila. It was the link between northern Mexico and the immense land of conjecture across the river; the fort, the hospice, the temple, and it soon became too the gateway, the trade center, the crossroads and the supply depot when the river ceased being a boundary and became a station on the only way to Texas.

And if this way went northeast, it also went southwest, as the ancient Comanche Trail led out of the buffalo plains to Mexico. The Trail crossed the river at two points, widely separated. One was near the Junta de los Rios above the river's big bend; the other at France Way near Fort St. John Baptist. Other travellers than Indians could use it.

One day in 1704 a young white man twenty-five years old accompanied by a handful of scouts, both white and Indian, appeared at France Way from the Texas side. He saw the stone bulk of San Bernardo in the distance across the river. Going over the river he met Indians and spoke to them fluently in their own tongue. He had trinkets for barter which he showed them. When he came to the mission he presented himself with courtesy. He made remarks about the great mineral riches of Mexico, the mines of Chihuahua and Parral. He had been across all of Texas and had seen no mining country, though he spoke with animation and fondness of the beautiful wooded glades where the traveller could rest, and of the friendly Indians who responded to invitations to trade with him. He had a map of his travels. The Spanish Franciscans examined it. The journey traced upon it started in Louisiana. The traveller believed that peaceful trade should be established between Louisiana and Mexico, through Fort St. John Baptist. He spoke in French. His name was Louis Juchereau de St. Denis, and he had come down the Mississippi from Canada a few years before. He saw bright possibilities of prosperity for himself and his remote settlement in Louisiana. In a sense, he was the future, and the future could wait. His visit was brief. Refreshed by the hospitality of the friars, who at the time were without policy as to what to do with him, he returned with his party to France Way, made the ford and disappeared into Texas.

But Fort St. John Baptist had not seen the last of him, and would not forget what he signified.

34.

Early Towns

Way up the river in the kingdom of New Mexico the haciendas were resettled. Irrigation water once more ran across orchard floors in shady flood, and produce gardens were weeded, and all awoke from the bad dream of the rebellion and the reconquest. New farms were settled about the old ones. Several Spanish families living and working side by side made the pattern of a town, with everything but official organization, armed protection, and the Church. In 1705 the New Mexican governor had the authority to found towns, though in the next century this power was reserved for the home government in Spain. A village was granted in the name of a family at Los Padillas in 1705, on the west side of the river above Isleta, and on April 23, 1706, Santa Fe decreed the establishment of Albuquerque on the east bank amidst deep cottonwood and willow groves on a wide sweep of rich bottom land enclosed by a long curve of the river fifteen miles from the mouth of Tijeras Canyon which cut between the Sandia and Manzanos mountains. The new town centered about the hacienda of Don Luís Carbajal which had been ruined in 1680. If the river Indians were now at peace, the transmontane Apaches were still a menace. With all its other municipal forms the town needed an armed guard, for it was New Mexico's destiny throughout nearly four centuries to live "gun in hand." Albuquerque, named in honor of the Duke of Albuquerque, had its patron saint, Francis Xavier, "the glorious apostle of the Indies," chosen by the governor, who told the King in his report that "as regards land, water, pasture, and fire-wood," the town was in "a good place." The church was already built; it was "very capacious and decent," and the priest's dwelling was nearly finished. The governor contributed vestments, a bell and altar fittings for the church, though chalices and other sacred furnishings were needed, and the King was asked for these. Work had begun on the royal municipal buildings, the settlers' houses were done, corrals were ready and the irrigation ditches already carried water from the river to the fields, which were sown. Thirty-five families, totalling two hundred and fifty people, adults and children, were settled. Everything was "in good order," and there had been "no expense to the royal treasury." It was of great importance to the kingdom to have a new fort "at a middle station along the road on one of the best sites which the said northern kingdom affords."

Soldiers were stationed in presidial squads to protect the new towns. At Santa Fe several Flying Companies of cavalry were garrisoned to take to the field when danger threatened. Bernalillo was already six years old. Santa Cruz upriver was older still. No longer were El Paso and Santa Fe the only two royal towns in the river system. All was in order except that —in a few months—the Madrid government commanded that the Patron of Albuquerque be changed from Saint Francis Xavier to Saint Philip of Neri as a gesture of courtesy to Philip V, the new King of Spain. Otherwise, "the kingdom," said the governor, "has attained the quiet, peace and tranquillity which it now enjoys."

Even the erring children longed to come home. Far to the east still lived most of the Pueblo Indians of San Lorenzo of the upriver country who had deserted their town during the revolt and had sought asylum with the "various heathen nations who inhabit the wide provinces of the plains." But their flight turned into captivity. Ever since the Rebellion they had been held as slaves. They had several times appealed for help from the reinstalled Spanish powers; and now in 1706 their pleas were answered when forty soldiers and a hundred Christian Indians marched to the east as rescuers. Claiming for the Crown all lands they crossed, they came among the heathen tribes, whom they treated "with much affection, flattery and cordiality," and managed to take custody of seventy-four Pueblo men, women and children, including two important chiefs, and to bring them home. Once there, a "ceremony of delivery and reception" was held, the apostates were absolved "with great solemnity and tenderness," and the local chiefs were given their offices again, to the satisfaction of all the kingdom.

In 1708 a new governor was "pleased to take away" the armed garrison at Albuquerque. There were immediate consequences. Albuquerque had been watched from the mountains. As soon as the squadrons withdrew in April, the Apaches came. The royal subjects of the town met to compare losses, and two of them drew up a petition which they presented in person to the council in Santa Fe on the fourteenth. They declared that the plains raiders came every day, even into the very corrals of the farms, and drove off the Spanish livestock with impunity. Seeing that there were no soldiers to prevent them, they could now be expected to fall upon the families and destroy them in their turn. The council was implored to present the case to the governor, that he might restore the Albuquerque garrison.

The old complaint—the governors were "concerned deeply with nothing save their own lawsuits"—was heard again. The missions had begged for help in re-establishing themselves, but without much luck. Mission bells were silent, for the Indians in the revolt had taken the clappers from which to make spear points. The churches, though clean, were bare. The sacred ornaments, vessels and paintings had been burned and never replaced. In some of the poorer parishes the Indians had made crosses and had painted them "according to their own style." In place of silver cruets were others made of clay, and still others of tin. There was hardly a complete set of vestments of one color in the whole province, and even at Santa Fe, Masses for the dead had to be said without a black cope, for the old one there was so worn and patched that it could no longer be used. These were large matters to those who complained of them.

And yet the towns took root, and their spiritual element made a society and a tradition out of life thinly drawn along the river. Los Lunas, south of Albuquerque, was founded in 1716, and, near El Paso, the Isleta, the Socorro and the Senecu of the South, all three founded when the loyal Indians of the upper towns of the same names had retreated with Otermín in 1680, now had their own missions. San Lorenzo, where the refugee governors had maintained their state in reed huts, also had a mission, and all were dominated by the Guadalupe of El Paso. "In these places," said a contemporary account, "Indians and Spaniards live commingled." From the river came the main irrigating ditch which the Spaniards controlled. It had two floodgates which could be opened to release water into other ditches that flowed, at Spanish pleasure, to the Indian fields. The farms were lush. There was "excellent wheat, free of all darnel, and with a remarkably large grain." The fine velvety soil of the south bank had to be plowed extra deep in order to hold up the heavy stalks of maize, for when the hard wind blew, as it so often did in growing season, the clattering plants were uprooted and laid flat on the ground. Beans, chick-peas, and "especially large, white sweet onions" grew well.

Such good things could be shown and handled and believed. Up the river where ice formed every winter, often so thickly that loaded

carts could cross over upon it, the mayor and the pastor of San Juan
wrote down what happened in the river nature of the early eighteenth
century. To the river's banks there would come eagles with white heads
and necks, who at sunrise would "perch on the trees nearby. In a little
while, circling in the air, they fly to a great height, whence they descend,
head downward and wings drawn back, with the swiftness of a shooting
star. The noise that they make is so great that it sounds like thunder, and
while they are still more than a hundred yards away the ice makes loud
cracking noises, and when they reach it a large hole is already open. The
eagle enters by it and seizes in its claws a fish weighing four, five, or more
pounds, which it eats upon the ice if no one prevents it. The most
remarkable thing is that in a short space of time the ice is already closed
up." The account was filed away among the official papers of the kingdom, where coming across it later someone added, "Although this note
has been copied as a marvelous incident of natural history, we cannot
set aside the distrust inspired by the observations of LaFontaine of
Grenoble upon the Phoenix, and other fables. . . ." The big sweet onions
of El Paso, the fabulous bald eagles of San Juan, both helped to make
the river's tale.

35.

Colonial Texas

Like all other frontier commanders, Captain Domingo Ramón at
Fort St. John Baptist received in 1713 clear orders from the Viceroy not
to admit foreign traders or foreign merchandise into Spanish lands. If
any foreigner crossed the frontier he was to be arrested and the Viceroy
notified. Mexico City would then decide the disposal of the prisoner.
Though France and Spain were precariously allied in the old world
through their Bourbon kings, Louis XIV and Philip V, in the new they
faced each other across the wastes of Texas as aggressor and defender.

It was a position darkly imaged by the Spanish temperament. The French
saw it somewhat differently; or so, with rippling plausibility, they strove
to show in the autumn of 1714.

For then there appeared again at France Way out of Texas, bearing information, merchandise and high good manners, the Colonial
Frenchman Louis de St. Denis, with three French and three Indian
companions. Now ten years after his first visit he was thirty-five years
old, and still in love with Texas. He reported to Captain Diego Ramón
at Fort St. John Baptist. He was full of stories—his party had set out to
buy cattle and other supplies for Louisiana from the Spanish missions
that were supposed to be in East Texas, but having heard these were
long since abandoned, he had come to the Rio Grande to make his purchases. He had travelled a year and nine months from Mobile. On the
way he had been obliged to fight a pitched battle against Indian enemies
of the Texas. He had seen a beautiful site for a mission, a fort and a
town—the San Antonio River. He gave flourish to his purpose, which,
he made plain, was to open trade with northern New Spain. He wanted
to draw the two frontiers together, not separate them with barriers. If
he was a wilderness master, he was also a merchant of state, and if he was
in a position of risk he seemed not to recognize it. He handed his French
passport to Captain Ramón, whose orders were clear. Captain de St.
Denis and his friends were placed in arrest, while news of their presence
on the river went by fast courier to Mexico City.

It was a comfortable arrest, for the prisoners were lodged in the
home of the commander. They could easily have escaped, but St. Denis
chose not to, saying, "I fear nothing from these people or from Mexico."
The post commander's granddaughter, Doña María Ramón, was to be
seen. She had been a little girl ten years before, during the ruddy,
muscular young Frenchman's first journey to the river. If she saw him
then, he saw her now. His captivity lasted several months at Fort St.
John Baptist. There were little rides that could safely be taken, from one
to the next of the three missions. There were grassy shadows where to
lie by the rocky pool with its waterfall near Saint Bernard's. There were
dangers to share that like any shared emotion left a certain commitment between people. In March, 1715, the Indians of Fort St. John
Baptist revolted. At midnight they attacked the fort, throwing down
bars and chasing out horses and cattle, flourishing torches and crying
death. The garrison arose to fight. Friars took refuge in the stone granary
of Saint Bernard's. Others went for aid from a mission farther inland.
Indians set fire to what they could. Help arrived from the south, the

revolt was subdued, never to recur, and Captain de St. Denis declared his love to Doña María Ramón, to which her grandfather gave his consent. The prisoner was in excellent favor.

In June a company of soldiers arrived from Mexico to take him and his comrades to the Viceroy. He departed in all confidence, the prospective grandson-in-law of the frontier captain who was duty-bound to oppose the French. He was the smiling embodiment of a force that would not be denied. The Spaniards spoke of him as a menace, and yet with grace submitted to his intention.

He was back in the following April to take his bride at St. John Baptist. After long inquisitions before the viceregal authorities, he ended as a Spanish officer, in charge of supplies for an expedition immediately ordered by the Viceroy. If the French came as traders and as suitors, it was clear that Spain must once again occupy East Texas to prevail against them. The missions abandoned in 1693 were ordered re-established, yet the alarming Frenchman himself who occasioned the move was to serve as quartermaster to the Spaniards on their eastward march. St. Denis faced his loyalties both ways. Through secret letters carried by Indian couriers to the Governor of Louisiana, he kept his own home government informed of his successes, and proposed that France extend the borders of Louisiana to the Rio Grande. The nearer New Spain moved to New France the easier were chances for commerce to sustain the needs of Louisiana. This fulfilled French policy. France inviting, Spain extending defenses, both acted through the imperative medium of St. Denis. He had several weeks with his bride at St. John Baptist before the supply forces, soldiers and missionaries were assembled at the river for the departure to the east.

In March, 1716, the expedition under the command of Captain Domingo Ramón crossed the river at France Way. The ford was unusually easy, as the river was low. Along with arms, building tools, food and sacerdotal supplies, the train carried certain items that had a French air in the wilderness, reflecting St. Denis's accent on trade for his own colonists: silk hosiery for ladies and gentlemen, bolts of laces and ribbons, four dozen pairs of shoes. The train camped on the north bank of the river for a week. A soldier married a girl of a settler's family, and the festivities lasted two days. Fray Francisco Hidalgo, founder of the missions abandoned twenty-three years before, was now joyfully returning to reopen his chapels and see his Texas people again. On March 27 the little army—there were twenty-five soldiers—and all the other company passed in review before Captain Domingo Ramón and his second-in-command, Captain de St. Denis, and with their thousand animals drew away from the Rio Grande over the south Texas plains in the season of wild flowers. The scent of the flowers was aloft in the air for weeks, and the ground exhaling after spring rains was dazzling with fields and meadows and miles of white and pink poppies, blue flax, bluebonnets, magenta phlox, yellow and white daisies, orange gaillardia, in exquisite profusion. The entry was made in peace. Once among the Texas people, St. Denis served as interpreter, presiding over the exchanges between Indian and Spaniard with satisfaction and dispatch. All smoked in turn a peace pipe nearly three feet long. Volleys were fired, the Te Deum was sung, Fray Francisco Hidalgo embraced his children and their new children, and during the first ten days of July four missions were settled in what long later was known as Nacogdoches County. Spain had its living claim to Texas, face to face with Louisiana.

On the journey eastward from the Rio Grande, in slow travel the marchers saw the need of another settlement between the river and the missions nearly a thousand miles away. At a suitable distance from the two ends of the journey, they passed through lush, low-rolling country where a small river wound its way through shady groves and flower-starred meadows. It was a stream that earlier travellers had named after San Antonio. In the following year, at Fort St. John Baptist, the religious and lay powers of Colonial Spain were once again assembling to cross into Texas to found a community, this time on the San Antonio River. Fray Antonio de San Buenaventura Olivares was the chief missioner of the enterprise, and the new governor and captain-general of Texas, Don Martín de Alarcón, was the commander.

Fray Antonio reached the Rio Grande ahead of the Governor. What he found there enraged him. The discipline of the frontier was lax. Indians were insolent and indifferent. After the example of the garrison, they had lost respect for the friars, and even flouted the authority of the troops. Thievery and revolt were everywhere. The corruption of society went right to the top, for the Ramón family, so long in charge at Fort St. John Baptist, gave only nominal observance to the famous regulations against foreign trade, and had actually been enriched by dealing with the French through St. Denis, who had married into the family. To be sure, St. Denis, on appearing for the third time over France Way in April, 1717, had been arrested by his grandfather-in-law, and had had his rich cargo of merchandise impounded; but what good were such measures when there seemed to be evidence that organized contraband trade on a large scale was going on between him and the

Ramóns? Moreover, in spite of the requirement that every Frenchman crossing the river was to be clapped into prison, plenty of them came and went as they liked, and even paused comfortably at the Fort. Three were quite openly digging a mine in Coahuila. St. Denis had been sent to Mexico for questioning again, leaving his goods at the river frontier post.

In August the Governor arrived at the Fort, and conducted a personal investigation into affairs. The French seen there by Fray Antonio vanished, but the Spaniards remaining seemed much influenced by French ideas. The Governor though he was unable to find proof of actual wrongdoing on the part of the Ramón family and St. Denis recommended that they be relieved of their posts. But with an artfulness that recalled the sprightly talents of their French relation, they continued to pursue their double course, and engaged in helping the Spanish Governor assemble his expedition that was to establish San Antonio and to serve as a vital supply link in the chain that would contain the French. The foundation of San Antonio knew another urgent reason: unruly Indians of the Rio Grande were to be moved to the new community, and there resettled about their missions, which would be officially transferred with them.

Burning with zeal and faith in Providence, Fray Antonio tugged at the Governor's establishment to take to the trail over the river. But Alarcón had problems of recruitment, supply and legal authorization that took time to solve. Anxious letters came to the Rio Grande from the East Texas missions, where now the French seemed actually to be hostile to the Spaniards whom they had called to the east for commerce. St. Denis in Mexico, after being questioned and briefly jailed, was at large on bond and free to return to the river to sell his goods. He came, disposed of all his cargo, and returned to Mexico City with money and a plan to arrange a government post for himself. The winter passed, and still the expedition did not leave, and the Two Majesties became acrimonious toward one another, the one over delay, the other over importunity. But finally, on April 9, 1718, Governor Alarcón crossed at France Way, and nine days later, having refused to travel with him, Fray Antonio followed. The two parties followed different routes, through a season of cloudbursts and risen streams, but by May first, they met at the head of a spring creek in "a thick wood of . . . elms, poplars, hackberry trees, oaks, and many mulberries, all of them being thickly covered with wild grapevines," and with proper ceremonies in the following days the town and the first missions of San Antonio were secured. There in the next few years would rise five mission churches, with their cells for dwelling and storing, all made of the rich limestone that lay under the black soil of the grand plain of South Texas, and all beautifully illustrating different graces of the Franciscan baroque style —San Antonio de Valero (the Alamo) with its scrolled façade; La Purísima Concepción with its perfect dome; San Francisco de la Espada with its richly modified Moorish arch at the main door; San Juan Capistrano with its uprolling façade pierced with arches for bells; and San José, with its dome and its carved tower and embrasures and huge barrel-vaulted granary. From the great clay coffins of the upper river, to the mighty walls of St. Bernard's at Fort St. John Baptist, and ending with the temples of San Antonio in their misty meadows, the Franciscan style knew a century of wonderful change that yet expressed unchanging faith.

On January 29, 1719, Governor Alarcón heard a startling piece of news that came wandering overland with whatever traveller might be crossing Texas. It had to do with St. Denis, last believed safely in hand at Mexico City. His money was all spent. The government post he sought had been denied him, and he was in consequence heard to be saying about town that he intended to avenge himself by inspiring a revolt among the Rio Grande Indians. The government heard of his mutterings and threatened his arrest. On September 5, 1718, he vanished, barely escaping a royal order that he be deported with his wife to Guatemala. Had he returned to Louisiana? No one knew in Texas, but the French attitude seemed less inviting.

In fact, the official French policy had never been quite so hospitable as St. Denis had made it seem. So long before as 1715 Governor Cadillac of New France had determined to order St. Denis "to engage all the savages on Red River to oppose the establishment of the Spaniards." And yet they had been established, and with St. Denis's grace. Was it possible that if he had two national policies to dance between, he had also a third which engaged him the most, which was his own? While he could be everywhere, he and his relations grew rich, and to all concerned he could toss what each desired—the Spanish friars their converts, the French settlers their imported finery, the Viceroy of New Spain his fortified frontier, the Ramón family their profits. When he vanished, it was with the effect of broken promises.

In June, 1719, at the Spanish mission outpost of Los Adaes in East Texas, the French attacked. The size of the demonstration—eight Frenchmen made war on a Spanish lay brother and a private soldier and upset the henyard—was less disturbing than its mere fact. The lay brother escaped to the next mission, and as soon as news could travel, the whole Spanish eastern frontier was in panic. St. Denis was blamed for the attack. The missions felt their isolation and insecurity. In the autumn they withdrew to San Antonio, and for the next year all the aching machinery of Spanish viceregal government worked at organizing a return to East Texas. The Marquis of Aguayo came to Fort St. John Baptist in December, 1720, commanding a restorative expedition. There he heard that St. Denis was assembling a great Indian horde to attack San Antonio. Reinforcements were sent ahead, and the Marquis presently followed, but the threatened battle was only a nervous rumor. The Marquis marched eastward, and in August, 1721, at the Neches River a horseman swam his mount across to meet him. It was St. Denis, prepared to observe the peace that had been concluded between France and Spain in Europe. The Marquis agreed, provided France might abandon Texas, and Spain reoccupy it to her former limits. St. Denis withdrew, but reluctantly, somehow preserving intact for as long as he might live his nuisance value as an unsettling presence on the Spanish eastern border.

The flow and counterflow of France and Spain against one another reached from the northern river kingdom of New Mexico out to the north central plains in the same period. Santa Fe heard that the French were intruding westward with Pawnee Indian allies. New France claimed that Spanish forces were mobilizing to march from Santa Fe to capture Illinois. In the summer of 1720 Captain Pedro de Villasur led some of the presidial company of Santa Fe—forty-two soldiers—and a party of settlers and Indian fighters out to the plains. With him was L'Archevêque —the Frenchman who had helped to murder LaSalle—who was now a Spanish subject. Like St. Denis he acted as interpreter between Spaniards and Indians when the two forces met at the North Platte River. The Pawnees were French-trained in the use of arms and tactics. They feigned not to understand L'Archevêque. Negotiations came to nothing. A battle followed in which the Santa Feans were overwhelmed. Only thirteen escaped to return to the New Mexican capital. L'Archevêque was among those killed. It was rumored that French soldiers, disguised as Pawnees, were among the victors, and that to avenge LaSalle they had singled out his assassin. The unsettled plains claimed their dead, but with little to fight over but space, the northern campaigns came to nothing, and hostilities, if not vigilance, died out with the signing of the peace between France and Spain in the homelands.

After the early years of the religious and military missions that crossed the Rio Grande into Texas, the civil authority must follow; and in the winter of 1731 there appeared at Fort St. John Baptist a party of fifteen families numbering fifty-six persons, accompanied by armed escort. These were people from the Canary Islands, removed by royal decree to resettle at San Antonio, there to establish the first civil organization in Texas. They stayed for two days on the Rio Grande. While there one of their company, a little girl of five, died. She was the only casualty of a journey lasting many months. In March all arrived at San Antonio, where the missions and the fort would thenceforth serve a royally chartered city. All the settlers were granted patents of nobility under which they were to enjoy the same privileges, dignity and prerogatives as the Hidalgos of Castile.

Over the river at Fort St. John Baptist went the life stream of Texas. For decades this ford was the beach-head for invasions, the supply depot, the station of reinforcements, the ecclesiastical headquarters, the wayfarer's haven, and the starting point for explorations, like that of Berroterán who was sent northwest along the Rio Grande in 1720 to examine the unknown river country between St. John Baptist and the Junta de Los Rios. In the early half of the eighteenth century Fort St. John Baptist and El Paso marked the extremes of Spanish settlement on the river's lower thousand miles. Between them lived only one other—that of the missions at the meeting of the rivers.

But its life was fitful, now flickering high, again low, for unlike other frontier mission outposts, it had no fort and garrison for its defense. The Indian temper blew hot and cold, and the friars responded accordingly, bringing conversion when it was asked for—and it was asked for repeatedly; and fleeing, often in rags and starving over deserts, when savages backslid. So it was in the time of Fray Nicolás López, the founder of the Junta in 1683, and so it continued to be into the eighteenth century. The Indians were described as "very clever and politic," the country of the junction of the Rio Grande and the Concho was seen as productive and desirable, and the passage of the river there was one of the two grand ways to Texas—as the plains Indians had long demonstrated. Settled missions at that gateway would do much to prevent plundering raids into northern Mexico. The governors of New Biscay and Coahuila sent a number of expeditions (the first of these was that of Trasviño Retis in 1715) to pacify the region permanently, and to bring back information of value to the north Mexican governments. But they sent no garrison to remain. Friars accompanied the march, the missions were reopened, new ones were added, soldiers withdrew, and for a year or two all was well.

And then, usually in the nighttime, with scream and brand, the converts would rise against their peaceful fathers and kill them, or try to, or drive them away. In 1725 two friars were seized and tied. Their heads were to be cut off and the Indians were going to dance about them. Granted time for their own confessions, the missioners gave each other absolution. Suddenly a force of soldiers appeared. They were from Chihuahua. At sight of them the Indians fled. The friars were lifted up and taken to Chihuahua, where their delivery was celebrated with public rejoicings.

In the following year there was talk of establishing a fort with a garrison at the Junta, but nothing came of it, and resident missionary efforts were not resumed. Occasional visits from inland missions during peaceful interludes were all that seemed possible. In 1736 a garrison was stationed in a new fort—the Presidio Sacramento—on the San Diego River that entered the Rio Grande south of the later Del Rio. But with the whole Big Bend in between, it was too far from the Junta to be the source of any protection. Three efforts were made in 1747 to assimilate the Junta into the civilized influence of northern Mexico. Pedro Rábago y Terán led a party from Monclova; Fermín de Vidaurre set out from Durango; and Captain Joseph Idoyaga came with his men from a hundred and fifty miles up the Conchos. They all described the beauty of the confluence, its rich farm lands, the eight Indian villages in the flat valley; and strong recommendations were made again for the establishment of a fort, without which no permanent colonial life could be expected to cling to the river of the Fish Indians, as they were called there.

But government had its maps, and what lay not on the river but beyond it was what induced forts and garrisons and town charters. North of El Paso lay the whole settled kingdom of New Mexico. Northeast of Fort St. John Baptist lay the central Texas kingdom with its steadily developing communities and trade. Both sites called alive important gateway settlements. But across the confluence at the Junta was only the Comanche trail leading to and from the wild plains. Eastern New Mexico and western Texas yet held little but empty wilderness and roving hostility. No garrison was ordered to the Junta for another ten years. There was another immense stretch of the river still unoccupied, hardly visualized, that had to be mapped and settled. It was valley land that reached from Fort St. John Baptist all the way to the river's mouth at the Gulf. Spanish life was pushing north toward the Texas river frontier.

Indian raiders threatened it, in spite of the Spanish settlements in Texas.
While in New Mexico, the valley was the road, in Texas the Rio Grande
had been known principally by its fords, where colonial life leaped the
river and left it behind. It was not until 1747 that the last valley of the
lower river came to be understood and used, in a large gesture devised
by an able colonizer.

He faced difficulties; but one long familiar to earlier Spanish
officers was already ended. "St. Denis," declared a Spanish administrator
in 1744, "St. Denis is dead, thank God, and now we can breathe easier."

36.

Mexico Bay

In 1746 Don José de Escandón was corregidor—mayor, or chief
magistrate, of Querétaro. For seven years the Mexican government had
been looking for the right man to command the settlement of the last
Spanish frontier. Several applied for the post, but some were not plausible enough and some were too much so. The Crown weighed all applications, and was not satisfied. A man was wanted who, with a flawless
record in public affairs, a history of known piety and a proper family
life, could combine large gestures of imagination and of courage. The
great conquerors all seemed to love their enemy the wilderness; to
understand its dry and poisonous and illimitable reaches. To such men
the unknown was an invitation that made their heads swim with desire.
They were inclined to simplify their visions, but many of them had the
genius to make their visions come true after all. If they could see the
terra incognita as thought it were on a map, and in the air could trace
with a finger just where they would go and what they would do, it was
astonishing how often on the land itself they kept their promises.

The great Mexico Bay made a vast crescent, and in the habit of
speech in 1746, the term included the wide shore lands that lay inland

from the low beaches. For miles from the sea the lands plainly referred
to their old life as ocean floors. There were jungles in the southern
arc of the crescent and sand wastes on the northern. The Rio Grande
flowed into the ocean at the center of the arc encompassing Texas and
the Mexican coastline. It was a region that recalled though it did not
equal in size the old kingdom of Florida whose western boundary two
centuries earlier was the River of Palms. Now with the province of
Mexico Bay reaching both north and south of the river, and from the
river's mouth upstream to Fort St. John Baptist, the country had to be
seen comprehensively, and all its sweep called for sweeping plans to
conquer it. On September 3, 1746, the Viceroy of New Spain made his
appointment of the commander for the job. He chose the corregidor
of Querétaro, who had never applied for it.

But Escandón's record was excellent. He was forty-six years old, a
native of Spain, son of a highly respected family. Eager like the conquerors of the Golden Age to create his own glory, he came to the
Americas as a youth. He served as a cavalry cadet in Yucatán for six years,
fighting renegade Indians and meeting the tentative English thrusts
against Mexico made from the sea. Promoted lieutenant, he was transferred to Querétaro for duty against the unpacified Indians of the Sierra
Gorda. Local campaigns lasted for years there, with the mountain Indians
ensconced in their vast natural castles, and the missions, ranches and
towns of Querétaro in periodic danger when the Indians swept down
from the heights. At the age of twenty-seven, Lieutenant de Escandón
went to Spain to marry. He brought his wife back to his frontier station
and resumed his service in the field. In the next dozen years he rose
rapidly as an Indian campaigner. By 1740 the Indians of the Sierra Gorda
were subdued, largely through his efforts as commander. He was promoted to the post of Lieutenant General, or military governor, of Sierra
Gorda, and confirmed his field victories by establishing missions and
villages where the Indians, intransigent for two centuries, were now
gathered in peace. He was the very officer to understand the problem
of Mexico Bay where, noted the government, the Indian nations "live
without religion, without fixed habitation, without dress, who like wild
and wandering beasts, occupy the coast of the Mexican Gulf, its ports, its
famous salines, rich rivers, healthful plains, fertile lands, and valuable
minerals. With their murders, thefts, fires, and all kinds of inhuman
atrocities, they desolate entire jurisdictions, provinces, cities, villages, and
Christian settlements along the southern, western, and northern confines
of their haunts. They obstruct the roads, paralyze commerce, and occa-

sion incalculable losses to the royal treasury daily with the increased annual costs involved in the maintenance of presidios and the organization of campaigns."

The Lieutenant General lost no time in organizing his moves upon Mexico Bay. He studied reports and maps. He weighed earlier schemes, and came to his own. He was made a viceregal lieutenant general which meant that his authority was superior to that of the provincial governors and commanders whom he put to work in certain orders that went in many different directions by fast couriers in the autumn of 1746. All of northeastern New Spain came alive with the new enterprise, and provincial governors and frontier garrisons looked toward its realization with the New Year.

For in January, 1747, from seven different posts on the outlying perimeter of the arc of Mexico Bay seven different armed detachments began to move simultaneously toward the mouth of the Rio Grande, which required about a thirty-day march for each. In one great, co-ordinated movement, Escandón brought all of Mexico Bay under comprehensive examination, which, he said, would "cause great wonder to the natives to see Spanish soldiers entering from all directions, before the news of their presence can be transmitted by smoke signals." There were seven hundred sixty-five soldiers in his seven divisions. They reconnoitered a region of almost a hundred and twenty thousand square miles, which Escandón described as "a sort of bag lying between Tampico, Pánuco, Villa de Valles, Custodia de Rio Verde, Neuvo Reyno de León and the Bahía del Espiritu Santo," where stood the farthest Spanish fort of coastal Texas. Two hundred and twenty-eight years after the first attempt to settle the River of Palms—by which was meant the lower Rio Grande—the Spanish power at last embraced all of the river but its source country above New Mexico.

Escandón arrived at the mouth of the river on February twenty-seventh with his detachment from Jaumave, which had begun its march in January. He saw the marshy lands and the palms, and no other trees but willows. He saw how in wide shallow lagoons beside the river the water flowed in and out according to how the wind blew. Upstream the river's meanders could be tapped for irrigation. Wild onions—delicious to taste—grew in abundance. Wild horses and cattle grazed on the seaside flats. On the beach were empty bottles and broken planking cast up from shipwrecks. Escandón saw people—various Indian nations, and one whose people were negroid. Where had these come from? The wild Negroes believed that their ancestors, all male warriors, carrying spears and

shields, had come by sea, swimming, or, some said, in boats, and had
taken Indian women to wife. Escandón wondered. Perhaps they had
come from islands between Mexico Bay and Africa. Perhaps a slave ship
had been wrecked and the survivors cast ashore at the River of Palms.
Or had they been left behind by the first Spanish ships that had touched
the river between 1519 and 1523? Who could say? The beach Indians
were friendly, and so were others from the river inlands, who declared
that they would welcome the settlement of missions in their country.
Gifts were distributed—Spanish tobacco, biscuits, tin jewelry. Escandón
and his men built a barge by which to cross to the north bank and
sound the river. There was no bay at the mouth, but only a sand bar
hardly four yards deep. The stream was so abundant that its waters
flowing into the gulf were noticeable for more than a league offshore,
and "the waves being unable to thwart them, they maintain their sweetness." If the river had a main channel reaching the sea, there were also
others that cut through the low dunes to make little mouths. The river
showed change. "I suppose," said Escandón, "small ships could enter
the river." But he added that the land was so flat and the banks so low
that small protection was offered to navigators.

One of the other divisions in the radial descent upon Mexico
Bay started from Fort St. John Baptist, crossed the ford there, and
marched to the Gulf along the north bank. They soon came to the end
of the river's rocky character, and entered upon the silty lands that went
flatter and lower as they marched. The country then as they saw it had
little vegetation other than scattered mesquite groves. They said there
was little or no water. Nine different Indian nations lived along the
river's low reaches and allowed the Spaniards to pass by in peace. Early
in March the detachment reached the ocean, following the northernmost branch of the river, which they tried to sound but without success.
They reported to Escandón at the mouth of the river's main channel.
The co-ordinated expedition was a success, as one detachment after
another completed its march and brought its reports to the Lieutenant
General. Not a soldier was lost. The vast bag of Mexico Bay was mapped,
and the Rio Grande was seen as the central vein for strategic exploitation. Escandón dismissed his divisions to return to their home garrisons,
and led his own back to Querétaro, where throughout the summer he
worked over his data and wrote his official report and recommendation.

Let the new lands, he said, be settled from the very same frontier
forts from which the soldiers of his seven divisions had marched to the
river. Offer those soldiers the first chance to become settlers. Give them

tracts of land and furnish them with funds up to certain amounts so
that in moving and settling they might not suffer undue financial hardship. Choose experienced missionaries to go with the settlers. Do not
establish fortresses in each new settlement. Rather let the settlers themselves plant their fields and then defend them if need be; for men with
families and fields at stake will defend them with greater devotion than
paid soldiers in a frontier garrison, so many of whom were under legal
sentences that had to be served in the wilderness instead of in prison.
If for the first or second year, while the settlers were putting down
their stakes, an armed guard were needed, then a few soldiers might be
sent along; but only temporarily. Under these proposals, there were
fourteen settlements and missions to be established. Of these, six were to
take root along the Rio Grande. The region of Mexico Bay had looked
to him like Santander, the province of his boyhood in Spain; and
Escandón suggested that the Gulf kingdom be called New Santander.
His report went to Mexico City, and there entered into the toils of government. It aroused admiration, his proposals were approved, he was
appointed to make good his exploration by undertaking the colonization,
and the Viceroy recommended him to the King for some suitable form
of royal recognition. He accepted the appointment on June 1, 1748, and
immediately sent out word in his famous seven directions to enlist five
hundred volunteer families to found the first fourteen towns of New
Santander. Seven hundred families applied. Those accepted were given
free land, a gift of money amounting to between one and two hundred
pesos, and a ten-year exemption from taxes.

In February, 1749, the first of the lower Rio Grande settlers came
out of Nuevo León to make the town of Nuestra Señora de Santa Ana de
Camargo. Forty families and a squad of soldiers built a town of straw
huts thatched with palm leaves on the Mexican San Juan River near its
confluence with the Rio Grande. On March third Escandón arrived from
the interior where he had already assisted at the establishment of other
towns. Two days later Camargo was formally dedicated with Mass celebrated under an arbor. Spirits ran high. The land was good for farming
and cattle raising. The neighboring Indians were eager to settle alongside the Spaniards. Wood for building was plentiful up the San Juan.
The settlers built flatboats to cross the river. Salt could be had near-by.
Two friars were in residence, and a mission was established, and within
a few years would have its stone church. Escandón gave the settlers a
supply of corn to tide them over until their first harvest, and moved
downstream to join another group of settlers from inland posts. With

them on March fourteenth he established the community of Reynosa
on the south bank. He gave them food, farming implements, clothes and
oxen. The pattern of Spanish settlement on the river's last reaches was
being fulfilled rapidly and peacefully. Escandón travelled from one to
another of his new communities watching them come alive all according to his plan. In October, 1749, at Madrid, the King expressed his
approval of Escandón's service by creating him Count of Sierra Gorda,
and appointing him a Knight of Santiago, Spain's highest military honor.
News of such striking royal favor reached him early in the following
year, and he assumed his new style that had been won in the field, far
from palaces and courts.

About halfway between Fort St. John Baptist and the mouth of
the Rio Grande the town of Dolores was founded on the north bank
during the summer of 1750. It clustered about the ranch of Don José
Vásquez Borrego, a cattle raiser who asked Escandón to include him in
his colonization plans. Borrego maintained a ferry service for his own
people and herds, running two flatboats which were attended by four
peons. Down the river in the same summer Revilla (later Guerrero) was
established on the south bank, at the site of the ranch of Don Nicolás
de la Garza. Like Dolores, it was a cattle town, whose herds were grazed
in the vast pastures across the river. Friction between the two towns
occurred now and then as their herds mingled.

Mier near the south bank was founded in 1753, and Escandón
remarked soon that "the entire frontier on the opposite bank of the Rio
Grande del Norte is settled . . ." out of which came the later towns
of Roma and Rio Grande City. On May 15, 1755, on the north bank,
with the benefit of an excellent ford and easy access over flat country
on either side, a handful of families were settled by Escandón, who
named their grant the Villa of Laredo.

And now the lower river towns gradually drew the traffic to
Texas away from the crossing at Fort St. John Baptist. Dolores and
Laredo, with their ferries, Reynosa with its access to the salt deposits
over the river to the northeast, saw more and more of the slow but persistent travel between the older Mexican states and New Santander.
Royal couriers and military inspectors and missionaries went back and
forth over the river on their duties. Wagon trains, cattle herds and
trading convoys chose the more peaceful routes of the river's mild southeast country in preference to the rocky fords, deep walls and Apache
menaces upriver, where in 1749 a priest and his party were murdered
as they neared Fort St. John Baptist. The six lower river towns encour-

aged ranchers to take their headquarters farther into Texas. If the lower
river settlement came late, in relation to the old river kingdom of New
Mexico, it came fast. The straw huts were soon replaced by earthen
houses, stone churches, and plastered walls with carved wooden doors,
all squared around a central plaza. Floods rose and towns were removed
to safer ground near their original sites—Reynosa and Camargo were
moved once, and Revilla three times. Indian settlers took second thoughts
and ran away, but were mostly recovered and resettled. Smallpox epidemics struck during the 1750s, there were seasons of drought, and at
its best life was hard and meagre. But it was tenacious, and the river was
its home. Vast as it was, the province of New Santander had little wealth
in the great world's terms of money, purchasable beauty, luxury, or even
comfort. Its material values were all reckoned in the earthiest terms—
hides, horn, beef, mutton, wool, salt, fish, fruit. Distances were very
great, summers were violent with heat, drought or deluge, winters were
subject to wild icy storms out of the north. A lower river town made a
little geometrized chequer of wall and tower, faintly pink, yellow, blue,
white and earthen, at the end of a straggle of road on the river's high
bank. For the rest, there was abstract dimension—the plains dimming
to sea-blue in a wilderness of light, north in Texas, or south in Mexico,
where for all life that came after, the hard, modest toil of the Count of
Sierra Gorda remained ancestral.

37.

Forgotten Lessons

Even in the eighteenth century there was but one seaport in
Mexico open to ships from the Old World, and that was Veracruz. Every
effort was made to exclude trade and traffic from any country but Spain.
Spanish America, north and south, tried unceasingly with mission and
fort to keep her incredibly extended boundaries everywhere closed. And

yet across distance and every imaginable obstacle of geography the immense empire was knitted together by the royal mail service with its couriers. Mail was delivered, however slowly, to any farthest Indian outpost where a Spanish addressee was known by name. To reach the Rio Grande, the post came to Mexico City, and if destined for the lower river towns was forwarded by way of Querétaro or Monclova; and if for New Mexico, by way of Chihuahua and El Paso. With the mail came the news gazettes, late but, for all practical purposes in a limestone mission or a clay fortress on the Rio Grande, absorbingly current. An editor printed in his *Mercurio de México* a notice which begged "the Presidents, Governors, Mayors and other Prelates of the chief towns to let him have the news of their districts, first nights of plays, foundations, origins of miraculous images, and other things worthy of the public light, for him to print it in the coming month," along with the "General News from the Kingdoms of Europe as well as from New Spain." The fringed leather saddlebags were emptied of their consignments of personal and public news at settlements of New Santander; at Fort St. John Baptist where the missions now attended only a handful of Indian families and a constantly dwindling stream of travellers; at the Junta de los Rios, where in 1759 a protective fort was finally established among the missions, and abandoned under pressure from the northern plains in 1767; and at El Paso where life was busy, prices were scandalously high, and the river flooded every summer from May to July.

During the high-water season, traffic for the north forded in peril with the aid of Indian swimmers, or waited among the five towns until the muddy runoff of melted snow from far northern mountains was by. How could melted snow be muddy? they wondered. The river was always muddy. They shrugged. It was its nature, coming through deserts where the earth was loose, and vegetation sparse, so that water rolling over it took along what could be moved. So the riverbed was always being built up by dragged earth, until the river rose above its own walls and fell into new, lower courses, or encountered rock canyons which contained it. There was a dam at El Paso to be rebuilt each year. With willow wands, said a traveller, the El Pasoans made "large cylindrical baskets. These they fill with small stones and gravel and when the flood subsides they roll them into position." Then the less violent flow could be diverted from backwaters into irrigation canals and taken to the Spanish and Indian fields of the south bank. The trade caravans for Chihuahua and Santa Fe crossed in safety, taking to the south such commodities as dressed hides, Indian slaves, peltries of beaver and muskrat, woven blankets and rugs, piñon nuts, salt and turquoise; and to the north, imports from Europe through Spain and Veracruz, and from China and the Philippines through Acapulco.

Describing the five missions in the vicinity of El Paso in 1764, a Franciscan inspector called the Guadalupe "the flower of them all, both on account of its fruits and garden products and of its climate." But all of the other missions there—San Lorenzo del Real, San Antonio Senecu, San Antonio de la Isleta and San Francisco del Socorro—had their gardens and vineyards, their communal orchards and fields. The Indian farmers, under their Spanish masters, harvested pears, peaches, apples and grapes. The friars made their own sacramental wine; the citizens their brandy. Wheat and corn were piled in the granaries, and doled out to the Indians in lean seasons. Indian servants fulfilled the duties of bell ringer, cook, porter, sacristans, "grinding-women for the wheat." The clustered settlements of El Paso were already a busy and strategic junction point on the traffic lane north and south across the river, "the great Rio del Norte," which was "a beautiful image of the celebrated Nile, for if mortals, urged by necessity, are enlisted under the banner of the waters of the Nile, so also are other mortals for the same reason settled along the banks of the Rio del Norte."

In "that old and unfortunate province" of New Mexico, as a Mexican civil servant called it, a census of the mid-eighteenth century estimated a population of 771 households, comprising approximately ten thousand people. The greatest towns were Santa Cruz in the north, Santa Fe, Albuquerque and—the largest—El Paso. In these were congregated rather more than half the Spanish population. The remainder lived in the river haciendas, now grown from the bosky homes of one or two families each to clusters of families in a village, where one family usually dominated with wealth or lineage those others who furnished labor, servants, soldiery or artisans. These were conservative settlements. Tradition made them so, and so did the slowness of any vehicle of change. Above all, the central idea of life was unchanging, as it contained the society in its explanation of the hard world, and freed in each person his individual dignity, worth and communication with the divine. The Franciscan clergy maintained twenty-five missions; though not without difficulties.

For many churches destroyed in the terror of 1680 had never been restored, and many of those that had been were still impoverished and bare. With so little of the world's goods to go round in the "old and unfortunate province" the missions were often denied their barest needs, and worse, the poorest and most subject people—the pueblo Indians—were exploited for the gain of the official class, from governors at the top to local functionaries at the bottom, who held the whip hand of legal and military force. The lessons in human relations of an earlier century were forgotten; and the old complaints resounded again, as friars who had chosen poverty for themselves cried out against official injustices that befell those who were guaranteed protection by the law of the Crown, which was mocked by its very guardians.

Governors and local officials alike, stormed a New Mexico mission friar in 1750 after forty years of struggle in the river kingdom, "have hated, and do hate to the death, and insult and persecute the missionary religious, causing them all the troubles and annoyances that their passion dictates, without any other reason or fault than the opposition of the religious to the very serious injustices which the said governors and alcaldes inflict upon the helpless Indians. . . ." The friars were able to specify their complaints. In the harvesttime, soldiers came to the pueblos in the guise of traders, bought the whole local crop, ordered Indians to load it and carry it to Santa Fe "where the Governor lives," and paid them, if at all, in little heaps of childish trash—chuchumates, or glass beads, cheap knives, awls, tobacco dregs. In consequence, Indians must hunger and, hungering, go to the mountains after game, or hire out to work on farms, and in any case leave the missions. Spanish officials were still putting Indians at forced labor on building projects, and sending them down to Chihuahua with cattle drives, and causing them to produce blankets and cloth which were taken without proper pay.

As Indian property was stolen, Indian persons were abused. From the river pueblos, five men and five women were designated to go to the Palace at Santa Fe every Sunday. It made no difference whether or not they were enrolled in classes for religious instruction. They had to set out on foot or horseback, and "whether the weather is good or bad, they must be in the Palace on Sunday, to do which they have to cross the frozen Rio del Norte, and this has cost many lives, abortions, and convulsions among the women." When they arrived, the men had to "haul wood and perform other services, and the women to grind wheat and corn by hand." If they were lucky they brought along something to eat, for nothing was given them at the Palace. Mere unkindness was not all. "Such girls as come to this work with their virtue unsullied lose it there, for they are very strongly moved by desire for gain, so that they easily fall. The married women who go there pregnant have miscarriages for the most part, both on account of the excessive labor, and of the long journey. . . ."

The civil authorities permitted buying and selling of Indian slaves. The friars reported that in the case of Indian women or girls, "before delivering them to the Christians who buy them, if they are ten years old or over, they deflower them and corrupt them" with the auction crowd looking on, "without considering anything but their unbridled lust and brutal shamelessness." After such an act the girl was handed over to her purchaser with the remark, " 'Now you can take her—now she is good.' " Once when some friars were talking to the Governor, an Indian woman came to him and accused him of raping her daughter. Hardly noticing her, the Governor interrupted his conversation long enough to direct that the woman be paid off with a buffalo hide he had handy. Even the Indian dead were not sacred. After killing an Indian, "the sergeant ordered him hung up on a plain, where he stayed until the fathers came to take the body down and give it sepulture."

Why was nothing done against such evils? There, said the clergy, "we are coming to the spool on which the thread is wound." For if the Indians were helpless before the material power of the governing class, the clergy were helpless before its cynical reprisals. When friars made complaints to a colonial official, he replied with insults and charges of disturbing the peace. If they were lucky that was all; but all too often they were accused of crimes of which they were innocent, their reputations were destroyed, and false witnesses were paid to appear against them in the inquiries conducted by the Father President, who dared not ignore the formal legal complaints of the civil authority. Justice was corrupted. The law was a private convenience for the magistrate. The only recourse for the guardian priests was to write to Mexico, hoping that their tales would reach the proper listener. For, as a Franciscan said, he and his brothers were "the mystic watch-dogs of the house of God," and if at times they were remiss, they yet awoke when the need for alarm was great, and "now I bark . . . in this paper I make an outcry, and God grant that my barks may reach the ears of the most excellent lord viceroy. . . ." In summary, "the Indians are indulged in their vices, dances, estufas, superstitions, witchcrafts, and idolatries in the mountains, while we receive no favor but on the contrary are interfered with when we try to compel the vicious and rebellious to receive their instruction and catechism. On the one hand"—and here was the heart of the matter—"they give them protection in their disobedience to us, and on the other they harass and oppress them. . . . Now what can we expect . . . ?" The father missioner looked over his shoulder and with a shudder recalled the terror of 1680.

Everywhere on the river the tasks of civilizing and converting the Indians had to be done over and over, often for the very same people. Christianity was not a tradition that struck deeply and sustained itself among them. From one extreme of bloody rebellion to another of trivial but exhausting annoyance—Indian women talked so loudly in church that the Mass could hardly be heard and so they had to be separated by kneeling men—the friars knew every reason for discouragement. But their sense of purpose endured, even in grimly realistic terms. If the lord viceroy is going to send new missioners as requested, let him "for the love of God . . . see that they are over forty years of age, mild and humble, stripped of all property, and that they know how to endure many hardships." The friar who wrote that was a veteran in the river kingdom. "I am sixty-seven years of age, but, judging by the strength that I feel in myself I would say that I have seven and sixty spiritual arms to defend this holy province from so many enemies. They will be conquered, for envy and greed never prevail. . . ."

Rivalry, actually, in his own field threatened the Franciscan. For some time there had been talk of introducing another order of priests— the Jesuits—into New Mexico. Perhaps at first the Jesuits would undertake only certain specified missions. The Moqui Indians of the west were mentioned. But who knew to what such missions might lead? For two centuries the brothers of St. Francis had given themselves to the river, usually alone, and when necessary had walked barefoot into martyrdom. The Jesuits proposed certain conditions to the Viceroy. They even indicated that the Moqui Indians "wanted black fathers to convert them," meaning priests in black cassocks, instead of friars in blue, and would refuse to receive the blue while awaiting the black. It was unsettling, and it brought forth from a Franciscan the sardonic remark, "It is not the color that converts, reverend father, but the substance of the word of God," and the friar added that if the Jesuits came, he would oppose their entrance. But he thought they would not come. If the Two Majesties were again at odds, one of them was not at peace with itself either.

But in another image of life during the decades that bridged the eighteenth and nineteenth centuries along the New Mexican river there seemed to breathe the peace of a long ending. It was an image that presented much of Spain and that modified all things Spanish with the ways of the river land and its earliest Indian people. It was the life of the

haciendas in their riverside pastures and classic glades. Spain was far
away and had to be imagined, now, instead of remembered. But tradition
was strong, even as with each generation it encountered slow change;
and in a last golden light the pastoral life of the river kingdom stood
clear in all its details of habitation and family, its beliefs, customs,
works and ways.

38.

Hacienda and Village

i. land and house

The riverside groves were deep and cast a sweet chilling shade.
In their silence, their dampness in the low ground, the composite sound
of the river reached far along the cottonwood or poplar aisles. Silky flow
could be heard, and little incidents of suck and seep, and the murmur
or ducks talking, and the blurred clap of his wings as a blue heron
clambered slowly from mud bar to sky. Willow stands made little green
rooms open to the air. Cutting through the boskies, the main ditch opened
its mouth upstream at the riverbank to take in flow for irrigation. It
was a ditch perhaps six feet broad, four feet deep. It had wooden gates
and sluices. From its artery ran narrow shallow veins to the various
fields. When the light was low and the earth was darkening these little
channels looked to hold quicksilver. In full noon, their water was seen
to be heavy with mud, brown and sluggish.

But their work was visible in the green of the fields, which gave
cool air to anyone who rode by them. Feed for animals grew there, and
vegetables for the families who lived beyond the fields that separated
them from the river. Orchards lay at the end of the field. Facing anywhere, the immediate land was flat. A few miles away mountains rose

up, and against their hazy screens the slim poplars and broad cotton-woods of the foreground were dark. The clear deserts beyond the valley were cooked by the sun to give off an herby sweetness in the air, which travelled to the groves and the fields and, mixing with their blue damp-ness and the rich muddy breath of the river, made an earthy smell that caused a pang of well-being and memory of place in those who now and then inhaled with sudden awareness.

The farms lay in narrow strips inland from the river. The earliest New Mexico grant under title was given in 1685. Where several clustered side by side, there were common enterprises. Cattle and sheep were grazed in the foothills rising away from the bottom lands, and tended for all by herders from not one farm but several. Corrals lay near to the house.

The house of a big hacienda was an image in earth of the family. Through generations it grew as the family grew. Its life faced inward. The outer walls were blind against the open country with its Indian dangers, and were entered by wide covered passageways as deep as a room, and barred with heavy wooden doors that were secured with massive iron locks. Within, the rooms all opened on a patio in which trees grew, that in time towered over the roofs. Where the clay hives of the classic Indian towns grew upward in terrace above terrace, the hacienda, built of the same materials, and using many of the pueblo's details in style and method, expanded along the ground in a single storey. Beginning with one system of rooms about a square patio, the house, as new lives came, grew into another patio, and even another. The walls were often three feet thick, built of massive adobe blocks and plastered with earth mixed with straw. Ceiling beams were peeled tree poles, and between them were laid peeled sapling sticks, often in a herringbone pattern. Windows facing the patio held sections of selenite or small panes of imported glass, and were shuttered with carved wooden panels hung from iron or leather hinges, or upon round wooden pegs fitted into carved wooden rings. The floors were of packed earth. Within the patios, an extension of the roof made a porch on all sides that was supported with wooden pillars and carved, scrolled corbels. In their plan—a succession of squares, either extended in line or grouped in checkerboard—the great earth houses might recall in their humble way the grille of the Escorial Palace.

In feudal containment, the river house threw its high clay wall around all the purposes and needs of its life. There was a great room, or sala, for grand occasions—dances, receptions, family gatherings. A family

chapel sat at one corner of the oldest patio, and over its door might be a
belfry with a bell from Mexico. Each parental bedroom was also a sitting
room with its own fireplace. The kitchen was a long room where the
family sat down to meals. Near it were long dark storerooms in one of
which meat and game were hung. In another, dried fruits were stored,
and piñons in bags, and grain of wheat and corn in jars. Beyond the
walls of these rooms, and reached by a heavy rear gate, sparkled a little
ditch bringing a vein of water from the main ditch that drank of the
river. Rooms for servants ran along the rear. A blacksmith shop with
forge, anvil and leather bellows and a tool house with carpentry supplies
and hides stood side by side in a work patio, where pens for chickens and
sheep, a stable for horses and a shed for milk cows closed the square. The
soft lumber of the cottonwood, that yet weathered so well, turning a
silvery gray, and drying to hardness, was used for posts, rails, pegs and
joists.

The interior walls of the dwelling rooms and the inside patio
walls were finished in a glowing white plaster of gesso, or gypsum, which
occurred in deposits near the river, as at Cochiti. It was powdered and
mixed with water, and applied by the family women with a soft pad of
woolly sheepskin, in a craft that was common to the Moors of North
Africa, the Spaniards of the homeland, and the Indians of the river
pueblos. Around the base of the walls, rising two feet above the floor, a
dado was painted with plaster made from the most colorful hue of
the local earth—red or yellow or sienna—as a shield for the pure white
walls against the dust of the floor. Where black earth could be found, it
was mixed with fine sand and moisture until it could be spread on the
floors in a smooth thin surface. When it dried hard, it was polished with
the bare palm of the hand until it shone again.

In its essential form, the room was simple, and very close to the
Indian's. The Indian at first lived on his floor. Later he made an earthen
bench that hugged his wall, and if he sat he had his wall to lean against.
His very house was his furniture. The humble Spaniard made his earthen
bench too, and in using it was tied to his wall. But the rich Spaniard
moved away from the wall to the free center of the room, where he placed
furniture, which was heavy, dark and formal. Its character reflected his.
If he sat in his chair, he must sit bolt upright, for the seat was narrow
and shallow, its back straight, its arms high and hard, its legs tall. No
matter how rich the materials that shaped it—carved wood, polychromed
leather, Valencian velvet, Italian fringe and gold bullion lace, Peruvian
serge—his repose was fixed in a discomfort that seemed proper to his

decorum. His luxuries, even if he was rich, were spiritual, not material. Even the greatest of his kings had preferred to live and work in a bare stone room, taking little physical comfort in the midst of the magnificence that was his to command. In penance—an opinion that could be detected in many Spanish ways of life—in penance resided virtue. It was only suitable that even wealth brought its discomforts to be suffered in patience.

What grandeurs he allowed himself represented the Spanish colonist's pride more than his joy in luxury. There were beauties to be enjoyed in many of the objects accumulated in the river valley by a patriarchal family, and sentiments to be told over as heirlooms descended. Placed against the stark earthen walls of a valley house, imported furnishings and precious objects even at their richest never seemed out of place. Inlaid woods, gold leaf, velvets, crystal, pure silver, turned the master's rooms, which in form were exactly like those of a pueblo, into the apartments of a Castilian palace. Profuse trade with the Indies brought European articles to New Spain, and some of these found their way to the northern kingdom, where they made references of nostalgia, pride and respect for the past.

In the sala was a pair of Castilian vargueños—Spain's only invention in furniture—which were wooden chests honeycombed with little drawers and compartments, supported by high legs, and carved, inlaid with ivory and nacre, and studded with worked metals. There were tall straight chairs with leather seats, and stiff armchairs in crimson velvet rubbed pale at the edges. A long narrow table, so high that it could not be slouched over, recalling the style and discipline of the monastery, stood in the middle of the room. Along the unbroken whitewashed wall facing the patio windows across the room was a continuous bench made of wall-earth. It was covered with Indian-made blankets. Above it, for its whole length, fixed to the wall, was a strip of Dutch cotton cloth to protect from the whitewash the shoulders of those who leaned back as they sat. At one end of the room was a wide, deep fireplace. Its hearth was made of flagstones. Heavy iron fire tools stood by its maw. In its chimney face there might have been a design of Valencian tiles, showing birds, leaf and flower forms in dark red and white, or an animal drama, such as a wolf eating a rabbit. If the family had armorial bearings, these were displayed in Valencian blue and white tile. Near the fireplace, on the floor, sat a Mexican chest with heavy iron hinges, lock and handles. Its panels were like little scenes in a theatre, painted in brilliant colors, and illustrating stories of common knowledge. Many mirrors hung along the walls, some framed in gold leaf over carved wood, some in tortoise shell and ivory, some in little facets of mirror set in mosaic along the frame. The Mexico-Orient trade brought curious, gleaming fabrics from China, and for its rarity and strange richness of gold and silver thread, a strip of Chinese brocade was sometimes hung flat on the white wall. By daylight the room was cool and dim, for the patio windows were deep and low, and shaded outside by the overhang of the porch. The room was lighted at night by candles, held in iron candelabra, or others carved of wood, covered with gesso, and finished with gold leaf. Every· thing was always clean.

This was because there were enough servants and because the lady of the house was an energetic and demanding housekeeper. The bedroom that she shared with her husband revealed her duties and her preoccupations. The bed was big enough for two, thinly mattressed, covered with a richly embroidered spread done in native yarns by the mistress who copied flowers off a Chinese shawl, and presided over at its head by a blue and gilt statue of Our Lady of Guadalupe. Clothes were kept in chests of leather studded with brass nails or of carved unpainted wood. Indian rugs were on the hand-rubbed floor. There was a fireplace, and by the window stood a small worktable and a chair where the matri· arch spent hours at her work. On the table was her mother-of-pearl needle case. Next to it was a Moorish box of tortoise shell, ivory and teakwood which held her silver scissors, a little penknife, her spools of thread, her gold thimble, and a magnifying glass in a silver-gilt handle. There she embroidered altar cloths, bedspreads, tablecloths, linens, and taught her daughters her skill. If they married, each must know, as she had known, how to work on handkerchiefs with strands of her own hair the name of her husband. They must be able to embroider with beads. She kept little glass phials filled with beads of different colors and with them made scenes, flowers, birds, and sentiments on muslin strips. Vestments had to be embroidered and repaired. There was a rage for poodles in eighteenth-century polite society, for the King of Spain was a French Bourbon and the poodle was a French dog. Ladies—in Mexico and New Mexico—sewed elaborate little backgrounds into which tiny china poodles could be stitched, and the whole framed and displayed in the sala. Callers admired these objects and spoke of them as "very European"—always the highest compliment a colonial could pay. A pair of silver daggers lay on the bedroom table. On the deep window sill were a copper bowl and pitcher, and by them stood a dark blue drinking glass ornamented with golden roses and an inscription in gold that said "My Love." In a corner was a long row of boots belonging to the master, a pair for every task, as they showed, from walking in the river mud, to riding spurred, to dancing in the sala. In the same corner leaned a musket that was always loaded. On a wall of the bedroom hung a likeness of Our Lady of Remedies, embroidered on red velvet in lifelike colors, her robe studded with baroque pearls. She was the patroness of the river kingdom. It was impossible to pass her a dozen times a day without each time in half-awareness wafting to her a thought, a prayer, for protection for the house, its lives, and all its possessions.

The kitchen was in many ways the richest room in the house. Its graduated copper pots, hanging above the fireplace and its iron oven, shone like treasure. On its wooden shelves gleamed rows of dishes and glass. There was blue glass from Puebla—pitchers, mugs, goblets. There were cups and tumblers and vases of glass, milk-white and clear and colored, from La Granja de San Ildefonso in the province of Toledo. There were deep cups and saucers of Talavera pottery out of which to drink chocolate, and large breakfast bowls of the same ware. Porcelain from China, Majolica from Mexico, jugs and bowls from the pueblos of the river stood on wooden shelves or tiled ledges in the kitchen. Wood was used for utensils, too, long trough-shaped bateas, or bowls, in which clothes were washed, or vegetables, or dishes. Large trays and bread plates were fashioned out of cottonwood, and after use were washed and set on edge to drain and dry. From much handling through many years, they were good to touch—smooth, softly polished, and loved through work. The kitchen furniture was not so grand as that in the sala. It was of plainly made, unfinished wood—long table, chairs and benches. Against a wall stood several trasteros. These were tall cabinets with locked double doors whose upper panels were latticed, or pierced in designs, and inlaid with mosaic patterns of common straw that gleamed like gold. Through these openwork panels shone the highlights of the family silver. When the trastero doors were unlocked and swung open, the shelves revealed large silver platters, trays and bowls standing on edge. There were piles of silver dinner plates, and rows of cups and saucers, mugs, pitchers, chocolate pots; knives, forks and spoons. Some of it was made in Spain, and bore Spanish hallmarks; much of it in Mexico. All of it was heavy, almost pure in its silver content and, except for any blazons of arms belonging to the family, plain. Light struck from its surface as from water, with a faint suggestion of ripple that added richness of texture to weight of substance. Though massive, the silver pieces had grace, and though treasured, they bore the little pits

and dents of daily use. To eat in the kitchen, off silver—in this were both
the Spaniard's earthy simplicity and his pride.

His spirit he took across the main patio to the family chapel,
entering through panelled doors that held the carved keys of Saint
Peter and the Spanish Crown, side by side, the Two Majesties. The chapel
was a small, plain room with an altar at the end. A crucifix of dark wood
stood on the altar between candlesticks. The body of Christ was carved
to show His agony, with drops of blood in relief and painted red, at
brow, side, hands and feet—symbol of a sacrifice never to be forgotten
by the family, and lesson to sustain them in their own commonplace
daily sufferings. The altar was clothed in a frontal of imported velvet
or brocade; or if such was not to be had, in a colcha embroidery done at
home, of dyed yarns, representing large flowers, leaves and fruit. The
family's favorite saints, in various representations, stood on pedestals or
hung on the walls in paintings. To them in mute appeal for aid in particular causes were affixed little votive images called *milagros*. If a hand
was injured, if an ear ached, if rheumatism crippled a leg; if a cow was
sick; if sheep were threatened by mountain lions, little silver likenesses
of these members or creatures were pinned to a saint in perpetual intercession for relief. A thoughtful household obtaining these from Mexico
kept a supply on hand in a little velvet-covered casket and produced
them as needed. The head of the household conducted family prayers in
the chapel, and when the priest came, the altar was dressed with wild
flowers and lighted with extra candles, and a set of vestments kept for
the purpose was produced, and all heard Mass. Those families who lived
near towns went on Sunday to the town church. Albuquerque in the
latter half of the eighteenth century was empty all week, but on Sunday
was alive with the families who rode or drove from the river farms to
attend services at Saint Philip of Neri's.

ii. fashion

They wore their best for such an occasion. Indian servants kept
their traditional dress which showed little change since the Spanish
colonization, except for woollen blankets which they had learned to make.
Half-castes, and the poor soldiery serving time in New Mexico instead
of in prison, and an occasional trail-driver, and the valley farmhands,

appeared in red, blue or brown suits made of jerga, a coarse woollen serge woven in the province. Their hats were flat-brimmed like those of Cordova. The Spanish cloak was replaced by the Mexican serape, which in turn came from the Indian's shoulder blanket. The men's jackets were long-skirted and full-sleeved, and their trouser legs now reached to the foot, having dropped from the knee. All wore boots. A sash wrapped several times about the waist replaced a belt and held small weapons of blade or barrel. The wives of such humble men wore voluminous skirts of jerga, and shirts as elaborate as they could afford, over which were sleeveless little coats. On their heads and shoulders the women wore shawls, or rebozos, of bright solid colors, which they folded in a large triangle, and whose points they crossed at the throat to be thrown over the shoulders. The shawls were fringed, and the length of the fringe determined the worth of the article, and the wealth, the position, of its owner.

The leading families—those who called themselves *gentes de razón*, "those who use reason," "the educated ones," "the right people,"—had a handsome variety of dress to choose from, with many colors and precious materials. The men wore fine linen shirts and underclothes. Their suits were of velvet, or of thin soft leather, or French serge, heavy with gold or silver cording in elaborate traceries, and buttoned with gold or silver or diamond paste buttons. A skirted coat, a short waistcoat, and long skintight trousers buttoned the whole length of the leg from waist to ankle made up such a suit. With it went small arms—dagger, pistol, short sword; a tightly woven serape large enough to cover the whole body when unfolded and slipped over the head by a slit in the center; and a hat, whether a tricorne edged with ostrich plumage, or a cordovan hat with a high crown banded in many rows of gold lace, either sometimes worn over a silk kerchief tied tightly over the head like a cap, and recalling the scarf worn under a steel helmet.

Women of the rich houses followed the fashion of Spain, which changed slowly, so that even if they were far away in time and distance from Madrid and the court, they were in the style in their tight bodices and long sleeves, their low necks, their pinched high waists and their spreading, shining skirts of heavy silk or satin, over which laces were cascaded and looped. They had a choice of rebozos, whether one of white lace, or one of China silk heavy with embroidered scarlet and yellow flowers and green leaves and blue shading and long red fringe, or one of silk that fell like water in plain solid colors, including black, or finally, one of black lace with its designs like the shadows of rose leaves. From

their little ivory and velvet caskets they could choose their jewels—
emerald and pearl and amethyst and gold earrings, bracelets, rings and
pins; and rose-cut diamonds from Ceylon set in clusters like bouquets;
and a Paris-style lorgnette with mother-of-pearl and gold handles with
which to follow the Missal and edify an Indian; and gold chains and
flexible gold fish and pure gold tassels by the cunning goldsmiths of
Germany. If such finery picked up its share of dust in the far valley, still
it spoke formally of the proper way to live, wherever.

iii. family and work

For in its own scale the family was as rigid and formal as the
court of the King in respect to authority, reverence, and responsibility.
So long as he lived the father was the lord, to be obeyed, respected and
loved. In turn he must provide the goods of life to those for whose lives
he was responsible, and lead them wisely, and guide their work. The
mother, in rich family or poor, was the lady of all, and worked harder
than any at the endless household duties. Reverence was due to her for
she brought life and gave it to the world, and in doing so through the
years received wisdom to which all would do well to listen. If her
lord died before her, she until her death was the head of the family,
and to the love and respect paid to her was now to be added obedience.
Her ways were the right ways, no matter what the world tried to teach.
She knew them without learning. Often in the colonial family, if the
father represented the earth's life and its work of seasons and its secrets
of strength, the mother was the fire and the spirit, the divined imagination at the heart of things, which she seemed the older she lived to per-
ceive the more brightly. Her sons and daughters dared to risk humor with
her, though rarely with their father. The grandchildren and great-grand-
children—for the families in their homemade sustenances were long-
lived—stood in awe of their august forebears.
    Relationships were stabilized, and each had its appropriate man-
ner. Matrons of equal age and degree on meeting leaned their faces side
by side and each kissed the air murmuring a politeness. Men, in greeting,
formally folded each other in their arms, making two quick little slaps
on the shoulder. Once a man declared himself *compadre*—"co-father" or
fellow godfather—with another man, he was bound in a friendship that

had a sacred duty to remain unbroken. A community in which such fellowships were intershared by all the men was certain of its own harmony, for to break it was almost sacrilegious, and could occur only through tragedy or passion.

When prayers in the chapel were finished for the day, all filed out past the senior member of the family who had led the prayers, and kissed his hand, genuflecting, in veneration of age. Arriving in a jolting, heavy carriage slung on leather straps, a great-aunt would come to stay with a rich family. She was received by the assembled relatives to whom she gave the most formal greeting. She stiffly put the tips of her small fingers, heavily jewelled, on the shoulders of each in turn. Her Indian maid followed her from the carriage, and men carried her shallow trunk of tanned rawhide that was stitched together in lozenges and squares, showing red flannel in between. The household soon learned her eccentric custom of crying out "Ave Maria" to anyone who took her notice. Who heard her was supposed to pause, cross his arms, and recite the whole prayer silently. She invited certain ones to join her in a compact of the Ave Maria. Hooking her right little finger in that of her friend, she led in reciting a charm:

> "How many hours has the day,
> Has Hail Mary that we pray."

If she made a compact as *comadre,* or "co-mother," "sister god-mother," with another woman, they chanted together:

> "Flower basket, scatter never,
> In this life and in the next,
> We'll be comadres forever.
>
> Tra-la-la and tra-la-loo,
> Whoever becomes comadre
> Divides her heart in two."

To repudiate a shocking statement or action, the cross was invoked by putting the right thumb upright across the right forefinger held level, and saying *"Pongote la cruz"*—"I put the cross on you!"

Children, who wore miniatures of their parents' clothes, early echoed their parents' formality. They soon learned to stop crying over trifles. In their grave dark pearly faces with their large black eyes were reflected the animal repose, the spiritual certitude and the mind's govern-

ment that so generally marked the temperaments of their elders. These
were qualities of order that could be shattered by passion or debauched
by folly; but they survived, if not in the individual, then in the ideals of
the conservative life he came from, in which the family, however large,
remained tightly woven together; and in which a pride of inheritance
gave rich and poor alike a dignity becoming to the heirs of Columbus
and Cortés and Coronado and Oñate and Vargas whose deeds and
graces begot not only kingdoms but characters. In even his simplest acts
the colonial Spaniard seemed to proclaim his proud heritage. For his
beliefs and ways required a certain accompaniment of style; and in a
remote land, poor in itself, style took effort to maintain. Behind the
style of the big river households there was much work, for the men out of
doors, for the women within.

While children played in the patio, under the prattling cottonwoods, and talked to their parrots, the mother had many tasks to over-
see. For her embroidery and knitting, there was wool to be dyed. Favorite colors came in the Mexican trade—reds and blues from cochineal,
indigo and brazilwood. But these were scarce, and the old Indian dyes
used for centuries on sacred feathers and kachina masks now colored the
threads for embroidering bedspreads, altar cloths, upholstery and clothing: yellow from the rabbit brush, blue from larkspur, pink from the tag
alder, blue-green from copper ore. Wool from brown and black sheep
was used unchanged. With homespun yarns the women knitted stockings, and wove brown and white rugs for the slippery floors. They made
toilet soap from animal fats, adding melon seeds, rosemary, wild rose
leaves and bran starch, and grinding the whole mixture to paste, forming
it in cakes, and setting them in the sun to dry. To make pomade for
their hair, they mixed strained beef marrow, powdered rose leaves and
rosemary. If their skin was too swarthy, they bleached it with a paste
prepared from wild raspberry juice mixed with powdered eggshells or
ashes of elkhorns, soaked rice and melon seeds. To hold curls in place,
they used thick sugar-water. The women made candles, dipping a long
cotton string into melted tallow or beeswax and hanging it up to cool.
When it was cool, they dipped it again, and again, until the candle was as
big as they liked. In the spring, they gathered up the blankets in the
house, heaped them on a cart and drove them to the river to be washed.
By the riverside a fire was built, water was heated in big copper kettles,
and yucca root was beaten and thrown into a long wooden trough into
which hot water was poured. The women, bare-armed and barefooted,
knelt by the trough and flailed the water until they made suds. The

blankets were then immersed, rubbed and wrung until the country's unfading dye colors came clear again. At the river's edge, while mocking-birds, larks and blackbirds swept above them with excitement, they rinsed the heavy clothes in the current, and then spread them in the meadow grass to dry.

If extra help was needed, women came from near-by families, but never to work for pay. Their men would have been offended to have money offered to their women. When the work was done, and the visitors returned home, they were willing to accept a little gift, of "whatever was handy." This had pride, remembering the pretensions of the starving hidalgos of long ago, and also good sense, if on another day the helpers needed help.

Food and drink took much work to produce. The women made spiced wine, simmered in an earthen pot for a day with spices and sugar, sealed with a ring of fresh dough. Sweet cookies were made with twenty-four egg yolks. On a heated metate stone, dense chocolate was made by grinding cocoa beans, stick cinnamon, pecans and maple sugar—all imported—into a paste which was dried and cut into cakes. Cooked with thick whole milk, these made the black chocolate drink which was served at breakfast, and at four in the afternoon with cookies. The finest tor-tillas—large, thin, round corncakes—were made from blue corn meal. Three of these, layered with slices of pink onion and curls of yellow cheese and sprinkled with green lettuce and swimming in cooked red chili pepper sauce, made a favorite dish. When men butchered beeves or hogs in the work patio, the beef was cut in strips and dried in the sun, the pork was sliced and soaked in a juice of red chilis sharp with garlic and salt. Pork fat was diced and fried in deep fat to make cracklings which were used in place of bacon. A soupbone was used not once but many times, and was even passed from one poor family to another to boil with beans. Women harvested grapes which they washed, drained in a basket, and hung in a storeroom from the beams to dry into raisins. In the fall, as the Pueblo people had done for centuries, the hacienda women cut up sweet pumpkins and melons, setting the pieces out on stakes to dry. Squashes and plums were dried on cloths spread over the flat roofs. When the cane was mature in the fall, it was time to make syrup, and all helped. Against an outdoor wall near the kitchen was a long oven made of earthen bricks. In its top were six round holes under which a fire was kept hot. The days were often cool and the evenings cold, and as the work was long, bonfires were kept burning to give warmth and light while men with wooden mauls pounded the fresh cane on fat logs, reducing it to a pulp. The pulp was put into a wide barrel, into which a round heavy press was fitted. To the press a long slender timber was attached so that it could rock free like a seesaw. Here now was boys' work, and two climbed on each end of the timber, and as they rode up and down in privileged delight, the press rose and fell, squeezing juice from the pulp which ran through a hole in the barrel's side into a wooden trough. Women took up the juice in dippers made of cut gourds, strained it into clay jars, and set these, six at a time, to boil on the oven until the juice was red and clear. In the bonfire-light after dusk all was animated, purposeful and satisfactory, and when the first jar was ready, a sample of the syrup was passed about to be tasted by those who had helped to produce it.

The great families had Indian slaves. These were housed with the paid servants, and given lessons in catechism, and promised their freedom so soon as they might be, in the judgment of their owners, civilized enough to sustain it. They were allowed to marry, and their children were born free under the law. Female slaves were ladies' maids and kitchen helpers. Male slaves worked in the fields and among the animal herds. So few goods came by wagon train that the province had to sustain itself, and the raising of cattle and sheep, and the growing of food were the main concern of all. Crops, said a Franciscan survey, were "so limited that each inhabitant scarcely raises enough for himself." But by the middle of the eighteenth century there were millions of sheep grazing on the sparse slopes of the watershed. Between two hundred thousand and five hundred thousand sheep were driven every year to Mexico for sale. The grasses struggled for life in ordinary years and in dry years barely showed. The colonials looked at their hills and shook their heads. It was all very much like Spain, a condition of natural life that seemed impossible to govern. The tilted lands were growing more barren, the torrents —when it did rain—swept faster and cut deeper, the earth ran into the tributaries and into the river, piling up silt on the river floor, the river spilled over its old banks and made swamps on good farm land, and a man could only bow his head and invoke patience. Inherited practice had a firm hold upon him, at the expense of understanding the forces that his use of the land released in violence. Rain made grass, and he lifted up his eyes to look for rain. No other answer occurred to him. Animals had to eat. They had to stay on his own range or be stolen by roving Indians. He watched his sheep for signs of rain, for though they rarely gamboled, they would do so if rain were in the air. Before a rain, said the shepherds, a sheep would draw himself up and bleat and shake himself as though already wet. Before a rain, said the cowherders, a cow would throw her hind legs and bawl.

In May men rode out from the hacienda to help with lambing at the sheep camps. There were always goats with the herds, and when the men returned they brought home kidskins of long, silky white hair. These were delivered to the mistress, who had them washed with soap and water. When they were dry, cooked sheep brains were rubbed into the hairless side. Set into the sun, the skins became soaked as the brains melted. Washed again, they were dried and worked by hand until they were soft as cloth and pure white. Some were dyed in brilliant colors and used as little hearthrugs in the bedrooms, to keep the feet warm while dressing and undressing by the fire.

All houses kept horses to ride, burros to carry packs, and mules to pull the massive wagons and carriages. Wheels were greased with a homemade lubricant of fat mixed with pine tar. When a family carriage went travelling, it was accompanied by armed outriders and postilions, not for style but for protection against waylaying Indians.

Where water power could be had from a ditch brought close to the house, a mill was set up in a room twelve feet square. The ditchwater turned a wooden wheel outside the walls, and beyond it fell booming into a pool shaded by willows and huge hairy sunflowers where the youths of the household bathed and swam. Inside the walls an axle from the wheel turned a massive wooden gear that revolved a pole fixed to a grinding stone. Hanging from the ceiling was a stiff bullhide hopper from which grain fell in a steady stream into the hole of the turning stone and was ground against a circular flat stone eighteen inches thick that was bound to the floor, and enclosed in a bin. The meal was taken from the bin, sacked, and sent to the house, where kitchenmaids spread it out on a large white cloth upon the floor. They sifted it through a swiss-cloth sieve that was made to rise and fall on a smooth pole held upright. One sifting prepared the flour for whole-wheat bread; a second, through a finer sieve, for pastries. This work began with a prayer, before the maids loosed their prattle. Later, setting the dough for bread, they murmured the name of the Holy Trinity, and marked the soft loaves with a cross, to insure a good baking.

After the harvest in the fall, and the threshing of beans, peas and grains, orders were given by the master for a wagon to set out for the salines beyond the eastern mountains, where the household would obtain its year's supply of salt. As winter came on, outdoor work lessened, and wandering laborers were seen no more till spring. But others came.

A tailor might stay for weeks, while he made suits for the family men.
A shoemaker might appear with his boxes and tools to repair boots and
make new ones with tough bullhide for the foot, and fine Cordovan
leather for the tops. Now and then a startling creature or two would
appear, dressed in wild stripes and shimmering and chiming with
jewelry. These would be gypsies—Turks or Arabs—who came selling
medals and rosaries which they swore came from the Holy Land. Glaring
strangely, they smiled over the secret which all knew they had, which
was the power to put evil spells. Apprehensively they were made guests,
their holy trash was purchased, and presently they moved on to the
mingled relief and regret of the family, who saw so few visitors. An occasional government officer would appear from the Viceroy's court in
Mexico on his way to Santa Fe, and make himself at home. He was
treated with respect, for Spaniards accepted authority. They might be
skeptical and willing to change the authority under which they lived,
but authority there must be. Even if the travelling official gave himself
airs, which the farther he went from the capital seemed to grow grander,
his hosts smiled. Many odd things came with the law, but the law was
powerfully implanted in them from long ago, and its flourishes were in
fact a pleasure instead of a nuisance. In any case, hospitality to the
visitor was a sacred tradition, and every comfort, all exquisite courtesy
were his no matter who he might be. And when off the dusty riverside
trails there came a guest who brought with him more than his own
simple claim as a man, who in fact was a legal and spiritual descendant
of the Twelve Apostles, then the household outdid itself.

Three times during the eighteenth century the successive Bishops
of Durango travelled from their cathedral city in New Spain to Santa
Fe, the most outlandish town in their province. Each moved by heavy
carriage, accompanied by baggage carts, a mounted guard and various
clergy. The Bishop made use of the hospitality of the great river houses.
The chapel was thrown open, decorated and lavishly lighted. His mitre,
crozier and cope were taken from their leather hampers, he was vested,
he gave Benediction at the altar, and touring the premises, he blessed
the house. Children were told off to be prepared for confirmation, which
he would administer on his return from Santa Fe. The kitchen buzzed
like a hive and steamed like a hot spring. The whole house sparkled and
shone. It was like receiving royalty to have the Bishop and his train.
Every last finery from the great cities to the south and over the seas was
brought out, and every local grace was displayed with anxiety. The Lord
Bishop was gratified, and weighed homage for its true value, which was

the pleasure it brought the giver, not the receiver. When he entered his carriage again in his worn black with edges of purple, he looked only like a country priest, and when he drove off on his squealing wheels, he left whirling eddies of thought behind him. According to their temperaments, some members of the household, at this contact of the great world, were more content, others more dissatisfied, with the homely labors, loves and beauties of family life in the valley.

In late November the yearly market caravan began to assemble, starting at the northernmost river towns, and coming down the valley to pick up wagons at each stop on its way to Mexico. The wagons were loaded with goods and covered with lashed wagon sheets. The cargoes included woollen blankets, dried meat, tanned buffalo and deer hides, strings of red and green chili. These articles would be sold or traded for products of Mexico, the Philippines, China, South America and Europe. Silver and gold money found its way each year into the province when the train returned. But for the most part, transactions in New Mexico were completed in goods of the country, for almost no hard money circulated. A system of four kinds of pesos, dollars, came to custom among the people: silver dollars, which were very scarce, worth eight *reales,* "royals," or about an ounce of silver; "dollars of the future," worth six royals; "old" dollars, worth four royals; and "dollars of land," worth two royals. As all were called dollars, the Indians and simpler people accepted all as equal; but the traders always reckoned what they bought in "dollars of the land," or cheapest value, and what they sold in silver dollars, or highest value. It was a monetary system based on coinage but activated through barter. Blankets, hides, livestock changed hands instead of money.

iv. mischance

It was a picture of commerce somehow in harmony with the basic terms of production and survival in the valley estates. For in any day over the fields where the long thick low house sat in its boxes of light and shadow the thin distant cry of "Indios!" might be raised. The chapel bell would swing full circle and its clapper would now and then cleave to silence like a dry tongue in the mouth. All work was dropped. The men came running in a crouch from the fields. Children were angrily

and dearly hauled up from their ditchside play. All streamed to the
house, and once within the walls, they shut and barred the thick cottonwood gates. The men took to the roofs where they lay down by the
waterspout openings with their muskets. The plumed line of dust that
had started to make a circle beyond the fields and close in toward them
now was drawing nearer and the nodding gallop of Apache horses could
be seen and the naked sprawl of their riders. "At the expense of our
blood, with arms in hand," the household were ready to defend their
common life. The attackers might have both arrows and firearms. If they
wounded or killed a fellow on the roof, the household swallowed its
grief, though confronting death the women usually sought comfort in
screams. Muskets fired from the roof. The crazy thieves took casualties.
One might come close with a brand hoping to fire the house. Another
one or two might attack the rear gate or try to enter by the mill wheel.
A man or a child from the house who had not gained sanctuary with
all others might be found in the groves, dragged forth to view, and killed
and killed, once in body, many times in idea, while the rooftops could
only watch, and fire muskets, and rage. But the great house usually stood,
though death and suffering had come in, and fields, if dry, might be
burned, and ditches be broken and wanton flood result. The attack
would be over as quickly as it had come. The swinging line of riders
broke apart and their long dust plume died down. Each marauder
streaked for the distant mountains by himself. Each made a column of
dust that danced over the plain eastward like the little desert whirlwinds, the "sand devils," of hot afternoons. Long later, still watchful,
the guards came off the roofs, and damage, wound and death were
reckoned, as mischances were reckoned under the weather, or any other
large, hard, and inescapable condition of living.

v. feast days

There were more joyful occasions, and these they made for themselves in the river households. Religious feast days were celebrated with
gaiety as well as devotion. In March there were prayers to San Isidro,
patron of farmers, when the irrigation ditches were cleared of their
golden winter stubble. If a ditch served several families, men from each
came to do his share. The weeds were ignited. All day the ditches were

watched to see that fire did not spread to the fields. Food was taken out to the watchers, and picnics for all the family sometimes followed. The ditch fires showed after dusk and were guarded all night. At home, the children before going to bed went to the heavy patio gates and looked through the cracks at the magic glow across the fields. On June twenty-fourth, the water in the river and the ditches was declared holy, for this was the feast day of St. John, who had baptized Jesus in the river Jordan. Early after sunup the women and girls went to the ditches or to the river and bathed. Good health would follow. When they returned, little children went and then youths and men. This order was observed out of decency, for they were people extremely modest and would not go to bathe in mingled sexes.

The great feast of Christmas was celebrated with food, song, prayer, theater and firelight. Special delicacies came out of the kitchen—fried tarts of mincemeat and piñon nuts, white corn tamales, sweet cakes. Little bands of young singers, called the Oremus Boys, went from house to house in the villages, or in a hacienda toured the living quarters, knocking at each door, before which they sang Christmas songs. When their song was done, they received freshly baked sweetmeats. The house-top was illuminated with dozens of lanterns burning candles. All day before Christmas special fires were laid of piñon sticks, in squares of four, and rising to eight or ten rows high. These were placed to outline the plan of a rambling house, or the road of a village, and even the profile of near-by hills. When darkness fell, they were lighted, and in their orderly distribution, gallant columns of spark and smoke, and spirited crackle, they made a spectacle that delighted all. But they had more purpose than this. By the very signal of that firelight, the Holy Child born that night was to find His way to the homes of those who had made the fires. Boys ran among the bonfires, jumped over them, and dared rebuke. It came, in the form of the Abuelo, or Bogeyman, who appeared once a year, always at Christmas, to threaten boys with punishment for badness. He carried a great whip which he cracked after them over the bonfires. He was a fright in tatters, with a false voice, and a made-up face. They dreaded and dared him, laughingly. He chased them home where he made them kneel down and say their prayers. When he left they burst out again into the sharp clear night where the aromatic piñon smoke smelled so sweet under a whole sky quivering with stars of Bethlehem.

It was not a season of personal gifts. The greater gift of the infant Jesus came to all in joyful renewal. In the great sala, by candlelight,

after much whispered preparation, at one end of the room a company
of family players appeared in costume to enact the tale of the Nativity,
in many scenes, before the rest of the household and guests and neighbors. The shepherds told in verse of the star in the sky. The three kings
appeared in finery with their gold, frankincense and myrrh. At the door
of an inn, someone knocked and sang, and all knew it was Saint Joseph:

> Where is there lodging
> For these wandering ones
> Who come so tired
> From long hard roads?

To this the landlord replied:

> Who knocks at the door
> In imprudent disturbance,
> Forgetting how late,
> And awakes all the house?

In the audience all knew what was coming but the littlest ones, and
they learned and would never forget, as Saint Joseph sang:

> Sir, I beg of you
> In all your charity
> To give shelter to this Lady.

It was anguish to know the sufferings of that small and Holy Family when
the landlord, reminding all of what mankind was capable, answered in
his hardness:

> My house awaits
> Him who has money.
> May God help him
> Who has none.

So the scene shifted to a stable, where through a window an ox and a
mule put their heads, and where attended by angels and visited by the
three kings the Child of the world was born again in the midst of homely
music and passionate belief.

At midnight the patio was alight with fires and all moved to the
chapel for services. Sometimes a priest from the town church was on
hand, and held midnight Mass. At the elevation of the Host, the bell

was rung, and with a hot coal a special salute was touched off from gunpowder poured on the blacksmith's anvil and covered by a big flagstone.

vi. wedding feast

Other than fixed feast days, marriages were the highest occasions.
There was no courtship. One day the father of a promising youth, accompanied by the boy's godfather or best friend, called upon the father of
a suitable girl and presented a letter, or made a formal speech, proposing
marriage between the two young people. No answer was expected immediately. Pleasantries were exchanged over cups of chocolate, and the
callers withdrew. After a few weeks, the call was returned, with a refusal
or an acceptance. If accepted, the bridegroom may have heard something earlier that told him of his happiness, for the house of the bride's
family would be redecorated throughout for the wedding, and news of
unusual activity in her household perhaps travelled. Neighboring families might be joined by the marriage, or families living far apart. Cousins
in the second and third degree frequently married, for the great families
took pride in keeping intact their pure Castilian blood, and to do so,
where there were fewer Spanish than mixed strains, would marry within
the clan. Once the date had been agreed upon preparations went forward
too in the groom's family, until at last they were ready to set out for the
home of the bride. They went in their jarring carriage. In a wagon
behind them came the groom's contributions to the wedding—all the
food for the feast and cooks to prepare it; the leather trunks carrying
the bride's wedding gown and her whole trousseau; and other gifts.
    When they arrived, the groom's parents were given the freedom
of the house, for they were to be in charge of the whole wedding festivity.
The godparents of both bride and groom were there too, and would
serve as best man and matron of honor, and counsel the young couple
until they were married. Marriage was a sacrament. The godparents had
solemn duties in connection with such a great stage in life. The betrothal
took place as soon as the wedding party was complete. All relatives
gathered in the sala, where the families came together. The bride's father
brought her forward and presented her to the groom's father saying,
"Here is she whom you sought." The groom's father introduced her to
all his own people, and then introduced the groom to all her family. It

was possible that this was the first meeting of the betrothed. All then
turned toward the bride's godfather, before whom the young couple
knelt down on white cushions, while he solemnized the engagement by
putting a rosary of corals or pearls—the two precious sea growths from
the faraway Pacific—first over the groom's head and then over the bride's.

Now the trunks were brought in from the groom's wagon and
presented to the bride. They were taken unopened to her bedroom,
where a few privileged girls could see their contents with her. Happiness
and importance filled the air now as the preparations for the wedding
went rapidly ahead. It would follow the next day. The bride stood for
her godmother to see if the wedding dress needed alteration, and tried
on all the other clothes. The visiting cooks went to work, helped by the
resident cooks. The mud ovens outdoors were heated up. The groom's
comestibles were noticed, to determine if he was generous or stingy.
Musicians arrived. Lanterns were put everywhere in the open. If the
time of year permitted, the patio was decorated and used. Pine boughs
were tied to the posts of the *portal* all around the court. Guests kept
coming to stay. Kegs of wine, flagons of brandy from El Paso were set
about. If the chapel was large enough for all, the wedding would take
place there, but if it wasn't, an altar was set up in the patio or the sala,
where the priest could administer the sacrament of holy matrimony. He
would do this only with the provision that at the first opportunity the
married couple must come to town, bringing their godparents, to hear
a nuptial Mass and receive the blessing in church.

At last all was ready, and the engaged youth and maiden, who
though under the same roof since their betrothal had kept away from
one another, now met again before the altar in the evening, accompanied
by their godparents. They were married in candlelight, with the hand-
shaped earthen walls of their family about them, and a burden upon
them of solemn commitment. Tensions broke when the vows were done.
All gathered in the sala for the wedding feast. Now a river house had
put forth another reach of growth and promise of the future, all in
proper observance of ways that were as old as memory. In her white
silk wedding dress the bride went on the arm of her husband in his
rich silver-braided suit and his lace-ruffled shirt. Everyone came past to
embrace them, and then the feast began. Roast chickens basted in spiced
wine and stuffed with meat, piñons and raisins; baked hams; ribs of beef;
fresh bread of blue meal; cookies, cakes, sweets; beakers of chocolate
and flasks of wine; bowls of hot chili; platters of tortillas, all stood upon
extra tables draped to the floor with lace curtains. All feasted.

Then came music, and dark eyes fired up. The sala was cleared, while the musicians tuned up on two or three violins, a guitar and a guitarrón, or bass guitar. Servants came to spread clean wheat straw on the earth floor to keep dust from rising, or stood by with jars of water from which to sprinkle the floor between dances. In the candlelight the faces of the women, heavily powdered with Mexican white lead, looked an ashen violet, in which their eyes were dark caves deeply harboring the ardent emotion of the occasion. The orchestra struck up. They danced quadrilles and minuets, whose figures drew all dancers into fleeting touch with each other. There were paired dances, like la raspa, with its heel thunderings and its laughing fast walk. There were marching dances accompanied by spoken verses invented on the spot by someone who was famous as an improvisor. He would go to stand before a guest, bow, and without an instant's groping for what to say, recite an improvised ballad of eight-syllabled lines paying compliment to his subject whom he faced. He celebrated the beauty, charm and talent of the bride, weaving in episodes of her childhood, alluding to her gallant ancestry, and promising her a dazzling future. The groom he saluted in another decima as a superb horseman and buffalo hunter, or trail-driver, or heir of an illustrious house. Sometimes he sang a riddle poem, and all tried to guess the answer.

While the dancing went on, the bride had an obligation to fulfill. Retiring from the floor in her wedding dress, she reappeared presently in another gown from her trousseau, and later in another, and another. Everyone was eager to see what she had been given. Politely and proudly she gratified them. They fingered her silks and examined the set of jewels given her by the groom—matching earrings, necklace, bracelets, combs, brooches, of gold inlaid with enamel, or seed pearls, rose diamonds, amethysts or garnets.

Before midnight the bride retired not to reappear. Her maiden friends and her godmother went with her. The groom drank with the men in whose company he now belonged, while boys watched and nudged. The dancing continued, and humor went around. The groom's father calling above the noise in the hot, hard-plastered room, urged everyone to keep right on enjoying themselves. Presently the groom managed to slip away. In the bridal chamber the ladies admitted him and left him with his bride. Across the patio the merriment continued. Voices were singing. Someone shouted a refrain. The violins jigged along in a remote monotonous sing, and the gulping throb of the guitarrón was like a pulse of mindless life in the night.

So the river society renewed, celebrated and blessed itself.

On the following day the groom took his bride home to his father's house, where new rooms would be added as their home, in which they would have privacy, even as they shared the communal life of the hacienda.

When the children were born of the marriage, they were baptized as soon as possible. There was no greater token of love than to dedicate them to God. If they died in infancy, grief was put aside for a sort of exalted rejoicing that in their christened innocence they had been gathered straightway to God in Heaven. If they lived, they were cherished.

> Lullaby, little one,
> Lullaby, baby.
> For your cradle
> I give you my heart.

As they grew, like all children, they aped in their play what grownups did; but very early they were given tasks to do, and a little boy worked at a miniature share of his father's work, in field, corral or shed, and a little girl learned at sewing table, or in kitchen. They were an observant part of all the family's large or small occasions. The largest of these was death.

vii. mortality

There were sombre relish and conviviality in how death was received in the river kingdom. The Spaniard had a black mind and a morbid tradition. Philip II lived in him for centuries. Death was the gateway to an eternal life, whether, by his own choice, in heaven or hell. Its symbols were always before him. They clattered in gaiety on All Souls' Day—toy skeletons, candy skulls, tiny trick coffins like a jack-in-the-box—and they presided over him daily in all the painted and bloody agonies of his household saints. He did not fear death more than most men, but more than most, he was an informed critic of the emotions of mortality, and at proper times summoned them forth for their own sake, gave them style, and so became their master.

When death from natural causes was seen to be coming the family could only do its best to make the victim comfortable. There were no physicians anywhere on the river excepting the pueblo medicine doctors, and their concepts were too alien to Spanish life to be taken seriously. The parish priest was sent for if he was within reach. To die in sanctity was the most real of necessities. All prayers and observances were made. If the dying belonged to the sodality of Our Lady of Mount Carmel (who was the divine inspiration of Saint John of the Cross as theologian and poet) he knew that he might not die until once more he felt the earth. At his request a brick of clay was brought him to touch. Touching it, he believed his final struggles would be eased. His dear ones watched by his bed. When the last hour came they sent for the resador, who always led prayers aloud at devotional services. He now had a duty to perform, and he came to join the watchers. He was an expert at knowing the exact moment of death. Relying on his wide experience and his natural gifts, he kept his gaze upon the dying face; and when he recognized the first veil of final mystery as it came, he cried loudly three times, as was his duty, the name of Jesus. At the moment of death, the soul took flight to its Savior's name. The best friend of the deceased or the oldest man present closed the eyes. Men dressed the corpse if it was that of a man; women if that of a woman, or a child.

And now that death was among them, the bereaved women screamed in grief. They did it as a form of artistry. They threw themselves from side to side and wailed formless words. This was expected of them, a mortal politeness that was understood and even judged. In obscure wisdom they set out to exhaust, to cure, grief through its own excesses. Now and then in the midst of their working clamor, their interest might be seized by something beyond. They paused and gazed while their shrieks fell to whimpers. They were lost like staring children; and then, as always, life moved, their fixity was broken, and with a shake of the head they came back to their duty and redoubled their lamentations. Private loss became an experience to share in full measure with all who would partake of it. A woman shrieking and throwing herself required other women to hold her and give comfort. These in turn needed friends to relieve them at their enervating work. The whole society of women worked toward the seemliness of the event.

Men built the coffin of raw wood. The corpse was laid in it, and then with lighted candles at head and feet was placed on view in the sala for the wake, or velorio. All who could, attended to watch all night, while prayers were recited in unison, hymns of devotion to the patron saint were sung, and memories of the dead were exchanged. At midnight supper was served. The household was thronged and busy. Such an occasion was so much enjoyed that wakes were held even without death present. These were solemnized in honor of appropriate saints throughout the year. Men singing traditional laments in procession brought saintly statues from the church or the chapel, and communal meditations on death were observed as for a recent bereavement. A wake for a deceased person sometimes continued for two nights and was ended with burial. If the family lived near town, the coffin was borne to the parish church for a Requiem Mass, after which it was buried in the floor of the church while all present sang dolefully together. If the family lived far in the country, burial took place in the family chapel or in a cemetery upland from the river, out of reach of swampy soil. A fence of wooden pickets with ornamental tips stood around the family graveyard. A cairn of stones was put at the head of the grave to support a wooden cross. Late in the eighteenth century itinerant stone carvers sometimes appeared in the river settlements, and were hired to make a monument. One family, at Belén, had a carved stone mausoleum, built by sculptors brought from Italy. The funeral of a child was gay and impish, reflecting the happy fact that it died without sin. Dressed in white and decked with flowers and bright ribbons, the corpse was carried along in a procession that all but danced. The local musicians played furiously on their violins the tunes which everyone knew at their fandangos. The marchers chattered and laughed. Grief was out of place for one who had left the temptations of the world and already knew heavenly bliss.

For if life was a battle between good and evil, then the moment of decision came at the moment of death. Evil lived in the flesh, which would in the end lose the fight; but it also accompanied the spirit, and unless exorcised in piety before death promised eternal damnation. In the power of this conviction, Rio Grande Spaniards, like their most august forebears in Spain, strove to put down evil by punishing their own flesh. The flail of the Emperor Charles V, inherited and used by his son Philip II and willed in turn to his kingly heir, sounded in echo through the centuries amongst the villages and estates of the river kingdom. Their particular discipline in piety came alike to monarch and colonial from the thirteenth century, when self-flagellation in atonement was widespread amongst European religious orders and individuals, including the Third Order of Saint Francis. Searching for the river in the spring of 1598, Oñate's colony had paused in northern Mexico on Holy Thursday to seek redemption through pain, and "the night," wrote Captain Pérez de Villagrá later, "the night was one of prayer and penance for all. The soldiers, with cruel scourges, beat their backs unmercifully until the camp ran crimson with their blood. The humble Franciscan friars, barefoot and clothed in cruel thorny girdles, devoutly chanted their doleful hymns, praying forgiveness for their sins. . . . Don Juan, unknown to anyone except me, went to a secluded spot where he cruelly scourged himself, mingling bitter tears with the blood which flowed from his many wounds. . . ." By 1627, processions of flagellants in the Spanish river lands were mentioned as a matter of course in official reports of the Father President. When Vargas took the crown back to Santa Fe, "The Third Order of Penitence"—not to be confused with the Third Order of St. Francis—was established in the 1690s at Santa Fe and Santa Cruz, and legally recorded. In 1794 a cathedral document at Santa Fe named the same brotherhood, saying that it had "been in existence since the earliest years of the conquest." First administered under sacerdotal guidance, the brotherhood became more and more the responsibility of laymen, until in the latter half of the eighteenth century and throughout the nineteenth they alone conducted its ceremonies. For by then the Franciscans were rapidly losing their independent control of New Mexico's religious affairs, under pressure from the Bishops of Durango who worked, in the end successfully, to bring the river kingdom under their dominion. The Franciscan authorities were as a consequence withdrawing more and more of their friars from the vast province where few enough had ever been assigned.

Men of the Spanish villages and haciendas joined the fraternity to do bodily penance in atonement for their own sins and for the death of Jesus upon the cross. Calling themselves the Penitent Brothers, they were subdivided into two groups—the Brothers of Light, who administered the sodality, and the Brothers of Blood, who as the rank and file carried out its precepts. A village or a group of haciendas supported a morada, a chapter house of the Penitents. This was an earth chapel set away by itself. It had no windows, rarely a belfry, never more than one storey, often only one room. It was as secret and as plain as a kiva. It was closed to all but initiates. Within was the bare furniture of piety—an altar, a wooden cross great enough for a man, lengths of chain, blood-spattered whips bearing thongs of leather studded with cactus thorns, locally made images of saints painted flat or carved and colored, and various representations of Christ, and a life-sized figure of death in a cart. Here the chapter met for business, in secrecy, and, as the calendar demanded, in pain spiritual or pain physical. The members discussed good works that they might perform, together or individually. Apart from the great houses, there was deep poverty in the valley of the haciendas, and much suffering, and if charity could be done, it must be. The brotherhood met for prayer, and thinking of the poor souls in purgatory, prayed for their delivery into heaven—an act, under their faith, of supreme charity.

A young man taken into the chapter was initiated through memorized ritual and ordeals of pain. He came after dark on an appointed night to the morada, remembering and awed at what he was told to do, that would soon sweep his humdrum life into new wonder, prestige and expression of its deepest self. In the pathos of those who longed to conform, he lifted his hand and knocked upon the morada's door, and said,

"God's child knocks at this chapel door for His grace."

"Penance," replied a solemn voice from within, "penance is required by those who seek salvation."

"Saint Peter will open the gate," recited the novice, shivering at the analogy of heaven, "bathing me with the light in the name of Mary, with the seal of Jesus. I ask this brotherhood: Who gives this house light?"

"Jesus," answered the leader within.

"Who fills it with joy?"

"Mary."

"Who preserves it with faith?"

"Joseph."

The door was then opened to him. He was taken within and led to kneel and bend before a bench. His back was bared by the attendant Brothers of Light. He was exhorted in the duties of membership and secrecy. The sangrador, an officer empowered to draw the blood of the initiate, came to the kneeling youth and with a knife of obsidian cut three deep gashes the length of his back, and three more the width. Laying down his knife the sangrador took up salt which he rubbed into the wounds and stepped back expectantly. The novice remembered what he must now say.

"For the love of God bestow upon me a reminder of the three meditations of the passion of our Lord."

Nodding in propriety, the sangrador marked the three meditations with three lashes of a rawhide whip on each side of the kneeling man's bare body.

"For the love of God," begged the novice, "bestow on me the remainder of the five wounds of Christ."

And when these were given with the whip, he asked for the

bestowal of the Forty Days in the Wilderness, and the Seven Last Words of Christ, which were laid upon him. Then he was taken up and led aside, and his wounds were bathed for him, and he was by now lost in rapt endurance, and on his back were the welts of membership, as proofs of manhood, marks of prestige, and of faith.

When Lent approached, the Penitents made plans for its observance. In the whole Lenten canon of atonement they found the passionate theme of their own society, and led all others in public avowals of contrition and acts of penance. The tragedy of Christ's Passion was the central motive of their entire spiritual life, their art, and their acceptance of human estate. Through it they found the power to bear their own worldly sufferings and by it they were liberated from the burden of sin. Possessing so certainly a divine Champion they attained a strong dignity that was their consolation no matter what their material or social estate in life. If they were for the most part poor people without education save that which came from their daily experience and from the lessons of the pastor, they yet knew in a philosophical achievement of a high order that man's nature, capable of evil as well as of good, needed to be redeemed for his inner peace. Such a conviction was a universal commonplace in the Spanish society of the river kingdom.

Each year at the beginning of Holy Week the Penitents began their most intense demonstrations of faith. They retired to the morada, and were not seen to emerge for four days, while women prepared and brought food to the door for them. With the stripping of the altars on Holy Thursday came the tenebrous thoughts that prepared all for Good Friday. Litanies and prayers were heard in the morada. Plain song, far removed from the glories of old-world compositions, modified by strange accidental dissonances, and accompanied by the thin wailing of a home-made flageolet, rose above the praying brotherhood. In the darkness of Good Friday eve they emerged from the chapter house. Chanting in procession, while their countrymen watched in kneeling rows or walked beside them holding torches of pitch, they whipped themselves with chains and flails until their backs ran red. Girls, called Veronicas, ran to wipe their faces with cloths. In the valley, the tributary canyons, of the northern river, such nights were cold. Returning to the morada, the processional members watched all night, at intervals renewing their flagellations, and crying out the psalm of the Miserere.

> Deliver me from blood, O God!
> Thou God of my salvation,
> And my tongue shall extol Thy Justice!

And on the following day, Good Friday, within the walls of the
morada an ordeal of spiritual pain was enacted. From infancy the Spanish people were poignantly aware of the whole drama of Calvary, and
in various ways strove to share in humanity's guilt for the death of
Jesus, and to claim the redemption promised to them by that very death.
The Penitents of the river in passionate earnest sought to identify themselves with the sacrifice of Christ, and to renew in themselves the blessings to be drawn from it. They elected one of their number to the awful
role of the Saviour. He was chosen for his goodness in life. Like any
man, he knew fear when his life was in danger, and it was in danger
now. Yet he was honored, and to face what was coming he was empowered
by a sense of glory in his identity with Godhead. If the sweat stood out
on his brow his soul rose within him. He was ready when within the
blind walls of the morada his brothers seized him roughly, as soldiers
had seized Jesus, and brought him to judgment. While the reader of the
brotherhood intoned the Passion of Christ from the gospels, the events
he narrated were acted out by men who knew and deeply believed in
what they were to do. Christ was questioned before the High Priest and
He answered, that He was the Son of God. The high priest cried, "He
has blasphemed," and demanded of the populace what they desired,
and they cried out for death, and struck at their brother in the morada.
They took him a step or two elsewhere and faced him to Pilate, who
washed his hands of him, and asked what was to be done with him? and
they replied out of centuries and for all men, "Let Him be crucified!"
The scene shifted in the narrow hall of the clay chapel, and was in the
palace of the Procurator of Judea. There in mankind's reduction of all
its victims to their animal being, the persecutors denuded the Christ
and exposed him. They then put on him a royal scarlet robe, a crown
of thorns made from wild rose branches, gave him a rude sceptre, and
paid him mocking honor, while the hearts of the brothers were moved
at what they did—to jeer as a false king the one who was King of all
creation. Their ire rose with the gospel. They took his sceptre from their
brother and beat him with it. They spat at him. He stood for them,
entranced. They stripped him again and put his own clothes on him.

Outside the morada all knew what was transpiring within. History
recorded in the gospels told them, and local memory, and sounds that
came on the cold night. The weather was often bitter in Holy Week on
the river, and snow fell on the little foothills that rose from the valley,
and the sparse bushes looked black in daylight. One of the hills near

the settlement stood a little higher than others. A path led to its top. This was Calvary.

Late in the morning on Good Friday the Passion within the morada came into daylight. A procession was formed. The Penitents went barefoot in their black hoods and white trunks. A group of flagellants led the way. The Christ followed, bent under the man-sized cross which he carried from the morada. A little group of honored brothers pulled the morada's rough wooden cart in which sat a wooden skeleton with gaping jaws—the carved image of Death. It held a drawn bow with a real arrow. Spectators from the settlement knelt to watch, and if the cart jolted against one of them this was counted a blessing. It was left to chance and the roughness of the cold ground whether Death's arrow would be jarred free from its stretched bowstring and fly away. The arrow, they said, once did so, and quivered into the flesh of a spectator, killing him. Death was everywhere. In fierce irony and challenge the people exposed themselves to its caprice, and ways of forgotten origin stirred in them out of the cultish death rituals of medieval Europe, as they now approached on the village Calvary the scene of the supreme death of their inheritance.

The mount was studded with rocks that pierced bare feet and with bushes that tore at bare bodies. Up a path worn by many generations that had walked the same hill for the same purpose the village Christ made his way, followed by all his neighbors. He fell three times and rose again to drag the cross to the appointed station at the top. The Veronicas wiped the faces of those who suffered in their imitations of Christ. The sound of whips on bleeding backs smote the air. To the cracked whistle of the flageolet, voices made their way in unison through the penitential psalms. With the marchers walked not only the history of Jesus Christ, but also the whole past of Israel, and Israel's whole past of Asiatic myth.

At the summit of the hill overlooking the lower river lands, the Christ was laid supine upon his cross, to which he was tied with bands of cotton cloth. His cross was raised against the white sky of the horizon. Those who watched saw a living bare body hanging upon the cruel tree and knew again what had been suffered for them in love at Golgotha. They fell to their knees at the instant of the crucifixion and beating their breasts cried out together, *"Peccado! Peccado!"*—"I have sinned! I have sinned!"—lost in the identity of the crucified. As the brother Christ hung on his cross wearing only black head-bag and white trunks, his

body turned blue from the bindings that held him to it so tightly that
his blood ceased to move in him. He was watched to detect the moment
when he could endure no more and must die. When they saw it his
brothers lowered the cross and took him from it, bearing him away to
the morada to restore him if possible.

With that moment the village Christ had enacted the giving up
of the Ghost, and out of the Gospel of Saint Matthew the words came
back to all who watched—how "the earth did quake, and the rocks rent,
and the graves were opened: and many bodies of the saints arose," and
how for three hours there was darkness. And so on Good Friday night
the brothers gathered in the morada to imitate the anguish and darkness
of all nature, in the service of the Tinieblas. Twelve candles were lighted
upon the altar. The Brother Reader recited twelve psalms. At the conclusion of each, one candle was extinguished until there was total darkness. With that, sounds imitative of the world in anguish and upheaval
broke out in terrifying volume. All roared and groaned, while chains
clanked, and wooden rattles whirred, and sticks thumped on drums,
and hammers struck metal. After minutes, came sudden silence, and
a single voice cried out asking for a sudario—the cloth that covered the
face of a corpse. This was an elevated idiom, meant to signify a prayer
for a soul in purgatory. The prayer was recited by a leader, to which
all responded. The quaking uproar broke out again, and again a sudario
was given, and for an hour in alternating clamor and prayer, the ceremony of darkness was observed, and at last the purifying terrors were
over.

If the village Christ died he was buried by his brotherhood in
secrecy, and his shoes were put the next day on the doorstep of his house
to notify his family that he was dead. Grieved, they yet rejoiced, for
they believed that in his ritual sacrifice he had gained for himself and
them direct entry into heaven. His cross was left to stand all year on the
summit of his hill, and sometimes two others were placed, one on each
side of his, to recall the thieves who had died on Calvary with the Son
of Man. From a distance they looked like twigs against the sky. Year-
round they had the power to prick the thoughts of anyone who had
sanctioned why they were there.

viii. the saints

For the crosses were in fact a form of monumental art at its most bare and artless. As such they stated starkly the whole purpose of visual art in the lives of the river people. That purpose was hortatory, not ornamental or esthetic. Rather than primarily to delight the eye, it was to compel goodness, which it did by means of images of the cross, the Deity and the saints, whose presence reminded the people of sufferings on earth that led to glories in eternity. And in their art—the art of the *santo,* or represented saint—the people revealed alike their longings and their own images, for the saints they fashioned were self-portraits.

In their first century on the river, Spaniards had brought their saints from Europe—large church paintings and carved images in the styles of the High Renaissance. In them along with piety echoed the civilized richness of court and cathedral, and through them shone conventions of drawing, modelling, and painting that adored the human body in its beauty, and strove to immortalize it with every elegance. The exuberance of patronal society was raised in works of art, even on religious themes, to a dazzling splendor, through superb techniques. Greek ideals of pagan beauty were revived to celebrate the persons and events of the Christian church. Through imported works of art, European sophistication presided over the worship of the river Spaniards and Indians in their rude adobe churches—until the terror of 1680. And then in one overwhelming gust of hatred, the Indians destroyed every vestige of the Spanish spirit that could be burned, ripped or uprooted, and the European likenesses of Christ, the Holy Family and the saints disappeared from their places of reverence in the homes and churches of the river. After their return to their impoverished kingdom, the colonists and the friars restored what they could of their property. But the Crown had lost interest in spending money on New Mexico. The Franciscan order on its own could afford only the most meagre of supplies to keep the missions alive. The barest necessities of life were all that came north in the wagon trains. The river kingdom began to recede more and more into its northern remoteness with every year as the home government in Spain found itself increasingly absorbed and on the defensive in European affairs. Imperial Spain was slowly bled of its life flow, and almost all the goods of life along the river were now created locally. Among these were the very saints themselves.

For, one way or another, there had to be saints in every house, chapel and mission, and if there were no saints from Europe, once again, the Franciscan friars, who when necessary could do anything, filled the need. They painted sacred pictures on buffalo skins. They remembered mannerisms of drawing and of coloring out of Europe, and their first efforts reflected these. On little tablets of wood they painted saints that could be hung up on a wall. Out of columns of cottonwood they carved statues which they colored. The friars fiercely preserved the seemliness of religious places by founding a local school of saint makers. They taught what they knew about drawing, painting and carving to those among their people who showed aptitude. As the eighteenth century passed, and the friars were gradually withdrawn, the work was left wholly with laymen. Born in the river world, they knew no direct European influence. A recognized profession of saint maker grew up, to create an original contribution of the Rio Grande to the art of the world.

It was an art that sought the universal divine, and expressed it through the humble daily likeness of the saint maker's own people. If this was the inevitable formula for the artist anywhere, then it was the qualifying locality, and the nature of the style, that made the Rio Grande saints unique. The faces and postures of those saints were those that prevailed in the bosky farms of the river—little cramped gestures without grace and yet tense with spirit; poor thin faces with great eyes that had always looked on poverty and in the mystery of hardship had found an identity with the divine. If the actors in the penitential events of Holy Week were fixed suddenly in their stark attitudes, with their dark eyes, their angled arms, their gaunt bodies, black hair, pale olive skins and brilliant lips, there, suddenly, would be seen the attitudes of the religious art of the Spanish Rio Grande. The santos at once gave and received a staring piety that exactly expressed the spirit of faith in all its vast, yet intimate, simplicity.

In time the saint maker became a familiar figure as he travelled up and down the river with his pack mule whose panniers contained a selection of saints to be sold at the rich houses or in the poor villages. He had tablets, or retablos, ranging in size from about four by six inches to about twelve by eighteen. He made these by first smoothing the wooden surface, then coating it with several washes of gypsum like that used on the walls of rooms. He ground his own pigments. Black came from charcoal, reds, browns and orange from iron ochre, yellows from ocherous clay, blue and green, which faded, from the copper ores used by the Indians for their kachina painting. For his medium he used water and egg yolk, and, much later, oil. He drew the outline of his saint in black or dark brown, and then filled in the color. His tablet often had an ornamental painted border, and at the top, a lunette carved in shell-like flutings. He tied a rawhide thong through a little hole by which to hang the tablet on the wall.

In his pack there were wooden figures fashioned in the round that stood from a few inches to several feet tall. These he called bultos. He made them like dolls. The torso was of one piece, the arms and legs of others that were attached, sometimes by sockets, sometimes by strips of muslin pasted as hinges. He covered the face and body with his gypsum wash, and then painted the features and the flesh. Every saint had his attribute by which he was recognized—Michael with his sword and the scales of justice, Raphael and his fish, Peter and his keys, Veronica and her veil, John with his long cruciform staff and his lamb. The saint maker carved such attributes separately, and affixed them to the figure. He worked to make his creations as lifelike as possible. If his bodily proportions were inaccurate, and the modelling of face and hands and feet faulty, it was only because his skill was not equal to his intention. But the passion that begot his works had more power to express than his technical ignorance had to constrain. His failures in realism did not deny life to his works—the life that he breathed into them out of the depth of his feeling, the power of his faith, and his desire to please his customers. He was an artist for whose productions there existed a lively demand throughout the society he was part of. This condition gave him dignity and fulfillment as man as well as artist. Fully integrated among his fellows, he gave in his work not only his own vision but theirs; and when he re-imagined their life in the presence of their reality, he became the means by which their society perpetuated its own image in art.

It was odd, but it was true, that though he had a set of severe conventions for painting faces, they never came out exactly alike, but had striking originality in characterization; and yet however individual they might be, all his faces were unmistakably Spanish. He gave them deep porched eyes, heavily rimmed with black, and thick, arching black eyebrows, and coal-black hair. The women's faces he finished with a paint that made them look like matrons made up for fandangos, with the ash-violet complexions that came from their lead powder. To his portraits of Christ and other masculine saints he gave beards, painted in shiny black. He often attached real hair to the heads of both male and female statues, and sometimes did not carve their clothing but made it out of cloth soaked in gypsum wash, arranged in folds when wet, and painted when stiffly dry.

Looking at the Mother of God bought from a saint maker, the owners could often see the living mother of their mud house in the valley. One statue showed her in sorrow, with a black rebozo, her brows lifted in pity above mica eyes, her full mouth trembling on the very taste of the grief that swelled in her round cheeks, with their touches of pink paint, and her full throat. Her dress was painted and so were its buttons, embroidery, and the rosary about her waist. Her hands were unduly large, and looked rough with work. Another divine-and-earthly mother had a calm, knowing gaze, above a great nose and a mouth shadowed with a wise smile, that seemed to rest upon daily concerns of husband, children, cooking pots and domestic animals. A Saint Raphael holding his fish was a heavy-browed youth with huge eyes full of the joy of the fisherman who has taken his catch out of the river beyond his family fields. In the right hand of a Saint Joseph was his flowered staff that bore a cluster of yucca blossoms. In his other arm he held the infant Jesus whose almond eyes and painted smile recalled the Mongol antiquity of the river Indians. The saint himself wore a look of grave, untutored wisdom in Indian fixity. In a crucifix were all the exhaustion, dryness, filthiness of caked wound and scab, the rivulets of painted blood, that countless people had seen on the village Christs of their own hill. His arms and legs were bound to the cross with miniature strips of cloth. In another carved Christ with real hair hanging lank the local face was focussed in staring rapture upon universal mystery unseen but believed. In another Christ, recumbent in a wooden cage symbolic of the tomb, the carved and painted mouth with a row of revealed tiny teeth was fixed open upon a silent unending scream. The power in his face was like that in the openmouthed masks of those clay figures buried with the dead in ancient Mexico. The Holy Trinity was represented by three bodies, joined, and three heads, as identical as the saint maker could make them, and the face of all was the square face of a handsome bearded farmer with roughly chiselled features who in obedience and patience drew the terms of his life out of the river earth. So in countless examples, stiff, angular, almost coerced into eloquence, the saints in tablet and statue spoke with passionate directness of the daily life whose daily need had called them forth in all their anguished divinity.

Though they had an awesome character, they had also an intimate personality. A favorite household saint was almost a member of the family, constantly included in the making of decisions, and consulted a dozen times a day in the comfort of half-thought and daydream. "What shall I do?" The santo would send the right answer. "May my harvest be good!" The santo would arrange it. "If the baby would only get well!" The santo must save it. "If I could only be loved!" The santo— if was a legitimate love—might bless it. Living as such a personality, the santo was subject not only to reverence but on occasion to displeasure, when prayerful requests were not answered. Then the santo was turned with its face to the wall, or put away in a trunk, until the request was answered, or its purpose dwindled through passing time. Addresses to the saints now and then took on an Indian character. When storms came, an Indian cook in a Spanish house went out the door and recalling the sacred use of corn meal in the pueblos threw a handful of salt to the sky, making the shape of a cross, and praying:

> Saint Barbara, holy maid,
> Save us, Lady.
> In thunder and lightning afraid.

ix. *provincials*

So in simplicity of spirit, and in direct productive life upon the land, with the most laborious of methods, the life of the hacienda valley took its way far from the great world. Out in the world, revolutions in psychology, and government, and science, were creating new concepts of living. But Spain, the mother country, consciously closed herself to these; and barely a ripple of late eighteenth-century European movement reached the river kingdom. The machine was being discovered as a power in civilization. Technology was born. Industry entered upon violent growth. But not in Spain, and not in the far valley of the Spanish river of North America. The Spanish had no gift for technology, generally speaking. Though the pure sciences were studied, their application was left to other nations. But even Spain's rich tradition of scholarly education did not reach to the river frontier. There were no schools for the haciendas, and no colleges. Even the Franciscan classes in the pueblo missions were disappearing in the last colonial century, as the teachers were withdrawn. Children of the river families learned what they could from their parents. This meant a sufficient skill at the jobs

of working the land, and saving the soul. But it brought little for the
life of the mind. There were no printing presses in New Mexico. The
only books that came in the trade caravans went to the friars, and were
of a professional religious nature, with perhaps a copy or two of the
poems of Sister Juana Inés de la Cruz, Mexico's intellectual nun. An
occasional youth was taught to read, write and consider philosophy by
a priest who guided him toward a vocation in the religious life and
presently sent him to a seminary in Mexico. For the rest, only sons of
the richest river families could hope for a formal education. Such young
men were sent to Mexico City to college, or to Spain. They were promising scholars. Baron von Humboldt in Mexico found "that the young
men who have distinguished themselves by their rapid progress in the
exact sciences came for a great part from the northernmost provinces of
New Spain," where because of constant guard against wild Indians they
had led "a singularly active life, which has to be spent mostly on horseback." When they came home, they might become leaders in local politics, and enjoy the prestige of having seen the world. But the local
horizons and ways of the river prevailed over the sons as over the
fathers. Now and then a proud daughter of a hacienda was taken south
with the autumn wagons to be educated in a convent where she would
learn the crafts of ladyship. In due course she would return to her
family, ready to marry an eligible young man, and maintain with him
the combination of domestic grace and primitive husbandry that characterized all life in the river estates.

For the rest, it was a life that had its arts. If these did not blaze
and tremble with the peculiar acrid glory of Spain at her greatest, they
yet glowed behind the sombre patience of the people like coals dying
under ashes. If their spirit longed for poetry, it had to be content with
the doggerel rhymes at dances, and in the nomenclature of the land,
like the name given to the mountains between Galisteo and the Rio
Grande, which were called the Sierra de Dolores. In such a place name
the Spaniards met the landscape of their souls. Their theatre was made
of the artless plays enacted by amateurs at Christmas and in Holy
Week with deep religious meaning. Their music sounded in the simple
scratches of violins at parties, funerals, the wail of the flageolet in the
Penitential passion, the singing of High Mass, the celebration of love
and adventure in ballads. Their painting and sculpture showed in the
saints made in the valley. Their architecture rose out of earth forms in
the universal style of the adobe house and church. All expression in art

was integrated in the occasions and forms of local living in the long valley. It was all unprofessional and traditional, and none of it was produced for its own sake, but always to serve primarily an intimate function of the society. As the ways of life were taken from the local earth, the texture of living more and more showed the face of local tradition with its Indian source. The river house, Indian dress, dyes, articles of trade, seasonal ceremonies like the opening of the ditches in spring, the drying of succulent foods, the kivalike form and secrecy of the morada, the bogeyman who benevolently scared children into goodness—such details stood for the gradual absorption of the Spaniards into the ancient environment where they came to conquer and remained to submit.

Did they see themselves in their long procession through the colonial centuries—thirsty for discovery, but often scornful of what they found; bearers of truth which all too often they bestowed with cruelty; lionhearted and greedy-minded; masters of great wildernesses that yet mastered them in the end?

Those who lived in the haciendas and villages of the river illustrated a last chapter of what it meant to be provincial in the Spanish empire. Through three centuries the colonials knew first how it was to move farther away from Spain; and then from Cuba, then from Mexico City, then from Culiacán; and from the big monasteries of New Biscay and Coahuila to the Rio Grande. Every stage brought reduced movement, less color, luxury, amenity, worldly importance in all things. In time, remote from their sources, the colonists lived on hearsay instead of communion. Folk artisanship replaced skilled professional craftsmanship. Barter substituted for money. Home-butchered animals instead of prepared commodities sustained life. Custom overshadowed law. It was a civilization falling asleep—remembering instead of creating, and then forgetting; and then learning the barest lessons of the new environment, until their meagre knowledge had to serve in place of the grandeurs of the source. As they were native lessons, so were they appropriate, but as their products in objects and ways were primitive, they were matters of marvel at what was produced not with so much skill, but with so little. A grand energy, a great civilization, having reached heights of expression in the arts of painting, poetry, architecture, faith and arms, had returned to the culture of the folk. Defeated by distance and time, the Rio Grande Spaniards finally lived as the Pueblo Indians lived—in a fixed, traditional present.

What they preserved were their distinction and grace of person and manner—all that was left of the Golden Age whose other attributes had once been so glorious, so powerful across the world.

And yet in their daily realities they found content. Escorials and armadas and missions over the seas were all very well, but now there was enough to do just to sustain life. All about them was a land whose forms of mountain, desert and valley seemed to pre-figure eternity. The brilliant sky called out life on the hacienda by day; and at night, with tasks done, and reviewed in prayer, and promised for the morrow, all seemed as it should be, with the sound of frogs and crickets, and the seep and suck of the river going forever by, and the cool breath of the fields, and the heavy sweet smell of the river mud, and the voluminous quiet of the cottonwood domes. The haciendas fell asleep under a blessing of nature.

39.

The World Intrudes

The Spanish community, scattered along the river for nearly two thousand miles from Taos to Reynosa, knew increasing trouble in meeting its own simple needs, whether of ceremony or material growth. In the 1750s there was only one man who knew how to beat a military drum, and at the end of the century there were no more than thirteen skilled carpenters, in all the New Mexico valley. Poverty ruled. It ruled in Spain, where monetary disasters followed upon wars long since bereft of adventure and triumph; and it ruled in the colonies, where the Crown could no longer afford to pay for far-flung garrisons, and missions, and new enterprises. Aside from the ancient pueblos, there were less than twenty villages and towns on the whole river. As royal support for the river frontier lessened, the haciendas and towns were more exposed to Indian dangers. Comanches swept over Taos in 1760, carrying

off fifty Spanish women and children, who were never recovered. Even
so, once a year, Plains Indians came to Taos to attend the fair, and the
Spaniards from downriver met them there, and a Frenchman now and
then appeared from the east. Loot from plains warfare changed hands
in New Mexico. "They bring captives to sell," noted Bishop Tamarón
of Durango after his visit to Taos in 1760, and "buckskins, many buffalo
hides, and booty that they have taken in other parts—horses, guns,
muskets, ammunition, knives, meat, and various other things. No money
circulates in these fairs, but articles are traded for each other and in
this way those people provide themselves."

Even such primitive energy in commerce was lacking on the
Texas river, for in 1762 the government of New Spain relaxed its efforts
to colonize Texas as a protection against the French. The French threat
to Texas was removed when France ceded Louisiana to Spain. The
lower river towns founded by Escandón were left with more local
problems. At Laredo, in 1771, dispute raged as to which side of the
Rio Grande was to be permanently settled. The original community
had been established on the north bank, but safety from increasing
Indian raids called for removal to the south bank. If the debate went
beyond words, there were stocks in the old plaza into which the alcalde,
José Martínez de Sotomayor, could clap offenders. Compromise resulted
when some families moved across the river, while others remained on
the north bank, and sought shelter on the south bank only when Indian
alarms were given.

They came often. The big ranches on both sides of the Texas
river were repeatedly raided, and the river towns knew one siege after
another, with fire, pillage, and death. What could be done? The central
government had neither money nor troops to add to the meagre garrisons of the Mexican river states. An effort was made to combine the
forces of New Biscay, Coahuila, Tamaulipas and Nuevo León, so that
a continuous patrol of the river frontier would be possible. New Mexico
could add no troops to such a force, for the old river kingdom had all
it could do to survive its own Indian troubles, falling back mainly upon
attempts to pit one wild tribe against another so that warring they
might leave the valley pueblos, farms and towns in peace. It was a forlorn policy.

But appeasement seemed all that was left to the lower river
commanders and the governor of Texas at the end of the eighteenth
century. To tribes agreeing to be friendly, annual tribute was paid. It
seemed like a nightmare when each year the inert enemy came to be

paid for a peace that was at best precarious. Who knew how long the
bribes would satisfy, or when the recipients might become critical of the
gifts they were offered? In one shipment to San Antonio meant for
Indians there were one hundred English rifles, one hundred thirty dozen
knives, some with horn handles, sixty hatchets, sixty dozen scissors, fifty
dozen combs, thirty dozen little mirrors, fifty pounds of copper wire
and fifty pounds of beads to string upon it, twenty pairs of braided and
buckled short trousers, sixty-two copper kettles and sixty dozen jingle
bells. In a typical year the Governor of Texas received one thousand
nine hundred seventy-three Indians to whom he gave such nervous
bribes.

New Mexico in the 1770s suffered under concentrated Comanche
warfare which swept down the Rio Grande under the command of
Cuerno Verde. An able governor, de Anza, transferred from Sonora,
ended such hostilities for the time being by chasing the Comanche
captain over the plains to Kansas and there destroying him and many
of his warriors. Politics, in the same decade, persisted. From his hacienda
near Albuquerque, Don Eusebio Durán y Chaves went to Spain in 1774
to see King Charles III, who as the empire's bonds wore thin had time
for collections of birds, musical clocks, ingenious gardens and the re-
decoration of palaces. It was Don Eusebio's purpose to acquire for life
by royal grant the post of alcalde of the river pueblos of Sandía, San
Felipe, Santo Domingo and Cochiti, with the right of succession for his
son. He was received by the King, who listened to a recital of the Durán
y Chaves family's achievements through many generations on the river;
and in the end granted the petition. The personal exchange was one of
the last between a Spanish monarch and any of his subjects from the
Rio Grande. Don Eusebio made his long way homeward to New Mexico,
where the reach of the Old World was losing its grasp.

But the river world was reaching out to tie itself to the life, east
and west, of the North American continent. In 1776, Fray Silvestre Vélez
de Escalante set out from Santa Fe and travelled up the Chama River
from its Rio Grande confluence at Española, to find a path west to the
missions at Monterey, California. His course was indirect. It took him
to Mesa Verde, where he saw the silent cliff houses of the Indian ancestors
of the Rio Grande pueblos, and in eight months of travel, he failed to
reach the Pacific. But he returned with new knowledge which later
pathfinders could use. In another direction, the Spanish capital of San
Antonio sought to establish a regular route between that point, Santa Fe
and St. Louis on the Mississippi. The roads were found, and if regular

commerce was not yet possible, the future was waiting nearer than anyone knew, with its new energies. Across the lower Rio Grande at the end of the century an increasing trade in horses came and went. Foreigners—Frenchmen, Englishmen, Americans, even a few Irish— crossed Texas from Louisiana and entered the north Mexican provinces where they bought or traded for horses which they drove eastward for sale; and an old Indian trail was worn wider and deeper. Even Indians from the plains now and then went peaceably southward, pausing at the river to obtain permission to seek audience with the Viceroy in Mexico. And why? asked the Count of Sierra Gorda in Laredo and was told that the Indians wanted to establish colonies of their own over the Rio Grande in Mexico. Their request was humored. The Indians toured Mexico and went home again to the plains having seen what they had seen, which later could find use in their border warfare against the settlers who had let them pass by.

Lessons in human relations came hard—and late. In 1785 the Governor at Santa Fe received an official letter notifying him that the custom of branding Negroes on cheek and shoulder had been abolished. Under the guise of granting Indians their full privileges as subjects of the King, a government decree of 1794 took away from the Texas missions and placed under the care of civil justices all those who had been for ten years or longer the wards of the friars. Where the Indian had farmed his field and bred his cattle under the selfless teaching of the missionary, he was now to act alone. He could sell his crops, choose his occupation, and live where he pleased. Liberty was his. He was free to live like any Spaniard. The decree was a curious mixture of enlighten- ment and irresponsibility, and its motives were too bald to remain long hidden by rhetoric. In fact, there was no longer enough money to sub- sidize the missions, and their secularization was inevitable. No missions had ever been self-supporting. Part of their support had come from the Franciscan order, and the greater part from the Crown. Now the chapels were to become parish churches, to be supported by local population, or left empty to the weather. In many a mission friars would no longer teach Indians to read and write and work for the communal support of the settlement in modern fashion. There was no one else who holding duty and faith above worldly gain disinterestedly loved an Indian. In being granted with a flourish his equal status with the lay Spaniard, the Indian was in fact abandoned to a life of misery and exploitation. The civil justices assigned as his guardians were officially enjoined to guard the Indian against drunkenness, for drunk, he made a fool of

himself and sold his meagre goods for a gulp of liquor. It was a fact
used to advantage by Spanish traders. An Indian hiring out to labor
was to be protected against unjust payment, but if he chose, he might
accept commodities instead of cash, and their value was of course fixed
by his employer. With no education for a gradual assumption of civil
status, the Indian was abruptly required to be self-supporting and self-
governing in the alien society of the Spaniard.

A bishop of northern New Spain saw the inevitable consequences
and warned against them. He cited the corruption of the colonial and
local governments, and he spoke of the nature of the Indian still so near
to its savage inheritance. He pleaded that the friars lived and worked in
close community with Indians, and gave to them guidance and love that
no civil agent, however dedicated and honest, could ever match. The
plea was useless. The missions were secularized, the Indians were cut
adrift, many of the lower river chapels fell into disuse. The Texas-
Coahuila parishes came under the jurisdiction of the Bishop of Linares,
just as those of the New Mexico river became the responsibility, in due
course, of the Bishop of Durango.

The act of secularization was the last blow for such a community
as Fort St. John Baptist on the Rio Grande. Traffic crossing by its ford
was long since diminished, as Laredo and other downstream towns grew
to provide nearer gateways between interior Mexico and inhabited Texas.
But a little cluster of mission Indians still lived at Saint Bernard's, and
the fort still had a flying company in station to protect river ranches
against wild raiders. Now asked to maintain the great stone temple with
its convent, its granary, its baptistry, as a local parish church, the few
families, the underpaid and often criminal soldiers of the garrison, could
not do so. The friars were withdrawn. The other two missions of the
triangle at St. John Baptist were abandoned also. These two of earthern
structure weathered rapidly away. Saint Bernard's with its beautiful
tapestried stone survived the elements, but in time lost much of its
sound splendor to other uses, for as the decades passed, and a remote
northern Mexico town was settled where the fort had stood, the
townspeople tore at its walls to build their own houses, corrals and
market shops out of the stones quarried by the Franciscans so long ago.
The first and the finest stone mission of the Rio Grande gaped open to
the weather when the roof of the nave fell in. Grass appeared in the
high cracks of the walls where dust was packed by wind. Snakes came to
cast off their micalike skins in the open rooms amid the warming stones
of spring. The irrigation canals broke and the water ran idly. The fathers'

pool still mirrored its gray and yellow rock cliff. Saint Bernard's returned
to the wilderness from whose needs and materials it was built.

Up the river its first bridge was being erected at El Paso in 1797.
The wood for it had to be brought from far away in the north, and
was delayed in arriving, thanks to incompetence on the part of the engineer in charge. But in October three years later the bridge was completed, though it seemed to require constant repairs. More pine beams
were sent from Santa Fe in June, 1802, with a warning—wood was
precious—not to entrust it to the man in charge of the bridge, and a
strong suggestion that someone more suitable be found locally to direct
the work. A few weeks later the receipt of the timber was acknowledged
from El Paso, and a new engineer named. The governor himself, Fernando de Chacón, went to inspect the bridge, and finally took charge
of its repair. It gave him much trouble. He suffered injuries at the
bridge, there were no medical facilities in El Paso, or anywhere in New
Mexico, to cure him, and he ended by petitioning King Charles IV in
November, 1802, to relieve him of his post as governor and give him
an appointment in Spain. Fourteen months later the King granted his
petition. The bridge needed additional repairs in the following year,
and a party was sent to the Sierra de la Soledad from El Paso to cut
wood. Placed as it was, at the entrance of New Mexico, the bridge was
important to the whole kingdom. As late as 1819, Indians "and other
poor people" of Taos were pressed into service to haul mountain lumber
all the way down the river to the bridge at El Paso, often to their
personal hardship. In that year, the resident Franciscan of Taos wrote
to the governor at Santa Fe appealing to him to excuse the Taos farmers
from furnishing oxen for hauling timber to El Paso for the bridge until
late summer, so that they might work their crops. The governor scratched
his approval on the edge of the friar's letter, and ordered hauling
suspended.

But it was one thing to build a bridge for internal commerce,
quite another to allow foreigners to use it. At all her frontiers, New Spain
tried to exclude strangers. The Count of Revilla Gigedo, Viceroy, in
1792 issued an order received in New Mexico that required innkeepers
to report every day to the local magistrate who their transient lodgers
were. After the battle of Cape Saint Vincent in February, 1797, when
England's navy defeated Spain's, and followed this by raiding Spanish
possessions at home and in the Indies seas, a secret governmental dispatch
came to Governor de Chacón at Santa Fe in July with alarming news
and grave warnings. Spain believed that the English were readying an

expedition that was to sweep across North America from Halifax, Nova
Scotia, aimed particularly at an invasion of New Mexico by way of the
Mississippi and Missouri rivers. Observe every precaution, advised the
dispatch, to protect Indian and Spanish subjects against English and
American designs upon their loyalty. Intensify military reconnaissance
at the borders. Arrest all foreigners. Go so far even as to employ Comanches and other erstwhile Indian enemies as allies in an unceasing
vigilance. The home government was greatly exercised; but if its efforts
could ever have stayed what it feared might come, they were already
too late.

For the frontiers had been crossed not by a fantastic expedition
from Nova Scotia, or a French army from Louisiana, but a handful of
men here, another there, bearing passports in some cases, in others
nothing but enterprise. Traders came to Texas, trappers entered northern New Mexico, and by 1804 sixty-eight foreigners had come to Texas
to stay. They included Frenchmen, who arrived from Louisiana in 1778,
Englishmen in 1783, Irishmen in 1786, and United States Americans in
1789. Spanish frontier officials had their orders against foreigners, but
the spaces of the country were vast, the Spanish garrisons meagre, and
occasional officers corrupt. Intrusions over the eastern border of Texas
had the effect of shock-waves that travelled all the way to the Rio Grande
and beyond into northern Mexico.

Louisiana, New Orleans, were Spanish in 1800, but the city was
a turmoil of mixed foreigners, languages and intentions. Adventurers
from the states were already to be seen there, and their intrigues overheard. In November, the principal towns of the lower Rio Grande were
alerted by news that flew across Texas. An American of New Orleans,
Philip Nolan, with thirty or forty followers, most of whom were from
the United States, was making his way illegally toward Mexico on what
he announced as an expedition to capture wild horses in New Santander,
bring them back across Texas and sell or trade them in the southern
States. But he had been in Texas before, and there was a standing order
for his arrest. In the face of it, he persisted in his new adventure. It
was known that his company was now heavily armed. He himself carried
a double-barrelled shotgun, a carbine and a brace of pistols. In spite of
Spanish protests to American officials against his violation of American
neutrality agreements, Nolan was allowed—or was he encouraged?—to
set out on his venture. The Supreme Court of the Territory of Mississippi, which heard the Spanish complaint against him, declared that "it
is beyond our power and contrary to the constitution of the United

States to prevent one or more citizens from leaving their country when it cannot be proved with evidence that their intentions are hostile." Nolan gave assurances that his purpose was wholly commercial and peaceful. He was planning to be gone only three months. As for the heavy armament he and his men carried, the arsenal was solely to bring down game on which to subsist, and to repel Indians and bandits. He proceeded with his plans, many of which, in the rude unrest of New Orleans, became known to Spanish spies who sent rapid dispatches to San Antonio, the Rio Grande and Mexico City. Nolan was going to the Rio Grande by the Gulf Coast, dodging Spanish outposts. Then his plans were changed, he was entering Texas farther north, and would proceed to Revilla, on the Rio Grande, where, he said, he had things already well arranged so as to meet no resistance. What was behind it all? The Spaniards were distracted. Nolan evidently had the implicit support of the United States in his movements that were so formally unwelcome to the government of the Rio Grande. Did he seem to presage a future gathering of larger forces behind him to the East? If he were successful, would greater companies, with more on their minds than horse trading, move across Texas, and take the river, and perhaps northern Mexico? The Rio Grande was a strategic barrier, in any case. The garrisons stationed there received their orders when word came that Nolan, after a skirmish with royal troops on the Wichita River in north central Texas, was on his way.

The garrison commanders at Laredo, Revilla, Mier, Camargo, Reynosa and Refugio (a mission that stood on the site of later Matamoros) were ordered by the governor of New Santander to arrest any foreigner entering their posts without a passport. The towns were to mobilize their militia to two-thirds strength, and soldiers from each were sent to Reynosa as a large guard to hold Nolan when he should appear. For he was believed to be marching down the Gulf Coast in November to the mouth of the Rio Grande, and Reynosa was the most important river town near to the Gulf. He was expected to follow the river upstream and try to cross into Mexico at Reynosa. But the other river garrisons were not idle. All of them sent out daily scouting parties up to ten men each, while appeals went to the governor for trained officers, more men, better arms, and military supplies. The provincial governor, unable to send help, could only call for redoubled vigilance. At Laredo the horses of the cavalry were usually stabled on the north shore of the river. Fearing surprise attack and theft of the mounts, the commandant had them moved to the south bank.

Out of Texas came continued rumors—but no Nolan. For the last weeks of November, all of December and half of January, the river towns braced and waited for the thirty or forty invaders whose captain so insolently defied the official will of New Spain. What were the river Spaniards so afraid of, in their towns, and on their huge ranches? If their garrisons were poor, they yet outnumbered the invaders so far from home in so immense a land. The Spaniards in defending their sovereignty which already was losing its power from within seemed to know that the future was upon them already, from within and without. No effort was too great if Nolan could be halted, and with him, even for a moment, the energies that in so little time had swept from the Atlantic states to the Mississippi. The governors of northern Mexico in person moved with troops to the Rio Grande to take up the defense. Hererra of Nuevo León with a hundred men was at Revilla, where Nolan had airly said he would "not be detained two days." Cordero of Coahuila threw a line of a hundred and sixty men from Laredo inland to Monclova to intercept Nolan if he should penetrate south of the river. Blanco of New Santander marched with a force from San Carlos to the mouth of the river to find Nolan, but failed to encounter him. The Governor combed the coast for him, and then marched up the river all the way to Laredo. News had come that the Comanches, led by the invaders, were gathering for frightful descents upon Laredo and Fort St. John Baptist. For three months the whole lower river frontier was on a war basis to repel the first organized intrusion from the United States.

But it never came to the river. In March, 1801, the Rio Grande commands heard how on the twenty-first, Spanish troops from Nacogdoches in East Texas had surrounded Nolan in his camp near the Brazos river. The American expedition was now reduced to twenty-five members. Far from being a powerful invasion force, they were dug in at a permanent camp in the midst of hostile Indian country. Their defenses consisted of crudely made log bulwarks. They were hungry and hairy. They had been subsisting on horse meat. All their rumors and threats suddenly fell down like torn banners. The Spanish troops attacked and by midmorning it was all over. Nolan was killed. His ears were cut off to send to the Spanish governor at San Antonio. His survivors surrendered. On the Rio Grande, the militia were demobilized. Over four hundred soldiers had been waiting for nearly five months to repel the invasion. For the first time the river towns had known the posture of defense against another threat than that of horse Indians.

Their accustomed peace and poverty settled again over the towns and ranches of the Texas river.

But not for long, for in the following year a compact made by the home government of Spain gave Louisiana back to France. Once again, but now in vastly greater meanings, the dangers of an unprotected eastern border swept over the weakened governments of northern New Spain. The Rio Grande was again a political line on a map. LaSalle in 1682 had claimed the River of Palms as the western boundary of French Louisiana. In "Secret Instructions for the Captain-General of Louisiana," dated March 26, 1802, the French government set forth a claim to the Rio Grande "from its mouth to about the thirtieth parallel" as the western boundary of Louisiana. Alluding vaguely to former agreements with Spain, never substantiated, the document went on to note that "the line of demarcation stops after reaching this point, and there seems never to have been any agreement in regard to this part of the frontier. The farther we go northward, the more undecided is the boundary. This part of America contains little more than uninhabited forests or Indian tribes, and the necessity of fixing a boundary has never yet been felt there." The French claim took in almost half of the Rio Grande inland from the Gulf.

It was a claim that the French did not press; but its existence in 1802 created an horizon at the Rio Grande for all those who looked westward across Texas in the following decades, from the successive owners of Louisiana to the three republics of Texas, and ending with Texas as a state of the American federal union. The return of Louisiana to France was a shock to northern Mexico. Already impoverished by failing governmental support, and distracted by Indian troubles, where would the Rio Grande states find the means to guard the frontier, now moved so much closer by the treaty of 1802? The treaty did contain one crumb to allay anxiety for the future. It specified that if France ever gave up Louisiana, she must yield it only to Spain. From this clause the governors of New Spain took comfort while they could.

But secretly in the following year to raise monies to finance his war against England, Napoleon Bonaparte, dictator of France, sold Louisiana to the United States for $15,000,000. Once again, and with violence sure to come, the status of Texas, and the Rio Grande, was thrown in doubt. United States troops were mobilized along the Mississippi to support the American commissioners who entered New Orleans to take possession from the French. The question was soon raised as to

how far, having bought Louisiana, might the Americans consider the
territory to extend? The French had claimed all the way across Texas
to the Rio Grande. Why should not the Americans? President Thomas
Jefferson in fact did so. East Texas was agitated. Spanish garrisons were
reinforced—but how pitifully. Border incidents occurred. New Spain
made desperate plans to establish physical defenses, living possession, of
the coastal wastes of Texas. The resources of Cuba and Mexico together
were to be used for naval power and for the raising of colonial families.
New sites inland in the Texas wilderness were to become towns and forts
that would discourage the United States. But all such plans came to
little or nothing, while the author of New Spain's latest trouble assumed
in December, 1804, the crown of emperor in the metropolitan church of
Notre Dame de Paris. His state was immense. It revived Roman splendors
and improved them with designs by Isabey, involving miles of blue
velvet, and millions of embroidered golden bees, and columns of upstart
peers and peeresses in plumes and diamonds, and a captive Pope, and
a clarion reminder that a field soldier could lead a revolution and make
himself a throne that the world would acknowledge. It was a lesson that
was to have its echo in Mexico one day, and as such exotically enough it
had a waft of meaning for the Rio Grande. More immediately, off Trafalgar, in 1805, the navy of Spain, in bondage to Napoleon, was destroyed
forever by England's Nelson. The lifeline of the Indies, thinning for so
long, was ready to break.

Reduced to moral force, Spain agreed to arbitrate with the United
States in conversations at Madrid the actual boundary between Louisiana
and Texas. But these diplomacies had no outcome. The boundary was
still the old western line of Louisiana on the Red River, or the Rio
Grande, depending upon which party looked east or west. In February,
1806, the United States General Wilkinson moved with troops to
Natchitoches, in disputed territory. An agreement was presently reached
between New Spain and the United States to respect a neutral zone
between the Arroyo Hondo and the Sabine River—despite the words
of General Wilkinson that he would "soon plant our standards on the
left bank of the Grand River." To believe Wilkinson, he had been
working the whole broad West through his imagination "for sixteen
years." The routes to Santa Fe from St. Louis; the strength of life along
the Rio Grande; the interior empire of the prairies with its wealth and
its possible independence through access to the sea by the Mississippi—
what dreams did he have, and how far was he hoping to go to externalize
them? There was no sure answer, but he was not far removed from the

restless affairs of Aaron Burr, and at one time he received monies as an
agent for Spain while wearing the uniform of an American general officer.
In 1806 advancing from the Arroyo Hondo to the east bank of the Sabine
with triumphant airs, he halted there and with him halted whatever
ill-imagined glory he had been brooding alive. The royal governor of
Texas, Salcedo, earnestly worked to keep the peace, while war sentiment
was alight in the United States. When the issue of American sovereignty
was talked of east of the Mississippi, it was focussed on Texas, and
the lower Rio Grande. Nobody yet gave much thought to the rest of
the river.

New Mexico was lost in the north, far removed from the fears
and urgencies that kept all of Texas and the Rio Grande Mexican states
in agitation. The death agonies that were beginning at the Gulf seemed
hardly real or meaningful in the old river kingdom. Something of their
tremors came up the river, as along a dying nerve, from time to time,
in the form of official papers. These were examined at Santa Fe, noted,
tied, and put into a box in the ancient governmental palace on the plaza.
The general drift of policy was grasped; but there were more local
matters that had to be given attention.

Periodically since the first coming of the Spaniards, epidemics of
smallpox had swept through the river pueblos taking a fearful harvest.
Now in 1805, with vaccination a proved preventative, the government
sent Surgeon Larrañaga, of the Santa Fe garrison, among the settlements.
He was the only doctor in hundreds of miles. His present task was difficult. Parents, both Indian and Spanish, were ignorant of science. The
medium of vaccination seemed to them cruel and dangerous. They
resisted him. On his travels, it was not easy for the doctor to preserve
the vaccine under proper conditions. Moreover, he encountered epidemics of whooping cough, measles and dysentery in several pueblos,
and was reluctant to vaccinate children already ill. But he did what he
could, and reported mass vaccinations at El Paso, Cebolleta, Albuquerque, Santa Fe, Laguna and even Zuñi. In the same year, the governor
of New Mexico proposed that an annual fair be held at El Paso in September. He invited skilled weavers to come from New Biscay, and he
pointed out how unsatisfactory the present commercial organization of
the province was.

Commerce had its oddities—and dangers. In June, 1805, there
appeared in Santa Fe a man named James Pursley with two Plains
Indians. They came from the Rocky Mountains to the north, as scouts
for a great band of horse Indians who sent them to discover whether

trade relations with New Mexico could be established. The main body of Indians—there were two thousand of them, and they had ten thousand animals—lurked in camp on the plains that were later called South Park, Colorado. The Governor of New Mexico, Joaquin Real Alencaster, agreed to "enter into a trade." The Indian messengers went back to their people, but Pursley remained in Santa Fe, among, as he thought, civilized people. A Kentuckian, he felt equal to the whole open West. But at Santa Fe he encountered persons and conditions that made him regret bitterly his decision to stay. He was not a prisoner, but he was told that he might not leave the province without a passport. He was free to ask for it at any time, but until he did so, he was under bond not to escape. He was forbidden to write letters. He knew that if he had but two hours' head start, "not all the province could take him." He was allowed to keep his gun. At home, in Kentucky, he had made his own gunpowder when needed; but when he did the same in Santa Fe, he was nearly hanged when discovered, for it was a capital crime to make explosives in the old kingdom. All he could do was resign himself to make a living at his trade, which was that of carpenter. When he worked for the Spanish officers, they paid him poorly and he was powerless to complain. But "he made a great deal of money" working for others, for his kind of skill was rare in New Mexico. He was the first citizen of the United States to penetrate the land of the upper Rio Grande, where no one might pass either way across the Spanish colonial frontier.

Everywhere on the river affairs all looked inward. Among the lower river towns a new colony was gathered together in 1806 from the people and resources of Mier, Camargo and Refugio, near the Gulf, to cross into Texas and found the town of San Marcos as an outpost against organized American intrusion. It was the old design that had been followed over Texas so often before; and it suffered a familiar fate. Harried by Indians, the settlers at San Marcos abandoned their town in 1812 and returned to the Rio Grande. Their purpose had never been tried in a dramatic resistance of American invasion. Not that invasion did not come—but it came through infiltration rather than frontal attack. Settlers arrived in modest little parties. If they entered Texas as travellers or traders or hunters, they yet contrived to stay. Wherever they put themselves on the earth, the American newcomers seemed able to take root against the wilderness. French settlements, Spanish outposts had come and gone. But the wilderness dweller from the United States clung to his advancing frontier at all its stages and never retreated.

Spanish intelligence travelled often and fast. Warnings were relayed from presidio to military district headquarters to provincial governor, and orders came back down the line.

Chihuahua learned, presumably from agents at St. Louis who sent their reports down the Mississippi and over Texas to the Rio Grande, of a venture approaching the river kingdom at the north, and warned Santa Fe in 1806. An American lieutenant with a small band of men travelling as traders, and perhaps even as settlers, had been dispatched by General Wilkinson to examine the plains and enter New Mexico from the north. His name was Pike, and with his men he should be intercepted and returned to the States, or captured and taken to Santa Fe. In a last marshalling of power, the old river kingdom gathered one hundred regular troops, and mobilized five hundred New Mexican militia, all mounted. In command was Lieutenant Don Facundo Melgares who with his two officers next-in-command rode black horses. All the troopers rode white horses, and the animal train totalled two thousand. With provisions for six months the party moved out eastward in June, 1806, to find Pike; to reconnoitre the wild land between New Mexico and the supposed plains boundary of Louisiana, which had not been fixed even by the United States; and to establish alliances with Plains Indians against the eastern Americans. In October Melgares was back in Santa Fe with his troops. He submitted his personal expense account immediately, and was obliged to report that he had not found his man.

Though his man was willing, even eager, to be found. On his own, he was trying to reach the New Mexico river and Santa Fe. As winter came Zebulon Montgomery Pike and his men were in the Rocky Mountains where they suffered greatly. On January twenty-eighth, probing southwestward through sand dunes and following a sandy creek, Pike made camp, and then "ascended one of the largest hills of sand" from which with his spyglass he "could discover a large river," which he "supposed to be Red River." But it was not the Red River, it was the Rio Grande, winding placidly through the vast open San Luis Valley of Colorado. In the mountains to the west, high on the towering slopes of the Continental Divide, the river had its source in three main branches. Gazing through his telescope, Pike could be sure of his mission now.

According to his orders from General Wilkinson he was like Melgares to make binding treaties with horse Indians (whom he addressed with some grandeur in French), and to make notes on the

natural history, terrain and peoples of the areas he crossed. Mineral
and botanical specimens were to be collected, and a careful log of
mileages and astronomical observations recorded. Most important—and
least covered by written orders—was the job of entering among the New
Mexicans, discovering their temper, noticing their defenses, and considering means, including the military, of opening a way to Santa Fe.
He was to avoid making trouble when he at last reached his goal: "Your
conduct," wrote Wilkinson, "must be marked by such circumspection
and direction as may prevent alarm or conflict, as you will be held
responsible for consequences."

Travelling westward in September, 1806, Pike came to a Pawnee
settlement on the twenty-fifth. The Indians said that a great troop of
soldiers on white horses had been there a month before. They were the
Spaniards from Santa Fe who had been looking for him. The Pawnee
Chief showed Pike flags, medals, mules, and commissions written with
a flourish which the Spaniards had given him. The Spanish commander
was a young man—too young to make binding agreements, said the Chief;
he had come only to open the way for further dealings later. But there
had been certain courteous threats, and Pike wrote to Secretary of War
Dearborn that the Spaniards had mounted "an expedition expressly for
the purpose of striking a dread into these different nations of the Spanish
power, and to bring about a combination in their favor," and he called
the Spanish dealings with the Pawnees "an infringement of our territory."

Pike treated with the Pawnees for a fortnight. He tried to induce
them to give over their Spanish trophies, but they would finally yield
only the Spanish flag in trade for that of the United States. But it was
possible that the Spanish troops might return, and finding that the
Indians had disposed of their colors, give them trouble. Pike explained
this, and returned the Spanish flag to the Indians, who were moved to
"a general shout of applause."

Advancing westward with the autumn the Americans entered the
mountains and encountered every hardship in wind, snow, cold and
hunger. By the time Pike came to the river five men with frozen feet on
which they could not walk had been left behind in the mountains. The
remaining ten were exhausted but determined to establish a base from
which they could go back to rescue their companions. Three days after
viewing the river for the first time, they came to its bank. The first thing
they looked for was timber with which to make boats for a descent of
the river. Finding none, they marched downstream thirteen miles and

came to the mouth of a confluent—the Conejos River—that flowed from the west. They turned up this stream for five miles and found a "small prairie" with cottonwoods within reach where Pike ordered a halt. On his map he marked the Rio Grande as the Red River. For the next several days he led his men in building a stockade against "the insolence, cupidity, and barbarity of the savages." It was a stout little fortress, thirty-six feet square, twelve feet high, built of cottonwood logs and protected at its open top by a crown of sharpened stakes that projected outward at a slant beyond the walls for two and a half feet. The lower ends of the stakes were lodged in a ditch that ran around the inside of the walls. There was no gate. The occupants moved in and out by a tunnel under the walls and a plank laid over the moat. Gunports were opened in the walls eight feet above the ground, and raised interior walks were built for riflemen and sentries.

For a week the party worked, rested, read, hunted—and schemed. With Pike travelled a young physician, Dr. John Hamilton Robinson, who had been assigned to the expedition by General Wilkinson. He was adventurous and personable, with "blooming cheeks, fine complexion, and a genius-speaking eye." He possessed "a liberality of mind too great ever to reject an hypothesis because it was not agreeable to the dogmas of the schools; or adopt it because it had all the éclat of novelty. His soul could conceive great actions, and his hand was ready to achieve them; in short, it may truly be said that nothing was above his genius." The problem now was how to make contact with the New Mexicans without arousing suspicion. Pike and the doctor developed an idea. Why not use Morrison's claim? This was a paper in Robinson's possession which had been given him by a friend in St. Louis to present for collection if he should ever come upon a trader named Baptiste LaLande, who now lived at Santa Fe. Under treaties between Spain and the United States, a mutual guarantee protected "the right of seeking the recovery of all just debts or demands before the legal and authorized tribunals of the country." The two schemers resolved to make "this claim a pretext for Robinson to visit Santa Fe." They gave the paper "the proper appearance." The doctor would take it to Santa Fe to collect Mr. Morrison's claim against Monsieur LaLande; would give over information about the party on the northern river; and after that it would not be long until Spanish officials came to the river fort. Pike's company would be taken to New Mexico, and their purpose—"to gain a knowledge of the country, the prospect of trade, force, etc."—would be near fulfillment. Dr. Robinson set out alone on February seventh to find

Santa Fe, and on the same day, a party went back into the mountains
to rescue the soldiers who had been left behind a hundred and eighty
miles away.

The doctor walked up the Conejos River on the first day, and
on the second, bore south. Soon on the slope of a mountain he met two
Yuta Indians with bows and arrows who were afraid of him, but he
overcame them with some small gifts, and they agreed to take him to
Santa Fe. On the following day he reached the village of Agua Caliente,
where he spent the night on a mattress on the floor of the local commander's house, while word of his presence went to the capital by
courier. He was escorted south on the trail early the next day, and
before nightfall found himself in the presence of Governor Joaquin
Real Alencaster, who saw in him a *"joven de presencia fina."* But even
if he was "a young man of fine presence," the Governor was hard with
him. He took possession of all his papers, interrogated him austerely, and
learned readily that he came from a party of Americans, under a first
lieutenant named "Mongo-Meri-Paike," whom he had left in their
"excellent retrenchments" on a river to the north. For himself, the doctor
said he had come to Santa Fe seeking a certain Baptiste LaLande, against
whom he had a claim for monies due. He handed over the claim. The
Governor said he would look into it. The interrogation proceeded.

When had he set out, with his friends, on the expedition that
brought them here?

Last July.

And what had been their experience with Indians whom they
must have met on the plains?

As to that, they had made friends with the Indians, and were
authorized to make alliances with certain tribes on behalf of the United
States.

Which tribes, in particular?

It seemed that the Comanches were included.

At this period of New Mexico's unstable Indian relations, the
Comanches were formal allies of the Santa Fe government. The doctor's
revelations were disturbing. He was ordered to a room in the Palace
ordinarily used as a cell for officers in arrest and a noncommissioned
officer was assigned to remain with him, though the doctor was not
denied permission to walk about the town. Food was sent to him from
the Governor's table.

On the next day he was taken again to the Governor, who had
examined the LaLande affair, only to discover that LaLande had no

property. The debt could not be paid, though at some future time the Governor would see what could be done.

The doctor now made "a spirited remonstrance." He invoked treaties and he spoke bitingly of any foreign government that gave asylum to a man evading his creditors.

The Governor scowled; but with more courtesy than before, he invited the doctor to dine with him, which was a welcome gesture. In the course of the meal, the Governor brought up a matter that troubled him. As his guest was a man of medicine, he could not forbear to mention that he suffered from dropsy, and though he was being treated by a certain reverend father who practiced medicine in the city, he would be glad now of professional advice. The doctor "prescribed a regimen and a mode of treatment." His prescriptions differed from those of the local physician, who as a result showed his enmity later.

With the next day, the doctor was told he would be taken south to Chihuahua, for further interrogation by the Commandant-General of the Interior Provinces. He resigned himself, and on the following day, glad of the opportunity to see more of the country, for which he was "willing to run the risk of future consequences," he marched south under escort.

It was not long until Pike, at his stockade, knew that Dr. Robinson's job was done. With one of his soldiers he was out hunting on February sixteenth when he met two armed horsemen, a Spanish dragoon and a civilized Indian. Both parties "acted with great precaution," but drew together to talk and all sat down on the ground. The strangers told Pike that they had left Santa Fe four days before; "that Robinson had arrived there, and been received with great kindness by the governor." Presently the spies—Pike knew they were spies—went to the stockade with him and spent the night. In the morning, after cordial exchanges, they left, and Pike with his little garrison fell to reinforcing the stockade, for they knew that they would presently have other visitors.

One morning ten days later a sentry at the cottonwood fort fired his musket in the air. Two strangers were approaching. Pike received them in the stockade. They were Frenchmen, from Santa Fe. Conversations began in which evasions were exchanged with every air of polite frankness.

The Governor, they said, had heard that Pike's little defense work in the wilderness was about to be attacked by Yuta Indians; and accordingly he had sent troops out to protect him—fifty regular dragoons, and fifty militia, all mounted. They would arrive in two days.

Pike answered nothing.

Two days? In a few minutes the main body of the Spanish detachment appeared, all armed with lances, carbines and pistols, with two
officers: Lieutenant Ignacio Saltelo, in command, and Lieutenant Bartolomé Fernández. Pike sent word that the officers might enter the fort,
leaving their troops halted in the cottonwood grove a little distance
away. They agreed, entered by the miniature drawbridge which astonished them, and joined Pike for a breakfast of deer, meal, goose and
some biscuit. After breakfast Lieutenant Saltelo got down to business.

"Sir," he said to Pike, "the Governor of New Mexico being
informed you had missed your route, ordered me to offer you, in his
name, mules, money, or whatever you might stand in need of to conduct
you to the head of Red river; as from Santa Fe to where it is sometimes
navigable is eight days' journey. . . ."

"What!" cried Pike, interrupting, "is not this the Red river?"

"No, Sir! The Rio del Norte."

As if in chagrin Pike ordered the United States flag to be hauled
down. He knew also that in spite of manners, the Spanish officers had
orders to take him to the capital regardless of his wishes. Lieutenant
Saltelo said:

"The Governor has provided one hundred mules and horses to
take in the party and their baggage. He is very anxious to see you at
Santa Fe."

Pike explained that some of his men had not yet rejoined the
party at the fort, and he could not leave without them. He said further,
with every appearance of a free man, that his orders did not justify his
entering Spanish territory. The Spanish officer insisted; Pike grew hot;
and Lieutenant Saltelo mildly assured him that "not the least restraint"
would be used. The Governor only had to have an explanation of
Pike's business on the frontier. (This was the third new reason given for
the Governor's solicitude.) Pike finally agreed to leave for Santa Fe,
provided a large party were left behind to await the coming of the
invalid soldiers and their rescuers to the stockade. Pike felt a certain professional regret as affairs calmed down. After all, he was confident of his
military situation. The stockade was stout. "I could so easily have put
them at defiance," he mused. He hated to see lost all the work he and
his men had put into the defenses. The Spanish soldiers seemed overjoyed that the intruders did not intend to resist; but Pike's men felt
otherwise, for they mistrusted the Spaniards, and besides, said Pike, they
wanted to raise "a little dust."

But friendliness soon prevailed. The Santa Fe soldiers gave food and blankets to the eastern Americans. By eleven the next morning, February 27, 1807, the Santa Fe column set out. Fifty Spaniards stayed behind with Lieutenant Saltelo to await the men from the mountains; Pike and the rest were escorted by Lieutenant Bartolomé Fernández, of whom Pike made a good friend, referring to him always as Bartholomew. They marched up the Conejos, struck off southwestward, and four days later reached the Rio Grande from the west, coming down the Chama to San Juan. They had come from a country of deep snow to a land of plains where there was no snow and vegetation was sprouting. As they passed by villages, the inhabitants stared at the visitors, who were in wretched circumstance. Pike himself was "dressed in a pair of blue trousers, mockinsons, blanket coat, and a cap made of scarlet cloth lined with fox skin; my poor fellows were in leggings, breech cloths and leather coats." All were unshaven and thin, and none had a hat but the leader, and few had shoes.

Pike observed the Pueblo Indians of the region. He found that they were not slaves of individuals, but of the state, for they were "compelled to do military duty, drive mules, carry loads, or, in fact, perform any other act of duty or bondage that the will of the commandant of the district, or of any passing military tyrant, chooses to ordain." Nor was this all. "I was myself eye-witness," said Pike, "of a scene which made my heart bleed for those poor wretches, at the same time that it excited my indignation and contempt, that they would suffer themselves, with arms in their hands, to be beaten and knocked about by beings no ways their superiors, unless a small tint of complexion could be supposed to give that superiority." It seemed that one night on the way to Santa Fe, two of the Indian riders with the Santa Fe troops ran off to a near-by pueblo which was their home. In the morning, all Indian riders were turned out in mounted formation to tell who had gone absent without leave in the night. All refused to speak. At once, for their silence, several were "knocked down from their horses by the Spanish dragoons with the butt of their lances." The Indians got up and stood like stone. Their faces streamed with blood. They held weapons in their hands. But they gave no sign of what they must have felt—"the boiling indignation of their souls at the indignities offered by the wretch clothed with a little brief authority! The day," said Pike, who knew nothing of 1680 and 1696, "the day of retribution will come in thunder and vengeance!"

On March second the company came to San Juan on the Rio

Grande and were received by the Father President, who had lived there
for forty years. He gave them coffee and chocolate to drink, and asked
Pike back to dinner, and saw to it that his men had a place to stay.
Pike on his way to visit the soldiers' quarters was accosted at the door
by a man who said to him in broken English,

"My friend, I am very sorry to see you here; we are all prisoners
in this country and can never return; I have been a prisoner for nearly
three years, and cannot get out."

Something about the creature, plucking and fawning, repelled
Pike.

"As for your being a prisoner," said Pike, "it must be for some
crime. As for myself, I feel no apprehension. And when you speak to
me, talk French. I can hardly understand your English."

Pike turned to join his men in their room, and at his heels a
stream of questions followed. How had Pike come into northern New
Mexico? Why? Where was he going? The importunate wretch followed
him into the billet, and Pike ordered his men to shut and lock the door
and faced him. He was sure now that the man was sent to worry some
damaging admission out of him.

"You are a spy, sent by the Governor, or someone, to trick me,
aren't you? All men of that description are scoundrels, and should never
fail to be punished, while I have the power to do it . . . " and he ordered
his soldiers to grasp the man. "If you make a sound, or resist, I'll be
obliged to make use of this . . . " and he drew his sabre.

The man broke down. Yes—only let him for God's sake not be
harmed—yes, he was an agent of the Governor. He had been told to meet
Pike and by raising complaints against the Spaniards, inspire him to
pour forth all the information the government hoped for. He was a
miserable man who harmed nobody, but whose goods had all been taken
by the New Mexicans, who would not even turn him loose to go back
to St. Louis. He was Baptiste LaLande.

Pike ordered him released, and said to him,

"I consider you as too contemptible for further notice. But you
may tell the Governor, the next time he employs emissaries, to choose
those of more ability and sense. Moreover, I question whether His
Excellency will find the sifting of us an easy task."

Pike saw to his men, and returned to the priest's house. LaLande
accompanied him; but not to make any complaints about his rough
handling. Instead, he announced that Pike was a former governor of

Illinois. The effect of this absurdity was a marked increase in the respect shown by the old priest, who now gave dinner to Pike—"the first good meal, wine, etc."—that he had had in eight months. He overindulged, while the father talked for two hours about his hobby, which was botany. Later, in exchange, Pike demonstrated his sextant to the pastor out of doors, to the astonishment of the hundreds of San Juan Indians who surrounded them, and, indeed, of the pastor himself, who shook his head. He knew no mathematics and would never be able to use a sextant. How was this? wondered Pike. The Father President explained that it was Spanish governmental policy to prohibit the study of science in the Indies so that the colonial inhabitants would have no basis of comparing their conditions with those of other lands.

The march was resumed the next day. As the party drew nearer to Santa Fe, Pike thought of his papers. It would be awkward if certain of these came into the hands of the New Mexicans. Since he was likely to be the one who would be most thoroughly examined, he found it wise to distribute some of his documents among his five men to conceal inside their clothing. The rest of his papers he placed in "a little chest" where in innocence they could be revealed if asked for. The party with horse and pack mule jogged on, now on the east bank of the river. Passing on through Pojoaque and Tesuque, they came in late afternoon within sight of Santa Fe. (In his field notes he spelled it "St.Afee.") "Its appearance from a distance," said Pike, "struck my mind with the same effect as a fleet of flat-bottomed boats which are seen in the spring and fall seasons, descending the Ohio river." As he entered the city he saw that it straggled along the Santa Fe creek for about a mile, and that it was only three streets in width. The streets were narrow—twenty-five feet across. A great crowd accompanied the cavalcade to the Palace where Pike and his people were taken through a long vista of several rooms that had rugs of buffalo, bear or other skins, into a far room where they sat down. After a wait, Governor Joaquin Real Alencaster entered, and everyone stood. Pike's new friend Bartholomew was present. The Governor spoke to Pike in French.

"Do you speak French?" he asked brusquely.

"Yes sir," replied Pike.

"You come to reconnoitre our country, do you?"

"I marched to reconnoitre our own."

"In what character are you?"

"In my proper character, an officer of the United States army."

"And this Robinson," said the Governor, "is he attached to your party?"

Pike thought for a moment. Robinson was already a prisoner. What if, unknown to either of them, their country and Spain might now be at war over boundary issues? Under the rules of war, Robinson might be subject to execution as a spy. To protect the doctor, Pike replied, "No."

And now it was the Governor who grew thoughtful. Why should the eastern American lie so brazenly if there were not something equivocal about his whole presence within these borders?

"Do you know him?" asked the Governor.

"Yes; he is from St. Louis."

"How many men have you?"

"Fifteen."

"And this Robinson makes sixteen?"

"I have already told Your Excellency that he does not belong to my party, and shall answer no more interrogatories on that subject."

"When did you leave St. Louis?"

"July fifteenth."

"I think you marched in June."

"No, sir!"

There was bad temper in the air. The Governor dismissed Pike, ordering him to go to Bartholomew's house, and return in the evening at seven with all his papers. As they went out, Pike saw that his friend Bartholomew "seemed much hurt at the interview."

In the evening at seven they returned to the Palace.

"Where are your papers?" demanded the Governor.

"I understand my trunk has been taken possession of by your guard."

The Governor received this with surprise, sent for the trunk, and a new interpreter, who when he arrived turned out to be Sergeant Solomon Colley, one of the prisoners taken from Philip Nolan's abortive invasion of Texas six years before. The Governor permitted all to sit down, and through the interpreter began to question Pike, starting all over again, with his name and birthplace. Pike answered Sergeant Colley in English, and then spoke directly to the governor in French, and with energy. All this narrow questioning, he said, was useless. Only let the governor read Pike's commission from the United States, and his orders from his general, and he would see that he came with no hostile intentions toward the Spanish government. On the contrary, urged Pike, he had express instructions to guard against giving offense or alarm. Do this, and His Excellency would be convinced that far from deserving treatment as undesirables, Pike and his men would be "objects on which the so much celebrated generosity of the Spanish nation might be exercised. . . ."

The governor seemed mollified. The trunk had arrived, and he glanced through its contents, noting a diary, and "an exact map, in ink, of all the rivers and lands that they had reconnoitred," and some official papers. Which were the commission and the orders? Pike read them to him in French. The governor sprang to his feet and for the first time gave his hand to Pike.

"I am happy," he said, "to know you as a man of honor and a gentleman," and added kindly that Pike could go now, and take his chest of papers with him. They would make other arrangements tomorrow. Pike retired with his trunk. He found now that his soldiers were drinking with some hospitable citizens of St. Afee. He was alarmed. His men still carried papers that least of all he wanted the local authorities to see. Taking his men aside, he retrieved all his documents, went to his room at Bartholomew's house, and with relief put them into his chest, where they would now be safe, for he was convinced that "the examination of papers was over."

But he was deceived; for early the next day an officer brought orders from the governor for Pike to appear before him, and to bring the trunkful of papers, as he wished to make some observations on Pike's route, and other matters. There was no chance to remove any of the papers. The governor's messenger waited for him. Pike was helpless. Bringing the trunk he came before the governor.

In silence the governor went through the enlarged collection of documents. There was much to consider. The box held letters to and from Wilkinson and Pike; maps; diaries giving carefully observed data of the journey to this province, and of New Mexico itself; a pasteboard folio quarto, "containing copies of official communications to the Secretary of War and to General Wilkinson, and various observations relative to the mission of the said lieutenant, with 67 used folios"; and other significant materials. Surely it was in itself significant that the lieutenant had tried to hide some of the now revealed documents? With the evidence of such mysterious behavior, and of the documents themselves, Real Alencaster resolved to send Pike and his men to Chihuahua in their turn. He told Pike of his decision, and added, "You have the key of your trunk in your own possession; the trunk will be put under charge of the officer who commands your escort."

"If we go to Chihuahua," asked Pike, "must we be considered as prisoners of war?"

"By no means," answered the governor.

"You have already disarmed my men without my knowledge; are their arms to be returned or not?"

"They can receive them at any moment."

Now something else troubled Pike. It was a professional matter of some delicacy. His reputation as an officer was involved. He said,

"But, sir, I cannot consent to be led three or four hundred leagues out of my route, without its being by force of arms."

The Governor understood.

"I know you do not go voluntarily; but I will give you a certificate from under my hand of my having obliged you to march."

He then asked Pike to dine, and said that arrangements were already made for him to set out immediately afterward on his journey down the Rio Grande. On the river, below Albuquerque, a relief escort was waiting for him, said the Governor, with "the officer who commanded the expedition to the Pawnees."

Pike did not want to be impertinent; but he had to ask:

"Pray, sir! do you not think it was a greater infringement of our territory to send 600 miles in the Pawnees', than for me with our small party to come on the frontiers of yours with an intent to descend Red river?"

"I do not understand you," said the governor coldly. Pike rejoined with sarcasm:

"No, sir! any further explanation is unnecessary," and took his leave for the moment, returning to Bartholomew's house. Presently he received by messenger from the Governor twenty-one dollars in cash for his current expenses, which would be charged against the United States, and a gift of a shirt and a new neckcloth that had been made in Spain by the Governor's sister. At midday he returned to dine at the clay Palace. The meal was "rather splendid, having a variety of dishes and wines of the southern provinces." The Governor, enjoying his own wine, "became very sociable." It was soon time to go. Pike left a note for his men who were yet to come from the northern stockade, bidding them to "keep up a good discipline and not be alarmed or discouraged." In the plaza Sergeant Colley, "the American prisoner, came up

with tears in his eyes," and begged Pike not to forget him when he
arrived home in the United States. Pike had also seen and talked with
James Pursley, who was still a prisoner at large in New Mexico, and not
fated to leave until 1824. The Governor's coach was waiting. They
climbed in—the Governor, Bartholomew, Pike and Captain D'Almansa,
who commanded the escort—and drove out in a snowstorm for three
miles, drawn by six mules and attended by a guard of cavalry. When it
came time to say good-bye, the Governor struck an attitude, and
declaimed:

"Remember Alencaster, in peace or war!"

He then returned to the city, and the travellers, mounted on
horses, rode on through the heavy snow as darkness fell. At ten o'clock
that night they found their way with great difficulty down the escarpment of La Bajada and came to a village where they were taken in for
the night by the resident priest, and given supper. After supper Pike
and the two officers talked for a while. D'Almansa—he was an elderly
native of New Mexico—complained sadly that he had been a soldier of
the King for forty years. In all that time he had risen only to the rank
of first lieutenant of the line, and captain by brevet; while many a
youngster from Spain, serving in the colonies, had been promoted over
his head. After the old man went to sleep, Bartholomew in his turn
bared his heart to Pike. He was one of those New Mexicans who "longed
for a change of affairs, and an open trade with the United States." He
believed that the United States would invade New Mexico by the next
spring. In vain Pike denied this. Bartholomew insisted, and wondered
how he would fare when the time came. Pike ended by solemnly writing
out for him "a certificate addressed to the citizens of the United States,
stating his friendly disposition and his being a man of influence." The
paper was a comfort to Bartholomew.

As it was still snowing hard the next morning, the march was
delayed. Bartholomew took Pike to call on an old, infirm Spaniard who
received them hospitably, gave them chocolate, and asked many questions about the United States, drawing comparisons with Spain. "What
appeared to the old veteran most extraordinary," noted Pike, "was that
we ever changed our president." The old Spaniard was astonished to
hear Pike say that "there was a perfect freedom of conscience permitted
in our country. He, however, expressed his warm approbation of the
measure." But once again it was time to march, and now Bartholomew
had to return to Santa Fe. He embraced Pike and the other eastern
Americans, and Pike "could not avoid shedding tears" as they parted;

his friend had been good to him. The southbound column set out once more.

Pike examined everything and kept a journal, for his information would be of vital importance to the men and women of the United States who fulfilling individually some pressing instinct to enter new lands to the west fulfilled together what all felt to be the historic destiny of their country. At Santo Domingo pueblo, now situated on the east bank of the Rio Grande, Pike saw rich paintings in the church, and a life-sized statue of the patron saint, ornamented with gold and silver. The view from the church roof was "one of the handsomest" in New Mexico. The next day at San Felipe he made notes on a bridge over the river. It had eight spans, with "pillars made of neat woodwork, something similar to a crate, and in the form of a keel-boat, the sharp end or bow to the current; this crate or butment was filled with stone, in which the river lodged sand, clay, etc., until it had become of a tolerably firm consistency. On the top of the pillars were laid pine logs, lengthways, squared on two sides; being joined pretty close, these made a tolerable bridge for horses, but would not have been very safe for carriages, as there were no hand-rails." With the bridge at El Paso, this was one of the only two on the whole river. At Albuquerque on March seventh Pike received animated entertainment at the priest's house, where beautiful orphan girls waited on the company, and embraced the guests "as a mark of their friendship." It was the season of opening the ditches after winter, and he saw men, women and children at work in the fields by the haciendas, giving "life and gayety to the surrounding scenery." The scene put him in mind of what he had read of the irrigation works of Egypt. Downstream at the next village, in the house of the local commander, Pike saw someone sitting by the fire reading a book, who arose and spoke. Pike searched him with his eyes for a moment, and then exclaimed,

"Robinson!"

"Yes."

"But I do not know you!"

"But I know you. . . . Yet, my friend," said the doctor, "I grieve to see you here and thus, for I presume you are a prisoner."

"No! I wear my sword, as you see; all my men have their arms, and the moment they dare to ill-treat us we will surprise their guards in the night, carry off some horses, make our way to the Apaches, and then set them at defiance."

But he could not get over Robinson's improved appearance. When he had last seen him, Robinson was "pale, emaciated, with uncombed locks and beard of eight months' growth." And now he was well-fed, smooth-faced, and ruddy, with sparkling eye. Captain D'Almansa entered, and Pike introduced the doctor, saying that he had been a member of the party from the start. The Captain smiled. It was plain that he had known as much all along. Pike was sheepish, and resolved to write to the Governor, when he could, to explain why he had denied the doctor as one of his group. Robinson told Pike of his adventures, and ended with a word about Lieutenant Don Facundo Melgares, who was to command the escort from that point on. In him, said the doctor, Pike would find "a gentleman, a soldier, and one of the most gallant men you ever knew."

But when Pike and Melgares met, there was constraint. Pike was chagrined to be delivered after all, and by his own actions, into the hands of a Spanish officer who had been away from home looking for him for ten months, and had spent for his government over ten thousand dollars on the mission. But Melgares received him "with the most manly frankness and the politeness of a man of the world," and seeing Pike out of sorts, "took every means in his power to banish my reserve, which made it impossible on my part not to endeavor to appear cheerful." The young Spanish officer did not affect the haughty manners of the Castilian, but behaved more like an urbane Frenchman. He confessed himself to be one of the few Spanish officers in the New World who still remained loyal to the King, and deprecated the idea of revolution. Melgares and Pike soon became warm friends—as befitted the past and the future.

In the afternoon, the escort commander sent a note to the alcaldes of nearby villages:

> Send this evening six or eight of your handsomest young girls to the village of St. Fernández, where I propose giving a fandango, for the entertainment of the American officers arrived this day.
> (Signed)   Don Facundo.

The command was obeyed. Pike observed that such obedience "portrays more clearly than a chapter of observations the degraded state of the common people." The girls arrived, they were indeed beautiful, and the ball was given. But as to women in New Spain, Pike noted primly: "Finding that the men only regard them as objects of gratification to the sensual passions, they have lost every idea of that feast of

reason and flow of soul which arises from the intercourse of two refined
and virtuous minds." They were, in fact, like creatures in a Turkish
harem. He believed that their men actually thought more of their
horses than of them. Yet he was eager to record the "heaven-like qualities of hospitality and kindness" with which he was received in his
march down the Rio Grande, when at overnight halts in villages, there
were banquets, fandangos and cockfights. But soon there were no more
villages on the route, for the column had come to the Dead Man's
March. They crossed to the west bank and stayed with the river, and
Pike noted the great difficulty of the trail. Fording again where the
river turned east at the end of the desert passage, they continued on
the east bank until they came to the bridge two miles above El Paso.
There they crossed, and entering El Paso were surrounded with hospitality, and pleased with the river lands. Gambling was rampant. Pike
watched Melgares play cards during three days in a row, and win so
heavily that to keep his luck he gave away five hundred dollars to the
ladies in whose house they were billeted. After several days at El Paso,
the march was taken up across New Biscay to the south, and in nine
days the prisoners were pleasantly received at Chihuahua, where they
were detained for many weeks while Pike's documents were translated
and studied.

Finally he and his men were expelled from New Spain, granted a
loan of a thousand dollars by the commandant-general at Chihuahua,
and escorted across northern Mexico to Coahuila and the lower Rio
Grande. Pike's records were rich, despite the trouble he had in making
and keeping them in Spanish territory—toward the end he concealed his
daily pages in the rifle barrels of his soldiers. His whole journey and its
observations brought the Spanish west for the first time into the knowledge of the United States. With him the source country of the Rio
Grande entered history. The Spanish instinct to exclude him—and his
kind—was from its own point of view correct, even if it was fated never
to succeed. A veiling mist had been blown away from the map, and there
before the gaze of the United States lay shining the mountains of New
Mexico, and the Rio Grande, and farther away, and just visible, but
real, the Pacific. . . .

The departing guests came to the Rio Grande on June 1, 1807,
at Fort St. John Baptist. They stayed only one night there. Pike thought
there were twenty-five hundred residents, and he saw "three or four
handsome missions," and a powder magazine, and barracks for the garrison, and as the defenses of the fort, "a few iron field-pieces on miserable

truck carriages." The place made a poor impression. There was trouble finding supper. Pike's compass was stolen from him there. He heard of an American who stayed at Fort St. John Baptist practicing medicine, and sent for him. The man told a long, adventurous tale, of hardship and misfortune, playing on the sympathies of his hearers; but when one of Pike's men recognized him he turned out to be a murderer and an imposter, and Pike delivered him over to the local authorities. A troupe of entertainers were in town for the moment, and in the evening gave a show. They were slack-wire artists. Everyone went to see them. But they were "in no wise extraordinary in their performances, except in language which would bring a blush on the cheek of the most abandoned of the female sex in the United States." Late in the following day the Americans with their escort crossed the river and camped at a ranch on the other side. The next morning they set out across Spanish Texas, and in three weeks reached Louisiana, where on July first, at four in the afternoon, at Natchitoches, Pike felt his heart leap when he saw the United States flag.

At Santa Fe, Governor Real Alencaster did his duty by calling attention once again to "the necessity of putting this Province on a respectable basis and of maintaining advanced forts and establishments on the principal rivers in order to contain the ambitious ideas expressed by the Anglo-American government." He could do no more. His superiors did nothing. In the following year, his successor ordered the military commander at Taos to conduct scouting expeditions, in order to keep out foreigners; and not long later the pastor of Taos sent a report marked "Private" to Santa Fe to tell that Indians of the pueblo were holding secret meetings in their kivas with white men, who were thought to be French or American.

While such local matters blew hot and cold the dying Empire knew a major change at its heart. In 1808 the legitimate King of Spain, Ferdinand VII, brutalized by Napoleon, gave up his crown. Napoleon at once bestowed it upon his brother Joseph Bonaparte. Ferdinand, whose name with a "Viva" was carved in the ceiling beams of a high stately room in the town of St. John Baptist on the river, was jailed in Talleyrand's French château while Spain became a theatre of war. For contrary to Napoleon's contemptuous guess a great body of Spaniards resisted the conquest which he had taken for granted, and established beyond his reach a legitimist capital at Cádiz on the short Atlantic coast of southern Spain. Soon the Spanish patriots had the powerful wits of Wellington leading their defense. And for the first time in history, and

even in the midst of war against the master of Europe, who whether as
enemy or ally was Spain's sorrow, the motherland gave to the Indies what
they had never owned: a right to representation in the national governing body. In January, 1809, the Cádiz parliament decreed that delegates
were to be elected in the colonial states, which now received full membership as partners in the government. In 1810, the Rio Grande provinces
of New Mexico and Coahuila-Texas named their deputies and sent them
to take their seats in the parliament of Cádiz. From Coahuila-Texas went
Don Miguel Ramos Arizpe, who held the degree of doctor of laws from
the university in Mexico City. From New Mexico went Don Pedro
Bautista Pino. Both provinces of the Rio Grande grasped eagerly at their
first chance to present their needs directly to the home government.

Dr. Ramos Arizpe carried with him a great list of instructions.
He was to ask the parliament to unify the many local jurisdictions of the
lower Rio Grande states; to improve the wretched roads that precariously
connected the wilderness communities; to stimulate agriculture, cattle
raising and industry; to provide for a cigar factory at Saltillo after all
the centuries when it had been forbidden to Spanish colonials to utilize
their own tobacco crops in local manufacture; to abolish the odious
tariffs on wool and cotton and with funds thus available to set up various
textile mills; to grant the status of incorporated city to Saltillo; and to
found a college where the youth of the provinces could be taught
grammar and philosophy.

Don Pedro Bautista Pino, who owned great estates east of the Rio
Grande along the Galisteo Creek in New Mexico, sailed from Veracruz
with a party of several persons, including his private secretary. During
his three years in Spain he presented an urgent program of recommendations on behalf of the upper Rio Grande province. He addressed his
papers to King Ferdinand VII, and quoted the instructions under which
he came to the córtes from New Mexico: "The function of our representative is not limited to looking after the welfare of this province; he must
at the same time guard the general welfare of the monarchy." Within
this frame of political orthodoxy he proposed, then, "1. The establishment of a bishopric at Santa Fe; 2. The establishment of a seminary
college of higher learning, and of public schools for the instruction of
the youth; 3. Uniformity in military service, the addition of . . . five
presidios . . . and payment of salaries to all settlers who may be enlisted
. . . as is done in Durango, Sonora, Texas, and other adjoining provinces;
4. The establishment of a civil and criminal court in Chihuahua." By
what was asked it could be seen what was missing. The nearest bishop

was at Durango; the nearest civil and criminal court was at Mexico City. Don Pedro spoke proudly in his sense of injury and justice. "These four petitions, Sire, should not be called petitions, for, could any other province in the monarchy claim to have existed fifty years without having seen a bishop? Is there any other province six hundred leagues from the seat of the administration of justice? There is no such province, no matter how miserably poor it may be. Consequently, the requests made by my province as petitions should be called claims and not petitions."

Don Pedro went to Paris before his return home, and to London, where he bought a beautiful and very costly landau in which for years he was to be seen riding over the frightful roads of New Mexico. No one ever asked in vain for a ride if Don Pedro had a seat empty.

As for what he and Doctor Ramos Arizpe had presented to the parliament—nothing came of any of it. With acid wit, the people of Santa Fe in after years sang a popular couplet that expressed what the river province felt about the politics of the homeland and the gullibility of the colonies:

> Don Pedro Pino went;
> Don Pedro Pino came back.

Deputies from all the Indies answered the call; but if she had counted on them to hold the Empire together, Spain had called them too late. Three centuries of taking without giving in proportion had done their work. The Spanish Americas found their opportunity for freedom in the distracted exhaustion of their motherland. Out of the wedding of the old world and the new had come a new people on their own lands, where in the end they must be their own masters. Freedom's work was already making. Don Pedro Bautista Pino closed his state papers to the King by saying in alarm, ". . . America and Spain must work in closer and closer co-operation, without permitting any difference to arise whereby the colonies might become victims of the great and horrible misfortunes now suffered by some of the provinces of New Spain, which in regard to the glory and prosperity of the nation are deceived by a few malicious enemies."

It was a loyalist's gallant effort to dismiss the power that was abroad in the new world; but no such effort could any longer succeed. No misfortune seemed so great to people hungry for freedom as the weight of the dying yet grasping hand of Spain upon them; and those were more than malicious reports that told how Spanish glory and pros-

perity were things of the past. In the very year when the Rio Grande
deputies took their seats at Cádiz the first revolution of Mexico broke
out, and spread fast to the dusty towns and brush-grown ranches of the
lower river.

40.

The Shout

On September 16, 1810, at Dolores in the province of Guanajuato,
a proclamation of liberty was made by the parish priest, Father Miguel
Hidalgo. The "grito de Dolores"—the shout from Dolores—rang out over
Mexico, and overnight won a tremendous response, especially in the
internal and northern states. Priests, soldiers, ranchers, merchants,
Christian Indians, laborers, adventurers and fortune hunters—men of
every class threw in their fortunes with the revolution. They marched
under the banner of the patroness of Mexico, the Virgin of Guadalupe.
For the first time there was a powerful, organized movement, under an
inspiring leader, to express the hopes of the Mexicans for their freedom, though there had been little uprisings earlier, local in nature and
quickly suppressed. A month after Hidalgo's shout the royal council in
Spain issued an offer of amnesty to rebels in New Spain who bowed again
to Spanish authority. As it still took from two to three months for official
business to pass either way over the ocean, the government in this order
referred to earlier rebellions, that lacked the scale and fury of Hidalgo's
movement with its hundred thousand volunteers, many of whom came
from the lower Rio Grande.

These were recruited by the lively efforts of two brothers. One
was a blacksmith and merchant named José Bernardo Gutierrez de
Lara who came from New Santander. Aroused by Hidalgo's cry, he
threw himself passionately into the fight. In the 1750s his ancestors had
founded the river town of Revilla under the Count of Sierra Gorda;

and his brother José Antonio Gutierrez de Lara was a priest well known in the river settlements. With Hidalgo sweeping through the interior towns and cities, Father José Antonio Gutierrez de Lara went back and forth along the Rio Grande in the autumn of 1810, visiting Laredo, Revilla, Mier, Camargo and Reynosa with such effect that in the following February the governor of New Santander, who had fled his capital before the revolutionists, reported to Mexico City that "revolution and terror rage in the settlements along the Rio Grande."

While Hidalgo's forces, styled the Army of America, after a feint at the capital of Mexico, turned north again and spread toward the Rio Grande, the river towns heard of how the revolution had sprung into flame in Texas. At San Antonio the royal governor, Manuel Salcedo, and his officers were captured by army rebels and forced to proceed in heavy chains to the Rio Grande where at Fort St. John Baptist they were jailed. With a Bonaparte on the throne of Spain, the Latin Texans feared that future diplomacy would see them thrown to the French by the royal Spanish government. A strong belief in Mexican independence ruled the Texans. They took the United States for their model, and called themselves Americans, and spoke of setting up for their own a government of Americans by Americans. Spanish by inheritance, they hated both Spain and France. In the great urge of the hour they forgot their frontier troubles with the United States and turned to Washington hoping to find an ally in the struggle.

In February, 1811, the rebels were feeling the rallied strength of the royalists; and when two emissaries of the revolution, General Ignacio Aldama and Father Juan Salazar, came to Laredo on their way to the United States to raise men and munitions for their cause, they found the local garrison loyal to Spain. Captain José Días de Bustamante, in command of all government troops on the river, declared that he would sooner turn his forces over to the French, the English, the murderous Indians, than to the rebels. But he let Hidalgo's messengers pass. On their mission rested Hidalgo's hopes, for his Army of the Americas was already on the run. Not long since, with nearly a hundred thousand men, Hidalgo had been ready to take Mexico City; and now, turned back from the capital by his own doubts and beset by swiftly gathering royalist troops, he was coming north with only five thousand ragged men and a straggling supply train. His one great resource was a treasury of two millions in gold and silver bullion that he carried along. His sympathizers were in power in Texas, and he would join them, restore his forces, and return to the liberation of Mexico.

But after only three months, the revolutionary regime was over-thrown in San Antonio. In March royalist deputies arrived at St. John Baptist. This old river fort was now ardently royalist. The deputies were on their way to find and deliver the imprisoned Governor Salcedo, who was held on a ranch near Monclova, and who soon would resume his duties in San Antonio. The river line knew every move made by loyalist and insurgent, as the fortunes of each surged back and forth between in-terior Mexico and Texas. At Saltillo on March sixteenth Father Hidalgo and his commanders held council. With two millions in gold and silver they would be able to do good business buying arms and influence in the States. Texas, over the river, was to be the floodgate for the great tide of help that would win the revolution. While in the midst of their starving army they made plans, they were joined by an unexpected guest. It was José Bernardo Gutierrez de Lara, who came to offer to the failing revolt all that he owned—his fortune, his services, his life. The rebel staff took heart from his fiery spirit. He was accepted as one of them, he was given a commission as lieutenant colonel, he was charged with raising an army in the river states and bringing them to Fort St. John Baptist. Perhaps by now, the messengers Aldama and Salazar already had arms, men and money promised in the United States. The Shout would sound again with new power.

But now came word that Aldama and Salazar had been taken when the royalists overthrew San Antonio. Gutierrez de Lara offered to carry out their mission. He would go to Washington himself. The rebel chiefs thanked him, and authorized him to do so, but first, let him go to the Rio Grande and recruit men. The Army of America was dying away by desertion. Gutierrez de Lara saw the need and obeyed. When Hidalgo and the staff moved out for Texas, only a thousand men were left to escort them. On March twenty-first, near Baján, in the desert, by ambush and treachery, the Army of America was cut to pieces by royalist forces. Hidalgo and almost all the rebel leaders were taken, and their supplies, and their gold and silver, and their hopes. In four months Hidalgo and all his commanders would be executed. The libera-tion would seem to be a lost cause. There was a flurry at Laredo, there was a spark of hope at Fort St. John Baptist with most of its garrison absent, but only from Revilla came action that kept the revolution alive.

For Bernardo Gutierrez de Lara managed to get away unseen by the royalists, cross the river, and vanish into Texas. With him he had twelve men and Captain Miguel Menchaca, who seemed to be an ardent revolutionist. If the revolution lay shattered, it had the sympathy of

most of the civilized world. Gutierrez de Lara refused to see it abandoned.
He now set out to accomplish the mission for which he had applied
before the disaster in the Mexican desert. Menchaca, who knew the
trails, guided him across Texas to Louisiana where, after passing
through great dangers from royalist troops who searched for his party,
he arrived in August. He immediately found sympathizers for his cause.
A plot was hatched. While he went to Washington to enlist aid from the
United States, Menchaca was to return secretly to Texas, recruit an
army, and overthrow Governor Salcedo. Once done, this deed would
permit Menchaca to establish a new revolutionary government, and
to send Gutierrez de Lara its credentials, and money, and proof that it
was a reality worth supporting. They were great dimensions of belief
and daring which Gutierrez de Lara took with him when he left for
Washington—"Guazinton," as he wrote it—in October.

He arrived on December eleventh and encountered policy on two
levels, as its spokesmen might have said. One was official, whereby the
Government of the United States observed strict neutrality in the affairs
of Spain and her rebellious colonies. The other was private and unofficial,
whereby aid and encouragement were to be given to the Latin American
rebels. In spite of his odd status, for he had no credentials to submit, and
he could speak of himself though with pride only as a "Lieutenant-
Colonel, an American of the Kingdom of Mexico," Gutierrez de Lara
was warmly received at the State Department. His position deserved
respect, for who knew what was at stake if war should break out between
the United States and England? Who knew what would be the key that
would unlock Spanish America to the trade of the United States? He
was not an experienced statesman; but his blacksmith shop, his small
mercantile ventures on the Rio Grande did not benumb him in high
circles now.

He told of Menchaca's activities, which he felt sure would succeed.
So soon as they did, there would be a new government in Texas to deal
with. When that day came, let the United States permit the shipment
of arms and supplies to the Rio Grande and the north Mexican states.

He proposed that in return for such waiving of neutrality, a
newly free Mexico would ship silver, wool and other exports to the
United States. The trade impasse would be broken. Perhaps in time the
Western Hemisphere would be wholly independent of European trade.

Finally, with a touch upon the most raw nerve of all, he pointed
out the disadvantages to the Americas if upon local political disagreements there should suddenly intrude "any malignant effort that might

come from Europe"; and to prevent any such possibility, he asked for military aid from the United States to join forces with the revolutionary movement.

The chief clerk of the State Department heard him on December twelfth, and much impressed, brought him to the Secretary, James Monroe, with whom he had three interviews. The Secretary was interested to hear of Captain Menchaca's great enterprise that was even then launched in Texas. He urged Lieutenant Colonel Gutierrez de Lara to remain in Washington until such time as would see the stabilization of the Menchaca government at San Antonio, when proper credentials could be issued to him. Speaking for his government, the Secretary could agree that freer trade relations between the United States and Mexico were most desirable. As for outright aid in men and arms—this was a matter with many aspects. One of these had to do with the *pretext* under which the United States could move troops into Texas. Luckily, there was an old issue available. The Secretary, wrote Gutierrez de Lara in his diary, ". . . told me that it would be easy to send an army to the Rio Grande under the pretext that they were going to take possession of the lands which France had sold to them." As the Mexican patriot listened his heart sank within him, for he saw then the price of help. The Secretary continued his argument, and pointed out as though to a questioning world that once on the Rio Grande, the American army could then, more or less incidentally, "help the Creoles."

Gutierrez de Lara thought quickly, and made a despairing counter-proposal that might just gain him American troops and leave his land free. He would accept the plan, he said, provided the United States forces would come under his command.

At this, the Secretary lost interest in his own proposition, and Gutierrez de Lara was obliged to reject it himself. He could not trade all of Texas for the support he so greatly wanted. He saw vanish the aid he had come to enlist; but the price was too great, and in any case he had no authority to agree to such a bargain. Indeed, he must go further than rejection of it, if what lay in the thoughts of the State Department people really constituted a threat. He proposed new agreement upon the old idea of a neutral zone "to separate the two nations, or Americas, for thereby would be obviated many discords which commonly result from the close contact of two powers." This idea aroused no interest, though Monroe was cordial, and ordered arrangements to be made for Lieutenant Colonel Gutierrez de Lara's expenses while in Washington, and for his return passage when he should depart.

Between his second and third conferences with Monroe there were evidently further discussions in the State Department. A crisis was approaching in British-American relations. When he returned for his final talk with Monroe, Gutierrez de Lara was amazed to hear the Secretary say that if war were declared between the United States and Great Britain, the United States would send an army of fifty thousand men to Mexico on the side of the revolutionists. Gutierrez de Lara could scarcely believe his ears. It was a prize of undreamed-of proportions to take home to the struggling liberators of Mexico. They would never believe him. He would have to carry proof. He asked the Secretary for a copy in writing of what he had just promised.

The Secretary regretted that he would be unable to provide this.

Gutierrez de Lara lost his elation. What he felt was plain in his diary when later he made notes on the interview. "Mary Most Holy!" he ejaculated, "help me and rescue me from these men!"

The Secretary dismissed him kindly, urging him to return home, to pursue his plans, to assure his associates that the United States regarded favorably their intentions; and indicated that there was no reason now to wait for credentials from Captain Menchaca and the new government of Texas. For Menchaca, with three hundred American volunteers, entering into Texas to win a new nation, had met a large Royalist patrol, whom he had joined immediately, abandoning his adventurous followers. The Americans had fled without casualties. Gutierrez de Lara so was left alone in his determination. But the State Department gave him every assistance in making his way homeward, and presently he had the powerful help of new friends—one of them the American agent William Shaler, another a Cuban patriot called José Alvarez Toledo, who was ready to die for the freedom of the Indies. In January Gutierrez de Lara sailed from Philadelphia for New Orleans with new plans for the independence of Mexico, while Spain, if she had lost the power to nourish, seemed also to have lost the wits to understand the Indies. In January, 1812, with revolt in the whole air over the Western Hemisphere, she issued a state edict calling upon the colonies for their aid in her war against Napoleon, that *"moderno Atila,"* with his *"ferocidad,"* his *"crueldad calculada,"* his *"arte infernal."* Come, cried Spain to the embittered colonials, restore *"las dulces ideas de fraternidad y de unión"* which had marked *"nuestra común felicidad"* throughout three centuries. . . .

Aid? What aid? Mexico, riven by battles over many a dusty city, was poor and hungry. Food, all commodities, became scarce. Local merchants at Laredo agreed with others in other towns: if supply ran short, prices had to rise. The alcalde of Laredo, Manuel Dovaline, took measures in March, 1812, against the inflation and profiteering that resulted from the revolution and caused hardship to so many of his citizens. Prices were fixed on such items as meat, beans, candles and hay—green or dried. Those who came to market at Laredo to sell were required by law to offer consumers a fair chance to buy. All produce had to be displayed for sale at fixed prices in the public plaza for three days before it could be offered for sale wholesale or in bulk to jobbers. Not long later the same officer established, for Laredo, a bureau of standards. Sellers were required to bring their measuring sticks and bulk measures to be checked and approved. Europe and its strivings seemed very far away.

Throughout the spring and summer of 1812 rumors of Gutierrez de Lara came to his own part of the river. He was in New Orleans. He was in Nachitoches. He was coming down the Gulf Coast with fifteen thousand soldiers and eight thousand Indians. He was marching for San Antonio. He was in a rage because his property at Revilla had been confiscated by the royalist government, his family had been imprisoned. Surely he would come to their rescue? Not all such rumors could be true at the same time, but actually he was moving into Texas, and ahead of him went a cloud of printed manifestoes and proclamations. A printing press, and a wandering American printer who fed his own rickety radicalism into the clanking platens, seemed to be indispensable articles of equipment to the filibustering armies that reached across Texas toward the Rio Grande in the last royal decade. Gutierrez de Lara, said a broadside, was on his way to free "the hemisphere of Columbus." Another entitled "The Friend of Man" exhorted the "sons of Montezuma" to unshackle themselves from Spain. These papers of sedition reached their goal. Captain Bustamante, the royalist commander on the lower Rio Grande, was obliged to write to the governor at San Antonio that in spite of every precaution to intercept the agents of Gutierrez de Lara and confiscate their revolutionary pamphlets, the flood of dangerous ideas had rolled through. River Indians were openly discussing, for all the world like Rousseau's savages, the philosophy of government. What right, asked the Indians, had a King to rule over other people? All people must have, they asserted, the right of self-government. Liberty and freedom were the natural states of man. It was uncanny to hear murdering horse Indians at large with such opinions. Near Revilla an Indian shepherd was often seen driving his sheep up and down the river.

As he went he left behind him the pamphlets of Gutierrez de Lara, who was coming, said the shepherd, back to Revilla.

And in fact a large force sprang to arms under Gutierrez de Lara, though nothing so large as it was rumored to be. But all those who by neutrality laws had been stayed for years in Louisiana, gazing with hunger toward the spare and beautiful land of Texas, now saw their chance to make their fortunes. What did the pretext matter? Let the printer grind out the passionate ideals of the revolution. Texas was waiting for the settler. Gutierrez de Lara took for his second in command the American officer Augustus Magee. The men of the "Republican Army of the North" were on their way by August, 1812, to Nacogdoches. The town received them as liberators. Texas had been breached. On the seventeenth, Governor Salcedo wrote in desperation to the Viceroy. He mentioned the two battalions of soldiers who had recently been sent to Mexico from Spain to help defeat the revolution, and he asked for a thousand of those men at once. The Viceroy's reply was not drafted until seven months later, when no matter what it said it would be of no use. On the same day, Salcedo sent couriers to the Rio Grande states asking for immediate reinforcements. Only one out of four commanders of royal troops sent aid. The royal governor of Texas waited with his doom at San Antonio.

In October a familiar figure reappeared at Fort St. John Baptist, travelling toward Chihuahua. He was Dr. Robinson, Pike's old comrade. His purpose now was secret, though he carried credentials from both the United States government and the new regime of Gutierrez de Lara. He disappeared into Mexico, and four months later was again at the river outpost, having spoken for Secretary Monroe to the Mexican authorities on behalf of better relations between the United States and the loyalist Mexican government. It was a strange message, for Washington was openly supporting Gutierrez de Lara's agitations. Dr. Robinson, with his usual animation, spoke to proponents of all points of view; and returned without bringing any official satisfaction. At St. John Baptist on his return trip, he proposed himself as mediator between the revolution and the royal government. His spirited offer was declined, and he returned to the United States across Texas in March.

On his way he paused briefly at San Antonio. He found the Governor bitter against the royal officials in Mexico who had sent him no help. Gutierrez de Lara and Magee were advancing fast, now. By late March San Antonio was under siege, and news of the end came to Laredo on April eighth when an escaped royalist officer rode into the

river city to tell of what he had seen. The Republican Army of the
North took San Antonio on April second. On the following day a trial
was held at which Governor Salcedo and sixteen of his officers were
sentenced to be shot. Gutierrez de Lara, some said, pardoned them; but
before they could be taken safely away, they were led on horses out on
the southern road of San Antonio by one hundred rebels in the darkening evening. They were ordered to dismount. They were tied hand and
foot. Their throats were cut. They were stripped naked. They were
left to lie waiting dead for beasts of prey and carrion birds. Gutierrez
de Lara at once set about drafting the declaration of independence and
the constitution of the first Republic of Texas, which he proclaimed
with grandiloquence on April seventeenth, 1813.

Four months later the Republic was in ruins. Spanish royal forces
converging on interior Texas from Laredo and Fort St. John Baptist
brought down the republic in the battle of Medina on the eighteenth
of August. Gutierrez de Lara was already in the discard. His American
allies had shelved him in favor of the Cuban Toledo. Royal government
was officially restored in Texas, and everywhere on the Rio Grande, in
September.

At Santa Fe the French were still a menace to upper Rio Grande
officials, and in April a certain José Antonio Casados of New Mexico
was interrogated as to whether or not he had given "topographical
information" to a Frenchman resident at Santa Fe. In 1813 King Joseph
Bonaparte fled Spain before the allied armies led by Wellington, and
Ferdinand VII was brought back from his French prison to Madrid to
occupy his throne once more. In his absence the Cádiz parliament had
preserved the frame of a legitimate Spanish government, and had sought
to conciliate the Indies with liberal decrees, including declarations of
equality for Indians and colonials, and the abolition of the Inquisition.
Now the returned King repudiated as many as he could of the parliament's reforms, and in 1815, with the tireless concern for trifles that was
his inheritance on the Spanish throne, he approved a circular—a copy
reached Santa Fe—regulating the mustaches of army officers.

The energies of the nineteenth century colonies, straining for
freedom, were not conciliated by Spain. Authority was if anything
drawn tighter by the hands of the home government. If new towns
struggled to come alive on the Rio Grande, the colonial administrators
were referred to the Laws of the Indies, which provided clearly that no
one, neither viceroy, nor council, nor governor, nor "any other officers
of the Indies, however high they may be," might grant city or town

titles in the New World, "because this favor must be asked of our Council
of the Indies" in Spain. Any such title granted from within the New
World was declared void in advance. For the rest, all the old precise
conditions still had to be met if a colonial desired to found a town.
He agreed by contract to gather "at least thirty persons," each of whom
was to have "a house, ten breeding cows, four oxen, or two oxen and
two yearlings, one brood mare, one breeding sow, twenty Castilian
breeding ewes, and six hens and one cock." The founder was also to
choose a priest, and provide a church, and equip it. All this was to be
established and ready by a certain fixed time. If he failed to finish his
enterprise by the date agreed upon, the contract with the royal power
said "he shall lose all that he may have built, cultivated or earned,
which we shall apply to our Royal Patrimony, and he shall also incur
the penalty of one thousand dollars in gold for our Chamber. . . ." If
he completed his contract in order, he was to receive four square leagues
of land; and he retained the powers that had been granted to him; for
he received "the civil and criminal jurisdiction . . . for the days of his
life and for those of a son and heir; he also received authority to appoint
alcaldes of ordinary jurisdiction, aldermen, and other officers of the
council of the town. . . ."

Such exhaustive paternalism played its part in the early periods
of conquest, when the first responsibility was to transplant intact in the
new land the image of home; but home long since had taken a new defi-
nition; and oversea names were scrawled in blood on the whole map
of that New World which Alexander VI had given forever to the Spanish
kings and queens.

Along the Rio Grande after 1813 the revolutionary spirit was
not extinguished. Occasionally its flicker and glare showed like watch
fires on the horizon of royal north Mexico. Mischief harassed the government from many quarters. A seditious courier was taken on the river
and made to reveal that in New Orleans Gutierrez de Lara, Toledo, a
party of pirates and a band of ambitious traders were concocting plans
for a co-ordinated attack by land and sea against northern Mexico. In
a larger affair there seemed to be relief, for by royal order the Te Deum
was sung in the river chapels in September, 1813, to celebrate the disaster that had overwhelmed Napoleon in the snows of Russia in the
previous autumn, news of which had just come to Santa Fe. But the
relief was short, and after Napoleon's escape from Elba, Ferdinand VII
circularized the New World with warnings against possible surprises by
Napoleon's agents in the Americas.

In fact, Joseph Bonaparte was now living at Point Breeze, on the Delaware River in New Jersey, and was said to be interested in various movements against Spanish Texas and Mexico. At Philadelphia, in 1816, he met with conspirators headed by a young Spanish revolutionary named Francisco Xavier Mina. He listened to Mina's plan. With the volunteer forces he was raising—his support drew upon adventurous men from England, Spain, Cuba, Haiti and the United States—Mina intended to go by sea to the mouth of the New Santander River in the Gulf of Mexico, disembark, march overland and capture Mexico City. Joseph, the ex-king, gave Mina a letter of credit on a London bank for one hundred thousand dollars. Was it not possible that the crown of an independent Mexico might descend upon this Bonaparte if, aided by his letter of credit, the conspirators should succeed? In April, 1817, Mina's fleet, headed southwestward, dropped anchor off the mouth of the Rio Grande. There were two frigates, two brigs, and two schooners carrying about four hundred motley troops. On shore was the royalist outpost, consisting altogether of a corporal and four privates, to defend the entrance to the river. Mina flew the Spanish flag. When he sent an officer and some men ashore they were unsuspectingly received by the corporal. Where were they from? The officer replied that they were "a Spanish squadron from the Havannah for Vera Cruz." And what did the landing party require?—and the corporal helped the filibusters to round up some cattle and slaughter them. Other boats came inshore. One was upset, an officer was drowned. The water casks were filled from the fresh if muddy river, while the corporal in command of the river's mouth cheerfully chatted about the positions of other government troops on the Mexico Bay. Along with his nine cannon, Mina had a printing press. On it while at the mouth of the Rio Grande he had a bulletin printed, under the date of April 12, 1817, which was afterward believed to be the first Texas imprint. In a few hours the little squadron set sail; and in a few weeks its mission was a failure, its forces divided and scattered, its leaders dead.

But Joseph Bonaparte backed another venture in the following year when he put money at the disposal of a Bonapartist general, Charles Lallemand, who had plans for a colony in Spanish Texas. The Viceroy of Mexico countered with secret orders to his outposts, including those of the Rio Grande, to exclude the French general. There was a rumor —it was enough to appall the Spanish colonial government—a rumor that said if Napoleon were rescued from St. Helena, he might very well take up his residence in General Lallemand's Texas settlement. And was Joseph Bonaparte still looking for another crown in Spanish America? In spite of orders from Mexico City, Lallemand, with his followers, came to the Texas coast in 1818, to establish the colony known as Champ d'Asile. But under Indian pressure and before rumors of Spanish power gathering to expel the intruders, it was abandoned in six months.

So for the better part of two decades Texas, with its part of the Rio Grande, was regarded as fair game by any person or faction able to muster enough strength to invade her territory. By far the greatest interest was shown by Americans of the United States; and with each repeated attempt against the soil of Spanish Texas the Americans, as though sanctioned by habit, seemed to feel that their claim to Texas increased in power and virtue. There was a shred of precedent for American claims to all of Texas as far as the Rio Grande—the famous, and ambiguous, French view of the territory involved in the various sovereignties of Louisiana, beginning with that of Louis XIV. So long as the issue remained in doubt, frontier struggles to settle it by seizure were inevitable. But now in 1819, the instrument known as the Florida Treaty settled all disputes between Spain and the United States over boundaries and territories. Among its other provisions, the Treaty gave Florida to the United States, fixed the Sabine River as the western boundary line of Louisiana and—most significant of all—established that the United States ceded to Spain and renounced forever all its "rights, claims and pretensions" to Texas, with the long Rio Grande boundary.

If the agreement seemed acceptable to the northern and eastern regions of the United States, on the frontier west it produced roars of fury. The land-hungry adventurers lingering in Louisiana, the frontier fighters of many races and nations who answered every cry, wherever raised, for the freedom of Texas, saw themselves betrayed. Once again a small volunteer army came together, now under the leadership of James Long, in the summer of 1819. Against active discouragement by the United States their plans proceeded, and by June they were across the Sabine, conventionally accompanied by a printer named Eli Harris, who struck off on the twenty-third a declaration of independence for the second Republic of Texas. Long was named as president, and gathered about him a supreme council whose membership included José Bernardo Gutierrez de Lara, as a sort of elder statesman of border revolt. The royalist powers opposed Long's venture; but the opponents never came to serious battle. Texas was a waste, after a decade of march and counter-march by invaders and defenders. The whole immense province had scarcely four thousand inhabitants of the white race. For those who tried to live there outside the struggle, there was a third foe who took advantage of it on his own ground: the Indian.

For to him the manifestoes of liberators and the retaliations of royal militia meant only a chance to sweep down upon isolated ranches and border towns and wilderness trails, to kill, steal and burn. The Rio Grande garrisons were frequently off on expeditions against filibusters, and their home stations were left open to Indian attack. At Laredo the north-bank settlers abandoned their side of the river and gathered on the opposite, where they built watchtowers and kept vigil. Indians entered into the illicit commerce in stolen horses between the Rio Grande states and East Texas, dealing with American traders who paid them well for the wild herds they drove north over the river and all the way to Louisiana. Such trade relations did not make the Indians into allies of white Americans at large. Party to neither side in the struggle for Texas, the Indians preyed upon both. In 1818 the Comanches staged their greatest raids upon the lower river. They drove off thousands of head of livestock, and murdered settlers, and burned down towns—among them, the Villa de Palafox, which had been founded thirty miles above Laredo on the north bank of the river in 1810. They left it depopulated and destroyed. It was never resettled. Several coal mining settlements in the same region were also wiped out. If the Florida Treaty gave Texas to Spain, the Spanish authority had little left with which to keep it in peace and safety.

On January 1, 1820, the home government suffered a blow that paralyzed it further. A Spanish army mutiny, led by Colonel Rafael Riego, gathered popular support. Spain's last military power had been exhausted in attempts to put down the revolutionary outbreaks in the colonies. The home army declared against any such further service. It was believed that out of forty thousand troops recently sent to the Americas, north and south, not a man had returned. Spain was shaking apart, and the effect of this was felt in the New World. It was with some hope of success that Henry Clay attacked the Florida Treaty in Congress on April 3, 1820, for the treaty had not yet been ratified by Spain, and sentiment in the American West was wild against it. Clay demanded that the treaty be repudiated, and that by the division of Spanish lands the United States must take in all of Texas, all the way to the Rio Grande. John Quincy Adams disagreed with him. "The appetite for Texas," he declared, "was from the first a Western passion," and he added that it was "stimulated by no one more greedily than Henry Clay," who, he said, "preached the doctrine that we should have insisted upon our shadow of a claim to the Rio del Norte. . . ."

While such passions affecting the destiny of the Rio Grande were felt in Madrid, and Washington, and over Texas, the acting governor at Santa Fe, Facundo Melgares, Pike's old royalist friend, summoned the alcaldes of New Mexico to convene on November first in the Palace of the Governors. Their purpose was to consider ways and means for the journey of Don Pedro Bautista Pino who was once again readying himself to return to Spain and take his seat in the parliament. Ferdinand VII on his release from France had abolished colonial representation; and now, as a consequence of Riego's revolt, it was restored. As in the old days, when service to the Crown was undertaken so often by great figures of the Indies conquest "at no expense to His Majesty," the colonial delegate was obliged to pay his own way, or have it paid for him by his province.

The meeting was symbolic of what had been. Presided over by a royalist governor, it soberly went to work on a routine matter that tied the Spanish Rio Grande to Spain—for almost the last time.

In the same autumn, and symbolic of what was to come, a mild but tenacious man from Missouri named Moses Austin appeared in San Antonio to request official permission of the royal authorities to settle a group of Anglo-American families in Texas. After some hesitation, he was granted approval of his petition on January 17, 1821, and he returned to Missouri to make preparations with his people for their exodus. They would surrender their United States citizenship, and enter Texas as subjects of the King of Spain. But the nature of that sovereignty was soon altered in a series of events that when it began moved swiftly.

41.

The Broken Grasp of Spain

At Washington on February 22, 1821, Spain ratified the Florida Treaty. But two days later, at Iguala, a town halfway between Mexico City and Acapulco, the rallying call of a new Mexican revolution was sounded by Colonel Agustín de Iturbide, an officer of the viceregal army, and the days of Spain in Mexico were numbered. Riego's mutiny in the home country had provided a precedent, and Napoleon's airs had provided a manner, for Iturbide's sudden rise to eminence.

His revolutionary call was the Plan of Iguala. It consisted of three points to which all the dissident parties of Mexico could rally—clergy, people of property, the American-born colonials. It proposed, first, the continuation of the Catholic Church as the established church of Mexico; second, the establishment of an independent limited monarchy; and third, equal rights for Spaniards and creoles.

With only twenty-five hundred troops to support him at Iguala, Iturbide soon had overwhelming approval from the mass of Mexicans. He won his revolution with an idea. Not a shot was fired. He marched across the country taking on volunteers in great numbers. The popularity of his Plan spread like wildfire. In vain, orders were dispatched on March third by the viceregal office to all its branches warning against Iturbide's propaganda, and calling for loyalty to the government. All circumstances—turmoil in Spain, long-frustrated desire for freedom in Mexico—created an atmosphere of success for Colonel de Iturbide. There were signs that he saw in his destiny a repetition of that of another field soldier who had suddenly become more than a commander—had embodied a glorious ideal—had swept a nation into ardent dedication to himself—and had finally consented to wear a crown. For Bonaparte he was willing to read Iturbide.

By summer one province after another was taking the oath supporting the independence of Mexico. On July third orders went to the river provinces from one of the last royal strongholds sanctioning the oath to the new regime and giving instructions for its form. All people were to assemble before a crucifix and a book of the Gospels, and swear—the military on the hilts of their swords, the civil on the cross— to uphold the holy, Roman, Apostolic faith; to defend the freedom of the empire of Mexico; and to keep the peace between Mexicans of European and Mexicans of American blood. Later in the month New Biscay was urged to capitulate, and, up the river, New Mexico on September eleventh took the oath by order of Melgares, the last northern royalist.

He had every legal right, now, to give his order; for in August the tremendous act of separation had been done. A new viceroy, General O'Donojú, had arrived from Spain to mollify the rebellion and to urge Mexico to await the action of parliament which assuredly would recognize her claims to independence. But he found that Mexican freedom had gone beyond claim and was fact. Iturbide met with him at Cordova, in the province of Vera Cruz. It was soon clear to the last Viceroy that unless he accepted at once the fact of Mexican independence, a massacre of Spaniards living in Mexico, a civil war of fearful dimensions, must come. On July twenty-fourth he signed away Spain's dominion over Mexico and all the outlands she embraced—the Central Americas, California, New Mexico, Texas. The Florida treaty would hold—but now between the United States and Mexico. The grasp of Spain was broken at last, and forever.

Mexico's first Consul now proceeded to the capital, where he was ecstatically received. He named a provisional governing body, and appointed a regency of five members, including General O'Donojú, with himself as president. On September twenty-second the "Act of Independence of the Mexican Empire" was solemnly proclaimed. Its creator was styled "Most Serene Highness." In Texas James Long was captured with what remained of his filibustering group, and claimed that he had heard nothing of all Iturbide's works in Mexico. Far from admitting that he was an aggressor against Mexican soil, Long declared that all he had ever worked for was the liberation of Texas from Spain, and the further freedom of Mexico. He was taken to Mexico City for examination of such doubtful statements, and there not long later was shot to death in a scrape with a Mexican sentry.

Meanwhile the Empire was coming into its new state. The Most Serene Highness in November sent out to his far-flung provincial gover

nors the news that he had founded an order of merit—the Order of
Guadalupe. He asked Santa Fe for confidential nominations of those who
deserved to receive the cross and ribbon of the new honor. News still
came slowly to the New Mexico river. At Santa Fe they heard on
December twenty-sixth how the liberator had entered his capital city,
and on January sixth, led by Governor Melgares, who was now a passionate servant of the new Empire, New Mexico celebrated the triumph.
Santa Fe at dawn heard artillery salutes. A parade was held. The post-
master, Juan Bautista Vigil, painted new decorations for a ball held in
the Palace, at which the alcalde, Pedro Armendaris, led a cotillion. Later
in the evening a brilliant tableau was staged, in which the Plan of
Iguala was dramatically represented in all three of its exhilarating
clauses, with Father Juan Tomás Terrazas as The Church, Alférez Santiago Abréu as Independence, and Chaplain Francisco Hocio as The
Union of Spaniards and Creoles. The whole affair recalled the eloquence
of Governor Melgares spoken a few days earlier: "New Mexicans . . . let
us show tyrants that although we live at the very extremity of North
America we love the holy religion of our fathers; that we cherish and
protect the desired union between Spaniards of both hemispheres; and
that, with our last drop of blood, we will sustain the sacred independence
of the Mexican empire!"

It was not long before the empire had its crown. The Most
Serene Highness was proclaimed as Emperor Agustín I, with his wife
as Empress, by the Mexican congress on May nineteenth, 1822. Like any
proper Bonaparte he promptly created his father and mother, his sons
and daughters, all princes and princesses. It was a satisfying gesture for
one who had once resigned from the Army in the face of official charges
of squalid misconduct in military and private affairs. All turned now
to him, even those who had hopes in his far provinces. A worried provincial was in Mexico City, and on May 21, 1822, wrote to the Emperor
Agustín I:

>   Sir:

>   Having become a citizen of this Empire, by the formation
>   of a settlement of three hundred families from the United States
>   of America in the Province of Texas, under authority from the
>   Deputation in the Internal Provinces; and participating in the
>   Sentiments of Joy manifested by the nation at the recent political
>   change, I respectfully approach His Imperial Majesty, and offer
>   my congratulations on the happy consummation of the inde-

pendence of Mexico, by the election of the hero of Iguala, the
Liberator of his Country to the Imperial Throne—

I make a tender of my services, my loyalty, and my fidelity
to the Constitutional Emperor of Mexico; a tender which I am
ready to verify by an oath of allegiance to the Empire.

This solemn act cuts me off from all protection or dependence on my former government—my property, my prospects, my
future hopes of happiness, for myself and family, and for the
families I have brought with me, are centered here— This is our
adopted Nation:—We look to the Sovereign Congress as the pure
fountain whence those blessings are to flow which will diffuse
peace, improvement, intelligence, and happiness over this new
born Nation:

We raise our eyes and hearts to him, whose virtues have
elevated him to the station he merited, as the Father, who is to
distribute those blessings to his people with a firm, impartial,
and benevolent hand—

I therefore supplicate that his Imperial Majesty will have
the goodness to take the Settlement I have formed under his protection, and that we may be received as Children of the great
Mexican family.

The prostrate appeal was signed by Stephen F. Austin, who had succeeded upon his father's death to the leadership of the Missouri exodus.
The future of Texas and the river hung upon his letter; though in terms
which none foresaw.

For two months preparations went furiously ahead toward the
coronation of the emperor. The Napoleonic analogy there reached its
climax; for in great engraved folios by Percier, the designs of Isabey for
Napoleon's fabulous coronation had been preserved, and Mexican de-
signers, artisans, couturiers and masters of ceremony must have had access
to them. Improvising desperately, they did what they could about red
velvet, and golden bees, and precedence, and state coaches. But the
results, with an emperor and empress in borrowed diamonds, served
mainly to reveal ambition and poverty together; and foreign observers
smiled with terrible tact, as the President of Congress placed a crown
upon the head of Agustín I, who in turn crowned the Empress Ana
María with a diadem, while a memory of Joséphine moved in the
shadows. The American consul wrote home that the affair, lasting five
hours, was "a most tiresome Pantomime," and General Wilkinson, who
also attended, fell asleep twice, and later said it had all been "clumsy
and tinselled."

And everywhere along the Rio Grande—from the mountain towns and pueblos of the north, and the high bosky valleys of the farming haciendas, and the gravelly garrison villages of the turn of the river, and the dusty little cities of the thorned brush country, to the lone sentry outposts in the sweet heavy air of the Gulf beaches—the Spanish colors were down; and for a little while in their place hovered the first imperial eagles of modern Mexico.

Sources for
Volume One, By Chapters

APPENDIX A

Sources for
Volume One, by Chapters

RATHER THAN INTERRUPT THE FLOW OF THE NARRATIVE by the use of footnotes on each page, or of superior numbers referring to a later listing of notes, I have adopted a simplified form of reference in order to identify my sources. I hope my system will provide relief for the general reader who is not concerned with authorities, and yet will reassure the scholarly reader with respectable evidence, given here, of my efforts to make my long story a true one. Each source is here noted in brief form which corresponds to its alphabetical position in the General Bibliography (Appendix C), where the reader will find full bibliographical particulars.

prologue

1. Creation: Croneis; Milham; Talman.
2. Gazetteer: Bartlett; Emory, *Report;* Federal Writers Program, WPA, *Colorado,* and *New Mexico,* and *Texas;* Lane, F. C.; Peyton.

book one: the indian rio grande

1. The Ancients: Coolidge; Huntington; Martin, P. S.; Watson; Wissler.
2. The Cliffs: Bandelier, *Delight Makers,* and *Final Report;* Benedict; Bryan; Fergusson, E.; Fewkes, *Two Types;* Hewett, *Ancient Life;* Kroeber; Lummis. *Mesa;* MacClary; Martin, P. S.; Renaud; Twitchell, *Leading Facts.*
3. To the River: Bandelier. *Final Report;* Benedict; Bryan; Fergusson, E.; Gilpin, *Pueblos;* Hewett, *Ancient Life,* and *Pueblo Indian World;* Hoffman; Martin, P. S.; Reagan; Renaud; Twitchell, *Leading Facts;* USDA, *Survey Report (Rio Puerco)*, and *Tewa Basin Study;* Watson.
4. The Stuff of Life: Alexander; Bandelier, *Delight Makers,* and *Diaries* and *Documentary History,* and *Indians of the Rio Grande Valley;* Benedict; Brand; Bryan; Castetter; Coolidge; Crane; Davenport; Denver Art Museum, *Leaflet Series, 1936,* and *1939;* Dobie, *Vaquero;* Douglas; Fergusson, E.; Frazer; Harrington; Hewett, *Ancient Life,* and *Pueblo Indian World;* Hrdlička; Jeançon, *Pueblo Indian Clothing,* and *Pueblo Indian Foods;* Kelley; Kidder; Lummis, *Mesa;* MacClary; Martin, G. C.; Martin, P. S.; Palmer, R. A.; Parsons; Renaud; Smith, V. J.; Thoburn; Twitchell, *Leading Facts;* USDA, Field flood control co-ordinating committee, *Survey Report . . . Rio Puerco;* USDA, SCS, *Report on Rio Grande Watershed,* and *Tewa Basin Study;* USDI, *Reclamation Handbook;* Watson; White; Wissler.

book two: the spanish rio grande

1. The River of Palms: Bandelier, *Hemenway Southwestern Expedition;* Benavides; Castañeda, C. E.; Hoffman, Fritz L., in Céliz; Watson.
2. Rivals: Castañeda, C. E.; Cortés; Diaz del Castillo.
3. Upland River: Bishop; Bolton, *Coronado,* and *Spanish Borderlands,* and *Spanish Exploration;* Hallenbeck, Álvar Nuñez; Hodge; Nuñez Cabeza de Vaca.
4. The Travellers' Tales: Bandelier, *Hemenway Southwestern Expedition,* and *Historical Introduction;* Bishop; Díaz del Castillo; Foscue; Hallenbeck, *Álvar Nuñez;* Hammond, G. P., *Narratives of the Coronado Expedition;* Hammond, G. P., and Rey, in Montoya; Hodge; Nuñez Cabeza de Vaca; Wright.
5. Destiny and the Future: Bolton, *Coronado;* Castañeda de Náxera.
6. Faith and Bad Faith: Bolton, *Coronado;* Castañeda de Náxera.
7. Facing Battle: Bolton, *Coronado;* Castañeda de Náxera; Díaz del Castillo.
8. Battle Piece: Bolton, *Coronado;* Castañeda de Náxera.
9. The Garrison: Bandelier, *Historical Introduction,* and *Indians of the Rio*

Grande Valley; Bolton, *Coronado;* Castañeda de Náxera; Díaz del Castillo; Gilpin, *Pueblos;* Hammond, G. P., *Narratives of the Coronado Expedition;* Towne; Watson.

10. Siege: Bolton, *Coronado;* Castañeda de Náxera; Hammond, G. P., *Narratives of the Coronado Expedition.*

11. The Eastern Plains: Bandelier, *Historical Introduction;* Bolton, *Coronado,* and *Southwestern Exploration;* Castañeda de Náxera.

12. Prophecy and Retreat: Bolton, *Coronado;* Castañeda, C. E.; Castañeda de Náxera; Cervantes Saavedra; Hammond, G. P., *Narratives of the Coronado Expedition;* Vásquez de Coronado.

13. Lords and Victims: Bolton, *Coronado;* Castañeda, C. E.; Castañeda de Náxera; Hammond, G. P., *Narratives of the Coronado Expedition;* Hammond, G. P., and Rey, in Montoya; Sanford.

14. The River of May: DeGolyer.

15. Four Enterprises: Bandelier, *Historical Documents;* Bolton, *Spanish Exploration;* Castañeda, C. E.; Gonzales de Mendoza; Hackett, in Bandelier, *Historical Documents;* Hallenbeck, *Land of the Conquistadores;* Hammond, G. P., Hodge, Rey, in Benavides; Hammond, G. P., in Montoya; Hewett, *Pueblo Indian World;* Hodge, in Nuñez Cabeza de Vaca.

16. Possession: Bolton, *Spanish Borderlands,* and *Spanish Exploration;* Hackett, in Bandelier, *Historical Documents;* Hammond, G. P., and Rey, in Montoya; Pérez de Villagrá; Trend.

17. The River Capital: Artiñano; Bandelier, *Documentary History,* and *Historical Documents;* Benavides; Bolton, *Spanish Borderlands,* and *Spanish Exploration;* Fergusson, E.; Hallenbeck, *Land of the Conquistadores;* Hammond, G. P., and Rey, in Montoya; Montoya; Oñate, in Bandelier, *Historical Documents;* Oñate, in Montoya; Pérez de Villagrá; Towne; Vega.

18. Collective Memory: Armstrong; Artiñano; Bell; Buckle; Cervantes Saavedra; Columbus; Crane; Díaz del Castillo; Fitzmaurice-Kelly; Gautier; Gibson, C. E.; Goldscheider; Hanke, *First Social Experiments,* and *Spanish Struggle;* Hewett, *Ancient Life;* Hume; Huntington; Leonard; Madariaga, *Fall,* and *Rise of the Spanish American Empire,* and *Spain;* Martialis; Maugham; Meier-Graefe; Prescott; Priestley; Trend.

19. Duties: Bandelier, *Indians of the Rio Grande Valley;* Benavides; Bolton, *Spanish Exploration;* Crane; Hallenbeck, *Land of the Conquistadores;* Oñate, in Montoya; Pérez de Villagrá.

20. A Dark Day in Winter: Hallenbeck, *Land of the Conquistadores;* Horgan, *Habit of Empire;* Montoya; Pérez de Villagrá.

21. The Battle of Ácoma: Hallenbeck, *Land of the Conquistadores;* Horgan, *Habit of Empire;* Pérez de Villagrá.

22. Afterthoughts: Pérez de Villagrá.

23. Exchange: Bandelier, *Final Report;* Benavides; Bolton, *Spanish Exploration;* Bourke; Burkholder; Denver Art Museum, *Leaflet Series,* 1940; Hewett, *Ancient Life,* and *Pueblo Indian World;* Montoya; Oñate, in Montoya; USDA, SCS, *Rio Grande Watershed in Colorado and New Mexico.*

24. The Promises: Bandelier, *Historical Documents,* and Hackett, in same; Hallenbeck, *Land of the Conquistadores;* Hammond, G. P., and Rey, in Montoya.

25. The Desert Fathers: Bandelier, *Historical Documents;* Bell; Benavides; Bourke; Crane; Dickey; Fergusson, E.; Francis of Assisi; Gilpin, *Pueblos;* Hammond, G. P., Hodge, Rey, in Benavides; Kubler; Leonard; Leonard in Siqüenza y Góngora; Madariaga, *Fall,* and *Rise of the Spanish American Empire;* Maugham; Siqüenza y Góngora; Towne; USDI, Reclamation Handbook.

26. The Two Majesties: Armstrong; Bandelier, *Historical Documents;* Benavides; Díaz del Castillo; Ellis; Hanke, *First Social Experiments,* and *Spanish Struggle;* Hewett, *Pueblo Indian World;* Madariaga, *Fall,* and *Rise of the Spanish American Empire;* Trend; Underhill.

27. The Hungry: Alessio Robles; Bandelier, *Historical Documents;* Benavides; Castañeda, C. E.; Crane; Hewett, *Ancient Life;* Morfi; USDI, NPS. *San Buenaventura Mission.*

28. This Miserable Kingdom: Bandelier, *Historical Documents;* Crane; Hackett; Hallenbeck, *Land of the Conquistadores.*

29. The Terror: Bandelier, *Historical Documents;* Burkholder; Chavez; Crane; Gilpin, *Pueblos;* Hackett; Hammond, G. P., Hodge, Rey, in Benavides; Kubler; Madariaga, *Fall of the Spanish American Empire;* Peyton; Underhill; USDA, *Rio Grande Watershed in Colorado and New Mexico.*

30. Limit of Vision: Hackett; Hallenbeck, *Land of the Conquistadores.*

31. A Way to the Texas: Bandelier, *Historical Documents;* Benavides; Bolton, *Spanish Exploration;* Castañeda, C. E.; Hammond, G. P., Hodge, Rey, in Benavides.

32. The Great Captain: Bandelier, *Final Report,* and *Hemenway Southwestern Expedition,* and *Historical Documents;* Chavez; Crane; Espinosa, in Vargas; Hallenbeck, *Land of the Conquistadores;* Hammond, G. P., Hodge, Rey, in Benavides; Twitchell, *Spanish Archives;* Vargas; Wallace, S.

33. Fort St. John Baptist: Bandelier, *Historical Documents;* Céliz; Hammond, G. P., Hodge, Rey, in Benavides; Hoffman, Fritz L., in Céliz; McKellar; Morfi; Priestley.

34. Early Towns: Alessio Robles; Bandelier, *Historical Documents;* Burkholder; Hallenbeck, *Land of the Conquistadores;* Pino; Twitchell, *Spanish Archives.*

35. Colonial Texas: Castañeda, C. E.; Céliz; Hoffman, Fritz L., in Céliz; Morfi.

36. Mexico Bay: Alessio Robles; Castañeda, C. E.; Wilcox, *Conversations.*

37. Forgotten Lessons: Bandelier, *Historical Documents;* Bolton, *Spanish Borderlands;* Bryan; Castañeda, C. E.; Chavez; Conkling; Díaz del Castillo; Dougherty; Fergusson, E.; Kubler; Madariaga, *Rise of the Spanish American Empire;* Priestley.

38. Hacienda and Village: Bandelier, *Final Report,* and *Historical Documents;* Benedict; Benavides; Beshoar; Bevan; Bolton, *Coronado,* and *Spanish Borderlands;* Boyd, E.; Castañeda, C. E.; Chavez; Dickey; Dougherty; Fergusson, E.; Fisher; Forrest; Hackett, in Bandelier, *Historical Documents;* Horgan, *Colonial Life;* James, G. W.; Jaramillo; Kincaid; Kubler Madariaga, *Fall,* and *Rise of the Spanish American Empire;* May; Pérez d Villagrá; Priestley; Salpointe; Twitchell, *Spanish Archives;* Underhil USDA, Field flood control co-ordinating committee, *Survey Report* . . *Rio Puerco;* USDA, SCS, *Rio Grande Watershed in Colorado and New Mexico;* Wilder.

39. The World Intrudes: Alessio Robles; Altamira y Crevea; Castañeda, C. E.; Dickey, Dougherty; Grant, B.; Hollon; Pike; Pino; Rives; Sibley; Sitwell; Twitchell, *Spanish Archives;* Watson; Wilcox, *Conversations.*

40. The Shout: Barker, *Austin Papers;* Castañeda, C. E.; Cox; Gutierrez de Lara; Rives; Twitchell, *Spanish Archives;* Wilcox, *Conversations;* Wortham.

41. The Broken Grasp of Spain: Barker, *Austin Papers;* Castañeda, C. E.; Percier; Rives; Robertson; Twitchell, *Spanish Archives;* Wilcox, *Conversations.*

BOOK THREE

The Mexican Rio Grande

I.

A Colony for Mexico

THE DISTANCE WAS GREAT—twelve hundred miles—and overland travel from the middle Gulf Coast of Texas to the Mexican capital was toilsome and dangerous. The roads were appalling. Robbers abounded along the way. As the southbound traveller drew closer to the Rio Grande two dangers became intensified. One was the lack of support and habitation for him in the countryside, which became a wilderness of mesquite and chaparral where water and fodder were hard to find. The other was the roving presence of mounted Indians from the North American prairies. Beyond the river, provincial capitals lay on the way to Mexico City, but their comforts were meagre, their garrisons concerned with guarding governors rather than voyagers, and their societies exiled from great affairs by rocky and sandy distance. The mails were irregular, and a letter dispatched from the river crossings at Laredo or St. John Baptist or Reynosa might well have to be entrusted to a private traveller going its way. Any such place was "as poor as sand bank, or drought, and indolence can make it," in the words of a letter that went from Laredo to the Texas Gulf Coast in March, 1822. It was the first of a stream of papers that Stephen Austin wrote to his people while on the mission that took him to the Mexican capital for the first time.

He had left the early settlers of his colony on the Brazos and Colorado rivers of coastal Texas. Eight families were there. A hundred fifty-one men were already at work making houses out of what they could find, and planting fields for the time when they could send for their families out of Louisiana. They had come in good faith, under permission granted by provincial administrators of the Spanish Crown. But by the time they arrived, Mexico was independent, and the colonial

grants made to the Austins were meaningless without confirmation by
the nascent Mexican government. It was to obtain this that Stephen F.
Austin went to the capital.

There would, he felt certain, be little difficulty over the matter.
A few interviews, an exchange of papers, some signatures—and the trick
was done. His case was clear. Anyone with the smallest sense should be
able to see it. The grand sweeps of Texas could only mean anything
to Mexico if they were populated and developed, loyally, ably and at
once. Austin and his people were ready to swear allegiance to the new
Emperor Agustín I, and renounce altogether their United States citizenship. There was work in the new homes to be done, and in his dedicated
zeal Austin counted on starting for Texas ten or twelve days after his
appearance in Mexico City.

But if there were delays, he was patient. The Mexicans, absorbed
with the thousand details of making a new government, were preoccupied with the Emperor's accession. Austin wandered observantly about
the streets. The city was "magnificent," though most of the population
lived in misery. He lived frugally. With him he had brought four hundred dollars in doubloons that had to last him. He was earnest and
polite, and Mexicans formed an agreeable impression of him. He studied
their language—his own new national tongue. He launched his petition
on its way in various offices. There he heard hints of further delays.
It appeared that while the government was glad to hear him, his enterprise, great as it might look to him, was but one of a number of applications already received from other colonizers; and all these together
were only details of a much greater question—the whole question of
Mexico's colonial policy under her new empire. There were indications
that the large policy must be framed before any of its parts could be
approved. It was encouraging that the Mexican Congress was at work
in committee. It was time to be reasonable, and wait in calm for the
new fathers of the empire to act. The Emperor was, he felt, "a very
good man as well as a great one," who had the happiness of the nation
much at heart.

Though how slowly moved the Congress; and what unsettling
rivalries began to show plain. The Emperor had enemies who began to
be heard. July passed, and the colonial question waited until in August
the old patriot from the Rio Grande, José Antonio Gutierrez de Lara,
spoke in Congress for the colonial bill. He let himself go, saying that,
based on North American patterns, the bill with its enlightened provisions would call to settlers who would pour into the new Empire, bring-

ing prosperity and civilization to outlands presently owned by animals
and savages. The great isthmus of Mexico, connecting two continents
and standing across the path between Europe and Asia, would become
the center of the world's commerce. The bill in its details even embraced
Austin's humble case, and he had every hope of seeing it passed and
himself on his way home within the month, at last free to get on with
his foundation, officially confirmed by the law of Mexico.

But the proud new machinery that would make this possible
suffered a violent shock toward the end of August, when the Emperor's
soldiery seized fifteen deputies of the Congress under a charge of treason.
The nation was outraged, and the colonial question was lost in tumult
over the government's condition. The new Empire was economically
prostrate. The Emperor's court style was already a great burden finan-
cially. The Congress was paralyzed. A military tyranny was being born
under the Crown, and swept along in the current of patriotic opposition
to it were other energies less disinterested; for the unrest of the moment
released the ambitions of men who strove to turn the new freedom of
Mexico to their own advantage. In the largest sense the constitutional
crisis was a legacy from Spain. For by centuries of rigid paternalism,
the fatherland had denied the colonial Mexicans any fair share in their
own government, had failed to educate them in public affairs, and had
so deeply bred in them the hunger for freedom that a man's personal
fate—human life itself—seemed trifles to spend recklessly if they could
buy a share, whether just or not, of Mexico for a Mexican. All governments were ponderous, all were drugged with the petty satisfactions of
daily policy making, all knew inner conflict, and divided opinion, and
the centrifugal tendency to fly apart through partisan loyalties to opposed
individuals or beliefs. But the Mexican government at its birth knew
these tendencies to extremity and faced almost a century of effort to
overcome them.

There were sharp differences in form, style and motive between
the Spanish and Mexican concepts of government. The Austins, in
founding their colony, were prepared to deal with Spain's colonial government. Tenuous as it may have become, it was yet experienced and
established in its own elaborate authority. Its systems could be studied.
Its principles were known and plain and rigid. And then Mexico broke
free of Spain, and the official relationship of settler to government had to
be redefined and newly approved. At first it might seem that the Mexicans, with their new empire, would merely change the actors and keep
the old play. There would be a new set of bureaus, titles, insignia, but

surely all would otherwise be the same. But what was profoundly different was what determined all—the Mexican character. Under the Castilian forms that the colonial society had for so long been trained to
perpetuate, the Mexican character was not the same thing at all as the
Spanish character.

For the people of Mexico, when they found themselves in possession of their own nation, brought with them to power all the qualities
of temperament and inheritance that for centuries had been subordinate
under the Spanish Crown. These were now dominant over the land, and
even where refined in a fragment of the population by Spanish training,
were greatly modified by the buried Indian past of Mexico. Between
two lost disciplines—the ancient Indian and the formal Spanish—the
Mexican character given freedom to express itself did so intemperately.
The politics of the new nation seemed to care little for the individual
human life. Such indifference was deeply rooted in the sacrificial rites
of the ancient sun priests, and in pagan identification with pitiless earth
deities, and in savage hunting ways, and in untold Indian centuries of
inert impersonality for the mass of people, under which the individual
was crushed into conformity with nature's pattern that wasted him in
order out of decay to perpetuate the type, all heedless of his human
capacities of mind and soul. Spain brought the individual to society in
the New World, though she did not bring for him even the modest degree
of freedom in representative government that Spaniards knew at home.
Independent Mexico looked to the United States for a new pattern of
government. A new dimension of freedom had come into the world
with the creation of the young and amazingly dynamic nation in North
America—it was barely fifty years old—whose constitution and laws and
westward expansion Mexico's new statesmen examined with mixed longing and alarm.

But constitutional forms were not absolute, and what a citizen
of the United States meant by independence and its methods and what
a Mexican meant were not altogether the same thing. The difference
in understanding that lay there was another of the difficulties that
Stephen Austin began to encounter, along with the paralysis of Mexico's
congress, and the stalling of the Texan petition in one after another
bureau, and the furies that swept the capital at the Emperor's absolutism.
Austin could only redouble his patience, and examine his purse.

His four hundred dollars' worth of doubloons was melting away.
Unable to abandon his purpose in Mexico, he drew a draft on one of

his colonists, and filled his time with sober enterprises that would both demonstrate his serious intention to enter into Mexican national life, and, he hoped, prove useful to the struggling government. Writing for hours, he produced memorials to the Congress that proposed organization plans for legislatures and law courts and colonies. He was invariably polite when he called upon officials to invest them with his greater political experience as a former citizen of a free country. His progress in the Spanish language gratified them. Earnestly he exhorted his younger brother John by letter to study, study, and prove progress by writing him back in Spanish, the language, he was certain, of their whole future in Texas.

Stephen Austin was a small, fastidious man, with a head rather large for his body. His clean-shaven face was full, crowned with disarrayed dark curls. Below the intense scowl of his domed brow gazed his great eyes—the right, level and calm; the left, alight and piercing. He had a large nose that inclined a trifle to the left, and a full mouth, sensitively modelled. It was a visionary countenance, with something of the facile good looks of an actor, through which his intensity could flare in calculated animation. In his dress he courted a sober elegance. His skirted dark coat sat on his narrow shoulders and lifted its rolled collar up beside his smooth cheeks, and higher yet rose the white points of his shirt collar, enclosing his chin above his white stock and bow cravat. He wore a light waistcoat and tapering trousers and squared-toed boots. If there was general fashion in all this, there was also much of his nature—modest, decent and without any touch of personal style that suggested humor or lightness of spirit. For of these traits he showed no sign. In all the thousands of pages of his preserved letters there was hardly a smile, or a revealed love—except for the establishment of the colony that was his life's trouble and necessity. In Mexico waiting upon the distracted government he was a bachelor thirty years old.

By November the Emperor's autocratic actions seemed on the way to acceptance, and the general colonies law once again moved in channels. Austin heard that it would soon go to the Emperor for signature, and on the twenty-second, he wrote to Texas that "in less than ten days I shall be dispatched with everything freely arranged." A quill, a flourish, "Agustín" and a rubric— But suddenly in the ancient coastal city of Veracruz on December 2, 1822, a republic was proclaimed and once again the Emperor turned aside from the colonies bill. It appeared that, as Austin wrote, the Veracruz revolutionary leader was a "General

Santana"—a name he was fated to spell, though no more correctly, for years to come in the struggles that would flow back and forth over the Rio Grande between Mexico and Texas.

The uprising at Veracruz was not a mere provincial disturbance. As December passed, the republicans of Veracruz won the ear of other Mexicans; and though the Emperor sent forces against them at Jalapa that defeated Santa Anna there, the nation had heard with eagerness of the uprising, and as fast as they had swept to the support of Iturbide a year ago, they now turned their support to his opponents. A fight for the crown was looming. The Emperor was preoccupied with it. Austin wrote to John on Christmas Day that Agustín had not yet approved the colonies bill, and held out little hope of action for "at least three weeks more." But at the New Year, word came from the Moncada Palace that the Emperor had read the bill, was returning it to the Congress with minor revisions, and by January fourth the bill was law. Austin took pride in the fact. "I am certain," he wrote, "that if I had not remained at the capital to agitate this subject . . . the law would never have been passed." But one heavy task led only to another. The bill provided the legal terms under which Austin's petition might be approved, but the petition itself now must be acted upon separately. Once again all hung upon the Emperor's attention. This was a restless faculty. Abroad in the nation, provinces and garrisons fell to the rebels, whether in terms of armed allegiance or vehement pronouncement. While the empire crumbled, Austin, again delayed, was obliged to sell his watch for one hundred dollars. His clothes were giving out. His privations were honorable, but tiresome. They contrasted soberly with the talk that was going around concerning the imperial court.

The Emperor—it was said—was drunk every day. The cost of his household was unreasonable—the Empress Ana María ordered chocolate in the amount of 480 pesos, and the Emperor spent too much on his wardrobe. There was a matter of a saddle fashioned from bearskin, green velvet, tooled leather and gold. Debts running to over two millions of pesos were already contracted by the imperial government. There were more officers and bandsmen in the imperial army than there were soldiers. Think of it: the Emperor might destroy his reign in one final burst of folly, such as a "murderous, bacchanalian orgy. . . ." Austin's purpose seemed lost in such confusions surrounding the "very good man as well as a great one" whom he had courted at the beginning with so much hope. Nevertheless he pressed his petition until with certain revisions it was signed by the Emperor on February 18, 1823. By then the

Emperor's dominion had shrunk until he controlled only the capital of Mexico and its environs. What if the government fell? Would its acts in behalf of the colony be valid? Austin saw too clearly what must follow upon Agustín's "violations" and "usurpations" not to know how these would affect his plans for Texas. The inevitable came to pass on March nineteenth, when the Emperor abdicated, and a delegate in the abused Congress cried, "Agustín! Agustín! you gave us independence but deprived us of liberty!"

At once the Congress passed a resolution declaring that "all governmental measures resulting from the coronation were . . . illegal," and orders went to the provinces that henceforth anyone was a traitor who acknowledged Agustín as Emperor of Mexico. The decree went to the outlandish Rio Grande towns, while the central government moved to establish a republic, and Austin wrote to Congress, who must now once more act upon his colonial grant, "I have already witnessed, with the greatest pleasure, the . . . entire change of the government . . . ," and asked once again for a ratification of his claim. He was rewarded at last. On April fourteenth, the Congress, though suspending the general colonies law, approved Austin's establishment. The way was open to the settlement of Texas by immigrants from the United States. It was the most fateful single act of the Mexican nation in the nineteenth century, for by it were released forces that must clash in always increasing energy until in the end they would meet in bloody battle along all but the whole course of the Rio Grande.

The deposed Emperor and the provisional government made certain arrangements for the future. He was to be known as Don Agustín de Iturbide, with the style of "Excellency." He was required to agree that he would depart for Italy, where he was to spend the rest of his life. So long as he lived, he was to receive a pension of 25,000 pesos annually. At his death, his widow would receive a pension of 8,000 pesos during her lifetime. In a matter of a few weeks the exiled family sailed from Veracruz on the British armed merchantman *Rawlins,* Captain Quelch. Their luggage indicated both imperial nostalgia and anxiety for the future. It contained paintings by old masters, personal jewels, hampers of silverware—and the ermine and embroidered velvet, the batons, stars and crosses of the imperial state regalia. In addition to their Excellencies Don Agustín and Doña Ana, the party included their eight children, and a number of chaplains, secretaries and servants. The *Rawlins* set out under sail to cross the Atlantic for Leghorn (it was not far from Elba) and once ashore, the exiles hoped to make their way

to Rome, where—surely?—they would live, looking westward, forever
after.

◦

2.

A Wild Strain

The mountain system of the northern Rio Grande was a vast,
secret world. Wandering Indians there made shrines of twig and feather
and bone, and went their ways. Close to the high clouds that made their
rivers, the inhuman peaks doubled the roar of thunder, or hissed with
sheets of rain, or abided in massive silence. Below them lay every variation of park and meadow and lost lake; gashed canyon and rocky room-
like penetralia in the stupendous temples of the high wilderness. Along
hidden watercourses and in little cupped lakes lived and worked the
family of a small creature destined to be the first cause of great change
in the human life of the river during the early nineteenth century. It
was the beaver.

In still pool or mild current the beaver made his house of mud
and twig. Its doorway was under water. The occupants dived to enter it
and came up beyond into the dry shelter of their lodge that they had
built of sticks and mud, where their food was stored and where they were
safe from animal predators. The backwater before the den had to be
three feet deep, and if this did not exist naturally, the beavers built
dams to collect it. They chose a tree by the edge. Sitting upright, they
chewed away bark in a belt, eating of it now and then from their paws.
Down to bare wood, they gnawed away until the tree was ready to fall.
Often it fell into water where it would make a stout beginning for a
dam. Working in concert they brought from near-by woods bundles of
stick and bush and starting out from the bank began to shore up their
barrier. They dived to the bottom of the water and brought up loads
of mud. This was plaster. With their broad tails they trowelled mud

over the laid timbers, layer upon layer, always extending the reach of
the dam until it touched the opposite limit of the course or cove where
they worked. At times they paused to play, racing each other in the
water, diving, and loudly slapping the water with their tails.

When house and dam were finished, it was time to lay up provisions within against winter when there would be no green sprouts of
willow and cottonwood and fresh grass to eat in season. The beaver clan
went foraging, often far inland from their water, in search of bark. The
best bark was on the smaller branches high out of reach. The beavers
brought down the tree, and then stripped the tender young bark off the
branches laid low. They cut the bark into three-foot strips, pulled them
to their water, and there floated them to the lodge. They made little signs
to guide them as they went—mounds of twig and earth which they im-
pregnated with castorum, a musk secreted by the animal itself, that
attracted their sense of smell and reassuringly meant *beaver* and told
them where the road lay. Once in the lodge and eating, they were neat
and fastidious. They took out through the water doorway all the refuse
of a meal and threw it into the current. Drifting away, it lodged down-
current out of their way—bits of gnawed stick and knotty branch and
hard root.

In the spring came the young. Leaving the mother during gesta-
tion, the male went travelling, often far away to other water, where
he swam and frolicked, ate tender greens at the bank, and did not return
home until the offspring were born. Then he took them in charge,
trained them in work, and in the late summer led them out to forage
before the sharp frosts and the thickening of their fur against the cold.
Everywhere in the secret lakes and along the tributaries and in the
quieter passages of the main river this lively cycle was continued by
beavers in incalculable thousands, and wherever mountain and water
met, evidences of it were scattered and lodged undisturbed—until the
last Spanish and the first Mexican years of the Rio Grande.

For by then the beaver's fur was in great demand for the making
of men's hats. The hatters of London and Paris, New York, Boston and
Philadelphia consumed great cargoes of beaver pelt, and the fur trade
moved westward out of St. Louis over the American continent to Astoria
and the northern Rockies. While Stephen Austin was completing his
organized arrangements with the new government of Mexico to bring
new settlers from the east nearer to the lower Rio Grande, the river's
upper reaches knew another sort of growing infiltration by men who
whether they came alone, or with a few companions, or many, still came

without formal approval by the Mexican government, and with no resounding program of colonial loyalty or pious hope.

They came to take beaver in the mountain waters, in spring and autumn up north, or all through the winter in New Mexico if the season was mild. Many of them were French Canadians; the rest were from anywhere in the United States, though mostly from the frontier settlements. They outfitted themselves at St. Louis, and remembering what was commonly known out of Pike's reports, crossed the plains and entered the mountains by the hundreds in the 1820s. Among their number were men who made the first trails beyond the prairies, that led overland so early as 1826, to the Pacific. Jedediah Smith, Charles Beaubien, the Roubidoux brothers, Céran St. Vrain, Bill Williams, the youthful runaway Kit Carson for whose return a reward of one cent was posted by the employer to whom he was apprenticed—such men went to the mountains after beaver skins to sell for a few dollars a pound, and all unwitting showed the way across the continent.

The movement had already had its pioneer in James Pursley, the Kentuckian, who had been detained at Santa Fe in 1805 under the Spanish governor. Others entering New Mexico from the plains were arrested, to be marched down the Rio Grande to El Paso and the prisons of Chihuahua in 1812, after confiscation of their goods, and were not released until the freeing of Mexico in 1821. Another party of trappers were taken by the provincial Spanish government in 1817, jailed in irons for forty-eight days at Santa Fe, and were finally released after being stripped of thirty thousand dollars' worth of furs and supplies. Such actions by the government were meant to protect the trapping industry already worked on a small scale by the Mexicans of the valley. Regulations declared that only permanent residents might hunt beaver. They were required to buy a hunting license, their number in any party was carefully fixed and recorded, and so were the length of time to be spent in the hunt and the weapons to be used—traps, firearms, or snares. If the early American trappers could not buy official licenses, they soon found a way to get around the law. "The North Americans began to corrupt the New Mexicans," noted a Santa Fe lawyer, "by purchasing their licenses from them," and so risked arrest.

But still the trappers came, and against other hazards. The greatest of these were the roving Indians on the prairies and the eastern upsweeps of the Rocky Mountains. For an Indian hunter could read the menace that came with the white hunter; and he moved with every savagery to defend his hunting grounds. The trapper retaliated. He fought the Indian with Indian ways, and took scalps, and burned tepee villages, and abducted women, and pressed westward. He fought distance, hunger, and thirst, and if he was unwary enough to be bitten by a rattlesnake, he cauterized the wound by burning a thick pinch of gunpowder in it. Once in the mountains he met his second greatest adversary in great numbers. This was the great grizzly bear, who was curious, fearless and gifted with a massive ursine intelligence. With lumbering speed the grizzlies could travel forty miles between dawn and dark through mountains. It was not unusual for trappers to kill five or six in a day, or to see fifty or sixty, and one hunter declared that one day he saw two hundred and twenty of them. The grizzly towered above a man. His forepaws were eight or nine inches wide, and his claws six inches long. He weighed from fifteen-to-eighteen hundred pounds. His embrace was certain death. So steadily did he smell and find the trappers that in a few decades by their guns his kind was made almost extinct.

The earthen village of Ranchos de Taos near the Rio Grande was the northern town nearest the beaver waters of the mountains, and there came the mountain men to organize their supplies for the trapping seasons. They found that some men of the Ranchos de Taos already, though to a limited degree, followed the trapper's life. Seeing how swarthy they were, the newcomers thought they must be of mixed Negro and Indian blood. It was astonishing how primitive were the ways of life in Taos—the farmers used only oxen in cultivating their fields, and a miserable plow made of a Y-shaped branch from a tree, with an iron head to its end that turned the earth. Hoes, axes and other tools were all old-fashioned. There were no sawmills; no mechanical ingenuities to speed up work; and—what was oddest to the squinting and raring trappers from the East—the people seemed to have no desire for such means to change their slow, simple ways.

The mountain men encountered at Taos their first experience of the Mexican government. Taos was the seat of the northernmost customs house of Mexico. As the trappers brought little to declare in goods for sale, they were evidently allowed to go about their preparations for departure into the mountains. They bought what flour and produce they could, and recruited an occasional Taoseño to join their parties, and made ready their equipment. In the far northern Rockies the trapping parties were often large, numbering from fifty to a hundred men. Most of these were camp personnel who maintained a base for the trappers and hunters who went forward into the wilderness. The "Frenchmen" from Canada sometimes kept Indian wives, and estab-

464 Book Three: The Mexican Rio Grande

lished in the mountains a semipermanent household with rude domestic amenities. Other parties were smaller, and instead of working for the great fur companies as contract employees, went their ways alone, as "free" trappers. Those who descended to the Rio Grande's northern reaches were more often than not in small units of a dozen, or three or four, or even a single man, who meant to take their furs and sell them to the highest bidder at the season's end. But all the trappers shared aspects of costume, equipment and even character, many of which grew from the tradition of the forest frontiersman of the late eighteenth century.

The mountain man was almost Indian-colored from exposure to the weather. His hair hung upon his shoulders. He was bearded. Next to his skin he wore a red flannel loincloth. His outer clothes were of buckskin, fringed at all the seams. The jacket sometimes reached to the knee over tight, wrinkled leggings. His feet were covered by moccasins made of deer or buffalo leather. Around his waist was a leather belt into which he thrust his flintlock pistols, his knife for skinning or scalping, and his shingling hatchet. Over one shoulder hung his bullet pouch, and over the other his powder horn. To their baldrics were attached his bullet mould, ball screw, wiper and an awl for working leather. When he moved he shimmered with fringe and rang and clacked with accoutrements of metal and wood. The most important of these were his traps, of which he carried five or six, and his firearm with its slender separate crutch of hardwood. It was always a rifle—never a shotgun, which he scorned as an effete fowling piece. Made in the gun works of the brothers Jacob and Samuel Hawken, of St. Louis, the rifle had two locks for which he kept about him a hundred flints, twenty-five pounds of powder and several pounds of lead. The barrel, thirty-six inches long, was made by hand of soft iron. The recoil of its blast shocked into a hardwood stock beautifully turned and slender. Peering vividly out from under his low-crowned hat of rough wool, he was an American original, as hard as the hardest thing that could happen to him.

Alone, or with a companion or a small party, he packed his supplies on two horses and, riding a third, left Taos for the mountains in the autumn. He was wary of roaming Indians, dangerous animals— and other trapper parties. For nobody could stake a claim on hunting country, and every trapper party competed against every other. He did his best to keep his movement and direction secret, to throw others off the trail, and find the wildest country where he would be most free from rivalry. Following the groins of the foothills, the mountain men came

among high slopes and rocky screens. If two worked as a pair, they
sought for a concealed place where they could make camp and tether
their horses, near beaver water. There they built a shelter, and if their
goal was a mountain lake, or a slow passage of stream, they set to work
hacking out a cottonwood canoe. In natural forest paths they looked for
the little musky mounds that marked beaver trails. They searched
currents for the drift of gnawed beaver sticks. Every such sign took them
closer to their prey. When they were sure they had found its little world,
at evening under the pure suspended light of mountain skies they
silently coasted along the shores of quiet water to set their traps.

They laid each trap two or three inches underwater on the slope
of the shore, and, a little removed, they fixed a pole in deep mud and
chained the trap to it. They stripped a twig of its bark and dipped one
end into a supply of castorum, the beaver's own secretion that would
be his bait. They fastened the twig between the open jaws of the trap
leaving the musky end four inches above water. The beaver in the nighttime was drawn to it by scent. He raised his muzzle to inhale, his hind
quarters went lower in the water, and the trap seized him. He threw
himself into deeper water; but the trap held him, and the pole held the
trap, and presently he sank to drown. In the high, still daybreak, the
trappers coasted by their traps again in the canoe, and took up their
catch.

Working a rocky stream from the bank the trappers lodged the
trap and its chained pole in the current, where the beaver found the
scent. In his struggles he might drag the trap and pole to the shore,
where his burden became entangled in "thickets of brook willows," and
held him till found. Sometimes he struggled to deeper midstream water,
where the pole floated as a marker; and then the trappers putting off
their buckskins that if saturated would dry slowly and then be hard as
wood, went naked and shivering into the cold mountain stream to swim
for their take. And some parties rafted down the whole length of the
river in New Mexico, all the way to El Paso. Their method astonished
the New Mexicans, to whom it seemed suspect because it was new. Was
it proper to use a new kind of trap, and float noiselessly to a beaver site
taking their catch by surprise, and spend the night in midstream with
the raft moored to trees on each bank to be out of the reach of wild
animals? And at the end of the journey, to sell the timbers of the raft
for a good price at El Paso where wood was so scarce, take up the catch
and vanish overland eastward without reporting to the government? The
New Mexicans frowned at such ingenuity, energy and novelty.

When in the mountains they had exhausted a beaver site the trappers moved on to another. With their traps over their shoulders they forded streams amidst floating ice; or with their traps hanging down their backs, they scaled and descended the hard ridges between water-courses where the harder the country the better the chance that no others had come there before them. The trap weighed about five pounds, and its chain was about five feet long. A full-grown beaver weighed between thirty and forty pounds. The catch was an awkward burden to carry back to camp for skinning. Removing the pelt from the animal, the trappers stretched it on a frame of sprung willow withes to dry. The flesh they cooked by hanging it before a fire from a thong. The carcass turned by its own weight, roasting evenly. The broad, flat tail they liked best of all. They cut it off, skinned it, toasted it at the end of a stick, and ate it with relish, as a relief from the usual hunter's diet of deer, elk, antelope, bear, lynx, or buffalo meat, or buffalo marrowbones, or buffalo blood drunk spurting and warm from the throat of a newly killed specimen.

All through the winter-fast months the mountain men worked, obedient to animal laws and themselves almost animal in their isolation, freedom and harmony with the wilderness. Their peltries were cached and the piles grew, in the end to be baled with rawhide thongs. A trapper took in a good season about four hundred pounds of beaver skins. Sometimes his cache was invaded and destroyed by prowling animals, or stolen by mountain Indians; and then his months of hard-ship went for nothing. But if he kept his pile, he was ready to come out of the boxed mountains whose cool winds brushing all day over high-tilted meadows carried the scent of wild flowers down the open slopes where he descended with his haul. At five dollars a pound it would bring him two thousand dollars in the market.

But once again in Taos, he might then meet trouble with the Mexican authorities. Now that he had his cargo, they showed an interest in him. If he was unlucky, they questioned him, examined his bales, and invoking regulations that nobody mentioned when he started out months before, confiscated his whole catch. If he resisted he was taken to Santa Fe and jailed, with official talk about the Mexican decree of 1824 that prohibited trapping by foreigners in Mexican territory. Since there were no public warehouses hunters could only store their catches in towns by making deals with local citizens for storage space on private premises. If a Mexican citizen gave protection to a foreign trapper he was in danger from his own government. At Peña Blanca on the Rio

Grande in 1827 one Luís María Cabeza de Vaca hid in his house the "contraband" of beaver skins left there for safe keeping by a trapper named Young. From Santa Fe a corporal and eight soldiers of the presidial company came to seize it. Cabeza de Vaca resisted them, firing upon them in protection of his home. The soldiers returned the fire and killed him. The official report of the affair stated that "the deceased died while defending a violation of the . . . rights of the Nation," and asked exoneration for the corporal and his squad.

But local officials might be bribed, and a license trumped up, and the catch restored to the trapper. In any case, after his mountain months, he was ready to burst his bonds of solitude, and he did so with raw delight. All his general passion and violence that his mountain work required him to suppress while moving lithe and crafty after watchful creatures he now broke free in the clay village where he returned among men and women. He had a frosty look of filth over him. His hair was knotted and his beard was a catch-all for the refuse of months. His clothes reeked like his body. His mouth was dry with one kind of thirst and his flesh on fire with another. If the one tavern in the town was full, he went to a house and asked for a corner of the packed mud floor where he could throw his gear, and was granted it. The family knew what he came to seek with his comrades. The women took kettles out of doors and built fires around them to heat water. When it was hot they brought it in, and found him waiting in his crusted skin sitting in a wooden tub. The women poured the water over him. He thrashed. He was as hairy as an animal and as unmindedly lustful. The water hit him and he gave the recognized cry of the mountain man—"Wagh!"—a grunt, a warning, and a boast. Bathing as violently as he did all other acts, he began again to know forgotten satisfactions. As he emerged with wet light running on his skin, white everywhere but on face and hands whose weather would not wash off, he was a new man.

The whiskey of Taos—they called it "lightning"—now warmed him within. He drank until he had fire under his scowl. The women did what they could to improve his clothes. He rattled his money and they made him a supper that burned him inside with chilis and spices. Early in the evening he stamped his way to the tavern in the plaza where a fandango was about to start. All benches and tables were pushed back against the walls of the large room. Tin lanterns pierced with little nail holes in a design hung from the raw beams of the ceiling. Two fiddlers, a guitarist and a flutist began to make up the music together. They played popular ballads—the same ones that at slower tempos also served

for accompaniments to the Mass and to processions. As the crowd grew
the room was hazed with blue cigarette smoke from the mouths of men
and women alike. The women were powdered till their faces looked
pale lavender. They clustered together at one side of the room. From
the other the men came and took them somewhat as cocks took hens—a
dusty pounce met by a bridling glare, and then an impassive harmony
between the sexes suggesting absent-minded enjoyment. Lacking milled
lumber the floor was a hard and polished cake of earth. The couples
moved with expressionless faces—all but the mountain man. In his face
there glared a starved animation. His heels made muffled thunder on
the ground. The Mexican dances were set pieces, with evolutions and
patterns. He did not heed them. He threw himself in baleful joy through
whatever movements occurred to him, "Wagh!" The lightning jug went
around. The music scratched and squealed. The windows of the tavern
hall were like lanterns in the pure darkness below Taos Mountain.
When the fandango was over, all went home. The mountain man took
a woman from the ball to her house. At rut like a big, fanged mountain
cat—"Wa-a-a-g-h!"—he spent the night with her to nobody's surprise or
censure; and, as one such man said, he had no reason afterward to bring
"charges of severity" against her.

Presently he travelled to a trading post on the prairies, or to St.
Louis, to sell his catch. In the frontier cities of the United States he
was a prodigal spender, uneasy in their relatively ordered society, loose
as it was compared to life in older and more easterly places. When the
season rolled around again, he was off again to his lost lakes and rivers
where obscurely content he felt most like the self he imagined until it
came true.

For over three decades the trapping trade flourished. At its height
the annual shipment of beaver skins from Abiquiu on the Chama and
Taos on the Rio Grande was worth two hundred thousand dollars. But
in the 1830s the market for beaver began to break, for the China trade
out of England and New England was growing, and the clipper ships
were bringing silk in great quantities to the manufacturing cities of the
world. Fashion changed. Silk was offered for hats instead of fur; and
the change brought the decline and finally the almost virtual abolishment of the Rocky Mountain fur trade. The trapper was cast adrift to
find new work. He could abide it only in the land of his hardy prowess,
and there he found it, whether he joined the overland commercial caravans as a wagon hand, or the American Army's later surveying expeditions as a guide, or amazingly settled on river land as a farmer. He knew

the craft of the wilderness and he made its first trails for the westering white man. Some of the earliest venturers in the Mexico trade were trappers; and as the trade continued to grow and establish its bases ever farther west, the trappers met it with their wares; and what had been a memorized path became a visible road; and along it moved another of the unofficial invasions of the Mexican Rio Grande that could only end by changing nations. The first sustained effort toward that end was made by the individual trapper. His greatest power to achieve it lay in his individualism. Where the Mexican was hedged by governmental authority, the trapper made his own. Where the Mexican was formal, he was wild. Where the one was indolent, the other was consumed by a fanatical driving impulse. The invasion, unorganized as it was, commercial in purpose, wild and free in its individuals, seemed to express some secret personal motive beyond the material. The trappers forecast a new, a wild, strain of human society to come to the northern river.

3.

The Twin Sisters

Stephen Austin, after three hundred and fifty-five days in Mexico, left for Texas on April 18, 1823, having "determined to fulfill rigidly all the duties and obligations of a Mexican citizen." But these he saw as a nineteenth century rationalist, not as a Mexican. Nothing could better illustrate the difference than the subject of religion. One of the conditions of obtaining his grant imposed upon Austin the preservation of Roman Catholicism as the official religion of the colony, as it was of all Mexico. All colonists were to be "Roman Apostolic Catholics." Having ostensibly bowed to this requirement in order to obtain his charter, Austin's real views of the matter stung his thoughts as he travelled homeward. Finally at Monterey, his spite could no longer be contained. In a letter from there he wrote of the clergy—the "Fryers"—that they were "miserable drones" and "the enemies of liberty." His bias turned toward the Mexicans. "There never was a people so dreadfully priestridden and enslaved by superstition and fanaticism as the great part of this nation. The clergy literally [sic] suck the blood of the unfortunate people. . . ." And in another letter he poured out contempt upon his new countrymen to whom he had sworn to be loyal: ". . . to be candid the majority of the people of the whole nation as far as I have seen them want nothing but tails to be more brutes than the Apes. . . . but keep this to yourself, it wont do to tell them so—thank God there are no fryars near the Colorado and if they come there to distress me I shall hang them to a certainty. . . ."

As these were bigoted sentiments, he concealed them under the better part of valor when he arrived at Matamoros on the Rio Grande. He showed his grants to the local authorities, who did not question them, and went on his way to the colony. Once home, he addressed his colonists, and after assuring them that his mission to Mexico had been entirely successful, and that "the titles to your land is indisputable . . . perfect and complete for ever, and each settler may sell his land the same as he could do in the United States," he touched upon the subject that so inflamed his private letters. "I wish," he stated, now for publication, "I wish the settlers to remember that the Roman Catholic is the religion of this nation . . . we must all be particular on this subject and respect the Catholic religion with all that attention due to its sacredness and to the laws of the Church. . . ."

Was this conflict of views, private and public, to be taken as a sign of cynical expediency, of vulgar contempt for the other party to a bargain, whom it was proper in mean selfishness to outwit at any cost, including honor? There was nothing to indicate that any of the settlers were, or became, Catholics; and later advertisements in the East calling for additional emigrants to Texas failed to set forth plainly the full conditions of the Mexican law in respect to the religious requirement. From the beginning, the equivocal attitude of the settlers toward their hosts foreboded much for the future ownership and character of Texas. Austin was empowered to establish and administer his own civil government, pending final extension of the Mexican authority over the northeastern provinces. When this came, with San Antonio de Béxar confirmed as the provincial seat and a Mexican administrator established there, government in Texas took form in the odd mixed image of remembered Spain, Mexico, New England and the prairie frontier. It was a mixture among whose strains conflict was ordained from the beginning; for government could only be the expression of human character in the aggregate, and where that character arose from hopelessly different traditions, one must eventually triumph, by whatever means, until conflict should give way to peace under the stronger. The individualism of the trapper in the north had its counterpart on the great empty littoral of Mexico Bay at the river's end.

News of the work of the Mexican congress came slowly to the lower Rio Grande towns; they were hardly more in the stream of things in 1823 than when they were founded by the Count of Sierra Gorda in the 1750s. The river frontier was still thought of at times by the official mind as a place of exile. Far upstream, near Ojinaga, a penal colony called Vado Piedra—Rocky Ford—was established. It was peopled by criminals in a Condemned Regiment. Under a soldiery hardly superior to themselves in record and type, they guarded the cattle and horse plains of northern Chihuahua against raiding Apaches and Comanches, and worked the prison farms with water from the river, and marched by armed guards went out in hunting parties to take game in the empty plain of San Esteban north of the river. On one such hunt they found a herd of buffalo and looked forward to a supply of good fresh meat. They made the surround, the drive began, and the slaughter followed. Busy at the jobs of skinning and butchering their supply, they did not know what watched them from the hills that bounded the plain. It was a band of Comanches, who when the meat was ready flowed at full gallop down upon the Mexicans, killed them, scalped them, and made off with the supply. Such an episode was but one of countless examples of how the central government was without power, resources, or even imagination, to protect its far marches. In the summer of 1823, a group of northwestern provinces moved to acquire statehood for themselves, under the federal system even then coming to pass under debate in the Mexican congress.

Coahuila, Nuevo León, Tamaulipas and Texas sent delegates to Monterrey to draw up their claims and argue their cases for local government under the federal union. They hoped to reproduce the autonomous system of the United States. A measure of the autonomy enjoyed by the States was indicated in the general American usage of the plural verb in state papers and correspondence with reference to the several states. "The United States are," they said, over and over again—never "the United States is." The concept of the sovereign state dwelling in harmony with her sister states, but with proud local rights, internal powers and traditional if young privileges, was the chief element in the

design of federal union. It was a design that was to meet an early test
in relations between Texas and Mexico, and Mexico and the United
States.

The Mexican congress adopted the federal system; and in January,
1824, the northern states were granted what they asked for, with Nuevo
León, Texas and Coahuila as one vast state. The constitution provided
that each of the three units might petition for separate statehood if its
condition appeared to justify further separate incorporation. In May
Nuevo León was divided from the others under its own state government,
leaving Texas and Coahuila under a common governor. A precedent
had been established, and almost from the first the "Twin Sisters," as
Texas and Coahuila were called, listened to talk of their own separation,
and people wondered where the dividing line between them lay. Was
it the Mesina River? The Nueces? Or was the clumsy make-up of the
state separated naturally by the Rio Grande that so often before was
claimed as a boundary between nations? Saltillo was the capital of the
Twin Sisters. Much travel was required between Texas and Coahuila
on the state's business. The arrangement was awkward. Certain Texas
officers even found it hard to spell the name of their commonwealth. On
a legal paper offered in Texas court, it was given as "State of Cowehey
and Taxus." If the unembarrassed phonetics of the frontier owed something to illiteracy—for few of the Texan settlers, by the evidence of their
papers, had more than the simplest schooling—there seemed to be also a
touch of exasperation with the outlandish words and names with which
the Mexicans affronted their new citizens from the American prairies.
Again much explosive power lay buried under primitive attitudes.

And certain self-protective acts of the Mexican government were
ominous for the colony above the Rio Grande. In 1824, Mexico was
troubled with sectional uprisings and gatherings that threatened the
authority of the new government. A decree was published by the Congress forbidding assemblies or juntas of citizens. What sort of republic
was this that denied its people the right of free assembly? It was—whatever the current phrase would have been—un-American. But the point
was, it was not un-Mexican, and the new Texans did not grasp the fact.
It was more easily understood and accepted in the Rio Grande towns—
the same Mexican towns where the Gutierrez de Laras had lighted the
brands of revolt for Hidalgo—and life along the river continued to turn
itself to older interests and dangers. In 1824 a mission of the Oblate
Fathers established a chapel on the north bank across from Reynosa,
where the missioners set out in their cloister a grove of orange trees that

flourished prophetically, the first citrus plantation in the lower river
meadows. And a few months later word went to Texas from across the
river that Comanches were on the rampage, stealing horses and mules,
killing soldiery, and committing "excesses against some poor women"
who were alone on a ranch far removed from the last upriver fort of
Saint John Baptist.

4.

Last Return

At the Mexican east coast port of Soto la Marina on July 17,
1824, the British ship *Spring* put in with passengers whose arrival created
excitement, and brought swift action by the government. The passengers
were the ex-Emperor Agustín I, his wife, and their two youngest children.
After thirteen months of exile, Don Agustín was ready to resume his
throne. On board the *Spring* was a printing press that had been turning
out manifestoes during the Atlantic crossing. In the ship's hold were guns
and munitions, and in the personal hampers of the travellers were the
imperial state robes. "My return," recorded the exile, "has been solicited
by different parts of the country, which considers me necessary to the
establishment of unanimity there and to consolidation of the government." He also feared that Ferdinand VII of Spain, supported by the
Holy Alliance, intended to reconquer Mexico. The months in Europe
had been unsatisfactory. The College of Cardinals had denied him permission to settle in Rome. In England, where he had gone to place the
ex-Crown Prince in school, Don Agustín had conferred with San Martín,
the liberator of Peru, who was skeptical of an imperial return to Mexico.
It seemed to him, he said drily, that the Mexicans "had made known their
opinion when they banished" Iturbide. To this Iturbide replied, "This
exile was a work of violence, and the wish of only four persons. . . ." He
proceeded with his intrigues. He was watched. A Dominican friar who

followed him to Europe reported his movements to the Mexican government; and by the time he was ready to return, they were ready for him. The Congress had passed a decree denouncing him as a traitor if he should ever again appear on Mexican soil, and a sentence of death lay over him and all Mexicans who might in any way assist him.

Leaving his wife and children on the *Spring*, Iturbide landed from a small boat, and was immediately arrested by General Garza. The legislature of Tamaulipas was sitting at the time, and he was taken before it. The presiding officer was a famous priest who in his own time had preached the revolution of Hidalgo along the Rio Grande. It was Father José Antonio Gutierrez de Lara. He permitted Iturbide to speak to the legislators, who immediately voted under the Congressional decree to carry out the death sentence on the designated traitor. Father Gutierrez de Lara served not only as judge but also as confessor. He heard Iturbide's confession three times, and on July nineteenth, the rifle squad came, and took the prisoner away, and shot him to death under an act of Congress of which he had not heard until his return. On the twentieth, burial was held in the cemetery of the parish church of Padilla. Accompanied by her children, Doña Ana María was disembarked and her future discussed. In the end, on the pension of 8,000 pesos guaranteed to the Emperor's widow, she agreed to live out of Mexico, and left for Philadelphia to spend the rest of her days.

5.

The Spark

In March, 1825, another and more abiding threat to Mexico from without her boundaries made talk. A citizen wrote to Stephen Austin from the States concerning the outcome of the recent presidential election. "Mr. John Q. Adams had been Duly Elected . . . thare is great hopes of the United States becoming Peaceable possession of the

Province of Texas as far as the Rio Grande. . . ." Texas suddenly took on new promise for the North Americans. A father in New Orleans advised "his son to not sell his land claims in Texas," for the talk in New Orleans was that "our Minister to Mexico is about to conclude a Trety with the Mexican Republic for the Province of Texas—the Rio grande to be the line between the two governments. . . ." The writer ended by asking Austin to reserve him some good land on the Brazos or the Colorado. It was a sudden revival of Henry Clay's old demand for Texas all the way to the river, and now it was pressed by John Quincy Adams, who had opposed it during the debates of 1819 on the Florida Treaty.

There was more than frontier rumor to the report that the United States hankered after Texas and the Rio Grande. It seemed expedient to examine again, this time with Mexico instead of Spain, the terms of the Florida Treaty that had defined the Sabine as the western limits of Louisiana. United States policy desired to see the whole eastern drainage of the Rocky Mountains above the Rio Grande as American territory. Mexico would be asked to redefine the northeastern limits of her country. Discussions would take place in Mexico between the government and Mr. Joel Poinsett, the United States minister, who was empowered to offer certain reassurances such as a guarantee that in territory newly ceded by Mexico the States would provide measures to overcome the Comanche warfare that harassed the Rio Grande provinces. But rumors were not only current in Louisiana—they swept through Mexico; and the very suggestion by itself that the United States wanted to discuss boundaries, after she had in 1819 renounced forever "all rights, claims and pretensions" to Texas and the Rio Grande, created an atmosphere in which Poinsett found it difficult even to raise the question. For the time being he let it lie, and so did Mexico, while in Texas the colony toiled away in hardship and remoteness at the job of establishing a fragment of the only life they knew—that of the United States—under the Mexican flag.

Eighteen twenty-five was a wet year along the lower river. Commercial and official communications between the colony and the state capital at Saltillo were more difficult than usual. From Reynosa a colonist wrote to Austin, "All the water courses are up so that mules with Cargo cannot proceed . . . there has been a great deal of Rain in this Country . . . the Rio Grande is very high. . . ." Another wrote later, from Camargo, ". . . from what I can learn there are a grate many goods in this part of the Country,—the Indians are still doing Mischief . . . they Stole forty Horses from here a few days before we arrived here." He added a warning that a certain Nixon, also a colonist, was busying himself up and down the river in efforts to do harm to Austin, "writing against" him to the Mexican government. "My nearves," concluded the uprooted American, "are very weeke."

Such news was only an added discouragement to Austin in his labors, and at times he broke out in his letters with bitter denunciations of those whom he led, and gloomy predictions for the future. "You always," wrote his brother James to him, "you always put the worst construction on things and thereby render yourself fretful and melancholy." But colonial stresses were continuous, both from within and without. A Choctaw informant alarmed Austin in 1826 with word that "Comanches are going to make a grand effort, next Fall, against Bexar and the Rio Grande frontier," and he forwarded the warning to Saucedo, the Mexican administrator at San Antonio. The remorseless Nixon persisted in his defamations, even though a Mexican friend assured Austin that his protestations were "falso y falsisimo." But every whisper of ill will only increased the mistrust with which the central government viewed affairs above the river, and in December, 1826, a crisis came.

It arose between the Mexican government and the settlement made near Nacogdoches by American immigrants under Benjamin Edwards, who had obtained a Mexican grant after Austin had received his own. The two colonies were far apart, but, in the scale of Texan distances, they were still neighbors, and both groups of newcomers were American. The trouble was that Edwards and his followers settled on lands already occupied by a scattering of Mexicans. From the first, there were two factions—one American, one Mexican, in outlook and sympathy—in the Edwards colony. Disagreements were frequent and bitter. The local alcalde, Samuel Norris, favored the Mexican population, and upheld the Mexican claims to previous land grants. American settlers saw their hard work of establishment about to go for nothing. Mexicans seized their property, had them arrested on false charges, jailed and fined. Edwards appealed to Austin for advice on how to proceed. Austin counseled him to write Governor Blanco, at Saltillo, setting forth his complaints, and appealing for justice. This he did in September.

A few weeks later came the governor's reply. It annulled Edwards's contract, and expelled him from Mexican territory, even if he desired to appeal his case to the central government in Mexico City. It was too much for the settlers to accept. Edwards proclaimed freedom in a series of fiery broadsides and letters, alluding to the ills suffered by his followers. "Our properties daily seized by violence and injustice, our persons violated, our liberties trampled underfoot, and ourselves the destined and immediate victims of Spanish or Mexican bayonets; we have sprung to arms for our safety" from the works of "this imbecile, this faithless and perfidious government. Great God!" he cried, "can you any longer hesitate, fellow citizens, what to do?" He announced the founding of Fredonia, a new republic, and he called for aid from the United States, from Austin and his colonies, and from a coalition of Indian tribes. Of all these, only the Indians responded. "Twenty-three Nations of Indians," he announced, "exclusive of the Comanches, are now sacredly *pledged* to aid us in our *Independence—*". The price was great, and it was promised on a basis of no real authority. The Indians were to be given ownership of a vast area of the prairies, for Edwards had designated "a line North of this, running westwardly to the Rio Grande; securing all individual rights within their territory" to the Indians.

Austin saw it all with regret. He had worked hard enough to convince the Mexican government that he and his people intended to be loyal and were in fact so. He saw the Fredonians as the "Nacogdoches madmen," and he could only believe that they were inviting Indians to rise and sweep the frontiers with a reign of terror. Far from helping the Edwards movement, Austin called his militia to arms, and proclaimed that one hundred of his men would march to support the government against Nacogdoches. "I know nothing," he wrote icily to a correspondent in East Texas, "I know nothing positive as to the particular acts of oppression or injustice which you complain of against the local authorities of Nacogdoches. If report is to be believed you have cause to complain against the local authorities, but my Dr Sir the local authorities of Nacogdoches is not the whole Govt. What would you say in the U. S. if a party were to rebel against the Govt. because a Justice of the peace, had done wrong—"

Within a month Fredonia collapsed. The Mexican army sent troops. Austin's colony abided firmly loyal to their Mexican allegiance. Austin was commended by the government for his stand. New settlers entered East Texas to replace those cast out with Edwards. The Indian coalition was broken up, and the "twenty-three Nations" once more agreed to subsist under Mexican rule. The crisis was over; but a demonstration had been made of how difficult it was to hold together in peace two opposing national temperaments; and once again the cry of "to the Rio Grande" had been raised by men from the United States. It had hardly subsided when from a higher quarter the general idea was raised

again, for later in 1827, Henry Clay as Secretary of State authorized
Poinsett to offer Mexico $1,000,000 if she would permit the extension of
the North American boundary to the Rio Grande. Poinsett, in the prevailing atmosphere in Mexico City, did not submit the offer. But its
terms were known even in the colony, and J. E. B. Austin wrote to his
sister that if the United States were to buy Texas, the family "would
not take less than $500,000" for their "interest in the Country. . . ." in
any settlement by the United States of individual claims following such
a purchase.

On a more personal level, relations were at times touch and go.
A colonist travelling through Matamoros wrote back to the Brazos: "We
remain as usual with now and then a little difficulty, as hapened at
a Ball the other evening, but since we have had fine dancing. . . . You
know I am not in favor Spanish (except the Women of this Country
they do verry well when that is said all is said) for the men are the
damdest rascals in the world. . . . We had a frolick on the 8 January and
got a little foxy."

Mexicans in their turn had their own views. In 1828 a certain
José María Sánchez saw the Austin settlement. It was a scattered little
town of about two thousand people, and its forms were new in Texas.
The Rio Grande frontier had towns built of earth and rock, tinted
plaster, and rocky streets laid out at right angles to a square central
plaza dominated by a church. They were towns that rose from the river
landscape like parts of it. At San Felipe de Austin on the Brazos, Sánchez
saw forty or fifty little wooden houses. They were built in the image of
the forest and cabin life of the North American frontier, out of logs
interlocked at the corners, and chinked with mud plaster. Rock chimneys
rose at the end of each house. Many houses had only one room. Those
that had two displayed a new mannerism of the American forest primitive style, for the two rooms were separated by an open breezeway under
the same roof that covered the rooms. Such a dwelling was called a
dog-run house. Later it would know modifications in rock construction
and stucco, and remain characteristic of Texas living. Austin's own
bachelor quarters were of this design. Sánchez remarked "two wretched
little stores" where the settlers bought their goods. One sold "only
whiskey, rum, sugar, and coffee; the other rice, flour, lard and cheap
cloth." There was no coherent plan to the village. The houses lay scattered at random on the low rolling land. Sánchez observed Austin at his
labors, and learned something of the views and temperaments of the
colonists. He shook his head over the whole spectacle, and wrote that

Austin "in all his action, has, as one may say, lulled the authorities into a sense of security, while he works diligently for his own ends." There was something in the air, and Sánchez felt it. "In my judgment," he concluded, "the spark that will start the conflagration that will deprive us of Texas, will start from this colony."

What was it that promised such trouble? Was it the energetic impatience of the Americans? They were accustomed to acting for themselves. They did not wait, anywhere, for central authority to justify them in what they sought and how they sought it. When men came together on the frontier to make a common life, they *were* the government, at once, and energetically. The colony saw only its own wants and problems. Austin could not help feeling exasperation at the miserable, poor, confused doings of the Mexicans. The Mexican government, he told a distinguished American who was considering a move to Texas—it was Commodore David Porter—"may easily make Texas a very flourishing and advantageous member of the confederation   it is now a dead weight —Texas once settled and the whole of the frontier of the Rio Grande from New Mexico to Matamoros would be effectually protected from the indians which would be an incalcutable advantage. . . ."

But if he and his work suffered by the very remoteness of Texas from the heart of government, he was unable to comprehend the furies that swept through Mexico periodically. In the eight years since gaining independence from Spain, Mexico knew three revolutions and a shuttling of presidents by force of arms, from old General Guadalupe Victoria, the first—"one of Plutarch's Romans," as he was gloriously called in the usual elation that swept new officers into the Moncada Palace— to General Guerrero, while Santa Anna alternated between discreet obscurity on his ranch and armed uprisings in the posture of a hero. And in the summer of 1829, as Texas struggled to establish laws, and justify her growing sentiment for separate statehood, and resist discriminatory customs regulations at Mexican ports of entry, Mexico faced a preposterous threat from over the Atlantic.

For Ferdinand VII, bearing out the dead Iturbide's prediction, undertook to reconquer Mexico with thirty-five hundred troops who were embarked from Havana in July. It was the year's worst season in Mexico Bay, with hurricanes and rain. If Cortés had managed with fewer invaders, he did not have seven millions of inhabitants to face who could meet him with his own weapons. The Spanish fleet steered clear of San Juan de Ulloa and Veracruz. Instead, the miserable army was put ashore at Tampico, after which the ships sailed away for Cuba. The incredible monarch at Madrid was confident that once in Mexico, his forces would be met with legions of Mexicans who eager to throw off the disorders of self-government would spring loyally to the Crown and help put down the upstart republic overnight. The royal calculations were inexact. Seizing the opportunity for one of his emergences, Santa Anna rallied troops about him without help from the republican government and led the campaign against the Spaniards, who without reinforcement or support, and riddled by fever, surrendered to him on September 11, 1829. The invasion was over. Fewer than two thousand Spaniards survived to be shipped back to Cuba. Santa Anna was a national hero. Biding his time, he modestly retired to the country, and a few weeks later a revolution broke out in army garrisons in Yucatán and elsewhere, and the national government was overthrown. The new president was Anastasio Bustamante who after attending to the spoils of victory looked north to the colonies with new plans.

During that same summer the coastwise shipping of the gulf, plying between New Orleans and the Mexican east coast ports, put in and out of the anchorage at the mouth of the Rio Grande, carrying passengers, money and merchandise. Matamoros was the first considerable town upriver. Gulf vessels could not come to her riverbanks, for the river's last reaches were shallow, full of difficult bends and bars. Cargo had to be landed on the beaches of the estuary and hauled overland to the customs houses, and to the start of the long desert journey to the interior in wagons and on pack mules. Other towns farther upriver—Reynosa, Camargo, even Saint John Baptist, now called Presidio del Rio Grande—were terminal points for better roads to the interior than the one from Matamoros. But to reach them by water had never been tried, and the only boating upriver consisted of a ferry crossing here and there at the most populous routes, where a brown ferryman, who worked naked in readiness to jump into the water to push if his skiff went aground, poled his fares over the muddy current unchallenged—until August, 1829.

6.

The "Ariel"

On the third of that month, a letter was handed at Matamoros to an overland traveller leaving for San Felipe de Austin on the Brazos. It was addressed to Stephen Austin, and it said "I am here with a Steamboat and some goods for the purpose of ascending the River del norte to open a commercial intercourse with the interior if practicable and taking up land for future benefit— It is extreemly doubtfull whether the enterprise will result in success. I shall however give some months attention to it . . . It will be some weeks before I can get ready to start from this and Should the opportunity offer I should be pleased to hear from you. Your council after so much painfull experience would be valuable. . . ." In its calm determination and tractable realism the letter carried a certain familiar tone. It had the Austin touch, and in fact, it was signed by Captain Henry Austin, Stephen's cousin. Characteristically, it was obliged to add, in the North American obsession with a familiar topic, "before leaving the US I laid before the Govt a Memoir on the western boundary pointing out the advantages of an exchange of the territory west of the Rocky Mountains for the land between the Del norte and the US giving the Mexican Govt one or two millions to enduce the exchange—" If President Andrew Jackson, newly elected, had anticipated him by already sending an emissary to Mexico with an offer of five millions for the territory to the Rio Grande, Henry Austin nevertheless was thinking continentally, like a man of his time, and of his family; and he now proceeded with his venture as master of the first Rio Grande steamboat.

She was called the *Ariel* and was, so her captain said, "a boat of great speed and power," and perhaps could run as fast as seven knots an hour. She carried one hundred thousand pounds of freight. She burned wood in her great furnaces that made her bulge amidships, where she bulged again at each side with the paddle wheels that looked as if they

had been taken from a millstream. According to her type, the *Ariel*
carried a single tall black smokestack directly above her boilers and
engines. Her decks were wide, her hull narrow below them, taking a
draft of between three and four feet of water. The pilothouse forward,
and the cabin amidships, were high and narrow, with upright wooden
ribbing through which gaunt little windows looked out darkly. Against
her white paint two small brass cannon sparkled at bow and stern. These
were on guard against pirates in the Gulf or robbers on land. She pad-
dled along bustily like a heavy, changeling swan that could never leave
the water, though giving to the sky from her tall black neck a proud and
billowing banner of dense smoke shot through with huge sparks of
burning wood that crackled upward when the boilers were stocked
anew. Her fuel she took on board anywhere along the banks where
enough wood grew, and piles of it were stacked at the engine-room
door. She brought new sounds to the river. Her paddle wheels hissed
and foamed when she backed water, and chopped along sweetly dripping
when she was on a clear run. Blowing off steam she split the brilliant
air, and sounding her steam whistle with a jet of white plume she made
travelling music, and with her brass bell atop the pilothouse she commanded in marine propriety her changes of speed and the passing of
hours. Around the endless loops and bends of the lower river she
searched in caution for enough water to bear her and above the flood-
cut banks her stack moved slowly by to be marvelled at from the few
cultivated fields, the pastures, the grazing land of the brush, until she
put in at a little town of stone and clay, where all swarmed to see her
in the beating heat of a Rio Grande summer.

The Captain's letter took twenty-four days to be delivered, and
Stephen Austin answered it at once, and with measured pessimism. He
feared that his cousin's doubts about the enterprise were "but too well
founded." He had been working on a map of Texas, and was full of his
subject. The Rio Grande and its country were "entirely unfit for steam
navigation." Captain Austin had asked for "council" and it came dutifully. "As regards the country on the Rio Grande, so far as my information extends it is calculated entirely for pastoral purposes and can never
be valuable as an agricultural section The soil is rich and fertile, but
the seasons are dry and so very iregular as to destroy every thing like
certainty in crops, unless where there are facilities for irrigation, and
those can only be obtained by means of machinery for raising the water
out of the river—an expedient which would be expensive and I think
inadequate—tho many have had it on contemplation, as I have been

told, to use steam for this purpose—" A thought occurred to him. Perhaps, if the climate and soil were suitable, a coffee plantation might be tried somewhere on the river, and he left it politely with Captain Austin, who was much travelled, adding, "Your observation in all quarters of the world, will enable you to form a much more correct opinion as to this, than any one who has ever visited there." Still, he would say one thing. "As regards lands for future benefit, I am decidedly of opinion that one league of land well situated in Texas will be worth more than ten on the Rio Grande— The Sun and moon are not more dissimilar than the two countries. . . ." He had really given it much thought, while making notes for his map. Texas teemed with natural products— beef, dairy fats, grain, garden crops, cotton, sugar, tobacco, timber, and lumber; and industries could readily be set up to turn out cotton and woollen fabrics, distilled liquors; and the horse and mule trade could be developed. What was needed was more immigration by civilized persons, and the establishment of Texas as a separate state under Mexico. Given these, the "citizens of Texas would deal with the Indians, and protect the whole Rio Grande frontier at no cost to the government." One vision led to another, and to his cousin he added that he had "in contemplation to open a road direct from here"—the Brazos—"to *Passo del Norte* and Santa Fe." The idea was to turn, in one sweeping gesture, the Missouri-New Mexico trade southward to Texas, where between a city which he might found at Galveston and the ancient pass into northern Mexico a new highway could be stretched across all of Texas. If this could be managed, and if Henry's "views incline this way," wrote Stephen, "I would join with you on equal terms—"

But Henry Austin, occupied with the poor realities of the river, was learning them fast. He had been "induced to embark in this operation by the hope of retrieving my ruined fortune and of laying a foundation for an estate for my family by Securing a large tract of land." His contract with the Mexican political authority empowered him to colonize "any of the vacant lands on this river but there are none vacant that are worth having or that can be got at conveniently." By September he had been upriver nearly as far as Revilla, where he found "the river so dangerous in low water" that he "did not think it prudent to proceed up at this late season." Only in wet season could the *Ariel* go above Mier, (by which he really meant Roma), and below Mier all the good land was already taken. He had to decide to spend the winter plying between Camargo and Matamoros, making two or three trips a month, depending upon how much business was to be had. The outlook was not encouraging. If it came to failure, he said, "I should only be able to save my self from ruin by taking the boat to some place where She could be Sold or employed to advantage." Could Stephen tell him whether there might be enough wealth, travel and shipping from the Brazos to justify taking the *Ariel* there?

Even when there was enough water, the *Ariel* knew misfortune. In late September a great flood came down the river, and Captain Austin remarked that it "would have enabled him to go quite to Santa Fe," but for one thing. The very flood that would float the *Ariel* far upriver brought with it "a pestilence which prostrated everybody." He was the only member of the *Ariel's* crew to escape the epidemic. For nearly three months, during which the high water would have taken the *Ariel* most profitably up and down the river, his men were all incapacitated, and she lay idle at Matamoros, while salaries continued, and expenses of upkeep. Morosely he discussed with a group of local merchants the idea of selling them a half interest in the steamboat, to keep it running between the river's mouth and Matamoros. But he found it a sore trial to negotiate with the Matamorans. "There is such an inveterate jealousy of strangers," he said, "and so much perfidy in the Mexican people that nothing conducted by a stranger can succeed if they can prevent it." All he could do was make plans for withdrawal from the river without too great a loss. Even that would take months more of steaming up and down the restricted river to earn freighting fees. If he could not in the end sell the *Ariel* and leave her behind, he would have to run to New Orleans and sell her there. It would be as well to dispose of some of her original cargo in any case. He asked his cousin about an item of that. "I have a printing press, and types. is it wanted in Texas. It will not sell here as the people cannot read. the value is 1500$." There was something absurdly valiant in taking a steamboat where there was no water, a printing press where none could read. . . .

Though business improved early in 1830, and for three months the *Ariel* "more than paid her expences," until the merchants of Matamoros were convinced that "a Steamboat to facilitate the transportation of goods is all important to the prosperity of the place," Captain Austin was firm in his resolve to depart as soon as he could "quit with credit. . . . Nothing," he said, "nothing but my pride and the censure to which I should expose myself by abandoning a project of my own proposing has induced me to continue here so long— At all events I shall extricate myself with a few months—"

7.

Slavery

Meanwhile affairs in Mexico were producing high feelings in Texas, and the effects of these were increasingly to be met with on the Rio Grande. Captain Henry Austin kept abreast of issues that developed in the utmost gravity for the future of Texas—both immediate and ultimate.

Chief among them was the issue of slavery.

From Matamoros at the end of January, 1830, Captain Austin wrote to his cousin, ". . . We have many rumors here of a revolutionary disposition in the people of Texas on account of the decree freeing all slaves in the Republic." He referred to an action taken by President Guerrero in September, 1829, abolishing slavery throughout Mexico, excepting the Isthmus of Tehuantepec. The president acted under dictatorial powers that the Congress had granted him during the attempted invasion by troops of Ferdinand VII. The decree was seen in Texas by Austin and all his people, and by members of the several colonies scattered to the east, as a mortal blow to their existence; for the economy of the settlements rested upon slave labor, and ever since their foundation they had had to resist Mexican attempts to abolish slavery by law. What could be done now? Austin counseled moderation. "There ought to be no vociferous and visionary excitement or noise about this matter. Our course is a very plain one—calm, deliberate, dispationate, inflexible firmness; and not windy and ridiculous blowing and wild threats, and much less anything like opposition to the Mexican Constitution, nothing of this kind will do any good. . . ."

What he warned against revealed what was already the temper of the settlers. There was time for reflection, for the Mexican political chief of the Department of Texas had already, on his own authority, suspended the execution of Guerrero's edict in Texas, and had appealed to the President that Texas be added to Tehuantepec as exempt from the

new law. Let the government have time to reconsider. Austin himself
was sternly resolved to fight for the right to hold slaves, for though he
owned only one, "an old, decreped woman, not worth much" whom he
had bought the year before for $350, he declared the whole thing was
a matter of principle, and he intended to protect his constitutional
rights in the matter so far as he was able. He was not at once obliged
to do so, for in December came word that the President "has been
pleased . . . to declare the department of Texas excepted. . . ." Slavery
was secure for the time being in the settlements.

Its presence there was legal under the Mexican grants originally
given to Austin in 1822. One of his continuing troubles in Mexico City
during the trying months of pressing his petition through government
channels had been a disagreement about the terms under which settlers
could introduce slaves into Mexico and keep them. The new government's feeling was that slavery should be done away with, and prescribed accordingly, under a gradual process. Austin wrote in 1822, that
his "principal difficulty is slavery, this they will not admit—as the law is
all slaves are to be free in ten years. . . ." He was working for arrangements more to the advantage of his colonists. ". . . I am trying to have
it amended so as to make them slaves for life and their children free
at 21 years. . . ." He was afraid that he would not succeed in his efforts,
but in the turmoil of Mexico City politics, he came off better than he
had dared hope. The colonies law finally provided that "After the pro-
mulgation of this law there shall be neither sale nor purchase of slaves
who are brought to the empire; their children born in the empire shall
be free at the age of fourteen." The slave trade, of course, was prohibited
by these terms, and the children would be lost just as they reached a
useful age; but the parents until their death were secured to their owners
as economic machinery. It seemed like a piece of good business, and
after all, laws could be modified. For the next decade Stephen Austin
never stopped trying to modify them—though his attitude toward slavery
at times wavered oddly, and for curious reasons.

In 1824 the colonists were alarmed by talk that all slaves were
to be freed in Mexico. Austin headed a committee that filed a protest,
pointing out how ruin would befall the colony if the original three
hundred families could no longer rely on their slaves for farming, defense
and propagation of involuntary labor. The committee went further than
a request that the current regulations be undisturbed; they asked that
these be revised to declare that "the slaves and their descendants of the
300 families . . . shall be slaves for life. . . ." The provisions freeing

children at fourteen were thus to be abolished, to insure unending generations of slave labor from which there was to be no escape in perpetuity. Commercial traffic in slaves, however, the committee did not ask for, but courteously bowed to the current provision banning it. Austin was busy all year with letters and petitions to hold fast to the institution that provided property holders with human chattels.

Not that he would have Mexican officials think he approved of slavery—perish the thought. ". . . por me parte," he declared to one of them, "no soy en favor de la esclavitud en ninguna manera qe. sea. . . ." But if he was not in favor of slavery in any possible form, he was able to go on to say that slavery, having been legally recognized by the central government in the colonies law, and being so vitally necessary to the prosperity of the colony, should be maintained. How else could new colonists be induced to enter Texas from Louisiana? It was a vexing matter, as he indicated by questions he put to the authorities. What was he authorized to do if slaves ran away from their owners in the United States and came to Texas? "If the runaway remains here he is a nuisance to the Country—if his owner claims him and he is not given up it will destroy all harmony between the Citizens of that State and this—" And another tedious aspect of it all: what was he to do with "a free man who steals a Negro from that State and brings him here?" How was that crime to be punished?—for it was "certainly a very high Crime," and as punishment he could only propose whipping, a heavy fine and imprisonment. He busied himself with exhaustive drafts of how slavery could be maintained and regulated, and when he heard that the legislature of Coahuila-Texas was considering a measure to prohibit slavery "absolutely and forever in all its territory," he warned in wounded accents that the settlers could only regard its passage as "una acta de mala fé" on the part of the government, since they had come in with their slaves under the law. But he did not see his own strenuous effort to modify the law as an act of bad faith, and again and again he warned that the colony must face ruin if its slaves were freed. Now and then he gave ground, and to save slavery a while longer, asked that children of slaves be emancipated—though only at reaching the age of twenty-five.

So the struggle went on through the 1820s, and nowhere was heard a voice like that of Bartolomé de las Casas lifted on behalf, not of property, or the liberty of a restricted few, or of legalistic guarantees, but of the inherent humanity of men and women and children, who must not be owned like implements of work, and used as such. The arguments were all expedient, the reasons grubby, the eloquence geared to anxiety over material investments. Clumsy as it was, and even corruptible and at times bloodthirsty, the Mexican government, speaking with the voice of the Indian who had known the meaning of slavery under the early Spaniards, alone held any sort of moral posture in the long struggle whose stake was a measure of man's dignity.

Finally in 1827 Coahuila-Texas adopted a law freeing at birth children born to slaves, and permitting a period of only six months after the adoption and publication of the law during which additional slaves might be brought into the state. It was severe, but not so severe as the legislature's first draft of the bill, and it owed its final form to agitations led by Austin and his settlers. Austin wrote hastily to his brother-in-law to come to Texas at once, bringing his slaves, before the six months' period was over. But as with so many laws of the Republic, this one was not enforced in such an outlying land as Texas. Stephen Austin himself, in the face of the laws of 1822 and after, barring slave trade, bought his "decreped old woman" in 1828. New colonists poured into Texas from the East, and by 1830 the American population numbered thirty thousand—twice the number of the Texas Indians and Mexicans together. On the river in January, 1830, Captain Henry Austin told his cousin what he was hearing in Matamoros.

". . . The Mexicans appear to be very jealous of your increasing strength," he wrote, and he reflected another current topic: "I think the conviction that Texas cannot long remain theirs may determine them to sell to the U S now they have an opportunity." For though nothing had been accomplished officially, the United States minister to Mexico was known to have five million dollars available for the purchase of Texas, and perhaps a little over, if certain individuals in the capital could find ways to receive North American dollars quite privately—or so the minister hoped (though without the knowledge or approval of President Jackson). But his intrigues had little chance to develop. The government at Mexico City took alarm at the swelling immigration in Texas, and the growing establishment there of a society made in the likeness of the United States. Intelligence went from the Rio Grande to the capital, accompanied by various recommendations for the control of the North Americans and the reaffirmation of Mexican authority above the river; and in April, 1830, the government acted to repress the Anglo-American colonies in Texas. On the sixth, President Bustamante signed an Act of Congress that closed the frontier to Anglo-American settlers, though it held out inducements to Mexicans and immigrants from any foreign country other than the United States to take up claims in Texas. No travellers from the United States could enter even temporarily without a Mexican visa. Any settlement already in process of movement from the United States was cancelled. Existing colonies were not to be disturbed, but no slaves were to be brought into them henceforth. Texas coastal commerce was thrown open to foreigners for four years and at certain seaports the customs regulations were suspended to the advantage of Mexican and oversea colonists. These measures were to be enforced by military power, and at Matamoros, General Manuel Mier y Terán mobilized troops to march into Texas to do the job. The Texan settlers were to have their comeuppance.

After reflection, Stephen Austin wrote to the President and to General Mier y Terán, and drafted though did not send a letter to Lucas Alamán, the Mexican vice-president, who held jurisdiction over the colonies. He argued hotly against the exclusion measures of the new law, and especially its decree that cancelled settlements undertaken but not completed. Speaking for the colonists, and protesting their good faith, he asked, "Is it good policy to sour their minds and alienate their affections?" Already there were new settlers on the road from as far away as New York. They had sold their property at home, and had made all the complicated arrangements necessary for a new life in a new nation. From the moment of his acceptance of their applications, Austin considered them already members of the colony. He would not apply the new law to them. ". . . Immagine," he charged the government, "immagine for a moment the situation in which some hundreds of families had to be placed, by being stopped on the road to this colony after having sold all their property where they formerly lived and incurred heavy expences, they would be totally ruined, and"—let the government take note—"the odium would of necessity fall on the Govt that caused their ruin—public sympathy would be excited to a very high degree and public indignation would immediately follow. . . ." He asked flatly that orders be sent to "the Com^t Genl of this section not to stop the emigrants to my colony—". His protest was effective. In a few weeks he was assured by General Mier y Terán that his colony was not indicated under the article affecting settlements in progress.

But the rest of the Congressional act was to be prosecuted. It was plain to Austin that the article on slavery, confirming the state law already passed by Coahuila-Texas, could not be argued against; and he made no reference to it in his letters to the government—though in the one he wrote but did not send to Alamán, he took a mollifying line that reflected his sense of the expedient. "I have to say that I have always been opposed from principle to slavery and that I am well satisfied with the prohibitory laws on that subject." It was a statement hardly in accord with his earlier acts and protests. These he tried to explain away. "I have advocated the toleration of slavery in the infancy of the settlement because I at one time totally despaired of getting emigrants without allowing them to bring slaves." Having worked to implant slavery in the colonies it was difficult to know how he could ever hope to uproot it by a simple reversal of his own opinion. Still, he tried. "The country is now sufficiently advanced and as far as my influence extends I shall forever oppose slavery in Texas—I have made this declaratory to the settlers in public manner. . . ."

He even wrote to Henry Austin about his new mind. ". . . I am myself opposed to a union with the U.S. unless we first receive some *guarantees,* amongst them I should insist on the perpetual exclusion of slavery from this country. . . ." In 1830 union with the United States was already a real possibility to the Anglo-Texans.

But if he was now against slavery, suddenly in a scattering of letters written in June, 1830, he revealed why. It was the exposure of a morbid obsession. "The idea of seeing such a country as this overrun by a slave population almost makes me weep— It is in vain to tell a North American that the white population will be destroyed some fifty or eighty years hence by the negroes, and that his daughters will be violated and Butched by them." He shuddered to think of it, and he agonized over the answers he got when he gave warnings. The settlers dismissed him saying that "it is too far off to think of—" and "they can do as I have, take care of themselves—" and "something will turn up to keep off the evil, etc, etc,". Such, he said, "such are the silly answers of the slave holder." For the first time Stephen Austin gave a word to the ethical aspects of slavery. "To say anything to them as to the justice of slavery, or its demoralizing effects on society, is only to draw ridicule upon the person who attempts it—"

Luxuriating in the horrors of orgiastic explosions in the future, he rode ahead with his theme. "To those who do not reflect, I would say, 'take your pen—put down the number of slaves now in the slave states—calculate their increase for eighty years at the known rate of augmentation—Calculate the extent of country to which they are, and must be confided, and its capacity to support human beings—Then calculate the number of white population and their increase—deduct from said increase, the emigration of whites to other countries; (no such

deduction can be made from the increase of blacks, for they cannot
emigrate,) compare the two sums, and then suppose that you will be
alive at the period above mentioned, that you have a long-cherished
and beloved wife, a number of daughters, grand daughters, and great
grand daughters . . . would no fears for their fate, a horrible fate;
intrude themselves upon your pillow, and overcloud the evening of your
life'? . . . If Texas is wisely and prudently managed, it will be saved from
the overwhelming ruin which mathematical demonstration declares must
overtake the slave states. . . ." What would the solution be, in wisdom
and prudence? He seemed to see only one. "A few years more and
Mexico will be the only resting place left for the whites South of Illinois,
unless"—not that he advocated it, but there it was—"unless the blacks
are exterminated by a general massacre by the Whites; and afterwards
excluded from being brought into the country—In a century more either
the whites, or the blacks must cease to exist in the southern States, or they
must intermarry and all be placed on an equality."

8.

Bad Blood

But in 1830 there were other problems, too, for Captain Henry
Austin reported from the Rio Grande that General Mier y Terán desired
a meeting with Stephen, whom he did not deceive for a moment. It was
Mier y Terán, and no one else, who had designed the government's
measures against Texas, and Stephen Austin had "always known it."
They were on the best of terms, of course, and observed all amenities,
but just the same Stephen wished Henry would write him when "the
long-expected army of Texas is to be on, and its number, etc.—" This
referred to the movement of troops over the Rio Grande to enforce new
revenue laws at customs houses to be established at various points in
Texas, and to see that other provisions of the Act of April sixth were

carried out. Enjoining calm at home, Stephen Austin reported that "The most perfect peace and harmony reigns over all Texas and will no doubt so continue—"

Henry saw otherwise on the Rio Grande. Mier y Terán on taking his army into Texas was planning, according to what Henry heard, to remove Stephen from the colony, because his influence with the colonists was "dangerous to the security of the province." It was a shocking rumor, and Henry dismissed it, "supposing it to be impossible for the Gen¹ to meditate so rash a measure." But soon he was not so certain. He wrote to Stephen that Mier y Terán was overheard saying that "he viewed the foreigners in this part of the country as the Most dangerous enemies of it particularly the North Americans whose sole object was to wrest from the Mexicans their property and so much of their territory as they could get— . . . You know," continued Henry, "You know the duplicity of the Mexican character—their general want of faith in all transactions and the necessity of being guarded against their villainy. . . . It may therefore be wise to keep yourself under cover of your own rifles, which Gen¹ Teran has not the nerve nor the power to encounter. . . ." and Captain Henry Austin added "you must take good care not to let it transpire that I communicate with you on this subject as it would probably consign me to the Calabose. . . ."

In Matamoros there were troubles for North Americans engaged in shipping in and out of the Rio Grande. A new state law required all foreign merchants except the English, the German and the Dutch to pay a tax on their capital in trade and on all importation during the previous year. The specific exceptions left only United States shipping subject to the tax. The regulations permitted the Texas colonies to ship goods to Matamoros, Veracruz and Tampico; but they had to pay the revenue. It may have been a measure in retaliation for abuses of the customs laws by the Texans, who for years had taken advantage of exemption from duty on goods to be used for building the colony to introduce all sorts of other goods in great quantity which they illegally used in commerce. Bad blood stirred at provocation from both government and settlers. "The Govts and people of Mexico appear to become more hostile daily to the citizens of the US.," as Henry Austin saw affairs on the river, "and I am of opinion will ultimately drive them from Mexico or reduce the U S to the necessity of compelling them to respect the rights of her Citizens—"

Matamoros was an armed camp. Mier y Terán's soldiers were on guard at every point. The customhouse was a fort, and collection of duties was accelerated, and its revenue was poured into the Commandant General's hands. It was the only source of funds with which to pay his troops. There were three hundred soldiers in town, and sixteen hundred more were expected to arrive soon, to be drilled and trained for the Texas entry. The army was raised through levies made on the Mexican people. The law stated that "vagabonds and disorderly persons shall be taken in preference for military service, recruits may be obtained by entrapment and decoy." Henry Austin did not expect the army to move north. He believed that affairs in central Mexican politics concerned Mier y Terán far more than the problems of Texas, and in fact, the General was changing his tune, protesting that he favored the Texans in all things. Perhaps there was a new reason for this, and Henry wrote, "I think he has more apprehension of a Grito for Centralism in the South and a separation of those northern states which are federal, than of the US or Texas. . . . I also suspect he counts upon much support from Texas in such an event. . . ."

But in that summer the vagabond army did move across the Rio Grande. Mier y Terán established a dozen or so military posts in Texas whose presence was an affront to the colonists, and returned to his headquarters at Matamoros. It was a hot summer, parched with drought. Henry Austin looked at the river to see it go drier and lower. Was he trapped with the *Ariel?* The searing winds came, and lifted sand into the air. It was choking, even while the air was sticky and humid. The land was flat and the lower sky presaged the sea and freedom and rescue, but the *Ariel* had to be readied, and there were officials to see, and six or eight thousand dollars to retrieve. Where was the image of the future that he had brought to the river—prosperity, and an estate with green lawns to the bank, and a heritage for a family? "Poor fellow," noted his brother Archibald in the East when it was plain that the Rio Grande steamboat venture was doomed, "he has traversed the world, beat the Bush, in every Hemisphere, contended with almost unexampled perseverance, with the freaks of fortune, had a fortune at various times as it were in his grasp, and have frustrated, Blocade, Wars and peace have so intervened as destroy his well-founded hopes of success, the all powerful ingine Steam does not appear to enable him to stem the current that has set against him. . . ."

But at last, in late August, he took the *Ariel* down the river and up the coast to the Brazos. He met Stephen Austin in due course, and discussed taking up a league of land. The prospect was not filling. He said it would "be folly for me to devote the remainder of my life to the

occupation of a league of land." His past stirred in his memory, his scale
of imagination would not let him be, and he shared with Stephen as
with a kindred spirit the vague creative longings that made them both
active, unhappy and relentless. "I must do something on an extensive
scale with prospects of ultimate advantage of magnitude," he declared,
"or do nothing. . . . You and I may indulge our imaginations with the
pleasing prospect of passing the remainder of life in the tranquillity
which a snug stock farm appears to offer, but neither you nor I could
exist in such a state. . . ."

It was true; and Henry planned to move on to New Orleans and
the States. He had a last word of advice for Stephen. There was political
rumor that Mexico's federation was about to break apart into independent provinces. General Mier y Terán in such a case had his eye on
his choice of land. "I strongly suspect Teran looks to Texas for his share.
Flatter him in that point and make him believe the people of Texas
look up to him as their political Savior and you may do anything with
him. . . ." After this word, he was ready to go; but once again the *Ariel*
was delayed by bad luck, for the beef rations packed for the homeward
voyage spoiled overnight, and four crewmen deserted in the dark. He
set about repairing his supplies and crew at the mouth of the Brazos,
while "Farewell," wrote Stephen from San Felipe upstream, "I hope you
may have a calm run to the U.S.—it is more than I expect to have for
the next two years, and God knows whether I shall ever see much
quiet—" And then the *Ariel* was ready, with her woodpiles replenished,
and she set out to cross the bar into the Gulf. But she had taken on too
much wood, and to lighten her for the crossing, the Captain set ashore
to leave behind him his two brass cannon and other weighty cargo. The
Ariel tried the bar again. This time she ran aground. In getting off, she
was damaged. She ventured on, but her troubles had been too much for
her; she sank and was abandoned in Galveston Bay. It would be sixteen
years before steam came back to the lower Rio Grande. Captain Henry
Austin, though still plagued by "prospects of ultimate advantage of
magnitude," settled in his cousin's colony in Texas after all.

The head of the colony was also head of the militia, with the
rank of colonel. The law required him to have the uniform of colonel in
the Mexican army, of navy blue, with gold epaulettes, a scarlet waistcoat
with gold round cord on the edges, a gold-mounted sword and belt,
and a yellow sash; a set of holsters, a pair of boots and yellow spurs;
pantaloons trimmed with black silk braid; a military surtout with a
standing collar, that was to be "handsomely though plainely trimmed

with black silk cord"; and a yellow-bitted bridle. Colonel Stephen F.
Austin ordered all this out of New York in the summer of 1830. It was
months in coming, for the embroidery of gold bullion on the coat took
time, and cost forty-one dollars. It finally left for Texas by ship on
December twentieth; but it would arrive too late to be taken to Saltillo
by Colonel Austin, who was obliged to attend the next session of the
legislature of the Twin Sisters, that would open in January, 1831. He
travelled by way of Béxar, and struck out from there for the Rio Grande,
which he crossed at France Way, as it was still called. He passed through
the Presidio, where the population continued to take down grand
yellow-gray stones from the ruins of St. Bernard's to make their shops
and houses and corrals, and proceeded with an armed escort to Monclova and Saltillo. There was much to debate in the session, much to
prove; her own identity for Texas, without loss of loyalty to Mexico.
Behind the immediate issues loomed and pressed more relentlessly every
day the energy of the United States as it reached toward the Rio
Grande's two extremes of terrain, at the Gulf and in the Rocky
Mountain north.

9.

The Mexico Trade

"We are caraing on a smart Trade with St. tefee from the boons
lick country," wrote a Missouri merchant as early as 1824. For three centuries the flow of colonial life had moved by the compass needle north
and south, from Mexico to the river and back again—captains and friars
and householders; convicts paroled as colonists; an occasional bishop
in his large, upholstered wagon; merchant trains with their Indian
drivers; military inspectors of the Spanish Crown visiting frontier garrisons of forty men and four hundred horses and twenty firearms; journey-
man artisans and now and then a student travelling between wilderness

and a Spanish university: all in their slow glisten and wonderful persistence travelled north and south.

And then, with the nineteenth century, in a swing of the needle,
the compass began to show life flowing toward the river along a new
axis, from east to west, in a new measure of knowledge, and at a quickened pace. New paths were imagined. One much speculated upon in 1825
was the Red River, in spite of the immense "Raft" of tangled timber
that hung over its course like a low thick canopy for almost a hundred
miles, so that the river ran unseen as if in a subterranean current. But
its upper end pointed generally toward Santa Fe, though its source fell
short of there by a hundred and fifty miles, and the talk was that if the
Raft could be cleared away, as men were now planning to clear it, then
"Steam boats will be able to assend within a day or two's Journey from
Sta Fee," and "if this is done the whole current of the Intercourse with
New Mexico will be by way of Red River and the whole valley of it
will Soon be settled. and the time may come when more cotton may
go out of Red River than now goes out of the mississippi. . . ." For
many reasons the Red River undertaking never materialized. For one
thing, the clearing of the Great Raft was too difficult to do. For another,
the upper reaches of the Red River could not float steamboats except
perhaps in storm water. And finally, the Mexico trade already in progress
overland to Chihuahua by way of the prairies and Santa Fe grew so
fast that the Santa Fe trail quickly became the established route.

It had been Spain's firm policy to exclude all trade from the
United States except through the severely controlled port of Veracruz.
There came North American goods by sea, and, if any reached the Rio
Grande and Santa Fe, went northward by the old cottonwood carts from
Mexico. By the time it arrived, merchandise cost the New Mexicans
dearly. One common item—calico and even "bleached and brown domes-
tic goods"—sold for two or three dollars a yard.

But with the independence of Mexico in 1821, the restrictions
were, if somewhat capriciously, relaxed. The trappers of the mountains
showed the way to the Rio Grande overland. Both Anglo-Americans and
Mexicans wondered whether trails might turn into roads; and in 1824,
a group of citizens from Mexican Santa Fe crossed the plains to invite
trade from the Mississippi valley. Stephen Austin's brother wrote to
him about it: "A Deputation from Santa Fe arrived a few weeks ago
at the council Bluffs—the object of their visit was to ascertain the most
eligible Situation for a road to be cut from Santa Fe—to that place—and
also to enter into some arrangement to Secure traders (to and from the

Province of New Mexico) —from attacks of the indians—and to appoint agents for the purpose of facilitating an intercourse and commerce to the United States—".

By then the Mexico trade was a reality. In 1821 William Becknell had taken out to the plains "a company of men destined to the westward for the purpose of trading for Horses and Mules, and catching wild animals of every description," as his announcement stated in the *Missouri Intelligencer*. His intention was to trade with Indians; but on the prairies he met a wandering group of Santa Feans who persuaded the Missourians "to accompany them to the new emporium [Santa Fe], where, notwithstanding the trifling amount of merchandise they were possessed of, they realized a very handsome profit. . . ." The expedition was equipped only with pack animals, and so were those few that went out again in the following year. In May of 1824 Becknell introduced an important innovation on the trail to Santa Fe, when taking out another merchandise train, he hauled his goods in wagons for the first time. The wagons were a success, for "no where else on the American continent," observed a trader, "can be found a route of 800 miles in extend more easily traversed by wagons than the one between Independence and Santa Fe."

The volume of traffic grew faster than the Mexicans had expected. Ready to measure by their own experience of the single, dawdling, annual train of the Rio Grande valley, and their own unhurried natures, they were hardly prepared to see so many caravans, and so many traders, and so much merchandise rolling past their vaguely defined boundaries. It was alarming. So much business could only mean so much power eventually in the hands of the Anglo-American visitors. Mexico went no further with deputations to the States to establish roads and propose commerce. But it was too late. The gates had been opened, and the flood had started, and would increase.

The first trade road led to Taos, where the trappers had gone. It was the port of entry for New Mexico, where papers were examined. The customs house was at Santa Fe, and there the serious business of taxation, and sometimes of confiscation, was done. As the trade grew, if Mexico could not exclude it, she could at least bear upon it every tedium and elaboration of government control that a Spanish heritage could suggest. Months before setting out, the trader had to have his entire bill of merchandise made out and translated into Spanish. This was copied in duplicate, and sent by traveller, or by mail if possible, to the point of destination, whether Santa Fe or Chihuahua, or any point between them. Once entered, the invoice could not be altered in any way, and any error in further copying it, even to a slip of the pen, was enough to subject the cargo to confiscation when it later arrived. The invoice was stamped, and a copy was returned to the trader with a "guia," or clearance. The guia was permitted to name three points of destination for the shipment, which thereafter could go nowhere else. There was a time limit on the validity of the guia. If its return to the trader were delayed by the officials, or by uncertainty of mails, the trader was sure to be late in his travel, for he could not start without the clearance in hand. And if he was late in arriving, then he was taxed double the duty levied on his goods.

But at last, if he had his papers, the trader could depart. The wagon train commander carried a document issued by the Superintendent of Indian Affairs at St. Louis, showing the names of all men in the trading party, and granting them permission "to pass into and through the Indian country, &c . . . to the province of Mexico." The trail to Santa Fe soon found an easier way than going by Taos, and down the black rocky canyon of the river west of the Sangre de Cristo mountains. It took a diagonal on entering New Mexico and came around the southern prow of the mountains and passing through San Miguel del Vado entered Santa Fe from the southeast. If the question was raised why the wagon trains, whose cargo was destined chiefly for Chihuahua, did not go directly there instead of so far out of the way as Santa Fe, a trader gave the answer. "I answer, that we dreaded a journey across the southern prairies on account of the reputed aridity of the country in that direction, and I had no great desire to venture directly into a southern port in the present state of uncertainty as to the conditions of entry." El Paso and Presidio del Norte were ports of entry on the Rio Grande below New Mexico, but received little traffic.

Every summer saw the traders come in sight through the blue-green hills southeast of Santa Fe. The long wagon trains gritted and creaked their way into the plaza, and the traders inhaled on the cool air the poignant scent of the piñon smoke that always hovered over the old royal city. An arrival was a great event. The Santa Feans came flocking to see the newcomers, who stared back at them, while both thought they had never seen such outlandish creatures. In the trading company there were many diverse men whom the taverns, gambling rooms and certain Mexican women prepared to entertain—city merchants, frontiersmen, wandering tinkers, farmers, hunters, wagoners. They often represented many nationalities, and in one train there were men of "seven distinct nations, each speaking his own native tongue," and a trader noted a voluble Frenchman who was given to "curious gesticulations," and "two phlegmatic wanderers from Germany," and two Polish exiles of a "calm eccentricity," and various Indians including a Creek and a Chickasaw, and "sundry loquacious Mexicans," and Americans who "were mostly backwoodsmen, who could handle the rifle better than the whip, but who nevertheless officiated as wagoners." Santa Fe had never seen the like.

They wore anything and everything. The merchant was the most elegant, in his dark, fustian long coat with its many pockets in which he could carry so much, his light trousers, and his round hat. The backwoodsman wore a shirt of linsey, that was made of mixed wool and flax, or a fringed leather jacket. The farmer's coat of twilled cotton cloth was already known as blue jean. The wagoner's vest had flannel sleeves. The party bristled with arms until they gave a "very brigand-like appearance." The hunter had his long rifle, and derided the "scatter-gun," as he called the double-barrelled fowling piece carried by Americans who back home went shooting for sport. But the scatter-gun had its serious uses, for on the prairies among enemy Indians "a charge of buckshot in night attacks (which are most common) will of course be more like to do execution than a single rifle-ball fired at random. . . ." Almost everyone carried pistols and knives. Now and then a large, rich train brought along artillery: "We had two swivels mounted upon one pair of wheels . . . one of these was a long brass piece made to order, with a calibre of but an inch and a quarter, yet of sufficient metal to throw a leaden ball . . . a mile with surprising accuracy. The other was iron, and a little larger."

The freight wagons of the train were long, heavy and narrow, with wheels higher at the rear than at the front, and double hoods of Osnabrück linen stretched over arched bows. From a little distance and seen from the end, such a wagon seemed to be wearing a great sun-bonnet. The most popular wagons were made in Pennsylvania, first at Conestoga, later at Pittsburgh. Each could carry a load of about five thousand pounds. To pull it took three span of oxen, horses or mules. Each of these wore a collar of bells. The cargo was remarkably various, containing textiles of all sorts, from calico to velvet; clothes for men and women, including ribbons, handkerchiefs, hats, suspender buttons, rhinestones and kid gloves; building materials, cutlery, glassware, tools, baskets, furniture, paper, ink and paints; foods and spices of every kind and medicines and tobacco and almanacs and champagne and candles and colored lithographs and—a popular item—jew's-harps.

The wagons crowded into the plaza like fishing boats in a small harbor after long hazard at sea. The journey had taken ten weeks from Old Franklin in Howard County on the Missouri River. The eastern terminus moved westward for decades, to Independence, and then Westport, and then Westport Landing which became Kansas City. The road was an extension of the long westward walk of Daniel Boone, that had ended near Boone's Lick with his life. In the fourth year of the trade Congress authorized the President of the United States to "cause a road to be marked out from the western frontier of Missouri to the confines of New Mexico," and the government treated with Plains Indians for the right to cross to Santa Fe, paying the Osage and Kansa tribes eight hundred dollars each. Early encounters with Indians were peaceful; but it was not long until traders, regarding the Indians as inferior creatures, abused them; and Indians replied with all their ancient skill in savage warfare. Trading trains could not have protection by United States troops west of the Arkansas River because of treaty conditions. A trader of the 1830s thought that "such an extensive unhabitable waste as the great prairies are, ought certainly to be under maritime regulations," and considering the principal destinations of the trains, he recommended that "some internal arrangements should be made between the United States and Texas or Mexico, whereby the armies of either might indiscrimminately range upon this desert, as ships of war upon the ocean. . . ."

Traders often thought of the sea in their great prairie crossings. The vast open land looked like the sea, and the sky over it rimmed the world at the horizons without obstruction. "Seas of grass," they said, and "prairie schooner," and "prairie ocean." They found the journey, like a sea voyage, a giver of health, and many a frontier doctor sent a sickling on a prairie "enterprise" and saw him come alive of it. It was an affirmative experience. The voyagers believed in their work, which few others had performed; they had a sense of their worth and need; and they knew health of body and spirit. One said, "The insatiable appetite acquired by travellers is almost incredible, and the quantity of coffee drank is even more so. . . ." Each man did full justice to the rations he was required to bring—fifty pounds each of bacon and flour, twenty pounds of sugar, ten pounds of coffee, and salt, beans and crackers—and to the game he brought down with his rifle or scatter-gun on the way. His job was hard, and the bonneted wagons rarely made more than eleven to fifteen miles a day. He came through Indian alarms and terrifying storms and prairie fires. If he and the wind moved in the same direction a prairie fire ahead of him was no great trouble, for "fire burns so slowly back against the wind even through tall grass, wagons can be driven through it with safety." But if the wind came driving the fire from ahead, "it would often (particularly in tall grass) set both wagon and team in flames." Under a favoring wind a train once passed safely through a fire; but at night the wind changed, and the fire caught up with the wagons the next day.

At the end of the first lap of the journey, as night came down over Santa Fe, it was time to let go. The public rooms of Santa Fe were crowded early in the evening, and private ones later. Monte games—one trader of severe tastes called them "pandemoniums"—raged, and a fandango was called, and Taos whiskey and El Paso brandy flowed, and music, yells and ebullient salvos from firearms broke the mountain-clasped night. Tomorrow would come the ordeal of the customs house, with its rattle of papers, long official silences that chilled the hearts of the traders, and the glitter of greed in the eyes of the motley Mexican soldiers who watched the checking of the cargoes. The process might take several days; but once the papers were declared in order, and the duties paid, it would be time to tear the traders away from the rude joys of Santa Fe, and take the train down the river to El Paso, and beyond, to the city of Chihuahua.

They took the old road on the east bank all the way. After the empty plains the narrow valley with its many little villages of earth, its separate estate farms, seemed like civilization; and so it was, though odd to Yankee eyes. Yet the valley in the second quarter of the nineteenth century was so much terrorized by Apaches and even occasional Comanches that the traders could not hope to strike out on their own, however plain the road and frequent the settlements. If they staged few battles against riding Indians, it was because the trains made a great show of force and circumstance that discouraged attack.

The wagons wracked their way down the escarpment of La Bajada off Santa Fe plain, and along the valley road, soon passing in and out of cottonwood shade, a river grace. The bridge at San Felipe had long since been washed away by storm water, and all the way on the river until near to the mouth fifteen hundred miles away there was not a single ferry. This troubled few who wanted to cross, for during three quarters of the year, the river could be forded wherever there was an easy bank. Troubles mostly came otherwise, and took official form; for in any town where there was a squad of soldiery and an alcalde who saw his duty as a confusion of his personality, the long toiling train was apt to be halted by authority of the Mexican nation, and the whole customs inspection repeated, while the train commanders held their breaths, and wagoners bathed in the sweet-scented muddy river, and animals grazed, and summertime slipped away. It was no use to look for back roads that bypassed the little garrisons; for any train discovered off the main highway was, however orderly its papers, subject to immediate and entire confiscation.

But at last they moved on again, and saw how one little river town after another, only a few miles apart—Peralta, Valencia, Tomé, Adelino—seemed isolated from one another, with local differences in building style, costume and church furnishings. None of the river towns below Santa Fe had an inn or public house. Stopping for the night, the traders parked their train on the outskirts of a village, near water, and under trees, and built their fires and put down their blankets on the ground. The townspeople came to look at them as they pastured their animals and cooked their supper, and heard them talk, and sing, and recite to amuse one another, and watched them dance to fiddles and clapped hands under upward firelight on green leaves, and perhaps saw them take a man and bare his back and tie him to a tree to give him lashes with a bullwhip; and if they asked why this was done, they were told that the man was a bad debtor who was being made to pay off what he owed at a dollar a lash. In the morning with bellow and bray and holler, the rankle of harness bells, and the grind of axles and the complaint of wagon wood, the train moved on into the deserts above Socorro and below. There were no towns in that stretch but many camping sites that had been used for generations by riverside travellers—Pascual, El Contadero, Alemán, Robledo, San Diego, Fray Cristóbal—before entering the Dead Man's March. Such places had no permanent habitation or structure; but filled and emptied as travel went by.

The Mexican postrider carried the mail between Chihuahua and Santa Fe over this route, though since the raiding Indians had become active, he could not keep his schedule of two trips a month. Most writers sent their letters by private hands, to avoid loss, and also to keep them from being opened, and their business aired, in the post offices of Albuquerque and Santa Fe—the only ones in New Mexico. The postrider carried the leather post bag. It was locked. But because there was a shortage of keys on deposit at the post offices, he also carried the only key. His life was dangerous, and making a living was hard, and it came to him that a little extra silver would be his if he gave to inquisitive persons the privilege of ransacking the mail in his charge. One day in the Dead Man's March a Missouri trader saw a New Mexican ride up to the postrider who was passing by on his service. They conversed briefly, coming to an agreement; and then the postman unlocked his pouch and dumped its contents on the ground. His client searched the mail, and for the privilege handed him "the moderate price of one dollar."

Pressing on through the Dead Man's March as fast as they could, for water was still scarce, and their emergency casks were emptied all too soon, the traders returned to the riverside again and came upon one after another settlement that "had formerly been the seat of opulence and prosperity" but which had "long since been abandoned in consequence of the marauding incursions of the Apaches." Nearing El Paso, if the river was high at the ford six miles above town, they faced a hard job. Nowhere was there a sign of a bridge—the old one had gone in flood. The traders now had to unload the cargo and take the wagons apart, and using a thirty-foot dugout "canoe" that was at hand, float the wagon parts one by one across the river, and assemble them again on the opposite bank. The cargo followed. Sometimes they met quicksand at the ford, and then had to work fast to "drag mules out by the ears," and "to carry out the loading package by package," and "to haul out the wagon piece by piece—wheel by wheel."

Once across the river, the train rolled on, and in about three miles came to a dam of stone and brush that diverted the waters to the El Paso settlements for irrigation. Three miles farther loomed the tower of Guadalupe, at one corner of the plaza. Again the customs inspection delayed progress. The inspector was exacting and disagreeable. While he did his duty, the traders who could be spared from the ordeal wandered about the district, and ate local grapes "of the most exquisite flavor," and drank "Pass wine" and "Pass whiskey," and saw how the town hardly extended beyond the plaza, though as they resumed their march into Mexico, they realized that the settlements continued for ten or twelve miles down the river in a "series of plantations," with cornfields, orchards and vineyards under cultivation. At their end, the road left the river, and the train headed due south for the city of Chihuahua, and the southern terminus of the long journey from Missouri.

In an early year the Mexico trade did a business of about fifteen thousand dollars. Twenty years later, the total annual value of cargoes was nearly a million dollars, and a single enterprise brought back one hundred and fifty thousand dollars. Traders were paid by the Mexicans in gold and silver for their merchandise—gold dust from a placer mine near Santa Fe, silver bullion from the mines of Chihuahua. Silver was moulded into ingots weighing between fifty and eighty pounds each, and worth fifteen hundred dollars. Rich men in Chihuahua stacked silver bars in their cellars, where a Missourian saw such cords that looked like "a winter's supply of firewood." If the payment was made in specie, the traders poured their coins into newly made sacks of green rawhide, which as it dried stiff and hard compressed the money in a tight bale.

If all went well for a train, the traders could dispose of their wares in Chihuahua and return to Santa Fe in time to leave for Missouri in the autumn. But if beset by accidents, too many official delays, slow markets, or a wet summer that kept the rivers at flood, they might have to spend nearly a year on the round trip, staying the winter in Santa Fe; for once winter was on the mountains and on the plains, the men could not venture homeward. Pasturage was poor as autumn advanced, and the open road that was so passable in summertime was in winter a terrible passage exposed to the drive of blizzards. The traders hurried their business and their return to Santa Fe up the river. In addition to their bales and bars and buckskin sacks of silver and gold, they brought Mexican cargoes to sell at home—buffalo rugs, furs, wool, coarse blankets of Mexican and Indian make; and they drove herds of Mexican mules and asses. The wagonloads were kept light, with no more than two thousand pounds of goods in each, to ease the pull on animals who would feed poorly on the autumnal forage, and to make fast marches possible as the days became short and cold and promised trouble in a prairie winter. The westward drive to Santa Fe in early summer had taken seventy days. The return trip, with light wagons and increased knowledge, took forty. With every summer the number of trains increased, and with every trip, the traders, fixed upon their own concerns, and aware of no larger purpose, advanced the process that would in time make foreigners of the Mexicans in their own long valley of the Rio Grande.

IO.

Tormented Loyalties

In June, 1832, returning home by way of Matamoros from another of his annual trips to the legislature at Saltillo, Stephen Austin declared that he had had "a very hard and hot trip." The whole country was "all parched up," and at many places in northern Mexico no rain had fallen for eight months. It was fatiguing to travel so far from the Brazos to Coahuila in vain efforts to bring order and government for Texas out of the near-anarchy that prevailed in the northern provinces. All of Mexico was in political turmoil, and the outlying districts wavered between national and local problems, troubled by both and unable to compose either. Texas was viewed with fixed suspicion. Her people had resisted bitterly the repressive policies that followed the enactment of the laws of April 6, 1830, and her delegate to Saltillo was obliged again and again to protest loyalty, even while he argued in measured tones for justice. It was therefore gratifying to Stephen Austin to find that in his crossings of the Rio Grande he was treated "with more attention and respect" than he had "any reason to expect." True, he still had enemies who roved the river frontier trying to discredit him and blacken the character of Texas. His reply to this was firm. "My character belongs to the colony and any unjust attack upon me situated as I now am, is in fact an attack upon all," he declared, and continued to examine frontier problems. It was a disgrace that the river towns were still without protection by the central government against Comanche attacks. The mails were uncertain, and a connection must be made between the United States and Mexican postal systems. There was a serious threat to Matamoros, the Rio Grande's largest commercial port, in a petition before the Mexican Congress, to favor Veracruz by closing the mouth of the Rio Grande to shipping. Matamoros was spiritedly defended by a colonist. "The natural advantages, which this place possesses, in point of health, over the Southern port; the superior facili-

ties in the transportation of merchandise into the interior; its contiguity
to the frontier; and its importance as a military port, claim the consideration and protection of the general Government. . . ." It was a
touching view of a town that was beaten either by dust or downpour
the year round, along a river that was either an exhausted meander of
last waters among sand bars or a wide sailing flood.

Such extremes brought to mind the condition of the colony amidst
its opposing hopes and frustrations. To lead the way forward through
them called for nerve. "It has," said Austin, "it has been my policy to
slide along without any noise." It was galling that in his task he met with
difficulties not only from the Mexicans, but from among his own people,
and he was ready with another bitter opinion. "I fear (judging by my
own experience) that the predominant traits in the North American
character are ingratitude, selfishness, and avarice. The people of this
Colony have caused (what I formerly said was impossible) a shade of
misanthropy to pass over me. . . ." Of himself he had few doubts. "I
can with truth and clear conscience say that none of the sordid and
selfish motives which influence the mass of adventures had any weight
in determining me to attack the wilderness. I commenced on the solid
basis of sound and philanthropic intentions and of undeviating integrity." But when the Government pressed him to follow one course, and
his people another, he suffered. Did people not know how he toiled for
them? Lonely and isolated by his severe temperament and his flatness
of spirit—the wages of rationalism—it seemed that he must at times
reach for popularity by sudden changes of belief. Swayed by opinions
contrary to his, and that he despised, he must contradict himself in
crisis after crisis on the major issues of his world—slavery, statehood,
independence itself.

"Our situation is extremely delicate and interesting," he told
his sister in 1831, in an odd mixture of passion and objectivity. "To
remain as we are, is impossible. We have not the right kind of material
for an Independent Government and an union with the United States
would bring Negro Slavery—that curse of curses, and worst of reproaches,
on civilized man; that unanswered, and unanswerable, inconsistency
of *free* and liberal republicans"—and yet he had brought slavery with
him. "I think the Government will yield, and give us what we ought
to have. If not, we shall go for *Independence*"—the very idea of which
he denied indignantly when addressing suspicious Mexican officials—
"and put our trust in our selves, our riffles, and—our God. Adios."

It was true that the confusions all about him were greater, more violent, than his own. At Matamoros in the dry, hot June of 1832 he heard the latest news from both sides of the Rio Grande. For six months Santa Anna had been leading a revolution against President Bustamante. It had started in Veracruz and was now inflaming all of Mexico, and though Austin had hoped to keep Texas above the battle—"what is needed there is a *dead calm*"—in that very June, and in his absence, the colonists had met and passed resolutions supporting Santa Anna. Hastily Austin wrote home from Matamoros counselling "prudence and harmony and legal proceedings—no violence."

But violence was already bursting upon Texas. In rebellion against exorbitant duty charges and other abuses, three unarmed schooners in Texas colonial trade were sailed out of the Brazos River without clearing the Mexican port authority or paying tonnage fees. Presently one of the schooners, the *Sabine,* returned, bringing two brass cannon. They were the *Ariel's* old cannon that had been put ashore to lighten her for her last attempt to cross the bar of Galveston Bay. The Texans now possessed artillery. Ill feeling grew, and in the late spring the Mexican authority arrested seven colonists and took them into the fort at Anáhuac on Galveston Bay. Their neighbors took up arms and attacked the fort, to obtain the release of the prisoners. Negotiations ended in charges of bad faith on both sides, and the settlers sent for the *Ariel's* cannon. These could not come by land, and so were mounted on the schooner *Brazoria* behind bulwarks of baled cotton. To reach Anáhuac, she must sail past Fort Velasco, at Galveston. The garrison there refused her passage, and a land-sea battle followed that ended with the surrender of the fort, the disablement of the *Brazoria,* the release of the prisoners of Anáhuac, the abandonment of that post, and the withdrawal by summer's end of all Mexican troops from Texas. Most of them pronounced their support of Santa Anna and went to join him. It was the first victory of Texan arms against Mexico. Quiet was restored for the moment, and Stephen Austin once again from the Rio Grande proclaimed adherence to Mexico and the Mexican confederation.

At Matamoros in late June he saw the local effect of the Santa Anna campaign. "We have had a revolution here, or rather a change of garrisons and of officers. The Govt. troops very quietly marched off at one end of the town, and Col. Mexía with 300 marched *in* at the other end—he is of the Santana party. . . ." Mexía brought his troops from Tampico by water, accompanied by the Governor of Tamaulipas. They landed at the mouth of the river, marched overland without

incident except the firing of three cannon balls at a small party of
government cavalry that quickly dispersed itself, and many of the ten
thousand people of Matamoros and near-by settlements escorted the
invaders into town. "I have never seen anything conducted with so
much good order," Austin said. " . . . the ordinary business of the
merchants was not interrupted one hour—not one cent of private
property has been touched—not one act of confusion or even of disorder
has occurred since Mexía arrived. . . . he is . . . I think quite a liberal
and good man. I am much pleased with him." There was some concern
over reports that General Mier y Terán, who adhered to the government,
was in the neighborhood with an army; but this was dissipated presently
by news that Santa Anna had engaged him in battle and defeated him.
Austin presently heard what had followed on July third. "Teran killed
himself at Padilla on the 3—he ran his sword through his heart on the
very spot where Iturbide was shot." Santa Anna continued to drive his
way to the capital and the presidential palace.

Austin addressed him from the Rio Grande. " . . . I have
expressed my opinion," he said with vehemence that mounted with his
latest thought, "to the government of the Nation and to General Santa
Anna from Matamoros, with a particular notice of the slanderous, unjust
and Machiavellian lie, of that imaginary ghost raised by the aristocratic and designing enemies of the immigration of republican
settlers—that the inhabitants of Texas wish to secede from Mexico." In
a few days he took ship with General Mexía for the Brazos, and once
home, put himself on record in support of the current revolution. "The
colony and all Texas have but one course left which is to unite in the
cause of the Santana party, and if necessary fight it out. . . ."

For it was clear that the party in power under President Bustamante would grant little that Texas wanted. Bustamante's laws of
April 6, 1830, reduced Texas to a mere source of revenue that was to
be wrung from her by soldiery. New immigration was illegal under
Article II of the law. The appeals of Texas for loyal autonomy were
ignored. Bustamante actually threatened to make Texas into one vast
penal colony for the ejecta of Mexican society. No wonder the Texans
turned hopefully to Santa Anna, whose drive now looked certain of
success. He could not possibly do worse for Texas than Bustamante; he
could only do better. In the main, Texas wanted two things. One was
relief from the laws that cut off further North American settlers from
entering. The other was separation from Coahuila into statehood for
herself under the Mexican federation.

Many of the Texan complaints were like those laid before the Spanish córtes by the colonial delegates of Coahuila and New Mexico seventeen years before. Again the colony was too far from the view of the government for colonists to receive the most ordinary official services. Stephen Austin in 1832 stated that in all of Texas there was not one civil court, or even a lawyer, while the "supreme tribunal of Justice is at Saltillo, a distance of 300 leagues. The legislature understands neither the situation nor the wants of Texas, nor can it understand them. The military powers under the anti-republican anti-liberal administration of Guerrero's assassins . . . have treated the government and constitution of the State of Coahuila and Texas with a complete contempt. If the authorities of the State have borne such insults, there is no reason why the people should do so. . . ."

There were other conditions that tended to make a natural separation between Coahuila and Texas. Texas with her great Gulf Coast had access to foreign commerce, while Coahuila, all inland, lived on a straggle of internal commerce. Inhabited Texas with her meadow-lands and rains from the Gulf was mainly farming country, while arid Coahuila was mostly given over to cattle ranges and mining. When Coahuila dealt with commerce and industry she provided for her own conditions, not those in Texas. "In short," said Austin, "you may say that Texas needs a *government,* and that the best she can have, is to be created a State in the Mexican Federation." And to justify, support and administer her own state government, Texas needed to grow: " . . . We want more population, and to obtain it the Article 11th of the law of April 6th, 1830 must be abrogated," concluded Austin.

As though to prove intentions of complete loyalty to Mexico, the Texans would ask that San Antonio de Béxar become the state capital. It was the oldest settlement, the seat of Mexican authority, in Texas. Its town council should be the nucleus of a Texas legislature. Let the council, urged Austin, "represent against the laws preventing imigration from other countries . . . let it complain against the maritime tariff, a barbarous contrivance ruinous to agriculture; let it expose clearly the abuses of the military power, and above all, let it be the first to urge a seperation from Coahuila and the formation of a seperate State." The San Antonians, if they would do these things, need not fear a lack of support. "The character of the people of Texas is interprizing and decided, they scorn dangers and laugh at obstacles; therefore if Béxar wishes to be at the head of these people, it must be decided in its course, it must be *Mexico-Texan.*"

There was little time left to make such decisions. The Texan colonists were in no mood to wait much longer for recognition and accommodation of their needs by the mother government. "Things have now come to such a pass," said Austin, "that lukewarm measures are ruinous, it is necessary to adopt a party, and to declare it publicly, otherwise I apprehend that it would be difficult to avoid difficulties, divisions, and local ill feeling throughout Texas." But the summer of 1832 passed, and no sign of official interest in the Texas question came either from Mexico City, or Saltillo or even San Antonio, and in September, the colonists acted. Boldly breaking the law of 1824 that prohibited citizens of Mexico from holding assemblies, the Texan aldermen of San Felipe de Austin on the Brazos called a convention to meet on October first to discuss ways and means to achieve separate statehood, and to take up other public questions.

The convention sat from Monday to Saturday in the first week of October. It was attended by only fifty-six delegates, for not enough time had been allowed for many more men to be present. But they aired their great principle in free debate. Among the delegates were native Mexicans who lived in Texas, and other foreigners than the Anglo-Americans. When they rose at the end of the week they had a sense of having done a momentous act. But "our consciences are clear," declared Austin. "Should the future drive us into an attitude of hostility in defense of what we have so dearly earned, the public opinion of good men, I think, will acquit us of wrong—we shall *then* expect that the sympathies which cheered the struggling Greeks and Poles—that sanctioned the independence of Spanish America—that applaud the liberals of France, and the reformists of Great Britain, will also cheer the humble watch fires of our undisciplined militia, and if necessary soon swell their ranks to a respectable army. . . ." But he hastened to make clear that separation from Coahuila was all that was wanted, not separation from Mexico. And yet—and yet when the first convention had risen and its members gone home, he could not help revealing in that autumn of 1832 a dreamlike possibility. Separation from Mexico, he said, was not to the interest of Texas "if such a thing can be avoided, unless"—and he underlined what came next—*"unless indeed we should float into the Northern Republic with the consent of all parties, ourselves included."*

It was like the completion of a design for another man and his purpose when Stephen Austin received a letter written from Nashville, Tennessee, September 10, 1832, by one of Austin's colonists, who was travelling. It came by hand, and on its cover bore the inscription,

"Politeness of Genl. Houston," and it introduced the bearer: "Genl. A. [sic] Houston of this town is going to depart for Texas in a day or two, he is going by the way *Arkansas Territory,* it will take him until in the month of Decr. sometime to reach you, I have given him a letter of introduction to you which he will hand you on his arrival there, I am not informed of his views in Visiting that country, I think he would be a great addition to Our country as a Citizen, he is a very intimate friend of the Presidents . . . I think it would be well worth your trouble to try and Make him a Citizen of your Colony. . . ."

The second statehood convention assembled on April 1, 1833. On the same day in Mexico General Santa Anna was inaugurated as President of Mexico. The Texans had guessed right in the recent revolution, and now prepared their address to the new president. Their labors were mainly given to two great matters. One was the drafting of a state constitution, and the committee to do this was headed by General Sam Houston, who had come to stay. The other was the framing of a petition to the national government appealing for statehood under the law of 1824 that said, "So soon as Texas is in a situation to figure as a State she shall inform Congress thereof for its resolution." For a fortnight the delegates worked on their papers; and ended by appointing three commissioners to proceed to Mexico with the Texan case. Of these, only one, Stephen Austin, went. He was confident of the outcome.

"I go with considerable—I may say—strong hopes of success," he declared. The petition was well argued from a legal point of view, its tone was respectful and dignified, and surely the government could neither take offense at it nor refuse what was asked. Every constitutional approach to the affair would be followed so long as there was hope of official agreement in the end. Stephen Austin hoped for a harmonious solution, for this mission was the last he intended to perform for the colony. He had worked tirelessly, and had launched a great enterprise, and now he hoped to retire with one more success behind him. "If however I fail,"—and he now reflected what was already in the minds of his people—"and war is the result, I will take a hand in that, and enter the ranks as a soldier of Texas." Who knew? In any case, on the eve of departure, he was not sorry for all the large impulses that had brought him through trouble and the ingratitude of small minds. "I had rather at least be capable of being moved by bright visions, never realized, than to pass through the world without being touched by the recollections of the past, the events of the present, or the anticipations of the future," he meditated, leaving for the Rio

Grande and the capital, and hoping to be home again in four months, if not sooner.

News of the convention had reached Matamoros in garbled form. It made much excitement. Along the Rio Grande it was believed that Texas had declared national independence and was raising an army to fight Mexico. Austin hastened to see the new Commandant General, Vicente Filisola, whom he reassured, with the result that Filisola ended by thinking well of statehood for Texas. The Commandant General was shocked by conditions as he found them on the Rio Grande, where smuggling was arrogantly carried on by officials, traders and clever lawyers. He discussed his problems with Austin, who was not well. Epidemics were sweeping the whole country in the summer of 1833, and Austin was a victim in May—"much debilitated by Dysentary or *Cholorina.*"

Waiting to take ship for Veracruz from the river's mouth, he was troubled by an old obsession that once again and in another sweeping veer of his convictions agitated itself into his correspondence. "I have been adverse to the principle of slavery in Texas. I have now, and for the last six months, changed my views of that matter; though my ideas are the same as to the abstract principle. Texas *must be* a slave country. Circumstances and unavoidable necessity compels it. It is the wish of the people there, and it is my duty to do all I can, prudently, in favor of it. I will do so." The dark dream of 1830 had passed off; and the climate of the society he had founded now prevailed over the justice and terror with which he had once viewed slavery, and over the morbid hatred he had then shown for the Negro. In the end he seemed like an individual torn asunder by the matter as a whole nation was later to be. He shook himself together for the trip to the capital—down to the river's mouth, up over the side of "a little schooner," and off for an expected voyage of six days to Veracruz, whence he would proceed overland to Mexico City, and the prompt dispatch of his business with Santa Anna and the government.

I I.

"God and Texas"

Nothing worked as so reasonably planned.

First, the week at sea—"I had a wretched trip. *One month* from Matamoros to Veracruz in a little schooner—ten days on short allowance of water—none but salt provisions—and sea sick all the time. But I am well now." He was in Mexico City by then, only to find that President Santa Anna was in the field with troops, putting down civil war. Vice President Gómez Farias was acting executive, and Austin called on him, and on appropriate cabinet ministers, on July 19th. He was cordially asked to return in four days to make a formal, oral presentation of his case, and when he did so, he was politely requested to submit his appeal in writing. In nine days he had it ready, and the hearings proceeded, while he felt by turns elated and hopeless. In his exhaustion, the cholorina returned to him, and he was "so weary that life is hardly worth having. . . ." But he was soon about and busy again, working on his great questions of statehood, and the repeal of the ban on immigration; and taking up other pendant matters opportunely, such as establishment of regular mails for the colonies and relief from import duties.

But however hard he worked, his little gains seemed to vanish in the toils of government—committees, interviews, debates in the Congress, all aggravated by the suspicion with which the Mexicans regarded the intentions of the United States. President Jackson's envoy in Mexico was once again pressing the purchase of Texas all the way to the Rio Grande, with a repeated offer of five million dollars. Beyond that, and in clumsy intrigue, the envoy was erecting a system of bribery that was an insult alike to Mexican pride and the dignity of the United States. Jackson in Washington, like Austin in Mexico, hoped to accomplish his different aims for Texas by legal means, with candor and good will. But all Mexico could see in either's approach was an insatiable appetite for her vast province of Texas; and in her alarm, which was entirely justified, she took refuge in the hesitations and elaborations of her bureaucracy; and Stephen Austin felt his patience run thin.

He heard from Texas. The news grieved him sadly. Cholera was spreading, his brother John was dead of it, and many close friends. He longed to go home, and one day in the fall while calling on the Vice President his taut nerves betrayed him, and he spoke sharply.

Either, he said, Texas must be made a state by the government, or she would make herself one.

Señor Gómez Farias was enraged. Was this a threat?

Austin replied that it was not a threat, only a statement of fact which he felt it his duty as a good Mexican to give to the authorities, that they might act wisely.

He thought the Vice President was mollified by his explanation, and he went to his lodgings. Once there, his own words echoed in his ear, and he sat down and wrote a furious letter to the Town Council of San Antonio de Béxar. It was dated October 2, 1833. In it he said that civil war conditions in Mexico made it impossible for anything to be accomplished. Nothing had been done for his mission, and nothing would be done. In such a state of affairs, he called for the settlements of Texas to combine without delay to form their own state government under the law of 7 May 1824. The central government was going to do nothing for Texas. "If the people of Texas," he wrote, "do not take their affairs into their own hands, that land is lost," and he was powerfully convinced that the course he urged was the only one that would save them all from total anarchy and ruin. Let them not lose an instant in uniting to form a local government independent of Coahuila even if the general government refuses its approval. "Dios y Texas," he concluded, and dispatched the paper which would travel for almost a month before being delivered in San Antonio, while he lingered in the capital.

The civil war suddenly took a new turn, resistance collapsed, and in early November the President returned to town and resumed his office. Austin soon gained access to him, and once again his volatile hopes rose. Santa Anna in gold lace and decorations was small, compact and stocky, with a large head and a gravely sensitive expression in his fine eyes, and a delicate smile that seemed to comment upon his own blood-won eminence with some detachment. If Austin was ready to face him with impatience, the President disarmed him. He seemed "very friendly about Texas," and quite as though he had never written his fiery letter of October second, Austin wrote home after his interviews with the

President—he saw him twice—"I am of opinion that if you all keep quiet and obey the state laws that the *substance* of all Texas wants will be granted. The appearance of things is much better than it was a month or even two weeks ago. . . ."

And in fact the government now moved swiftly to compose the Texas question. The ban on immigration was formally lifted. While statehood was not granted out of hand, and in any case would have to be voted on by all the other states of the federation, the government pledged itself to bring Texas as rapidly as possible to it, or to the status of a territory, and Austin sent word that "all will go right." Lesser questions of tariffs, mails, and establishment of local courts were, in government's timeless gestures, referred to appropriate offices for study. Eager to be off, Austin told the colony that "Texas matters are all right. Nothing is wanted there but *quiet.* . . ." But yes, there was one more thing. "It is now very important to harmonise with Béxar. . . ." for at all costs his letter of October second must not be acted upon now. He left Mexico City on the tenth of December.

At Saltillo, on January 3, 1834, on his way home he called on the local commandant to discuss Texan affairs, and was immediately placed under arrest by order of Vice President Gómez Farias. For the Town Council of San Antonio de Béxar, horrified even to receive the revolutionary letter of October second, had sent copies of it everywhere, and one had reached Gómez Farias, together with a copy of their reply, which groaned with loyalty and begged to be read by the government. "It is certainly regrettable," stated the San Antonians to Austin, "that you should breathe sentiments so contrary and opposed to those of every good Mexican. . . . This corporation neither can nor ought, or even wishes, to follow your suggestion, and it begs that you cease writing to it in regard to this matter"—they shuddered—"because you know very well what these communications render one liable to. . . ." The evidence was damning, and the prisoner could but recognize the fact.

"In a moment of irritation and impatience I wrote an imprudent letter to the Aynta. of Texas in October last," he informed a colonist, "for which I have been arrested and ordered back to Mexico . . . as a prisoner. I do not blame the govt at all for this—my treatment has been very good since my arrest . . ." and he asked the Town Council of San Felipe de Austin "that there may be no excitement about it." Looking back, he could not help listing the "calamities" of the past year in Texas —"floods, pestilence and"—what had brought him to jail—"conventions." It was an odd view to take of the democratic process by which his colony reached for new life. For the rest, he declared that all he had done was work "arduously, faithfully . . . and pationately" for statehood. . . . "This is all, and this is no crime. . . ."

He was kept for ten months in various Mexico prisons. One of them was the dreaded Accordada that had been used by the Inquisition, and there he knew solitary confinement. His only friend was a mouse who regularly came to see him and learned to eat out of his hand. "I . . . laughed at his antic miniature comedies," remarked the prisoner with one of his rare smiles, "and talked to him for hours." After seven months of confinement Austin saw his great mission to Mexico with new, and sad, eyes: "I hope the State question is totally *dead* and will remain so." His friends at home took to heart his requests that they do nothing to agitate for his freedom. No word, no plea, no funds, came from Texas. Presently he was moved to another prison, and then to another. His bitterness overflowed when he heard from one of his guards that certain Texans were at work arranging for him to be in prison for years and years. What if he *had* asked them to stay out of the case? They should have overruled his impulse toward self-sacrifice to make a gesture in his behalf. "A frank, manly, but mild and respectful representation from the people of Texas in my favor would have set me at liberty long since and would do it now . . . my situation is desolate. . . . I expect to die in this prison. . . . When I am dead," he threatened luxuriously, "justice will be done me. . . . This is man and mankind—a picture of human life."

It took months, a year, but finally Texans pleaded for him, and, touched, he declared that he had never believed a word of the stories about colonists working against him. He was released on bail, his trial was scheduled through many changes of venue and postponements, and he occupied himself with memorials on matters of government. He found time—there was plenty of time—to sit for two portraits in miniature on ivory, one in rich formal dress, the other in buckskin hunting costume with rifle, dog, books and leafy savannah, and both fashionably Byronic in feeling. Actually, suspended between the law in Mexico and his responsibilities at home, he was at liberty to amuse himself for the first time in fourteen years. He went to the play; to the opera; to assemblies and balls. He frequented drawing rooms. He wished he could take a long pleasure trip after his scrape was disposed of. Texas seemed curiously far from his thoughts. There, at home, forces were still growing that had sent him to Mexico, and a powerful new personality was increasingly known through the settlements, as General Houston, established in a law practice in East Texas, made himself felt in public questions.

"The little Gentleman," he ironically called Stephen Austin; and after reading one or two of Austin's mournful and suspicious letters from prison, he felt "pity mingled with contempt," and added that Austin "showed the disposition of the viper without its fangs."

But after so many delays of the law, Austin's enforced holiday was suddenly at an end, and under a general amnesty applying to participants in the civil wars, he was at last after two years given his passport and allowed to go home in July, 1835. He sailed from Vera-cruz for New Orleans, where he would take another ship for Texas. He believed he was bringing one more chance for Texas, if she would be patient and if the President had made his compromises in good faith, to win the place she wanted in the Federation. It was true that Santa Anna had mentioned a plan to send a corps of four thousand infantry, cavalry and artillery to San Antonio de Béxar to control Texas; but Austin thought he had dissuaded him.

Yet Santa Anna's victories in the civil wars were not comprehensive; and as rebellion broke out in one state or another, he was forced to put it down again; and he ended by suspending the federation, dissolving legislatures, and appointing his own creatures to governorships. When such revolution flared in Coahuila, he sent his brother-in-law, General Martin Perfecto de Cos, to the northern provinces to restore order. An army moved into position on the Rio Grande at Matamoros, facing Texas. Was Cos with his troops along the river ready to execute Santa Anna's armed occupation after all?

Texans seemed willing to give him provocation to do so. A customs garrison of forty men and a captain had been re-established at Anáhuac. Early in the summer of 1835 they were taken prisoners by thirty Texans under William B. Travis, and ordered out of Texas. They went. Once again Mexican arms had been thrown back across the Rio Grande. General Cos made his report, and was ordered to capture the five ringleaders of the latest Anáhuac affair, together with Lorenzo de Zavala, who was a refugee from the personal and political enmity of Santa Anna. Cos accordingly directed his subordinate commander at Béxar to arrest Zavala by force if necessary, and requested the peaceful delivery of the Anáhuac filibusters. It was an act that touched off all the latent explosive power in the Texas colonies. Rumors flew across the settlements. Mexico was coming to invade Texas and take the demanded men by force. The colonies were to be deprived of slaves. The Mexican constitution of 1824, which was the last refuge of Texan hopes, the actual charter of their contract, was nullified. Settlers who had arrived since April 6, 1830, were to be expelled. Texans who had resisted Mexican soldiery were to be court-martialled. A military despotism was about to descend. . . . The colonists encouraged one another with promises of defiance, and war was in the air.

It hovered over the Gulf. The government maintained a revenue ship called the *Correo de México* to patrol the shipping for Velasco, with orders to capture contraband vessels. In August she took an American brig. American captains thereafter vowed vengeance. The chance for it came on September first, when the schooner *San Felipe,* of United States registry, sighted the *Correo de México* off the mouth of the Brazos. The *San Felipe* closed in and fired on the Mexican. The fire was returned. The engagement lasted three quarters of an hour, until the *Correo de México* withdrew.

One of the passengers on the American ship was Stephen Austin, returning from Mexico. It was his first view of battle, and it told him, after his long absence, how bitter were the animosities to which he had come home. He landed from the *San Felipe* and all night long he "walked the beach, his mind oppressed with the gravity of the situation, forecasting the troubles ahead to Texas." How many more armed encounters, however small, could there be without an actual state of war? He was hailed on his return as the only leader who could unify Texas and show her where to go. What was there left to hope for from a Mexico too ravaged by civil war to order her own national, let alone a provincial, government? Santa Anna in destroying the federation of the states had established a centralist government with himself as absolute ruler. Who could deny to Texans the liberty of deciding whether or not they would rest content under such a government? Who could tell the Texans not to defend their rights under the 1824 Constitution? Who could tell them not to oppose with a militia under arms Cos and his troops from the Rio Grande if they should come? Austin found that another convention—was it to be another "calamity"?—had already been called to decide on the issue. It was plain that if they decided against the dictatorship, war must follow. Many counselled keeping the peace, at least until Texas might organize for war. Many others called for immediate war.

Austin was asked to address his colonists at Brazoria on September eighth, when they wanted to hear his counsel in their trouble. If he asked them to defer or withdraw the call to the convention, they would know he was against war. If he approved it—they would follow him under arms. He rose to speak; and in a very few minutes, all knew the answer. Only a gathering of the people of Texas, he declared, could justly determine whether they would accept the abandonment of the republican for the centralized government. The convention was to be held. The decision was made. Under its implications, a call to arms sounded throughout Texas; and facing the Rio Grande, the North American colonists made ready.

12.

From Mexico's Point of View

What had to be done was familiar enough to be thoroughly understood by General Cos and the citizens of the Rio Grande. It had been done often enough in the states below the river. When pronouncements were made against the government, and arms were brandished in revolution, there must follow long marches in prickly dust; passages and encampments in gritty mountains where a column of government troops was lost like any lizard; sightings of distant towns like images in mirrors of heat, approaches in wide circlings, and then contact, firing, a cavalry charge, confusions of personal valor; and whether after one day, or many, an end in some plaza with the reading of an official paper, a dropping sword, a volley, men crumbling dead and leaking crimson, while from arched shadows framed in white plaster the non-military residents of Mexico regarded with fixed and fated eyes what an army was for.

Above the river, Texas—up to now the least troublesome of all Mexican political districts—invited suppression. The action that followed, seen from the Mexican point of view, was that of a sovereign national government doing its duty. It was a point of view to be maintained, in the way of nations, by force of arms, as long as possible.

In September General Cos again demanded the delivery of Zavala and the perpetrators of the Anáhuac outrage; and when they were not surrendered, he hurried his preparations to go and take them. He mustered five hundred soldiers at Matamoros. Some of these were trained and uniformed. Most were recently arrived criminals herded north for frontier service. He did what he could with them—issued arms, conducted drills, assigned them to units. They were of predominantly Mexican Indian strains, like all the soldiery of the nation. In their own village units lost in rock or jungle or desert with primitive weapons they were willing warriors and remorseless familiars of death. Now in squads, under heavy rifles, and subject to other authority than that of magic ancestors, they wondered at being soldiers. General Cos embarked them on small ships at the mouth of the Rio Grande on September 17, 1835, to sail up the coast on the Laguna Madre inside Padre Island for Copano on Matagorda Bay. He intended to go ashore, march inland to San Antonio de Béxar to join the Mexican garrison there, and by a show of power, to reduce the Texans, take his prisoners, and restore order above the Rio Grande. It was not known how long the general commanding the northeast provinces would be absent from his Matamoros headquarters; but information would be sent back from time to time, and as soon as the Texans had been brought to their senses, certain long-range plans would take effect. President Santa Anna was absent from the capital, preparing regiments that would in due course immensely reinforce the garrisons of Texas, and in any case, he had informed the Texans that he proposed personally to visit them in the following March—"as a friend." Meanwhile, the acting President had issued a circular from the capital which came to the Rio Grande forces to show them their duty, the reasons for it, and the promise of their own triumph. It was read with interest from Matamoros to Fort Rio Grande:

"The colonists established in Texas have recently given the most unequivocal evidence of the extremity to which perfidy, ingratitude and the restless spirit that animates them can go, since—forgetting what they owe to the supreme government of the nation which so generously admitted them to its bosom, gave them fertile lands to cultivate, and allowed them all the means to live in comfort and abundance—they have risen against that same government, taking up arms against it under the pretense of sustaining a system which an immense majority of Mexicans have asked to have changed, thus concealing their criminal purpose of dismembering the territory of the Republic.

"His Excellency the President *ad interim,* justly irritated by a conduct so perfidious, has fixed his entire attention upon this subject, and in order to suppress and punish that band of ungrateful foreigners, has directed that the most active measures be taken, measures required by the very nature of what is in reality a crime against the whole nation. The troops destined to sustain the honor of the country and the government will perform their duty and will cover themselves with glory."

The government made a strong case for the people and the army, and showed every confidence, even though it was a long march into Texas and the seat of the trouble. What if there were over twenty thousand settlers there now? They were not organized, their communities were scattered, and the two largest ones—in East Texas and along the Brazos—had few dealings together, and no political connection. Matamoros and its environs alone totalled around ten thousand people; and below Matamoros were the other states of Mexico where even in times of trial (the national treasury was empty and troops lived off the lands they crossed or the cities they invested) the sheer weight of numbers would certainly overwhelm the Texans, if they persisted in forgetting who owned Texas, after all. . . . News from General Cos was awaited with confidence and interest.

It was incredible when finally, by courier, and traveller, and scribbled field dispatch, it began to filter through the brush country into the sovereign Mexican establishments of the Rio Grande; and when, on Christmas Day, 1835, General Cos himself with an exhausted brigade appeared out of Texas at Laredo upriver, crossed, and settled his followers to lick their wounds. His campaign of four months could now be seen in its entirety from the Mexican point of view.

Entering Texas from the shore in September, General Cos heard how the Texans were organizing everywhere under committees of public safety; yet no one opposed him as he marched inland toward San Antonio, going by way of La Bahía, now called Goliad. He arrived there on the second of October and at once learned of a clumsy performance that had developed a few days before at Gonzales, a settlement east of San Antonio. The settlers there possessed a brass six-pounder that had been given them by the army four years before as a protection against Indians. Now in the unrest that prevailed so widely, Colonel Ugartechea, the commander at San Antonio, remembered the cannon, and even though it was known to be unmounted, he sent a small detachment to take it away. The settlers refused to give it up, captured the detachment, sent word to their neighbors that the government was about to attack them, and a force of Texans gathered fast preparing for battle. They removed their women and children to safety. They commandeered all the small boats on the Guadalupe River where Gonzales stood. They were ready when eighty soldiers under a lieutenant appeared from the garrison at San Antonio to free their comrades, take the brass cannon and arrest those responsible for outright revolt. The lieutenant held discretionary orders. If the Texans outnumbered him so far as to make it seem likely that he would be repulsed, and the national dignity impaired, he was to retire. Upon examining the situation he concluded that he must do so, and withdrew his position to "a slight eminence" six miles west of the Guadalupe River.

But that night—it was about eleven o'clock on October first—the Texans crossed over the river and then waited until dawn, which came over heavy fog. And then coming within a range of about three hundred and fifty yards, an advance party of Texans fired upon the army and were at once pursued by soldiers. The six-pounder was brought forward and set off with a load of grapeshot. As the fog lifted the army saw a piece of insolence. Over the cannon the Texans had placed a sign reading "Come and Take it!". The lieutenant from San Antonio gave an order to his trumpeter, who sounded a parley, which was held. No agreement resulted. The army would not surrender, and the rebels would not give up the old brass piece that was the cause of all the trouble. Instead, after the truce was over, the Texans fired it again, and then charged. There were over a hundred and fifty of them, fifty mounted. A loyalist soldier was killed. The army became disorganized, turned, and hurried off to San Antonio.

It was hardly a battle; yet the Texans had deliberately prepared for it as if it were to be one, and with effrontery had actually taken the initiative in attack. It was clear that the colonists had determined on war, were now enemies, and had fought their first engagement as such, with results unfortunate for the national dignity. General Cos had not arrived a moment too soon.

He inspected the supplies stored in the ruined mission of La Bahía at Goliad, which would serve him as an important base between San Antonio and the sea, and would also command a strategic road to Matamoros and the Rio Grande. In the old mission were stored for the large punitive operations planned by General Cos a number of pieces of artillery, three hundred rifles, ten thousand dollars in strongboxes, and plentiful supplies. After estimating the situation, General Cos stationed thirty soldiers and a colonel to guard the base, led his forces through the heavy autumn air over rolling hills and past green meadowlands threaded by bright little creeks to San Antonio, where he would hold consultations with Colonel Ugartechea. He hardly reached there before an exasperating report reached after him.

On the night of October ninth the Texans had descended upon Goliad, killed a sentry, chopped their way through a door with axes, and had captured the colonel commanding, all his men, and everything stored in the mission of La Bahía. It was bad, but what made it worse was that the outrage had been committed by only forty Texans, one of whom was a known troublemaker named Milam, who had in fact escaped from prison at Monterrey. With Goliad lost to him, General Cos had no base for either the lower Rio Grande or the seaports of Texas. The campaign was opening inauspiciously for the government. It was time to do something to reverse the trend.

General Cos established his men at San Antonio, and for two weeks examined the situation in staff discussions with Colonel Ugartechea; and then—was the initiative always to be in the hands of the enemy?—an army of many hundred Texans was reported to be approaching San Antonio. On September twenty-seventh a large advance party took up a position in the river hollows by the empty mission of the Immaculate Conception—one of the five clustered along the San Antonio river. The Texans were about a mile and a half across an open plain from garrison headquarters. Their very position was a challenge—almost it seemed like a threat of siege to the garrison. General Cos met it with decision.

When the Texans woke up on the morning of the twenty-eighth they found themselves surrounded by four hundred government troops. There was no escape for them, and no sensible course but surrender. Instead, under the heavy morning fog they formed two elements down in the river hollows, which afforded them natural breastworks, and there when the fog rose the army advanced upon them with blazing volleys, that seemed, however, to take little effect. It was the enemy fire that was effective—dreadfully so. It was amazing how the Texans handled firearms, they aimed like hawks, they fired with extreme deliberation, and all too often they hit their mark. They had a sort of drilled system. One man loaded while another fired, by pairs, so, along the lines, so that there never was a gap of silence and vulnerability while all loaded at once. The government force charged three times, supported by a brass six-pounder that hurled grapeshot into the shallow ravine; but the rifle fire from the river was so terrible that a hundred soldiers were killed or wounded, and it was not long until the rest were retreating to San Antonio, leaving behind them the cannon which became a prize for the enemy. There could be no doubt that this, the Battle of La Concepción, was another defeat for the properly constituted authority of Mexico.

An hour later the remainder of the Texan army appeared from down the river course, where they had marched and camped by the other missions—Saint Francis of Espada, Saint John of Capistrano, Saint Joseph—and joined their victorious men who had been captained by Texans named Bowie and Fannin. The fifth mission was within the town, it was the one commonly spoken of as the Álamo, and though partially ruined, served as a useful storehouse, shop building and fortress for the garrison. There was every possibility in the encampment across the plain to the south that the Texans would not be content until they took the Álamo also. There were now about a thousand men gathered beyond the Concepción mission with its arched cloister and its beautiful dome, and their commander was discovered to be Colonel Esteban Austin, the chief of the Brazos colony. General Cos still held the road that led back to Laredo on the Rio Grande. Acting decisively, he dispatched Colonel Ugartechea and a hundred garrison soldiers to Laredo to return by forced marches with reinforcements of as many as five hundred conscripted convicts who were stationed there. Left with eight hundred men in the town, General Cos directed operations, erecting barricades, placing batteries and strengthening all defenses.

In the following days the Texans were everywhere. Twice they moved their position closer. They patrolled the approaches and kept supplies from coming into San Antonio. They sent a demand for surrender which despite his shrinking stock of food and other supplies General Cos disdained, just as he disdained breaking forth to give battle. For nearly a month the garrison waited for the return of Ugartechea and the conscripts, and the Texans in little sallies rode around the town trying to force combat. It was plain that they had no heavy guns with which to reduce the garrison from afar. They seemed restless and confused, and reports came in from their bivouacs that many of them were leaving their camp in disgust because there was no fight. But they received reinforcements now and then—three companies of volunteers from the United States, one from East Texas—and their intention seemed to be to hang on.

What they were determined to fight for was meanwhile being declared in a civil assembly held in San Felipe de Austin early in the same month. Those settlers who were not serving in the field with the armed party met to create a state government, swearing loyalty to

Mexico under the constitution of 1824, and electing a governor, a commander-in-chief, and other officials. They had the idea that they were not pronouncing against Mexico, or sending men to fight against her, but only against the present government of Don Antonio López de Santa Anna and his system. They were supposed to believe that their policy would have the sympathy and support of many thousands of Mexicans below the Rio Grande who also preferred to cling to the abandoned constitution. But the President had more than once disposed of such Mexicans, and in any case, the Texan affair was rebellion against him, and the army, and the powers that were, and would be handled accordingly, as General Cos was handling them.

At San Antonio, General Cos faced increasing difficulties over supplies. Even fodder was scarce, and one day he sent a column of one hundred muleteers and soldiers out on the old Rio Grande road to cut grass for the hungry horses of the garrison. They gathered a pack-train load of grass in safety and were coming back to the town when a hundred mounted Texans attacked them, evidently thinking they were attacking Colonel Ugartechea with his reinforcements, and his saddlebags loaded with silver with which to pay troops and conduct the war. More Texans rushed to join the fight when they saw it developing, and the foraging party was obliged to break and run for the town, leaving behind all the mules, and fifty soldiers dead and a number wounded.

It became known later that a day or so before the grass fight Colonel Austin resigned the command of his forces to journey to the United States as a commissioner to raise money and support for the Texan revolt. Colonel Edward Burleson was elected, as North Americans always elected their officers, to succeed him in command. Shortly afterward events began to move more rapidly.

First, General Cos was betrayed by the escape of three Texan prisoners of the Anáhuac affair, and the desertion of a Mexican lieutenant. These men conveyed to the enemy camp news of how things were inside the besieged headquarters. The Texans evidently took much encouragement from what they learned of the state of the troops, supplies and defenses of San Antonio and the fortified Álamo mission. On the night of December fourth, the enemy moved to a new position by the old mill northeast of town, and just before sunrise on the fifth they attacked in three columns. One entered the town by way of Acequia Street, another through Soledad Street, both coming swiftly to the northern entrances of the main plaza. At the same time, the third attacked the Álamo east of the river, and a battle of four days began.

Every street and rooftop was fought for. Every house was the scene
of a delaying action. The Texans used their small arms with fearful
accuracy, and raked the narrow streets with their handful of small
cannon. It rained on December eighth and the day was cold. When the
Texans gained entry to the first room of a row of adobe houses, they
used battering rams to break through into the next, and the next, until
they held the whole row, and then a whole street. Even the arrival of
Colonel Ugartechea with men from the Rio Grande on the night of the
eighth could not hold San Antonio against the wildly fighting invaders.
General Cos withdrew from the plaza to the Álamo, which his men still
defended, and prepared to rally for a great effort that would make the
best use of Ugartechea's troops and save the town and the flag. But it was
a night of further betrayals. Three officers led their companies out and
left for the Rio Grande, and when the desertions were known, the remaining soldiers began to cry "Treason! Treason!", and the civilians joined
them in creating a panic. General Cos went among them calling out
counsels of courage and calm; but he was unrecognized or ignored, and
suffered brutal maltreatment in the darkness and the confusion of his
own people. He came to his final decision that night, and at sunrise, he
sent his Adjutant-Inspector forth from the Álamo with his surrender.

A treaty was signed on the eleventh, and on the fourteenth
General Cos began his return to the Rio Grande, having agreed for himself and his officers upon his honor not to oppose further the re-establishment of the Constitution of 1824. The conscript criminals were to be
removed from Texas beyond the Rio Grande, while the remainder of
the government troops were at liberty to remain in Texas or follow
their commanding general as they chose. All were allowed to keep their
arms and equipment. The wounded and sick were allowed to remain in
Texas until they should recover. No prisoners were kept by the Texans,
or shot. The campaign had taken a little less than four months, and
had cost Mexico hundreds of casualties in killed or wounded, the Texans
two killed and twenty-six wounded. The Texan army, its disloyal task
finished, scattered its units to their home neighborhoods. General Cos
on December fourteenth with eleven hundred and five men began the
march that ended on Christmas Day, 1835, at Laredo on the Rio Grande.

No proper adherent of the Mexican party in power could see
the Texans' revolt as anything but a personal affront to the President.
But if they were in revolt against his system, he was already arranging
to deal with them. It was known on the Mexican frontier that he was
raising ten thousand soldiers to take to Texas, and the news filtered over

the river to the rebels themselves, who hurriedly and with great confusion between military elements and political began in December to dispose their defenses. They secured the port of Copano, and bases at Goliad, Refugio, Matagorda and Velasco. Travellers still came and went between Texas and Coahuila, and there were also couriers and spies who brought news to the river. By such means it was learned that the Texans, after much dissension in their own councils, were preparing to mount an expedition against Matamoros. To do so they made a decision that could only be satisfying to the President and his generals; for to obtain troops for the invasion of Mexico at Matamoros, they withdrew all but sixty men from the garrison at the Álamo in San Antonio, and in two divided parties, started for the Rio Grande metropolis in winter weather of freezing mists and cold rains over the long stretch of barren country parallel to the coast. They moved slowly, which gave time for the Mexican northeast command to send heavy reinforcements to Matamoros throughout January, 1836.

Both the uprisen colonists and the generals of the republic considered making their opposing movements by sea; but neither had enough ships in which to transport their troops. The Texans had four precarious, if armed, schooners that gave them command of the Mexico Bay. The President, therefore, proceeded with plans for a land campaign. General Fernández was already at Matamoros with his reinforcements. General Urrea was ordered to join him there and cross the Rio Grande immediately, to seek out and destroy the Texan expedition. General Santa Anna with the main body of five brigades numbering just over six thousand men marched for Laredo by way of Fort Saint John Baptist and arrived on February twelfth. On the same day General Ramírez y Sesma crossed the river by the ford of France Way and headed for San Antonio de Béxar. After attending a ball at Laredo, the President took his troops across the Rio Grande on rafts and in his turn left for San Antonio on February sixteenth. On the next day General Urrea crossed the Rio Grande at Matamoros. The multiple invasion was launched. Mexico again watched her sovereign duty being done, this time by the President and his forces.

The main body was stretched out for miles, with distances between its brigades that would take days to close. It was a miserable march. The forces on leaving the Rio Grande had to cross hard brush wastelands until they came to the Nueces; and then began the difficulties created by the succession of rivers that looked on the map of Texas like veins in the half of a great leaf, all running more or less parallel, and equally separated, to the edge, which was the coast. Away from the rivers there was little water to be had for so great an army. Supply was complicated and the soldiers were forced to accept half rations. The country was too poor to feed them as they went. It rained and snowed; wagons and caissons were repeatedly mired. Or on other days the sun poured down its heat, and men and animals suffered from thirst. Soldiers fell ill and many had to be carried on the wheeled vehicles, adding to the burdens of the already punished draft animals. It was not long before wagoners recognized signs of dangerous disease in the horses and mules of the army. Many animals were stricken with the mal de lengua that was a swelling of the tongue from thirst and dry fodder; many others with the telele, a fever taken from drinking polluted water activated by the hot sun. Many soldiers died and were left in the wastes. There were few settlements where relief could be found, and what population he did encounter the President found to be apathetic in the face of the grand issue that was about to be settled by force of arms.

But he pressed forward, expecting to fall upon the rebels in San Antonio just before dawn on February twenty-second in a stunning surprise. His plan was ruined by a matter beyond his control. The heavens opened, a cloudburst fell, and his advance was mired down. It was not until the twenty-fourth that forward elements of the army entered the town. They met no opposition, and he joined them there two days later. A reconnaissance revealed that the only enemy position in the vicinity had been taken up in the structures of the Álamo, where artillery defenses on earthworks and behind the walls as established by General Cos in December were still in place. Barricaded behind them, and presumably with rations gathered to withstand a siege, was a body of Texans. Their cooking fires sent smoke above the walls, and their blinded gates and windows gave notice of their intention to remain. Above them stood their own version of the flag of Mexico—the red, white and green, with two stars, that represented Coahuila and Texas. In the face of General Santa Anna it flaunted the Constitution of 1824, under which the Twin Sister state had been founded.

The mission of San Antonio de Valero was of the usual pattern. It stood east of the river from which meandering acequias flowed past its enclosures. Built in the early eighteenth century it had stood empty since 1793, except for occasional use as a military depot. It had a great walled plaza, fifty-four by one hundred and fifty-four yards; a convent with a large patio; thick stone rooms used as a jail; a corral; and a church, whose roof had fallen in, filling the interior with hillocks of rubble. It took its popular name from the fact that a company of soldiers from El Álamo, a garrison post in Coahuila, had once been stationed there. The outer limits of the whole establishment, whether plaza, patio or church wall, enclosed about two and a half acres, and measured over a quarter of a mile. It did not seem possible that the party of Texans within the walls was large enough to man them effectively. General Santa Anna was in no hurry to open a full-scale attack, pending the arrival of other troops behind him on the long straggled march from the Rio Grande. He placed his batteries pointing across the river toward the Álamo, and established encampments with earthworks about the settlements of San Antonio at ranges measuring from three hundred to a thousand yards from the mission. His guns were light fieldpieces that could not be expected to break down walls; but he ordered cannonading, and for several days shells were lobbed into the mission enclosures, and cavalry detachments rode the perimeter to prevent escape of the occupants.

Yet a certain amount of passing in and out went on. Messengers got away, presumably asking for reinforcement by other Texas militia. One night a group of these managed to come in and join the defenders of the mission. During another night a small party dashed out to collect firewood and set some houses on fire near one of the army's batteries. By day they all worked at strengthening their works. From the walls, sharpshooters picked off soldiers who exposed themselves. It was an intermittent duel between six-pounders and small arms.

Intelligence reports indicated that a large force—two hundred men or more, under the Texan Fannin—were gathered in the neighborhood of Gonzales, and might advance upon San Antonio. General Ramírez y Sesma was ordered out with a cavalry regiment and an infantry battalion to find and dispose of them. What he was to do with them was plainly indicated in General Santa Anna's orders to him: *"En esta guerra sabe vd. que no hay prisoneros. . . ."* But if in that war there were to be no prisoners, Ramírez y Sesma found not even an enemy on the old road to Gonzales. He advanced eight miles, as far as the Espada mission, and returned on the following day to San Antonio. It was later learned that Fannin's column had started to the support of the Álamo but had turned back.

While General Santa Anna was waiting for his reinforcements, and the bombardment continued, and the defenders of the mission tried to build their safety out of the rubble within, the Texans took a fateful and defiant step on March second at the village of Washington on the

Brazos. Fifty-eight delegates, of whom three were Mexicans, signed a declaration of national independence from Mexico. They elected a full slate of national officers, including a commander-in-chief of the armed forces, and drew up a constitution, and set down their pretexts for their actions in a long bill of complaints against the mother country. For something over three months they had claimed to be a self-constituted state under the Mexican republic; now they claimed to be an independent and sovereign nation among the nations of the world. Far from the siege of San Antonio, the new government solemnly sent forth their resounding declarations against the power and authority of Mexico. If before the Texans had been guilty of serious civil disturbances, they were now guilty of outright treason, with its terrible terms of justice.

At last on Friday, March fourth, reinforcements arrived from the third brigade on the Rio Grande road, and the President called a council of war and heard his generals. Cos—who did not feel bound by the parole given to the Texans in the December treaty—was present, and urged that a full-scale attack on the Álamo should be delayed until the arrival, expected by Monday, of two twelve-pounders. Others disagreed. The President kept his own counsel until the next day, when he gave out a plan of assault to be staged before daylight on Sunday, March sixth. Of his five thousand troops, he assigned twenty-five hundred to the attack, divided into four columns, and equipped with axes, iron bars and scaling ladders in addition to the usual arms, to swarm against the walls simultaneously from the points of the compass. The President would direct operations from the headquarters of the reserve—with the river between himself and the Álamo.

Late Saturday night a silence fell when the cannonading, the sniping, were ordered to be stopped. Only meadow sounds, the low rattle of frogs in the river, and the random stirrings of bivouacs where many men and animals were awake in darkness were heard where for days and nights past the artillery had continuously thumped and the rifles had rung. At four o'clock the assault columns began to move into place in a silence severely preserved until some soldiers in one of them raised a shout—the kind of noise that soldiers made to stiffen one another and terrify the enemy. In this case it warned the enemy; and when at dawn on that Sunday the bugle split the heavy calm of the meadows about San Antonio, and the massive attack began, the army in all its four approaches was met with tremendous fire from the artillery and the rifles on the walls. The columns fell back and attacked again, and again, while the massed bands of the brigades across the river played the

"Degüello" to inspire their troops, for it was a word, and a tune, that meant the "throat-cutting," and when played in battle it signified that there was to be no quarter given to the enemy.

The Texan marksmanship, the speed, continuity and fury of their fire, were frightful. Soldiers fell by the score. But the number of their comrades was great, and gaps were closed, and presently there was a great swarm so near the bases of the walls, that the artillery above could not be traversed downward to bear on them. Suddenly a breach was made on the north side, and another on the south, and soldiers poured in to capture the Álamo plaza. The defenders fell back to the convent and its patio, and to the roofless church. The army turned their own cannon on them, and squad after squad advanced to take room after room in the convent cells, killing all whom they trapped in each. The Mexican bayonets whistled and darted in the early sunlight that rayed into the convent patio. The ground was strewn with dead attackers and defenders. But still the army strove and, when all was silent in the outer courts and rooms, threw its remaining power against the church, which was the last stronghold of the Texans. The main doors were forced, and everywhere—in the nave, the baptistry, the transepts, the sacristy, with their heaps of long-fallen stone and weedy mounds of earth, under the light morning sky within the open walls—the victory was won man by man until after an hour not one defender was seen alive anywhere in the profaned and mouldered mission.

But five who had hidden themselves were found and hauled out half an hour later, just as President Santa Anna, summoned from across the river by news of his triumph, arrived before the mission, where his troops were formed into line to receive him. General Castrillon showed him the prisoners, suggesting clemency. The President was shocked. Prisoners? How incredible. What had he already published in orders? "In this war, you understand, there are no prisoners." In a fury he turned his back upon Castrillon, and seeing his attitude, the formation broke ranks, took the unarmed prisoners, and killed them. The President's secretary, who was there, felt with certain others that this was a horror *"que reprueba la humanidad";* but by an order that followed the President's policy was once more made clear.

The corpses of the Texans, numbering one hundred and eighty-two, were dragged from where they had fallen within walls and on floors that were pungent with burnt gunpowder and hardening blood to the open ground before the mission. There they were stacked in layers alternating with dry brush and branches and the whole was heaped with

wood and set on fire, and left to burn and fall to the fingerings of the
wind. The mission graveyard was reserved for the fallen among the
Mexican troops. But so many had died in the battle that there was not
room for them all in the consecrated ground, and the officer charged
with their disposal ended by having the remainder thrown into the San
Antonio River. He estimated that the army had lost sixteen hundred
men in the hour's engagement. If this was exaggerated, the figures compiled by the President's secretary were studied. He spoke of three hundred dead after the battle, and another hundred among the wounded
who died later. The President disagreed with all such tallies, and dictated to his secretary that while over six hundred Texans had perished,
the army lost only seventy killed and three hundred wounded, out of
an attacking force of only fourteen hundred. But however far such
figures were open to question, the day had brought a victory, and Santa
Anna moved energetically to exploit it against other Texan operations
farther and south.

One had already come to its end—the expedition against Matamoros. General Urrea advanced from the lower Rio Grande in search
of the invasion force, and learned that a large part of it was in barracks
at San Patricio. Marching even at night through the freezing winds
of a norther off the plains, he came before the village at three o'clock
on the morning of February twenty-seventh and within half an hour
attacked the garrison. All but four of the Texan enemy were taken. A
few days later another portion of the invasion force was discovered returning from the Rio Grande where the Texans had gone to capture horses
for their expedition. There was a running fight over the prairies twenty
miles from San Patricio in which General Urrea held the field command
in person. With lance, lasso and rifle his troops destroyed the enemy
resistance and took many prisoners. The descent upon Matamoros was
completely turned, and troops from her strengthened garrison were free
to join General Urrea in Texas.

The President at San Antonio received news of Urrea's victories
in the field, and felt much satisfaction in knowing that in all probability
the Texan revolt was crushed. He disposed troops among the seacoast
settlements and inland towns. Some he sent to Goliad, where they reinforced Urrea, who had been told of Texan forces there and at Refugio
about twenty-five miles away. Urrea attacked Refugio first—again there
was an assault upon a fortified mission, and again the Texans were defeated, though a great number of them escaped toward Victoria. But
there they found the town in Mexican hands and, after a fight, were

forced to surrender. They were marched to Goliad, which Urrea had captured. By the twentieth of March all enemy forces operating on the Guadalupe and San Antonio rivers were taken, and a force of prisoners numbering over three hundred, including the Texan commander Fannin, was under guard at Goliad. Word of the triumph was dispatched to the President.

Gratified, he was at the same time astounded that prisoners had actually been taken. When, when would his subordinates understand his orders? There was even a law, passed in 1835, requiring that all foreigners appearing in Mexico under arms should be considered as pirates, and treated as such. With some impatience he sent peremptory orders to Goliad that the prisoners were without exception to be put to death immediately. This command caused certain misgivings in General Urrea and other officers, for the surrender of the Texans had been accepted with an agreement that they would be paroled. But it had to be obeyed, and arrangements were made on the evening of March twenty-sixth to do so. The prisoners suspected nothing, and a number of them entertained themselves and their companions with music on several flutes, playing a nostalgic air popular with them entitled "Home, Sweet Home." At daybreak—the next day was Palm Sunday—the prisoners were turned out and formed in three groups under guard of the entire garrison. They were puzzled. What was the formation for? To preserve order it was thought wise to reassure them. One group was told that they were to be marched to the coast to take ship for their home settlements; another, that they were a work party to help with the slaughter of beeves; the last, that their barracks were needed to accommodate General Santa Anna and his escort who were expected in Goliad. They were marched out of town in three different directions for half a mile, in columns of twos, with guards flanking each column on both sides. The same action followed for each column. At the halt, the file of guards on one side moved through the column to the other, so that all guards were on the same side. And then before the prisoners knew what to expect, the guards fired, and the executions began. The first volley brought down almost all of the Texans; but a few ran away and there followed little localized pursuits for the next hour or so. In the end, only twenty-seven got away, so that, on the whole, the President's order was carried out successfully. Over three hundred were executed. Their bodies were jerked out of their clothes, flung naked into piles and with winter brush as fuel were set to burning. Days later there were still hands and feet to be seen among the ashes. With clemency that amounted to daring insubordination, the commandant of Goliad, troubled by his orders to effect the punishment, had spared the lives of four Texan doctors of medicine and a handful of others. Word of his mercy did not reach the President for some time, when other events absorbed his attention, and the survivors were safe.

Moving from success to success—the Álamo, the Matamoros movement, Refugio, Victoria, Goliad and its mass executions—General Santa Anna now laid plans to return to Mexico with news of his brilliant reduction of Texas—the Texas that called itself a nation. He meant to travel by sea, sending back to the Rio Grande by road the artillery and supply trains for which he might again have use in Mexico. But his generals persuaded him to remain until troop dispositions had been securely made through the humbled province, where now confusion and panic among the Texans created uncertainty for army and enemy alike. A great flight eastward began in all the Texas colonies, evidently in hopes that the power of the United States on the Louisiana border would protect the colonists. Their arms were scattered, their forces were in disagreement about how to organize further defense against punishment, and at best they could have had miserably inadequate numbers to hold the immense territory they claimed as their own. Their national government was ineffectual, and even their first and best-known leader, Stephen Austin, was absent from Texas, soliciting aid in the North American states. Another figure became known as the dominant leader of Texas; and as the nature of the crisis was military, so was he a military man. He was, as the President referred to him, "the so-called General Houston," who had been appointed commander-in-chief of the Texas national armed forces at the convention of independence.

It was he who led the remaining Texan forces eastward in a scattering retreat after the crucial news of the Álamo, Refugio and Goliad. When the settlers heard of his flight they fled also, crossing rivers that had risen in spring floods. In spite of the labors of travelling overland in heavy rains, the President determined now upon a vigorous pursuit of Houston and, so soon as he should bring him to bay, the destruction of the Texan armed forces once and for all. Accordingly he left San Antonio de Béxar on March thirty-first. His confidence was great. He assigned various brigades to occupation and policing duties apart from the main purpose of overtaking Houston, and with the remainder of the troops, he hurried eastward. In his advance he enjoyed one satisfaction after another. He came to the Brazos, and the town of San Felipe de Austin, on April seventh, to find this seat of trouble empty and in ashes. He caught a glimpse of enemy troops on the opposite shore of the Brazos, but he could not reach them, for the river was in flood, and the Texans had all the boats. Somewhere beyond them was Houston with his main body. The President marched down the Brazos, and crossed on the eleventh, at Thompson's Ferry. There he heard interesting information. At the town of Harrisburg, thirty miles northeast, the Texans who called themselves president and vice president of their nation, together with other prominent civilian leaders of the rebellion, were said to be; and General Santa Anna resolved at once to push ahead to take them as important prizes of the campaign. But they had fled when during the night of the fifteenth he arrived at Harrisburg. All he found were three printers, who said the Texan officials had left for New Washington. Wherever they were, there was the capital of Texas; and General Santa Anna learned later that they had made their way to Galveston Island, where in their persons they constituted the government.

The printers had other information. It seemed that Houston with eight hundred troops was falling back northeastward, attempting to put the Trinity River between him and the relentless chase that had moved so swiftly, in the face of such difficulties, over two thirds of the way across Texas. The President ordered Harrisburg put to the torch, and marched for New Washington, a wretched community of half a dozen houses on a spit of land jutting from the west into an estuary of Galveston Bay. Lynch's Ferry over the San Jacinto Creek was slightly to the north. In all probability Lynch's Ferry would be the escape route of Houston and his forces fleeing toward the Trinity farther east. The President ordered reconnaissance operations. If Houston was coming from the northwest down to Lynch's Ferry, he would have to cross Buffalo Bayou, a large inlet of Galveston Bay into which the San Jacinto Creek emptied. It would be a difficult crossing. The President resolved to reach Lynch's Ferry first, and when Houston's people came out of the swamp toward the crossing, to destroy them and end the war.

He prepared to set out, then, on the morning of the twentieth, first seeing that New Washington was burned. He then turned to the trail that led through a thick woods from the village to open prairie beyond, and was about to pass the word for the advance when a scout galloped into camp to report that Houston and his troops were fast approaching upon the rear guard of the army, and had already taken prisoners.

There were times when responsibility and power cost dearly in the lives of those who bore them.

Such a moment now came for the President, lonely in his awful position, and bending every skill and strength to the successful completion of his design. On hearing that Houston was about to trap him at the very exit of the flaming village of New Washington, General Santa Anna lost command of himself and by his actions cast the entire army into disorder and fear. He threw himself upon his horse, shrieking that the enemy was at hand and disaster imminent, and spurred his way wildly down the column of troops and animals waiting to depart. He scattered his own men right and left, trampling some in his fury to pass through the woods and out to the prairie. Others maintained order, brought the men through the copse, and formed them in battle order in the open land. But Houston was nowhere to be seen. The report had been false. Once again in control of himself, the President conducted a proper advance upon Lynch's Ferry, and at two in the afternoon of the nineteenth made the first contact with the "so-called General Houston," whose pickets were sighted near the junction of the bayou and the creek. Fire was exchanged. There was a sense of two major forces feeling each other out, wheeling for advantage, and wary of precipitating any action prematurely.

General Santa Anna took up his position on a low eminence crowned with a woods. There opposite to him at a distance of about a thousand yards was a screen of brush along Buffalo Bayou, with open ground between. The General described his position as an excellent one, "with water in the rear, a thick wood on the right down to the banks of the San Jacinto, a broad plain on the left, and open ground in front." With additional defenses worked up during the night of the twentieth, General Santa Anna felt confident in the face of any attack from the Texans, who were somewhere to the north and west. One thing was certain. The President and his troops lay squarely across the approaches to Lynch's Ferry. The whole place was a pleasant piece of country. The little creek, the deep bayou, were like scenes in a park. Wonderful trees lined their banks, magnolias eighty feet high, and evergreens, rhododendrons, arbutus, laurel, bay and firs. In the dense air against the varying dark greens of the background, drifts of musket smoke, and volumes from cannon, showed blue before vanishing in the afternoon and evening of the twentieth.

The President had sent Gaona, Cos and Urrea off to coastal missions with their brigades, but lately, about to close with his quarry, he had ordered Cos to rejoin him, and expected him momentarily. Early on April twenty-first the President directed the building of a further defense on the left of his line, facing the distant wood screen behind which the Texans at a distance of thirteen hundred yards were known to be concentrated. This breastwork was most ingeniously devised out of heaps of baggage, packsaddles, bags of hard bread and loose brush, to the height of five feet. A gap was left in its centre for a fieldpiece to speak through. While these preparations went forward, General Cos appeared with four hundred troops, having marched all night. In their exhaustion, they were considerately ordered to stack arms, dispose their luggage, and take their rest.

In fact, the whole army was fatigued. The entire campaign had been one of hardship; and it was a mercy that the day—it was April 21, 1836—was calm and without sustained disturbance. The President's encampment, with all the advantages that reassured him—including that of a retreat route across Vince's Creek to his rear, where for his convenience should he need it stood the only bridge over any watercourse between him and the Brazos—was quiet. It seemed the first day in months to allow soldiers to go about little chores for themselves. Some built lean-to shelters of brush. Others took unsaddled horses down to water. Many—most of the army, in fact—slept with the first ease in weeks. A few cooked themselves what they liked, and talked, and ate. The usual pickets were stationed about in the afternoon silence. General Santa Anna himself was in his tent, asleep, after the arduous duties of so many days. It was an open April day with light dancing on the varnished leaves of the magnolias and rhododendrons.

Suddenly, at half-past four, alert pickets observed movement opposite to the left of their line, and made report. A front of Texan cavalry was seen emerging into the clear, and feinting forward. The alarm given, troops on duty opened fire on the cavalry. Scarcely had they done so when from the timbered screen across the open area there broke forward a disciplined advance of Texan infantry.

They came fast and in silence. When they were three hundred yards from the President's breastwork of twigs, leather and stale bread, the Mexicans who manned it let go with a fearful broadside of musket fire.

The Texans did not pause or kneel to return the fire. They did not fire at all, but kept coming. Their faces and hands were white with tension.

The barricade fired again, and still the Texans did not reply but only came on, breaking into double-quick time. The Texan artillery advanced and poured in grape and canister over the breastwork. And then—it seemed to have been managed in an instant—the Texans were at point-blank range of the soldiers before the President's camp, and there they cried out in shaking unison, "Remember the Álamo! Remember Goliad!" and with their rifles all but in the faces of the soldiers, they fired then for the first time and swarmed through the crumbling breastwork in wild power.

When the federal soldiers, unable to reload and fire at such close quarters, swung their bayonets into play, the Texans, having none, grasped their own rifles as war clubs and broke them over bayonet blades, and heads, and bodies, with sharp crackings. The line at the barricade fell apart though General Castrillon came forward to rally it. He was soon killed. The barricade was lost. Panic seized the entire encampment. Within twenty minutes the men of the commander-in-chief's army were fighting each other to escape to the rear, before the white rage of the Texans, who fought like creatures possessed of demons, so that the federal troops had to face not only surprise, skillful use of arms, and superior knowledge of the country, but also some quality more terrible by far—a vengeful fury for which there was no match.

And now the President's advantaged position was seen to be disastrous; for the soldiers running away had nowhere to go but down the rear slope toward water of the bayou; and there they were shot, clubbed, and trampled, until whole companies of them were drowned in mud and dandled by the water's drift. Those who managed a safe crossing streaked for the bridge at Vince's Creek. But when they reached it, they found it burned away. Texan scouts had destroyed it before the attack; and once again there was slaughter on the banks and in the stream. The President's secretary was there and made a note of what he saw: "There were an infinite number of dead piled one upon the other, till they might have served as a bridge." The Texans pressed their victory full into evening. The war was ended with those few hours. Out of the President's battle force of thirteen hundred men, only forty managed to avoid being killed, wounded or captured. The Texans lost two men killed, and twenty-three wounded, out of seven hundred and eighty-three in the engagement.

If his soldiers asked that night where the President of Mexico might be, the story was soon told. Harshly awakened from his rest, he had taken a powerful horse and had ridden furiously for the bridge at Vince's Creek. Miraculously he escaped death. Eluding the fire of pursuers, he came to the crossing; and when he saw that the bridge was gone, he urged his mount down the steep bank into the water. There his horse was hopelessly mired down, and he left it, and disappeared in the gathering twilight. Night covered the confusions of the day and ended the fighting.

In the morning, Texan scouts ranged the surrounding country to make sure that no further resistance was possible. They came upon fugitives here and there, and took them prisoner. About ten miles west of the creek a scouting party came upon a Mexican hiding in tall grass. They ordered him to stand, but he lay prone. A scout said:

"Boys, I'll make him move," and aimed his rifle at him.

"Don't shoot," said another, and dismounting, gave him a kick, adding, "Get up, damn you!"

The fugitive slowly arose. His clothes were muddy. He was dressed in a leather cap, a laborer's blue cotton jacket over an expensive shirt, cheap linen trousers and red worsted slippers. Speaking in Spanish he addressed his captors, one of whom could translate what he said. The man said he was not an officer, but a plain cavalry soldier. A Texan hauled him up on the croup of his horse and the party returned to camp. As they neared General Houston's headquarters they passed by other prisoners who regarded them. Suddenly the mounted prisoner was recognized by his compatriots.

"The President!" they cried, and some saluted him, "Santa Anna!"

It was he. He was rapidly taken before General Houston, who had been wounded in the battle. The President's position was most serious. He had heard the terrible cries of "Álamo" and "Goliad" on the day before, and he knew he was held personally responsible for what they recalled. His agitation now was so great that before he could speak with General Houston he was obliged to ask for opium. This was given to him, and presently he was able to conduct affairs as President and commander-in-chief of Mexico.

First, with reference to the episodes at the Álamo and Goliad, he wished to make plain that he personally should not be blamed for the severe measures taken there, as he had only been the instrument of carrying out the clear provisions of Mexican law.

Second, upon being granted his freedom, he would, speaking for Mexico, arrange for the recognition of the national independence of Texas.

General Houston, replying only to the second point, stated that as military commander he could not discuss a matter that must be concluded by the civil authorities of Texas; and in any case, before further negotiations, he required General Santa Anna to order his remaining troops to retire from Texas soil, which meant withdrawal beyond the

Rio Grande. Accordingly, the President dictated a dispatch to General
Filisola, who was at the Brazos, which said: "Your Excellency, The small
division under my immediate command having had an unfortunate
encounter yesterday afternoon, I find myself a prisoner of war in the
hands of the enemy, who have extended to me all possible consideration."
After this restrained remark, he went on to direct that all divisions of
the army still at large immediately fall back, some to Béxar, some to
Victoria, there to await further orders. He ended by saying, "I have
agreed with General Houston upon armistice pending certain negotiations which may put an end to the war forever."

This was not true; the war was already over; and Filisola, Urrea
and Gaona had not waited for orders to retreat, but immediately on
hearing the news of San Jacinto, had begun their withdrawals toward
the Rio Grande. Again the rivers of Texas were hard obstacles to armies
with heavy equipment; for the spring rains stormed daily during the
weeks of the marches, and the retreat was harder than the entry had
been. But finally, on May twenty-eighth, the first units crossed the Rio
Grande to Matamoros under Urrea; and there, on June eighteenth, the
last, under Andrade, completed the evacuation. No national Mexican
troops were left in Texas, other than prisoners of war.

Of these, General Santa Anna was in the gravest danger of harm.
Citizens and soldiers of Texas demanded his life in return for the slaugh-
ters he had wrought among their comrades. Texan officials protected
him with difficulty, and proceeded with treaty negotiations. Under these
—there was one public and one secret set of agreements—he promised
that he should never again "during the present war of independence"
wage war, or encourage others to wage war, against Texas; that all
fighting would stop; that Mexico's armed forces should leave Texas; that
prisoners should be exchanged; that all property, "including horses,
cattle, negro slaves or indentured individuals" captured by the Mexicans,
should be returned to the Texan owners; that Texan independence
should be recognized; that President Santa Anna should be returned
safely to Veracruz; and that, as the boundary between Mexico and
Texas, the Rio Grande should be accepted.

When news, first of the disaster in Texas, and second, of the terms
of the President's treaties, came to the government in Mexico City,
dismay gathered around a hard core of refusal ever to agree to the
independence of Texas or the establishment of the Rio Grande as the
boundary. But as Texas in her disputatious energy, and Mexico in her
poverty and political instability, took steps to recover from the campaign

of the President—he had gone free—it was plain to see which of the two nations remained the stronger. Texas, with twenty thousand people against the nine millions of Mexico, held her independence; and when her nationhood was recognized first by the United States, and then by England, France and other powers, her mother country, if she would not recognize, yet was obliged to accept a great portion of the Rio Grande as the actual boundary between the two nations that had for so long been one.

Within Texas, the Mexican point of view ceased to be significant.

13.

Fortunes of New Mexico

i. peoples and towns

Only along the Rio Grande above El Paso was the determining point of view still altogether Mexican, and it seemed more natural there than in Texas. Spanish life, the influence of Mexico, had been alive in New Mexico for three centuries as they had never been in Texas. The farthest forts and missions in Texas had been repeatedly abandoned by the Spanish power, while on the upper river, however poorly, they had lived even to overcome the terrible Indian revolt of 1680. The very land of New Mexico was more familiar to the Mexican memory than the land of Texas. New Mexico recreated the images of Spain and Mexico with bare mountain, tawny plain and narrow river grove; while for Mexicans in Texas few determining memories sprang to life out of the Texas landscape, with its wide coastal greenery, its prairies vaster than all Spain, and its belts of rolling green hills. In the 1830s, under Mexico, as for three centuries under Spain, organized life clung to the valley of the Rio Grande from Taos to El Paso, leaving the rest of the huge territory

virtually without population except for the travelling Indians who had
made their trails across it for so long, leaving hardly any other mark
of life.

Along the New Mexican river lived about forty thousand Mexicans and ten thousand Pueblo Indians. Though the census was irregular,
and records were ill-kept, the impression was that the Mexican population was growing, while the Indian was diminishing. An observant citizen
was convinced that the loss of numbers among Indians must be blamed
on only one thing. It was, he declared, "an abuse which is deeply rooted
among Indian women; they refuse to bear more than four children;
they succeed in this matter by drinking certain beverages which they
prepare for that purpose." He called for the proper authorities—governmental or ecclesiastical—"to drive this practice out by any available
means as soon as possible."

No new pueblos and only a few Mexican towns were founded
after the turn of the nineteenth century. Above Taos, Arroyo Hondo,
in 1823, and Questa, in 1829, were added to the Mexican communities.
At El Paso, through the early 1820s, all settlement clung to the south
bank of the river. James Pattie, the trapper, saw the old community
as it lay spread out among its vineyards and wheat fields. He thought the
town had a breadth of about three miles, but he did not know whether
to call "the Passo del Norte a settlement or a town. It is," he said, "in
fact a kind of continued village, extending eight miles on the river.
Fronting this large group of houses, is a nursery of the fruit trees, of
almost all countries and climes. . . ." In 1827 the settlement put out its
growth in another direction—it crossed the river. A householder named
José María Ponce de León made himself a new home on the north bank.
Before long he had neighbors who followed his example. The result was
a nucleus for the later, the American, El Paso.

But as new towns came to be, old ones endured through the years
without much change of character, though with differences in detail.
In 1832 "the wall of Santa Fe" was spoken of as crumbling . . . "an
obstacle to the beauty of the city because it is becoming more dilapidated
every day, and within a short time only its ruins will remain." It adjoined
the old palace, which was itself "in partial ruins and in a general state
of neglect." All towns were of earthen construction, with wooden beams,
and were built around a central plaza from whose four corners the principal streets wandered off toward the open country. On these were
situated shops and places of entertainment, and of supply, such as wood-

yards. Behind the plaza, dwellings were disposed between the arms of the streets and followed no town plan, but found their places rather by the natural course of an irrigation ditch than by any severe grid laid out. Each house with its truck garden, its trees and its animal yard, was like a little plot of country life that showed the seasons. In spring pink and white blossoms of fruit trees sparkled in bright air beside pale tan adobe walls. In summer, when shade trees were leafed out, there were grand, slow-moving washes of shadow over the house whose rooms for their deep walls and thick earth roof stayed cool all day. In autumn when trees went bare, and sunlight thin, blue pencilled shadows of branch and twig played on the packed swept yard, and smoke from fires of piñon wood seemed to stand bluer and longer in the golden air. And when winter came, and snow fell, seen from the height of a valley slope the town, with all its boxlike shapes at odd angles about the formal oblong of the plaza with its continuous roof, looked like a scattering of great ingots of snow in sharp relief against their own shadows that lay like stripes on white ground.

The winter was long, for the river ran in high land, and towns were backed by hills, and hills by mountains. In some years the river froze almost to the bottom, and men working or travelling were able to cross without bridges or fords, for the ice was solid, and bore the weight of loaded oxcarts, pack trains and men on horseback from bank to bank. Even when the snow stopped falling and days were clear, the air was so cold that men could hardly work in the open, and women at their milking in the cowshed saw the warm milk freeze as it sprayed upon the cold pail.

But as the house stayed cool in summer, so it stayed warm in winter. The windows were small, the clay fireplaces deep and elevated so that they threw great heat, and the house was thick. People were comfortable if they stayed indoors; and if they went out, they were wrapped in furs that came in abundance from the creatures of the surrounding mountains. Barring disasters, men and women lived long— often to the age of ninety, or a hundred, or over. Age was honored. Old people when their days of physical usefulness were past yet had other uses, and gave of them to their own satisfaction and the continued creation of family law—the oracular wisdom of long experience, the power of tradition, the lessons that lay in conscious respect for the earthly source of life. These were values that knew little change throughout Christian Mexico. In the Rio Grande towns they abided late.

ii. politics

But if the family as a unit of human life seemed secure in its inherited ways, and was able to fulfill its precepts, the towns as the smallest subdivisions of political life had greater difficulties to meet in their need of order. A Rio Grande town was governed in the pattern of Mexico life—but in skeletal form. Mexican customs prevailed—but without a flow of refreshment through full contact with their source. Mexican ideas moved the people—but weakened by distance from their point of origin. For hundreds of years the northern river province had begged the central authority in Mexico, first under the Spanish viceroy, and now under the president and congress of the republic, for more troops, more money, more administrators, more clergy, more courts of law, more educational facilities; and had never received much more than an occasional visit by an inspector general, a bishop or a customs collector. The province had to be content with maintaining certain governmental forms, without the means to give them substance.

The New Mexican river province under the republic was ruled by a political chief appointed for an undefined term by the central government. Once he was in residence, he was answerable to no one else; but if his post was coveted by a man of influence, he might suddenly lose it, no matter how well he served. If his successor served ill, there was little recourse for the people under a ruler who alone had the ear of the government. His work was not easy—the budget of his office did not even provide for him a permanent secretary. His time was mainly taken up with the review of legal decisions made in the largest towns by their mayors, who served also as justices of the peace—though his duties were not supposed to include such a function. But in their inherent trust in and need for authority, the people could turn to no one else to appeal their cases. Thoughtful citizens saw the dangers in such arrangements— injustice, corruption, the impossibility of finding able men to accept public office under capricious tenure.

There were only sixteen towns considerable enough to have their own local government. These were grouped into three departments. Each department had a capital town from which lesser towns drew their authority. The capitals were Santa Cruz, Santa Fe and Albuquerque, and these alone had town councils and mayors. The lesser towns were commanded by a military officer who held no judicial powers. If an affair at law came up in his town, he referred it to the powers of his capital town for decision; and if they could not settle it to satisfaction, it must go to the political chief of the province at Santa Fe. If there it was not adjudicated to an end, there was one more recourse; but few citizens were able to spend what was required in time and money to make the last appeal, for the nearest practicing civil and criminal court sat at Guadalajara, distant almost two thousand miles through months of travel from the upper Rio Grande. There was no one in the long valley of New Mexico who was sufficiently trained in the processes of law to "conduct an examining trial, to prepare a defense, or to prosecute a case." Crime went unpunished and injustice had no orderly redress. When a man was arrested and put in jail, he entered an ordinary adobe room where with his cellmates he spent his time "in noisy revelry and conversation." He enjoyed free meals, and was not detained if during the day he thought of errands that must take him abroad, or if at night hearing the music of a fandango he resolved to join the dance. At his own pleasure he returned to his filthy cell and the congenial company of his fellow prisoners, all of whom took "their imprisonment with the greatest nonchalance."

iii. defense

If the province was unable to maintain internal order, it was even less equipped to face armed threats from beyond the frontier. A presidial company of a hundred men was stationed at Santa Fe to protect the northernmost boundaries of the republic, and to deal with civil disturbances throughout a province of over a hundred thousand square miles. What—intelligent citizens often thought of it—what would happen if an armed invasion, say three or four thousand strong, should appear from the United States? Even if the whole population of forty thousand sprang to defend New Mexico, how effective could they be without training, discipline, or adequate arms? The presidial company would be overwhelmed. The nearest important military headquarters was at Chihuahua, five hundred miles from Santa Fe, with stark deserts between. How could intelligent command be exercised over New Mexico from so remote a commandery general? Before a courier could reach there to report an invasion or a major Indian uprising the province of New Mexico could be lost.

Citizens saw what was needed and made urgent recommendations. New Mexico should be granted its own commandery general separate from Chihuahua's. Troop strength should be greatly increased to control the never-ending assaults by riding Indians who came from east and west of the river. The main garrison should not be stationed in Santa Fe, which was too far from the usual scene of Indian depredations, but should be located at Valverde, on the Rio Grande, just above the northern entrance to the Dead Man's March. There, where a ruined hacienda stood, a fort should be established, from which, as a midway point, troops could range forth upriver, downriver, or inland on either side, to meet internal disorder promptly. If this were done, the whole road to the south would be so well policed that in a few years along "the delightful banks" of the Rio Grande there would be "an uninterrupted cordillera of flourishing settlements!" The prospect was stunning. "Farewell, Dead Man's March! Farewell, gloomy and fearful desert, you would vanish forever . . . !" The citizen who urged this course even proposed a way to pay for it. Since the wall of Santa Fe was falling apart more every day, let the government sell its earthen bricks to people who wanted to build houses, and use the funds to erect the new presidio at Valverde. Thus there would be no drain upon the treasury of New Mexico—which in any case was empty.

With more troops, more officers would be needed. Where might they come from? A military academy was proposed, to be established at Santa Fe, for the training of cadets under a full curriculum embracing "military tactics, regulations . . . economy of administration, methods of conducting a trial, manner of directing a defense . . . procedure in a council of war . . . arithmetic . . . the elements of geometry, geography, and fortifications." The superintendent should be a gifted officer who would be paid a salary of one thousand pesos, which would be raised from tuitions and company funds.

And finally, the organization and training of a civil militia was strongly urged by those who took thought for New Mexico. "What a powerful defense would be presented by eight or nine thousand New Mexicans, expert in the use of weapons, equipped and ready for war!" Of all Mexico, the northern river frontier most needed such defenses. Those who lived in New Mexico knew that "the army is more useful and necessary on the frontier, as our unfortunate history proves"—for they were mindful of what had lately happened in Texas. They knew that the United States concentrated most of her standing army on her western frontiers. Could not the Mexican government read the significance of that fact? New Mexicans could read it even as long ago as 1810: "Once this territory is lost, it will be impossible to recover it. . . ." Such representations were made in vain. The Mexican government, though smarting under Santa Anna's loss of Texas, did nothing to reinforce the remaining province of the Rio Grande.

iv. church and school

Other defenses were crumbling, too, in a society that profoundly believed in the need of them. These were the ministrations, public and corporate, private and personal, of the Church. For seventy years there had been no visit by a bishop in the province. When Don Pedro Bautista Pino went from New Mexico to the Spanish córtes in 1810 he was already an old man; but he never knew "how bishops dressed" until he reached Spain. At last, in 1833, Don Antonio Zubiria, Bishop of Durango, came to tour the parishes of New Mexico. His progress was a triumph. Bridges over arroyos on his road were repaired and decked with wild flowers. He entered towns under ceremonial arches. For his passing, houses were dressed with whatever finery their owners could hang out the window—rugs, brocades, curtains. People knelt under his blessing in newly swept streets as his coach lumbered by. The only ones who were sorry to see him come were the few Franciscans who remained in the province, for the secularization of the missions, begun at the end of the eighteenth century, was nearly completed, and the Bishop was a symbol of the process, for now New Mexico came under the jurisdiction of his see of Durango, whose seat was four hundred leagues south of El Paso. Bishop Zubiría spent many weeks inspecting his northern parishes; and a year after his return to Durango the Franciscan system was gone from New Mexico; the secularization was fully accomplished.

With the Franciscans gone, secular priests were supposed to come from Durango to replace them in all the missions of the pueblos and the parishes of the towns. But they did not come in proper numbers, and the handful that came seemed to preside over a rapid dissolution of the church. In the pueblos, mission premises reverted to their Indian owners, and like the missions of Texas when secularized in the eighteenth

century began to fall into ruin through neglect. Only five pueblos had
resident priests. The town parishes were not much better off; for the
secular clergy had no funds behind them such as the Franciscan Order
had made available to its friars to supplement local support. Parish
priests now lived, and church properties were maintained, wholly on
what their parishioners could contribute. This was in most places miserably little. Few parishes had resident pastors. Most were vacant, to be
visited two or three times a year by a travelling priest. Church buildings
went to ruin without annual replastering with adobe. Pastors lived in
misery and faced the old age and death of paupers. Some yielded to
human failings and coveted a better living. Others valiantly pursued
their duties through every hardship and deprivation. Still one or two
others, far from ecclesiastical authority and the source of discipline,
betrayed their vows and while still professing priesthood adopted ways
of life they were supposed to correct in others. Such clergymen shocked
foreign travellers who saw them at their genial indulgence. Devout New
Mexicans also shook their heads, and bitterly regretted that in their
province there was no administrative head of church affairs, a bishop, a
vicar general, who would govern the clergy, preserve discipline, and let
flower the faith that was so deeply rooted in the people.

It was to them a "truly doleful" matter "to see an infinite number
of the sick die without confession or extreme unction." Regular Sunday
Mass was said in only a few churches. Baptisms were arranged only with
infinite difficulty. When death came, and a funeral Mass was needed, the
corpse often remained unburied for days, until a priest could be found
and brought to officiate. The penalties, and contrasts, of distance from
the capital were severe: In 1838 the remains of Agustín de Iturbide
were removed from Padilla to Mexico City, where they were reinterred
in the cathedral with the highest pomp—the street outlining the grand
plaza of the capital was entirely shaded by scalloped canopies, the populace made a lane through which the cortège passed, there was a black-
plumed hearse drawn by six horses with outriders and followed by
troops in a column of company fronts, while in the center of the Zócalo
artillery fired a paced salute. But in New Mexico, where each parish and
mission worked to pay its meagre tithe out of the year's labor with
field and flock to support a religious, people more often than not died
and were buried without his solace. As for the tithes—local corruption
had its ways, and they went "only to enrich three or four private persons,
without any spiritual benefit to New Mexico or temporal profit to the
republic."

Another trouble to the view of a good citizen was the state of education in the province. There were primary schools in only six towns in the early 1830s, and the total annual expenditure for teacher salaries was only 1,850 pesos—and even so, it was reported that "relatively speaking, there is no better pay in the territory than that received by schoolteachers." But many of the teachers were indifferent and ignorant, the authorities paid no attention to the schools, and it could only be concluded that "no noticeable results are achieved by primary instruction." There were scarcely any books anywhere. Here and there the vocation of the teacher found expression when a priest took a class of young men to teach them a scrap of philosophy, or a young layman gathered others about him to study Latin and Spanish grammar. In 1834 the public schools were closed for lack of funds to maintain them. In the same year there was a glimmer of hope for public enlightenment. On the first printing press to reach New Mexico, a weekly newspaper entitled *El Crepúsculo*—The Dawn—appeared in a foolscap sheet for the benefit of fifty subscribers. But after one month, publication was suspended, and the only newspapers seen in the province were months-old copies from Mexico or the United States.

v. foreigners

For the traders, with their news, came all through the '30s in increasing numbers, and saw the poverty of the towns, the unworked capacities of the country, and the primitive methods of a nontechnical and incurious people. Food was raised only in the narrow straggle of farms along the immediate valley of the Rio Grande. Each family grew only what was needed to support its own members during the year. If hard times came, with drought or unseasonable freezes, or if the family had miscalculated its needs, there were months late in the year when hunger came as a familiar of life in New Mexico. The only commercial crops were cotton and tobacco, raised for trading within the province and for shipping down the river road to Mexican markets. Beyond the mountains on each side of the cultivated valley lay immense empires of unworked soil. There fortunes could be made, agriculture on a vast scale undertaken—but for two factors. One was the never-ending menace of the roving Indian; the other was that strain in the colonial character that had never recovered from the dream of Quivira, with its promise of free wealth, and its waking rejection of hard work as the price of its fulfillment.

And yet there were no paupers, for if a man did not have his own patch of land from which to gain a bean or an ear of corn for his family, he had recourse to an owner of large herds of sheep, proposing himself as a shepherd. Given a thousand ewes and ten rams to tend, he received as his pay a percentage of the lambs, with the remainder going to the owner. In time, after his own little flock had grown by the almost daily birth of lambs the year round—for the rams and the ewes were never separated—he was able to leave his employer and take on shepherds of his own whose work would yield him the owner's percentage in his turn. Sheep provided milk, meat and wool to the family; and lambs that were sold for the drive to Mexico. An American trader estimated that about a quarter of a million sheep and goats grazed on the valley slopes, and up to half a million sheep were walked to Mexico every year. In spite of such a great figure, sales brought little, for the price of sheep was very low, and the individual sheep was not heavy. As for cattle, the same trader believed that only about five thousand were maintained.

The Rio Grande Mexican was a rude craftsman. Where his work held primitive beauty of feeling or design, he was unaware of it; and when the United States traders kept coming, he turned to them for the products of their country, glad to buy instead of to make. Soon the province was served by foreigners who were expert craftsmen and adroit bargainers—carpenters, blacksmiths, tinsmiths, gunsmiths, tailors, hatters, shoemakers. The Americans set up water-powered mills. One spent a winter in Santa Fe building a public clock—the first one in an ancient city that previously took the time of day from a stone sundial at the old Palace. Others established a distillery up the Rio Grande at Arroyo Hondo, using water power in its machines. In a very few years all fabrication industry and commerce in the province were led by the foreigners. These men became a familiar sight in the towns and along the roads of the province. They had for sale services and objects that the natives wanted, they obeyed such laws as they could, and when the laws were unreasonable or administered with caprice, they circumvented them as cleverly and as quietly as possible. Gazing at them, the natives had a sense of what was inevitably coming; and seeing the Americans as agents of change and usurpation, they could not forbear expressing their bitterness. There were occasional brawls, attacks, robberies and murders. The American traders and tinkers kept a sharp eye out, especially when they travelled the well-worn roads on which New Mexicans were safe from banditry.

Yet even there the traditions of New Mexican hospitality showed themselves when the strangers stopped for a meal or a lodging for the night; and New Mexican women were gentle with the tall, energetic, and often blond men from the East, some of whom fell in love with the country, and resolved to stay, marry, and make their fortunes along the valley. A farm here, a flour mill there, a lumberyard, a brickkiln, a tannery—such establishments brought the techniques of the United States frontier far from home, and using the bountiful raw materials of New Mexico made so much visible change in the commercial life of the province that an upper Rio Grande Mexican cried out, "How long shall we continue to be foreigners on our own soil?"

14.

Revolt Up River

On this background of the New Mexican Rio Grande, with its natural beauties and its social poverties, there flared in 1837 a surge of violence whose causes bore some resemblance to those behind the uprising of the Texans in the previous year. New Mexico, too, was far from the seat of central government, and yet was denied full local government. With Santa Anna's revocation of the federal constitution of 1824, New Mexico lost the position of statehood and was demoted to the status of territorial department. New Mexico, too, was subject to an always-increasing population of busy citizens from the United States, who brought new notions of individual liberty and state autonomy. For the first time since Mexican independence, the political ruler of New Mexico, appointed by Santa Anna, was not a native New Mexican, but an officer of the Mexican Army. He was Colonel Albino Pérez, and he came to rule with Santa Anna's centralist principles. And finally, as

Texas had been seen by the capital chiefly as a source of revenue and as
a vast compound for the criminal discards of Mexican society, so New
Mexico in her wretched subsistence economy was suddenly in 1837 subjected to new taxes that would feed directly to the bankrupt national
treasury.

Colonel Pérez laid about him with his taxations. Some of his
levies affected the foreign traders, who had no recourse but to submit—
though, it was said, not without seditious whispers that may have fanned
the fires that were already taking light amongst the people. Others struck
directly at the native occupations and pleasures. A woodcutter was subjected to a new license costing five dollars a month. A drover or a shepherd taking his animals through Santa Fe to market had to pay a tax
of about twenty-five cents a head. A showman was taxed two dollars for
each performance he gave, and to give a dance cost the proprietor fifty
cents. All who lived without regular lawful occupations were to be
arrested. It was not long until rumors, spread by the enemies of Colonel
Pérez, enraged humorless citizens with stories of how a tax was to be
laid upon every barnyard fowl, and how a husband was to be taxed for
each performance of his marital duty. A new law re-established the
public schools, but with elaborate requirements of parents that in many
respects amounted to invasion of privacy and imposition of police rule.
Popular resentment grew rapidly, and only awaited an incident to touch
it off violently.

Among the enemies of the political chief was a certain Don
Manuel Armijo, a man of substance who lived at Albuquerque. For a
few months he had held an appointment from Colonel Pérez as a minor
official of the territory, substituting for another who had been tried for
peculation in office. When the peculator was restored to office, Armijo
was turned out, and in discontent began to intrigue against the government. He found powerful allies who resented the new regime; and an
underground movement was organized in the river communities, especially among the pueblos. In Taos, an upriver citizen, Jose Gonzáles, was
a leader of the Armijo movement. The terrible days of Otermín and
Vargas seemed to be looming once more, when the pueblos would rise
again. But this time, the Indians were in league with Mexican leaders,
and both were turned against the national authority.

Colonel Pérez was encountering troubles in maintaining his government. Having no public monies with which to buy supplies for his
presidial troops, he turned to the American traders who were in town
for the summer. They granted him large credits, and purchases were

made; but they were filtered through graft, and the Governor was
obliged to dismiss various grafters. When he disciplined native New
Mexicans, his popularity sank again. There was a case in the north. A
local official of Taos was put in jail at Santa Cruz by the Governor's
prefect of the northern district. At once there was an outcry against
tyranny. Organized rebellion sprang into the open. "Taxes! Taxes!" cried
the rebels, gathering at Santa Cruz in great numbers from the northern
pueblos. They marched on the jail and released the prisoner early in
August, and on the third held a convention out of which they published
a "pronouncement," a "plan," a "shout," in the familiar tradition of
Mexicans in revolt. After several clauses that protested piety and valor,
the plan of Santa Cruz became specific, and resolved not to accept for
New Mexico any status of department or territory instead of statehood;
not to submit to taxation, and not to obey those who would impose it.
The milling throng grew. It was led by Juan José Esquivel, the mayor
of Santa Cruz. Santa Fe was only twenty-five miles away to the south.
Loyal agents hurried there to Colonel Pérez, with a warning of the
numbers, the temper and the armament of the rebels.

The Governor decided from this information that what existed
in the north was merely a state "of exaggerated unrest." He was a regular
officer. Mobs were not armies. Still, he called for town officials to mobilize
the militia at once, and made plans to march up the river to scatter the
rioters. Response was apathetic; only a hundred and fifty men were
mustered, most of whom were warriors from Santo Domingo. With these,
and a wheeled cannon, and such presidial troops as were adequately
equipped, Colonel Pérez marched from Santa Fe on August seventh. He
camped that night eighteen miles from town, amongst the pale rosy
fantasies of the eroded Rio Grande bottom; and proceeded on the
following day toward Santa Cruz.

The enemy had come down the river to meet him and, breaking
upon him from ambush near the black mesa of San Ildefonso, disorganized his force with surprise. He tried to parley, to listen to grievances;
but the rebels fired and his troops deserted him. The Santo Domingo
warriors joined their fellow Indians of the northern pueblos. Colonel
Pérez and his few loyal men fell back about their cannon, which they
fired. But numbers were too great for them, the rebels charged, killing
six or seven men, and the Governor with twenty-three soldiers abandoned
the fieldpiece and hurried south to Santa Fe, arriving at three in the
afternoon.

He found the city in a state of general anxiety. The New Mexican

residents expected a general sack if the rebels should be victorious. The
American traders, having supplied the government troops, feared for
their stock and their persons if the rampage reached the capital. They
barricaded their wagons, and hid merchandise in the houses of friends,
and carried arms. The Governor was powerless to protect his capital or
to advise his people. He went through his desk, packed a few things,
and with a handful of friends and defenders left Santa Fe at ten o'clock
that night for the river road, and the south, and safety, like Otermín a
hundred and fifty-seven years before him. Riding hard through the
night he came to the hacienda of El Álamo near the river, and slept
there.

But others were abroad in the night too—Indian couriers from
the battlefield up the river who rode to advise other pueblo warriors
along the road that the Governor with friends was trying to escape to
Mexico, and that it was the command of the victorious rebels that he
and his followers were to be caught and killed.

In the morning Colonel Pérez rode out again, and soon saw that
the way ahead of him was guarded by Indians. He dispersed his party,
letting each man save himself. Asking one to lead his saddle horse away,
he dismounted and began to walk back to Santa Fe up the trail of La
Bajada and over the wide Santa Fe plain where moving along on foot
he might be inconspicuous. He walked all day, the ninth of August,
toward the capital. From the opposite direction, the city was filling all
day with the hordes of Santa Cruz, who came to take possession of
property and government. Toward sundown Colonel Pérez came through
fields to the farm of a friend where he sought refuge. But he had been
followed all day by Indians from the river flats. They entered, seized
him, beheaded him, and when he was dead, performed his symbolic
unmanning by stripping him naked, and throwing him awry on the
ground where they left him. Pushing on to the city they took his head
along, and, meeting the victorious insurgents, with it entered upon a
game of football.

Soon others who had sought to escape with the Governor were
found in hiding among the farms on the outskirts of the capital. They
were hauled forth, denuded, and run through with lances at leisure
until they died. Another captive was taken to Santo Domingo and put
into the stocks overnight. On the morrow while they execrated the
crimes of the government, the Indians cut off his members one after
the other and showed them to him in derision until they cut out his
eyes and his tongue. After a long time dying, he was removed from the

stocks and flung over the ground as carrion. In all a dozen supporters of the dead Governor were destroyed with protracted enjoyment.

On August tenth the rebels held a conclave for the election of a new, a native, governor. Don Manuel Armijo could not but hope that his efforts at rebellion, already so successful, must bring him the governorship. But the meeting elected Jose Gonzáles, the northern leader—"a good honest hunter, but a very ignorant man," as a trader said. Don Manuel Armijo, though repudiated, remained in Santa Fe to work with the new government. There was much to accomplish. All the property of the assassinated officials had to be divided among the new leaders. One of the rebels who had led the football game with Colonel Pérez's head on the day before found it hilarious to strut about in the Colonel's bloody coat. Lists of people to put in jail must be considered, and confiscations of property sketched out. Governor Gonzáles desired the convention to discuss the startling idea that help and alliance for New Mexico's new government should be sought in the Republic of Texas.

The citizens of Santa Fe and the visiting traders watched events with uneasiness, but a sack of the city did not develop, and the traders were not attacked. True, some of them faced great loss if not ruin, for they had given large credits to the defeated government, and could not hope that the rebels would honor the debts of their victims. A party of traders wrote to the United States minister in Mexico, asking him to obtain redress for them from the central government; but never received any. For in Mexico it was angrily believed that the insurrection had been fostered by the foreign Americans, even though they had supported the legitimate government of Colonel Pérez with goods and credit.

All in good time, Don Manuel Armijo came to his own plans. For several days he served the new government on committees, and attended a session of the new Governor's party in Santa Fe on August twenty-seventh, at which certain confiscations of property were made official. Many of the rebels out of the north were muttering about moving into the downriver estates and taking what they liked. Don Manuel Armijo's properties were downriver at Albuquerque. Suddenly the whole affair displeased him. He left Santa Fe, hurried to the Downriver, and began to gather about him a new party in opposition to Gonzáles. Most of the Santa Cruz army had been disbanded and its members had returned to their pueblos upriver. From Albuquerque, Armijo moved on south to the river village of Tomé, where on September eighth he issued a new pronouncement in defiance of the Gonzáles party. He had with him a parish priest, a mayor or two from downriver towns, and a number of citizens who had discovered with him a burning devotion to the con-stitution and laws of Mexico. They drafted a paper. It noted with belated horror the "iniquitous measures" being planned by the rebels of Santa Cruz "to destroy the peace, harmony, and good order of the citizens," and it repudiated their authority, naming instead as the one surviving legitimate officer of Mexican government in the river province the Prefect of Albuquerque, who had escaped the massacres. The counterpronounce-ment went on to declare that "no one shall be molested in their property or privileges; if they have any," and that an armed force was to be raised under the command of Don Manuel Armijo. Further, the pueblo Indians were advised to "remain tranquil, and not mix in Mexican affairs." To make certain of this, the pueblos were promised that they might govern themselves until the re-establishment of legitimate au-thority in the province. Finally, the army headquarters at Chihuahua would be asked for reinforcements, and the central government in Mexico City would be apprised of all that was now being done—chiefly by Don Manuel Armijo—in loyal efforts to recover the province from the rebels who had forsworn allegiance to Mexico, and who had made plans to ask Texas to protect them.

In Santa Fe, another loyalist movement was daring to show itself. General José Caballero, the federal troop commander, who at the moment had no troops, since the presidial company had been disbanded, issued a call for resistance in the face of the Gonzáles government. The new regime was a mockery. All was confusion in the capital, and "the chieftains of the unsurrection, swollen with triumph, continued figuring in the scene, and without any respect to the government which they themselves erected, constantly concocted new machinations which they have put into practice in an equally alarming manner. . . . Wretches!" cried General Caballero. "Their savage ignorance precipitates them from abyss into abyss in search of the punishment which divine justice cannot forgive, but will prepare for them." It was clear that in this civil strife, north was against south—Upriver against Downriver. General Caballero called for the united effort of the downriver people, recognized Don Manuel Armijo's title to command the volunteers, and proudly announced that the old presidial company was re-enlisting without pay to drive the rebels out of power.

All through September the forces gathered downriver; and toward the end of the month Armijo led them north along the river road and up the escarpment of Santa Fe plain. Governor Gonzáles fled before them. The northern rebel authority cracked wide open, and Armijo took possession of the capital without a battle, "the just cause of order and laws," he declared, "rapidly triumphing, in defense of which I grasped my sword, without the effusion of a drop of Mexican blood." He promised, pending the will of the federal government, to maintain law and order, and more: "if in order to attain these ends, it becomes necessary for me to make some examples of severity, I shall, without doubt, dictate them, although in sorrow. . . ."

Already in jail, incomunicados, were four leaders of the rebellion—though Governor Gonzáles was not one of them. He had escaped to the north where at Santa Cruz the rebellion was still in formal existence. Armijo assumed the office of political chief, and shuttled offices and duties about among his followers, and formed a government after the manner of Santa Anna, whom he resembled in such qualities as flexibility of conscience, political adroitness and an unusually strong instinct for self-preservation. The rebels were still to be dealt with in their northern country, but he was waiting for the Chihuahua reinforcements, and meanwhile, he composed an inflated report of his activities for the federal government, and sent it flying down the river road by courier, to earn him his confirmation as governor—which came from a grateful government in due course.

In the middle of October his private interests downriver called him, but before taking a few days' leave from his absorbing and agreeable duties he went into the matter of the prisoners in their filthy earth cells at the old Palace. On the whole, it seemed best to dispose of them without trial, and as examples. Accordingly, he left orders with General Caballero to have them shot, and rode out of the capital on the seventeenth for Albuquerque.

But something about the order gave General Caballero uneasiness, and he deferred carrying it out. Was the capital strongly enough garrisoned to withstand an assault when the rebels heard of the executions? Would it not be prudent to wait for more troops? Possibly he knew his man, though without expressing himself openly; but was it not conceivable that if in the future there should come a time of reprisals, it would be the actual executioner rather than the judge who might be paid off savagely? Governor Armijo would be out of town during the execution if it were performed as ordered. An order could be repudiated; not a volley from a firing squad. Whatever his reasons, General Caballero called a meeting of the chief officers of the government, and laid his problem before them on September twenty-first. They unanimously resolved that while the Governor's order must be carried out, the garrison must first be "strengthened by all the force necessary to repel any attempt that may be made. . . ." However, they provided that if news of an impending attack should come, then the prisoners were to be instantly decapitated in their cells.

The Governor returned as these policies were formulated. He accepted them, and advised the prisoners to put their affairs in order. This amounted to a reprieve of nearly three months; for the suitable strengthening of the garrison did not appear until early January, 1838, when two hundred dragoons from Zacatecas and two hundred regulars from Chihuahua at last arrived to join the Governor. They came opportunely, for another defiant proclamation of rebellion sounded forth from Santa Cruz, accompanied by threats to rescue the prisoners in the Palace. With the added troops from Mexico now under his command, the Governor felt strong enough to assume personal responsibility for the executions he had ordered months before. On January twenty-fourth, 1838, the four rebel chieftains were taken out of the Palace, and at the site of a sentry post three hundred yards from the plaza, were beheaded, while the Governor breathed in a state paper, "May God grant that this spectacle, so sad for peaceful New Mexico, be the last to present itself to its natural humaneness and good sense. . . ."

He was then ready, in the last week of January, to take his augmented forces into the field. As they marched out for the upper river, the capital was once more thrown into anxiety. The American traders made their wagons ready for immediate flight eastward, even through winter weather, if the rebels should win the impending battle; and the citizenry once again waited for the sacking of their town.

They were not long left in suspense. A courier came galloping in from Santa Cruz, where the rebels had met the army, and the capital breathed easy at his news—though the engagement had opened with a change of heart in the Governor. Seeing thirteen hundred Indians massed before him in their paint, pricked feathers, and bristled weapons, he wondered if perhaps after all he should not fall back with his five hundred and eighty-two soldiers. He had a familiar saying that his actions frequently illustrated—"*Vale mas estár tomado por valiente que serlo.*" But if it was better to be taken for a brave man than to be one, his reputation was saved for him by a certain Captain Muñoz of the Zacatecas dragoons, who seeing the Governor's faintness of heart, came to him and said:

"If your Excellency will allow me, I will oust that rabble in an instant with my little company alone."

The Governor superbly assented; the captain charged; the Indians fled, losing a dozen men, including José Gonzáles, the rebel governor, who was captured and brought before his old accomplice. Now Governor Armijo, with a great victory in his pocket, was once again a man of decision as he received Gonzáles, who extended his hand.

"How do you do, my colleague," said Gonzáles as between governors, if not accomplices.

"How do you do, my colleague," replied Don Manuel Armijo, and added, "Confess yourself, my colleague,"—for Chaplain of Dragoons Antonio José Martínez was present to hear the ex-Governor's confession. Don Manuel Armijo then turned to Don Pedro Muñoz and a squad of soldiers, and commanded, "Now, shoot my colleague."

The command was immediately obeyed, the rebels of the north were defeated for good, and the Governor returned to Santa Fe from the Upriver to reign for most of the next eight years in absolute power over what was left of the Mexican Rio Grande.

15.

The River Republic

Periodically, ever since her full retreat below the Rio Grande in 1836, Mexico threatened to return to Texas to punish the upstarts and regain the great province. But the shock of her defeat threw Mexico deeper into civil war, and the struggle between centralism with its dictatorship and federalism with its longing to re-establish the states under the Constitution of 1824 lasted for years and took all her official energies. Texas went unpunished, her independence was confirmed by leading powers of the world, and even in the midst of the agitating problems of creating her government, there were counterthreats on the part of Texas factions to invade Mexico. These were sporadic and largely matters of a familiar Texan temperament; and Texas too had her internal social troubles which consumed all her armed power for some time, and spared Mexico in her turn further chastisement.

For in the wake of victory, the Texans spread themselves increasingly over lands and privileges belonging for centuries to some of the most predatory Indian tribes in North America. Clashes resulted. Indian warfare with all its shock, speed and horror tried to arrest the widening of pioneer settlement; and the new republic to save its life was obliged to mobilize armed forces for relentless campaigns against Cherokees, Comanches and other tribes. The job would take generations to complete, but by 1839 the worst of the formal Indian warfare was put down, and many demobilized Texans who fought for the simple joy of fighting—the temperament—looked elsewhere for satisfaction.

They found it in the country of the Rio Grande, for there in 1839 swelled a movement of the Mexican civil struggle with a stunning objective, in which the Texas government was earnestly invited to join. Federal Mexican revolutionists proposed that an independent republic be fought for and formed, to reach from ocean and ocean, and to consist of Texas, Nuevo León, Tamaulipas, Coahuila, Durango, New Mexico and the Californias, upper and lower. Though lively sentiment to join in the venture arose in Texas, President Lamar and his government declined, and even counselled Texans as individuals—an often precarious undertaking—to hold their peace. Some hoped that the federal scheme would soon burst into open warfare, for so long as Mexico's central government was occupied with revolt below the Rio Grande, it could not hope to plan for invasion above. In any case, the North Mexican movement was a real one in 1839, and to fight its coming battles, it brought together the strangest combinations of men.

For Mexicans were readying to fight against Mexicans; and, footloose and spoiling since their release from Indian frontier campaigns, Texans swarmed to help them. The Mexican revolutionary army was commanded by a border lawyer. This was General Antonio Canales who had been moving amongst the ranches of the wastelands raising a force of volunteers who brought their own weapons and horses. For ten years, off and on, he was to devote himself to the cause of an independent border republic. Its outlines varied from time to time, but the general idea possessed him, and he pursued it with everything but talent. Like many Mexicans he was a man of double vocation, the more absorbing part of which was to be a general. His lawyer's work could have detained him but little. To have like-minded supporting commanders—Colonels José María Gonzáles and Zapata; to lead horsemen who, like the

Mexicans, had little to lose, or like the Texans, simply went for the ride; to match wits with the weather, and one kind of brutality with another, and power with guile—that was the life. It was incredible how they moved about—how much ground they covered, and what ground! It lay vast, empty and gray under an empty sky. Its hard spiny growths lost their green under clinging dust. Dry earth ravines showed where storm water ran and would run again but all too briefly. An occasional trail, hardly a road, ran away into infinity to be lost southward in mountain passes of naked rock, hot by day and cold by night. The sun made vision into a narrow slit of distance where the land itself was an enemy and where clicking across the ancient dust like desert insects the enemy troops would move toward battle.

The one earth feature by which all places were oriented was the Rio Grande; and quite as though it were not the stated boundary between two established nations, General Canales took his way freely across it in either direction according to the urgencies of the moment. It was an eloquent comment on the condition of Texas that Texans did not stop him when he ranged north of the river as far as the Nueces. But he came not against Texas but to gird his forces and recruit Texans. In Texas territory at Lipantitlan on the Nueces where in the late summer of 1839 he maintained his headquarters, his little army was joined by a hundred and eighty Texans officered by Colonels Reuben Ross and S. W. Jordan. Each Texan was promised twenty-five dollars a month, a half league of land, and an equal share in the loot of war. Together they were ready to go, so soon as they should know whom they were to fight, and where.

Northeast Mexico was held by widely separated centralist garrisons. General Canalizo was at Matamoros with fifteen hundred troops, guarding the Rio Grande outlet to the sea. General Pavón with five hundred regulars and four cannon was at Revilla to control the immediate upriver towns. General Arista commanded Monterrey, the main inland approach to Saltillo and the capital. To fight these dispositions Canales had six hundred men—Texans, one hundred and eighty; two hundred and fifty mounted rancheros; one hundred and ten footmen; and sixty Indians with primitive arms. He organized them into two divisions, with Jordan and Zapata in command of one, and himself and Ross of the other. Of the three government garrisons, he picked Pavón's at Revilla to attack first; and on September twentieth he left the Nueces with all his men and marched for the Rio Grande. It took ten days to cross the wilderness between the two rivers. On the thirtieth the federalists crossed the Rio Grande planning to fall upon Revilla in a surprise attack. But federal informers saw Jordan's division at the river, where he had trouble crossing his horses, and hurried to warn Pavón. Surprise was gone; and when the centralists entered Revilla two days later, so was Pavón, with most of his forces, who were retreating inland toward Monterrey. Canales pressed after them, sending out scouts, while the hankering to fight thickened in the Texans, so far denied what they had come for.

At eleven o'clock in the morning of October third in the rolling, rough country beyond Mier, near the Alcantro Creek, General Canales found the centralists in battle formation. On sighting him in their turn, they fired a ball from a nine-pounder, and Canales with his three colonels agreed upon a plan of battle. It was never used. The Texan elements under their command on seeing the enemy did not wait to bother with orders. Leaving the Mexicans, the Indians and the high command behind, they raced forward in wild zest until they were within point-blank range of the enemy, took cover behind mesquite bushes and in a little arroyo, and began to throw effective rifle fire at the regulars. Colonels Jordan and Ross waited for General Canales to support the Texans, but with his Mexicans he only watched the battle from the rear, and did not move. The Texans were already committed; and their two colonels went forward, commanded a charge, and after twenty minutes of fierce, close fighting, forced the centralist lines to break and run.

It was the moment to press a full-scale pursuit; but still Canales hesitated, and Pavón was able to withdraw his cannons and wagons out of range. Presently he sent a flag asking for a truce of twelve hours, to which Canales agreed. When night came the centralist army pulled back five miles to a lone ranch with stone corrals and established a strong position. On the next morning, when the truce lapsed, Canales marched again to overtake the enemy. The Texan troops were in advance, and astonished Pavón when they appeared outside his walls. Major Joseph Dolan demanded a surrender. General Pavón came forward. His men were without water or provisions. He gave over his sword to Major Dolan, who indicated that he would better surrender it to General Canales.

"No, sir," replied the centralist commander, "I surrender to the brave Texans. They are my conquerors!"

He had lost a hundred and fifty men in the battle of the day before in killed, wounded or missing. The remaining three hundred and fifty of his command were taken prisoners, and in the amenities of north Mexican warfare, these promptly joined General Canales to fight on the other side, with their own four pieces of artillery which now were his. The Texans lost fourteen killed and wounded at the battle of Alcantro.

It was a promising victory for the army of the proposed federation. News of it went down the river and inland to Monterrey, causing dismay. The population loved a victor. Sentiment would always swing to him, and bring him recruits, food, money and the atmosphere of success on which revolutions fed and grew. All wondered where Canales would strike next. Another such swift triumph, and another, and the new river republic might spring alive. But Canales, if not exhausted by the efforts of his Texan allies, was inclined to take his ease at Mier, where he established himself and his augmented forces for forty days, as October whiled away, and part of November, and the old brown stone town glistened and rang with the colors and music and chatter of the autumn fair with its carnival, and the government forces downriver and inland caught their breath and had time to prepare their defenses, and the Texans fumed at inactivity, and some went home.

Finally in the middle of November Canales proceeded downriver against Matamoros. It took twenty-eight days of hard marching to make the hundred and sixty-five miles from Mier. Canales now had one thousand and sixty men and his four recently captured fieldpieces. He intended to lay siege to Matamoros, where General Canalizo with eighteen cannon and fifteen hundred regular troops awaited him. On December twelfth the federalists reached Matamoros and laid down their siege.

There soon followed two gestures of extreme caution that had the air almost of an exchange of courtesies.

On December fifteenth Colonel Zapata took a platoon, half Mexican and half Texan, against a Matamoros outpost, killed thirteen of its defenders, and retreated. In consequence, Canalizo immediately withdrew all his other outposts into the city.

On the next day, Canales announced to a council of war that since the besieged government forces in Matamoros would not come out to meet him in battle, he did not think it proper for him to attack them in their city; and that therefore he intended to abandon the siege and withdraw. The Texans were thunderstruck at such reasoning, protested, offered to storm the city by themselves. General Canales refused their offer, and with that, Colonel Ross detached fifty Texans from the federalist army and in disgust led them across the Rio Grande and home to Texas.

Abandoning Matamoros on the same day, General Canales turned southwestward to Monterrey. He had heard that the town was garrisoned by only four hundred troops under Arista, and he counted on taking their ammunition stores to supply his own men. Somehow he still managed to give an air of success, for on the way his men were provisioned, and each received a contribution of five dollars, out of the resources of the population of Caderita. Near Monterrey the defenders, heavily reinforced, awaited the rebels in rough country. Arista did the handsome thing and came out to fight. Canales, freed of his recent qualms, judged it proper under the circumstances to reply; and artillery let go on both sides. The duel was continued bravely through the whole day. Swabbers and gunners labored to produce their roars and drifts of smoke. No shot from either side took effect, though the forces were only eight hundred yards apart. It was in many ways a satisfactory battle. It ended with nightfall.

On the following morning Canales found that Arista had fallen back a mile nearer the city to a strong position, and pressed forward in a double play. He sent three hundred cavalry on a feint to the line, while with the rest of his power he detoured Arista and came to the city itself. Monterrey was his if he but entered. But in another of his complicated decisions he settled in the large patio of a convent on the outskirts and fortified it, while his troops stared at each other in bewilderment. Late in the afternoon Arista returned to the city, placed artillery, and on the following day—it was Christmas Day—another artillery exchange began that lasted for two days and hurt nobody. On the twenty-seventh a cavalry skirmish took place during which Colonel Gonzáles turned and ran, leaving his colleague Zapata in the field. The gestures were all fierce—the spirit, if not frivolous, then preoccupied. The Texans again were scandalized.

It was their presence, in fact, that made Arista as reluctant as Canales to engage in real combat. He knew their powers. But he believed more than they in cleverness. On the night of the twenty-seventh he sent agents among the federalist bivouacs. There by campfire and over coffee and in shadows his winning scheme was carried out. Out of the twelve hundred and fifty men in the Canales command, Arista managed to bribe seven hundred Mexicans to desert to him. Canales now had a real pretext for a retreat and with energy he acted upon it. Arista's cavalry chased after him, a skirmish threatened but did not develop, and another hundred and sixty Mexicans abandoned Canales. The retreat continued to the Rio Grande with Arista's cavalry snapping at its heels like coyotes and turning to run if threatened with a fight. On the seventh of January, 1840, Canales brought his column across the river and on the next day forty-five more Texans said good-bye and went home.

And now, having ranged for five months over thousands of square miles of comfortless land, and with his forces at their lowest ebb in numbers and sense of motive, Canales chose the moment to proclaim to the world the purpose of his scattered campaign that had accomplished nothing. On the banks of the river in his character as lawyer he framed a proclamation calling for delegates to spring forth from the dusty wastes to organize the Republic of the Rio Grande. Horsemen took copies of the document up and down the flat valley and inland to ranches, villages and towns. On January eighteenth enough delegates were assembled to give form to deliberations and, at Canales's field headquarters on the Texan side of the river, were set to work. They drafted a constitution modelled on the long-lamented Mexican Constitution of 1824. A capital was selected—Laredo. A president was named—Jesús Cárdenas. A commander-in-chief and secretary of war was appointed— General Canales. A flag was devised. Various offices were filled. There was by its own statement a new nation on the Rio Grande. Its boundaries were yet to be determined by battle, its existence yet to be granted by the mother country and other nations. But those who created it felt, and behaved, like a government, and granted the armed forces of the Republic of the Rio Grande extra rations and an issue all around of mescal, with which to celebrate. On the twenty-eighth of January President Cárdenas was inaugurated at Revilla amidst whatever pomp and ceremony were afforded by the resources of a little river town made of earthen boxes and willow-edged acequias and jacals of brush and wattles.

The army stayed at Revilla for three weeks and then pushed upriver to capture old Fort Saint John Baptist from the regulars, who had retired before their approach. Canales now had only seventy-four Texans in his command, and Colonel Jordan proposed that the army retire to the Nueces to obtain many more Texan volunteers and to reorganize. Canales did not approve the suggestion; and for the third time lost a sizable body of his best fighters, for Jordan with sixty Texans quit the adventure and took the road home over France Way. The loss cost the army of the Republic very heavily. Twelve days later Canales, marching inland from the presidio, was found by Arista with a large force and whipped so badly that he was barely able to run for the Rio Grande and cross to safety.

After all, then, Canales, with his president, was obliged to retire to Texas to raise new strength to continue the struggle, for without Texans they could not seem to win battles. Cárdenas went to Victoria on the Guadalupe River, Canales to Austin, to spread their offers. Canales later established his headquarters and raised the flag of the Republic of the Rio Grande at San Patricio, using Texan soil as casually as Mexican for his purposes. Response came. Though warned by President Lamar that Texas refused to recognize the new republican movement, and in spite of previous experience with its conduct of campaigns, four hundred and ten Texans, with three colonels, including Jordan, who returned to the new flag, joined Canales at San Patricio. Three hundred Mexicans from both sides of the river also rallied to him. With seven hundred and ten men, he began the slow movement back to the Rio Grande.

Jordan, with a hundred and ten Texans, and Colonels López and Molano, with a hundred and fifty Mexicans, were ordered to carry the revolution down the river towns of the right bank in advance of Canales and his main body. In June, 1840, they made demonstrations and signs of victory at Laredo, Revilla, Mier and Camargo. Now López and Molano announced new orders to Jordan which, they said, had been given them by Canales. They were to leave the river and strike southward, to raise new companies, and collect arms, ammunition and money. Jordan acceded, and the march began. It soon took on the character of a triumph. In one town after another the new republic was hailed with cheers, bells, artillery salutes, and the fat of that lean land. Victoria, the capital of Tamaulipas, fell, and the new republic vanguard installed a new state government.

Now followed a series of curious movements directed by the two Mexican colonels, López and Molano. Though Colonel Jordan and the Texans could not see any real purpose in these orders, they obeyed, moving through the Sierra Madre by an unlikely route which the Mexicans said would lead to Saltillo. But soon suspicions of treachery on the part of López and Molano occurred to the Texans. These were confirmed when they realized that the column was being taken not to Saltillo but to San Luis Potosí. Jordan insisted that the march change its course and head for Saltillo where an enemy force was stationed. One day's march from Saltillo a courier brought Jordan a message from a loyal friend at Victoria de Tamaulipas that López and Molano were maneuvering the Texan force into a position where for a cash payment they would deliver the Texan volunteers to the enemy.

Jordan could not bring himself to believe this. He faced the Mexican colonels with the accusation. They were horrified. How could he even think such a thing of them? Bitterly they said that it was a personal enemy of theirs who desiring to ruin them had sent the wicked message. Jordan was moved. He reassured them of his faith in them, and preparations for an attack upon Saltillo began. The city, too, was busy in the golden October weather. Its flat roofs were prepared for spectators of the coming battle, and hillsides too were occupied by civilians. Everyone was an amateur of the arts of battle. Opposing forces moving in tight formations made grand patterns that were easy to follow. The spectacle would have amplitude, with land for a theatre, bullets for dialogue, and death for many climaxes much to the Mexican taste. Women shawled against the sun came out bringing children for a glimpse of their future. Merchants and clerks and old men came to let their blood stir at what they missed in their days. The Saltillo garrison had promised them a victory to watch.

Unknown to Jordan, Colonel Molano had been in town conferring with the local commander about the price of betraying the Texans. The theory behind the deal was true and simple—break the Texans, and you break the revolution and the Rio Grande republic. Colonel López was fully informed of the arrangements. The plan was ready. The regulars, a thousand strong, defended Saltillo in trenches on top of a hill three miles south of the town. The Rio Grande force faced them from another hill six hundred yards away. A ravine was between the positions. Late in the morning of October twenty-third the regulars moved forward. It was the signal, and Colonel López, commanding for Rio Grande, began to execute the plan of betrayal. He ordered the Texan elements to march from the line toward a gorge in the mountains. If they entered it, they would be in a box that could be closed behind them till they were all shot to death. As Colonel Jordan moved unsuspectingly to follow the order, one of his officers rode up to him and shouted,

"In the name of God, sir, where are we going? If you take us to that gorge over there, the enemy will not leave a man to tell what became of us!"

Jordan suddenly saw it all. He gave a command, the Texan march was reversed, the column rode down the ravine passing the garrison trenches only a hundred and fifty yards away, and threw his men quickly

into an abandoned hacienda in the direct line of fire from the enemy. It
was the only cover to be had. The regulars began to fire, and with that,
López, crying out, "Long live the Supreme Government!" broke for the
enemy lines. All the Rio Grande infantry also deserted at about the
same time. The Texans were left with the Rio Grande rancheros behind
the broken walls of the old hacienda.

In short order they were surrounded on three sides. For a couple
of hours the centralists poured rifle fire and cannon fire upon them. The
Texans waited in silence. Their silence convinced the regular commander
that they were wholly reduced by his furious salvos, and at four o'clock
he ordered an advance. The hilltops quickened as the spectators saw the
great last act approaching. The centralists charged—and at thirty yards
were received with the usual Texas blast of terrible accuracy, and another,
and another. In a little while it was all over. When over four hundred
of the attacking regulars had been killed by the cold control of the
Texan fire, panic broke on the field. The regular soldiers turned and
fled to town. On the hills, the audience scrambled for home and safety
in dismay. The play had had an unexpected last act. The Texans lost
five men, won the battle, and embittered by treason gave up the war.
Organizing for retreat, they marched away home on the road to Monclova and France Way, holding off a force of regular cavalry that pursued them as far as the Rio Grande. The river republic lost another
defender when Colonel Antonio Zapata was captured near Morelos, and,
having refused to turn traitor to his cause, was executed and beheaded.
The Centralists brought his head in a barrel of brandy to Guerrero
on the river, his home; and there, on a pole set up opposite to his house,
his head was exhibited for three days for his wife and family to see.
Meanwhile, General Canales, far from marching in support of his various
divisions in the field, had moved aimlessly against San Marino in Tamaulipas, had retired hastily to Camargo on the San Juan, and there had surrendered to Arista.

With that act the Republic of the Rio Grande with its spacious
notions—its constitution, its president, its commander-in-chief, its army,
its two-room adobe and stone capitol building on the high north bank
of the river at Laredo—was suppressed; though the separatist idea in
north Mexico was to be revived under varying forms and names for many
years. In imagining the success of his scheme, Canales had proposed the
eventual annexation of his Republic of the Rio Grande to the Republic
of Texas, with the Texan southern boundary extended to the Sierra
Madre—the rocky scales of the double continental spine that made Mex-

ico resemble on the map a great iguana curving southward through the tropics. The Rio Grande remained as the actual, if disputed, boundary of Texas on the south; and soon the Texas boundary question turned westward to the long upper course of the river in New Mexico.

16.

The Santa Fe Pioneers

It fell to Governor Manuel Armijo to deal not only with all the old internal hostilities—raiding Indians and civil complaints—but in the autumn of 1841 with a new threat that loomed across New Mexico's vague eastern border. The New Mexican rebels of 1837 and 1838 had thought of turning to Texas for support and alliance; and while formal appeals may not have been sent by Gonzáles, news of the strong disaffection of the northern Rio Grande communities reached the Texans through traders and other travellers. Even after rebellion had been put down, the Upriver remained resentful of defeat and the execution of its leaders; and elsewhere in the province the airs and tyrannies of Governor Armijo created an atmosphere of opposition to the government. The discontent was not organized, its expressions were responses to long-suffered hard times, and the Governor heard few threats to alarm him unduly from within his domain. But if American traders in general felt superior to the New Mexicans, and optimistic over future possession of the river country, the Texans felt even more so, and moreover could point to what they regarded as a legal support of their attitude toward the New Mexican Rio Grande.

For in 1836, after the defeat of the Mexican armies, the Texan Republic by an act of its congress laid claim to the entire Rio Grande, from source to mouth, as the western boundary of Texas. Under such act, all of New Mexico lying east of the river was held to be Texan territory. But a great wilderness six hundred miles wide separated inhabited

Texas from New Mexico, and the claim was not put to the test of action during the first five years of the Texan Republic, which had other, more immediate internal problems to meet.

But now in the summer of 1841 there came urgent warnings from Mexico City to Governor Armijo that an expedition was forming in Texas under the sponsorship of the Texan President Mirabeau Bonaparte Lamar with the object of crossing the high plains wilderness northwest to Santa Fe. It was to be a large party, and volunteers were openly solicited through the pages of the *Austin City Gazette*. The purpose of the enterprise was announced as mercantile, but its character was to be overwhelmingly military, in order safely to "escort the merchandise through the Comanche territory." Volunteers received assurances. "All who arm, mount, and equip themselves will receive the pay of mounted gunmen—will serve for six months, or until the return of the expedition, and will be supplied with subsistence, &c. The companies will consist of fifty-six, rank and file, and elect their own company officers. The Field and Staff Officers will be appointed by the President. Ten large road-wagons will be furnished by the government to the merchants who desire to send their goods to that market, and the troops will secure their transportation. As this expedition will not only furnish an ample field for adventure on the march, but conduce, by a successful result, to the benefit of our common country," the advertisement anticipated "on the part of the young men whose crops are already in the ground, a readiness to unite . . . and contribute by their discipline, as well as their courage, to sustain the interest and the glory of our young Republic." The announcement was signed by William G. Cooke, who with three others, was commissioned "to represent our government with the people of Santa Fe."

Represent? For what purpose? Why did a wagon train full of goods need commissioners? The Mexican authorities were exercised by the news. It seemed plain to them that Texas was about to test her claim to the country of the upper Rio Grande. Mexico City promised reinforcements to Governor Armijo. The expedition was to be guarded against at all costs.

Meanwhile in Texas all preparations went rapidly forward. Volunteers mobilized at several encampments. The parties called themselves the "Santa Fe Pioneers." Enthusiasm ran high. It was believed in Texas that the New Mexicans were eager for the enterprise to be launched. A letter was circulated that gave encouragement to the expeditioners. It was written from Santa Fe, and it stated that the Texans would be welcomed by two thirds of the Rio Grande Mexicans, and all the Pueblo Indians and American traders. The Governor, it asserted, knew all that was in the wind, and he was quoted as saying that if the Texans came he neither could nor would resist them. The pioneers gathered—six military companies totalling two hundred and seventy men with a cannon, under the command of Brigadier General Hugh Mc-Leod; ten leading merchants from San Antonio de Béxar and their necessary employees; the commissioners; and a handful of guests and observers, including a young English lawyer named Thomas Falconer, and George Wilkins Kendall, a journalist from New Orleans. All men were mounted, there were fourteen wagons loaded with goods, two wagons that hauled the effects of the commanding general, another for the baggage of each of the six companies, and a doctor's wagon. These were each drawn by six to eight span of oxen, and the single cannon was pulled by mules.

President Lamar made careful preparations for the reception of his Texan commissioners. He chose three American residents of New Mexico then in Texas to serve as joint commissioners with his own men, and he addressed to the citizens of Santa Fe in Spanish and English a printed communication that revealed the real purpose of the whole undertaking. This was the annexation by Texas of the upper Rio Grande.

"We tender to you," declared President Lamar paternally, "a full participation in all our blessings. The great River of the North, which you inhabit, is the natural and convenient boundary of our territory, and we shall take great pleasure in hailing you as fellow-citizens, members of our young Republic, and co-aspirants with us for all the glory of establishing a new and happy and free nation. . . ." What greater gift could a Texan offer than to belong to Texas? The President continued, "This communication I trust will be received by you and by your public Authorities, in the same spirit of kindness and sincerity in which it is dictated," and if encouraged, he promised to send along later in the summer his commissioners who would "explain more minutely the condition of our Country, of the Seaboard and the co-relative interests which so emphatically recommend and ought perpetually to cement the perfect union and identity of Santa Fee and Texas. . . ." The copies of this proclamation were packed and confidently taken along by the Pioneers. If in the face of it there were any doubt about their purpose, a letter from the United States representative in Texas to Secretary of State Daniel Webster dispelled it on June 22, 1841: "An expedition . . . under the controul of three commissioners, left Austin, on the 6th instant, for Santa Fe. The object of the Republic is to open a trade with the people of that country, and induce them, if possible, to become an integral part of Texas."

All through the summer Governor Armijo received news of the Texan movements and made his own arrangements to deal with them. He had reason to suspect that many of his citizens might use the moment of the invasion to rise against him, and indeed, there was a plot in Taos to assassinate him when the Texans should appear. Many suspects were thrown into jail. The American traders and businessmen were watched narrowly by the Governor's people. Stories were put out that were calculated to terrify the New Mexicans into self-preservative loyalty. The Texans were coming to pillage, to murder, to usurp. Life and property would be in peril. If the Texans should succeed, they would profane and suppress the Holy Faith of New Mexico. Only the Governor could save all. His propaganda was poured forth, and as the Texans drew nearer toward the end of August, he had the satisfaction of observing that popular feeling in many quarters ran with him. It was not that he was loved—quite the contrary, for his oppressive and self-indulgent government was an offense to all who were not directly its beneficiaries in office. But a danger from without—this was enough to make his opposing measures seem like statesmanship, as his ragged men at arms were gathered to be drilled and provisioned and equipped out of the bottom of the barrel.

For his part, Governor Armijo, who was devoted to the good things of life, gave himself a certain state. He was always described as a fine-looking man, six feet tall, though inclined to stoutness that increased with the years until he was seen as "a mountain of fat." There was something Roman about his large head, with its dark, level-shadowed eyes, its long nose that emerged flush from the brow and sailed downward in a slight curve, its straight mouth with the thin upper lip that suggested timidity or worse, and the full lower lip that reached in appetite for the feasts of the flesh. His jaws were heavy and round. He was clean-shaven, and he wore his dark hair shorter than most men around him. His taste in uniforms ran to the lavish. In dress, he wore a cocked hat, braided heavily with gold lace, and crowned by a white ostrich plume that waved above his right eye. His blue tail coat had a high collar that rose against his jaws and revealed a white stock at his full throat. Epaulettes of thick gold discs with massive gold fringe weighed upon him as shimmering reminders of rank, and a silken sash bearing a grand medallion crossed his breast from his left shoulder. He had a heavy, simple charm of manner. Strangers opened up to him with pleasure at the pains he took to be agreeable. He disarmed them with confessions of genial rascality on his part—what was it about the sheep? Now well-to-do, he had founded his fortune by stealing sheep, and— the listener was expected to laugh, and think of wicked but amusing acts out of his own past—once upon a time he had sold a ewe to a man, not once, but fourteen times, the same ewe, stolen back to sell again to the same dupe. A sociable man, he loved to gamble, and did well at monté in the rooms of *La Tules,* Doña Gertrudes Barceló, who queened it over the society of Santa Fe. Moving about his functions in the long house of earth whose dust fell a little more each day, Governor Armijo was a focus of color and grandeur amidst poverty, a living and opinionated symbol of what government was like in the Mexico of 1842.

For in the capital itself, President Santa Anna was once more returning to the absolute power he was to hold nine times over Mexico before Mexico was done with him. While splendors were heaped on him with his own approval, he bore his exalted condition with an air faintly deprecating and surprised. When he dined in state, six colonels "stood the whole time of dinner behind his Excellency's chair," as an ambassadress observed, and when he was scheduled to appear at an opera gala—they were giving Donizetti's *Belisarius* (it was thought to be most appropriate)—the preparations were very grand. Two second-tier boxes were thrown together and lined in red and gold to accommodate the President and his party. The stairway leading to them was lined with solid rows of footmen in red and gold. On his arrival accompanied by a suite of generals uniformed like himself in red and gold, the President was handed a libretto of *Belisarius* in a special red and gold binding. The house was jammed, the "boxes were very brilliant— all the diamonds taken out for the occasion," the ambassadress noted further. The President took his chair, and the generals "sat like peacocks" surrounding him. He looked "modest and retiring, and as if quite unaccustomed to the public gaze"—an effect that took much experience to attain. "Knowing nothing of his past history, one would have said a philosopher . . . one who had tried the world, and found that all was vanity—one who had suffered ingratitude. . . ." When he passed through the capital, it was to travel "very much *en roi.*" There were outriders, a great escort of cavalry, a string of coaches with his own drawn by four white horses, and all proceeding at full gallop through dirt streets and lanes of staring, dusty people.

His proconsul far to the north at Santa Fe proclaimed his own

state with what was to be had locally. Governor Armijo if he lacked
an opera house and a sumptuous household guard yet had a gang of
hard riders in ragged serapes, and a state coach—though this was really
nothing more than a long wagon—"a curious specimen of Mexican taste
and workmanship." The axles were widely separated, and to them were
heavily affixed two massive timbers on which, without springs, the body
of the coach rested. But to make up for its jolting unwieldiness the
coach carried on its front a brave display of gilt work. If it had none
of the lightness and elegance of the carriage brought to the Rio Grande
from England in 1813 by Don Pedro Bautista y Pino—the English
understood such affairs better—it told all who saw it that General Don
Manuel Armijo was coming. And if there was no corps of liveried footmen in the old Palace, and little red and gold, the Governor had his
own way of decorating his executive office. Tacked to its walls were
scalps and pairs of ears sliced from killed Indians or other enemies
of the state and brought to him as proof of duties done or bounties
claimed.

In August the Governor sent Captain Damasio Salazar, a trusted
officer, to the east to scout the approaching Texans. Almost at once he
made contact. On September fourth three prisoners arrived in Santa Fe
under guard. Captain Salazar had sent them. They were the commissioners Howland, Baker and Rosenbury who in all good nature and
confidence had come ahead of the Texan party, bringing copies of President Lamar's ardent invitation to treason. They were cast into jail, only
to escape a few days later, and to be pursued. After a skirmish in the
country during which Rosenbury was killed, Howland and Baker were
recaptured and imprisoned at San Miguel del Vado, on the eastern
frontier, to await the Governor's arrival.

For he was going in person to meet his enemies. First, however,
he wooed the loyalty of any New Mexicans who may have planned to
throw in with the Texans. Referring to the "ever accredited mildness
that in all epochs and circumstances has characterized the benignity of
the Mexican government, which as a guide, has ever been followed by
him who addresses you," he offered amnesty to any citizens who "seduced
with or deceived by coaxing words" had promised to aid the Texans,
provided such citizens from that day forward would "accredit their
patriotism, adhesion, loyalty and fidelity" to Mexico. He could not for
a moment believe that if they but gave thought to "the danger of losing
your religion, your country, and your property," they would come back
under the Mexican flag; and promising them a great victory over the

Texans, he concluded convivially, "with this, your fellow citizen and chief drinks to your health."

Next, he gave orders to guard against any sudden move of the North American merchants to join forces with the invaders. To the United States consul at Santa Fe, the Governor sent a stern command. "As Commanding General of this department, and, in the name of the Mexican nation I warn you, as Consul of the United States of the North, that neither yourself nor any one of the strangers staying or dwelling in this Capital leave it under any pretext or motive; that you all must remain in the city till my return. . . . Acknowledge to me at once the receipt of this precept. God and Liberty, Santa Fe, September 16th, 1841."

The North Americans had reason to be alarmed. A group of them met and composed a letter to Secretary Webster at Washington on the same day. "Sir:—In a moment of extreme excitement and danger we, a few isolated American citizens, together with a few other citizens of other nations, feel it to be our duty to inform the Government of the United States of the circumstances which surround and oppress us in these moments. It has been learned here that an invading expedition composed of 325 men from Texas is approaching this Territory; on that account, all the inhabitants and all the officials of the government have become so exasperated against all strangers in this place that we deem ourselves in danger of our lives and destruction of our property; there is danger imminent; and we fear that before this reaches Washington we shall have been robbed and murdered.

"The governor marched off today with his troops to repel the invaders. . . ." But the Governor's army had hardly gone when, with the effect of yielding to an afterthought of enraged self-righteousness, one of his officers suddenly returned to town with several soldiers, went to the house of the American consul, entered, and "grievously insulted him striking him on the face." Mexican citizens gathered for the fun, but a few "of better dispositions" intervened and stopped it. The officer and his men returned to the street, and there he announced for all to hear that once the Texans were disposed of, he "would return with his troops and would destroy all of us, the strangers. . . . We, therefore, hope that, with the presentation of these circumstances to our government, measures will be adopted that will avoid the recurrence of similar injuries to our citizens. . . ."

The Consul protested officially to the Governor, who sent back assurances from the field that provided they behaved themselves, the foreigners would be protected in their rights. The Governor, in his

character as commander-in-chief, continued his march along the old
Missouri trail that skirted the forested mountains southeast before it
turned northeast at San Miguel. He was mounted on a huge mule that
bore a magnificent saddle and a gorgeous caparison. With him were
about a thousand men-at-arms—Mexicans with guns and cutlery, Indians
with lances, bows and arrows. Just after sundown as he approached the
ruined Pecos mission in the cold twilight that fell swiftly he came to
a turn in the road to see Captain Salazar with a hundred soldiers and
five Texan prisoners. The Governor's trumpeter sounded the flourishes
that always announced him, and the Captain drew up his force in line
by the roadside. The Governor rode forward to the prisoners showing
all his hearty charm. Without dismounting he shook their hands—the
prisoners were roped together—called them "friends," and remarking
that he had been informed of their capture, asked who they might be.

One Texan—it was a Captain Lewis—nervously replied that they
were merchants on the Santa Fe Trail from the United States.

Another—Van Ness—contradicted him by saying that all but one
were Texans, and the last was Mr. Kendall, from New Orleans. But
the Governor ignoring Van Ness leaned down to Lewis, took a handful
of his collar and hauled him roughly up beside his mule and growled:

"What does this mean? I can read—Texas!" and he pointed to
the word on the buttons of Captain Lewis's uniform that carried also
a single star. Lewis trembled, and the Governor, outraged at being lied
to, added, "You need not think to deceive me: no merchant from the
United States ever travels with a Texan military jacket."

It was a bad start. The prisoners were in trouble. The Governor
asked more questions. Where was the rest of the Texan column? How
many were there in it? What were they after? He listened while they
assured him that the Texans came on mercantile business with peaceful
purposes. He considered the case of Mr. Kendall, who had a Mexican
passport, and was merely travelling with the column to enjoy its protection. Mr. Kendall's papers were in order, but he would be left with
the prisoners until his intentions were somewhat better understood. The
Governor gazed at them, and reading in their faces what they had heard
about him, he blurted out that he was a man of honor; he was no
assassin; he would have them know moreover that he was a great soldier.
They returned his look and held their tongues. He then asked who of
the prisoners could speak Spanish, and Captain Lewis, who had lived in
Mexico, came forward eagerly. The Governor ordered him untied from
his fellows, mounted him on a mule, motioned him to a place in his

company, and turned to Captain Salazar, to whom he bawled an order to march the prisoners that night to San Miguel where they had just come from. The Captain was astonished, and dared to remonstrate with the Governor.

"But they have already walked nearly thirty miles today, your Excellency, and are hardly able to walk all the way back tonight," said Captain Salazar, not entirely able to conceal his own distaste for the return march that he must endure with the prisoners.

"They are able to walk thirty miles more," replied the Governor with a mock-heroic gesture. He was of that order of men whose self-satisfactions—and these must be large if they would satisfy—were all taken at the expense of others: in money, honor, or, quite simply and commonly, in the blood and breath of life. "The Texans are active and untiring people—I know them." And then, in the constricted voice of a furious fat man, he added, "If one of them *pretends* to be sick or tired on the road, *shoot him down and bring me his ears! Go!*"

And with a blast of bugles and a command to his troops he rode by the prisoners on the darkening trail to San Miguel. The exhausted Texans took up their march in turn. At midnight they were halted in a meadow when a cloudburst fell. They slept till dawn in the rain and after two more hours on the trail reached the village of San Miguel which was now teeming with the Governor's soldiery. The prisoners were confined in a house on the plaza, there to reflect on what had befallen them since leaving home, and to wonder what was happening to the rest of their expedition, and to imagine the fate that was taking shape for them in the capricious vapors of the Governor's mind.

In miserable truth, the Texans had to acknowledge that the expedition was a failure even before it encountered the New Mexicans. It had started too late in the season, for by the time the train was out on the high plains, the best pasturage was gone—burned away by the terrible summer sun. Nobody knew much about the route to follow except two Mexican guides, who deserted one night. Indians harried the pioneers—in one attack they killed five Texans, stripped them, and cut the heart out of one. Supply was badly planned, and food ran out. The travellers ate insects, reptiles, anything. A large part of the force was detached and sent ahead under Colonel Cooke, the commissioner, to find San Miguel and buy food to bring back to the starving main body. Other groups—Harland, Baker and Rosenbury in one, and Kendall with his four companions—were sent ahead at various times to scout the New Mexicans and make cordial overtures; but with mournful results.

Colonel Cooke did not return, and neither did the others. Indians raided the main body one night and stampeded the animals, making off with eighty-three horses and all the cattle except the draft oxen and mules. As the train crawled slowly forward a great part of the company now had to walk. Many threw away their arms and ammunition, greatly reducing the company's power to defend itself. Many men fell ill for lack of salt to replace what they sweated away. Discipline crumbled, and the brisk intention of the expedition became a farce. Conquer a province, annex the upper Rio Grande? All they wanted now, the Santa Fe Pioneers, scattered in two large parties on the plains and one small party in cells at San Miguel, were rescue and something to eat.

On the morning of their arrival at San Miguel, Kendall and his three fellow prisoners looked out the window of their cell and saw a man led out blindfolded and pounded down to his knees against a plaza wall and shot in the back by a squad of soldiers at three paces. So close a fusillade did not kill him, and the corporal of the squad dispatched him by putting his pistol to the man's breast and shooting him in the heart. The flash set his shirt on fire. It burned until his blood seeped into the little flames putting them out. The victim was Baker, executed for running away from captivity at Santa Fe.

In a few minutes Kendall and his group were taken out to the plaza and lined up facing a window through which they could see the Governor wearing a blue uniform and a sword. Talking to someone out of sight in the room, he pointed to the prisoners outside, listened, spoke, nodded. The unseen individual within answered him about each prisoner. It gave them the feeling of being on trial. With Baker's body smouldering on the ground a few paces away they saw themselves grimly. And then the door opened, the Governor came out and weighing his own majesty with satisfaction on each step walked slowly to the prisoners and faced them. He was pleased to be gravely magnanimous. His charm was sobered, but it was there.

"Gentlemen," he said, "gentlemen, you told me the truth yesterday—Don Samuel has corroborated your statements—I save your lives."

Don Samuel? they thought, the unseen informant in the room? Who could he be? The Governor continued:

"I have ordered Don Samuel to be shot—he will be in five minutes. He ran away from Santa Fe, and, in attempting to reach Colonel Cooke's party, has been retaken."

They felt a shock of recognition. Don Samuel was Howland, the third of the advance commissioners.

"You now see the penalty of trying to escape," concluded the Governor, "his fate will be yours if you attempt it.—Sergeant of the guard, conduct these gentlemen back to prison."

But before they moved, Howland was brought forth to die. His hands were tightly tied behind him. He passed closely in front of the others. They blanched at what they saw. His left ear and left cheek were cut wholly away, his left arm was grossly hacked where the sword had finished its strokes. He turned to his friends, and their hearts beat when with the other side of his face he gave them a strong, sweet smile. They tried to go to him, were stopped by guards, and he said to them gently, "Good-bye, boys; I've got to suffer. You must—" but he was walked past them and that was all they heard. He was taken to see Baker's body, and then a blindfold was put over his ruined face, he was made to kneel and was shot dead by the squad, while the other prisoners watched sick with rage. They were then marched back to their cell.

The plaza was now gradually emptied of troops, and they wondered why, and were told that Governor Armijo with a thousand warriors was marching on Antón Chico, a village thirty miles away, where Colonel Cooke and his detachment of ninety-four men were encamped. All day couriers came and went—there were reports of a battle, and then of a surrender, unconditional surrender, which the prisoners could not believe. Surely Cooke and his men would put up a fight—but the report was true, and the plaza walls echoed with salvos, ringing of bells in the church tower, outlandish music on guitars, fiddles and trumpets, and cries of "Long live the Mexican Republic!" and "Long live the brave General Armijo!" and "Death to the Texans!" There was a procession, the tutelar saint of the village was carried from and to the church, a Te Deum was sung, and the celebration went on all night. Every ten minutes the prisoners heard the sentries dolefully cry out, "Centinela alerta-a-a-a!" in relay from post to post.

In the morning the Governor received the prisoners again. It pleased him to be candid. He said that of course he knew they were gentlemen—Howland had told him so, and indeed, they looked it; he had given orders that they must be treated accordingly. He waved them to seats. He then quizzed them about General McLeod and the main body of the Texans who were yet to be taken, and in fact he was about to go and take them, and if they put up a fight, he would kill them all. As his prowess reminded him of himself, and his department, his native talents rose within him, and he improvised a little epic, an aria, on the subject of his own valor, the splendor of his army, the glory, strength and richness of New Mexico, while his captives could hardly believe their ears. In time he dismissed them to new quarters, and in a few minutes they heard trumpets, the clatter of a mounted column, and watched him dash by on his great mule, leading his troops, in a superb blue serape heavy with gold and silver bullion.

Three days later—it was September twentieth—Cooke's people began to pass through San Miguel on their way to Mexico City under guard, and roped together. The San Miguel prisoners, hungry for news, were not permitted to talk to them; but could only speculate upon their own destiny. But their spirits rose in the next few days, for they were kindly waited upon by the women of the place, who brought them good food, and amused them with attentions, and listened to their jokes, and exclaimed at their general good nature. The young priest of the parish was good to them, too. As the days passed the prisoners saw several caravans go by on their way to Santa Fe. If only, they thought, if only they might escape and make their way to the United States by the Santa Fe Trail! But they were closely guarded. For three weeks they waited for news of McLeod and the main body; and then, in driblets, a few Texans were brought in at a time, and finally on October ninth the bells rang again, and a procession was formed, and guns were fired, and they knew that the Governor's victory was complete. Within the next few days all the remaining Texans were driven into San Miguel. They were in a frightful state. Most of their clothes had been taken from them, they had only one blanket each to protect them from the sharp mountain weather, they were starving. Their merchant wagons followed, in the possession of the Mexicans, and once ranged in the plaza, were emptied of their cargo which was promptly distributed among the Governor's people, with great shares going to himself and to Captain Lewis.

For it now came clear what Lewis had been up to. Kendall and his friends had been wondering where Captain Lewis had been during their captivity which he had been spared; and now they heard how, beginning as interpreter for the Governor, he had succumbed to a cruel weakness of his own character, and had served as a traitor, inducing his fellow Texans to put down their arms and submit to the Governor under false promises of good will. The Texans, as soon as they gave up their rifles, were tied together with lariats, and robbed of their personal valuables, knives and baggage. It was a sad discovery.

October seventeenth came as a warm day. Little showers of rain fell. The Texans were all turned out together into the plaza and counted

—nearly two hundred of them. For the first time in many weeks they were reunited—all but Cooke's party who had been taken through town without pausing a few days before—and they exchanged their news, while waiting to hear what was now to become of them. This they soon learned; for Captain Damasio Salazar was put in command of a guard of two hundred soldiers, for the purpose of marching the Texans on foot two thousand miles to Mexico City and the mercies of Santa Anna, while Governor Armijo flushed with achievement rode back to Santa Fe and the triumphal welcome of a hero.

Many of the marchers already knew Captain Salazar for what he was. Their hearts sank now. He drew his tradition from impulses deep in humanity at its most inhumane. His view of authority, and the value of life, and the meaning, and uses, of pain, was not unique. It had shown itself in his superiors—the President of Mexico, the Governor of New Mexico. If he was a man who could not read, so that subordinates had to make sense for him out of written orders and passports, yet in sustained effort he could bring his faculties to bear on other matters of quite respectable complexity—how to wound the human mind and body, how to torture them, how to kill them, how to dishonor them when killed, and all nicely devised to slake his own hearty appetites.

He now gave an order and marched the column out on the old Pecos road. By sundown he brought them to Pecos and without feeding them, turned the prisoners into the ruins of the mission to spend the night. After the warm day and its dancing rain showers the night was icy, for there was snow on the Sangre de Cristos and its breath came driving down on the wind. Having been robbed of most of their clothing, the prisoners had only one single blanket each. It was not enough. Nobody slept all night. In the morning, before the cold mists of the Pecos canyon began to thin, they looked hungrily to their custodian for food, and leaped with joy when he called them—all one hundred eighty-seven of them—to gather about him. When he was surrounded, Captain Salazar reached into a receptacle he had, and took from it a small cake. The men looked at it. He tossed it into the air above them, and they scrambled over each other to reach for it. He laughed to see the sight, and tossed another, and another, until he had thrown up fifty cakes—all he had for the whole party. He had the joy of making animals out of men who were comrades. The more they fought each other for the cakes the more his glee showed itself. When there was nothing left, and with more than two thirds of the men still sick with hunger, he fell them in and started the day's march. He was taking them to the Rio

Grande by way of Galisteo Creek. The ground was rough. Their feet bled, for many had no shoes. They passed the second night in an open corral after a pint of meal for their day's ration. The Captain would not resist what wells of rich humanity dwelt deep in him—he told the prisoners that his orders from the Governor were to keep them tied throughout every night; but as he knew they might be tired, he dared to disobey the order. Of course, if any man tried to escape, not only he, but every one of his companions would be shot to death.

On the third day he marched them into Santo Domingo on the Rio Grande, and a few hours later into San Felipe downstream. In both pueblos the Indian women were kind to them, bringing them food and sympathy. But Salazar pushed on as soon as possible, improvising tortures as he went. At Algodones, on the river, when the prisoners begged to be given house shelter against the cold, he thrust them all into two connecting rooms so small that they would hold scarcely twenty in ordinary comfort, and listened to their yells and thuddings with satisfaction, for they were slowly suffocating. In his own good time he released fifty to sleep on the ground. At Sandía pueblo he issued rations of one ear of uncooked corn per man. At Albuquerque he marched them through the streets. At Los Placeres ranch he gave out no rations, and when the men begged, he pointed to pastured horses and mules near-by and remarked that the "grazing was excellent." At Valencia on the old river road he issued a pint of flour around, but few men had energy enough to cook it into anything edible, and most sank to stupor while frost gathered on their blankets. In the morning the Captain found one of the Texans dead, and as an accounting for the Governor, cut off his ears, and threw the body into a ditch. Then calling the morning's roll, he was asked by another Texan for permission to ride in a cart for he had become too lame to walk; and granted it. A mile later the cart broke down, and the Captain ordered the Texan to walk, then, or be shot. "Then shoot, and the quicker the better!" said the Texan, and Captain Salazar did so, then cutting off the man's ears, taking his shirt and trousers, and leaving another body for dogs or coyotes.

The Captain could only relieve the tedium of his mission by rapid progress. At times he turned the command over to a subordinate and snatched a few hours of sleep in a wagon by day to supplement his night's rest. At Socorro he allowed a day's halt, and then pushed on toward the Dead Man's March. He was obliged to shoot another man who was falling behind, and take his ears. It did not suit him to permit any of the ailing prisoners to ride on any of the unburdened mules that

were led by the escort. Reaching the Dead Man's March he announced
that the crossing would be made without the usual overnight stops.
They entered it after a heavy snowfall that came during the night and
left five inches of snow on the sleeping prisoners. Once again a member
of the stumbling and dragging detachment lagged in the rear, and the
Captain ordered a soldier to make him keep up. The Texan was unable
to do so, and the soldier knocked out his brains with a clubbed rifle,
remembering to bring the ears to the Captain. During the crossing of
the Dead Man's March the Captain met northbound troops from
Durango—the reinforcements promised to the Governor to help him
deal with the Texans. Already dealing with the Texans, Captain Salazar
pushed them on to the end of the desert crossing and once more came
to the Rio Grande, with the loss of only one more Texan, who died of
pneumonia, complicated by a piece of drollery on the part of a Mexican
soldier. The sick man, supported by friends, who heard the death rattle
in his throat, came to a moment of lucidity and asked for water. Just
then, the soldier, smiling for his joke, pointed a rifle in his face and
pulled the trigger. The gun was not loaded, but the sick man was con-
vulsed by the action, and threw out his arms in self-protection. The
soldier could not resist repeating his success. He again took aim and
snapped the trigger. It was too much for the patient. He shuddered
once and died. His ears were cut off and taken to Captain Salazar, who
now had a collection of five pairs.

Now that they were nearing El Paso, the Captain and his men
found a new enjoyment—describing to the Texans what their fate must
be once they entered the jurisdiction of Chihuahua. All that had passed
before would be trifling compared to what awaited them farther south.
It was a pleasure to torture the minds, as well as the flesh, of weakened
men. The thought was left with them that upon the arrival of orders
from President Santa Anna, they would all be executed. Pushing dutifully on, the Captain caused his charges to ford the Rio Grande, which
at its deepest came to their chins. The water was bitter cold. Only a
few miles ahead lay El Paso, where Captain Salazar was to turn the
prisoners over to the commanding general of the Chihuahua department,
Don José María Elías Gonzáles.

What followed was like a dream. The transfer was made, and
within two hours the prisoners were billeted in small squads at different
houses of the El Pasoans. After five months of never seeing a table or
a chair, they were seated to partake of "well-cooked meats, eggs, the finest
bread . . . even the wines of the place." General Elias was in a rage at

the treatment they had endured. Salazar, coming to make his report to him, proudly stated that he had delivered every prisoner safely but five who had died on the way, and to prove the accuracy of his tally, threw down on the General's desk five pairs of ears strung on a thong. The General by now knew all, and held Salazar for the murder of three of the men, and for an accounting of what he had stolen from the prisoners.

El Paso could not do enough for the miserable Texans. The citizens fed them, let them bathe, gave them money, clothes and beds. The young parish priest, Father Ramón Ortiz, endeared himself to everyone with his handsome face, his sympathetic expression, and his openhearted help. General Elias ordered that they remain for three days of rest in El Paso. When it was time to resume the march, the whole city turned out to see them off, and many residents—the commanding general, the priest, several other leading citizens—rode part of the way with them and hoped that they would come safely to Mexico City and speedy liberation, and took an "affectionate farewell." So the Santa Fe Pioneers left "the lovely town or city of El Paso," in its "delightful situation in a quiet and secluded valley, its rippling artificial brooks, its shady streets, its teeming and luxurious vineyards, its dry, pure air and mild climate, and above all, its kind and hospitable inhabitants. . . . Surely," pleaded a prisoner, not one of the Texans could "ever think of El Paso, or the dwellers therein, without lively gratitude."

But El Paso was only an interlude of mercy. On arrival overland in the capital, they were distributed among several prisons—the dreadful Accordada and the Santiago convent in Mexico City, another in Puebla, the grimly isolated fortress of Perote. Those in the Santiago were objects of curiosity for fashionable residents of Mexico City. The Spanish Ambassadress—a former American—noted that "a good deal of interest has been excited here lately about the Texian prisoners taken in the Santa Fe expedition. . . ." She had heard that they were stripped of their hats, shoes, and coats. One day she went with a party to see them. The common soldiers were in the courtyard, the officers in the convent's large hall. She understood that President Santa Anna planned to "have them put in chains, and sent out to sweep the streets, with the miserable prisoners of the Accordada." But an officer with her pooh-poohed the idea. Actually, she found that there seemed to be "very little if any vindictive feeling against them"; and in June, 1842, the President to celebrate his birthday gave the bulk of the prisoners their freedom—though one singled out for severe treatment was isolated in the fortress of San Juan de Ullóa until January, 1845, when he made his escape and

returned to Texas. The Texan attempt on the upper Rio Grande—
General Andrew Jackson writing in retirement to General Sam Houston
called it "the wild-goose campaign against Santa Fe"—was done with.
The upper river faded into remoteness again; and the Texas Rio Grande
came into view through the smoke of little battles between Mexicans
and Texans over the boundary claims, and the sovereignties, that
divided them.

17.

Border Smoke

For vastly the greater part of its twelve hundred miles, the
border country of the Rio Grande was bare and ungrateful. Below the
El Paso settlements was the old village at the junta de los rios, called
Presidio del Norte, where amidst crumbling missions a garrison guarded
the river crossing and a port of entry. Then, reading downstream, came
the fantastic country of the Big Bend, where only Indian wanderers
penetrated. Old Fort Saint John Baptist and the half-dozen Escandón
towns and the Gulf settlements for river commerce were the only formal
communities below the Big Bend. Ranches and haciendas were scattered
along the valley, many of them established under Mexican grants after
1821—but the Texas rebellion, and Indian raids, and the scorching of
the land under demands of volunteer armies in civil conflict caused
many to be abandoned. Where once near the river sheep and goats were
raised, and farther inland, mules, horses and horned cattle; and where
after 1817 corn was grown and after 1830 cotton and sugar cane, the
lower valley was "turned into a desert." Commerce was reduced to a
trickle, and in the 1830s at Matamoros after the smoky withdrawal of
Captain Henry Austin with the *Ariel,* "wagons were almost as scarce
as steamboats." The great tract between the Rio Grande and the Nueces
was an empty wilderness buffer between populated Texas and the

boundary she claimed. Mexico had never recognized the independence of Texas, much less her Rio Grande border. Mexicans still freely used the north side of the river as far as the Nueces, and Texas was powerless to prevent them.

Under her first president, General Houston, Texas did not actually make a do-or-die issue out of the Rio Grande. After the victory of 1836 she asked the United States to annex her and grant her statehood, even going so far as to propose a new boundary, if it would expedite action. The boundary was to be the watershed between the Rio Grande and the Nueces, and the New Mexico Rio Grande was to be abandoned as the western limits. But the United States did not welcome the proposal to annex Texas, and the old boundary claim stood. It was emphasized in armed raids on Mexican establishments on the river—in 1837, when Texans attacked Laredo without results, and four years later in the Lamar project of the Santa Fe Pioneers. Again in 1837 Texas asked for annexation, and again the United States refused, finding the request "inexpedient, under existing circumstances." For Texas and Mexico were officially still in a state of war, while the United States was at peace with Mexico, and bound to her by a trade treaty to be observed scrupulously so long as it could be "reasonably hoped" that Mexico would "perform her duties and respect our rights under it." The Texas Republic was obliged to be content with recognition by the United States, which came on March 1, 1837, under a joint Congressional resolution.

Of all the factors that kept the annexation issue in a turmoil for twelve years the most emotional, and for a long time the most decisive, was in a sense a legacy from Stephen Austin. It was the institution of slavery, on which he had founded the working economy of his settlements. If, for a period, he had wavered in his view of the justice and the usefulness of slavery, the Texas Rebellion by its successful outcome confirmed his last view of the matter; for among the first laws drawn up by the Texan convention of independence in March, 1836, were those conserving and regulating the holding of slaves. What had Austin said? Texas "must be a slave country. Circumstances and unavoidable necessity compel it. . . ." By the time he died of pneumonia as secretary of state of the Republic in December, 1836, his slave policy was firmly embodied in Texan life.

As a fixed feature of that life, it became in the United States a hot issue between the northern abolitionists and the slaveholding masters of the south. Their respective views were expressed in Congress. If her system of slavery would come into the Union with the rest of

Texas, the abolitionists would fight against annexation, and the south would fight for it. The central struggle for power in the United States in terms of opposed views of living human property remained for almost a decade the dominant factor in all discussions of the annexation of Texas, and prevented any resolution of the matter.

After her early rejections by the United States, Texas, particularly under the presidency of Lamar, turned away from the idea of annexation toward a more vibrant nationalism. In 1839 she tried to bring about a state of peace with Mexico with an offer of five million dollars in exchange for national recognition and acceptance of the Rio Grande as the boundary between the two nations. The Mexican Congress was indignant at the proposal, and refused to consider even a truce that did not reaffirm Mexican sovereignty over Texas. But if a state of war continued, little indicated the fact. Private trading expeditions moved across the Rio Grande between northern Mexican towns and San Antonio, exchanging Mexican sugar, flour, beams, and leather goods for Texan tobacco and American calico and hardware—until early in the second presidency of General Houston.

In December, 1841, at Austin, General Houston was inaugurated as president for the second time, appearing "on the stage in a linsey-woolsey hunting shirt, and pantaloons, and an old wide-brimmed white fur hat. In this," thought an observer—it was Dr. Josiah Gregg, the Santa Fe trader, now roaming far afield in Texas with opinions tart as ever—"Gen. Houston demonstrated more vanity than if he had appeared in an ordinary cloth suit. He knew it would be much remarked, and thought it would be popular no doubt, with [the] body of the people." His vice-president, General Edward Burleson, "also appeared and was sworn in in his fancy Indian leathered hunting shirt—probably more for the purpose of being in unison with the president than for vanity. . . ." The president's speech was "rather dry and monotonous." Much of it was taken up with praising his own previous efforts on behalf of Texas, and much with severe criticisms of Lamar, his predecessor, who had sent the Pioneers against Santa Fe.

The issue was not dead; for in January, 1842, news reached Texas of the defeat, capture and treatment of the Texan Santa Fe expedition; and the public temper raged at the barbarisms of Governor Armijo and other Mexicans. Congress was in session under the new administration, and in a fury passed a resolution demanding that the boundary of Texas leap across the Rio Grande, and take in Sinaloa, Durango, Coahuila, Tamaulipas, Sonora, Chihuahua and the Californias

—in effect, the old huge design of the Republic of the Rio Grande that had been fought for and lost by Canales and his Texan volunteers two years before. Houston vetoed the resolution, and Congress passed it again over his veto. When word of such wild lust for Mexican territory came to Mexico, it was to inflame Santa Anna, supremely forgetful of the last scenes of 1836, with desires for a punitive war. In Texas there were two parties of sentiment. One was hot for an offensive war against Mexico. The other, represented by Houston, saw that defensive measures were the best Texas could manage at the moment. Both Mexico and Texas were without funds or credit. The scene of any possible warfare between them—the immense, starkly beautiful but barren lands of the Rio Grande —could hardly support a handful of towns and ranches, let alone mounted armies with their need of forage and their levies of money, food and animals of burden. The armed forces of Texas were not organized or trained. War seemed unlikely.

But suddenly, as a flourish against Texan designs on the eight vast states of north Mexico, on March 5, 1842, Mexican troops descended upon Refugio, Goliad and San Antonio. The Texan garrisons of all three places were too small to make any effective resistance, and all surrendered. For their part, the Mexican forces were too far from base, and too few, to do more than raise the Mexican colors over the three Texan towns; and after proclaiming the laws of Mexico to their enraged citizens, withdrew two days later and retired below the Rio Grande.

So after six years of preoccupied restraint, both Texas and Mexico again made the gestures of war toward one another. Houston alerted all military manpower in Texas. The Texan navy—five schooners and two brigs—was ordered to blockade Mexico's east coast ports and the mouth of the Rio Grande. Santa Anna promised to march across Texas and plant the Mexican flag on her eastern borders at the Sabine. Houston, in a letter addressed to Santa Anna and released to the world, told him his statement was a "silly gasconade," and in his turn pledged that Texans "will march across the Rio Grande, and—believe me, sir—ere the banner of Mexico shall triumphantly float on the banks of the Sabine, the Texan standard of the Single Star, borne by the Anglo-Saxon race, shall display its bright folds, in Liberty's triumph, on the isthmus of Darien."

Deeds fell short of such an exchange of rhetoric. Neither nation had funds to pay a full-scale army. Texas tried to borrow a million dollars in the United States and failed. The navy's expenses for over-hauling could not be met and the blockade was never enforced. When the Texan congress voted an offensive war against Mexico, Houston felt obliged to veto the bill. All he could propose were defensive schemes along the border, and small forces were mobilized only to be infuriated by restraining orders.

In early June a Texan volunteer defense force of one hundred and ninety-two men under General Davis was attacked by five hundred Mexican cavalry with two hundred infantry and one cannon under General Canales, who was now in the national service against which he had plotted and danced about on horseback two years before. There was a ragged and enthusiastic cavalry charge, a feint or two, and a Texan bullet killed the Mexican officer commanding the cannon, whereupon General Canales flew back to the Rio Grande with his detachment, and the Texan volunteers disbanded.

Seen from far away in Washington, the state of affairs was a nuisance, and pressure was exerted by the annexationists in the United States to bring the war officially to an end. Once done, this would permit the United States to intervene in the Texas question without taking sides in a war—if an occasional brief scuffle between unsupported armed bands could be called a war. On June twenty-second, Secretary Webster asked the American minister to Mexico to lay before the Santa Anna government certain observations. After all, realities had better be faced: Texans and Mexicans were wholly different in their traditions, languages and ways; a vast distance separated their seats of government; they had now been disunited for many years; Texas was recognized as a nation by many other nations of the world, and maintained diplomatic and commercial relations with them. It did appear on the face of it that any future return of Texas to Mexican sovereignty "was among the things most to be doubted." The prevailing situation was harmful to commerce everywhere in the Gulf. To be sure, if the war must be continued by its parties, the United States could not interfere; but if she could help to compose a peace, she would be most willing to do so. Mexico must see that peace would bring the United States an opportunity to enter legitimately into the matter of Texan annexation. But Mexico rejected the offer, and in further repudiation set out to show by another armed thrust across the river that the war was far from over.

Like the others, the latest attack was little more than a brandishing of arms. It came on September 11, 1842, against San Antonio, where General Adrian Woll appeared with twelve hundred Mexicans. There was little local resistance; but the Texan militia was ordered to the counterattack, and volunteers marched from Gonzales to take back the old battle-pitted city. On the thirteenth there was an engagement on the Salado Creek six miles east of town between the Gonzales volunteers and Woll with eight hundred men. The Mexicans lost sixty killed and many wounded, the Texans ten wounded and none killed. "Huzza! Huzza for Texas!" cried the Texan commander in writing after the fight. But Texas suffered other losses that day when another volunteer band attempting to reach the Gonzales detachment was surrounded and destroyed with about forty-five killed and fifteen taken prisoners. Woll retired to the city and organized his train for retreat. By the eighteenth all his people were pulling back to the Rio Grande, taking along fifty-three prisoners, plunder, and a number of San Antonio citizens of Mexican blood who threw in their lot with Mexico. The Texans pursued the retreating troops for thirty or forty miles and then gave up to return homeward.

The Woll exploit was the signal for retaliation. The Republic's various bands of volunteers were ordered to meet in rendezvous at Medina, under the command of General Alexander Somervell. They were in high temper. Immediate invasion of Mexico was their hot hope. Seen from the ranks, any concern for the problems of supply, transport and military organization looked like merely irritating caution. Somervell had almost nothing with which to equip his men. There were intrigues and rivalries over the command positions, including the highest. The volunteers were not interested in making an army—they wanted to whip Mexico, at once, and many a man felt equal to the job alone, and became a corrosive malcontent at being restrained until some small show of order and discipline was achieved. But finally, after what a chafing officer called a "week of breeches-making," Somervell set out for the Rio Grande with seven hundred and fifty men. His orders from President Houston read: "When the forces shall have assembled, if their strength and condition will warrant a movement upon the enemy, it is desirable that it should be executed with promptness and efficiency." This left much to the discretion of the commanding general—a discretion that was the very opposite of the spirit of the volunteers.

On December seventh, at night, after seventeen days of difficult marching, the Southwestern Army of Texas reached the vicinity of Laredo on the north bank of the river. General Somervell kept the troops mounted, enjoined quiet, and "all was dead silence." The men noticed the "mysterious whisperings and grave concealments" of their commander that night, and concluded that plans were building for an attack at dawn. But with daylight, when they entered the town, all they encountered were "some women, children, and old men," for the Mexican garrison of one hundred troops had withdrawn across the river to the town's other part. The volunteers "felt they were badly humbugged," and sarcastically spoke of "the siege of Laredo."

Dissatisfaction with the campaign grew. Somervell first encamped his men a mile above Laredo, then three miles below it. He did not here cross the river into Mexico. His men were badly fed. In a day or two a large number of them broke restraints, entered Laredo and plundered it of "many articles of a useless character." Somervell collected the loot and restored it to the mayor. What sort of warfare was this against people who had murdered and robbed and burned their way in and out of Texas? But spirits rose with an order to march. All expected that now at last they would cross the river and sweep down the Mexican side taking town after town. Instead, Somervell led them down the Texan side, and presently edged away inland, through thickets of thorny brush that tore the men's breeches and legs. It was not long until they understood that he was leading them homeward. After protests, the General paraded his men and called for a vote. Of seven hundred and forty men present, two hundred voted to go home. They were released to do so under a colonel. The rest elected General Somervell to lead them into Mexico. A few days later, back at the river, he crossed them to Guerrero, and soon made contact with three hundred of General Canales' cavalry, who quickly retired. On the next day Somervell began to cross the Southwestern Army back to the Texan side of the Rio Grande on six large, flat-bottomed skiffs, and when the movement was complete, he ordered the boats to be sunk behind him. On December nineteenth his adjutant published an order: "The troops belonging to the Southwestern Army will march at ten o'clock this morning for the junction of the Rio Frío and the Nueces, thence to Gonzales, where they will be disbanded." Under his discretionary instructions, he had his reason for issuing it: ". . . Having been eleven days on the river, and knowing the various positions of the enemy's troops, I was satisfied that they were concentrating in such numbers as to render a longer stay an act of imprudence."

A large part of the army was astounded at the order, and, after hurried debates, refused to go with him. He departed inland with about two hundred officers and men, leaving three hundred and four, under five captains, to decide upon their own next moves.

18.

To Mier and Beyond

If they were not to invade and destroy Mexico, they would in any case use the Rio Grande settlements to obtain horses and provisions for themselves, before in their own good time they too should turn homeward. Their first move was to elect a commander. They chose Colonel William S. Fisher, who having served under Canales two years before knew something of the Rio Grande country. Among the other officers was Thomas J. Green, a spirited young veteran of the Texas Rebellion.

The river was at high water. It was decided to take most of the force downstream by boat, while the rest marched parallel on the Texan bank. Despite Somervell's orders, his skiffs had been hidden instead of destroyed, and now they were found and put to use. The men spoke humorously of them as their "navy." Tom Green was put in charge of them. His "flagboat" displayed a red banner with the Texan star. There were not enough men to fill all the boats, and the empty ones were left burning as the flotilla started downstream. They came to riverside ranches where they took provisions. The marching horses ate in corn-fields. Scouts probed the Mexican bank for news of the enemy. The land and river-borne forces joined together each night. One night they found and disarmed a band of Karankawa Indians who had been on a raid into Texas. On the twenty-first of December the camp was made on the Texas bank opposite the way to Mier, which lay seven miles inland in Mexico. An officer was sent into the town for information, and re-turned to report that General Canales had just evacuated the place, but local residents told how General Ampudia and a large force was hourly expected to come to the city. It was, next to Matamoros, the largest town of the lower river, and would be able to supply the needs of the Texans.

On the next day, Tom Green accompanied Colonel Fisher to Mier and presented the mayor, whose name they understood to be Don

Juan, with a requisition for whatever government supplies might be stored there, "including cannon, small firearms, powder, lead, munitions of war of every kind, &c." In addition, the levy—giving an inflated estimate of the Texan strength to impress the Mexicans—demanded "5 days' rations for 1200 men, to wit: 40 sacks of flour of 6 arrobas each, 1200 lbs. sugar, 600 lbs. coffee, 200 pairs of strong coarse shoes, 100 pair of do. pantaloons, and 100 blankets." The mayor parted his hands. Though he would fill the requisition for the Texans as he had had to fill so many for Mexican armies, it could not be done instantly. The levy had to be apportioned among the citizens, who would patiently bring what they could afford.

All day the supplies piled up, and by nightfall were nearly complete, when it was found that teams and wagons to haul them had not yet been provided. Delivery to the Texan camp across the river must wait till tomorrow. The Texan commanders agreed, but inventing their own guarantee took Don Juan with them across the river. Tom Green assumed charge of him. He gave him a supper of mutton. It was a cold night. A "heartless norther" was blowing. Don Juan, said Green, was "a far more decent man than the majority of Mexican officials." To protect him against any temptation to escape, Green drolly thought of a milder restraint than chains. He took Don Juan under his blanket, and— mocking the episode later in the editorial first person plural—"gently placed one of his legs between ours, and though there was no community of language between us, yet we seemed to understand each other's motions, for when one turned over the other turned, we always maintaining his leg in the same affectionate position." When morning came Don Juan showed "a haggard countenance," and all day watched anxiously for the requisition train to appear. It did not appear, and at night "the norther continued to blow, and we again had the mutual honour of sleeping with each other in the same affectionate manner. . . . Don Juan, not knowing what the non-compliance of his order as to the provisions would bring about, grew still more restiff. His dreams were anything but pleasant, if we were to judge from his nervous excitability, and sleeping exclamations. . . ."

On Christmas Day the mayor's worries were given substance. A captured Mexican reported that the supply delivery had been halted by General Ampudia and General Canales, who had arrived at Mier with seven hundred troops and two fieldpieces. Five Texans who had been in the town were held prisoner. At their river camp the Texans held a council of war and all voted to attack the city. Green went to his

boats and found Don Juan asleep. He did not wake up until most of the
Texans had been ferried over the river a mile or two above the village
of Roma. He was astonished at the activity all about him, and asked
what it meant, and was told that his city was about to be invaded. In
the name of his wife and children he begged not to be carried into
battle. He was promised a position well in the rear. The crossing was
completed by four o'clock.

Shortly afterward gunfire was heard downstream. Scouts reported
that the Mexicans had taken up a position to prevent a lower river
crossing, had captured two Texans, and had retreated to the city. The
Texan main body pushed forward as twilight came. A mile from town
they met enemy pickets who fired and fled. By seven o'clock the winter
darkness brought a cold, drizzling rain that kept up all night. The
Texans moved to the crest of a meandering bluff that followed the left
bank of Alcantro Creek. Before them across the creek was the eastern
face of the town. The creek was about sixty feet wide, running rapidly
over stones with a watery roar that was all that could be heard, for the
town was quiet, and the Texans kept a hush. Scouts went out in the
rain to find a way down the bluff and over the creek. Above and below
the town there were easy fords. These were guarded by Mexicans, for
the scouts in the dark could hear the chime and creak of cavalry gear
when horses shook themselves. The crossing would have to be made
almost straight down the bluff and over the creek.

While their scouts threw a scattering of diversionary fire across
the regular fords, the bulk of the Texans keeping strict silence climbed
forty feet down the bluff, moved up the creek a little distance, and forded
it waist-high. During this movement Don Juan, the mayor, made his
escape. Coming up to the town they met a Mexican picket, opened fire,
and followed with a rush upon a steep street that led to the plaza. Mexican artillery was placed at the head of the street. The Texans fired upon
it, and took cover behind houses at a street intersection to reload. The
Mexicans replied with grapeshot, and pausing to reload in their turn,
were again fired upon by the Texans; and so the duel continued.

Mier was built of a river sandstone that weathered to a rich
brown. The houses, all one storey high, were contiguous in each block
of streets. At their street intersection the Texans forced entry to a corner
house, and once inside, found a crowbar with which they tore passageways from room to room until they were only fifty yards from the plaza.
Breaking ports in the walls they bore their aim on the artillery and all
through the night kept up a harassing fire; and with dawn, when they

could see the artillerymen, they picked them off until the enemy field-pieces were silenced. Ampudia's soldiers then took to the housetops, threw themselves down on the flat roofs, and continued the battle against Texans who hugged walls and fired from behind windows and broke through roofs to level their "astonishing marksmanship."

Late in the morning the Texans looked across the creek and saw the eight men left in charge of the camp on the bluff receive a furious attack by first sixty, and then several hundred, Mexican cavalry. The camp guards fought well; but three were killed, including the son of Captain Henry Austin; three were taken prisoner, and the last two by supreme valor managed to run to join their comrades fighting in the town.

Many were wounded in the Texan main body, but Tom Green and others had the sense of moving close to victory, for the enemy fire slackened, and after one more furious charge, fell silent. In the charge Colonel Fisher was wounded in the right thumb. It seemed like a slight wound, but the shock to him was great, and he was seized with vomiting. Tom Green came to him and found him unable to exert his command. It was an awkward moment. Green was certain they were "in the midst of victory." He assumed command, and gave orders that would place the Texans for their final triumph. Just then a white flag was borne to them from the Mexican positions by one of the Texans captured shortly before on the Alcantro bluff—Dr. Sinnickson. The Texans were jubilant. Here was the white flag of surrender. Colonel Fisher received Dr. Sinnickson, who brought messages from General Ampudia.

But what he had to say was not at all what they expected to hear. Ampudia, far from surrendering, was offering the Texans a chance to surrender or be destroyed. If they should surrender, Ampudia promised that "they should be treated with all the honors and considerations of prisoners of war; that the Santa Fe prisoners should be treated so likewise"—there were several Santa Fe Pioneers present who had been released by Santa Anna the year before—"and that our men should not be sent to Mexico, but kept upon the frontier until an exchange or pacification were effected." Ampudia further assured them "that he had 1700 *regular* troops in the city, and 800 fresh troops near by from Monterrey, which would be up in a few minutes; that it was useless . . . to contend longer against such odds. . . ."

Most of the Texans were amazed to hear these terms repeated by Colonel Fisher. Some few officers and a number of men murmured that they should be accepted. Green stared at Fisher, who seemed seriously to consider making the surrender. Under cover of the truce the Mexicans infiltrated the Texan positions. Every moment was precious and Green pleaded for authority to renew the battle or at least to make a fighting retreat over the Rio Grande to safety. But Fisher, sickened by his wound, and shaken by thought of the losses that must come in fighting a way home, hesitated, spoke to the men, vouched for the honor of General Ampudia, and ended by taking Green with him to make the surrender. Green, miserable with rage, reflected upon the "effect of gunshot wounds upon the nerves, which, unlike those from the sword or knife, show a fall of countenance and a corresponding depression of spirits," and concluded bitterly that "in future the advice of a wounded commander should be received with great caution, if at all." In a short while, the Texan arms were laid down in the plaza, the men were herded into small stone rooms under guard, and General Jesús Cárdenas, the prefect of Tamaulipas, who had appeared in the city, wrote from Mier on December 26, 1842, to the mayor of Laredo—for the river towns were apprehensive—that "today at three o'clock in the afternoon the Texans surrendered after seventeen hours of continuous fighting . . . the only guarantee being that their lives would be spared."

For no sooner had the Texans given up than the Mexican commanders changed the terms of the capitulation. The guarantee that they would be treated as prisoners of war was left out of the written articles of surrender drawn up by General Ampudia. The Texans were apprehensive; and in the following days their bitterness had reason to grow. With only two hundred and sixty-one men in the battle, they had brought the enemy force of over two thousand to the moment of defeat— only to see it thrown away by their sick and frightened leader; for they heard from Texan prisoners who had been taken by Ampudia before the surrender that at the moment he sent out the truce flag, he and all his high command were ready to run away down the river road if the Texans refused his overture. The horses of the Mexican staff, saddled and ready, had been held waiting for flight at the south streets opening off the plaza. The Texans lost sixteen dead and about thirty badly wounded, while the Mexican losses were in excess of seven hundred. The victory had been wasted. Only the Texans left behind at the Rio Grande camp escaped: forty-two, warned by a good ruse of Tom Green's, marched for home.

The rest soon saw how the terms of capitulation were to be enacted. On the last day of December they were marched out on the Mexican river road toward Matamoros, with artillery leading and closing the column, and their files closed on the flanks by infantry with fixed bayonets and beyond these by cavalry. The weather was still bitter. The captives had lost their best blankets to the cavalry. One cold night they made little fires in camp, and when the flames died the men raked away the coals and laid themselves "in piles in the ashes" to keep warm. Their feet were raw. They were thirsty, having no canteens. The march was rapid, with few stops for water. As they entered the river towns— Camargo, Reynosa, Guadalupe—they were walked around the plazas to be exhibited like live trophies of a menagerie hunt, while bells rang, salvos were fired, fireworks were let off, and slogans of valor on strips of paper were pathetically shown by children—"Glory and gratitude to the brave Canales," "Eternal honor to the immortal Ampudia." In one town a company of naked painted Indians joined the jubilee, yelling, and firing blank charges into the faces of the prisoners. These were followed by a band of dancers—twenty little boys led by a tiny old man, "not larger than a boy of twelve," and all dressed in a profusion of colored scarves and ribbons, and wearing headdresses of small mirrors fastened to make obelisks. Shaking gourds filled with gravel, the dancers cut figures in time to music played by several marching violinists, "always keeping good time in step and motion," jigging first on one foot, then the other.

The Texans dismayed their masters with humorous commentary at times. One evening they were thrust into a cattle pen to spend the night in ankle-deep manure, and, treated like cattle, they "were determined to complete the character. They would get down upon their all-fours, bow their necks, paw up the dirt, and low like bulls." Another night corralled in a sheep pen, they "bleated more like sheep than any sheep in Mexico."

At Matamoros they were driven through streets under triumphal arches. It was, they observed, "the only American-built town" they saw in Mexico, with "many frame houses with shingled roofs . . . and built of combustible materials as most Southern towns in the United States." It was situated about half a mile from the Rio Grande, and thirty from its mouth, contained a population of about ten thousand, and was "the most defenceless city in Mexico." There they learned that despite General Ampudia's promise to the contrary, they were to be marched inland to Mexico City where—terrible thought—Santa Anna reigned. On January 14, 1843, in several detachments, the prisoners left the river for the interior, by way of Monterrey and Saltillo.

It was twenty months before those who survived saw Texas

again. Their story came across the river piecemeal. Much of it was
shocking, even beyond the conventional brutalities expected of certain
types of Mexican officers. Ordinary decent treatment was such a welcome
contrast that when it came Tom Green was invariably moved to compose a letter of courtly gratitude to the responsible official. He was just
as ready with stern letters of protest when—in repeated betrayal of the
prisoner-of-war agreement—the men were thrown into rooms so small
and airless that suffocation was a danger, or when they were badly fed
or not fed at all, or when at the caprice of a Mexican detachment commander they were all threatened with assassination. They went along
tied together by lariats, and plotted escape. A chance came at the
Hacienda Solado, a hundred miles beyond Saltillo. Led by Captain
Ewing Cameron, the Texans overpowered their guards one morning in
February, took their weapons and horses and dashed away for freedom,
leaving five dead and several wounded prisoners behind.

For two days they kept to the roads, heading for Monclova, France
Way and Texas; but afraid of being overtaken by soldiery, they turned
off the road into mountains to the west, hoping to find a secret way
across them to the open plains of Coahuila and finally the river. For
five days they struggled against rock and thirst and hunger. Always the
mountains opposed them. On the third day they were forced to kill their
horses for meat. Many of the men wept in the act. The party pushed
ahead on foot. Some fell behind dying of thirst and were left. The sun
was fierce by day, the thin mountain air bitter cold by night. Only a few
scraps of thorned plants grew amidst the unwatered rocks. Eating of
their puffy leaves, the men tasted fire, and drank worse, for in desperation
they drank their own urine and knew in consequence "a consuming
agony." Some scratched up cool earth from the shade of the bushes and
applied it to their bare bellies and throats for a second of relief. On the
fifth day they saw camp smoke and those who could went for it. It was
smoke from an army campfire. Excepting five who had died, four who
individually managed to escape homeward, and three who had vanished
never to be heard of again, all the prisoners were once again in the
hands of the Mexicans.

Driven back to the Hacienda Salado handcuffed in pairs, they
came under the touch of President Santa Anna, who had sent orders
that every tenth man was to be shot. One hundred and fifty-nine white
beans were placed in a small clay jug, and seventeen black beans were
added on top of those. The black beans meant death. The beans were not
stirred up. In a courtyard with high walls on which uniformed Mexican

dragoons in shakos and crossbelts stood guard, the prisoners were lined up to come two-by-two for their beans. Cameron, the leader of the escape, was told to draw first. "Well, boys," he said, "we have to draw, let's be at it." He drew. The first bean was white. He was spared. The prisoners shuffled up in turn. "Boys," said one, "this beats raffling all to pieces." Another remarked, "This is the tallest gambling scrape I ever was in." Drawing a black bean, another showed it to his fellows with a smile and declared, "Boys, I told you so; I never failed in my life to draw a prize." Another who drew black said lightly, "Well, they won't make much off me, anyhow, for I know I have killed twenty-five of the yellowbellies." He then asked for his dinner and smoked a cigar. A young man who drew a black bean said to the Mexican officer with the jug, "After the battle of San Jacinto, my family took in one of your prisoner youths, raised and educated him, and this is our requital." When the drawing was done, Captain Cameron, weeping bitterly, asked the Mexican officers to kill him and spare his fellows. The afternoon was failing. Those who drew death were roped together and taken to another courtyard beyond the high wall. Their comrades in the first courtyard could hear preparations, and then volleys, and dying groans, and then repeated shots—one prisoner had to be shot fifteen times before he died— and a scramble amidst the Mexican soldiery as one fainted at what he saw and as he fell was caught by the others. So evening came on March 25, 1843. In the morning the prisoners were once again placed briskly on the road to Mexico City. As they were marched out of the hacienda they saw the broken bodies of their friends scattered on the ground.

A month later they were near Mexico City when an order came from President Santa Anna to execute Captain Cameron, even though he had drawn a white bean. The execution was promptly carried out. In a sense, it was done as a courtesy to General Canales, who, having nursed a private grudge against Cameron since they had served together in the Rio Grande republican campaign of 1840, had requested it.

The Texans were assigned to various prisons—most of them to the formidable castle of Perote on the road to Veracruz. They heard that efforts were being made in behalf of their release by foreign governments—Britain and the United States. Their own government also made appeals for them; but they were embittered to hear that President Houston refused to accredit their invasion of Mexico as an official and authorized movement of the Texas army. ". . . They went without orders," he wrote, and "so far as that was concerned the government of Texas was not responsible, and the men were thereby placed out of the protection of the rules of war." Left at that, their situation would seem almost hopeless. But Houston went on to ask the British chargé d'affaires in Texas, who was negotiating as a neutral for the release of the prisoners, to plead a further point: ". . . The Mexican officers, by proposing terms of capitulation to the men, relieved them from the responsibility which they had incurred; and the moment the men surrendered in accordance with the proposals of capitulation, they became prisoners-of-war, and were entitled to all immunities as such. . . . Upon this view of the case, I base my hopes of their salvation, if it should be speedily presented, through the agency of her majesty's minister, to the Mexican government." The British and American ministers did what they could, an individual prisoner or two was released now and then, a daring escape from Perote was managed by Tom Green and some companions, but it was not until September 16, 1844, that all were finally set free by order of Santa Anna, who felt constrained to mercy while mourning his wife, recently dead.

Texas made only one more armed effort against Mexicans—another abortive one, commanded by Colonel Jacob Snively who led a company out on the north plains in the summer of 1843 to attack and rob a rich caravan out of Santa Fe which on its return trip from Saint Louis was accompanied by Governor Armijo in his amplitude. As a consequence of all the Texan incursions of the past three years, Santa Anna in August, 1843, closed the customs houses of the Rio Grande at Taos, El Paso and Presidio del Norte, ending the Santa Fe and Chihuahua trade from over the plains. But once again Mexico acting against the North Americans was too late; for events had moved into larger channels; diplomatic and political currents long agitated began to move fast and soon grew to flood, gathering to pour the great energies of the United States of North America across the plains toward the long Rio Grande shore of Mexico and Texas.

19.

Diplomacies

In 1843 political debate in the United States was sharpened over slavery, which promised to be a bitter issue in the coming presidential campaign of 1844. The abolitionists of the North made their strength felt throughout the nation; and the slaveholders of the South saw that only by the creation of new slaveholding states could their cherished feudal institution survive. Texas, with her system of slavery already established, would bring new strength to the Southern position; and proposals to annex Texas were again heard in Congress.

Now Texas became the object of rivalries between powerful European influences and the United States. England and France had already served Texas as mediators with Mexico. Fears and rumors in Washington gave color to incredible, and yet conceivable, possibilities—was Texas to become a British colony? would a French Bourbon prince govern a Texas pendant to France? President Houston seemed to favor annexation to the United States, if to any other power; but his republic had fared poorly in previous attempts to bring about American statehood; and in his second term he was willing to throw a scare into the Congress at Washington by accepting the good offices of Great Britain in diplomatic representations to Mexico. As a result of British services, an armistice between Mexico and Texas was at last after eight years of a state of war agreed to on June 15, 1843. Andrew Jackson wrote to Houston, "I see you are negotiating with Mexico, but be careful of the designing English." The press was full of alarms about the Texas-British intimacy, and Houston enjoyed it all, even assuring the British representative in Texas that in the midst of wild surmise in the newspapers, he was ". . . as cool as a shoemaker's lapstone in an open shop at Christmas. . . ."

His strategy of a European bias in diplomacy was successful in the United States, where annexation became a major battle cry in the

gathering presidential campaign. Mexico was not deaf to the sound.
Two days after the proclamation of the Texas armistice, Mexico issued
a general statement of policy meant specifically for North Americans,
reaffirming the old Mexican law that dealt with armed foreign intruders
on Mexican soil. It did not matter whether any such foreigner "be accompanied in his enterprise by a few or by many adventurers . . . all such
persons taken with arms in their hands shall be immediately put to
death." This notice was reinforced by a note handed to the United States
minister in Mexico saying that the Mexican government would consider
any act of the American Congress to annex Texas a declaration of war
against Mexico. Over the shoulder of Mexico gazed the British, and in
the foreground, in newly found composure, reclined Texas, now for a
brief interlude in a position to make her own choices among international partners.

These positions meant more than allegory. The political contenders
in the United States suddenly saw that an issue more critical than slavery
was now visible in the midst of all the turmoil over annexing Texas.
The issue was whether Texas was to be allowed to come under the influence, and possibly even the dominion, of a foreign power—Great Britain
The Monroe Doctrine was seriously threatened by the possibility. The
Southern slaveholders had an additional motive for fearing the encroach-
ment of Britain, for if she gained control of Texas, avowedly she would
put an end to slavery there. They redoubled their efforts to hasten
annexation, while much of the hitherto immovable abolitionist strength
that had resisted Texas-with-slavery came around to the view that the
greater evil lay in permitting Europe to extend new colonial power to
the Gulf of Mexico. As the campaign mounted in 1844, the fight was no
less bitter over annexation and its terms, but the lines were more clearly
drawn than before. The Democratic candidate, Mr. James K. Polk of
Tennessee, was firmly in favor of annexation, and of denying the British
claim to Oregon, which was also being agitated at the time.

As the campaign mounted in 1844 the Whigs held their national
convention first. They nominated Henry Clay, and in their platform
they failed to take notice of the leading issue before the people—annexation. A month later the Democratic party convened and concluded its
platform with the statement that "the re-occupation of Oregon and the
re-annexation of Texas are great American measures, which this Convention recommends to the cordial support of the Democracy of the
Union." It was a realistic sounding of the public sentiment, which was
expressed pungently in another way by General Andrew Jackson who

in retirement had not lost his gift for reading the popular temper: ". . . You might as well, it appears to me, attempt to turn the current of the Mississippi, as to turn the democracy from the annexation of Texas." There was a clear choice before the American people, to be made by torchlight as the campaign summer went by, while Mexico was treated to the pleasure of watching the North Americans choose their president on the basis of annexing some two hundred and forty thousand square miles of what she still considered to be Mexican territory.

At one moment the matter seemed close to settlement even before the election. A treaty between Texas and the United States was signed on the executive level on April 12, 1844, granting Texas the status of a territory of the United States, with all the defense measures that might be necessary under that condition. But the Senate failed to ratify the treaty ten days later, the Texan Congress took no action on it, and the moment of decision passed. The vote in the presidential election would after all determine the outcome. General Jackson wrote to President Houston, "The rejection of the treaty filled me with regret; but the effect of this movement brings the subject directly to the attention of the people; and we shall, in the course of a few months, be enabled to understand what their verdict will be." President Houston replied, "It is now the duty of the United States to make an advance that can not be equivocal in its character; and when she opens the door, and removes all impediments, it might be well for Texas to accept the invitation."

For Texas needed help. The Mexican armistice had run its course without the achievement of peace. True, a peace conference had been held at Salinas on the Rio Grande near Laredo by commissioners of Mexico and Texas; but when its conclusions were presented to President Houston he refused to sign the treaty because in it Texas was described as "a department of Mexico." The nominal courtesies of the armistice were cancelled, and in June the central Mexican government instructed General Woll in north Mexico to resume any necessary acts of war against Texas. The Rio Grande was made a boundary in an odd new way, a line across which Texans were dared to step. If one did so, to the distance of a league south of the river, he was to be found guilty at a summary court-martial and shot. He was not to try to run away, either, for if he were "rash enough to fly at the sight of any force belonging to the Supreme Government," he was to be chased until he fell dead or was captured to be killed. A few days later General Woll dispatched to President Houston a formal declaration of war, and news came out of Mexico all summer of how armies were being trained for a new invasion of Texas. This was plainly to be Santa Anna's reply to the open agitation in the United States for annexation. With so much strength behind it, the movement seemed too powerful for Britain and France to oppose with further colonial plans for Texas. Though still cordial, they offered no strength to Texas in her decisive year.

Meanwhile in the United States sentiment ran high. It was made more acute by the publication of George Wilkins Kendall's *Narrative of the Texan Santa Fe Expedition,* which told a large public for the first time what Mexicans had done to North Americans in that scrape. As election neared, with internal struggles in the major parties, the issues were compounded—slavery and abolition, free trade and protection, the "Know-Nothing" movement, Oregon, and again the Bank of the United States—but dominating these was the issue of statehood for Texas on which the Democrats campaigned. As the campaign proceeded, Henry Clay also spoke up for annexation if Texas could be acquired "without dishonor, without war, with the common consent of the Union, and upon just and fair terms." But when he said further that slavery was not an issue in the annexation debate he lost the votes of the Liberty Party in New York State, and in consequence Polk was elected in November. The voters knew that "the election of Mr. Polk means that Texas will be annexed to the United States," as a Whig politician and editor put it.

Texans understood the same thing, and General Houston, now succeeded in the presidency by his secretary of state Anson Jones, saw that his hopes of many years must be fulfilled with the union of his second country to his first. In the early weeks of 1845 the press and public made annexation its own passionate topic while Congress debated. The Free-Soilers spent their last efforts to prevent so vast a new slave territory as Texas from entering the union and securing the Southern dominance in Congress—for one of the provisions of annexation was to be that Texas could divide itself into five states at her pleasure—and the annexationists rang every change possible on the theme of the Monroe Doctrine. But the Democrats had a Congressional majority safe in hand, and the matter moved toward the vote in Congress, while in Mexico Santa Anna was dethroned and banished into exile, and the new government under José Joaquín Herrera proposed to recognize the independence of Texas at last, in a desperate trial at winning Texas away from the United States. It was late. On February 25, 1845, the House of Representatives at Washington voted the resolution offering statehood to Texas, and on March first the Senate passed it. President John Tyler, about to leave office, signed it the same day, and the invitation to union was trans-

mitted to Texas on March third. On the following day Polk was inaugurated, ready to face the implications of the major plank in his platform.

At the end of March, Mexico broke off diplomatic relations with
the United States, and in May passed a law declaring peace with Texas,
on a basis of Texan independence. A treaty was drawn up in discussion
with the Texan Secretary of State that was to be offered to the people
of independent Texas for their ratification. England and France again
figured as the mediators. But Mexico was too late, and for the last time.
Texas sentiment for annexation was so strong that when the Mexican
treaty was submitted to the Texan Senate in June, a scandal resulted.
The Texan Secretary of State was twice burned in effigy and, under a
rain of abuse for having treated with Mexico in opposition to the spirit
of annexation, fled the republic for Europe. On July fourth, a convention
called by President Jones met at Washington on the Brazos to discuss
the invitation from the United States and the Mexican treaty. The
treaty was ignored, and with only one delegate dissenting, the convention recommended to the citizens of Texas that the invitation to statehood should be accepted.

On the same day certain cautionary army and navy orders went
out from Washington on the Potomac. If, as she had promised to do in
the event of annexation, Mexico should declare war against the United
States and try to hold Texas, then Texas must be defended, like any
other United States possession. General Zachary Taylor was at Fort
Jesup, Louisiana, with United States troops. He was ordered to take his
force to Corpus Christi on the Gulf Coast and establish a base from
which the land defense of Texas might be managed. Commodore David
Conner was ordered to patrol the Gulf ports of Mexico with the United
States Home Squadron. By the end of the month Taylor was landing his
soldiers over the difficult bar before Corpus Christi.

His mission was nonaggressive. His men had plenty of time to
satisfy their curiosity about the new land. A soldier rode a mustang for
the first time—"the animal was lively and frisky enough, but a mere rat
compared with our northern horses." Many men traded for mustangs to
use on pleasure rides over the flat coastal country. An odd thing happened to the mustangs during a horse trade. "The best look as if they
had lost all the fire they possessed in a state of nature. Their look is one
of regret. . . ." There was curiosity, too, about the putative enemy. Late
in the summer a Mexican spying for the American service returned from
Matamoros, a hundred and fifty miles distant on the Rio Grande, with
a report that gave relief, and yet too a tinge of disappointment. "He

reports no warlike preparations, and that the two thousand men at Matamoros have again dwindled to five hundred. He says the people in that vicinity are opposed to the war."

On October thirteenth, in a general election, the people of Texas voted all but unanimously to ratify the annexation resolution, and adopted their new state constitution. Among the provisions for annexation made by Congress was this one: "Questions of boundaries with other nations are to be adjusted by the United States." Texas was relieved of making good her claim, now, to the Rio Grande. Having brought the claim with her into the Union, she laid it at the feet of the United States.

President Polk had made earnest diplomatic proposals to Mexico that any dispute over Texas be composed through peaceful negotiation, and on October fifteenth came a change in the sentiment of the Mexican government. President Herrera agreed to receive a United States diplomatic representative on condition that Commodore Conner withdraw his forces from the waters off Veracruz. Conner withdrew immediately, and on November tenth, John Slidell was appointed as the United States envoy extraordinary. He arrived at Veracruz on the last day of the month. He was instructed to offer Mexico these terms: for a boundary following the Rio Grande from its mouth to El Paso, and from there due west, taking in the present areas of California, New Mexico, Arizona, Nevada and Utah, the United States would pay twenty-five million dollars (though President Polk declared himself "ready to pay forty millions for it"); and in addition, if Mexico would recognize the Texas boundary claim of the whole Rio Grande from mouth to source, the United States would assume the debt of paying all claims of her citizens against Mexico, to be calculated at a minimum of two million dollars.

Slidell set out for the capital only to encounter the afterthoughts of President Herrera, who had discovered that his agreement to negotiate with the United States was violently opposed by a new revolutionary party in Mexico. Herrera fought a delaying action of excuses—Slidell was not properly accredited; Slidell was coming as a "minister," which implied that annexation was already recognized by Mexico, and Mexico could receive him only as a "commissioner"; it was not proper for Mexico to hear any Texas matters from anyone but the Texan government; and under these conditions, Slidell could not be received by the President of Mexico. The American minister sent word of his rebuff to Washington and lingered in Mexico hoping to persuade the government to receive his credentials. By the end of December he had a new

Mexican president to deal with—General Mariano Paredes y Arillaga, for Herrera had been overthrown because of his conciliatory attitude toward the Americans. Paredes took office on January 4, 1846, as leader of the war party. He declared an aggressive policy—Santa Anna's old claim to Texas all the way to the Sabine at Louisiana; and he promised to defend it. On January twelfth when Polk received Slidell's message of an impasse, he saw that despite repeated efforts to negotiate, war had come closer. On the next day he sent orders through Secretary of War Marcy to General Taylor at Corpus Christi to march for the Rio Grande.

It was a wet winter on the Gulf Coast. The American troops were delighted when a new indoor diversion was ready for them—an army theatre built in Corpus Christi, "a capital building," according to a soldier, "capable of seating some eight hundred persons. The scenes were painted by officers of the army. A very clever company was engaged, and many an otherwise dreary evening was spent by many of us with infinite pleasure within its walls." Taylor received Polk's new orders on February third; but he could not immediately execute them, for the whole coastal plain was a mire, and before he could move wagons, ordnance and columns of troops, he must know more about marching conditions. On February ninth he sent out an experimental wagon train to make a test of travel in wet weather. By the sixteenth he had his report, and could plan the movement. In the state capital of Texas, on that day, the flag of the single star was hauled down and in its place rose the colors of the United States, to complete the official annexation.

While Taylor's officers and men went about preparing for the southward march along the coast, there were opposing views among them about the task they were sent to do. Though they knew that the General was to "avoid any acts of aggression" against Mexican forces across the river "unless an actual state of war should exist," many believed that the United States had stung Mexico into defense of her rightful possessions. They saw that between the Nueces and the Rio Grande there was nothing but unsettled wilderness and that, as a soldier said, "so far as actual occupation was concerned, the Texan claim was tenuous indeed." Lieutenant U. S. Grant thought the armed march to Mexico was "unholy." He "had a horror of the Mexican War," but lacked "moral courage enough to resign." One of Taylor's regimental commanders recorded similar views. "As to the right of this movement, I have said from the first that the United States are the aggressors. We have outraged the Mexican government by an arrogance and presumption that deserve to be punished. For ten years we have been encroaching

on Mexico and insulting her. . . ." A Pennsyl
"How unjust! The march to the banks of the Rio
an act of hostility," and the United States behin
virtue goaded Mexico to assume "the odium of beg
views were not mollified even by Taylor's orders
from Polk, that required all personnel "to observe
respect the rights of all the inhabitants who may
prosecution of their respective occupations. Und
any way will any interference be allowed with the
principles of the inhabitants. . . . Whatever may
of the army will be bought . . . at the highest pri

Not all, or even most, of the army had do
What they had heard of Mexico's actions—the inhum
Armijo, and their imitators heaped upon Anglo
prisoners—and what they began to learn of Mexic
the border gave them strong motives, beyond thei
job ahead. Rumors reached the army that notherm
a revolutionary temper. "No lover of freedom can
tears to witness the deplorable, degraded state
Mexican is cast. It is in the natural course of things
the northern states will declare themselves indepe
vision of the Republic of the Rio Grande, or of tl
loomed again. A north Mexican emissary even rod
to persuade him to hold back his advance and give
ists one more chance to declare their independen
General Arista was mentioned—and spare the new
of being a battleground between Mexico and the
many years hence," added an American officer, "tl
state still further west [than Texas] begging to be
the immediate justification of the American occup
Texas to the union," he concluded, "we were boun
was . . . Texas with her prescribed limits. She
Grande."

Finally, another, and coolheaded, American
whole story through his own experience as a Mis
decades, disposed of his own qualms in a majestic p
when the subject was first agitated, I had my misgi
quences and policy, and I also thought the rights of
some degree respected, the discussion of the matte
first difficulty, and the deportment of Mexico the se

20.

The United States to the River

"We are off for the Rio Grande!" wrote an American diarist on March 8, 1846.

The diplomacy was done with, the high policy was released into action, the national energy was beginning to pour out, and the reality of the experience came into the scale of men who embodied it individually. If the stakes were continental, the terms, in the long columns that struggled through the bare country, were personal. The soldiers saw, felt, gave, endured and suffered. Much was new and strange; much—at times—beautiful; and they were moved to know in their personal experience what the nations more abstractedly opposed to one another.

The sober tenacity of Stephen Austin, the tormented loyalties of the early Anglo-Texans, the wild self-regard of the trapper, the organized and systematic ways of the Missouri trader, the physical power that served Texans ready to die for freedom or adventure—all these prophetic American qualities taken together seemed stronger than their sum; suggested destiny; and now approached their larger fulfillment as the Army of the United States every day drew nearer to the disputed border.

After the heavy rains the land was already dry. Water holes were sometimes a day's march apart. Prairie grass, recently burned off, left a quilt of black ashes through which the army marched, and the ashes rose and lodged on the soldiers' faces and made them "resemble Africans." But they were equal to all annoyances. They endured all, as Lieutenant Grant saw, "without a murmur," and another officer remarked that "there is a 'physique' and 'morale' about our 'little army' of which they never dreamed; well clad, well fed, and well armed; moving forward with an enthusiasm and 'sangfroid' which carries victory in their face. I feel more and more convinced that we can successfully contend with an immensely superior force."

There were things to stare at on the way—one day "a mustang taking it into his head to be a little restive, relieved himself of his load, a demure-looking campwoman." And there were sights to delight the eye. After the heavy rains of winter and early spring, the Gulf lands were bright with an illimitable reach of wildflowers. ". . . The flowers during today's march were gloriously rich; conspicuous above all were the Texan plume, a beautiful scarlet flower, the Mexican poppy, and the indigo. . . ." The very air in the Texas spring was wonderful. "I do not think I have ever felt a sweeter or fresher morning," wrote a soldier on March twenty-fourth. "The morning star and moon were about setting; the former, even as day broke, looked like a diamond set in the clear, blue sky. . . . We marched through a wilderness of mesquite and acacia thickets, fragrant with the blossom of the latter; the grass was rich; the peavine, with bits of delicate blossom, abundant. . . . The air from the sea was delightful, and everything in nature appeared so happy that it was perfectly exhilarating." The thickets were alive with singing birds. One day a mirage in the distance made the prairie look on fire; and once past the belt of mesquite thickets, they saw open prairie, with no trees, reaching all the way to the hazy Gulf. The nearer they came to the river the faster flew rumors that a battle awaited them; but still there were pleasures of the country to record. The country "was really beautiful; such grazing was never seen before. The ground appeared alive with quail, and every waterhole turned out its flock of ducks. As you approach the river chaparral increased in density. The soil is very rich. . . . The country is perfectly level, and the roads are in capital order. . . ." They had not seen a single habitation since leaving Corpus Christi.

As the army marched along the coast, a fleet of supply ships steamed down the Gulf toward Point Isabel, a little port nine miles up the coast from the Rio Grande, in a harbor formed by reaches of low land divided by a narrow entrance from the sea, called Los Brazos de Santiago—the Arms of Saint James. Here General Taylor intended to establish his base of supplies. Point Isabel, though in Texas territory, was used by Mexicans as a port of entry. Sea traffic put in there to unload cargo that was taken overland to the Rio Grande, in preference to anchoring off the mouth of the river and taking cargo inland over the far-reaching shallows by lighter. As General Taylor approached Mexico, two hundred and fifty Mexican troops of artillery and infantry, commanded by General García, defended Point Isabel, and its customs house, and the private trade in bribes that comfortably sustained the captain of the port, a certain Señor Rodríguez, who ruled over fifty or sixty residents in their shacks of twined reeds, timber from wrecked ships, and grass thatching. The customs house, though the largest, was "a miserable hovel."

On March twenty-fifth Captain Rodríguez saw stands of smoke far out above the Gulf approaches to the Arms of Saint James. In a rage, he concluded that these announced the vessels of the United States. A handful of his residents went inland to meet the army. Point Isabel was bracketed from sea and land. Saying good-bye to his little monopoly, Captain Rodríguez set fire to the customs house and as many other huts as possible, and with General García and the Mexican troops, ran away down the beach to Boca Chica, at the mouth of the Rio Grande.

Looked at again, the American ships were standing in closer; and almost on the heels of the port captain, General Taylor arrived with his cavalry and his wagons. Soldiers went to work putting out what fires they could, saving a few of the sea-grass houses. The General saw that his base was well-chosen, for in that low, level sea land, Point Isabel stood up, a bluff about twenty feet high, and made a prow out into the bay, commanding all approaches, and giving a clear view southward toward the Rio Grande. Sail now showed under the sea-borne smoke, and three hours after the General's arrival, the fleet entered the Arms, escorted by two brigs-of-war and a cutter—though with trouble. A high wind was blowing, the passage was unfamiliar, the *Monmouth* went aground and the *Neva,* fighting strong currents of air and sea with extra steam pressure, blew a hole in her boiler. But supplies came off at once, including four eighteen-pounders. The life line for the army was established, and two days later General Taylor, leaving a garrison, resumed the march with full wagons to join the bulk of the army that was camped waiting for him in a wide meadow edged by ridges of chaparral and mesquite that in flat land showed high, and gave its name, Palo Alto, to the place. It lay about halfway between Point Isabel and Matamoros, eighteen miles apart by road. With the return of the General and his detachment, the army was reunited in bulk, and pushed ahead immediately to the south. A few miles farther on they passed through an old dry lagoon edged with palms where the river had once run. It was called the Resaca de la Palma. They were stirred by rumors that four thousand Mexicans would cross the Rio Grande on the morrow and give battle.

And at last, late in the morning of March 28, 1846, the Americans came to the river. They saw its shallow brown waters forever taking the wide bend around the town of Matamoros, and there across the stream were two hundred people to return the stares of the American army, and in the town a Mexican army band marched and played, as sentries were disposed on both banks. After noon, and with first bivouac duties done, a number of young American officers eased their way down the north bank of the river and throwing off their uniforms went into the water to bathe. Across the river they were seen by a group of Mexican girls. In a few minutes with light laughter the girls came down to the water on the opposite bank and entered into it in their turn. The young men and women called to each other; and in answer both moved forward. Shining with water and sunlight the hard white and the soft earthen bodies approached to meet in midstream. Suddenly the rifles of the Mexican sentries took aim at the young men. The American soldiers kissed their hands at the Mexican girls and returned to their proper riverside. The allegory of life seeking itself through love before battle was broken and scattered; and other furies long gathering awaited release on the Rio Grande.

BOOK FOUR

The United States Rio Grande

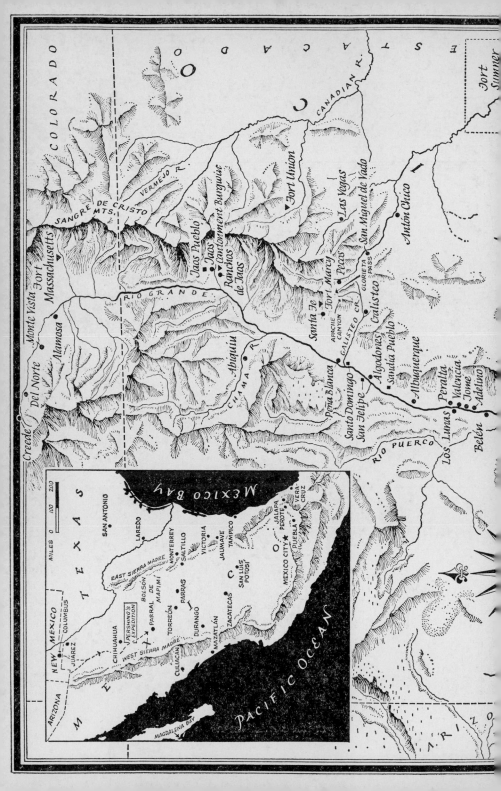

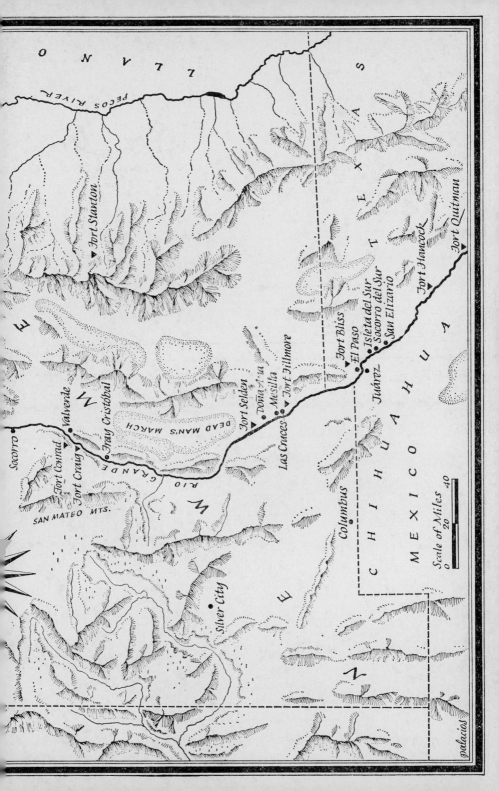

I.

"Way, You Rio"

"GOOD-BYE. COME BACK A MAN," said an Indiana father to his son, a volunteer for the Rio Grande in 1846. The young man "gave him a shower of tears" and left for the war. It was the nation asking for fulfillment of the first significant task of its early maturity. The national policy on the river was at the start in the hands of the regular army—Taylor's three brigades, that represented only a small segment of the American people, and even included representatives of foreign populations. But it would not be long until, through expansion of the army by volunteers, the whole people would feel the war that was fought in their name. On town hall and courthouse the recruiting notices would soon be tacked up, and soon gaunt little coaches connected by swaying chains behind stovelike locomotives would haul volunteer companies to concentration points, and regiments would go down the wide tributaries on scroll-sawed steamboats to the Mississippi that led to the Gulf. Out of the eastern harbors already sailed other transports and supply ships under raked masts and tall funnels, to the tune of a capstan song:

> Oh, say, were you ever in the Rio Grande?
> Way, you Rio.
> It's there that the river runs down golden sand.
> For we're bound to the Rio Grande.

> And away, you Rio!
> Way, you Rio!
> Sing fare you well,
> My pretty young girls,
> For we're bound to the Rio Grande!

The electric telegraph did not yet touch across Texas. News by fastest Army courier took two weeks to come from the river to Washington, and mails by steamer were even slower, and most newspapers came out only once a week. The families at home could only repose their confidence in what lay behind the whole people who had already turned to the west in so many other enterprises. The move to Mexico was full of anxiety; met with unpopularity in various quarters of the nation; and, from a certain political view, violated international morality. But its general direction seemed natural, for on an official and national scale it was but one more step in the westward march hitherto taken by individuals, and families, and business associates, and private communities. There was no surprise in its sudden call upon the country to go to the West and Southwest with the largest home army assembled since General Washington's. What had William Becknell printed in a Missouri newspaper so long ago as 1821? Calling for men to join him in a plains trading expedition after horses and mules, he had without intending eloquence or a heroic tone simply announced men "destined to the westward." Whether he meant immediate destination or large destiny, the effect was the same, and his countrymen after him showed no more uncertainty than he.

> Oh, New York town is no place for me—
> Way, you Rio!
> I'll pack up my bag and go to sea.
> For we're bound to the Rio Grande!

> And away, you Rio,
> Way, you Rio! . . .

Even if almost nothing was known about far Texas, and Mexico, and the problems waiting in distance, climate and the Mexican nature, the United States was confident as the war opened that it would be a short one.

> We'll sell our salt cod for molasses and rum—
> Way, you Rio!
> And get home again 'fore Thanksgiving has come.
> For we're bound to the Rio Grande!

> And away, you Rio! . . .

General Taylor's army on the north bank of the Rio Grande in March, 1846, represented the third of the three great peoples who came to the river. The American soldiers, taken together, were prophets of a time to come. The collective prophecy they carried was not plain to all its carriers, but it stirred in them like their own seed, and sow it they must. Its nature could be read from fragments out of the ancestries of idea, issue, motive and way of life that had created them in a society new to the world—a society formed around a central passion: the freedom and equality of democratic man. A taste of this—the American theme—had already come near to the river with the Texan settlers in the south, and the trappers and traders in the north; but now once again change, coming with a final sovereignty, was about to make its way along the whole river with an energy and a complexity unknown in the earlier societies of the Indian, the Spaniard and the Mexican.

2.

Collective Prophecy

i. new man and new principles

Until 1846 it was the frontier people from the United States who had made new life in the Far West. In that year the whole nation began to take part, through the national army, in the life of the West, which was tied to all the United States by longing, and letters, and hope. But what had made the frontiersmen had also made their successors; and out of the past of the seventy-year-old nation, and of the impulses—some of them as old as the great ages of Mediterranean life—that had created it, marched the Americans, who with all their differences showed common traits and beliefs that seemed to the rest of the world like the marks of a new order of associated men. In America, ideally, a man was an individual not merely to himself, but to all his fellows, under restraints and aids agreed upon by all, in the interest of each.

The settlement of eastern North America was not an expression of the parent state, like the colonial acts of Spain in Mexico first done eighty-eight years before the founding of Virginia. It came as a movement of various individuals and minorities out of England, the Netherlands, the German States and France who even under crown charters and with various motives—religious, commercial and adventurous—soon revealed if they did not first proclaim that their essential desire was for self-government, under a system of social equality. When this desire came plain in the various scattered colonies of the eastern seaboard, even with their differing localisms it seemed to draw them together to reinforce one another in their essential drive for realized individualism for their people. For whatever reason, they had all come to feel in the old world that they had reached the limits of their hopes for growth, freedom and self-expression. To attain these they proved themselves willing to take great risks and undertake great labors. They were plants turning toward the light and space of a new Eden. Cotton Mather said "the whole earth is the Lord's garden—why should men not tend its empty places?" The idea of liberty separated the early settlers from other people in European societies. Were there two kinds of men—those who feared liberty, and those who held it above earthly authority?

They who left "all the pleasant accommodations of their native country" to pass over "a terrible *ocean,* into a more terrible *desert*" in search of freedom under God brought an energy that was more powerful than any already established in the New World. The Indian society had always been arrested in an anonymous communal arrangement by the absence of the idea of the individual. The Spanish society was built on an inertia which allowed the high cultivation of the individual yet denied it any expression that was not in harmony with the prevailing official position of the state. Now imagining new experience until it occurred, the American settlers brought a frame of life in which the individual was not only permitted but obliged to create himself socially. The forces that obliged him so were the unexampled frontier environment, the swift emergence of a self-made culture, the extension of democratic doctrine, and the joyful sanction of anyone who grew to his own individualism, comely or rude. A poetry of action was inherent in all such obligational forces; and it both contained and exposed a mighty volume of spiritual strength.

That strength was great enough to bring the colonies together to make a new nation, and to survive the terrible hazards of the struggle to design a government for all citizens that would not destroy the essential freedom of each. That this was achieved, and swiftly, as the lives of nations were reckoned, was a matter of fame. European observers came among the Americans, to live their life, and record what they examined, and return with a book manuscript to Europe.

"The happy and the powerful," remarked one thinking about the occasion of the colonies, "do not go into exile, and there are no surer guarantees of equality among men than poverty and misfortune." And another seeing in his mind's eye the migration over the ocean, reflected of the Americans that "everything has tended to regenerate them: new laws, a new mode of living, a new social system. Here they are become men. In Europe they were so many useless plants, wanting vegetative mold and refreshing showers. They withered; and were mowed down by want, hunger, and war. . . . The American is a new man, who acts upon new principles. . . ."

When before had a new land and a new idea of man been brought together in their newness? Even the vast soil of America in its primeval bounty and beauty and untouchedness seemed ordained—"in this state it is offered to man," observed Tocqueville; man who was "not barbarous, ignorant and isolated, as he was in the early ages, but already in possession of the most important secrets of nature, united to his fellow men, and instructed by the experience of fifty centuries. . . ." He saw that in older migrations—say, at the fall of Rome—peoples scattering for new places carried with them destruction and death; while in America, each settler brought "the elements of prosperity and life." They knew full well the nature, and the might, of their achievement. They paid reverence to one of its humblest symbols, and moved Tocqueville as they did so. It was Plymouth Rock. "Here," he said, "is a stone which the feet of a few poor fugitives pressed for an instant, and this stone becomes famous; it is treasured by a great nation, a fragment is prized as a relic. But what," he asked, remembering Europe and its symbols, "what has become of the doorsteps of a thousand palaces? Who troubles himself about them?"

It was not to build palaces or make vast conquests that the Americans went to work on their new lands. Tocqueville saw that all they then wanted to do was to add a few yards of land to a farm, put out an orchard, build a room or two—and always to make life easier. He marvelled at how hard they worked to gain such ends—what "feverish ardor" and "avidity" they spent to improve their material circumstances. Indeed, there was a danger in their zeal, their "vague dread . . . lest they should not have chosen the shortest path" that might lead to their own welfare: for such a pursuit might "at last shut out the rest of the world," and even come between "itself and heaven." This was a meditation for a philosopher; it did not deter later emigrants from Europe.

For in swelling numbers they came to the American coast, and established themselves for hire, so freeing countless American-born citizens for their plunge into the interior of the continent. This "double migration was incessant," wrote Tocqueville. "It begins in the middle of Europe, it crosses the Atlantic Ocean, and it advances over the solitudes of the New World. Millions of men are marching at once toward the same horizon; their language, religion, manners, differ; their object is the same. Fortune has been promised to them somewhere in the West, and to the West they go to find it. . . ."

For in the early nineteenth century the American West was already the world's marvel. With the Louisiana Purchase Jefferson had committed the nation to a continental reach. But more, in his whole concept of democracy he had opened political frontiers in the thoughts of men that only the West, in its sheer space, could contain. "In early youth," said a pioneer toward the end of his days, "we removed to and settled in a country universally known over the continent as the 'Great West'. . . . Towns, steamboats, post offices and children were named 'Far West' in honor of that wonderful country. . . ." It was there for the taking. After 1820 land was to be bought from the government for $1.25 an acre. In most American families, as well as in the newer arrivals from oversea, the memory was still keen of how the old-world society was based on great landlords and their holdings. Space was narrow in Europe. Hierarchies and classes constricted men in fixed places into which they had been born. Who could simply go forth anywhere in Europe and take land to make a new life for himself out of it? And even if land were so available, how little of it was there at best, compared to what lay between the Alleghenies and the Rockies, and beyond. . . .

In their constant search for better, easier ways of life, the Americans as they moved on westward repudiated one past after another—that of Europe, that of the Atlantic coast, that of their first inland settlements. A Frenchman at the end of the eighteenth century saw this as "complete proof of the American indifference to love and friendship and of failure to form attachments to anything. . . ." The American abandoned, "without reluctance, the place where he first drew breath, the church in which he first perceived the idea of a supreme being, the tombs of his ancestors, the friends of his infancy, the companions of his youth, and all the pleasures of his society"—all for land, new land. If this was a desire deep in the individual, it must reappear as an element in the national character; and it was seen by some as a driving force behind the march of General Taylor's army to the river. Abraham Lincoln, who opposed the Mexican War, supported his point with a joke about an Illinois farmer who said, "I ain't greedy about land. I only want what jines mine." That farmer's self-pardoning greed suggested the temperament of some of the earliest settlers to cross the Alleghenies, who struck Tocqueville as "only an agglomeration of adventurers and speculators . . . we are amazed at the persons [there] invested with authority," and he asked how from such settlers could a proper life be made to grow.

But such pioneers were not for long alone on the frontier. Others—all kinds—kept coming; and among the adventurers who pushed out beyond the settlements were various Europeans of high degree who appeared to view the West as a great park where they might hunt, and explore, and record marvels new to the inquiring and cultivated intelligence. There were German princes with grand suites and striped canvas pavilions and personal physicians; British sportsmen elaborately armed and staffed with frontier scouts; and hired artists who sketched and painted for their noble patrons the Indians, the game, and the landscapes of the prairies and the Rocky Mountains. They took away with them after their grand tours a body of information to be published or exhibited abroad; while the settlers remained to enact the freedom they had designed for themselves.

As each succeeding frontier was settled, it was resolved into the form of a state government; and its most significant act was to give form to the convictions of liberty for which it had been populated. The new states spread their energy and influence not only westward, but eastward; for their new constitutions popularly adopted universal manhood suffrage, and under their example the old Atlantic states were required by their people to set aside religious and property qualifications for the vote and in their turn to adopt universal manhood suffrage also. The same impulse that thrust individual Americans westward returned a fuller democracy to the states they had left behind them.

But if liberty was not a new idea in mankind, then it was new to equate it with comparative solitude. The Americans brought distance with them as a virtue, dragging it along to separate them from their fellows, in an endless appetite for freedom. In Louisiana Audubon came upon the wilderness cabin of a Connecticut family. When he asked

why they had moved to such a "wild and solitary spot," the husband
replied, "The people are growing too numerous now to thrive in New
England." The very nation was founded on the concept of the integrity
and self-sufficiency of the individual. The frontier attitude was perhaps
a caricature of this—its lines all too black, its features too coarse, its
sentiments rising in balloons of comment too fiercely rude, and its
shading too rough in its crosshatching; but, like many a wood-engraved
political cartoon of the period, it was true in its essential quality. Freedom meant not only independence of spirit and belief; it meant also a
chance to dominate the material environment. This was new in North
America, where before the environment had dominated the Indian and
the Spaniard.

Passing over the eastern mountains, taking the rivers if they
flowed west or southwest, and coming to the forest frontier, the settlers
took down trees if necessary to let their road go on. Almost at once
organized communication followed them. The mail travelled by small
cart, in a green darkness by day, and by night through firelight cast all
about by torches of pine cut and held by the driver. Every so often the
cart reached a hut in the woods. This was the post office. There, a
bundle of letters was thrown off, the cart galloped on and, when they
could, the forest settlers came from their hidden cabins to leaf through
the folded, sealed papers for their mail. The cart now and then carried a
passenger. One of them marvelled at signs of how fast and how soon
settlers had deserted their recent clearings and cabins as they moved
westward to look once more for a better life. And soon, too, the woods
took back what they had lost to the clearings. The post traveller would
come upon a little opening of light through the green density and there
see a chimney in the woods, standing alone above its blackened hearth;
or the remains of a cabin whose logs were sprouting anew, while vines
and flowers hung like veils from the corner uprights, making a bower.
The only sounds to be heard in the high green aisles were dove song and
woodpecker drillings. The traveller asked himself if ruins, then, were
already there; and like many who came after him, he tried to recreate
in his mind the character of the men to whom the woods had allowed
passage, only to spring up behind them as they went.

The Americans were

> "Those that look carelessly in the faces
> of Presidents and governors, as to say,
> *Who are you?*,

Those of earth-born passion, simple,
never constrain'd, never obedient,

Those of inland America,"

sang Walt Whitman. The people, he said, were "ungrammatical, untidy, and their sins gaunt and ill-bred," and yet they had "measureless wealth of latent power and capacity, their vast, artistic contrasts of lights and shades, with . . . entire reliability in emergencies, and a certain breadth of historic grandeur, of peace or war . . . the peaceablest and most good-natured race in the world, and the most personally independent and intelligent. . . . Grand, common stock! to me the accomplish'd and convincing growth, prophetic of the future; proof undeniable to sharpest sense, of perfect beauty, tenderness and pluck. . . ."

From the first, the frontiersman saw himself as a new breed of cat, and behaved accordingly, in cutting himself off from the past. Whenever he saw that he was regarded as rude and coarse, he at once acted more coarsely and rudely. He jeered at any of his fellows who echoed the manners and tastes of the East, or of England. His patriotism was deep and true, but he pounded Eastern or foreign visitors into exhaustion with his defiant assertions of it. Yankee Doodle was a figure in a piercing little song, but he was more. He was a reality who made actual appearances among frontier crowds, when some fellow felt like dressing up in striped trousers, a blue tail coat and a tall beaver hat, to remind himself and all others of what an American looked like. He was regarded without surprise or question. Any man had a sanction for oddity. Audubon saw a man in New Orleans on the levee wearing a flop-brimmed hat, a bright green coat, wide yellow nankeen pants, a pink vest, and a frilled shirt. In his shirt was a bunch of magnolias from which the head of a live baby alligator swung to and fro. He carried a loud silk umbrella with one hand, and with the other a cage of brightly feathered birds. Stalking grandly, he was singing "My love is but a lassie yet" in a Scottish dialect; but when he talked, his speech was native American. He was a one-man drama, and his right to create a spectacle was granted. He was exaggerating his individualism, and his observers let him be in his dreamlike commitment, that was haunted by his passion—arising from buried discontents dimly understood by all—to be distinguished among his kind, in any way he desired.

In certain ways, the American not only created a new kind of society; he also began to look like a new kind of man. His inner likeness

gave him a new and characteristic outer bearing, and his physical experience in overcoming a virgin land brought to him and his sons rugged
health and taller, broader, harder bodies. Drawing contributors from
many old-world nationalities, the American race in a few generations
through common experience, spirit and belief, shaped them into a general
type that even with its myriad variations yet stood forth as a recognizable
ideal figure for Western democratic man. This American was tall and
rangy, and he walked with a long stride, pressing his legs against the
unknown distance and future in a steady gait that gave a breathing swing
to his upper body. Beyond physical dimensions and details, it was his
quality of movement that gave him his most characteristic appearance;
for movement expressed nature and will. His nature was to be free, strong
and original; his will was to succeed in these aims, against obstacles of
tradition and wilderness country; and all that he had in mind and met
in nature helped to make his aspect new among mankind.

Going West, he clothed himself in few garments, all designed
for work. As such, they not only covered but revealed his body, ignoring
style and ornament for the simpler value of leaving him free in the
gestures of labor. If he worked in open prairies or on wide rivers his
hat was wide-brimmed to shade him from the sun. If he worked in
mountains or woods he had a fur cap for warmth, and for kinship with
the animals he hunted and loved in their defeat. Now and then he wore
a felt hat wetted and dried in the shape of the tricorne of the Revolution.
His shirt was loose, cut to hang over his shoulders front and back, with
sleeves seamed to the rest between shoulder and elbow, and tightened
around the wrist with a lace or a button. His trousers were tight from
waist to knee, and made either to hang over or fit inside his boots with
their thick soles and squared toes. For jacket he often wore a cloth or
hide vest, and for coat on occasions of leisure a long-skirted affair with
pockets inside the tails. The materials were mostly homespun, and were
often left undyed. When colored, they showed the colors of berries or
spices—frosty blue, dark cranberry red, sassafras yellow, cinnamon or nut
brown, leaf green. The trapper or scout in buckskin was deer-colored
and from a little distance in a wood if he held still was hardly to be
mistaken for anything but another deer. The farther he went from
settled life the more he tended to resemble a creature of the wilds,
until an occasional one could only be spoken of in animal terms, like
the man who was observed "mounted on a mountain mustang, his face,
what little of it could be seen besides hair, looking very much like a

small piece of buffalo meat, and with hair standing out like porcupine quills. . . ."

Embracing the farthest wilderness, the first settlers struck an occasional cultivated observer as men who reverted to savagery. Crève-coeur said they had "an instinctive fondness for the reckless savage life, alternately indolent and laborious, full and fasting, occupied in hunting, fishing, feasting, intriguing, amours, interdicted by no laws, or difficult morals, or any restraints, but the invisible ones of Indian habit and opinion." Again, "these men appear to be no better than carnivorous animals, of a superior rank, living on the flesh of wild animals when they can catch them, and when they are not able, subsisting on grain." And again, "remote from the power of example and the check of shame, many families exhibit the most hideous part of our society. They are a kind of forlorn hope, preceding by ten or twelve years, the most respect-able" who "come after them. In that space, prosperity will polish some, vice and law will drive off the rest, who, uniting with others like them-selves, will recede still farther, making room for more industrious people, who will finish their improvements. . . ."

What showed in a later light was the prophetic persistence of image of a new life which led the forerunners to enact their own folk-lore as they thought of it amidst surroundings for which there was no previous pattern. The real binder of the new society was a willingness on the part of all to endure poverty for the sake of independence—"Poverty & Independence," as Audubon wrote in his journal for 1820, ". . . the only friends that will travel together through the world." The nation had begun as "a people of cultivators, scattered over an immense territory," as Crèvecoeur saw. But among the Western settlers every level of social position was represented, and every degree of development in cultural aspect and expression, from the wildcat primitive to the classical scholar, the tinker to the craftsman, the lawless scout to the maker of communities of calm and organic order, the man who governed his fellows by a spirit of fire to the one who led them by rational science. Together they might seem to glisten and seethe inseparable as sands in light, but in their ways and manners, they could be remembered as separate grains each shining sharply for itself.

ii. frontier attitudes

As the individual felt equal to the vast wilderness, so he was able to get on with the job of turning a continent into a neighborhood. Despite the fifty centuries of social cultivation behind him, the instant he had to be ready to practice wilderness craft he was ready. An ancient atavism of man against animal sprang close in time and memory; and a fabled breed of hunters was the result across the Appalachians. As marksmanship was their craft, it became their art and their entertainment, even their inducement to waste what sustained them. General William Henry Harrison, writing to the Secretary of War and Marine from Fort Saint Vincent, Indiana, in 1801, said, "One white hunter will destroy more game than five of the common Indians, the latter generally contenting himself with a sufficiency for present subsistence, while the other, eager for game, hunts for the skin of the animal alone." The hunters, tenacious, wasteful, wilful, were men who would kill one bounty of nature to obtain another, and in taking the wilderness with violence would not be stayed by moderation or thought of the future's needs. Merely to take a treed raccoon, they would chop down the tree, at night, by a woods pool or bayou, with torches guttering and dogs dancing.

Compared to others, they were a nation of sharpshooters. Their skill was what won Texas, and plains battles against riding Indians. To prove their skill men held contests to show their wonderful handling of the long rifle. Audubon saw them at it. The rifleman first cleaned his barrel. He then took a ball from his leather pouch, cupped it in the palm of his hand, and from his slung horn poured just enough powder to cover the ball. He poured the powder into the tube, set the ball in after it, and wadded it with a patch of six-hundred-thread linen, and rammed it all home with a hickory rod. He then faced the target. Sometimes this was a nail, driven two thirds into a board forty paces away. In one of three shots, he was able to finish driving the nail. He could trim the wick of a lighted candle at fifty paces without putting it out. At a hundred yards he could cut off a turkey's head. At comparable distances, he could hit the eye of an enemy. He could bark a squirrel, as Audubon saw Daniel Boone do it. The hunter aimed at a branch just where a squirrel sat, and hit the bark. The concussion killed the squirrel and sent him spinning in the air, to fall to the ground with his fur and flesh undamaged. The report of the long rifle made a crack like a whip. Men who could shoot like that, and who otherwise knew how to use themselves against the wilds, made a close community.

They gave later comers a hard time until able to prove themselves in the same terms. This habit sometimes showed itself in a comic hostility that masked a process of shrewd appraisal and suspended judgment until the newcomer could earn acceptance in the occupations and diversions of the initiated. Such hazing sometimes went to the limits of test and danger. Dimly it wanted to prove that a stranger could take care of himself or if need be do his part for the common safety in situations of peril. But further, the attitude was so exaggerated, so preposterously more than itself, that it suggested some obscure but grinding necessity to enlarge and insist upon all the masculine attributes that were taken for granted by most men in most other environments. It seemed as though a predominantly male society like that of the frontier was obliged to accentuate its maleness to make an outsize virtue of it, and so preserve in eternal boyhood the secrets and discoveries of essential virility that in the boy's first awareness of them assumed such proud, obsessive and exciting value. In many of its social expressions the early frontier West resembled a vast boys' club whose members dealt with puzzling perils and uncertainties by shouting them down with incantations of prowess.

Wildcats? Such a man could lick his weight in wildcats, and so stated with truculence and often. He would cry that he was a blacksnake, the longest, slickest, wisest of all. He was a weasel, clever enough to steal whatever he wanted. He was a raccoon, a tornado, an earthscreamer, a river at flood, a gamecock; he used a pine tree for a toothpick and he drank a lake if he was thirsty; he was cocked on a hair trigger and it was sure death merely to look at him in a certain way. He would as soon fight as eat; and—he sighed like a gale and belched like a geyser —he just loved to eat. He would take anybody on with a gun, or a knife, or bare hands with thumbs to gouge out eyes, and all for the pleasure of it, both received and given. If anyone thought he was just fooling, let him take up the ultimate challenge, and consent to fight him naked, straddling a bench or a log and strapped to it within a few inches of each other, and armed with a knife each; and see who finally fell over cut and bleeding, and who still sat there able to spit when the onlookers came forward to untie the both of them, one live and one dead. It was a challenge that was actually given and taken when doubt or boredom reached desperation.

Aggressive humility was another frontier attitude, perhaps less to be trusted than open truculence. It suggested envy, and private schemes to take what was wanted. Many frontiersmen could manage their faces with an actor's control. This was a technique of shrewdness, to wipe off any expression from which another could read intention or attitude. It was the poker face, and it could conceal either a teeming mind or one absolutely empty and at a loss. If a man felt ignorant he did well to conceal his feeling; and in any case, who knew everything? If men believed in equality, then what one man didn't know was just as good as what another didn't know. Out of tact, knowledge was often as carefully concealed as ignorance. It appeared that the ideas of the democratic citizen either dealt exactly with small matters, or vaguely with large ones, with no thoughts in between.

But if there were few learned men in the new society, there were few ignorant. The American cared "more to know a great deal quickly than anything well," Tocqueville said, and further noted that "the habit of inattention must be considered the greatest defect of the democratic character." The citizen's mind was always busy with his own concerns—chiefly those of business, his own situation, the assertion in thought of his own plans. These were his diversion as well as his livelihood; and they left little room for the charms of useless but delightful ideas. Like all generations, those of the early republic went in for rages and fads of belief that seemed to enlighten the people even while giving them a thin authority in obscure affairs, which they could display with elegance. Among the most gratifying of these were phrenology and its offshoots, which seemed to provide a penetrating key to human capacities. It was a period accomplishment to know with finality the secrets of personality by a glance and a touch upon the skull; and it was a popular pleasure to say, as if it meant something, that Fauvel-Gouraud's system of Phreno-Mnemotechny operated "through the intellectual and not the mechanical action of the mind."

Gravely accepted at the time, such imported fantasy seemed to give tone to the society. But there were more local notions of fantasy that really caught something of its likeness. David Crockett passed from life into legend before his death, and was quoted in a body of literature written down long after its invention. One time, out hunting, when the sun rose he lighted his pipe from it, shouldered his bear, walked home, "introducin' people to the fresh daylight with a piece of sunrise in my pocket." The expression held something of the blitheness, the sweet fresh primality, the sense of outset as at dawn, of the early nation.

Confidence dwelled in such a large view, and reflected the trust with which Americans moved alone through solitudes. When they met one another, they fell into easy, immediate fellowship, a habit they would never lose. Despite natural dangers, Audubon said ". . . So little risk do travellers run in the United States that no one ever dreams of any to be encountered on the road."

—Though one night putting up at a forest cabin where he was allowed to enter and scrape a cake out of the ashes to eat for his supper, and make a bed of skins from a heap in the corner, he was seen to possess a handsome gold watch. Later in the night he heard his hostess, "an infernal hag," plotting with her drunken sons to murder him and steal the watch. He was saved by the arrival of other travellers and had the satisfaction of seeing the murderous family executed, their goods given to a wounded young Indian who also had taken refuge under the same roof, and their cabin burned. Justice so swift proved how rare was such a crime against a traveller's faith; and how trustworthy was the ordinary forest home.

iii. woman and home

It was woman who gave it grace and amenity, with whatever materials were at hand. Her courage was as great and her work as hard as her husband's. Her satisfactions were all tacit. Unlike the European who flattered women but did not treat them as his equal, the American almost never complimented his wife, but showed her in other ways how fully he valued and counted upon her partnership in a wilderness venture. If as a figure she was idealized in countless impersonal episodes of frontier lore, she was, like the men, also projected in the grotesque vein. Mike Fink, the river boatman who was translated into myth, had an incredible daughter. She was so huge she tamed a full-grown bear; and all at once she could chew with one side of her mouth, whistle with the other, and scream with the middle. Grandeurs and amenities abandoned with the East merged with the talents and symbols of the West in a description of another frontier maiden, whose bonnet was a hornet's nest. Her gown was a whole bear's hide, with the tail for a train. She could drink from a creek without a cup, shoot a wild goose flying, wade the Mississippi without getting wet, outscream a catamount, and jump over her own shadow. She had good, strong horse sense, knew a woodchuck from a skunk, and could dance down any fellow. . . . Such monstrous views of woman were in a perverse way a proof of her equality with men whose experience she wholly shared in the job of making the new life. After the troubles of migration, it was she who gave heart to the cabin home.

"A pleasing uniformity of decent competence," said Crèvecoeur, "appears throughout our habitations. The meanest of our log houses is a dry and comfortable habitation." It was put together of trees felled by axe to make a clearing. The stumps were burned away in a long chore that boys could do. Seedlings showed in the rubble, and were cut down or allowed to grow, depending on where they sprang. Larger trees with heavy foliage were circled through the bark to kill their shade and let light through upon patches of corn sowed between them.

The house was about thirty feet long, fifteen feet wide, and fifteen feet high. It was all one room, and it had a single window hung with a muslin curtain. At one end rose the chimney made of stones hauled from a creek near-by or dug out of the ground. The hearth was of packed clay. The fireplace was wide and high, to hold an immense fire, that not only heated but lighted the whole room. Over the hearth hung a long rifle on iron hooks, and above it, for decoration, perhaps a deer- or bearskin, and a clutch of eagle or hawk feathers. On the wall to the right of the chimney was tacked an engraved map of the United States on Pennsylvania laid paper. From its eastern parts where it showed dense hatching of towns, roads, waterways and mountains in lines of black ink, the map faded toward the Mississippi until beyond the river westward it showed little but the names of Indian tribes bitten into spaces of white paper, with a straggle of the Rocky Mountains like a spine of tiny pine cones, and a tentative broken curve for the empty Pacific coast. Near the map hung a single plank shelf on which rested the family's books—a Bible, the first six books of Milton, a volume of Shakespeare, an almanac. Along the wall instead of closets stood wooden chests. In the center of the room was a long table built in the clearing. Its legs still held bark. On the table was a teapot of English china, a handful of silver spoons by Revere or Hurd of Boston, some teacups, and a little pile of old newspapers. Such a dwelling as Tocqueville saw it was "a little world, an ark of civilization amid an ocean of foliage. . . ."

Here was enclosed all the life of the family, for parents, children and dogs; here ate and slept the traveller in the common firelight under the protecting rooftree made by the father; and here presided the mother. She was in many cases a woman of gentle cultivation who had left the home of prosperous parents to risk with her husband the trials of the Great West, bringing with her as best she could all the graces she had learned. Her life was hard. She bore children frequently and in countless cases without any aid but that of her husband. Her day began with sunup and until her daughters were old enough she did its womanly tasks alone. She aged fast. Her appearance was inclined to be "at once sad but resolute." If she seemed exhausted, yet it was with pride, that her life should be so insatiably used by her man, her children, and her place on earth; and when travellers came, she and her husband gave what they had of shelter, food and floor. This was done as a duty, impassively, with no pretense that uninvited guests were in every case occasions of joy.

Like an Indian woman, the mother cooked out of doors except on the coldest winter days, when she set her kettles and skillets in the great indoor fireplace. She lighted her fire with flint and steel, or punk and tinder, until about 1829, when something else came along that was described with amazement. A tall red-haired young man—he turned out to be Alexander William Doniphan who would appear on the New Mexico Rio Grande in 1846—"took from his pocket the like of which I had never before seen . . . rubbed it on the sole of his boot and lo! there was combustion fire." The phosphorus-tipped friction match quickly sprang into wide use. On a spit the mother cooked all sorts of game brought in by her husband and her sons. When they went on a bee hunt they came home with plenty of wild honey. In deep kettles she made a variety of stews, seasoned with herbs for which the woods were combed. Out of corn and wheat flour ground at home she baked bread and cakes. From wild berries and fruits she made sweets. In time she would be able to gather produce from her own orchards, after her little trees began to bear. Out of the woods she took her medicines, from which she mixed a general remedy called bitters. To a draught of whiskey she added sarsaparilla roots, dock roots, black snakeroot, the bark of dogwood and of wild cherry, and a few beads of black pine gum. This was fed to grownups and children alike when indicated.

When she wasn't cooking she was working toward cloth at her spinning wheel or loom; or making new garments; or mending old ones. It was said on the frontier that the first thing a young man did was to get him a wife so's to have her make him some clothes. When she wasn't sewing she was teaching the children their ABC's, and how to read, and how to cipher, and who the Lord Jesus was, and where their

grandparents were, and what America was, and how a living was made.
She had very little money and needed no more, for her husband obtained goods by trade; and what money they had was enough to pay
the government, "as there were no unreasonable taxes." The mother
told her young ones of what was dangerous in the surrounding country
—wolves, snakes, big cats, bears. She made it plain that not all Indians
were to be feared, for many went by on camping and hunting trips,
and though queer and with outlandish notions, and a shock to see with
all the cranky nakedness they showed, many of them were almost friends.
She spoke of other kinds, of whom all had heard, who came with brand
and scream and arrow and stolen rifle, to kill all who lived in a cabin
like hers. Thinking of it, she raised her head, and put her hand under
her children's chins and made them raise theirs, and said that fear was
no excuse not to stay where you wanted to stay, if you did no harm
there, and bore your share of work. There were days when she even
found time to surprise the children with a cornhusk doll, dressed and
painted, or a rag doll that she had made for the girls; for the boys,
perhaps a little horse made of twigs and a spool, or a toy bear stuffed
with pine needles, or a beanbag, or a buckskin ball worked and worked
until its seams met just right to create the sphere.

She kept her girls by her till late; her boys she lost early. The
boys had hardly a cubhood. They went from boy to man; for as soon
as their bodies were lengthening and filling to meet physical toil, they
were ready to do a man's work; and were granted leave to do it. None
could read the prickling thoughts of a youth or guess where they would
turn him. The father watched his sons come to independence; and he
saw this with pride, as an extension of the national ideal of equality
and democratic opportunity. If the son wanted to stay at home to work,
he was welcome; he was equally at liberty to do what many did at fourteen or fifteen—make a bundle of what he owned, take a rifle from the
family's armory, and with a sweet bloom of ignorance on his confident face, go out on his own to a still farther West than the one he
grew up in. He went with trading trains, or trapping parties, or with
exploring expeditions of the Army, or joined a wild and dissolute crew
of rivermen; and what he learned he measured by the gaunt, strong
image of life to which he was born in the forest clearing, where in
little he saw the community of work that in the large held America
together. Everyone worked, and no job for man or woman was high or
low, but all were respectable if honest. No one was embarrassed to work
for pay. The President himself was paid.

iv. community expression

As neighborhoods took form, and the habits of a family were united with those of others, a sense of community governed all; and after the time when every day required ceaseless work, the neighbors at last were able to keep the Sabbath. They came together for worship in a clearing, or presently built a meetinghouse where they could be enclosed with the spirit of holiness that, they felt, arose more powerfully from all than from each. Going to church they carried in hand their shoes and stockings to keep them clean and only when near the meetinghouse did they sit down on a log and put them on to enter into worship presentably. Democracy spoke through a frontier hymn of 1800:

> Come hungry, come thirsty, come ragged, come bare,
> Come filthy, come lousy, come just as you are. . . .

And when they were gathered, it was one of their number who emerged to speak for them. There was always one who could "preach a pretty fair backwoods hardshell sermon." His expression was geared not to vaults and ambulatories and transepts but to groves and clearings and roughhewn rafters. Emotion—raw, contagious—was what they came to release, in the name of God. When the spirit was on them, they worshipped somewhat in the vein of the frontier fantasy that gave them identity with wildcat, tornado, ring-tailed roarer, and earth-screamer.

For daily close to violent peril and the large acts of birth, life, and death with no specialized skills to meet them, when they gathered to deal with human destiny under God their prayer took violent forms in the forest revival meetings of 1800 and after. The wildcat was licked over and over in testimonials given in meeting against Satan. The earth-screamer rose and jabbered sounds that if they were words belonged to an unknown tongue; but their message of guilt and release was understood by all. Shouting people fell to the ground in convulsions of humility and brief lost-mindedness. They writhed, jerked, crawled and trembled, while their tears streamed into the dust, and those who watched and heard felt strange longings begin to shake within themselves, and soon they too were lost to the hard world and were thrown down by a power greater than each—the power of all together. Crying of David's dance before the Ark of the Covenant one would suddenly

leap into the air, crack his heels as for a hoedown, and start to jig like
a man on a river boat. Born of the intention to worship, there took form
among them the essential acts of theatre, dance, and concert—every satisfaction, however rude, of the desire to find through formal emotion a
delivery from the limitations of the flesh, in its connotations of hardship, suffering and sin. So led by one of their number they gave themselves up to each other in the name of the Lamb; and purged by spectacular emotion in which all took part, returned to their ordinary selves
with sighs of renewed innocence and strength.

It was a mood, then, proper to other Sabbath pastimes, against
the misted blue distances beyond woods, and river hills, and creekside
meadows; the lyric, gold-washed afternoons of the frontier landscapes.
A man would bring a horse to the meeting; and for hours the horse was
judged by a ring of critics who squinted at his general conformation,
felt his withers, counted his teeth, stroked his coat. Another, prosperous,
donated a beef or a turkey as a prize for the best marksman; and the
long rifles cracked like whips in a shooting contest. Others—men and
women alike—fished at the edge of a stream with thoughts upside down
in clear water. Others sat and "visited," feeling the past week in bone
and flesh, and letting their weight rest till tomorrow. Someone sang—
"The Soldier's Tear," "Long, Long Ago"—

> Now that you've come, all my griefs are removed,
> Let me forget that so long you have roved,
> Let me believe that you love as you loved
> Long, long ago,
> Long ago.

From the long-ago, drifts of the national heritage glowed and faded in
memory, hearsay, and gossip—how General Washington used to hold a
levee at Philadelphia in his black velvet court dress wearing a beautiful
little sword and an expression of calm elevation, while Lady Washington
watched him to see whom to speak to; how a man who when lightning
struck a tree was reminded that as a boy-sailor on the U.S.S. *Constella-
tion* he saw the foremast of the French frigate *Insurgente* crack and fall;
how another who had sailed with Decatur never forgot the burning of
the *Philadelphia* before Tripoli; how a woman watched Madam Madison
carry a picture and a parrot out of the White House when the British
came to burn the capital; how Daniel Boone tried out his coffin—there
was a picture of him doing it—before he died; how you could ride from
Lockport to Albany on the Erie Canal so smoothly; how the remark-

able new hotels of New York, five stories tall, had parlors for ladies, and music in the dining rooms; how the word "Slavery" had best not be mentioned till you knew which side you were talking to; how the public still took passage on river steamboats even though so many burst their boilers and sank on fire; and the railroads—how you not only got cinders in your eyes from riding on them, but just from standing in your own field and watching them go by; how printing presses, if you could believe what you heard, would all be run by steam in the end; and why didn't Daniel Webster go the whole hog and go to England to live, where the whiskey was better, and he would feel at home if he loved them so; and if Santy Anno did what they said he did in Texas why did they let him go; and if so many men had seen the famous white mustang wild on the prairies how come nobody ever took and caught him; and how the women in Santa Fee, every one of them, young or old, pretty or plain, smoked what they called seegaritos and blew the smoke in the faces of men at dances; and—sooner or later the talk all got around to it —who ought to be thrown out of office, and why, and who was going to be elected. . . .

For, as to politics, every American was an expert. He knew this was true, for he *was* the government. To make him so his forebears had fought and died; and to keep him so, he would fight and die himself. He saw himself as the people at large, and the people as embodied in himself. He, the voter, projected into the people, was the source and object of everything. The people, observed Tocqueville, reigned in the world of the United States politics as the Deity did in the universe. If, as Crèvecoeur thought, the American was a new man who acted upon new principles, "he must therefore entertain new ideas and form new opinions." Politics was the supreme topic for American conversation; and its object was liberty. "In this country," wryly declared the French Bourbon royalist Montlezun, "where the word liberty is never omitted in conversation, there is the greatest tyranny of opinion; that is, of political opinion, for that is the only kind that seems important." What this royalist authoritarian failed to note was the immensely important fact that the opinion was not that of a single controlling individual, but of a majority of individuals who controlled. An art of collective living was at birth; and as it would govern the destinies of all, so it took the energies of all, at the expense of other values that in older societies were exquisitely developed as ornaments of life—the fine arts, the abstract pleasures of philosophy, all the tones of aristocratic systems that had for so long hidden matter under manner.

For man himself was the proper heart of the matter of life; and
when the Americans rediscovered the fact, and the world heard them
talk about it, they were listened to with a sense of recognition. Tocqueville observed that "the political debates of a democratic people, however
small it may be, have a degree of breadth that often renders them attrac-
tive to mankind. All men are interested by them because they treat of
man, who is everywhere the same." America seemed to stand not only
for equality of opportunity; but to be also the land of mankind's second
chance. To the degree that the Americans were interested in each other,
the world was interested in them.

And indeed, Americans took a lively, sometimes a prying interest
in one another's affairs. It seemed to one student of the new democracy
that "if an American were condemned to confine his activity to his own
affairs, he would be robbed of one half of his existence; he would feel
an immense void in . . . life, and his wretchedness would be unbear-
able." What saved all was again the general consent to the will of the
majority; and the majority on occasion not only made the laws, but even
reserved the right to break them. For once law was established, if it
appeared to bear too closely upon the rights of the individual, he was
free to enlist others with him in an effort to change it to resist the power
of central authority, and to remake, over and over again, the image of
the nation in the likeness of his view of life. The citizen's training began
early—schoolchildren made up rules for their own games and clamored
for their observance among themselves. In any contingency developing
in public—a traffic upset, a quarrel, a complaint against a merchant or
innkeeper—the onlookers formed themselves into a deliberative body,
and resolved upon what to do. Committees met to decide upon all
manner of things—even to the drinking of alcoholic beverages. In the
early nineteenth century temperance societies with over two hundred
and seventy thousand members carried a stern influence. Their cheerless
sway in Pennsylvania alone in one year reduced the consumption of
alcohol by five hundred thousand gallons.

v. language

Such effect could arise only from an inexhaustible outpouring of
speech. The Americans were talkative. With opinions sharply ready,

they spoke their pieces freely. To rise and be heard was not only essential to their system of life; it was almost the only social joy they knew. In the absence of well-established theatrical life, and opera companies, and museums, the debating societies of the Americans had to serve as substitutes. They were popular. In their meeting rooms citizens rehearsed the postures and appeals that must serve them if they ever went to Congress; and the habits of debate became so satisfying that even in intimate conversation the member was likely to forget that he was talking to an individual and to fall into the larger airs of one who swayed a meeting, and if his style rose with his opinion, so that he became heated, he swept the air with his arm, and, carried away by his own sound, he addressed his lone listener as "Gentlemen. . . ." For oratory could always sweep him away, his own most of all. Newly the possessor of the parliamentary arts, he sometimes lost himself in them to the point of forensic nonsense. But more important to the habit of democracy than the nonsense of manner was the right of all citizens to be heard.

"Eloquence is, in fact, after gold, their highest ideal," said Father Grassi, an Italian Jesuit who gazed at the Americans during his five years as president of Georgetown College from 1810 to 1815. He went on to say that New World orators paid less mind to the inner values of a speech—originality and beauty of thought, weight of ideas, force of argument and logical development—than they did to its manner. They knew their success with a public waiting to be edified rested upon other details—florid metaphor, elegant words, grand periods. The American speaker confessed that he was impatient of "a vulgar and sterile state of facts." What the people wanted must be offered. "A people who have fresh and lively feelings will always relish oratory." The oratory of the West was "free, lofty, agitating, grand, impassioned. . . ." It was a people's art; and like a people's art, it had a curious double spirit. It both derided and imitated the richness of more aristocratic or better-educated models. It was aware of the idiom of a donnish class, an élite in whom all elevated expression was reposed by older societies; and rejected it in the name of a whole population who shared equally the joys and powers of making utterances that could sound splendiferous, whatever on earth they might mean. Much frontier oratory in its inflation took to kidding on the level. The inflation was perfectly conscious and was often meant to be comic—and yet at the same time, it hoped to intoxicate with its reminders of large acts, projected fantasies of patriotism, and a new historical spirit. For metaphor it drew freely on the marvels of the unfolding continent—the might of Niagara, the sweep of the prairies, the noble rise of the Rockies, the blaze of Western starlight, the arc of heaven that embraced America from coast to coast, and endlessly the scowling American eagle who dwelt on pinnacles and crags, and soared in freedom above the restraints of earth. Like all the arts of the people, their oratory expressed desire and character. Its inflations and exaggerations were brandished in reply to the vastness of the West, the bulk of mountains, where man was so little. If there was vulgarity in its expression, there was also pathos; for what showed plain was the violent dancing of a spirit that must assert or be lost.

As the country—its land, political purpose and united energy—was new, so must its most common means of expression—language itself—be new. For the old forms of English the people laid down new rules and made up new words. Inventing his character, and adopting wilderness ways with which he had to achieve physical victory, the American needed new means with which to express himself. By 1815 he had a new dialect that was a distinct tangent of the mother tongue. Much of its vocabulary was consciously fantastic; and any man was privileged to coin vivid, homely, and extravagant locutions, and might even become a virtuoso of the process. The frontier talked the raw materials of a new literature. Politics, work, and daily character in shrewd masquerade stimulated the most vigorous flow of new speech expressions. Those that had a real spark of aptness, a truth in their color, passed into current use. Stump speakers flung them back at their creators; they were picked up by newspapers; and in time passed into general acceptance as correct. It was a language that sought understanding at the level of least education. It reflected a general suspiciousness of studied correctness, and in the beginning it even disdained formal recognition of different social levels. "Our dictionary," noted Crèvecoeur before the nineteenth century, "is short in words of dignity and names of honor." But it was not long until the frontier granted titles to anyone whose calling or whose knack of impersonation seemed to demand them—Judge, General, Colonel, Doctor, Reverend. . . .

Tocqueville found American speech full of abstract terms which enlarged and obscured the thoughts they were intended to convey, and he concluded that democratic nations preferred obscurity to labor—the labor of speaking and writing correctly and clearly. His observation again caught something of the essential character of people working out a great experiment in equality. Make it *sound* grand, they seemed to say, and you *are* grand. Keep it loose, and you are not committed. Generalize, and you are delivered from the concrete which in terms of your own life may be hard and graceless. Roar, and inconvenient truth or painful accuracy may be stilled. To the untutored ear, the accents of education sounded fancy. So, without education, adopt the fanciness, and you will sound educated. Upon such a trait much comic character was based—the itinerant preacher, the courtly Negro, the windy swindler.

American humor rested less on inherent wit or sharp observation of human failings than on rough drolleries full of exaggeration and strange usage for its own sake. The speech became noisy and profuse. It imitated sounds of sucking and smacking and cracking and slicing and chopping and sawing and thumping and poking and digging and clap-ping and exclaiming and hushing. It stuck in extra syllables for elegance and comic surprise. It liked to repeat in the same word the sound of dental consonants that gave a jerky, droll effect. It made comedy out of mouth-widening vowel sounds and speech-yodels whose effect depended upon a swallowed *l*—the gobble of the North American turkey. It was at times almost abstract sound. Its character, stripped of known words and their meaning, and left only with sound, might still suggest the meaning intended, along with the hard, simple, and at times lyrically beautiful life from which it came.

To throw fits into someone was to cornuck him. To mean huge was to say monstropolous. A total abstainer from alcohol abstained teetotaciously. An angelical character was angeliferous. Someone who wanted to flee skedaddled, which meant that he absquatulated. Something complete was bodaciously so. To defeat or overcome was to ram-squaddle and to obliterate was to obflisticate. A strong man was a screamer, and an important one a ripstaver. If a fellow took off his clothes he shucked himself; and a woman suffering from a certain nervous disorder had the peedoodles. If there was a kettle of meat and vegetable stew for supper, it was known as burgoo. To cheat someone, or to deceive with false love, was to honeyfogle. . . . It took only a few such words salted through an otherwise conventional passage of speech or writing to change its character into something entirely new in effect. The effect was that of imaginative enlargement of experience. Even place names reflected the tendency. Audubon on the Mississippi recorded in 1820 that "many places on this River are rendered More terrible in Idea by their Extraordinary Names than real difficulties—". And if the native speech could evoke pictures of rough, hilarious or absurd experience, it could also summon forward much of the accidental beauty that pervaded the memories of the westering people. Again it was Audubon who noted a lovely usage that made a picture of countless frontier encampments: firelight, he said, "is named in some parts of the country, *forest light. . . .*"

In both the grotesque and the lyric lay predictions of the national literature that was to come.

vi. arts and utility

With the open secret of the whopping lie the frontier made its own first conscious literature. Competitions of tall tales were held in which the people tried to create their own myths. Boasts of prowess, marvels of animal origin or reincarnation, farces of anthropomorphism, fabulous reversals of the natural order, minglings of Indian, Gaelic and huntsman's lore—these were typical raw materials for the made-up stories with which improvisers in camp hoped to entertain and stun one another. As they dealt highhandedly with the mysteries of nature, they were in great contrast to the mythologies of all Indians, who stood in awe before the elements; and as they celebrated the rebellious triumphs or howling humiliations of a man alone in the fantastic world, they were opposed in spirit to the decorousness of the Spanish character. So long as there were new sights to behold, new endurances to encounter, the frontier's own literature held the character of a mythology. But it was not long—a matter of a generation—before experience seen in those terms from the inside became the subject of a commercial literature that saw the West from the outside, and found for it a huge national audience. In the end, the commercial literature came back to the frontier, and there the living subjects of its formularistic romances read with credulity and love what it told about the West, very little of which was real or true.

The novels of Fenimore Cooper grafted the frontier forest upon the conventions of European romanticism, and soon a flood of imitations of Cooper's popular creations poured forth from the steam printing presses of the East, and were known as "steam literature." If these were full of wild inaccuracy, they met the desire of whole populations at home and abroad to participate in the early nineteenth century's only new physical adventure.

But truer meanings of the American adventure were gathering to be heard, and would proclaim through Emerson the American mind, that must convert the world, and through Whitman the American body,

that must father upon it a new breed. The Yankee philosopher spoke
for the freedom of the individual intellect and its responsibility in a
democracy. The crowd-roaming poet, revealing the true polarities of the
feminine and the masculine in himself, passionately celebrated the body
of the recumbent land and the body of the democratic man who possessed it. In the central ideas of these two interpreters of the new nation
lay seeds that would grow throughout all significant American literature
after them; for they were mystically sensitive to the essential quality in
the early national experience, and like prophets, spoke it forth to the
future, over the heads of the people, as it were, to their common heirs.

Meanwhile, the people, close to what they had known on the
frontier, gratified in countless ways the memorial impulse, creating the
"old-timer." At a settlers' meeting in Missouri someone read a metrical
catalog of early families, written in a tradition if not in a meter that
recalled Michael Drayton and the Battle of Agincourt, with the names
of common heroes standing forth to kindle the minds of those who had
helped to win a wilderness, a century, a nation:

> Sam Lucas, Boggs and Swearingen,
> The Nolands and the Fristoes, then,
> The Greggs, with Owens two;
> The Davises and the Flournoys,
> The Kings and Staytons and McCoys,
> And Dailey with his twenty boys—
> All these and more we knew. . . .

In such a purpose, however humbly, literature came to the service of
the people.

It was a service required of all the arts in early America. "Nothing," declared Dr. Franklin, "nothing is good or beautiful but in the
measure that it is useful: yet all things have a utility under particular
circumstances. Thus poetry, painting, music (and the stage of their
embodiment) are all necessary and proper gratifications of a refined
state of society but"—and here was suggested an admonitory glance from
aside his small curlicue spectacles—"but objectionable at an earlier
period, since their cultivation would make a taste for their enjoyment
precede its means." But Franklin was looking east, not west, and thinking of opera houses, theatres and museums in the cities of Europe. He
saw that utility must be a determining value for the arts of a forming
democracy; but having little of the creative temperament he forgot that
the arts would never wait for ideal conditions or a refinement of society

to bring them forth. Even as the frontier took its westward course they came forth because it was in their nature never to be denied; and as they appeared in the context of democracy they spoke both to the people and for them.

vii. light in the clearing

By river and by road troupes of theatre players followed the settlers. Floating along waterways actors rehearsed in costume on deck, to the astonishment of people working in riverside fields or travelling along towpaths. In their costume hampers were stuffed the wrinkled habiliments of their repertoire—the blacks of Hamlet, the stripes of Yankee Doodle, the crowns and swords and ermine and velvet for Richard III, plumes for Pizarro. When they came to towns, they played in halls, meetinghouses, later in theatres; and the actors eddied in and out of the public life offstage in grand strangeness, ample of manner, of swelling speech, and garbed in bright colors that would not bear close inspection after hard travel and measly pay. Every frontier American was a hot critic, for he knew something himself about making a character and the art of dissembling. The roving theatre brought with it the magic of a heightened life, and in its freedom of movement and fancy, probed into the longings of its audiences, revealing to them the hidden discontents and shortfallings of the selves that glowed in their desires and that were never so disturbing as when they watched the enactment of a heroic play, however ragged its character, or poor its scenes. Many a playgoer, facile with the emotions of revival and tall tale, fell into confusion watching the actors, and forgetting what was imaginary and what was real, had to be restrained by neighbors from intervening in the acted drama. In the face of such familiar transports the actors were patient; for it was, every time, the greatest tribute they could receive; and for what it signified they stoutly and willingly fought like other pioneers the dangers of frontier travel—Indian attacks upon their little troupe, an occasional robber, uneasy threats by backwoodsmen who resented the appearance of actors with their silky airs, their humbling literacy, their swagger and color, their way with women. . . .

But towns were far between, and the theatre company was ready to play wherever anyone would attend. A cluster of cabins on a riverside, a clearing in a forest—anywhere. In such places the play was given out of doors, with no curtain, and for scenery, only what the woods provided. A space between thickets served as stage, with real trees for "wings" from behind which the actors could enter. Scene and location and date were affirmed, in Elizabethan style, in the spoken text. Tallow candles held in potatoes made footlights, unless the settlement was too poor to spare these, when the lights were made out of old linen rag wicks burning in pans of fat. If not even these were to be had, then the play was given in the dark, and imaginary life rode forth on the voices of actors unseen but speaking with doubled intensity to pierce their listeners who sat on benches facing them, or on the ground. But perhaps the moon was out, and then silvered in common magic the forest, the animated figures striving with one another, the spectators, were united in a creation of spirit as powerful as it was mysterious, and as poignant as it was fugitive; a little point of light shining one night in the deep continental darkness.

The wandering players had their specialties, turns of song, recitation or dance which they gave between the acts of a play, or put together in a whole program as a minstrel show. Their plays were expedient versions of those popular in established Eastern theatres, and sometimes included a vehicle for a famous star, like Junius Brutus Booth, who found on the frontier a certain fulfillment of his mystical and libertarian nature. Some of the plays were of American origin, and many of these were written around a central stock character. They were Yankee plays—*Jonathan Postfree*, or, *The Honest Yankee* (1807); *The Saw-Mill*, or, *A Yankee Trick* (1829); *Solon Shingle, The People's Lawyer* (1839). A recurring figure in plays improvised within a strict convention was the rube who for four acts served as the dupe of clever, rich, educated and cruel men, such as lawyers, bankers, and land speculators; and who in act five turned upon them with blinking innocence that got the best of them every time. The hick in the city presented variations of this democratic passion in which the central figure—in his carrot-red wig, his blacked-out teeth, his baggy pants into which he kept looking with a squirm to see if what he lost was to be found in there, only to be embarrassed to discover the audience watching him in the act—raised the people by impersonating someone laughably lower than their lowest specimen. There were plays on episodes of early American history—*The Arab Chief and the Pirate of the East* (1834), which recalled naval adventures in the Barbary wars; dramas in which Washington appeared; and adaptations of Cooper's novels.

But the most popular native theme was the Indian. In the theatres
of the East, and in the very clearings and at woods-edges where the
people had killed and known killings by Indians, Indian plays were
acted in such profusion that in time it was said that they had become
"perfect *nuisances.*" They presented the tragedy of the Indian, and
recalled promises made by white men and broken. In their explorations,
and perhaps expiations, of the betrayals of human relations and rights,
they accepted the Indian as a human being, with none of the legalistic
debate as to his nature that had for so long occupied the colonial Spaniard. The Indian of the early American theatre was an ideal figure of
natural man, echoing Rousseau's concept of the savage. In *Metamora,* or,
The Last of the Wampanoags, written by John Augustus Stone in 1829,
and played for decades by Edwin Forrest, the Indian hero ended the
play with an apostrophe to the white soldiers who have killed him: "My
curses on you, white men! May the Great Spirit curse you when he speaks
in his war voice from the clouds! Murderers! . . . May your graves and
the graves of your children be in the path the red man shall trace!
And may the wolf and the panther howl over your fleshless bones, fit
banquet for the destroyers! Spirits of the grave, I come! But the curse
of Metamora stays with the white man! I die. . . . [Falls and dies]."
With this play, and in nearly forty others on Indian themes, the audiences who made them so popular seemed to make gestures of poetic
redress, and to bring into the light a sense of guilt toward the Indian
who had suffered the destruction of his liberty and the loss of his land.
Audubon's view of the Indian in 1820 found its echoes in the theatre of
the people for many decades: "Whenever I meet *Indians* I feel the greatness of our Creator in all its Splendor, for there I see the Man Naked
from his Hand and yet free from Acquired Sorrow. . . ." By what they
responded to and thus made profitable the people shaped their own
democratic image in the creative arts of America. The theatre seemed
to make one further gesture in self-portraiture, for even as they continued to take the continent from the Indians, the people used the
theatre as a medium of confession.

viii. sons of harmony

In their music, too, they found community, whether in joining together for religious, political, social, or working occasions. American music was essentially an art of performance rather than of invention. The Puritans brought their hymns with them; and as North American life became more polite than pious, grand musical societies with serious purpose were founded in the cities to produce works of Haydn, Bach, Pleyel, Mozart, Handel, Purcell, Dr. Thomas Arne and Sir Henry Bishop. The Revolution, with its achievement of freedom through martial valor, was followed by a new popularity of music. Francis Hopkinson of Philadelphia came forward as the first sophisticated native composer, composing songs that echoed the manner of Dr. Arne, and reflected the simple sweetness of morning light. His works for harpsichord were given in proper concerts, and a company came to present French opera in New York and Philadelphia, and soon there were attempts to shape dialogue-and-ballad operas on native subjects.

In a more popular vein the fife became the rage. Its shrillness and panic legerity suggested the state of the national feeling. With little stinging scales it challenged the conservatism of the past, forcing an animated vision of a future as brisk and insistent as its own voice. The fife presided at the head of parades and at rallies. If the fifer went travelling, his instrument provided a walking skirl to keep him company and announce him when he arrived at inns, fairs or parties, where being asked he would play solo airs and tweedling songs.

William Billings in the late eighteenth century brought a new formal excitement into the prevailing church music of Puritan psalms sung in unison. In primitive imitation of the high contrapuntal style he arranged them in harmonies for part singing. His tunes made an immediate appeal and on being published in engraved sheets sold widely. They were, he declared, "twenty times as powerful as the old slow tunes," and calling them "fuges," he described their new character in terms of contest between the parts, "each part striving for mastery and victory, the audience entertained and delighted, their minds surpassingly agitated and extremely fluctuated, sometimes declaring for one part, and sometimes for another,"—for all the world like partisans in democratic politics. "Now the solemn bass demands their attention, now the manly tenor;

now the lofty counter, now the volatile treble. Now here, now there; now
here again—O ecstatic!" he cried to his creations, quite carried away by
the sense of movement in his art, "Rush on, you sons of harmony!"

As music went west with the frontier settlers it lost the opportunity for formal performance offered by the cities. In the mountains
and forests, it took the form of traditional songs from the British highlands and, through the Negro, from the west coast of Africa. The frontier
made up few new songs, for the settlers were already past the phase of
civilization in which primitive people originated a folk music. Appala-
chian and savannah and prairie song were all modifications of old
expressions long before developed over the Atlantic in the British Isles
and Africa, and were often corruptions of these. But they were augmented by accidental beauties of tonal expression that Western life produced in its work. On the crystal rivers when a flatboat or keelboat came
to a bend, a boatman sounded a warning on a horn, playing a vagrant
tune that drifted on the water and was lost in the trees—

> O, Boatman! wind that horn again
> For never did the listening air
> Upon its lambent bosom bear
> So wild, so soft, so sweet a strain!

In the golden mists of river perspective it made a signal of wonder,
nostalgia and the stir of going over America, much as the sound of the
railroad whistles would do in later times. Steamboats put the boatman's
horn to rest, for with them came steam screams, a new sound in the
nation's work that must in time find expression in its music. And so too,
the ringing of anvils, the chinking of harness, the locust song of the
power saw. . . .

If music in America drew all its substance from the Old World, and
made little if any gift to the creation of new music, then the rhythms
of work and simple social occasion led to a style of instrumentation and
accompaniment that made do with materials caught up out of common
life. Rough, witty, percussive, the style, listened to fastidiously, might
have seemed almost antimusical; yet in the primitive sense it performed
an essentially musical task—to make rhythm and beat with many percussive means, and assign melody to a single line for violin, flageolet,
voice or group of voices. Western music devoted itself to a lively function—the levitation of the body. To hear it was to see physical gesture—
cakewalk, dance figure, the waggles of convivial drollery. There was
little contemplative or serious role for music. But in its simple repetitive

drive there lay translations of work beats, the blows of mauls and axes and hammers which in a group of working men always fell into accidental syncopation that even more than Negro rhythms may have prefigured the jazz idiom of a century after. Of all percussion instruments, hands were the easiest to use. The gesture again prefigured the form, and evoked the scene with the rhythm of handclaps, either on the beat or off, with single clap or double to the beat—people in a ring, or in line, or in a square, dappled by sunlight through shade out of doors, or shown by the bloom of lanterns indoors, when intense conviviality erased distance and void and wilderness, with choral shrillings and the threeked echo of handclaps in the eaves; in high musical terms a performance rude and graceless, but worthy of respect as a means to let the people stand forth in their hunger for exchange and delivery of spirit. For popular music (like all other popular arts) held little abstract artistic value, but was wonderfully eloquent in describing its makers and users.

Percussion effects to express the simple rhythms that dominated frontier music came from anywhere and everywhere. George Caleb Bingham drew a young riverman sitting on a sawhorse and holding a skillet in one hand while he stroked and struck it with the knuckles of the other, to accompany the sound of a fiddle played by another man sitting on a keg. Negro musicians brought their drum-headed banjos into the people's music, and also taught countless boys how to hold polished pork rib bones between their knuckles, and shake, rattle and roll them with brilliant effect. The jew's-harp though capable of giving an illusion of different pitches made a humming monotone whose only variations were percussive. Drumsticks like knuckles performed on any surface. Flute, flageolet and violin sang melody—if they survived egocentric drives encountered on the frontier: Audubon hearing "a great uproar" one night in his guest room went to find Rafinesque, the naturalist, "running about the room naked, holding the handle of my favorite violin, the body of which he had battered to pieces against the walls in attempting to kill the bats"—of a rare species—"which had entered by the open window." The violin, a Cremona, was demolished. But Audubon still had his flageolet, and when he travelled, staying overnight with strangers, he repaid their hospitality with "a few airs" before taking his leave in the morning.

Popular songs heard in theatres brought together verse and music in strong declamation that swept the audience into joining the refrain, as in a piece that kindled every patriot with its narrative of Jackson's victory over the British in Louisiana:

But Jackson he was wide awake, and wasn't scar'd at trifles,
For well he knew what aim we take with our Kentucky rifles;
So he led us down to Cypress Swamp, the ground was low and mucky;
There stood John Bull in martial pomp: *but here was old Kentucky.* . . .

The actor, dressed in buckskins, threw down his fur cap, and took aim
with his property rifle, and the audience, with handclaps, foot-stamps
and roaring voices, crashed out the chorus between stanzas:

> Oh, Kentucky!
> The hunters of Kentucky!
> Oh, Kentucky!
> The hunters of Kentucky!

Such a song, in both its subject and its clean, hard style, would have the
power to evoke its singers and stompers long afterward.

Group song was a popular pleasure, and the singers developed
their own kind of literacy through a simplified system of musical notation. It was a system that employed notes of distinctive shape repeated
for the several intervals of the scale—some square, others triangular,
others oval, so that they looked like little scatterings of buckwheat
heads on the staff lines. From this resemblance the system, which originated in Lancashire, was called "Buckwheat Notation," at first in derision, later in simple acceptance, as its use spread fast among singers who
found conventional musical notation difficult for sight reading. With the
turn of the eighteenth century, when religious revival meetings swept
the West, shape-note singing became a general accomplishment that was
never to be lost among untrained but fervent folk singers of America.
Songbooks sold widely, and westering travellers took along copies of such
as *The Western Lyre,* issued at Cincinnati in 1831, and *The Missouri
Harmony,* at St. Louis in 1837. Even blank music books went with the
emigrants, who when they heard new songs wrote down text and tune
in buckwheat notation to share them with new friends when their journey allowed. In the hoot and glee of their mingled voices the early
travellers celebrated the community of their hopes, the power of their
faith, and an eternal trial at rising above sin. If what they sang was not
transcendent as music, it served a purpose in harmony with what they
were, taking the voice of each, and for a little while making them all
one, in still another image of the equality and democracy they strove
to create together with their lives.

ix. knacks and crafts

A frontiersman "boasted that with only hickory withes and a jack-knife he could make a very good wagon."

In such a statement lay the seed of all the arts and crafts—the "practical arts" as they were called—in early America. Dr. Franklin's concern for the marriage of beauty and utility was unconsciously answered by the men and women who in successive settlements were obliged by scarcity of rich materials to equip and ornament their daily tasks with objects of their own making. It was natural that the practical arts in a democracy were first of all functional. If the conditions of their lives denied to the settlers access to the fine arts, there was also in the crotchety plainness of the people a hint that the fine arts were suspect. Puritan bleakness was partly responsible for such a view. But another and overriding sense had effect too. This was a democratic suspicion that the fine arts had always been identified with aristocratic patronage. Palaces crammed with splendors, artists appointed to court, prestige and expense attached to the work of master-artists—such airs of luxury seemed highfalutin, and to partake of them called for a whole world of experience, education and allusion in which the democrat could only feel at a disadvantage. In their gnarled self-respect the people must earn their own evolvement of the arts. If at first they must be content with making a beautifully finished rake handle that felt good to the grasp, or a plain little chair that looked polite as it sat empty and felt good as it was occupied, or a wooden decoy duck carved and painted to fool a game bird in early daylight and otherwise to ornament a shelf with its sleek green, brown, gray, black and white reminders of sport and sustenance, then what they fashioned so honestly had the authority of answering honest needs.

In the pattern of ordinary social development the settlers would have climbed through primitive generations or centuries toward a flowering of refined art based on their utilitarian creations. But there were two reasons why such a sequence was not necessary. First, the settlers were not socially primitive people, but civilized people taking new land with a new social idea; and second, to their new idea of man and to new land in which to realize it there was soon added a third newness that swept the first two along at an amazing rate of historical develop-

ment. This was the discovery and spreading use of technological methods
—many new means of making corporate life closer, and individual life
easier, so that united to his fellows the individual was to be relatively
free from toil. The frontiering and completion of the American continent took place during the first years of a world revolution in technology.
The effect of this coincidence upon the people's expression in the arts
was to drive home more deeply than ever the love of usefulness over
beauty—if it came to a choice. The handicraft of the settler would soon
exert itself in designing for machine crafts. Machine crafts would make
possible through duplication of copies a widespread use of what before
had been limited to an original and its user, who was so often its maker.
The spirit of the copy said, My value is in serving as many people as
possible, to help in their lives. Has this work not its own beauty? The
spirit of the original said, I am unique, and my beauty lies in my
rarity, for the touch of my creator is on me everywhere. What matter
that I serve only one?

But there the matter came to a point. For the democratic impulse
sought to bring the goods and beauties of life to as many people as
possible, in contrast to the aristocratic impulse that granted patronage
to art forms for an élite. If traditional fine-art forms were the highest
expression of creative spirit in civilization, then the Americans seemed
to have forgotten the fact; and to have busied themselves with an expression of creative spirit for which the raw material was mankind itself,
in a powerful belief that the arts of living together must come first.
Their masterpiece of creative spirit was the forging of human liberty
and equality in a coherent society. In the process they illustrated the
difference between the practical arts and the fine or inutile arts, considered as historical records.

Through articles made for use, the practical arts left an uncritical
likeness of the society that produced them. On the other hand, the fine,
or inutile, arts always made a conscious criticism or interpretation of the
life from which they grew. This was one of their chief intentions. The
record they left was formal, and while it suggested the taste of the times,
it suggested even more sharply the personality of the designer. The position and character of the arts in America seemed to equate utility with
the anonymous people, and formal beauty with the individual creator
in the fine arts. And as it was the body of the people together who made
the conditions of life, it was their popular expression in the arts and
crafts that achieved originality, style and freshness; while to the scattered few "fine" artists was left the task of treating American subject

matter in techniques and visions imitative of European models. The universal American tinker became a maker of machines for work, the whittler became a sculptor of workaday signs, artisan and artist were one; and their genius for the practical became a national characteristic that would lead to a standard of material life new to the world.

In their conviction of purpose there could also be delight in how they worked; and in countless objects made for use they celebrated their own gaunt graces, and left a record of how, in their spirits, fancy and patience and good sense could meet.

Where color was used, they used it exuberantly, on wood, metal or in fabrics. On the other hand, form was frugal, as the gestures of labor were frugal, with the inference of meeting a purpose with not too little, or too much, but just enough energy. The Conestoga wagon illustrated both idioms of color and form. Shaped like a great open coffer, and slung on wheels to go away, it was just a plain receptacle; but with its bright blue sides, vermilion wheels and dazzling creamy hood of Osnabrück linen, it recalled the painting palette of the Pennsylvania Germans, who made flowers in such frank colors, and stars, fruit, doves, parrots, on their boxes, furniture and certificates of occasion.

Wood was the commonest American material. The continent had a seemingly inexhaustible supply. The frontier American craftsman used it for most houses he built; and for most of the objects that went into a house or served business. He made all manner of chests, none exactly alike, but all sharing a common plainness. If he made a tall clock case, it was severely plain. His benches, beautifully surfaced, remained as close as possible to their original parts of plank and branch. Such severity suggested not only that the maker was a plain man, for religious or other reasons unsympathetic toward rich ornament; but also that he was in a hurry, with many another task awaiting him. But when he came to make machines of wood, his pace of work must have been measured and easy; for what resulted sometimes were such masterpieces of functional design that their beauty would satisfy long later any interest in abstract art. Such machines were a Shaker spinning wheel, with its large delicate wheel suspended above a base remarkably light on slender legs; and a fork for pitching barley and straw that extended four wooden tines in repeated tapering curves in a gesture of work that combined exquisite efficiency with elegance. Something of the same beauty brought thoughtlessly to life out of a grave concern for a good feel and a perfect usefulness could be seen in the wooden stocks made to support the cast metal parts of American rifles. Their tactile appeal, combined out of

finish and shape, was so great that no man could see a good one without
wanting to run his hand over it, even if he wasn't thinking directly about
how a white morning came over whitening water where game must
rise with the day.

Wooden crafts and painting came together in various needs for
painted sculpture, and for outdoor commercial signs. Ships built in the
Eastern yards were given carved figureheads that were portraits of real
men or women, great figures out of the young national history, or
idealized allegorical creations. In their proud realism, these were often
heroic in scale, and carved with wonderful, wavelike freedom of scrolling
design. They were brightly painted and heightened with gold leaf, and
when installed under the bowsprit leaning over the bosom of the waters,
they made visible the personality with which men have always endowed
ships. At the stern, there was often opportunity to create carving and
gilding, where the ship's name and home port were shown. In such long
horizontal panels a peculiarly American style of decoration, using letters and ornaments, treated space with the balance and grace of the
printer's art.

Other figures of popular sculpture were life-sized wooden Indians
or Turks or Negroes to stand before tobacco stores in bright paint and
arresting stare. It took twelve days to make such a figure—six for the
carving at a foot a day, and six for the finishing. To produce hanging
signs for inns, shops, barbers, the craftsman again allied woodworking
to painting, and often called again on the serene severities of typography
to govern the spacing of his symbols and letters. Many such signs were
beautifully contrived and when they called to the customer, did so
calmly, offering, at inns, the one word, "Entertainment," and displaying, for shops, carved likenesses of wares in bas-relief.

Painting was allied to metal crafts in the production of such
articles as tin utensils, canisters, pots, trays and boxes; andirons and
bootjacks and hitching posts that represented human or animal figures;
and various toys. The metal craftsman made weather vanes in every
kind of symbol. The conventional cock was joined by new designs, with
certain ones recurring to reflect the interests of the public—a fish, a
whale, a grasshopper, a trotting horse, a horse in extended racing stride,
a frigate in full sail, a locomotive and tender. These were painted or
treated entirely with gold leaf or left in the black silhouette of wrought
iron. Lanterns and candlesticks and trivets; locks, hinges and latches;
firemarks in iron with designs that again recalled typography—all had
simple grace and the occasional appealing falter whereby the hand of

the originator could be detected. It was in duplicated objects of cast metal that the impersonality of the coming steam power era was suggested—rifle barrels, spread eagles for flagpole and cornice finials, plain iron kettles with their three little legs cast on the pouchlike belly.

In weaving, embroidering, rugmaking, quilting, women contributed to the idiom of American crafts. The richly colored floral and vinelike designs of crewel embroidery derived from Jacobean England were succeeded by plainer patterns in hard homespun cloth. Weaving tablecloths and bedspreads and coverlets, the housewife developed simple geometries that repeated variations based on squares and triangles, frequently in colors of blue and white. Her most personal style appeared in quilting. Here was an exercise in thrift, for she used patches of cloth saved from every which source; and in ingenuity, for her hope was to achieve symmetrical patterns out of scraps that came along with no rhyme or reason; and in patience, for a quilt was big, to fit on a man-and-wife bed, and to make only one six-inch-square patch of the ten dozen or so needed would call for thousands of stitches. But she persisted, and produced an original work whose simplicity and modesty told much about her life and the joys of her labors throughout many hours made up of a few minutes here, a few there, when in repose she was not idle.

x. first interpreters

Little—almost none—of the formal art of painting told as much about American life as such workaday crafts. Before the 1840s only two painters—Edward Hicks and James John Audubon—brought together matter and manner in styles that yielded out of imagination and experience true images of the new America. Hicks was a native artist whose painting arose from two other prepossessions—religion and his trade as a coach builder. He was a Quaker preacher, and the austere tenets of his church gave simplicity to his vision, and educated him in terms of Biblical literalism. His working trade called for decorative painting on the panels of carriages, and for it he learned to grind his own color, and to make his own brushes. Moving from Pennsylvania to New York, and on to Maryland, and Ohio, he worked as house painter, sign painter, and carriagemaker, rising in Quaker meeting wherever he might be. Something in his spirit told him that painting pictures was ungodly, yet

something else told him more strongly that it was a delight and in the
end a necessity. He tried to compose his warring spirits by devoting his
paints to religious themes. His pictures took well with the public, and
in time even the Quakers encouraged him in his art, provided he pursued it "within the bounds of innocence." Self-trained, his talent developed until in his most famous subject matter he gave forth in composed
enchantment his vision of life. It described the human and animal
worlds as he would see them, and it identified the act of colonization in
North America with the ultimate equality of creatures promised by
the prophet Isaiah:

> The wolf also shall dwell with the lamb, and the leopard shall
> lie down with the kid; and the calf and the young lion and the
> fatling together; and a little child shall lead them. And the cow
> and the bear shall feed; their young ones shall lie down together;
> and the lion shall eat straw like the ox. And the sucking child
> shall play on the hole of the asp, and the weaned child shall put
> his hand on the cockatrice' den. They shall not hurt nor destroy
> in all my holy mountain; for the earth shall be full of the knowl-
> edge of the Lord, as the waters cover the sea.

The Reverend Mr. Hicks painted a picture of that vision. If he had
painted it only once, it would perhaps not have furnished sufficient
evidence for his general emotion. But he painted it over thirty times,
and its idyllic democracy stood for what he felt in his nation, believed of
his God, and desired of his fellow creatures. His treatment of Isaiah's
vision was perfectly literal. There were the animals, clustered together in
peace—he called his subject "The Peaceable Kingdom"—and yes, there
a little child led them, and other little children set their hands over the
serpents' pits; and upon the animal faces lingered bewitched expressions
that seemed to veil yet reveal human thoughts. In the middle distance
was an allegorical group representing William Penn making his treaty
with the Indians, and on a lovely bay beyond lay a ship with pearly
sails. Come, said the painting, let all manner of men, as well as all
manner of animals, dwell together in peace. Let this occur, it implied
further, in our great land of North America, with its waters, mountains,
and endless depths of forest. With one huge oak set against dense
shadowy foliage Hicks suggested inexhaustible America; and in the
prim, sweet compliance of his animals and Indians and colonists with
the spirit of peace and equality he captured the desire that had con-

ceived America. Everything in the work was "within the bounds of innocence"—the concept, the drawing, the design, the color scheme; nothing
in it owed a debt to European conventions of art.

The reverend carriagemaker illustrated in his career how in
America's early arts they best saw and captured America who sought her
humbly, through crafts and other acts of work.

A number of beautifully gifted artists before Hicks painted
American portraits and historical subjects, but by the spirit of their
training and technique, they remained colonials. Copley was the American Reynolds, Stuart the American Romney, Sully the American Lawrence, and so on. However rich and copious their productions, they
could not suggest the new America so well as the work of another artist
who when he went to work had no conscious plan to catch a likeness
of America. But that was what he caught, in the general passion of his
first purpose, which was scientific. That he was not a native American
made no difference to his capture of the American essence in his work.
Beginning with Asiatic migrations after the ice age. America was always
peopled by foreigners. What mattered was how he saw a new land in
its new lights:

"Imagine," wrote a French critic who saw a first showing of his
work in 1827 at Edinburgh, "imagine a landscape wholly American,
trees, flowers, grass, even the tints of the sky and the waters, quickened
with a life that is real, peculiar, trans-Atlantic. On twigs, branches, bits
of shore, copied by the brush with the strictest fidelity, sport the feathered races of the New World, in the size of life, each in its particular
attitude, its individuality and peculiarities. Their plumages," and it
was of course Audubon's birds of which he wrote, "sparkle with nature's
own tints; you see them in motion or at rest . . . singing, running,
asleep, just awakened, beating the air, skimming the waves, or rending
one another in their battles. It is a real and palpable vision of the New
World, with its atmosphere, its imposing vegetation, and its tribes
which know not the yoke of man. The sun shines athwart the clearing
in the woods; the swan floats suspended between a cloudless sky and a
glittering wave; strange and majestic figures keep pace with the sun;
. . . and this realization of an entire hemisphere, this picture of a
nature so lusty and strong, is due to the brush of a single man; such
an unheard-of triumph of patience and genius! . . ."

If the French critic did not know America, it was likely that he
knew Europe; and the important thing in his impression of Audubon's
world was that it was strange and new, in its golden stands of light,

its vast river prospects, its blue perspectives stepping away into woods and mountains; all incidental to the bird or animal so studiously arrested in the foreground—incidental, but again, as though early America had to be seen obliquely lest she vanish, standing forth in the truth. Over his shoulder, so to speak, and beyond his scientific purpose, Audubon saw the land and fixed it forever in its spacious morning sense.

There were other painters who combined scientific interests with the arts, like little Leonardos. The Peales of Philadelphia operated a museum of curiosities that included scientific specimens. Samuel F. B. Morse along with his telegraph and Robert Fulton with his improved steamboat were literate painters in conventional styles. The American forerunner in any craft of life seemed required to possess various knacks, if he would be self-sufficient, and also serve his countrymen with all the talents needed to throw together a new culture.

xi. the american art

"It is not," wrote John Adams to his wife Abigail from Paris in 1780, "it is not indeed the fine arts which our country requires; the useful, the mechanic arts are those which we have occasion for in a young country." Wandering about Paris, he could have filled volumes with descriptions of temples and palaces, paintings, sculptures, tapestry, porcelain, and so on, if he only had the time. But this, he said, he could not do without neglecting his duty. And what was his duty? "The science of government is my duty to study, more than all other sciences." And as for the arts—"the arts of legislation and administration and negotiation ought to take the place of, indeed, to exclude, in a manner, all other arts. I must study politics and war, that my sons may have liberty to study mathematics and philosophy. My sons ought to study mathematics and philosophy, geography, natural history and naval architecture, navigation, commerce, and agriculture, in order to give their children a right to study painting, poetry, music, architecture, statuary, tapestry and porcelain. Adieu."

In 1817 he still had qualms about the general subject. "Is it possible to enlist the 'fine arts,'" he asked, "on the side of truth, of virtue, of piety, or even of honor? From the dawn of history they have been prostituted to the service of superstition and despotism." He even graded the arts in the order of their perfidy, "History and epic poetry are worse than architecture, sculpture, and painting, because they are more lasting deceptions." But though he felt that the sciences and arts, for all their failings, had "vastly and immensely ameliorated the condition of man, and even improved his morals," there seemed actually little to be done about disciplining them. "It is in vain to think of restraining the fine arts," he concluded. "Luxury will follow riches and the fine arts will come with luxury in spite of all that wisdom can do. . . ."

John Adams did not see how widely characteristic of the American people was Dr. Franklin's notion that beauty depended wholly upon utility. If what the people made for usefulness had beauty, it lay in abstract qualities that recalled the gestures of human purpose and use. Every act of building and equipping of America for work was admittedly a worthwhile social achievement. But was it any the less an aesthetic achievement to create the very subject of America at work than to comment upon the subject afterward in the formal processes of art? This was the question that America asked of the traditional arts, and would continue to ask in creating all forms of technological design. To make the society itself flower and sprout color and fulfill purpose—this was the American art, and its medium was the liberty of the individual citizen.

In the immense neighborhoods of the frontier the settlers came together from their scatterings in field and forest to help each other at tasks too great for a single family. And when they gathered, they made entertainment out of their work, at husking bees, flax-scutching bees, house-raising bees. Whiskey flowed, and great meals were cooked out of doors in pits of embers, and not only many hands, but shared ideas of how to do it, made light work. Holding strong desires for freedom from all bondages, including that of primitive labor, the Americans became virtuosos of convenience in living. What they discovered about the conquest of manual labor they were able to share by the same means that would in the end make them neighbors in common knowledge over the whole continent—instruments of communication such as those that came into being and use at the very time of the westward movements of the first half of the nineteenth century—the steamboat, the electric telegraph, developments in printing methods, the steam locomotive. An American song gave a sense of exhilaration that came with the railroads:

    Singing through the forest,
    Rattling over the ridges,
    Shooting under arches,
    Running over bridges. . . .

There was a national genius for "make-do." The boundaries of material development seemed to be pushed back in a new dimension of ingenuity; and the nation felt the brisk joy of working all technical limitations to their utmost limit. Common sense was put to work with uncommon energy; and Dr. Franklin's imported rationalism, the seed of technology, appeared to become an American trait. In its spirit of inquiry, it faced the Americans not only to the west, but also to the morrow. If the Indians in their dateless time had been bound by the present, and the Spaniards by the past in their collective memory, then the Americans had a passion for the future. The future was the American theme. To make a better life today, yes, they strove; but there would be tomorrow a still better one, right there on earth; and to achieve this, as surely it would be achieved, every citizen believed he had his chance, in his own way. Because enough people believed so, they created a nation of the many, governed by all, for the benefit of each in his own terms of life, liberty and the pursuit of happiness so long as these did not undo the voted will of the majority.

3.

Bivouac

  This creation was the inheritance of the troops gathering on the Texas river in the mildness of March, 1846; and in all their separate persons and various fashions they bore living evidence of the national character. If it was a complex character, yet through all the common expressions of its owners—their vision of human life, their energy and materialism, their politics and oratory and language, their dominant

religion and mythology, their theatre and music and crafts, their dedication to the affairs of work and business—shone a single faith. It was
faith in democracy, whose power in national terms was about to meet
another test facing Mexico.

> Oh, say were you ever in Rio Grande?
> Way, you Rio!
> Oh, were you ever on that strand?
> For we're bound to the Rio Grande!

The song was heard on the supply ships standing in for General
Taylor's depot at Point Isabel; and in a plowed field on the north bank
of the river opposite Matamoros on March twenty-eighth where the
Army was camped in a square with its wagons in the middle which
seemed to a young officer "a very bad position for defense." In the afternoon a flag staff was planted on which the Stars and Stripes were run
up "in a prompt and spirited manner while a band of music struck
up our National air," creating "a momentary stir among the spectators
on the opposite bank." Presently General Taylor sent Brigadier General
William J. Worth across the river to make representations to a Mexican
general officer who "viewed with great indignation our flag planted on
Mexican soil." A United States lieutenant read a paper, prepared in
French, stating for General Taylor that his troops were present under
orders of President Polk to take peaceable possession of the country as
far as the left bank of the Rio Grande and that General Taylor hoped
the Mexican commander would see nothing in the act to produce hostility between the two countries. The Mexican general—it was R. D. de la
Vega, who represented General Mejía, the commander of Matamoros—
listened while a subordinate translated the message into Spanish, and
then asked,

"It is the intention of General Taylor to remain with his army
on the left bank of the Rio Grande?"

"Most assuredly," replied General Worth, "and there to remain
until directed otherwise by his government."

General Worth now asked to see the American consul at Matamoros. The request was refused. Worth frowned. Was the consul a
prisoner? he asked. No, Vega said, not at all, he was "in full exercise
of his functions." Moreover, no American in the city was in arrest.
Worth drew himself up.

"I have now to state," he said, "that a refusal of my demand to
see the American consul is regarded as a belligerent act; and in conclu-

sion, I have to add, the commanding general of the American forces
on the left bank of the river will regard the passage of any armed party
of Mexicans in hostile array across the Rio Grande as an act of war,
and pursue it accordingly."

The interview was over. Worth and his officers were ferried back
across the river by Mexican boatmen. Evening came in like sea mist
from Mexico Bay. Soon there was formations of firelight outlining
the American bivouac. In the darkness no lights showed in Matamoros.
Through rain that fell all night long the American soldiers heard men
digging and piling earth across the river; and when morning came saw
that there were new earthworks facing them with a Mexican twelve-
pounder siege gun in position.

4·

The Army of the Rio Grande

Matamoros seen from the opposite bank in morning light appeared
to be embedded in a great garden, with the unfinished plaster towers of
the church rising out of greenery. Beyond the town lay gardens and
cotton fields. The settlement reached up and down the river for a mile.
It was still the river of palms, though no longer so named. Tall ranks
of palm trees stood along the banks, and inland, along the ridges of old
resacas, that were former beds of the river. The river's course in 1846 made
deep meanders about Matamoros. The town lay half a mile back from
two wide sandy lobes of ground into which fitted a single lobe of the
opposite bank. In the center of the Texas lobe that bulged into Mexico
American soldiers on the morning of March twenty-ninth began to build
a defensive position for the first battery to be placed. They named it
Fort Texas. Its guns stared straight at the headquarters of General
Mejía across the way. Earth was hauled and piled by a different regiment each day, as the design of a fortress was laid out with six bastion

fronts. In plan, the fort looked like a great snowflake. It was large enough to hold four or five regiments. The flagpole rose from within its massive sloping walls that went higher every day.

The Mexicans were busy too. Following the river bend opposite Fort Texas they too raised earthen banks to protect newly placed batteries of mortars and bombs. Upstream they threw together another defense, a hollow square of piled earth, that they named Fort Paredes. Over the town flew four Mexican flags; and the flags of England, France and Spain, to locate their national consulates, and in the event of bombardment to proclaim immunity. It was easy to see both ways across the river; even to hear. The two armies watched each other over the shoulder, as it were, while each continued preparations for what to do to the other. Mexicans were confident of winning if war broke out. Mexican troops greatly outnumbered American forces, and even to European observers the United States seemed to be risking defeat in Mexico's great northern deserts.

United States troops wandered about off duty on their side of the river and saw their first scraps of Mexican life. About twenty houses stood in the fields near the bivouac. Most of their families had fled across the river after the arrival of the army. Every family had a goat in the house, and a gamecock tied under every bed. Up and down river were gardens where grew lemons, oranges, figs, peaches; and lines of palms bearing plantain and cocoanut. From the little farms came those few Mexicans who had stayed home, and who now brought chickens, vegetables and milk to sell to the troops. After a day or two, vendors from Matamoros came and went freely among the Americans, selling food and oddments. Among them, the Army was certain, there were many spies who saw and heard all they needed, while "we are doing nothing," observed a young Kentuckian early in April, adding that "an enterprising general might have cut us to pieces any night since our arrival here." He sighed. He did not want to censure General Taylor who, he could only assume, had information denied to others.

Watching each other prepare for war, the armies kept up a social tone across the river. Work and drill were plainly visible both ways, and were observed with interest and often with admiration. The Mexicans made frequent rumpus with drums and trumpets during the day. Detachments were marched and countermarched, and American regulars lounged on their bank and applauded. The Mexican river front became a promenade where in open carriages the best society drove along to greet the Americans. Gallant conversations were held across the stream.

Compliments flew. Friendships were pledged. Many of the Mexican officers were handsome, beautifully uniformed and wonderfully graceful in their manners. Beside them, their soldiers were "half-starved-looking devils" who excited in the Americans "only feelings of contempt." Both armies loved band music, and gathered to listen to each other's at sundown. While the women of Matamoros dawdled by in their lacy rebozos on the opposite shore, the hungry men so far from home gave them music. "We played 'Yankee Doodle' because it made a loud noise, the 'Star Spangled Banner' because it waved over us, 'Hail Columbia' because it was inspiriting, and the sweetest airs from the operas for the beautiful señoritas." But when the Mexican music came, it was "exquisite . . . surpassing anything ever heard from a military band." And then the warm April night was on them in darkness, and the riverside amenities were done, and back in camp, at tattoo, the American soldiers heard how a large force of Mexican cavalry was thought to have crossed the river below them, and all were ordered to memorize the watchword— "Texas"—and to sleep on their arms without undressing. But morning came without incident, and work went on, and in the afternoon, perhaps, there was something curious to be seen at Fort Paredes, where the work was nearly done. There, if they would stroll to the river, the Americans could see the Mexican soldiers kneeling on the ramps and parapets of earth they had thrown up, while a priest in a white cope heavy with gold bullion blessed the fort, scattering holy water everywhere on it, that it might with divine assistance stand with them against wound, death and defeat in their cause. In the mystery of the blessing there lay somewhere embedded the mystery of the common soldier's thought of war—how little he might gain for himself, how much of himself he might lose.

Some thought about it until it made them change their minds. One afternoon early in April both armies heard rapid volleys of rifle fire downstream from Fort Texas, below the central ferry crossing. On hearing the fire, the Mexican pickets at the ferry ran away "like scared dogs" to Matamoros. Soldiers from Fort Texas swarmed to the bank and saw that their own sentries were firing at a deserter who was trying to swim the river to escape to Mexico. He was hit. He sank and drowned. It was a scene to be repeated many times. Upward of thirty men deserted the American flag in the first few weeks on the river.

While work went forward at Fort Texas the depot at Point Isabel was daily growing. Dispatch riders and wagons moved back and forth between the two posts. Troops built quarters and warehouses and dock facilities at Point Isabel. The installation was called Fort Polk. New shipping came in almost daily. The bar at the entrance of the Arms of Saint James was only eight feet under water, and the broad side-wheeler steamers took it gingerly. There was a story that in ancient times one of the largest and richest of Mexican cities stood at the entrance only to be swept away by the sea in a storm; and another that a later Mexican village with a fort and a garrison of sixty Mexican soldiers was wiped away in a single night by a hurricane, leaving only the low, bare sand islands that paralleled the coast. The only other settlement on the nearby beaches was a village called Bagdad that stood on a sandspit on the last Mexican bank of the Rio Grande at its mouth. There came Mexicans from as far away as Monterrey to enjoy bathing in the sea. It was subject not only to Gulf storms, but to high water when the river overflowed its low dunes in flood, and the waters shifted back and forth in dispute over ocean floor and beach. The bar at the river's mouth had even less water than the Brazos entrance, and the Army had not yet received vessels shallow enough in draft to enter the river, where no steamboat had entered since the departure of Captain Austin's *Ariel* in 1830. All supplies in the first weeks of April, 1846, came over the road from Point Isabel to Fort Texas. On the fifth, the Army's heavy guns, eighteen-pounders, arrived from Point Isabel to be emplaced in the fort.

General Taylor regarded in patience the preparations made at his command. Certain of his officers wished he might move a little faster. It had taken over a year since annexation was approved by Congress to bring an army to the Rio Grande. And now that it was there, could not something more be done, if not to give battle, then at least to smarten up the camp, guard against spies, drill the troops . . . ?

But the General was calm. He rode his horse, old Whitey, among the tents, the working parties, the soldiers lounging off duty, and gave homely reassurance just by his looks. His face was wrinkled and dark yellow, and he took less trouble about a uniform than any of his private soldiers. Now he wore an old oilcloth cap, and again a farmer's broad-brimmed straw hat, or even a big Mexican sombrero. His coat was either of blue-checked gingham, or a faded green homespun, or a linen roundabout duster, or a brown fustian. Sometimes he wore linen trousers, or attakapas pantaloons, or "a common soldier's light-blue overalls," or blue Army pants without braid. Someone said he looked rather like Fenimore Cooper. The men knew his goodness of heart, for like them he felt as "honest and as good as anybody." He lived in a

plain unguarded tent under a cottonwood tree a little way from a pond
that had an island in it. From it he could watch Fort Texas and the
granular glisten of camp life under the Mexican sun.

Some of his officers chafed under his limitations of mind and
education. "Slow of speech," with "a stammering voice," he could make
his wishes known, but before they could become official, someone had
to put them into readable English. If he took a dislike to a man, he was
passionate and implacable forever after against him. For most men in
the American government he had a suspicious contempt, like any voter
jealous of power held over him even by his consent. Theoretical refinements of strategy and tactics were foreign to his mind; but "a certain
bull-headed obstinacy" in his character gave him the force—the slow,
undeviating force—he could throw into a fight; and the common Army
received it through his presence in his wanderings among them; and
through what they heard of him in his headquarters. Missing nothing,
giving a minimum of orders, he waited for the American position on
the north bank of the river to develop; while he sat in his camp chair
and told and listened to stories that would make him laugh till the tears
ran down his face—preferably the same stories, over and over, by the
hour—in the comforting drone of a simple man who had no love and
no brilliance for anything but his uncomplicated vision of duty.

The troops of General Taylor's command were regulars. Volunteers would join him later. For the present he had not more than twenty-
three hundred men, while his staff estimated that the Mexicans could
certainly oppose them with three or four times as many. More than
one American officer thought it "a mistake to come with so small a
force . . . no one seems to think a disaster to our Army a thing possible,
and most of the Army are disappointed and impatient that General
Taylor does not create a pretext for taking the town." True, it did not
seem plausible that the Mexicans had any discipline; but the Americans
also labored under a disadvantage—some of the senior officers were incapable of drilling them. "We ought to have the best-instructed troops
in the world," sighed a brilliant lieutenant colonel commanding the
Third Infantry, "but are far from it." General Taylor knew nothing of
army movements, and only one brigade commander out of three could
"give the simplest command . . . 'break to the right or march to the left,'
for instance—" without the prompting of an adjutant. The common drill
of the battalion was impossible to execute, much less the movements of
a brigade or an army. It was a comfort that the Third Infantry, at least,
was well-trained, "for every officer and every man knows his place and

duty." Lieutenant U. S. Grant did not agree entirely with such an estimate of the army as a whole, for he believed that "the officers of the regular Army, from highest to lowest, were educated in their profession." A more efficient army for its number and "armament" never "fought a battle than the one commanded by General Taylor on Mexican—or Texan—soil." But then Lieutenant Grant was not yet of the line; he was a quartermaster, to whom an infantryman would deny an opinion on the fitness of troops.

The enlisted soldiers were men who had gone into the Army in peacetime to serve for seven dollars a month. At that rate few officers expected to find a very superior breed of individual in the ranks. The opportunities of American civil life drew men of ambition with their expanding rewards; and only when volunteers later came to the Army, to fight for patriotic reasons, was the quality of the enlisted soldiers improved. Among the regulars were many soldiers of foreign birth—English, Irish, French, German, Polish. Many of these were veterans of the Napoleonic wars. To them Mexico offered free land—three hundred and twenty acres to a private soldier, more to holders of higher grades—and immunity if they would desert. Enough did so to form what was called the San Patricio Battalion of the Mexican forces.

Except for a few companies that carried recently developed percussion-cap muskets, the infantry under General Taylor was armed with flintlock muskets that were charged with paper cartridges packed with powder, buckshot and ball. Their range was only a few hundred yards. Everyone wore blue—the men, jackets, trousers and fatigue caps of light blue; the officers, dark blue frock coats and light blue trousers with braid. In the artillery was vested most of the dash and prestige of United States arms. Taylor had four twelve-pounder howitzers that threw shell, and four deep-voiced eighteen-pounders for siege. Beyond these, he commanded the latest glory of the Army, which was the mobile, light, horse-drawn cannonry trained to maneuver fast in the field, and which was known as the "Flying Artillery." Its weapons were brass six-pounders that fired solid shot. Its officers—Ringgold, Duncan, Bragg, Ridgely—were young men all trained at West Point. They had the spirit of those who knew they belonged to a corps d'élite: and who swore that their new weapon—the Flying Artillery—was the key to victory in all future warfare. Even their vocabulary reflected their high style: in 1846 a shot from a cannon was called a "blizzard."

As April wore on, preparations continued on the river. Soldiers soon found it dangerous to explore the countryside. One, Colonel Cross,

the chief quartermaster, rode out alone on the tenth of April and did
not come back. All the American power was concentrated in Fort Texas,
with its heavy guns. Outside its bastions loomed a battery containing
two howitzers. The Mexicans completed six batteries, strung along the
river, and—it was somewhat dismaying—planted in deep pits protected
by high embankments in front, until it seemed that "they could not be
knocked out, or only with luck or difficulty, by the American fire." From
such hidden positions the Mexican fire, if it came, would rise in high
lobs to sail heavily across the river and fall from almost directly above
into Fort Texas, and upon the tenting grounds gathered about it. The
weather was odd—warm nights and cold, alternately; and one afternoon
a sheeting rain came in on a sudden gale and swamped the camp. Tents
were blown down in the company streets, and everything in them was
soaked. If General Taylor went on waiting, so did the commander in
Mexico.

5.

The Cannonade

What General Mejía was waiting for became clear on April
eleventh, when the Americans heard the bells of Matamoros suddenly
clamoring in jubilee and a salute of twenty guns going off. They piled
toward the river to observe a grand affair. With two hundred new troops,
General Pedro de Ampudia, the old North Mexican campaigner, was
arriving in Matamoros to relieve General Mejía of command. The
Mexican garrison paraded in honor of their new commanding general,
while the Mexican bands of music "excelled all former efforts." Late in
the afternoon Ampudia came down to the riverside to inspect the fortifications. On his left breast he wore a decoration awarded to him for
his triumph over the Texans at Mier. Stories about him came across
the river by pedlar, and flew through the American camp: he was a

great general, he was a brave man, he was a bloodthirsty fiend who in marching to the river just now had refused to be encumbered by sick and straggling soldiers and had ordered such wretches to be shot.

The next day at three o'clock two Mexican officers came down to the ferry on their bank with a trumpeter and sounded a parley. Matters were beginning to move. Ampudia's representatives were brought across. They were taken to General Taylor's tent under its cottonwood. There they handed a document to the commander of the Army of the Rio Grande. General Ampudia, it stated, would not insult the good sense of General Taylor by explaining "the many grounds for just grievances felt by the Mexican nation," but required him "in all form, and at latest in the peremptory term of twenty-four hours" to break up his camp and retire to the north bank of the Nueces river, so allowing the two governments to regulate "the pending question of Texas." If General Taylor insisted "in remaining upon the soil of the department of Tamaulipas," war must follow.

General Taylor accepted the message, and said that he would answer it at ten o'clock the following morning. The Mexican officers were escorted back to the ferry, and the staff went to work that same afternoon to elevate General Taylor's wishes into a proper dispatch. He wanted it said that as an Army commander he could have no truck with another government in diplomatic affairs. He would remind Señor General Don Pedro de Ampudia, though, that the United States government had done its best to settle the Rio Grande dispute by peaceful means, but without any success. Meantime, he was ordered to occupy and hold the country up to the left bank of the river until the whole shebang was definitely settled, and in obeying his orders, he had made no hostile moves. To wind up the argument, he could not, under his orders, back up from where he was—or, as the educated adjutant put it, "to retrograde from the position which I now occupy." The General wanted it added in there somewhere that he was sorry for the other choice left to him by General Ampudia, with "the individual suffering that may result"; but he wanted it understood that he would "by no means avoid such alternative, leaving the responsibility with those who rashly commence hostilities." He had the honor to be—and here the adjutant nodded—"very respectively, your obedient servant."

Promptly at ten o'clock in the next morning the answer was delivered across the river; and at two o'clock an American dragoon patrol rode up to headquarters to report that Mexican troops were crossing the river into Texas some miles below camp. Nothing further was heard of this Mexican movement. But if the enemy was receiving supplies by ship at the river's mouth where there were no American troops yet posted, access to the sea was denied Ampudia by General Taylor's next move, when he requested Commodore Connor to blockade the entrance with units of the United States Home Squadron.

The General had a Mexican man of affairs on his staff, a certain Chapita, who had connections in Matamoros. On April fifteenth Chapita flourished a piece of information—Ampudia, so lately installed as commander of the north, was soon to be displaced by another veteran of Texas and north Mexican campaigns, General Mariano Arista, a tall, redheaded soldier who having lived in Cincinnati, Ohio, presumably knew how to treat with Americans. The opinion went around the American officers' messes that his appointment indicated peace for a while— "the war is put off till June. This ends the chapter. There will not be a hostile gun fired, but we shall have to drag through a hot and tedious summer here without our families, infinitely worse than all the horrors of war. It is nonsense," declared an American major, "for our government to temporize any longer with Mexico." Were there not provocations enough?

Colonel Cross, for example—what had become of him? Were Mexicans responsible for his disappearance? On the seventeenth of April a detachment was ordered to the field under the command of Lieutenant Theodoric Porter (son of Commodore David Porter) to find out. Two days later men from Porter's detail came straggling into the camp to hack out a sobering story. In a hard rainstorm at night they had been attacked by Mexicans, members of a guerilla band led by a border bandit called Roman Falcón. In the downpour, the Americans found most of their powder wet. Lieutenant Porter was killed, with several of his soldiers. The survivors came home sure that just so had Colonel Cross been killed, though his body had not been found. But in another two days it was discovered by another scouting party. There was nothing left but his skeleton and a few scraps of equipment. Coyotes and buzzards had picked the bones clean. Was nothing to be done about such an outrage? But a state of war did not yet exist.

And then, on April twenty-third, President Paredes appeared before the Congress of Mexico to declare that "from this day defensive way begins," and was received with enthusiasm.

His statement was timed to give strategic—and legal—support to the command at Matamoros; for on the following day Mariano Arista arrived to relieve Pedro de Ampudia, with orders to go into action immediately. One day later a large force of cavalry under General Anastasio Torrejón crossed the Rio Grande above Fort Texas. The movement was met at Carricitos Ranch by a scouting party of sixty-three men under Captain Seth Thorton. Eleven Americans were killed, several wounded, and the rest captured to be taken to Matamoros. It was the first engagement of the war, and word of it was sent by express courier to the President and the Cabinet at Washington, who still hoped to make their point by peaceful means.

Close on such a first success, the Mexican forces now crossed the river, above and below Fort Texas, by-passing the American main body, and manoeuvring to close behind it to cut it off from the supply base at Point Isabel. Communications with the base were already precarious. So many Mexican troops were massing on the coast that reports came into camp telling how Point Isabel had already been attacked. Not Chapita, but his nephew, had the best story—how two regiments of Mexican infantry and one of cavalry had been "cut to pieces" by American artillery. The whole story was false. Point Isabel was still safe, and Commodore Connor had sailed for the Arms of Saint James to land five hundred marines and sailors, having left another large detachment on land at the river's mouth. On April twenty-eight for an hour before nightfall there was a continuous fire of musketry in Matamoros. American officers wondered if a revolt had broken out across the way. But the matter was never explained. General Taylor informed his staff that evening that he would march in six days—on May third—with the bulk of the Army to protect Point Isabel and throw back the enemy, "wherever he found him." To defend Fort Texas, he would leave the Seventh Infantry behind, and the "sick, lame and lazy, with Land's and Bragg's artillery." Major Jacob Brown was assigned the command of Fort Texas. His orders from General Taylor were clear: he must maintain his post, he must on no account risk his position by making a sally, and if he were surrounded and besieged he must inform the General by firing the eighteen-pounders of Fort Texas at regular intervals, which would be heard at Point Isabel through the heavy sea air. At last a young officer was able to exclaim to his diary, "Glorious times these!"

He left for glory three days sooner than the Commanding General had planned, for on the morning of May first a large Mexican force crossed the river below Matamoros, moving up the coast toward Point Isabel. General Taylor alerted the army and at two o'clock began to pull away from the Rio Grande on the narrow road that was bordered by old river beds edged with palms. "I go to meet the enemy," recorded the young officer, "with my feelings all schooled to do my duty regardless of personal consequences." They marched for eighteen hours and encamped at midnight without having seen the enemy. At daybreak the long column of infantry, flying artillery, dragoons and wagons moved out again. By noon they were arriving at Point Isabel where across the low dunes tufted with sharp grass they could see the etched black spars and idle smoke of the fleet in the harbor. The troops were hungry. They'd had no coffee and little else to eat or drink since leaving Fort Texas. Soon they found oranges and lemons to suck for thirst, but there was only one water well—a new one dug by the army—to meet the wants of nearly two thousand men. They slept on the ground that night without fires or blankets, and only the officers had tents. Pickets strained for sign of the enemy in the dark.

None came.

A little while after day broke over the sea, and before reveille, the sleeping camp was awakened by heavy sound from far away. Men lifted their heads to listen. They heard cannonading from the Rio Grande, and knew Fort Texas and its little garrison were under bombardment. The stifled thumps of the distant cannon "were listened to with feelings so intense that our soldiers fairly ceased for a moment to breathe." In a few minutes the "camp was wild with excitement," for as Lieutenant Grant said, "The war had begun." Worried by what they could hear, they yet dreaded to have it cease, for continued cannonading was the "best proof that the Fort" had "not fallen. . . ." It kept up all day; and at night, riding hard with four voluntary companions, Captain Samuel H. Walker, of the Texas Rangers, on orders of General Taylor, returned to Fort Texas for news.

6.

Fort Texas

He approached the fort early the next morning and made his way carefully into the dry moat that surrounded it. There he signalled and was recognized by Major Brown, who had him brought up by a ladder. They exchanged their news. The bombardment beginning at five that morning, said Major Brown, must have thrown over fifteen hundred shots and shells at Fort Texas throughout the day. Remarkably little damage was done to the fort, though one soldier was killed. Even the tents of the Seventh Infantry, set up within the walls, and the horses of the dragoon company, tied to picket lines there, were not hit. The garrison's gunners knocked out two of the heaviest Mexican cannon, and most of the bombardment from across the river thereafter was laid by mortars. The fort seemed secure. Captain Walker was glad to be able to take such good news back to Point Isabel. In his turn he described to Major Brown how coming overland he had found the country "literally filled" with Mexicans. To communicate between Point Isabel and Fort Texas was "desperate service." Walker snatched some rest and spent the day—May fourth—with the garrison.

As the day wore on, the Mexican artillery resumed its fire. The ramparts of the fort were manned by riflemen, but it presently seemed safe to assume that the Mexicans were not going to storm the position with troops. Major Brown ordered his men off the parapets, but kept them immediately below their positions on the alert. Because his magazine held very little ammunition, he decided to conserve what he had "to use against assault"—should it come—"rather than spend it against enemy batteries." Work continued on bombproof shelters near the rifle posts. These were made by setting out barrels close together to form small rooms, with timber laid across their tops and packed with earth to a thickness of several feet.

The artillery observers in the fort could plainly see each Mexican battery over the river before Matamoros. One was a little way upstream in a grove of trees. One tree towered above the rest. In it was a Mexican observer with a spyglass. The next one downstream held mortars in a pit; the next was protected by sandbags; the next, by a line of piled earth; and the last was enclosed in a large earthen square. From these positions came sailing either shells of bronze or iron balls. They came slowly enough to be seen in their heavy rise and fall. The shells were round, like bombs, with protruding fuses, and they hissed and whirled in their trajectories. On landing they exploded, and reflected by the ground their force was spent upward in the air, throwing metal, and showers of sand that settled back slowly. When a battery fired over the way, the observers in Fort Texas called out which one it was—"Sand-bag battery," or "Lower fort mortar battery," or "Tree mortar battery," and if it sent over a bomb, easily identified, that too was called out, and the men fell face down on the ground to take open shelter under the narrow point of the cone-shaped explosion at impact. In his high tree the Mexican soldier with his spyglass saw the Americans falling every time a shell went off, and reported, "so it looked to him," that those who fell were killed. His reports were repeated in Matamoros and soon it was believed that the Americans were "dying by scores." Encouraged, General Arista considered plans for taking the fort by assault. Late in the afternoon of May fourth Captain Walker left Fort Texas to find his way through the enemy movements inland and report to General Taylor that the river garrison was holding well.

Soon after Walker left, Major Brown's attention was suddenly turned from the river to the country in the rear of the fort when musket fire was heard from there. Mexican troops were established about four hundred yards away, firing toward the fort. Though at that distance their fire fell short, Major Brown concluded that they were making the frank gesture of an assault. He ordered the parapets and all bastions manned to repel attack. Evening fell, and no storm came, but the defenses were ready all night. In the dark there were sounds of activity inland— the gear of moving horsemen, murmur of men massing, the grunt and scrape of shovels. There would be something to see at dawn.

With daybreak on the fifth the garrison saw that an "immense force of thousands," both horse and foot, was aligned behind Fort Texas with its left end anchored on a point of the river below the fort and its right on a point above, for a distance of a mile. In the country behind the line was a new battery emplacement—the "Country Battery," as the Americans immediately called it. The fort was now encircled by the enemy. The garrison went to work training eighteen-pound and six-pound batteries on the new line from their positions in the two south-easterly bastions of the fort.

At five o'clock in the afternoon all Mexican guns on both sides of the river opened on the fort with "a galling crossfire of shot and shell." It was returned by all batteries of the fort, until after an hour the enemy barrage ceased on both sides as if by prearrangement. Presently a Mexican informer, named Valdez, made his way to the gate of Fort Texas and asked to be admitted, for he had news. Glittering with a native talent for intrigue he was taken to Major Brown.

What was his news?

He replied that in Matamoros they were telling how a party of United States dragoons on a foray out of Point Isabel had been driven back to the base.

Was that all?

No, there was more: General Arista's troops were "becoming dissatisfied, and were deserting in great numbers."

Anything else?

Yes, it was said that a revolution had broken out in Mexico.

While there may have been general encouragement in some of this, Major Brown faced harder information at hand. In the last evening light a party of Mexican cavalry made a reconnaissance within eight hundred yards of the fort. One of Brown's junior officers came to ask permission to take dragoons and sally out to "return the reconnaissance at closer view." Major Brown approved; and in a few moments the lieutenant and his men rode out of the gate of Fort Texas. They were gone for an hour, and returned with all safe to report that they had ridden close to the Country Battery forcing Mexicans to retire behind it. There were thousands of enemy soldiers deployed about the open plain behind the fort. General Taylor's headquarters under the tree near the pond was occupied by the enemy, who had posted guards along the ditches thrown up by the General's detail. The garrison's situation was now unstable. It was time for Major Brown to think about signalling over the dunes with paced salvos of the eighteen-pounders to General Taylor, twelve miles away as sound travelled.

The sun was hardly up on Wednesday the sixth when the eighteen-pounders began their heavy intervals. Their pace was so measured that the enemy as if understanding their message began to reply with salvos from the Lower Fort Mortar Battery and the Country Battery. Mexican guns found the range that day. Their shot and shell tore down tents within the fort, and wounded many horses on the dragoon picket lines. If there were too few men in Fort Texas to offer a strong defense, they were lucky in one way; for in the great area of the fort they were also too few to offer compact targets. All they could do was watch for the sailing cannonballs and shells, and avoid them if they could. They had so little ammunition that Major Brown held the fire of his batteries, hoarding what he had against a mass attack. His men made a game of the bombardment. They laughed and jeered and hopped aside when the balls landed. An old mess cook making coffee for his fellows saw a ball roll into the ashes of his cooking fire. It spilled his pot. He walked up and kicked the spent ball, saying in disgust, "There! Those [profane] Mexicans have knocked over my coffee."

After nearly four hours of shelling the fort was showing damage. Major Brown, with his adjutant, went on a round of inspection. He came to a bomb shelter on which soldiers were making repairs. He stopped to direct them. Amidst the general shelling a bomb struck on the parapet just above the work party. It threw up a curtain of sand. The soldiers fell waiting for the explosion; but none came. The shell buried itself as a dud. The men rose again—all but one. They turned to see Major Brown who lay among them with his right leg blown off by a direct hit from another ball. They saw the end of his thigh bone bluish white amid raw muscle. He was conscious. As they took him up to carry him to the hospital tent he said,

"Men, go to your duties. Stand by your posts. I am but one among you."

While surgeons operated, amputating his leg above the knee, his command was taken over by Captain E. S. Hawkins. After the operation the Major remarked that it was fortunate for the United States that the wound had come to him instead of to a younger man. He was put to bed in a bomb shelter. The shelling continued.

At about four o'clock it ceased, and at half-past, two Mexican officers advanced with a white flag. They halted before the fort. To meet them, Captain Hawkins sent two officers, who brought back a proposal made by the Mexicans "on humanity's grounds" that Fort Texas surrender, and spare further bloodshed and destruction. Captain Hawkins examined the proposal. It would have been useful to know, just then, where General Taylor was, and whether he had heard and understood the signal salvos of the heavy guns, and what conditions were governing his own decisions across the seaside plain. Fort Texas was in trouble. It could be only a matter of time until—but Captain Hawkins disposed

of the surrender demand without solving his own uncertainties. At
five o'clock he sent his spokesmen out to reject the Mexican advice.
The garrison made ready with what they could. The Mexican shelling
was resumed immediately, but Fort Texas could not reply. As darkness
came the assault was expected. It did not develop, but the bombardment
continued for the first time into the night. It made a picture, as a soldier
saw. "As the shells rose into the air, the burning fuses gave them the
appearance of fiery comets, and at times so rapidly did they fly, that
streams of seemingly continuous, hissing light, formed magnificent arches
from the Mexican batteries to our fort, where they found a common
centre. The continued reverberations of the heavy discharges, the constant explosion of shells, the sheeted flame from the mortars and howitzers,
that in the darkness of night seemed bursting volcanoes, formed a picture
of war at once sublime and terrible. . . ." Quiet did not come till late.

It came only to be broken at dawn of Thursday, May seventh.
The garrison was feeling the strain of fatigue and uncertainty. There was
no word from the General. Who knew how long they would have to
keep on dodging shells? They noticed that the Mexican shells this morning were not of the usual bronze, but were now of iron. It was something
for the soldiers to talk about. Firing continued intermittently all morning. A number of horses were killed. In the afternoon the firing grew
steady and went on till sundown. One shell smashed through a tent and
blew up in a chest that held all the instruments of the Seventh Regiment
band. Bits of brasses and woodwinds flew into the air.

That afternoon in Matamoros a formation was held to commit
and encourage Mexican infantry to lead the long-expected assault on
Fort Texas. It was to take place at midnight. General Arista's assurances
were conveyed to the small brown soldiers who stood in ragged garments,
listening immovably. The time was excellent, said their officers, for
the attack. It was well known that vast numbers of the North American
soldiers in the fort had been killed: resistance would be weak. Moreover,
those wretches who somehow had survived the tremendous artillery
demonstrations of the Mexican army were by now so exhausted and worn
down that they could never make a proper defense. The assault troops
had the honor of leading the arms of Mexico to victory. An inspiring
name for the detachment was therewith bestowed upon them—they
were to be called the "Forlorn Hope," in the spirit of those who dare
the powers of fate by voluntarily recognizing hazard so great that only
the greatest of soldiers could overcome it. The ranks of the Forlorn
Hope sent up no cheers, while their leaders continued "to nerve them

for the work," and "every passion was appealed to, and prejudice consulted. . . ." When midnight came, and the hour of attack, the Fort Texas garrison heard sudden discharges of muskets, and then bugles in the darkness sounding the charge, and all braced to meet what must come—but it did not come. The Forlorn Hope remained impassive in the dark. Was it true, then, that General Arista was having trouble with his troops? Now instead of a swarming assault from all sides against the fort, artillery fire was resumed and lasted till day broke, and the garrison did not sleep, and looked at one another, and wondered where the General was.

The firing went on all morning, Friday, May eighth, in hot, sticky weather. The garrison was tired. They had not even the satisfaction of returning the bombardment of the enemy. The soldier's greatest privation—not to know what was going to happen to him—troubled the men. Their apprehension fed on idleness. They were not yet starving or thirsting—but who knew when they might be, especially if General Taylor had not heard the eighteen-pounders, or having heard them, could not for various reasons come back to the river? And still the Mexican batteries threw in shot and shell, until it was impossible to think, day or night. It sometimes seemed that not another explosion could be endured—and then, sometimes, suddenly there was quiet, like an answer to a mortal need, and the firing stopped.

It stopped at two o'clock that Friday, and in the deep relief of silence, the garrison heard nothing, for a few moments. And then, from far away, a great meaning trundled through the hot, dense air. The soldiers of Fort Texas jumped to their feet and listened, staring at each other. What they heard was "a severe cannonading towards Point Isabel," whose sounds "continued to roll on the plain," and they knew what they were hearing, and they pounded and hugged one another for joy, and sent up together a "simultaneous shout . . . that must have sounded in Matamoros more terribly than our severest cannonade." The General, somewhere, out there on the sandy plain, was coming back to the river, and in his march had met the enemy, and was giving battle.

At the shout that went up from Fort Texas, the Mexican batteries on both sides of the river opened again with a harder barrage than they had ever thrown before. Every time there was a momentary silence on the river, the sounds of the battle on the inland plain came through, and the garrison cheered. They cheered that afternoon when they saw great numbers of Mexican infantry and cavalry crossing the Rio Grande above and below the fort to head rapidly inland toward the battle. The

movement could only mean that Mexicans were badly needed to reinforce their comrades who were trying to stop General Taylor's army from
coming back to Fort Texas.

Shortly before sunset the bombardments ceased, both near and far;
and a little while later an accommodating Mexican, carrying a white
flag, approached Fort Texas and was admitted. He had news. It was
true—the United States forces had engaged the Mexicans at a place
called Palo Alto, and had pushed them back toward the Rio Grande.
Nightfall had ended the battle, which perhaps would be resumed in
the morning. Who could say?

It was quiet all night that night on the river. At two o'clock
in the morning, when Major Jacob Brown died in the bombshelter, the
quiet seemed stiller. The night sounds of the river pressed closer.
Crickets asked and asked in the rushes. Now and then a catfish came up
for air and strenuously slapped its way underwater again. A goat bell
sounded faintly on the other side. Voices were talking somewhere. Someone waded the river—thighs, coming slowly, and creating two new
skeins of current. Jacob Brown was enfolded in an army blanket. His
garrison slept and would soon awaken.

7.

The Listeners

The ninth of May, Saturday, was a day of wilting heat, worse than
any other so far. The distance everywhere was lost in a pale milky haze.
Blurred ranks of palm trees seemed to float upright without touching
earth; their thick stems were cut by the shimmer of heat at the sandy
ground. There was fine dust over greenery until all looked pale olive in
color, under a sky more white than blue. Fort Texas was still surrounded,
though only an occasional shot was lobbed into it. Many of the siege
troops from behind the fort were gone to reinforce the Mexican lines

farther inland to the north. The garrison listened for sounds of renewed battle. None came all morning, and they wondered again where General Taylor had gone, and what General Arista was doing. They watched upriver and down, and the road leading from the main ferry across the open country toward Point Isabel. From the elevated banquettes of the fort they could see the whole countryside and all the river approaches—the sandy flats, and the easy slopes to the river, and the river itself with its sand bars, and its deep and shallow channels, marked by difference in the current, and the banks about a hundred yards apart. No carriages rolled along the Mexican bank now, and no gallant banter flew across. Matamoros was oddly quiet, as though a carnival of war and jubilation had been interrupted by an announcement not yet quite understood. Here and there someone crossed the river, a handful of soldiers, a vendor in his white shirt and his wide white pantaloons wrapped almost twice about his frank brown belly. If a horseman went off at a gallop up the road to the north, in the odd stillness of the simmering day he seemed momentous: but only because the soldiers who watched him from the fort strained so hard to see, and to hear, where there was nothing to see or hear, that their thoughts ran away with them after such a simple event as a rider vanishing up a dusty road.

Noon passed, and there was no news, and the hours of early afternoon, until at last, somewhat after three o'clock the garrison once more heard the opening claps of battle from over the plain. There were statements from the artillery—but today few and far between when compared with yesterday. Now it was the flat sputter of musket fire that seemed incessant. The listening soldiers said to each other that the fight today was closer in—they could not be sure, but under such sustained rifle fire and with so little cannonading, there must be rushes of small units of men, maybe even fighting hand to hand. There was not much wind on a day of such wet heat, but now and then it shifted, with the effect of a great, distant door opening or shutting on far decisions, and the listeners remembered marching from that quarter, and some estimated that the battle was happening about five miles away from Fort Texas, at the place where the Point Isabel road passed through the old dry lagoon where once the river had run edged with palms—the Resaca de la Palma. Anyone who remembered it and how the road ran there saw that it made a natural situation for ambush. The Mexicans outnumbered the General's troops by nearly four to one; and furthermore, knew the country well. The garrison's fate depended on which soldiers would return to the river from the plain.

At about five o'clock they saw what looked like the first sweepings of a coming storm. Dust rose in a long line to the north and east; the whole line seemed to come toward the river before an impelling wind. Presently they heard sounds—little scraps of audible indignity, and then saw the mortal humility of men running for their lives, who had thrown away anything that would hinder their flight, the Mexican army of the north in rout and terror breaking as fast as they could for the Rio Grande. The garrison roared with joy. They could not see the whole force in retreat, but the portion they saw, in its panic and volume, was enough to assure that upstream and down, out of sight, more thousands were in a wild scramble for individual survival. The river front was jammed with men who fought to slide down the softly caving bank into the water and across to Mexico. Their voices cried for safety. They climbed across one another to swim. Many were drowned, including wounded who were carried in sacks on muleback. It was like a mindless swarm of brown-skinned animals that ran breathless before a prairie fire.

It was not long until what they ran before could be heard and seen—the United States Dragoons, Artillery and Infantry "in one mass at full run, yelling at every step," and firing whenever they could as they came. In the midst of their cheers that "reached high heaven" as they swept toward the river, they faltered only once, when three shots from an eighteen-pounder broke toward them, and narrowly missed them. They stared toward Fort Texas, thinking their own men had mistakenly opened fire on them; but the eighteen-pounder was across the river, and as it did not speak again, perhaps its crew had run away with the soaking-wet fugitives who went by it. The Americans rushed on, "yelling like mad." General Taylor's Army of the Rio Grande was once again at the river. The siege of Fort Texas was lifted.

Before nightfall the army was formed into improvised marching order and withdrawn to make camp near their supply wagons that were established on the day's battleground. So complete was the rout of the enemy that few security measures were needed along the north bank of the river that night. "Thus," recorded an officer, "thus ended the day in the most brilliant victory of the age."

By late afternoon of the next day, the army was making its encampment once again around Fort Texas by the river; and the Seventh Infantry and the other garrison troops, free among their countrymen again, listened to the stories of the two famous battles which they had heard but had not seen.

8.

Palo Alto

First, the Battle of Palo Alto.

They heard how General Taylor with two thousand men left
Point Isabel for Fort Texas, on the evening of May seventh, bringing a
train of two hundred and fifty wagons loaded with stores. He knew from
the signal guns that he was needed, and soon. The army made seven
miles that night and pushed on early the next day, the eighth of May,
crossing a great open prairie where on their right and left were ponds of
fresh water. Ahead of them three miles rose the ridge of tall ancient
mesquite trees—the place called Palo Alto where General Worth and
the rest had camped on the first march to the river. Everybody remembered it. Now, right before that background of gnarled greenery, the
army saw the Mexicans, drawn up in line a mile wide, with their cavalry
on the right, artillery in the center, and infantry on the left. The enemy
arms sparkled, for it was light and hot in the early sky. Between the two
forces there was nothing but long, dry grass.

The General ordered a halt between the ponds, and the men after
stacking arms were sent to fill their canteens and water the horses, half
a regiment at a time. The water was sweet, after the brackish water of
Isabel. The soldiers drank and washed. They stirred up dust from the
long grass and in their bellies were knots of wonder before battle. In
half an hour the regiments were reassembled. The wagons were ordered
to remain in the rear at the ponds when the army was formed in a solid
square and ordered to advance.

Breaking from solid square into line, the army moved forward in
an order of battle that put the Fifth Infantry on the right, and then
reading to the left, Major Ringgold's Flying Artillery, the Third Infantry,
the Sixth Infantry, two eighteen-pounders, the Dragoons, Duncan's battery, and the Eighth Infantry. The grass was so thick that marching
tread and roll of caisson were muffled. In some places the prairie grass

reached as high as a man's shoulder, and was stiff, each blade "pointed at the top, and hard and almost as sharp as a darning-needle!" It was dry and brittle.

The Mexican ranks made a long blur of color reaching from wing to wing of the woods of Palo Alto. It was useful to know their number, and, to count it, Lieutenant J. E. Blake of the Topographical Engineers rode out ahead of the Fifth Infantry and, coming opposite the Mexican left end, turned parallel to the Mexican line and rode alone, in full view and at brilliant speed, down its whole length. An embodiment of the spirit rising in the Army of the Rio Grande as it sparkled and creaked and tinkled its way on the grassy plain, Lieutenant Blake returned, safe and admired, to report to the General.

Captain May's Dragoons left the line to gallop forward and mark the spot at which the Flying Artillery would establish their batteries. Shortly afterward the Mexican cannon let go with ball and grapeshot. The range was about seven hundred yards, and the salvos fell far short of the advancing troops. Clouds of dust came up, and sulphurous smoke. The army pressed on, and coming into the Mexican range, soon learned, with jokes and laughter, to watch the enemy cannon balls come rolling on the ground and dividing the thick grass, and to break ranks to let them rumble harmlessly by. The Flying Artillery leaped forward to their planned positions. The line was halted behind them. They fired, and in a few minutes the General's two eighteen-pounders opened up, and the battle was on. It was two o'clock. For over an hour the cannon duel kept up, with twenty or thirty pieces of artillery raging. That was the fury whose sound travelled to Fort Texas.

Soldiers were always accompanied by dogs. At the first exchange of cannon fire, two army dogs turned and with tails tight went yelping for Point Isabel. Another, belonging to a battery officer, watched his cannon fire, and started to chase the ball every time, but always lost it to the airy distance in bewilderment. The infantrymen were too far removed to use rifles, and so stood at order arms as spectators, "watching the effect of our shots upon the enemy, and watching his shots so as to step out of their way." Though some suffered wounds from the enemy fire, the rest stood their ground "with a coolness and steadiness almost incredible, cracking jokes the whole time and sending up, whenever one of our guns made a big gap in the Mexican lines, a shout that must have struck terror to their hearts. . . ." The battle began, and continued, as an artillery duel, with rushes by the dragoons to head off enemy cavalry thrusts. The infantrymen were ready with General Taylor's order of the day before in mind: "The General . . . wishes to enjoin upon the battalions of Infantry that their main dependence must be in the bayonet."

While the artillery exchange raged in the center, the Mexicans sent out two flank attacks. On the left, lancers under General Torrejón made a wide circle at full gallop to attack the supply wagons in the rear of the ponds. It was thrown back by Ridgely's Flying Artillery who raced around the line to take up a new position. There they let go with blizzards of shot. On the right, enemy artillery and cavalry tried to circle behind the line, but were met by the Fifth Infantry, supported by the Third, to be scattered by muskets fired from square formations. Major Ringgold's light batteries pressed this advantage and took a new position to rake the enemy lines from the left. To meet the threat, the Mexican front was forced to shift into a new angle, and General Taylor ordered a corresponding oblique march in his line to face it. While this formal evolution took place, both lines ceased fire.

In the sudden silence a new sound was heard over the plain—the hiss of flames. For a wad from an American battery had set the grass on fire, and now, banking upward from a fast-moving front of flame, heavy clouds of black smoke rolled between the forces and hid them from each other. Lieutenant Duncan drove his battery under the smoke to establish a new position only three hundred yards from the Mexican right. From behind the wavering protection of the smoke cloud, he "opened so unexpected and destructive a fire" upon the enemy that "their ranks were broken and hundreds of them moved down and the whole right wing of their army was thrown into utmost confusion."

The sun was beginning to set, and the coolness of the coming night was forcing the smoke down on the plain. Major Ringgold rode to the rear to order up more ammunition for his battery. An enemy six-pound ball struck him, cutting off his right leg at the thigh. He was laid upon the ground. Quietly he gave over his watch and his purse to be delivered to his sister. He then "appeared to have closed his connection with the world, and calmly to await death." Another officer was grievously wounded: the whole of his lower jaw was shot away. A veteran of Napoleon's armies was killed when both his legs were blown off. The army rolled forward against the haze, and the Mexicans were lessening their fire. They made one more infantry advance, in full pomp, under the deepening sky, with a band playing—such music as had sounded a week before out of Matamoros, in the idle evenings. The band was struck by a salvo of shells that silenced it. The musicians fell. Their brave instruments were torn like paper. It was the day's last fight. Dim beyond the smoke the whole Mexican force that survived fell back into the Palo Alto along the low ridge that bounded the plain to the south, and night came, and ended pursuit, and brought silence.

General Taylor encamped his men that night on the enemy's original battle line. His staff came together to reconstruct a coherent pattern of the battle. The enemy had fought with six thousand, the Americans with two thousand troops. Three hundred and twenty Mexicans had been killed, over four hundred wounded. General Taylor lost nine men killed, and forty-seven wounded. The enemy's greatest mistake was his first—opening fire at a range of seven hundred yards, at which he could not hope to be effective, so allowing the Army of the Rio Grande to gauge his strength and take up positions of advantage at will. It was clear that "the manoeuvres of our corps were made with great coolness and precision," and that the "management of our batteries" was "skillful and prompt." While the staff conferred by torchlight, surgeons moved among the wounded of both nations on the field, and burial squads dug graves for the dead, and all night long, the United States Dragoons were on guard, riding in a circle about the army that slept victorious.

9.

Resaca de la Palma

Morning came hot again. The dead were still being buried. Soldiers, as they had a chance, wandered over the rubble of battle left on the field—scraps of uniform, abandoned weapons. The wounded were still being brought in. One party of Americans came upon a startling sight. They saw a handsome young Mexican officer in a beautiful uniform lying down with his head resting against his reclining horse, with its splendid saddle. They were like sleepers who had forgotten to leave the scene of battle. Were they asleep? The soldiers leaned closer, and swore they were asleep; but when they touched to awaken the serene young officer, they saw that the back of his head had been shot away, but without disfiguring his face; and that the horse must have been killed at the same instant by another shot; so that both fell together. The soldiers wondered.

The enemy forces were seen moving amidst the Palo Alto to the south early in the day, but they soon vanished beyond it. General Taylor called a staff council. What went on in it leaked out afterward, and the troops knew that seven out of ten commanders had voted to desist from battle, preferring to entrench where they were and await reinforcements by volunteers who surely would soon land at the Arms from New Orleans. The General listened, and turned to the three who voted to pursue the enemy at once. He agreed with them. He dismissed the council with orders to establish the supply train there in camp, and to assign the two eighteen-pounders and a twelve-pound battery with artillerymen as its guard. He then sent out a reconnaissance in force to locate the enemy, and after that assembled the main body in one massive column and started forward at the pace of the foot soldier.

The army was soon past the ridge of Palo Alto on the road that led to Matamoros. After marching for three miles, the General received information from his advance party. The Mexican Army of the North was in battle position at the old lagoons that flanked the road. It was an ideal position, for they commanded the only road to the Rio Grande in that vicinity. The lagoons were long and shallow, three of them, lying end to end, and linked by natural little causeways over the nearest of which passed the highway. The road ran beside the first lagoon, and then turned to cross before the second. The third lagoon lay broadside to the road within musket range. All three together made a natural fortification as if designed to control any passage on the road. The lagoons were edged on both near and far sides with thickets of chaparral and stands of palms that gave cover to entrenched troops. In the lagoon beds here and there stood stagnant ponds where once long ago the Rio Grande flowed. The old river bed—the Resaca de la Palma—was now bristling with Mexican troops. Ranks of them stood below the breast-high, near rim of the beds, and other ranks of them crouched on the far rim as a second line of defense, and past them must go the United States troops if they wanted to take the Rio Grande road.

General Taylor moved forward a detachment to draw the enemy's artillery fire and so reveal his battery positions. In half an hour the contact was made. The Flying Artillery was sent ahead on the road and ordered to engage the Mexican batteries. Two infantry regiments were deployed on each side of the road to move forward in support of the artillery. The artillery flew, and working hard under the beating sun the cannoneers pulled off their clothes to their breeches and let go with terribly sustained fire. The infantry regiments swept forward in line on each side of the road, and met the Mexican rifle fire as it ripped out across the near parapets of the resaca. The defensive fire was heavy, but it did not stop the oncoming infantry, who in a little while were pouring down over the rim of the resaca into the lagoon bed, to force the Mexicans in close combat to run for cover behind the second rim.

Meanwhile the American artillery was having less effect. The enemy batteries protected by dense thickets continued to rake the main approach of the road. One Mexican battery in particular was placed squarely on the road where it led through the far side of the resaca. Try as he might, Ridgely (who had succeeded to Ringgold's command) could not silence it. General Taylor jogged up the road on Old Whitey to examine the situation. All about him "the balls were falling like hailstones," and when he was cautioned that he was too close to the enemy, he answered, "Let us ride a little nearer, the balls will fall behind us." He sent for Captain May of the Dragoons, and ordered him to attack the troublesome battery, saying "Charge, Captain, *nolens volens!*" May took his mounted squadron down the road. He wore a gold tassel on his blue cap, above long hair and beard. His men, like the cannoneers, had stripped to their bellies. They rode up to the position of Ridgely's batteries, that blocked the road. May indicated that he must go by, and Ridgely answered,

"Wait, Charley, wait until I draw their fire!"

The Dragoons remained at the halt while the Flying Artillery threw in blizzards. The Mexican guns replied. And then, working by hand, Ridgely and his fellows pulled their guns off the road, and at full gallop May led the Dragoons out on the causeway with their sabres whistling and their bare sweated skin flashing. They came down, up and over the lagoon bed and drove the enemy gunners from their guns. As the Dragoons swept down the other side of the resaca, the gunners returned to their posts, and General Taylor, from his place on the road, sitting with one knee cocked over his pommel, shouted,

"Take those guns, and by God keep them!"

By the time May and his riders had turned and formed to charge the battery from the rear, elements of the United States Eighth and

Fifth Infantry regiments were already charging it, and soon took it for good. The resaca was crossed at the most important place.

Elsewhere in the other lagoons the fighting took the form of rifle volleys followed by rushes of infantry in small units that threw the Mexicans back from the near ridges down through stagnant pools, and across the beds, and up the far ridges into tangled chaparral. Suddenly, first in one quarter, then another, the battle seemed to go against the enemy. The Mexican batteries, in turn, ceased to fire. Nerve seemed to ebb away from the Mexicans. No longer hearing their cannon, and pressed by the United States infantry, they went wild. There were courageous thrusts by isolated groups of Mexicans, but a moment came when both forces, in the midst of absorbing individual combat, realized that the way to Fort Texas at the river was breached. "A deafening shout of triumph went up from the whole of our men," noted an American officer, "which struck such terror into the Mexican ranks that they fled in all directions."

The combat surged beyond the resaca into flat country studded with chaparral groves. Daylight was changing as the sun came lower. The Mexican cavalry and artillery horses broke and ran away. Mexican officers ran like their men. The pursuit became a race. Behind the Mexican lines was General Arista's field camp. The Americans found it abandoned, but full of signs of surprise. There was a sumptuous canvas marquee displaying every comfort and crowded with chests and chests of administrative equipment and trunks of personal possessions. About it lay piles of supplies—thousands of musket ball-cartridges in boxes, and about five hundred packsaddles, and many stands of small arms. Near the headquarters tent simmered great vats of stew in pepper sauce, and mounds of half-butchered animals, all suggesting preparations for a grand victory celebration. General Arista was gone—barely in time. In his tent he had left his personal portfolio of papers, "containing the most important information." It was taken by an American staff officer, along with a stack of the General's personal stationery, on which letters afterward went home to families in the United States. The order was given to pursue the enemy, "and on we went," said a man who was there that day, "yelling and firing with the Mexicans in full run before us until we reached the river and found their General, officers and cavalry had outrun us. . . ."

The engagements of the two days were really episodes of the same battle. In the second, the Americans lost thirty-three killed, eighty-nine wounded. The Mexican losses were, in proportion, frightful—almost

two thousand men killed or wounded, eight cannon captured and one
dismounted, more than a thousand stands of small arms and all ammunition in about twenty wagonloads, all pack mules of which there were
nearly seven hundred, all provisions and the personal baggage of officers,
all drums and a great many colors. Among the prisoners was General de
la Vega, who would be sent by ship to New Orleans.

Prisoners gave a piece of curious information. The Mexican
army went into the Battle of Resaca de la Palma depressed by "rumors
of treachery in the high command." General Arista knew nothing of
them, for they had been circulated by his political enemies, including,
some said, General Pedro de Ampudia, whom he had superseded.
General Arista, further, knew little of what his army would face that
day, for when word came to him that General Taylor was moving upon
him, he dismissed the report, "insisting that the advance was a mere
skirmish." Throughout the battle of May ninth, he sat in his marquee
absorbed and happy, hard at work on piles of official papers, undisturbed by the "skirmish" that cost him sole possession of the Rio Grande
—though not, some years later, the presidency of Mexico.

I O.

The River Dead

The American commanders had much comment to make on the
two-day battle. At ten o'clock at night General Taylor worked on his
report, the heart of which lay in the statement, "The enemy has re-
crossed the river, and I am sure will not again molest us on this bank."
His officers all agreed about one thing: "It is a glorious fact for the
army," as one put it, "that there were no volunteers with us." The
greatest victories since New Orleans belonged entirely to the regulars.
They were justly proud, for the officers, especially the subalterns in the
Army of the Rio Grande, were mostly out of West Point, which at the

very time was threatened with abolishment by a Congress that had listened to charges that the military academy was a school for aristocratical popinjays who cost their country much and could give it nothing. The first Rio Grande battles would change the tune, for it was soon known everywhere that "on their first encounter, the subordinate officers, chiefly from West Point, executed their orders with the precision of a field day exercise, showing beyond all question the utility of military education and discipline, and putting to rest at once the attacks on the Military Academy which had become so formidable that few believed it possible to sustain the institution a year longer. . . ."

The officers discussed the qualities of the enemy. How odd that all through the dripping heat of the day, while American soldiers threw off every stitch possible, the little Mexicans wore their heavy quilted overcoats buttoned tight or tied about their shoulders. What a difference, noted the military critics, there was between the Mexican officers and men! The officers were elegant, elaborately uniformed, full of style and address—and almost to a man incompetent. They did not really lead their troops, or see to their welfare, or use their endurance wisely. The common foot soldiers were marched thirty miles a day, sometimes fifty, while the American infantryman averaged perhaps fifteen. The dark little Mexican Indian was courageous, and "with an able general would make a good fight," as Lieutenant Grant said. But what could he do if even his weapons were faulty? Why, even at close range, was his marksmanship so poor? American officers examined the Mexican ammunition, and found the answer: the Mexican cartridge held twice as much powder as was necessary, and because of that, a fired rifle kicked bruisingly, and because of the excessive kick the Mexican aim was poor and the cost, to Mexico, terrible.

The United States had its own failures at the high administrative level. If anyone asked the officers why, when the Mexican forces were driven yelling across the river a few hours ago, the American army did not cross, pursue and wholly destroy them, the answer came with the bitterness and scorn which the field always felt for the War Department: there were no boats, no materials to make a bridge, to take the pursuing troops across. Why had nobody foreseen the need? But someone had. A year ago, General Taylor had written to ask the War Department to equip him with "a ponton train" for river crossings. The request was never acted upon in Washington; and he now wrote that if he had had what he asked for, it "would have enabled the army to cross on the evening of the battle, to take Matamoros, with all the artillery and stores

of the enemy, and a great number of prisoners; in short, to destroy
entirely the Mexican army."

Still, there was enough glory to go around, and even Lieutenant
Grant, of the Quartermasters, got his share, for during the battle at the
resaca he was given temporary command of an infantry company, ". . . an
honor and responsibility I thought very great," as he said. He smiled
later over the flourishes he executed in the fight. He led his company
at a charge, captured a Mexican colonel, and then learned that the
ground he fought over had already been taken by the Americans. He
could only conclude "that the battle of Resaca de la Palma would have
been won just as it was if I had not been there. . . ."

Matamoros had been decorated with cloths and garlands to celebrate a Mexican victory. On the night of the retreat the women of the
city tore down the festive array and ripped their ball gowns. Violent
disorder broke out in the streets. Crime and confusion gratified distracted
appetite in every way.

For the next two days, squads were at work burying the dead of
both armies. On the battlefields lay bodies mouldering open to all
nature, as it worked to purify corruption—the sun, the sky, the buzzards,
the burrowing insects, the coyotes. "Already," wrote a soldier, "the
vultures were at their widespread feast, the wolves howling and fighting
over their dreadful meal. . . ." The scent of decay was dense over the
land and along the river; it was what many young soldiers would most
remember for a long time after the battles. For several days the river
fell, and as it went lower it revealed many bodies of Mexican soldiers
drowned while trying to escape on the ninth. Some of the bodies were
lodged in low tree branches lately submerged but now high and dry;
and hung there in the air until they dropped "piece meal into the river
below." The river itself, for a while, became offensive; and the awed
soldiers watched how the mutilated corpses drifting downstream would
be attacked by catfish, "causing them to twitch and roll about, as if still
in the agonies of death. . . ."

General Taylor rode over to Fort Polk at Point Isabel on the
eleventh of May, "on public business." A steamer stood out for New
Orleans. On board were General de la Vega, with other prisoners of
high rank. Courier officers sailed with General Taylor's news of the
great victories. From New Orleans it would be relayed by express
messenger until within reach of the telegraph; and then by wire, to
Washington and New York.

II.

The Nation's War

The cabinet met with President Polk in Washington on May ninth—the day of the second battle—and, as he noted in his diary, "All agreed that if the Mexican forces at Matamoros committed any act of hostility on General Taylor's forces I should immediately send a message to Congress recommending an immediate declaration of war. . . ." The President adjourned the meeting without having had any word of encounters on the Rio Grande.

But about six o'clock in the afternoon of the same day the Adjutant General of the Army appeared at the White House with dispatches for the President that had just arrived by the southern mail. They were from General Taylor, and they told of the attack made on April twenty-sixth by General Torrejón's lancers, in which Captain Thornton and his men had all been captured or killed on Texas soil. The cause for war was established. The President immediately prepared his war message, which was passed by the House two days later, and by the Senate on the day following. Polk signed it on May thirteenth, as Congress voted a war appropriation of ten million dollars and authorized the President to call for fifty thousand volunteers.

And now the national position toward Mexico was immensely shifted from a localized stance on the lower Rio Grande in protection of a border claim, to an all-embracing purpose of defeating Mexico wherever she could be touched. The President already had his grand strategy in mind. His first move toward its execution was to order an expedition to be organized out of Fort Leavenworth, to march against Santa Fe and the north Mexican provinces all the way to the Pacific. Colonel Stephen Watts Kearny was to have the command.

On May sixteenth the President presented his plan to the cabinet. A huge pincers movement was to embrace Mexico simultaneously with many claws. In addition to Taylor on the lower river and Kearny on the

Rocky Mountain Rio Grande of the north, an army was to march from San Antonio to Chihuahua crossing the Rio Grande at old Fort Saint John Baptist—a move that was later to inspire Doniphan to meet it by marching down the New Mexican Rio Grande to El Paso and from there to Chihuahua City. Naval forces in the Pacific were to capture the coast of California, as General Kearny went west from New Mexico to take California from inland; and other naval forces in the Atlantic would blockade Mexican east coast ports from Tampico to Yucatán. Finally— though it was a later addition to the plan—an invasion would be mounted with landings at Veracruz and an overland sweep to Mexico City. Four of those movements would take in the Rio Grande at widely separated places along its great length. The plan in its spacious strategy comprehended a vast portion of the continent. It was at once approved by the Cabinet, and before the day was over, also by Senator Thomas Hart Benton, the Senate leader, for whom the President sent in order to make certain its support by Congress.

The raising of volunteers next came up for discussion. The President saw that a truly national effort would be required by the war, and he knew how to call it forth. He had already sketched a "distribution among the States of the 50,000 volunteers authorized to be raised," and he now submitted it to the Cabinet, who approved his scheme. "A portion of this force was assigned to each State and Territory in the Union," he explained, "so as to make each feel an interest in the war. . . ." By this decision Polk made the Rio Grande a household word, a family concern, in the nation. As the whole nation had debated—taken sides— passionately on the Texas issue, so the war for the Rio Grande was in everyone's awareness, and the river was a national feature. But not until their men went to it in great numbers from every quarter of the land would the Rio Grande become personal—the property, the sorrow, the pride and the romance of the whole American people. Its name acquired an evocative power it was never to lose, even though people might forget in later generations how this came to be.

With the publication of the news of Torrejón's raid, the war spirit began to rise at home. Recruiting began at once, and in many states the quotas were filled immediately, with immense overflows—in Tennessee thirty thousand volunteered for the three thousand who were called; in Indiana, where four regiments were authorized, fourteen could be formed. With his volunteer program launched, the President considered other problems of winning against Mexico. He sent for Bishop John Hughes of New York, the Roman Catholic primate, to enlist his advice and support on how to assure the Mexicans that their religion was safe under the Constitution of the United States. "The false idea had been industriously circulated by interested partisans in Mexico," explained the President, "that our object was to overthrow their religion and rob their churches, and that if they believed this, they would make a desperate resistance to our army in the present war." Could not Spanish-speaking priests accompany the American troops as chaplains, and even "visit Mexico in advance of the army," to reassure the Mexican clergy, who would thus be less inclined to encourage resistance by their Mexican parishioners? The Bishop thought this an excellent idea, and offered to do all he could to help solve the problem—even to paying a visit himself to the Archbishop of Mexico, whom he knew personally. "I found Bishop Hughes," noted the President, "a highly intelligent and agreeable man, and my interview with him was of the most satisfactory character. . . ." In spite of Whig opposition in Congress, the President's war program was finding popular support everywhere.

It received tremendous response when the next news came from the river. On May twenty-third, "the southern mail this evening brought intelligence of two decided victories obtained by General Taylor's army over the Mexicans on the Del Norte," recorded the President, adding that "no official account of these battles was received." But Taylor's reports arrived a day or so later, and meanwhile the papers had the stories. Bells rang out in the Eastern cities, and men and women danced in the streets, and by torchlight gifted citizens delivered orations as was their right and need, and bonfires flared in downtown squares. If so many rose with enthusiasm to the national commitment, no one was obliged to, and some didn't. A New York lawyer told his diary, "Great news from the frontier; two great victories; the Mexicans smitten hip and thigh and General Somebody"—it was Vega—"taken prisoner. 'Nothing equal to it,' said my extra, 'in all Napoleon's campaigns.' Hurrah, hurrah, crow and cackle . . . and no end to the glorification. I do believe we're the windiest people extant. . . ." But he was a Whig, and a skeptic, and his wry view was a lonely one.

For in every salable medium the war and its leading personalities were kept before the public. Fashion, with its reflection of what the people thought about, took up war subjects for lithography, glassware, china, fabrics, pottery. Print publishers rushed to press with scenes from the war lithographed in color. Sarony and Major presented the death of Major Ringgold at Palo Alto, who was shown reclining against two comrades, while his fallen horse turned its head to heaven with a look of intense sorrow in its welling eyes. Nathaniel Currier offered the Battle of Palo Alto, with General Taylor in the foreground, while United States Infantry advanced in solid ranks upon Mexican artillery shown eighteen feet away. Kellogg and Thayer printed the capture of General de la Vega, and both Currier and Weber issued gallant scenes of Captain May's charge at Resaca, with his gold tassel and hair tossed by his speed. In their emotional style, the prints told more about the people at home than about the events illustrated.

Some of the print subjects were issued on fabrics—silk kerchiefs and curtain materials. One chintz showed Zachary Taylor, in brown, green and ochres, wearing a stovepipe hat, sitting sidewise on "Old Whitey," with the American flag floating over battling troops in the distance, the whole wreathed in roses and leaves, and repeated mechanically. General Taylor was also fixed in likeness on jugs, cups, plates, snuffboxes, and on twenty-six different flasks made by the glassware craftsmen of Baltimore, Philadelphia, New Jersey and the Monongahela-Pittsburgh district. Presently from England came sets of Staffordshire china, known as "The Texian Campaigne," showing scenes of the Army on the Rio Grande. It was the theme of the day toward which all interest turned: ". . . me toward the Mexican sea . . ." said Walt Whitman for himself, and, poet as prophet, for everyone. The popular imagination could not have enough given to it about the war. Long later Ulysses Grant read "of deeds of heroism attributed to officers and soldiers, none of which we ever saw. . . . I do not suppose any war was ever fought with reference to which so many romances were invented."

But never before had the nation set out to extend its reach over so vast a theatre of war; or to use so many of its men in armed service. Its scale of operations was commensurate with its new sense of the continent; and so was its imagination.

12.

Invasion Summer

Once more after Resaca the army was massing on the Rio Grande's north bank, and the days were spent in re-establishing supply lines from Fort Polk, resting the troops, and consolidating a grip on the river's defenses. On the fifteenth American troops seized the village of Barita, their first conquest on the Mexican side of the river. The village lay a few miles upstream from the mouth, and consisted of a customs station and many huts. A breastwork was at once thrown up to command the river and all its approaches. For want of boats or bridging elements, no crossing had been yet possible upstream where the main bulk of the army was gathered. Fort Texas was now called Fort Brown, in memory of its dead commander, and would soon be the town of Brownsville. There were still Mexican troops in Matamoros, but Fort Brown commanded the river front now, and hostilities were all but suspended. General Taylor had every intention of crossing the river once he had the means. Again on May fifteenth a small element of his army moved against the Mexican shore. Lieutenant Richard Graham commanded a detail of soldiers who were given the job of swimming the river to the south bank where Mexican boats were moored. Covered by American guns, they crossed, cut free a number of boats and brought them back safely. The next two days were spent in examining the river for a suitable crossing place. Upstream three or four miles there was a Mexican ferry that was operated by pulling barges along a rope stretched over the river. It was noted by American scouting parties.

At noon on the seventeenth of May Mexican trumpeters sounded a parley on the opposite bank. It was clear that the enemy had recognized General Taylor's intentions to enter Matamoros, and now a Mexican general asked for an interview with him. He was brought over with his aide to make a proposition for General Arista.

Would General Taylor agree to an armistice while a courier could go and return from Mexico City "with a view . . . of settling our controversy by negotiation?"

No: General Taylor "peremptorily refused, saying that he had once offered that course to Arista, who, supposing that we were weak and an easy prey, refused it."

The Mexican General reviewed his instructions, and then "proposed to surrender the public property including arms and ammunition if General Taylor would promise not to cross the river."

On the contrary: General Taylor would take Matamoros and all the public property found there for the United States, and would establish his headquarters in that city. His mind was made up. He had been reinforced by "a large accession of troops from the United States"—volunteers were on the way—and he had ample armaments to batter the city down. He had already distributed orders to move up the river to the ferry, and his troops were alerted to start over at half-past one. However, he would make one concession: he would hold off crossing until three o'clock, to await General Arista's surrender.

The Mexican officers went to their boat and returned to their commander; and at half past one the Army moved out on the north bank to the ferry upstream, and halted there for General Taylor's next order. At sunset he appeared in the new riverside camp and declared that he had heard nothing from Arista. His officers at the ferry were able to give him news. All afternoon, Mexicans had been crossing to return to their homes on the north side of the river, and had told how the Mexican army had retreated from Matamoros, taking along all their artillery. The General was hacked. How could he ramsquaddle somebody who had skedaddled? He supposed the report was true enough. There was nothing to do but settle down for the night and cross in the morning.

The crossing began early on May eighteenth. It was slow, for the ferry could take only about fifty men at a time. A junior officer trying to swim his horse across was drowned, and so was a soldier of his company. At eight o'clock the ferry on a return trip to the north bank brought a deputation of Matamoros city officials to see General Taylor. He received them, spent two hours with them, and sent them back to town with assurances that he would treat all their people as he would American citizens. Meanwhile the Dragoons, Ridgely's Flying Artillery battery, the eighteen-pounders and a battalion of infantry were getting over the river. The General ordered them to march down the Mexican bank, while he set out downstream on the north side to the ferry opposite Fort Paredes, where he would take the main body across. There was no battle in prospect, for the Mexican army had all gone. Taylor's men were excited and jubilant to be entering Mexico as masters of an important town. The elements on opposite banks moved downriver, and just as the General's forces arrived opposite Fort Paredes, the American flag broke out from the flagstaff of the fort where on the evening before the Mexican flag had hung. As it went up, the lead regiment on the north bank "gave three deafening cheers which were taken up successively by those in the rear until the air was fairly rent by the glorious shout. . . ." The patriotism of soldiers was spontaneous, robust and loving.

At the Fort Paredes ferry there were three boats manned by Mexicans. The Army would have "the felicity of being *ferried across by the enemy.*" A ferryman worked at each end of the flatboat, which was hauled across by pulling at a rope tied to each bank. On one barge, a ferryman was naked, the other wore a scrap of shirt and something on his feet. The crossing went rapidly, the first troops went up the south bank, and over a sandy plain north of the city, and entered Matamoros to the tune of "Yankee Doodle." Only a few troops occupied the town; the remainder made camp on the plain precisely opposite Fort Brown where they had first encamped on the river. "Much has been accomplished today for the United States," wrote an infantry officer.

In the next few days the army went to see the sights. Matamoros was laid out in squares. The houses were mostly of brick, and few windows had glass in them, but were protected by iron grilles. It was a flat-roofed town. The Americans found it odd that there was so little damage from the bombardment by Fort Texas. The wounded, though, were everywhere. Public buildings and private houses held long rows of suffering Mexican soldiers lying on cowhides. Visitors could "tell at a glance the wounded of Palo Alto or Resaca de la Palma." The first showed many amputations, for Palo Alto was an artillery battle; the second, wounds from bullets, for Resaca was mostly a small-arms battle. An American officer saw a dying Mexican soldier who held "in his hand the grapeshot that had passed through his breast. He showed it to us with a sad countenance." The town was orderly, though one night a Kentuckian disarmed several Mexicans who were "cavorting about the streets with drawn swords."

If the conquerors had entered Matamoros expecting to find an exotic atmosphere and a colorful society they were disappointed. The town was dusty, hot and still. The best society had fled with the Army. The air and ground, especially at night, were alive with stinging insects. There was little stir of commerce amongst the population of eight thousand. "It is not," wrote Lieutenant Grant, "a place of as much business importance as our little towns of 1,000." The odor of sickness and suffering drifted everywhere from the improvised hospital wards. There was little to fulfill the "glowing pictures of Spanish beauty and grandeur" that had filled the heads of the invaders before they crossed the river. They accepted what they found quietly. "The behavior of our army after victory," an officer found, "is as highly honorable as the victories themselves." The Americans invaded neither the civil nor religious rights of the residents. Mexican judges still sat in their courts, law and order prevailed, and if an American soldier disturbed the peace he was punished. "The army, instead of entering the city as conquerors, encamp quietly in the suburbs. . . ." Their tents stretched "out before you for miles, until they grow into seeming white spots, looking like snowballs resting on the bluish sward."

Such conditions reflected the temperament and the mild power of the commanding general over his regulars. His new headquarters were set up in four tents under a clump of stunted and ill-shaped trees overlooking a bend in the river. No sentinels were posted near him. While the camp trained to make ready for his next movement of the Army, he sat and worked and told stories in his tent. Whatever was to be done with General Arista's captured marquee with its magnificent appointments, he didn't want it. For a table he used two rough blue wooden chests set together. It was covered with papers in which he could burrow after an idea he needed. When he had visitors he yelled for Ben, his servant, who brought refreshments—a pitcher of Rio Grande water and tumblers on a tin tray put down on a stool. To visitors seated in canvas camp chairs, the General waved an invitation to drink, saying "Help yourselves." They saw him as "a very thickset, farmer-looking old gentleman, in a linen roundabout, and remarkable for short legs and long body." His eyes shone brightly in his seamed face. Behind them, they soon saw, his mind missed nothing.

It was not long before visitors came, in profusion and great circumstance. General Taylor was the national hero. The Congress and various state legislatures voted him medals and swords of honor, and delegations arrived to make presentations with appropriate remarks, hampers of champagne and delicacies. An ode was offered to him in Latin, which he could not read. Two French artists went at him with odd squintings and crayons held forward to take measurements in the air, and reporters from the Eastern papers besought him for interviews. To such, he said, "Help yourselves," and retained a sandy composure, for he knew honeyfogling when he saw it, and what it was worth; while at home, the Albany *Journal* predicted that he would be the next President of the United States.

He was more at home in the immediate problems of command. On crossing the river he had sent a mounted force to pursue Arista and the escaped Mexican Army. After a thrust of sixty miles south of Matamoros, the pursuit was abandoned because there were so little water and forage to be had in the harsh country. When he was ready to take up his campaign again, he would have to devise other measures than marching inland from Matamoros. On May twenty-fourth appeared the first sign of a solution to the problem. It was the high-pressure steamboat *Neva* which arrived from the estuary to tie up at Matamoros. The troops went down to see her. She was of light draft. With enough like her, high enough in the water to get over the bar at the river's mouth, the Army could in large part be carried up the river to invade Mexico from such a point as Camargo, a hundred and thirty miles upstream, and to move against the important cities of Monterrey, Saltillo, Victoria. With the arrival of the volunteers, General Taylor would have ten thousand men, four thousand animals, and all commensurate supplies to transport upriver. He ordered the quartermaster to send to the United States to procure light-draft river steamers in use there. The mission left within four days, to go up the Mississippi, and up the Ohio as far as Pittsburgh, and along the Alabama, the Chattahoochee, the Apalachicola, to find steamboats. Within a few weeks the first of them were already churning their way down to the Gulf, and across to the mouth of the Rio Grande— the *Big Hatchee,* the *Hatchee Eagle,* the *Troy,* the *Corvette.* Captain Austin's *Ariel* was remembered. General Taylor was assured that steam navigation, under certain conditions, was practicable on the river.

Until the ships came, and the volunteers in greater number, there were other matters for him to ruminate in headquarters—even one or two about which to feel a shaking anger beneath a calm, blinking exterior. On May twenty-seventh the mail expected from the States was "lost by the express who got drunk on the way up from Point Isabel." The matter was not merely awkward, it might also give a dangerous advantage to the enemy, for the mail contained instructions from Washington for the next moves against Mexico—possibly even the President's whole continental design for the war. A few days later headquarters believed what it heard next—that General Winfield Scott, the commander of the whole United States Army, would presently arrive on the Rio Grande, with all his spacious ways, and his bludgeoning opinions expressed in rhetoric as majestic as his uniforms. General Taylor hated to think of it. He could not abide him. Perhaps—if the boats came, and the volunteers—he might be able to take the Army up the river before the terrific General-in-Chief could arrive.

13.

Recurrent Frontier

Meanwhile, he mildly presided over what was happening to Matamoros, imposing restraints only when public order required them. Through the first weeks of occupation, the city had kept its formal Mexican character. Officers dined with friendly local families, and learned to drink wine at table. Some studied Spanish for "several hours in the forenoon, and then fell asleep"—after the local custom. Attendance at Mass was a novel diversion for non-Catholics who at home had never risked it. In the town the General had found a huge storage of seegars—eleven or twelve wagonloads. He caused them to be distributed to everyone in the Army who smoked. The troops drilled, held target practice, and late in the hot afternoons found their steps taking them out of increasing habit up the river a little way to Fort Paredes, where they would sit down on the bank to watch with swollen thoughts as the girls of Mexico, unembarrassed by an audience that exuded longing, bathed in the warm stream, and called, and played. In the evenings the soldiers dawdled in the streets, now and then catching a glimpse of a private garden through a patio gate, to see flowering vines and orange and lemon trees heavy with ripe fruit. Sometimes at the grilled windows women lounged smoking their seegaritos, willing to talk to lonesome men. In the plaza regimental bands played after evening mess, and on Sunday mornings Ridgely's Flying Artillery Battery gave exhibition drills. Now and then a trooper whiled away time training a donkey. The Army of the Rio Grande was nearly bored out of its wits.

But then, in a few weeks, the commerce of appetites arrived to assuage the Army; and in a very short while Matamoros was a bear pit. A powerful strain of the United States energy came into play, with high animal spirits, rowdyism, bright lights and noise and waste and extravagance and arrogance that pardoned itself with a marvelling smile that grown men could be so boyish. The Army society soon presented another picture of an American frontier in its first, most awkward age; but here superimposed on an existing civilization. Wherever they went in great numbers, the Americans re-enacted the frontier experience. Out of the violent humor of boredom, and with the new resources of American commerce, they made of Matamoros a raw American town in the summers of 1846 and 1847.

Gamblers and saloonkeepers from the States swarmed up from Point Isabel and opened their shops to a rush of custom. Dance halls, equipped with musicians and girls and upstairs rooms, found a large trade. All the classic trash of a displaced society looking for pleasure was soon visible. Discipline suffered. Local jails and military compounds were crowded with arrested officers and men. The volunteers were arriving now in numbers, and a regular officer declared that they were "playing the devil and disgracing the country in Matamoros." Sutlers came with stores of goods, to be sold at sky-high prices. "A long step toward civilization" was taken when shipments of ice arrived, and whiskey juleps could be had at the bars. An American vaudeville company, true to the tradition of the pioneer theatre, appeared and occupied the old Spanish opera house, playing to a "most motley audience," according to one of the actors—young Mr. Joseph Jefferson. A playbill announced, for Sunday evening, August ninth, *The Dumb Girl of Genoa* in a world première, and *The Desert Rose,* and "a great variety of dancing; the whole to conclude with a dance in wooden shoes, that will be a caution to corns and cockroaches." After a few profitable weeks the company was disbanded when its manager ran away with all its cash. Mr. Jefferson next found employment selling seegars and tobacco at Mr. William Foyle's "Grand Spanish Saloon," whose most prominent rival was a saloon called The Resaca House. Drinking was so general and troublesome that General Taylor in midsummer issued an order forbidding the sale of spirits after August fifteenth. In honor of the order, Mr. Foyle convened a "sarcastic meeting" of the "Friends of Temperance" in his drinking parlor. Another businessman had already done well with a soda fountain, where he sold "soda water with syrups" to another great appetite of the troops. And presently arrived four thousand Bibles, shipped out by the American

Bible Society, and soon the moan and stammer of the voluntary revivalist were heard amidst the carousing. Two Catholic priests, appointed chaplains to the Army in line with the President's discussion with the Bishop of New York, arrived early in July. There was plenty of work for all, as the volunteers continued to join the camps.

Over the river camped the Texas Ranger companies that had volunteered as separate units. They made their own shelters out of reed and brush, for the Quartermaster issued them no tents, or any other equipment. Some of the Rangers were veterans of the Mier fiasco; and having marched over much of north Mexico, were valuable guides to General Taylor on conditions of the country and surprises of the Mexican character. Wondering yet if it were possible to march against Monterrey from Matamoros without first going upriver to turn inland, General Taylor was advised by the Rangers that it was not: the country, dry, was too barren—the country, wet, was impassable. He proceeded with the Camargo plan. The Rangers were, in their tradition, "not only the eyes and ears of General Taylor's army, but its right and left arms as well." Their view of Mexicans was deplored by the General, however; and after a number of cool outrages committed by Rangers against their hereditary enemies, he trusted them less with missions in north Mexico.

It seemed for a time important to work for the good will of the northern provinces, where sentiment was still active for secession from the central government, and for revival of the independent Republic of the Rio Grande. "By judicious management," thought an American officer, "nothing would be easier than to separate all the Northern provinces from Mexico." Coming while the American forces were preparing deep invasion of Mexico, such a political loss might be a fatal blow to the enemy government.

One day very soon after the Army was settled on the Mexican side, a man arrived to present to the staff a plan that would, he felt sure, help to divide Mexico against herself. He was General Hugh McCleod, the late commander of the Santa Fe Pioneers and released prisoner of the Mexicans. He proposed to publish a newspaper in Matamoros, in both Spanish and English, called *The Republic of the Rio Grande And The People's Friend,* whose job it would be to persuade "the people of the states of Tamaulipas, Nuevo León, Coahuila and Chihuahua to an appreciation of the merits of a separate Northern Mexican federation." The Army approved the idea as an instrument of propaganda and psychological warfare, and the first issue of the paper appeared on June second. It was "very well received by the Matamorians," and would surely open the eyes of the northern Mexicans "to the degradation of their condition under the existing and former Governments and the contrast presented to them of what they might be under a Government of equal and just laws and free institutions." A week later the second issue was out, and "the Mexicans read it with much avidity." After another issue, however, the paper passed into new hands, and the new owners while promising to continue publication—"single copy, one bit"— stated editorially that they did not "feel themselves altogether qualified to work out a republic on the Rio Grande." The paper's name was changed to *The American Flag*, and publication continued for two years, all in English, with straight news. The great secession above the Sierra Madre once again faded away.

It was a summer of tremendous storms over the Gulf and the Rio Grande littoral. Time and again the huge American encampment was beaten down by wind, rain, thunder and lightning. The issue tents were unequal to the tempests—even if they stood, the tents "afforded but little shelter from the rain," wrote a field soldier. "The Army is treated shamefully with regard to tents. There is unpardonable neglect somewhere." Not only comfort was at stake—the very armament was in danger. "Inspected my company and found the muskets in bad order. Can't be helped, the frequent rains and no tents to protect the muskets must rust them. . . ." And still the furies blew, screaming through the swayed palm trees, and bringing up the river in sudden flood, and darkening the whole sky to the color of smoke over half of Tamaulipas and Gulf Texas.

If the regulars, with their old soldier ways, were baffled by the weather, the volunteers found it even more discouraging. Untrained and hardly disciplined, the volunteers soon found that their patriotic fervor faded out as they encountered the daily realities of their service on the river. Everything was strange—strange, but without interest. What had been undertaken as adventure soon became miserable duty. If there were occasional beauties to see, not every man could see them, though one soldier would never forget his last night on shipboard nearing the river's mouth under a summer moon. "The moonlight . . . was of a whiteness to shut out the stars. . . . A strange object within pistol-shot was moving swiftly in a direction the opposite of ours. It seemed infinitely large and high. The silence of its going deepened the mystery. It acted as if self-controlled. Then I realized that it was permitted me to see a spectacle fast disappearing, and the most imposing and majestic of the

apparitions of the sea—a three-masted merchantman full-rigged, every
sail set, and laden so deep that the light waves gave it no lateral motion.
On it went, glacial white, mountain high, deathly still, a spectral, glid-
ing glory of moonlit space. . . . It passed, vanished, and made no sign. . . ,
My standards of the sublime are few—it is one of them." The soldier was
Lieutenant Lew Wallace, of the first Indiana Volunteers, who over thirty
years later at Santa Fe would be governor of the New Mexico Rio Grande.

But with the daylight landings, the volunteers saw the muddy
stream of the river pouring angrily into the Gulf, and nothing but
dunes north of the river, and the village of Bagdad south of it, where
smugglers trafficked, and along the shore only wreckage silvered and
rotted by the furious sun and the sandy wind and the salty tides. All
through the summer the volunteer camps were built upon both sides
of the river from the mouth to Matamoros until over twenty thousand
soldiers were in the Rio Grande theatre of operation. Sick from the
crowded, tedious voyage the volunteers landed to find confusion. As one
regiment arrived another pulled out for upriver, vacating an unsanitary
camp. The volunteers elected their own officers, few of whom had military experience. Command was infirm, and obedience, even co-operation,
whimsical. The regiments gave themselves great airs, with brave titles—
the Killers, the Gunmen, the Guards—and fanciful uniforms recreating
the styles of the Revolutionary War and the War of 1812 and the Napoleonic adventures. Some wore thigh-boots tricked out in red morocco,
and tunics of brilliant color faced in bright contrasts, and tricorne hats,
or shakos with pompons, or plumed sugar-loaf caps. In the moist heat—it
was often over 120 degrees—sweat poured down under such headgear,
and after seeing General Taylor ambling about on Old Whitey, or a big
gray mule, "like an old man a-going to mill," wearing his straw sombrero,
many threw away their elaborate caps and bought Mexican hats for
themselves; and if their officers ventured to object, the volunteers, "as
honest and good as anybody," made hard faces and cited the General.

All their equipment and provisions were unsuitable for men in
that climate. Rations, issued three times a week, were beans, coffee, sugar,
pickled pork, and flour or hard biscuits. There were no vegetables, "not
even onions." The biscuits were "alive with brown bugs . . . the men
frequently substituted pieces of them for gunflints." Now and then
against orders men went to shoot beef cattle and sneak them back to
mess. When this was not possible, they dragged the river for shrimps
to supply fresh meat. The only drinking water to be had came from the
river, "a tepid mixture about thirty per cent sand and the rest half

yellow mud." A full draught of it was a sure purgative. Now and then a
ship put in from Boston with ice which could be bought for a dollar a
pound—while it lasted. Firewood was scarce on the dunes. Most cooking
was done on coal brought from Pennsylvania or Ohio. For the thousands of men sifted along the banks it was life in unrelieved wilderness.
By night, they tried to sleep in spite of blowing sand, stinging flies, burrowing chiggers and "night fowls," as they called mosquitoes. By day,
fellows had little to do but walk along the beach, chasing the huge white
crabs that jumped like great spiders, or swim in the surf, or pick up
shells, open them, pull apart the sea creatures within, and throw them
to gulls and curlews. When the fun wore out, "there was nothing left to
do except speculate upon what was to become of them."

Comrades sickened of each other. Some actually died of home-
sickness. And soon there were epidemics of physical illness—smallpox,
mumps, measles, and worst of all, violent intestinal infections. If drinking the river water led to dysentery—the familiar Rio Grande "cholerina"
—unsanitary conditions in camp, and unrefrigerated food, and improper
diet brought enteric fevers to a fearfully increasing number of men.
Over and over Lieutenant Wallace saw it happen. "The soldier may
have been in perfect health the day we went into camp . . . ; at rollcall,
three weeks having passed, I notice the change in his appearance. His
cheeks have the tinge of old gunny sacks; under the jaw the skin is
ween and flabby; his eyes are filmy and sinking; he moves listlessly; the
voice answering the sergeant is flat; instead of supporting the gun at
order arms, the gun is supporting him. . . . The surgeon gives him an
opium pill"—or calomel and jalap—and "another week and his place in
ranks is vacant. A messmate answers for him. . . . There is no hospital
of any kind. It will go hard with him, one of six in a close tent, nine
feet by nine, for the night will not bring him enough of blessed coolness
to soothe the fever made burning through the day. His comrades not
themselves sick are his nurses. They do their best, but their best is wanting. . . . A delicacy of any sort would be a relief; he prays for it pitifully,
and they bring him the very food which laid him on his back in the first
instance—bean soup, unleavened flapjacks, and bacon. Another week
and he is giving his remnant of strength to decency. At last he has no
vigor left; mind and will are down together; the final stage is come. . . ."

One regiment lost five hundred men in six months. There were
too many to bury in daytime, so funerals were held at night. Lumber for
coffins was soon exhausted, and the burial squads used gunboxes and
the staves of cracker barrels; and when these gave out, army blankets,

and then nothing. "And then, the poor men," wrote Lieutenant Wallace, "the poor men were not always allowed their natural rest in the sands of the dunes where we laid them, for the winds, blowing fitfully, now a 'norther,' now from the Gulf, thought nothing, it seemed, of uncovering a corpse and exposing it naked." In their tents the living could not shut out the sound at night of the dead march played by fife and muffled drum "heard first faintly and scarcely distinguishable from the distant monotone of breakers." It sounded incessantly, and even when the burials were briefly interrupted the soldiers were not free of its tune, for hearing it all night long in the pouring moonlight, the mockingbirds of the Gulf whistled snatches of it in the hot daytime. The nation heard with growing anger of the number who died in the river camps all summer.

In desperation many volunteers gave in to mischief, license, and finally crime. The Mexican residents came to hate and fear them. They foraged recklessly for Mexican corn, cattle and women; they stole Mexican fence posts to burn in campfires; if a Mexican displeased them, he was in great danger of being killed. Murders were common. The soldiers in river camps drank even more liquor than those stationed at Matamoros. It was their need to do violence. Volunteers camped opposite Matamoros amused themselves by coming down to the north bank with their muskets and firing at random across the way at the American camps opposite until a staff officer at headquarters said a day in his tent was like a day in battle. The Texas Rangers accepted recruits many of whom were "desperados and ruffians and renegades from the States" as wild and dissipated as "Russian Cossacks." Such men, it was noted, were not Texans. Spoiling for action against the enemy, which was denied to thousands in the summer encampments, volunteers fought one another. One day a soldier of the Baltimore Battalion and a soldier of the Ohio regiment, fishing at the river, both claimed the same catfish. The quarrel nearly became a pitched battle with loaded rifles between the two organizations, and was ended only when the colonel of the Ohio used the flat of his sword on the Baltimore fisherman. Stories of all such disorders went to home newspapers, and Whig editorials in opposition to the war called the volunteers a national disgrace.

In vain General Taylor issued orders commanding proper conduct—soldiers were to pay for what they took from Mexicans, firearms were not to be discharged off duty, the men were not to fight one another, and so on. But still the outrages persisted, and the Army took little disciplinary action. The volunteer officers held command only by a sort of hair-triggered compliance on the part of their men, who had elected them, and who could undo them as well. Now and then an officer—most probably a regular serving with volunteers—tried strong measures to subdue in an individual example the general insubordination. A French priest assigned as chaplain saw with pity and shame how "the most barbarous chastisements are inflicted for offences which in France would be fully expiated by a few hours' imprisonment. I have seen soldiers suspended by the arms from branches of trees for drunkenness. Sometimes, too, they tie their arms and legs, and fling them repeatedly into the river, and then drag them to the bank with a cord. A soldier, stricken with a severe malady, lay on his bed of suffering in chains. He died in his chains; and, perhaps, in consequence of being kept chained." He was happy to add that "such cases of cruelty . . . are rare. They are individual acts for which, ordinarily speaking, the American officers, who in general are men distinguished alike for their high intelligence and accomplishments, are in nowise responsible."

Of all the river camps, the one—never given a name—at the mouth was the most wretched. The First Indiana were supposed to guard the important entrance, but there wasn't a Mexican to be seen except an occasional smuggler scratching himself, and the beach, at Bagdad. Twenty men could have held the strategic location, according to Lieutenant Wallace. New regiments would arrive overland from landings at Point Isabel, and if the First Indiana thought relief was at hand, they were wrong. The sight of the new troops bound upriver "marching by, flags flying, drums beating, and hurrying aboard boats as if they smelled the contagion in our camp or feared an order for them to stop and take our place, was maddening. . . ." They heard little from upriver, and what they did hear was mostly distorted. "A steam-boat man would stray in among us with the news. . . . Occasionally, too, an inspector came down and took a snap-look at our tents from the guard of his steamer. . . . There was not a soul among us so simple as not to see that we were practically in limbo. . . ."

14.

Upstream and Inland

On his level, too, the Commanding General had special problems. Late in June General Taylor received an infuriating letter. It was from Major General Winfield Scott, at Washington, and if it held any welcome note it lay in the implication that Scott might not after all appear on the Rio Grande, but remain in Washington, content to issue plans for the defeat of Mexico. But what plans! Working with maps, and making grand assumptions about the geography of Mexico, he issued a stupefying command to Taylor on June twelfth, 1846:

"Take up the line of march beyond the Rio Grande, and press your operations toward the heart of the enemy's country. . . . The high road to the capital of Mexico will, of course, be one of those lines."

How easy he made it sound! A brisk walk, the cutting of an arterial highway, and Mexico City must fall. But where was any knowledge of the scale of Mexican distance, or understanding of the north Mexican desert, or recollection of what it took to feed, water and shelter an army?

General Taylor replied at once to the Adjutant General at Washington, determined, "nolens volens," to describe certain realities. He was already planning to move upriver to Camargo. But "from Camargo to the city of Mexico is little if any short of 1,000 miles in length. The resources of the country are, to say the best, not superabundant, and over long spaces of the route are known to be deficient. . . . I consider it impracticable to keep open so long a line of communication. It is, therefore, my opinion that our operations from this frontier should not look to the city of Mexico, but should be confined to cutting off the northern provinces—an undertaking of comparative facility and assurance of success." His strategy meant to capture Monterrey, Saltillo, and other key cities of the northeast, just as he had been planning all along.

He received another letter from Washington by the middle of

July which gave some comfort. It came from Secretary of War Marcy, and, written before the Secretary had seen Taylor's reply to Scott, it indicated that there were some in the War Department who could look at a map and see more than the Army's General-in-Chief: ". . . If it should appear that the difficulties and obstacles to conducting a campaign from the Rio Grande . . . for any considerable distance into the interior of Mexico will be very great, the Department will consider whether the main invasion should not ultimately take place from some other point on the coast—say Tampico . . . or Vera Cruz. . . . The distance from Vera Cruz to the city of Mexico is not more than one-third of that from the Rio Grande. . . ."

General Taylor replied, somewhat stiffly making reference to General Scott's design, that he could not determine whether he could win the war alone in his northern frontier campaign. Practice alone would show whether his army could subsist beyond Monterrey. As for Tampico, he felt it was impossible, and about Veracruz he had no views. He was not disposed further to extend his advice. He knew what he could do with his present resources, and he intended to proceed. Did Washington aim to catch him in a trap? Get him to give advice, then take it, and if it went wrong, blame him? He knew what was behind their attitude—Scott, and Polk, and who else: they were trying to kill the sentiment that was building up all over the country—Taylor for President. They were scared by the Whig mass meetings that had been held at which in spontaneous demonstrations he had been acclaimed as the necessary nominee for '48. That was part of it—the other part was the enraging ignorance of politicians in walnut-panelled offices on the Potomac of what actualities governed the Army of the Rio Grande, two thousand miles away. It was, in the face of these, almost an impertinence for the War Department to have an opinion, way back there, on the staff level, when the reality was here, on this muddy ditch, in this heat, with soldiers dying of their bowels. General Taylor told his fellow field-soldiers, speaking of those safe in Washington, "They have an intention . . . to break me down." His army was to be thrown away, and the venture wasted, "for all of which I shall be made the scapegoat."

But the high pressure steamboats were already on the river, and on July twenty-sixth the first detachment had gone upstream on the *I. E. Roberts*. The rains had continued, the river was running almost at flood level, and on August fourth General Taylor boarded the *Hatchee Eagle* with his staff for Camargo. He arrived on the eighth and at once reviewed the troops that had preceded him. The rest of the invasion forces were coming up both by river and by land for the jump-off into Mexico. Like ten thousand others back home, the wife of a young major felt her heart turn westward. "My thoughts," she wrote in a diary kept for her husband's return, "my thoughts have wandered to the Rio Grande."

After the fall of Matamoros, upriver towns were occupied by small infantry forces without opposition and as the heavy movement by road began and continued in late July and early August, the troops found their flag already flying over Reynosa and Mier on their way to Camargo. The march was an ordeal that lasted eight days, through rain and mud, or blasting sunlight and dust. The old Escandón towns offered little shelter—they looked deserted but the men soon saw that "there is scarcely an old wall standing that some family does not live behind." In many places the river road was flooded, and the columns had to make detours to the south. Water holes at evening were brackish and some were contaminated by cattle who to escape the extraordinary heat of that summer stood in them for weeks. There were few reliefs for the troops, though now and then they passed little ranches where young girls gladdened them with waves and laughter. After passing a little beyond Mier, they saw their first mountains—faint blue crowns on the southwest horizon. They started up coveys of plover and sent bands of wild horses glaring and plunging away. One regiment met a Mexican driving his cart full of fresh melons to Matamoros, and in a few minutes, to his delight, bought his whole load at high prices. The heat was presently so frightful that the troops were halted to rest after midday. Reveille sounded at midnight, and the march was taken up again by moonlight, while fifers and drummers, "with a perfect *vim*," did their best to inspirit their fellows with the tune of "The Girl I Left Behind Me." It was necessary, though dangerous, to rely on Mexican guides: an infantry regiment was taken astray on the road to Linares, which was a Mexican army station, and was saved only when the treachery of their guide was discovered. Finally, after a march of one hundred and thirty miles—the air-line distance was eighty—the columns came up the rise of land that enclosed the San Juan River and saw Camargo lying below on the near bank, a little way above the confluence with the Rio Grande.

As the army made its way down into the valley, one of its officers was moved by the sight of it. The Rio Grande, "seen in stretches, had the appearance of so many lakes embedded in green foliage. The smoke from several ranchos curled gently and lazily upward . . . and a steamboat—a *high-pressure steamboat*—true emblem of an American, lay moored at the bank. . . . lazily working off steam. Add to this the long line of covered wagons—the troops, upon whose bayonets the sunbeams glistened, marching on their winding way, and you have a picture unsurpassed. . . ." Entering Camargo they heard that General Canales had just evacuated it, "after inflicting numerous pains and penalties upon the good people," who "hailed with great joy" the new occupation troops.

The steamboat voyage up to Camargo took from four to seven days. By the middle of August there were twenty vessels in service. They were officered by American masters, mates and engineers from the inland rivers, and manned by hired Mexicans. None of the steamboats drew more than five feet of water, some as little as three and a half loaded, and eighteen inches light. They burned wood, gathered every evening at the banks. The green mesquite was a slow fuel, and many a boat had to pull into the bank during the day to get up steam before resuming her voyage. If the river was free of snags, it presented a channel that shifted among soft sand bars, so that a master had to feel his way on each trip. Even so ships went aground all too often. One—the *Neva* —sank one night while tied up to the bank, and everyone believed she had been scuttled. The voyage was slow, and men were crowded together amidst bales of supplies, but progress was sure, and it was better than the overland march. The Rio Grande was "a noble river at the present stage of water," and the country along its banks "decidedly pleasing," where mesquite thickets alternated with open cornfields and little ranches or villages whose people came down to watch the little steamers puffing amazingly along. When the soldiers took off their hats and kissed their hands to the girls, they would all "shout and laugh and make themselves most merry." In general the upriver inhabitants were friendlier than those at Matamoros, and at Reynosa especially, said an officer, because of two facts: "first, the Texas Rangers have not been let loose on them, and [second], only Canales has . . . committed outrages upon them, which have rather turned the current of their feeling in our favor." The river voyages of that summer had interludes of high spirits and antic pleasure for soldiers who crowded the little steamers. One night a boat tied up near a solitary hut as darkness fell. An old Mexican came out of the hut to see the arrival. A fiddler, he was soon playing for the soldiers. They begged permission of their commander to go ashore so they could hold "a stag dance." This was granted. The men swarmed to the bank, where some built a fire and began to roast a goat. It was almost like a symbolic sacrifice to the pagan deity who soon inspired them all. An American fifer joined the Mexican fiddler in making music. A soldier who heard them play said they "imagined themselves possessed by the spirits of Pan and Paganini." Scratching and squealing away, they seized the troops with their tunes, and soon all the men were dancing. They danced "by couples, but without much regard to time or order. . . . The dancing . . . became stronger in proportion as the wild strains grew louder" and the soldiers "vied with each other in the extent and singularity of their saltations." Every so often something swept over the whole detachment, and to the light of the goat-roasting fire and the banked furnaces of the moored steamer, they all "indulged in a promenade or rather *gallopade* of two or three *heats* around the hut." In a scene of color, smoke, glow and animation like a lithograph of the period brought to life, the men feasted and danced and galloped on the riverbank—and then suddenly "a heavy rain terminated the sport on a seasonable hour, and the men returned to the boat much amused and refreshed by their exercise. . ."

The high water lasted all summer between Camargo and the sea. Regular navigation was more difficult farther upstream, though later in the year the *Major Brown* arrived at Laredo with supplies for a new army station there; but before she could cast off to go downstream, the river fell, and she was unable to sail for two years.

And now at Camargo the army repeated the spectacle of Matamoros. On a little stone and clay town with its squared streets and central church and plaza and peach-laden trees descended some fifteen thousand soldiers, with all the animal trains and heavy equipment and greedy hangers-on that accompanied them on the river. Before they could make camp the soldiers had to clear dense mesquite off the ground. The summer floods had swelled over town and field, and receding, had left heavy silt that dried as fine dust. When the wind blew, dust sifted everywhere.

And as always, after flooding, the Rio Grande bred disease. The new base of operations in a matter of days was pest-ridden. Thousands of men went down with the cholerina and hundreds died. The epidemic had come upriver with the transport of troops, and conditions at Carmargo spread it. Men bathed and animals drank in the San Juan River that was the camp water supply. Sanitation was poorly regulated, and hospital facilities were limited and little was known or understood of germs, or antisepsis, and though in Camargo there was a druggist's shop—it was the only shop in town—it sold only soda water. Once again

deaths were so numerous that military funerals became a mere shuffling
of wasted bodies into sandy troughs, while the dead march was sounded
by fifers and mockingbirds. Camargo was known as the "Yawning Graveyard." Tremendous heat by day and noisome fogs by night and insects
persistent in their millions made matters worse; and the Army, through
appropriate officers, attributed the epidemic to "noxious gases and deadly
miasmas."

But still the slow work of supply build-up went on, and until it
was done, General Taylor would not budge, though he had sent advance
elements toward Monterrey on reconnaissance. He was in an odd mood,
as one of his officers recorded. "The general was advancing in a strangely
divided frame of mind—had supreme confidence in his men, but he
had little confidence in the movement on which he was embarked."
Were those people in Washington trying to cornuck him? If he thought
so, it might take the starch out of him, until the time came to move
into action, and then a man would get back to where he felt like himself again. . . .

The rains went on, and soldiers were so wet all day that whiskey
was issued to them. Tent canvas was rotted till it resembled a sieve.
Sometimes after a storm the air was cool for hours—a delicious change,
and one night there was a brilliant display of meteors over the immense
Mexican plain. The camp heard that Comanches were on the loose
near Mier—three hundred were said to have killed the mayor, even
though an American infantry company was stationed there. Letters came
from home. One from his wife so moved an officer that his heart leaped
"at the reflection that she does not outdo me in devotion. Never for
one moment has my fidelity been tempted to give way." In an atmosphere of pathetic license, he had his own resources: "Have been all
afternoon on my bed reading 'King Henry the Fifth,' one of Shakespeare's
best plays"—best, even though it trembled with the soldier's lust:

> And the flesh'd soldier, rough and hard of heart,
> In liberty of bloody hand, shall range
> With conscience wide as hell, mowing like grass
> Your fresh fair virgins. . . .
> What is't to me, when you yourselves are cause,
> If your pure maidens fall into the hand
> Of hot and forcing violation?
> . . . Why, in a moment look to see
> The blind and bloody soldier with foul hand
> Defile the locks of your shrill-shrieking daughters. . . .

Many volunteer units had enlisted for stated, short terms of service. Now at Camargo when all the energy of the army was needed for the coming campaign in the interior, hundreds of men said good-bye and returned downriver on the steamboats that were headed for the Gulf to bring up more troops and supplies. Of those going home, "the great majority" were "pretty well disgusted with their service," which for them had meant only heat, and illness, and inaction on the outlandish river. But enough were left with the General to make a great display, and on August seventeenth he reviewed them, all drawn up in order of battle. Their line was over three quarters of a mile long —"one of the most magnificent military displays we have had since the last war." With General Taylor four other general officers inspected seven regiments of infantry and two battalions of horse artillery. All were in dress blues, the officers with gold stripes, except the General, who rode the line "in plain undress." He was himself again. He "never looked in better health or spirits," for action was soon to be resumed.

On the following day the first division moved into Mexico, by way of Mier, to be followed by one division a week until all but small holding forces were gone from the Rio Grande. The transport problem over the deserts had been solved—nineteen hundred pack mules with Mexican drivers took the place of most of the horse-drawn wagons. General Scott should have witnessed the difficulties of loading tent poles and canvas and mess chests and sheet-iron kettles and a hundred other articles on the little beasts, which took several hours at the outset of each day's march, so that the first-packed grew tired of standing, and broke and ran, sometimes bucking or rolling till they managed to scatter their burdens. Still, there was no better way to cross the wastes with an army's duffel.

As the movement got under way, the staff at Camargo heard that Mexico was in a state of revolution. President Paredes, who had marched toward the frontier as far as San Luis Potosí with eight thousand troops, was thrown out of office, and a provisional president had sent for the one man who despite his record could unite all Mexicans under his familiar name—Santa Anna. Under a safe-conduct honored by the United States, Santa Anna on his way home from exile in Cuba had landed at Veracruz an August sixteenth, and was proceeding to the capital to take charge. General Taylor now had his principal adversary.

Monterrey lay a hundred and fifty miles southwest of Camargo. The last of the Rio Grande divisions moved out on September first

and camped that night under a young moon. The General with his
staff accompanied the Fourth Infantry on September fifth. He was now
in such high spirits that his people wondered if perhaps he were over-
confident. Mexicans whom they met assured them that there would be
"Mucho fandango á Monterrey," and wondering what this meant, the
Americans—correctly—translated it to mean that there would be something of a fracas at Monterrey. The country they passed over was dead
level, with unending clumps of mesquite. Those who kept up their
journals every night had to write by the light of the new moon—there
was too much wind to let them light a candle. So under a wide movement of air over the great empty plain the combat forces of the Army
of the Rio Grande slowly faded out of sight into Mexico.

15.

The Army of the West

     Meanwhile, at Santa Fe, Don Manuel Armijo was once again
established in the Palace. After six years as governor, he had been succeeded in turn by two Mexican generals sent from the interior—Mariano
Martínez de Lejanza and Francisco García Conde, during whose terms
the civil and military conditions of the province fell off miserably. For
a time progressive New Mexicans held hopes that prosperity was at last
come to sustain commerce and feed the government. The fur companies
of Taos alone spent up to sixty thousand dollars a year for supplies,
and taxes were paid on a hundred thousand dollars' worth of skins
shipped out of Abiquiu. But envy led certain businessmen to seek a
larger share of such profits, and a new law was proclaimed to require
that trapping parties would be licensed only if composed of equal
numbers of native New Mexicans and visiting Americans. It was no:
long until the Americans by-passed the government to deal directly with
Indians.

The results were wretched—doubly so, for not only was revenue lost, but also relative peace with Navajo Indians, to whom the American trappers traded firearms, giving them the awful power now to attack the Mexicans with superiority of weapons. Depredations increased sharply, and the Mexicans were in general powerless to resist, for their laws prohibited the introduction of firearms among the population. But for a handful, ranchers, farmers, and town dwellers were armed only with bows and arrows. It was clear that the government feared to give them weapons for self-defense that could as well be turned against corrupt officials. And when outlying communities pleaded with Santa Fe for troops to be send to protect them, the answer was always no, as what few soldiers there were had to be kept in Santa Fe to defend the governor and his crowd. If the militia—with bows and arrows—were called out to avenge an Indian raid, it was noted by observant New Mexicans that it was not "by any means usual that the rich go out to follow the savages when they commit depredations."

And if at last the governor did happen to take steps against raiding Indians, he was more likely than not to create trouble instead of quiet it. The administrators sent from Mexico did not understand the problems that they had to deal with, especially those of the Indian nature. To General Martínez de Lejanza all Indians looked alike, and when he went to chastise a band of murdering Navajos, he seized with them a party of innocent Utes, with whose nation the New Mexicans had never known any organized trouble. Bringing his prisoners to Santa Fe, he punished Utes along with the others. Ute chieftains came to ask for the release of their people. The Governor received them in the Palace, and mistaking their vehement protests of injustice for personal threats, he called for his guards to defend him. Their defense was extreme: they assassinated the chiefs in the audience chamber; and it was not long until Utes swept down the Chama from the Rio Grande headwaters country to kill and burn. Enraged New Mexicans demanded troop patrols on the northern frontiers to give them security against the Utes, but the Governor proposed instead to march out and "chastise them severely in the spring, carrying the war to their country." There spoke the Mexican administrator who had no knowledge of the land he governed. "All his great imaginary movements had to be made, if done at all," said a disgusted New Mexican, "in the Ute country, rugged and mountainous, where there are no trails except those made by the mountain sheep and rabbits." Meanwhile, to those who asked for troops where the raids came, the governor "was so weak at all times as to try to persuade them that the point of peril was Santa Fe . . ." where he lived.

If the New Mexicans hoped for relief when at last General Martínez de Lejanza was "removed to the sweets of private life," his successor, though he reigned briefly, was a disappointment. General García Conde openly misappropriated public funds to his personal uses; and upon his departure, the return of Don Manuel Armijo positively seemed like a blessing. At least Armijo was a native who as such knew what he had to deal with, and if his failures resounded, he was like Santa Anna another phoenix of disaster—a personage with a gift for the spectacular, for which the Latin soul could forgive much. He returned to preside over a bankrupt citizenry who had been permitted no means and no experience of self-defense, and who found themselves in the early summer of 1846 at war with the United States. Already he had acted in response to news of how the North Americans were advancing to the lower Rio Grande. To Albert Speyer, a Prussian resident of Santa Fe who operated wagons in the Missouri trade, the governor gave an order to bring back on his spring trip two wagonloads of arms and ammunition.

Speyer made his purchases at St. Louis and prepared to turn West again. Trailers for Oregon were gathered there too—among them young Francis Parkman with his notebook, and many others who looked past the Mississippi with the hungry American eye. One was a young midshipman bound for the Columbia River with dispatches, who in spite of his immediate destination had "a wild plan of raising a body of men, and *taking Santa Fe*." The travellers left for all points west from St. Louis by river, floating down to Independence, where the trails began—northwest, southwest. "Speyer," noted Parkman, "had an immense number of goods on board," tended by "piratical-looking Mexicans" who wore "broad, peaked hats." There were others bound for Santa Fe—"a vulgar New Yorker, with the moustache and the air of a Frenchman," and a young man who had "one brother on the Atlantic, another on the Pacific, and a third on the Mississippi, while he is going to Santa Fe. So much for American wandering." There was also a young fellow from St. Louis who when the steamer tied up near Independence "harnessed his mule into his waggons, and drove off for Santa Fe, bent on seeing. He seemed about eighteen years old, open, enterprising, and thoughtless. He will come back a full-grown man." Speyer pulled out on the Santa Fe trail in early May for his ten-week crossing of the prairies. Three weeks later, at Fort Leavenworth, Colonel Stephen Watts

Kearny, after he had his orders to march against New Mexico, heard of Speyer's consignment of arms and ammunition for the enemy, and ordered out two troops of dragoons to overtake the train and seize its military supplies. But slow as it was, the train had enough of a start, and went safely on to Santa Fe.

There, by the end of June, the citizens knew of General Taylor's victories at the seacoast; but even if those were Mexicans troops whom he had whipped, the whole thing had happened far away, and a travelling scientist wrote that "The people at Santa Fe appeared indifferent to the defeat at Palo Alto; only Governor Armijo felt alarmed, because he had been informed that troops would be sent over the plains to occupy New Mexico." News came to the Governor "by extraordinary express" that Mexicans out on the plains had seen United States military forces at the Vermejo River headed for New Mexico. They were described as six hundred men, "the advance guard of the Army destined to invade this Department." The main body was said to be at the Arkansas River. The Governor immediately issued a call for the militia to arm. Two companies were to report to Santa Fe, one to remain on guard at Taos, with their pikes, spears, bows and arrows, and a few antiquated muskets. A light scouting party was sent to Vermejo to bring further details of the advance invasion force.

The detachment was back in a few days with an easing report. They had found traces of an encampment on the Vermejo, but these reflected only a small party, and could have indicated either hunters or soldiers. The Governor was relieved. On July eighth he disbanded the militia, but with a cautionary order to "hold themselves in readiness at the first notice." But two days later—it was exasperating—he received more serious news. It came in a letter to him from four Santa Fe traders who were not Mexicans. Writing from Independence, they told him that a "considerable body of the North American army was on the march" for New Mexico with "the purpose of occupying the same, by order of the United States." The American commander had assured the merchants that "their mercantile interests would be in no danger," and that they might even send this letter with his permission, announcing his advance; and that all he required of them was that they not precede the army, but travel in its rear. There could be no doubt about the truth of the letter; and Governor Armijo was forced to heave his thoughts from position to position in search of what to do.

He chose to ask for a solution of the difficulty by someone else. He called a meeting at Santa Fe of leading citizens, officials, and two solicitors from Chihuahua who happened to be in New Mexico. First he read them the merchants' letter; and then he astounded them with what he said next. He asked the opinion of the meeting "whether he ought to defend the Department or not." One of the lawyers rose to say that "a question of that nature should not be propounded." The Governor held the inherent power and obligation to defend New Mexico. All that should be asked was how "the defense should be made." The other lawyer and the rest agreed vigorously. In danger of being misunderstood, the Governor scrambled to protest, not once, but twice, that he was "ready to sacrifice his life and property . . . on the altar of his country," and he thanked all for their "most sincere patriotic sentiments," asked them to "be in readiness at a moment's notice," and adjourned the meeting.

His position was impossible and no one seemed to understand it and feel for him. It was easy enough to cry for valor—but where were money, arms and troops? Reports kept coming into town of the advancing army—how powerful, how steady their approach, how familiar the land they so strangely moved across. If citizens asked why the Governor did nothing, he could reply that they were wrong—he had told all to hold themselves in readiness, and moreover he was preparing a proclamation.

On August eighth he issued the latest of his state papers. "Fellow Patriots," he trumpeted, "the moment has, at last, come when the country requires from her sons, the unlimited decision, the reserveless sacrifices, which circumstances, extreme under any point of view, claim for its salvation." He went on to refer to the eagle of Iguala, the value of unity—"a house divided against itself cannot stand," he declared—the illustrious President of Mexico, and the god of armies. But if the citizens looked for a plan, an order as to what to do in the face of the threat that every day drew nearer, they found none. True, he did hope for victory, but his hope was qualified: victory "if it be possible," he said, and added, with an eye to his future, "for no one is obliged to do what is impossible. . . ." Thereupon, he heavily shrugged off his burden of leadership onto those who only waited to be told what to do: "Your governor is dependent upon your pecuniary resources, upon your decision, and upon your convictions." In conclusion, he assured the New Mexicans that "he who actually governs you is ready to sacrifice his life and interests in defense of his beloved country." It was an excellent proclamation in every respect but one: it said nothing.

Two days later the Governor asked the New Mexico Assembly,

then in session, to vote one thousand dollars for the support of the regular troops. The Assembly could not vote him the actual money. There was none in the public treasury. But they authorized him to float a loan for the sum, to be guaranteed by future revenues of the government, and then adjourned, never to meet again at Santa Fe. If the Governor tried to raise the loan among the local men of business, he did not record any use of the monies. Meanwhile, into Santa Fe thronged volunteer militiamen "to be ready." And as they came, leaving their ranches un-protected, the Navajos struck at the outlying frontiers, and killed or captured people of at least twenty families. The capital was in an uproar. The question was asked: Why had the Governor not assembled his men through the weeks of July, and moved out to meet the enemy on the plains long before now? There now remained only one natural position of defense between Santa Fe and the relentless progress of the American force. This was Apache Canyon, where the road passed through a rocky defile. Fifteen miles distant, it was the eastern gateway to Santa Fe. If it were breached, all would be lost.

16.

The Secret Agent

But if there was reason to think that the Governor believed all was lost already, his views were not shared by his second in command, Colonel Diego Archuleta, who for himself—and many others—favored a furious defense. First reported as four thousand strong, the Americans were now known to consist of only twelve hundred regular and volun-teer troops. Properly inspired and energetically led, over four thousand New Mexicans could be raised to save the province even now, even with bows and arrows, even in the face of the impossible. But it was late—how late was made clear on August twelfth when under safe-conduct an officer and a civilian, with a guard of twelve dragoons, appeared in Santa Fe as emissaries from Colonel Kearny, and presented themselves at the Palace.

They were Captain Philip St. George Cooke and Mr. James Magoffin. Captain Cooke brought a letter from Kearny to the Governor, which he was to present at a suitable moment. Magoffin, as a Santa Fe trader and resident of Chihuahua, knew Spanish, and was an old acquaintance of the Governor. But to protect what he must do later he resolved not to go with Cooke for an official interview, and left with him an interpreter to manage introductions. While Magoffin went to see friends among the traders, Cooke entered the Palace and was soon conducted into "a large and lofty apartment, with a carpeted earth floor." He saw Governor Armijo "seated at a table, with six or eight military and civic officials standing. There was no mistaking the governor, a large fine-looking man . . . he wore a blue frock coat, with a rolling collar and a general's shoulder straps, blue striped trousers with gold lace, and a red sash." He received the Captain agreeably.

In the meantime Magoffin sought out Henry Connelly, a prominent trader who also lived in Mexico, whom he had known well. The two could talk frankly.

What did Connelly think the Governor intended to do about resisting the invasion?

The Governor, Connelly replied, "was not determined to resist," as things stood.

That was gratifying. What about others? Was there strong sentiment elsewhere to give battle?

Connelly, "being intimately acquainted with Colonel Diego Archuleta & and having opportunity of conversing with him on the subject of impeding the entrance of the U.S. forces into that city," was able to answer for him: "the Col. was decided in making a defense. . . ."

Magoffin was glad to have the information. He now knew how he must proceed. Leaving Connelly, he presently paid his respects to the Governor without having shown himself publicly as a member of Kearny's mission. Official affairs were over for the moment, and when the Governor invited his old friend Magoffin, and the American captain to dine with him, they accepted. It was such an occasion as the Governor always enjoyed. Turning on all his old, florid good-fellowship he beamed upon his guests. Captain Cooke was an able officer, well-educated, and a credit to any man's table. James Magoffin was a handsome Kentucky Irishman with a robust wit and a stock of hilarious stories. The candlelight was bright, the wine flowed, the food was rich and hotly spiced,

Indian servants moved silently in and out of the shadows, and presiding as the first gentleman of New Mexico, the Governor was in his element, among men, with his general's tunic unbuttoned, his duties forgotten along with tomorrow, and other morrows.

But a little before ten o'clock, when dinner was over, the Governor rose and accompanied his guests to Cooke's quarters, and there, in private, they got down to business. Magoffin was fluent in Spanish. He knew the country and its ways and its chief. He carried now a private authority that came from intimate councils with the great; for a few months ago, in Washington, Senator Benton had taken him to see President Polk and Secretary Marcy, who appointed him to accompany Colonel Kearny as a secret agent, with the mission—proposed by the Senator—of persuading the powers of New Mexico, by whatever means, to submit to conquest without resisting. His work was to be unofficial, done in shadow, but nonetheless binding in its results. For the official gesture of the occasion, Magoffin now nodded to Captain Cooke, who produced Colonel Kearny's letter. To the Governor's heavy face with its eye for the main chance, Magoffin translated it.

Fully written in official style, it contained really only two ideas.

The first announced that by the annexation of Texas the boundary between the United States and Mexico was now the Rio Grande from its source to its mouth. The United States Army of the West was now marching to take possession of New Mexico as far as the east bank of the river.

The second advised the Governor "to submit to fate," and surrender peaceably. If he should do so, all would go well with him and his people. If he should not, he and his government would be treated as enemies. They would be overcome and would receive the curses of their countrymen.

There followed a long conversation. Magoffin was able to use powerful arguments. He was pleased to say that the President of the United States himself had sent him to bring assurances to the distinguished Governor of New Mexico and his good people. The United States hoped "only to give peace and prosperity to the inhabitants." Why not take a realistic view of the situation? Kearny was coming with enough troops to defeat any resistance, and even stronger reinforcements were to follow. It was possible to use the tone of one reasonable man talking to another, for Magoffin already knew from Connelly that the Governor was not disposed to fight. Possibly, even probably, there was offhand mention of financial embarrassments that so often visited a gifted public servant who retired from office having suffered heavy personal losses in consequence of living up to his position; and there was evidence in time that a large sum may have changed hands in the sealing of Magoffin's argument; for he later asked the United States government for fifty thousand dollars to reimburse him for "secret services rendered during the war." It was known that the Governor suffered from a fatalistic venality. Already convinced that there was nothing he could do to save his state, he would show a business sense compatible with his nature if he consented to be paid for what must inevitably come.

As everyone knew, the only strong defense of Santa Fe lay at Apache Canyon.

The Governor now "promised not to make a stand at the defile, after which the invaders would have no difficulty." It was an entirely satisfactory interview. The Governor's only remaining problem was how to keep up a plausible show of resistance to satisfy public sentiment while avoiding a real fight. There were gestures that he would have to make—mobilization, levies of supply, a sortie to the canyon—but somehow, when the time came, he would manage to go through with his deal. Captain Cooke was strongly impressed with James Magoffin's skill in using his old influence over the Governor. The meeting broke up with cordial exchanges.

It was now Colonel Archuleta's turn. Magoffin conversed with him separately—probably on the following day. Magoffin immediately saw that "fight was in him." He was a young man, a veteran of service as captain of the New Mexican rurales. He would have to be "drawn off," or his influence might control the Governor, and a smooth design might turn into nuisance and bloodshed. Magoffin had a suggestion for him, and the fiery colonel listened. He listened with increasing attention as Magoffin touched home to the heart of personal ambition. What had Kearny proclaimed? Only that he was coming to occupy New Mexico as far as the Rio Grande's east bank. Nothing was said about what lay beyond—the immense empire west of the river. Why should not Colonel Diego Archuleta give up the costly and in the end useless defense of the eastern part of the province, retire to the west bank of the river, and there pronounce himself chief of state over a great province in which the United States had no interest whatsoever? Surely he would succeed in holding such a position. Speaking as a presidential agent, Magoffin added that the western half of New Mexico would be "too far off to be protected by the central government" at Washington. The opportunity was stunning. Colonel Archuleta was shaken. Magoffin pressed his advantage, and went on to suggest that in addition, or perhaps even as a substitute arrangement, Archuleta might well be given a post of responsibility under the United States government in its own area of New Mexico. He could rest assured that Magoffin would recommend him to Kearny for such appointment, if he liked. A quick light of a great future in the Colonel's eye, a moment's pause for the sake of dignity, and it was all over. The Colonel submitted. "The Colonel would have fought," Magoffin could say. "I quieted him."

Magoffin then, with these successes behind him, dropped in on a number of the other leading citizens of Santa Fe, "many of the rich" with whom he "had ample intercourse." He repeated his courteous threats and appealing arguments—"the only object of our government was . . . to give peace and quietude to the good people of the country"— and was glad to see that he "gave them entire satisfaction." If the promises he had received were sincere, the battle of Santa Fe was already won. He took pains to hide his arrangements, and even assured his friend Connelly that a "strong stand would be made a few miles from the city." Out of caution, Connelly and a number of other American businessmen left Santa Fe under permits issued by the Governor. Magoffin— they could not imagine why—stayed in town; and Captain Cooke returned to join Kearny, who was almost at Las Vegas, to bring him the favorable news.

And now the Governor entered upon a bustling program of public measures for defense. He commandeered horses and mules. He dispatched a large force toward Apache Canyon to make camp and await his arrival. He ordered every male citizen between the ages of thirteen and fifty-nine to spring to arms and march to the front. In the end, four thousand New Mexicans would be posed at the defile. The father of a boy not yet thirteen asked that the child be excused from service and the Governor answered, "No, sir, he is a cadet, and is, therefore, subject to the ordinances, and he is a military officer, and, therefore, must go to the front." The little boy reported long later that "Armijo placed at my disposal a piece of light artillery with its equipage and artillerymen under my orders; we marched to Apache Canyon. . . ."

Others were more fortunate in their requests to be excused: those who paid the Governor any sum between twenty and one hundred dollars were let off. At the same time he opened a subscription for a public war chest. Patriots gave what they could. He turned his eye to the church, and ordered the pastor of Santa Fe to give over all the money,

plate and livestock in his possession. Ignoring the right of succession of
the lieutenant governor he secretly signed over control of official as well
as private affairs to a business friend, who could protect his interests if
the time came for him to absent himself. His old henchman, Damasio
Salazar, risen to the title of general since the happier days of the Texan
Santa Fe Expedition, now demanded—as though he suspected the Governor's intentions—the command of the defense forces.

But he was denied the glory, for on the sixteenth of August
Governor Armijo rode off to join the encampment in Apache Canyon.
Las Vegas had fallen. In another day or two the Americans would be
upon him. He brought with him a guard of dragoons, the last of the
militia, and—to their astonishment—the members of the legislative
Assembly of New Mexico. He found the armed citizenry barricaded
behind evergreen branches, and he heard how among them there had
almost been mutiny. Once with them, he gave an energetic display of
leadership. First he planted his artillery out in the open one hundred
yards away from the mouth of the canyon, "by which he evidently
intended that the gorge should be passed before his fire was opened,"
as an American officer later observed. It was a gesture of defense that
would yet prove convenient for the invaders who had bought him off.
Then in a great sweat to shift responsibility from his own shoulders to
those who later could be vilified as traitors, he had recourse to a familiar
habit. There in the canyon he called a series of meetings to demand
indignantly what his people would have him do. The answers were not
what he hoped for.

He first convened the legislative Assembly on the red hillside
with its cedar clumps, and asked them "to say whether he should defend
the Department or treat with the enemy." An assemblyman answered
for his colleagues that the question was improper: they were there not
as legislators but as soldiers, "and their duty was to act as such, and
obey orders." The Governor dismissed them. He could not pin the
blame for a retreat upon his Assembly.

He next sent for the officers of the militia and volunteers, and
repeated his question. A citizen replied—and his reply was allowed to
stand by his fellows—that they "had assembled in camp to fight, and that
was what they should do and it was their wish to do so." Again the Governor was denied the pretext he longed for. But someone, either then
or a little later, brought up the proclamation issued by Kearny from
Las Vegas, in which New Mexicans were promised every consideration
in their way of life and religion if they would submit peacefully, and

the Governor was able to seize the opportunity to insult his citizen soldiery.

"Cowards!" he shrieked, and went on to declare that he "would not compromise himself by going into battle with people who had no Military Discipline." Forthwith he commanded them to disband and go to their homes—with the enemy five leagues away and advancing steadily. The regulars, he stormed, with the regulars he would meet any situation that approached. He tried desperately to seem like a victim of fate. But he was acting. In turn he kept showing all the tricks of his repertory—the man of decision, the fearless patriot, the reasonable democrat, the statesman in command of a high rhetorical style if not of an army; and all the while he was obliged by his profitable secret commitments to keep his gestures hollow. Giving every appearance now of being "very much exasperated" at what he chose to regard as his betrayal by the bewildered volunteers, he saw them begin their immediate retreat from the canyon. All was confusion. Each man took any horse he wanted, and galloped away home.

Lastly the Governor and Commanding General assembled the regular officers and once again asked his famous question. They replied that "they should march at once, meet the enemy and give them battle." He hastily dispersed them, but a few minutes later, hearing cheers from the troops who had been told what their officers had said, he was obliged to announce that he would attack. But not yet, not quite yet, for he had a letter to write. Dating it "Camp in the Canyon, August 16, 1846," he addressed Colonel Kearny with sentiments that were plainly intended to be seen afterward, to the writer's credit, by the central Mexican government. Step by step, he described the measures he had taken to save his province. He recorded how ardently he desired to defend it; he made plain that defense was impossible because reinforcements could not come in time from central Mexico, so far away; and he announced that he was withdrawing to the left bank of the Rio Grande, there to await decisions made by the two warring governments. He then launched into the flourishes that came so naturally to him: "I protest to Your Excellency before God and man that I do not recognize the Department of New Mexico as the land of the Republic of the North"—but what did that matter, since he had sold it out privately? "My heart is grieved with pain, on seeing that from my hands the country in which I first saw light passing to another nation"—which was another way of assuring Kearny that the deal held. "I do not deliver to Your Excellency the Department, and I only make my military retreat, until I shall receive orders from my gov-

ernment"—but he closed by tacitly recognizing the new authority that
was coming along the old Pecos road: "I recommend to your Excellency
the inhabitants of this beautiful country. They are most worthy, as your
Excellency will see, of the kind consideration of the government."

He gave the letter to Colonel Archuleta to deliver, and in spite
of his announced intention to fight, or to retire to the west side of the
river to keep vigil, he ordered the regulars to accompany him at once
to Santa Fe, where he gathered up all the money, plate and supplies he
could load on pack animals, herded the requisitioned horses and mules
of the defense forces into a private band for himself, and with hardly a
pause, fled down the river taking all the regular dragoons along as his
personal bodyguard. Over a doorway of the Palace was an inscription,
Vita fugit sicut umbra. If life fled like a shadow, so did the Governor.
News of his desertion flew through the city, and many of the proper-
tied residents in panic ran away also. One who remained stated bitterly,
remembering Francis I, "It can be said that Mr. Armijo did absolutely
nothing, nothing, and can say 'All is lost, including honor' . . ." His
accomplice Archuleta also ran away, taking refuge on his downriver
ranch, probably without delivering the Governor's letter. He had not
proclaimed himself political chief of the west bank of the Rio Grande.
Perhaps the time for it was not yet ripe. Perhaps he should wait and see
what office would be offered to him, under assurances of the presidential
agent, by the new masters of Santa Fe.

17.

Bloodless Possession

For the moment, Lieutenant Governor Juan Bautista Vigil y
Alarid assumed office as provisional governor in the midst of the popular
terror caused "by the flight of General Manuel Armijo, the desertion of

his soldiers . . . and the fear brought . . . by the approach of the military forces of the United States. . . ." His first act was to post everywhere copies of Kearny's letter to Armijo promising kindness to the New Mexicans. His second was to send his acting secretary of state, "quite a youth, and dressed in the fashion of the Americans," to meet Kearny with a letter announcing the governor's abandonment of his post, and extending a welcome to Santa Fe. Various Americans in the city also went out to meet the Army.

August eighteenth was a rainy day and the road was muddy. In midafternoon the first troops of the advancing column were seen from the edge of town moving along the base of cedar-covered hills. Most of the Santa Feans who were left went indoors. A few Mexicans lingered to peer around adobe corners as the army arrived among the houses. Not yet certain that there would be no resistance, the soldiers came with "drawn sabres and daggers in every look." The column was in close formation. At five o'clock General Kearny—he had just received his promotion—rode to the plaza. The artillery rolled on by him to take up a position on a hill that commanded the town from the north. The officers of Vigil's provisional government were waiting at the Palace. As the General arrived before them and dismounted, the sun broke through the heavy sky in a waft of splendor, Vigil greeted the General and turned over to him the office of governor, the United States flag was run up above the Palace, and from the north hill sounded a "glorious national salute" of thirteen guns. Soldiers still marching through the earth-walled lanes of the town heard a "wail of grief" from the men and women within their houses. A lieutenant noted that "there was not the least show . . . of resistance in any way," Magoffin, Cooke, Armijo and Archuleta had done their work well.

While the troops wound up to camp on the artillery hill, the General and his staff entered the Palace where they were given El Paso wine. They were hungry and thirsty. They had marched twenty-nine miles with nothing to eat since five in the morning. The staff went to dine at the house of a Mexican officer, "very much after the manner of a French dinner, one dish succeeding another in endless variety." Later, "in fine spirits," General Kearny showed his officers through the Palace. They saw a long ballroom with a dirt floor, and doors panelled in buffalo hide painted to resemble wood, and offices, bedrooms, guardroom, kitchens and prison cells and the patio garden, all "suitable to the dignity of a governor in New Mexico," though many parts of the building were "in a state of decay. . . ." Up on the hill the soldiers found little wood to burn, and in the sharp night kept their fires flaring with the tops of green cedars.

As soon as they could on the following days soldiers ranged through the town and some wrote notes on what they saw. Santa Fe was shabby, with no signs of either taste or wealth. There were no gardens— but the visitors had not yet looked within patio walls. Cornfields were laid out in the very center of town. Everything was a queer jumble of the clever and the primitive. Public walks enclosing the plaza were covered by a continuous roof, which was capital in case of rain; but there were no "public lights" anywhere in the streets at night. Delicious fruits were to be had at the market—peaches, grapes, melons, apples. The residents were poor and beggarly, and if the women were not handsome, they were "rather more intelligent than the men" and all loved parties, for there were "phandangoes almost every night." The army erected a hundred-foot-high flagpole in the plaza for the American colors. Odd little discoveries were made now and then. One brought to light Governor Manuel Armijo's state coach, with its now shabby gilt. A young officer examined it, and concluded, "as to going out in it, no one in his senses would risk his neck in such a clumsy and crazy affair." If there was one general impression shared by all, it was about the bells. There were five in the main church, and the other two had one or more each, and they all rang, it seemed, all the time, night and day. Dawdling about the famous old city, a soldier decided that in what he saw there was "nothing to pay us for our long march. . . ."

The General saw it all with a different set of values. It was no small matter to have taken the capital of the upper Rio Grande province at so little cost and in such good order. He could be well satisfied with the completion of the first phase of his mission. Stephen Kearny was fifty-two years old, a small man with a plain, thoughtful face that with its large, pale eyes and seamed cheeks suggested the looks of Andrew Jackson. His hair was gray, brushed forward on his brow and temples in the style of his youth—the period of the War of 1812, in which he had first seen service. The wings of a narrow white collar were folded across a high black stock under his jaws. His long blue coat piped in gold and bearing gold bullion epaulettes and twelve gold buttons fitted his trim figure closely. He was "very agreeable in conversation and manners," he conducted himself "with ease," and with gallant charm he could both "receive and return compliments." Candid and plain-speaking, he was an immediate success with new friends in Santa Fe, and with much to occupy him, he found time for both official and social affairs.

On the day after his entry he delighted the public with a speech he made before the Palace, in which again he pledged his government to honor the civil and religious rights of all. He called for peace and harmony, and announced that "being in possession of Santa Fe, I am therefore virtually in possession of all New Mexico. Armijo," he said, "is no longer your governor. His power is departed; but he will return and be as one of you. When he shall return you are not to molest him. . . . I am your governor—henceforth look to me for protection."

Vigil y Alarid replied to the address. With dignity he gave New Mexico's allegiance to the new flag, and added, "To us the power of the Mexican republic is dead. No matter what her condition, she was our mother. What child will not shed abundant tears at the tomb of his parents? I might indicate some of the causes for her misfortunes, but domestic troubles should not be made public. It is sufficient to say that civil war is the cursed source of that deadly poison which has spread over one of the grandest and greatest countries that has ever been created. . . ."

The conquest was completed on the following day when chiefs came from the river pueblos to declare their allegiance. The General had a "long and interesting" interview with them, "a fine, hardy, robust-looking set, with bows and arrows and Indian dress." They fascinated the staff with a recital of their tradition that had long promised how "the white man would come from the far east and release them from the bonds and shackles which the Spaniards had imposed" upon them. "Three hundred years of injustice and oppression" had "failed to extinguish in this race the recollection that they were once the peaceable and inoffensive masters of the country." A deputation of the clergy also appeared and joined in the new allegiance. In the evening a message arrived from Don Manuel Armijo, hinting that he might return, and "asking on what terms he would be received." But this turned out to be only a dodge to give him time to make good his escape to the south, in case pursuit and capture were planned. As he went he ravened upon his countrymen, driving off their cattle and horses with those he had previously stolen. A dedicated, and scared, materialist, his philosophy knew no limits. Scrambling toward Chihuahua he did not know that five hundred Mexican troops under a regular colonel were marching north to help him to defend New Mexico. With them, and supported by the rich resources of the Downriver district, he might have—but it was idle to imagine an act of duty and fidelity by which he might have defended the river kingdom; for its easy loss was long since determined by the facts of his character.

On August twenty-second General Kearny issued another procla- mation to the New Mexicans. In it he repeated all his previous assur- ances protecting their rights. And then he went one step farther in defining the limits of New Mexico now under his command. He an- nounced his intention "to hold the department, with its original boundaries (on both sides of the Del Norte), as a part of the United States, and under the name of 'the Territory of New Mexico.' " There vent, at one stroke of the pen, the old fiction about the Texas boundary at the east bank of the upper Rio Grande; and with it went Colonel Diego Archuleta's chance for a personal empire. Kearny was acting in accordance with confidential orders issued to him on June third by the Secretary of War, which stated that in case he conquered Santa Fe, with it would be "included the Department or State of New Mexico." The news was quietly taken, though it remained to be seen what Colonel Archuleta's reaction would be.

The citizens saw with pleasure through the following days that the General meant quite simply what he had proclaimed. Their habits, religion, civil rights and unofficial customs were left undisturbed. He was able to give brisk attention to details. He abolished the use of "stamp paper" which the Mexican government had sold for eight dollars a sheet, on which, to be legal, all business and official transactions had to be drawn up. He went to Mass as a gesture of courtesy. He called on the American traders, and he dined with Mexican families. He worked on plans for a march to California, in which he would be followed by a battalion of Mormons who had volunteered on condition of receiving their discharges once they reached the Pacific coast. With him in Santa Fe, in addition to his regulars, was a volunteer Missouri regiment under Colonel Alexander Doniphan, which, in the grand strategy of the war, would march down the Rio Grande and on to Chihuahua in an attempt to meet American forces under General Wool.

All through the last two weeks of August Santa Fe was alive with rumors that Governor Armijo had not, after all, gone very far south, and that indeed he was busy raising five or six thousand men in the Downriver, and would soon return to his capital, force it to surrender, and resume his station in the Palace. The citizens watched the General to see if he would send soldiers out against Don Manuel. But even though he did nothing, the rumors were believed by many of Armijo's former followers, who fled the city, "lest on his return they should be considered as traitors and treated accordingly."

James Magoffin was still busy at the center of things, still dis-sembling his true purposes behind his character as Chihuahua trader—a disguise that had the virtue of truth. His brother Samuel was in Santa Fe, headed south with his caravan, and had brought along his new wife, Susan, who was much in love and interested in everything—conditions that she revealed in her diary. "Brother James" came to supper frequently, and the military came to call, including the General, who made a flutter at the end of August by announcing that he was about to take a strong force and march to the Downriver for a look around. It would be as well to examine the rumors of Armijo's activities there, and meet the population, and know the country better. James Magoffin was to precede him by one day, and once again prepare the way; after which—though this was still a secret design—he would go on to Chihuahua, where before the arrival of General Wool with his American troops he would undertake to "quiet" the Mexican authorities just as he had done at Santa Fe.

James Magoffin still had Colonel Archuleta on his mind, and sometime before the departure of the downriver reconnaissance, he made a point of seeing General Kearny about him. He reminded the General of the private agreement with Archuleta, and recommended him for an official post under the new Territorial government—some job "which would compromise him," and bind him to the United States cause. Yes, the General remembered. Yes, of course, he intended to take care of the matter. Magoffin left it with him, and spent his last two evenings with Samuel and Susan, and "cracked jokes and spun yarns, laughed, drank &c." There was a supper of "oysters & champaign," and at night on September first he left for Downriver.

On September second the General led seven hundred soldiers out for the country below. "We passed through S.Fé with our banners flying to the breeze," said a volunteer, and "the Ladies looked intently from the housetops as we passed—" Three days later an army grazing detachment out on the plain to the south heard cannon fire from the direction of Albuquerque. It was a salute to the General on his arrival there. He sent word back to Santa Fe that "all was quiet and no armed force of any kind in the field." By the eleventh he was in the capital again, well-satisfied with what he had seen. As soon as he had time he called on the Samuel Magoffins and amused Susan with his description

of life down the river. At Santo Domingo the Indians, mounted, costumed and painted, gave a stunning exhibition of a sham battle; and
later the resident pastor gave a collation to the staff, while behind his
back the young soldiers and the Indian servant girls flirted in a "little
exchange of the artillery of the eyes." On down the valley people turned
out to offer melons and other fresh fruit. The soldiers bought quantities,
using their uniform buttons for money. A button passed for twenty-five
cents. Hundreds of Mexicans and Indians trailed along after the Army,
and seemed "well pleased with the change of government." At Albuquerque the General called on Mrs. Manuel Armijo, who seemed to be
"a good-looking woman and rather cheerful." Another traveller saw her
a little while afterward as "a comely dame of forty, with the remains of
considerable beauty, but quite passée." Her husband, said the natives,
had "gone to the Devil," and a volunteer entered a mysterious rumor
in his diary: "Don Manuel emasculated."

The troops went as far as Tomé. They saw large flocks of ducks,
geese and swans on the Rio Grande, and plenty of fish. The weather was
pleasant until the last few days, when sandstorms came up. At Tomé
there was a fiesta in honor of the Blessed Virgin Mary, with processions,
bonfires and fireworks. The volunteers gave trouble and seventy or eighty
of them had to be given extra duty to discipline them. The staff took
part in the fiesta, walking in the procession, and the General carried a
lighted candle, "making," as he said to amuse Susan Magoffin, "a fool
of myself." The whole tour was reassuring, in its pledges of loyalty, its
"most flattering treatment," with some of the towns exhibiting fireworks
and theatrical entertainments, and giving balls. If Armijo had been busy
raising a force, there was no sign of it, or of him. New Mexico seemed
secure, and as soon as final plans were ready, the General could leave
for the West.

He ordered Colonel Doniphan to remain at Santa Fe until relieved
by another volunteer force that was coming from Missouri under the
command of Colonel Sterling Price for occupation duty. In his reports
to Washington the General, after noting the satisfactory state of the
population, went on to describe the Rio Grande. It was a stream, he
said, that needed engineering controls; and he recommended that the
War Department plan them. He attended to the final details of his movement across Arizona toward California, and fixed his departure for
September twenty-fifth. The night before leaving, he was the guest of
honor at a ball given in the Palace by the merchants of Santa Fe. Many

of those invited did not attend, said Mrs. Magoffin, "owing to the death of an old gentleman a few days before, who was related to half the city." But the company was sprightly, and wearing her scarlet Canton crepe shawl, Susan was "soon surrounded by the Gen. and his officers." The local ladies were turned out in the Mexican style, "large sleeves, short waists, ruffled skirts, and no bustles." They all smoked seegaritos, and one who made a flashing appearance was "the old woman with false hair and teeth"—Doña Tules, who ran the leading monte game of Santa Fe. The dancing was lively. They danced the *cuna*—"the cradle." Susan Magoffin thought it beautiful. It was somewhat like the waltz. A couple stood face to face, encircling each other's waist with their arms, to make the sides of a cradle. As they swung around, both leaned back, to close the bottom of the cradle. The music of a violin and a guitar scraped and thumped, clouds of cigarette smoke hung under the ceiling, and in a corner a local matron of position sat with her foot on a human foot-stool—her servant, who crouched before her.

The Army marched out at noon the next day. The General was busy with last-minute details, one of which "for some reason" he had neglected until it was now too late. He had not made any arrangements for the future of Colonel Diego Archuleta. It would prove to be a costly oversight. The command of New Mexico was turned over to Colonel Doniphan.

Eleven days later, opposite Valverde Mesa on the Rio Grande General Kearny was preparing to leave the river and turn westward when he met "Mr. Kit Carson with a party of sixteen men on his way to Washington City with mail and papers—an express from Commodore Stockton and Lieutenant-Colonel Fremont, reporting that the Californias were already in possession of the Americans . . . ; that the American flag was already flying from every important position in the territory, and that the country was free from Mexican control, the war ended, and peace and harmony established among the people." Two large phases of President Polk's grand strategy were accomplished with the taking of New Mexico and California. General Kearny, offering to detail a substitute courier, persuaded Kit Carson to turn right around and guide him to California. Keeping with him only his battery of two howitzers and a hundred dragoons, the General sent the rest of his force back to Santa Fe, and pushed on for the Pacific. James Magoffin took leave of him and rode for El Paso on his way to Chihuahua, where, if all went well, he would do for General Wool what he had done for General

Kearny. It was for him a satisfaction to be able to say, in simple truth, "Bloodless possession of New Mexico was what President Polk wished: it was obtained through my means. . . ."

18.

The Army of Chihuahua

Another thrust in the American grand strategy of the war came to the river on October eighth, 1846, at France Way. The old ford of St. Denis, and the Spanish founders of Texas, now saw Brigadier General John E. Wool's Army of Chihuahua coming to Mexico at a point about five hundred river miles inland from the Gulf. Wool came on the old trade route from San Antonio that skirted at great distance the highlands rising from the deep coastal plain. As they neared the river his soldiers saw passages of purple and yellow limestone, occasional canyons, and far-reaching surfaces of pale gray dust broken by thorny brush; and to men marching in war so far from home, at the end of day after day, over so great a waste, night came like a vast sinking of the heart.

They had taken eleven days to march about one hundred and seventy-five miles from San Antonio. As they neared the river their order in column read first, four companies of dragoons; and then, six infantry companies, both regulars and volunteers from Illinois; General Wool and his staff; the Arkansas volunteer artillery regiment; the wagon trains, and a rear guard. Each soldier was issued twenty cartridges, and all guns and cannon were heavily loaded. Across the river, old Fort Saint John Baptist was now called the Presidio del Rio Grande. It was known to be garrisoned by Mexican troops. Wool's men expected a fight. There would be no long interval of posed yet suspended hostilities on both sides of the river such as had delayed General Taylor's operations downstream for so long; for General Wool, before undertaking his march, had made certain to equip the division with a "flying-bridge," the parts of which were hauled in wagons—framed timbers, and spans of various lengths, and pontoons—under the charge of two engineer officers, Captain William D. Fraser and Captain Robert E. Lee.

It was like General Wool to insist upon extraordinary preparations for a campaign. He had been for twenty-five years Inspector-General of the Army, and had formed a habit of furious interest in details and a dear love of uniformity. He required all personnel to shave daily, even beardless volunteer boys, no matter where the Army of Chihuahuas might find itself. Units that took his smallest order less than awesomely he disciplined with hardness, and when the Arkansas Volunteers insisted on behaving like frontier democrats in military matters he conducted a running feud with their colonel, Archibald Yell, former governor of their state. He brawled primly with other senior officers, too, and with Dr. Josiah Gregg, whom he had engaged at San Antonio as an expert on Mexico to accompany the Army in the post of interpreter. If Gregg saw him at first as "an amiable gentlemanly man," it was not long before he was calling him a man "of a very unpleasant, whimsical temperament—decidedly old-womanish"; and the volunteers referred to him as "the old Woolly Devil," and "Old Granny Wool." But he continued to demand strict order on the march, proper sanitation in camp, and sustained training; and in the end his troops remained more healthy than those in other invasion units, and when they were tested in battle proved to be well-prepared.

They were on the alert now as they came to the Rio Grande on October eighth and looked across at Mexico, expecting to see the Presidio garrison drawn up to fight. But, as a young volunteer German immigrant noted, "with the exception of two Mexicans who held up a white flag, and waved their hats, there was no one else to see." The Presidio garrison had abandoned the town and retired to the interior. The mayor of Presidio del Rio Grande crossed and gave his old stone town into "the protection of the United States." The men dismissed from ranks broke for the river, whose water "was muddy, but good to drink." The current was "very rapid," and the stream "about as wide as the Ohio at Cincinnati." The troops found refreshment by bathing at once.

The engineers went to work on their flying bridge, and also assembled ferry barges, while the troops waiting to cross hardened their spirits with grim little jobs. "There has been," wrote Captain Lee to his wife, "a great whetting of knives, grinding of swords, and sharpening of bayonets, ever since we reached the river." Within three days the flying bridge and the ferries were ready, and under a hard rain the Army of Chihuahua crossed to Mexico and marched over brushy bottomland to Presidio five miles inland. "We were lucky," scribbled the German youth, "to find cornbread instead of bullets awaiting us. . . ." The residents were friendly, but charged "exorbitant prices for everything." The Mexican officials sought out General Wool with a great piece of news. A hundred miles southeast beyond mountain and desert General Taylor with the Army of the Rio Grande had captured Monterrey in engagements lasting from September twentieth to twenty-fourth. It was not so much to rejoice the Americans with this news that it was given them by the Mexican town authorities, as to report further that General Taylor after his victory had agreed to an armistice of eight weeks. The Presidians gave General Wool a copy of the articles of capitulation of Monterrey, in which the cease-fire was clearly provided for. Surely he would honor it?

The General found nothing in the articles to keep him from continuing his march, and he agreed to abide by the armistice after arriving at Monclova, another hundred and seventy-five miles away. Meanwhile he took a few days to rest his men, replenish supplies, and consider possible routes for his descent upon Chihuahua, should the war continue. In another day Brigadier General James Shields arrived from Camargo to command the Infantry brigade and confirmed the news of Taylor's third big victory. General Shields—who later quarrelled with Wool—earned a line or two in Dr. Gregg's notebook: ". . . a military monomaniac—crazy—his head addled by his elevation . . . one of the veriest *military* simpletons." The Army of Chihuahua had its notables. Another was the wife of Major David Hunter, Paymaster USA. Amidst the small but varied crowd of women on the campaign, most of them attached to enlisted men, Mrs. Paymaster Hunter loomed as "a very amiable, meritorious and remarkable lady who is truly the heroine of Gen. Wool's campaign, having been the only respectable female in the army," as Gregg saw her. She had marched from San Antonio, and she would proceed into Mexico, to suffer "innumerable sacrifices, privations and dangers—and all for affection to her husband." If Dr. Gregg heard some "contend that she has been out of place," he thought this was possibly true in one sense. "Nevertheless," he insisted, "I must consider that there is at least no *demerit* in her course: in fact"—his head swam with generosity—"in fact, I think it merits more than a mere negative. . . ."

Few of the soldiers saw Presidio, for their camp was four miles west of town, and they were marched to it without pause, much as they would have liked to gaze about. But "I always forget," sighed a volunteer, "that I have no will of my own but that I am a part of a machine." Still, in glimpses, the Army could see that Presidio, with its stone town gate, was colorful. Its earthen houses carried architectural ornaments frescoed in pale earth colors. Weeds worked on the ruin of Saint Bernard's. Private gardens of sugar cane, cotton and fig trees attracted the invaders. Two thousand people belonged in Presidio, but now in the war only about half were still in town. It was not a healthful spot, for swamps and bogs stood on all sides, caused by overflow from irrigation canals. In their brief stay, the Army picked up "considerable chills and fevers."

One day two starving men lurched their way into camp to be taken care of. They were Texas Rangers who had been captured a few weeks earlier in a previous American touch at the river. It was an episode unauthorized by the Army, and it ended in recall of the troops, and reprimand for its commander—Colonel William S. Harney, who had been unable to contain himself at San Antonio until General Wool's arrival during the summer. He had taken Presidio in August with only a few companies of rangers and regulars. When he was ordered to withdraw his impulsive invasion, the Mexicans returned, and fired at his rear guard over the river, and took a few prisoners. One man, a civilian sutler, had a strange story to tell, and he came in his turn among Wool's men to tell it.

With seven companions he had been ferrying supplies for Colonel Harney when the Mexicans fired upon him in the river. He jumped overboard. He couldn't swim, but crawled underwater to the Mexican bank where he hid till dark, when he pushed a log out in the current to bear him across to the American bank. But he could not make it, and ended by floating thirty miles downstream before he could manage to land. He walked up to the campsite opposite Presidio only to find that the Americans had left. Mexicans then captured him, and the night before he was to be marched to the interior with other prisoners, he escaped, and again entered the river, found another log, and floated down again, this time for eighty miles, to Laredo. Hoping to meet Wool's Army at France Way, he walked up from Laredo, found the encampment, introduced himself—he was a Mr. Riddle—and told his story.

In camp, volunteers greased the wagons, and regulars let them do it "—the volunteers have to do all the extra work," one of them observed—and got on with their washing and everybody prepared for inspection which meant, under General Wool, buying new clothes if old ones were worn or unpresentable. A regimental sutler asked "10 dollars for a pair of coarse boots, and 6 dollars for linen trousers." On the private soldier's pay of seven dollars a month, it was hard to meet the General's standards. Sardonically the private soldiers referred to themselves as "seven-dollar targets."

And yet there was pride in the Army, and a sense of affirmative purpose, for at Presidio a young private recorded quite simply, "I had the honor of doing guard duty soon after our arrival in Mexico. The guard parade of 300 men make a grand appearance. They parade daily under command of the staff officers, Captains, etc." He did not see the ceremony as merely a formal flourish of arms that took up his time and set him to trudging at somebody else's pleasure. He noted further that "Our lieutenants have the least to do, and can take it easy." And when it was time to go to work, the Division could respond swiftly. On October fifteenth, "this morning at 9 o'clock the alarm was sounded, and then a call to arms. In ten minutes we were in readiness to meet the enemy. In the distance . . . shots were heard. The Dragoons went out to investigate, but soon returned to report that the Mexicans at Presidio were celebrating a feast day, and were shooting volleys in honor of the day." But the Army was leaving the next day for the interior, and General Wool must review them all before starting, and so "We had a big review in the afternoon. . . . Later," about to leave for the unknown, and obscurely aware of how poignant might be the idlest words if they were the last from a soldier who might never return, "later in the day I wrote two letters to the home folks. . . ."

At four in the morning on October sixteenth the advance elements of the Army of Chihuahua moved away from the river, on the Monclova road, over a land perfectly level, and without water in a day's march. Some of the soldiers had picked up at Presidio a "kind of scurvy" that made "lips, teeth, gums and tongue sore," so that it was agony to eat. There seemed nothing in prospect for days but the repeated chores of marching overland, for no enemy forces appeared, and Dr. Gregg, on his mule, with his red parasol, riding beside the marching men who were heavy-belted and pendulous with scabbarded blades, remarked, "Verily our war-seeking soldiers are becoming desperate for want of an enemy upon whom to display their valor."

Once at Monclova, General Wool waited four weeks under the terms of Taylor's armistice. While he waited, he studied obstacles and solutions to his proposed move upon Chihuahua City. To his west lay the great and all but impassable Bolsón de Mapimí, an elevated desert shaped like a huge pouch and rimmed by mountains. Dust-gray, water-less, silent, it rose between five and ten thousand feet in altitude, and covered nearly ten thousand square miles. He could not cross it with an army, but would have to detour around it to capture Chihuahua City and paralyze north central Mexico—if the armistice were lifted and hostilities resumed. It was lifted, suddenly, for the Washington government ordered General Taylor to rescind it; and Taylor notified Santa Anna, who was now in the field as Mexican supreme commander, that the war would be renewed on November thirteenth. Three days later Taylor's Army of the Rio Grande occupied Saltillo, basing Worth's division there.

And now, studying his most suitable route to the west, Wool saw that he must march south from Monclova to Parrás in order to skirt the Bolsón de Mapimí before turning west and north toward Chihuahua. He saw further that Parrás was only ninety miles from Saltillo, and the United States forces there. It seemed to him that, coming so close to the main body of invasion, his division would be more useful as a part of it than as a lone expedition crawling through weeks of wilderness travel on a mission whose success was by no means certain. Accordingly, he sent an express to General Taylor at Monterrey suggesting that orders be issued to change his objective, attaching him instead to the Monterrey-Saltillo-Parrás line. Taylor promptly approved; and the Army of Chihuahua marched on November twenty-fourth for Parrás, to go no farther west.

But Colonel Doniphan at Santa Fe knew nothing of the change in plan, and proceeded with his part of the design against Chihuahua City, which he had persuaded General Kearny to approve.

19.

The Free Missourians

Colonel Sterling Price and his Missouri regiment had been in Santa Fe since October third, preparing to take over from Doniphan. The Mormon battalion was also there, outfitting under Captain Philip St. George Cooke to march for California. Their condition appalled their new commander. They were hardly a military force. They were "too much enlisted by families," as he saw. "Some were too old, some feeble, some young; much embarrassed"—in the Mormon style—"by too many women." They were "undisciplined; much worn by travelling on foot . . . from Nauvoo, Ill.; . . . clothing scant, no money to pay them . . . or clothing to issue." Another officer observed that "A more ragamuffin looking set than the Mormons it would be hard to find. . . . From the officers down I could see nothing like a genteel-looking man. . . ." There was a general eagerness to leave Santa Fe and be on the move. Out of various motives—freedom for the Mormons, adventure for the soldiers, business for the traders—everyone wanted to be up and going. The troops were all "anxious to get away, each one wishing to be the first." A lieutenant said, "Some prefer an expedition to California, some south, and all are fearful they will not get to go where they wish."

On October seventh many of the traders at Santa Fe started downriver, including the Samuel Magoffins, with their wagons for Chihuahua. Their march was planned to take advantage of protection by the Doniphan column, and they would make rendezvous with the troops at Valverde before driving on for Mexico and—who knew?—perhaps battle. On the same day Colonel Doniphan received a dispatch from General Kearny ordering him to take a crack detachment and enter the Navajo country to wring pledges of peace out of the Indians who had taken advantage of the unsettled conditions of a change of government in New Mexico to ravage the countryside.

Preparations were stepped up. On October fifteenth and sixteenth the Mormons moved out. Soldiers knowing they were about to depart suddenly felt nostalgic about what they would leave. One made a note of the "artillery band at tattoo, who play several tunes every evening between the calls. To hear the martial notes of a bugle on a clear calm lovely evening is always soul-stirring, but to have three or four good musicians in a land destitute of taste or rational amusements nightly play some old and favorite air, when one's mind is running upon home, friends, and the many luxuries and enjoyments we have deprived our-selves of, is certainly a pleasure . . . one of the few enjoyments I have in Santa Fe is the music. . . ." And then came darkness, and the lively nighttime, until the army's curfew at ten, when "the gun fires." Then the citizens "can be seen running in all directions, the monte tables are deserted, and the merry fandango is no longer heard . . . and the stillness only interrupted by the tread of the sentinels, the rattling of their arms, or the reliefs going on post. Occasionally a sentinel is heard calling the corporal of the guard, having taken a prisoner, some unlucky individ-ual who is caught straying from home or returning from a gambling house. . . ."

Colonel Doniphan with three hundred mounted troopers left Santa Fe on October twenty-sixth. The rest of his force—some five hun-dred men—would follow on the river road to await him at Valverde while below Albuquerque he turned west for the Navajo plains. On the day of his departure the Navajos, as though to confirm the need of his discipline, raided the old river villages south of Albuquerque—Tomé, Valencia and the rest—killing many people and driving off five thousand sheep from the valley farms. The Mexican ranchers, now territorial citi-zens of the United States, sent their remaining herds and flocks to the eastern mountains for safekeeping, and organized bands of "voluntarios" to chase after the Navajos in their western wilderness, where Doniphan would soon force a great roundup of chiefs for a council of peace.

The rest of the First Missouri Volunteers toiled down the river in their own free style. Their column stretched out for miles—at one time for as far as a hundred. Parties of traders were intermittently scattered along their line, until at times soldiers could not be told from civilians. Their uniforms were incomplete, and such as they had were of summer weight. There was already snow on the mountains above Santa Fe, and winter followed the marchers down the valley. Many suffered, for they had thrown away their tents to make light their loads. The nights were hard. One morning the troops awoke to find themselves under four inches of snow. In the valley they saw great passages of geese flying south, and shot a few, but the weather was "too cold for sport." Large blocks of ice floated down the river. Fording was difficult. The river road was sandy in spots, and gave trouble to teams and teamsters. Soldiers "had to spend half of their time at the wheels." Oxen died on the trail and men took ill and were sent back to Santa Fe. Soldiers foraged in mountains twenty-five miles away from the road to bring firewood to the column. The human climate was not pleasant, either; for as they marched south the troops felt that "the people generally have hostile feelings and would be able to render efficient aid to any force sent against us from below. . . ." The spirit had changed from the first enthusiasm for the new regime. There were powers at work in the dark to change it. But so far, in early December, the Americans, only sorry that as conquerors they were not better loved, suspected nothing.

Presently, at Lemitar, and below, at Socorro, the column came into what seemed like a new climate. The weather moderated. Soldiers found diversions in Socorro, if at high prices. An English traveller, George Frederick Ruxton, was also there in December, 1846, and made notes on what he saw of the old river town. Its appearance was "that of a delapidated brick kiln, or a prairie dog town, indeed from this animal the New Mexicans appear to have derived their style of architecture." The people seemed to him dirty, mean, lazy, beggarly. ". . . In his rabbit burrow," with his tortillas, his chile, and his corn shuck cigarette, "the New Mexican is content; and with an occasional traveller to pilfer, or the excitement of a stray Texan to massacre now and then, is tolerably happy—his only care being that the river rise enough to fill his acequia . . . that sufficient maize may grow to furnish him tortillas for the winter, and shucks for his half-starved horse or mules, which the Navajos have left, out of charity, after killing half his sons and daughters and bearing into captivity the wife of his bosom. . . ."

Ruxton had come up the Chihuahua Trail, and now in December he was among the traders and Missouri volunteers. He marvelled at the loose formation of the column, and its disorders, and its lack of uniformity in all things. Even the ammunition and provision wagons, he noted, were travelling through enemy country without an escort. At Valverde, where the camps of the soldiers and traders were made while awaiting Colonel Doniphan, Ruxton, an officer in a British regiment, could hardly believe what he saw. "From appearances no one would have imagined this to be a military encampment. The tents were in line, but there all uniformity ceased. There were no regulations in force with regard to cleanliness. The camp was strewed with the bones and offal of the cattle slaughtered for its supply, and not the slightest attention was paid to keeping it clear from other accumulations of filth. The men, unwashed and unshaven, were ragged and dirty, without uniforms, and dressed as, and how, they pleased. They wandered about, listless and sickly looking, or were sitting in groups playing at cards, and swearing and cursing, even at the officers if they interfered to stop it (as I witnessed). The greatest irregularities constantly took place. Sentries, or a guard, although in an enemy's country, were voted unnecessary; and one fine day, during the time I was there, three Navajo Indians ran off with a flock of 800 sheep belonging to the camp, killing the two volunteers in charge of them, and reaching the mountains in safety with their booty. Their mules and horses were straying over the country; in fact, the most total want of discipline was apparent in everything." It was all true, and shocking to a cultivated observer with professional military standards. What a foreigner could not see was that the volunteers were frontier individualists, enacting a primitive stage of democracy, even if it often proclaimed the self to the disadvantage of its fellows. But in the end, what did it matter, mused Ruxton: "These very men, however, were as full of fight as game cocks," and when a fight was coming, that was what was wanted.

For Mexican troops were massing in northern Chihuahua. Ruxton had seen them. There was every sign that they would defend El Paso, the gateway. He brought news, too, of others he had seen—Ex-Governor Manuel Armijo, travelling southward with Albert Speyer, the Santa Fe trader, and all their wagons. Speyer's large consignment of arms and ammunition, so laboriously hauled from St. Louis, was seized by the Mexican army, in spite of a hired escort of "thirty strapping young Missourians, each with a long rifle across his saddle."

Armijo had other worries. Ruxton told his listeners at Valverde about him. "A mountain of fat," the fugitive governor "rolled out of his American Dearborn," and asked,

"What is the price of cotton goods at Durango?" He had seven wagonloads with him to sell. Next he asked,

"What are they saying in Mexico of the doings at Santa Fe—" its capture by the Americans without any resistance?

"There is but one opinion," replied Ruxton, "expressed over all the country—that General Armijo and the New Mexicans are a pack of arrant cowards."

"Oh, my God!" shrieked Armijo. "They don't know that I had but seventy-five men to fight three thousand. What could I do?"

Other news came to Valverde. Traffic through El Paso was closed. Traders camped farther down the valley sent word that a large force was coming up from Chihuahua to capture all travellers and goods. Drivers made corrals of their wagons, sinking their wheels to the hubs "for a breast-work in case of attack." Worse, a party that had managed to get through to El Paso had been captured and jailed, and one—it was James Magoffin—had been led away to Chihuahua City where he was tried for his life as a spy. His secret work at Santa Fe had been discovered. He was in great danger. Samuel and Susan Magoffin heard this with distress at Valverde.

Colonel Doniphan returned to the river from the Navajo country on December twelfth at Socorro, bringing with him a treaty signed by the chiefs with X's, promising "permanent peace, mutual trust and friendship." He hurried down to Valverde to join his main body of troops, and set to work preparing "our train," as he said, "to obey the order of General Kearny, requiring me to report to General Wool." He animated the command, took them down to Fray Cristóbal, and without incident led them through the Dead Man's March. They emerged from it at the river on December twenty-second and found the last traders camped downstream. There was no communication with El Paso. Mexicans living at the new settlement of Doña Ana would say nothing. There was battle in the air. The Colonel shook together his units for regular inspections. Ammunition was passed out, and without recourse to voting, pickets were stationed at night. The fighting strength of the long, scattered column totalled eight hundred and fifty-six men—all riflemen. There were no cannon at hand for, as Wool's forces were well-equipped with a regiment of artillery, the Missourian batteries had been left behind at Santa Fe.

20.

Brazito and the Pass

It seemed odd not to have news of General Wool. Presumably, by now, he should have drawn near to the city of Chihuahua, if he had not actually entered it. News of so striking an event would surely have come north, despite all the Mexican army might do to censor it. And yet there was not even a rumor of his invasion. But in any case, Colonel Doniphan's orders read to report to General Wool at Chihuahua City, and there he must go to find him. The column straggled on past Doña Ana—the last settlement above El Paso forty-five miles away. The weather was pleasant as the march began on December twenty-fifth. It was to be a short march, perhaps out of respect for the great feast of Christmas. Coming near to a fine camping site with leafy river bottoms and an easy approach for leading horses to water, the Colonel ordered a halt and a camp made around one o'clock. He sent out scouts to survey the neighborhood, and south of the campsite they suddenly saw and chased a small party of Mexican observers who as they ran away left behind a fine horse. The horse was captured and taken back to camp.

The Americans were being watched, then, and Colonel Doniphan had his first direct warning, and his first captive—the horse. While the wagons were being unloaded, and the teams and cavalry mounts were led to the river to drink and forage, the Colonel called for a deck of cards, and sat down to play the scouts for the ownership of the Mexican mount. It was a gesture in the democratic volunteer style. The game was not yet finished when to the south on the flat valley a cloud of dust was seen to appear and grow. The Colonel estimated its size and behavior; and gave the order to sound "boots and saddles." In another moment he cancelled it, for the cavalry mounts were all at the river. There was not time to bring them back and saddle them. He commanded everyone to form in infantry line, and established the teamsters as a guard around their wagon park.

In less than half an hour the dust was near enough to reveal its source—a Mexican army of eleven hundred men—lancers, cavalry and infantry—with a howitzer. They advanced steadily, coming along a high level parallel to the river and to mountains that rose a few miles away as the eastern limit of the valley. Once opposite the camp, whose site was called Brazito, they wheeled into front and halted on the elevation half a mile away from the Missourians, who were drawn up in line with the Rio Grande in their rear. The Mexican front reached north and south for two miles. The regulars among them were uniformed in red "& made quite a cavalier appearance," as a volunteer saw. The American Army of the West had not yet fired a shot in battle. Now with the moment of decision upon them, they drew together out of their rambunctious disorder as volunteers, and presented a hard, clear, disciplined force, waiting for the command to fight. The scene on the riverside plain had a third group of observers: a large party of Apache Indians who from the mountains in the rear of the Mexican line proposed to watch the encounter.

The day was sunny, and the valley's winter colors shone in the clear air—pale russet reeds, silver grass, and gold straw; gray-violet mountains above the speckled bench where the Mexican arms glimmered; and in the river groves, copper, gold and bronze leaves clinging to the cottonwoods like trophies of beaten metal waiting for conquerors. From the Mexican lines emerged a rider who cantered to within a hundred steps of the Missourians. There he halted and displayed a flag. It was black, with two white skulls above crossbones on one side, and on the other, white lettering that read *"Libertad ó muerte!"* Doniphan's adjutant with an interpreter rode out to meet him.

"Let your commander come to our line and speak to our General," said the Mexican.

"If your General wants to see our commander," replied the Missourians, "let him come here."

"We shall break your ranks, then, and take him there!"

"Come and take him!"

"Damn it all, we will neither give nor ask quarter," said the Mexican waving his flag, "prepare for a charge!" and galloped back to his line.

Colonel Doniphan passed an order down the ranks: "Prepare to squat!" The men laughed, but knew he was in earnest, for he followed it up by ordering them to hold their fire, and let the Mexicans shoot over their heads until their advance was so close that the volunteer marksmanship could take terrible effect. The Mexicans moved. Their infantry was on the American right, their howitzer in the center, and their cavalry on the left. As they came they fired and paused, fired and paused, five times, without any return fire from the ranks before the river. They turned to ask one another what kind of people were these who stood up to be shot at without shooting back. They shrugged. It was clear that the Americans meant to surrender.

But the long rifles were cocked, and the officers were watching the Colonel, and the files were already told off, one and two, one kneeling to reload while the other stood to fire, and when the Mexicans had come within a hundred and fifty yards, the word came, and "number one fired, and then number two . . . and it was well done and had a fine effect, their cavalry reeling under it, and their whole line giving," recorded a Missouri lieutenant. The Mexican cavalry charged around the end to get at the parked wagons, and there too the teamsters held fire until it could be given with maximum damage. When it came, the Mexicans veered away in confusion.

At the same time, the Missourian right charged the enemy howitzer and captured it. It was at once put to work by volunteers who formed a battery of artillerymen about it. The whole Missouri line now surged forward at the command to charge, and the Mexican front rolled back at some distance before it, as though blown over the ground by a shock wave. By the time the Americans reached the high level of the first Mexican stand, the Mexicans were nowhere to be seen. At a full run they had retreated out of sight. Some who fled to the mountains were stopped and killed by the Apaches there. Others headed south to flee through El Paso. One was a woman who had followed the Mexican soldiers into battle. At the defeat, she jumped on a mule and whipped it into a frantic trot southward. Another woman was killed at the capture of the howitzer, and her body carried away. There were Mexican dead over the field, and much abandoned property.

The soldiers were allowed to pick up what they could find; and soon retreated to the Brazito camp, loaded with wine, and trinkets, and garments, and little crosses, and scraps of equipment, and dropped weapons. All were in roaring spirits. They had come ably and safely through their first battle. They had proved that frontier democrats were capable of discipline when the necessity for it was presented in terms of life and death. "Our men behaved like veterans," declared an officer, "and exhibited a coolness and obedience to orders worthy of any troops." Once again in camp, they knocked open the Mexican wine jugs and

took the day as a "Christmas frolic." Colonel Doniphan was amused at
the Mexican aim with the howitzer. It was always high, and he said that
"about a bushel of copper ore" from the howitzer must have passed
over his head "by at least ten feet." He settled down to resume his interrupted card game, finished it, and agreed that the Mexican horse was
won by one of the scouts. The losers had the last laugh when it turned
out that the horse had been allowed to escape during the battle. "It
was late at night before all was quiet in camp," noted a lieutenant,
"being greatly exhilarated by our victory without the loss of a man. . . ."

Leaving camp early the next morning they wore their trophies
of victory. "One had on a Mexican dragoon cap, another a serape, some,
beads and crosses, almost everyone something. . . ." The volunteers
were themselves again. They marched south, passed the Mexican base
camp of the day before, found "some of the fires still burning," and
came upon a handful of Mexican dead left behind. "We thought only
of reaching El Paso," wrote a soldier, "and solving the problem whether
we shall have another fight or not."

It was solved the next day when in sight of the earth city on the
south bank they were met by a deputation come "from El Paso to surrender the place, and to inform us that the Mexicans were totally
defeated and never stopped but continued on to Chihuahua in squads,
dispersing in all directions." The conquerors crossed the river by a ford
between two vineyards, marched through the town accepting "grapes,
apples, wine, pears, peaches, etc., in great abundance" from the residents,
and camped in a vineyard at the far side, with open country beyond.
The wind was blowing, and the fine alluvial soil of the valley's old riverbeds came up in long hauls on the air against the exposed camp. At the
end of December at El Paso the river was a meagre stream winding by
the dusty violet mountains of the pass, and between groves of valley
cottonwoods with their hammered dark-gold leaves. Above the banks
rose freckled sandhills, and bare trees in the distance looked like arrested
gray smoke. The earth, and the houses that came up from it, were of a
pale, skin-brown color. Washed sunlight bore down through thin white
cloud, and flocks of huge crows made commotions in the fields. The
country was dusty and flat; and in its open winter airs all things, even
the low, extensive town, were absorbed, from a little distance, by golden
space.

The regiment found El Paso very different from Santa Fe. The
old northern capital seemed in retrospect to be rude and graceless by
comparison with the charms of the wide irrigation canals of El Paso,

and its beautifully set vineyards, orchards and fields, and the patios with so much greenery, the fine workmanship of the houses, and their superior furnishings and—presently—their hospitality. For at first the populace had run away, but soon began to return when it was plain that the Americans, while they might be infidels and heretics, as Governor Trias had proclaimed in Chihuahua, were not barbarians, as he had also called them. But neither were they notably virtuous. As the people returned, and enterprise saw opportunity, victor and vanquished combined in the commerce of appetites; for the regiment was in town to stay until Colonel Doniphan's plans and equipment were complete.

Now in the northernmost city of Chihuahua, he was positively assured by surrendered Mexican soldiers that General Wool had made no move at all against the state. Here was a dilemma. Should he advance to Chihuahua hoping that in time Wool would appear? Should he undertake such a march deep into enemy country without artillery? Or should he ignore his orders from Kearny and not proceed? In a sense the decision was not his alone, for the men under his command were all volunteers with decided views. He explained the problem to them and put the decision to a vote. All but two or three voted to continue the march. One, "a blacksmith in Company F, was shoeing a horse when told of the result of the vote," reported a Missouri cavalryman. "It frightened him. He was opposed to going on. He dropped the shoe of the horse upon which he was at work, and began to talk of the foolishness and danger of the march. He talked of nothing else and talked incessantly. It preyed on his mind and deranged his reason. In two weeks he had talked himself to death, and was buried at El Paso. . . ."

Now with his answer firmly provided, Colonel Doniphan "determined to order a battery and a hundred artillerists from New Mexico." Until they should arrive from Santa Fe, there was nothing for it but to wait at El Paso; for lacking the certainty of meeting Wool and coming under the protection of his cannon in the event of a fight deep in the interior, it would be foolhardy, in the Colonel's judgment, to march without heavy guns. He sent an express to Colonel Price at Santa Fe with his requisition, and the volunteers unbuttoned themselves for a high time during the pause.

"The army," saw a lieutenant, "was composed of men of a restless and roving disposition, and the little discipline which prevailed was totally insufficient to prevent rioting and dissipation, which endangered the health of the troops as well as their efficiency. . . ." While some officers and men did the jobs of setting up supply, taking possession of

the primitive gristmills of the town, and sequestering captured arms and
ammunition in warehouses, others thronged the old plaza where amidst
the market stalls were the stands of "perpetual gambling—monte-dealing,
chuck-luck, &c," at which Mexicans and soldiers blocked the street.
Fandangos were given for the officers. Three soldiers were arrested to
be court-martialled for ravishing a Mexican woman. Horse and mule
racing for high stakes drew enormous crowds. The native wines and
brandies poured forth. By the middle of January Colonel Doniphan, like
Taylor at Matamoros, was obliged to issue orders curbing the opportunities for excesses. Gambling, fandangos and racing were officially
suppressed, but without practical success. Drills and inspections were
held, and men were trained in the mounted charge with sabres.

Rumors came into town of Mexican forces mustering in the south,
at Carizal, and of movements downriver near the old presidio at the
Junta de los Rios. The Colonel sent scouts in both directions. At the
end of the first week of January the Carizal scouting party returned
with three prisoners one of whom was the parish priest of El Paso,
Father Ortíz, who had been so kind to the captured Texans five years
earlier. He was questioned by Doniphan who gave him a furious lecture,
for if he had not been acting as a spy, he had at any rate been taken
in the company of spies reporting to Carizal on American affairs at
El Paso.

But if the pastor was a patriot, he was still a figure of charity
and even elegance in the hospitality he bestowed on foreigners. The
Samuel Magoffins were taken into his rectory to stay, and were served
by his two sisters who kept house for their popular and charming brother.
"We have chocolate every morning on rising," Susan told her diary,
"breakfast about 10 o'k, dinner at two, chocolate again at dark, and
supper at 9 o'clock, all are attentive, indeed we are so free and easy,
'tis almost a hotel, meals are served in our own room, one of the ladies
always being in attendance. . . ." The weather was so mild that trees
were coming into leaf. In patios hidden from the streets visitors took
their ease surrounded by flowering plants in pots, and rose bushes and
beds of lilies, and tropical birds in wicker cages, and nibbling pigeons,
and cats eyeing them. Business was bustling, and the residents were "well
pleased by the conduct of the American Army." The troops had received
no army pay since their enlistment. Their clothes were in tatters, but
with what funds they had brought along, or had made in gambling or
in other improvised ways, they bought what they needed from local
merchants at high prices. The wind blew on some days, and on others

a fine crystal sunshine warmed everyone with a sense of common well-
being. At night, in the January cold, sentries were bothered by "a great
many wolves, which come down from the neighboring mountains into
the suburbs of El Paso" to kill sheep and feast on "the offal about the
shambles and slaughter-pens." The wolves, keeping up "a dolorous
serenade during the nights," frequently attacked the sentry posts, where
the soldiers shot at them. Hearing musket fire from the outskirts, the
town woke up to fears of battle; but then quiet could come again, and
morning, and Colonel Doniphan would wonder why the artillery from
Santa Fe had not yet arrived. There was a reason—a highly disturbing
one; but he did not know it yet. All he could do was wait in the early
weeks of January, 1847.

21.

Counterdance

On December twenty-eighth—the day following Doniphan's entry
into El Paso—a majestic arrival occurred twelve hundred miles away at
the Arms of Saint James on the Gulf, when a steamer put in to deliver,
with his staff, a major general six feet four inches tall, of glaring eye,
heavy build, and a manner of solemn amplitude, all sumptuously uniformed in blue and gold. It was Winfield Scott, at sixty years of age the
General-in-Chief of the United States Army.

His journey had been crammed with inconveniences most unsuitable to the progress of a major general. It was impossible to imagine
how so many "cruel uncertainties" could seek to impede him who so
loved the splendid comfort of high rank, even with its unending duties
of manner, rhetoric and ceremony. He had left from New York, where
he caught a heavy cold. Sailing for New Orleans, he had been delayed
almost a week at sea by vexatious head winds. In New Orleans for four
days, he held official conversations, and dined with Senator Henry Clay,

and—it was astounding and supremely impertinent—the purpose of his journey which was the highest strategic secret of the war appeared in print in a Spanish language newspaper of the city, and was at once copied by other papers, and sent off to the Eastern press as vital news. In a trice a public that grew by hours knew that General Scott was on his way to the Rio Grande to confer with General Taylor, and to lay down the final arrangements for a landing of American troops at Veracruz to invade Mexico from the east coast. It was hard to know which would be worse—the embarrassments or the dangers that might result from the leak.

Where it had come from, nobody could imagine. He had been particularly careful in writing to General Taylor from New York on November twenty-fifth, announcing his coming, but not to identify Veracruz as his objective. To do so would not have been "prudent at this distance." All he had said was that he was "not coming to supersede you in the immediate command on the line of operations rendered illustrious by you and your gallant army. My proposed theatre is different. You may imagine it. . . ." It was awkward that some Mexican had also imagined it, and had printed a story absurd in detail but correct in general. The letter went on to state that the writer would proceed to Camargo in order to be "within easy corresponding distance from you." It said further, "But, my dear general, I shall be obliged to take from you most of the gallant officers and men (regulars and volunteers) whom you have so long and so nobly commanded. I am afraid that I shall, by imperious necessity—the approach of yellow fever on the gulf coast—reduce you, for a time, to stand on the defensive. This will be infinitely painful to you, and for that reason distressing to me. But I rely on your patriotism to submit to the temporary sacrifice with cheerfulness." If the letter had been intercepted—though nobody knew —the yellow fever at the Gulf and the diversion of troops from one to another theatre may also have told too much. Perhaps the leak occurred at Washington, where the plan had been laid down. What would President Polk think?

He had been most cordial to General Scott of late. Certainly the President had no confidence in General Taylor, and spoke out freely against him. "I am now satisfied that anybody would do better than Taylor," he stated even after the victories of Palo Alto, Resaca and Monterrey. "Taylor is no doubt brave and will fight, but is not fit for a higher command than that of a regiment. I have no prejudice against him, but think he has acted with great weakness and folly. . . ."

General Scott could but concur—though earlier his opinion of General Taylor had been favorable. But now it seemed discreet to agree with the President, with whom he had "many long personal interviews on military matters," and to accept the command of the great expedition to come. In only four days of staff discussions throughout "the great bureaux" of the War Department, the grand campaign had been mapped, and before leaving for the Rio Grande, the General-in-Chief magnificently wrote a circular to the leading Whigs in Congress commending the President and the Secretary of War for their handsome treatment of him in his hour of added responsibility. He left Washington "highly flattered with the confidence and kindness the President has just shown me." At New Orleans on December twentieth he wrote again to General Taylor, enlarging upon the campaign plans, and now calling him to a meeting at Camargo. He marked his dispatch "most confidential . . . outside and in," and sent it by officer express to General Taylor at Monterrey, and prepared to sail from New Orleans for the Rio Grande on December twenty-fourth.

There was one last exasperation at New Orleans before sailing. General Scott was informed that on the heels of his departure from Washington, the President had sent to Congress a bill creating the office of lieutenant general of the Army, and proposing its bestowal upon Senator Thomas Hart Benton, who would thus supersede all other general officers. The President had remarked to a legislator that he had been "compelled to send Gen'l Scott to take command of the Army as a choice of evils, he being the only man in the army who by his rank could command Taylor." The news was incredible. General Scott dismissed it with grandeur.

"If the rank were asked for," he stated, "it could only—remembering Mr. Polk's assurance of support and reward—be intended for me on the report of my first success," and left for Point Isabel.

When he arrived, he found no word from Taylor, and resolved to go upriver without delay. He was in a genial mood as he renewed old acquaintances among the officers, even, in a general amnesty, restoring to favor such as had once felt his ire. One, Lieutenant Colonel Ethan Allan Hitchcock, who had served under him in Washington, hardly expected to meet him now, remembering that General Scott had once "found a place for a flare-up and did flare up in the highest sort of style" against him. But now the General sent for him at Point Isabel, rose, offered him his hand, and made him "a very complimentary speech," ending up with an appointment to his staff.

"Are you ready to move forward?" asked the General.

"Perfectly," replied Colonel Hitchcock.

"Got a horse?"

"Two, General."

"Glad! Glad! You will join me tomorrow?"

"With great pleasure."

"Clever! Very clever! Right! Right! We start early."

"I will be ready, General."

They boarded the *Big Hatchee* the next morning and steamed along the wide loops of the Rio Grande through dunes and marshes, coming to Matamoros by nightfall. There was still no word from General Taylor. Nobody knew what was happening at Monterrey. Matamoros was "wild with rumors," one of which spread the word that Taylor's communications had been cut by the enemy. Transferring to the steamer *Corvette,* the staff continued its progress the next day, with observations upon the natives who seemed the next thing to "Indians in mud huts," who came to sell wood for $2.50 a cord to the captain; and a pause for an exchange of intelligence with a down-bound steamer, whose news was that Mexican troops were massing below Saltillo under the command of Santa Anna; and hours on deck, when the little ship moved slowly between the banks, while General Scott was "particularly civil," lolling immensely and rumbling on in the satisfactions of high-level reminiscence, amidst subordinates who could not take away the topic, but who remained content under the tall funnel to breathe of smoke and sparks and greatness.

General Scott explained at length the orders which brought him there. He outlined in detail the "ultimate objects of his movement." He re-enacted with relish his many interviews with the President—"what Mr. P. said, what he said," back and forth, back and forth. If there were brief, ever so brief, moments of silence in which the General undertook to "look so wise as the Sphinx," it did seem that he accomplished only "a puzzled, dubious gaze into vacancy." And then, perhaps in "bad French," he would resume his satisfied soliloquy, or sober his hearers with a "flat joke," or treat them to "agonizing pedantries of connoissership in wine and cookery." Since his temper was uncertain, all he said was taken with deference, even, in some cases, with fondness, for those who worked closely with him knew his qualities of bravery, skill and warmheartedness.

The anticipated conference with General Taylor was odd to contemplate. There could be no two men more antithetical. General Scott exploited every massive grace of high position; General Taylor in rumpled overalls shambled about on a yellow mule. Where one condescended, the other fraternized. If one delighted in exercising his mind and displaying its florid contents, the other—but it was General Scott himself who said of General Taylor that "few men ever had a more comfortable, labor-saving contempt for learning of every kind. . . ." Their opposed qualities were never more sharply stated than by the soldiers themselves, who with their timeless knack for truth in caricature, spoke of Scott as Old Fuss and Feathers, and of Taylor as Old Rough and Ready—nicknames joyfully taken up by press and public.

Given such differences, the conference at Camargo, with its delicate issues of command prerogative, the distribution of troops and the opportunity for victory, seemed likely to be difficult. And there was even one further bone of contention buried under more official matters: each man, with much popular reason to do so, saw himself as the next President of the United States.

But on January 3, 1847, when the *Corvette* arrived at Camargo, General Taylor was not there, and there was still no word from him directly. It was the staff at Camargo who gave General Scott the information that General Taylor, far from coming to meet him at the Rio Grande as ordered, had instead pursued a project of his own—an extended march eastward into Tamaulipas. He was out of reach for the time being. It seemed to the General-in-Chief that—really—he had done all he could to invite General Taylor's participation in the next immediate decisions; and he now acted with firmness. He wrote orders to General Butler, who was in command of the Monterrey-Saltillo line in the absence of Taylor, to abandon Saltillo, hold Monterrey for defense only, and detach and send at once to the Brazos under General Worth's command a whole division of General Taylor's army. Certain others of Taylor's troops were ordered to Tampico. The dispatch included further details of the Veracruz campaign plan, and closed with General Scott's reflection that though Providence might defeat him, he thought the Mexicans could not. Marked *Private and Confidential,* the papers went not only to General Butler, but in duplicate to General Taylor, for his perusal when he could receive them. There was little more to do at Camargo. General Scott and his people looked over the town and camp the rest of the day, and one of the staff remarked it as "one of the most miserable places I ever saw, dirty and dilapidated and but little better than a Seminole village." They returned to the *Corvette* with relief and the next day started downriver. Five days later they were again at the Arms of Saint

James, where General Scott pushed preparations for the armada he would lead to the Mexican coast.

All his communications to General Taylor so far ran into trouble. The first, from New York, which was delivered, Taylor dismissed saying, "a more contemptible and insidious communication was never written." The second, from New Orleans, was never delivered, because of what Scott later called "gross neglect of the officer who bore it." The third, from Camargo, reached Taylor on January fourteenth upon his return from the Tamaulipas reconnaissance. On reading it, he was outraged in every personal and professional consideration. General Butler had already acted on the orders it contained. But there was also a dreadful probability that the Mexicans were reacting in their turn, for the copy sent by Scott to Taylor had been intercepted, its officer courier killed, and its contents hurried on to Santa Anna. The copy that eventually reached Taylor was sent to him by Butler.

General Taylor at once saw the implications of the orders, and their effect upon the enemy. If all the best troops of the Army of the Rio Grande were to be pulled out and sent to Scott, then what an opportunity was left for Santa Anna, with his forces massing below Saltillo! It could lead to a disastrous defeat for General Taylor. He saw it all as a wicked affront, with overtones of persecution. Scott's demands for his troops were leaving him with only eight hundred regulars and less than seven thousand volunteers without battle experience. Six general officers were also removed from his army, leaving him only two or three none of whom had had command experience in combat. Once again the bland decisions of the War Department, and the incomprehensible and therefore hateful personality of General Scott intruded upon the bleak realities of the front lines of the desert war, with all its labors, its experience and its human stakes. Washington! What could they know there, where everything was reduced to papers in a conference room, "with its long, official, green-covered table and chairs ranged in official order around it," as another public servant saw, "and official stationery in front of each chair. One could not sit there a moment without official sensations of dignity and red-tapery. . . ." General Taylor's responses were lively.

He wrote to Scott declining to report for a discussion, as he would be busy with matters at Victoria and later at Monterrey. He declared that if Scott had relieved him of his whole command, he would have registered "no complaint." But to reduce his forces so radically, and then to leave him to face over twenty thousand men under Santa

Anna, this was hard to understand—or perhaps it could be understood only too well. "I feel," he wrote bitterly, "I feel that I have lost the confidence of the government, or it would not have suffered me to remain, up to this time, ignorant of its intentions. . . ." Nevertheless, "however much I may feel personally mortified and outraged . . . I will carry out in good faith . . . the views of the government, though"—his darkest suspicions welled over—"though I may be sacrificed in the effort." To his son-in-law he raged, "It seems to me the great object so far as I am concerned . . . is to keep me as much in the dark . . . as it was possible to do; particularly as far as the authorities at Washington are concerned." And as for Scott's orders to pull back from Saltillo and cool his heels at Monterrey, General Taylor flatly informed the Secretary of War, "I shall do no such thing without orders to that effect from proper authority." So much for his recognition of the powers of the General-in-Chief.

General Scott continued to be "the most urbane of conquerors." Replying to Taylor, he said, "There are some expressions in your letters which, as I wish to forget them, I shall not specify or recall. . . . If I had been within easy reach of you . . . I should . . . have consulted you fully on all points. . . . As it was, I had to act promptly, and, to a considerable extent, in the dark. . . ." Elsewhere, and later, he commented that his orders for the reassignment to him of Taylor's troops "began to sour [Taylor's] mind in proportion as he became more and more prominent as a candidate for the Presidency," and he spoke of "the senseless and ungrateful clamor of Taylor, which, like his other prejudices, abided with him to the end. . . ." But General Scott was not to escape his own sense of betrayal, and to speak of "the perfidy of Mr. Polk," for it turned out to be true that the President had made every effort to appoint Senator Benton to the supreme command and had only been thwarted by Congress; and furthermore, the President had suspected General Scott himself, "from his inordinate vanity or from some other cause," of having given out at New Orleans the story of his coming invasion of Mexico. In the President's view, "the truth is neither Taylor nor Scott are fit for the command of an army in the great operations in progress and which are contemplated."

General Taylor, in another statement to his son-in-law, set the tone on which the formal counterdance of vanities ended. "One of the expectations of those who perpetrated the outrage against me was, that I would at once leave the country . . . in disgust & return to the U States which if I had done so, would have been used by them to my disadvantage. . . . But in this"—his countryman's ire crackled—"in this I shall disappoint them, as I have determined to remain & do my duty no matter under what circumstances until I am withdrawn. . . . I recd an answer from Genl Scott to a communication I wrote him from Victoria, in which I did not disguise my feelings; he is somewhat tart in his reply. . . . He & myself now understand each other perfectly, & there can for the future be none other than official intercourse between us."

The whole scene of the Rio Grande appalled General Scott. He could not forbear writing to the Secretary of War his impressions in which lay a strong if implied rebuke of General Taylor's management of volunteers. He was "agonized" by what he had heard from reliable witnesses. "If a tenth of what is said be true" the volunteers "have committed atrocities—horrors—in Mexico, sufficient to make Heaven weep, & every American of Christian morals *blush* for his country. Murder, robbery & rape on mothers & daughters in the presence of the tied up males of the families, have been common all along the Rio Grande. . . . The respectable volunteers—7 in 10—have been as much horrified & disgusted as the regulars, with such barbarian conduct. As far as I can learn"—where was Taylor?—"not one of the felons has been punished, & very few rebuked—the officers, generally, being as much afraid of their men as the poor suffering Mexicans themselves are afraid of the miscreants. Most atrocities are always committed in the absence of regulars, but sometimes in the presence of acquiescing, trembling volunteer officers."

But at Point Isabel, General Scott's problems were more immediate. At the War Department he had ordered all the complicated gear for his amphibious invasion—troops, ships, supplies and equipment, including one hundred and forty-one surfboats for the landings, and casks of drinking water from the Mississippi, and enough firewood to last sixty days. But all these were slow to arrive. There would hardly be time for training in the tactics of putting an army ashore for battle. The weather was foreboding—northers and high seas. But at last on January 22, 1847 the build-up began. Worth arrived downriver with his division. His men were jubilant, thinking they were homeward bound until, at the mouth, they discovered that they were assigned to the invasion. Inland at Saltillo, they were replaced by Wool's brigade. On the same day the first detachment of new volunteers arrived at Point Isabel from the East. Presently, out of New Orleans, the transports began to appear. Their character was disappointing—they were brigs and schooners of light tonnage that rode the stormy Gulf with difficulty. On February fourth a steamer brought the surfboats—not all that had been requisitioned, but only sixty-five. Five days later General Scott suffered a more severe blow yet—he heard that the Mexicans had captured his third letter to General Taylor, and were in possession of his plans for the assault. It was imperative now to move fast, and he redoubled the efforts of the Army. Even without sufficient ships or all his supplies, he must move. But one more woe beset him. A furious norther blew in on February twelfth. Sand flew, the shipping strained at anchor, the Army shivered amidst the dunes, until finally on February fifteenth General Scott was able to embark with the advance detachments for rendezvous, first at Lobos Island, then at Tampico on the Pánuco, and the massed descent upon Veracruz. In a few days the site of the invasion jump-off at the Rio Grande beaches was once again occupied by only the garrison at the Fort Polk supply depot, and the forgotten regiment on the tide-washed wastes at the river mouth.

All through the weeks of preparations on the coast, Santa Anna, far inland, was moving up with twenty-five thousand troops, from San Luis Potosí to Encarnación, and finally to a mountain-sided plain below Saltillo. General Taylor, having been pressed, had agreed to run for President if nominated in 1848, had taken and abandoned Victoria, and had retired to await Santa Anna at Buena Vista. There on February twenty-second and twenty-third the desert armies met; and in a great if costly victory Taylor with his weakened forces won northern Mexico— and the Presidency. Ten days later General Scott's men began their landings near Veracruz. On March twenty-seventh the city surrendered, and on April eighth the coastal army began its march inland over the route of Cortés to the heart of Mexico.

22.

The Avengers

Meanwhile Doniphan's Missourians waited at El Paso for the
artillery to come from Santa Fe. Suddenly on January tenth there was
news from the north. "A New Mexican taken up" by a patrol near
El Paso, jotted a volunteer, "states that a revolution is on foot in
Santa Fe." For over a week Colonel Doniphan heard nothing further;
and then on the nineteenth two lieutenants rode into El Paso with
more information. There had been rumors of revolt ever since Kearny's
departure. The sentiment of the people toward the Americans seemed
to have changed. Even the Pueblo Indians, at first glad to see their
Mexican masters overcome by new powers out of the legendary east,
soon told each other that they had been "outraged—their lives at stake—
their possessions in danger." New Mexicans complained of the "bullying
and overbearing demeanor" of the conquerors. There was tension in the
air. Colonel Price, in command at Santa Fe, and Governor Charles Bent,
who had been appointed to rule the territory by General Kearny, felt it.
It looked to his troops as though "indecision" ruled Colonel Price. He
was not given anything to act upon until one day just before Christmas
1846 he learned of a visit paid to Lieutenant Governor Vigil by the
figure who presided over much of the vice of Santa Fe. It was Doña
Gertrudes Barceló, La Tules, with her wig and false teeth, who whispered that a large group of conspirators—men who had voted against
the surrender of New Mexico under Armijo—had been meeting secretly
to plan a revolt for Christmas Eve. All over the territory, as well as in
the capital, native patriots were to rise and capture or murder every
North American in New Mexico. The preparations had been going on
for months—whispering campaigns, encouragement of malcontents, and
organizing of armed bands. Even El Paso was included in the pattern
of rebellion, and Father Ortíz was its agent there. The whole scheme

was led by an angry man to whom promises had been made—and broken: Colonel Don Diego Archuleta, who had been left with neither an empire west of the Rio Grande nor an official post under the new government. His vengeance had deep roots and but for La Tules it would have burst forth on Christmas Eve, in the style of the terrible revolt of 1680.

The territorial government moved swiftly. Fifteen of the ring-leaders were arrested, though Colonel Archuleta made his escape, along ,with one or two others. All the artillery of the Army was parked at all entrances to the plaza, and sentries were everywhere. After a nervous day vigilance was relaxed, for with the leaders in arrest the rebel organization seemed to melt away. Colonel Price again spoke of sending the artillery downriver to Doniphan. An officer observed, "The artillery are making ready to march . . . ; the clanking of the anvil is incessant; caissons and gun carriages are strewn around the forges." He had an afterthought: "At this juncture it is almost doubtful whether the safety of our citizens does not require that the artillery should remain. . . ." But Doniphan had waited long enough, and Price ordered the ordnance and its men to be ready to depart January eighth. The report of success in the Battle of Brazito later encouraged him in his decision. Any threat from Chihuahua by Mexican forces now seemed remote.

Governor Bent said as much, among other things, in a proclamation to the New Mexicans in early January. "You are now governed by new statutory laws and you also have the free government promised to you. Do not abuse the great liberty which is vouchsafed to you by it, so you may gather the abundant fruits which await you in the future. Those who are blindly opposed . . . also those persons who dream that mankind should bow to their whims, have become satisfied that they cannot find employment in the offices which are usually given to men of probity and honesty, exasperated have come forth as leaders of a revolution against the present government. . . . Their treason was discovered in time and smothered at its birth. Now they are wandering about and hiding from people, but their doctrines are scattered broadcast among the people, thereby causing uneasiness, and they still hold to their ruinous plans. . . . There is still another pretext with which they want to alarm you and that is the falsehood that troops are coming from the interior"—Chihuahua—"in order to reconquer the country." But what, asked the Governor, what help could a Chihuahua torn by internal weakness and opposing factions bring to the far north? He advised the New Mexicans to remain quiet and attend to their work, while he pre-

pared to leave for Taos to visit his home there. Warned that his life
was still endangered by the extremist followers of the absent Archuleta,
he shrugged off all concern and went home.

Days passed, until at El Paso on February seventh two artillery
officers riding in advance of the batteries and their troops hurried to
Colonel Doniphan and reported that "Gov. Bent & all the Americans at
Taos were assassinated," and that soldiers from Santa Fe were ordered
to march up the Rio Grande to Taos to destroy a rebel force composed
largely of Indians of the pueblo there.

It was heavy news for the Missourians; but when by the following
day the remainder of the artillery column had arrived, there was nothing
for Doniphan to do but give the command for the departure southward into the Chihuahua desert, where—who knew?—he might find safety
with General Wool in all his power, or alone might face destruction
by a Mexican army before Chihuahua City. With his eight hundred
opinionated volunteers he left the Rio Grande at El Paso on February
8, 1847.

Far to the north, nearly the whole length of the river away in New
Mexico, the after-convulsions of the Taos Massacre were still being felt.

23.

Massacre at Taos

For on January nineteenth—the very day when Doniphan at
El Paso heard that the revolt of Christmas Eve had been smothered—
Archuleta's latest plans had erupted at Taos with pitiable results. He
was not personally on hand to witness or to pay for the horror wrought
by his infuriated vanity, which was enfolded in the rags of his patriotism.
His local accomplices had aroused the Indians of the pueblo and the
Mexicans of the village of San Fernando not only against all Americans
but also any natives who had joined the new government. Even the local

pastor, Father Antonio José Martínez, was said to encourage the rebels.
All day on the eighteenth the rebellious Indians crowded into San Fernando; and throughout hours of drinking the fiery whiskey of Taos their
vague sense of injury became a clear and inspired vision. The uproar
grew until Governor Bent was advised to leave town for his own safety.
He declined. The rebels made drunken speeches to one another far into
night; and before dawn of the nineteenth were ready to enact their
evil dream.

The family of Governor Bent were all awakened in the dark by
the noise of a mob crowding into the plaza where his house stood in a
row of connected buildings. Under his roof with him were his wife, his
children, and two friends, Mrs. Christopher Carson and Mrs. Thomas
Boggs, whose famous husbands were absent from Taos—Carson still with
Kearny in California, Boggs on his way home bringing United States
mail over a newly established route. The Governor rose from his bed
and went to the *portal* to face the shouting faces under torchlight.

What did they want?

They told him that "they did not intend to leave an American
alive in New Mexico; and as he was governor, they would kill him first."
They surged toward him.

He tried to calm them, appealing to their "honor and manhood."

They laughed. They drew their bows, lightly so as not to kill
but only hurt him, and let fly their arrows, aiming at his eyes, his
cheeks, his breast. He fell back into his house. They followed. They
took him, threw him down, and tore away his scalp with knives. In the
next room the women were digging a hole with a poker and an iron
spoon through the earthen wall into the adjoining house. When they
could they thrust the children through and followed. The Governor
crawled to join them, "holding his hand on top of his bleeding head."
Indians came after him through the hole. Others swarmed down over
the flat roof into the yard and broke into the house next door. Throwing
aside his wife who would protect him they killed him with guns. Someone brought a board and brass nails. Spreading his scalp they tacked it
to the board and glaring with joy went through the village to show
their trophy. The women and children of the Governor's household
were left behind with his body. It was secretly buried at three o'clock
in the morning of the following day by Mexican friends who risked
much to bring such a mercy, and food and clothing, to the family.

From the Governor's murder the rebels moved on to others.
Sheriff Stephen Lee was killed on his own rooftop. Young Narcisse

Beaubien, home from study at Cape Girardeau College on the Mississippi, was tortured, scalped and killed. J. W. Leal, the United States
District Attorney who had accompanied the Governor to Taos, was
awakened, denuded, marched through the village before the rebels who
sang as they pricked him with lances and arrows, and scalped alive.
Praying them to kill him, he instead received arrows that drove delicately
into his eyes, mouth and nose. He was thrown broken and alive to freeze
in a ditch for several hours. At last the rebels in their terrible sense
of virtue returned from other work and killed him with a few final
arrows. His body was given to hogs who feasted upon it until in the
afternoon Mrs. Beaubien, who had lost her son, dared to see that it
was buried. Upriver at the same time seven Americans were killed and
their property burned at Arroyo Hondo, and two at the Red River. In
all, twelve were massacred in the uprising of the nineteenth, and at
once similar outbreaks followed in other northern towns. Their successes encouraged the conspirators to hold meetings, organize a government, collect an army to march against Santa Fe, and send dispatches
to the Downriver urging more revolts. An Indian loyal to the American
authorities hurried down the river canyons and over the plateau of
Santa Fe to notify Colonel Price of the catastrophe. There in the capital
Donaciano Vigil assumed office as acting governor, and worked with
Price to organize strong counterblows to the revolution.

While the rebels were gathering forces from the countrysides,
Colonel Price called into Santa Fe various units that were scattered as
grazing parties and as town garrisons. By January twenty-third he was
able to move upriver with three hundred and fifty troops and four brass
twelve-pound mountain howitzers. The rebels had come downriver
from Taos as far as Santa Cruz. There during the next afternoon all
about the once-important town surrounded by broken hills Price's regiment fought two thousand rebels, and drove them to retreat into the
Rio Grande canyon through which at the river's edge wound the road
to Taos. Before giving pursuit the American soldiers, wrote one of their
officers, "destroyed the grain, wood and residence" of Don Diego Archuleta, who was "one of the richest and most influential of the leaders. . . ."
The Taos road was primitive and the snows obliterated it entirely in
many places. Encumbered with heavy equipment the American troops
struggled northward breaking trails as they went, while the insurgents
swarmed as individuals among the carved hills and faces of the canyon
keeping out of range until they could assemble again to make a stand
on the east side of the river, behind a little mountain shaped like a

funnel without its stem from which the place took its name—Embudo. On the twenty-ninth in bitter cold amidst the tumbled black walls of volcanic rock brushed with snow and spotted with the dark olive green of piñon trees, Price found the enemy massed against him and attacked. Once again he drove them upriver, and followed at his slower pace until on February third he brought his power up from the river on to the windy sweep of Taos Plain.

No obstacle remained now, and later the same day coming through groves of silvery trees he arrived before the ancient twin pueblos of Taos that faced each other across a wide plaza where Taos Creek ran under broken ice. The howitzers were run forward to bombard, but night fell before a battle could be fully mounted. The main body camped for the night at the village of San Fernando de Taos a few miles southward. In the cold, sunny morning, all companies moved on the pueblos to surround them. Taos Mountain, streaked with snow, rose in the north as a background for the fury that followed. Many of the seven hundred warriors of Taos were collected in the pueblo church that stood at the northwest corner of the plaza. It was manned as a fort, with holes on the parapet and in the walls through which the defenders could shoot. The great terraced steps of the two pueblos were silent and empty, their ladders drawn up, their occupants waiting within like creatures in burrows listening for a favorable change of weather. In the fields on all sides the troops were drawn up, facing the clay wall that surrounded the town area. The howitzers were planted to effect a cross fire at a range of four hundred yards. Cannonading opened the battle, with flashes of fire, drifts of brown smoke, and black explosions over the snow. Dismounted soldiers charged in waves, the artillery moved up between salvos, and all converged toward the church. Its earthen walls were stout. "An attempt was made to cut through the walls of the church . . . with axes," reported a young artillery officer who commanded a six-pound howitzer in the battle, "but they were so thick and the fire so deadly that it was found to be impracticable." Still, the axes had thinned the three-foot thickness of the walls, and the young officer brought his howitzer up within sixty yards of the church and fired at the hacked part of the wall and "soon made a breech large enough for five or six men to enter abreast. The roof of the church was then fired, and I ran the 6 Pdr. up within 30 feet of the breech, and poured grape shot into the church. Lighted shells were also thrown in, which bursted handsomely." The attackers could see the interior. It was teeming with Indians, great numbers of whom fell dead and wounded. Rafters caught fire from the explosions.

The noise was fearsome, chorded together with the cannonades, the rattle
of muskets, the shouts of the attackers, the cries of those hurt inside the
church, and the roar and crack and tumble of burning timber. "The
order to storm the church was then given . . . and the storming party
rushed it, so as we entered we found the smoke and dust so dense, that
it was impossible to exist in it unless near the openings, and that the
enemy had all retired except from the gallery, as we entered they fled,
and were shot down by our troops from the neighboring walls." Soon
the roof fell in, and blackened beams hung down, and the cold sunlight
poured in from the bright blue sky. The church was a ruin and a charnel
house. "In 20 minutes we had possession of the church and the houses
in that part of the town, and the white flags were flying from the two
Pueblos . . ." Before sundown the north pueblo was abandoned, and
the soldiers took to it for the night.

It was still dark the next morning when in the acrid air of smoking timber and spilled blood the elders of the pueblo, bringing their
women and children and sacred objects, came before Colonel Price to
plead for peace. He granted it on condition that they surrender the
leaders of the insurrection, who were given to him. In his three battles
he had lost ten men killed and fifty-two wounded, some of whom later
died. The rebellious Indians and Mexicans lost a hundred and fifty
killed and more than that number wounded. The engagements of the
Taos Rebellion were the last to be fought near the Rio Grande in the
War with Mexico.

24.

Chihuahua

While the rebel leaders were marched to San Fernando de Taos
for imprisonment and trial, Colonel Doniphan and the Missouri Volunteers were finding their way deep into Chihuahua. The traders waiting at

El Paso to hear of the outcome of his march, upon which would depend their future business on the Chihuahua Trail, heard throughout the month nothing but rumors. Most came from Mexican sources, and told of heavy reverses put upon the Americans by Mexican arms—Santa Anna had defeated the Army of the Rio Grande at San Luis Potosí, and General Taylor was a prisoner of war; General Wool was surrounded at Monterrey; a great force was marching from Durango to destroy Doniphan and recapture New Mexico; Santa Anna was about to invade Texas—not one of which was true. But such reports had power, and the Samuel Magoffins, waiting at the Pass, were troubled by them, especially the latest which promised that the residents of El Paso were about to rise up and murder all Americans in the place. They were sure the end had come when early in March a Mexican friend came to them "with his hair somewhat in ends and features ghastly. At once our minds were filled with apprehensions," wrote Susan, "lest the dread sentence had been passed. Without seating himself . . . he took Mr. Magoffin by the hand and led him out of the room in haste, and with tears in his eyes told him that 'he was a Mexican, and it pained him to the heart to know that the American army had gained the battle and taken possession of Chi.' "

For on February twenty-eighth, without Wool, who never came to the western interior, and with traders pressed into service to help him, Colonel Doniphan and his thousand citizens had met four thousand one hundred and twenty Mexicans in the valley of the Sacramento Creek north of Chihuahua City at noon, and after a fight lasting three and a half hours, had defeated them. On the next day he took formal possession of the city of Chihuahua and freed all American prisoners including James Magoffin. Among his spoils was "the black flag which cut such a conspicuous figure at Brazito." When news of his triumph reached the United States, William Cullen Bryant compared him to Xenophon for his great self-sustaining march through so many thousand miles; and the President, in his diary, was proud of what the soldiers under both Price and Doniphan had accomplished: "The number of troops engaged was comparatively small, but I consider this victory one of the most signal which has been gained during the war. . . . The truth is our troops, regulars and volunteers, will obtain victories wherever they meet the enemy. This they would do," he added like any proper Western democrat, and out of his scorn for such as Scott and Taylor, "if they were without officers to command them higher in rank than lieutenants. It is injustice, therefore, to award the generals all the credit."

25.

Trial at Taos

In Taos the war on the river entered upon its last scenes when the rebel leaders were brought to trial before Judge Beaubien, whose son had been one of their victims. The hearings were opened at nine in the morning on April 5, 1847, in a "small, oblong apartment" with adobe walls and two narrow windows. The judge's bench was at one end, and near it were chairs for witnesses and jury, all divided from the rest of the room by a thin railing. The room was jammed with spectators who stood. The prisoners faced the judge. On a plank bench at one side sat the three main witnesses, Mrs. Bent, Mrs. Boggs and Mrs. Carson. All three were Mexican women. A young American onlooker from Cincinnati stared at them. "Señora Bent was quite handsome . . . good figure for her age; luxuriant raven hair; unexceptional teeth, and brilliant, dark eyes, the effect of which was heightened by a clear, brunette complexion. The other lady"—Mrs. Boggs—"though not so agreeable in appearance, was much younger." He looked longest at "the wife of the renowned mountaineer, Kit Carson," and a century later what he felt still moved with life. "Her style of beauty was of the haughty, heart-breaking kind—such as would lead a man with a glance of the eye, to risk his life for one smile. I could not but desire her acquaintance. The dress and manners of the three ladies, bespoke a greater degree of refinement, than usual. . . ."

The jury included Mexicans, French Canadians, and Americans. Six prisoners were on trial. The prosecuting attorneys were an American twenty-two years old and another from Missouri who in the blowsy longing of frontier eloquence had "fought, bled and died" for his country in the war. The counsel for defense was a volunteer private on furlough to serve the court. The trial lasted two days, and seemed to the young man from Cincinnati "a strange mixture of violence and justice," for "it certainly did appear to be a great assumption on the part of the

Americans to conquer a country, and then arraign the revolting inhabitants for treason." (President Polk was later to agree with him, in principle.) The three main witnesses told their stories of the sorrowful night. "When Mrs. Bent gave in her testimony . . . pointing out the Indian who killed the Governor, not a muscle of the chief's face twitched, or betrayed agitation, though he was aware her evidence unmistakably sealed his death warrant—he sat with lips gently closed, eyes earnestly centered on her, without a show of malice or hatred—an almost sublime spectacle of Indian fortitude, and of the severe mastery to which the emotions can be subjected. . . ."

When the jury retired, a Canadian juror could hardly wait to cast his verdict, and needed only to know what it should be. Dancing with excitement, he asked the foreman,

"Monsieur Chad*wick!* Vot sall *I* say?"

"Keep still man," said the foreman with a sense of propriety, "until we talk awhile to the rest about it. Don't be in such a hurry."

"Oui! Oui! c'est bon; très bien! Mais, monsieur vot sall ve do avec sacrés prisonniers—sacrés enfants—"

The foreman was not troubled too far by niceties of procedure. He replied,

". . . Why, hang them, of course; what did you come in here for? Wait till I'm done with these Mexicans"—part of the jury—"and I will tell you what to do."

The jury returned to the courtroom in less than fifteen minutes with verdicts of guilty "in the first degree—five for murder, one for treason." Judge Beaubien, recalling that the jail was "overstocked with others awaiting trial," fixed the following day for executing the sentence of death, saying solemnly, "Muerte, muerte, muerte." There was a moment of terrible silence, and then the guards came forward, the prisoners "drew their serapes more closely around them," and impassively returned to jail.

The next day was Friday, the death day, the day of Golgotha. A few clouds drifted in a brilliant sky. Convivial interest in San Fernando de Taos brought a crowd of morning drinkers to Estes's Tavern where Metcalfe the sheriff—a son-in-law of the saloonkeeper—was glad to see them. Needing ropes for his day's work, he had none, and must borrow them. From traders and a teamster he obtained what he needed and went to a room next to the bar to tie the hangman's noose on one end of each rope or lariat. One or two mountaineers helped him. One found the lariat too stiff to work. Metcalfe brought a royal's worth of Mexican soap with which to soften all the ropes. He did not forget to note in his bill of expenses,

To soft soap for greasing nooses . . . 12½.

After they had washed the sticky soap from their fingers the helpers were given a drink of Taos whiskey by Mr. Estes.

Then lighting cigarettes and carrying their nooses, they all accompanied Sheriff Metcalfe to the jail. Seeing the nooses, onlookers exclaimed. The jail was at the edge of San Fernando. There were no houses between it and the fields to the north. A hundred and fifty yards away in a field a scaffold of two uprights and a crossbeam now stood. Not far from it was a large tree. The mountaineers with their lariats went into the jail. Across the patio they saw a brass howitzer with its muzzle four feet from the room in which the prisoners were held—a long, cold room, badly ventilated by one small window and the open door where the sun came in on the earthen floor. In its patch of light two prisoners were lying on a *serape,* wearing brightly colored shirts, open on their brown skin showing "a wilderness of straight black hair." They were filthy. They were silent to greetings. They were to die in two hours. Leaning about the room were the other prisoners—eighty in all— ragged, lousy, miserable.

At nine o'clock there was a stir. The soldiery were being mustered. Priests came to administer the last rites. A crowd collected outside. Soon the word passed that the condemned were coming. Eighteen armed men made a square at the gate to receive them. They were marched to the scaffold in the field with their hands tied behind them. On the backs of their heads were white cotton caps that would be pulled over their faces when the moment came. At the nearest houses the roofs were crowded with spectators. On the jail roof was a mountain howitzer—the same one used in destroying the church. It was loaded and trained on the gallows. A soldier stood by it with a lighted match in his hand. Two hundred and twelve soldiers were formed in the field. Under the gallows waited a government wagon with two mules in harness.

The condemned were marched to it. The escort of soldiery made an evolution, forming a hollow square about the scaffold, from which the soaped lariats now depended. Strongly shadowed by the clear sun the condemned men were placed in the wagon. The scaffold was so narrow that they touched one another as they stood on the wagon bed— men waiting for other men to do mortal things to them, while hundreds

watched in bated quiet. Now the nooses were set loosely about their
throats. They were asked if they would speak. *"Mi padre, mi madre—"*
the little words were scarcely heard. Their white caps were pulled forward from rakish angles until their heads, all covered, were six white
stumps. Harness was twitched and slapped, the mules started forward,
the wagon was drawn out from under what weighted it. The rawhide
ropes creaked and straightened and swung in narrow compass. Con-
vulsed, the bodies swayed and turned and bumped one another, and
two gripped hands, and held so, till dead.

Forty minutes later the soldiers were marched away, the howitzer
came down from its roof, and the population broke forward toward the
gallows. The ropes were slacked off. Some of the knots, despite the
sheriff's soap, were hard. A hunter was cutting one such knot when the
owner of the rope, a teamster, came forward and said,   ..

"Hello, there, don't cut that rope. I won't have anything to tie
my mules with. . . . I'm in government service, an' if them picket
halters was gone, slap down would go a dollar apiece."

The hunter desisted, worked the knot loose, and gave him his
halter whole. Relatives claimed the bodies. Indian widows went to their
dead men and each took hers up, tied him to her back, and set out
walking in grief to the pueblo three miles away, to bury him at home,
with ghostly Indian honors. The Americans who had helped with the
whole affair took up a collection of five dollars and sent it ahead to
Mr. Estes's bar to have eggnog prepared. When dismissed they took their
rifles and walked to the tavern where in the back room by one o'clock
they were drunk on eggnog, made with real American brandy. One of
them danced an Indian dance till he fell down unconscious, while the
rest roared with laughter. At the end of April when five more Indians
and four Mexicans were hanged at Taos, the war on the Rio Grande
was over.

26.

All on the Plains of Mexico

All summer long in 1847 troops were homeward bound along the Rio Grande. They were volunteers whose terms of enlistment were completed. It was safe to let them go without replacement, for the war was all but won with General Scott's inland battles to the South—Cerro Gordo, Puebla, Contreras, Molino el Rey—though in the atmosphere prevailing at home not everyone was confident, and some were critical. A New York diarist, George Templeton Strong, expected in March to hear "that Taylor and his force are prisoners of war and that we're driven across the Rio Grande (and I can't see what's to hinder)"; and in May he recorded "Rumor of a defeat in Mexico: 'Col. Doniphan' licked somewhere near Chihuahua. . . . Hope it's true, for the only way of bringing the war to a close is to prosecute it totissimus viribus, and a little defeat or two will open up the administration"; and in August, "Nothing further from Mexico; everybody waiting with mouth wide open for the first reliable statement of what Scott's doing; there are about three new lies every day. . . ."

As the American movements of the whole Mexican War, but for the California naval campaign, had been based on the Rio Grande, so now in the summertime many of the forces came back by the river. The Missouri thousand, who had entered upon the Rio Grande in the New Mexican north, now completed their great loop from Chihuahua to Coahuila, Nuevo León and Tamaulipas, and approached it again through Mier, Camargo and Reynosa. Doniphan's men kept their character to the end. A homeward-bound soldier of Wool's division saw them: "They look wild and have a peculiar manner, and don't seem to have any discipline." Their commander, at the end of his campaign, was satisfied with them. "High spirits and a bold front," said Colonel Doniphan, "is perhaps the safest policy. My men are rough, ragged, and ready, having one more of the R's than General Taylor himself . . . all have done their duty, and done it nobly. . . ." The volunteers were not to be judged by the occasional individual whose exuberance took a wrong turn—like Ben Leaton of whom Dr. Josiah Gregg spoke as "a desperado." Leaton with three other men deserted from Doniphan's force to live as bandits on the Rio Grande near Presidio del Norte. They established themselves in one of the large ruins of the early eighteenth century missions at La Junta de los Rios, called their stronghold Fort Leaton, and preyed on the Indians and Mexicans of the region until Leaton's death in 1852.

Coming out of Mexico to the river, soldiers urged their officers to hurry the march, for steamboats were scarce, and the first units to arrive at the little river towns would have first chance to go on board for the long journey home. One regiment marched all night to beat another to Reynosa; and when they reached there, secured the only two boats on hand. Three other ships were mud-bound below the town. The river was alternately high and low that summer. When a steamer went aground the troops had to wade ashore to lighten it. If it did not come off the mud, the troops had to wait for wagons from upstream to carry their supply, and the trip was resumed by land. And then it might rain, and for hours, for two days, even, the men without tents "stood like cattle in the mud both day and night" until steamers floated down to pick them up. A change in weather brought a change in travel, with shifts from muddy roads to ships, or stranded ships to dusty roads. Roads and steamers were rarely used at the same time.

The boats were so crowded that on the lower decks men could not lie or sit, but had to stand; while those on the upper decks spat their tobacco juice upon those below. Only officers were allowed in the cabins. Guards were posted to keep the rank and file out. As well as they could, the men played cards, drank whiskey and talked all night. The weather was hot. Many had fevers, and all felt "depressed and ill." They longed to be clean of the vermin of Mexico. A river captain said to a soldier,

"I took up some New-Yorkers not long since; they scratched themselves in a leisurely sort of way. But you fellows scratch with great earnestness—scratch yourselves all over—scratch rapidly—violently —scratch all the time. What's the matter with you? Got fleas?"

The veteran replied in the vein of frontier grandeur,

"Fleas! Do you think we are dogs, to go about infested with fleas?" He snorted. "These are lice! We work harder than the New-Yorkers because we have more to do. Our lice are big handsome fellows, and we have plenty of them—got them in Mexico!"

But there were satisfactions, too. It was heartening to clean guns
for the last time and turn them in to the ordnance companies; and to
be paid off for the first time in months; and to burn "saddles, and other
horse rigging"; and on a road-march to come upon a company of tight-
rope walkers at an isolated ranch—the men were "especially interested
to see Preciosa, the prima donna, perform," who with her troupe "displayed fine talent. . . ." Soldiers went to bathe in the river during a
halt, and now and then were shot at from bushes along the bank. But
the river was generally at peace ever since March, when "depredations
of the guerrillas, and the large force under General Urrea, in the Valley
of the San Juan, caused much uneasiness and alarm throughout the
Valley of the Rio Grande." When they could go ashore for a little while
at a river town, the soldiers tried to buy a meal. All they found was
"bread and ginger pop." They hoped for better at Matamoros, the
the river metropolis, where they must surely find "newspapers, bread,
cheese and cigars." But if rain did not keep all on board, the steamboats would pause only an hour or two, and the soldiers would get
up their hopes for the next stop, at the river's mouth. Matamoros had
begun to "assume quite an American appearance—brick and framed
houses, with shingled roofs." The population of the Mexican period
—ten thousand—was reduced to between three and five thousand. The
steamboats took the bends among the dunes, and came to the mouth,
where on the left bank was a roaring American army depot which the
soldiers called Sodom, and on the right down the beach a quarter of a
mile was Bagdad, where in an eating house they ordered up breakfast
and "ate potatoes for the first time in a year." There was only one
stage left before leaving for home—a walk up the nine-mile beach to
Point Isabel where the Gulf steamers docked.

Waiting, the men filled the days with bathing and running on
the beach, picking up shells, and eating oysters, and the nights with
gambling, drinking, and fighting to pay off old scores of enmity accumulated during the year of serving together at close quarters in arduous and
boring duty. Some units were discharged from the service of the United
States before embarking at Point Isabel, others after arriving at New
Orleans. In either case, they were treated to a ceremony, when an
orator—an officer of their regiment or a civilian master of the high
style—rang in their ears the martial sounds of their story. "Bearded
and bronzed as were the soldiers" who listened hungrily to what they
had done, "they cried till the tears left glistening paths down their
cheeks." Lieutenant Lew Wallace declared after hearing the oration

on the occasion of his discharge, "I alighted from my perch sore and cramped; but from that day to this I have never regretted the year left behind me as a soldier in Mexico. . . ."

And all through the long hot summer while the armies of the northern campaigns were turning homeward, the troops under General Scott were toiling across central Mexico toward the capital. "We had to throw away the scabbard and to advance with the naked blade," stated the General-in-Chief in the style of Clarendon. As his army swept inland he ordered distribution among the Mexicans of a broadsheet that adroitly summarized the issues of the war and the purpose of the United States. It reminded the natives that in 1824 Mexico established a government after the model of the United States, in which each state elected its own governor, and that in 1834 Santa Anna destroyed the federal constitution, proclaiming a central government and taking to himself the appointment of governors. Zacatecas and Texas resisted such usurpation of local power. Texas declared her independence and fought for her rights. In the Texan war, Santa Anna's subordinates, under his order, massacred five hundred Texans at Goliad after they had surrendered. The Texans defeated Santa Anna at San Jacinto and took him prisoner. Texas, independent, applied for admission to the United States, which denied and postponed annexation for ten years. The war between Mexico and Texas abolished all boundaries. The United States sent a minister to Mexico to negotiate a boundary. He was repelled. The United States then having accepted Texas as a state ordered an Army of Occupation to the Rio Grande. Mexican troops crossed the river and attacked the American army, were beaten, and had been beaten ever since, though Santa Anna boasted of victories. The United States had only good will toward Mexicans. The broadsheet concluded, "We are here for no earthly purpose except the hope of obtaining peace." The battles of the summer having brought Scott to the Valley of Mexico, peace seemed as desirable to the Mexicans as to him; and on August twenty-fourth he granted an armistice during which peace negotiations were undertaken.

Nicholas P. Trist, chief clerk of the State Department, arrived from Washington under commission by President Polk to deal directly with Santa Anna, president and military chief. The move gave General Scott another opportunity to "flare up in the highest sort of style" but in time he forgave Trist his intrusion, sent him a gift of some guava jelly, and thenceforward co-operated with him in efforts for peace. The armistice was abruptly ended by Scott on September sixth when it was clear that the Mexicans were using its period of grace to reinforce their troops, newly fortify Chapultepec Castle, and arouse public sentiment to support renewed fighting; and further when the Mexican peace commission proffered terms that were patently unacceptable. There were dealings backstage in which Santa Anna accepted ten thousand dollars as a down payment on a bribe for surrender that, it was whispered, might go as high as a million. Hostilities were at once resumed, the battle of Molino el Rey and the storming of Chapultepec followed, and on September fourteenth Scott and his generals led the army into Mexico City. Mexicans continued to resist elsewhere—Puebla, Huamantla, Atlixco. Santa Anna's government fell, and he was superseded in command of the army. It was not long until all major military resistance ceased, and once again, but now more realistically, peace talks were undertaken by the Mexicans. For it was plain who must prevail: Mexico had only 8,109 men under arms, and of these less than three thousand were on guard at Querétaro, the temporary capital; while the American forces numbered 43,059, of whom thirty-two thousand were under Scott's immediate command in support of his position at Mexico City.

All through the fall of 1847 and into the winter of 1848 the peace talks continued, with discussions of boundaries and lands as the spoils of war. New Mexico was suddenly taken out of consideration for outright cession when in December at the order of Colonel Price delegates of her citizens gathered at Santa Fe to organize a territorial government under the United States. The act amounted to a voluntary annexation which Mexico would be powerless to undo.

The rest of Mexican territory was in jeopardy from other forces; for with the suspension of the fighting, sentiment in the United States spoke out from every quarter with violent and even virtuous appetites for Mexico's land. The President told Congress in December that the United States "might have to take the full measure of indemnity into its hands"—which all understood to mean the annexation of the whole of Mexico. The possibility had wide support in the press and among the more radical members of the President's party. There were cries of "Destiny"—"God ordained that Mexico should be an integral part of the Union." A mission of terrible sternness lay upon the conquerors— "The Mexicans are aboriginal Indians and must share the destiny of their race—extinction!" Without a qualm feelings of racial superiority were brought to support greed: "Look at the gold and silver glittering there in masses that await the pick of the Saxon." The issue was seen through many bigotries—religious, political and educational. Mexico's religion was attacked as the enemy of republicanism, and Mexico must be rescued from it. The clamor was heard in Mexico, where General Scott while reserving his personal views stated that "two-fifths of the Mexican population, including more than half of the Congress," would favor annexation of their whole country to the United States. Polk's opponents were outspoken in their turn: "It is folly to absorb such a country into our own, to exhaust such a nation into the healthy veins of a republic like this," and Daniel Webster declared that California and New Mexico were "not worth a dollar."

But what Trist was asking for, upon instructions from Washington, were terms that fixed the United States boundary at the Rio Grande from the mouth to the thirty-second parallel, and thence west to the Pacific; and through weeks of meetings he gained substantially what he asked for, with only a small concession to modify the boundary between the Californias a little north of the thirty-second parallel. For all of New Mexico (which then included Arizona) and upper California, he agreed to pay fifteen million dollars, and he further pledged the United States to pay the claims of its citizens against the Mexican government. His task was accomplished under extraordinary conditions, for after the collapse of the armistice in September he had been recalled by Washington, but had refused to obey, certain that he would be able to resolve the meetings into an acceptable treaty. General Scott appeared to agree with him, and with reason. On February second a treaty was signed at Guadalupe Hidalgo, a suburb of Mexico City, and the commissioner hurried to the States to submit it to the government.

News went through Mexico that peace was made, though official notification of the outpost garrisons could not be managed with dispatch. In the same week, Colonel Sterling Price, at El Paso, heard that a Mexican army in Chihuahua was preparing to march north to reconquer the central Rio Grande. At once he began to lay plans for an expedition of his own to follow Doniphan's path and once again subdue Chihuahua.

In Washington, though the public exulted at a settlement, the Treaty of Guadalupe Hidalgo met a mixed reception. The President accepted it with reservations: "If the treaty was now to be made," he wrote on February twenty-first, "I should demand more territory, perhaps to make the Sierra Madre the line." But with minor adjustments in articles dealing with land titles in Texas and other ceded areas, he sent it to the Senate, where it encountered stormy fortunes, mostly equated with party sentiment. Daniel Webster and Sam Houston opposed it outright. Jefferson Davis called for the acquisition of most of Tamaulipas and Nuevo León, all of Coahuila, and much of Chihuahua. Secretary of State Buchanan hoped for the Sierra Madre partition, and the extremist Democrats demanded all of Northern Mexico. But as the Preisdent had noted, it was doubtful whether additional territory "could ever be obtained by the consent of Mexico," without which renewed war would be necessary to gain more land. The nation was done with war for the time, and even though a soldier in Mexico wrote home that "Some one said that we ought to continue the war and whip them"—the Mexicans—"until they consented to take back all Texas," Trist's Treaty was ratified on March 10, 1848, by the United States.

The last military gestures of the war were made by Colonel Price's force, which moved south from El Paso on March first. At Doniphan's battlefield of Sacramento they were met under a flag of truce by Governor Trias, who announced that a treaty had been signed. Colonel Price did not accept his statement. Trias retired, Price entered Chihuahua City without opposition and drove on to pursue Trias to Santa Cruz de Rosales sixty miles to the south. Once again Trias tried to convince him that a state of peace existed. In reply, Price mounted a blockade of the town to await reinforcements of cavalry and artillery. When these appeared, he attacked without choosing to verify the protestations of the Mexican commander. The battle for Santa Cruz ended in victory for Colonel Price just after sundown with the loss of four Americans killed and nineteen wounded, and an uncounted but much greater number of Mexican casualties—all suffered forty-two days after the signing of the treaty. At Querétaro on May twenty-fifth the treaty was ratified by the Mexican government—now again rid of Santa Anna, and for the second last time—and ratifications were exchanged by spokesmen for the two nations. In the same month, just as an impoverished Mexico was about to deliver over her lands in North America by ratifying the treaty, gold was discovered at Sutter's Fort in the California she was signing away.

And now there was settlement at last of the old disputes over the southeasterly Rio Grande as an accepted boundary. The Emperor Charles V had first posed the river—the Rio de las Palmas—as the western boundary in 1525 of the great, the imagined, province of Florida. In 1682 La Salle had claimed for France all lands east of it, and in 1716 St. Denis urged his government to designate the Rio Grande as a French boundary. In 1802 the French declared it the farthest limit of Louisiana, and Jefferson had repeated the claim in 1803 after his purchase of

Louisiana from Napoleon. Monroe in 1811 had terrified Gutierrez de Lara with the same notion, which persisted untried until in the Florida Treaty of 1819 the United States renounced it "forever." Henry Clay in 1821 attacked the Florida Treaty and again claimed all of Texas to the Rio Grande for the United States, though inconclusively. In 1824 the river was debated as the dividing line between the Mexican provinces of Coahuila and Texas, in the event of their political separation. Many Americans in 1825, with the accession to office of President John Quincy Adams, expected that Texas would be acquired peaceably all the way to the Rio Grande. Henry Clay as Secretary of State in 1827 attempted to buy it so from Mexico for a million dollars. In 1832 and 1833 the Texas Statehood Conventions under Mexico saw the Rio Grande as the new state's southwestern border. President Andrew Jackson, like Clay, tried to buy Texas to the river, though for a higher figure—five millions—in 1833. An independent Texas fought for the river line and won it in 1836, though without the agreement of any Mexican official except Santa Anna's, and his—once his skin was safe—he repudiated. In the early summer of 1848, what so long a sequence of claims had labored over and over to effect was now confirmed by overwhelming power: that the southeasterly Rio Grande had always seemed a natural boundary between different sovereignties, kinds of country and types of society. Under the sense of destiny of the American people, and their weight of arms, the issue—passed from trappers to traders, traders to soldiers, soldiers to citizens—was at rest. The Rio Grande in Colorado and New Mexico, and its left bank in Texas, belonged to the United States. It was won by the whole nation. Walt Whitman in New Orleans in 1848 remarked that "Probably the influence most deeply pervading everything at that time through the United States, both in physical fact and sentiment, was the Mexican War. . . ." It was won by the tradition, the skill, of the frontier rifleman. And it was won by a spirit drawn from deep in the national character. As a volunteer in the war concluded, "There was a *national* feeling in the army. . . . Every soldier felt he was a *freeman;* that he was a citizen of the MODEL REPUBLIC; and that he ought to look upon the disgrace of the AMERICAN ARMS AS INDIVIDUAL DISHONOR. . . ."

While Winfield Scott remained at Mexico City throughout the peace talks (later with many fulminations against the President and the administration he would make his way to the United States and two unsuccessful stands as presidential candidate), Zachary Taylor returned to the river in November, 1847, for the long journey home. At Mier he was honored by the officers of the Third Dragoons with "a light colla-

tion." Going downstream on the steamboat *Major Brown* he was received
with artillery salutes at Camargo, where he reviewed the Tenth Infantry.
Continuing his voyage on the *Colonel Cross* he came to Matamoros
where he found that leave of absence had been granted to him, and
boarding the *McKee,* he wound down to the Gulf and up the beach to
Point Isabel, where on Friday, November twenty-sixth, he entered the
Monmouth and sailed for New Orleans, a hero's reception, and—a year
later—the Presidency, which would give him an opportunity to pasture
his horse on the front lawn of the White House. "The only respectable
female in the army"—Mrs. Paymaster Hunter—thought of travelling to
the United States in his company; but at the last minute she was unable
to leave her husband, and at Matamoros "she resolved to remain—being
now, as she remarked, within 'striking distance' so that she can go home
when she may wish. . . ."

In vessels drawing away from the river, the Gulf, with homeward-
bound troops, the sailors sang a new song:

> When Zacharias Taylor gained the day,
> Heave away, Santy Anno;
> He made poor Santy run away,
> All on the plains of Mexico.
>
> So heave her up and away we'll go,
> Heave away, Santy Anno;
> Heave her up and away we'll go,
> All on the plains of Mexico.

After the marches, the battles and the camps, the ingenuities, the lawlessness, the energies of the army and the steamboats, the river gradually
went back to quiet. The little river towns of earth and rock, baked at
some seasons, icy-winded at others, had been suddenly awakened by
the arrival of the army to know a year or two of prosperity, violence,
change—the world passing through; and now they fell back into their
sempiternal dust to serve only as hubs for the life of rancherias in the
countryside, where only the elements made motion amidst the daily cycle
of color in the skies, above the slow-circling birds, the obscure snakes,
and the silence broken only by the slide and roll of the heavy river water.

> General Scott and Taylor, too,
> Heave away, Santy Anno;
> Have made poor Santy meet his Waterloo,
> All on the plains of Mexico.

> So heave her up and away we'll go,
> Heave away, Santy Anno. . . .

Captain Robert E. Lee of General Wool's brigade bought his little son a mustang pony in Mexico, and had it shipped to Baltimore. The pony's name was Santa Anna. At the abandoned wastes of the river's mouth rooted in sand and the white dust of shells lay the blackened wreckage of "the numberless vessels" grounded during the war. The beach was now an empty prison, where once troops had been sent to be punished—yet not quite empty so long as there was someone to remember what lay there. For a young officer waiting for the ship that would take him home from the Rio Grande made a note of what he saw. ". . . I strolled out to the dunes so thickly peopled with our dead. The revelations were shocking." Wind and wash had hauled away the covering of the graves, exposing their contents. His colonel ordered him to "take a working party and rebury all remains." As he did so, the lieutenant wondered if the government would ever take home the bodies of the fallen. It was not done in his lifetime, or after. "The poor fellows are abandoned," he thought, remembering his comrades. "Only the Great Gulf lifts a voice for them—an inarticulate, everlasting moan." Soon his ship was ready in its turn, and with the living he sailed away from the Rio Grande.

> Santy Anno was a good old man,
> Heave away, Santy Anno;
> Till he got into war with your Uncle Sam,
> All on the plains of Mexico.

27.

El Dorado

Of the war's consequences, some were small, of concern to perhaps only one or two. At noon one day in February, 1848, President Polk had a caller—the ex-Empress Ana María Iturbide who came from Philadelphia with her friend, a Miss White, to interpret for her, to ask about her pension from the Mexican government which owing to the war she was not receiving. In her anxious isolation of language, Doña Ana gathered from Miss White that the President would do what he could. He would ask for a grant from Congress, and did so. There the matter was lost in committee, until thirteen years later the exiled and so briefly imperial matron died in Philadelphia.

Other consequences were national. When the terrific news of the discovery of gold came from California, Mexico knew what she had lost with the war, the Americans what they had gained—the Golden Land, El Dorado, at last—and, as an American magazine put it, "then began the rising and the rush." It rose in such appetite and fury that Henry David Thoreau was moved to groan, "Going to California . . . it is only three thousand miles nearer Hell. . . . What a comment, what a satire on our institutions! The conclusion will be that mankind will hang itself upon a tree. And who would interfere to cut it down?" In a sense, the rush was never to end for the rest of the nation. With varying objectives in the popular imagination, there would always be something lying in wait to be taken on the golden strand. Once again the Western frontier called, and the United States replied with movement.

Some travellers went by clipper ship from the Eastern ports, sailing to Panama for a jungle passage to the other ocean and a precarious coastwise shipping to the north; or continuing around Cape Horn and up the west coast of the Americas. Some landed at the Arms of Saint James in the Gulf, sailed up the Rio Grande in rusty steamboats left over from the war, and went overland across northern Mexico from

Camargo or Mier. Other overland routes spanned the continent at the waist, or again touched out from San Antonio toward Eagle Pass, a march across Mexico to Mazatlan, and a northbound vessel. Another reached from San Antonio to El Paso, to follow the river up to a ford north of the new town of Las Cruces, and turn west. And still another came from over the prairies to find the river below Santa Fe, follow it southward to Socorro or Doña Ana, and take the westward turn there. The stakes looked enormous, but in the end, they seemed only a pretext, for relatively few of the tens of thousands of emigrants made great fortunes out of gold. But all found new land, new opportunities in life according to their tastes and abilities; and to satisfy what compelled them within, all endured troubles and even perils, in the classic frontier style.

The journey by the Gulf and the river took in the new town of Brownsville, that had grown up around Fort Brown. In 1849, along with all the lower river towns but Mier, and with only one doctor of medicine in the valley, Brownsville was swept by an epidemic of cholera. Upriver California travellers lost many of their companions, who died in Rio Grande City, Roma, Camargo, and on river steamboats. Some of those who escaped the disease fled home to the Eastern States. Others who went on westward saw services of intercession at Mier, where the cholera had not come—a Te Deum and Mass in the old brown stone church, with the organ shaking the air through the open doors, and bells ringing, and a procession of the Host to the plaza which was decked with bright cloths, and children waving little flags made of kerchiefs tied to sticks, and rockets rising into the sunshine.

One emigrant coming up from Brownsville to Roma to strike inland across Mexico travelled the river by "the splendid, fast-sailing, high-pressure steamboat 'Tom McKinney,' propelled by an engine of four crab power, the steam being furnished from two enormous boilers formerly used on a first-class Mississippi boat . . . she was of very light draught. . . . ." He had advice for "all parties coming by this route. Do not form parties to exceed fifteen in number, as it will be difficult to procure subsistence en route for larger ones. . . . Do not encumber yourselves with unnecessary baggage. No man's ought . . . to exceed 150 lbs; and it is folly to bring any amount of provisions. A few cooking utensils are necessary, and also saddles and bridles. . . ."

A party of gold seekers crossing Mexico for Mazatlan was attacked by Indians, their stock and horses were stolen. The animals were recovered by soldiers from Fort Duncan on the river. The travellers rested near the fort. Their place was called California Camp. Used by later emigrants, it became the town of Eagle Pass, named for the great bird who for several years lived on the river, and was seen to make his way slowly from one bank to another always by the same airy course.

Overland parties from San Antonio for El Paso helped to incise the road that later stage lines would use. American society awheel, carrying all its amenity and structure with it, found it reassuring amidst daily strangeness to hold meetings, elect caravan officials, and to celebrate patriotic anniversaries with oratory, recitations and "readings." When it was necessary to pause to "let the oxen blow," the train made camp and voted a social evening. Coming to the river at the site of Fort Quitman the emigrants found shade—their first in hundreds of miles—with cottonwoods and willows. The road was sandy, and if a horse sprained an ankle, its owner dismounted to join "what the boys call the walking committee." The river in June, 1849, was often in flood, and one morning "rose from fifty feet wide to five hundred," at the rate of "nearly a foot a minute." To ford it a man had to tie his clothes and firearms with his belt to his horse's neck, and swim hanging on to his horse's tail.

At El Paso the travellers camped near the town but on an island— La Isla—made by a division of the river's flow round a sandspit "from 2 to 4 miles wide & about 20 miles long." On it were the three ancient mission towns of Isleta del Sur, Socorro del Sur, and San Elizario. By another change of the river's course the island later became part of the American bank. The emigrants traded with the Mexicans for fruit and vegetables—"250 large onions for an old sword which cost about ten shillings in New York new"—and shot ducks and quail, and cleaned river water with a filter made of prickly pears. Six pecks of wheat cost five dollars, and of flour, seven. The Americans rendered their own tallow— "invaluable"—and were watched with interest by Mexican men dressed in white muslin shirts hanging open and pants "tight around the thighs" but wider down the leg and wide-leafed straw hats, and Mexican women in scarves and separated blouses and skirts, and smaller children "nearly naked."

The El Paso valley was more than ever a crossroads. By late August, 1849, four hundred wagons had passed through on the way to the gold fields, and even though "accounts from the gold region is good," many travellers had become discouraged and had lingered there at loose ends. Another emigrant said they "look blue," listening to rumors of the hard passage ahead. So many talked of wintering at El Paso that he declared "The Pass, no doubt, will be a great place this winter, as gambling, drinking, &c, are all the rage," and "The Pass this winter will be the theatre in which many a horrible scene will be played. . . ." Already, displaced emigrants had abused the Mexicans, demanding houseroom, and turning into horse thieves, gamblers and even murderers. One set up a business killing Apache Indians and selling scalps to the Mexican government for two hundred dollars each, and collecting two hundred and fifty for each prisoner. If Indians were scarce, he even killed Mexicans to profit from their scalps.

But those who went on followed the river up from El Paso. A few miles north of town they met a man and a boy who sold "wiskey & gin" for fifty cents per third of a pint—"extravagantly low." They passed a ranch house fenced with "timbers from the wagons brought from Missouri by Col. Doniphan in 1846," and came to Las Cruces with its few houses, and a few miles later saw the American flag for the first time in "many a day" flying above Doña Ana. Turning there toward San Diego, California, they forded the river—there were no longer any bridges on the whole course of the Rio Grande—and continued their passage westward.

The overlanders who came across the central prairies to the Rio Grande below Santa Fe had much to do every evening when camp was made. One left a record. "Now comes the busy scene of pitching tents, collecting wood, preparing food, etc. The sound of the axe, the metallic ring of the blacksmith's hammer, the merry voice of children, the braying of mules, is heard. Some children are playing near the water . . . ladies are attending to their domestic concerns, the preparing of a good meal for their families." Music rose, and the "sweet sound of the flute . . . will come floating on the ear, or the well accorded voices of a band of vocalists, or the merry notes of a violin accompanied with the tripping sound of feet. . . ." Another left practical warning. "The march down the Rio Grande was most arduous and difficult; the road is very bad after reaching the river. . . ." The only good thing was that for a large part of the way "before leaving the river, green corn, onions, grapes, fresh meat, and fish" could be "procured in abundance," and there was "no scarcity of wood, water and grass." One party in the summer of 1849 paused near Socorro to celebrate the Fourth of July. "Our messes all joined together and purchased 20 lambs at a rancho nearby our camp, which made us a good dinner. We had the Declaration of Independence read, and an oration, after which we drank the health of our friends at home and the prosperity of our country. . . . One mess brought out some of the best Hollands [gin], another cognac, while your humble servant

and a few others were lucky enough to find at the bottom of a trunk
some sparkling champagne, reserved for this occasion. At sunset we fired
a grand salute, and in the evening we had a fandango at which, by special
invitation, there were present a crowd of the fair señoritas. They waltz
'devinly' and their dancing is 'dem foine'. . . ."

Not far from Socorro, at Lemitar, a year later, ex-Governor
Manuel Armíjo, established on one of his properties, was hoping for
political preferment under the American government of New Mexico.
His eyes were on election to the post of delegate to the Territorial Assembly. He supposed it was necessary to swear loyalty to the United States
in order to occupy any position. He had not done it, but he could not
believe that that would "militate against [him] in receiving votes as
delegate." Others "whose names it would be a shame to mention" had
received votes. Why not he? "I would to God," he cried, "they would
vote for me for President of the United States." But if nothing came of
his unbounded ambitions, he could sigh, "I am here as a saint whose
day has passed—but well content, because I know how to philosophize."
Though rumored to have buried much treasure, he was out of funds,
and was forced to offer his silver table service to an American lieutenant
for three hundred dollars.

28.

Contraband

Brownsville began as a scattering of huts and jacales that were
soon brought into a grid of streets at right angles by order of the local
sheriff, who destroyed any dwellings that were not in line by a certain
date. The first population was made up of French and American merchants and Mexican families. Four years later there were five or six
thousand residents, "chiefly Mexicans." New houses were built of brick,
and the streets were edged with rows of Chinese lilac, willow and acacia.

On windy days both Brownsville and Matamoros, opposite, were obscured by a flying haze of the river's fine pale sand, and on rainy the
streets were runnels where little rivers ran down to the town quay,
which was shaped like an amphitheatre, where bales of goods came and
went with the steamboats. It was a busy town, alive with horsemen, and
ranch carts, and aguaderos in loose white cotton who sold water brought
from the river in little casks with axles fixed to their ends so that casks
were drawn like rollers.

Once again the society enacted the extreme individualism of the
frontier. Bankrupts, escaped criminals, deserters from the armies of the
recent war, gamblers and swindlers set the tone. The barrooms were
fighting pits. Pistol duels added style to murder. Murderers and other
offenders were lynched at the town shambles by hanging from the timbers on which beeves were butchered. The place was "without roof or
shade, roasted by the sun, and the resort of dogs which fought for the
bones of the animals." The sheriff—a huge man of great strength and
a brutal force—usually killed the men he set out to arrest. Bloodhounds
guarded the gate of his jail. One prisoner who served time under him
and was discharged alive was a drummer boy who had deserted in the
war, had been sentenced to be shot, but because of his extreme youth
had instead been drummed out of the army. He lived at Brownsville as a
boy-drunkard, terrorizing the streets with his threats and oaths. One day
he appeared naked on horseback, riding in and out of stores and saloons,
defying arrest. The sheriff shot him in the arm and lodged him behind
the bloodhounds. On being released, he found a rifle, shot the sheriff
with a ramrod still in the barrel, and fled to Eagle Pass, where he continued to enact his doom as a public nuisance until a quartermaster's
carpenter of Fort Duncan shot and killed him, to the general applause
of the upriver authorities and citizens.

Local elections at Brownsville were held with violent partisanship.
Opposing parties staged parades with the colors of their candidates worn
by supporters, horses and even dogs. On election day voters were offered
free whiskey from tables set up in the streets. By comparison, Matamoros
across the way was calm. On the last three days of Holy Week, no vehicles
ran there, and all year the Mexican customs guard, with its well-uni-
formed officers who had "a very distingué air," had so little to do that
its soldiers slept "nearly the entire day in a grove of the *Palma Christi*
planted near the shed."

They slept not because the cross-river traffic in goods was small.
It was large—but almost all unofficial, for everywhere on the lower river

the smuggling of contraband goods was highly organized. Matamoros might be the official port of entry for Mexico on the lower Rio Grande, but upstream, whole towns were established as stations for the illegal passage of merchandise by enterprising Americans. Davis Landing, where wartime steamboats refueled, was soon transformed into Rio Grande City, which was seen as "a vast assemblage of American stores and Mexican huts, where smuggling progresses on an extensive scale." Several companies of the United States Army were stationed a little south of town at Fort Ringgold (later Ringgold Barracks). There was no customs office on the Mexican side, for Mexico had no funds to pay for adding to her border ports. The smugglers operated on so great a scale that their calling was accepted as respectable business. They prospered so long as they were willing to suffer inconveniences, one of which was the climate. "Trees and verdure are rarely seen," noted a visitor to Rio Grande City, "so that the heat reflected from the river sand, and from the rocks and gravel of the hills, makes the place a veritable furnace. One should possess the incombustible nature of the Salamander to live there. . . ." Roma, farther north, suddenly grew after the war with "fine houses and warehouses" for the American exporters. An American boundary surveyor was puzzled to explain how so remote a little town could support such prosperity. One night while he was out in the open away from Roma taking observations he found the answer. In spite of the calmness of the night, the mercury of the artificial horizon in his instrument was "very tremulous." Calculations were useless in such odd conditions. He packed up his case and started to town through the dark only to meet a "long train of mules, heavily laden, going toward the Mexican side. The motion of the animals caused the disturbance of the mercury, and their rich burden of contraband goods, intended for the Mexican market, explained the prosperity of the town. . . ."

American and Mexican businessmen collaborated in breaking the customs regulations. At Roma in a certain period of two months over a hundred thousand dollars' worth of goods went across the river illegally and efficiently. Cotton cloth was the main article of sale, and there lay the reason for the whole contraband trade. For the Mexican government maintained a monopoly of cotton manufacture. The industry was large. At its peak it employed over two hundred thousand workers, and produced over a million bolts of cloth a year. To protect this business, the government placed an exorbitant tariff on imported stuffs, and along the border, this amounted to an invitation to cheat the garrisons at Matamoros, Mier and Camargo.

But officials there were not above the battle. Winking at the official duty rates, the customs houses of the three towns bid against one another for the American trade; and—in a typical instance—if Mier offered a lower rate than Camargo, Mier prepared to receive the custom, pass the American goods, and keep the fees for her officers. But watching what went on, Camargo's soldiers were waiting for the American merchants as they crossed near Mier. In a flourish, the soldiers captured the pack train and its men. Camargo took that trick from Mier. But the game was not over, for a party of Texas Rangers and mustang hunters were paid two thousand dollars by the American exporters to spring across the river and rescue the goods. This they did, returning with the cargo, together with the clothes and firearms of the Camargo troops.

Such conduct of business held much to recommend it to the border spirit. It was illegal, it was adventurous, it was a game. But it was also expensive and complicated, and much could go awry in the process. How much better, thought the merchants of Brownsville and Matamoros—the largest business towns on the river—if the Mexican government, or better yet, a new government established by revolution, were to abolish the intolerable monopoly, and establish a system of competitive trade with a reasonable duty fee! There would thus be legitimate markets and fair profits for both American exporters and Mexican merchants. A committee of businessmen from Brownsville and Matamoros was organized to arrange for a revolution, calling upon an instrument already at hand.

For ever since the war the mirage of the separatist republic had intermittently appeared over the Rio Grande states of north Mexico, and its champion now was a certain General Carvajal, who had fought under Canales in the earlier campaigns to establish it. Carvajal had the nucleus of an army whose ranks included veterans from the American forces of the Mexican War who were not yet done—might never be done—with the binding miseries and the sandy little glories of warfare on the thorny deserts below the river. "Of middle size, symmetrically formed," General Carvajal "had regular features: his lively eye spoke at once address and energy—" and now before it clearly loomed once again his vision of the Republic of the Sierra Madre. If he received financial support from the merchants who came asking him to lead the revolution and end once and for all the tiresome contraband laws with his new republic, he could not fail. He agreed to make war on the Mexican government along the river, whose troops were commanded by General Ávalos at Matamoros. Carvajal's first target was Camargo. He captured it readily and paused to recruit his ranks, and to wait for hard cash and supplies from his backers down the river.

But the days passed, and no funds arrived, and presently it was known that the merchants were no longer with him. They were instead dealing with Ávalos, whom they invited "to a grand entertainment, at which they discussed the measures to be taken against Carvajal." The merchants had won their point in a deal with Ávalos by which—over the protests of the Mexican customs chief—American cotton could enter Mexico at a low duty, with a suitable extra fee for the general himself. It seemed that the merchants could not wait for the successful issue of a revolution, for huge shipments of goods had accumulated on the American shore, and must be moved. Now under their new arrangements they pacified Carvajal with promises for the future, if he would but hold his fire. He camped at Reynosa waiting for his promised support once again; and while he waited, for eight days cotton shipments worth half a million pesos went over the Rio Grande. It was a great stake of business for the big operators, and it was done quietly—and at the expense of the smaller frontier brokers who now had no prospect of selling their goods to a flooded market. The little operators told Carvajal what had been done to them, and he saw his own betrayal too. He attacked some of the pack trains bearing the goods to the interior, burned what he could, and then marched to besiege Matamoros.

The siege lasted twelve days during which Carvajal twice occupied Fort Paredes and once penetrated into the city with sappers and skirmishers. But when news came that his old commander and fellow revolutionary, General Canales, was on the march to relieve the city, he retired upriver to Rio Grande City. Canales followed him, and after circular retreats executed with great spirit, both armies, by the inexorable laws of Mexican border revolutions, "found themselves face to face by their very efforts to escape each other." A battle resulted near Camargo with many casualties until Carvajal's ammunition was exhausted, and Canales seized the opportunity for retreating in "a strategical movement," taking with him a number of American prisoners who a few months later under pathetic circumstances were executed "rather as rebels and assassins than as prisoners of war." Smuggling was continued undisturbed. The Republic of the Sierra Madre was once again done for. Its Mexican veterans scattered to their ranches in the wilderness on both sides of the river.

29.

A Thread of Spirit

During many decades after the war, life on both sides of the river held the same flavor, without sharp differences resulting from the American ownership of the left bank. Settlers and vagrants from the United States attached themselves to the towns, to engage in trade and wagon-driving. Almost none took up ranching or agriculture. The back-country life of the rancherias continued in the Mexican tradition, apart from the world of commerce, news and ideas. There was only one thread that bound together the isolated families on their ranches lost in dusty space, and it was an invisible one—the thread of spirit that tied them to their religion, and that was traced for them whenever he could do it by the parish priest from Brownsville, who every year or so rode out on his horse, alone, to find them so far apart, and yet so close to him, in the bitter brush deserts.

Such a man in the 1850s was a missioner from France, cultivated, patient, courageous and inexhaustibly curious about the outlandish country where he found himself. He was happy to receive a warm welcome from "Catholics, Protestants, Jews all alike", who "offered their best services," wherever he went. First he went to work on his church. He planted a garden beside it, and trained a wild boar to serve as a watchdog to keep people from picking flowers during the sermons which they moved out of doors to escape. He ordered an organ from Mexico. The church was ugly, and he "contrived, after a time, to cover . . . the walls with certain paintings on cotton." He took his place as a vigorous citizen of Brownsville. On his errands he was often chased by the sheriff's bloodhounds. He warned the sheriff to keep them chained, but to no avail. One day he was obliged to shoot the dogs. He regretted having to do so, for he liked animals, and even for his own pleasure and the instruction of others developed a small zoo.

When he had time he wandered over to Matamoros and was

charmed with what he saw—the plaza with its lilac hedges, the patio gardens with their orange, pomegranate, peach, palm, and fig trees, the quiet hot days, and then the lively evening when as the Angelus rang out before sunset the shuttered doors and windows opened, the streets filled, ladies in bright muslins came to their iron balconies, and promenaders drifted among the lilacs, to chat, laugh and smoke till midnight. All was animation. Chocolate and coffee were served everywhere. "Conversations," he recalled, "turn mostly on poetry, on religion, on love, horses, music and dancing. Scandal and politics engage but little this sequestered people, favoured with a sky the most beautiful, a climate the mildest in the world."

Again, he ventured down the river to the mouth, where he remarked that "the Spaniards of the 16th century well designated this coast by calling it *Costa Deserta.*" When he saw Bagdad he was not reminded of "the abode of Harûn-al-Rashid." A dozen Mexican families lived there in reed huts plastered with mud and oyster shells, with no trace of near-by cultivation to provide food for them. On the other shore of the mouth in half-ruined wooden sheds left over from the war abided a group of American beachcombers who fished and hunted by day, and by evening, met "to smoke, to read the papers aloud, and to discuss politics." The busy pastor concluded that "eccentricity and feelings of independence must be pushed far enough to make people live thus in deserts, without name or shade, and spend in solitude and inaction a life without aim." Now and then a sloop arrived at Bagdad from Tampico, bringing bananas, ananas, cocoanuts and lemons, which were sold upriver in the towns.

It was not long until the father missioner found that church relations in his vast parish of the lower Rio Grande were decayed where not simply abandoned. In the last Spanish years visiting priests had made their rounds amongst the ranches every year or two. But after the achievement of Mexican independence such visits almost ceased; and—as happened in New Mexico during the same period—"all pertaining to doctrine and morality fell into the shade," and only "what struck the senses was more tenacious in its hold. The substance was lost in the form, and external practices, as is natural to the Mexicans, became the chief objects of attention. This religious decadence was a sad sight. . . ."

A month after his arrival from France he went up the river to start setting matters right. He packed a set of light silk vestments from Lyons, a chalice, a pyx, a catechism, a chrismatory containing holy oils, certificates of baptism, first communion and marriage, and a few personal necessities, and sailed upstream on the steamboat *Comanche* until she stuck fast on a sand bar. Thenceforth he proceeded on horseback.

The land was empty, silent and wavering in glassy heat. The only living thing he encountered in the early stages of his journey filled him with pleasure because it lived. It was—must he say it?—a rattlesnake, and were its bite not mortal, he reflected, he could have dismounted "to embrace the creature." In the little towns he found the Mexicans were poor and few in number, and "most anxious to have a priest to instruct them in their duties, to support them in their misery, and to close their eyes at the supreme moment of death." His riverside road was intersected by straggling trails made by cattle going to water. In the waters of Alamo Creek he saw "people of every age and each sex" bathing. He visited Mier, and found it a beautiful town, "with its church spire, palm and aloe trees, cut in profile against the azure firmament." The local pastor gave him information, and he called to see various families in town, with whom he smoked a cigarette, ate a sweet cake and drank a mug of chocolate. It was a pleasure to see how "strikingly handsome" were the men and women of Mier, and to hear what good Spanish they spoke, "less corrupted with Indian words and phrases."

One time when he left Mier it was late at night. Lost in the dark, he kept wondering where to turn to reach the Rio Grande across the markless plateau. Suddenly out of the night appeared "the shadow of a man," quite naked, making his way home to Mier after working in the fields all day. The missioner asked him the way to the river. Without a word the peon took the bridle of the missioner's horse and led him for ten minutes across the plateau, and then said, "Let the horses take their own course," and "vanished like an apparition." At Camargo the traveller encountered simplicity of another kind no less deeply Indian. He assisted at high Mass in the parish church. Sacred music "was played on a large drum, a trombone, two clarionets, and several violins. . . . A great surprise awaited me. During the elevation they commenced playing the *Marseillaise*." True, he recalled, "throughout all America the *Marseillaise* is quite the rage. . . ."

If he wanted to progress from one ranch to the next on the Texan side of the river, he found that the only roads were the old Spanish trails in Mexico. "Often the shortest and even the only route between two Texian *ranchos* is to cross the Rio Grande and travel the Mexican territory, and to recross the Rio Grande again near one's destination." But whichever side he was on, the back-country life was the same, for the ranchers were all Mexicans. They seemed "just as indolent as their

countrymen in town," with "all the characteristics and all the defects
of an infant people." He studied them with a professional eye, and came
to a conclusion. "Voluptuousness is surely their damning vice." But he
added that this came not so much from depraved morals as from ignorance and enervation. He could not imagine how a ranchero made a
living, overpowered as he was by the mere notion of effort—"save in
pleasures." The Mexican rancher could sleep anywhere, better under a
tree than a roof. Poor ranchers lived on coffee, chocolate, tortillas and
sun-dried beef; the rich on rice, spices, lamb cooked with raisins, tamales.
Neither walked, even to go half a mile, but always rode. He might live
in "a wretched hut," but on his horse the Mexican lavished every
splendor, with gold and silver studdings on saddle and bridle. His horse
was his inseparable companion. Riding out, the rancher wore his best—
a broad-brimmed hat trimmed with gold lace or a gold chain, and lined
with green; an embroidered shirt; velvet trousers with broad facings of
black braid slashed at the calf to show his long white cotton drawers;
a bright scarf of China crepe at the waist; and silver spurs.

The missioner saw many a company of such horsemen on high
occasions. Going to a feast celebrating a baptism, a marriage, or a fandango, they rode "like a horde of madmen let loose, or of Indians. . . ."
Their women rode with them. At full gallop, they went shouting, singing, in a cloud of dust, and pulled up at a cluster of ranch buildings
made of stakes and reeds laid out in a miniature plaza, with a long
street intersecting it. If the ranch was decked for a wedding, tables with
food were set out under brush arbors. The missioner was pressed to partake of the feast. He nearly choked on the "horrid sauce of beef-suet,
pepper and spices," which tasted like melted tallow. There was nothing
to drink but whiskey, which he refused, though the hot sauce made
him think he could "quaff the Rio Grande at a draught." After the
feast and a siesta in the shade there were horse races down the long
dusty street between the jacales; and after the races the riders linked
arms and strolled around in groups, singing to the music of a guitar or
an accordion. Though none had musical training, everyone played and
sang "with no less taste than talent." Now and then a young fellow took
a woman en croupe and in a flourish of violent gallantry galloped her
to the end of the street and back, then seizing others in turn, repeated
his strenuous compliment.

When evening came, the horses were tethered, lanterns were
lighted in the trees, and benches were set out to make a square. The
women laid aside their mantillas and formed a line while the men came

to make a row behind them. When two violins, two clarinets and a bass
drum began to play, the fandango was on. The missioner watched for
a while, and then withdrew to seclusion behind a hut, wrapped his
blanket about him and lay down to sleep. It was useless. "During the
whole night, the bum-bum of the big drum, the shrill discordant notes
of the clarionet, the roars of merriment, and the thundering acclamation
of the dancers" kept him "from closing an eye." And if the dancers
rested for a moment, others sang. It was true that their voices were sweet
and their songs "racy with the poetry of nature." Still others sat under
the trees smoking and "relating fantastic stories as history." An "itinerant troubadour" might be present in his wanderings from ranch to
ranch, and in return for a meal and a corner in which to spread his
serape for the night, told stories—making a hit with tales of witches
who lived in the river country—and sang ballads to the sound of his
guitar. At one such wedding feast the bride was admitted to be the
"living descendant of Montezuma." She was an orphan, and of all her
immense family wealth nothing was left to her but vast lands in Texas,
whose title since the war it was impossible to hold. Offered six thousand
dollars in settlement, "she accepted this miserable sum, and married the
man she loved,"going with him "to continue in obscurity, her existence
unknown, indeed, to the world, but withal peaceful and happy. . . ."

Resuming his rounds, the missioner came to his remote families
after long, hard rides, to bring them the blessing of God upon their
stages of life, temporal and eternal. He baptized new children. He sat
with the older children and gave them their lessons in catechism. He
instructed them for their first communions. Through him they learned
the true meaning of the stories of the Holy Family and the saints told
them by their parents in fragments half remembered and half invented.
If young people waited to be married he performed the sacrament of
matrimony for them. If old people were ready to die he brought them
the grace of a happy death, while the ranch women wept and shrieked,
striking their breasts and tearing their hair in propriety. He was an
honored guest and he became a friend. He was the world, with its news,
its powers, and its sense of form. Through him the lost clusters of
humanity scattered about the blinding prickly wilderness were brought
into the great design of life, and given dignity, and their rightful share
of an all-enfolding love, and salvation through it. When he had renewed
their understanding of these things through an explanation of the Mass
which they could attend so seldom, he prepared to celebrate it for them.

Taking two meal tubs, he set them at the foot of a large sycamore

tree under its embracing shade. Over the tubs he laid a door from a hut.
This was his altar. He dressed it with two bottles covered with moss to
serve as candlesticks, and he took the crucifix he wore and hung it on the
stem of the tree. With muslin mantillas and shawls fixed to branches
he made a drapery about the altar. Then—it was still early in the hot
day—he went to the bank of the Rio Grande to read his breviary. After
that it was time to call everyone to Mass. He walked through the settlement of the ranch ringing a little bell, and they came. They knelt on
a patch of green grass in the sycamore shade, all silent, and attended
the repetition of the Holy Sacrifice first done and now done again in
their behalf; and vastly away the plain was gilded by the sun, and overhead in the branches birds sang.

The missioner, so far away from the cultivated graces of life in
his beloved France, learned to know different graces in the people he
came so far to serve. One night he had a companionable visit from
the old Mexican soldier who was his man of all work—"cook, butler,
sacristan." It was a lovely night, and the missioner was taking his ease
in the garden of his rectory where he had contrived a gallery of board
from which depended a hammock. There he liked to doze, or consult
his thoughts, or gaze at his flower beds in the summer starlight, or watch
the lights of Fort Brown as they went out one after another when the
bugle ended the day. The sacristan sat down on the ground near the
hammock and for a while neither he nor the misioner spoke, but simply
dwelled together in the night. Then puffing at a cigarette, the old campaigner launched in a loud voice a monologue "on the beauties of the
heavens and the earth."

"See," he said, "what a charming night it is! what sweet mellow
temperature! what pure and balmy air! what silence in all nature! How
this silence of night ravishes my soul!" And yet all was not silence. "Do
you hear the cry of the widow"—the great-tailed grackle that made hilarious clatter in the treetops everywhere on the lower river—"as she flies and
flutters in the distance? Why does she not sleep beneath the broad shade
of the ebony tree? Mystery of God," he said, and fell silent under it.
And then he was moved to continue. "Do you see those myriads of stars
whose twinkling splendor lights the plains like the timid doubtful twilight? And those majestic palm-trees, whose graceful branches gently
poise themselves against the clear sky, seeming as if at night-time they
bear fruit of fire, suspended from every branch? And those stars that fall
and fade away, leaving behind them a light narrow cascade of diamonds?
Oh!" he cried, "how wonderful are the works of God!"

However much the misioner may have elaborated the translation of what he heard that night, he could still say, "I was wrapt in amazement and delight at the poetic rapture of my old soldier. . . ."

30.

Boundaries

Words put forth in campaigns—military or political—sometimes had to be overcome. Though General Kearny on approaching New Mexico had said that he proposed to take only the lands lying east of the Rio Grande, soon afterward he swept his claim across the river all the way to California. With the signing of the peace, Mexico succumbed to the terms of the United States; but not Texas. Texas in 1836 claimed all New Mexico's area east of the river, amounting to some ninety-eight thousand square miles. In 1848 she reaffirmed the claim by another act of her legislature, and sent a Texan judge to hold court in New Mexico. This was Spruce M. Baird, who travelled along the New Mexican valley agitating the Texan cause. Near Socorro he made an ally of a returned refugee. "Genl. Armijo," he reported to Governor George T. Wood of Texas, "Genl. Armijo espouses our cause with some zeal and is decidedly the first man in that region." Baird soon measured him. "I bought him out lock stock and barrel." Armijo was living on past glories, and could not refrain from showing the Texan certain spoils left over from the victory over General McLeod's Santa Fe Pioneers of 1841. "He showed me General McCloud's regimentals and says no other Mexican general can exhibit such trophies."

But New Mexico was now a ward of the United States, and her citizens—though without prior approval by the national government—moved to achieve territorial status. Ignoring the claim of Texas and the presence of her jurist, they held an election to choose a New Mexican delegate to Congress, with voters eligible in the vast disputed area. The

Governor of Texas drew his sword. Texas, he declared, would seize New
Mexico to the east bank by force. But he was not dealing now with an
Armijo whom earlier Texans had even so not been able to overthrow;
he was dealing with the United States, and the government at Washington assured him promptly that if he sent Texan troops to New Mexico
they would be received and disposed of as aggressors.

The local quarrel suddenly flared into larger significance when
other Southern states threw in with Texas in her sense of injury, and
against the government made bitter charges of an overreach of federal
power. The Northern states as automatically sided with the national
government; and a premonition of tragic things to come could be read
in the argument. For embedded in the question of states' rights against
federal authority was the issue of slavery. Texas had long since been
committed to slavery by the policies of Stephen Austin. Texas held a
further promise of value to the Southern faction, for at the time of her
acceptance into the Union she had been guaranteed the right to divide
herself by vote of her citizens into as many as five states, all of which
would presumably declare for slavery. The possession of immense new
tracts taken from New Mexico would make such a sub-division not only
politically powerful in national questions, but also locally rich in
material resources. Again in 1850 Texas by joint resolution of her
legislative chambers asserted her New Mexican claim and promised
that "the State of Texas will maintain the integrity of her territory."

The question was taken up by Congress in the summer, and an
omnibus bill—the Compromise of 1850—was passed with provisions that
settled the local status of new lands won by the Mexican War, and
postponed the ultimate challenge to the union inherent in sectional
animosities. California became a state without slavery. New Mexico
was separated into two federal territories, one of which embraced the
later statehood areas of New Mexico and Arizona, the other comprising
those of Utah and Nevada. Both were to decide for freedom or slavery
upon becoming states. Fugitive slave laws were tightened, and in the
District of Columbia, while slavery was continued, the slave trade was
outlawed. And the disputed lands between Texas and the upper Rio
Grande were given to New Mexico, with a payment of ten million
dollars awarded to Texas. President Millard Fillmore promptly signed
the bill and sent it to Texas.

It created a furor in Austin. The Governor convened the legislature in a special session to take action. The bill had many features to
infuriate the Texan houses. It required their acceptance of its provisions

by a deadline—December 1, 1850. It assumed that Texas interests could be disposed by the federal government. And its proposal to pay the ten millions was hedged with conditions that seemed to reflect upon Texan honor, for only half the great sum was to be paid outright, the other half to be held until Texas herself had paid off claims against the United States that accompanied Texas into the Union. Were Texans to conclude that Texas could not be trusted to meet her obligations if she obtained the ten millions all at once? Focussing the furies of his legislature, the Governor proposed the immediate occupation of Santa Fe by force of arms, and then made another suggestion—that the disputed lands be sold to the United States, but with the reservation that Texas retain jurisdiction over them. The halls at Austin echoed much high feeling in debate: but in the end, opposition collapsed, and on November 25, 1850, safely before the deadline, the terms of the United States were accepted and affirmed by act of law in the Texas legislature. The New Mexican Rio Grande was not to be an interstate boundary after all, except for a little jog of a few miles above El Paso on the modern map.

But in addition to marking Mexico off from Texas, a portion of the river as it turned north from El Paso was indicated as the boundary between New and old Mexico. A precise survey of the international boundary was still to be made under the articles of the Treaty of Guadalupe Hidalgo. These provided that the line "shall commence in the Gulf of Mexico, three leagues from land, opposite the mouth of the Rio Grande, otherwise called the Rio Bravo del Norte, or opposite the mouth of its deepest branch, if it should have more than one branch emptying directly into the sea; from thence up the middle of that river, following the deepest channel, where it has more than one, to the point where it strikes the southern boundary of New Mexico; thence, westwardly, along the whole southern boundary of New Mexico (which runs north of the town called *Paso* to its western termination; thence, northward, along the western line of New Mexico, until it intersects the first branch of the river Gila; (or if it should not intersect any branch of that river, then to the point on the said line nearest to such branch, and thence in a direct line to the same; thence down the middle of said branch and of the said river, until it empties into the Rio Colorado; thence across the Rio Colorado, following the division between Upper and Lower California, to the Pacific Ocean." In these provisions the river's habit of changing its course was taken into account. For centuries the channel had wandered, creating the old resacas of the littoral; and, more recently, the isla at El Paso; and, a hundred years later, leaving

as farmland—marked "No Dumping"—the site of the steamboat dock at
Davis's Landing half a mile from the new bank. Far into the twentieth
century the vagaries of the river's course would keep an international
commission at work adjusting problems of ownership and sovereignty
raised by sudden storm changes in the channel.

In 1849 President Polk offered Lieutenant Colonel W. H. Emory
the post of boundary commissioner if he would resign from the Army to
conduct the survey, which he "respectfully declined" to do. Colonel
John B. Weller was then appointed, and Emory became his chief astron-
omer and commander of the escort troops that would accompany the
survey expedition. They embarked from the east coast for the Isthmus
of Panama with the news of California gold ringing in their ears—news
that made trouble for the survey when later in California many members
of the party quit to seek their fortunes in the gold fields. The boundary
commission in 1849 and 1850 was able to accomplish little. The commission was repeatedly bankrupt because the government failed to send
the monies appropriated, promised and needed for the field work. John
Russell Bartlett was appointed to replace Weller, and once again the
expedition was organized. The new commissioner had a lively interest in
the country he went to study, and was proud to see gathered by eminent
scientists under his leadership much striking new scientific information,
and quoted his experts to the effect that, "It will be perfectly safe to say,
that one hundred undescribed species of North American vertebrate
animals have been added to our fauna. The entire annals of zoological
history scarcely present a parallel to this case."

He took delight in the social amenities of the Pass, at Magoffinsville on the north side of the Rio Grande—one of three American settlements there. It represented "the American El Paso," and consisted of
"a large square, around which" were "substantial adobe buildings of a
better description than usual, embracing some six or eight large stores
and warehouses, well filled with merchandise." The commissioner found
the town "admirably situated," and belonging "wholly to James W.
Magoffin, Esq., an American, long resident in Mexico, whose energy
and public spirit will undoubtedly make it the principal place on the
frontier. . . ."

Magoffin had lost none of his savoir faire since the war. With
"delicacies prepared in New York and Paris for the foreign markets"
he could serve "a cold collation . . . that would have done credit to the
caterer of a metropolitan hotel." Bartlett stayed in quarters on the
Mexican side three or four miles away, and when James Magoffin gave

an evening party, the guests forded the river in carriages, sometimes getting stuck fast in midstream until Mexicans came to carry them ashore. The company remained at the party till the next morning, returning home by daylight. When the commissioner in his turn desired to give a party, Magoffin invited him to use a large hall at Magoffinsville. It was a success, even to four great "new-fashioned chandeliers improvised for the occasion" out of sardine tins fixed to a hoop off a pork barrel, wrapped with Apache calicoes and supplied with a "dozen burners each," that "shed such a ray of light upon the festal hall, as rendered the charms of the fair señoritas doubly captivating. . . ."

But if the impromptu delights of El Paso broke the monotony of a hard job, Commisioner Bartlett still seemed unable to get it done. He was a man of many gifts—scholar, antiquarian, bibliographer—and his interests yielded much of value about the nature of the new country taken by conquest. But there were complaints that he spent too much time away in Mexico, and in February, 1853, he was relieved of office. Colonel John C. Frémont who was named to replace him never assumed active part in the direction of the survey. Colonel Emory was still a member of its staff. Presently he appeared in Washington to complain vigorously about the government's handling of the commission; and after all, he was appointed as commissioner, and undertook his command in 1854.

It was his mission to survey another and final southern boundary of the United States, for in 1853 the Gadsden Treaty had been concluded with Mexico which for a consideration of ten million dollars gave the United States new lands in southern New Mexico and Arizona. This was an important acquisition. It embraced a great east-west strip of high flat country ideal for the course of a railroad. If the United States had not bought it, her southernmost rail lines to the West would have had to pass through Mexican territory.

In his survey report Emory made a striking picture of the character of the land by imagining it as a passage by sea. He found that the "depression" of the continent from east to west was wide, stretching from the confluence of the Pecos with the Rio Grande to the Gulf of California. "If the sea," he said, "were to rise to 4,000 feet above its present level, the navigator could cross the continent near the 32nd parallel of latitude. He would be on soundings of uniform depth, from the Gulf of California to the Pecos River. He would see to the north and to the south prominent peaks and sierras, and at times his passage would be narrow and intricate. At El Paso he would be within gunshot of both shores"—the gap through which the Rio Grande ran. He had noticed "this remarkable depression in the continent, in an exploration made by me in 1846," while he was campaigning as a lieutenant in the Army of the West. He had pointed it out to James Buchanan as a basis for fixing the boundary under the Mexican peace terms, and the Secretary of State had instructed Trist "not to take a line north of the 32nd parallel." The instruction had been ignored, and only with the Gadsden Treaty was Emory's original recommendation carried out.

Emory's border mission took two years to complete. He was harassed not only by Indians but also by the raids of Rio Grande free-booters—Carvajal and others—who were still making dust along the river. It was his impression that conditions in the long, speckled valley had "steadily gone backwards since the days of the Spanish rule." With his small party and all their topographic gear he followed the river line between vast stretches of unknown land; and in some places even the river itself had to be taken on conjecture, notably in the Big Bend. He was an able and orderly soldier, "calm, dignified and firm," with all the versatility of so many officers in the mid-century army; and it was particularly exasperating that again and again the government let his men go without pay—once they mutinied in protest—and repudiated his scrupulous requisitions on monies appropriated for his work. He tried to resign but his resignation was refused, and, despite all, he was able to finish his duty. There were compensations. The longer he worked the more he seemed interested in the harsh country that slowly yielded itself up to his knowledge. James Magoffin—an old friend with whom he had campaigned in '46—gave him much help. Best of all, the Mexican officers on the boundary commission who worked with him were intelligent, co-operative and courteous. The interpreter who officiated at joint sessions of the survey was Don Felipe de Iturbide, "the younger son of the late Emperor." In the journals of the joint commission, the daily entries were signed alternately in first place by the Mexican and United States commissioners, to balance the precedence of the two nations in their common effort. The survey was harmoniously concluded, to the satisfaction of both governments.

The youngest river town to be affected by the final boundary was Mesilla, New Mexico. It was established in 1853 through Mexican land grants just across the first boundary between the nations. Las Cruces and Doña Ana lay a little way to its north in United States territory. Those two towns were suddenly crowded after the war by "Texans and other Americans who exercised Texas 'head rights' and took up grants of land" so thickly and forcibly that native Mexicans living there were obliged to move away. Mesilla was founded by those Mexicans who sought safety and peace in the near-by Mexican territory, protected by the line of the first treaty. The town was made entirely of adobe. Its roof lines on one-storey houses rose and fell gently like natural earth contours, on a valley background of willows, cottonwoods and cat-tails. Principal houses in the plaza were developed in a style that could be called Rio Grande Palladian. Wooden windows and door frames, topped with beautifully proportioned classic pediments in miniature, were let into the earthen walls. Square panelling on shutters or doors accompanied them. Such refinements could turn a long, uneven, hand-plastered mud wall into the façade of a palace. The line of inheritance was clear through centuries from Rome to Spain, to Mexico, and up to the Rio Grande. Spirit moved. It survived, as it always survived materials. It would ring, too, in the bells of Mesilla, when two decades later they were cast there of articles of bronze and silver brought by the parishioners to be melted down.

The Gadsden Treaty, carrying the boundary farther south to Magoffinsville, included Mesilla in the United States—and also Lemitar, where General Manuel Armijo had died on December 12, 1853. He was buried in the northwest corner of the parish church at Socorro, and shortly afterward was memorialized as one of New Mexico's "greatest benefactors" by the Assembly at Santa Fe, which having forgotten certain details of his career then adjourned out of respect for the "memory and distinguished services" of the enterprising sheep-thief who had risen to govern and to betray the upper Rio Grande. He did not live to see his remaining property formally annexed with southern New Mexico.

Residents there were at first apprehensive at the change in sovereignty, but the new government protected the grants they had received from Mexico, and on July 4, 1855, Governor David Meriwether of New Mexico, escorted by General John Garland and United States troops from Santa Fe, arrived to take formal possession of the town and valley of Mesilla. After entering the little town with his parade the Governor made a speech which was translated into Spanish. The United States flag was raised in the plaza while the soldiers cheered three times. The Third Infantry Band played "Hail Columbia," "Yankee Doodle" and "The Star-Spangled Banner." Local Mexican officials came forward to swear allegiance to their new government. Any who did not want to live under it were "notified to leave and to take refuge in Mexican dominions," said a soldier from New York state, and he added, "This was the best 4th of July I have passed since I have been in the Army. . . ."

31.

Flag and Lamplight

But there was yet another reason why the Gadsden Purchase was necessary. In the great strip of land which it comprehended there had been since the war an unremitting terror laid down by Apache, Comanche and Lipan Indians, who preyed on Mexican residents and American settlers and travellers alike. Since many of the Indians raided from within American territory, Mexico filed huge claims for indemnity against the American government. But lacking sovereignty in the terrorized borderlands, the United States could not there make its power felt. The only answer was to acquire the strip—and continue to add links to the chain of army posts all the way up the Rio Grande from the Gulf to the headwaters country. From the eighteen-fifties to the eighties, when the Indians were finally pacified on government reservations, the immense river empire was policed by only a score of little garrisons. A flag by day, lamplight in a window by night, signalled from these posts often hundreds of miles apart a ready and thoughtless valor that stood against the alien faith of the Indian in his own cause that was now seized by the destructive convulsions of a dying mythology. To guard a fifteen-hundred-mile frontier containing fifty thousand Indians—of whom over twenty thousand were actively hostile—New Mexico in 1854 had a total of sixteen hundred and fifty-four officers and men, scattered among less than a dozen forts.

The forts of the Rio Grande system fell into two general groups —those in Texas and those in New Mexico. Many of the Texas river forts had been established during the war, and after 1849 were main-

tained "to protect the peaceable inhabitants," observed the Army's Inspector General in 1856, "and preserve our own neutrality in all revolutionary movements in Mexico for some years to come."

The military headquarters of the Department of Texas was at
San Antonio. From there orders were relayed to the little regimental
components stationed together for garrison duty at outland forts. A
complete regiment was almost never held together at a single post. Its
companies were assigned separately to different stations. Each fort on
the border river had units of artillery, infantry and mounted infantry,
a band, quartermaster's and ordnance departments, occasionally a
chaplain; and invariably a component of laundresses—some of whom
were soldiers' wives—living in a row of tents behind their respective
companies.

Some of the lower river posts were adjacent to towns—Fort Brown
at Brownsville, Ringgold Barracks at Rio Grande City, Fort McIntosh
at Laredo, Fort Duncan at Eagle Pass—and were named for officers who
had died in the river campaign. Others—often named for veterans of the
war in the Mexican interior—were alone in the wilderness, like Fort
Inge, Fort Clark, Camp Hudson, Camp Peña Colorada, Fort Quitman,
Fort Davis and Fort Hancock, and, far back from the river, guarded
its approaches.

They were all examined by the Inspector General in 1856. On the
whole he found officers and men in good shape, in spite of comfortless
living conditions. Desertions were few and discipline was good, even
though there was much sickness—yellow fever and dysentery—in the river
forts. The companies turned out everywhere to show him how "handsomely" they could execute the "broad-sword exercise," or bayonet drill,
or battalion drill, or artillery practice, though on the target range at
one post rifle fire was not what it should have been. Repeatedly he noted
that barracks lacked "iron bedsteads," and that the men's bunks were
"miserable," and the kitchens "worthless." It was shocking to find that
the powder magazines at Ringgold Barracks had leaking roofs, and that
the lightning rods "want pointing." If there was a useful small library
in the quartermaster's house, there was no school for the handful of
children on the post. Lumber was the most scarce of materials, with
barely enough to make coffins. Water was hauled from the river into
settling tanks.

No station on the Texas river was "ever considered desirable,"
wrote an officer's wife, "on account of its unfailing sand and heat."
There were "no comfortable houses at Fort Duncan," the laundresses

lived in "hackales," the hospital windows had cloth in them instead of
glass, and the summers were so hot that the Inspector General recommended for the men, instead of their issue tunics of thickly lined broad-
cloth, a light summer jacket that could be washed. At McIntosh the
entire garrison lived in tents, except for two officers who built and paid
for a little house themselves. Everyone else suffered by heat in summer
and cold in winter. Noting that a bastioned field fort had been built
of stone and earth on the high river bluff of Fort McIntosh, the Inspector General wryly recommended that before any further effort and
money were spent on fortifications and officers' comforts, the men
should be given adequate barracks. There was no shade anywhere on
the post.

"The Troops have been extremely exposed to the burning sun
on the Rio Grande," he commented, "for instance at McIntosh and
Duncan, where they have not been allowed by their own labour to cut
posts & make shades & elevate their tents." The reason was that "the
population on that river expect pay for all trees & stakes cut," and the
department commander "prohibited any expenditure for the temporary
accommodation of the troops." Even the "horses of the mounted men,"
he found, "have been much exposed without shades." He must have
seen, if he did not record, how little wood there was to cut in that
rocky passage of the river.

And another thing: the post sutler sold "ardent spirits," though
there existed a regulation against the practice. It seemed that the post
commander considered it preferable to condone the sale of spirits rather
than face the inevitable cluster of bootleggers who would meet the needs
of soldiers just outside the fort. The Inspector General observed that
"the regulation should be either rescinded or enforced. . . ." He found
that there were no Indians on the north side of the river, and that depredations were traceable to Lipans who crossed out of Mexico. It was
gratifying that "A very good understanding exists with the people and
authorities on the Mexican side of the river"—a circumstance that
through the century became a tradition for the border cities that faced
each other across the Rio Grande. A final cordiality complimented the
Inspector General at McIntosh when the enlisted men's theatrical
society gave a play "whose performance was very creditable to them."
Hoping that the post gardens could manage to produce more vegetables
and so hold down the scurvy, he was off to see other forts and the same
problems.

Though he ran into occasional variations on the military theme and these made his tour more amusing. One was about the system of supplying the river forts by boat. The head of steam navigation in the 1850s (and in fact until the twentieth century when the last steamer ran in 1907) was Roma. Goods were transshipped upriver to the forts by pack and wagon from there. But the report of an early quartermaster of Fort Brown was extraordinary, even though his claims and recommendations came to nothing, as so often happened with Army reports. First of all, until steamboats were released from wartime troop duty, he supplied the river garrisons by keelboat. And then in 1850 he sent an expedition up the river with orders to navigate to the farthest possible place. He hoped to discover that shipping could utilize far more of the river's length than it had so far done. A keelboat and a skiff, manned by sixteen men, ascended the river by channel to a point a thousand miles above the head of steam travel, or about thirteen hundred miles above the mouth. It was an astonishing penetration for a river with so little water, and the expeditioneers came back, all safe, to report optimistically that if the channel were improved in certain passages, steam navigation would be entirely feasible all the way "up to Babbitt's Falls." These falls were described as "not perpendicular, but a rapid descent of some 200 feet in about half a mile." They were walled in by a perpendicular gorge hundreds of feet high—so high, with such rocky darkness below the slit of sky overhead, that "the stars could be seen at mid-day." It was a new piece of knowledge of the Rio Grande, and it may have described one of the canyons of the Big Bend. In his enthusiasm the leader of the expedition could see steam navigation having its terminus in the profitless canyon. But even though such pioneer quartermasters argued how practical it would be to fit the river for steam commerce, nothing was done to extend the steamboats' range; for by the international treaties of peace, both Mexico and the United States were bound to consult each other in any engineering works on the boundary river. Such combined action would have to wait for a new century, and then it would turn not to meandering travel by channel, but to irrigation and power projects, such as the international Falcón Dam, which would be dedicated by the American and Mexican presidents in 1953.

In another notion, the Army's quartermaster department hoped to transplant a form of transportation suitable for desert operations, and the Inspector General was in a position to report on its progress. In May, 1856, an American officer arrived at Indianola on the Gulf bringing with him from Smyrna "a drove of Camels of 34 in number, as follows,—1 Tunis Camel a mule, Bactrian Camels mules, I male Booghdee Camel a mule, 4 Arabian male Camels of burden, 14 Arabian female Camels of burden, 1 Arabian male calf camel, 1 male Senaar Dromedary, 1 female Muscat dromedary, 2 male Siout dromedaries, 4 female Siout dromedaries, 1 male Mt Sinai dromedary, and 1 female and 1 male calfs." In addition to American personnel, his staff included three Arabians and two Turks. "I inspected these animals," declared the Inspector General. He had no doubt they were "designed by the Creator for beasts of burthen." But he could not yet say, "before a fair experiment," whether they would answer the needs of the Army for durable pack animals in long hauls over waterless lands in the Southwest. He noted their obvious advantages—they were convenient to pack as they crouched on the ground, and the humps on their backs made it easy to keep in the saddle—and approved the first stage of the experiment, which was to keep them for breeding. In later stages, the desert beasts were to be marched across the Southwest into Arizona. Their military practicability in their new environment was never conclusively established; and the drove gradually perished—though in the tourist mythology of another century, reports of wild camels seen amidst the illusory rocks of Arizona would recur with some regularity.

As the Army brought its organization with it, so the form of its frontier forts reflecting this tended to be repetitious. But there were local variations, and between the river posts of Texas and New Mexico there seemed to be one general difference. Those in Texas were laid out in an open order of buildings and tents, arranged for the living convenience of a small community rather than for defense against attack or siege. Those in New Mexico were typically fortresses, one-storey castles of earth, which even when not actually surrounded by revetted walls were guarded by the placement of the outermost square of buildings in a design for defense. Fort Bliss in its early sites and Fort Thorn were enclosed by walls, Fort Craig had many interior squares enfolded by an almost continuous quadrangle of buildings, Fort Marcy showed in clay the classic flanks of a crenelated field fortification. But whatever their variations, they were all, upriver and down, created in remarkably short times by the men who would first garrison them. Their materials were mostly those to be had on the ground. These were put to use without imagination in detail, but certainly in response to imagination in the large, that projected the nation's task over the immense river empire, and brought there the Army's likeness, in all its rigidities of order, duty and hardship.

The Army's first style along the upper Rio Grande was Mexican—
adobe construction, long rows of rooms opening out on a plaza, one-
storey high. Later, as posts became permanent, and decades of duty
seemed certain, the New Mexico Territorial manner succeeded. Milled
lumber took the place of stripped logs, and fired bricks of sun-dried
adobe, and even two storeys of one. Windows and doors came from lum-
beryards back East, and the buildings of an important post assumed the
look of a segment out of a small city east of the Mississippi, with the
frank, neighborly gesture of the wooden front porch, a grassed yard and
a picket fence, and a central parade ground like a small park. The Army
was the medium through which the airs and manners of life in the
United States came to the river frontier to stay.

Early in their establishment the scattered garrisons, particularly
in Texas, seemed to Commissioner Bartlett to be misdirecting their
efforts. It was the policy of the Army to grow at each fort as much of
its food as possible. Soldiers farmed while Indians ranged. In his
boundary report the Commissioner urged that "a change should be
made in the system pursued at the frontier posts. Soldiers should not
go into quarters, and then quietly remain devoting themselves to agriculture. Better would it be for the government to pay double the price
it now does for its wheat and corn than to employ the soldiers for cultivating it; for the consequence of the present system is, that by their
attending to the fields, they become unfitted for and neglect their proper
duty as soldiers." The Commissioner suggested that "with the opening
of the spring, the soldiers should leave their quarters, and be kept moving
from one point to another. Let them be a few days in a mountain pass,
next at some oasis in the desert whither the savage must resort to satisfy
his parching thirst, and again in some of those beautiful valleys covered
with luxuriant grass, which are also his resort after his predatory excursions, that he may recruit his animals. This active life," he concluded,
writing in comfort far from the scene of his proposals, "would be much
more agreeable and healthy for the men than the inactivity of a garrison, and would tend more to overawe and subdue the Indian. . . ." In
any case, it was not long until the Indian's own tactics called forth the
frontier Army's constant movement in and out of the river forts for endlessly repeated parleys, battles and punishments.

Until 1851 most troops in New Mexico were garrisoned in Santa
Fe, Albuquerque and other towns. But in that year the new department
commander, Colonel E. V. Sumner, was appalled at what he found of
soldier life in the towns, particularly Santa Fe, a "sink of vice," and for

both moral and administrative reasons, he ordered the department headquarters moved from Santa Fe to a new site near Las Vegas, where Fort
Union was immediately established and construction begun. For thirty
years Fort Union was to be the headquarters and supply depot of the
Army in New Mexico. All Missouri trails converged there. It was the
eastern gateway to New Mexico. The river posts were provisioned and
governed from it.

For two years after the war American troops were quartered in the
ruined church and presidio of San Elizario on the long sand island below
El Paso. In 1851 Fort Bliss was founded—though it was not so named
until a little later—at Smith's Ranch, the site of the village of Franklin
near Magoffinsville, and was to know two other adjacent locations before
its final one. Upriver near Mesilla, Fort Fillmore was erected on the east
bank in 1851, and three years later with the arrival of new troops it
received four officers' wives "who had the courage to accompany the
army on its toilsome march of three months across the plains." They
were "the only American ladies" seen by Commissioner Bartlett between
San Antonio and the Pacific, and he believed they were "the only ones
on this portion of the frontier" in 1854. Fort Thorn was established
on the west bank opposite Doña Ana in 1854, and guarded the San Diego
road as it turned away from the river for California. At the foot of
Valverde Mesa, Fort Conrad was built in 1851 but two years later was
abandoned and its garrison moved a few miles south to found Fort Craig
with a spread of twenty-two buildings—"the best and prettiest fort in
New Mexico," according to a soldier, who added, "It is situated on a
table land beside the Rio Grande. It is set in a grove of cottonwood
trees." Only small garrisons were left at Albuquerque and Santa Fe.
Cantonment Burgwin, eight miles south of Taos in a mountain canyon,
and Fort Massachusetts, in the San Luis Valley through which the river
wound after its passage out of the mountains of its source, were the
northernmost of the riverland posts at mid-century. In later decades
Fort Macrae (whose site would be covered by the waters of Elephant
Butte Dam in the twentieth century) and Fort Selden were added to
valley defenses.

On all sides, invisible until they acted, were the enemy people—
Navajos north and west of the river, Apaches in its mountain flanks,
Lipans along its southeast stretches, and Comanches who wintered in
the Bolsón de Mapimí and ranged from Mexico to the buffalo plains
north and east of Santa Fe. Movement according to the seasons and the
presence of prey or spoils was their medium of life. They used the deserts

as no soldier ever could; for their very identity lay in that land, and
knowing its common secrets they could make its thinnest resources feed
them, and hide them, and answer their beliefs of spirit, and give them
power.

In that great open country where the Army's forts and wagon
trains were so small, the Indians crowded upon them unrelentingly.
No one could safely venture alone more than three miles from Fort
Bliss in 1852. Every small party travelling the road from San Antonio
to El Paso was attacked by Comanches, and the prairies along its course
were burned by Indians to deprive the trains of grass for their animals,
so that the Army had to haul extra feed in wagons. An Indian fighter
said that in twenty years of raiding in New Mexico and Arizona the
Apaches cost settlers over fifty million dollars in destruction and theft.
New Mexicans, between 1846 and 1850, according to figures of United
States Marshals, lost 453,293 sheep, 12,887 mules, 7,050 horses and 31,581
horned cattle. The Apaches perfected a method of making off with
flocks of sheep. They shaped the flock into an oblong pattern never
wider than thirty feet, and as long as required. Choosing the strongest
sheep they lashed them together by the horns two by two, forming
them into a living fence that enclosed the flock on each long side until
the sheep within could not stray. Indian drivers strode along beside
and behind the flock, and at its head a squad of young, hardy Indians
set the pace. Running night and day, the desert thieves could take twenty
thousand sheep from fifty to seventy miles in a day, sometimes making
swift marches of up to fifteen hundred miles, far out of reach of organized
pursuit.

In the face of such tactics the Army tried to establish order by
treaty. It seemed that each new commander as he came to take over a
Department tried to parley with the enemy. Indians were generally
willing to accept an invitation to a conference at some bare place in
the wilderness. There came the mounted Army column with its blue
wagons under their white tops, each drawn by six mules and escorted by
six cavalrymen. The soldiers made camp with tents, and strung picket
lines for horses, and established the precise, frugal and unchanging
order of their housekeeping in the field.

All about at a little distance camped the Indians in their own way,
with tepees, arranged according to no order, hundreds of them, alive
with warriors, their wives, children, old men and women, horses for
the best fighters, and countless dogs. While the bulk of Indians sat in
a great demilune facing the soldier camp, watching but pretending

not to watch, and the troopers lounged at hair-trigger ease with their
weapons, the commanding officer and his staff deliberated with the
chiefs. The commander made gifts to the chiefs which they appraised
expertly and in silence unless they felt more was due to them, when with
injured dignity they would say so. If one chief received more than
another trouble flickered and if it broke out hasty adjustments had to
be made. And then the discussion proceeded to the agenda.

The commander recited a list of things to be recovered—stolen
horses, sheep, cattle, and even children. The Indian spokesman understood him through an interpreter, and in his turn replied, with little
gestures of the chin that poked at places faraway and dim, and speaking
in sounds that exploded in the throat, or drilled against his teeth, or
yelped like the mindless voicings of a coyote, he said that he had no
knowledge of stolen horses, sheep, cattle or children, but that if he discovered any such, he would—and here with his fingers bundled together
he made a dabbing motion of delivery—he would give them to the commander. Strange things did happen, he conceded. He was an old man,
and the other chiefs were old men in their wisdom. If what the commander said was true, then the blame must be put on the young men
of the Indian nation, for who could control them in the years of their
pounding blood, animal splendor and pricking desire to do great deeds?
The commander sighed. So the excuses always went. All he could do was
propose pledges of future peace, and make impressive to the meagre
degree possible in the surroundings an act of scratching a large sheet
of paper with an X whereby some part of the signer would seem forever
to be held captive to ceremony and honor. The commander could only
reflect that some day, such an act, such a document, would turn out
to be the last one necessary; and only hope that this might be it.

The parley was adjourned.

The soldiers relaxed, and a few drifted among the Indians to see
them closely, and discover if they carried gold bullets, and if so, as
many did, to trade a dozen leaden balls for one gold. By dark the soldiers
were back in their own camp, behind sentries; and in the night, looking
out of the bivouac toward the Indian positions, what they saw was
written down by a young sergeant: "At least 1000 little fires were to be
seen about us. . . ."

In the morning, if they were camped near the river during a cold
month, soldiers might see how Apaches hunted ducks. From a brushy
shore several large gourds went bobbing on wavelets toward ducks who
swam on the shallow water. Lightly, randomly the gourds moved among

the ducks who murmured and circled but did not fly. Suddenly a duck
here, another there, and another, vanished below the water, while
alarmed at last the remainder went to the air, and the hunters arose to
stand in the river. They wore the gourds over their heads with holes cut
for their eyes. For days they had practiced floating empty gourds among
the ducks until the ducks were no longer alarmed by them. Then the
hunters wearing their gourds entered the water unseen and perfectly
imitating the motion of the empty gourds bobbing on the river waded
in a crouch on the river floor until they could seize their game from
below, pull them underwater, and stuff them into the bags. The
soldiers knew too that Apaches wearing the horned heads and tied skins
of antelopes could go in perfect masquerade among those sensitive
animals and at close range kill their quarry. Such craft at hunting wild
creatures compelled admiration and wonder. But more—it measured too
the skill of desert Indians at their other work of surprising and destroying their human enemies. It was a skill never to be matched in kind by
the Army. It had to be overcome by other techniques and the compounded courage of fellows-at-arms who, outnumbered in the wilderness, yet put forward in a conviction of massed power the policy of the
United States when there came a time for battle.

For after parleys and treaties, when the soldiers returned to
their forts and the Indians to their light-stricken and distant country,
troubles began all over again, with raid, thieving, murder and fire. From
the fort nearest to the trouble a column of troops moved out in pursuit
of the enemy. Often they had with them an Indian scout in the service
of the Army. With his help they read the vacant land. They watched
the horizon for smoke of campfires. If they came upon the trail and
found campfire ashes they studied these to learn how long ago the fire
had been put out, how much stirred by winds, what kind of desert fuel
had been burned, how many people it had served by its size. If grass grew
at the site, was it trampled, and how widely? Were there animal droppings and evidence of animal urine? These by their condition might
tell passage of time. Were there signals for other Indians—little markers
of twig and stone? If there were even a single bush near-by, throwing
a lacy shadow, was there an enemy scout hiding there?—for soldiers
recorded how using the barest ground an Indian plainsman could wholly
conceal himself from unpracticed observation at a distance of only a
few feet.

And then, sooner or later, perhaps in a rocky canyon, or a shallow
in the plains, or the shadow of a mesa, the war party was found posed

for battle. Sometimes they had with them their rag-bundled women. The
warriors were polygamous, and their striding women were fiercely contentious for the man who owned them. Aprowl like cats across the thorny
land, they clawed their way after their thieving, murdering, lying lords.
When the troopers formed for battle, they would see an occasional
Indian rise up out of cover in jeering defiance. He turned his back and
showed his naked posterior, clapping it obscenely as he shouted words
of challenge and contempt. When the battle came, it might be brief.
Both parties were accoutred for light, rapid movement. A siege was
rare. Leaving their transport and supply guarded well behind them, the
soldiers advanced using what cover they could find. Their rifles sounded.
The Indian fire was returned with both arrow and bullet. Twenty
minutes, an hour, more or less, and the skirmish was over, with dead
and wounded on both sides. Sometimes the greater part of the Indians
escaped while the rest fought off the attack. Again, the whole war party
might be taken. And again, the troopers might have to retire or all be
destroyed. However the issue went, what all knew beyond its decisive
moments was that though the battle might be final for men who fought
it, there were many more battles to come before the prairies and deserts
would be at peace.

   When the fight was over the soldiers buried their dead. They
dug a common grave and lined it with pack tarpaulins. They wrapped
the fallen in their bedding rolls and laid them in the grave. An officer
read or repeated prayers for the dead, and earth was closed over the dead
troopers. The bugler sounded taps. A squad fired a salute. Sometimes
the commander's tent was pitched over the grave. Sometimes fires were
built on the grave to blacken all marks of burial. But if the Army column
moved on to pursue escaping Indians, and returning days later passed
by that way again, they might find that the fire-scarred grave had told
all too plainly what lay there, and that another Indian party had thrown
it open to steal the burial blankets, tossing the bodies about to be picked
by carrion birds and animals. Then the soldiers would gather the
remains and reduce them to a stern safety. "We built a large pile of
pine wood; put on bodies; burned the flesh; took the bones away,"
observed a young cavalryman. He helped to bring the bones of an
officer back to a Rio Grande fort in 1855. The captain's wife was waiting
there for him. She was one of the only four American ladies stationed
between San Antonio and the Pacific. In her doorway she asked where
her husband was when the troops returned. They evaded her questions.
But she knew, and in some persistence of a desire both to deny what

must come and to leave others their ease for yet a little while, she
accepted their poor evasions, and spoke lightly, and went about her
tasks in quarters, until an hour later at their duty and in their time the
others came to tell her what she knew they would tell, and she wept.
Later, a new post in the mountains was named for the captain—Fort
Stanton.

Along the lower river some of the Texas forts had their counterparts in Mexican garrisons across the way, as at Matamoros, Laredo and
Eagle Pass. Courtesies and entertainments were exchanged by officers
and their families. At Piedras Negras, opposite Eagle Pass, American
officers and ladies went to eat Mexican food, and see bullfights, and
hear the music of the Mexican army band "—so sweet and thrilling—",
and watch the "superb drilling of Mexican soldiers, who marched and
countermarched for at least an hour without a single order being
spoken, they responding merely to a tap of the drum as each new
movement was initiated." American troops, thought an officer's wife,
"could never be kept in such slavish subjection." Sometimes the Mexican
band came across to play at Fort Duncan, serenading the ladies—perhaps
a little dangerously—who "listened as in a dream to its rendering of
various operas and Mexican national airs, played with such expression
that all the sentiments they indicated were aroused."

And once during the 1850s there was another sort of excitement
to discuss, when an American border freebooter named Callahan crossed
the Rio Grande with a band of followers to recover some Seminole
Negro slaves who had escaped from him into Mexico. He was met by a
force of seven hundred Mexican troops whom he defeated. They fled
the city of Piedras Negras, which he occupied and looted. A citizen of
Eagle Pass saw some of Callahan's men. "Every one that I saw had more or
less of jewelry displayed about his neck and breast"—gold earrings, necklaces, finger rings, watches. The raiders stole food, and other supplies,
and silver-mounted saddles. When the Mexicans showed signs of returning to fight, Callahan as an American citizen appealed for support to
Major Burbank, commanding at Fort Duncan. The major replied that
the raiders had no business in Piedras Negras, and should withdraw. All
he would agree to do would be to cover their retreat with the guns of
Fort Duncan. Callahan was pressed by the returning Mexican force.
With a single round of grapeshot from a four-pound cannon, he discouraged the Mexican attack and returned to Eagle Pass where the
whole town had watched his affair from the riverbank.

But most of the Rio Grande forts stood in isolation. Cantonment

Burgwin near Taos was so remote and dull that when an officer and his
wife had a chance to visit Fort Union with its complement of a hundred
residents, they exclaimed that "the post seemed very gay to us, with
the band and so many people." Coming back to the river from the
Indian country in 1856 an officer paused at Fort Bliss, which seemed to
him a "most unmilitary" post, and went on to Fort Fillmore, where
matters were far better conducted. On his way upriver to Fort Craig
he and his command were overtaken by a blizzard, and made camp
hurriedly. They built a great ring of fires within their circle of parked
wagons, and there, in their own climate, the soldiers were almost as
warm as in spring, while the commander spent the evening reading in his
tent by the warmth of his small portable stove, and the norther clapped
away outside. It was a joy to arrive at Craig in a day or two, and dine
at the officers' mess, and play poker, and run into Army talk again—who
was getting married, which way the last promotions had gone, was there
any hope for a new pay bill in Congress, would an officer always have
to pay his own travel expenses on leave and put up with half-pay to
boot, was that a new daguerreotype over there of the General's youngest
daughter—all the enfolding and reassuring trifles that held together
an isolated society between its occasions of hard, and at times heroic,
professional duty.

Enlisted men talked of other things. Once in dangerous Indian
country the entire command of three hundred men were put on guard
all night, while their five officers slept in tents pitched at the center of
the camp. "Oh," said an enlisted man, "oh that our government only
knew the courage of some of her officers! Nothing happened during the
night." They talked about a colonel who with his sword cut a soldier
who fell in the field from thirst and could not march further. "The
man fell, bleeding profusely. We went on and left him . . . a poor victim
of an inhuman tyrant." They talked about a captain who enraged by
clumsiness shown at drill "ran his sabre into a man's back, injuring him
for life. The captain says it was accidental. I don't know." They talked
about troubles between enlisted men, too—the soldier at Fort Craig who
refused to obey an order by his corporal, drew a knife, was shot through
the heart by the corporal, and was buried "without the honors of war,"
while the corporal received no blame. . . .

Both officers and enlisted men and any women stationed at a
fort did what they could to lighten the weight of wilderness. A melodeon
was shipped in by cart, and someone played it for chapel. Someone else
organized burro races and everyone took part either as jockeys or laugh-

ing spectators. On holidays and Saturday nights a committee cleared the
floor of mess hall or armory, put up decorations of paper and lights,
arranged a bay for an orchestra of band musicians, and all came to enjoy
a "social hop," for "nothing now offers the soldier more joy," said a
soldier's letter to a newspaper, "than when he is carried away by the
excitement of the dance," in the polka, the schottische, the lancers, and—
an intoxicating innovation—the "glide waltz." It was a convention that
the enlisted men should form a dramatic society to present in one gala
evening a number of specialty acts, an exhibition of gymnastics, and a
play. One post theatre was always referred to as the "opera house." Its
offerings were watched by all of the garrison not engaged in the performance, and earnestly overpraised at the last curtain. Any soldier
gifted with a public accomplishment was in demand, like a young sergeant who wrote in his notebook at a Rio Grande post: "Stopped with
Company I, 1st Dragoons, at Fort Thorn. By invitation recited Plato's
'Soliloquy on the Immortality of the Soul' at a kind of theatre established here." Out of the *Phaedo* he repeated for other men in the wilderness whose business it might be to die of their duty, ". . . if the soul is
really immortal, what care should be taken of her, not only in respect
of the portion of time which is called life, but of eternity! . . ." In such
ways the tedium of garrison life was relieved. But soon the forts of the
Rio Grande would have a mission larger than guard duty.

32.

The Rio Grande Divided

Just as the election of Polk in 1844 had signified that Texas
would join the Union, so the re-election of Lincoln in 1860 made it
inevitable that she would leave it. Following the lead of South Carolina
and other states early to secede, Texas called a convention to give form
to the views about human relations with which since the troubled times

of Stephen Austin she had justified her slave-operated economy. On February 2, 1861, the convention "passed an ordinance dissolving all political connection with the government of the United States, and the people thereof," and called an election for February twenty-third at which Texans would ratify it.

How unnatural, cried Texas, that the Northern states should feel hostile toward the "Southern states and their beneficent and patriarchal system of African slavery!" How could the North proclaim "the debasing doctrine of the equality of men, irrespective of race or color—a doctrine at war with nature, in opposition to the experience of mankind, and in violation of the plainest revelations of the divine law"? Forgetting the passion for equality that had led to the founding of the nation, the statesmen of Texas labored to clothe their pretext for disunion in self-righteous and finally in pious terms: "We hold, as undeniable truths, that the governments of the various states, and of the confederacy itself, were established exclusively by the white race, for themselves and their posterity; that the African race had no agency in their establishment; that they were rightfully held and regarded as an inferior and dependent race, and in that condition only could their existence in this country be rendered beneficial or tolerable: That, in this free government"—only a few white Texans wondered how the word "free" could be used if it did not apply to all human beings—"ALL WHITE MEN ARE, AND OF RIGHT OUGHT TO BE, ENTITLED TO EQUAL CIVIL AND POLITICAL RIGHTS; that the servitude of the African race, as existing in these states, is mutually beneficial to both bond and free, and is abundantly authorized and justified by the experience of mankind, and"—though no scripture was cited—"by the revealed will of the Almighty Creator, as recognized by all Christian nations; while the destruction of the existing relations between the two races, as advanced by our sectional enemies, would bring inevitable calamities upon both, and"—here was exposed the material motive behind earlier, more elevated protest—"and desolation upon the fifteen slaveholding states. . . ."

Sentiment for secession was so clearly formed in Texas that even before the public voted on it, preparations for war went forward. General David Emmanuel Twiggs, commanding United States troops in the Department, repeatedly asked Washington for instructions to follow if Texas seceded. None came. At last, when a "committee for public safety" demanded that he surrender all Army posts and property in Texas to the state government, he agreed. For this "treachery to the flag of his country" he was dismissed from the service. A few months later he was solaced with a commission as major general in the Confederate Army. On February 23, 1861, Texans voted overwhelmingly to quit the Union, and when word came of the Confederate attack on the garrison of Fort Sumter at Charleston whose commander had refused to act like Twiggs, Governor Clark of Texas, like President Lincoln at Washington, called for volunteers and moved into war measures. Lieutenant Colonel John R. Baylor with Texas militia occupied the forts west of San Antonio, even as far up the Rio Grande as Fort Bliss, and, later, Mesilla. Loyal citizens fled before him. One, a native of Maine named Babbitt, with two other men, escaped from El Paso in two dugout canoes lashed together by which they floated on the Rio Grande all the way to Brownsville—some twelve hundred miles—in the first known continuous voyage of the boundary river.

New Mexico meanwhile remained loyal to the United States, and the Rio Grande was divided between its own north and south, like the nation at large. Many memories helped the old river kingdom to abide with the federal authority. Her population was largely Mexican. The decision of Texas to default her statehood aroused little sympathy among a people whose traditional relations with Texas had been marked by earlier Texan disloyalties and aggressions—the Texan revolt, the Texan border adventures, the Texan attempts to annex New Mexico first by arms and then by boundary claims. Further, when Mexico, displaying a degree of social and political maturity, outlawed slavery by the decrees of 1829, New Mexico as her province was governed by them. After New Mexico became United States territory it was with the provision under the Compromise of 1850 that on reaching statehood she would vote for or against slavery within her limits. But she was not to wait so long. Though in 1859 her legislature passed a law protecting slave property already introduced into the territory, at the next session, in 1862, she would repeal the law and thereafter support the antislavery philosophy of the national government in both form and spirit. That New Mexico even under her brief legal sanction did not encourage modern slavery was indicated by the small number of Negro slaves there at the outset of the war—some twenty-two in all.

As war came in the spring of 1861 Colonel William W. Loring, commander of United States forces in New Mexico, left his command and joined the Confederacy. He was succeeded by Colonel Edward R. S. Canby to whom fell the preparation of the river garrisons and other outposts for defense. Resources were few, and though militia men of Latin blood responded to his call, they were untrained and unready for battle.

In July he was obliged to remain inactive when Colonel Baylor, with several companies of artillery and mounted rifles, marched up the river from El Paso as far as Mesilla to give battle to the Union garrison at Fort Fillmore.

The fort commander was Major Isaac Lynde, a kindly, gray-bearded veteran of thirty-four years in the Infantry, who soon heard that the Texans were coming. In spite of what he knew, he ordered no extra precautions against surprise. "Great God, what brainless imbecility!" exclaimed his post surgeon, who clearly saw present danger and later raged at what followed. On the night of July twenty-fourth Baylor's troops camped six hundred yards from the fort intending an attack at daybreak. Two of his men deserted to enter the fort and give warning. Major Lynde ordered the long roll on the drums, the garrison awoke— but not to action. No scouts were sent out to measure the enemy, and the next morning, Baylor and his men were calmly permitted to ford the Rio Grande near the fort and occupy Mesilla, where they were received with "vivas and hurrahs" by the people. Soon afterward Major Lynde ordered almost his whole force of seven hundred men to form for an advance upon Mesilla. If its purpose was worthy, its execution was, as the post surgeon declared, "one of the most extraordinary, imbecile, and childish military movements ever perpetrated. . . ." Lynde demanded the surrender of the invaders. It was refused. He then ordered cavalry out on a frontal instead of a flanking movement, with the result that four men were killed and several wounded. On a near-by hill were clustered women, children and unarmed men of Mesilla who came to watch the fight. Lynde ordered his artillery to fire upon them, and luckily the fire fell short. Presently the Major rode up to the post surgeon at his field hospital wagon and ordered,

"Doctor, get your wounded ready to retreat."

"Where to, sir?" asked the doctor, thinking the battle was about to begin in earnest.

"To the fort," replied the commander.

"Great God!" thought the doctor, "is this the disgraceful finale . . . ?", but he must obey. The garrison withdrew to the fort two miles away to the amazement of most of its officers. The next morning the Major ordered another retreat, now to Fort Stanton in the mountains a hundred and fifty miles northeast of Mesilla, leaving Baylor, with only two hundred and fifty troops, in possession at the river.

The summer weather was merciless. The high plains east of the river were dry. There were the Organ Mountains to cross. The retreat

was a misery—and in another day the Confederates came after the fleeing command. In a "sublimity of majestic indifference" Major Lynde
was taking lunch at San Augustín Springs when his officers came to
beg him to fight. He exercised his authority, refused their protests, and—
"suicidal, cowardly, pusillanimous"—in a little while surrendered his
force unconditionally to Colonel Baylor. A few days later on August
first Baylor issued a proclamation announcing southern New Mexico and
all of Arizona as a Territory of the Confederate States, with Mesilla as
its capital and himself as its military governor. On the following day
Fort Stanton was abandoned by Union forces that withdrew to Albuquerque. The garrison of Fort Thorn retired upriver to Fort Craig,
which was now the only strong United States defense below Albuquerque.
Major Lynde's surrender yielded all of southern New Mexico to the
Confederacy, and along the Rio Grande opened the way to objectives of immense, perhaps decisive, importance to the whole Southern
cause.

For the Rio Grande invasion was not merely a matter of subduing
a handful of earthen towns along a drought-parched river, and of converting a primitive, scattered population of Indians and Mexicans to
a belief in states rights, and ownership of certain human beings by certain
others. It was a matter of gaining a pathway to vast lands and resources
whose possession—so argued Southern strategists—might actually tip the
scales in the struggle for power between the South and the North. These
were the gold fields of Colorado and California, the mountain west
running to the Pacific from Denver through Salt Lake City, the ports
of California, all of Arizona and New Mexico, and even—either by conquest or purchase—Chihuahua, Sonora and Baja California. Such a huge
acquisition would give the Confederacy a transcontinental scope with
world outlets in two seas; and by taking in the gold fields, which Lincoln
called "the life-blood of our financial credit," it would go far toward
crippling the Union's power to sustain the cost of war. The first move
in such a grand design was to secure New Mexico. The river was the land
vein along which that mission must be pursued.

While Baylor with his little force was opening the southern gateway, another Confederate commander was preparing a larger army to
execute the grand strategy. This was Henry H. Sibley, who as a United
States officer had served with the Army in the Rio Grande Valley before
the war. Because of his knowledge of the river country he was commissioned brigadier general by President Jefferson Davis at Richmond and
given command of the Ar..., of New Mexico, a brigade in strength,

which he undertook to raise in Texas during the summer and fall of
1861, to the number of almost thirty-five hundred men.

Colonel Canby, working at his defenses, had one thousand New
Mexico militia to start with in support of his components of regular
troops. He now raised five regiments of volunteers to be commanded
by prominent New Mexicans, including Kit Carson, and distributed
them to strengthen the garrisons. He heavily provisioned Fort Craig.
He improved the defenses of Albuquerque, Santa Fe and Fort Union.
And as Sibley began to move across Texas toward Fort Bliss, Canby
asked Governor Gilpin of Colorado for a re-enforcement of volunteers.
Their first detachment arrived, two companies strong, and joined the
force downriver at Fort Craig where Canby was massing four thousand
men for a campaign southward to recapture Fort Bliss. But before he
could move, Sibley's brigade began to march up the river on February 7,
1862, and by the eleventh was within twenty miles of Fort Craig. The first
major battle of the Civil War on the Rio Grande was shaping up, with
the Confederate invaders holding the initiative.

Isolated probing actions by scouts of both armies followed, but
without clashes. Late in the day of February nineteenth the main body
of the Texan brigade began to draw into view across the river from Fort
Craig, and by nightfall a large force was marked out by its campfires,
and soldiers watching from the fort could hear voices across the water
when the wind came from the east. The Confederates were camped on
an open plain on the river's east bank opposite the fort. It was the only
clear ground between black lava beds and ravines to the south and the
abrupt mesa of Valverde two miles to the north, which sent the river
on a wide bend toward the west. Two miles farther north, the mesa
ended at another open plain with easy banks at each side of the river,
where russet reeds clustered at the water's edge, and golden winter
cottonwoods stood in groves. On the west side were fields where Fort
Craig soldiers grew feed for their horses, and the place—once the site
of Fort Conrad—was now called the Hay Camp.

Canby at Craig expected an attack upon his strong position, perhaps a siege. But when on the twentieth he could see that the enemy
supply train, a mile and a half away across the river, was moving north,
he concluded that Sibley was about to by-pass him, taking his way
around the mesa's eastern end. Canby ordered an attack. His troops
forded the river and came up the opposite shore toward the Confederate
camp in the face of rifle and cannon fire. Unable to advance or find compact cover on the mild slopes of the open plain, the Union troops scat-

tered to cling to isolated positions. There they spent the night, and returned across the river to the fort at dawn of the following day. By then the Texans had moved in strength to the upriver side of the mesa. Canby provisioned his men and hurried them off to the Hay Camp. When they reached it, they saw the Texans on the open land north of the mesa, and fired on them. The battle of Valverde was opened at nine o'clock in the morning, to last all day.

It was a hot winter day, with a strong wind blowing that hauled long shifts of dust, and tore away smoke from the muzzles of cannon, rifles and shotguns—for the Texans carried many of these. The Union forces charged through the river in strength early in the fight, and met a terrible fire that killed many in midstream whose bodies floated away in the gentle current of winter's low water. Artillery duels continued across the river until the Union cannon were dragged to the east bank, where from a strong position beyond the range of Confederate small arms they drove the invaders back from the river toward sandy ridges that marked a former bed of the river. The Texans made flanking charges with cavalry, but were thrown off. Three times the Texans tried to charge from their sand hills, and each time were forced back.

After noon more Union troops were ordered across the river, including the Second Regiment of New Mexico Volunteers, five companies of which refused to obey out of fear of the furious capacities of Texans in battle. In the course of the day occurred shifts in the commands of both sides. Colonel Canby came to take personal charge of the Union troops, relieving Colonel Ben S. Roberts, and General Sibley, becoming indisposed—some said drunk—turned the Confederate command over to Colonel Tom Green, who though older by nearly twenty years since the Mier adventure, was still a spirited and original soldier.

The battle seemed a draw until late in the day, when the strongest Union battery of six guns established at the northern end of the battleground was charged first by cavalry, and then in a fury of daring ordered by Tom Green, by the whole Texan force that had been pinned down most of the day in the sand hills. The charge was tremendous, and the fighting for eight minutes "was terrific beyond description." But the Union battery was inadequately supported; and all its officers and men were killed at their guns. It was the turning point. Seeing their crack battery taken, the Union forces broke toward the river, "more like a herd of frightened mustangs than men." Many more were slaughtered in making the ford. The rest were hastily formed once they reached the west bank. The Confederates gathered a cavalry force to charge after them and complete the victory, but before it could ride through the river, a truce party came from Canby's command asking for a cease-fire to permit burial of the dead and care of the wounded. It was granted. Under its protection, then, Canby's army hurried south to Fort Craig in entire defeat, while on the field of their victory the invaders camped that night, eating luxuriously of captured "Yankee light bread and other most delicious eatables," and drinking the whiskey they found in many a Union canteen, and believing the story they heard—how the canteens of the Union battery that had fought so hard had been "tinctured with ether." The first phase of Sibley's mission to conquer the mountain West was accomplished, for with the main New Mexican forces disposed of at least for the time being, he could now turn his back on them, march north to the chief cities of the territory and prepare to take its last major garrison at Fort Union.

On the very night of his defeat, Canby sent orders by courier to the northern posts announcing Sibley's victory, and giving orders that all public property, "and particularly provisions," were to be destroyed if necessary to keep them from falling into the hands of the invaders. So it was that Sibley, coming into sight of Albuquerque a few days later, saw three great columns of smoke standing above the town, and knew that a rich depot of supplies had been burned in anticipation of his arrival—and his need. "If it could have been possible for us to have hindered this," said a Texan soldier, "the Confederate Army of New Mexico would never have experienced any inconvenience for the want of clothing or commissaries." The Union quartermaster officer who gave the order to burn all public property in Albuquerque at half-past six on the morning of March second said that all was destroyed but supplies of "molasses, vinegar, soap and candles, and a few saddles, carpenter's tools, and office furniture." Most of these were pilfered by New Mexican residents. The Union garrison fled to Santa Fe, and Sibley's men took Albuquerque unopposed.

From Santa Fe a Union inspector-general sent a gloomy report to General Halleck at St. Louis. ". . . It is needless to say that this country is in a critical condition. The militia have all run away and the New Mexican volunteers are deserting in large numbers. No dependence whatever can be placed on the natives; they are worse than worthless; they are really aids to the enemy, who catch them, take their arms and tell them to go home." It had not been possible in one generation to erase the effects of the long periods of Spanish and Mexican rule when poverty and corruption had denied the people any proper lessons in self-defense. But help was coming. Another "force of Colorado volunteers is already on the way to assist us," added the inspector, "and they may possibly arrive in time to save us from immediate danger." The Federal troops at Santa Fe were too few to defend the capital; once again Army property went up in smoke, and the garrison pulled out for Fort Union.

There on March tenth the First Colorado arrived in tearing spirits after a brilliant march through heavy winter. The Colorado volunteers were mostly recruits from the frontier mining towns. They had come West to make their fortunes, and now they had marched South to earn their fame. They drilled and trained for two weeks at Fort Union, where the territory's last defenses stood. Colonel Canby, still immobilized downriver at Fort Craig, had sent orders that a supreme effort must be made to hold Fort Union. If it went, the whole territory went, and Colorado would be next. Meanwhile, the seat of New Mexican government had been moved to Las Vegas, and between March sixteenth and twenty-fourth three Texan regiments moved into Santa Fe. Other Texan forces were based at Galisteo twenty miles to the south. "We felt like heroes," wrote a Texan soldier to his wife, telling how his army had swept past Fort Craig leaving it cut off from its supply source in northern New Mexico. "We marched up the country with the fixed determination to wrench this country from the United States government. . . ." Fort Union was the great prize to be taken next. The Texan was confident. Fort Union, he said, "was ours already; and then New Mexico would belong to the new government of the South, and it would then be so easy to cut off all communication with California. . . ." A Texan picket of six hundred men left Santa Fe on March twenty-second to stand guard at the entrance to Apache Canyon. Las Vegas lay beyond, and Fort Union. Soon the main body of Texans would join the camp at the mouth of the canyon, and the sweep to the northeast would continue.

But on March twenty-sixth in the afternoon the Confederate picket heard that a small force—"200 Mexicans and about 200 regulars" from Fort Union—was coming through the canyon on its way to attack Santa Fe. It sounded like folly, and it constituted a nuisance to be brushed off as lightly as possible. The Texan camp sprang to arms and taking two field guns marched up the canyon to meet and dispose of the foolhardy Union troops. Four miles up the canyon they saw the Federal column coming at the double time, and opened fire. The trotting column halted and the Texans went about forming into proper battle line. But before they could manage this, every expectation was upset, for the Federal infantry "were upon the hills on both sides of us," wrote the Texan to his wife, "shooting us down like sheep." In the rocky trough of the canyon the Texans retreated, and their attackers pressed along above them—"they could be seen on the mountains jumping from rock to rock like so many mountain sheep." Time and again the Texans retired to new positions and delivered fearful fire. Nothing could stop their enemies. How could this be, wondered the Texans; when had New Mexicans ever fought like this? But they soon discovered whom they were facing. "Instead of Mexicans and regulars, they were *regular demons,* upon whom iron and lead had no effect, in the shape of Pike's Peakers, from the Denver City gold mines. . . ." Falling back beyond a deep arroyo near the canyon's entrance, the Texans made a last stand. Surely there they would be safe—but a company of Union cavalry came flying down to the arroyo, jumped it, and with drawn sabres and revolvers and in incredible immunity won the battle. The Texan picket surrendered, losing seventy-one prisoners, while the rest fled toward the rear.

Two days later, on the twenty-eighth, the battle was renewed, now between the main bodies of the two armies. The Confederates moved up from Galisteo into the canyon, and met the Federal forces who were much augmented by reinforcements from Fort Union, between the slopes of Glorieta Pass. The fight in the Pass surged through the day without decided advantage to either side. From high ground amid red rocks the batteries exchanged their salvos, and dismounted soldiers fought among clumps of cedar and mountain oak on the gritty slopes. The contest looked like a draw—until the Texan commander received word late in the day of a disaster that had overtaken him in his rear, at the west end of the canyon. There a Federal force under Major John M. Chivington, a Colorado preacher, had come by a hidden march behind hills above the canyon to fall upon the Confederate supply train of eighty-five wagons and nearly six hundred horses and mules which had been left lightly guarded. Charging down on the supply camp, Chivington and three hundred men of the First Colorado captured the guards, burned the wagons with all their contents, and bayonetted all the animals. News of this calamity came to the Confederate commander in the canyon during an armistice he had requested in order to bury his dead and attend to his wounded. The battle was adjourned until noon of the following day. It was never resumed, for without his supply, the Texan colonel knew he could not sustain his forces for another engagement. He led them away to Santa Fe. Word of his defeat went to General

Sibley, who was still at Albuquerque. The losses in the two phases of the battle cost the Confederates about three hundred and fifty killed, wounded and captured; the Union forces, about one hundred and fifty.

The Coloradoans were eager to press on after the retreating Texans and wipe them out; but direct orders had come from Colonel Canby to retire to Fort Union and keep it "at all hazards, and to leave nothing to chance." He feared an attack on the fort from the East, if a Confederate force was still available to move out of the Rio Grande valley and up the eastern plains of New Mexico. Further, he was himself once again in the field, for he was able to leave Fort Craig on April first to overtake Sibley at Albuquerque. There were now assembled the remnants of the Texan brigade. Santa Fe was once again free. On April eighth Canby arrived before Albuquerque, exchanged artillery salvos with Sibley, and then retired to the Sandía Mountains to await reinforcements from Fort Union.

Sibley looked upon his own situation. His artillery ammunition was gone. He ordered his brass fieldpieces buried. His supply train was destroyed, and could be replaced only by capturing another from the Union forces. But they were now victorious, thanks to the First Colorado, and could hold on to their wagons and animals. The countryside was too poor to offer the invading army subsistence for a long campaign, such as had for its purpose the capture of the whole mountain and desert West. He was not the military governor of a conquered territory whose resources he could wring dry at will. He was the leader of a now hungry, tired and ragged army. On April twelfth he ordered a retreat to begin. His main body crossed the river at Albuquerque and went down the west bank to Los Lunas. During the next day the remainder straggled down the east bank and camped at Los Pinos, the ranch of Henry Connelly, then Governor of New Mexico. The ranch stood at Peralta, almost opposite to Los Lunas. On the same day Canby's reinforcements arrived, and on the next, he marched to pursue the retreating Texans, whom he overtook at Peralta on the fifteenth, and engaged in a skirmish before nightfall. "As we galloped across the bottom towards them they fluttered like birds in a snare," wrote a Colorado volunteer. During the night the Texans forded the river, and came up with their main body on the west side. They left behind them their sick and wounded "without attendance, without medicine, and almost without food."

For the next several days the retreat continued on the west bank, while the pursuit paralleled it on the east bank. Both armies were within cannon shot of each other, but no battles followed. Union troops wondered why Colonel Canby did not cross the river and destroy Sibley's Texans once and for all. Was it because Canby was Sibley's brother-in-law? Or was Canby content to save his own men, and let the earth do his work for him? For Sibley, without resources, was crossing some of the hardest country in the river kingdom, where back of the narrow valley benches there lay nothing but desert. To shake his pursuers Sibley turned, after a few days, into even harder lands. He left the river terraces and detoured westward into the San Mateo Mountains. Lost to sight, he continued southward then until he arrived at Fort Bliss, where before sending his broken forces home across the western wastes of Texas he composed his impressions.

Reporting to the Confederate government at Richmond, he was convinced "that, except for its geographical position, the Territory of New Mexico is not worth a quarter of the blood and treasure expended in its conquest"—forgetting how in that very geographical position rested the whole hope of the Confederate design for empire, now lost. Able to ignore the very purpose of his mission, he went on to cite further exasperations. In New Mexico, "the indispensable element, food, cannot be relied on. During the last year, and pending recent operations, hundreds of thousands of sheep have been driven off by the Navajo Indians. Indeed, such were the complaints of the people in this respect that I had determined, as good policy, to encourage private enterprises against that tribe and the Apaches, and"—he was a consistent Confederate—"and to legalize the enslaving of them." In the face of the record, he managed to sound like a conqueror. "We have beaten the enemy in every encounter and against large odds. . . ." In the act of retreating, he thought it wise to smother any hopes for a return to New Mexico. ". . . I cannot speak encouragingly for the future, my troops, having manifested a dogged, irreconcilable detestation of the country and the people. . . ."

On May fourteenth, at James Magoffin's, he assembled his troops and took leave of them. He told them what they had been through, he congratulated them upon "the successes which have crowned their arms . . . in the short but brilliant campaign." He listed their engagements. "The boasted valor of Texans has been fully vindicated, Valverde, Glorieta, Albuquerque, Peralta, and last, though not least, your successful and almost unprecedented evacuation, through mountain passes and over a trackless waste of a hundred miles through a famishing country, will be duly chronicled, and form one of the brightest pages in the history of the Second American Revolution. . . ." It was a commander's valedictory in the style of the Mexicans he so despised, for it referred to everything but his total defeat. In early summer of 1862 the Texans were gone, Colonel Baylor's Confederate Territory of Arizona was undone, the threat against the whole Federal Far West was lifted, and the Civil War, so far as it concerned the Rio Grande in New Mexico, was over.

33.

The Desolate

But not every problem that had come with it. "The whole country was a theater of desolation," wrote a newly arrived officer of what he saw in the summer of 1862. "What the Confederates failed to appropriate, the Apaches destroyed. The inhabitants were literally starving and utterly demoralized." He came to the river at Mesilla in August, 1862, with Brigadier General James H. Carleton's column of troops ordered from California to reinforce New Mexico against the Texans. When they arrived the Texans had departed, and New Mexico was struggling with her old internal enemies, the roving tribes—and extreme hardship complicated by a ten-year drought. As the California Column came to take the ford at Mesilla they found that the river was so empty that they "crossed the river-bed on foot, dry-shod."

Plenty of stories about the river's exhaustion were heard during the 1850s. At El Paso people dug holes nine feet deep in the dry bed in order to tap a little groundwater for domestic uses. Herds of goats and sheep were driven up from Presidio del Norte to El Paso in the river bed which when dry made a fine path. Once when the river was revived by a little runoff a few miles above the Pass, residents on the Mexican side diverted all the flow to their fields and orchards. The people of Franklin on the American side "raised the question as to their right." The matter was "compromised" through a division of the waters between the users in both nations. In the winter of 1855 the river "disappeared

about 25 miles above Las Cruces (about San Diego Crossing) sunk in
the sand and did not appear again until it reached the . . . fall about
3 miles above El Paso." Here was the same curious concept as that held
by the Spaniards in 1541, when one of Coronado's officers reported
that the lower New Mexico river "disappeared underground like the
Guadiana in Estremadura . . . while farther on it reappeared as a large
stream." But there was no flowing subterranean passage; only an exhaustion of surface flow, and a lowered level of groundwater unable to seep
above to make channel water. Here and there in such an interrupted
passage the people might find deep holes or pools where quantities of fish
gathered to survive; and they fished for these all they liked. But fish out
of a few pools could not sustain the population, and Carleton's troopers
found that "instead of being able to furnish us supplies, we were compelled to afford them occasional assistance." Luckily the Californians
had been well-provisioned by their commander with rations that included
pemmican, which they hated, and they were "consequently in a condition
to be independent until such protection could be granted as would
induce the resident population to re-commence farming operations."

For if there were no Confederates to fight, Carleton soon found
that his well-trained soldiers would have plenty to do to control Indian
raiders. He made a rapid reconnaissance of the Pass country, and then
hastened to Santa Fe to become commander of New Mexico, relieving
Canby who departed for the East and the star of a brigadier. Carleton,
with the support of Governor Connelly, soon resolved under martial
law to throw every resource of the Territory into controlling the Indians.
For the first time in New Mexico they were to be confined on a reservation. The site chosen by Carleton was on the Pecos River in southeastern
New Mexico, where a cottonwood grove sixteen miles long and half a
mile wide at its widest bordered the red, muddy stream. A fort was
constructed and named after General Edwin V. Sumner, and there first
the Mescalero Apaches and later the Navajos were gathered and guarded.
There were no Mexican or American settlements anywhere near the
Bosque Redondo, as the reservation was called after its grove that
curved along the Pecos. The Indians were encouraged to raise their food
now instead of steal it. They took glumly to such a life. To the Army
all Indians looked alike—but the Apaches and Navajos were hereditary
enemies, and combining them on a single reservation caused extra problems of supervision. They were dispirited. When the Apaches had finally
surrendered to Carleton their leader told him, ". . . We are worn-out; we
have no more heart; we have no provisions, no means to live; your troops

are everywhere. . . . Do with us as may seem good to you, but do not forget that we are men and braves." It was an affecting speech, but soldiers remembered how relentless and how clever the Apaches had been for generations in their thieving. "These Indians are a decided institution in New Mexico," noted a trooper, "they seldom kill their tenants the Mexicans. It would be bad policy. Dead men raise no stock. . . ." As for Navajos, soldiers concluded that in addition to their terrible warfare the Navajos could claim a curious distinction. "Persons who speak the Welsh language find no difficulty in understanding them and being understood by them. . . ." It seemed obvious to soldiers that Navajos were descended from Welsh families who long before had been cast away on the Texas Gulf Coast.

The Apaches in their hundreds and the Navajos in their thousands suffered from cold and hunger at the Bosque Redondo. General Carleton inspected Fort Sumner and found they were not raising enough food for themselves, and ordered full government rations to be made available to them. Further, he organized a cattle drive to bring stock animals to the reservation. The first movement of its kind under American administration, it was the forerunner of the cattle trail industry of New Mexico. One member of the inspecting party with General Carleton was Juan B. Lamy, first bishop of Santa Fe. He reviewed the misfortunes of the Indians, and of these the one he felt able to relieve was the lack of education for their children, of whom there were nearly three thousand at the Bosque Redondo. The Bishop offered to find teachers for them. It was the best hope for the future, as he always felt. But though the Army authorities might agree with him in general, they made nothing of his offer.

The Fort Sumner experiment lasted for five years. It was abandoned because of many difficulties. The two tribes could not learn to live in harmony at close quarters. Their hardships were discouraging. They were not pastoral people who took naturally to farming. Government policy in Washington knew little of the realities that had led to the captivity of the Indians, and saw only its effect upon them as inhumane. When first the Apaches and later the Navajos broke out of the reservation, they were allowed to return to their old lands. The Apaches were to make trouble for many more years; but the Navajos were for the most part pacified. Going west across the rivers, they were exiles coming home, and one old man among them said, "When we saw the top of the mountain from Albuquerque we wondered if it was our mountain, and we felt like talking to the ground, we loved it so. . . ."

The interlude had its value. Farming and ranching, the settling of towns, greater safety in travel, had opportunity to develop. Further, Carleton, a stern administrator of martial law, put down disturbing elements in the civil population. For during the years before the Civil War, and after its suppression in New Mexico and Arizona, the territories had been "cursed by the presence of two or three hundred of the most infamous scoundrels it is possible to conceive. Innocent and unoffending men," said one of Carleton's captains, "were shot down or bowie-knived merely for the pleasure of witnessing their death agonies. Men walked the streets and public squares with double-barrelled shotguns, and hunted each other as sportsmen hunt for game. . . . Since Carleton's occupation of those Territories with his California Column, a great change for the better has taken place, and this melioration promises to gain ground. . . ."

34.

Confederate Border

Private inspiration was also the cause of much public disorder and suffering on the Texas river in the years that bracketted the Civil War—but with a difference from the pattern of trouble in New Mexico. Along the Texas Rio Grande it was organized into bands of outlaw Mexicans (sometimes allied with Indians) that killed ranchers and travellers, destroyed property, and stole stock animals. Chased by United States and Mexican authorities, they were seldom inconvenienced by both governments at the same time, and to escape had only to cross the river in either direction, depending upon which nation pursued them at the moment. Sanctuary always lay over the river. When the law pursuing a criminal asked "Where is he?" the famous answer on the lower Rio Grande was always, "al otro lado—on the other side." The design of pursuit and escape, with repeated tales of boldness, quick wits and inventive cruelty, led to a confused tradition among the people. Through long experience as connoisseurs of border butchery, they came to glorify the more expert criminals who made victims of their kind. When out of the welter of torture, murder, burning and theft there emerged an occasional Mexican virtuoso of remorseless savagery, he was celebrated in folk songs, for mingled with the terror which greeted his sudden appearances was a sigh of admiration. His type, with few variations, was the reigning folk hero along the boundary river for a century.

One such who played his character about the river towns of Mier, Roma, Reynosa and Camargo in the early 1860s was Abram García. As it was his whim always to ride a white horse, he was known as the White Cavalier. He and his band of followers were as handsome as they were brave, and as vain as they were cruel. They rode superb horses, saddled in gear that flashed with silver and gold mountings. Their immense hats heavy with gold and silver threads threw capes of shadow over their upper bodies and in the shadow flashed brilliant eyes and dazzling teeth. Their short jackets and tight trousers were made of velvet or the thinnest buckskins, loaded with silver buttons and bullion lace. They bristled with weapons. It was their convention to affect an elaborate courtesy of manner while hot with lust they reduced their victims to an animal state, and in the process gave pain. The White Cavalier enjoyed causing men to dance or have their feet shot off. When they had danced enough, he saw that they were stripped and beaten until almost, or—what could it possibly matter?—or in fact, dead. Then taking their horses, money, merchandise, or other portable possessions he spurred his mount till it bled and with marvellous grace vanished in a cloud of dust.

An even more ambitious example of the type was Juan Nepomuceno Cortina who beginning as a private murderer, later, like Canales and Carvajal, sometimes took whole towns and even provinces for his game. His title in the folk convention of his time was "Red Robber of the Rio Grande." In 1859 he captured Brownsville after a battle and in the following year he was pursued by Lieutenant Colonel Robert E. Lee, who was then still an officer of the United States Army on duty in Texas. He eluded Colonel Lee, who was restricted in his efforts by international policy governing the penetration of United States troops into Mexico. After another year Cortina made a brilliant reappearance on the Rio Grande to burn the little river town of Roma. It was his specialty to posture as the defender of Mexicans in Texas, which gave a spurious dignity to his passion for destruction. His career was to know strange periods of official sanction, when after revolutionizing Tamaulipas he became its governor, and when under President Juárez, and the later republic, he was to serve as a general officer. For fifteen years or more he was intermittently the scourge of the lower river—and he became the subject of a ballad that would survive to commemorate him.

The two governments at the river, with whatever help from orderly American and Mexican citizens, could not overcome the outrages of Indian and bandit raiding parties. It was the Confederate state of Texas that controlled the troubles better than any earlier authority. In 1861 a regiment of cavalry was raised by Texas to patrol the border. Its troopers rode the main routes of travel to police Indian trails and keep constant watch on the towns. They kept outlaws from coming in organized bands over the river from Mexico; and they searched for travellers crossing south out of Texas who were escaping from the conscription of Texans for armed service, or who were deserting the Confederate Army, or who were Northern sympathizers seeking refuge. In the early period of the war there was a large traffic of such people for whom the river was a boundary beyond which lay freedom. Doing their duty, the troopers of the Texas cavalry captured many of them. A further duty of the regiment was to keep order on the Confederacy's only international border outlet to world trade; for cotton from Texas was marketed across the Rio Grande in immense quantities.

From 1861 to the end of the war, the Texas Gulf ports were blockaded by the United States Navy. The West Gulf Squadron—commanded from 1862 to 1864 by Admiral David Farragut—patrolled the ancient Spanish kingdom of Florida from Pensacola to the Rio Grande. Confederate blockade-running ships sailed between north Mexico ports, including Bagdad and Matamoros at the mouth of the Rio Grande, and Atlantic ports of transshipment in the West Indies. The blockade-runners were built for invisibility and speed. With long slender hulls they sat low in the water displacing about five hundred tons. They were powered by steam and propelled by side paddle wheels. Their raked funnels were built with telescopic joints so they could be lowered to escape sighting. Their boilers were stoked with hard coal to show as little smoke as possible. Over their foredecks was a turtle-back shield to throw off heavy seas, and they were painted sea-gray to escape notice by day. Running the blockade by night they showed no lights, and blew off steam through underwater exhausts. Eastbound they carried cotton for the Europe trade, and westbound they brought crucial war materials such as lead, mercury, sulphur, and woven goods. If they passed the Gulf

Squadron safely, they were free to use the Rio Grande ports of Bagdad
and Matamoros quite openly; for as Mexico was neutral her ports, under
a convention honored by the United States Supreme Court, could not
be directly blockaded. Even vessels destined for Matamoros, if captured
by the Union squadron, had to be released to proceed on their way—
though in at least one such case the war contraband cargo was seized.

In 1862 the Confederates held Brownsville, which meant that
cotton shipments could be most conveniently made across the river there.
Shallow draft steamers of many foreign nations came direct to the docks
of Matamoros. Larger ships anchored in the Gulf off Bagdad and their
cargoes were landed by lighter to be carried up the riverbanks to the
Matamoros customs house, and transshipped into Texas. The southernmost Rio Grande towns became the greatest cotton markets in the world.
Cotton was sold at fifty cents a pound, or more, in gold. Once again
Matamoros experienced sudden growth, now to a population of thirty-
five thousand, until she became Mexico's most important doorway to
North America. In 1863 there was suddenly a prospect that through
Matamoros the Confederate States might receive new and substantial
support for their cause.

For the French were in Mexico. Since 1861 French troops had
been arriving in increasing strength—at first with the support of Spain
and Great Britain who soon withdrew—for the purpose of establishing
a Mexican government that would pay up Mexico's huge and defaulted
foreign indebtedness. Struggling to maintain his revolutionary regime,
Benito Juárez worked to settle national economic problems without
foreign intervention, and resisted the French. It was soon apparent that
the fortunes of France in Mexico were linked with those of the Confederate States of America. If the South were successful, and if in her
success she should receive aid from French Mexico, then the Monroe
Doctrine would be nullified by the natural alliance that would follow.
Once again there would be European power in the western hemisphere.
The United States while honoring the neutrality of Mexico, recognized
the Juárez government and opposed the French invasion. But occupied
by the Civil War, Washington could spare no resources for active intervention. Resistance to the French had to be made within the strategic
limits of the war at home. These, extending everywhere in the states,
included Texas and the border; and there, in November, 1863, a force
of six thousand Union troops under General Banks arrived from the
Gulf to capture Brownsville. Fort Brown and the river shore and the
old sea meadows all the way to Point Isabel were once again occupied

by an army. Its first purpose was to take part in the large-scale Federal invasion of Texas from her two borders, by way of the Red River and the Rio Grande—a scheme that was never executed. Its next move was to discourage by its presence any effort of the French—who now had almost forty thousand troops in Mexico—to reinforce the Confederacy through Matamoros. No French troops threatened Matamoros during the Union occupation of Brownsville.

The occupation interrupted the cotton trade out of Brownsville. Cotton was now hauled overland from San Antonio warehouses to Eagle Pass far upriver, where remained the only Mexican port of entry above Matamoros. Confederate troops, in garrison at Fort Duncan, preserved the secessionist authority of the town, though out of eighty-three votes cast there in the Texas election on secession, eighty went for the Union. Those loyal to the United States fled to Piedras Negras across the river, and were joined by others from elsewhere in Texas, and all knew every trouble of exile. Few of them could speak Spanish. All found it hard to get jobs. Many who tried to return over the river on their way to the United States were captured, and some were hanged.

Immense cotton shipments were crossed from Eagle Pass to Piedras Negras. A founding citizen of Eagle Pass saw in 1864 how at one time "the whole river bottom from the bank of the river to the edge of town was covered with cotton." It was a fine volume of business for the Mexican customs officers, who took an export duty from the Confederacy of one bale for each bale passed through the port. From Piedras Negras the cotton was transported by road down the Mexican side of the river to Matamoros or Bagdad, where the ocean-going ships waited.

In the summer of 1864 the affairs of Mexico touched toward the border river with increased energy. On June twelfth the Archduke Maximilian of Austria arrived in Mexico to ascend the throne as emperor. The French troops that armed his régime—for he was the candidate of Napoleon III for the crown of Mexico—pressed closer to the border and forced Juárez to transfer his roving government to the extreme north, at El Paso on the Mexican bank. In July the Union forces at Brownsville were withdrawn and only a small garrison was left to hold Point Isabel and the Arms of St. James. The Juárez forces held Matamoros, where Cortina, in one of his periods of official respectability, was the commanding general under the republic. He was, extraordinarily, now tacitly an ally of the United States, in opposition to the Confederate garrison that moved into Fort Brown when the Federal forces left it.

Late in the summer a French army of five thousand men landed at Bagdad and marched inland to take Matamoros from the republic. General Cortina led three thousand men and sixteen cannon down the river to meet them, drove them back to the sea, and then turned to defeat a Confederate force from Brownsville that had supported the French by attacking his rear guard. On the ninth he captured Brownsville, ran up the United States flag, and offered the city to the Union commander at Point Isabel, who with his troops was unable to accept it. Presently General Cortina was off on other campaigns in northern Mexico, the Confederates were back in Fort Brown, the Emperor Maximilian's power was established at Matamoros under General Mejía, whom the river populace knew of old, and the spring of 1865 saw the Confederacy fall into ruin. As Lee surrendered on April ninth at Appomattox, the Confederate Trans-Mississippi Department consisting of Arkansas, Louisiana and Texas, continued to resist. It was not until May sixth that the three states were surrendered. But even after that, on May thirteenth, Confederate troops from Fort Brown and Union troops from Point Isabel met in battle near Taylor's plain of Palo Alto. The Confederates forced the Union detachment to retreat, but could not break their line, and when evening fell overland from the Gulf the engagement ended— and with it all Civil War hostilities on the Texas river.

35.

The Second Mexican Empire

There remained under the command of General Kirby Smith a large Confederate army in Texas to be surrendered or captured. On May seventeenth, at Washington, one Rio Grande veteran issued orders to another for the final pacification of Texas. Lieutenant General U. S. Grant, the quartermaster-officer with Taylor in 1846, wrote to Major General Philip H. Sheridan, who had served at Fort Duncan as a lieutenant in 1854, to "proceed without delay to the West to . . . restore

Texas, and that part of Louisiana held by the enemy, to the Union. . . ."
Sheridan was to "place a strong force on the Rio Grande, holding it at
least to a point opposite Camargo, and above that if"—the supreme commander well remembered the river country—"if supplies can be procured. . . . I think," he added, "the Rio Grande should be strongly held,
whether the forces in Texas surrender or not, and that no time should
be lost in getting troops there. If war is to be made, they will be in the
right place; if Kirby Smith surrenders, they will be on the line which
is to be strongly garrisoned. . . ."

Was it odd that even after all resistance in Texas was ended there
should still be a need there for a great army? Grant mentioned the Fourth
Corps, the Twenty-fifth Corps, and thirty-seven thousand other troops
as available to occupy Texas and hold the Rio Grande. General Sheridan
hastened to see him and soon heard him speak of what could not be
written in orders. The United States still maintained official neutrality
toward France and her invasion of Mexico, while actually holding every
sympathy for Juárez and his republic. It was to show great potential
strength in support of the Juárez army that the river line was to be held
in force by United States troops. "As a matter of fact," wrote General
Sheridan later, General Grant said that he "looked upon the invasion
of Mexico by Maximilian as a part of the rebellion itself, and that our
success in putting down secession would never be complete until the
French and Austrian invaders were compelled to quit the territory of
our sister republic." Grant cautioned Sheridan "to act with great circumspection, since the Secretary of State, Mr. Seward, was much opposed
to the use of our troops along the border in any active way that would
be likely to involve us in a war with European powers."

Sheridan left at once for Texas by way of New Orleans. Near the
mouth of the Red River he heard from Edward R. S. Canby—now a
major general—that General Kirby Smith had surrendered to him on
May 26, 1865, under terms like those offered to Lee, by which the defeated officers might take home with them their animals, side arms and
possessions, to apply them to the needs of peace. With that act, Sheridan's
second, and unofficial, mission became his first. He hurried on to Brownsville, arriving June first, to animate his river command with every
scheme short of battle to harass Imperial Mexico. The task was well
within his grasp as an able professional. "That bold dragoon," he was
called by a New Yorker who once entertained him at dinner. His host
saw him as "a stumpy, quadrangular little man, with a forehead of no
promise and hair so short that it looked like a coat of black paint. But

his eye and his mouth shew force" and "his talk is pleasant. . . ." This diarist saw him as "a brilliant practitioner" in military affairs, and—a connoisseur in his mountainous antiquity—General Scott said of Sheridan's battles in 1864 against Early that they were "among the *most finished* affairs of this war. . . ."

Once at the river, Sheridan saw that if he was to supply a great army along its valley he must do better than haul supplies by wagon and mule over the Point Isabel flats. There was no railroad anywhere on the Rio Grande. He immediately began to build the first one—a narrow-gauge line running from Point Isabel to Brownsville, that used wood-burning locomotives with extravagant cowcatchers and commodious wooden cabs. He soon heard disagreeable news. General Kirby Smith's command, though surrendered, was making an effort to remain intact, with the object of fleeing to Mexico to serve under the Emperor. Sheridan sent troops in force up the river to "make demonstrations" that would discourage the Confederates from crossing. Already they had delivered to General Mejía in Matamoros a supply of munitions. Sheridan sternly demanded the return of these. He saw a perfect pretext for invasion if Mejía refused. He was not alone in his sense of a possible war against the Emperor. The Eastern papers were saying that Napoleon III was about to send heavy reinforcements to Mexico, and readers noted that the United States would have a hundred thousand troops on the Rio Grande to oppose him, and war seemed "clearly in the cards" to an observant civilian who had served in Lincoln's administration. He thought it not entirely undesirable. Like all intelligent and sympathetic citizens, he was grieved by what the war had done to the nation. Was there a cure waiting at the Rio Grande? "Six months," he mused, "six months of campaigning by Virginians and Mississippians and Texans, shoulder to shoulder with New Englanders and Westerners . . . might be wonderfully reconstructive in its effect and reunite our fractured young national bones faster than any other treatment could possibly do. . . ."

Still the Secretary of State refused to sanction direct intervention at the border, even though after General Sheridan's "demonstrations" the French everywhere in northern Mexico, demoralized and agitated, seemed about to withdraw to the south. But General Mejía delivered up the Confederate munitions, and "a golden opportunity was lost," as Sheridan said, "for we had ample excuse for crossing the boundary." Encouraged once again by Seward's policy, the Emperor, said General Sheridan, "gained in strength till finally all the accessible sections of

Mexico were in his possession, and the Republic under President Juárez almost succumbed."

The General admitted to "growing impatient at this," and decided to "try again what virtue there might be in a hostile demonstration." First he reviewed the Fourth Corps at San Antonio in September as though to prepare "with some ostentation for a campaign," and then "escorted by a regiment of horse" he dashed to Fort Duncan at Eagle Pass on the river. He hadn't been there since he was a lieutenant fighting Lipans, hunting for turkey, geese, deer and antelope, and observing the bird life of the valley. Now he made contact with agents of Juárez in Piedras Negras, "taking care not to do this in the dark," and in a day or two all north Mexico was convinced that the American general was only awaiting the arrival of a great force of troops to cross the river and fight for Juárez and the Republic. The results were most promising. The Emperor's army abandoned all of north Mexico as far south as Monterrey. The only imperial garrison was the handful left at Matamoros with Mejía, and they were confined there by "that unknown quantity" General Cortina, who harassed the town so that none dared venture out of it. Republican troops were collected at Camargo, Mier and other river towns.

The moment was ripe for a crushing blow at the Empire—but once again the State Department, after protests from the French Ambassador, ordered "a strict neutrality," and Sheridan was obliged to stay on his side of the river.

He could only spend his energies on lesser excitements than invasion. He put down a colonization scheme organized by ex-Confederate personages who had been promised titles of nobility, land grants and the comforts of a new system of peonage by the Emperor if they would migrate to join him. He worked to compose the rivalries of General Cortina and General Canales who while fighting for the Republic "were freebooters enough to take a shy at each other frequently," and to unite them in a single command he recruited General Carvajal to come from Washington. But Carvajal, "the old wretch," was quickly unseated by Canales, and efforts at harmony failed. Matamoros was again in the hands of the Republic. General Sheridan sent frequent shipments of munitions "by the most secret methods" to the Juárez forces—in one shipment there were thirty thousand muskets—and by midsummer of 1866 the republican armies held the entire Mexican Rio Grande, and "in fact," wrote General Sheridan, "nearly the whole of Mexico down to San Luis Potosí."

Such news changed policy at the Tuileries in the following winter. Napoleon III cabled to his commander in Mexico—Sheridan saw a copy of the cable—to withdraw French troops under Maximilian. The message was sent at the very time when at Saint-Cloud the despairing Empress of Mexico was beseeching the French Emperor to send more aid to her doomed husband. By February, 1867, all French soldiers in Mexico were gone, some having embarked from Matamoros for the voyage home. Through the spring Maximilian fought his last battles until at Querétaro in June he was taken prisoner and the Empire was lost.

When the news of his capture reached the river, a ball was given in the Customs House at Piedras Negras to which "all the foreigners in Eagle Pass were invited . . . together with all the best people in that part of the country." The next word that came was spread there by a Mexican colonel who coming to the river from the interior told how the Emperor had been condemned to death, and how after his sentence the people of Mexico felt great sympathy for him. In Mexico City—had they heard this at the river?—five hundred ladies dressed in mourning marched in procession to present a petition for clemency to the authorities. It was denied. On the morning of June nineteenth everybody went up the hill at Querétaro—the Colonel had been there and had seen it all—to watch the Emperor as he was brought out by platoons of soldiers. When the Emperor and the two generals who were to die with him—one was Mejía—were lined up facing the firing squad "Maximilian advanced and presented each of the firing party with a gold doubloon, with the request that they would take good aim until he gave them the signal to fire by removing his hand from his breast. After resuming his position he eulogized his generals and resigned to them the honor of dying first. After they fell he calmly confronted the death that awaited him and met it with a fearlessness that became him. . . ." The news shocked the world, and a New Yorker made the wry comment that Juárez's Liberal party ". . . could hardly be expected to depart from the settled practice of all Mexican administrations in their hour of victory. . . ."

If there were few battles, or even skirmishes, on the Texas Rio Grande in the Civil War, its final phase was its most important one. General Sheridan observed, "At the close of our war there was little hope for the Republic of Mexico. Indeed, till our troops were concentrated on the Rio Grande there was none. Our appearance in such force along the border permitted the Liberal leaders, refugees from their homes, to establish rendezvous whence they could promulgate their plans in safety, while the countenance thus given the cause, when hope was well-nigh gone, incited the Mexican people to renewed resistance. Beginning again with very scant means, for they had lost about all, the Liberals saw their cause, under the influence of such significant and powerful backing, progress and steadily grow so strong that within two years Imperialism had received its death-blow. I doubt," concluded the General with satisfaction, "I doubt very much whether such results could have been achieved without the presence of an American army on the Rio Grande, which, be it remembered, was sent there because, in General Grant's words, the French invasion of Mexico was so closely related to the rebellion as to be essentially a part of it."

In the Civil War campaign of the New Mexico Rio Grande the Rocky Mountain and Pacific West was saved for the Union; while the Federal occupation of the Texan Rio Grande helped to sustain the Monroe Doctrine and Mexican autonomy. Soon the United States troops were pulled away from the river in great numbers, with only small garrisons left in the river forts; and across the way in Mexico, those who had fought the Empire returned to their prewar occupations. Among them was General Cortina, who with refreshed vigor resumed his career of raider and destroyer in and out of Texas.

Of all Western problems remaining after the Civil War the greatest one was that of the unpacified Indians. It loomed in menace behind every growing expression of civilized life in the river empire, where it was estimated that the Comanches, the Apaches, the Navajos, and the Lipans with their allies totalled eighty thousand. But as early as 1866 there was promise of a solution—of sorts—for it appeared that "the government in Washington," as a New Mexican churchman noted, was "contemplating a plan, which if carried out with prudence and humanity" would lead to the conversion of the Indians, "particularly of their children. . . ." Under the power and need of the whole nation in its westward reach the freedom of the Indians was about to be lost. Its last expressions glared the more brightly and terribly for the twilight that gathered to close over the long Indian day.

36.

The Mexico Moon

To the old Spanish question, "What is an Indian?", the Americans found various answers, depending upon their nearness to frontier experience. The Washington government, farthest away, when appealed to time and again for help, either replied, like Madrid or Mexico City in their periods of sovereignty, that local troops must suppress the savages, or sent Congressional commissions to investigate rumors of Indian outrages. One such commission, sitting in Texas in 1873, summoned any who had complaints, and many responded. "Several of these men," stated the executive document of the hearing, "while appearing before the commission to record their losses by Indian raids, were called away by the news of fresh attacks upon their residences and property. . . ." So at the very instant when unwieldy government at last was listening, though not yet acting, the human reality and trial of the people was dramatically proved. It was important that this was so, for removed far from the scenes of depredation, the government at times seemed skeptical of the alarms and supplications it heard so often from the West. The whole problem was confusing, for not all Indians were murderous aggressors—the Pueblos of the Rio Grande abided in peace, and their governors each held an ebony cane headed with silver that had been bestowed as symbols of authority in 1863, bearing the engraved name of the bestower: "A. Lincoln Pres. U.S."

But the others, the nomads? What hope was there for peace with them? Commissioner Emory in the 'fifties said they had "but two settled principles of action—to kill the defenceless and avoid collision with a superior or equal force." Some reformers proposed a gentle approach, in Quaker courage and passivity, on the grounds that the Indian hardly knew right from wrong, and could not be held responsible, really, for what he did not consider criminal. An Indian fighter of long experience bitterly disposed of such a view, to his own satisfaction, anyway.

"It is all very well to argue that the Indian knows no better," he wrote of the Apache, "that he merely possesses the teachings of his race, that his cruelties are the results of untaught savage disposition, etc.; but . . . is it true policy that intelligent, christian people should be sacrificed, year after year, and their massacres excused on the ground that the murderers were only Indians? . . . Must we forever continue to accept the wild and impracticable theories of parlor readers on Indian character? Can we continue to pay millions annually for the short-sighted and pernicious policy which has heretofore"—he was writing in 1867—"regulated our Indian affairs?" As for the old question about the Indian nature, he had a grim and certain answer. "The American savage is no idiot. He knows right from wrong, and is quite as cognizant of the fact when he commits a wrong as the most instructed of our race. If the reader should feel a particle of doubt on this point, all he has to do is to commit a wrong upon an Apache, and he will very soon become convinced that the savage is quite as much aware of the fact as he can be. . . . The capacity to discriminate between right and wrong is not the exclusive property of christianized people. . . ." The Apache understood his own acts. What he misjudged was their effect on the white man. "When an Apache mutilates the dead body of his enemy, he knows that he is doing a wrong and cowardly act; but he persists in doing it, because he judges us from his stand-point, and imagines that sight of the muti· lated corpse will produce terror in the beholders"—a mistake. The Indian "has not arrived at that amount of information which would instruct him that disgust and anger, with a determination for redress at the earliest opportunity, are engendered instead of dread. Like the rest of mankind, he is apt to measure other people's corn by his own bushel."

Many observers conceded that the Indian had his provocations to resist the white man. The earliest settlers broke promises made to him, and later on a great scale so did the government. As the frontiersmen were individualists by necessity, they made their own first laws, and destruction of an Indian was hardly treated as a crime. If there had ever been a time to handle the Indian with Quaker gentleness—and after all this had a simple resemblance to the Franciscan touch upon the Indian—that time was at the very first contacts with the Indian plains-men. But it was now too late for a policy of trustful brotherhood. When one after another the governors of Texas were refused substantial in-creases of the Army garrisons along the river, Texas recruited three battalions of rangers and did what she could to patrol the river plains above Laredo where the Indians came and went on their terrible business against American settlers above the left bank and Mexican on both.

There was nothing new in the warfare now pursued by the Indian—except its scale. Where in the Spanish and Mexican periods Apaches, Comanches, Lipans, had all been famous for raids, these were occasional strikes against a few obvious settlements scattered in a great empire largely Indian in its ownership. But after the Civil War every continental gesture, every new reach for natural wealth of the United States drove the Indians a whole nation at a time from their accustomed haunts, and Indian nations in solid though not co-ordinated response swarmed out on the offensive as their world was contracted about them. Exploitation of gold discoveries in the Rocky Mountain territories drove them from some of their best hunting grounds. Buffalo drives on the prairies forced them southwest toward the river, and so did the thrust of railroads across the land, followed by new American towns. Cattle trails cut across the ancient Indian paths and interrupted their free travel. The essential nature of the Plains Indian life—movement—was in jeopardy. To a Comanche warrior who said, "I know every stream and every wood between the Rio Grande and the Arkansas," the American expansion plainly meant the death of his nation as he had known it. Everywhere in the whole immense region of the arid lands of North America, of which the central vein was the Rio Grande for nearly two thousand miles, the Indian atrocities rose to a new intensity.

Indians out of Mexico raged over the river into Texas, and Indians from the plains crossed in the other direction. From Arizona on the west and from Texas on the east Indians descended upon New Mexico. Ten thousand horses a year were stolen from the north Mexican frontier, and cattle stolen in Texas were driven to New Mexico to be traded along the pastoral river. Comanches and Apaches fought each other for their spoils. Mexican wagoners if captured might be tied upsidedown to their own wagon wheels with their heads a foot off the ground, where small fires were built to boil their brains until they burst from their skulls. A red and yellow American coach lettered "Butterfield Overland Dispatch" above windows that gave a glimpse of an interior lined with pink brocade and biscuit-tufted leather seats might be overtaken in its journey, and its occupants turned out to die, and its animals stolen, and the coach itself burned. Children—especially boys—were stolen, and both boys and girls were beaten and otherwise abused, and if they cried were killed, and a surprising number survived to grow up as tribesmen. Women, American and Mexican, were taken away into

concubinage and slavery. Adult white men were killed rather than captured. The dead were dishonored by mutilations that hideously mocked
their reduction to final impotence. If destroying Indians rarely entered
the center of a remote town, they were bold and brilliant about striking
at its loose ends where streets faded into open country, and stealing,
killing, burning and vanishing all in a moment. At Eagle Pass when an
avenging party rode out in pursuit, its men gave "the Terrible Texas,"
which was "a concert of sounds before entering an Indian fight accompanied by volleys of pistol shots. . . ." A man, knowing there were Indians
about, once whistled to keep up his spirits, and a friend hearing him
remarked that "there was no tune to his music," and did not blame him.
In the American river towns where Indians struck there was bitter feeling
toward the Mexican authorities on the other side, who sometimes did
less than their share to take and punish the raiders. Citizens riding out
after escaping raiders might see nothing of them but a line of smokes
standing across the plains at intervals as signals to show other Indians
where rode success and safety.

It was the Comanches who in the beginning had brought captured wild horses from the Spanish lands to the plains, and they remained
the leading nation in the swift, always shifting warfare against the growing power of the Americans. As constant enemies they became familiar
to the settlers, who saw them not only with rage and fear but also with a
sense of wonder at many details of their mysterious life.

Their visions were like the weather over mountain and plain,
their laws came from the creature powers of the earth. Needing assurance or protection from life beyond himself, an Indian plainsman went
alone into the open land to undertake an ordeal of thirst, hunger or
other suffering, that would bring him a vision. When he was worthy, it
came to him as another man who spoke to him, giving him a song for
his own, or a sacred ritual. He was both prostrated and exalted when
the vision on leaving took animal form so that he would know what
creature had blessed him, and whose feathers or fur or bone he must
ever after keep by him as sacred protection. When an Indian drew pictures of what he knew, he left out some things it would be dangerous to
set down, for in itself a drawing could exert wicked power. To the white
strangers, some of the daily realities of the Indians seemed poetic—the
very name of the largest division of the Comanche nation, the one that
ranged about the river, was "the Honey-Eaters."

From the horse they took their style. Dismounted they were
awkward and sluggish, but the moment they were on a horse they showed

every ease and grace, as if they took lordship from the animal who was lord of the prairies. Comanche children learned to ride early. The warrior would never ride a mare. Maleness was superior, and any expression of its attributes enhanced his own. War chiefs each owned great bands of horses, by the hundreds. Even apart from what they would bring in trade, these represented wealth and splendor—and yet more, they carried in them their master's essence; for when he broke a wild mustang, the Comanche roped and threw it, and then made it his in another way. He put his mouth to its nostrils and exhaled his breath into them and, with it, his controlling spirit.

In September every year the Honey-Eaters in great numbers went to the Rio Grande and deep into Mexico to take horses. Then the heat of full summer was waning, and the rains were over so that no marks of travel would be left in mud for pursuers to follow, and the nights were fragrant and clear, and the grass was still succulent before winter. Because of where they went, and when, they called the month of September the Mexico Moon.

The raid was carefully organized. It began with ceremony—dances and songs and tales in honor of war, around a great fire, at night. Of the men, only the warriors going on the raid took active part. Each had a woman to dance with him. Leaving the firelight some vanished into the trembling shadows to make love, while men too old to accompany the raid told of their great days and struck drums for emphasis. The raid leader was absolute in his command. He said where they would go, who would be the scouts, who would do the camp work, where they would camp. Gathering his lieutenants, he mapped for them on the bare ground the trails they would take, and designated natural features, and showed the distance and time to be passed between halts. He knew the spaces, the trees, the water, the canyons, the mesas they would pass; and where in Mexico were the best animals and women and children ripe for taking. Preparations were soon completed—often in a single night; and at dawn the party moved south. It included enough women to perform the usual menial services—pitching and striking the tepees, gathering fuel, dressing or undressing the horses with their riding blankets.

Comanche women were short-haired. Their dress was voluminous, exposing only face and hands. On their long tunics they embroidered designs of flowers or animals in colored porcupine quills. When travelling exposed to sun and wind they covered their faces with red ochre. It seemed their only vanity, for they spent little attention on clothes or ornaments. It was their men who took trouble over appearance. They made themselves magnificent in every possible way. Their hair was braided in two queues that hung to their thighs, and studded with silver discs graduated in size as the queue narrowed, or interwoven with bright cloth strips or scraps of fur. Earrings of silver, gold, shell or bone hung from their pierced lobes. Soft, wonderfully tanned buckskins provided their long shirts, and the tight leggings that reached from foot to waist, and the breechclout drawn through the belt front and back. A wide strip was left where the buckskins were seamed, and this was sometimes cut into long fringes and tipped with silver or bead ornaments. Well-cut moccasins, a buffalo robe or a blanket from New Mexico, a cap of swept-back feathers finished the dress. The Comanche man had many suits of such a costume—so many that he kept a particular bag to carry them in. For special occasions he painted himself—black for war, and otherwise bright reds, blues, yellows and white, in any designs that pleased him. The general effect was so grand and so careful that an American traveller said of the men in a Comanche encampment that he had "never seen as much foppery displayed in our cities," and concluded that the "adjustment of toilet must occupy several hours of each day." Some of the young lords even "carried umbrellas to protect them from the sun."

Superbly mounted, they used cured sheepskins or pieces of buffalo hides to ride on, and their bridles were made of rawhide. They were armed with bows made of bois d'arc, metal-tipped arrows, ash-wood lances, shields of stiffened buffalo hide edged with turkey feathers, a flint-stone battle-axe, and sometimes with rifles, bowie knives and machetes.

In camp their tepees rose and fell as if by magic—the women were expert at handling the long poles and skins with which the shelters were made. The tepee seemed like a great garment, as it were, drawn about the shoulders of a seated Indian giant. In the evening on the trail when the leader lighted his sacred pipe all his aides smoked it with him. They ate game taken during the day's travel, or if none was to be had, they killed a horse and cooked it. They drank from a water bag made of a buffalo paunch, or a whole antelope skin. To obtain a great delicacy they cut the udder of a cow or goat and sucked the mixed blood and milk. Their active life and diet of lean meat kept most of the warriors slender, though there was one Comanche chief so fat that he could not heave himself upon any of his fifteen hundred horses, and was obliged to travel sitting on a travois.

Scouts journeyed a day ahead of the main war party. They would select the site for a temporary base camp from which the actual raid

would be sprung, and the attack would be timed to come at night during
or just after the full moon. The upper Comanche Trail to Mexico was a
famous thoroughfare. To a resident of the lands it crossed it seemed in the
nineteenth century like "a great chalk line on the map of West Texas
from the Llano Estacado to the Rio Grande." Nearing the river, it forked
westward to cross about forty miles below the junta de los rios, where
the Conchos entered the Rio Grande; and it forked again to cross the
river about thirty miles farther east. There was a garrison at Presidio
del Norte near the junta. Both forks were well to the southeast of it.
Going into Mexico, the warriors took the western fork. Returning they
took the eastern. Their objectives were ranches, farms, villages, mines in
northern Mexico, even as far as Durango.

When September came, the Mexico Moon, the residents of the
river lands took their annual precautions. Sentinels were sent out to
stations on the highest peaks and crags of the western approaches to the
Big Bend. There they set up piles of brush and faggot to light as signal
fires when the time came. They stood guard night after night as the
moon rose later and fuller, until in its fall of turquoise light the whole
fantasy of the rocky night seemed visible in sharpest detail and distance.
Mountains were clear on the horizon, and declivities of the earth far
away were like shadows, and even the colors of rock—yellow, rose, purple
—were discernible in the calm shower of moonlight.

And then one night, far across the land, a pinpoint of rosy light
would show like a fallen star burning on the ground; and near it
another, and another, in the order of campfires; and the farthest sentinels on their cold platforms would know that they saw what they were
watching for—the advance elements of the Honey-Eaters. Striking life to
their fire high in the sky they gave the signal that was awaited by
watchers on the next height, who in turn lighted their wood; and soon
the news was taken south all the way to the river by the chain of watch-
fires, telling men and women on their scattered ranches to gather their
children and their animals and go to the river villages for protection.

In another day and a night came the rustling and glittering
front of the war party, standing forth in the pour of the moon. Progress-
ing amidst pointed rocks they bristled with gleaming points of their
own, and passing over dry ground crusty with mica they winked and
flashed with their silver jewels. The land they crossed was banded with
every color, and so were their painted faces and breasts, their arms and
bellies. If mystery was suspended in the very landscape of the Big Bend,
it also clung around their spirits; and as they contended with a land of

the utmost hardness, hardness hung like conviction in their hearts. In oddly stirring ways they seemed like direct expressions of the fantastic lands where they roved.

They approached the river whose sandy slopes were made of powdered mountains. There they would camp; water the horses; smoke and rest and ignore the poor settlements upriver and down, at least on the southerly journey, for they were after greater spoils than those huddled about the darkened jacales and earthen huts near-by. At day-break they would cross over the Rio Grande and be on their way, together a living embodiment of the land they called their own.

It would not long be theirs.

In 1867, either by treaty, or by direct order of the President of the United States, the Plains Indian nations were limited to reserved lands. The borderland tribes were assigned to the Indian Territory, to share it with the Five Civilized Tribes who had been moved there in President Jackson's time. Land was to be held by the tribe rather than owned by the individual, until 1887 when an act of Congress opened the way for individual Indians to hold title to property.

The "Peace Policy" of the government, with its negotiation of treaties as between two sovereignties, was not wholly a success. Indian leaders were eloquent in opposing the idea of reservation lands. "The world was made for all to live in," said a Kickapoo chief to a govern-ment commission, and ". . . the white man has no right to encroach on the hunting grounds of the red man, and has no right to cut the land up into little squares. . . ." A Comanche statesman declared, "My people have never first drawn a bow or fired a gun against the whites. . . . It was you who sent out the first soldier and we who sent out the second." So much for the past. As for the future, he said to the American com-missioners, ". . . You wanted to put us upon a reservation, to build us houses and make us medicine lodges. I do not want them. I was born upon the prairie, where the wind blew free . . . and everything drew a free breath . . . we only wish to wander on the prairie until we die. . . ."

Government gave the Peace Policy a chance to work. But the Indians could not observe the terms of treaties voluntarily, and raids and strife continued when war parties broke away from their reserva-tions. In 1871 the Congress took the Indians into legal custody as wards of the nation. They were to be supported by the government, with their affairs administered by Indian agents. The system had its failures. "What," demanded an officer long experienced in Indian warfare, "what can a political camp-follower, who has done party service in our cities, and been appointed Indian Agent as reward for such service, possibly know of Indian character?" Again the Indian met bad faith on the part of his conquerors. If he was a great enemy the white man had made him so, thought many of those who had borne the battle against him in the realities of the frontier. And—national policy was sometimes incredible— if the Indian was corrupt and slow to throw off his dangerous ways, then again it seemed clear that he had been greatly tempted: when the government announced that a ransom of one hundred dollars would be paid for the return of each white captive held by Indians, the Indians, becoming used to the value of money, were only induced to arrange for more captives. It would take two decades for the forcible pacification of the Indians to be successful. In the same period, an intermittent war of depredations was laid down over the river lands from Laredo to the Gulf, not by Indians, but by white men, of Mexico and Texas.

37.

Bad Men and Good

The Indian terrors represented an effort by a whole society, in the full power of its sanctions, to carry out an essentially conservative mission. Indians in trying to save their empire and their ancient ways were not outlaws. On the contrary, they were obeying their own laws to the utmost. It was the American and Mexican bandits of the river lands who broke the laws, even of their own countries. Their mission was one of private lawless gain, and in the crazy desperation of the vicious acts of a leader and his band lay an expression of human character adrift from its natural foundations of society and nationality. After the period of relative calm during the Civil War on the border, river outlaws came back to dominate the country with more violence than ever. Some of them were lost to society as a result of the war—men who came to the river owning nothing, and reflecting the spiritual displacement from which great sectors of the nation had to recover. Some were Texans embittered by the hardships and indignities of reconstruction within their own state. Others were children of adventure who had to be nourished on excitement at no matter whose expense of property and life. All these came in such numbers that in 1877 the Texas government published a list of five thousand "men wanted in Texas" by the law.

From the Gulf to Laredo; in the passes of the Big Bend; over the river at El Paso; in the Mesilla Valley of New Mexico the outlaws worked. They were gamblers, smugglers, stealers of horses and cattle, and all too often murderers, some of whom in a suspension of moral values came to be admired as the ablest of their vocation. One of these was William Bonney, called Billy the Kid, with his succession of dazzling murders, brilliant escapes from jail, and languid insolence in the face of the law. Of many a domineering outcast it was often said on the border river, "He's killed several men and no telling how many Mexicans. . . ."—for his victims were often those who lived over the river.

These retaliated in kind, in a spirit illustrated by the remark of a Mexican at Matamoros: "Shoot the first gringo who comes over here and tries to look at a hide." Depositions by the hundreds made before government commissions testified to the volume and fury of raids by Mexican marauders on the Texas side of the river. "Throughout the valley of the Rio Grande," declared an Army report of 1875, "and for a hundred and forty miles back from it, crops and herds have been abandoned; people dared not travel except in armed parties; civil law outside of the towns was suspended, and sheriffs and judges reported . . . that it was unsafe to attempt to execute processes of law outside of the towns, unless the officers of the law were accompanied by soldiers to protect them. . . ." A United States customs official at Edinburgh, Texas, wrote to General E. O. C. Ord, commanding the Department of Texas, ". . . We, the Americans living in this county, live all the time in dread. It has become so common for the bandits to cross the river and murder Americans, that we think it is only a question of time as to ourselves."

Overland traders were attacked and robbed—one lost "over four thousand in gold" near Mier—and the horses, cattle and lives of ranchers were taken by thieves who struck and raced for the Mexican bank, where lay complete sanctuary. "In an area of fifteen thousand square miles," said a deponent, "from the Nueces to the Rio Grande, and from San Antonio to the Devil's River, they have stolen nearly all the stock at different times and taken it to Mexico, selling it there, with the knowledge and sufferance of the local authorities. . . ." A Mexican army captain who was seen on his side of the river driving a herd of four hundred stolen cattle remarked, like an Apache speaking of New Mexican farmers, "The gringos are raising cows for me." Mexican bandits sometimes went disguised as Indians. The mayors of Mexican river towns admitted that the trade in stolen cattle was immense, with the average price of five dollars a head paid by buyers in Mexico. The illicit trade found complete protection in a "Free Zone" officially established by Mexico along her entire northern border, from the Pacific to the Atlantic Gulf. The limits of the Zone were loosely defined. Its purpose was to grant relief from customs fees to northern Mexicans, but its freedom was taken to grant immunity to any fugitive from Texas, against whom the local Mexican authorities refused to move if he were in the Zona Libre.

Volunteer parties of American ranchers went to the river in pursuit of their lost animals, and some ransomed them for three dollars apiece. If such a bargain could not be struck, they might resort to battle at fords where cattle trails crossed the river. The Mexican federal government stationed two or three companies of troops on the river, ostensibly to control bandit parties. They were a poor lot, and a Texas militia captain told Congress, "The Mexican cavalry is very indifferently armed and mounted. The men are armed with all sorts of guns. I believe they all wear a uniform cap, but they wear hardly anything else; they are shamefully naked." Even under such an able officer as General Falcón, the miserable troopers were unable to succeed in their mission.

If raiders were deterred by the American military escorts that accompanied a commission from Washington on a tour of the river lands, it was only briefly, for no sooner had the commission closed its hearings and returned to Congress than "an increase in the number of raids occurred," with the cattle thieves more furious than ever "in bitterness and determination." General Ord found a parallel in history for the conditions that so incensed border Americans. "It seems to me that the circumstances of the plunder of the stock ranches on the Rio Grande are almost identical with the piracies committed on our commerce at one time by the Algerines, who fled in safety to their own ports with their prizes. There the offenses were committed on the open sea; here they are committed with the same ease on the open plain. In both cases the pirates found a ready sale for their captures in the ports where their expeditions were fitted out, namely, Algiers and Tripoli, &c, for the Moors; Matamoros, Reynosa, Camargo, Mier and Guerrero for the Mexicans. And in both cases the pirates were rewarded by promotions

and honors." Sure of their power, the desert pirates hardly bothered to
hide. An Army officer going upstream as a steamboat passenger in 1876
said that his vessel passed right through a herd of stolen cattle "that the
Mexicans were driving across the river. Part of the cattle were on one
side of the river and part on the other, and the Mexicans were stripped,
and had the saddles off their horses, and were in the river driving the
cattle across."

When Americans on the border hoped for war against Mexico
to force an end to the outrages, they considered how the cure might be
worse than the ill; for the Mexican side was far more populous than
the Texan side, and, said a Texan witness before Congress, "We are not
so foolish but that we know that a war with Mexico, unless premedi-
tated and our Government fully prepared for it, would result in the
immediate occupation by Mexicans, for a time at least, of all that country bordering on the river, and would, consequently, involve the loss of
the larger part of our stock and the destruction of all our property."
Certainly the Army was not "fully prepared" for war on the border in
1876, when out of his Departmental troops General Ord could assign
only four hundred to the Rio Grande, of which only three hundred were
cavalry. It was all he had to work with, though in the previous year
he had asked for a regiment of cavalry "for service on the lower river,
and, if practicable, a light-draught iron clad" to be sent to Point Isabel
by the Navy "provided with a sufficient number of steam-launches to
patrol the river Rio Grande." He was sure that the vessels would be
even better than a regiment "to stop the marauding." Cruising launches
"could show continually where parties had recently crossed into American territory, or might be crossing, and as the telegraph" was "being
laid on the banks, cavalry stationed along the river (an exceedingly
crooked one) could get notice to the point and take the trail. . . ." The
river's own action made the task of patrolling hard and the pursuit
difficult, for in flood or freshet the river chopped away banks, and
destroyed roads and trails, and in the lower flats inundated great tracts
with mud, so that troops were forced to keep to the high ground. Further, as the river changed its course after storm, it also changed the
boundary, so that soldiers were not always certain where they might
act on their own ground.

On both sides of the river the "bad man" ruled. If he was a Mexican, he was, at his most impressive, a "general," like Cortina or Canales,
both of whom were busy at the congenial task of combining theft with
revolutionary gestures, and with fighting each other. If he was an

American, he was typically an unreconstructed Civil War veteran, or a displaced outcast of Eastern American cities who displayed to exaggeration the frontier trait of extreme individualism that once had mastered a continental wilderness, and now remained to terrorize it. There was much in his nature—even as it was misdirected—that was typical of the pioneer settler in the river wilderness. "Well," said a rancher who joined a volunteer band to invade Mexico illegally in hazardous pursuit of cattle thieves, "we loved living more than we loved life." And, he noted, the American bad man "got no mail." In such a detail there was a glimpse of how the bad man was divided from society and personal ties.

Every activity was affected by violence in an atmosphere where it so often prevailed. Elections in American river towns were signals for riot, destruction and even "little wars," as a peace officer said, and— revealing something of the river frontier character—he added that they gave him, a "hot-blooded youngster . . . a thrill that was hard to beat."

Political violence had an international setting. The 1870s saw many revolutionary movements organized by Mexicans conspiring in American river towns—Las Cruces, El Paso, Ysleta, Laredo, Brownsville. In 1874 the frontier was occupied with the revival of the old Rio Grande revolution of the north, that sought once again to create the Republic of the Sierra Madre. Twelve north Mexico governors signed a declaration of independence, and for a year the desert republic again struggled to be born, while the central government sent a few troops, and Canales and Cortina fought them as well as one another, and an American Army observer noted that in his opinion Mexico City would "undoubtedly be glad to get rid of most of the territory, which yields nothing but pronunciamentos and revolutions," and would "promptly accede to what it will be plain it cannot prevent."

But again, after its repeated apparitions throughout thirty years, the desert glimmer of a new nation faded away, and a year later, at Brownsville and Piedras Negras another pattern of revolution took form under Porfirio Díaz, which opened with the capture of Matamoros and flared all across Mexico to success at the capital. A merchant upriver at El Paso said, "Everything is quiet here," though he was certain that the Díaz revolution in Mexico would "kill business there and probably make it bad here. Our business in Paso del Norte, Mexico, will be levied for taxes in advance," and he knew these would have to be paid again at the regular taxation period. "Politics," he sighed, "furnishes the excuse for the revolutions in Mexico, but the real purpose of the revolution is robbery and the enrichment of new elements. . . ."

Meanwhile, the larger affairs of Mexico left the frontier north
to its own impulses. Early in 1877 Cortina threatened new raids over
the river into lower Texas, and to discourage him, the United States
gunboat *Rio Bravo* was moored to the riverbank opposite Matamoros.
She could not patrol upriver waters because she took too deep a draft
except in floodtime. The vessel knew a further disadvantage—her captain
was a drunkard, and his removal was advised by General Ord. But if the
Army could proceed against an indiscreet naval officer, it could do little
against the Mexican raids that continued unchecked along the river.
Lieutenant General Philip H. Sheridan, commanding the Military Division of the Missouri, that embraced the Southwest all the way to the
border, knew why: American troops were without authority to cross
the border and on Mexican territory overtake and punish the raiders.
"As I have heretofore had occasions to observe," he wrote to the Adjutant General in May, 1877, "the Rio Grande is a very long and difficult
frontier to protect." Under the circumstances, all he could recommend
was that Washington "take some steps to require the Mexican government to aid in the protection of that frontier."

Three weeks later a vigorous solution was at last ordered by
President Rutherford Hayes, at whose direction the Secretary of War
told General William T. Sherman, commanding the Army, "You will . . .
direct General Ord that in case the lawless incursions continue he will
be at liberty . . . when in pursuit of the marauders and when his troops
are either in sight of them or upon a fresh trail, to follow them across
the Rio Grande, and to overtake and punish them, as well as retake
stolen property taken from our citizens and found in their hands on the
Mexican side of the line." The President, "while anxious to avoid giving
offense to Mexico," was "nevertheless convinced that the invasion of our
territory by armed and organized bodies of thieves and robbers to prey
upon our citizens should not be longer endured."

The presidential order brought furious objection from Mexico.
Her foreign office declared—with some justice—that raids came as often
from Texas into Mexico as the other way round. About El Paso in the
early summer months of 1877 still another revolution against Mexico
had been organized by Lerdo de Tejada, whose troop commander,
Colonel Macharro, gathered an army in the great natural fortress of
the Hueco Tanks, where spring lakes were walled in by sheer castellated
rocks. In his forces were many Texans. Again it was difficult to know
who of the confused border population were the aggressors—Texans or
Mexicans. United States troops were sent from New Mexico by Colonel

Edward Hatch "with the intention of breaking up" the revolutionists who organized on American soil. But Macharro succeeded in taking the Mexican El Paso, though he held it only briefly. "One of the 7 day revolutions ended last night," wrote a young German storekeeper to his family in Europe in early June, 1877. He resisted the revolutionists throughout, even when they threatened to jail him for refusing to contribute a hundred dollars to their funds. His protection lay in the power and prestige of the United States. "I fastened the U. S. consul's shield above the door which was sufficient notice to them that they had to respect the American flag. . . ." His gesture gained power from the sudden tension that had developed between Mexico and the United States during that summer. Rio Grande Mexicans were at last face to face with the realities of their northern boundary. For nearly thirty years after the Treaty of Guadalupe Hidalgo, and forty after the Texan revolution, they continued to view the lands divided by the river as one grand unit—from the Sierra Madre to the Nueces, and from the Conchos to the Pecos—and to treat them as such. Old loyalties, old joys, old spirits of strife and brio made the official boundary seem insignificant. Blood, language, mores were stronger than law, nationality, and order.

But now there were strengthened powers at work to enforce the implications of the boundary concept. One was the policy of the Hayes administration. Another was the enlarged and resourceful operations of the Texas Rangers. And another was the effort—Mexico's first real one—by Porfirio Díaz to keep the peace on the border by armed force. It was General Ramon Treviño, governor of Nuevo León under Díaz, who "more than any other man below the Rio Grande," said a Texas rancher of the period, "was responsible for quelling the *bandidos.*" Still, through the summer, American cavalry columns crossed into Mexico after raiders, in the face of Mexican official protests.

In the border cities more was anticipated. "We have been expecting a declaration of war by the United States against Mexico all summer," said a citizen of El Paso in August. "If this came about it would be the best thing that could happen and of great importance to us." In October, he believed "war was at hand," and if it was, he had second thoughts about it. He had been following the news of the Russian campaign in the Caucasus against Turkish troops and their Circassian mountaineer allies, and if war came in Mexico, he wondered how professional American soldiers would prosper. "It is not at all improbable that the Americans will fare as the Russians are now doing. The more one despises one's enemy," he remarked with an eye open on an occasional

American attitude toward Latin neighbors, "the greater the danger of
being defeated. It is very difficult and dangerous to invade a country
that has no railroads, no roads, no bridges and very little water. On
the other hand it is ideal country for guerrilla warfare. The Mexican
has lots of endurance. He can take long trips and hard marches with
only corn and sugar for food. If the American soldier does not have his
rations of bacon, coffee and sugar for a couple of days he easily becomes
exhausted. . . ." But by mid-November the war sentiment was much
abated, and he saw it for what it was. "The demand for war in many
of the American newspapers and especially in Texas is caused by speculators who want to make fortunes furnishing war supplies. The freedom
of the press is abused and many of the papers pay no attention as to
whether they print the truth or not. . . ."

In the autumn of 1877 a disturbance arose in the El Paso region
that set in motion all the opposed powers of border loyalties. Eastward
of El Paso about a hundred and ten miles lay a group of saline lakes from
which Mexicans of both sides of the river had taken salt since 1863. They
took it free from what they saw as a resource of nature open to all, and
they hauled it in cartloads to the Rio Grande about ninety miles away
to sell it to the boundary settlements. The salt trade became the livelihood of several river villages. In 1866 and in 1873 attempts were made by
Texans to file legal claim to the lakes, but their claims were not valid,
and it was not until 1877 that other Texas interests acquired a legal
right to the saline deposits. The new owners at once established a fixed
fee to be paid by all who came to gather salt. The traders who had used
the deposits as a free public commodity raised bitter complaint, and in
the social climate of the time and place, the outcome inevitably was
civil violence. The Mexicans—greatly in the majority—had energetic
leaders, including their parish priests and an Italian settler with political
gifts. Opposed to these, the Texan interests, with a stubborn and reckless representative on the spot, held grimly to their legal right to the lakes.

Every classical element of a borderland dispute was present in
the situation. The affair was international. It grew up around an issue
of profitable property and enterprise. It posed Texans against Mexicans,
and since the Mexicans involved lived on both sides of the river, it
created a "racial" issue of Anglo-Saxons against Latins. It pulled in
politics and the Church, and when the dispute was laid before the courts
of law, these had no immediate means to enforce the peace. On one side
the Mexicans formed a mob and on the other the Americans were represented by a force of volunteer rangers. There were no Army troops in

garrison at El Paso, and when a detachment came from another post, its members were under orders to maintain order—but without taking sides in a local conflict. Threats of assassination were exchanged by the factions, and presently one came true when the Texan claimant killed the Italian politician who championed the Mexicans. These, inflamed by the advices of their pastor—who was later removed by the Church for his unworthy behavior—organized their revenge in the villages downriver from El Paso, and ended by killing the Texan leader and two of his supporters, and taking most of the volunteer ranger force as prisoners.

The American El Paso feared an attack, for the Mexicans seemed to expand their discontent to include hatred of all Americans, and additional troops were called to the scene from New Mexico. When they came, under the command of Colonel Edward A. Hatch, they succeeded in preventing further organized violence—but not individual violence on the part of other Americans who came to help in putting down the troubles. Rape, robbery and murder went unpunished on the American side, and across the river Mexican lawbreakers seeking immunity found it when Mexican officials in El Paso del Norte refused to bring them to justice. A United States Army commission arrived to make an investigation for President Hayes. The re-establishment of Fort Bliss at El Paso on the American bank resulted. For the rest, after nearly six months of uproar, bloodshed and suffering, the troubled residents of the El Paso valley once again knew comparative quiet, and the very cause of the Salt War was accepted, under superior force, by the people whom it had inflamed. Now when they went with their cottonwood carts over their ninety-mile desert trail to procure salt, they paid for every load after all.

Some of the Americans who had hurried to El Paso during the height of the troubles to fight Mexicans looked elsewhere for a release of their compelling energies, and found it in New Mexico, where the Lincoln County War was developing between rival cattle interests. It continued with such disruption of civil peace that the territorial authorities seemed unable to enforce order. In Washington General Sherman, echoing the remarks of a veteran of '46 about Texas, said, "We should have another war with Mexico to make her take back New Mexico," and General Lew Wallace, the Rio Grande veteran of Taylor's campaign, was sent to Santa Fe as territorial governor to restore the influence of law, which he managed to do only after Washington gave reluctant approval to his request for permission to use United States troops against the outlaws. In 1881 Texas Rangers were in the Big Bend to deal with bandit raiders from New Mexico, and as part of their severe duty made partial surveys of the huge, secret canyons of the river there.

Slowly, then, but inevitably, all such extensions of society in its order came to prevail over the vicious tedium of fear and destruction laid over the river frontier by the lawless. If it seemed inescapable that the successive frontiers of the American West had first to endure periods of terrorism imposed by irresponsible outcasts, it was true that at the same time, all the elements needed for organized social life made their courageous first bids in the new lands. Among the most effective of these were pioneer merchants, who came to set up their stores in the river cities of New Mexico and Texas, and by importation of goods began to link them to the great complex world of manufacture and production. Many such men were German immigrants who brought with them not only an understanding of business, but also a background of good education. One of them was a youngster who came to the towns of the North Pass in 1876. His experience was typical, and in letters sent to his relatives in Germany he shared it.

He left home to escape the militarism of the Bismarck empire. Its antithesis was the American West with its freedom. There he had relatives—earlier immigrants—for whom he was going to work. Crossing the sea he encountered new wonders—porpoises, whales, gamblers and luxury. In America as he travelled westward he met family friends and connections at New York, Chicago, St. Louis, Las Cruces. He found his journey by stagecoach from Kansas interesting but strenuous. The coaches were light and strong, with gray canvas sides and leather straps instead of iron or steel springs, which would break on the rough roads. The coach stopped three times a day for twenty minutes to let the passengers feed, and at other times, for five minutes to change mules. Otherwise the coach never stopped, day or night, but was pulled at a steady gallop, up hill or down, over good road or rocky. The passengers got no sleep. When the coach by a freak of the road was upset, which happened often, the driver did not seem to mind. Once arrived in New Mexico over the Santa Fe Trail, the passengers found the road better. It followed the river, and at Las Cruces made a junction with the highway to California, which ran through Silver City, Tucson, Yuma to San Diego, where travellers took a steamer for San Francisco. A coach ran daily from Santa Fe to El Paso, and an optimistic petition was being circulated to ask for the building of a railroad—"they are not asking much," observed the young German, "only the little stretch from St. Louis via San Antonio, Texas, [and] El Paso to San Francisco, California."

The young apprentice merchant reached El Paso—now a community on the American bank—a few days before Christmas. Ten minutes after his arrival he sat down to eat the last scrap of a sausage given to him by his mother. It had fed him all the way from Hamburg, where he cut the first piece. On Christmas Eve he was forlorn. The German tradition of Christmas meant nothing here. Mexicans observed the feast only as a religious event. For himself, he wrote, "there does not seem to be much to do about it." Looking at the valley cottonwoods he noted that their dead golden leaves were still on the branches. He hoped for letters, and asked that they be addressed to El Paso, New Mexico, instead of El Paso, Texas, in order to pass them over a shorter route to earlier delivery.

Looking about him at first he concluded that he was not likely to "make a fortune in a short time." The country was poor, the river carried very little water, and what flow there was seemed hardly enough to irrigate the farms and supply the urban needs of the eight thousand people who depended on it. There was a dam of brush and stones two miles above the town, but it was too porous to divert much of the flow, and he heard that when floods came the dam was swept away every time. He thought a new and stronger one should be built upstream. Of his fellow citizens he saw that many were "fugitives from the States." He missed his beer. Few of the Americans and Germans drank it because it was too scarce and too expensive. Whiskey and tequila were the usual beverages.

It was not long until he made friends, for he was young, energetic and personable, and through his uncle who employed him as a clerk he had a respectable introduction to society. He enthusiastically attended dances given at private houses. Beginning at nine o'clock in the evening, the dance was held in the patio whose swept earth floor was covered first with carpets and then with large tarpaulins. He was proficient in quadrilles and other dances known at home, and he learned a new one—a native dance called "la chubana." Supper was laid after midnight. Mexican gentlemen served the ladies first, standing behind their chairs until they were done. Then the men sat down to eat. The party lasted until eight o'clock in the morning. On other evenings he went calling, and stayed to play lotto and sixty-six. He thought he was doing very well at learning English, and already spoke some Spanish.

His prospects in the general mercantile business soon looked better to him. "It will not be long before I have made a fine place for myself," he wrote, even though he was not to receive any salary during his first six or twelve months. "I will try and make $100,000," he told his family grandly, "and then things will boom." The store carried nearly every class of merchandise, and he handled "everything from a corn plaster to a wig"—including dry goods, shoes, hardware, grain, feedstuffs, medicines, textiles from San Ildefonso and Chihuahua. Most women wore dresses of calico, and even in January he saw men in pants and shirts of unbleached muslin. Business had its extraordinary aspects. The prevailing interest rate was from ten to eighteen per cent annually. One day he saw a wagon train crossing out of Mexico on its way to San Antonio that carried one hundred and ninety thousand dollars' worth of coin and silver bars, and three thousand pounds of copper, some in coin, the rest in bars, for export to England. On another day he put his hand in the mail chute at the United States post office and found a snake. Wagon freighters taking goods from El Paso to Santa Fe were sometimes attacked by Indians, in spite of patrols from the recently established Army post at Fort Selden up the river. Now and then a band of freebooters swarmed into town from Mexico. One such consisted of a hundred Mexican cavalrymen. The young clerk had "never seen so many cut-throats together at one time." Even their officers knew their kind, for they confined them in billets except when accompanied by a sergeant. One night some of them broke out and stole a brass clock from a house thinking the brass was gold. When they discovered their mistake they threw the clock in bits "on the roof of the church." What odd creatures they were! "The complexion of these soldiers who come from the states of Sinaloa, Zacatecas and Durango (as well as that of some of our local inhabitants) is that of dry wood-ashes, neither black, nor brown, but grayish." The troop stayed for two days, and after damages, levies and pilferings were reckoned, would end up costing the store two hundred dollars.

The apprentice knew his family wanted to hear how he lived, and he wrote, "I am going to enumerate the members of my household, *1st* my old woman Doña Andrea who attends to my food and drink, *2nd* my porter who keeps the flies off me while I eat and is good for many things, a boy who helps in the store, 1 horse, 2 dogs, 1 rooster, 2 hens, 9 chicks and also countless bugs. . . ." He was being newly shaped by such a new life. Did he look any different? They would want to know at home. When a photographer "drifted into El Paso" he intended to have his picture taken for them, though he did not do so. But no matter how he looked, he felt different. He was becoming an American. They sent him some newspapers from Germany, full of "Your Excellencies" and "Your Highnesses," and the like. He could not help saying, "As this sort of address and cringing are not known here the whole thing makes a funny and ludicrous impression. . . ." When he was given a commission as a vice-commercial agent of the United States consulate at Paso del Norte, his family back home preened themselves and bridled proudly at his success in the new world, which had brought him an official title. To their congratulations he replied drily, "To tell the truth I do not consider being vice-commercial agent of very great importance. I look upon this honor very much like the title of an obscure book, 'Sad But True. . . .' "

His tradition was general along the Rio Grande wherever a business community was evolving out of primitive beginnings of trade in Mexican earth towns. The immigrant took his place with the American merchants and he seeded their society with memories of European styles and ways that added a degree of grace to the pursuit of gain. Such memories could have visible embodiment. At Albuquerque a successful German merchant built a Schloss on the marshy sweeps of the river bottom. It was made of adobe, wood and stone, with a central tower, and several wings, all painted white, set amidst a park of trees with fountains, arbors and meandering acequias. It contained a ballroom at one end of which was an organ with gold pipes. The castle's high narrow windows brought in dim daylight upon dark wooden panelling. There was materialized a propriety that echoed sentiment out of Schiller, and the courts of provincial Highnesses, and the dreams of Wagner; and it was all paid for by the freighting of goods over the trail from Missouri and down the river. The castle's owner watered his park with river water in summer, and in winter took his children on a sled over the river when it froze solid. He wore skates. The sled had wooden runners, and a board bed with a small chair fixed to it. He used to freight goods over the ice to the small stores and trading posts in the villages on the opposite bank below Albuquerque. A romantic castle in a river grove became possible only as civil peace began to prevail on the Rio Grande frontier.

Already the work of civilization had reached far into the wilderness of Indian savages, Mexicans and Anglo-Americans through the one institution that was able to make its benign energy felt in hacienda, pueblo and city. This was the Church in New Mexico, and in its effect upon the civil good of the whole river empire there rested an image of a man. He was the first bishop and archbishop of Santa Fe, Juan Bautista Lamy. When he came to the river in 1851 as vicar apostolic he found a sorry state of affairs. The nearest bishop had always been at Durango, fifteen hundred miles away. The Franciscans had been removed altogether. The handful of secular priests sent from Durango—there were only nine in New Mexico in 1851—were all too often dispirited and indifferent at their duties. The population lacked not only for spiritual help but also for civilizing aids in other matters. There were no schools, no hospitals, no agency to provide a sense of the future to the young in terms of their rightful growth of spirit and mind. The churches were almost all in ruins. An immense task faced the young bishop. He attacked it with a sort of grave passion, and for the rest of his life he was to see grow under his touch a revived society that found its connection with the great world.

He began his teaching at the simplest point of contact with his diocese—any point, across desert and mountain, which he could reach by going on foot or mounted on a burro or a horse. He travelled tens of thousands of miles in order to find his people and know their country. Finding and knowing these, he loved them, whether in a remote pueblo, a forgotten river town, or a mining camp. He took his knowledge of their needs to Baltimore, where the Council of American Bishops sat, and to Rome, where the Pope gave him encouragement and support, and to France, his homeland, where he enlisted scores of young priests to join him in the toil that waited in America's oldest frontier. His thoughts and deeds were woven in and out of the life of the river frontier like fine threads among coarse. He stood as a man of mind and spirit in a society of physical, often brutal, preoccupations. He represented knowledge and charity where all too often prevailed ignorance and self-interest. In opening the window of New Mexico upon the world, Archbishop Lamy expressed his own belief in freedom through enlightenment, without which her people would continue to live as victims instead of as masters of their environment. A willingness to advance the condition of man through social change was first expressed through him of all those who ever governed in the river kingdom. Such advance had been excluded by the Indians through ignorance, by the Spaniards through policy, and by the Mexicans through poverty. The Archbishop by his works seemed to anticipate the precept of a later teacher of his faith who said, "All our raw material of sanctity is in the now, just as it is."

So with the raw materials that he found he created the image of a life that had its design in the all-encompassing terms of his Christianity. His love of enlightenment came to show in the form of schools. He founded conventual academies in several cities all the way from Santa Fe to El Paso. He established a college in Santa Fe and led the citizens'

support for New Mexico's first system of public education. His love of
charity created the first hospital and orphanage in the Southwest, to
which he gave up his own house. Where he had come to find nine poor
and indifferent priests, in a few years he had over forty who strove to
match his exquisite example of probity and dedication. He built eighty-
five new churches, repaired the old ones and ended with almost a hundred and fifty altogether, including the cathedral of Santa Fe which
he raised in the likeness of the romanesque temples of his native
Auvergne. His good, clear sense of the uses of the world led him to do
all he could to bring the railroad to Santa Fe and to foster the establishment of industry. He encouraged the slowly learning population to
answer the call of new opportunities of work under new forms of commerce and to be provident with their honest gains.

If he loved growth for itself he revealed this faculty most simply
in his garden behind the cathedral of Santa Fe. There within meandering walls he grew wonderful fruit of many varieties and planted several
species of imported trees, hoping by his example to lead his fellow
citizens to find joy for themselves and others in bringing shade, flower
and fruit to a land so sparing of its own offerings of these.

Not the least of his personal contributions to his people was his
plain, tall presence among them. When he would walk about the plaza
of Santa Fe, or ride into an earthen town on a burro, or step off an
afternoon train at Albuquerque, or an early morning train at Las Cruces,
he seemed to lift up every heart by his encompassing smile, that so
wholly changed his gaunt face and deeply shadowed eyes. He was spare
and weathered like any other plainsman, the worst of whose endurances
and dangers he had learned for himself. There was no other way in which
he could have come to grips with the great duty of his life, and the land
that embraced it.

In 1875 when he was created archbishop the whole territory
celebrated the honor with him—the plain citizenry, the government, the
army, men of business and industry, the students in his colleges, and the
Indians in their pueblos. Upon his death in 1888 he was mourned both
as a humble missionary priest and as a creative citizen who by his
double example gave to the severe land that he loved its first secure
sense of the values that could not fail no matter how complex the world
of the future might become.

38.

The Last Wagons

And now, during the 1870s, the nation showed recovery from the effects of the Civil War. In this recovery it expressed the national genius for technology, by which, even in the unfinished West, ways of living would soon be changed as though in response to new laws of faith. The troubles of reconstruction were largely modified. The roving Indians were in process of recession. Law and order, if not entirely effective, were at least organized in frontier communities. The nation was getting on with its work. It would not be long until the Rio Grande line would begin to feel the energy of the machine in life, which would bring to the river societies their last and most pervasive change. Meanwhile, even with the old resources of animal power, there was a quickening of communication over the Rio Grande empire.

For all peoples the problem of overland travel had always been the same—the making of roads that followed the shortest, easiest way to a destination. So, from the time of the first, lonely walkers, had Indian trails been made, and so the primitive Spanish and Mexican roads, and the trade routes of the United States, and the paths of cattle drives that crossed New Mexico and Texas. Stagecoach travel continued along the river in New Mexico, and another route came from San Antonio, Texas, to cross the Rio Grande at Eagle Pass, on its way to Monterrey. In dry weather the road was good, and the trip took six days. Muddy ground prolonged the passage to seven or eight days. Seventy-two good mules were kept at post stations along the way. Six mules pulled the coach in United States territory, and eight in Mexico, where the going was harder. Moving along through a landscape dazzled with light and emptiness, the equipage maintained a steady, rapid pace, in spite of its great weight. The coach weighed three thousand pounds, its carrying capacity was four thousand pounds, and the harness of the team weighed twelve hundred pounds. The vehicle was built by Abbot, Downing and Company, of Concord, New Hampshire, and cost its Texan proprietor $1,250. It was commodious—eighteen passengers of average size could be seated "very comfortably." There were three seats inside, each with room for three people. Three more seats of the same capacity were on the roof, one close behind the driver, one in the middle, both facing forward, and one at the rear, facing backward. The coach's flat top was covered with heavy waterproof duck, and guarded on all sides by an iron railing two feet high. The body was built of the choicest hickory, and was slung on leather braces. All metalwork was of the best steel—axles, door handles, hinges, angle irons, bracings. The seats were upholstered in fine brown calfskin over horsehair and steel coil springs. At the rear was a capacious boot in which trunks and other heavy luggage were carried.

Indians presented a constant danger in the Texas part of the trip, but once at Eagle Pass, the passengers were sure of comforts; and over the river in Mexico, at the stage's overnight stops, a dance was sometimes given in honor of the travellers. The most respected people from the country around were invited. Mexican ladies came dressed in their finery, carrying French fans in little brocaded scabbards, and when the fans were opened out, they sparkled with brilliants and gold threads. At daytime stage stops in Mexico, native musicians came to serenade the passengers, for a few cents, with flutes "made of burnt clay and cane. . . ."

In the 'seventies trade over the Missouri trail to Santa Fe served chiefly to supply the New Mexican Rio Grande, while shipments for the interior of Mexico were for the most part drawn from Europe. After the two great river wars of the 'forties and 'sixties Mexican commerce turned away from the United States, until European nations held virtual monopolies. Texan freighters rarely heard English spoken in Mexico. Foreign business agents were German, French, or British, all of whom worked in the language of the country. Many cargoes from Europe were landed on the Texas coast to be freighted across Texas under bond. The wagons crossed the Rio Grande at the old ford of France Way, where the town of Guerrero now stood; or at Eagle Pass, Presidio del Norte, or El Paso. Texas freighters used huge blue wagons with beds twenty-four feet long and four and a half feet wide, with sides almost six feet high. They weighed four thousand pounds and carried a full load of seven thousand. On irregular roads they rocked steadily from side to side, until the weight was carried by two wheels at a time, which lightened the drag on their teams of mules. To control the heavy momentum of a wagon going downgrade the teamster hauled on a stout hickory brake that reached from his seat to the rear wheels. Mexican freighters used carts of

cottonwood balanced on two wheels seven feet high. Their axles were
of pecan or live-oak wood, and worn by rough travel, often took to
making an intolerable screech. To stop the noise by lubrication, the
Mexican carters fed the fat, succulent leaves of the prickly pear one at
a time into the wheel housing. Such a cart carried five thousand pounds
in its bed, that was fifteen feet long and six wide, with a shade cover
thatched out of straw. Its cargo was equally distributed so as to balance
on the single axle, and the whole was pulled by five or six span of oxen
lashed to their wooden yokes by rawhide straps.

At each end of the freighting trip, whether at Matamoros or in
the interior, the Texan teamsters were always astonished at the skill
and strength of the little Mexicans who loaded their cargo. The cargador,
who rarely weighed over a hundred and sixty pounds, conquered his
burdens with ingenious means. Across his brow he wore a loop of strap
that passed over his shoulders and down his back. Just between his hips
it held a muelle, or pad, six inches thick, ten wide and fourteen long.
It was a cushion upon which his load would rest as he bent forward, and
lodged against the top swell of his buttocks it moved up and down
with them in time with his steps. In that movement lay the secret of
his power. About to receive his load, he turned his back to it and began
to step up and down in place, like a soldier marking time. The several
men who were ready to put his load upon him also took up the rhythmic
step in time with his and, at a signal, gave the load on to his pad. He
held the load with a steel hook in each hand, and as soon as he felt it
secure, and without stopping his light, rapid steps he trotted off with it.
The cargador was able to carry a load of five hundred pounds or more,
so long as he received it in motion and never halted until he was relieved
of it. A Texan freighter who never ceased marvelling at the little brown
figures in white cotton, pumping their legs up and down under their
tremendous burdens, said he "never saw one of them use the least
exertion."

Taking European goods from the Gulf to upriver crossings,
Texan freighters sometimes found themselves halted on the American
shore by north Mexican revolutions on the other side. Then there was
nothing to do but wait until the little war was over. After such an experience, one wagon master entered Mexico, delivered his cargo, and returned
with three hundred and fifty thousand dollars in Mexican silver and
forty thousand pounds of copper, addressed to Europe. To protect his
train he engaged a Mexican officer with thirty men for a thousand
dollars to escort him to the border. For his round trip which took him

back to the seaports of the Gulf, the freighter earned $17,500. Young, hardy and adventurous, he found the freight-trail life not only profitable but enjoyable, for in camp every night, the freighting company, whenever possible, held a dance after supper. They "laid several wagon sheets on the ground inside the corral made by the surrounding wagons." On the tall wagon wheels they stuck lighted candles. If they were near a town, Mexican musicians came with stringed instruments to play, and otherwise, teamsters made music with what they might have—a violin, a banjo, bones, and hands to clap. The wagon sheets "on the level, hard ground furnished a splendid surface for the dancers," who enjoyed themselves "to the utmost." They danced all night, until the train corporal drove in the herd to be hitched at daybreak. Whenever possible they invited guests from ranches in the open country, and "after breakfast in camp, 'the best people' returned through the wilderness to their homes. . . .", and the freight train rolled and pitched slowly off on its way on the great flat lands through which the river ran. As they went, they encountered other long movements of men and animals in the open territory—herds of cattle and bands of horsemen who represented the largest and most characteristic industry of the nineteenth century on the Texas Rio Grande, and the last of the forms of life peculiar to the West.

39.

The Last Frontiersman

Ever since the eighteenth century the raising and tending of large herds of beef cattle had been practiced on the Texas river's wide, flat borderlands. All descended from animals brought to Mexico in the sixteenth century by Spaniards, there were several types of cattle on the river plains, of which the most distinctive had tremendously long horns doubled up and backward for half their length; heavy thin heads; tall legs, and narrow, powerful flanks. They were haired in various colors, with white patches. By the hundred thousand, wild cattle roved at large over the uninhabited land on both sides of the border, and constituted its prevailing form of wealth. As such they were always prizes for Indians, Mexicans and Americans who in an unbroken tradition of border violence raided the herds—preferably those already gathered into ownership by other men—and drove away thousands of animals to sell on the hoof, or to kill for their hides which were bailed and sold to traders, while the carcasses were left to carrion, and the bones to workers who gathered them up and hauled them for sale as fertilizer to Texas farming towns.

Even in the face of such hazard a few cattle traders drove herds east to New Orleans, north to Missouri, and west even as far as California, before the Civil War. But the trade was unorganized, and the principal markets, New Orleans and Mobile, were supplied by cattle steamers that sailed out of the Texas Gulf ports. The longhorn cattle they carried were called "coasters" or "sea lions." The coastwise cattle trade was limited by a monopoly held on Gulf shipping by the Morgan Line. "To anyone outside of the ship company," wrote an early cattle trader, "an enormous rate of freight was exacted, practically debarring the ordinary shipper." And when the Civil War took levies of man power from the cattle business, the trade was further constricted. In consequence of such conditions, "for a quarter of a century or more," the trader remarked, "the herds of Texas continued to increase much faster than the mature surplus was marketed. In fact, no market accessible existed sufficiently to consume this surplus, and of course the stock [became] less valuable in proportion as it became plentiful." But shortly after the Civil War the cattle trade was revived, and by the 'seventies, the herds of Texas owners were the largest in the United States. Of these, some of the largest belonged to great companies operating where the nation's range cattle industry had its origin—along the Rio Grande between the Pecos and Mexico Bay.

It was the brasada, the brush country, stretching from the Nueces to the Rio Grande. It was profuse in growths—but almost all were thorned. It was either swept with gray dust borne on blistering winds or beaten by deluges that hissed as they first struck the hot ground or raked by blizzards that came whistling out of the north. In its interlocking thickets that enclosed small clearings where grew curly mesquite grass, cattle could graze by thousands and hardly be seen by horsemen who sought them. There cicadas sang of the heat, and sharp-haired peccaries rooted among the thorns, and blue quail ran amidst the wiry shadows, and rattlesnakes sought the cool and sometimes were drummed to death by wild turkey gobblers at whose destroying wings they struck and struck with no effect on nerveless quill and feather. It was a land of hard secrets, the best kept of which was the location of water. Its few rivers ran in abruptly cut trenches walled with pink or yellow or slate blue limestone, and could not be seen except from their very brinks. In every direction the wilderness looked the same. There were no distant mountains to be seen. The land swelled away toward the white sky in slow rolls and shimmered in the heat that blended the ashen color of the ground with the olive greens of the brush until across the distance there seemed to hang a veil of dusty lilac.

It was astonishing how much human activity there was in a land so hostile to man's needs. It was the scene of habitual Indian travels, and of the military campaigns of the Mexicans and Texans in their wars, and of the United States Army in its Rio Grande movements, and of travelling traders, missioners and criminals. In its thickets there was even an occasional small ranch, locked in isolation by sun, distance, and the poverty of its occupants, who possessed even few wishes. And it became the scene of organized work in the cattle business. Animals born and grown there were taken in herds to the milder prairies above the Nueces, and across the rest of Texas and Oklahoma to beef markets in the north. ". . . The cow boys, as the common laborers are termed," said a cattleman who saw the industry develop, "go in squads of four or five scouting over the entire range, camping wherever night overtakes them, catching with the lasso upon the prairies every young animal found whose mother bears their employer's brand." It was "legal and a universal practice to capture any unmarked and unbranded animal upon the range and mark and brand the same in their employer's brand, no matter to whom the animal may really belong, so be it is over one year old and unbranded. . . ."

The cow boy was the last of the clearly original types of Western American to draw his general tradition and character from the kind of land he worked in, and the kind of work he did. His forerunners were the trapper of the mountains and the trader of the plains. Of the three, he left the fullest legacy of romance and to see him as he first was, it would be necessary in a later century to clear a way back to him through a dense folk literature of the printed page, the moving picture film and the radio that in using all his symbols would almost never touch the reality that supported them.

His work was monotonous in hardship and loneliness, and occasionally it was shot through with excitement that rose from danger. The
country where he worked was in its dimensions and character his enemy;
and yet it was also in an intimate way almost a completion of his nature,
that revelled in vast vacant privacies, and fixed its vision on the distance
as though to avoid any social responsibility. He had for his most constant
companion not a man or a woman, but an animal—his horse, on whom
his work and his convenience and even at times his life depended. His
duties took him endlessly riding over range country, where he sought for
cattle to capture, calves or yearlings to brand, herds to drive to water,
individual cows or bulls of a proper age or condition to cut out of a
herd for segregation into another group. Such a group would then be
driven to another location—a different pasture or a market.

In dealing with cows through the consent of his horse, the cow boy
needed to know much of the nature of both animals. Through experience he learned to anticipate the behavior of cattle, and to judge the
effect upon them of every stimulus. He saw that the laws that governed
them were the laws of the crowd; and he developed extraordinary skill
in handling great crowds of cattle at a time. His horse, broken to riding,
and subject to his will, he had to know as an individual creature, and
dominate relentlessly its nature by turns sensitive, stubborn and gentle.
Living with these two animal natures, the cow boy seemed to acquire in
his own certain of their traits, almost as though to be effective at living
and working with them, he must open his own animal nature to theirs
and through sympathy resemble them. If he could be as simple as a cow,
he could also be as stubborn; as fearless as a wild mustang, and as suspicious of the unfamiliar; as incurious as an individual bull, and as wild
to run with a crowd when attracted. Even in his physical type, the cow
boy might tend to resemble his animal companions—a certain flare of
nostril and whiteness of eyelash could recall the thoughtless face of a
calf; a leanness of leg and arm was a reminder of a horse's fine-boned
supports and further suggested the physique best adapted to, and developed for, the horseman's job—the hard, sinewy body, light of weight
but powerful, tall for high vision over the animal herd, long-legged
for gripping the mount around its breathing barrel. His state of body
and nerve had to be ready to fight, for his job sometimes included battle,
when Indians or organized cattle and horse thieves came down upon
his herd. Then like any soldier he had to shoot to kill, under the sanction
of his duty. For his labors, he was paid in the 1870s from fifteen to twenty

dollars a month in gold or silver. He saw himself at his task, and his self-image survived in his anonymous folk literature:

> All day long on the prairie I ride,
> Not even a dog to trot by my side:
> My fire I kindle with chips gathered round,
> My coffee I boil without being ground.

In any group of nineteenth century cow boys, more were bearded than clean-shaven. Their costumes were much alike, though with individual variations. But all their garments were "coarse and substantial, few in number and often of the gaudy pattern." The cow boy wore a wide-brimmed hat with its crown dented into a pyramid or flattened. If the brim in front was sometimes turned up off his face, it could be turned down to protect him from the pressing light of the sky under which he spent all day. Around his neck he wore a bandana of tough silk. It served many purposes. Tied over his face it filtered dust before his breath. It served to blindfold a calf or tie its legs. It was a towel, a napkin, a bandage, a handkerchief, or simply an ornament. His shirt was of stout cotton flannel, in a bright color or loud design of checks or stripes or plaids. Over it he sometimes wore a cloth or leather vest but rarely a jacket. His trousers were either of heavy denim, dyed dark blue, sewn with coarse yellow thread, and reinforced at points of great wear with copper rivets; or were of odd colors and materials, mostly dark, that could stand tough use. They fitted tightly. The trouser legs were stuffed into boots that reached almost to the knee. At work, the cow boy often wore leggings of thick cowhide. They were made after the pattern of Indian leggings—two long tubes, with wide flaps at each side cut into fringes or studded with silver disks, that reached from ankle to groin, and were tied to a belt as though to the string of a breechclout. Their purpose was to shield him against thorns in the brush he rode through, and the violent rub of haired animal hides, and the burn of rope when he pulled it against his leg as he turned his horse to control a lasso'd creature. On his boots he wore large spurs, of silver or iron. He wore gloves to work in, and around his tight hips he wore a cartridge belt from which depended his pistol—most often a Colt's single-action, 45 caliber revolver called the Peacemaker. He had no change of clothing. He went unwashed and unbathed unless he camped by a stream or a pond. "I wash," he said in his multiple anonymity,

I wash in a pool and wipe on a sack;
I carry my wardrobe all on my back. . . .

Like the object of his work and its chief instrument—the cow and the horse—his Texas saddle, in its essential form, came from Spain. Its high pommel and cantle, heavy stirrups and great weight suggested the squarish, chairlike saddle of the jousting knight, though its design was modified by Mexican saddlers until all contours were rounded and smoothed, and the pommel, of silver or other metal, was developed to serve as a cleat about which to secure the lariat whose other end was noosed about a captive cow or horse. When not in use the lariat was coiled and tied to the saddle. There was little other baggage on the saddle, except now and then a leather scabbard containing a short rifle. If two cow boys travelled together they carried their camp equipment and bedrolls on a pack animal. Otherwise, when a large group worked daily out of a central camp, their equipment was carried in the camp wagon to which they returned during the day for meals and at night for fire, food and companionship.

The wagon, pulled by four horses and driven by the camp cook, was a roving headquarters for the grazing party. Its form was invented by Charles Goodnight in the 1850s, who adapted an Army vehicle to the needs of the cow camp. Rolling in movement, it had a compact look, with its sheets over bows, that concealed the contents, which consisted of bedrolls for the workers and at its free end a high, square chest standing upright. Parked, free of it horses, and with its tongue propped level to serve as a rack for harness, and with its sheets extended and supported by poles to make a generous pavilion of shade to one side, the wagon seemed to expand into several times its own size. It was amazing how much it carried, and how much immediate ground its unpacked equipment could cover. The chest at the rear was faced with a wooden lid which when opened downward became a worktable supported by a central leg. Then were revealed in the chest many fitted drawers and hatches in which the cook kept every necessity for cooking and every oddment, including medicines. Behind it in the wagon bed, along with the bedrolls, he carried his heavy pots and skillets and tin dishes. Beneath the wagon frame hung buckets and to its sides were lashed water barrels.

The cooking fire, which at night served also to give its only light to the camp gathering, was made a few feet from the wagon and its profuse scatter of equipment. There the cook prepared his meals, always the same. If brush or wood were scarce, he made his fire of dried animal droppings, like the Spanish soldiers who centuries before had found these the only useful product of fabled Quivira. If he had no matches he could start his fire by pouring gunpowder into his pistol, wadding it loosely, and firing it with its muzzle close to a scrap of cloth or other dry kindling. He prepared a great pot of coffee boiled from whole beans. A cow boy drank a quart or more every day. Of such coffee it was said that "you would hesitate, if judging from appearance, whether to call it coffee or ink." It was drunk without cream or sugar. There was a kettle full of stew in which using his pocketknife—his only table service—the cow boy probed for a lump of meat. With thick biscuit or cornbread he soaked up the gravy and like an Indian ate from his fingers. There were no green vegetables to be had. A pot of kidney beans finished the meal. The cow boys squatted near one another, or stood idling by the wagon, and ate in silence and with speed. A meal was not an occasion of social interest. It was an act of need, disposed of without grace or amenity. Inseparable from it were the taste and smell of dust and cow-hair and horse sweat and leather—sensory attributes of everything in the cow boy's working life.

> For want of an oven I cook bread in a pot,
> And sleep on the ground for want of a cot.

But before the bedrolls were opened up from their heavy canvas covers, and the work party went to sleep, there was a little while for talk and other diversion. Such a miniature society created its own theatre. There was always someone who would be moved to perform, while the rest gazed at the intimate, never-failing marvel of how one whom they knew—a man just like them—became before their very eyes somebody else. The campfire put rosy light over the near faces of the gathered men and their cluttered possessions, and threw their shadows like spokes out on the flat ground until the immense darkness absorbed all. At the very center of light a fellow rose. He had a joke to tell. He acted it out. It may have been well known to all, but they listened in fixity. It was likely to be an obscene jape. The cow boy, observed a cattleman of the 'seventies, "relishes . . . a corrupt tale, wherein abounds much vulgarity and animal propensity." His delight was a practical joke on one of his fellows. The joke was good if it made a fool of someone. It was better if it mocked the victim's personal peculiarity, and it was even better if it played upon "animal propensity"—for the sake of symbolic relief of the enforced continence under which the work party lived on the range. There were other stories to hear—many dealt with experiences

in the Civil War, to which the early cow boys were still close in time.
There were wrestling and other trials of strength to perform. There were
songs to sing, some of whose texts were lewd parodies of sentimental
ballads. All knew the songs of the cattle trail, and could sing them
together. If in one of his cubbyholes the cook carried a violin for its
owner, there would be fiddle music of an astonishing legerity that yet
managed to seem tuneless, while a cow boy danced a clog in firelighted
dust, and the rest clapped hands. Often a mournful piety stirred in
someone, and when he began to sing a hymn, others joined him, and
like a sigh of innocence, their united voices rose over their lonely fire
where they camped, a little knot of men with every potentiality, to one
or another degree, for every human attribute. The bedrolls came out of
the wagon and were spread. Nobody had a book to read, and in any case,
the firelight was dying and would soon be down to coals.

> My ceiling's the sky, my floor is the grass,
> My music's the lowing of herds as they pass;
> My books are the brooks, my sermons the stones,
> My parson a wolf on his pulpit of bones. . . .

As his artless song implied, the cow boy belonged to the type of
man who was not, actually, domesticated. He chose freedom in the wilds
over responsibilities of hearth and home. He thought more about work
than he did of a family. He made love on almost a seasonal schedule,
as though in rut. He visited a prostitute, or took a sweetheart, only to
leave her, with sighs about how he must go roaming, as though all would
understand his natural state. He departed for work or went off to fight
wherever he would find other men like himself. He preferred the society
of men to that of women: for only with men could he live a daily life
that was made up of danger, and hard exposure, and primitive manners.
These did not seem like disadvantages to him, for he liked them for themselves, and, further, they brought into his life excitement, freedom and
wilderness, all of which he sought.

If he saw himself as a simple creature, and if tradition so accepted
him, both were wrong. His temperament and character were full of
tempestuous contradictions and stresses. The life he chose resembled the
Indian's more than any other, but it lacked the sustaining spiritual
power of the Indian's nature-mythology, and so it could not really hold
for him the unquestioned dignity of a system that tried to explain—in
whatever error—the whole of human life. He was close to the frontiersman many of whose ways he repeated, but he was neither innovator,

builder nor explorer. His love of hardness and primitive conditions could be turned either to serve his comrades in unbreakable loyalty, or to lead him, as it did in individual cases, to a career as gunman or cattle thief. His longing for love was so great that he felt an exaggerated chivalry for womankind, but in his worship he made women unreal; and yet through his song literature he lamented, ". . . between me and love lies a gulf very wide." He sanctioned his state by romanticizing it in ballad and story; but he refuted it symbolically by his periodic violent outbreaks of gunplay, drunkenness and venery. And with all his hardness, he gave in to a soft core of sentiment whose objects were the animals he worked with, and the comrades who worked with him.

"I and they were but creatures of circumstance," said a cow boy of his fellows in his domesticated old age, "—the circumstances of an unfenced world." From their unfencedness came their main characteristics. Solitude was put upon them by their chosen environment, which thus modified their character. "Adhesiveness," in the jargon of the nineteenth-century parlor science, was a human trait. The nearest living being to whom the cow boy could turn with affection was his horse. It was his daylong companion and helper. It obeyed his orders and made him master of distance and took him in and out of danger. Responding to his signals, it seemed to him to possess more than animal intelligence. His horse, a masterpiece of anthropomorphism, joined him in a partnerhip, and was paid every honor due to such a position. "My horse," continued the retired cow boy, "my horse was something alive, something intelligent and friendly and true. He was sensitive, and for him I had a profound feeling. I sometimes think back on . . . remarkable horses I owned in much the same way that I think back on certain friends that have left me. . . . I went hungry sometimes, but if there was any possible way of getting food for my horse or if there was a place to stake him, even though I had to walk back a mile after putting him to graze"—and cow boys hated to walk—"I never let him go hungry. Many a time I have divided the water in a canteen with a horse." If it was expedient to take care of his horse in order to assure his own mobility and safety, and if it was ordinary human kindness to care for a dumb creature, there was yet more than such promptings in the cow boy's devotion to his mount, as many a song and story attested. The professional cow boy rarely had a cultivated mind; and in his incurious thought he was lowered and his horse was elevated until they drew together in common identity. It was a process typical of a juvenile stage of character, and it may have suggested why the cow boy and his legend should appeal forever after as a figure of play to little boys. In much the same sort of emotion the cow boy felt a mournful fondness for the animals he herded—the little "dogies" to whom he sang on the trail to keep them quiet, and to whom he attributed something of himself as they were objects of his vigilance and labor, day and night. In its innocence and pathos his system of projected sentimentality for his animals suggested that only by making of them more than they were could he have survived his lonely and arduous duty with them. One of his songs said of the cow boy that "his education is but to endure. . . ."

Another song celebrated the life of cow boys together in their wandering yet coherent community. "The boys were like brothers," they sang of themselves, "their friendship was great. . . ." Alike in their extreme individualism, their self-reliance, their choice of a life wild, free and rude, the companions of the cow camp gave to one another an extreme loyalty. It seemed like a tribute to the hard skills they had to master to do their jobs. A man who proved himself able at it deserved membership in a freemasonry unlike any other. Its physical tasks caused a high value to come upon the life of action, in which there was no place for the values of mind and spirit. These were relegated to the world of women; and in the towns and cities that later completed the settling of the last frontier West, for the better part of a century it would be the women's organizations that would try to rescue the fine arts, education, religion, and social amenity from being held as simply irrelevant to civilized life—an attitude even more withering to mankind's highest expressions than one of mere contempt. For its purpose in its time, the brotherhood of the cow camp was all that was needed to make an effective society. Diverse like all individuals, and sprung from various backgrounds and kinds of experience, the cow boys taken together seemed to merge into a type more readily than most workers in a common job. Their environment directly created the terms of their work, and their work in its uncomplicated terms created their attitudes and points of view. And if they were like one another in their principal traits, it was because so many of them chose their calling for the same general reason.

This—it was attested to again and again in the cow boy's anonymous ballad literature—this was flight from one kind of life to another. Many cow boys left home, "each," said a ballad,

"Each with a hidden secret well smothered in his breast,
Which brought us out to Mexico, way out here in the West."

In this lay a suggestion of doom, a rude Byronism that was echoed in other songs by allusions to unhappiness, guilt, escape. Some were driven to the new society of the cow range by a faithless girl at home, or a dissolute life, or a criminal past; others by inability to become reconciled to their home societies following the Civil War, or by bitterness in family life, or even by a cruel stepmother. Romantic conventions of behavior in the nineteenth century could move the cow boy, who punished those who had betrayed him. "I'll go," he threatened,

> ". . . to the Rio Grande,
> And get me a job with a cow boy band."

He did not mean a band of musicians, for not until the next century would the cow boy's public identity be chiefly that of an entertainer who in a commercial adaptation of the cow boy costume would spend more time with a microphone than with either horse or cow. No, with companions on the cattle range, the cow boy, deaf to dissuasion by loved ones who had proved faithless, promised to go

> ". . . where the bullets fly,
> And follow the cow trail till I die."

Unable for whatever reason to accept the bindings of conventional society, within the one he sought and helped to make on the last frontier, he was capable of sure dependability in any cause for the common good of his comrades, whom he did not judge, even if sometimes a propensity to go wrong should overtake them in the very land where they had thought to escape their doom. Who knew when a man might encounter the moral frailty of one of his friends of the brushlands?

> As I walked out in the streets of Laredo,
> As I walked out in Laredo one day,
> I spied a dear cow boy wrapped up in white linen,
> Wrapped up in white linen as cold as the clay.

It was a dirge for a young man who in his dying words revealed a longing for a gentler land than the dusty empire of his work, and confessed his errors. "Oh," he said,

> "Oh, beat the drum slowly and play the fife lowly,
> Play the dead march as you carry me along;
> Take me to the green valley, there lay the sod o'er me,
> For I'm a young cow boy and I know I've done wrong."

Unashamed of their grief that sprang from their close living, his bearers saw themselves in him, and if he had sinned, they could not condemn him.

> We beat the drum slowly and played the fife lowly,
> And bitterly wept as we bore him along;
> For we all loved our comrade, so brave, young and handsome,
> We all loved our comrade although he'd done wrong.

For here was a clan feeling, a solidarity, with a realistic view of character and its capacity for error. Idealizing one another in the all-male society of their work and play, the cow boys remained loyal above, or even because of, the weaknesses they shared and assuaged with violence. In conclusion, the dirge moved from the individual to the group.

> Then beat your drum lowly and play your fife slowly,
> Beat the Dead March as you carry me along;
> We all love our cow boys so young and so handsome,
> We all love our cow boys although they've done wrong.

In another valedictory the cow boy spirit, after reciting the perils of "some bad company" which could only lead to being "doomed for hell," ended in the presence of the hangman with an admonition to morality.

> It's now I'm on the scaffold,
> My moments are not long;
> You may forget the singer
> But don't forget the song.

In the cow boy's lonely character there were extremes of feeling and behavior. If in his work there seemed to be a discipline of dedicated steadfastness, a purity of vocation, then when he went to town, he threw himself into indulgence. Perhaps the town was a reminder of the coherent social life he had fled at home, and perhaps it was now a guilty joy to outrage it by his behavior. Certainly the town was the very opposite of the desolate open range from which even the cow boy needed periodic change.

His best chance for it came when men of the range party were told off to drive a herd of cattle to the marketing and shipping towns. The main trails along which he drove went north from the Texan Rio Grande to Kansas, and another—the Goodnight-Loving Trail—led westward to New Mexico and California. It passed the Pecos River at Horsehead Crossing about a hundred miles above the Rio Grande, and presently divided into two forks. One pointed north to Colorado. The other crossed the Rio Grande at Las Cruces and followed the old road to San Diego.

The cattle made trails that showed many narrow grooves side by side—marks of the strict formation in which the animals in their thousands were driven for upwards of a thousand miles. A cow boy said that trail life was "wonderfully pleasant"—this in spite of continuing hazards. There still might be trouble with Indians. All the cattle were wild, and were easily stampeded by attacks, or by thunderstorms, or by hail. If the weather was wet, rivers rose, and to take thousands of cattle across swollen waters was at best a tedious job, and often a perilous one. Against the drovers on the move there pressed at one period a whole organized enterprise of thievery. Outlaws captured drovers, tortured them, sometimes killed them, and stole their herds. When one drover was captured, he tried to talk his way out of his trouble, but the bandits were immovable and a reporter of the incident said bitterly that "it was like preaching morality to an alligator."

But in swelling volume the animal trains passed through to their destinations, and the cow boys were happy on the trail. They played tricks on one another, and shot game on the prairies, and after supper sang, told stories, danced to a fiddle, lay back to look at the stars and speculate about them, and listened for the sounds of the herd settling down for the night. "I do not know anything more wholesome and satisfying," mused a cow boy long after his trail days, "than seeing cattle come in on their bed ground at night so full and contented that they grunt when they lie down." It was like a communion of creature comforts in which man and animal could meet. Three shifts of night guards were posted over the herds. A sleepy cow boy rubbed tobacco juice in his eyes to keep awake. Morning must come, and another day to be spent at the pace of cattle walking with odd delicacy in their narrow grooved trails, and after enough such days, the shipping town would take form like a few scattered gray boxes on the severe horizon, and the cow boy would feel his various hungers begin to stir.

It was in town that he got into most of his trouble. Every facility was there to help him do it. As a cattle shipper observed, in frontier towns "there are always to be found a number of bad characters, both male and female; of the very worst class in the universe, such as have fallen below the level of the lowest type of brute creation." These pandered to the cow boy's howling appetite for dissipation.

Sometimes he rode into town and without cleaning himself or

changing his clothes but just as he had dismounted in hat, damp shirt,
earth-caked trousers, and boots and spurs, he strode into a dance house,
seized a "calico queen" or a "painted cat," as he called the dancing
women, and with Indian yells and a wild eye went pounding about the
dance floor under a grinding necessity to prove in public, most of all
to himself, that he was at last having a good time. The music to which
he danced was "wretched . . . ground out of dilapidated instruments,
by beings fully as degraded as the most vile. Few more wild, reckless
scenes of abandoned debauchery can be seen on the civilized earth,"
remarked the cattle shipper, "than a dance house in full blast in one
of the many frontier towns. To say they dance wildly or in an abandoned
manner is putting it mild. . . ."

And sometimes the cow boy, at large in town with his accumulated pay, went first to improve his looks. In a barbershop he had a bath,
and then had his three to six months' growth of hair trimmed, and his
full beard cut down, shaped and dyed black. In a clothing store he
bought completely new clothes, from hat to boots, and then, strapping
on his pistol, he was ready to impose himself like shock upon the town.
Gambling rooms, saloons, a theatre, a row of prostitutes' quarters like
cattle stalls, dance houses—from one to the next the cow boy could make
his explosive way, to be catered to by "men who live a soulless, aimless
life," and women who had "fallen low, alas! how low . . . miserable
beings." Among the conventions of the cow boy's town manners was
free use of his firearm, whether he might harm anyone or not. The
pathos of folly long done and half forgotten would make his murderous
antics seem unreal to later view. But they were real enough in the frontier towns of the 1870s. "It is idle," sighed the cattle shipper in that
decade, "it is idle to deny the fact that the wild, reckless conduct of the
cow boys while drunk . . . have brought the *personnel* of the Texan
cattle trade into great disrepute, and filled many graves with victims,
bad men and good men. . . . But by far the larger portion of those
killed are of that class that can be spared without detriment to the good
morals and respectability of humanity. . . ." And "after a few days of
frolic and debauchery, the cow boy is ready, in company with his comrades, to start back to Texas, often not having one dollar left of his
summer's wages." All he had was a memory that found its way into one
of his songs, about "The way we drank and gambled and threw the
girls around. . . ."

The cow boy triumphed at a lonely work in a beautiful and
dangerous land. Those of his qualities that did the job were the good

ones—courage, strength, devotion to duty. His worse traits, exercised for relief, were not judged in relation to his task. All aspects of his complex nature entered into his romance. He saw himself for his own achievement, and like the earliest individuals of the frontier, he consciously created his character and his tradition, and whether his emotion was honest or not, it was so energetic that by it he made his nation see him in his own terms. In him, the last American to live a life of wild freedom, his domesticated compatriots saw the end of their historical beginnings, and paid him nostalgic tribute in all their popular arts. Soon, like them, he would lose his nomadic, free and rough form of life before the westward sweep of machine technics by which Americans made their lives physically more easy—and socially less independent and self-reliant. In the very exercise of their genius for convenience in living, the Americans sacrificed to the social and commercial patterns of mass technics some part of the personal liberty in whose name the nation had been founded. The cow boy in his choice of solitude held on to his whole liberty as long as he could. But domestication of his West by machine technics began in the 1860s and, once started, went fast.

For in response to such technics, the cattle industry grew with suddenness, and then became stabilized. The first of these was the westward advance of the railroads with which the northbound cattle drives could make a junction. It was not easy to arrange for the earliest rail transport of western cattle. A young Illinois cattle shipper who was the first to establish a livestock market in Kansas was astonished to have his new idea rejected by two railroad presidents and the leading businessmen of several Kansas towns to whom he went in turn. Finally the Hannibal & St. Joe Railroad gave the young shipper a contract "at very satisfactory rates of freight from the Missouri River to Quincy, thence to Chicago." He selected Abilene, Kansas, as the site for his stockyards, and in 1867, the first cattle were driven there from Texas. During the next four years 1,460,000 head of cattle were brought to Abilene. Other trails and shipping centers were soon established, and it was estimated that during a period of twenty-eight years nearly ten million cattle worth almost a hundred million dollars were moved from the Texas ranges to market. In the process of developing so great a business, the whole practice of cattle raising became formalized through changes that sought greater efficiency.

One of these used a technical machine product that soon conquered the open range where wild cattle once drifted according to weather. It was barbed wire, first used in 1875 to fence pastures in which

with fewer and less skillful cow boys the herds could be restricted and
more easily managed. When land was enclosed, ranch dwellings were
needed. Permanent headquarters buildings followed. Cattle no longer
were driven to rivers but found their water in earth tanks supplied by
dug wells, with still another machine product to keep it flowing—the
metal windmill. The main trunk lines of the railroads ran east to west
across the continent; but soon feeder lines were built—sometimes following the flat terrain of the old trails—and machine transportation reached
nearer and nearer to the great ranches of the border where the whole
cattle industry had had its beginnings. The Missouri, Kansas and Texas
Railroad was the great Texas cattle line. It tapped the Rio Grande
brush country ranges. The Atchison, Topeka and Santa Fe main line
crossed New Mexico and a branch line ran from Belen on the Rio
Grande all the way down the valley to El Paso. The Texas and Pacific
reached eastward from San Diego to El Paso in 1877, and bridges now
came back to the Rio Grande to stay. The whole river empire was soon
tied to the rest of the nation by rails. When packing houses were established at Kansas City, Fort Worth and other Southwestern cities, the
final pattern of the organized beef cattle industry was realized. In it
there was little room for the figure, the temperament, of the original
cow boy, with his individual lordship over great unimpeded distances
and his need of freedom as he defined it. His cow camp literature
recorded yet another stage—the last—of his history. "The cow boy has
left the country," he could sing, "and the campfire has gone out. . . ."

On barbed wire fences, like symbols of the new order of affairs
over the controlled range lands, dead, skinned coyotes were impaled in
a frieze—twenty or thirty of them at a time. They were stretched in midair with a lean, racing look of unearthly nimbleness, running nowhere;
and their skulled teeth had the smile of their own ghosts, wits of the
plains. In the dried varnish of their own amber serum they glistened
under the sun. The day of unrestrained predators was over.

40.

Treasure

Illusion was the very nourishment of treasure seekers. Watching westward in 1858 for their first sight of mountains a party of prospectors entering Colorado saw on the horizon what one of the company said looked "like a thunder cloud." What he saw were the Spanish Peaks in the Sangre de Cristo range. His party turned north and followed the base of the mountains to the camps of Pike's Peak and Cherry Creek, where first discoveries of gold were followed by disappointment. Early stories in guidebooks and newspapers, all too often written by men who had never been west, told how gold was lying "on the plains, in the mountains, and by the streams, only waiting to be gathered up." The realities were different. Mineral treasure was present, but it had to be found in its secret lodgments and taken out by hard work. Many immigrants turned away homeward in disgust, making a wish in a popular jingle to

> "Hang Byers and D. C. Oakes
> For starting this damned Pike's Peak hoax,"

and some drifted southward to New Mexico, where one couple, "with wagon and mess," settled at Taos when the wife was offered a position teaching school. But others persisted, and the Colorado gold fields soon flourished. For about its first decade Colorado mining was located in the great central ranges of the Rockies, far removed from the Rio Grande and the San Juan Mountains of its source.

For though the New York *Herald* declared in 1857 that in "the Sierra San Juan, where, if we recollect rightly, both Pike and Frémont lost their way, gold, silver, cinnabar and precious stones are found in immense quantities," there was no mining of any significance in the Rio Grande basin of Colorado until after the Civil War. Settlement was limited to a few farming communities in the grand San Luis Valley,

whose mild slopes and level floor recalled its origin as a huge lake.
Through it the river ran a gentle course along which a handful of
Mexican families established themselves in 1853 distant from the most
northerly New Mexican settlements by only a few days' march. Using
the river to irrigate their little fields, and the wide grassy valley to graze
their small herds, they recreated the scene of slow water, bounteous
cottonwood tree and earthen house that was so familiar in the river's
New Mexican passage. They looked no farther for treasures of the
earth.

In 1860, as though re-enacting in miniature an earlier pattern
of conquest, a small party of Americans passed through the Mexican
settlements of the San Luis Valley and followed the Rio Grande out
of sight into the mountains of the source. They were looking for gold
in the San Juan. Their search took them through summer and autumn,
until they were caught in the snows of winter. In the following spring
they were joined by other prospectors and all spent. the next summer
in the San Juan Mountains, but without finding gold. Before another
winter could trap them they returned eastward to Fort Garland, where
they heard that the Civil War had broken out; and the leader of the
prospectors hurried to Virginia to enlist.

At the end of the decade other attempts were made to find the
riches of the San Juan, and scattered strikes led to the establishment
of mines on the western slope of the continental divide. By 1870 there
was enough traffic along the headwaters of the Rio Grande to call alive
the town of Del Norte as a supply point, at the gateway of the river
between the San Luis Valley and the mountains. In the same year gold
was found at Wightman's Gulch and other sites in the Del Norte region,
the most thriving of which was Summitville to the southwest. The population of the district grew to six hundred. Stamp mills were set up at
the largest camps. During the short summers pack trains bringing ore
came from over the divide by way of Stony Pass which was over twelve
thousand feet above sea level. On the eastward road out of the mountains a new town was founded in 1878—Alamosa.

It came as the new western terminus of the Denver and Rio
Grande Western Railroad. The town itself came by rail, for from the
old terminus of Garland City houses, churches, stores and other buildings
were hauled on flat cars to be set up at the new end of the line. With
heavy transportation now available, a new commercial interest was
developed in the San Luis Valley that soon overshadowed mining as the
main business of the region. Large-scale irrigation projects were organ-

ized and supported by foreign capital—principally British. Between
Alamosa and Del Norte a huge grid of irrigation canals reached out
from the Rio Grande for thirty or forty miles north and south. A land
boom resulted. Speculation in land values and water rights went wild.
As in so many other Western localities toward the end of the nineteenth
century, company promoters preached a new paradise and trainloads
of colonists came in response to the dazzling promise. For a little while,
so long as competition was fresh and vigorous, the San Luis prospered
in the vision of a future nourished by inexhaustible resources. Monte
Vista, a third railroad town, was founded in 1887. But within a decade
the vision bagan to pale, for what ended so many other organized
Western dreams elsewhere presently took effect in southern Colorado—
there was not enough water. Sapped by the greatly overextended system
of canals, the river could not supply all. The euphoria of the pioneer
faded, many immigrants abandoned their hopes and went away, and
those who remained came to a regulated sharing of the waters whose
stabilized flow was made possible by the building of reservoirs at the
head of the valley. In the same period the mining ventures of the San
Luis Valley began to lose energy. The camptowns of the Summitville
region were left to the weather, and turned into silvered ghosts. Raw
pine boarding turned gray, and weeds climbed the rusting machinery,
and the character of the wide valley became wholly agricultural, supplied and drained by the railroad in a stabilized economy.

But farther up the river a major find of precious minerals was
made in 1889 that suddenly brought the Rio Grande source country
into the national news. For several years prospectors had been scratching
at the rocks beyond Wagon Wheel Gap—where Kit Carson had once
fought the Ute Indians—but without making significant discoveries. In
that country they saw diamond clear creeks that were shadowed all day
by narrowing mountains but for a little while at noon, when straight
fingers of sunlight reached down through forest. On slopes open to the
sun in summer, groves of quaking aspens showed here and there, creating little gardens of their own within immense wild parks. In winter
the only green was that of the evergreens, solemn and frowning amidst
the silver and brown of lichens—the colors of age—set off by heavy banks
of snow. Far above, at timberline, like fixed images of the winds on the
inhumane peaks, the last trees clutched the naked rock with gestures of
agonized survival. Emerging from between two flat-cliffed mountains of
flesh-colored stone streaked with olive lichens came a little stream which
the prospectors named Willow Creek. They saw that it was a tributary

of the Rio Grande, and that it had its own smaller tributary which they
called West Willow Creek.

On a summer day in 1889 two experienced prospectors who had
made successful discoveries elsewhere walked up Willow Creek through
its formidable gateway. Presently one of them—Nicholas C. Creede—saw
in the stream what surely seemed to be evidence of silver ore on the
washed sandy bottom. He followed the creek and turned into its west
branch, and when he reached the head of it, found rocks flecked with
quartz and stippled with silver. Creede and his partner George L. Smith
staked a location and went to work sinking a shaft at the spot. They
were soon rewarded, for they struck a silver vein so rich that Creede on
first making certain of it, exclaimed, "Holy Moses!" The mine was given
that name. Winter would soon close in. Creede and Smith gathered specimens of their mine, and went to Denver where word of the discovery
presently reached David H. Moffat, president of the Denver and Rio
Grande Western Railroad. With other investors, Moffat bought shares
in the Holy Moses after inspecting it when travel became possible the
next spring. Creede was retained to continue prospecting for the new
syndicate. In the summer of 1890 a rush began to Willow Gap, and by
October there was a town of tents ready to survive the winter.

A year later the Denver and Rio Grande Western tracks reached
Creede, as Willow Gap was now called, and by December trains ran
regularly up the Rio Grande canyon past Wagon Wheel Gap and the
confluence of Willow Creek, which entered the river along a peninsula
of heavy gravel. Twenty months after it was founded, Creede displayed
an energy that reached far beyond its own rock-bound limits. A gentleman journalist felt it in Denver on his way to examine the new camp.
The word Creede "faced you everywhere from billboards, flaunted at
you from canvas awnings stretched across the streets, and stared at you
from daily papers in type an inch long." In Denver shops there were
photographs of Creede, and "the only correct map of Creede," and ore
specimens from the Holy Moses. Miners' outfittings were advertised
everywhere. A druggist pleaded in the newspapers for an investment of
five hundred dollars with which to start a drugstore in Creede. Wherever the visitor met other people—in hotel lobbies, or the Denver Club—
"Creede" was in the air. On the train from Denver to Creede every
passenger "showed the effect of the magnet that was drawing him—he
was restless, impatient, excited." The daily train had fifteen or twenty
cars, and even so there were not enough seats for all its two or three
hundred passengers. Some of the men sat on the others, while women

of a certain class "smoked with the men and passed their flasks down the length of the car." As the train pulled into Creede the journalist jumped from his car "into two or three feet of mud and snow," and saw that "the ticket and telegraph offices on one side of the track were situated in a freight car with windows and doors cut out of it." The next thing noticed by the incoming passenger was that Creede already had electricity. A single electric light burned high against the pink cliff of Willow Gap at whose base huddled the town, and incandescent carbon "glow-lamps" shone in white, red and blue brilliance along the street front.

As a familiar of the great clubs and smart restaurants and polite drawing rooms of the world's capitals, the journalist was entranced by the simple rudeness of all he found in the mining camp. The approaches and slopes of Willow Gap were "covered with hundreds of little pine boxes and log cabins." It was "a village of fresh pine." There was "not a brick, a painted front, nor an awning in the entire town," which looked "like a city of fresh cardboard." The street was all confusion and movement. He saw "oxteams, mules, men, and donkeys loaded with ore . . . sinking knee deep in the mud," and "furniture, and kegs of beer, bedding and canned provisions, clothing and half-open packing cases, and piles of raw lumber . . . heaped up in front of the new stores—stores of canvas only, stores with canvas tops and foundations of logs, and houses with the *Leadville front,* where the upper boards have been left square instead of following the sloping angle of the roof." At the base of the superb rock panels rising above the town, all such clutter looked to him "impudent and absurd"—more like a "gypsy camp in a canyon," really, than a town. And the nomenclature of the establishments!—The Holy Moses Saloon, The Théâtre Comique, The Keno, The Little Delmonico. . . .

And the accommodations!—there were dozens of hotels, most of which afforded the traveller only a cot in a common room teeming with other sleepers. Beds were so scarce that the railroad company often left a number of Pullman cars on a siding to provide a lodging for the night. The population by now was about ten thousand, and included every type of commercial frontier character. The journalist saw gamblers, prospectors, miners, engineers, bankers, bartenders, itinerant evangelists, actors, prostitutes, schoolteachers, family men and women, jobbers, merchants, and confidence men to whom in his observations he could condescend with easy bad manners, and adventurous younger sons of rich Eastern families, with whom he was more at home. Luckily, he was able to find a bed for the night with a group of these young men who, like him, had come just for the lark. To go West to see such a spectacle as Creede was a gallant and correct thing for them to do, and he was their prophet, for his career had been full of just such fashionable exploits.

The night life, even though at the moment Creede was "not at all a dangerous place," with a lawlessness that was "scattered and mild," was worth an amused glance. There were things to see—a prize fight at Billy Woods's, a pie-eating match at Kernan's, a Mexican circus in the bottom near Wagon Wheel Gap, a religious service in Watrous and Brannigan's saloon where two electric lights hung in the middle of the room and a stove stood below them. The prayer meeting over, the house resumed its own character, and took in three hundred dollars an hour, while the women of the establishment, wearing "sombrero hats and flannel shirts and belts" above their long skirts, "were neither dashing and bold, nor remorseful and repentant." Actually, people seemed to use the gambling houses as clubs where they might keep warm and talk business and find company and gossip. One night Nicholas Creede was offered $1,250,000 for his share in the Holy Moses Mine, and refused. The journalist winced. How could anybody choose this life over what that much money would buy back East? But if the visitor read the Creede *Candle*—the local newspaper—he saw self-critical and outspoken opinion. Some of the citizens, it said, "would take the sweepstake prize at a hog show," and from time to time, it documented examples of the usual murderous antics of official "bad men" who in Creede as elsewhere on the recurrent American frontier enacted the dreariest convention of character in United States history.

The journalist went by day into the canyon to observe mining operations. Now he saw the prosperous, well-developed shafts, and again, "a solitary prospector tapping at the great rock in front of him, and only stopping to dip his hot face and blistered hands into the snow about him, before he began to drive the steel bar again with the help which hope gave to him." Long lines of burros went down the gulch "carrying five bags of ore each, with but twenty dollars' worth of silver scattered through each load." The voice of the driver echoed on the upright stone walls and the tinkle of the little burro bells carried far in the enclosed air. Other loads, often of ten tons, were brought down in sleds drawn by horses. The trail was slippery with packed snow and once their momentum was released, the sleds came flying heavily down the twisting canyon course and into town, where all scattered out of their way, for they must not stop until they stopped by the railroad tracks, which they reached in a great circle on the flat land where their cargo would be removed to freight cars.

Within a year after the mines were opened in Creede and its near-by camps of Sunnyside, Bachelor and Spar City, six million dollars' worth of silver was shipped out. In its sudden rise to fame and prosperity, Creede was typical of any mining town of the period in the West—and so it was, too, in its early fall to decay. After 1893 the price of silver declined, many mines were abandoned, and others if they were kept running were greatly reduced in operation.

Socorro on the river in central New Mexico knew much the same history. Silver was found in the Socorro mountains in 1867, and for over a decade was hauled upriver by mule train. When in 1880 the Santa Fe line went down the river toward El Paso, the Socorro region drew a new population of exploiters until Socorro itself was the largest town in New Mexico—one estimate fixed the total at thirty thousand. Magdalena, twenty-seven miles west of the river, was established by silver miners in 1884, and a railroad spur soon reached it. But again, in the familiar cycle of such mining towns, decline followed until both Socorro and Magdalena were primarily focal towns for agriculture—here, the supply and shipping points for cattle and sheep raisers. Only an occasional die-hard among prospectors continued to go alone with his burro, his pick, his skillet and his coffeepot into the blue rocks of his visions, determined, if he had one, to be faithful to his secret until the end.

One such was found in after years near Socorro when a group of students on a Saturday exploration came upon a jug pit or cave whose open mouth, invisible from a very little distance across flat ground, was narrower than its interior. The students knew that the cave like others in the area must be a repository of an ochreous dust so dense and fine that to breathe it freely was dangerous. Equipped with a respirator and a flashlight, one of the students was lowered into the pit by the others. In a few moments he was hauled up to tell what he had seen. His find was awesome. When he landed in the pit he disturbed from its floor a swiftly billowing cloud of yellow dust. It roiled in the air shutting off the sight of anything about him. He peered with his lamp toward the pit walls and suddenly through the suspended motes he was shocked to see at his very side the figure of a man that seemed to be molded of the dust, leaning on a sloping wall of earth with its brow on its forearm. It was the body of an old prospector, wearing a short coat hanging open and trousers poked into high boots, and over all a softening layer of

dust. Half buried near his feet was his pick. It seemed probable that
he had gone alone into the pit with no protection against the dust that
instantly rose to choke the air about him. Leaning his head upon his
arm against the wall as he struggled to breathe he had died of suffocation. Through the years he had been mummified by the dry air and the
little desert whirlwinds that having created the pit must have continued
to spin in and out of it now and again. In his open grave he was a
classic rendering of dust to dust itself, and a symbol of solitary man,
killed by the country of his love, faith and work.

41.

The Last Earth Secrets

For almost four centuries after the Spaniards first began to record
the river's history a long passage—over one fifth—of its course went undescribed. This was the country of the Big Bend, where one after another
great canyons and rocky deserts turned away travellers and settlers—all
but the few Indians who had once lived in cliffside caves and others
who migrated ceaselessly north and south and who may have seen most
of the secret river land that lay between the entrance of the Rio Conchos
into the Rio Grande and the confluence of the Pecos nearly four hundred miles downstream. But such Indians left no records of the country.

The Spanish settlements nearest to the blind channel were those
temporarily made by missioners in 1683 and 1684, and those by government forces in 1747, at the Junta. From there, looking downstream, the
Spaniards could see the first of the mountain fantasies that would have
closed off the river to ordinary navigation even if there had been enough
water to carry it. The Army quartermaster party that ascended the river
in keelboats in 1850 left a report that told how they had gone upstream
from Fort Brown a distance of about thirteen hundred miles and how
finally they had been halted by falls in a great canyon. But if they

reached one of the Big Bend canyons their record was not explicit. In 1852 and 1853 Colonel Emory's boundary surveyors followed the river's course wherever possible, but in the Big Bend they were forced to view the canyon system from a distance, or from the tops of the gorges, where precise measurement and description of the channel could not be made. The three men who declared that they had escaped the Confederate Army at El Paso in 1861 by floating all the way to Brownsville in two dugout canoes lashed together left no narrative of the unknown Big Bend country through which their voyage would have taken them. In December, 1881, and January, 1882, a detachment of Texas Rangers set out from Lajitas, below Presidio, to navigate the Big Bend in three boats. They worked their way downstream to the mouth of Maravillas Canyon and there, after fifty-two days, their expedition ended, with a great stretch of the river—all the way to the Pecos—still unobserved by boat. Having kept no daily record of their observations, they made their report from memory. If it was a testimony to adventure and courage, it did not serve the purpose of a survey.

It was not until 1899 that the last secrets of the river's conformation were penetrated and recorded in systematic detail. In the autumn of that year Robert T. Hill, an officer of the United States Geological Survey, arrived at Presidio bringing five companions and three specially built boats for an expedition down the Rio Grande through its entire Big Bend career. As they made their preparations the travellers—one of whom was Hill's nineteen-year-old nephew—examined the local character of the river.

Above Presidio the river in some years vanished in the desert. Colonel Emory had told of how a herd of goats was driven all the way to El Paso in the dry stream bed. But relief and replenishment came to the Rio Grande just north of Presidio from the waters of the Conchos. With this tributary came new power for the Rio Grande in the struggle of water against rock, and another of those beautiful easings of desert into bounteous pastoral land that recurred along its course. This relief was here so striking that earlier travellers familiar with only the border country spoke of the Conchos as "the mother stream of the Rio Grande," and said that it brought "the first permanent water to the main river." Such a limited view was often taken of the Rio Grande throughout its history; for along its great length, and in different times, on different missions, travellers discovered the river in segments, named them differently, found contradictory characters in them, and for many generations did not form a comprehensive theory of the river's continuity, variety

and use. After the bare and voracious desert in which it nearly died, the
river at Presidio came among willows again and cottonwoods, lilac mountains with attendant clouds, emerald-green fields and pink sand, through
a sweetness in the air made from all these together.

On October fifth Hill gave the order to start the voyage. Two
men entered each of the three boats. Soon after leaving Presidio they
heard a roaring noise and presently encountered rapids foaming over
huge rounded boulders of volcanic rock. They had to get into the water
to guide the boats. They all knew, with Hill, that "loss of balance or a
fall meant almost certain death." They were in the rapids all day. Other
dangers ran along the river course and against these they kept loaded
rifles beside their oars. "Every bush and stone was closely scanned for
men in ambush," for bandits and assassins abounded. The most famous
and frightful was a Mexican named Alvarado, who was called "Old
White Lip," as one side of his mustache was white, the other black.

In the hazy heat on the downriver horizon images of another
country began to loom, almost like premonitions. Fantasies were made
manifest. Unimaginably long ago, mountain nature had gone capricious
in stunning terms. The land had opposed the river before this passage;
but never on the scale of what lay ahead. The Rio Grande was heading
for all the old conditions of its course—desert, mountain, canyon—but
now raised to prodigious dimensions of height, depth, length and power
in furies of sky action, and earth response. The scene could be understood only in the scale of what created it. Continental dimensions and
eminences of the hemisphere itself must be invoked. North America
at its waist was twenty-one hundred miles wide. Along its eastern shelf
the mountain chain of the Appalachians ran almost continuously from
north to south. Along its western shelf the Rocky Mountains ran almost
continuously from north to south. Towards the ends of their courses
these, the two major mountain systems of the continent, threw out spurs
toward one another which, incredibly and immensely, intersected. A
cataclysm so great using elements so huge could only leave fixed signs
of colossal turbulence in rock and earth, fantasies of shape and color and
atmospheric temper, including the dead but enduring evidence of volcanic action. The whole rind of the earth in the Big Bend country was
dropped in a great tilted slab to a depth of two or three thousand feet
on the north, and six thousand feet on the south, as though a cut were
made in a watermelon, and the segment pushed in below the surrounding surface. Mesas, volcanic mountains, plains, interior basins, deserts,
badlands, lava flows, beds of dried rivers and dead and vanished seas, ·

profuse in number and fantastic in shape and often violent in color
made that country in its vast freaks of light seem like figment instead
of fact.

Upstream the river had always been in touch with mountains; but
they lay generally parallel to its course. In the Big Bend the river encountered mountains in a new and extraordinary way; for they lay, chain
after chain of them, directly across its course as though to deny its
passage to the sea. But the pull of the sea was stronger than rock. The
Rio Grande with its shallow flow did not turn aside, or dam itself into
a system of lakes, but for ages wore its way as an antecedent river through
the escarpments as they rose, some to a height of almost a mile above
its course.

Late in their second day's voyage Hill and his men entered the
Bofecillos Mountains with their chocolate-colored cliffs—"the first of
the series of canyons of the Rio Grande" in which they "were to be
entombed for the succeeding weeks." It was called Murderer's Canyon,
for in it had been found a supposed victim of "Old White Lip." A little
farther down they came into Fresno Canyon which like the first one was
made by vertical cuts six hundred feet deep through walls of red volcanic
rock. The river flowed muddy yellow. On the tops of the canyons was
desert, out of reach of the water below—a condition that moved Hill as
"shocking and repulsive."

Suddenly they passed out of the canyon, leaving behind vertical
walls which continued north and south of the river, and into a valley
with every variety of form and color. The outermost hills were of dazzling chalky white capped with black tufa. Slopes were vermilion foothills
of clay. Still lower were river terraces of yellow clay and gravel, all
threaded by the narrow green ribbon of river vegetation.

Hill's party included Mexicans who promised to kill White Lip
on sight, a distraction to which Hill was cold. "Only a most fortunate
mistake prevented my men from carrying out their threat," he wrote.
"Alvarado had a surname as well as a Christian name, and when they
were told that the next ranch down the river was Ordoñez's, they did
not understand that this was another name for Alvarado until after we
had passed him with an infant in his arms, serenely watching us float
down the stream. . . ."

Below the bandit's home came "great bluffs of a dirty yellow
volcanic tuff, which weather into many fantastic, curvilinear forms. One
of these, two hundred feet high, stands out conspicuously from its surroundings, an almost perfect reproduction of the Egyptian sphinx." In

late afternoon they came to another wall cut ahead of them by the river, and entering camped with a sense of safety, "hemmed in on each side by vertical walls and out of rifle range from above." In the morning they emerged from this mile-long canyon and entered a sinuous course through what they called Black Rock Canyon, cut a thousand feet below the summit of a level plateau, and lined with buttes whose tabled tops and lower slopes showed thick bands of white chalk, with between them an immense bed of black lava. At evening they sailed into an open basin and passed the mouth of San Carlos Creek, a meagre flowing stream, the first tributary of the river below the Conchos.

At this point they had come one hundred miles by water, though in air line they were only fifty miles from Presidio. They camped on the Mexican side, and regarded a mile downstream "a vast mountain wall, the vertical escarpment of which ran directly north and south across the path of the river, and through which the latter cuts its way."

They were face to face with the first of the three mightiest obstacles of the Big Bend. It was the Santa Elena Range, running fifty miles from north to south. Ten miles of it lay in the United States; forty miles of it, sawed off by the river, lay in Mexico. The range was half a mile high and twelve miles wide. Its top was a plateau, tilted slightly to the west. From the top the river's cut was so clean that—as other observers noticed—it could not be seen until they came to stand at its very edge. Even from the crest of the canyon wall the running water a quarter of a mile below was not always visible, and when it could be seen from overhanging ledges, the stream looked like "a mere thread."

The next morning Hill's party came to the awesome gateway in the face of the escarpment. The river made a sudden bend as it entered the canyon, "and almost in the twinkling of an eye we passed out of the desert glare into the dark and silent depths of its gigantic canyon walls, which rise vertically from the water's edge to a narrow ribbon of sky above." The channel was only twenty-five feet wide. They could almost touch the walls with their oars. There was a deathlike stillness all about them as they floated without using their oars on the slipping waters. "Their flow is so silent as to be appalling," noted Hill, and "the solemnity and beauty of the spectacle were overwhelming."

They had drifted in this mountain oubliette for a few miles when they were halted by a disheartening discovery. Part of the huge southern wall had fallen in a great rock slide to obstruct the path, not for the water, which pounded its way beneath a pile of fifty-foot boulders, but for the boats. The slide rose to a height of two hundred feet, and though it was only a quarter of a mile in length, it cost Hill and his men three days to cross it—for there was no way to go but forward. They hauled their boats and equipment over the slide with the hardest effort, climbing to a height of one hundred and eighty feet and descending the other side. Even as they passed their freight hand over hand up the rugged slope they could still regard the magnificence of the scene with awe. Yellow and red marbles in the cliffs; gigantic columns five hundred feet high that had been undermined by the river to drop a few feet without tumbling and to lean against the walls; great caves below the skyline, and others at the waterline; fortress and castle and bastion of natural making; silence—all worked upon them.

And so did fears. What if the river should suddenly rise with storm water? What if they should wreck one or all of the boats on the rocky portage? They called the place Camp Misery. "While buried in this canyon at Camp Misery" they were "constantly impressed by the impossibility of escaping from it" if their fears came true. "For its entire length there is no place where this cliff can be climbed by man." Acutely conscious of their situation, they struggled on, hauling at the boats, each of which weighed three hundred pounds, with lariat and bare hands, over the immense limestone cubes "around and between which the water dashed with the force of a mill-race, and where a slip of the foot on the smooth rocks meant certain death." But they prevailed, and at last made ready to take to the water again early one morning. But "before the boats were loaded a tremendous roaring sound like distant thunder was heard up the canyon, and we saw that what we most dreaded was happening—the river was rising." They hurried their preparations and sprang aboard the skiffs. "It was either stay and starve or go and chance it. Fortunately, this particular rise proved to be a small one"—and in this they were lucky, for the river could rise thirty feet in half an hour in the Santa Elena canyon—"just sufficient to give impetus to our craft, and our course through the canyon was rapid."

The skyline was of always changing interest. There was no animal life at all in the canyon except for a small species of bat, and a family of quail which had ventured into the deep slot and found themselves unable to soar out again. As the enclosing walls rose to their greatest height—seventeen hundred and fifty feet—the boats sailed suddenly out into desert sunlight, after their twisting and turning twenty-five mile passage. And now the travellers could pause thankfully on the shore to look back at the mountain from which they had escaped. They saw the east face of the Santa Elena—an escarpment of pale buff limestone with hardly a break in its vertical thrust except for a shallow and sloping bench about halfway up. Its horizon was flat and sharply cut, with great nicks in it where waterless canyons bit into the rock to remain suspended high up the cliff. As the mountain ended sharply, so the desert began sharply, reaching far inland, and going with the river for the next forty miles. The very rock of Santa Elena seen from the desert downstream looked like a shimmering image of the heat. Sand, orange-colored foothills, blue haze in the canyon's mouth, all spoke of waste and heat, in immense proportions. Such was its scale that for a week after leaving the Santa Elena Hill's men could see its face from down the river. Hill could proudly record that "as bold and extensive as is this mountain, it had hitherto found no place or name on published maps."

Now entering the desert the Rio Grande in crossing the forty-mile stretch wound for a hundred miles. Every variety of barren terrain was visible on both sides of the river—level plains, deep terraces, arroyos, lava-capped hills, summits and small mountain ranges. Hill said it was the "hottest and most sterile region imaginable." In full summer the temperature often rose to one hundred and thirty or forty degrees by day, and by night dropped close to freezing. Repeated enough, such violent contrasts cracked rock, so that much of the wild and furious aspect of the region could be traced to such earth action. Above the desert on the north the range of Los Chisos mountains rose to a total altitude of nine thousand feet, or sixty-five hundred above the river. "Wherever one climbs out of the low stream groove these peaks stare him in the face like white-cloud spirits rising from a base of misty gray shadow and vegetation," wrote Hill. Their name was said to be an Indian word for "ghosts." The highest peak of the Chisos was named for Commissioner Emory. Color was as extraordinary as form there—black, yellow, vermilion, white, brown, buff, all altered by distance and heat, and, after cloud-burst when the sweeping air held moisture suspended, all given mystery by every variation of light—ray, burst, or curtain.

Hill saw almost no human life along the way, except for one small band of cattle thieves "leisurely driving a herd of stolen cattle across the river into Mexico," and an outlaw called Greasy Bill with a straggle of followers who camped on the Mexican side. Surely the boats must be nearing the apex of the Big Bend?—for each time the river turned northward Hill thought they had come to it. But five times they travelled around southern bends of the river only to turn southeastward again on the course by which they had left Presidio. And when at last they turned northeastward to hold their new course beyond the apex, they saw ahead of them another mountain barrier athwart the river. As they drew near to it they could see what looked in the face of the sierra like a heavy black line drawn from top to bottom. This was the slit into which the Rio Grande vanished; and they thought the river seemed to plunge into a "seething hole without visible outlet." Again it was a limestone canyon, with strata tilted and bent into odd formations. Here the river made many more turns and bends than in the Santa Elena, and its course was varied with many side-canyons entering through "pinnacled and terraced cream-colored walls." It was the Little Mariscal Canyon, and was soon succeeded by Big Mariscal Canyon, of similar character. The voyagers saw in it "a Rocky Mountain sheep far above . . . upon an inaccessible ledge. Serafine took one shot at him, and he tumbled back in a majestic leap." The trip through these canyons was unimpeded, and after a few hours, at noon, the party was out in the desert again, where they saw on the Mexican side the ruins of an old fort called the Presidio de San Vicente. The next day brought the boats to another canyon, through mountains like those of the day before, but not so big. Emerging from it, they soon came to "the village of Boquillas" where they "encountered the first and only American civilization upon our expedition."

Just east of Boquillas the longest and deepest of the Big Bend canyons appeared between the Dead Horse Mountains in Texas and directly opposite in Mexico, the Sierra del Carmen. Fifty miles long and five thousand feet deep, it was Boquillas Canyon—"little mouths," for the narrowness of the towering gateways cut in the mountain rock. The river, said Hill, "in approaching this mountain, first turns from side to side in short stretches, as if trying to avoid the mighty barrier above it, and then, as if realizing that it is constantly becoming involved in the maze of foot-hills, suddenly starts across it."

Once in the canyon the voyagers found even more extraordinary formations, colors and vagaries of the river than before. They made many right-angle bends, each producing startling new vistas. Immense caves hung empty in the cliffs. In many places the sheer yellow walls were cut from top to bottom by wonderful fissures gleaming with chalk white or vermilion minerals. Gigantic tributary canyons opened into the main course. During the passage of the Boquillas, which took several days, the moon was full, and night after night the men were awed by the coming and going of the moonlight which would first glow on the topmost pinnacles and then start down the western wall, "gently settling from stratum to stratum as the black shadows fled before it, until finally it reached the silent but rapid waters of the river, which became a belt of silver. . . . I could never sleep until the glorious light had ferreted out the shadows from every crevice and driven darkness from the canyon." And then the moonlight would creep up the other wall until all was darkness again.

They met no obstruction in the Boquillas, and one day never knowing which turn of the dark chasm would at last show them a vista not of another wall deep in shade but of open sky and horizon, they came out into the last of the desert basins in their course. At the canyon mouth there were a thousand goats with their shepherds and dogs. Startled, all ran away. The flat valley rose in terraces to the bases of mountains on either side. Hill observed, "The human mind is almost incapable of conceiving the vast quantity of boulders which in times past have poured out of these vertical canyons into such open plains."

Once again, having passed so much canyon and desert in which there was none, the travellers began to see animal life. A lizard; two immense ravens, "half-hopping, half-flying"; beaver slides on the banks: three deer; blue quail; a mockingbird—"only one who is accustomed to the animal life of the desert can imagine the joy with which we greeted these lowly friends."

After a twelve-mile desert stretch they entered another canyon with broken walls, the cliffs receded, and they passed the mouth of a dead river on the Texas side. It was Maravillas Creek, "a horrible desert arroyo, leading northward for one hundred miles or more. . . . It has a channel sufficient for the Hudson, but is utterly devoid of water. Now and then, in the intervals of years, great floods pour down its stony bottom, giving the boulders and other desert debris a further push toward the Rio Grande and the sea."

At this point the river turned due east, continuing in a narrow valley far below the complicated forms of a great limestone plateau. Would there be no end to these enclosures? Hill and his people were weary of them. "In the steep canyons there had always been a tense feeling of anxiety, accompanied by a longing to escape their dangers as soon as possible." Their first hint of comfort in those weeks came one Sunday noon. "Shortly after making the turn to the east, and in the depths of a beautifully terraced canyon, we came upon [a] copious hot spring running out of the bluff upon a low bench, where it made a large, clear pool of water. . . . Here we made our first and only stop for recreation. After lunch, most of the party proceeded to the warm pool, and, stripping, we literally soaked for hours in its delightful waters, stopping occasionally to soap and scrub our linen."

They speculated upon the height of the cliffs. Nobody guessed more than five hundred feet. Hill found "a good place for the first time in all our course to scale the canyon walls," went up and measured the exact height. Like all travellers in the southwest they had been fooled by the clear air which like a lens acted to bring distance near. The height was sixteen hundred and fifty feet. "The view from the summit was superb, revealing the panorama of the uplands, which is completely shut out while traversing the chasm below."

They went on eastward in their boats through curious formations. "In this eastern stretch the immediate gorge of the river is generally a canyon within a canyon." As it continued easterly, the river gradually surmounted the great limestone formation that had made its prison walls and tried to frustrate its course. But this relief was short. At the 102nd meridian the Rio Grande again vanished between the walls of a rocky trough whose color was no longer buff and orange, but white "which weathers into great curves rather than vertical ledges." The effects were handsome—hundred-foot pillars, immense overhanging gables under which the boatmen sailed for hours, finding wild game on the banks and wild honey in caves. But they were exhausted in temper and body, and "no longer appreciated the noble surroundings. We longed only to escape from the walls, upon which we now began to look as a prison."

Time itself must have seemed hostile.

They had rowed ten hours every day for over a month. More than once they had to drag the boats over dangerous rapids, getting ducked and soaked. The sunshine in the open stretches was pitiless. They were bored with their limited diet. Never out of mind were the dangers of river nature, and, if they had to abandon the river, the hopelessness of reaching safety overland through desert wilderness without water, on foot. They watched for a landmark that would tell them they had finished their hard journey. It was a sign known for decades to the few first travellers of the region—"a huge pile of sticks skilfully entwined into what is perhaps the largest bird's nest in America," which clung to the edge of a small cave in the yellow river bluff on the Mexican side. It was the home of a pair of eagles which every year produced their young in it.

The travellers finally saw it and knew they were done.

They landed on a little beach opposite the nest. The village of

Langtry was a mile and a half away, a station on the Southern Pacific Railroad. They sent for a packhorse and took their equipment to town, and were received by Judge Roy Bean under his sign which proclaimed him to be the Law West of the Pecos, a Justice of the Peace, a Notary Republic, and a purveyor of San Antonio Lager Beer. Locked in some crevice of cranky romance proper to his country and his character, Judge Bean kept a glowing image of the actress Lily Langtry, the Jersey Lily, for whose photograph he had conceived a passion. His village, first called Vinegaroon, Texas, he renamed in her honor. After his death she paused on a transcontinental tour in her private "palace car" to look wonderingly for a moment upon a reproduction of her portrait by Sir John Millais that hung over the bar in Judge Bean's Jersey Lily Saloon, and to accept as gifts from his successor Judge Bean's gavel and rifle.

Robert Hill and his men had navigated and mapped "three hundred and fifty miles of a portion of one of America's greatest rivers which hitherto had been considered impassable." To discover the last earth secrets of the Rio Grande they had lived for weeks in a lost world created through incalculable time. On reaching Langtry, Texas, and its transcontinental railroad, they were immediately restored to the modern world of technology in power and communication.

42.

Revolution and Reflex

It was a world by which the life of the United States Rio Grande was already much modified. Now beyond the river in Mexico, under the rule of President Porfirio Díaz, the first industrial techniques and systematic exploitations of Mexico's great natural wealth were being developed together. Mexican railroads came to the river at Matamoros, Nuevo Laredo, Piedras Negras and Juárez during the Díaz reign, and symbolized, if in their operation they did not fully demonstrate, that sense of order in communication by which the machine world and its society kept the promises implicit in timetables and other conventions of commercial accord. Much in the American nature enjoyed such order, for efficiency in the use of time and man power and machine materials was becoming a matter of the national faith. On the other hand, much in the Mexican nature was indifferent if not hostile to such order, for to many Mexicans time meant only that tomorrow would come, and as for man power, it could be shot to death, and machines would break down sooner or later. Still, the Mexican president, proudly striving to bring his country into the company of modern world powers, imposed upon it with the aid of tax revenues derived from huge investments by foreign capital his own vision of society. Díaz brought to Mexico a long period of political order, industrial development, economic stability, and even some broadening of public education. It was a program that had resemblances to the systems of life in the great world powers. Foreign statesmen regarded President Díaz as their peer. Foreign capitalists, investing in Mexican oil and mining and ranching properties, could talk with him, for he spoke their language. Where had he learned it, born of Indian blood in a poor Oaxacan family, this ex-seminarian, this law student under Benito Juárez, this revolutionary soldier and one-time land reformer? But what did it matter, for Mexican bankers and landowners spoke it too, and approved the presidential achievement, with all its years of growing prosperity and order.

But it was a prosperity and an order brought about at the expense of the individual independence and political freedom of the Mexican people—and even their ownership of property. For under laws passed during the Díaz regime Mexico's natural wealth rested in the hands of less than four per cent of the population. It required no special knowledge for Mexicans at large to know that if under their absolute ruler they were living an orderly life, they were also hungry for the lands that their fathers had owned even in the unsettled times of such a recurrent national chief as Santa Anna, and the wars of his various glories and disgraces. Mexico, with her leaders laboring to bring her into the modern world, at the same time suffered a relapse into feudal inequities in her social structure that could lead only to revolution, with both its sacrifices and its crimes, its visions and treacheries. President Díaz, coming to power after his own successful revolution launched across the lower Rio Grande in 1876, began to consider, by 1909, the possible consequences of his repressive and efficient rule. He was already hearing talk of candidates to oppose him in his next election, a discourteous threat.

But it was more than that, for popular support, with no reason to be
loyal to the administration, was beginning to drift to those leaders who
dared to breathe a promise of land reform on behalf of those millions
who had no patch of earth on which to raise an ear of corn or a bean
for themselves and the children who must follow them even as hungry
and dispossessed.

President Díaz, at seventy-nine, had much experience of political
gesture. It seemed to him that if he were to demonstrate before his
nation how fully he enjoyed the confidence of the powerful republic
above the Rio Grande, with all attendant implications of prestige and
filtered wealth and perhaps even a hint of supporting force, then much
opposition in the election of next year, 1910, might fade away. He wrote
to President William Howard Taft of the United States to propose a
public meeting between them; and with gratifying swiftness the proposal
was accepted. President Taft in his first year of office was to make a great
swing across the United States from coast to coast; and on his way back,
would be pleased to stop over at El Paso to meet his colleague from
Mexico City, and, as it were, shake hands with him across the Rio Grande.

Relations along the border had been generally good since the
late 1880s when the last of the private bandit armies organized after the
style of Canales and Cortina had been suppressed by General Don Ramon
Treviño, to the satisfaction of President Díaz. True, there were still
individual masters of the bravura style of lawlessness at work, like Old
White Lip in the Big Bend, and Colonel Emory's remark of half a century before—"Property is very insecure all along the boundary"—was
still applicable. But depredations from below the border were now
frowned upon by Mexican authority, and the ruling temper above it
was far different from that which, in all respectability, moved General
Tom Green who like many Americans of his time was free in his thoughts
about Mexican territory. In his published account of the Mier adventure he proposed that if the abolition of slavery should ever come—he
shuddered to think of it—the United States should acquire all of Mexico
as far south as the twentieth parallel, which amounted to about three
fourths of the nation, and should deport all American Negroes to settle
there.

With the new century, the terms of disagreement between border
Mexicans and North Americans assumed new forms which had to do
with social attitudes rather than with open crime. The Anglo-American
technological society, with all its commercial originality, came to power
over the old combination of Indian and Latin ways of life, and rapidly

made a subject class of wage labor out of a population that for centuries had owned both sides of the river. The most easily recognized symbols of the respective positions of the North American and the Mexican peoples of the border were the white skin of the one and the brown of the other. The economic superiority of *white* over *brown* created corresponding social prejudice, until *brown* not only was dispossessed, but was made to feel inferior. It was a set of attitudes in which dwelt the seed of much trouble for later generations of the two Rio Grande peoples, one so heedless and energetic, the other so hapless and proud.

But as the two presidents approached their common frontier in 1909 all was courtesy and dignity, for good manners were easier to manage between heads of states than among simple citizens. President Taft was clear about what had occasioned the meeting. Díaz needed his public support, as the surge of liberal sentiment in Mexico might seem now to predict his overthrow. "I am glad to aid him," wrote President Taft to his wife as his special train trundled him dustily across the great spaces of Arizona toward the Rio Grande, "for the reason that we have two billions [of] American capital in Mexico that will be greatly endangered if Díaz were to die and his government go to pieces." It was an alarming prospect, for a turbulent Mexico would create in reflex agonizing problems for her neighboring government. "I can only hope and pray," added the corpulent American president, who thrived on comfort, "that his demise does not come until I am out of office. . . ."

The American presidential train came into the El Paso yards in the early forenoon of October sixteenth, while President Taft enfolded himself in his voluminous frock coat, as directed by State Department arrangements, which specified also that the Mexican president would appear in uniform. Waiting in the Tuscan-styled El Paso station was Colonel Pablo Escandón, the ADC to President Díaz, with greetings from his chief. Captain Archie Butt, the American ADC, descended from the private car with his president, and proceeded to the street where a cavalry escort from Fort Bliss was ready to conduct the commander-in-chief to the El Paso Chamber of Commerce. Once there, President Taft entered an empty back room, lay down on a black leather couch and went to sleep. But trumpets soon broke the distance with flourishes to announce that President José de la Cruz Porfirio Díaz was moving through the streets of Juárez. President Taft awoke to duty and rode to the international bridge. Advancing to the center over the cloacal drift of the shallow river the two presidents, while cannon salutes proclaimed their dignity, met and shook hands, as Captain Archie Butt

did the honors: "The President of the United States—the President of
Mexico!" President Taft, in English, said,

"I am very glad to welcome you, sir, here, I am very glad indeed,"
to which President Díaz, in Spanish, replied,

"I am very happy to meet you and to have the honor of being one
of the first foreigners to come over and give you a hearty welcome."

The old Indian president was dazzling. His stocky figure was
superbly uniformed and on his broad torso were spread the stars of a
dozen orders. President Taft felt "quite outshone," and observed further
that his aged colleague was "most remarkable in point of agility, quick-
ness of perception and dignity of carriage." After preliminary courtesies
the two chiefs moved to the American end of the bridge for a procession
through the streets of El Paso. The United States Secret Service had put
the city under augmented guard. An hour ago all citizens living along
the line of march were obliged to close and lock their doors, and as the
two presidents rode together to the Chamber of Commerce for a private
conversation the Secret Service kept clear a running space in the crowds
ahead and behind and on both sides of the state vehicle, and kept watching the populace for "sight of a drawn and set face," and, on seeing any
such, at once arranged to search the suspect person. A member of the
cortège reported that "over one hundred weapons were gathered in this
way, although none of them may have been intended for purposes of
assassination." Only one disorderly incident marred the day's arrangements—a dusty scuffle on the sidelines, a sob of passion, a flash of steel,
and an American boy fell dead under the knife of a Mexican youth
whose view of President Díaz he had obstructed. Amidst the cheers, who
knew whether the great men bowing along the lane saw it happen?

Once in the Chamber of Commerce the presidents, with confidential aides and interpreters, retired to a private room to talk business—the
business that had brought them both to the river. As it turned out, their
interests were not, after all, identical. True, President Taft offered to
President Díaz the benefits he had come to find; but there was now a
provision attached. The price of "full friendship and support," as a Mexican who was present later told, was the renewal by Mexico of leases
held by the United States Navy on basing facilities for the Pacific Fleet
in Magdalena Bay, on the west coast of Lower California. The old Mexican's eyes were "dark, unblinking, bright, spirited," and now behind
them moved thoughts that troubled him. He was already under hot fire
at home from the increasingly bold critics of his whole policy, including
the large concessions he had made to foreign powers. He was now forced

to choose between a further concession to the United States and a gesture of independence on behalf of Mexico. He shook his head. It would be impossible to renew the naval leases. The decision may have been more costly than he could have anticipated, for the Mexican witness to the interview believed that it was "one of the chief reasons the American government later winked its eyes" at the works of Madero in opposing Díaz.

The incident may have seemed small, yet it dealt in costly failure, for by it neither president fully gained what he wanted. There remained two thirds of the day's ceremonial program to carry out, but there was a sense that the heart had gone out of it. Still, amenity must be preserved, and President Taft was famous for his jolly nature, and soon further compliments and expressions of satisfaction were flowing, and after twenty minutes champagne was brought in and toasts were exchanged, and then the President of Mexico withdrew to his own soil over the river. He was followed at noon by President Taft, who called on him in Juárez where the public courtesies were repeated. In the evening sixty guests sat down with the two presidents to a state dinner at which the Mexican was host. Both were in civilian evening dress, the one monumentally plain, the other wearing the red, white and green ribbon of Mexico over his breast, and a profuse garland of miniature medals. The table service was the silver and gold plate from the presidential palace of Mexico City. There were jokes—the presidents in inquiring after the health of each other's wife made amusing remarks about the duties and activities of a political consort; and there were speeches—the host said the occasion afforded "a happy precedent for Latin-American republics to cultivate constant and cordial relations among themselves, with us, and with all other countries of the continent," and the guest replied that "the aims and ideals of our two nations are identical, their sympathy is mutual and lasting, and the world can be assured of a vast neutral zone of peace in which the controlling aspirations of either nation is individual and human happiness. . . ." Under the sound of such decorous revelries already moved the forces that all too soon must bring Mexico to bleeding misery and the United States to anger against her.

Before the evening ended a photograph was taken of the presidents and their military aides together. It would be an important piece of evidence for President Díaz to scatter about to show how he stood with the Americans. "He thinks," noted President Taft, "and I believe rightly, that the knowledge throughout his country of the friendship of the United States for him and his government will strengthen him with his own people, and tend to discourage revolutionists' efforts to establish a different government . . ." The party was over. President Taft with his aides returned to his train at El Paso. Noticing how nervous they seemed to be, he proposed a highball. They all took one, and after a deep drink one of the company said to the president,

"Thank God we're all out of Mexico and the day's over. We've been half crazy for fear somebody would take a shot at you."

The president chuckled and made a joke about the target he presented with his great bulk. The train pulled out eastward across Texas, leaving the Rio Grande and the border city where in a matter of months the conspiracy against Díaz would be centered in the ideas and the acts of Francisco Madero.

For Taft as president was not after all to escape the trials that came with the overthrow of the Díaz government. Madero opposed Díaz in the election of 1910, but his campaign proposals became so popular that he was arrested for sedition. He escaped, fled to El Paso, and from there, in the long succession of revolutionists who used the left bank as asylum and platform, he cried out across the river his plans for reform—chiefly agrarian. The people heard him, he returned to Mexico to lead a revolution, and in 1911 Porfirio Díaz resigned to go into exile in Paris. Once in power Madero, hoping to achieve internal peace for Mexico, made compromises with the remnants of the Díaz faction, and in his turn faced revolutionary opposition from the agrarian party. In 1912 President Taft supported him to the extent of prohibiting the shipment of arms from the United States to his opponents. At the same time the United States government advised its citizens in Mexico to come home, in order to avoid the risk of involvement in the disorders that spread rapidly in the wake of the new phase of the revolution, while President Taft was abused at home for his "surrender" of American rights. He could not have been sorry to yield the Mexico problem, along with the Presidency, to Woodrow Wilson after the election of 1912.

Barely a fortnight before the new American president was to take office Madero was forced to resign in Mexico, on February 19, 1913, and three days later, after having been refused sanctuary in the United States Embassy in Mexico City, was assassinated, along with Suárez his vice-president, by the adherents of General Victoriano Huerta, who seized the Mexican presidency for himself. Huerta, as a conservative, received early recognition by Great Britain, with her huge oil interests in Mexico that had been developed under Díaz. But President Wilson, refusing from the first to be influenced by American capitalists who held even heavier investments in Mexico, regarded Huerta—"the unspeakable Huerta," as he called him—as one who had seized power illegally and through violence, and denied him recognition by the United States, so arousing enmities both at home and in Mexico. By 1913 American investments in Mexico amounted to approximately $1,200,000,000, and American miners, oilmen, engineers, agriculturists and their families to the number of about seventy-five thousand were living in Mexico as custodians of such wealth. Must all this be endangered by President Wilson's fastidiousness? And without the enpowering recognition of the United States must General Huerta face the perils that rose against him?

For within a month after assuming the presidency Huerta was in his turn the target of a revolutionary movement that gathered in the north, where old comrades of the beloved Madero were making an army and a policy. The north—it was there that Díaz himself had gathered his power, and again it was the vast northern deserts whose people, as so often before, bursting from their isolation and impassioned by their poverty, bore the seeds of revolution. *"Nordismo,"* they said, making a philosophy out of their bleak land for which they had nothing to lose but life, and for which anything gained must be a relief. Huerta, knowing that he must assure himself of northern loyalties, called the governors of the Rio Grande states of Coahuila and Chihuahua to his support. Chihuahua joined the Federal cause; but not Coahuila. On March 26, 1913, her governor, Venustiano Carranza, refused allegiance to Huerta, proclaimed a new revolution, announced himself as "First Chief" of all those who remained true to the Madero reforms, and took to the field with a large and ragged army. His principal command he gave to one of Madero's most ardent lieutenants—a certain Doroteo Arango, who was better known by the name he had adopted years ago out of respect for an admired bandit called Francisco Villa. Becoming popular as a bandit in his turn, the new Francisco Villa was spoken of everywhere by the diminutive of his first name—Pancho—and as his military adventures earned him his command, they brought him the rank of general of brigade—General Pancho Villa.

If in the rapid turns and overturns of power in Mexico following the fall of Díaz there seemed to be many separate revolutions during the ensuing decade, these were more truly seen as successive phases of one long struggle. For what Madero had launched was the Grand Revolution against the feudalism of Díaz, and what followed, with so many different personalities in the murderous tug of war between the adherents of absolutism and those of constitutionalism, really revived the political polarities that had divided Mexico from the time of the Emperor Agustín until the triumph of Díaz. In pain and barbarism Mexico resumed the long civil war through which for the better part of a century she sought to find her independent character.

First Chief Carranza's initial move must be against the neighboring state of Chihuahua if *nordismo* was to present a united front. General Pancho Villa marched against Chihuahua City and drove the Federal defenders all the way to the Rio Grande at Ojinaga, opposite Presidio, Texas. Out of ten thousand troops only thirty-five hundred remained there to defend the Federal idea against *nordismo*. In their ragged white uniforms they dug trenches before Ojinaga facing south, and Texans watched them from Presidio, and an American reporter told how "when the sun went down with the flare of a blast furnace, patrols of cavalry rode sharply across the skyline to the night outposts," and how "after dark mysterious fires burned in the town." Ojinaga was almost wholly in ruins, stirring with wounded, hungry, sick people, while Presidio on the American side knew a brisk trade in gambling and merchandising and conspiracy—for "you could not walk around a corner at night without stumbling over a plot or a counterplot." Two troops of the Ninth United States Cavalry patrolled the riverside, and now and then a Mexican sentry opposite fired a stray shot at them, and was fired on in turn. What all expected came to pass after about three months, when General Pancho Villa with his forces appeared through the mountains from the south and drove the Federal army over the river into Presidio. The fugitives were interned afterward behind barbed wire at Fort Bliss. General Pancho Villa seized Juárez, offering an absorbing spectacle to the citizens of El Paso who clustered on the tops of tall buildings to view through telescopes the bivouac fires by night, and by day, the drag of cannon and the wander of little columns of revolutionary troops. Chihuahua now belonged to the Constitutionalist Army—or, more properly, to Pancho Villa. There was little that Huerta could do about it.

His recognition by Great Britain made the American position more difficult. President Wilson, hoping that "a refusal to recognize any government founded upon violence" would prove instructive to Latin American republics, asked the British to withdraw their recognition of Huerta; and when this was not done, he sent a personal emissary to Mexico to persuade Huerta that for the good of Mexico he must resign and permit a new election to be held from which he must bar himself as a candidate. The *de facto* ruler of Mexico was not equal to such a display of ethical objectivity. It was a disappointment, but President

Wilson in reporting to the Congress on his failure urged patience in the face of Mexico's disorders which promised such trouble for American property holders in Mexico. "We shall triumph as Mexico's friends sooner than we could triumph as her enemies," he said, "—and how much more handsomely, with how much higher and finer satisfaction of conscience and honor!" If to many the accent here seemed like that of a proctor, and the manner superior and dry, and the vision too ideal in an uncloistered world where competition was ruthless and massacre an admitted technique of government in Mexico, there was yet an uneasy recognition that here the forces of goodness were working at large in the cause of humanity in general. President Wilson was a strong as well as a delicate man, even if he lacked the humor that might have kept him from saying to a British statesman in 1913, "I am going to teach the South American Republics to elect good men!", for all the world as if the Southern nations were seated before him in his lecture room on the top floor of Dickinson Hall at Princeton, where on Monday and Tuesday mornings he used to meet his class in Jurisprudence and Politics. In 1913 he was sure that Carranza and Villa were the best choices among Huerta's opponents. "Villa," he thought, was "not so bad as he had been painted." In any case, he had not recognized any of the three, and there was a charming tact in the little story his ambassador to Britain wrote him on October twenty-fourth. Mr. Walter Hines Page "ran across" Prime Minister Asquith at the wedding of Prince Arthur of Connaught to the Duchess of Fife and had a lively little exchange with him.

"What do you infer from the latest news from Mexico?" asked the Prime Minister.

"Several things," replied Ambassador Page.

"Tell me the most important inference you draw."

"Well, the danger of prematurely making up one's mind about a Mexican adventurer."

"Ah!" murmured the Prime Minister and walked off.

It did seem that the British were unable to feel the true significance of American forbearance and American determination that Mexico should learn to solve her own problems like a proper democracy. A few weeks later Ambassador Page reported another exchange, this time with Sir Edward Grey, the Foreign Minister.

"Suppose you have to intervene?" asked Grey.

"Make 'em vote and live by their decisions," said Page, wholly in accord with the President's view.

"But suppose they will not so live?"

"We'll go in again and make 'em vote again."

"And keep this up for 200 years?"

"Yes, the United States will be here two hundred years and it can continue to shoot men for that little space till they learn to vote and to rule themselves."

Sir Edward Grey laughed. "I have never seen him laugh so heartily," reported the Ambassador. "Shooting men into self-government! . . . he comprehends that. But that's as far as his habit of mind goes." If the British Foreign Minister could not grasp the point of the American policy, it was idle to expect Mexican bandit politicians to do so. Early in January, 1914, Ambassador Page detected signs of a new approach to the whole Mexican problem. If the British would not withdraw their recognition of Huerta, they might—it was hinted by the head of the British oil concessions in Mexico—they might undertake intervention jointly with the United States.

But the reality lay elsewhere, in a shift from the great quiet rooms of ministers and ambassadors and presidents where in every accent of education and wit the embroilments of Mexico were discussed, to the glaring plains where hard as the rocks of their concealment and irresponsible as the dust that blew past them General Pancho Villa and his band went about making carrion of all who disagreed with either their whims or their idea of revolution—which in itself was not wholly clear to themselves. In February, 1914, an Englishman, William S. Benton, was murdered at Juárez in the presence of Pancho Villa by one of his men. Britain cried out for revenge, and even threatened taking punitive steps, but was prevented by the terms of the Monroe Doctrine. Page wrote to the President that he was glad "for us and for the world that it is *our* job and not theirs. They would India-ize and Egypt-ize Mexico forever. . . ."

On April 9, 1914, the United States received an official affront at the hands of Mexican troops. Unarmed sailors from the U.S.S. *Dolphin* picking up supplies in a routine fashion at Tampico were arrested by Mexican soldiers. They were released in two hours, and General Huerta hastened to explain that the dock used by the American sailors was in a restricted area, and that as Tampico was under martial law, his soldiers had only done their duty. But clearly the Americans had not known the dock was out of bounds, and he expressed his regrets over the incident. These explanations were not satisfactory to Admiral Mayo, commanding the American Gulf squadron. He demanded that the United States flag receive a special salute from the Tampico garrison commander. The demand was referred to Mexico City. On April thirteenth General Huerta refused to order that the salute be given. Both countries had now taken steps which dignity would not permit them to retrace. President Wilson ordered naval reinforcements to Tampico and served Huerta with an ultimatum to require Mexico to salute the American flag by six in the evening of April nineteenth. The hour passed without a sign from Mexico. A day went by, and part of a night, and then at half past two in the morning of April twenty-first, the President was awakened at the White House by a telephone call from his Secretary of State, William Jennings Bryan. Also on the line were Josephus Daniels, Secretary of the Navy, and Joseph Tumulty, the secretary to the President. Bryan had alarming news. A German ship was reported by Admiral Mayo as due to arrive at Veracruz at ten o'clock the same morning. It carried "large supplies of munitions and arms for the Mexicans." The Secretary of State asked the President's judgment "as to how we shall handle the situation."

"Of course, Mr. Bryan," said the President, "you understand what drastic action in this matter might ultimately mean in our relations with Mexico?"

"I thoroughly appreciate this, Mr. President," answered Bryan, "and fully considered it before telephoning you. . . ."

The President fell silent in thought for a moment, and then asked Secretary Daniels his opinion. Daniels believed that the cargo must not be landed. The President "without a moment's delay" said to him,

"Daniels, send this message to Admiral Mayo: *'Take Veracruz at once.'* "

The orders went out. "It's too bad, isn't it," said the President to Tumulty later, "but we could not allow that cargo to land. The Mexicans intend using those guns upon our own boys. It is hard to take action of this kind. . . ." Before the day was over American marines and sailors had captured Veracruz with a loss of four killed and twenty wounded, while Mexican casualties were reported "in hundreds." All Mexico was outraged—even Carranza, who opposed Huerta, demanded that the United States withdraw at once. But once committed, the President consolidated his position by ordering thirty-four hundred troops and twelve machine guns under Major General Frederick Funston from Texas to Veracruz. War was prevented from breaking out only by an offer of mediation on the part of Argentina, Brazil and Chile—the ABC Powers. Meeting at Niagara Falls they examined the whole Mexican state of affairs, hoping to find a solution in nominating a provisional president.

Meanwhile, the American garrisons of the Rio Grande border were under alert, and Brigadier General John J. Pershing was ordered to Fort Bliss, in April. He had won distinction and early promotion in the Philippine Islands fighting against insurgent Moros. His experience in putting down guerrilla fighters would surely be useful if war with Mexico should come. But in early summer there were signs that Huerta's position was growing precarious. President Wilson, seeing that Carranza and Villa made progress in their drive against Huerta, viewed them as "sincere patriots," and as for their British critics he said they were "radically mistaken. There has been less disorder and less danger to life where the Constitutionalists have gained control than there has been where Huerta is in control." In the face of the possibility that Villa might replace Huerta, Sir Edward Grey, with a nod to the moral position pre-empted for itself by the United States, thought that ". . . it was impossible to feel that morality was really to be secured by substituting him or his kind for Huerta. . . ."

If together Carranza and Villa had been successful in their drive against Huerta, now in the early summer of 1914 they began to fall out with each other. In June Carranza knew something that led him to write to Villa's supporters in the north, "I do not consider it advisable to promote Gen. Francisco Villa . . . excusing myself from giving the reasons which have determined this decision: I may add that at the proper time this promotion may be granted." Clearly, he was disciplining his military chief. Villa, though always ready with a fierce word in approval of loyalty, was used to having his own way. For the moment he was silent, while Carranza moved nearer to Mexico City. About Carranza there were at first glance all the signals of benevolence. He was a huge man, with an impressive head. His brow was open and broad. His white whiskers divided in the middle gave him a benign look. His eyes were shielded by blue-tinted glasses. His cheeks were ruddy and he had something of a paunch and he went about in modest and rumpled khakis. Mounted on a horse he sat like a bale of goods. A former senator and governor, he seemed at times diffident. But on closer acquaintance he showed a vanity so malignant and a nature so disagreeable that even his twinkling blue lenses could not conceal the hard black burn in his smallish eyes. A trancelike egotism seemed to inform many of his public acts. In July he had the satisfaction of seeing Huerta yield to him by fleeing Mexico City to seek sanctuary abroad.

After August 4, 1914, the affairs of Mexico became almost wholly a concern of the United States, for on that day the first World War began in Europe. On August twentieth Carranza made his entry as conqueror into Mexico City.

One of his early acts after assuming supreme control of the Mexican government was to demand the withdrawal of United States forces from Veracruz, where they had remained all summer. President Wilson found it possible to agree to the evacuation now that Huerta, the "unspeakable" wretch whose policies and actions had caused the occupation in the first place, was gone. The withdrawal was ordered on September fifteenth and was completed by November twenty-third. It was Carranza's first success in foreign affairs. Within his borders during the autumn he suffered a prompt demonstration of how the revolution, by a sort of cellular division, continued to perpetuate itself. On September thirtieth, in a manifesto issued from Chihuahua, the First Chief was repudiated by General Pancho Villa, who could not forbear to mention how he had been refused promotion to General of Division, while two others had been promoted over him. The manifesto then went on to declare a new revolution, with Villa pledging himself not to accept political office, and promising to establish a civilian *ad interim* president, and guaranteeing free elections. Calling on all to support him and his Division of the North, he cried. "Every Mexican citizen who does not contribute toward realising this freedom-bearing movement will feel remorse of conscience, in that he has not known how to love and how to serve his country." He signed it "Francisco Villa," and under that he promoted himself to "General-in-Chief."

Carranza answered him within a month, referring to the manifesto which he said was "written for Villa"—a sneer at the fact that Villa was illiterate. As for the promotion affair, the First Chief said "I did not deem it justified to recompense an insubordination with a promotion," for he had had evidence of Villa's disloyalty to him. Mentioning Villa's desire to refuse all political office for himself, Carranza remarked wryly, "we shall soon be able to ascertain whether or not he has this ambition." He knew his old comrade in arms, for within three months Villa proclaimed himself President of Mexico—though without seriously disturbing Carranza's claim to the position. Caught between the hatreds and rivalries of the two revoluntionary chiefs, and harried by the sideline activities of Zapata and others of his kind, Mexico entered upon the worst years of her internal struggles, of which Americans in growing numbers were victims.

President Wilson's Republican opposition and much of the press cried out for him to chastise Mexico. To what avail was the might of the United States if it must rest idle while her citizens were hurt, robbed, or killed by political bandits below the Rio Grande? Citizens bombarded their congressional delegations with offers to volunteer, to raise regiments of "Rough Riders" or of Negro soldiers, and many men proposed themselves for commisions in the Army or appointments in civilian war service. There was an outpouring of addresses to the President, printed in pamphlet form, that described the indignities and the horrors which Americans were suffering at the hands of Mexicans who were punished only with words from Washington. But he had supporters who though they made less outcry than his attackers outnumbered them greatly. "I have to pause and remind myself," reflected the President, "that I am President of the United States and not of a small group of Americans with vested interests in Mexico." But he did his utmost short of war for his countrymen beyond the border, continuing to bear upon Carranza with the pressures of world opinion and the weight of virtue. In March, 1915, he warned him against harming foreigners in Mexico, and "any apparent contempt for the rights and safety of those who respect religion—" for one of the revolutionary measures was to persecute the Church. "To warn you concerning such matters," wrote President Wilson to Carranza, "is an act of friendship. . . ." Such friendship seemed to mean nothing. Acts of depredation were continued, and at the end of March the President said "I am daily fearful that something imprudent may be done at Brownsville," and like his predecessor advised Americans in Mexico to come home. The advice was no more popular now than before.

United States Army garrisons along the border were augmented, chiefly by the cavalry in its last great service to the country. The lower river forts knew again some of the animation and importance of their first years, and bleak little stations of mounted troops were established in the Big Bend, and the border guard was intensified at Presidio, Fort Bliss, and Columbus, New Mexico, where the Thirteenth Cavalry watched over a vast plain that reached out of sight beyond the barbed wire fence of the boundary. President Wilson gave to the world a picture of what a wilderness Mexico had become by the acts of her own people. "Her crops are destroyed, her fields lie unseeded, her work cattle are confiscated for the use of the armed factions, her people flee to the mountains to escape being drawn into unending bloodshed, and no man seems to see or lead the way to peace and settled order. . . . Mexico is starving and without a government." One of her resources most ruined was the railroad system. Rebels used locomotives and chains to haul the railroad ties out of the ground, and to twist the rails into a tangle, and to make a heap of it all, which was then set on fire. All the railroad stations that could be reached were burned down. Rebel forces taking a town which had marshalling yards sent locomotives after freight cars on tracks in the near hundred miles. The cars were brought in and all burned. The destruction was so great that ten years would hardly suffice to set the lines operating again. Where trackage in parts of the north was allowed to survive, the army of Villa learned to use the railroad as a military instrument. The horses and cows of the army were put inside boxcars, the troopers in their huge hats and garlands of cartridge belts rode on top, and in time the signal of a rag of smoke on the distance came to mean terror and tribute in the hearts of the local people who could only snatch up a child, a chicken, a grandparent, and scratch their way to the mountains. "My poor Mexico," said Porfirio Díaz, in Paris, in that summer of 1915, and said no more, and died.

In midsummer one of Wilson's cabinet officers wrote of him, "These are times of terrible strain upon him. I saw him last night for a couple of hours, and the responsibility of the situation weighs terribly upon him." Now it was not only Mexico that heaped outrage upon insult, it was also Germany, for she was denying the open seas even to neutral shipping. On May seventh she had sunk the *Lusitania,* which—even if it was a legitimate target as a British ship—carried many American passengers; and war sentiment rose again in the United States. "How to keep us out of war and at the same time maintain our dignity—this is a task certainly large enough for the largest of men," concluded the secretary.

Carranza in his early acts of power had begun the restoration of certain land rights long taken from the communal villages by the Díaz laws. In consequence the Mexican revolutionary ranks closed behind him—excepting those commanded in the north by Villa. Carranza had, after all, a *de facto* government; and in the autumn of 1916 he was recognized by a conference of the United States and the other governments of the hemisphere as president of Mexico. The act of recognition sealed Villa's hostility to him. From now onward, the General-in-Chief of the northern deserts would go to any lengths to harass him. President Wilson, even though Carranza had refused to participate in the conference that had brought him respectability among the nations, saw the results in his own way: "The moral," he said to Congress, "the moral is that the states of America are not hostile rivals, but cooperating friends, and that their growing sense of community of interest, alike in matters political and alike in matters economic, is likely to give them a new significance as factors in international affairs and in the political history of the world." To the most thoughtful element of the Mexican people such words must have sounded reassuring; but the most thoughtful element was not in charge, and the ones that tore Mexico between them could only hear the message with imperfect comprehension of its generous humanity, and grow dull under its glow of high-mindedness.

A more understandable consequence, perhaps, of the new policy of recognition was an embargo declared on October twentieth on exportation of arms to Mexico, with the exception of territory controlled by Carranza. Villa and his other enemies were thus repudiated. It was a hard blow to General Pancho Villa and to the American arms manufacturers with whom he had been doing a great business. He was the lord of Chihuahua, now able to spend tens of thousands of dollars a month in purchasing American supplies. His agents and commissionaires swarmed in and out of El Paso. From now on if they wanted guns and bullets they would have to smuggle them—a duty they could manage with only a little bother. General-in-Chief Pancho Villa was well known in El Paso. Many men of business found it sensible to deal with him. At Fort Bliss his operations were watched. The cavalry drilled and trained against the day when they might be needed in action on the border.

General Pershing was a great believer in thorough training, and in the duty of example, down to the smallest details of an officer's bearing and deportment. He was himself a superb model of a soldier. If he seemed at times hard, he was fair, as he lived by the discipline which he required of others. He stood straight and his uniforms were cut in flat planes to fit the trimness of his figure. He spoke clearly in reflection of his clear thought, and so wrote. He was still too thin from the hardships suffered in the Philippine campaign, but he was gradually getting his full strength back, doing his job in command of his brigade with crisp respect for it and for himself. If he had feelings, few others, certainly none of his men, were permitted to know them. One morning in August, 1915, he met an occasion that called for all of his hardest self-discipline. He was told in a long distance telephone call that during the previous night his wife and three young daughters had lost their lives at San Francisco in a fire that destroyed their quarters. Of all his family only his infant son survived.

The young officer—young for a brigadier general—took leave to attend to matters that none could do for him. By midautumn he was again on duty at the Rio Grande. The training schedules went on as usual. He had been unable to bring himself to write even to close friends but this too he finally must do. On October fifth to one such he wrote, "I shall never be relieved of the poignancy of grief at the terrible loss. . . . It is too overwhelming!" He could not understand how he had lived through it all even thus far. He was trying to work and keep from thinking, but "Oh!" he confessed, "the desolation of Life! The emptiness of it all, after such fulness as I have had. . . ." He wrote again a month later. ". . . I cannot see that time makes the slightest difference. It is just as it was on the dreadful morning when the telephone message gave me the heartbreaking news." But he could see about him, and he saw how matters stood along the river. ". . . I shall be tied down with this border patrol indefinitely. I am working just as hard as possible and am really fortunate to have something to do." He was like a sword receiving through extremes of endurance its true temper.

Demands for national intervention in Mexico grew in volume throughout 1915. The hazards of intervention still seemed to President Wilson greater than the benefits, the injustice of it outweighing any possible material satisfactions. How, he considered, once having entered Mexico could the United States pull out? How ever convince Latin American neighbors that an invasion would be only a brief policing action? But many Americans did not want any such moderation. Citizens wrote to their congressmen and senators saying that the only way to make Mexico behave was to take her territory, whether only temporarily until quiet should be restored, or—why not?—in permanent annexation. And Mexico, hearing echoes of such sentiments, could remember what she had seen before across the Rio Grande, when North Americans came to live as Mexican colonists in Texas, and ended by owning Texas; and when soldiers singing "Green grow the lilacs, oh" came all along the Rio Grande and remained to own New Mexico, Arizona, and California. Would Mexico herself, like her northernmost states of yesterday, be turned now into a foreign land for her own people? President Wilson was a professional historian. He was not proud of the war of Mexican annexation of seventy years past. With all his sorrow and anger over Mexico's crimes, he could see some matters from her point of view.

Though it was true that she tried him sorely. In the late weeks of 1915 another hazard appeared out of Mexico. Secretary of State Lansing discovered that General Victoriano Huerta in El Paso was holding secret conversations with German agents, "looking toward the financing of a revolutionary expedition into northern Mexico." The Secretary declared that this "if it materialized" must end by involving the United States in active war "across the international boundary." It was clear, he said, that "the Germans were intriguing to cause trouble between this government and the *de facto* government of Carranza and also between the American authorities and the rebellious Villista generals. . . ."

There was an ominous quickening of affairs along the river. Mexicans were firing almost every day across the border at American patrols, among whom several were killed and wounded. In Carranza territory, down the river from Villa's empire, federal soldiers joined in outlaw raids on American settlements. On November twenty-sixth at Nogales, Villista troops fired into the American half of the town before withdrawing in a planned evacuation. After the New Year, General Pancho Villa, on January 10, 1916, threw an attack against a train on which American mining employees were riding near the Santa Isabel mines of Chihuahua, and murdered eighteen of them. If Villa had a policy that dictated his scattered pattern of outrages upon American citizens, it seemed to arise from his hatred of Carranza, and his desire at all costs to embarrass him, particularly by bringing down upon him, if he could, the full wrath of the United States. The most direct way to manage this—so Villa must think—was to continue his outrages upon American citizens. The work was congenial and he was a master at it, and so were many of his lieutenants, notably Fierro, "The Butcher," his greatest friend, who only made him sigh affectionately when he personally would shoot down a hundred prisoners for the simple pleasure of it.

The General-in-Chief was of medium height. He had the sort of figure that showed the baby in the body of the man, with thick shoulders, plump forward-hanging belly and short, light, curved legs. His face was deep-jowled. His short nose and wide nostrils and big lip suggested in a kind of good looks that nearness to the simian which was echoed also in his walk. When he walked, it was with a humped posture, and a somewhat pigeon-toed shamble. But like a Comanche Honey-Eater, the moment he was on a horse, he was a master of a physical style, whether to the sound of the shrill Mexican trumpet he rode at a smart walk along a troop-lined street in Juárez, or dirty and unshaven he picked his way at a gallop over the insecure footing of rocky foothills. It was his habit to say almost nothing, since he expressed his opinions in more direct ways, as so many dead men indicated. His mouth hung open under its thick mustache, and his expression was gentle but for his eyes, which an American journalist described as "never still and full of energy and brutality . . . intelligent as hell and as merciless." His bravery was famous. So was his short temper. He loved flattery and friendship, demanded loyalty and never gave it, except to Madero. He was the subject of many ballads which he could not hear often enough. He neither smoked nor drank, but—aside from killing—took his joys in venery and dancing. One time he danced steadily for thirty-six hours at a friend's wedding. In his savage infantilism he seemed to educated men who knew him more animal than man. "He is the most natural human being I ever saw," said one, "natural in the sense of being nearest to a wild animal." Another said ". . . he was as unmoral as a wolf." His general style was at least partly self-conscious, for like one of the frontier fantastics of early Western America, he once cried, "Qué chico se me hace el mar para hacer un buche de agua. . . ." In that boastful promise to use the ocean for a gargle there was a hint of the scale by which he measured himself. His land and people could measure him best by what he so often left behind him in his travels—a field full of dropped bundles of clothes that once had moved with the bodies inside them, or depending from a cottonwood tree clusters of hanged men like great bunches of gourds, and as hollow of life. Some of his countrymen saw him as the champion of the poor; others questioned the value of benefactions made possible by years of crime against humanity. As lord of Chihuahua he tried to make up a sensible government out of his own head. The effort was brave but erratic. Caged within the invisible bars of his ignorance he could escape them only through acts of violence upon others. This was the man who in January, 1916, was causing such grave concern to the United States, and to its officers on the Rio Grande border, including the young brigadier at Fort Bliss whose severe respect for life was to be measured by the sorrow he daily sought to overcome in acts of work.

In February the President told the United States Senate that seventy-six Americans had been killed in Mexico during the previous three years. Sixty-three of these had died in the last six weeks. In addition, thirty-six had been killed by Mexicans on American soil. For years feeling along the border had been against intervention, but now it shifted, and an American wrote, "As one striving to do business in the Republic of Mexico, I have been very hopeful that the next President of the United States might be a gentleman who did not hold such altruistic and ethical views as President Wilson. . . ."

General Pancho Villa continued to throw down his challenges. On March first an American family of ranchers south of the border in Mexico—their name was Wright—saw a band of horsemen ride up and

identified them by their red saddle blankets as Villistas. In very little
time the visitors did their work. They killed Wright, sent his infant son
off with a squad riding to Juárez, put the mother, Maud Wright, up on
a horse, took what they wanted of supplies, and circled off over the desert
toward the international boundary. Mrs. Wright rode with the column
for nine days on a forced march. She had nothing to eat but mule meat
and once for thirty hours had to go without water. She understood
Spanish and was startled to hear the bandits working out arrangements
to raid Columbus, New Mexico, which lay two miles north of the border,
and fifty west of El Paso. A town of four hundred people, it was the
station of six troops of the Thirteenth United States Cavalry. She knew
well enough what her captors liked to do to Americans. There was
nothing she could do to give warning. On March eighth she saw go and
return a squad of bandits and heard them report how they had crossed
the border and spied upon Columbus. They said that most of the garrison
were camping on guard near a ranch farther west, and that only a few
American soldiers were at the Columbus post. She could only wait to
witness further horrors.

On the same day a number of the officers of the Thirteenth were
in El Paso, playing polo at Fort Bliss. There seemed no cause for alarm
in the immediate situation at Columbus. The colonel of the regiment
took what information he could get from Mexican residents, but he was
prevented by orders from stepping an inch over the boundary to make
personal surveys. He heard rumors that Villa was in the neighborhood,
and was given the surprising, the even reassuring report that Villa was
coming to give himself up as a prisoner of war. He was said to have very
few men with him. The colonel continued his patrols along the American
side of the barbed wire fence that marked the international line. There
was a gate, of course, and the colonel stationed one troop there. Two
others were at the ranch farther along the line. Three troops and the
regimental machine gun were on post in Columbus. There was a late
train that came out from El Paso on the Southern Pacific and passed
through Columbus going west. Around midnight of March eighth-ninth,
a young officer of the Thirteenth arrived on the train to go on duty as
Officer of the Day. He had been at Bliss for the polo. It was a cold night,
but he was wakeful, and once established in the Officer of the Day's
shanty, he sat up reading. The rest of the post, and the town, were in
darkness and quiet.

It was a quarter of four when he heard a muffled sound from a
private on sentry post outside. He went to the door and saw a figure

moving in the dim fall of light from the O.D. shack. There was a shot, the sentry fell dead, and the Officer of the Day shot the Mexican who had killed him. In another second there was rifle fire from two sides of the camp and the town. Families were awakened by what at first they "thought was hail on the roof." Then bullets broke against the walls of houses, and screams sounded, and wailing cheers from the Mexican attackers. Some of the residents thought they heard General Pancho Villa's voice "everywhere." The Officer of the Day, nearest the attacking fire, took charge of the awakened troops and directed their defense. The machine gun jammed after a few rounds and became useless. For a while the darkness made a blind fight of it, but when the Mexicans set some buildings to burning, the glare showed the scene to the cavalry, and their resistance turned into attack. The raiders were amongst the streets now, killing and burning noisily. Soldiers' wives took their children and ran under the protection of shadowing alleys to gather for safety in a ser-geant's house that was defended by men of F Troop. The children were put under the beds and the women lay flat on the floor, while bullets swarmed above them through the walls. Everyone was quiet, even the children. Presently a sergeant of F Troop said to his soldiers outside, *"Pick your men,* there is hardly any more ammunition." In the wild firelight the battle hung for a little while longer at its peak, and then began to subside, for General Pancho Villa could not animate his men to another attack against such fire as they had finally faced. They began to fall away from the town. Dawn was near. Mrs. Wright, who had help-lessly watched the battle from a ditch outside, saw General Pancho Villa as he retreated. She asked him to turn her free. He jerked his head toward Columbus and told her to go. She entered the town and went to the house of friends. She found them. The husband was lying dead face down on his steps, his wife was near-by, badly wounded. Mrs. Wright was helped by an officer who sent her to his wife. As the raiders disap-peared into the early light of the desert, the officer's wife and all the others came out of the house where they had been safe. She saw "the dead and wounded everywhere." Nine townspeople and eight troopers had been killed, and many of Villa's men. She told later, "I did not know I could have such hate in my heart. I saw Mexicans horribly wounded and suffering terribly and did not care how much they suffered. . . ." She was soon "thankful to be busy" doing what she could for the wives, the children, of soldiers who had been killed or hurt that night. When Mrs. Wright came to her, she listened to her story, and judged her "a very strong intelligent ranch woman . . . a very remarkable person." Mrs.

Wright was able to give the officers much that was "valuable to know" about Villa and his band. She reported that he had between twenty-five hundred and three thousand men. Already convinced that she had lost everything, it would come as a great wonder when a few days later her baby would be restored to her.

In the growing daylight troops of the Thirteenth pursued Villa. They killed fifty of the raiders on the American side of the border, and following the rest over the line into Mexico, they killed another seventy in several little battles under the blazing sun. Lack of ammunition, food and water after eight hours forced the pursuers back to Columbus, while Villa and his men disappeared into their deserts, and decisions were taken in Washington and Mexico City.

Carranza made an immediate official apology for the Villa attack, promising to "use the most vigorous means to run this man to earth and avenge his horrible acts." Washington hoped he would indeed do so, but if Carranza's prompt apology was meant to prevent, or defer, American entry into Mexico, it failed of its purpose. The War Department ordered all garrisons on the Rio Grande to give chase into Mexico if attacked from over the border, and directed General Funston at Fort Sam Houston to send troops as soon as possible to overtake Villa and the raiders. "These troops will be withdrawn," commanded Secretary Baker, "as soon as the *de facto* government of Mexico is able to relieve them of this work. . . ." In a further detail, the Secretary wrote ". . . you are instructed to make all practical use of the aeroplanes at San Antonio, Texas, for observation." A new military age was upon the nation.

On the day when the American orders were issued—March tenth—Carranza proposed that "armed forces of either country might freely cross into the territory of the other . . . if the raid effected at Columbus should unfortunately be repeated at any other point on the border." It was the only possible move for him to make if Mexico's dignity was to be upheld. President Wilson approved the proposal, and Secretary Lansing telegraphed the State Department's acceptance of it. On March fifteenth a United States cavalry column crossed into Mexico under the command of Brigadier General John J. Pershing in pursuit of Villa and his men. The act was a signal for Carranza to fly into one of his furies. The "reciprocal pursuit" agreement, he cried, was meant to apply only to *future* raids—it was not to be applied retroactively to the Columbus raid. General Pancho Villa's policy of making trouble on an international plane was off to a good start. It effected corruption in simpler ways, too, for on the day after the attack, over a hundred thousand rounds of ammunition were sold in El Paso to Villa agents and taken across the river. "Fine doings," remarked the local citizen who reported the matter to Washington.

The American press expressed the rage felt by its readers. In New York, the *American* said "The American flag has indeed been saluted at last." The *Tribune* felt that "The Bryan-Wilson policy . . . has borne its perfect fruit," while the *Evening-Journal* demanded an immediate seizure of all Mexico and Central America: "What has been done in California and Texas by the United States can be done *all the way down to the southern bank of the Panama Canal and a few miles beyond.*" The *World* cried that "Nothing less than Villa's life can atone for the outrage," but the Chicago *Tribune* believed that in respect to the pacification of Mexico, "The death of Villa is a minor detail in such a program. . . . It is a condition—a chronic condition—of chaos, not a Villa, that confronts us." In another editorial, the New York *World* projected the real positions of the sovereignties involved: "So far as it is possible for a bandit to be at war, Villa is now at war with both Mexico and the United States. . . ." The hero of Chihuahua seemed really to feel like a sovereign power. His subjects had confidence in him, and said so in one of their songs, so touched with the acrid pathos of their land and its habits of life, death and war:

> Maybe they have guns and cannons,
> Maybe they are a lot stronger,
> We have only rocks and mountains—
> But we know how to last longer. . . .

President Wilson felt, at home, dangerous currents of opinion that if unchecked might bring war even closer. Two weeks after the Columbus disaster he said, "It is my duty to warn the people of the United States that persons along the border are engaged in giving currency to rumors of the most sensational sort, which are wholly unsupported by the facts. The object of this traffic in falsehood is obvious. It is to create friction between the United States and Mexico, to bring about intervention in the interest of the owners of Mexican properties. . . ." The Administration assured the country that the border was quiet; no preparations for war were necessary. This moved a businessman of the border to telegraph in a rage to a senator, ". . . I ask you to see that the Administration if it insists on being blind is forced to see the light and thereby stumble upon their duty. . . ."

The only note of satisfaction in the discussions of the hour came from the German Ambassador to the United States. In early April Count von Bernstorff reported to his government: "It seems to be increasingly probable that the punitive expedition against Villa will lead to a full-dress intervention. . . ." This suited Germany's plans precisely, for the agitation of the Mexican issue owed much to German enterprise, and "So long as the Mexican holds the stage here," continued Bernstorff, "we are, I believe, safe from an act of aggression on the part of the American government." This was a limited view of conditions that were seen in a larger frame by President Wilson. The Mexican chaos, he said, represented "a revolution as profound as that which occurred in France," and for his part he found that its aims were as valid, "no matter what the excesses committed. . . ." The President's point of view was faced with repeated challenges. General Pershing's command reached their point of farthest penetration into Mexico as the town of Parral in southern Chihuahua. There on April twelfth while buying supplies in town American cavalrymen were fired upon by Mexican federal troops. The attack was returned, and before it was over forty Mexicans and two Americans had been killed. Acts of war had been exchanged now not between a bandit and his pursuer but between the official forces of the two nations. Once again a state of war seemed near. To dispel it by agreement, and to allow to Mexico her full sovereignty in affairs of internal discipline, the United States proposed a conference between the military chiefs of both nations, to be held at El Paso. Major General Hugh L. Scott, chief of staff, and General Alvaro Obregón, Mexican secretary of war, met for talks in late April and early May. General Funston was on hand from Fort Sam Houston. The Mexican officer was received in state. He reviewed guards of honor, conferred with his hosts on a private car in the El Paso yards, and finally on May third agreed to a program—though not until General Scott had kept him in a room at the Paso del Norte Hotel for twelve hours of continuous, and secret, debate. It was just past midnight when General Obregón signed the concordat, after which General Scott, avoiding reporters, went out to telegraph his text to Washington. It was entirely satisfactory to the President, who made a public statement at once:

"The agreement drawn up and approved by officers of both governments contemplates the partial retirement of the American force toward the border, the prosecution of the search for Villa, and the dispersal of his remaining following by the Mexican forces, and the entire withdrawal of the American expedition" eventually. For American interventionists the formula gave too much respect to Mexico, for

Carranza, not enough. He refused to ratify the agreement because it fixed no date for the completion of the United States evacuation. And in the week of these discussions, Villa forces, striking in small and swift units, raided settlements in Texas near Dryden, and at Eagle Pass, and at Glen Springs and Boquillas in the Big Bend. The raids yielded the bandits little if anything in loot, and fewer than their usual captives or corpses, but were clearly intended to create further international mischief.

While Governor Ferguson of Texas urged the United States to "enter Mexico and assume control of that unfortunate country" for the purpose of establishing there a stable government "whether it takes 10 or 50 years to do it," troopers at Fort Bliss were called out to avenge the Glen Springs raid, where three American soldiers and three civilians had been killed on May fifth by a column of sixty raiders. On May sixth a second band of Villistas, twenty of whom were said to be residents of the American side of the Big Bend, galloped into Boquillas at dawn, looted a store and a neighboring mine, and captured eight men. News of the raids reached Bliss on Sunday, the seventh, while the officers were playing "an engrossing practice game of polo." By five in the afternoon two troops of the Eighth Cavalry were moving out by railroad for the Big Bend, and four days later, accompanied by two news correspondents and two motion picture cameramen in two Ford touring cars, and commanded by Major George T. Langhorne in his Cadillac "8"—his fellow officers knew he had "money on the outside"—crossed the Rio Grande at the old Spanish ford of San Vicente. The weather was fearfully hot and dusty. There was scarcely a road to follow. The motor cars made heavy going out of arroyos whose banks had to be dug away before they could be crossed on wheels, while the mounted cavalrymen chafed at the delays caused by their headquarters cars. Travelling at night the commander from his magnificent car would signal in an improvised code with a pocket flashlight to his soldiers following him—"good road," "bad road," "stop." When by day the pursuit force came upon Mexican settlements the cameramen took films of the residents, and "nearly frightened them to death by lining them up in front of their cameras. They had a pretty good idea," noted a young officer, "of what it meant to be stood up in a row and have a machine aimed at them. . . ." The cavalry sighted the bandits several times and gave chase, with "the Cadillac 8 bounding over the ditches and bushes like a steeplechase, to the tune of a cannonading." One time two American detachments manoeuvring unknown to each other in the same area nearly shot each other up in false dawn light. The chase lasted three weeks, and was called done when all prisoners had been retaken, the bandits dispersed, and several wounded and captured. Without having lost a man or a horse the Eighth Cavalry troopers returned to Fort Bliss on May twenty-eighth.

Meanwhile on May ninth the Carranzist forces in northern Mexico threatened to attack General Pershing's column. On the same day President Wilson called out the National Guard contingents of New Mexico, Arizona and Texas, even while he seemed to cling the more earnestly to his hope of avoiding a major contest with Mexico. On May eleventh he received Secretary of War Newton D. Baker and could not help speaking his innermost thoughts. "He said his Mexican policy," recorded the Secretary, "was based upon two of the most deeply seated convictions of his life. . . . First, his shame as an American over the first Mexican War, and his resolution that there should never be another such predatory enterprise. Second, . . . his belief in the principle laid down in the Virginia Bill of Rights that a people has the right to do as they damn please"—he really used the word "damn," said the Secretary—"with their own affairs. He wanted to give the Mexicans a chance to try. . . ." Furthermore, he seemed to see the country of Mexico in its vastness, and the vast effort needed to pacify it, for he said it would take "five hundred thousand men at least. . . ."

And there went Pershing, with a force that at its peak would not exceed fifteen thousand. An El Paso paper said that the pursuit of Villa was like turning a jackrabbit loose in Oklahoma and sending the El Paso police to hunt him. In the successive snows and winds, dusts and blasting sunlight of spring and early summer the Punitive Expedition creaked its way south on the plains beside the Sierra Madre. The General in order to travel rapidly between the scattered units of his widely deployed army went by motor. There were three light cars in his headquarters group. Early in the motor age desert travel was hard. Cars heated up and boiled over. Springs broke on the chucky roads. There was no roadside service. Keeping in touch with supplies of gasoline, oil, water and tires was difficult. The early movements southward were managed by rail—until Carranza denied the use of Mexican railroads to the American troops. Then an extended motor transport system had to be established with its base at Columbus, which became a boom town as the American source of all of Pershing's supply. In remarkably short time the quartermaster's motor truck supply lines were covering four thousand miles of Mexican trails, and penetrating to a distance of three hundred miles below the border. There were places where the trucks had to go as many as sixty miles in low gear. In all the strangeness of the country nothing was odder than the sudden appearance, along the motor lines, of little shops set up in booths by Chinese vendors who sold trifles and notions to American soldiers.

The Army brought many of its disadvantages with it. Equipment was inadequate, methods were all too often improvised. "Isn't this a great time," asked an officer, "for our cavalry to be going to war? No saddle and no drill regulations. . . ." He said that fifty-nine out of seventy-nine saddles in his troop were defective, and the trooper's regulation sabre was "an abomination," and ought to be thrown away. Others agreed with him, for a quartermaster later hauled two truckloads of discarded sabres all the way back to Columbus. The troops wore out their lariats and bandoliers. Shoe iron for the mounts was so scarce that the troop blacksmiths stopped to pick up a shoe cast anywhere along the road. The men carried horseshoe nails in a greasy rag to keep them from rusting. Troopers added kerchiefs to their uniforms against sweat and dust, and found "auto glasses" not a luxury but a necessity against the sun. Purchase of supply in the countryside was complicated. The colonel of the Tenth Cavalry had to resort to giving his personal cheques for purchases, and ran up a total of $1,680. Men grew so tired on the march that during short halts orders were given for "all to remain standing . . . otherwise men would immediately drop off to sleep, and there was much difficulty and delay in rousing them," and "horses . . . developed a hunger that caused them to chew the halter shanks," either of rope or leather. Was it the strange land itself that was trying to defeat these invaders? When the bandit trail led them into the Sierra Madre they found the temperature blazing hot by day, icy cold by night. "Men and animals had icicles hanging from their whiskers," and "canteens were frozen solid." In the canyons "darkness came on quickly. . . . The trails twisted and turned among the trees," and "a deceiving moonlight" changed all objects into fantastic shadows. But still, day after day, the packmaster rang his bell to call the animal train together, and the march would continue.

All along the extended line communications were all but impossible to maintain. The wireless and the telegraph were unreliable, and "the greatest deficiency," said an officer, "was the lack of an adequate air force." Eight open-seater biplanes from San Antonio were assigned to the expedition, and undertook a regular schedule of flights between the commanding general and his scattered units. A plane would fly in to a forward camp and land to deliver a message, and take one aboard, and rise off the scrubby desert to dwindle alone out of sight into the white

sky. All too soon six of the planes cracked up, and the last two were
left to cover the wilderness between Columbus and the commanding
general's farthest station four hundred miles south of the river. And
then those two gave out—one of them was fired at on the ground at
Chihuahua City—and the air force was done in Mexico. Debate sounded
throughout the service. Had the planes been properly employed? Should
they be used to fly messages, or to conduct forward reconnaissance? A
philosophy of the military air was being formed.

The ground troops remained. They persisted in their mission.
They hardened. It was clear that the land was not defeating them. The
United States continued its firm but mild pressure, and the National
Guard began to appear on the border, though only after one or two
false starts, for in Texas one hundred sixteen guardsmen refused to
muster and were granted discharges, and in New Mexico certain guardsmen reported for duty in derby hats and certain others brought their
feather beds. But still the border was strengthened and to Mexico
the sight seemed menacing. On May thirty-first Carranza issued a demand
to the United States for the instant removal of American troops from
Mexico. The note insolently charged that General Pershing's men were
being kept in Mexico to lend political value to President Wilson's campaign for renomination during the next few weeks. The President did
not answer it until after the convention which renominated him had
adjourned. Meanwhile, a number of scattered but possibly related acts
gave emphasis to Mexico's policy. On June sixteenth, in a communication
quickly ratified by Carranza, the Mexican commander of Federalist troops
in the north notified General Pershing that any movement of United
States troops further into the south, or to the east or west, or in any
direction but north to the border, would be considered by Mexico a
cause for war. On the next day bandits erupted near Brownsville and a
detachment from Fort Brown crossed the river to chase them. One day
later, across the great Mexican isthmus, two American naval officers of
the gunboat *Annapolis* were arrested at Mazatlan, and their boat crew
were fired on by Mexican troops on shore. On the following day, the
commander of the *Annapolis* radioed his government that the Mexican
state of Sinaloa had independently declared war on the United States.
And along the line of General Pershing's march Federalist troops were
gathering. Once more Carranza, having yet received no reply to his
arrogant note of three weeks before, formally demanded that the Punitive Expedition retire from Mexico. On June twentieth his answer
came: "The United States," it said, "cannot recede from its settled

determination to maintain its national rights and perform its full duty in preventing further invasions of the territory of the United States. . . ." On the same day General Funston wired Washington to ask for sixty-five thousand more National Guardsmen. One day later Carranza's troops opened fire on two troops of the Tenth United States Cavalry at Carrizal, in the state of Chihuahua.

Word of the engagement in the field before the town went to the border command from a wounded cavalry captain who wrote at nine fifteen in the morning on June 21, 1916, "I am hiding in a hole two thousand yards from the field and have one other wounded man and three men with me." At half past six that morning, having marched since before dawn, the troops came to an open field southeast of town. They were on their way to Ahumada, to the east of Carrizal. The senior officer, Captain Boyd of C Troop, sent a note into Carrizal asking for permission to take his men through it on their way. The permission was refused, with the admonition that the American troops could proceed to the north, but not to the east. Presently word came from the Carranzist general commanding in Carrizal that Boyd could bring his men into town for a conference. By now there was a line of about one hundred and twenty Mexican troops on the edge of town facing the Americans. Captain Boyd "feared an ambush." He formed his troops as skirmishers and moved toward Carrizal. "When we were within three hundred yards the Mexicans opened fire," wrote the wounded captain, "and a strong one, before we fired a shot; then we opened up." A battle of an hour ensued. Captain Boyd was killed, along with six other cavalrymen, and twenty-three were taken prisoner.

Immediately the United States demanded the release of the Carrizal prisoners and seized the international bridges of the Rio Grande to secure them in case of a full-scale invasion of Mexico. General Pershing was ordered to hold his ground. The entire National Guard was sent to the boundary. People in the river cities of Matamoros, Juárez and other border towns began to flee to the interior. In the indignant if miniature Sinaloan war, Mexicans fired again on American bluejackets without provocation. General Obregón began to talk about taking San Antonio, Texas, in two weeks. The Guard poured across the United States by troop train until there were fifty thousand men stationed at each of three border defense positions—at Nogales, El Paso and Brownsville.

Now at last Carranza was impressed by the policy of the United States. In the face of such swift and heavy mobilization, he ordered within a week the release of the Carrizal prisoners, and promised to undertake the pursuit of bandits. An equilibrium was restored to affairs between the two governments, and orders were issued at Washington for the Punitive Expedition to pull back from aggressive pursuit to assume guard duty in Northern Mexico. There had been skirmishes with bandits—mounted men coming off their horses to take cover behind mesquite brush, and now and then a bloom and fade of cartridge smoke over sandy wastes, and then some fellow lying inert on his own shadow. One detachment was sure it had come upon Villa and had actually wounded him, and in any case, no further major assaults upon American settlements had taken place. The Expedition had not been wasted, though in back-country tales Mexicans told one another how Villa had played hide and seek with his pursuers, as he crouched in brush or cave to watch the hot, dirty and tired troopers ride past him. The commanding general calmly resolved the whole adventure afterward. "After we had penetrated about four hundred miles into Mexican territory," wrote General Pershing, "and overtaken Villa's band and others, and scattered them, wounding Villa himself, the increasing disapproval of the Mexican Government doubtless caused the administration to conclude that it would be better to rest content that the outlaw bands had been severely punished and generally dispersed, and that the people of northern Mexico had been taught a salutary lesson. . . ."

The Chief of Staff agreed that Pershing's mission had been accomplished. He "made a complete success . . ." said General Scott, "from the War Department's point of view." Now in late June of 1916 "activities in Mexico were discontinued," reported General Pershing, "the more advanced elements were withdrawn, and the expedition thereafter held a line of communications reaching only about one hundred fifty miles south of the border. As there was then little work to do except to protect this line, a systematic scheme of training was inaugurated throughout the command." Without the preoccupations of the field, he had to find other barriers against his own thoughts. He would still think now and then that he had only to go home to find them all there—and then he would remember, and confess to an old friend, "One *never, never* can get over it." But the new training program was something to cling to, and he wrote, "Work is the only possible relief and I work like a slave all the time. We have had some of the most valuable instruction here I have ever seen in the army and I have laid out and conducted the most of it myself—just to keep busy."

The crisis was eased. "Peace with Mexico," said the New York *Times,* "now seemingly well assured, will be most welcome to all Americans, save for those few plotters of mischief who, for personal interest, have desired intervention." A Brazilian paper had its own view of American policy, though it seemed never to have listened to President Wilson: "The severity and the contempt with which Washington looks upon the revolutions of the neighboring countries are neither just nor Christian," declared the *Gazeta de Noticias* of Rio de Janeiro. And once again, the President reached out to Mexico as to an equal and independent power. In July he asked that a joint commission composed of three representatives of the United States and three of Mexico be convened to arbitrate their difficulties for the two nations. From the perspective of Europe, the news struck an American ambassador as a "light in the universal darkness! What an example to civilization in the midst of anarchy!" The commission undertook its work at New London, Connecticut, and presently moved it to Atlantic City. Secretary of the Interior Franklin K. Lane was chairman of the American delegation. He was hopeful of the joint commission's purpose. "It ought," he said, "to indicate the line of political direction in the New World for the next thousand years." But he soon encountered a difficulty familiar to those who dealt with the First Chief of Mexico. "Carranza is obsessed with the idea that he is a real god and not a tin god, that he holds thunderbolts in his hands instead of confetti, and he won't let us help him. . . ." There lay the real trouble. "The hardest part of all is to convince a proud and obstinate people that they really need any help." Mexicans, discovered Secretary Lane, "distrust us. They will not believe that we do not want to take some of their territory. . . ." But the conference persisted in its work through the fall and early winter of 1916, while rumors of Villa flew across the border—he was raising a new army of eighteen thousand men, he was about to lose Chihuahua, he was about to take Chihuahua back again, he was hiding in the Sierra nursing his wound and getting about on crutches, he was on the verge of driving Carranza from the National Palace.

There were other alarms—the State Department had evidence of German attempts to persuade Mexico to grant permission for the establishment of submarine bases in Mexican territory. President Wilson had long been convinced that a great part of the border troubles could be traced to German propaganda. In the atmosphere of growing tension between the United States and Germany there seemed to be some indication that Germany took the Rio Grande to be her new frontier.

The border saw a great revolving system of training in its camps. When ten thousand newly mustered guardsmen were sent there for active duty, ten thousand already there were relieved and sent home. The lessons of General Pershing's training program told along the river, and gave a great proportion of the nation's man power its first exercises in modern warfare. They were lessons that would bear fruit within a very few months overseas. Meanwhile, in echoes of 1846, American young men wandered about in the river towns after duty, and ate scalding messes in chili parlors and dawdled under glaring lights that showed the way to darker indulgences, though *The Rio Grande Rattler,* a soldier paper published by the New York division of the Guard, reported that when saloons were closed and bordellos declared off-limits by the command, soldiers accepted these prohibitions loyally. General Funston had a brush with a revival sect when he declined to permit revival meetings to be held in the camps, where after all the usual services of chaplains of all denominations were available. He did not, he said, "wish the emotions of the soldiers stirred," and he "did not accept the view that because a man put on his country's uniform he was necessarily lost. . . ."

And suddenly the whole adventure drew to its close. In November the joint Mexican-American commission made its final recommendation, proposing as the only solution that full diplomatic relations be re-established and the troops withdrawn altogether from Mexico. The United States should retire to the border, patrol it, and hold Mexico responsible for any encroachments. On February 5, 1917, General Pershing began his retirement from the other side of the Rio Grande, after eleven months in Mexico. A veteran of the national guard on the border wondered why Pershing's command was called the Punitive Expedition, "since"— so it looked from McAllen, Texas—"nobody got punished." In the fly-blown little bars of north Mexico, or by campfires, or amidst a column of horsemen crossing the desert, the song was still heard that could speak for Villa or any of his men.

> If some day I must die in a battle,
> If my body on the sierra must lie,
> Adelita, if God will allow it,
> You'll go to the sierra and cry. . . .

There, in the idea of the death that would bring to Villa and his men their first and all-claiming dignity, hovered the melancholy, the incurable lyricism of their harsh land.

For the United States, the Mexican involvement beyond the Rio Grande served a number of unforeseen but useful purposes. It steeled a commanding general and his citizen army for greater services in the first

World War. It gave the American air force its first trial at arms. In diplomatic co-operation between the sovereign nations of the hemisphere, it provided for the League of Nations and its chief architect a series of rehearsals that demonstrated a pattern of comity. Finally, it proved to Mexico that her neighbor above the river would suffer almost any lengths of indignity without resorting to an overwhelming retaliation whose aim would be acquisition of territory. Even though the time for it had not yet quite arrived, the way was open for full mutual respect between the countries of the Rio Grande.

All the old border troubles were resolved none too soon, if an unexpected new one was to be duly faced.

On February 27, 1917, the Secretary of State called at the White House to tell the President an astonishing story. As he listened to it, President Wilson several times exclaimed "Good Lord!", for it had become clear that the intentions of Germany—fantastic as it must seem—now included a plan to support Mexico in the seizure of the Rio Grande border states and Arizona if war should come between Germany and the United States. This was discovered through the interception of a telegram from Dr. Alfred Zimmermann, German foreign minister, to his minister to Mexico, Herr von Eckhardt. The telegram had come into the hands of the Allies through several channels. One copy was acquired by British agents in Mexico who sent it back to England where it was decoded—for the British had broken the German code months before, and were reading every official German dispatch that they could capture. Another transmission of the Zimmermann telegram, in partial form, was taken off the wireless. Another was intercepted out of Swedish diplomatic communication channels. And another, incredibly, was sent by telegraph attached to a telegram on a different, "open," subject, through the United States Embassy in Berlin, to Ambassador von Bernstorff in Washington, thus violating the diplomatic courtesy extended to the German Foreign Office by United States Ambassador James W. Gerard. "Good Lord!" exclaimed the President. This copy of the message had been forwarded by Bernstorff to Eckhardt on January nineteenth. As for what the message said, this was what it said:

"We intend to begin on the first of February unrestricted submarine warfare. We shall endeavour in spite of this to keep the United States of America neutral. In the event of not succeeding, we make Mexico a proposal of alliance on the following basis: make war together, make peace together, generous financial support and an understanding on our part that Mexico is to reconquer the lost territory in Texas, New

Mexico and Arizona. The settlement in detail is left to you. You will inform the President [of Mexico] of the above most secretly as soon as the outbreak of war with the United States of America is certain and add the suggestion that he should, on his initiative, invite Japan to immediate adherence and at the same time mediate between Japan and ourselves. Please call the President's attention to the fact that the ruthless employment of our submarines now offers the prospect of compelling in a few months to make peace.—Zimmermann."

"Good Lord!"

But wait—there was more. In a second telegram Dr. Zimmermann wanted his minister in Mexico to make it plain to Carranza that the alliance he was being offered was intended to dispose forever of the Monroe Doctrine, and that it represented Germany's long-range policy for Mexican relations, rather than merely a wartime measure to be repudiated with the end of hostilities. For the whole future, Mexico, Germany and Japan would present a joint power against the United States, who would have lost the old Spanish and Mexican provinces along with their old boundary river.

The whole affair seemed so incredible that President Wilson took extra steps to determine the authenticity of the messages. When this was established, he instructed the State Department to release them to the world as an example of German perfidy. Japan was horrified. She was already a member of the Allied nations, and her foreign office declared promptly, "Needless to say, Japan remains faithful to the Allies." To those in the United States who sympathized with Germany, and to those who prayed against American entry into the war, the messages could not seem true, with their cynical assumption that as a result of unrestricted submarine warfare the United States would most likely be drawn into the conflict; but the hopes of such citizens were punctured when Dr. Alfred Zimmermann publicly confirmed the authorship of the telegrams and their official character. Germany was dismayed by the exposure of her most secret plans, and, said an American diplomat overseas, "everybody is laughing at the frightful blunder the Germans made in proposing to Mexico to become an ally . . . the annals of diplomacy, I suppose, contain no filthier offer . . ." , and the scandal brought Dr. Zimmermann's fall from his exalted post.

Still, whether in secret or in public, Carranza was amenable to Germany's proposals. He asked if Germany could supply him with arms and ammunition—he specified the Mauser 7mm.—and with money. In the midst of talks with Germany he was constitutionally elected president of Mexico on March 11, 1917, while the Mexican congress was dominated by the pro-German "military party." Relations with the United States sank again. The United States Cavalry watched the border not only for bandits but for saboteurs; and after April second, when President Wilson, meeting the challenge that a nation believing in the freedom of the seas could no longer ignore, went to the Capitol to ask the Congress to declare that a state of war existed between Germany and the United States, the border guard was intensified. General Pershing was still there. "With the declaration of war against Germany," he observed, "there was much excitement in the southwest and many were the demands for protection against sabotage. Our first concern was to guard government property and railways. Military detachments were sent to the most critical points. . . ." It was not long before he was called to Washington and given a division—he was now a major general—to take to Europe, where he would be raised to the supreme command of all United States forces. The cavalry remained behind on the border, for bandit alarms were not all done with. The secret service, too, was active there, for as Secretary Lansing said, "The Mexican border was especially watched to prevent the spies and agents of the Central Powers from crossing into Mexico. . . ."

So through the years of the first World War the status quo was preserved, despite Germany's best plans. President Carranza continued to be hospitable to German propaganda, but no formal alliance came of it. In 1918 German agents were said to be at work on arrangements with General Pancho Villa. They would give him money and arms if he would raise a revolt and seize the Mexican government, thereafter concluding a formal alliance with Germany. Villa seemed amenable—but it was another plot that did not thicken, and in the end, with the defeat of the Central Powers, the United States retained the old Rio Grande and boundary territories which a victorious Germany was pledged to throw to Mexico.

Mexico's cycle of fury was not yet spent. In 1920 President Carranza, fleeing a new revolution, was overtaken and assassinated. The turn of General Pancho Villa came three years later when old enemies shot him to death on his ranch where he had lived in retirement. Through the next decades their successors slowly brought into realization many of the reforms postulated in the Grand Revolution of Madero. Some of these gave further suffering to the people. Most of them were no official concerns of the United States. One that affected American landholders in Mexico was Article Thirty-three of a certain modern law

of Mexico. It was that one which regulated the conditions of expropriation of foreign-owned property. A modern Rio Grande Mexican remarked
of it, "No, aquí en México hay no más dos artículos: el artículo treinta y
tres, y el artículo treinta-treinta—In Mexico there are but two articles:
article thirty-three, and article .30-30."

43.

Utility and Vision

1. utility

"Lot's things t'see," sang a character of youth in a twentieth
century folk opera of the Rio Grande Southwest,

> "Lot's things t'see,
> Gon' seem 'm all, and then some,
> Before I die.
> My granpa walked,
> My pappy rode,
> And me, I can fly."

It was an epitome of the cycle of change that came to the Rio
Grande with the machine, as it came to the rest of America and the
world. Previously, undergoing changes of predominant character with
each conquering race or nationality, the river societies had modified new
forms of social life with local circumstances and traditions—until the
coming of machine technics. And then, at a rate ever increasing, the addition of each machine technic in its turn made more swiftly certain the
domination of the environment through every technical means of the
modern age.

The difference of life along the Rio Grande from civilized human life elsewhere in the nation was at last only a matter of degree; for in kind, that life was established after the likeness of the corporate American character. In their various jobs and preoccupations the Rio Grande Americans—whether they passed by or stayed—revealed again their view of life through variations on the American theme—their materialism, their political vitality, their individuality, their passion for work, their tendency to make a recurrent frontier, and their devotion to an improved future on behalf of general humanity.

What remained to be seen of the river's past history were vestiges of its three old strains—those of the Indian epoch, the Latin centuries, and the American frontier—as they mingled with one another in forms often determined by commercial appeals addressed to residents and travellers moved by the local color. So in various places along the river were preserved together different illustrations of its earlier ways and times of society as if the river cut through the laminations of history as through those of the earth's crust. But finally all indigenous aspects of the river's three societies would be dissolved in the technological uniformity of the national life in the twentieth century.

The process was implicit in every step by which machine technics of energy and communication came to the river. It began when Captain Henry Austin brought the *Ariel* winding up to Matamoros in 1829 under its own steam power. It was furthered, at least in symbol, when in 1834 the printing press of Father Martínez produced for a few weeks at Taos the weekly newspaper *El Crepúsculo;* and when in 1865 General Sheridan brought the steam locomotive to the river at Brownsville. Electric telegraph lines reached Santa Fe from Denver in July, 1868, in what the acting territorial governor declared, in the first official telegram to be sent over the wires, addressed to President Andrew Johnson, to be "another advanced step of an enlightened age, bringing an old into instantaneous communication with newer though more advanced sections of our blessed Union, and with mankind in all civilized lands." The weekly Santa Fe *New Mexican* was immediately thereafter published as a daily, with wire service. Rail connections completed at Deming, New Mexico, in 1881 and at El Paso in 1882 brought the Rio Grande in the path of transcontinental commerce. The Rio Grande as the oldest vein of civilized life and communication in the area of the United States was unique in the settling of the West; for unlike other communities and areas of settlement, those of the Rio Grande were not born of the westward movement, but were already long established, with their own various patterns of life, when the recurrent American frontier reached out and put over them a new complex of living ways. After three and a half centuries of human life largely self-sustained the whole river line was drawn into the pattern of American national life and its material needs were increasingly met by distant sources.

The building of the railroads called for local labor; and a leading effect of this was to take men of Indian and Latin heritage from their little riverside farms and put them to work on the railroad right of way, while their farms were either cultivated by workers whom they hired, or were allowed to go untilled. And when the railroad work was done, native laborers turned to jobs in mining, or hired out to large-scale farming operations whose produce was shipped to commercial markets far away on the railroad lines. If in general the result of such change was a new prosperity, occasional dreams of a rich future faded away when the promises of a spellbinding promoter—the last frontier was full of the type—came to nothing. More than one small Western town, after the collapse of a railroad or land boom, celebrated the bitterness of disillusion in a gesture of mass irony when citizens came together in funeral style to bury the shovel that had been so hopefully used to break ground for a set of new tracks that would lead to the world.

Santa Fe had gas for lighting in 1880; electricity came not long afterward. The telephone was available in 1881, and ten years later in a little mining town of central New Mexico a machine arrived on the back of a burro to predict an industry devoted to the capture of the past in its most immediate expression. The burro was brought to stand before a mud-plastered log cabin while men, women and boys clustered around, listening to what the burro's owner promised. If it seemed impossible to believe him, only let them wait while he gave them a demonstration, for a modest fee. Here—let four of the boys come forward, and let him put into their ears the ends of small rubber tubes, and let them listen, as he started a small motor fixed to a little platform on the burro's back. The motor would turn a cylinder of black wax against which a stylus would play. In a moment they would hear a voice start to speak through the tubes, and then band music, and someone singing. He turned a switch, a spring creaked, and then, amidst whirring and scratching sounds, they were dazed to hear all that he had announced. Up a mountain trail the machine had come—it was a graphophone—bringing a trapped voice, and a new time, and a whole new way of communicating knowledge—the recording of sound. Motion pictures, radio and, finally, television would bring to mass audiences in the river empire, as to others the world over, a swift—often simultaneous—communication of images and ideas of experience that transcended the fixed limits of local traditions.

The last use of the river for water-borne travel ended early in the twentieth century. The last steamboat of the Rio Grande was the *Bessie*, a wood-burning sternwheeler, Captain Jesse Thornton commanding. She ran from the Gulf to the head of navigation at Roma. Like Captain Austin's *Ariel* and General Taylor's transports, she travelled only by day, tying up at night to the bank where piles of wood fuel awaited her at the end of a day's run. She carried freight and passengers— boys going to school at Brownsville, among others, and soldiers travelling between Ringgold Barracks and Fort Brown. In the summer of 1896 the commanding general of the Texas Department and his aide, a lieutenant, went on board to go downstream. Fifty years later, the aide, William J. Glasgow, then a retired general officer, remembered with musing joy how she was navigated through all the river's hooks and bends. It often happened that as the *Bessie* came to a bend, the wind would push her stern about in a grand arc until her bow was wedged into the bank. Then she would float free and sail on downstream stern first. At another bend a chance came to right matters. Captain Thornton let the leading stern take the bank, and the breeze and the current brought the bow around until the *Bessie* sailed once again like a proper ship, pointing her bow forward. The evolution was performed over and over, said General Glasgow, "and so she waltzed us all the way to Brownsville." She made her last trip in 1907, taking students from Roma to Brownsville, who when it was time to come home at the end of the school year, came overland; for the *Bessie*, worn out, was never replaced. Increased railroad and highway traffic on the littoral took the place of travel by river.

When the mechanization of private travel was made possible by the automobile, and the rapidly grown network of highways which it required across the nation, the great distances of the Rio Grande Southwest were contracted. With the interflow of increased personal traffic came a quickened interflow of local and national goods and experience and character. When mechanical flight—performing a myth fulfillment for mankind—was commercially established with an airport at every Rio Grande town of any consequence, the world's farthest reaches were only a couple of days away from the nation's oldest seats of civilized life. And when the demands of war required the development of a new

release of energy—nuclear fission—the Rio Grande valley in New Mexico
was the site of significant operations by the government's atomic scientists
at Los Alamos and Albuquerque.

If all such discoveries in the age of mass technics created changes
in material existence as great as those that came to the Indian with the
development of corn; and to the Pueblo dweller with the arrival of the
armored soldier with wheel, lever, gunpowder and horse; and to the
Spaniard and Mexican with the arrival of the Anglo-American political
system, then the American material triumph carried with it to the Rio
Grande the same question that accompanied the machine, wherever,
with all its implications, it was put to work.

The question was asked by a thoughtful American as he visited
the Paris exposition of 1900. "I . . . go down," wrote Henry Adams,
"down to the Champ de Mars and sit by the hour over the great dynamos,
watching them run as noiselessly and as smoothly as the planets, and
asking them—with infinite courtesy—where in the Hell they are
going. . . ." The more he thought about the problem of where the
development of mechanical power would lead, the more troubled he
became. "I apprehend for the next hundred years an ultimate, colossal,
cosmic collapse; but not on any of our old lines. My belief is that science
is to wreck us, and that we are like monkeys monkeying with a loaded
shell; we don't in the least know or care where our practically infinite
energies come from or will bring us to." For himself, he did not, he
said, care at all. "But the faintest disturbance of equilibrium is felt
throughout the solar system, and I feel sure that our power over energy
has now reached a point where it must sensibly affect the old adjustment. It is mathematically certain to me that another thirty years of
energy-development at the rate of the last century, must reach an
impasse."

ii. vision

But the answer that eluded Henry Adams seemed later to come
clear out of the spirit of the nation most energetic in the use of the
very technics that he questioned. "The useful, the mechanic arts are
those which we have occasion for. . . .", John Adams had said long
before his great-grandson felt such terrible doubts before the dynamos.

The old statesman, with his passionate belief in the American knack for utility, expressed the faith of his countrymen in their control over their powers. But the United States had no monopoly on the new social instruments of the age of mass technics. The world had them; and the world moved with them wherever they went. Among the implications of all new technics of communication and energy was the moral imperative to use them to serve rather than to destroy human society.

The Americans, westbound in the nineteenth century to fulfill their vision of a just society for their countrymen with the aid of their "mechanic arts," had once made a neighborhood of their continent.

Once again, in a process for which the American century on the Rio Grande was a typical western rehearsal, the spirit of the recurrent American frontier reached out; and halfway through the twentieth century the Americans, now with a vision of a just society for all the world's peoples, and with the aid of vastly expanded "mechanic arts," were trying to do their share to make a neighborhood of the world.

THE   END

Roswell, New Mexico,
1940–1942;
1946–1954.

Sources for
Volume Two, by Chapters

APPENDIX B

Sources for
Volume Two, by Chapters

Each source is here noted in brief form which corresponds to its alphabetical position in the General Bibliography (Appendix C), where the reader will find full bibliographical particulars.

book three: the mexican rio grande

1. A Colony For Mexico: Barker, *Austin Papers,* and *Life of Stephen F. Austin;* Dougherty; Robertson.
2. A Wild Strain: Cleland; Ferris; Irving; Pattie; Pino; Twitchell, *Spanish Archives.*
3. The Twin Sisters: Bancroft; Barker, *Austin Papers;* Rives; Robertson; Santleben; Williams, O. W., *Pecos Country.*
4. Last Return: Robertson.
5. The Spark: *Antiques;* Bancroft; Barker, *Austin Papers;* Rives.
6. The "Ariel": Barker, *Austin Papers.*
7. Slavery: Bancroft; Barker, *Austin Papers,* and *Life of Stephen F. Austin;* Rives; Webb.
8. Bad Blood: Bancroft; Barker, *Austin Papers.*
9. The Mexico Trade: Barker, *Austin Papers;* Cleland; Dickey; Dunbar; Gregg, J., *Commerce of the Prairies;* Pino; Rives; U. S. Government, *Passport.*
10. Tormented Loyalties: *Antiques;* Barker, *Austin Papers,* and *Life of Stephen F. Austin;* James, M.; Rives.

11. "God and Texas": Bancroft; Barker, *Austin Papers,* and *Life of Stephen F. Austin;* Green; Rives.
12. From Mexico's Point of View: Bancroft; Barker, *Austin Papers,* and *Life of Stephen F. Austin;* Gregg, J., *Diary and Letters . . . Southwestern Enterprises;* James, M.; Rives; Wortham.
13. Fortunes of New Mexico: Dickey; Pattie; Pino; Read; Robertson; USDA, SCS, *Rio Grande Watershed in Colorado and New Mexico.*
14. Revolt Up River: Armijo, *Counter-pronouncement;* Pino; Read; Tannenbaum; Twitchell, *Leading Facts,* and *Spanish Archives;* Vigil, *Minutes.*
15. The River Republic: Bancroft; Smith, J. H.; Yoakum.
16. The Santa Fe Pioneers: Bancroft; Calderon de la Barca; Carroll; Falconer; Kendall; Read; Twitchell, *Leading Facts;* Yoakum.
17. Border Smoke: Bancroft; Dobie, *Longhorns,* and *Vaquero;* Dougherty; Emory, *Report;* Gregg, J., *Diary and Letters . . . Southwestern Enterprises;* Rives; Webb, Yoakum.
18. To Mier and Beyond: Bancroft; Green; Rives; Webb; Wilcox, *Laredo during the Texas Republic.*
19. Diplomacies: Bancroft; Bill; Grant, U. S.; Gregg, J., *Diary and Letters . . . Southwestern Enterprises;* Henry, R. S.; Henry, W. S.; Houston; Lewis, L.; Rives; Santleben; Yoakum.
20. The United States to the River: Grant, U. S.; Henry, W. S.; Lewis, L.; Smith, E. K.; Webb.

book four: the united states rio grande

1. "Way, You Rio": Downes; Wallace, L.
2. Collective Prophecy: Adams, H.; Adams, J., and J. Q.; Audubon; Botkin; Butterfield; Christensen; Crèvecoeur; Curti; Dunbar; Grassi; Gregg, J., *Commerce of the Prairies;* Handlin; Kouwenhoven; Lipman; McCoy, J. C.; Mencken, *American Language,* and *Supplement I;* Miller; Montlezun; Moreau de St. Méry; Moses; National Capital Sesquicentennial Commission; Parkman; Quinn; Rice; Rosenfeld; Rourke, *American Humor,* and *Roots of American Culture;* Smith, H. N.; Stone; Tocqueville; Trollope; Whitman, *Leaves of Grass,* and *Prose Works.*
3. Bivouac: Barbour; Downes; Lewis, L.; Thorpe.
4. The Army of the Rio Grande: Barbour; Emory, *Report;* Grant, U. S.; Gregg, J., *Diary and Letters . . . Excursions in Mexico;* Henry, R. S.; Henry, W. S.; Lewis, L.; Wallace, L.; Whitman, *Prose Works.*
5. The Cannonade: Barbour; Bill; Grant, U. S.; Henry, R. S.; Henry, W. S.; Thorpe.
6. Fort Texas: Thorpe.
7. The Listeners: Henry, W. S.
8. Palo Alto: Barbour; Grant, U. S.; Henry, R. S.; Henry, W. S.; Thorpe.

9. Resaca de la Palma: Barbour; Grant, U. S.; Hamilton; Henry, R. S.; Henry, W. S.; Thorpe.
10. The River Dead: Barbour; Emory, *Report;* Grant, U. S.; Hamilton; Henry, R. S.; Henry, W. S.; Lewis, L.; Thorpe.
11. The Nation's War: *Antiques;* Bill; Hamilton; Henry, R. S.; Lewis, L.; Polk; Strong; Whitman, *Leaves of Grass.*
12. Invasion Summer: Barbour; Bill; Giddings; Hamilton; Henry, R. S.; Henry, W. S.; Lewis, L.; Thorpe.
13. Recurrent Frontier: Barbour; Bill; Domenech; Giddings; Hamilton; Henry, R. S.; Henry, W. S.; Kenly; Lewis, L.; Smith, H. N.; Wallace, L.; Webb.
14. Upstream and Inland: Barbour; Bill; Dobie, *Vaquero;* Dougherty; Giddings; Grant, U. S.; Hamilton; Henry, R. S.; Henry, W. S.; Kenly; Lewis, L.; Polk; Thorpe.
15. The Army of the West: New Mexico, Citizens; Parkman; Read; Vigil, D., *Speech, May 16, 1846,* and *Speech, June 22, 1846;* Wislizenus.
16. The Secret Agent: Armijo, *Letter to Gen. Kearny;* Benton, T. H., in Connelley; Crane; Hughes; Keleher; Magoffin; New Mexico, Citizens; Pino; Read; Vigil y Alarid.
17. Bloodless Possession: Bill; Emory, *Notes of a Military Reconnoissance;* Gibson, G. R.; Henry, R. S.; Hughes; Keleher; Magoffin; Nelson; Read.
18. The Army of Chihuahua: Bill; Butterfield; Ehinger; Freeman; Gregg, J., *Diary and Letters: Southwestern Enterprises,* and *Excursions in Mexico;* Henry, R. S.; Wilcox, *Laredo.*
19. The Free Missourians: Bill; Gibson, G. R.; Gregg, J., *Diary and Letters . . . Excursions in Mexico;* Keleher; Magoffin; Robinson; Ruxton; Wade, in Parkman; Wislizenus.
20. Brazito and The Pass: Connelley; Drumm, in Magoffin; Gibson, G. R.; Hughes; Kribben, in Gibson, G. R.; Magoffin; Ruxton.
21. Counterdance: Bill; Hamilton; Henry, R. S.; Henry, W. S.; Hitchcock; Lewis, L.; Polk; Smith, A. D. H.; Strong; Wallace L.
22. The Avengers: Connelley; Garrard; Hughes; Keleher; Ruxton; Twitchell, *Leading Facts.*
23. Massacre at Taos: Benton, T. H., in Connelley; Dyer; Garrard; Henry, R. S.; Hughes; Keleher; Ruxton; Twitchell, *Leading Facts.*
24. Chihuahua: Gibson, G. R.; Magoffin; Polk.
25. Trial at Taos: Garrard.
26. All on the Plains of Mexico: Adams, H.; Bill; Edwards, in Gregg, *Diary and Letters . . . Excursions in Mexico;* Ehinger; Emory, *Report;* Gregg, J., *Diary and Letters: Southwestern Enterprises,* and *Excursions in Mexico;* Hamilton; Henry, W. S.; Hitchcock; Hughes; Lee; Lewis, L.; Lomax, *Folk Song USA;* Polk; Rives; Rourke, *American Humor;* Strong; Wallace, L.; Whitman, *Prose Works.*
27. El Dorado: Armijo, *Letter to Donaciano Vigil;* Bartlett; Bieber; Durivage, in Bieber; Eccleston; Polk; Robertson; Sumpter; Thoreau.
28. Contraband: Bancroft; Bartlett; Domenech; Durivage, in Bieber; Emory, *Report;* Gregg, J., *Diary and Letters . . . Excursions in Mexico;* Smith, J. H.; Webb.

29. A Thread of Spirit: Domenech; Emory, *Report;* USDA, SCS, *Rio Grande Watershed in Colorado and New Mexico.*
30. Boundaries: Bancroft; Bartlett; Bennett; Bill; Binkley; Burkholder; Jones; Twitchell, *Leading Facts.*
31. Flag and Lamplight: Bartlett; Bennett; Boyd, Mrs. O. B.; Cremony; Crimmins, *Col. J. F. K. Mansfield's Report,* and *Two Thousand Miles by Boat;* Cruse; Dickey; Dougherty; DuBois; Emory, *Report;* Hughes; Keleher; Plato; Santleben; Stanley; Sumpter; Thomlinson; Toulouse, J. H.; Toulouse, J. H., Jr.
32. The Rio Grande Divided: Crane; Dougherty; Fulton; Hollister; Keleher; McKee, J. C.; Richardson; Whitford; Williams, E.; Wortham.
33. The Desolate: Cremony; Keleher; Hollister; Ronquillo.
34. Confederate Border: Bancroft; Corti; Coulter; Dobie, *Vaquero;* Freeman; Gonzalez, *Folk-Lore;* Santleben; Soley; Sumpter; Wortham.
35. The Second Mexican Empire: Bancroft; Coulter; Dobie, *Vaquero;* Hergesheimer; Santleben; Sheridan; Simpich; Strong.
36. The Mexico Moon: Benedict; Bieber; Cremony; Davenport; Dobie, *Mustangs,* and *Vaquero;* Emory, *Report;* Parsons; Pino; Ruxton; Santleben; Sumpter; Thomas, *Plains Indians;* U. S. Congress, 43rd Congress, 1st Session, *Executive Document no. 257;* USDA, Field Flood Control Committee, *Survey Report;* Wallace, E.; Williams, O. W., *Baja el Sol,* and *Untitled Pamphlet.*
37. Bad Men and Good: Archdiocese, Santa Fe; Crane; Defouri, in Howlett; Dobie, *Vaquero;* Federal Writers Program, WPA, *Texas;* Fergusson, Mrs. C. M.; Fulton; Gibson, G. R.; Gregg, R. D.; Howlett; Keleher; Kerbey; Kohlberg; Kubler; Lavelle; McKee, I.; Pike; Pino; Richardson; Ritch; Salpointe; Santleben; Townsend, *Early border elections,* and *Rangers and Indians;* Twitchell, *Leading Facts,* and *Spanish Archives;* U. S. Congress, 43rd Congress, 1st Session, HR, *Executive Document no. 257,* and 44th Congress, 1st Session, HR, *Report no. 343,* and 45th Congress, 1st Session, HR, *Executive Document no. 13;* Ward; Warner.
38. The Last Wagons: Dobie, *Vaquero;* Santleben.
39. The Last Frontiersman: Abels; Botkin; Brown, D.; Dobie, *Longhorns,* and *Mustangs,* and *Vaquero;* Kohlberg; Lomax, *Cowboy Songs,* and *Folk Song, USA;* McCoy, J. G.; Richardson; Santleben; Siringo, *Riata and Spurs,* and *Texas Cowboy;* Smith, E. E.; U. S. Congress, 44th Congress, 1st Session, HR, *Report no. 343;* Wadleigh.
40. Treasure: Burkholder; Conkling; Davis; Federal Writers Program, WPA, *Colorado,* and *New Mexico;* Simpich; Tierney; USDA, SCS, Southwest Region, *Sociological Survey;* Wolle.
41. The Last Earth Secrets: Casey; Crimmins, *Two Thousand Miles by Boat;* Emory, *Report;* Hill; Townsend, *Rangers and Indians.*
42. Reflex and Revolution: Austin, M.; Baker; Beals; Borah; Brenner; Callahan; Carranza; *Cavalry Journal;* Cramer; Dallam; Emory, *Report;* Glasgow; Gonzalez, *America Invades;* Green; Grey; Hammond, J. H.; Hendrick; Hill; House; Lane, F. K.; Lansing; Lewis, M.; *Literary Digest;* Millis; *Motion picture film footage; Outlook;* Palmer, F.; Pershing, *Letters,* and *My Experiences;* Powell; Pringle; Reed; Richie; Rose; Scott, *Papers,* and *Some*

Memories; Sullivan; Tompkins; Toulmin; Troxel; Tumulty; Villa; Walsh; Whitlock; Wilson.

43. Utility and Vision: Adams, H.; Adams, J., and J. Q.; Dobie, *Vaquero;* Federal Writers Program, WPA, *New Mexico;* Glasgow; Horgan, *Tree on the Plains;* Keleher; USDA, SCS, *Rio Grande Watershed in Colorado and New Mexico,* and *Sociological Survey.*

APPENDIX C

General Bibliography

APPENDIX C

General Bibliography

For the convenience of the reader as he refers to this list from the brief entries of sources as listed by chapters in Appendices A and B, I have here grouped alphabetically all sources materials, whether manuscript, primary sources, general works, periodicals, motion picture film or conversations. If this course may overlook certain conventions of bibliographical technique, it may have, through its single alphabet, a compensatory value in bringing the inquirer as directly as possible to the reference he seeks.

Abels, Robert. *Early American firearms* (*The American arts library*). Cleveland and New York, The World Publishing Co., 1950.

Adams, Henry. *Selected letters of Henry Adams,* edited with an introduction by Newton Arvin. New York, Farrar, Straus and Young, Inc., 1951.

Adams, John, and John Quincy. *The selected writings* . . . edited and with an introduction by Adrienne Koch and William Peden. New York, Alfred A. Knopf, 1946.

Alessio Robles, Vito. *Coahuila y Texas en la época colonial.* Mexico, D. F., Editorial Cultura, 1938.

Alexander, Hartley Burr. *North American* [*mythology*]. V. 10, of Mythology of all races, edited by Louis Herbert Gray. Boston, Marshall Jones Co., 1916.

Altamira y Crevea, Rafael. *A history of Spain from the beginnings to the present day.* Translated by Muna Lee. New York, D. Van Nostrand Co., 1949.

. . . . . . *Antiques.* Texas Issue, June 1948.

Armijo, Manuel. *Counter-pronouncement, Sept. 8, 1837, by Manuel Armijo* [*et al.*] *at Tomé, New Mexico* . . . *appointing a commission to prepare and present an address to the Supreme [Mexican] Government. . . .* Translated by Samuel C. Ellison, 1884. Original document. San Marino, California, Henry E. Huntington Library. (Excerpts quoted by permission of the Huntington Library.)

Armijo, Manuel. *Letter to General Kearny, written in Apache Canyon, August 16, 1846.* Translation. Original document. San Marino, California, Henry E. Huntington Library. (Excerpts quoted by permission of the Huntington Library.)

Armijo, Manuel. *Letter to Donaciano Vigil, written at Lemitar, New Mexico, July 16, 1850.* Translation. Original document. San Marino, California, Henry E. Huntington Library. (Excerpts quoted by permission of the Huntington Library.)

Armstrong, Edward. *The Emperor Charles V.* London, Macmillan and Co., 1910.

Artiñano, Pedro M. de. *Spanish art. The Burlington Magazine,* 1927.

Audubon, John James. *Audubon's America, the narratives and experiences of John James Audubon,* edited by Donald Culross Peattie . . . Boston, Houghton Mifflin Co., 1940.

Austin, Mary. *What the Mexican conference really means.* Reprint from *New York Times magazine.* New York, Latin American News Association, ND.

Baker, Ray Stannard. *Woodrow Wilson, life and letters. V. 6. Facing war, 1915–1917.* Garden City, Doubleday, Doran and Co., 1937.

Bancroft, Hubert Howe. *History of the North Mexican states and Texas.* 2 v. San Francisco, A. L. Bancroft and Co., 1884.

Bandelier, Adolph F. A. *The delight makers;* with an introduction by Charles F. Lummis. New York, Dodd, Mead and Co., 1916.

―――― *Diaries, 1880–1890.* Ms. 10 v. Santa Fe, Museum of New Mexico.

―――― *Documentary history of the Rio Grande pueblos.* Part two, of *Indians of the Rio Grande valley,* by Adolph F. A. Bandelier and Edgar L. Hewitt. Albuquerque, University of New Mexico Press, 1937.

―――― *Final report of investigations among Indians of the southwestern United States, carried on mainly in the years from 1880 to 1885.* Part II. Papers of the Archaeological Institute of America. American series, IV. Cambridge, printed by John Wilson and Son, University Press, 1892.

―――― *Hemenway southwestern expedition: Contributions to the history of the Southwestern portion of the United States.* Archaeological Institute of America. American series, V. Cambridge, printed by John Wilson and Son, 1890.

―――― *Historical documents relating to New Mexico, Nueva Vizcaya, and approaches thereto, to 1773.* Collected by Adolph F. A. Bandelier and Fanny R. Bandelier. Spanish texts and English translations. 3 v. Edited . . . by Charles Wilson Hackett. Washington, Carnegie Institution, 1923.

―――― *Historical introduction to studies among the sedentary Indians of New Mexico.* (In *Papers of the Archaeological Institute of America. American series. I.*) Boston, A. Williams and Co., 1881.

―――― *Indians of the Rio Grande valley,* by Adolph F. A. Bandelier and Edgar L. Hewett. Albuquerque, University of New Mexico Press, 1937.

Barbour, Philip Norbourne. *Journals of the late Philip Norbourne Barbour,* captain in the 3rd regiment, United States Infantry, and his wife, Martha Isabella Hopkins Barbour, written during the war with Mexico, 1846. Edited with foreword by Rhoda Van Bibber Tanner Doubleday. New York, G. P. Putnam's Sons, 1936.

Barker, Eugene C. *The Austin papers,* edited by Eugene C. Barker. *Annual Report of the American Historical Association, 1919.* 3 v. Washington, Government Printing Office, 1924.

——— *Life of Stephen F. Austin, founder of Texas, 1793–1836.* Nashville, Cokesbury Press, 1926.

Bartlett, John Russell *Personal narrative of explorations and incidents in Texas, New Mexico, California, Sonora, and Chihuahua, connected with the United States and Mexican Boundary Commission during the years 1850–1853.* 2 v. New York, D. Appleton Co., 1854.

Beals, Carleton. *Porfirio Diaz, dictator of Mexico.* Philadelphia, J. B. Lippincott Co., 1932.

Beazley, C. Raymond. *Voyages and travels mainly during the 16th and 17th centuries.* With an introduction by C. Raymond Beazley. "An English Garner." Westminster, Constable and Co., 1903.

Bell, Aubrey F. G. *Cervantes.* Norman, University of Oklahoma Press, 1947.

Benavides, Fray Alonso de. *Fray Alonso de Benavides' Revised Memorial of 1634* . . . edited by Frederick Webb Hodge, George P. Hammond and Agapito Rey. Albuquerque, University of New Mexico Press, 1945.

Benedict, Ruth. *Patterns of culture.* Boston, Houghton Mifflin Co., 1934.

Bennett, James A. *A dragoon in New Mexico, 1850–1856.* Edited by Clinton E. Brooks and Frank D. Reeves under the title, *Forts and Forays.* Albuquerque, University of New Mexico Press, 1948.

Beshoar, Barron B. *Western trails to Calvary.* Denver, The Westerners, Brand Book, 1949.

Bevan, Bernard. *Spanish art. The Burlington Magazine,* 1927.

Bieber, Ralph P. *Southern trails to California in 1849.* Glendale, The Arthur H. Clark Co., 1937.

Bill, Alfred Hoyt. *Rehearsal for conflict. The war with Mexico, 1846–1848.* New York, Alfred A. Knopf, 1947.

Binkley, William Campbell. *Reports from a Texan agent in New Mexico, 1849.* (In *New Spain and the Anglo-American west, historical contributions presented to Herbert Eugene Bolton.*) Los Angeles, privately printed, 1932.

Bishop, Morris. *The odyssey of Cabeza de Vaca.* New York, D. Appleton Co., 1933.

Bolton, Herbert Eugene. *Coronado, knight of pueblos and plains.* New York, Whittlesey House, 1949.

——— *The Spanish borderlands. A chronicle of Florida and the southwest.* New Haven, Yale University Press, 1921.

——— *Spanish exploration in the southwest, 1542–1706.* Edited by Herbert Eugene Bolton. *Original narratives of early American history.* New York, Charles Scribner's Sons, 1930.

Borah, William E. *Papers of Senator William E. Borah.* Mss. Washington, The Library of Congress.

Botkin, B. A. *A treasury of American folklore. Stories, ballads and traditions of the people,* edited by A. Botkin. New York, Crown Publishers, 1944.

Bourke, John G. *The folk-foods of the Rio Grande valley and of Northern Mexico.* (In *Southwestern Lore,* edited by J. Frank Dobie.) Publications of the Texas Folk-Lore Society Number 9. Dallas, The Southwest Press, 1931.

Boyd, E. *Saints and saint-makers of New Mexico.* Santa Fe, Laboratory of Anthropology, 1946.

Boyd, Mrs. Orsemus Bronson. *Cavalry life in tent and field.* New York, J. Selwin Tait and Sons, 1894.

Brand, Donald D. *Prehistoric trade in the southwest. New Mexico Business Review,* v. 4, No. 4, October, 1935.

Brenner, Anita. *Idols behind altars.* New York, Payson and Clarke, 1929.

Brown, Dee. *Trail driving days.* Text by Dee Brown; picture research by Martin F. Schmitt. New York, Charles Scribner's Sons, 1952.

Brown, Lloyd A. *Story of maps.* Boston, Little, Brown and Co., 1949.

Bryan, Kirk. *Pre-Columbian agriculture in the southwest, as conditioned by periods of alluviation. Annals of the Association of American Geographers,* v. 31, no. 4, December, 1941.

Buckle, Henry Thomas. *History of civilization in England.* 2 v. New York, D. Appleton Co., 1879.

Burkholder, Joseph L. *The middle Rio Grande conservancy district. Report of the chief engineer.* [State of New Mexico] 1928.

Butterfield, Roger. *The American past, a history of the United States from Concord to Hiroshima, 1775–1945.* New York, Simon and Schuster, 1947.

Calderón de la Barca, Frances Erskine Inglis. *Life in Mexico during a residence of two years in that country.* With an introduction by Henry Baerlein. New York, E. P. Dutton and Co., 1931.

Callahan, James Morton. *American foreign policy in Mexican relations.* New York, The Macmillan Co., 1932.

Carranza, Venustiano. *Reply of Don Venustiano Carranza to the chief of the Northern Division. The First Chief of the Constitutionalist Army, in charge of the Executive Power, to the Mexican people. Refutation of the manifest of General Francisco Villa.* Mexico, D. F., October 25, 1914.

Carroll, H. Bailey. *The Texan Santa Fe trail.* Canyon, Texas, Panhandle-Plains Historical Society, 1951.

Casey, Robert J. *The Texas border and some borderliners. A chronicle and a guide.* Indianapolis, Bobbs-Merrill Co., 1950.

Castañeda, Carlos E. *Our Catholic heritage in Texas, 1519–1936.* Prepared under the asupices of the Knights of Columbus of Texas, Paul J. Foik, editor. 7 v. Austin, Von Boeckmann-Jones Co., 1936.

Castañeda de Náxera, Pedro de. *Narrative of the expedition to Cibola, undertaken in 1540, in which are described all those settlements, ceremonies, and customs.* (In *Narratives of the Coronado Expedition, 1540–1542,* edited by George P. Hammond and Agapito Rey.) Albuquerque, University of New Mexico Press, 1940.

Castetter, Edward F. *The early utilization and the distribution of agave in the American southwest,* by Edward F. Castetter, Willis H. Bell and Alvin R.

Grove. Albuquerque, *University of New Mexico Bulletin,* Whole number 335, Dec. 1, 1939.

...... *Cavalry Journal,* July, 1916: *Notes on campaigning in Mexico;* November, 1916: *Cavalry equipment in Mexico; The cavalry fight at Columbus; Experiences in Mexico; Field notes from Mexico and the border.*

Céliz, Fray Francisco. *Diary of the Alarcón expedition into Texas, 1718–1719.* Translated by Fritz Leo Hoffman. Los Angeles, The Quivira Society, 1935.

Cervantes Saavedra, Miguel de. *Don Quixote de la Mancha.* Translated by Peter Motteux. New York, Illustrated Modern Library, 1946.

Chavez, Fray Angélico. *Our Lady of the Conquest.* Santa Fe, Historical Society of New Mexico, 1948.

Christensen, Erwin O. *The index of American design.* New York, Macmillan Co.; Washington, National Gallery of Art, Smithsonian Institution, 1950.

Cleland, Robert Glass. *This reckless breed of men, the trappers and fur traders of the southwest.* New York, Alfred A. Knopf, 1950.

Columbus, Christopher. *Discovery of the West Indies; journal of Columbus,* abridged by Las Casas. (In *Narratives of the discovery of America,* edited by A. W. Lawrence and Jean Young.) New York, Jonathan Cape and Harrison Smith, 1931.

Commager, Henry Steele. *America in perspective, the United States through foreign eyes,* edited by Henry Steele Commager. New York, Random House, 1947.

Conkling, Harold. *Water supply for possible development of irrigation and drainage projects on the Rio Grande river above El Paso, Texas.* Type script, 1919. Albuquerque, Middle Rio Grande Conservancy District

Connelley, William E. *Doniphan's expedition.* Topeka, Crane and Co., 1907

Coolidge, Mary Roberts. *The rain-makers, Indians of Arizona and New Mexico* Boston, Houghton Mifflin Co., 1929.

Cortés, Hernando, Marqués del Valle de Oaxaca. *Five letters, 1519–1526.* Translated by J. Bayard Morris. New York, Robert M. McBride Co., 1929.

Corti, Egon Caesar. *Maximilian and Charlotte of Mexico.* Translated from the German by Catherine Alison Phillips. 2 v. New York, Alfred A. Knopf, 1928.

Coulter, E. Merton. *The Confederate States of America, 1861–1865.* Baton Rouge, Louisiana State University Press; Austin, University of Texas, 1950.

Cox, Isaac Jolin. *Monroe and the early Mexican revolutionary agents.* (In *Annual Report, American Historical Association, 1911,* v. 1.) Washington, Government Printing Office.

Cramer, Stuart W. *Punitive expedition from Boquillas. Cavalry Journal,* November, 1916.

Crane, Leo. *Desert drums, the Pueblo Indians of New Mexico, 1540–1928.* Boston, Little, Brown and Co., 1928.

Cremony, John C. *Life among the Apaches.* Tucson, Arizona Silhouettes, 1951.

Crèvecoeur, Hector St. Jean de. *Letters from an American farmer* (extracts in *This was America,* edited by Oscar Handlin). Cambridge, Harvard University Press, 1949.

Crimmins, Martin L. *Colonel J. K. F. Mansfield's report of the inspection of the department of Texas in 1856. Southwestern Historical Quarterly,* v. 42, nos. 2, 3 and 4.

———— *Two thousand miles by boat in the Rio Grande in 1850. West Texas and Scientific Society Bulletin,* publication 5, bulletin 48, Dec. 1, 1933.

Croneis, Carey. *Down to earth, an introduction to geology,* by Cary Croneis, William C. Krumbein and Chichi Lasley. Chicago, University of Chicago Press, 1936.

Crow, John A. *The epic of Latin America.* Garden City, Doubleday and Co., 1946.

Cruse, Thomas. *Apache days and after,* edited and with an introduction by Eugene Cunningham. Caldwell, Idaho, The Caxton Printers, Ltd., 1941.

Curti, Merle. *The growth of American thought.* New York, Harper and Brothers, 1943.

Dallam, Samuel F. *The punitive expedition of 1916—some problems and experiences of a troop commander. Cavalry Journal,* July 1927.

Davenport, J. Walker. *Painted pebbles from the lower Pecos and Big Bend regions of Texas,* by J. Walker Davenport and Carl Chelf. San Antonio, Witte Memorial Museum, bulletin 5, ND.

Davis, Richard Harding. *The west from a car window.* New York, Harper and Brothers, 1892.

Defouri, James H. *Historical sketch of the Catholic church in New Mexico.* San Francisco, McCormick Brothers, Printers, 1887.

DeGolyer, E. M. *Across aboriginal America. The journey of three Englishmen across Texas in 1568.* El Paso, The Peripatetic Press, 1947.

Denver Art Museum. *Leaflet series,* 1936; 1939; 1940.

DeVoto, Bernard. *The Year of Decision 1846.* Boston, Houghton Mifflin Co., 1943.

Díaz del Castillo, Bernal. *True history of the conquest of Mexico, written in the year 1568.* Translated by Maurice Keatinge. 2 v. New York, Robert M. McBride, 1927.

Dickey, Roland F. *New Mexico village arts.* Drawings by Lloyd Lozes Goff. Albuquerque, University of Mexico Press, 1949.

Dobie, J. Frank. *Ballads and songs of the frontier folk.* (In *Texas and southwestern lore,* edited by J. Frank Dobie.) Austin, Publications of the Texas Folk-Lore Society, number 6, 1927.

———— *The longhorns.* Illustrated by Tom Lea. Boston, Little, Brown and Co., 1941.

———— *The mustangs.* Illustrated by Charles Banks Wilson. Boston, Little, Brown and Co., 1952.

———— *Tongues of the monte.* Garden City, Doubleday, Doran and Co., 1935.

———— *A vaquero of the brush country, partly from the reminiscences of John Young.* New York, Grosset and Dunlap, 1929.

Domenech, Emmanuel. *Missionary adventures in Texas and Mexico. A personal narrative of six years' sojourn in those regions.* Translated from the French under the author's superintendence. London, Longsmans, Brown, Green, Longmans and Roberts, 1858.

Dougherty, E. *The Rio Grande valley.* (In the *Magazine of History,* with notes and queries. Extra number, no. 138, 1867.) Tarrytown, New York, re-printed by William Abbatt, 1928.

Douglas, Frederic H. *Indian art of the United States,* by Frederic H. Douglas and Réné D'Harnoncourt. New York, the Museum of Modern Art, 1941.

Downes, Olin. *A treasury of American song,* by Olin Downes and Elie Siegmeister. New York, Howell, Soskin and Co., 1940.

DuBois, John Van Deusen. *Campaigns in the west, 1856–1861. The journals and letters of John Van Deusen DuBois,* edited by George P. Hammond. Tucson, Arizona Pioneers Historical Society, 1949.

Dunbar, Seymour. *A history of travel in America.* 4 v. in 1. New York, Tudor Publishing Co., 1937.

Dyer, Alexander Brydie. *Letter to Dr. Robert Johnston* [written at Santa Fe, New Mexico, February 14, 1847]. Ms. Santa Fe, Museum of New Mexico. (Excerpts quoted by permission of Museum of New Mexico.)

Eccleston, Robert. *Overland to California on the southwestern trail, 1849,* edited by George P. Hammond and Edward H. Howes. Berkeley and Los Angeles, University of California Press, 1950.

Ehinger, Augustus Frederick. *Diary of his travels from Illinois to Mexico and during his service as a member of Comp. H, Second Regiment Illinois Volunteers, July 1846–June 1847.* Ms. In the possession of Colonel Charles F. Ward, Roswell, New Mexico. (Excerpts quoted by permission of Col. Ward.)

Ellis, Havelock. *The soul of Spain.* Boston, Houghton Mifflin Co., 1924.

Emory, William H. *Notes of a military reconnoissance,* with introduction and notes by Ross Calvin. Albuquerque, University of New Mexico Press, 1951.

——— *Report of William H. Emory, Major First Cavalry and U.S. Commissioner, United States and Mexican Boundary Survey.* 34th Congress, 1st session, ex. doc. no. 135, Washington, Cornelius Wendell, printer, 1857.

Falconer, Thomas. *Letters and notes on the Texan Santa Fe expedition, 1841–1842 . . .* with introduction and notes by F. W. Hodge. New York, Dauber and Pine Bookshops, Inc., 1930.

Federal Writers Program, WPA. *Colorado, a guide to the highest state.* American Guide Series. New York, Hastings House, 1941.

——— *New Mexico, a guide to the colorful state.* American Guide Series. New York, Hastings House, 1940.

——— *Texas, a guide to the lone star state.* American Guide Series. New York, Hastings House, 1940.

Fergusson, Mrs. C. M. *Conversations,* at Albuquerque, New Mexico.

Fergusson, Erna. *Our southwest.* New York, Alfred A. Knopf, 1940.

Fergusson, Harvey. *Rio Grande.* New York, Alfred A. Knopf, 1933.

Ferris, W. A. *Life in the Rocky Mountains . . .* edited by Paul C. Phillips. Denver, Fred A. Rosenstock, Old West Publishing Co., 1940.

Fewkes, J. Walter. *The pueblo settlements near El Paso, Texas. American Anthropologist,* v. 4, 1902.

——— *Two types of southwestern cliff houses.* Washington, *Annual Report of the Smithsonian Institution,* 1921.

Fiock, L. R. *The functioning of a completed irrigation project as illustrated by the development and operation of the Rio Grande irrigation project.* Typescript. U. S. Department of Agriculture, Albuquerque, 1934.

Fisher, Reginald. *Notes on the relation of the Franciscans to the Penitentes.* Santa Fe, *El Palacio*, v. 48, December, 1944.

Fitzmaurice-Kelly, James. *New history of Spanish literature.* London, Humphrey Milford, 1926.

Forrest, Earle R. *Missions and pueblos of the old southwest.* Cleveland, Arthur H. Clarke Co., 1929.

Foscue, Edwin J. *The Mesilla valley of New Mexico: a study in aridity and irrigation. Economic Geography,* v. 7, no. 1, January 1931.

Frazer, James George. *The golden bough, a study in magic and religion.* New York, The Macmillan Co., 1935.

Freeman, Douglas Southall. *R. E. Lee, a biography.* New York, Charles Scribner's Sons, 1935.

Fulton, Maurice Garland. *New Mexico's own chronicle, three races in the writings of four hundred years,* adapted and edited by Maurice Garland Fulton and Paul Horgan. Dallas, Banks Upshaw and Co., 1937.

Garrard, Lewis H. *Wah-to-yah and the Taos trail.* Edited by Ralph P. Bieber. Glendale, The Arthur H. Clark Co., 1934.

Gautier, Théophile. *A romantic in Spain,* translated from the French by Catherine Alison Phillips. New York, Alfred A. Knopf, 1926.

Gibson, Charles E. *Story of the ship.* New York, Henry Schumann, 1948.

Gibson, George Rutledge. *Journal of a soldier under Kearny and Doniphan, 1846–1847.* Edited by Ralph P. Bieber. Glendale, The Arthur H. Clark Co., 1935.

Giddings, Luther. *Sketches of the campaign in northern Mexico in eighteen hundred forty-six and seven, by an officer of the First Regiment of Ohio volunteers.* New York, George P. Putnam and Co., 1853.

Gilpin, Laura. *The Pueblos, a camera chronicle.* New York, Hastings House, 1941.

—— *The Rio Grande, river of destiny. An interpretation of the river, the land, and the people.* New York, Duell, Sloan and Pearce, 1949.

Glasgow, Brig. Gen. William J. *Conversations* at El Paso, Texas.

Goldscheider, Ludwig. *El Greco.* New York, Phaidon Press—Oxford University Press, 1938.

Gonzáles de Mendoza, Juan. *A briefe relation of two notable voyages, the first made by frier Augustin Ruyz . . .; the second by Antonio de Espejo . . . taken out of the history of China written by Frier Juan Gonzales de Mendoça.* (In *The voyages, traffiques and discoveries of foreign voyagers . . .* by Richard Hakluyt, v. 10). London, J. M. Dent and Son, Ltd., 1928.

Gonzáles, Jovita. *America invades the border towns. Southwest Review,* v. 15, no. 4, summer 1940.

—— *Folk-lore of the Texas-Mexican vaquero.* (In *Texas and southwestern lore,* edited by J. Frank Dobie). Austin, Publications of the Texas Folk-Lore Society, number 6, 1927.

Grant, Blanche C. *When old trails were new, the story of Taos.* New York, Press of the Pioneers, 1934.

Grant, Ulysses Simpson. *Personal memoirs of U. S. Grant.* 2 v. New York, The Century Co., 1895.

Grassi, Giovanni Antonio. *Notizie varie sullo stato presente della repubblica degli Stati Uniti dell' America . . . (1819)* (Extracts in *This Was America,* edited by Oscar Handlin). Cambridge, Harvard University Press, 1949.

Green, Thomas J. *Journal of the Texian expedition against Mier . . .* [a facsimile reproduction of the original]. Austin, The Steck Co., 1935.

Gregg, Josiah. *Commerce of the prairies, the journal of a Santa Fe trader.* [Reprint from the edition of 1844.] Dallas, Southwest Press, 1933.

—— *Diary and letters of Josiah Gregg: Excursions in Mexico and California, 1847–1850,* edited by Maurice Garland Fulton, with an introduction by Paul Horgan. Norman, University of Oklahoma Press, 1944.

—— *Diary and letters of Josiah Gregg: Southwestern enterprises, 1840–1847,* edited by Maurice Garland Fulton, with an introduction by Paul Horgan. Norman, University of Oklahoma Press, 1941.

Gregg, Robert D. *The influence of border troubles on relations between the United States and Mexico, 1876–1910.* Baltimore, the Johns Hopkins Press, 1937.

Grey, Edward, Viscount Grey of Fallodon. *Twenty-five years, 1892–1916.* 2 v. New York, Frederick H. Stokes Co., 1926.

Gutierrez de Lara, José Bernardo. *Diary . . . 1811–1812.* Translated from the original Spanish by Elizabeth H. West. *American Historical Review,* v. 34, nos. 1 and 2.

Hackett, Charles Wilson. *Revolt of the Pueblo Indians of New Mexico and Otermin's attempted reconquest, 1680–1692.* Introduction and annotations by Charles Wilson Hackett. Translations of original documents by Charmion Clair Shelby. Coronado Cuarto Centennial Publications, 1540–1940, edited by George P. Hammond. V. 8 and 9. Albuquerque, University of New Mexico Press, 1942.

Hallenbeck, Cleve. *Álvar Nuñez Cabeza de Vaca, the journey and route of the first European to cross the continent of North America, 1534–1536.* Glendale, The Arthur H. Clarke Co., 1940.

—— *Land of the conquistadores.* Caldwell, Idaho, The Caxton Printers, 1950.

Hamilton, Holman. *Zachary Taylor, soldier of the republic.* Indianapolis, The Bobbs-Merrill Co., 1941.

Hammond, George P. *Narratives of the Coronado expedition, 1540–1542* [edited and annotated] by George P. Hammond and Agapito Rey. Coronado Cuarto Centennial Publications, edited by George P. Hammond. v. 2 Albuquerque, University of New Mexico Press, 1940.

Hammond, John Hays. *Autobiography.* 2 v. New York, Farrar and Rinehart, 1935.

Handlin, Oscar. *This was America,* edited by Oscar Handlin. Cambridge, Harvard University Press, 1949.

Hanke, Lewis. *The first social experiments in America, a study in the develop-*

ment of Spanish Indian Policy in the 16th century. Cambridge, Harvard University Press, 1935.

———— *Spanish struggle for justice in the conquest of America.* Philadelphia, University of Pennsylvania Press, 1949.

Harrington, J. P. *Old Indian geographical names around Santa Fe, New Mexico. American Anthropologist,* v. 22, 1920.

Hendrick, Burton J. *Life and letters of Walter H. Page.* 3 v. Garden City, Doubleday, Page and Co., 1922.

Henry, Robert Selph. *Story of the Mexican War.* Indianapolis, Bobbs-Merrill Co., 1950.

Henry, W. S. *Campaign sketches of the war with Mexico.* New York, Harper and Brothers, 1847.

Hergesheimer, Joseph. *Sheridan, a military narrative.* Boston, Houghton Mifflin Co., 1931.

Hewett, Edgar L. *Ancient life in the American southwest.* Indianapolis, Bobbs-Merrill Co., 1930.

———— *The Pueblo Indian world* . . . by Edgar L. Hewett and Bertha P. Dutton . . . Albuquerque, University of New Mexico; Santa Fe, School of American Research, 1945.

Hill, Robert L. *Running the canyons of the Rio Grande. A chapter of recent exploration.* Century Magazine, v. 61, no. 3, January 1901.

Hitchcock, Ethan Allen. *Fifty years in camp and field. Diary of Major General Ethan Allen Hitchcock, U.S.A.,* edited by W. A. Croffut, New York, G. P. Putnam's Sons, 1909.

Hodge, Frederick Webb. *Spanish explorers in the southwestern United States, 1528–1543,* edited by Frederick W. Hodge and Theodore H. Lewis. *Original narratives of early American history.* New York, Charles Scribner's Sons, 1925.

Hoffman, Fred L. *Why the Cliff Dwellers vanished. Scientific American,* v.123, 1920.

Hogan, William Ransom. *The Texas Republic.* Norman, University of Oklahoma Press, 1946.

Hollister, Ovando J. *Boldly they rode, a history of the First Colorado Regiment of Volunteers.* With an introduction by William McCleod Raine. Lakewood, Colorado, The Golden Press, 1949.

Hollon, W. Eugene. *The lost pathfinder, Zebulon Montgomery Pike.* Norman, University of Oklahoma Press, 1949.

Horgan, Paul. *Colonial Life in Latin America, an exhibition of history and art.* Roswell, New Mexico, Roswell Museum, 1949.

———— *The habit of empire* with landscapes by Peter Hurd. New York, Harper and Brothers, 1939.

———— *A tree on the plains,* Text for the opera by Ernst Bacon. Dallas, *Southwest Review,* v. 38, no. 4, 1943.

House, Edward M. *Intimate papers of Colonel House,* arranged as a narrative by Charles Seymour. 4 v. Boston, Houghton Mifflin Co., 1928.

Houston, Sam. *Proclamation by the President of Texas, announcing an armistice between Texas and Mexico, 29 July 1843.* Signed by Anson Jones, Secretary of state of Texas. Original document. San Marino, California,

Henry E. Huntington Library. (Excerpts quoted by permission of the Huntington Library.)

Howlett, W. J. *Life of the Right Reverend Joseph P. Machebeuf, D.D.* Pueblo, Colorado, 1908.

Hrdlička, Ales. *Physiological and medical observations among the Indians of the southwestern United States and northern Mexico.* Smithsonian Institution, Bureau of American Ethnology, *Bulletin 34,* Washington, Government Printing Office, 1908.

Hughes, John Taylor. *Diary* (in *Doniphan's expedition,* by William E. Connelley). Topeka, Crane and Co., 1907.

Hume, Martin A. S. *Phillip II of Spain.* London, The Macmillan Co., 1920.

Huntington, Ellsworth. *The red man's chronicle, a chronicle of aboriginal America. (Chronicles of America.)* New Haven, Yale University Press. 1921.

Irving, Washington. *The adventures of Captain Bonneville.* 2 v. New York, G. P. Putnam's Sons, 1895.

James, George Wharton. *New Mexico, land of the delight makers.* Boston, Page and Co., 1920.

James, Marquis. *The Raven, a biography of Sam Houston.* Indianapolis, Bobbs-Merrill Co., 1929.

Jaramillo, Cleofas M. *Shadows of the past (sombres del pasado).* Santa Fe, Seton Village Press, 1941.

Jeançon, Jean Allard. *Pueblo Indian clothing* by Jean Allard Jeançon and Frederic H. Douglas. Denver Art Museum, *Leaflet series 4,* 1930.

——— *Pueblo Indian foods* by Jean Allard Jeançon and Frederic H. Douglas. Denver Art Museum, *Leaflet series 8,* 1930.

Jones, Stephen B. *Boundary-making; a handbook for statesmen, treaty editors and boundary commissioners.* Washington, Carnegie Endowment for International Peace, 1945.

Keleher, William A. *Turmoil in New Mexico, 1846–1868.* Santa Fe, The Rydal Press, 1952.

Kelley, J. Charles. *Association of archaeological materials with geological deposits in the Big Bend region of Texas,* by J. Charles Kelley, T. N. Campbell and Donald J. Lehmer. Alpine, Texas, *Sul Ross State Teachers College Bulletin,* v. 21, no. 3, September 1, 1940.

Kendall, George Wilkins. *Narrative of the Texan Santa Fe expedition . . .* 2 v. [facsimile reproduction of the original edition.] Austin, The Steck Co., 1935.

Kenly, John Reese. *Memoirs of a Maryland volunteer, war with Mexico, in the years 1846–7–8.* Philadelphia, J. B. Lippincott and Co., 1873.

Kerbey, McFall. *Texas delta of an American Nile. National Geographic Magazine,* v. 75, no. 1, January 1939.

Kidder, A. V. *An introduction to the study of southwestern archaeology with a preliminary account of the excavations at Pecos.* New Haven, Yale University Press, 1924.

Kincaid, Edgar B. *The Mexican pastor.* (In *Texas and southwestern lore,* edited by J. Frank Dobie.) Publications of the Texas Folk-Lore Society, no. 9. Dallas, the Southwest Press, 1931.

Kohlberg, Ernst. *Letters, 1875–1877.* Translated from the German. Original documents. El Paso Public Library. (Excerpts quoted by permission of El Paso Public Library.)

Kortwright, Francis H. *The ducks, geese and swans of North America.* Washington, American Wildlife Association, 1943.

Kouwenhoven, John A. *Made in America, the arts in modern civilization.* Garden City, Doubleday and Co., 1948.

Kroeber, A. L. *Pueblos* (in *Encyclopedia Britannica,* 14th edition).

Kubler, George. *The religious architecture of New Mexico in the colonial period and since the American occupation.* Colorado Springs, The Taylor Museum, 1940.

Lane, Ferdinand C. *Earth's grandest rivers.* Garden City, Doubleday and Co., 1949.

Lane, Franklin Knight. *Letters of Franklin K. Lane, personal and political,* edited by Anne Wintermute Lane and Louise Herrick Vail. Boston, Houghton Mifflin Co., 1922.

Lansing, Robert. *War memoirs.* Indianapolis, Bobbs-Merrill Co., 1935.

Lavelle, Francis. *Archbishop Lamy, of Santa Fe.* (In *Family Annual* for 1889.) New York, Catholic Publications Society Co., 1888.

Lee, Robert E. *Recollections and letters of General Robert E. Lee.* New York, Doubleday Page, 1904.

Leonard, Irving A. *Books of the brave, being an account of books and men in the Spanish conquest and settlement of the sixteenth-century new world.* Cambridge, Harvard University Press, 1949.

Lewis, Lloyd. *Captain Sam Grant.* Boston, Little, Brown and Co., 1950.

Lewis, Macmillan. *Woodrow Wilson of Princeton.* Narberth, Penna., Livingston Publishing Co., 1952.

Lipman, Jean. *American folk art in wood, metal and stone.* New York, Pantheon, 1948.

. . . . . . *Literary Digest,* March–December, 1916.

Lomax, John A. *Cowboy songs and other frontier ballads,* collected by John A. Lomax. With an introduction by Barrett Wendell. New York, The Macmillan Co., 1927.

–——— *Folk song U S A, the 111 best American ballads,* collected, adapted and arranged by John A. Lomax and Alan Lomax; Alan Lomax, editor; Charles Seeger and Ruth Crawford Seeger, music editors. New York, Duell, Sloan and Pearce, 1947.

——— *Our singing country, a second volume of American ballads and folk songs,* collected and compiled by John A. Lomax and Alan Lomax; Ruth Crawford Seeger, music editor. New York, The Macmillan Co., 1941.

López de Gómara, Francisco. *General historie of the West Indies.* (Excerpts in Hakluyt's *Voyages, traffiques and discoveries of foreign voyagers.*) London, J. M. Dent, 1928.

Lowrie, Samuel Harman. *Culture conflict in Texas, 1821–1835.* New York, Columbia University Press, 1932.

Lummis, Charles F. *Land of poco tiempo.* New York, Charles Scribner's Sons, 1913.

———— *Mesa, canyon and pueblo.* New York, Century Co., 1925.

MacClary, John Stewart. *The first American farmers.* Art and Archaeology, v. 124, no. 3, September, 1927.

McCoy, John C. *Paper read before Old Settlers Historical Society, Jackson County, Missouri,* 1871.

McCoy, Joseph G. *Historic sketches of the cattle trade of the west and southwest.* [Facsimile reprint of the edition of 1874.] Washington, The Rare Book Shop, 1932.

McKee, Irving. *"Ben Hur" Wallace, the life of General Lew Wallace.* Berkeley and Los Angeles, University of California Press, 1947.

McKee, James Cooper. *Narrative of the surrender of a command of U.S. forces at Fort Fillmore, N.M., in July, A.D. 1861, at the breaking out of the Civil War . . .* second edition revised and corrected. New York, 1881.

McKellar, Mrs. S. B. *Conversations* at Eagle Pass, Texas.

Madariaga, Salvador de. *Fall of the Spanish American empire.* London, Hollis and Carter, 1948.

———— *Rise of the Spanish American empire.* London, Hollis and Carter, 1947.

———— *Spain.* New York, Creative Age Press, 1943.

Magoffin, Susan Shelby. *Down the Santa Fe Trail and into Mexico; the diary of Susan Shelby Magoffin, 1846–1847,* edited by Stella M. Drumm. New Haven, Yale University Press, 1926.

Martialis, Marcus Valerius. *Epigrams,* with an English translation by Walter C. A. Kerr. New York, G. P. Putnam's Sons, 1930.

Martin, George C. *Archaeological exploration of the Shumla caves. Report of the George C. Martin expedition, Southwest Texas Archaeological Society.* San Antonio, Witte Memorial Museum, 1933.

Martin, Paul S. *Indians before Columbus. Twenty thousand years of North American history revealed by archaeology,* by Paul S. Martin, George L. Quimby and Donald Collier. Chicago, University of Chicago Press, 1947.

Maugham, W. Somerset. *Don Fernando, or variations on some Spanish themes.* Garden City, Doubleday, Doran and Co., 1935.

May, Florence. *The Penitentes. Natural History,* v. 38, Dec. 1936.

Meier-Graefe, Julius. *The Spanish journey.* Translated by J. Holroyd Reece. New York, Harcourt, Brace and Co., ND.

Mencken, H. L. *The American language, an inquiry into the development of English in the United States.* Fourth edition. New York, Alfred A. Knopf, 1936.

———— Supplement I to the above, 1945.

Milham, Willis Isbister. *Meteorology.* New York, The Macmillan Co., 1929.

Miller, Alfred Jacob. *The west of Alfred Jacob Miller (1837),* from the notes and water colors in the Walters Art Gallery, with an account of the artist by Marvin C. Ross. Norman, University of Oklahoma Press, 1951.

Millis, Walter. *Road to war, America, 1914–1917.* Boston, Houghton Mifflin Co., 1935.

Montlezun, Baron de. *Voyage fait dans les années 1816 et 1817, de New-Yorck à la Nouvelle-Orléans et de l'Orénoque au Mississippi . . . (1818).* (Extracts in *This was America,* edited by Oscar Handlin.) Cambridge, Harvard University Press, 1949.

Montoya, Juan de. *New Mexico in 1602. Juan de Montoya's relation of the discovery of New Mexico.* Translated, edited, annotated, and with an introduction by George P. Hammond and Agapito Rey. Albuquerque, The Quivira Society, 1938.

Moreau de Saint-Méry, Méderic Louis Élie. *Voyage aux États-Unis de l'Amérique, 1793–1798.* (Extracts in *This was America,* edited by Oscar Handlin.) Cambridge, Harvard University Press, 1949.

Morfi, Fray Juan Agustín. *History of Texas, 1673–1779.* Translated, with biographical introduction and annotations by Carlos Eduardo Castañeda. In two parts. Albuquerque. The Quivira Society, 1935.

Moses, Montrose J. *The American dramatist.* Boston, Little, Brown and Co. 1925.

...... *Motion picture film footage,* showing Francisco Villa, General John J. Pershing, President Woodrow Wilson, President Venustiano Carranza, General Álvaro Obregón, General Frederick Funston, and desert fighting episode during the Punitive Expedition of 1916. New York, Lloyds Film Storage Co.

National Capital Sesquicentennial Commission. *American processional, 1492-- 1900.* Washington, The Corcoran Gallery of Art, 1950.

New Mexico, Citizens of. *Document addressed to President Santa Anna of Mexico, describing abandonment of New Mexico by Governor Manuel Armíjo.* Signed by various citizens, Santa Fe, September 26, 1846. Translation. Original document. San Marino, Henry E. Huntington Library. (Excerpts quoted by permission of the Huntington Library.)

Nuñez Cabeza de Vaca, Alvar. *Narrative of Alvar Nuñez Cabeza de Vaca,* edited by Frederick W. Hodge. (In *Spanish explorers of the southern United States,* 1528–1543.) *Original narratives of early American history.* New York, Charles Scribner's Sons, 1907.

...... *Outlook,* 30 October 1909.

Palmer, Frederick. *Newton D. Baker, America at war.* 2 v. New York, Dodd, Mead and Co., 1931.

Palmer, Rose A. *The North American Indians. The Smithsonian Scientific series,* v. 4. New York, Smithsonian Institution Series, Inc., 1938.

Parkman, Francis. *The journals of Francis Parkman,* edited by Mason Wade. 2 v. New York, Harper and Brothers, 1947.

Parsons, Elsie Clews. *Pueblo Indian religion.* 2 v. Chicago, University of Chicago Press, 1939.

Pattie, James O. *Personal narrative of James O. Pattie of Kentucky . . .* edited by Reuben Gold Thwaites. *Early Western Travels.* Cleveland, Arthur H. Clark Co., 1905.

Percier. *Le sacre de S.M. l'empereur Napoléon dans l'église métropolitaine de Paris, le xi frimaire an XIII, dimanche 2 décembre 1804.*

Pérez de Lúxan, Diego. *Expedition into New Mexico made by Antonio de Espéjo, 1582–1583.* Translated with introduction and notes by George P. Hammond and Agapito Rey. Los Angeles, The Quivira Society, 1929.

Pérez de Villagrá, Gaspar. *History of New Mexico.* Translated by Gilberto Espinosa. Introduction and notes by Frederick W. Hodge. Los Angeles, The Quivira Society, 1933.

Pershing, John Joseph. *Letters* (unpublished). Mss. 1915–1917. Private collection, Washington, D.C. (Excerpts quoted by permission of Mr. F. W. Pershing.)

—— *My experiences in the world war.* 2 v. New York, Frederick H. Stokes Co., 1931.

Peyton, Green. *America's heartland: the southwest.* Norman, University of Oklahoma Press, 1948.

Pike, Zebulon Montgomery. *The expeditions of Zebulon Montgomery Pike . . . during the years 1805–6–7,* edited by Elliott Coues. 3 v. New York, Francis P. Harper, 1895.

Pino, Pedro Bautista, *et al. Three New Mexico chronicles; the Exposición of Don Pedro Bautista Pino, 1812; the Ojeada of Lic. Antonio Barreiro, 1832; and the additions of Don José Agustín de Escudero, 1849.* Translated with introduction and notes by H. Bailey Carroll and J. Villasana Haggard. Albuquerque, The Quivira Society, 1942.

Plato. *Dialogues.* Selections from the translation of Benjamin Jowett . . . edited with an introduction by William Chase Greene. New York, Boni and Liveright, 1927.

Polk, James K. *Polk, the diary of a president, 1845–1849,* edited by Allan Nevins. New York, Longmans, Green, 1929.

Powell, Fred Wilbur. *The railroads of Mexico.* Boston, The Stratford Co., 1921.

Prescott, William H. *History of the reign of Philip the second, king of Spain.* Boston, Phillips, Sampson and Co., 1855.

Priestley, Herbert Ingram. *The coming of the white man, 1492–1848.* New York, The Macmillan Co., 1929.

Pringle, Henry F. *Life and times of William Howard Taft.* 2 v. New York, Farrar and Rinehart, 1939.

Quinn, Arthur Hobson. *A history of the American drama from the beginning to the Civil War.* New York, Harper and Brothers, 1923.

Read, Benjamin N. *Illustrated history of New Mexico.* [Santa Fe, New Mexican Printing Co., c. 1912.]

Reagan, Albert B. *Evidences of migration in ancient Pueblo times. American Anthropologist,* v. 35, 1933.

Reed, John. *Insurgent Mexico.* New York, D. Appleton Co., 1914.

Renaud, Etienne B. *Evolution of population and dwelling in the Indian southwest. Social Forces,* v. 7, 1928–1929.

Rice, Martin. *Old timers' poem,* read by the author Martin Rice at Old Settlers' meeting, Jackson County, Missouri, 1880.

Richardson, Rupert Norval. *The greater southwest . . .* by Richard Norval Richardson and Carl Coke Rister. Glendale, The Arthur H. Clark Co., 1934.

Richie, Ed. *Conversations* at Eagle Pass, Texas.

Ritch, William Gillet. *Article addressed to Editor, New York Herald, concerning establishment of archbishopric of Santa Fe. June 21, 1875.* Original document, ms. San Marino, Henry E. Huntington Library.

Rives, George Lockhart. *The United States and Mexico, 1821–1848.* 2 v. New York, Charles Scribner's Sons, 1913.

Robertson, William Spence. *Iturbide of Mexico.* Durham, Duke University Press, 1952.

Robinson, Jacob S. *A journal of the Santa Fe expedition under Colonel Doniphan.* Reprinted, with an historical introduction and notes by Carl L. Cannon, from the edition of 1848. *Narratives of the Trans-Mississippi Frontier.* Princeton, Princeton University Press, 1932.

Ronquillo, E. W. *Notes on "Rio Grande dry" in 1851 and 1863.* Written August 23, 1877. Original document. San Marino, Henry E. Huntington Library. (Excerpts quoted by permission of the Huntington Library.)

Rose, Stuart. *Conversations* at Philadelphia, Pennsylvania.

Rosenfeld, Paul. *An hour with American music. The One Hour Series.* Philadelphia, J. B. Lippincott Co., 1929.

Rourke, Constance. *American humor, a study of the national character.* New York, Harcourt, Brace and Co., 1931.

—— *The roots of American culture, and other essays.* Edited with a preface by Van Wyck Brooks. New York, Harcourt, Brace and Co., 1942.

Ruxton, George Frederick. *Ruxton of the Rockies.* Collected by Clyde and Mae Reed Porter, edited by LeRoy R. Hafen. Norman, University of Oklahoma Press, 1950.

Salpointe, Jean Baptiste. *Soldiers of the cross. Notes on the ecclesiastical history of New Mexico, Arizona and Colorado.* Banning, California, St. Boniface's Industrial School, 1898.

Sanford, Trent E. *The architecture of the southwest: Indian, Spanish, American.* New York, W. W. Norton and Co., 1950.

Santa Fe, Archdiocese of. *The old faith and Old Glory, 1846–1946, [the] story of the Church in New Mexico since the American occupation.* Santa Fe, New Mexico, 1946.

Santleben, August. *A Texas pioneer. Early staging and overland freighting days on the frontiers of Texas and Mexico.* New York and Washington, The Neale Publishing Co., c. 1910.

Scott, Hugh Lennox. *Papers of Major General Hugh L. Scott.* Mss. Washington. The Library of Congress.

—— *Some memories of a soldier.* New York, The Century Co., 1928.

Segale, Sister Blandina. *At the end of the Santa Fe Trail.* Milwaukee, Bruce Publishing Co., 1948.

Sheridan, Philip H. *Personal memoirs.* New York, Charles L. Webster Co., 1888.

Sibley, George Champlin. *The road to Santa Fe. The journal and diaries of George Champlin Sibley and others pertaining to the surveying and marking of a road from the Missouri frontier to the settlements of New Mexico, 1825–1827.* Edited by Kate L. Gregg. Albuquerque. The University of New Mexico Press, 1952.

Sigüenza y Góngora, Carlos de. *The Mercurio volante of Don Carlos de Sigüenza y Góngora. An account of the first expedition of Don Diego de Vargas into New Mexico in 1692.* Translated, with an introduction and notes, by Irving Albert Leonard. Los Angeles, The Quivira Society, 1932.

Simpich, Frederick. *Down the Rio Grande. National Geographic Magazine,* v. 76, no. 4, Oct., 1939.

Siringo, Charles A. *Riata and spurs.* Boston, Houghton Mifflin and Co., 1931.

—— *A Texas cowboy, or fifteen years on the hurricane deck of a Spanish pony, taken from real life* . . . with bibliographical study and introduction by J. Frank Dobie and drawings by Tom Lea. New York, William Sloane Associates, 1950.

Sitwell, Osbert. *Winters of content, and other discursions on Mediterranean art and travel.* London, Gerald Duckworth and Co., Ltd., 1950

Smith, Arthur D. Howden. *Old Fuss and Feathers* . . . *the life and exploits of Lt. General Winfield Scott.* New York, The Greystone Press, 1937.

Smith, Ephraim Kirby. *To Mexico with Scott; letters of Captain E. Kirby Smith to his wife,* prepared for the press by his daughter, Emma Jeanne Blackwood. . . Cambridge, Harvard University Press, 1917.

Smith, Erwin E. *Life on the Texas range.* Photographs by Erwin E. Smith; text by J. Evetts Haley. Austin, University of Texas Press, 1952.

Smith, Henry Nash. *Virgin land, the American west as symbol and myth.* Cambridge, Harvard University Press, 1950.

Smith, Justin H. *La república del Rio Grande. American Historical Review,* v. 25, Oct. 1919–July 1920.

Smith, Victor J. *A survey of Indian life in Texas.* Alpine, Texas, West Texas Historical and Scientific Society, Circular no. 5, 1941.

Soley, James Russell. *The blockade and the cruisers. (The navy in the Civil War.)* New York, Charles Scribner's Sons, 1903.

Stanley, F. *Fort Union [New Mexico].* Denver? [World Press], 1953.

Stone, John Augustus. *Matamora and other plays,* edited by Eugene R. Page Princeton, Princeton University Press, 1941.

Strong, George Templeton. *The diary of George Templeton Strong,* edited by Allan Nevins and Milton Halsey Thomas. 4 v. New York, The Macmillan Co., 1952.

Sullivan, Mark. *Our times. v. 4 and 5. The United States, 1900–1925.* New York, Charles Scribner's Sons, 1933.

Sumpter, Jesse. *Life of Jesse Sumpter, oldest citizen of Eagle Pass, Texas, commenced to be written down May 30, 1902. Taken down by Harry Warren. Finished June 14, 1906.* Original document. Typescript. Eagle Pass, Texas, private collection. (Excerpts quoted by permission of owner.)

Talman, Charles Fitzhugh. *The realm of the air.* Indianapolis, Bobbs-Merrill Co., 1931.

Tannenbaum, Frank. *Mexico, the struggle for peace and bread.* New York, Alfred A. Knopf, 1950.

Thoburn, Joseph B. *Ancient irrigation ditches of the plains. Chronicles of Oklahoma,* Oklahoma Historical Society, v. 6, 1931.

Thomas, Alfred B. *The first Santa Fe expedition, 1792–93.* Chronicles of Oklahoma, Oklahoma Historical Society, v. 6, 1931.

—— *The plains Indians and New Mexico, 1751–1778.* Albuquerque, University of New Mexico Press, 1940.

Thomlinson, Matthew H. *The garrison at Fort Bliss.* El Paso, Hertzog and Resler, 1945.

Thoreau, Henry David. *Journal.* Edited by Bradford Torrey [In collected edition of] *The writings of Henry David Thoreau.* Boston, Houghton Mifflin Co., 1906.

Thorpe, T. B. *Our army on the Rio Grande.* Philadelphia, Carey and Harte, 1846.

Tierney, Luke. *Pike's Peak gold rush guidebooks of 1859,* by Luke Tierney, William B. Parsons *et al.* Edited by Leroy R. Hafen. Glendale, Arthur H. Clarke Co., 1941.

Tocqueville, Alexis de. *Democracy in America.* The Henry Reeve text . . . edited . . . by Phillips Bradley. 2 v. New York, Alfred A. Knopf, 1945.

Tompkins, Frank. *Chasing Villa, the story behind the story of Pershing's expedition into Mexico.* Harrisburg, Military Service Publishing Co., 1934.

Toulmin, Harry A. *With Pershing in Mexico.* Harrisburg, Military Service Publishing Co., 1935.

Toulouse, Joseph H., Jr. *The mission of San Gregorio de Abó. A report on the excavation and repair of a seventeenth-century New Mexico mission.* Albuquerque, University of New Mexico Press, 1949.

Toulouse, Joseph H. *Pioneer posts of Texas,* by Joseph H. and James H. Toulouse. San Antonio, Naylor Publishing Co., 1936.

Towne, Charles Wayland. *Shepherd's empire,* by Charles Wayland Towne and Edward Norris Wentworth. Norman, University of Oklahoma Press, 1945.

Townsend, E. E. *Early border elections. Bulletin 44,* West Texas Historical and Scientific Society: Publications No. 4. Alpine, Texas, Sul Ross State Teachers College, 1932.

—— *Rangers and Indians in the Big Bend region. Bulletin 56,* West Texas Historical and Scientific Society: Publications No. 6. Alpine, Texas, Sul Ross State Teachers College, 1935.

Trend, J. B. *The civilization of Spain.* London, Oxford University Press, 1944.

Trollope, Frances. *Domestic manners of the Americans.* Edited . . . by Donald Smalley. New York, Alfred A. Knopf, 1949.

Troxel, O. C. *The Tenth Cavalry in Mexico. Cavalry Journal,* July, 1927.

Tumulty, Joseph P. *Woodrow Wilson as I knew him.* Garden City, Doubleday Page and Co., 1921.

Twitchell, Ralph Emerson. *The leading facts of New Mexican history.* V. 1 and 2. Cedar Rapids, The Torch Press, 1911.

—— *Old Santa Fe, the story of New Mexico's ancient capital.* Santa Fe New Mexican Publishing Corp., 1925.

—— *The Spanish archives of New Mexico.* 2 v. Cedar Rapids, The Torch Press, 1914.

Underhill, Ruth. *Work-a-day life of the Pueblos.* United States Indian service, *Indian life and customs, no. 4.* U. S. Department of the Interior. Phoenix, Phoenix Indian School Printing Dept., 1946.

United States Congress. 43rd Congress, 1st session. House of Representatives. *Executive document no. 257. Depredations on the frontiers of Texas. Message from the President of the United States, transmitting a communication from the Secretary of State, and a copy of the report of the commissioners to inquire into depredations on the frontiers of Texas.* May 26, 1874.

———44th Congress. 1st session. House of Representatives. *Report no. 343. Texas frontier troubles.* February 29, 1876.

———45th Congress. 1st session. House of Representatives. *Executive document no. 13. Mexican border troubles. Message from the President of the United States* . . . 1877.

United States Department of Agriculture. Field flood control co-ordinating committee. *Survey report. Run-off and water-flow retardation and soil-erosion prevention for flood-control purposes. Rio Puerco watershed, tributary of the upper Rio Grande.* Signed Hugh G. Calkins, Arthur Upson, Millard Peck. 1940.

United States Department of Agriculture. Soil Conservation Service, Region 8. *A description of the lands contiguous to the Elephant Butte Irrigation District of Southern New Mexico.* Typescript. Albuquerque, 1938.

———*Reconnaissance survey of human dependency on resources in the Rio Grande watershed.* Regional bulletin no. 33, Conservation economics series no. 6. Albuquerque, December, 1936.

———*A report on the Rio Grande watershed with special reference to soil conservation problems.* Prepared by Rio Grande District staff in collaboration with the staff of the regional office. Signed E. R. Smith, District manager, Rio Grande District. Albuquerque, November 22, 1936.

———*Rio Grande watershed in Colorado and New Mexico. A report on the condition and use of the land and water resources together with a general program for soil and water conservation.* Albuquerque, August, 1939.

———*The sociological survey of the Rio Grande watershed.* Typescript. Albuquerque, 1936.

———*Tewa Basin study. v. 1, The Indian pueblos; v. 2, The Spanish-American villages; v. 3, Physical surveys and other studies.* Mimeographed. Albuquerque, April, 1935.

United States Department of the Interior. Bureau of Reclamation. *Reclamation Handbook.* Washington, Superintendent of Documents, 1942.

United States Department of the Interior. Bureau of Reclamation, Region 5. *Brief descriptions of irrigation and multiple-purpose projects proposed for construction in the post-war period. June 1, 1945.*

United States Department of the Interior. National Park Service. *San Buenaventura Mission, Gran Quivira National Monument.* Santa Fe, Southwestern Monuments Association, ND.

United States [government] Office of the Superintendent of Indian Affairs. *Passport issued to a party of prairie travelers; signed by William Clark, Superintendent of Indian Affairs, July 23, 1820.* Original document. San Marino, Henry E. Huntington Library. (Excerpt quoted by permission of the Huntington Library.)

Vargas Zapata Luján Ponce de León, Diego de. *First expedition of Vargas into New Mexico, 1692.* Translated, with introduction and notes, by J. Manuel Espinosa. Albuquerque, University of New Mexico Press, 1940.

Vásquez de Coronado, Francisco. *Letter to the King of Spain from the province of Tiguex, Oct. 20, 1541.* (In *Narratives of the Coronado Expedition, 1540–1542,* edited by George P. Hammond and Agapito Rey.) Albuquerque, University of New Mexico Press, 1940.

Vega, Garcilaso de la. *The Florida of the Inca.* Translated and edited by John Grier and Jeanette Johnson Varner. Austin, University of Texas Press, 1951.

Vigil, Donaciano. *Minutes of a meeting held at Santa Fe, 27 August, 1837, by supporters of Governor Gonzáles . . . signed by Donaciano Vigil, acting secretary-sergeant.* Translation. Original document. San Marino, Henry E. Huntington Library. (Excerpts quoted by permission of the Huntington Library.)

———*Speech made before New Mexico Assembly, May 16, 1846.* Original document. San Marino, Henry E. Huntington Library. (Excerpts quoted by permission of the Huntington Library.)

———*Speech made before the New Mexico Assembly, June 22, 1846.* Original document. San Marino, Henry E. Huntington Library. (Excerpts quoted by permission of the Huntington Library.)

Vigil y Alarid, Juan Bautista. *Proclamation by Acting Governor Vigil y Alarid, Santa Fe, August 1846, to the citizens of Santa Fe, publishing General Kearny's proclamation of reassurances to the New Mexicans.* Original document. San Marino, Henry E. Huntington Library. (Excerpts quoted by permission of the Huntington Library.)

Villa, Francisco. *Manifesto addressed by General Francisco Villa to the nation, and documents justifying the disavowal of Venustiano Carranza as first chief of the revolution.* Chihuahua, Constitutionalist Army, headquarters, Division of the North, 1914.

Wadleigh, A. B. *Ranching in New Mexico, 1886–1890. New Mexico Historical Review,* v. 27, no. 1, January, 1952.

Wallace, Ernest. *The Comanches, lords of the south plains,* by Ernest Wallace and E. Adamson Hoebel. Norman, University of Oklahoma Press, 1952.

Wallace, Lew. *An autobiography.* New York, Harper and Brothers, 1906.

Wallace, Susan E. *Among the pueblos. Atlantic Monthly,* v. 46, August, 1880.

Walsh, Thomas J. *Papers of Senator Thomas J. Walsh.* Mss. Washington, The Library of Congress.

Ward, Charles Francis. *The Salt War of San Elizario (1877).* Thesis presented to the faculty of the graduate school of the University of Texas . . . Unpublished. Austin, 1932.

Warner, Louis H. *Archbishop Lamy, an epoch maker.* Santa Fe New Mexican Publishing Corp., 1936.

Watson, Don. *Cliff palace, the story of an ancient city.* Ann Arbor, Michigan. 1947.

Webb, Walter Prescott. *The Texas Rangers; a century of frontier defense.* Boston, Houghton Mifflin Co., 1935.

White, Leslie A. *The pueblo of Santo Domingo, New Mexico. Memoirs of the American Anthropological Assn., No. 43.* Menasha, Wisconsin, 1935.

Whitford, William Clarke. *Colorado volunteers in the Civil War; the New Mexico campaign in 1862.* Denver, The State Historical and Natural History Society, 1906.

Whitlock, Brand. *Journal.* Chosen and edited . . . by Allan Nevins. New York, Appleton-Century Co., 1936.

Whitman, Walt. *Leaves of grass.* New York, Heritage Press, ND.

—— *Prose works.* Philadelphia, David McKay, ND.

Wilcox, Seb. B. *Conversations* at Laredo, Texas.

—— *Laredo during the Texas Republic. Southwestern Historical Quarterly,* v. 42, no. 2, October, 1938.

Wilder, Mitchell A. *Santos, the religious folk art of New Mexico,* by Mitchell A. Wilder and Edgar Breitenbach. With a foreword by Rudolf A. Gerken. Archbishop of Santa Fe. Colorado Springs, The Taylor Museum, 1943.

Williams, Ellen. *Three years and a half in the army; or, History of the Second Colorados.* New York, Fowler and Wells, 1885.

Williams, O. W. *Baja el sol.* Pamphlet. Undated.

—— *Pecos county—its history.* Pamphlet. Undated.

—— *Untitled pamphlet in form of a letter, dated Alpine, Texas, March 16th, 1902, addressed to "My dear children."*

Wilson, Thomas Woodrow. *The public papers of Woodrow Wilson. The New Democracy. Presidential messages, addresses, and other papers (1913–1917).* 2 v. Edited by Ray Stannard Baker and William E. Dodd. New York, Harper and Brothers, 1926.

Wislizenus, A. *Memoir of a tour through northern Mexico, connected with Colonel Doniphan's expedition, 1846–47.* 30th Congress, 1st session. *Senate Miscellaneous no. 26.* Washington, Tippin and Streepen, Printers, 1848.

Wissler, Clark. *The American Indian.* New York, Oxford University Press, 1922.

Wolle, Muriel Sibell. *Stampede to timberline, the ghost towns and mining camps of Colorado.* Boulder, Colorado, The Author, 1949.

Wortham, Louis J. *A history of Texas from wilderness to commonwealth.* Fort Worth, Wortham-Molyneaux Co., 1924.

Wright, R. R. *Negro companions of the Spanish explorers. American Anthropologist,* v. 4, 1902.

Yoakum, H *History of Texas from its first settlement in 1685 to its annexation to the United States in 1846.* 2 v. New York, Redfield, 1856.

APPENDIX D

The Names of the Rio Grande

APPENDIX D

The Names of the Rio Grande

The Rio Grande has borne various names during different periods and along several different reaches of its course. These are the names I encountered in my study of the river:

Grand River (General Wilkinson, 1806).
P'osoge (modern Tewa—"big river").
Rio Bravo (Castaño de Sosa, 1590, and Oñate, 1598).
Rio Bravo del Norte.
Rio Caudaloso ("carrying much water").
Rio de la Concepción (Rodríguez expedition, 1581).
Rio de las Palmas (Pineda, 1519).
Rio de Nuestra Señora (Alvarado, 1540).
Rio de San Buenaventura del Norte (Fernando del Bosque, 1675).
Rio del Norte (Pérez de Luxán, 1582).
Rio del Norte y de Nuevo Mexico (Map, in Sigüenza y Góngora, 1700).
Rio Grande.
Rio Grande del Norte.
Rio Guadalquivir (Rodríguez, 1581).
Rio Turbio (Pérez de Luxán, 1581).
River of May (David Ingram, 1568).
Tiguex River (Jaramillo, 1540).

Index

Index

VOLUME I: *pages 3 through 440*

VOLUME II: *pages 453 through 945*

Abiquiu, New Mexico, 48, 468, 766
Abó, 154, 261, 263–64
Abreu, Alférez Santiago. *See* Santiago
    Abreu
Acapulco, 18, 348
Acordada Prison, 584
Ácoma, New Mexico, 113, 114, 154, 158,
    196–99
    massacre and battle, 200–09
    trial, 210–11
Adaes, Los, Texas, 336
Adams, Abigail, 658
Adams, Henry, 944
Adams, John, 658, 659, 944
Adams, John Quincy, 434, 474, 475,
    781
Adelino, 502
adobe, 48, 222, 224
Adrian, Cardinal, 182
advance to the river, by United States,
    609
Ágreda, María de (Mother María de
    Jesús), 232–38, 300, 304–05
Ágreda, Spain, 232, 235
agriculture. *See* crops; haciendas
Agua Caliente, 406
Agua de Santo Domingo. *See* Santo
    Domingo

Aguayo, Marquis de, 337
Aguilar, Captain de, 168, 196, 214, 216
Aguirre, Hortuño de. *See* Hortuño de
    Aguirre
Agustín (Indian), 315
Agustín I, Emperor. *See* Iturbide
airplanes, 943
Alamán, Lúcas, 489
Alameda, New Mexico, 322
Álamo, the (San Antonio de Valero
    Mission), 336, 524–30
    attack on, and taking by Mexicans,
    529–32
Álamo Creek, 795
Alamosa, Colorado, 888, 889
Alamosa Creek, 5
Alarcón, Martín de, 334–36
Alarid, Juan Bautista Vigil y. *See* Vigil
    y Alarid
Albernoz, Sosa. *See* Sosa Albernoz
Albuquerque, Duke of, 252
Albuquerque, New Mexico, 328, 330,
    348, 358, 392, 502, 544, 733, 734,
    743, 811, 812, 824, 826, 829, 865,
    944
Alcanfor, 115, 120, 122, 127–29, 132,
    136, 137, 139, 140, 154, 155, 159
Alcantro Creek, battle of, 562

alcohol. _See_ liquor

Aldama, Ignacio, 423, 424

Alemán, 502

Alemán, Juan, 121, 129

Alencaster, Joaquin Real. _See_ Real Alencaster

Alexander VI, Pope, and Bull of, 177, 241, 431

Almaden. _See_ Monclova

Almansa, Captain de, 415, 417

Alvarado ("Old White Lip"), 896, 897, 906

Alvarado, Hernando de, 111–17, 120, 121, 138

Alvarez de Pineda, Alonso, 85, 86, 88–91, 93

Alvarez Toledo, José, 427, 430, 431

American Bible Society, 702–03

American Flag, The, 704

Americans, North. _See_ United States

Ampudia, Pedro de, 592, 593, 595–97, 668–70, 689

Ana María, Empress, 439, 458, 460, 474

Anáhuac, 507, 519–20, 525

Anaya, Cristóbal de, 269, 275, 314, 389

Ancients, the, 13–80
   abandonment of cities, 19–21
   animals, 64
   caciques, 38–39, 47, 61
   children, 53–59
   clothing, 18, 51–53
   cult, medicine, 41–47
   cults, 38–39
   dances, ceremonial, 28–33, 39, 40, 46, 51, 76
   dead, 78
   death and personality, 75–79
   divorce, 53
   family life, 53–59
   farming, 14–16
   farming and hunting, 59–68
   food, 62–65

Ancients, the—_Cont'd_
   handicrafts, 17–18, 49–51
   houses, 17, 48–51
   kachinas, 29, 57–59, 65
   Keres and Tewa, 77
   kivas, 17, 26, 32, 39, 46, 47, 57, 64, 65, 76, 172, 209, 222, 223, 262
   koshare, 31, 47, 65–66
   life, communal, 37–47
   man, place of, 54
   matriarchy, 53–59
   medicine, cult of, 41–47
   mores, 37–47
   myths, 22–27, 35, 58
   names, personal, 76
   nature worship, 18
   origin, 13, 213
   personality and death, 75–79
   physique, 52
   play, 59
   population, 60
   pottery, 49–51
   priests, 38–39
   religion, 18, 21–23, 25–32, 73
   sexuality, 66
   societies, secret, 41–46
   speech, 77
   symbols, 50
   Tewa and Keres, 77
   travel and trade, 68–75
   war, 54–56
   war society, 47
   waters, sacred, 35
   witches, 41–46, 75–76
   women, 53–59

Andalusia, 178

Andrade, General, 540

Anian, Strait of, 92

Annapolis, U.S.S., 932

annexation of Texas. _See_ Texas

Anza, de, 392

Apache Canyon, 721, 724–27
   battle of, 827–29

Apaches, 61, 73, 198, 220, 234, 248, 249, 256, 257, 261–65, 269, 270, 272, 283, 285–87, 291, 306–08, 315, 319–22, 328, 329, 345, 368, 471, 501, 748, 749, 806, 812, 830–33, 844, 846, 847
  Mescaleros, 832
Apalachen, 101
"Apostle to the Indians." *See* Casas, Fray Bartolomé de las
Arango, Doroteo. *See* Villa, Francisco
Archevêque, Jean l', 304, 317, 337
architecture, 388
Archuleta, Diego, 721, 722, 724, 725, 728, 729, 732, 733, 735, 763, 764, 766
Arellano, Tristan de, 119, 127, 138, 140
Arenal, 116, 122, 123, 127, 130, 136
  battle of, 123–26, 146
Ariel (steamship), 481–84, 493, 494, 507, 585, 665, 700, 943
Arillaga, Mariano Paredes y. *See* Paredes y Arillaga
Arista, General, 561, 564–66, 568, 608, 670, 674, 675, 678, 680, 688, 689, 696–97, 699, 700
Aristotle, *Politics*, 240
  on slavery, 240–41
Arizona, 49, 800, 801
  Confederate States Territory, 823
  Gadsden Purchase, 803
  lawlessness, 834–36
  price paid for, with New Mexico, 779
Arizpe, Miguel Ramos. *See* Ramos Arizpe
Arkansas River, 500, 719
Arkansas Volunteers, 737
Armada, Great, 178, 185
Armendaris, Pedro, 438
Armijo, Manuel, 552, 555–59, 569, 570, 572–81, 587, 600, 608, 716–21, 728, 730–34, 745, 762

Armijo, Manuel—*Cont'd*
  negotiations with, 721–28
  proclamation, 720
Armijo, Mrs. Manuel, 734
Arms of Saint James. *See* Brazos de Santiago
Army, United States, in Mexico, 666–67, 689–90, 693
  as seen by an Englishman, 744–45
  forts and posts, 806–19
  See also Mexican War; names of forts
Arroyo Hondo, 400, 401, 542, 550, 766
art, North American, 651–59
arts, 388–90
Asquith, Herbert H., 913
Atchison, Topeka and Santa Fe Railroad, 886, 893
Atlantis, 107
Atlixco, battle of, 778
atomic energy, 944
Audubon, John James, 623, 625, 628, 641–42, 646, 649, 655, 657–58
  cited, 631
Austin, Texas, 587
Austin, Archibald, 493
Austin City Gazette, 570
Austin family, 478, 488, 506
Austin, Henry, 481–85, 488, 490–94, 585, 595, 665, 700, 943
Austin, J. E. B., 478
Austin, James, 476
Austin, John, 457, 458, 514
Austin, Moses, 435
Austin, Stephen F., 453–58, 461, 469, 474–79, 481, 484–86, 488–96, 505–19, 524, 525, 534, 586, 609, 800, 820
  arrest, 515–16
  death, 586
  letter to Iturbide, 438
  town named for him. *See* San Felipe de Austin

Avalos, General, 791–92
Ávila, Alonso Gil de. *See* Gil de Ávila
Ávila, Saint Teresa of, 191
A-wan-yu, legend of, 22
Ayala, Fray Pedro de, 264
Ayeta, Fray Francisco de, 268–83, 291–95
Aztecs, 49, 77

Babbitt's Fall, 809
Bachelor, Colorado, 893
bad men. *See* lawlessness
Bagdad, Tamaulipas, 665, 705, 708, 776, 794, 836–39
Bahía, La, Texas. *See* Goliad
Baird, Spruce M., 799
Baja California. *See* Lower California
Bajada, La, 312, 501
Baker, Commissioner, 574–79
Baker, Newton D., 930
bandits. *See* lawlessness
Barceló, Gertrudes (La Tules), 573, 735, 762, 763
Barita, 696
Barrionuevo, Francisco de, 138, 140, 172
barter. *See* trade
Bartlett, John Russell, 802, 803, 811, 812
battles:
  Ácoma, and massacre, 200–09
  Álamo, 529–32
  Alcantro Creek, 562
  Apache Canyon, 827–29
  Arenal, 123–26, 146
  Atlixco, 778
  Brazito, 747–50
  Buena Vista, 761
  Camargo, 792
  Cape Saint Vincent, 395
  Carrizal, 933
  Cero Gerdo, 774
  Chapultepec Castle, 778

battles:—*Cont'd*
  Chihuahua City, 769
  Concepción, La, 523–24
  Contreras, 774
  Eagle Pass, 257
  Hawikuh, 109–12, 115
  Huamantla, 778
  Medina, 430
  Mier, 594–97
  Moho, 146
  Molino el Rey, 774, 775
  Monterrey, 754
  North Platte River, 337
  Palo Alto, 679, 694, 698
  Palo Alto (second), 839
  Parral, 928
  Piedras, Negras, 817
  Puebla, 774, 778
  Quarai, 214
  Resaca de la Palma, 686–89, 694, 698
  Sacramento, 780
  Salado Creek, 590
  Saltillo, 566–68
  Santa Cruz, 780
  Santa Fe, 286–89
  Trafalgar, 400
  Valverde, 824–26
  Zía, 310
Bautista Pino, Pedro, 420–21, 435, 547, 574
Bay of Mexico. *See* Gulf of Mexico
Baylor, John R., 821–23, 831
Bean, Roy, 904
Beaubien, Charles, 462
Beaubien, Judge, 770, 771
Beaubien, Narcisse, 765–66, 770
beauty and use (American arts and crafts), 652
beaver, 460–62, 465, 466, 468
Becknell, William, 479, 618
Belén, New Mexico, 376, 886
Beltran, Fray Bernardino, 154, 156
Benavides, Alonso de, 233–37

Bent, Charles, 762, 765, 771
  murder of, 765
  Proclamation by, 763–64
Bent, Mrs. Charles, 720
Benton, Thomas Hart, 693, 723, 755, 759
Benton, William, 904
Bernal family, 318
Bernal, Gonzáles. *See* Gonzáles Bernal
Bernalillo, New Mexico, 115, 269, 275, 318, 322, 329
Bernstorff, Count von, 928, 937
Berrotéran, 338
Bertugo, Diego Dionysio de Peñalosa Briceña y. *See* Peñalosa Briceña
Bessie (steamship), 943
Béxar, 495
  See also San Antonio
bibliography, 949–53, 957–77
Big Bend, 5, 339, 585, 804, 809, 851, 894–98, 900–01, 918, 929
Big Hatchee (steamship), 700, 756
Big Mariscal Canyon, 901
Bigotes, 110, 111, 114, 117, 120, 132, 133, 135, 136, 140, 141
Billings, William, 647
Billy the Kid (Bonney), 854
Bingham, George Caleb, 649
birth control, Indian, 542
bison. *See* buffalo
Black Rock Canyon, 898
Blake, J. E., 683
Blanco, Governor, 398, 476
Blessed Virgin Mary, vision of, 264
Blue Range, 310
boats. *See* navigation
Bobole Indians, 258
Boca Chica, 611
Bofecillos Mountains, 897
Boggs, Mr. and Mrs. Thomas, 765, 770
Bolsa (Indian), 308
Bolsón de Mapimí, 740–41, 812

Bonaparte, Joseph, 419, 423, 430, 432, 433
Bonaparte, Napoleon, 399, 400, 419, 427, 431, 432, 439
Bonilla, Francisco Leyda de. *See* Leyda de Bonilla
Bonney, William (Billy the Kid), 854
book, earliest printed in America, 227
boom, land, 889
Boone, Daniel, 500, 628, 636
Booth, Junius Brutus, 645
Boquillas, and Canyon, 901, 902, 929
Borrego, Jose Vásquez. *See* Vásquez Borrego
Bosque, Fernando del, 258, 260
Bosque Redondo, 832, 833
boundaries, territory and state, 799–806
boundary:
  acceptance of, 540–41
  fixed at the river, 779
  Louisiana-Texas, 400
  Mexico-New Mexico, 801
  offer to Mexico by Clay, 478
  proposals by the United States, 606
  settlement, 780
  Sierra Madre suggested, 779
  Texas-Mexico, 475
  troubles, 585–91
Boundary Commission (1849), 802–04
Bowie, James, 524
Boyd, Captain, 933
Braba. *See* Taos
Bragg, Braxton, 667, 671
branches of the river. *See* tributaries
brasada, the, 872
Brazito, battle of, 747–50
Brazoria (schooner), 507
Brazos River, 453, 475, 478, 483, 484, 493, 505, 507, 510, 530, 537
Brazos de Santiago, Los (Arms of Saint James), 610, 611, 671, 686, 753, 757–58, 784, 838

Briceña y Bertugo, Diego Dionysio de Peñalosa. *See* Peñalosa Briceña
bridges, 416, 418, 501, 503, 787, 886, 933
    first, 395
Brown, Jacob, 671, 673, 675, 676, 679
Browne, Richard, 151–53
Brownsville, Texas, 696, 786, 788, 789, 791, 793, 807, 821, 837–41, 857, 895, 918, 932, 933, 943
Bryan, William Jennings, 915, 927
Bryant, William Cullen, 769
Buchanan, James, 780, 804
Buena Vista, battle of, 761
buffalo (bison), 55, 66–68, 111, 199
Bull of Alexander VI. *See* Alexander VI
Burbank, Major, 817
Burgos, Laws of, 229
Burleson, Edward, 525, 587
Burr, Aaron, 401
business towns, 791
Bustamente, Anastasio, 480, 488, 507, 508
Bustamente, José Días de. *See* Días de Bustamente
Butler, General, 757, 758
Butt, Archie, 907
Butterfield stagecoaches, 847

Caballo range, 98
Caballero, José, 556
Cabello, Juan Sánchez. *See* Sánchez Cabello
Cabeza de Vaca, Luís María de, 467
Cabeza de Vaca. *See* Nuñez Cabeza
Cacique, 110, 111, 117, 121, 132, 140, 141
caciques. *See* Ancients
Cadillac, Antoine de la Mothe, 336
Cádiz, 178, 185
California, 213, 217, 693, 732, 734, 742, 799, 801
    boundary, 779

California—*Cont'd*
    free State, 800
    gold discovery, and rush, 780, 784–88, 800
    possession of, 735
    price paid for, 779
    value decried by Webster, 779
California, Lower, 801, 823, 908
California Camp, 786
California Column, 831, 834
Callahan (freebooter), 817–18
Camargo, Tamaulipas, 344, 346, 397, 402, 480, 483, 568, 700, 703, 709–15, 738, 754, 755, 757, 774, 785, 790, 791, 795, 836, 840, 842, 855
    battle of, 792
Camargo, Diego de, 89–91
camels, 809–10
Cameron, Ewing, 598, 599
Camp Hudson, 807
Camp Misery, 899
Camp Peña Colorada, 807
Campo, Andres do, 146, 149
Canadian French trappers, 462–64
Canales, Antonio, 560–66, 568, 588, 589, 591–93, 597, 599, 712, 791, 842, 856, 857, 906
Canalizo, General, 561, 563
canals. *See* irrigation
Canby, Edward R. S., Major General, 821, 824–27, 829, 830, 832, 840
Caniedo, Sancho de. *See* Sancho de Caniedo
cannibalism. *See* Indians
Cantonment Burgwin, 812, 818
canyons, 5, 20, 71, 74, 809, 862, 894–99, 903
Cape Saint Vincent, battle of, 395
Carbajal, Agustín de, 269, 275
Carbajal, Luís, 289, 328
Cárdenas, Gárcia López de. *See* Gárcia López

Cardénas, Jesús, 565, 566, 596
Carleton, James H., Brigadier General, 831–34
Carlotta, Empress, 843
Carmen, Sierra del, 901
Carrança, Andres Dorantes de. *See* Dorantes de Carrança
Carranza Venustiano, 911, 913, 915, 917–20, 922, 926, 929, 930, 932, 935, 938
  assassination, 939
Carricitos Ranch, 671
Carrión, Luisa de, 234
Carrizal, 752
  battle of, 933
Carson, Kit, and Mrs. Carson, 462, 735, 765, 770, 824, 889
Cartagena, 178
Carvajal, General, 791, 792, 804, 842
Casados, José Antonio, 430
Casas, Fray Bartolomé de Las, Bishop of Chiapas, 240, 242–44
Casas Grandes, 257
Castañeda, Pedro de, of Náxera, *cited*, 3
Castaño de Sosa, Gaspar, 157–60, 171, 172, 191
Castillo Bernal Díaz del. *See* Díaz del Castillo
Castillo Maldonado, Alonso del, 99
Castrillon, General, 531, 538
Cathay, 92
Catholic Church. *See* Roman Catholic Church
cattle, 872–86
  country, 872, 873
  drives, 882–83, 885, 886
  ranches, 886
  stealing, 854–56, 883
  trails, 882–83, 885, 886
  war, 861
Caudi, 270, 296
Cavalier, Robert, Sieur de la Salle. *See* La Salle

Cavalier, White (García), 835
cave dwellers, 71–73
cave pictures, 71
Ceballos, Bernardo de, 247
Cerralvo, 256, 257
Cerro Gordo, battle of, 774
Cervantes, 133
chacan, 98
Chaco Canyon, 20
Chacón, Fernando de, 395
Chama River, 5, 36, 48, 63, 138, 172, 195, 392, 409, 468, 717
Chamuscado, Francisco Sánchez. *See* Sánchez Chamuscado
channels of the river, 259, 298, 343, 347, 712, 801–02, 856
Chapita, Señor, 670, 671
Chapultepec Castle, storming of, 778
Charles II of England, 253
Charles II of Spain, 276, 293
Charles III of Spain, 392
Charles IV of Spain, 395
Charles V, Emperor, 84–86, 92–94, 100, 105, 107, 111, 142, 147, 148, 180–84, 188, 238–44, 376, 780
Chaves, Eusebio Durán y. *See* Durán y Chaves
Chaves, Fernando Durán y. *See* Durán y Chaves
Chaves, Pedro Durán y. *See* Durán y Chaves
Chaves family, 321
Cherokees, 560
Cherry Creek, 887
Chihuahua City, 257, 339, 347, 420, 747, 751, 774, 864, 912, 917
  battle of, 769
Chihuahua State, 327, 462, 471, 496, 498, 502–04, 545, 546, 556, 768–69, 779, 823, 911, 912, 920, 922, 923, 935
  Army of, 736–41
Chihuahua Trail, 744, 769

children, Spanish-American, 361–62
Chilili, 263
Chisos Mountains, 900
Chivington, John M., 828
Choctaws, 476
cholera, 514, 785
cholerina, 713
Christ, Passion of; observance by Penitents, 319–82
Christianity, 111, 175–76
Christmas, 369–71
Christopher, 159, 168, 171, 172
Church. *See* Christianity; Roman Catholic Church
Church and State (The Two Majesties), 176–77, 238–56, 275–76, 278, 280, 281, 288, 290, 292
churches, 262
  design, 223–25
Cíbola, Seven Cities of, 103–08, 147
  See also Quivira
Cicero, 187
Ciqúique. *See* Pecos
Ciruelo, Fray Gerónimo, 227
cities. *See* towns; *also* names of towns
Cities of Wealth, Seven. *See* Cíbola
Civil War, 819–31
  Confederate States aims, 823
  desolation by, 831–34
Clarendon, Lord, 777
Clark, Governor, 821
Claros, Fray Juan, 197
Clay, Henry, 434, 475, 478, 602, 604, 753, 781
cliff dwellers. *See* pueblos
climate, zones, 6
coaches, stage, 847, 862, 868–69
Coahuila, 258, 260, 301, 302, 324, 326, 335, 338, 389, 391, 471, 505, 517, 560, 703, 911
Coahuila-Texas, 394, 420, 469–73, 487, 488, 495, 508, 509, 514, 528, 781
  law on slavery, 488, 489

coal mining, 434
coast, Gulf; blockade of, 836–37
Cochiti, New Mexico, 295, 296, 311, 354, 392
coffee growing, 483
college at Saltillo, 420
Colley, Solomon, 412, 414–15
Colonel Cross (steamship), 782
colonials, 388–90
colonies. *See* settlement
color of the river, 6
Colorado, 781
  mining, 887–94
Colorado River, 218, 453, 475, 801
Columbia River, 718
Columbus, Christopher, 175, 177, 241, 362
Columbus, New Mexico, 918, 930
  raid by Villa, 924–26
Comanche (steamship), 795
Comanche Trail, 327, 339, 851
Comanches, 61, 68, 73, 256, 257, 319, 390–92, 396, 398, 406, 434, 471, 473, 475–77, 501, 505, 560, 570, 714, 806, 812, 813, 844, 847, 848–52
  arms, 850
  dress, men's, 850
  "Honey Eaters," 848
  raids, 850–54
  tepees, 850
  women, 849–50
commerce. *See* trade
Commission, Boundary. *See* Boundary Commission
communication, 941–43, 945
Compostela, 16, 108, 131, 147, 208
Compromise of 1850, 800, 821
Concepción, La, battle of, 523–24
Conchos River, 5, 139, 153, 154, 156, 157, 199, 216, 299, 300, 338, 339, 405, 851, 894, 895, 898
junction. *See* Junta de los Rios

Conde, Francisco García. *See* García
    Conde
Condemned Regiment, 471
Conejos River, 5, 406, 409
Conestoga wagons, 499, 653
Confessions of Saint Augustine, 183
confluence of rivers. *See* Junta de los
    Rios; tributaries
Connelly, Henry, 722, 723, 725, 829,
    832
Conner, David, 605, 606, 670, 671
Conquistadora, La, 318
Contadero, El, 502
Continental Divide, 4, 403
contraband. *See* tariff
Contreras, battle of, 774
Cooke, Philip H. George, 722–25, 729,
    742
Cooke, William G., 570, 577, 578, 580,
    581
Cooper, James Fenimore, 642, 665
Copano, 520, 521
Copley, John Singleton, 657
Corchado, Fray Andres, 198
Cordero, Governor, 398
Córdoba, Spain, 187
corn (maize), 15, 20, 32, 49, 53, 55–57,
    60, 62–64, 79, 97, 257
Coronado. *See* Vásquez de Coronado
Corpus Christi, 605, 607
Correo de México (ship), 518
Cortés, Hernando de (Marquis of the
    Valley of Oaxaca), 85, 86, 89,
    91–93, 95, 100, 105, 107, 108,
    120, 123, 148, 164, 181, 229, 239,
    241, 243, 479
    death of, 148
Cortina, Juan Nepomuceno, 835, 838,
    839, 842, 844, 856–58, 906
Corvette (steamship), 700, 756, 757
Cos, Martin, Perfecto de. *See* Perfecto
    de Cos
Costa Deserta, 794

cotton, 792, 836–38
    manufacture, 790
cottonwood tree, 36
Council of the Indies, 242
courses of the river. *See* channels
cowboys, 877–86
    equipment, 876
    horses, 874
    songs, 875–88, 880–82
    wagons, 876
coyotes, 886
crafts. *See* Ancients—handicrafts
Creede (Willow Gap), 890–93
Creede, Nicholas C., 890, 892
Creede Candle, 892
Crescent, Great, 257
Crespúsculo, El, 549
Crèvecoeur, Michel Guillaume de, 627,
    637, 640
    cited, 632
Cristóbal Salazar, Fray, 146, 170, 195,
    198
Crockett, David, 640
Cromberger, Jacob, 187
crops, New Mexico, 228–29
Cross, Colonel, 667–68, 670
crossings. *See* bridges; ferries; fords
Cruz, Fray Diego de la, 160
Cruz, Fray Juan de la, 176
Cruz, Juana Iñes de la, 388
Cruzate, Domingo Jironza Petriz de.
    See Jironza Petriz
Cubero, Pedro Rodríguez. *See*
    Rodríguez Cubero
Cuellar, Pedro de, 269
Cuerno Verde, 392
Culiacan, 100, 108, 147, 389
Currier and Ives prints, 695
Custodia de Rio Verde, 342
customs and manners, 360–62
customs (tariff), 492, 498, 788–93

dams, 347, 503, 809, 812, 863

Dance of the Seises; church approval, 251
dances, 797, 863
dances, ceremonial. *See* Ancients; Indians
Daniels, Josephus, 915
Davis, General, 589
Davis, Jefferson, 780, 823
Davis Landing. *See* Rio Grande City
Dead Horse Mountain, 901
Dead Man's March (Jornada del Muerto), 196, 218, 246, 267, 279, 291, 311, 317, 418, 502, 546, 583, 746
Dearborn, Henry, 404
death and funerals, 374–76
Del Norte, Colorado, 888, 889
Del Rio, Texas, 157, 339
Deming, New Mexico, 941
Denver, Colorado, 890
Denver and Rio Grande Western Railroad, 888, 890
Deserted Coast, 794
deserts, 5
deviations of the river. *See* channels
Devil's River, 5
Días de Bustamente, José, 423, 428
Díaz, José de la Cruz Porfirio, 857, 859
    death, 919
    meeting with William H. Taft, 906–10
    resignation, 910
    revolution, 857
Díaz del Castillo, Bernal, 229, 239
diplomacies, 601–08
Discalced Nuns of Aragon, 232
diseases. *See* epidemics; names of diseases
Divide, Continental, 4, 403
Dolan, Joseph, 562
Dolphin (steamship), 914
Dolores, 345, 442

"Dolores, Grito de." *See* "Grito de Dolores"
Dominguez de Mendoza, Juan Domingo, 295, 300, 301
Doña Ana, New Mexico, 746, 785, 787, 804, 812
Doniphan, Alexander William, 633, 693, 732, 734, 735, 741–44, 746, 748–53, 762–64, 768, 769, 774, 775, 779, 780, 787
Don Quixote, 147, 191
Dorantes de Carrança, Andres, 99
Dovaline, Manuel, 428
Downriver district (Rio Abajo), 269, 287, 289
Drake, Sir Francis, 151–52
drama, the, 388
Drayton, Michael, 643
dress, Indian and Spanish-American, 359
drought, 19, 20, 36, 73, 97, 139, 195, 257, 260, 262, 263, 269, 272, 281, 303, 483, 505, 831, 902
Dryden, Texas, 929
duck hunting, Indian, 814–15
Durán y Chaves, Eusebio, 392
Durán y Chaves, Fernando, 322
Durán y Chaves, Pedro, 25
Durango, 339, 377, 394, 420, 421, 547, 560, 769, 851, 864
duties (customs). *See* tariff

Eagle Pass, Texas, 157, 785, 786, 807, 817, 838, 842, 843, 848, 869, 929
    battle of, 257
eagles, 331, 903
Early, Jubal, 841
Eckhardt, Herr von, 937
Edinburgh, Texas, 854
education, 387–88
Edwards, Benjamin, 476
El Dorado, 784–88
Elephant Butte Dam, 812

Elizabeth I, Queen, 185
El Paso (American town on right bank, and region of), 96, 166–74, 229, 248, 260, 264, 265, 271, 275, 278, 292, 294, 298, 300, 301, 305, 347, 348, 395, 418, 462, 465, 483, 498, 503, 541, 542, 584, 745, 746, 750, 753, 769, 785–87, 801–03, 831, 838, 857, 859–62, 906–08, 912, 920, 921, 926, 928, 933, 941
    fair, 401
El Paso-Juárez, Texas-Mexico, 166
Embudo, New Mexico, 767
emerald, 103
Emerson, Ralph Waldo, 642
Emory, W. H., 802–04, 845, 895, 898, 906
Empire, Spanish. *See* Spain
encomienda system, 241, 242, 244, 245
energy, atomic, 944
engineering works, 809
English-speaking visitors, early, 151–53
enterprises, four, 154–60
epidemics, 261, 263, 346, 401, 512, 514, 713–14, 754, 785
    See also names of diseases
erosion, soil, 364
Escalante, Fray Silvestre Vélez de. *See* Vélez de Escalante
Escalona, Fray Luís de, 128, 145, 146
Escandón (town), 585, 711
Escandón, José de (Count of Sierra Gorda), 340–46, 391, 393, 422, 471
    seven directions, 344
Escandón, Pablo, 907
Escorial, 186
Española, New Mexico, 392
Espéjo, Antonio, 154–57, 159
Esquivel, Juan José, 553
Espiritu Santo, Bahía del, 342
Espiritu Santo River (Mississippi), 319

Estabanico, 99, 105–07
Estes's Tavern, 771
ethnology, 13–80
Eulate, Governor, 246, 247, 250, 251
Europe and the Republic of Texas, 601–02
excommunication. *See* Roman Catholic Church

fair at El Paso, 401
fair at Taos, 391
Falcón, Ramon, 670, 855
Falcón Dam, 809
Falconer, Thomas, 571
falls, 809, 894, 896
family and work, 360–67
famine, 250, 256–68
fandango, 797
Fannin, James W., Jr., 524, 529, 533
Farfán de los Godos, Marcos, 196
Farías, Gómez. *See* Gómez Farías
farms. *See* crops; haciendas
Fauvel-Gouraud, 630
feast days, 368–71
federal union. *See* Texas-Coahuila
federation, pueblo, 306, 318
Ferdinand V, 239
Ferdinand VI, 419, 420, 430, 431, 435
Ferdinand VII, 473, 479, 485
Ferguson, James E., Governor, 929
Fernández, Bartolomé, 408, 409, 411–13, 415
Fernández, General, 527
ferries, 345, 480, 501, 503, 535, 696–98
Ferrol, 178
Fierro (lieutenant of Villa), 922
Filísola, Vincente, 512, 540
Fillmore, Millard, 800
Fink, Mike, 631
First Colorado Volunteers, 827–29
First Missouri Volunteers, 742–47, 774
First World War, 917
Fish Indians, 339

Fisher, William S., 592, 596
flagellation, self, 376–82
floods, 346, 347, 364, 475, 484, 501,
    503, 504, 506, 704, 713, 786,
    856, 863, 902
Florida, 85, 92, 93, 94, 101, 108, 180,
    300, 341, 780
Florida Treaty, 433, 434, 437, 475, 781
Flying Artillery, 683, 687, 697, 701
folklore. *See* pioneers
food, Spanish-American, 363
fords, 280, 324, 333, 338, 340, 343, 345,
    347, 394, 418, 471, 501, 503, 527,
    736, 744, 750, 787, 803, 822, 832,
    851, 869
foreigners, exclusion of, 395–96
Forrest, Edwin, 646
Fort Bliss, Texas, 810, 812, 813, 818,
    821, 824, 830, 861, 907, 912, 918,
    920, 929, 930
Fort Brown, Texas. *See* Fort Texas
Fort Clark, Texas, 807
Fort Conrad (Hay Camp), New Mex-
    ico, 812, 824–25
Fort Craig, New Mexico, 810, 812, 817,
    823, 824, 826, 827, 829
Fort Davis, Texas, 507
Fort Duncan, Texas, 786, 807, 808, 817,
    838, 842
Fort Fillmore, New Mexico, 812, 818,
    822
Fort Garland, Colorado, 888
Fort Hancock, Texas, 807
Fort Inge, Texas, 807
Fort Leaton, Texas, 775
Fort Leavenworth, Kansas, 692, 718
Fort Macrae, New Mexico, 812
Fort Marcy, New Mexico, 810
Fort Massachusetts, Colorado, 812
Fort McIntosh, Texas, 807, 808
Fort Paredes, Tamaulipas, 663, 664,
    697–98, 701, 792
Fort Polk, Texas, 665, 691, 696, 761

Fort Quitman, Texas, 786, 807
Fort Ringgold, Texas, 790
Fort Saint John Baptist (Presidio de
    Rio Grande), 323, 328, 331, 334,
    336, 338, 339, 341, 343, 345, 347,
    394, 398, 418–19, 423, 424, 453,
    473, 480, 483, 495, 565, 585, 693,
    736–39
Fort Saint Louis, Texas, 304
Fort Sam Houston, Texas, 928
Fort Selden, New Mexico, 812, 864
Fort Stanton, New Mexico, 817, 822,
    823, 832
Fort Sumner, New Mexico, 832, 833
Fort Texas (Fort Brown), Texas, 662,
    664, 665, 668, 671–79, 681, 682,
    688, 696, 698, 785, 798, 807, 809,
    837–39, 894, 932, 943
Fort Thorn, New Mexico, 810, 812,
    819, 823
Fort Union, New Mexico, 812, 824,
    826–29
Fort Velasco, Texas, 507
forts. *See* Army, United States
Fourth of July, 787
Foyle, William, 702
France, and Texas, 331–40
    claim to the river, 399
    threat to New Spain, 301–05, 324,
        391, 430
France Way (Paso de Francia), 324,
    327, 332–35, 495, 527, 565, 568,
    598, 736, 739, 869
Francis I, 84
Franciscans. *See* Roman Catholic
    Church
Franklin (town), 812, 831
Franklin, Benjamin, 643, 651, 659, 660
Fraser, William D., 737
Fray Cristóbal, New Mexico, 279, 280,
    746
Fredonia, 477
Free Missourians, 742–46

"Free Zone," 855
freight trains. *See* trains, freight
Fremont, John C., 735, 803, 887
French Canadian trappers, 462–63
French invasion of Mexico. *See* Mexico
Fresno Canyon, 897
friars. *See* Roman Catholic Church—
    Franciscans
Frijoles, Rito de los, 20, 213
Frio River, 591
frontiersmen. *See* pioneers
Fugitive Slave Law, 800
Fulton, Robert, 658
funerals, 374–76
Funston, Frederick, Major General,
    915, 926, 928, 933, 936
fur trade, and trapping, 460–69, 716–17

Gadsden Purchase and Treaty, 803–06
Galisteo, New Mexico, 827, 828
Galisteo Creek, 5, 22, 36, 220, 271–72,
    284, 285, 312, 388, 420
Galveston, Texas, 483, 507
Gaona, General, 536, 540
gap at El Paso, 804
Garay, Francisco, 85, 89, 91, 92, 94, 95,
    148, 153
García, Abram (White Cavalier), 835
García, Alonso, 269, 278, 279, 283, 290,
    291
García, General, 610, 611
García Conde, Francisco, 716, 718
García family, 321
García López de Cárdenas, 112, 115,
    116, 121, 123, 129, 130, 137, 143,
    144
Garland, John, Brigadier General, 805
Garland City, Colorado, 888
Garza, General, 474
Garza, Juan de la, 257
Garza, Nicolás de la, 345
gentes de razon, 359
Geological Survey, 895

geology, 3–4, 896–97
Georgetown College, 639
Gerard, James W., 937
German immigrants, stories of, 862–65
German views on Villa, 928
Germany and Mexico:
    alliance, proposed, against the
        United States, 937–40
    conversations, 921–22, 935
Géry, Jean, 303, 304
Gigedo, Revilla. *See* Revilla Gigedo
Gila River, 801
Gil de Ávila, Fray Alonso, 264
Gilpin, William, Governor, 824
Glasgow, William J., Brigadier General, 943
Glen Springs, 929
Glorieta Pass, 828
"God and Texas," 513–19
Godos, Marcos Farfán de los. *See*
    Farfán de los Godos
Godoy, Francisco Lucero de. *See* Lu-
    cero de Godoy
gold and silver, 120, 132, 140, 503–04
gold mining, 887–94
gold, Rocky Mountain, 847
gold rush. *See* California
Goliad (La Bahía), 521, 523, 527, 532,
    533
    massacre at, by Mexicans, 533
Gómez Farías, 513–15, 520–21
Gonzáles, José Maria Elias, 552, 555–
    57, 559, 561–62, 564, 569, 583–
    84
Gonzáles, Texas, 521, 529
Gonzáles Bernal family, 269
Goodnight, Charles, 876
Goodnight-Loving Trail, 882
governors, early; fate of, 148
Graham, Richard, 696
Granada (Hawikuh) and battle, 109–
    12, 115
Granillo, 283

Grant, Ulysses S., 607, 609, 667, 672, 690, 691, 695, 699, 839, 844
Grassi, Father, 639
Greasy Bill, 900
Great Britain and the Republic of Texas, 601–02
Great Raft, 496
Greco, El (Theotocopuli), 188
Green, Thomas J., 592, 593, 595, 596, 598, 825, 906
Gregg, Josiah, 587, 737, 738, 775
Grey, Sir Edward, 913, 914, 916
"Grito de Dolores," 422
gritos (shouts), 553
grizzly bears, 463
Grollet, Jacques, 304
Guadalajara, Jalisco, 258, 545
Guadalquiver River, 153, 178
Guadalupe River, 522
Guadalupe, Virgin of, 422
Guadalupe Hidalgo, Treaty of, 779, 801, 859
Guadalupe Victoria, General, 479
Guaes, 132
guardianship for Indians. *See enco-mienda* system
Guatemala, 93
Guerra, Fray Salvador de, 250
Guerrero (Revilla), 326, 345, 346, 397, 398, 422
Guerrero, Vicente, 479, 485, 486, 509, 855, 869
"guias," 498
Gulf of California, 218, 803
Gulf of Mexico, 5, 83, 85, 94, 340–46, 471, 479, 480, 482, 495, 509, 527, 589, 602, 605, 715, 836, 853, 872
Gutierrez de Humaña, Antonio, 159–60, 168, 173, 214, 216
Gutierrez de Lara, José Antonio, 423, 454, 472, 474
Gutierrez de Lara, José Bernardo, 422, 424–31, 433, 472, 781

Guzmán, Governor. *See* Nuño de Guzmán
gypsies, 366

haciendas, 268–69, 352–90
Halleck, Henry W., Major General, 826
Hannibal and St. Joe Railroad, 885
Harahey, 132
hardships, 101
Harney, William S., Colonel, 739
Harris, Eli, 433
Harrison, William Henry, 628
Hatch, Edward A., 859, 861
Hatchee Eagle (steamship), 700, 710
Hawikuh (Granada) and battle, 109–12, 115
Hawken, Jacob and Samuel, 464
Hawkins, E. S., 676
Hawkins, Captain Sir John, 151, 152
Hay Camp. *See* Fort Conrad
Hayes, Rutherford B., 858, 859, 861
Henry VIII, 84
Herrera, Governor, 398
Herrera, José Joaquin, 604, 606
Hicks, Edward, 655–56
Hidalgo, Miguel, 422–24, 472, 474
Hidalgo, Fray Francisco, 333, 334
Hidalgo, Pedro, 284
hidalgos, 190
highways. *See* roads
Hill, Robert T., 895–98, 900, 902–04
Hitchcock, Ethan Allen, Lieutenant Colonel, 755–56
Hocio, Francisco, 438
holidays, 368–71
Holy Moses mine, 890, 892
Holy Office. *See* Roman Catholic Church—inquisition
"Honey Eaters" (Comanches), 848
Hopis, 198
Hopkinson, Francis, 647
Horsehead Crossing, 882

horses:
cowboys', 874
Spanish, 109, 122, 434
trade in, 393
Horta, Juanes de la. *See* Juanes de la
Horta
Hortuño de Aguirre, 192
hot spring, 902
Houston, Sam, 516, 534–36, 539, 540,
585–90, 599–601, 603, 604, 780
Howland, Samuel, 574, 577–79
Huamantla, battle of, 778
Huerta, Victoriano, 910–13
Hughes, John, 693–94, 703
human sacrifice, 64, 139, 456
Humaña, Antonio Gutierrez. *See* Guti-
errez de Humaña
Humanos, 231, 233–35, 258
Humboldt, Baron von, 388
hunger. *See* famine
Hunter, Mrs. David, 738, 782
hunters. *See* pioneers

I. E. Roberts (steamship), 710
Idoyaga, Joseph, 339
Iguala, Plan of, 436, 438
illness. *See* epidemics; names of diseases
immigrants from Germany, stories of,
862–65
Independence, Missouri, 497, 500,
719
Independence Day, 787
Indian Territory, 852
Indianola, 809
Indians, 61, 74, 181
and liquor, 393–94
agents, white, 852–53
"Apostle to." *See* Casas, Fray Bartolomé de las
birth control, 542
burials, 73
cannibalism, 38, 263
character; dispute over, 239–45

Indians—*Cont'd*
Christianizing. *See* Roman Catholic
Church—missions
coalition, proposed, 477
dances, ceremonial, 250–51, 255
described, 845–46
dress, 358–59
encomienda system. *See encomienda*
exploitation, 215, 349–51
Five Civilized Tribes, 852
freedom, granting of, 393
guardianship. *See encomienda*
hunting, 814–15
incest, 250
in pioneer drama, 646
kachinas, 255
Laws of Burgos, 239
loss of freedom, 844–53
magic, 265
marriage contract, 249
massacre by, at Taos, 764–68
medicine doctors, 265
missions to. *See* Roman Catholic
Church—missions
mountain, 341
origin, 213, 239
pacification, 806
parley with, 813–14
"Peace Policy," government, 852
Plains, 68, 73, 847; reservations, 832–
33, 852
population, 844
Pueblo, 409, 542, 762, 845; federation, 306, 318; peace with, 319.
See also Ancients
outbreaks. *See* Indians—raids; Indians—uprising
raids, 220, 257, 258, 261, 263, 264,
270, 318–19, 321–22, 329–30,
332–33, 367–68, 390–92, 434, 475,
502, 503, 505, 560, 578, 721, 742,
743, 745, 806, 812–19, 831, 832,
845, 847, 848, 849, 850–54

Indians—*Cont'd*
riders, 848–49
runners, 296
slavery, 91, 93, 117, 211, 240, 241,
247, 248, 250, 258, 334, 350, 391;
abolition, 393
Spanish opinion of, 232
spoliation, 215, 349–51
Stinking Ones, 301
taxation, 248
tortures by, 263, 264, 554–55, 847
trade with, 212–15
treatment by Spanish, 239–45
tribute payments to, 391–92
uprising, 274–92; causes of, 289, 290
visions, 848
women; abuse by Spanish, 349–50;
Comanche, 849–50
See also names of tribes
Indies, 178, 185
admitted to Spanish government, 420
Laws of, 430–31
individual and State, 620–22
Infantando, Duke of, 144
Inferno, Plain of the, 322
Ingram, David, 151–53
Inquisition, the. *See* Roman Catholic
Church
irrigation, 60, 61, 212, 229, 325, 347,
352, 368–69, 394, 503, 739, 809,
888–89
Isabey, Jean Baptiste, 400, 439
Isla, La, 786
Islands, 786, 801, 812
Isleta, New Mexico, 113, 231, 233, 245,
250, 253, 288–90, 295, 297, 315,
328, 330, 348
Isleta del Sur, Texas, 297, 786
Isopete, 121, 132, 133, 135
Iturbide, Agustín I, Emperor, 436–40,
454, 455, 457, 479, 508, 548, 912
abdication, 459–60
return and execution, 473, 474

Iturbide, Agustín I, Emperor—*Cont'd*
revolt against, 457–59
Iturbide, Ana Maria de, Empress, 784
Iturbide, Felipe de, 804

Jackson, Andrew, 481, 488, 511, 513,
585, 601–03, 650–51, 730, 781
Jalapa, 458
Jamaica, 91
Japan, 938
Jaumave, 342
Jefferson, Joseph, 702
Jefferson, Thomas, 400, 622, 780
Jemez River (Creek), 5, 36, 138, 173,
198, 310, 314
Jersey Lily, the. *See* Langtry, Lily
Jesuits. *See* Roman Catholic Church
Jesus. *See* Christ
Jironza Petriz de Cruzate, Domingo,
297–99
John (Indian), 285–86
Johnson, Andrew, 852, 941
Jones, Anson, 604, 605
Jordan, S. W., 561, 562, 565–67
Jornada del Muerto. *See* Dead Man's
March
Joseph, 173, 214
Juan, Don, 592–94
Juan Luís, Captain, 284
Juanes de la Horta, 192
Juárez, Benito, 836–38, 840, 842, 843,
904, 905, 907
Juárez (town), 909, 912, 914, 922
Juárez-El Paso, Mexico-Texas, 166
Juchereau de Saint Denis, Louis. *See*
Saint Denis, Louis Juchereau de
junctions of rivers. *See* tributaries
Junta country, 299, 302
Junta de los Rios (junction of the
rivers), 153, 154, 156, 299, 327,
338, 339, 347, 585, 752, 755, 851,
894
Junta Indians, 302–04

kachinas. *See* Ancients; Indians
Kansa Indians, 500
Kansas City, Missouri, 500
Karankawa Indians, 592
Kearny, Stephen Watts, Brigadier General, 692, 693, 719, 721–28, 731–36, 741, 742, 746, 751, 762, 799
description, 730
Kendall, George Wilkins, 571, 576–78, 580
Narrative of the Texan Santa Fe Expedition, 604
Keres and Tewa, 77
Keres language, 197–98
Kickapoos, 852
king, Spanish, 176–77
Kingdom of Saint Francis. *See* Saint Francis, Kingdom of
kivas. *See* Ancients
koshare. *See* Ancients

Lajitas, 895
La Fontaine of Grenoble, 331
Lake Peak, 35
Lalande, Baptiste, 405, 406, 410–11
Lallemand, Charles, 432, 433
Lamar, Mirabeau Bonaparte, 560, 566, 570, 571, 574, 586, 587
Lamy, Juan Bautista, Archbishop, 833, 865–67
land boom, 889
land erosion, 20, 364
land occupation, 622
Lane, Franklin K., 935
Langhorne, George T., Major, 929
Langtry, Lily, 904
Langtry (Vinegaroon), Texas, 904
Lansing, Robert, 921–22, 926, 937, 939
Lara, José Antonio Gutierrez de. *See* Gutierrez de Lara
Lara, José Bernardo Gutierrez de. *See* Gutierrez de Lara

Laredo, Texas, 345, 391, 393, 394, 397, 398, 428, 433, 453, 521, 565, 586, 713, 807, 817, 847, 853
Larios, Fray Juan, 258
Larrañaga, Surgeon, 401
La Salle, Sieur de (Robert Cavalier), 301, 302, 304, 317, 337, 399, 780
murder of, 304
las Casas, Bartolomé de, 287
Las Cruces, New Mexico, 785, 787, 804, 832, 862, 882
Las Vegas, New Mexico, 725–27, 812, 827
lawlessness, 775, 834–36, 854–61, 896
Laws of Burgos, 239
Laws of the Indies, 430–31
Leadville front, 891
League of Nations, 937
Leal, J. W., 766
Leaton, Ben, 775
Lee, Robert E., 737, 783, 835, 839
Lee, Stephen, 765
legends. *See* Ancients—myths
Leiva, Pedro de, 274–77, 284, 289, 291
Lejanza, Mariano Martínez de. *See* Martínez de Lejanza
Lemitar, New Mexico, 744, 788
length of the river, 5
Leo X, Pope, 84
León, Alonso de, 256, 303
León, Diego de Vargas Zapata Luján, Ponce de. *See* Vargas Zapata
León, José María. *See* Ponce de León
León, Juan Ponce de. *See* Ponce de León
León, Pedro Ponce de. *See* Ponce de León
Leonardo da Vinci, 8
Lerdo de Tejada, 858
Lewis, Captain, 576, 580
Leyda de Bonilla, Francisco, 159–60, 168, 173, 214
Linares, 394, 711

Lincoln, Abraham, 819, 821, 823, 841, 845
cited, 623
Lincoln County War, 861
Lipans, 73, 806, 808, 812, 844, 847
Lipantitlan, 73, 561
liquor:
Army, 808
temperance societies, 638
use by Indians, 392–93
Little Mariscal Canyon, 901
Llano Estacado, 851
Lobos Island, 761
Long, James, 433, 437
López, Colonel, 566–68
López, Diego, 123, 126, 140
López, Fray Diego, 234, 237, 308
López, Fray Francisco, 172
López, Fray Nicolás, 299–301, 338
López de Cárdenas, García. *See* García López de Cárdenas
López de Mendizabel, Governor, 251
López de Santa Anna, Antonio, 458, 479, 507, 508, 511–15, 517, 518, 520, 525–27, 529–40, 551, 573, 581, 583, 584, 588, 589, 595, 597–600, 604, 607, 608, 715, 718, 720, 741, 756, 758, 759, 761, 769, 777, 778, 781, 905
deposition and banishment, 604
deposition, second, 780
dictator, 518
revolt by, 507
song about, 782–83
Loring, William W., 821
Los Álamos, New Mexico, 944
Los Lunas, New Mexico, 829
Los Pinos, New Mexico, 829
Louis XIV, 301, 302, 331, 433
Louisiana, 302, 324, 327, 333, 334, 391, 393, 396, 399, 433, 453, 475, 487, 623, 780
boundary with Texas, 400

Louisiana—*Cont'd*
sale to the United States, 399
Louisiana Purchase, 622, 780–81
Lower California, 801, 823, 908
loyalties, tormented, 505–12
Lúcas, Alamán, 489
Lucas (oblate), 145, 149
Lucero de Godoy, Francisco, 314
Lugo, Fray Alonzo de, 198
Luís (oblate), 128
Luján Ponce de León, Diego de Vargas Zapata. *See* Vargas Zapata
lumber. *See* Great Raft
Lunas, Los, 330
Lusitania (ship), 919
Luther, Martin, 84
Lynch's Ferry, 535, 536
Lynde, Isaac, Major, 822, 823

Macharro, Colonel, 858, 859
Madariaga, Salvador de, *Rise of the Spanish Empire*, 245, *note*
Madero, Francisco, 909, 911, 923
assassination, 910
Madrid, 194
Madrid, Francisco de, 25
Magdalena, New Mexico, 893
Magdalena Bay, Mexico, 908
Magee, Augustus, 429
Magellan, Ferdinand, 84
magic at El Paso, 266–67
Magoffin, James W., 722–25, 729, 733, 735, 746, 769, 802–04
Magoffin, Samuel, 733, 742, 746, 752, 769
Magoffin, Mrs. Susan, 733–35, 742, 746, 752, 769
Magoffinsville, 802, 803, 811
mail service, early, 347, 453, 502, 505
maize. *See* corn
Majesties, Two. *See* Church and State
Major Brown (steamship), 713, 782
Maldonado, Captain de, 123, 135

Maldonado, Alonso del Castillo. *See* Castillo Maldonado
Maldonado, Rodrigo de, 144
Manso Indians, 229, 260, 298
Manzanos mountains, 261, 321, 322, 328
Manzo y Zuniga, Francisco, 232, 233
Maravillas Canyon, 895
Maravillas Creek, 902
Marcus of Nice (Marcos de Niza), Friar, 105, 107, 108
Marcy, Secretary, 607, 710, 723
María de Jesús, Mother. *See* Ágreda, María de
Márques, Captain, 198, 199
marriages, 371–74
Martial, 174, 175
Martínez, Antonio José, 559, 765
Martínez, Fray Alonso, 163, 170, 197, 203, 207
Martínez de Lejanza, Mariano, 716–18
Martínez de Sotomayor, Jose, 391
martyrs. *See* Roman Catholic Church
Mary, Virgin, vision of, 264
Mary I, Queen of England, 178
Masewi and Oyoyewi, 25–26, 43, 47
masks, kachina. *See* Ancients—dances, Ancients—kachina, Indians—kachina
Massanet, Fray Damian, 304–05
masters of the ocean (Spaniards), 177–80
Matagorda, 527
Matamoros, Tamaulipas, 397, 470, 480, 483, 488, 489, 492, 505, 508, 521, 527, 532, 563, 597, 605, 606, 611, 662, 671, 690, 691, 696, 697, 701–02, 707, 711, 752, 776, 789–91, 793–94, 817, 836–39, 841–43, 854, 855, 857, 904
    siege, 792
    taking of, 698–700
    See also Refugio

Mather, Cotton, 620
Maximilian, Emperor, 838–44
    execution, 843–44
May, Charles, 687
May, River of, 151–53
Mayo, Henry T., 914, 915
Mazatlan, 785, 786, 932
McKee (steamship), 782
McLeod, Hugh, 571, 579, 580, 703, 799
medicine doctors. *See* Indians
Medina, battle of, 430
meeting of the rivers. *See* Junta de los Rios
Mejía, General, 508, 661, 662, 668, 839, 841, 843
Melgares, Facundo, 403, 417, 418, 435, 437, 438
Mena, Fray Marcos de, 151
Menchaca, Miguel, 192, 424–47
Mendez, Fray Hernando, 150
Mendizabel, Governor. *See* López de Mendizabel
Mendoza, Antonio, Viceroy, 100, 105–07, 112, 121, 145, 244
Mendoza, Fray Diego de, 274, 275, 296, 297
Mendoza, Juan Dominguez de. *See* Dominguez de Mendoza
men of the mountains. *See* fur trade
merchants. *See* trade
Mercurio de México, 347
mercury (quicksilver), 310, 315, 316
Meriwether, David, 805
Mesa Verde, 22, 392
mesas, 35
Mescalero Apaches, 262, 263, 832
Mesilla, 804, 805, 812, 821–23
Mesina River, 472
Metcalfe, Sheriff, 771
Mexía, Colonel. *See* Mejía, General
Mexican War, 459, 660–784

Mexican War—_Cont'd_
armistice, 777
army, United States, in Mexico, 666–67
Army of the West, 716–21
declaration of war by the United States, 692
Free Missourians, 742–46
hardships of the United States army, 705–07
invasion of Mexico, 696–701, 754–61, 774–84
peace talks, 778–79
peace treaty of Guadalupe Hidalgo, 779; ratification, 780
plan of operations, United States, 693
prints, 695
Veracruz campaign. _See_ Mexican War—invasion
volunteers, United States, 705, 707–08
See also specific entries—e.g., names of persons and places—in the Index
Mexico, 49, 69–70, 73, 77, 84, 85, 89, 90, 92, 94, 103, 122, 180, 183, 184, 186, 215
and Germany. _See_ Germany
and the United States: annexation and intervention by the United States, proposed, 921, 935; annexation considered after the Mexican War, 778–79; border disagreements, 906; capital from the United States, 907, 911, 913, 918; Commission, Joint, 935, 936; Conference, El Paso, and agreement, 928; diplomacies, 601–08; friction, 859–62, 914–20; Punitive Expedition of the United States, 930–32, 934, 936; threat to Mexico by the United States, 474–84; War. _See_ Mexican War
armistice with Texas, 601; arms importation embargoed by the United States, 920
civil war, 559
conquest, 191
controversy with Texans, 491–95
expropriation of foreign property, 940
federation; suspension by Santa Anna, 517, 518
Intervention by the United States and Great Britain, proposed, 914
Iturbide revolution and empire, 436–40
Nordismo, 911, 912
northern; separatist movement, 791
railroads, destruction of, 919
reconquest attempted by Spain, 479
Republic, progress of, 843–44
revolution, first, 422–33
revolutionary movements based on Texas, 857
revolutions, 479, 559, 715, 857, 858, 911
Roman Catholic Church, persecution of, 918
slavery, abolition of, 485, 821
States; annexation by United States proposed, 780
Valley of, 777
viewpoint on Texas, 519–41
War with Texas, 588–89, 603–04
See also specific headings—e.g., names of persons and places—in the Index
Mexico, Bay of. _See_ Gulf of Mexico
Mexico City, 107, 246, 709, 710
advance on, and entry, by Scott, 777, 778
Mexico Moon, 845–53

Micipipi River (Mississippi), 319
Michael, 217
Mier, Tamaulipas, 345, 397, 402, 483,
    563, 592, 594, 668, 703, 711, 714,
    715, 774, 781, 785, 790, 791, 795,
    835, 842, 854, 855, 906
  battle of, 594–97
Mier y Téran, General, 489, 491–94,
    508
Miguel, Fray Francisco, 197
migrations. *See* pioneers
Milam, Benjamin F., 523
Military Academy, United States, 689
Millais, Sir John, 904
Mina, Francisco Xavier, 432
mining, 887–94
miracles of Mother María de Jesús,
    232–38, 258, 304
missions. *See* Roman Catholic Church
Mississippi River, 157, 319, 399, 400,
    403, 496, 617
Mississippi Territory, 396
Missouri, 503, 504
  exodus from, 439
Missouri Harmony, The, 650
Missouri Intelligencer, 497
Missouri, Kansas and Texas Railroad,
    886
Missouri Trail, 869
Missourians, Free, 742–47, 774
Moffat, David H., 890
Moho, and siege, 121, 123, 129–36, 146
Molano, Colonel, 566, 567
Molino el Rey, battle of, 774, 778
Monclova (Almaden), Coahuila, 157,
    158, 302, 339, 347, 398, 738, 740
Monmouth (steamship), 611, 782
Monroe, James, 426, 427, 429, 781
Monroe Doctrine, 602, 604, 837, 844,
    914, 938
Monterey, California, 392
Monterrey, Nuevo León, 257, 258, 469,
    471, 561, 700, 703, 709, 710, 715–

16, 741, 754, 755, 757–59, 769,
    842
  battles of, 738, 754
Monte Vista, Colorado, 889
Montezuma, 85, 105, 120, 140, 270
Montlezun, 627
Moon, Mexico, 845–53
Moquis, 351
moradas, 377–82
Morgan line, 872
Morlete, Juan, 159
Mormon Battalion, 732, 742, 743
Morrison's claim, 405
Morse, Samuel F. B., 658
mortality, 374–76
Mothe Cadillac, Antoine de la. *See*
    Cadillac
mountain men. *See* fur trade
mountains, sacred, 35
mouth of the river, 5, 83, 88, 302, 303,
    480, 610, 611, 665, 670, 708, 794,
    801
mud in the river, 347
Muñoz, Pedro, 558–59
Murderer's Canyon, 897
music, Church. *See* Roman Catholic
    Church
myths. *See* Ancients

Nacogdoches, Texas, 398, 429, 476, 477
Nacogdoches County, 334
Nambé, 284, 319
names of the river, 21, 83, 88, 113, 115,
    127, 151, 153, 154, 257, 405, 662,
    780, 801, 895
  list of names, 981
Napoleon I, 399, 400, 419, 427, 431,
    433, 439, 781
Napoleon III, 838, 841, 843
Narrative of the Texan Santa Fe Ex-
    pedition, by Kendall, 604
Narváez, Pánfilo de, 92–95, 99, 123, 148
Natchitoches, Louisiana, 400, 419

Natividad, Fray Benito de, 251
Nava Brazinas, Marqués de la. *See* Vargas Zapata
Navajos (Navahos), 61, 74, 717, 721, 742, 743, 745, 746, 812, 830, 832, 844
of Welsh descent, reputed, 833
navigation, 492, 712, 809
last steamboat, 943
Navy, United States, base in Magdalena Bay, 908–09
Neches River, 337
Negroes:
early in Texas, 342–43
slavery, 393, 486–91, 512, 586–87, 601
Nelson, Lord, 400
Neva (steamship), 611, 700, 702
Nevada, 800
New Andalusia, 157
New Biscay, 273, 278, 282, 294, 300, 303–04, 338, 391, 401, 418, 437
New France. *See* Louisiana
New Galicia, 99, 105, 106
New Mexico, 5, 33, 49, 60, 157, 160, 168, 184, 186, 194, 213, 215–21, 225, 228–29, 244, 245, 248, 268–74, 337, 339, 346, 420, 437, 781
agriculture, 549–50
award of Texas territory, 800–01
boundary with Texas, 799–806
business; craftsmen, 550
church and school, 547–49
Confederate States Territory, 823
defense, 545–47
division, 800
education, 547–49, 552, 866–67
foreigners in, 549–51
Gadsden Purchase, 803
hospitality, 551
law, 545
lawlessness, 834–36
mission to Spain, 217–18

New Mexico—*Cont'd*
natives, as seen by an Englishman, 744
newspaper, first, 549
people, and towns, 541–44
politics, 544–45
population, 348, 542
possession, 160–66, 728–36
press, first, 549
price for, with Arizona, 779
revolts in, 551–59, 762–68; trial at Taos, 770–73
Roman Catholic Church in, 865
school and church, 547–49
slavery in, 821
taxation, 552
Territory, 732, 788; organized, 778
theatre, 228
towns and people, 541–44
value decried by Webster, 776
war, civil, 551–59
See also Republic of the Rio Grande
New Mexico Volunteers, 825
New Orleans, Louisiana, 399, 484, 494
New Santander, 34–47, 396, 397, 423
New Santander River, 432
New Spain. *See* Mexico
New Washington, Texas, 535, 536
newspapers, 347
Nievas, Francisco de, 199
Nogales, Arizona, 922, 923
Nolan, Philip, 396–98, 412
Nordismo. See Mexico
Norris, Samuel, 476
North Pass (El Paso del Norte), 166, 168, 251, 256, 260, 299, 311
North Platte River, 337
Nueces River, 471, 527, 561, 585, 586, 591, 607, 669
Nuestra Señora de la Concepción River, 154

Nueva Vizcaya. *See* New Biscay
Nuevo Laredo (Nuevo León), 904
Nuevo León, 157, 256, 261, 391, 471, 472, 560, 703, 774, 859
Nuevo Reyno de León, 342
Nuñez Cabeza de Vaca, Alvar, 99–103, 105, 107, 108, 111, 137, 139, 149, 154, 230
Nuño de Guzmán, 93, 99, 100, 103, 104, 148
Nuns, Discalced, of Aragon, 232

Oaxaca, Marquis of the Valley of. *See* Cortés
Oblate Fathers. *See* Roman Catholic Church
Obregón, Álvaro, 928, 933
ocean masters, Spaniards, 177–80
O'Donojú, General, 437
Office, Holy. *See* Roman Catholic Church—Inquisition
Ojinaga, Chihuahua, 471, 912
Okupi^{n}n, 35
Old Franklin, 500
"Old White Lip." *See* Alvarado
Olivares, Antonio de San Bonaventura. *See* San Bonaventura Olivares
Oñate, Count de (father of Juan), 163–64
Oñate, Juan de, 161–64, 167–69, 170, 172–74, 188, 195–219, 243, 307, 362
    proclamation by, 164–66
    recall, 218
Oraibi, 315
oranges, 472–73
Ord, E. O. C., Major General, 854–56, 858
Ordoñez, Fray Isidro, 245, 246
Oregon, 602, 718
Oremus Boys, 369
Organ Mountains, 822
Ortega, Fray Pedro de, 219

Ortíz, Father, 752, 762
Ortíz, Juan, 99, *note*
Ortíz, Ramon, 584
Osages, 500
Otermín, Antonio de, Governor, 271–73, 279–80, 282–87, 289, 292, 294, 295, 297, 298, 307, 554
Our Lady of Mount Carmel Sodality, 375
outlaws. *See* lawlessness
Ovando, Francisco de, 133–35, 138
Ovid, 192
Oyoyewi and Masewi, 25–26, 47

Pacific Ocean, 157, 198, 213, 392, 462
Padilla, 474
Padilla, Fray Juan de, 111, 114, 120, 128, 137, 145, 146, 149, 219
    death, 149
Padillas, Los, 328
Page, Walter Hines, 913–14
painters, early American, 655–60
painting, 388
Pajarito Plateau, 21
Palo Alto, Texas, 611, 698
    battle of, 679, 682–85, 694; second, 839
Palafox, Texas, 434
Palms, River of, 83–89
Pánuco, 149, 301, 342
Pánuco, Cacique, 89
Pánuco River, 89, 91–93, 150, 761
Pánuco-Victoria Garayana, 92
Paredes y Arillaga, Mariano, 607, 670, 715
Parkman, Francis, 718
Parraga, Fray Diego de, 29
Parral, Chihuahua, 259, 271, 273, 299, 311, 313, 316, 327
    battle of, 928
Parras, 741
Pascual, 502
Paso de Francia. *See* France Way

Paso del Norte. *See* North Pass; El
    Paso
Passion of Christ; observance by Peni-
    tents, 379–80
patrol of the river, 391
Pattie, James, 542
Paul III, Pope, 242
Pavon, General, 561, 562
Pawnees, 337, 404, 414
Peale family (painters), 658
Pecos Indians, 307
Pecos River, 5, 73, 117, 156, 157, 301,
    803, 832, 882, 894, 895
Peña Blanca, New Mexico, 467–68
Peñalosa, Eufemia de Sosa. *See* Sosa
    Peñalosa
Peñalosa Briceña y Bertugo, Diego
    Dionysio de (Count of Santa
    Fe), 251–53, 302–03
Penitent Brothers. *See* Third Order of
    Penitence
Penitents, 376–82
Penn, William, 656
Peralta, New Mexico, 502, 629
Peralta, Governor, 245, 246, 251
Percier, Charles, 439
Perea, Fray Estevan de, 233
Pérez, Albino, 551–55
    death, 555
Pérez de Villagrá, Gaspar, 170, 188, 198,
    199, 202, 207, 211, 376
Perfecto de Cos, Martin, 517–26, 528,
    530, 536, 537
Perillo, El, 267
Perillo Spring, 170, 246
Perote, 599, 600
Pershing, John J., General, 916, 920–
    22, 926, 928
    loss of wife and daughters, 920
    leader of Punitive Expedition into
    Mexico, 930–34, 936, 939
Petriz de Crusate, Domingo Jironza.
    See Jironza Petriz

Philip II, of Spain, 157, 161, 178, 182–
    86, 194, 238, 243, 293, 319, 374,
    376
Philip III, of Spain, 194–95, 217, 218
Philip V, 329, 331
phrenology, 630
pictures, cave, 71
Picuries, the, 198, 285, 286, 313
Piedras Negras, Coahuila, 838, 843,
    857, 904
    battle of, 817
Pike, Zebulon M., 403–07, 409–12, 414,
    415, 417, 429, 435, 462, 887
Pike's Peak, 887
Pineda. *See* Álvarez de Pineda
Piñero, Juan, 169
Pino, Pedro Bautista y. *See* Bautista y
    Pino
pioneers:
    arts, 654–60; and utility, 642–44
    communities, 635–38
    crafts and knacks, 651–55
    folklore, 627
    hardihood, 629
    home and women, 631–35
    humor, 641
    hunters, 628
    language, 640–42
    last, 871–86
    literature, 642
    music, 647–51
    oratory, 639
    painters, 655–60
    person and dress, 626
    plays, 644–47
    politics, 637
    recollections of history, 636–37
    religion, 634–36
    sharpshooters, 628
    spread to the West, 619–60
    theatre, 644–50
    utility and arts, 642–44
    women and home, 631–35

Pioneers, Santa Fe. *See* Santa Fe Pioneers
Piros (Indians), 48, 230, 236, 261, 264
Pius VI, Pope, 400
Plain of the Inferno, 322
Plains Indians, 68, 73
See also Indians; names of tribes
Plan of Iguala, 436, 438
plateau cities. *See* pueblos
Plato, 819
plays, 228, 338
Plymouth Rock, 621
Po-he-yemu, 270, 287–88
Pojuaque, and Creek, 36, 251
Poinsett, Joel, 475, 478
Point Isabel, Texas, 610, 611, 661, 664, 665, 671, 672, 675, 682, 702, 755, 760, 776, 837–39, 841, 856
Politics of Aristotle, 240
Polk, James K., 602, 604–08, 661, 671, 692, 693, 694, 700, 703, 710, 723, 735, 736, 754–56, 769, 771, 777–81, 784, 802
Ponce de León, Diego de Vargas Zapata Luján. *See* Vargas Zapata
Ponce de León, José María, 542
Ponce de León, Juan, 180
Ponce de León, Pedro, 184
Popé, 265, 270, 296, 306
Popes
Alexander VI, 177, 241, 431
Leo X, 84
Paul III, 243
Pius VI, 400
Porter, David, Commodore, 479, 670
Porter, Theodoric, 670
Posada, Fray Alonso de, 252
P'osoge, 113
postal service, early, 347, 453, 502, 505
posts, United States Army. *See* Army, United States—forts and posts
P'o-woge, 35
power projects, 809

prairies, 500
Preciosa, 776
precipitation, 6
Presidio de San Juan Bautista. *See* Fort Saint John Baptist
Presidio de Rio Grande. *See* Fort Saint John Baptist
Presidio de San Vicente, 901
Presidio del Norte, 498, 585, 775, 831, 851, 869, 895, 898, 912, 918
press, 347
Price, Sterling, 734, 742, 751, 762, 763, 766, 768, 769, 778–80
printing, 187
Priscillian the Heretic, 251
promises, 215–19
prospectors, 893–94
provincials, 87–90
Puaray, 154, 155, 159, 171, 199, 219
Puebla, Puebla, 357
battle of, 774, 778
Pueblo Indians. *See* Indians
pueblos, 109–12
abandonment, 306
population, 213
Puerco River, 5
Pursley, James, 401–02, 415, 462

Quarai, and battle of, 214, 248, 261,262
Quelch, Captain, 459
Querétaro, Querétaro, 326, 340, 341, 343, 347, 778, 780, 843
Questa, 542
quicksilver (mercury), 310, 315, 316
Quintana, 308
Quintillian, 174
Quivira, 103, 104, 122, 127, 132, 136, 138, 141, 143–47, 149, 214, 216, 217, 219, 261, 299, 550, 877
Quirós, Fray Cristóbal, 231, 236
Quixote, Don, 147, 191

Rábago y Terán, Pedro, 339

Rafinesque, Constantine Samuel, 649
Raft, Great, 496
rafts, trappers', 465
raids, Indian. *See* Indians
railroads, 803, 847, 862, 885, 886, 941,
    942
  first, 841
rainfall, 6
  See also drought
Ramírez y Sesma, General, 527, 529
Ramón, Diego, 324, 331
Ramón, Domingo, 333
Ramón, María, 332–33
Ramón family, 334, 336
Ramos Arizpe, Miguel, 420, 421
rancherias, 793, 795–96
  cattle, 886
Ranchos de Taos, New Mexico, 463
Rangers, Texas. *See* Texas Rangers
rapids, 896
rattlesnakes, 66, 72, 131
Rawlins, H.M.S., 459
Ray, Julian del, 192
Real Alencaster, Joaquin, 402, 406–08,
    411–15, 419
Red River, 5, 496, 766, 838
Refugio, Tamaulipas, 397, 402, 527,
    532. *See also* Matamoros
Regiment, Condemned, 471
religion, Mexican. *See* Roman Catholic
    Church
Renaissance, the, 177
reptiles, 66
Republic of the Rio Grande, 559–69,
    588, 703, 704
*Republic of the Rio Grande and the
    People's Friend,* 703
Republic of the Sierra Madre, 791, 857,
    930, 931
Resaca de la Palma, 611, 680, 686–89,
    694, 698
Retana, Juan de, 304
Retis, Trasviño, 338

Revilla, Tamaulipas, 483, 561–62, 565
  See also Guerrero
Revilla Gigedo, Count of, 396
revolt, Indian. *See* Indians—uprising
Reynosa, Tamaulipas, 345, 346, 390,
    397, 472, 480, 711, 774, 775, 792,
    836, 855
Riddle, adventures of, 739–40
Riego, Rafael, 434–46
rights, States', 800
Ringgold, S., Major, 694
Ringgold Barracks, Texas, 790, 807,
    943
Rio, Alonzo del, 283
Rio Abajo. *See* Downriver district
Rio Arriba. *See* Upriver district
Rio Bravo (U. S. gunboat), 858
Rio Frio, 591
Rio Grande City (Davis Landing),
    Texas, 345, 785, 790, 792, 801,
    807
Rise of the Spanish Empire, by Salva-
    dor de Madriaga, 245, *note*
Rito de los Frijoles, 20, 213
rivers, meeting of. *See* Junta de los
    Rios
roads, 943
  See also trails
Roberts, Ben S., 825
Robinson, John Hamilton, 405–07, 412,
    416–17, 429
Robledo, Pedro, 170, 502
Rock Creek, 5
Rocky Mountain men. *See* fur trade
Rocky Mountains, 4, 403, 462, 463, 475,
    495, 887, 896
  gold in, 847
Rodríguez, Captain, 611
Rodríguez, Fray Agustín, 154, 172
Rodríguez Cubero, Pedro, 319–21,
    323
Rodríguez de Suballe, Juan Severino
    de, 274, 275

Roma, Texas, 345, 785, 790, 809, 835, 836, 943

Roman Catholic Church
approval of dancing, 251
assignments, 197–98
churches, 262
excommunication, 245, 253, 254
Franciscans, 145, 146, 165, 172, 219–37, 254, 255, 268, 294, 325, 328, 336, 348–49, 351, 376–77, 383, 384, 387, 393, 547, 548; removal of, 866
in Mexico; attacked, 779, 918
in New Mexico, 547–49, 572, 865
Inquisition, 185, 246, 252, 254, 265, 516; abolition, 430
Jesuits, 351
martyrs, 219
miracles of Mother María de Jesús, 232–38
missions, 89, 150, 154, 156, 163, 165, 168, 181–82, 197–99, 202, 216, 219, 238, 244, 247, 254, 258, 260, 261, 305, 325, 344, 349, 472, 793–99; decay of, 394; secularization of, 394, 542; Texas, 305
music, 189, 227
Oblate Fathers, 472
official religion of Texas, under Austin, 469
Popes. *See* Popes
seminaries, 326
Rome, 174
Rosas, de, Governor, 251
Rosas, Fray Juan de, 197–98
Rosenburg, Commissioner, 574, 577
Ross, Reuben, 561–64
Roubideaux brothers, 462
Rosseau, Jean Jacques, 646
Ruíz, Fray Agustín, 219
Ruxton, George Frederick, 744–45

Sabeata, Juan, 299, 304

Sabinas River, 324
Sabine (schooner), 507
Sabine River, 400, 433, 475
Sacramento, battle of, 780
Sacramento Presidio, 339
sacrifice, human, 64, 139, 456
Sahagún the Elder, 192
Saint Augustine, *Confessions*, 183
Saint Bernard's Mission, Fort Saint John Baptist, 394
Saint Denis, Louis Juchereau de, 327, 332–37, 340, 780
ford of, 736
Saint Francis of Assisi, 219, 226, 228, 235, 236
Saint Francis, Kingdom of, 107
Saint Francis Xavier, 308, 328
Saint James of Compostela, 131, 208
Saint John Baptist, Fort. *See* Fort Saint John Baptist
Saint Lawrence, 186
Saint Louis, Missouri, 392, 462, 468, 498
Saint Michael, 236
Saint Philip the Apostle, 329
Saint Teresa of Ávila, 191
Saint Vrain, Céran, 462
saints, 383–88
makers, 384–86
Salado Creek, battle of, 590
Salado River (two rivers of the same name), 5
Salamanca, 112
Salas, Fray Juan de, 234, 236
Salas, Petronila de, 284
Salazar, Damasio, 574–77, 581–84, 726
Salazar, Fray Cristóbal de. *See* Cristóbal Salazar
Salazar, Juan, 423, 424
Salcedo, Manuel, 401, 423–25, 429, 430
Salines, 261–64
destruction, 264
Salineta, 280

salt, 70, 197, 198, 213, 214, 220, 247, 261, 322, 341, 344, 345, 365
Salt War, 860–61
Saltelo, Ignacio, 408, 409
Saltillo, Coahuila, 257, 420, 472, 475, 476, 505, 509, 561, 566, 700, 709, 741, 757–60
battle of, 566–68
San Antonio (de Béxar), Texas, 335–36, 338, 392, 424, 470, 476, 509, 514, 517, 530, 583, 589, 736, 785, 786, 807, 842, 926, 933
Álamo. *See* Álamo
missions, 336
San Antonio River, 332, 334, 523
San Antonio de Valero, Mission of. *See* Álamo
San Bernardo, 324, 325, 327, 336
San Buenaventura, Dionysio, 258, 259
San Buenaventura Olivares, Antonio, 334, 335
San Carlos Creek, 898
San Cristóbal, 313
San Diego, 502, 812
San Diego Crossing, New Mexico, 832
San Diego River, 339
San Elizario, Texas, 786, 802
San Esteban, Texas, 471
San Felipe (schooner), 518
San Felipe, New Mexico, 231, 318, 392, 416
San Felipe de Austin, Texas, 478, 510, 515, 525, 535
San Fernando de Taos, 767, 768, 771
San Francisco Solano, 324
San Ildefonso, New Mexico, 35, 48, 284, 553, 864
San Jacinto Creek, 535, 536
San Juan Bautista, Presidio de. *See* Fort Saint John Baptist
San Juan Capistrano, 336
San Juan de la Cruz, 219, 375
San Juan de los Caballeros, New Mexico, 173, 195, 196, 198–200, 202, 203, 205, 206, 208, 209, 213–19, 265, 269, 296, 313, 325
San Juan de Nuevo Mexico. *See* San Juan de los Caballeros
San Juan de Ulloa, Veracruz, 479, 584
San Juan Indians, 411
San Juan Mountains, 887–88
San Juan River, 302, 344, 568, 711
Valley of, 776
San Lázaro, New Mexico, 313
San Lorenzo del Real, New Mexico, 329, 348
San Luís Potosí, 769
San Luis Valley, Colorado, 403, 812, 888, 889
San Marcos, Texas, 402
San Martín, José, 474
San Mateo Mountains, 830
San Miguel, New Mexico, 286
San Patricio, Texas, 566
San Patricio Battalion, 667
San Vicente, Texas, 929
Sánchez, Cristóbal, 170
Sánchez, José Maria, 478
Sánchez Cabello, Juan, 292
Sánchez Chamuscado, Francisco, 159
Sancho de Caniedo, 93
Sandía, 154, 246, 275, 289, 392
Sandía Mountains, 829
Sandía Range, 35, 136, 321, 328
Sangre de Cristo Mountains, 312
Sangre de Cristo Range, 498, 581, 887
Santa Ana, New Mexico, 318
Santa Anna, Antonio López de. *See* López de Santa Anna
Santa Barbara, Mexico, 154, 199, 216
Santa Clara, New Mexico, 284
Santa Clara Peak, 35
Santa Cruz, New Mexico, 318, 321, 348, 377, 544, 553, 557, 766
battle of, 780
Santa Cruz Creek, 36

Santa Cruz de Rosales, 780
Santa Elena Canyon, 898–901
Santa Elena Mountains, 898
Santa Fe, Count of. *See* Peñalosa, Briceña y Bertugo, Diego Dionysio de
Santa Fe, New Mexico, 70, 219, 220, 227, 245–47, 261, 265, 266, 268–71, 273, 275, 279, 283, 287, 288, 306, 307, 310, 312, 313, 329, 347, 348, 377, 392, 401, 404, 411, 462, 466, 495–99, 501, 502, 542, 544–46, 550, 552, 555, 556, 573, 637, 692, 716–19, 721, 724–26, 730, 732, 735, 785, 787, 801, 805, 811, 812, 824, 827, 866, 867, 942
  battle of, 286–89
Santa Fe Creek, 36
Santa Fe Expedition, 726
Santa Fe line. *See* Atchison, Topeka and Santa Fe
Santa Fe Pioneers, 569–86, 703, 799
Santa Fe Range, 35
Santa Fe Trail, 862
Santa Isabel mines, 922
Santa María, Fray Juan de, 154, 155
Santiago de Compostela, Saint, 131, 208
Santiago Abreu, Alférez, 438
Santiestevan, 91
Santo Domingo, New Mexico, 158, 172, 261, 264, 284, 312, 392, 416, 734
Scott, Hugh L., Major General, 928, 934
Scott, Winfield, Major General, 700, 709, 710, 715, 753–61, 769, 774, 777–79, 841
  and Taylor; dissension, 754–61
  aspiration for Presidency, 757; candidacy, 781
  broadside to the Mexicans, 777
  victories in Mexico, 774
sculpture, 388

sea, masters of (Spaniards), 177–80
seasons, 6
Sebastian (oblate), 128, 146, 149
Seneca, 174, 251, 264, 271, 311, 330, 348
Sesma, Ramírez y. *See* Ramírez y Sesma
settlement, 89, 91, 92, 157, 158, 259, 260, 343–46, 348
settlements. *See* towns
settlers. *See* pioneers
Seven Cities. *See* Cíbola
Seville, Spain, 178, 187
Seward, William H., 840, 841
Shakespeare, William, 714
Shaler, William, 427
sheep, 335, 364, 550, 813
Sheridan, Philip H., Lieutenant General, 839, 841–43, 858
Sherman, William T., Lieutenant General, 861
Shields, James, 738
Shi-pap, Lake, 35
Shipapu, 39, 78, 262
shouts. *See gritos*
Sibley, Henry H., Brigadier General, 823–26, 829, 830
Sierra, Fray Antonio de, 278–79
Sierra Azul, 310
Sierra Blanca, 262
Sierra del Carmen, 901
Sierra de Dolores, 388
Sierra de la Soledad, 395
Sierra Gorda, Count of. *See* Escandón
Sierra Madre Range, 153, 566, 568–69
  suggested as boundary, 779
Sierra Madre, Republic of the, 791, 857, 930, 931
silt, 6, 347
silver, 890, 893
  and gold, 120, 132, 140, 503–04
Sinaloa, 864
  war on the United States, 932, 933
Sinnickson, Doctor, 595
Sisters, Twin. *See* Texas-Coahuila

slavery:
　Aristotle on, 240–41
　Fugitive Slave Law, 800
　in Mexico. *See* Mexico
　in Texas. *See* Texas
　law, Coahuila-Texas, 488
　See also Indians; Negroes
Slidell, John, 606, 607
smallpox, 261, 346, 401, 754
Smith, George L., 890
Smith, Jedediah, 462
Smith, Kirby, 839–41
Smith's Ranch, 812
snakes, 66
Snively, Jacob, 600
Socorro, New Mexico, 48, 264, 274,
　　　290, 311, 330, 348, 502, 744, 746,
　　　785, 787, 788, 893
Socorro del Sur, Texas, 786
Socorro Mountains, 893
Sodality of Our Lady of Mount Car-
　mel, 375
Sodom, 776
soil erosion, 20, 364
Somervell, Alexander, 590–92
Sonora, 143, 267, 282, 392, 420, 823
Sonora Valley, 112, 127
sorcery at El Paso, 266–67
Sosa. *See* Castaño de Sosa
Sosa Albernoz, 214, 216
Sosa Peñalosa, Eufemia de, 206
Soto, Hernando de, 99, 108
Soto la Marina, 473
Sotomayor, José Martínez de. *See* Mar-
　tínez de Sotomayor
sources of the river, 4–5, 887, 888
South Fork, Colorado, 5
South Park, Colorado, 402
South Sea. *See* Pacific Ocean
Spain:
　attempt to reconquer Mexico, 479
　Christianity, 175–76
　downfall, 436–40

Spain:—*Cont'd*
　Empire, decline of, 194
　kings, 180–87
　language, 187
　literature, 193–95
　memory of, 174–95
　swords, 192–93
Spaniards, 174–95
　coming of, 83–89, 96–99, 109–10
　description of, 86–88
　hidalgos, 190
　outfit, 167
Spanish Peaks, 887
Spar City, Colorado, 893
Speyer, Albert, 718–19, 745
spirits. *See* liquor
spirits, underworld, 270, 296
Spring (ship), 473, 474
spring, hot, 902
Spring Creek, 5
springs, 170
stage, the, 388
stagecoaches, 847, 862, 868–69
Staked Plain, 851
Stanton, Henry Whiting, Captain;
　and Fort, 816–17
starvation. *See* famine
State and Church. *See* Church and
　State
State and individual, 620–21
States, Western; formation of, 623
States' rights, 800
Stations, Army. *See* Army
steamboats. *See* navigation; *also* names
　of individual ships
Stinking Ones (Indians), 301
Stockton, Robert Field, Commodore,
　735
Stone, John Augustus, 646
Stony Pass, 888
strangers, exclusion of, 395–96
Strong, George Templeton, 774
Stuart, Gilbert, 657

Suárez, Vice President, 910
Suballe, Juan Severino Rodríguez de. *See* Rodríguez de Suballe
suffrage, 623
Sully, Thomas, 657
Summitville, Colorado, 888, 889
Sumner, Edwin V., 812–13, 832
Sunnyside, Colorado, 893
supply trains. *See* trains, freight
surveys, 894–904
swords, 192–93

Tabira (Gran Quivira), New Mexico, 261, 262
Taft, William Howard; meeting with Díaz, 906–10
Tagus River, 192
tales, travellers', 100–09
Talleyrand, 419
Tamarón, Bishop, 391
Tamaulipas, 391, 471, 474, 560, 566, 669, 703, 757, 758, 774, 830
Tampico, Tamaulipas, 152, 342, 479, 492, 710, 757, 761, 794
  incident, 914
Taos (Braba), New Mexico, 74, 114, 138, 173, 198, 219, 245, 252, 270, 283–86, 288, 313, 314, 390–91, 395, 419, 463, 464, 466, 467, 469, 497, 498, 541, 542, 552, 553, 716, 719, 764, 812, 818, 887
  fair, 391
  massacre, 764–68; trial, 770–73
Taos Creek, 36
tariff, 492, 498, 788–93
Tatarrax, 132, 140
Taxique, 251, 263, 322
Taylor, Zachary, 605–08, 610, 611, 617, 618, 623, 661, 663, 665–72, 674–83, 685–87, 689–92, 694–97, 699–703, 705, 707, 709–11, 714–16, 719, 736, 738, 741, 752, 754–61, 769, 774, 781, 839, 861, 943

Taylor, Zachary—*Cont'd*
  and Scott; dissension, 754–61
  aspiration to Presidency, 699, 710, 757, 759, 761; election, 761, 782
  description, 665–66
  honors, 699–70
  song about, 782–83
Tehuantepec, 485
Tejada. *See* Lerdo de Tejada
Tejada, Lorenzo de, 147
telegraph, 941
telephone, 942
temperance societies, 638
temperature, surface of the river, 6
Tenochtitlan, 93
Terán, Pedro Rábago y. *See* Rábago y Terán
Terrazas, Juan Tomás, 438
"Terrible Texas," 848
Terror, the, 274–93
Tesuque, New Mexico, 283, 284, 313, 323
Tewa towns, 198, 286
Tewa and Keres, 77
Tewas (Indians), 265
Texas, 259, 298–304
  annexation to the United States, approval by vote, 606–07; proposed, 586, 601–08; annexation of upriver territory, proposed, 571; annexation and the slavery issue, 587
  armistice with Mexico, 601
  Austin plan for settlement, 435
  boundary, 569, 799–806; claim to the river, 569; with Louisiana, 400
  civil organization, first, 338
  claim to, by North Americans, 433–35
  colonial, 331–41
  colonization by North Americans, 453–69
  cotton, 836–38

Texas—*Cont'd*
diplomacies over, 600–08
division, proposed, 604, 800
evacuation by Mexicans, 539–40
for Mexican independence, 423
"God and Texas," 513–19
government by Mexico, 509
in the Civil War, 819–31
independence, declaration of, 530;
    decried by Austin, 506, 508, 510;
    recognition of, 540, 559, 586;
    recognized by Mexico, 605
Indian raids, 560
infiltration by North Americans, 396,
    402, 488
law, Mexican, against entry of An-
    glo-Americans, 488–89
loss of territory to New Mexico, 800–
    19
loyalty, tormented, to Mexico, 505–
    12
missions, 305
nationalism, 587
nationhood, recognition of, 541
Negroes, early, 342–43
opening to settlement by North
    Americans, 459
part of proposed Republic of the
    Rio Grande, 560
peace conference with Mexico, 603
purchase by United States, proposed,
    513
reconstruction after the Civil War,
    854
renunciation of claim by the United
    States, 433
republic, first; proclamation and
    downfall, 430–31
republic, second, 433
republics, three, 399
revolt against Mexico, 519–41
secession from United States, 819–31
settlement, 429

Texas—*Cont'd*
slavery issue, 485–95, 506, 586–87,
    601, 800, 820; views of Austin,
    512
statehood conventions, 781
statehood issue in elections, 604
statehood, Mexican, 508–12, 514, 515
statehood, offer of, 604–05
threat to Mexico, 474–84
treaty, proposed, with United States,
    for territorial status, 603
war with Mexico, 588–89, 603–04
withdrawal of Mexican troops, 507
Texas and Pacific Railroad, 886
Texas-Coahuila, 394, 420, 469–73, 487,
    488, 495, 509, 514, 528, 781
law on slavery, 488, 489
Texas Rangers, 672, 703, 707, 712, 739,
    791, 846, 861–62, 895
theatre, the, 228, 388
Theotocopuli, Domenico (El Greco),
    188
Third Order of Penitence, 377
Third Order of Saint Francis, 376
Thomas, 159, 168, 171, 172, 207
Thompson's Ferry, 535
Thoreau, Henry D., 784
Thornton, Jesse, 943
Thornton, Seth, 671, 692
Tigua language, 197
Tiguex, 114, 115, 121–23, 127, 128, 133,
    135, 136, 139–40, 142–43, 145,
    146, 154, 318
Tiguex River, 137, 138, 142–44, 147,
    149
Tijeras Canyon, 322, 328
Tilini, 270, 296
Titian, 188
Tleume, 270, 296
tobacco, 420
Tocqueville, Alexis de, 621–22, 630,
    637, 640
    cited, 632, 638

Toledo (Cuban), 430, 431
Toledo, José Álvarez. *See* Álvarez Toledo
Toledo, Spain, 188, 192
Tom McKinney (steamship), 785
Tomé, New Mexico, 275, 502, 555, 734, 743
Torrejón, Anastasio, 671, 684, 692, 693
tortures. *See* Indians
Tovar, Pedro de, 143, 164
towns, 478, 480, 502, 802
   and haciendas, 353–90
   business, 791
   early, 328–31
   founding, 431
   number on the river, 390
trade, 331, 335, 347, 348, 355, 356, 367, 391, 396, 401–02, 492, 495–504, 791, 862, 868–72
   regulation of, 331, 334–36
   route, 736
   Spanish, with the Indians, 212–15
trails, 69–71, 74, 97, 99, 161, 324, 327, 339, 393, 469, 496, 561, 576, 718, 744, 769, 795, 812, 851, 862, 868, 869
   cattle, 882–83, 885, 886
trains, freight, 225, 229, 260, 262, 268, 269, 498, 499, 869–71
   wagon, last, 868–72
Trajan, 174
trapping, *See* fur trade
travellers' tales, 100–09
Travis, William B., 517
treasure (mines), 887–94
treaties:
   Gadsden, 803–06
   Guadalupe Hidalgo, 779, 801, 859
trees, dating by, 19–20
Treviño, Ramon, 859, 906
Trias, Governor, 751, 780
tributaries, 5, 22, 36, 63, 73, 138, 139, 153, 156, 172, 220, 299, 302, 312, 330, 338, 339, 344, 392, 585, 795, 803, 832, 851, 889, 894, 895, 898, 902
Trinchera Creek, 5
Trinity River, 535
Trist, Nicholas P., 777, 779–80, 804
trouble on the border, 585–91
Troy (steamship), 700
Truchas Peak, 35
Trujillo, Luisa de, 269
Tules, La. *See* Barceló, Gertrudes
Tumulty, Joseph P., 915
Turk, the, 117–21, 127, 132, 133, 135, 137, 139, 141, 214
   death, 140
turquoise, 70
Twide, Richard, 151–53
Twiggs, David Emmanuel, General, 820
Twin Sisters. *See* Texas-Coahuila
Two Majesties, the. *See* Church and State
Tyler, John, 605

underworld spirits, 70, 296
United States:
   and Germany. *See* Germany
   and Mexico; advance to the river, 609; annexation and intervention, proposed, 921, 935; border disagreements, 859–62, 906, 914–40; diplomacies, 601–08; Commission, Joint, 935, 936; conference, El Paso, and agreement, 928; Punitive Expedition, 930–34, 936; War. *See* Mexican War
   entry into World War I, 939
   infiltration into Texas, 396, 402
   negotiations with (1811), 425–27
   spread to the West, 617–60
United States Geological Survey, 895
United States Military Academy, 689–90

Upland river, 95–100, 269
uprising, Indian. *See* Indians
Upriver district (Rio Arriba), 95–100, 269
Urrea, General, 527, 532, 533, 536, 540, 776
Urrea, Lope de, 134
use and beauty (American arts and crafts), 652
Utah, 800
Utes, 717, 889
utility and vision, 940–45

Vaca, Alvar Nuñez Cabeza de. *See* Nuñez Cabeza
Vaca, Luís María Cabeza de. *See* Cabeza de Vaca
Vacas, Rio de las (Pecos), 156
Vado Piedra, 471
Valencia, New Mexico, 502, 743
Valencia family, 290
Valles, 342
Valley of Mexico, 777
Valley of Oaxaca, Marquis of the. *See* Cortés
Valley of the San Juan, 776
valleys, 5
Valverde, New Mexico, 546
Valverde Mesa, 735, 742, 743, 744, 746, 812
battle of, 824–26
Vargas Zapata Luján Ponce de León, Diego (Marqués de la Nava Brazinas) de, 305–23, 362, 377
Vásquez Borrego, José, 345
Vásquez de Coronado, Francisco, 105–08, 110, 111, 113, 121, 122, 126, 127, 129–32, 134–38, 140–47, 149, 153–55, 157, 159, 164, 172, 191, 212, 214, 318, 362, 832
prediction of career, 112
Vega, Lope de. *See* Lope de Vega

Vega, R. D. de la, General, 661, 689, 691, 694
Velasco, 518, 527
Vélez de Escalante, Fray Silvestre, 392
Veracruz, Veracruz, 85, 90, 93, 108, 149–51, 347, 348, 457, 479, 492, 496, 505, 507, 693, 710, 754, 761, 915
occupation by United States, 915–17
Verde Cuerno, 392
Vermejo River, 719
vermilion, 315, 316
Veronicas, 379, 381
Victoria, Mexico, 700, 758
Victoria de Tamaulipas, 566
Victoria Guarayana-Pánuco, 92
Vidaurre, Fermín de, 339
Vigil, Donaciano, 762, 766
Vigil, Juan Bautista, 438
Vigil y Alarid, Juan Bautista, 728, 729, 731
Villa, Francisco (Pancho Villa; Doroteo Arango), 911–14, 916, 917, 919–24, 934–36
assassination, 939
description, 922–23
German views on, 928
raid on Columbus, New Mexico, 924–28
raids by, 929
villages. *See* towns
Villagrá, Gaspar Pérez de. *See* Pérez de Villagrá, Gaspar
Villasur, Pedro de, 337
Vince's Creek, 537, 538
Vinci, Leonardo de, 84
Vinegaroon. *See* Langtry
Virgin Mary, vision of, 264
Virgin of Guadalupe, 422
Viseo, Bishop of, 232, 235
vision and utility, 940–45
visitations. *See* Ágreda; miracles
volcanic action, 896

volume of the river, 6, 343
voyage, first continuous, 821

wagon, Conestoga, 499
wagon trains. *See* trains, freight
Wagon Wheel Gap, Colorado, 889, 892
Walker, Samuel H., 672–74
Wallace, Lew, 705–07, 708, 776–77, 861
Walpi, 315
War Between the States. *See* Civil War
wars:
    cattle, 861
    Lincoln County, 861
    Mexican. *See* Mexican War
    salt, 860, 861
    Texas-Mexico, 603–04
    with the Indians. *See* Indians
Washington, Texas, 529–30, 605
water of the river, 347
wealth, Spanish and Indian, 142
Webster, Daniel, 571, 575, 589, 637, 780
    on "worthlessness" of California and New Mexico, 779
weddings, 371–74, 796–97
Weller, John B., 802
Wellington, Duke of, 419–20, 430
Welsh descent of Navajos, suggested, 833
West Point, 689–90
West Willow Creek, 890
Western Lyre, The, 650
White Cavalier (Garcia), 835
Whitman, Walt, 642, 695, 781
    cited, 624–25
Wightman's Gulch, Colorado, 888
Wilkinson, James, 400–01, 403–05, 439
Williams, Bill, 462
Willow Creek, 889–90
Willow Gap. *See* Creede
Wilson, Woodrow, 910–13, 915, 918–21, 926–28, 930, 932, 935, 937, 938

winter, 200, 543, 743–44, 871
witchcraft. *See* magic
Woll, Adrian, General, 589, 603
women, occupations of Spanish-American, 356–58, 362–65
Wood, George T., 799
Wool, John E., Brigadier General, 732, 733, 735, 736, 738–40, 746, 751, 760, 769, 774, 783
work and family, 360–67
World War I, 917, 919
    entry of United States, 939
Worth, William J., Brigadier General, 661, 662, 682, 741, 757, 760
Wright, murder by Villa; and Mrs. Wright, 923–26

Xavier. *See* Saint Francis Xavier
Xenophon, 769

Yell, Archibald, Colonel, 737
yellow fever, 754
Yucatan, 93, 480
yucca, 50–52, 54, 55, 57, 65, 70, 72, 74, 78, 114, 121, 213, 296, 313, 362, 386
Yunge Pueblo, 36
Yunque, 172
Yuque, 172
Yuque-Yunque, 138
Yuta Indians, 406, 407

Zacatecas, Zacatecas, 200, 258, 326, 864
Zaldívar, Captain, 140
Zaldívar, Juan de, 166, 171, 199–209
    death, 201
Zaldívar, Vicente de, 161–63, 166, 171–73, 191, 198–209, 213, 214, 217, 218
Zamora, Fray Francisco de, 198
Zapata, General, 917
Zapata, Antonio, 560–61, 564, 568

Zapata Luján Ponce de León, Diego de Vargas. *See* Vargas Zapata
Závala, Lorenzo de, 517, 519
Zía, 134, 198, 310, 314, 318
Zimmermann, Alfred, 937
"Zone, Free," 855
zones of climate, 6

Zubía, Diego de, 206, 208–09
Zubiría, Antonio, 547
Zumárraga, Bishop, 227
Zuñiga, Francisco Manzo y. *See* Manzo y Zuñiga
Zuñis, 109–12, 154, 198, 314–16
Zutucapan, 201, 208